HANDBOOK OF FAMILY LITERACY

Edited by

Barbara Hanna Wasik
University of North Carolina at Chapel Hill

LEA LAWRENCE ERLBAUM ASSOCIATES, PUBLISHERS

2004   Mahwah, New Jersey   London

Director, Editorial: Lane Akers
Executive Assistant: Bonita D'Amil
Cover Design: Sean Trane Sciarrone
Textbook Production Manager: Paul Smolenski
Full-Service Compositor: TechBooks
Text and Cover Printer: Hamilton Printing Company

This book was typeset in 10/12 pt. Times, Italic, Bold, Bold Italic. The heads were typeset in Helvetica Bold, and Helvetica Bold Italic.

Lawrence Erlbaum Associates, Inc., Publishers
10 Industrial Avenue
Mahwah, New Jersey 07430
www.erlbaum.com

Library of Congress Cataloging-in-Publication Data

Handbook of family literacy / edited by Barbara Hanna Wasik.
    p.   cm.
Includes bibliographical references and indexes.
    ISBN 0-8058-4307-8 (casebound : alk. paper)
      1. Family literacy programs—United States—Handbooks, manuals, etc.
  I. Wasik, Barbara Hanna.

LC151.H33   2004
302.2′244—dc22   2003027618

Books published by Lawrence Erlbaum Associates are printed on acid-free paper, and their bindings are chosen for strength and durability.

Printed in the United States of America
10 9 8 7 6 5 4 3 2 1

To my mother
Josephine N. Hanna
And the memory of my father
Frank J. Hanna, Sr.

Contents

About the Editor

Barbara Hanna Wasik, Ph.D., William R. Kenan Jr. Distinguished Professor, University of North Carolina at Chapel Hill, is a professor in the School of Education's School Psychology Program, a Fellow of the Frank Porter Graham Child Development Institute, and Director of the UNC-Chapel Hill Center for Home Visiting. A clinical and school psychologist, she has devoted most of her professional career to developing and evaluating early intervention programs for children at risk for social, emotional, or academic difficulties. She is the author or co-author of over 80 publications, including the book *Home Visiting: Procedures for Helping Families*, as well as assessment instruments for classrooms, problem solving, home visiting, and family literacy programs. She is one of the developers of Project CARE and the Infant Health and Development Program, two longitudinal early intervention experimental studies for at-risk children and their families. With her colleague Joseph Sparling, she is developing the Partners for Literacy curriculum, one of the two curricula to be used in the Classroom Literacy and Intervention Outcomes study, a national experimental study of the federal Even Start Family Literacy programs.

Preface

Researchers and writers have long been interested in the intergenerational transmission of literacy within families, including how families use language and literacy for communication and how families help children develop language and literacy skills. But over the past two decades, many have focused their attention on programs to help children and their parents who have low literacy skills, often referred to as family literacy programs.

Family literacy programs are a relatively new phenomenon within the broader scope of early childhood education and adult education endeavors. They have captured the attention of many practitioners, policymakers, and researchers because of their potential to address compelling issues of literacy and language for both children and adults. At the same time, they have fostered intense debates on the meaning of family literacy and efforts to provide intervention services to families.

This handbook was written to provide a comprehensive source of information on family literacy programs, a need that springs from the considerable expansion of these programs beginning in the 1980s. The authors address issues of importance for project directors, early childhood educators, parent educators, and adult educators. Topics include emergent literacy, storybook reading, cultural and language diversity, instructional procedures, literacy-rich classrooms, parent–child and teacher–child relationships, the home environment, and child and adult assessment. Authors discuss program issues, such as integrating across program components, service integration, home visiting, and evaluation. They also provide numerous recommendations for professional development. Researchers, policymakers, and local and state leaders will find current reviews that can inform future directions. Moreover, the handbook is suitable for students in a range of areas, including early childhood education, adult education, and parenting education. It can serve the needs of those who want a detailed introduction to this field as well as of those seeking advanced knowledge of the research, theory, and practice relevant to family literacy programs.

This handbook identifies and expands on major topics that have a direct bearing on family literacy, and it provides an in-depth look at many features of family literacy programs. At times, it gives very specific information for practice; at others, it provokes the reader with a discussion of broader social and cultural issues. Its focus ranges from parent–child relationships to procedures for evaluating local programs. Collectively, the authors provide an up-to-date account of the major dimensions of these programs and offer a strong foundation for moving forward.

Parts of this book were prepared under purchase orders number 43-31KV-7-A2-48 and ED-99-PO-4092 from the U.S. Department of Education to conduct a synthesis of research on family literacy programs. Support also came from the National Center for Early Development & Learning, established through a grant from the Office of Educational Research and Improvement to the Frank Porter Graham Child Development Institute at the University of North Carolina at Chapel Hill. The National Center for Early Development & Learning was funded under the Educational Research and Development Centers Program, PR/Award R307A60004.

Many people have contributed during one or more stages in the preparation of this handbook. Individuals with the federal Even Start Family Literacy Office, U.S. Department of Education, gave feedback on the initial set of research papers, especially Patricia McKee, Director of the Even Start Family Literacy Program, and Tracy Rimdzuis, and their help is appreciated. Grover Whitehurst, Director, Institute of Educational Science, was a contributor of the original research synthesis. I deeply appreciate the efforts of Lauren Dickson, Sharon Coleman, Kathleen Bueche, and Marie Butts on manuscript preparation; the editorial assistance of several individuals, including Eva Mamak, Suzannah Herrmann, Diana Kingsley, Leslie Moye, and Jennifer S. Hendrickson; and the contributions of two editorial consultants, Jonathan Wallace of Chapel Hill, NC, and John Swinton of College Station, PA. All of them helped this handbook become a reality. To Lane Akers at Lawrence Erlbaum Associates I give a special thanks for his constant support. My deepest appreciation goes to my husband, John, for his encouragement and patience during my long hours of work on this handbook, and to my three sons, Gregory, Mark, and Jeff, for our years of storybook reading.

About the Authors

Judith A. Alamprese is a principal associate at Abt Associates Inc., where she conducts research, evaluation, and policy studies in adult education and workforce development. Much of her research has focused on implementation of services in basic skills and job training programs, and the resulting adult outcomes. Ms. Alamprese has investigated the effects of comprehensive family literacy services on welfare recipients' development of basic skills and parenting skills, as well as their transition to economic self-sufficiency. She has also evaluated state family literacy systems and the delivery of professional development services. She has served on two National Research Council committees in adult literacy and was a member of the Expert Committee on Adult Education and Family Literacy convened by the National Institute of Child Health and Human Development. In 2002, she received the Kenneth J. Mattran Award from the Commission on Adult Basic Education.

Eunice N. Askov, Ph.D., is Distinguished Professor of Education and Co-Director of the Institute for the Study of Adult Literacy and of the Goodling Institute for Research in Family Literacy, The Pennsylvania State University. She has studied applications of technology in adult literacy programs at South Australia's Flinders University and the University of Western Australia. Named a Distinguished Fellow at Flinders University (1998), Dr. Askov has also received the University of Wisconsin, School of Education Alumni Achievement Award (1994) and the College of Education Career Achievement Award at Penn State (1999). She was the first Literacy Leader Fellow at the National Institute for Literacy in Washington, DC. Dr. Askov chairs the SIG on Adult Literacy and Adult Education in the American Educational Research Association. She is the author of four textbooks on reading instruction and numerous journal articles and book chapters.

Viv Bird has worked since 1994 at the National Literacy Trust, an independent charity that works with others to raise literacy standards in the UK. She was responsible for setting up the Trust's database and information service and launching its quarterly magazine, *Literacy Today*, which she edited until December 2002. Before working at the Trust, Ms. Bird worked in adult basic skills as an outreach worker setting up drop-in classes in disadvantaged areas as well as developing innovative family literacy programs. She is now project director of Literacy and Social Inclusion, a Basic Skills Agency National Support Project delivered by the National Literacy Trust. She is also a consultant to a National Research and Development Centre for Adult Literacy and Numeracy project on community-focused adult basic skills provision. Ms. Bird has been Chair of Governors for the last 8 years of a state secondary school.

Kathryn Bojczyk is a Ph.D. candidate in the Department of Child Development and Family Studies at Purdue University. She received her Master of Science degree in infant motor development from the Department of Health and Kinesiology at Purdue. She is a research assistant and data collection coordinator for Project Literacy, an early childhood educator professional development study at Purdue funded by the U.S. Department of Education. Her research interests include parents' beliefs and practices regarding children's language and literacy development, and the socialization of children's values.

Jeanne Brooks-Gunn, Ph.D., is the Virginia and Leonard Marx Professor of Child Development and Education at Teachers College, Columbia University. Her specialty is policy-oriented research focusing on family and community influences on the development of children and youth. She is the first director of the National Center for Children and Families, founded at Teachers College in 1992. She has directed the Adolescent Study Program at Teachers College and the College of Physicians and Surgeons, Columbia University, and is Co-Director of the Institute for Child and Family Policy at Columbia University. Dr. Brooks-Gunn is an author of over 400 published articles and 17 books. Her awards and honors include: the James McKeen Cattell Fellow Award (2001); the Urie Bronfenbrenner Award (2001); the Distinguished Contributions to Research in Public Policy Award (2001); and the Nicholas Hobbs Award (1997), all from the American Psychological Association; the Vice President's National Performance Review Hammer Award (1998); the John B. Hill Award from the Society for Research on Adolescence (1996); and the William Goode Book Award from the American Sociological Association (1988).

Donna M. Bryant, Ph.D., is a senior scientist at the FPG Child Development Institute at the University of North Carolina at Chapel Hill and a research professor in the School of Education. She co-directs the National Center for Early Development and Learning based at UNC-CH and funded by the Institute for Educational Sciences. She leads the evaluation team for North Carolina's Smart Start initiative and has conducted several studies of center-based child care, family child care, and family and health services. She has directed several studies of early intervention and prevention for children at risk for developmental disabilities. Her current studies with Head Start include the Head Start Quality Research Consortium and a study of mental health interventions for teachers and parents of children with challenging behaviors. She has authored many papers and chapters on early intervention and early childhood education and co-authored books on home visiting and early intervention.

John P. Comings, Ed.D., is a senior research associate and lecturer on education at the Harvard Graduate School of Education and Director of the National Center for the Study of Adult Learning and Literacy (NCSALL). Before coming to Harvard, Dr. Comings spent 12 years as vice president of World Education, a nonprofit agency that supports adult education projects in Asia, Africa, and the United States. He has served as the director of the State Literacy Resource Center in Massachusetts, assisted in the design of instructor training programs, and directed research and development projects in adult education programs. His research concerns the impact of adult literacy programs in the United States and in Third World countries as well as factors that support student persistence in adult education programs in the United States. He is an editor of the *Annual Review of Adult Learning and Literacy* and co-author of two reports on adult learning.

Sharon Darling is president and founder of the National Center for Family Literacy (NCFL). As a pioneer in education, Ms. Darling serves as an advisor on education issues to governors, policymakers, business leaders, and foundations. Her work has helped to shape state and federal policies and laws that address critical issues such as welfare reform, education reform, and workforce development. Her many awards and recognitions include: the National Humanities Medal, awarded by President and Mrs. Bush (2001); the Razor Walker Award from the University of North Carolina, for her contributions to the lives of children and youth (2000); Woman of Distinction Award, Birmingham Southern University (1999); Albert Schweitzer Prize for Humanitarianism, Johns Hopkins University (1998); Charles A. Dana Award for Pioneering Achievement in Education (1996); the Harold W. McGraw Award for Outstanding Educator

(1993); and several honorary doctorate degrees. She has authored numerous publications and articles on intergenerational education.

David K. Dickinson, Ed.D., is an associate professor of Reading and Language Arts at the Lynch School of Education at Boston College. In his research he has studied the contributions of homes and classrooms to the language and early literacy development of children from low-income families. Recently he has focused his energies on developing ways to help preschool teachers better support children's development in classrooms and more effectively help parents foster their child's language and literacy at home.

Dionne R. Dobbins, Ph.D., is a 2002–03 National Head Start Fellow working in the Office of the Associate Commissioner for the Head Start Bureau, where she focuses on issues related to the Head Start reauthorization process, the National Reporting System, Child Outcomes, family literacy, the STEP initiative, and various health initiatives. Dr. Dobbins is on sabbatical from the American Institutes for Research, where her responsibilities included providing support and expertise in the areas of training, child outcomes, adult literacy, qualitative research techniques, writing, and client interaction. Before her position at AIR, she was a Postdoctoral Fellow and served as Project Coordinator for the Carolina Family Literacy Studies in Chapel Hill, NC. In graduate school, she was a Research Assistant at the Linda Ray Intervention Center for Children Prenatally Exposed to Cocaine.

Sharyl Emberton is a director of Special Projects/Training at the National Center for Family Literacy, where she guides the training and technical assistance services provided to the Family and Child Education (FACE) Project, a family literacy program for American Indian families funded by the Bureau of Indian Affairs. Ms. Emberton has worked with families and young children for more than 30 years. Beginning with work in Eastern Kentucky for summer Head Start, she became a family service worker, and later coordinated Health, Nutrition, Special Education, and Family Services. She taught in the public schools, working with at-risk preschool children and their families, and team teaching 5- to 9-year-olds. An endorsed High/Scope Curriculum trainer, she holds degrees in Human Development/Family Studies and Early Elementary Education.

Lori A. Forlizzi, Ph.D., is lead trainer/developer at the TIU Adult Education Program in Lewistown, PA. She has 17 years experience in adult education doing teaching, research, evaluation, instructional materials development, staff development, and continuing education program planning. She has provided training, support, and technical assistance on assessment issues to Pennsylvania adult and family literacy educators for the past 5 years.

Allison Sidle Fuligni, Ph.D., is a research scientist at the UCLA Center for the Improvement of Child Care Quality. She was previously a research scientist at the Center for Children and Families at Teachers College, Columbia University. At the Center for Children and Families, Dr. Fuligni served as project director of the Early Head Start Research and Evaluation Project, a collaboration with Mathematica Policy Research, Inc. She also served as project coordinator for Columbia University's Head Start Quality Research Center. She has authored several review articles on the topic of early education and intervention for economically disadvantaged children and families. Current research topics include patterns of child-care use and quality of child-care settings, impacts of early childhood intervention programs, the transition to parenthood, caregiving in two-parent families, and applications of this work to workplace and social policy.

Vivian L. Gadsden, Ph.D., is associate professor of Education and Director of the National Center on Fathers and Families in the Graduate School of Education at the University of Pennsylvania, where she is Education Graduate Group Chair. Gadsden's research interests and projects focus on intergenerationality within low-income families and its intersections with literacy and learning, early childhood development, parenting, and health and mental health. She has studied low-income, minority fathers and the related problems of race, class, and gender bias. She has numerous publications on literacy within diverse communities, family development, and father involvement. She has testified before Congress on issues related to family literacy, and serves on several Congressionally mandated review boards and committees in organizations including the National Academy of Sciences, Society for Research in Child Development, American Education Research Association, National Reading Conference, International Reading Association.

Carol Scheffner Hammer, Ph.D., is an assistant professor of Communication Sciences and Disorders at The Pennsylvania State University. Her research interests include the language and literacy development of at-risk populations, parental beliefs about children's development, and environmental factors that affect the language and literacy development of children from diverse contexts. Her longitudinal research investigates the language and literacy development of bilingual children attending Head Start and the relationships among the environment and bilingual preschoolers' language and literacy outcomes. This project is funded by the National Institutes of Health-National Institute of Child Health and Human Development.

Peter Hannon, Ph.D., is a professor in the School of Education and member of the Literacy Research Centre at the University of Sheffield, England. His main research and teaching activity is in literacy and early childhood education. He has directed research projects on parental involvement in the teaching of literacy in the early school years, family literacy, preschool literacy development, and community-focused programs for children and adults. He is the author of *Literacy, Home and School* (1995) and *Reflecting on Literacy in Education* (2000).

Gloria L. Harbin, Ph.D., is a research associate professor in Education and a scientist at the FPG Child Development Institute at the University of North Carolina at Chapel Hill. Dr. Harbin directs three research projects that examine coordinated interagency systems of services. She is the lead researcher for collaborative systems and policies in two Research and Training Centers, one on service coordination and one on transition. Dr. Harbin is also the director of a leadership training project for local service system leaders. She has written nine articles and four chapters related to coordinated systems of services. Dr. Harbin has studied and consulted with states and communities across the country.

Darlene M. Head-Reeves is a doctoral student in the Early Childhood, Families, and Literacy Program in the School of Education at the University of North Carolina at Chapel Hill. She received her M.S. degree from Pennsylvania State University in 2001 after completing a master's thesis examining the history of family literacy initiatives in the United States. Her research interests include pathways to optimal cognitive, social, and emotional development of young children, with particular emphasis on the role of families and parents in promoting children's development.

Suzannah Herrmann, M.Ed. (Ph.D.) is a doctoral student at the University of North Carolina at Chapel Hill in the Educational Leadership program (received her doctorate from the Educational Leadership Program at the University of North Carolina at Chapel Hill in Educational Organizations and Policy Studies). She is a consultant to RMC Research Corporation on projects focusing on early literacy and family literacy. She has also worked as a coordinator of the Carolina Family Literacy Studies and the North Carolina Even Start Evaluation. She has participated as a fellow with the Putting Children First Program at Teachers College, Columbia University. Her research interests are child and family policy, family literacy, micropolitics of education, and service integration.

Kim Jacobs is a training and design specialist at the National Center for Family Literacy (NCFL) where she designs, develops, and delivers research-based training for family literacy practitioners. Ms. Jacobs worked as the lead content specialist to develop training for the Head Start Family Literacy Project. She has held positions in education for the past 23 years; she has taught child development, parenting, and family life education; and coordinated a high-school based, comprehensive early childhood school-to-work program. In addition, she has worked as a parent educator and a preschool teacher and has directed several parenting and early intervention programs. Ms. Jacobs holds a Master of Science in Education from the University of Kentucky. She is an NCFL-certified family literacy trainer and an early childhood educator trainer for the state of Kentucky. As a freelance writer, Ms. Jacobs has published numerous essays and articles and several works of novel-length fiction.

Peter Johnston, Ph.D., is a professor in the Reading Department at the University at Albany, State University of New York, and a senior researcher for the National Research Center on English Learning and Achievement. He serves on the editorial boards of *Reading Research Quarterly*, *Journal of Literacy Research*, *Elementary School Journal*, and *Literacy, Teaching and Learning*. He has published five books and numerous articles. His most recent books are *Knowing Literacy* (Stenhouse) and *Reading to Learn: Lessons from Exemplary Fourth Grade Classrooms* (Guilford, with Richard Allington). He chaired the International Reading Association (IRA) and the National Council of Teachers of English (NCTE) Joint Task Force on Assessment that produced the position monograph "Standards for the Assessment of Reading and Writing." He has received awards from the Educational Press Association and from IRA. His currently investigates the consequences of teaching practices for literacy acquisition and how teachers and students build productive literacy learning communities.

Kirsten Kainz is a doctoral student in the Early Childhood, Families, and Literacy program in the School of Education, University of North Carolina at Chapel Hill. Her research interests emphasize educational success and opportunity for all families. She has worked in the field of family literacy as a program director, home visitor, and teacher.

Wendy K. Lam, Ph.D., is a senior research psychologist at RTI International. She has more than a decade of clinical and research experience with underserved children and families at risk. At RTI, Dr. Lam is the principal investigator for a CDC-funded study of adolescent children of African American crack users. As a co-investigator for two NIDA-funded community-based intervention programs for African American substance abusers, Dr. Lam focuses on clients' parenting and child issues. She is involved with the National Evaluation of the Safe Schools, Healthy Students Initiative, assisting with study design, sampling, implementation, analyses, and dissemination. She also serves as a trainer for the Preschool Curriculum Evaluation Research program. Before joining RTI, Dr. Lam assisted with evaluations of community-based and comprehensive service systems for infant mortality and early childhood programs.

Christopher J. Lonigan, Ph.D., is a professor of psychology at Florida State University and associate director of the Florida Center for Reading Research. His research focuses primarily on the development of emergent literacy skills during the preschool period and how these skills affect later reading. He also studies evaluations of preschool interventions and curricula designed to prevent reading difficulties for preschool children who are at risk for later academic problems, psychiatric disorders in children, and the overlap between psychiatric disorders and problems in reading. His research has been funded from the National Institute of Child Health and Human Development, the U.S Department of Education, the Administration for Children Youth and Families, and the National Science Foundation. He has served on numerous boards and committees for the American Psychological Association, including the Committee for the Promotion of Evidence-Based Practice for Children. Dr. Lonigan is a member of the National Early Literacy Panel and serves on the editorial board of several journals.

Kimberly D. McDowell is a doctoral student in Communication Disorders at Florida State University. She is a licensed speech-language pathologist and former kindergarten teacher. Her research interests include emergent literacy, relations between expressive phonology and phonological sensitivity, and home-based interventions for preschool children with communication impairments.

Adele W. Miccio, Ph.D., is associate professor of Communication Sciences and Disorders and Applied Linguistics at The Pennsylvania State University and a visiting scholar at the Harvard University Graduate School of Education. Her research interests include phonological development and disorders and the phonological aspects of literacy development in children at risk. Dr. Miccio's current longitudinal research projects examine the relationship between phonological development and emerging literacy in children in poverty and second-language literacy acquisition and are funded by the National Institutes of Health-National Institute of Child Health and Human Development.

Lesley Mandel Morrow, Ph.D., is a professor at Rutgers University's Graduate School of Education, where she is coordinator of the literacy program. Her research dealing with early literacy development and the organization and management of language arts programs is carried out with children from diverse backgrounds. Dr. Morrow has more than 200 publications, including journal articles, chapters in books, monographs, and books. Three of her most recent are *Organization and Management of the Language Arts Block*; *Literacy Development in the Early Years: Helping Children Read and Write, 4th edition* (Allyn & Bacon), and *The Literacy Center: Contexts for Reading and Writing, 2nd edition* (Stenhouse Publishers). Dr. Morrow has received numerous grants for her research and has served as a principal research investigator for several research centers. She is an advisor to the High Scope Research Institute on Early Literacy. She is president of the International Reading Association for 2003 to 2004.

Lynn Okagaki, Ph.D., is professor of Child Development and Family Studies at Purdue University. Her research has focused on parenting among minority families, minority children's school achievement, and the socialization of children's values. Her work has been supported by the Spencer Foundation, the McDonnell Foundation, and the National Science Foundation. She has served on the National Science Foundation's Developmental and Learning Sciences panel, the National Research Council's Committee on Early Childhood Pedagogy, and on the editorial boards of the *Early Childhood Research Quarterly* and the *Journal of Applied Developmental Psychology.*

Barbara Alexander Pan, Ph.D., is a research associate and lecturer on education at the Harvard Graduate School of Education. She is trained as a developmental psychologist, and her major research interests are in language and literacy acquisition of first- and second-language learners in the broader context of their social and cognitive development. She investigates child, home, intergenerational, and sociocultural factors related to children's preparation for the language and literacy demands of school.

Julia Pettengill is a researcher for the Massachusetts Society for the Prevention of Cruelty to Children in their Center for Evaluation and Research with Children and Adolescents (CERCA). She has an academic background in languages, educational development, and literacy. Her professional experience ranges across various educational settings in Southern Africa and the United States. Ms. Pettengill spent 2 years working for the Education Development Center, Inc.'s Center for Children and Families. Her work with children and families on the Technology Enhanced Literacy Enriched Environment Program (T-LEEP) at EDC inspired her contribution to this handbook.

Beth M. Phillips is a doctoral candidate in clinical psychology at Florida State University. She received her M.S. in psychology from Florida State in 2000 and her B.S. in psychology from Duke University in 1995. Ms. Phillips' research interests are in the areas of assessment and intervention of early literacy skills with preschool children, behavioral regulation, temperament, and childhood anxiety disorders. She recently completed a 2-year research grant from the Head Start Bureau of the Department of Health and Human Services investigating behavioral inhibition and impulsivity in children. Ms. Phillips also conducts research on the overlap between preschool children's behavior and their emergent literacy skills. She is a co-author of publications on emergent literacy and child anxiety disorders.

Robert C. Pianta, Ph.D., is a professor in The Curry School of Education's Programs in Clinical and School Psychology at the University of Virginia and holds the William Clay Parrish Jr. Chair in Education. A former special education teacher, he is a developmental, school, and clinical child psychologist whose work focuses on how children's experiences at home and in school affect their development. He is interested in how relationships with teachers and parents, as well as classroom quality, can help improve outcomes for at-risk children and youth. Dr. Pianta is a principal investigator on the National Institute of Child Health and Human Development Study of Early Child Care and Youth Development, a senior investigator with the National Center for Early Development and Learning, and editor of the *Journal of School Psychology*. He has authored over 200 journal articles, chapters, and books on early childhood development, school readiness, and parent–child and teacher–child relationships.

Meta Potts, Ed.D., heads her own consulting agency, FOCUS on Literacy, and consults with the National Center for Family Literacy (NCFL) and the National Institute for Literacy as a National Certified Facilitator for the Equipped for the Future Initiative. She was the first director of Adult Learning Services for the National Center for Family Literacy and also served as director of the NCFL Family and Child Education (FACE) Program for the Bureau of Indian Affairs and as director of Training Research and Development.

Douglas R. Powell, Ph.D., is Distinguished Professor in the Department of Child Development and Family Studies at Purdue University. His research focuses on parenting interventions and early childhood educator professional development aimed at strengthening children's literacy development and academic competence. He is former editor of the *Early Childhood Research Quarterly,* former research editor of *Young Children,* and past chair of the American Educational Research Association's early education/child development special interest group. He is co-developer of the Even Start Family Literacy Program's guidelines for parenting education and author of numerous scholarly publications.

Victoria Purcell-Gates, Ph.D., is professor of Language and Literacy in the College of Education at Michigan State University. She conducts research on emergent and family literacy, adult literacy, and literacy learning in schools. She has published in numerous journals and is an active conference speaker on literacy issues. Her books include *Other People's Words: The Cycle of Low Literacy* (Harvard University Press, 1995), which was awarded the prestigious Grawemeyer Award in Education "for contribution toward making the world a better place," and *Now We Read, We See, We Speak: Portrait of Literacy Development in a Freirean-Based Adult Class* (Lawrence Erlbaum Associates, 2000). She is finishing a book on literacy development as it occurs both within schools and in use in the community, to be published by Harvard University Press in 2004.

Anne Ricciuti, Ph.D., is an associate at Abt Associates Inc. For the past 6 years, Dr. Ricciuti, a developmental psychologist by training, has been Deputy Project Director of the Third National Evaluation of Even Start. In addition, she has been a senior staff member on a study of the state administration of Even Start. Dr. Ricciuti has also been involved in evaluations of Title I and of the Comprehensive Child Development Program.

Flora V. Rodríguez-Brown, Ph.D., is a professor in Curriculum and Instruction at the University of Illinois at Chicago. She coordinates the teacher training programs for teachers of second-language learners and teaches courses in bilingualism and literacy, home-school connections, and learning in and out of school. She has been involved in family literacy with the Latino community in Chicago through Project FLAME since 1989. Her research interests are in literacy and second-language learning, learning at home, sociocultural issues in literacy learning, and the home–school connection.

Kathleen A. Roskos, Ph.D., is a professor at John Carroll University, where she teaches courses in reading education and reading diagnosis. She studies early literacy development, teacher cognition, and the design of professional education for teachers. Dr. Roskos has published research articles on these topics in leading journals, co-authored or co-edited several books related to early literacy development in children, and contributed chapters to books on early literacy, including several in research handbooks. She is a member of the IRA Publications Committee, a leader in the LDYC SIG of IRA, and a member of several local and regional professional boards. Dr. Roskos is the director of the Ohio Literacy Initiative at the Ohio Department of Education, and in this role coordinates K–12 literacy projects statewide and advises the Superintendent of Public Instruction on literacy issues and policy.

Catherine E. Snow, Ph.D., is the Henry Lee Shattuck Professor at the Harvard Graduate School of Education. She chaired the National Research Council Committee that produced *Preventing Reading Difficulties in Young Children* (1998), and the RAND Reading Study Group that wrote *Reading for Understanding: Towards an R&D Agenda for Reading* (2001). She is involved in research on the role of transfer from first- to second-language literacy, and in work to inform the design of teacher education for teachers of reading.

Joseph Sparling, Ph.D., is adjunct professor at Georgetown University and a retired fellow at the Frank Porter Graham Child Development Institute at the University of North Carolina at Chapel Hill. Professor Sparling was responsible for designing the child intervention component of three longitudinal intervention studies: the Abecedarian Project, Project CARE, and the Infant Health and Development Program. Each of these interventions produced improved literacy skills in young children.

Robert G. St.Pierre, Ph.D., is a vice president and principal associate in the Education and Family Support Area of Abt Associates Inc. Since 1975, he has been principal investigator for educational research, evaluation, and policy analysis projects spanning diverse areas such as family literacy, family support, child development, compensatory education, curricular interventions, school health education, and child nutrition. He is principal investigator for national evaluations of the Even Start Family Literacy Program and the Title I Preschool program and recently directed a national evaluation of the Comprehensive Child Development Program (the forerunner of Early Head Start). He reviews articles for several evaluation journals and has recently published in *Early Childhood Research Quarterly*, the *American Journal of Evaluation*, the *Future of Children*, and the *SRCD Social Policy Monograph* series.

John Strucker, Ed.D., is a research associate at the National Center for the Study of Adult Learning and Literacy (NCSALL) and lecturer in Education at the Harvard University Graduate School of Education. He is the principal investigator of NCSALL's Adult Reading Components Study and the NCSALL's Level 1 Project, a collaboration with Educational Testing Service. He teaches a laboratory practicum course at Harvard, "Developing Reading in Adults and Older Adolescents." Before joining NCSALL, he was an adult literacy and ESOL teacher for the City of Cambridge, MA, for 11 years, specializing in the diagnostic assessment and teaching of adults with reading disabilities. In addition to family literacy, his research interests include teacher training, adult vocabulary acquisition, and the application of technology to adult literacy.

Fumiyo Tao, senior associate at Abt Associates Inc., is working on several studies related to family literacy programs, including the Even Start Classroom Literacy Intervention and Outcomes Study and the Study of State Administration of the Even Start Program. For the last 10 years, Dr. Tao has played a key role in the Even Start national evaluation. She directed the second national evaluation, including the design and implementation of the evaluation data collection system in all local Even Start projects. Dr. Tao has also evaluated a program sponsored by the National Center for Family Literacy to provide work-focused family literacy services to families as a welfare-to-work strategy.

Jessica Temlock-Fields is a second-grade teacher in the Bridgewater, NJ, public schools and has taught both primary and intermediate grades over the past 7 years. She serves on the literacy team in her school and has published an article in *Highlights for Children Parent Involvement Newsletter.* She has been credited for her work in two books by fellow handbook contributor Lesley Morrow. She is completing her master's degree in Literacy at Rutgers University and will also receive a Reading Specialist Certification.

Sandra Twardosz, Ph.D., is a professor in the Department of Child and Family Studies at the University of Tennessee, Knoxville. Her current research focuses the resources of childcare environments to promote children's and teachers' involvement with books. Past research areas include the expression of affection in adult–child and peer relationships and the impact of environmental organization on behavior. Recent publications have appeared in *Early Education and Development, Early Childhood Research Quarterly, Journal of Research in Childhood Education,* and *American Annals of the Deaf.* She consults regularly with Head Start centers, is a board member of the Center for Children's and Young Adult Literature at the University of Tennessee, and is active in the International Reading Association and the National Reading Conference.

Barbara Van Horn is co-director of the Institute for the Study of Adult Literacy and Goodling Institute for Research in Family Literacy, both in the College of Education at Pennsylvania State University. Ms. Van Horn has directed Pennsylvania's statewide family literacy evaluation since 1998 and coordinated Pennsylvania's statewide Even Start Initiative. As part of the Even Start Initiative, she and her staff developed Family Literacy Indicators of Program Quality and drafted Family Literacy Performance Indicators based on data collected in the statewide evaluation. Prior work has included development of a manual on adult assessment within the context of the adult basic education system.

Lynne Vernon-Feagans, Ph.D., is the William C. Friday Distinguished Professor in Child Development and Family Studies in the School of Education at the University of North Carolina at Chapel Hill. Her research has focused on children's development of language and emergent literacy skills. She has had a particular interest in children's home and school experiences during the transition to school. Her book about the Abecedarian Early Intervention Project described the home and school environment for the children in this study during their first 3 years in school. She is the principal investigator of an NICHD program project that will document the individual differences in the early development of 1,200 very young children and their families who come from diverse ethnic and economic backgrounds with an emphasis on understanding the early language and literacy experiences of the children at home and in childcare.

Heide Spruck Wrigley, Ph.D., is senior researcher for Language, Literacy and Learning for Aguirre International, a social science research firm. She was the key content specialist for two federally funded studies, the National Study on What Works in ESL Literacy (completed in 2003) and Promising Practices in ESL Literacy, the only national studies in the United States focused exclusively on adult ESL. Her family literacy work includes a research and demonstration project on the U.S.–Mexico border that combines literacy for bilingual families with ESL and civics in a model focused on technology and project-based learning. She has provided technical assistance to many family literacy programs. Her international experience includes work in Poland, Egypt, Germany, and Canada, where she is the research director for a national demonstration project on Youth Literacy, funded by the Literacy Secretariat.

Elizabeth Yanoff is a doctoral student in Reading at the University at Albany, State University of New York, and a researcher with the National Research Center on English Learning and Achievement. She received her master's in education (1997) from the University of Illinois at Urbana-Champaign and her bachelor's in psychology (1992) from Swarthmore College. She has taught both preschool and elementary school, and her current research interests center on young children's literacy development in families and schools.

I

Overview of Family Literacy:
Development, Concepts, and Practice

This section looks at family literacy through a broad lens, covering concepts, developments, and practice in both the United States and England. It is intended to help the reader put into perspective 20 years of developments that have contributed to interest in family literacy practices and family literacy programs and to see a longer history of interest in family literacy.

In these two chapters, we define and expand basic concepts, including literacy, family, and family literacy, and we note how these have changed over time and influenced views of family literacy. Literacy is no longer a narrow concept that includes only one's ability to read and write, nor is it seen as a skill one develops only after entrance into formal education. Rather, literacy begins during a child's early years in the informal activities of everyday family life.

In chapter 1, we describe the range of services that fall under the broad heading of family literacy programs, including child-focused and adult-focused programs. Next we delve more deeply into comprehensive family literacy programs and especially the Even Start Family Literacy Programs, the largest comprehensive family literacy program in the United States. We discuss factors that contributed to the rise of family literacy programs, including concern over the relation between poverty and children's literacy skills; literature that shows the importance of the early years in children's literacy development; concern over low literacy skills among adults, including those who are parents of young children; and demographic changes that have brought large numbers of English-language learners to the United States. We also touch on conceptual frameworks behind family literacy programs, especially those of ecological theory, family systems theory, and parenting, as well as theories of emergent literacy. A description of family literacy programs covers both those that focus on one family member and those that provide more comprehensive services. Finally, a timeline notes the occurrence of significant funding, legislation, and evaluation efforts that have influenced family literacy programs in the United States over the last 20 years.

Peter Hannon and Viv Bird bring an international perspective to this overview by describing developments in England over a similar period. Though they note the considerable influence that U.S. models have had, they look at factors within England that have influenced both research studies and program implementation. They allow the reader to compare developments in the two countries, noting several parallels. For one, both have relatively constant funding streams and both have organizations that strongly promote family literacy. For another, leading programs in both countries define family literacy using nearly identical four-component models. In contrast to the United States, however, work in England is clearly built on a foundation of very strong early childhood education programs. Thus, work was needed to bring adult education and literacy into comprehensive programs.

English researchers have conducted a considerable amount of research on family literacy, but, as in the United States, many of these studies use a quasiexperimental design or pretest and posttest comparison. Nevertheless, the overall results show positive outcomes. Yet they also lack data to help determine whether programs offered in combination are more beneficial than those offered separately. Hannon and Bird identify challenges to family literacy in England that include funding, program flexibility, professional development, and the need for research and evaluation. Similar challenges face U.S. programs, and they are discussed in many of the handbook's chapters, particularly in the concluding chapters in Section IX.

These two chapters set the stage for more intensive examination of the components of family literacy programs, variables that influence child and adult literacy acquisition, conceptual issues, implementation issues, and recommendations for research on family literacy practices and family literacy programs.

1

Family Literacy: History, Concepts, Services

Barbara Hanna Wasik
Suzannah Herrmann
University of North Carolina at Chapel Hill

Our fascination with how literacy and language skills develop and our concern when children and adults experience difficulty in obtaining these skills have led to intensive studies of the roots of literacy. This exploration has taken us to families, the setting in which almost everyone learns the basic skills that form the foundation for later learning. Writers and researchers have examined family practices, beliefs, and resources to understand how families support literacy development. At the same time, they have studied these practices, beliefs, and resources to learn how literacy skills might best develop within families.

The authors of this volume take a look at family literacy from many different angles, providing a rich set of theories, data, and conclusions related to the development of literacy skills in both children and adults. Some examine formal and informal learning strategies that help both children and adults gain literacy skills. Others address related issues, including how family culture and language skills interact with literacy, the role of formal family literacy services, and assessment and evaluation. In this chapter, we address both historical and contemporary events influencing today's concepts related to family literacy and to family services focused on literacy acquisition. We reserve the phrase *family literacy* for literacy beliefs and practices among family members and the intergenerational transfer of literacy to children. We also use this phrase to describe studies of how young children become literate, including the relations between family literacy practices and children's literacy and language development (Leichter, 1984). We will use the terms *family literacy services* or *family literacy programs* to refer to interventions that enhance family members' literacy skills through an intergenerational focus. But before discussing those topics, we must consider how literacy itself has been defined.

LITERACY

Literacy is conventionally defined as the ability to read and write, and references to *a literate person* imply such ability. Literacy has also been conceptualized as a set of complex, multidimensional skills that begin at birth and develop over a person's life from childhood to adulthood. To be literate requires knowledge of letter–word correspondence as well as word

3

recognition, and includes knowledge of one's environment, which is necessary to comprehend what is read (Snow, Barnes, Chandler, Goodman, & Hemphill, 1991).

Though our culture puts considerable stress on acquiring literacy, we do not readily agree on literacy's definition, as illustrated by the conclusions of a symposium on preschool children and literacy held in the early 1980s. Goelman (1984) notes that participants came to the symposium with wide variations in definitions of literacy; some focused on what someone needs to know to be literate; others, on what someone who is literate can do. Rather than exclude any definition, participants agreed to define literacy as "patterns of discourse," a global definition did not lend direction to the field (Goelman, 1984).

During the past decade, as researchers have examined its mechanisms of social support, literacy has been recognized as a much more complex process than previously believed (Snow & Tabors, 1996); as a result, more detailed definitions have been considered. For example, a 1998 report of the National Research Council describes literacy as including not only reading and writing but also other creative or analytic acts (Snow, Burns, & Griffin, 1998). Other, broader definitions of literacy can be seen in federal legislation. In 1991, the National Literacy Act defined literacy as "an individual's ability to read, write, and speak in English, and compute and solve problems at levels of proficiency necessary to function on the job and in society, to achieve one's goals and develop one's knowledge and potential." The Workforce Investment Act of 1998 expanded this definition to include the ability to function in the family (National Center for Family Literacy [NCFL], 2000).

These legislative definitions reflect the adult learner's needs as worker, parent, family member, citizen, and community member. They are consistent with the expanded concept of adult literacy found in the National Institute for Literacy's Equipped for the Future (EFF) project. EFF identifies four standards, or categories of skills, that adults need in order to conduct their primary roles in life: communication skills, decision-making skills, interpersonal skills, and lifelong learning skills.

Although some have struggled to define the term, Gee (2001) questions whether there is such a general thing as literacy. Rather, he has argued that people adopt "ways with printed words" within different sociocultural practices for different purposes and functions and that these "ways with printed words . . . are always integrally and inextricably integrated with ways of talking, thinking, believing, knowing, acting, interacting, valuing, and feeling" (Gee, 2001, p. 30). Thus, views of literacy seem to be evolving away from a narrow focus on reading and writing toward a more encompassing definition that seeks to capture literacy's social and cultural aspects as well as individual characteristics and immediate contexts.

We see, then, that literacy can be described both as a natural or informal occurrence seen in everyday situations and experienced in home, family, and community life (Allison & Watson, 1994) and (the more common view) as a formal occurrence in the context of organized instruction in educational settings (Wasik, Dobbins, & Herrmann, 2001). Viewing literacy as a natural development is consistent with the view of literacy as a social practice integrated with other social practices (Delgado-Gaitan, 1994; Gee, 2001; Pellegrini, 2001; Street, 1984) and has direct relevance for family literacy research and services. Because many family literacy services include center-based educational settings for parent, child, or both, knowledge about literacy's formal occurrence is also pertinent to family literacy programs, as well as to those who study the intergenerational transfer of literacy. In the following section we describe the informal development of literacy within a developmental perspective.

Literacy as a Developmental Phenomenon

In 2 decades of studies on the development of natural literacy, researchers have constructed a set of beliefs about how children read and write before receiving formal instruction, a phenomenon now referred to as *emergent literacy* or *early literacy*. The term *emergent literacy* was derived from Clay's (1993) observational study of children's emerging reading behavior. Rather than seeing schools as the first or sole setting for children's literacy development, Clay and others recognized emergent literacy skills as developed during the preschool years and as influenced by both home literacy environment and parent–child interactions. More recently, the term *early literacy* has also been used to describe the same phenomenon (Neuman & Dickinson, 2001).

Emergent literacy encompasses the skills, knowledge, and attitudes believed to be the developmental precursors to reading and writing (Sulzby & Teale, 1991; Teale & Sulzby, 1986). Lonigan and Whitehurst (2001; Whitehurst & Lonigan, 1998) note the importance of supportive environments such as shared book reading in the development of emergent literacy skills. Emergent literacy is also based on the assumption that learning to read and write is a social and cultural process as well as a cognitive one. In Section II, Lonigan and Sparling each elaborates on the development of early literacy, whereas Morrow and Temlock-Fields show that through interacting with literacy events, children learn from adults who provide opportunities to experience literacy's functions and roles. Purcell-Gates also emphasizes the importance of knowledge about storybook reading in children's early literacy development.

The attention devoted to emergent literacy has produced an increased interest in variables that affect the child's literacy development, including parental, social, and cultural influences. In Section VII, Gadsden; Vernon-Feagans, Head-Reeves, and Kainz; and Wrigley examine how culture and literacy interact. In addition, researchers have studied how early literacy knowledge and skills are related to later reading and achievement in school. Research supporting correlations between children's literacy knowledge and skills at school entrance and their later school success (Wasik & Hendrickson, in press) has prompted additional attention to early literacy and the role of early childhood education in literacy development.

Concern that children were receiving less support at home than they needed for school success greatly influenced the development of early childhood programs, but these programs must be of high quality and must specifically address literacy in order to bring about significant child outcomes. In Section II, Fuligni and Brooks-Gunn take a detailed look at the characteristics and outcomes of stand-alone early childhood education programs and those offered as part of family literacy programs, noting the importance of ensuring high quality. Also in Section II, Dickinson, St.Pierre, and Pettengill review existing early childhood education in family literacy programs as well as Head Start early childhood programs and conclude that we must have intensive programs focused on growth in multiple dimensions in order to bring about significant outcomes for children.

Our country's increasing linguistic diversity has prompted analyses of the relations between acquisition of one's native language and acquisition of a second language by children and adults. In earlier years, less attention was devoted to helping English-language learners (ELL) acquire new skills and to helping them maintain their own language. Hammer and Miccio, in Section V, and Strucker, Snow, and Pan; and Wrigley, in Section VII, probe issues of language diversity, including how language and culture interact, the needs of second-language learners, and the importance of attending to culture as much as language when addressing the needs of ELL children and adults.

Literacy development is not limited to children. It occurs across the life span and, for adults, it can occur in the informal settings of home and community as well as in more formal settings. Think, for example, of a bilingual family in which one family member, a child or adult, translates a conversation for another member, labels objects, or helps with pronunciation. Think of when one adult asks another the meaning of a word. In Section IV, Comings, Alamprese, and Askov elaborate on the need for and the processes involved in adult education and literacy development in family literacy programs. Gadsden; Vernon-Feagans,

Head-Reeves, and Kainz; and Wrigley, in Section VII, illustrate many ways literacy is supported within families.

Family

Examining family literacy requires us to consider the meaning not only of literacy but also of *family*. For much of the 20th century, the term *family* referred to two parents and their children living in the same household. Our contemporary understanding is much broader. Two-parent families; one-parent families; blended families; extended families, adults, and children living in one household; and other individuals living together who call themselves family—All are captured by the term family. An understanding of this wider definition of family is necessary to understand how broad the concept of family literacy has become and to understand the breadth of services provided under the heading of family literacy programs.

The National Center for Family Literacy's description of families eligible for literacy services illustrates this broader view:

> For the families that [a] family literacy [program] intends to serve, boundaries of the traditional family structure are often expanded to include siblings and extended family members, custodial grandparents, neighbors and friends, or legal guardians . . . Families can encompass aunts, uncles, foster parents, grandparents, legal guardians, brothers and sisters, neighbors or other members of the community, grandchildren, nieces, nephews, cousins, and foster children; they can be of one ethnicity or several; they can live together in one housing structure, or sometimes they can live separate from one another, yet maintain a constant relationship. (King and McMaster, 2000, p. 14)

Thus, we see that references to family are increasingly inclusive, recognizing and accepting a myriad of constellations of people. This broader idea of family has a direct bearing on the study of literacy within families and the provision of family literacy services.

Family Literacy

For many years, anthropologists and sociologists have studied the family's role as educator, in societies ranging from nonliterate to highly literate. Furthermore, they have often used a broad definition of family, including extended families in their studies (Leichter, 1974).

In the past, educators varied in the weight given to the family's role in children's literacy acquisition. Indeed, there were times when the family was expected to help children begin to read (Mathews, 1966). In the mid-1900s, however, educators not only came to see parents in a more restricted role but also actually discouraged them from teaching their children. Educating children became the role of formal education, and schools were viewed as the place where children begin to learn to read and write. There was also an emphasis on children's readiness to read (Gesell, 1925). Educators believed that it was harmful for children to be taught before they were physically mature and ready to learn. Such beliefs affected decisions about when children should enter school; they were kept at home until they were considered physically ready to learn to read.

Our present understanding of children's literacy development—which recognizes the importance of home and community as settings for development prior to formal education—has received increasing support, beginning as early as the 1960s and 1970s. (Goodman, 1980; Leichter, 1979, 1984). Goodman was one of the first to describe the importance of the home environment, calling written language in books, letters, and newspapers the "roots of literacy" for children.

Throughout the 1980s, researchers who addressed questions of the family's influence on children's language and literacy provided additional support for the idea of literacy as an ongoing phenomenon of family life. These researchers produced important data on children's literacy development, but they also contributed to the theoretical shift toward an emergent literacy approach, emphasizing that children's literacy development takes place over time and that a considerable amount of literacy development occurs in homes and communities prior to entrance into school. Among these studies are the ethnographic works of Heath (1983), Taylor (1983), Taylor and Dorsey-Gaines (1988), Taylor and Strickland (1986), and Snow et al. (1991). These writings provide a rich depiction of how families communicate among themselves and with other groups and of the importance of family and community in literacy development.

Using ethnographic procedures, Heath (1983) studied children in three communities in the Piedmont area of North Carolina—including White working-class, Black working-class, and middle-class children who were learning to use language—observing strikingly different "ways with words" among children from different communities. Taylor (1983) provided insight into the ways children successfully learn to read and write through their participation in the everyday experiences of family life. Taylor and Strickland (1986) offered further valuable ethnographic accounts of family storybook reading time, showing the special role that storybook reading plays in family life as well as in the development of language and literacy skills. Snow and her colleagues (Snow et al., 1991) examined factors that influence literacy development in a group of low-income, ethnically diverse children, finding most families in their study were highly committed to their children's educational success. These early ethnographers changed our views about how literacy develops and about the role of family and culture in children's literacy development.

Other researchers also influenced our views about family and culture. Tharp and Gallimore (1988), writing in *Rousing Minds to Life*, pull from a rich array of theories in their culturally sensitive discussion of children in schools. In particular, they draw attention to the disparities between literacy interactions in the home and those in school. Moll (1990), Reese and Gallimore (2000), and Rogers (2002) have expanded our understanding of the need to consider the home literacy environment when planning for children in activities in school settings. Collectively these authors have influenced classroom instructional practices. Their ideas appear throughout the chapters in this handbook. An example is the chapter by Rodriguez-Brown, in Section III, in which she expands on these home–school relations as she discusses parenting education for Latino families.

As research on family literacy expanded, efforts were made to capture the concept's meaning. The Family Literacy Commission describes family literacy this way:

> Family literacy encompasses the ways parents, children, and extended family members use literacy at home and in their community. Sometimes, family literacy occurs naturally during the routines of daily living and helps adults and children "get things done." These events might include using drawings or writings to share ideas; composing notes or letters to communicate messages; making lists; reading and following directions; or sharing stories and ideas through conversation, reading, and writing. Family literacy may be initiated purposefully by a parent or may occur spontaneously as parents and children go about the business of their daily lives. (cited in Morrow, 1995)

A report summarizing a symposium for developing a family literacy research agenda again took a broad approach. It defined family literacy as both "the set of oral, graphic, and symbolic means by which family members exchange and retain information and meaning" and "the general level at which family members use their writing, reading, computing, communication, and problem solving skills to accomplish the various tasks of their daily lives" (Benjamin & Lord, 1996, p. 1).

In summary, although family literacy interventions are of relatively recent origin, family literacy as a phenomenon of family life has long been acknowledged and appreciated. Today there is relatively widespread recognition of the family's importance in children's development of early literacy skills and dispositions toward reading and writing, an appreciation for both informal and formal literacy practices in homes. In the following section we consider how family literacy services have been defined. Then we look at influences on the development of these programs.

FAMILY LITERACY SERVICES

Family literacy services are a fairly recent phenomenon within the broader scope of early childhood and adult education endeavors. They have captured the attention of educators, practitioners, policymakers, and researchers because of their potential to address compelling issues of literacy and language competence for both children and adults. At the same time, they have fostered intense debates on the meaning of family literacy and efforts to provide intervention services for families (Auerbach, 1989; Taylor, 1997).

As noted earlier, an important distinction exists between family literacy per se and family literacy services or programs. Family literacy refers to beliefs and interactions within families that have served across the centuries to foster language and literacy among their members. Most children will develop in their own homes the foundation needed to benefit from more formal literacy instruction in educational settings. Not all home settings, however, provide such opportunities for children. Even with school attendance, some children grow into adulthood without the reading and writing skills that are essential in contemporary society. Family literacy programs developed from an awareness that many children and adults were not well prepared for success in school or in the workplace.

Over the past 40 years, efforts have been made to address these concerns, including early childhood education, parenting education, and adult education. Many such efforts have been summarized in reviews or books. For example, Farran (1990, 2001), Barnett (2001), Bryant and Maxwell (1997), and Olds and Kitzman (1993), as well as Fuligni and Brooks-Gunn; and Dickinson, St.Pierre, and Pettengill in this volume, analyze early childhood education efforts.

Parenting education also has a long history. Included as part of Project Head Start from its beginning (Zigler & Valentine, 1990), parent education continues to play a central role in efforts to enhance child outcomes through parent–child interactions. It is at the center of almost all home-based intervention programs such as Early Head Start, Parents as Teachers, and Home Instruction for Parents of Preschool Children, and it is a basic component of the Even Start Family Literacy program. Powell, Pianta, Kelly, and Rodriguez-Brown, in Section III of this book, take a critical look at parenting education and offer strategies to make it relevant and effective.

Adult education and literacy services include adult basic education, adult secondary education for learners earning a high school diploma or the GED, and instruction for English-language learners. In Section IV of this handbook Comings, Alamprese, and Askov discuss the role of adult education in our society, noting changing views and needs. They address the interface of family literacy with adult education and workplace literacy and provide recommendations for improving adult education services within family literacy programs.

The term family literacy program describes a range of interventions devoted to child and adult literacy. These programs may address the needs of children, their parents, or both; provide direct or indirect services; focus on only one parent–child dyad or support a parent's interactions with more than one child; and take place in the home, in centers, in schools, or in the workplace. Interventions describing themselves as family literacy programs also include intergenerational programs in which nonrelated individuals participate (Smith, 1995), such as in a foster grandparent program.

Comprehensive family literacy programs, which offer all of the following components— early childhood education, adult education, parenting education and support, and parent–child literacy interactions—are a major focus of this handbook. They include the PACE program, the Kenan model, and the Even Start Family Literacy model. Before describing these more targeted programs, we will examine some of the influences that have fostered interest in family literacy services.

INFLUENCES ON THE DEVELOPMENT OF FAMILY LITERACY PROGRAMS

A number of factors have sparked interest in providing family literacy programs. They include the strong correlation among (a) literacy skills with parental education levels and poverty, (b) theoretical concepts about children's development and increased recognition of the family's role, (c) the growing body of evidence demonstrating a strong relation between the home environment and children's literacy development, and (d) the need for educational agencies to provide opportunities for learning English due to the increasing number of English-language learners. A thread that connects all these influences is the concern that when children do not develop strong literacy skills, they are at risk for school failure and for becoming adults who are not able to reach economic self-sufficiency or to promote literacy and language in their own children.

Literacy, Parental Educational Levels, and Poverty

One of the most frequently identified concerns behind family literacy programs is the large number of children and families living in poverty (Chase-Lansdale & Brooks-Gunn, 1995). Despite the economic successes of recent years, 13 million children still fall below the poverty line. In the areas of health, cognitive development, school achievement, and emotional well-being, children suffer from several negative life events associated with poverty (Duncan & Brooks-Gunn, 1997). Poverty is also associated with children's literacy levels; reading difficulties occur more often among poor, non-White, and non-native English-speaking children (Snow et al., 1998). This lower performance in literacy skills occurs at both the preschool and the early primary levels (Dickinson & Sprague, 2001). Furthermore, children with low literacy skills are not only less prepared for school but also perform poorly in later elementary grades (Juel, 1988) and high school (Cunningham & Stanovich, 1998). In this volume, Lonigan and Vernon-Feagans, Head-Reeves, and Kainz examine the relations between poverty and children's literacy.

   Many of these children continue to have low literacy skills when they reach adulthood. Adults with low literacy skills are more likely to be poor, earn a lower income, be frequently unemployed, participate in crime, and be in poor health. (Certainly, not all adults with low literacy skills have these characteristics. Many are gainfully employed, and many lead productive and satisfying lives, supporting their families and contributing to their communities.)

   Adults with low literacy skills are also parents of young children. According to a 1998 report by the National Institute for Literacy, 21 to 23% of American adults read at a low literacy level. Such adults can perform only tasks involving simple text and documents, and they display difficulty in reading, writing, and computational skills integral to everyday life (see Strucker, Snow, & Pan, Section VII). Providing an intergenerational program for parents with low literacy skills offers an opportunity for a more inclusive and integrated set of services that can enhance positive life course outcomes for their children as well as expand their own choices.

Theoretical Influences

Family literacy programs emerged more from a set of beliefs and assumptions about the intergenerational nature of literacy within families than from an explicit theoretical framework. One belief was that working with parents and children together would make it possible for parents to help their children, thus reducing the risk of school failure (Brizius & Foster, 1993). Another was that "a high-quality, developmentally appropriate early childhood program that is enhanced by parents who value the model of learning and being educated . . ." (Hayes, n.d., p. 17) would best meet the needs of children in low-literate families. Darling, in Section IX, identifies concepts basic to family systems theory and recognizes the importance of sound instructional practices in guiding initial program development efforts.

The belief that parents play an important role in children's literacy has influenced many efforts in the course of the last century, including the early intervention programs of the 1960s and 1970s (Brooks-Gunn, Berlin, & Fuligni, 2000). Many of these early efforts offered parent education as a way to reach children, often through home visiting programs, or provided center-based early childhood education services. Early intervention programs with an adult focus generally addressed parenting skills and not the parents' own literacy.

Although most early writers did not articulate a broad theoretical framework for family literacy research and comprehensive family literacy programs, Bronfenbrenner's (1979, 1986) ecological theory provides an exceptionally cogent one. Bronfenbrenner promoted a shift toward recognizing the family itself as a more appropriate focus of intervention than the child, arguing that "the family seems to be the most effective and economic system for fostering and sustaining the child's development. Without family involvement, intervention is likely to be unsuccessful, and what few effects are achieved are likely to disappear once the intervention is discontinued" (1974, p. 300).

Viewing family literacy from an ecological perspective, Bronfenbrenner (1986, p. 723) observed that although the family is the principal context in which human development takes place, "it is but one of several settings in which developmental process[es] can and do occur. Moreover, the processes operating in different settings are not independent of each other. To cite a common example, events at home can affect the child's progress in school, and vice versa."

Bronfenbrenner's (1986) well-known model provides both the organizing principle of this handbook and the theoretical foundation for many of its chapters. His ecological theory envisioned the child as nested within a set of increasingly complex environments. The inner circle of his model is the microsystem, where the family resides; it includes the neighborhood and community. The next circle is the exosystem, environments in which parents participate but where children seldom enter. Three of these are especially likely to affect the child's development: the parents' workplace, the parents' social networks, and the community's influence on family functioning. The outer circle is the macrosystem, where social and cultural beliefs reside. Of special interest to family literacy programs is Bronfenbrenner's conceptualization of the mesosystem, or the linkages and processes that take place between two or more settings. Authors in this handbook frequently focus on one or two of Bronfenbrenner's "circles" and sometimes incorporate all three into their discussion.

Bronfenbrenner (1989, p. 229) explains the macrosystem's importance by observing that the "patterns of belief and behavior characterizing the macrosystem are passed on from one generation to the next through processes of socialization carried out by various institutions of the culture, such as family, school, church, workplace, and structures of government." Throughout this handbook, but especially in those discussions in Section VII on culture and diversity, the authors use these overarching structures to describe and explain influences on children and their families.

We also explore the crucial home environment. The conceptual models of Leichter (1984), Britto and Brooks-Gunn (2001), Roskos and Twardosz, and Powell described in this handbook expand on the home environment's importance in children's literacy and language development. Leichter (1984) described home influences on children's literacy development with a three-part model. First is the environment, the physical resources that provide learning opportunities.

Second are the child's interactions with others in the home, including parents, siblings, and others. Third is the home's emotional climate and the support it provides for children's learning.

More recently, Britto and Brooks-Gunn (2001) have offered a similar set of three dimensions, based on their review of current research. They highlight language and verbal interactions; the learning climate—both its structural features and its functional aspects—and the social and emotional climate. They conclude that children "exposed to a richer linguistic environment earlier in life demonstrate a richer vocabulary and early acquisition of literacy skills."

Based on a review of existing research, Wasik and Hendrickson (in press) developed a model of home influences on literacy development that includes the following four domains: (a) parent characteristics, (b) child characteristics, (c) parent–child relationships, and (d) resources in the home environment. Elaborating on this model, we identified three areas of parent characteristics that have been empirically validated as relating to children's literacy development, including culture and ethnicity, parental beliefs, and socioeconomic status. In the present handbook, numerous authors address these parent characteristics and document their role in children's literacy development. In particular, Powell discusses parent beliefs and practices that contribute to children's literacy development; Emberton examines the role of culture in Native American families' parenting practices; and Rodriguez-Brown examines the role of culture and parenting in describing a parent education intervention for Hispanic families.

Our model also describes several key characteristics of children, including engagement, language proficiency, cognitive level, developmental level, social behavior, motivation, and medical conditions, that have been shown to influence their language and literacy skill acquisition. Developmental disabilities, oral language and vocabulary, and attention skills all contribute to how children will learn from their environment. In this handbook, Lonigan observes that in the emergent literacy domain, "individual differences are causally and powerfully connected to individual differences in reading achievement." He provides empirical support connecting children's attitudes, knowledge, and skills—especially oral language skills, print motivation, phonological processing skills, and letter knowledge—with later reading.

Many other researchers have explored how child characteristics affect literacy and reading, including Aram and Hall (1989), Rescorla (2000, 2002), Scarborough (1998, 2001), and Torgesen et al. (1999). This handbook, however, cannot provide a full accounting of this work. A forthcoming handbook will examine children's language and literacy development and disorders (Stone, Silliman, Ehram, & Apel, in press).

A third dimension in our model, parent–child relationships, is increasingly being shown to influence children's literacy skills. Children learn early language and literacy skills by interacting with others in the home, and the quality of these relationships is now being recognized as highly predictive of children's outcomes. Hart and Risley (1995) have provided additional empirical support for the relation between parent–child interactions and children's language and literacy outcomes. Pianta, in Section III of this handbook, offers a compelling case for the importance of parent–child relationships in all areas of child development, including literacy development. Kelly describes PACT Time, the family literacy program component designed to facilitate parent–child literacy interactions, noting that it also encourages positive parent–child relationships.

The fourth domain identified by our model is the home environment, a complex, multilayered, and multidimensional influence on literacy skills, not only for the child but also for the adult. In this handbook, many authors offer research and theory about the home environment, often focusing on storybook reading. Morrow and Temlock-Fields and Purcell-Gates address activities in the home that can influence children' literacy development; Gadsden notes the home's important influence on both adults' and children's literacy skills; and Hammer and Miccio discuss the home environment for Puerto Rican families.

Britto and Brooks-Gunn (2001) call for research that distinguishes dimensions of the home environment rather than studies global dimensions. Roskos and Twardosz expand on this need in Section V, showing through a detailed review of the literature that few researchers examine specific aspects of the home when discussing storybook reading, the most frequently studied home literacy activity. Spaces for reading, available time, and literacy resources are just some of the dimensions that need to be tackled in more depth.

Family systems theory sees the family itself as a social system, with interaction patterns that have been developed and maintained over time (Minuchin, 1985). Within family intervention programs, family systems theory provides a framework for identifying essential influences beyond direct program services (Minuchin, Colapinto, & Minuchin, 1998). Attention to family dynamics should be an integral part of any family-focused program. Basic principles recognize that change in any one family member can affect other individuals in the family. Family rules operate as norms and serve to organize family interactions. Thus, a person's increasing literacy skills may be welcomed by others in the family. But some changes can strain relationships or family traditions, such as when a parent wants to pursue further education but to do so would require financial sacrifice, someone else to care for children, or a change of cultural expectations.

Other theories that directly influence practice in family literacy programs include those on early literacy, referred to earlier and discussed in depth by authors in Section II; on early childhood education programs and parenting, a focus of Section III; and on adult learning and education, addressed in Section IV. Ideas about family diversity also affect program development, especially those that tackle the relations between culture and literacy and between language and literacy. Section V and several chapters elsewhere examine concepts about home influences as they relate both to program development and to instructional procedures for children and adults.

Other instructional concepts include integrating curricula across components, discussed by Potts in Section VI, and involving parents in developing the curriculum. Theories related to culture and families are addressed in depth in Section VII, with authors exploring race, ethnicity, culture, and language as they interact with literacy.

In concluding this look at theoretical influences on family literacy, we highlight the relevance of Vygotsky's theories for understanding family literacy practices and for developing effective instructional programs. As early as 1929, Vygotsky clearly delineated the contextual nature of learning and the importance of family and culture, writing that the developing child masters not only "the items of cultural experience but the habits and forms of cultural behavior and cultural methods of reasoning" (quoted in Bronfenbrenner, 1989, p. 206). Among his many influential tenets is that adults mediate young children's learning through their interactions, supporting and enabling children to move beyond their current level of functioning (Vygotsky, 1986). He observed that a zone of proximal development exists for children; when adults (or more competent peers) respond to this zone, challenging children to go just beyond their level of learning, they help children master new skills and knowledge. Such supportive interactions have come to be called scaffolding (Berk & Winsler, 1995). In this handbook, Sparling, Kelly, and Potts, among others, use Vygotsky's tenets to discuss the role of parents in children's development.

Changing Demographics

Many sources, including U.S. Census reports, demonstrate the linguistic changes in our society over the past 2 decades. Several authors in this volume describe efforts to help address the need of English language learners. (See chapters by Strucker, Snow, & Pan; Hammer & Miccio; and Rodriguez-Brown). Though assisting adults who are English-language learners was not an initial impetus for family literacy programs, the combination of services they offer is particularly appropriate for immigrant families who wish to advance their own literacy skills and employment options while also providing opportunities for their children to learn English. Related to this need is a growing acceptance of the idea that not only should we help adults and children learn English, but also we should help them maintain their home language and culture. This shift in thinking is significantly influencing debates about the kinds of programs that are most appropriate for children (Tabors, 1997). Hammer and Miccio explore findings from two instructional approaches for children who are English-language learners. Strucker, Snow, and Pan provide recommendations for instructors of children and adults; and Wrigley offers suggestions for working with families with many different home languages.

FAMILY LITERACY PROGRAMS

As the term family literacy gained widespread acceptance in recent years for describing programs, a number of ways to organize such programs have been proposed. For example, family literacy services can be categorized as direct or indirect for either adults or children (Nickse, 1990). Furthermore, programs can be described as either parent involvement programs (where parents learn to assist their children) or intergenerational family programs (where parents and children are co-learners) (Morrow, 1995).

Schools (Richardson, Sacks, & Ayers, 1995), libraries (Monsour & Talan, 1993), and work settings (Richards, 1998) have also incorporated family literacy objectives and procedures. Some use a model addressing child and adult needs directly. Others may emphasize family literacy by enhancing home–school linkages.

In this section, we describe intervention programs in which literacy is the primary or major focus. First, we describe efforts to enhance child literacy through early childhood programs or parent education. Next we illustrate programs that help adults develop literacy skills while offering vocational training, with the additional goal of providing parenting education to enhance outcomes for their children. We conclude with a description of comprehensive family literacy programs.

Emphasis on Child Language and Literacy

Some literacy programs address children's literacy and language development but do not directly address adults' literacy needs. They may provide assistance to children directly through preschool or day-care programs or indirectly by providing support to parents, thus enabling them to help their children.

Programs designed to reach children directly include High/Scope, the Abecedarian Project, Project CARE, and the Infant Health and Development Program (Infant Health and Development Program [IHDP], 1990; Ramey & Campbell, 1984; Wasik, Ramey, Bryant, & Sparling, 1990; Weikart, Bond, & McNeil, 1978). Reviewers of these and related projects (Barnett, 2001; Farran, 1990, 2001; Fuligni & Brooks-Gunn, Section II, this volume) have concluded that strong center-based programs can enhance children's literacy development and school performance. National programs that reach children indirectly through parent education include the Parents as Teachers Program, the Home Instruction for Parents of Preschool Children programs, and the Parent–Child Program, all home-visiting programs; and the Motheread Program, which can take place in a variety of settings. Research on these parenting programs has not demonstrated changes in children's literacy development and school readiness as definitively as research on programs that provide direct early childhood education. Below we briefly describe some of these child-focused early intervention programs.

Parents as Teachers Program.   Parents as Teachers (PAT) is an early childhood family education and support program created in 1981. The PAT program offers home visits in conjunction with parent group meetings, annual developmental screenings, and referrals to other community resources. In home visits, a certified parent educator helps families apply child development and child-rearing information (Wagner & Clayton, 1999; Winter & Rouse, 1990). Comprehensive parent training materials have been developed to address children from infancy through the preschool years. Bryant and Wasik present a more detailed description of PAT in their chapter on home-based programs and family literacy in Section V.

The Home Instruction Program for Preschool Youngsters.   Originally developed in 1968 in Israel and first implemented in the United States in 1984, the Home Instruction Program for Preschool Youngsters (HIPPY) is a 2-year, home-based early childhood education and parent involvement program for parents with limited formal education. The program features bimonthly home visits and bimonthly group meetings in which parents use HIPPY storybooks and educational activities with their preschool children (Baker, Piotrkowski, & Brooks-Gunn, 1999; Lombard, 1994).

Parent–Child Program.   The Parent–Child Program is committed to helping families challenged by obstacles such as poverty, low levels of education, and language to help their children be more successful in school. The program focuses on parent–child verbal interaction and developing critical language and literacy skills. Home visitors provide twice-weekly home visits over a 2-year period, modeling verbal interaction, parenting techniques, and educational play. Recent research shows positive educational outcomes for participating children (Parent-Child Program, 2003).

Motheread.   Established in 1987 in Raleigh, North Carolina, Motheread is a national nonprofit organization that serves counties in North Carolina and has programs in other states as well as the U.S. Virgin Islands. Components of this program focus on literacy classes, development of curriculum and instruction materials, and training. The program exists in a variety of settings, including women's prisons, libraries, schools, churches, and child-care centers (Barbara Bush Foundation for Family Literacy, 1989; Motheread, 1999, 2000).

Reading is Fundamental.   Reading Is Fundamental (RIF) founded in 1966, develops and delivers children's and family literacy programs that help prepare young children for reading through a national network of more than 310,000 community volunteers and through an extensive free book distribution program. In chapter 2 of this handbook, Hannon and Bird describe this program's implementation in England.

In summary, these programs and others are designed to provide direct services to children, and most of the intervention activities take place in the home setting. Earlier studies and reviews of such work have not produced strong documentation of child outcomes. Factors that might weaken outcomes include amount and quality of staff training, degree of adherence to program procedures, and low retention rates of participants. Some of these same factors also affect more comprehensive interventions, including Head Start and Even Start. Many home visiting programs are engaged in efforts to strengthen program characteristics, with the aim of increasing positive child and parent outcomes.

Emphasis on Adult Language and Literacy.   Some literacy programs focus primarily on adults' needs while also providing support for parenting activities that can promote children's language development. (Alamprese presents a comparison of adult education-only programs with adult education within family literacy programs in Section IV.)

Literacy Volunteers of America, Inc.   Literacy Volunteers of America (LVA) provides professionally trained volunteer tutors to teach basic literacy and English to adult speakers of other languages. Its goal is to help participants become better parents, workers, and citizens. LVA is a national network of over 350 locally based programs, supported by state and national governments. More than half of LVA affiliates support a family literacy component.

Collaborations for Literacy.   In 1983, the Collaborations for Literacy intervention model began at Boston University (Nickse & Englander, 1985). Undergraduate students learned to serve as tutors for more than 150 adults with low literacy skills whose children were participating in Chapter 1, the federal program funded to provide reading and language arts help to children with deficiencies (Nickse, Speicher, & Buchek, 1988). Parents received lessons not only to help improve their own literacy skills but also to acquire literacy activities they could use with their children (Daisey, 1991).

New York City Technical College Initiative.   Another university-initiated effort took place at New York City Technical College of the City University of New York (Handel & Goldsmith, 1988). Adults with low literacy skills participated in a program to enhance their own and their children's literacy. Activities included workshops for parents on how to read to children and parent participation in developmental reading classes to influence intergenerational transfer of skills (e.g., Kirsch & Jungeblut 1986).

Comprehensive Family Literacy Programs

In contrast to the kinds of programs described previously, comprehensive family literacy programs include educational programs for both children and adults, parent education, and time for parent–child literacy interactions. Table 1.1 presents a timeline showing the major events since 1984 that have contributed to family literacy interventions with direct emphasis on child and adult language and literacy.

Parent and Child Education Program.   Established in 1986, the Kentucky Parent and Child Education Program (PACE) is often recognized as the model for today's comprehensive family literacy efforts. It is the first major family literacy initiative that included direct child and adult services (though earlier programs addressed both child and adult literacy and language needs). The PACE program was based on the belief that providing literacy services to parents and their children had advantages over providing just one of these services.

Kenan Trust Family Literacy Project.   In 1989, PACE's success stimulated the Kenan Foundation of Chapel Hill, North Carolina, to offer additional funding to expand the program in Kentucky and North Carolina. The Kenan Trust Family Literacy Project began at seven sites in those two states. It was designed to bring together adult education programs and preschool programs in a coordinated effort with the goal of "breaking the cycle of illiteracy" for low-income families (Darling & Hayes, 1989). At first, parents and children rode together on a school bus to an elementary school 3 days a week. During the day, the parents participated in adult education activities, often attaining a General Education Development High School Equivalency Diploma (GED). They were also involved in parenting education, parent support, and vocational training. The children took part in an early childhood program. The parenting component included time for parents and children to engage in literacy or related activities. This model is the foundation for programs of the National Center for Family Literacy.

Because of their early Kenan Foundation funding, these programs are often said to use the Kenan model. The National Center for Family Literacy, established in 1989, has supported this

TABLE 1.1

Timeline of Significant Events in the Development of Family Literacy Services

1986	Kentucky's Parent and Child Education program is funded by the Kentucky legislature and begins in 6 rural counties.
1987	PACE expands to 18 rural counties in Kentucky.
1988	The Ford Foundation and Harvard University's Kennedy School of Government select PACE as one of 10 outstanding innovations in state and local government.
	William R. Kenan, Jr., Charitable Trust of Chapel Hill, NC, gives a major grant to expand the PACE program to three sites in Kentucky and to four in North Carolina.
	The Even Start Family Literacy Program is authorized by the Elementary and Secondary Education Act of 1965.
1989	The Barbara Bush Foundation for Family Literacy, a private nonprofit organization, is established to support the development of family literacy programs.
	The Even Start Family Literacy Program was first authorized in 1989 as Part B of Chapter 1 of Title 1 of the Elementary and Secondary Education Act of 1965 (ESEA), beginning with 4-year federal discretionary grants for family literacy programs ($14.8 million budget, 76 projects, 44 states).
	The Kenan Trust gives a grant to establish the National Center for Family Literacy in Louisville, KY.
1990	Congress passes the National Literacy Act (P.L. 102–73), amending the Even Start program by calling for improving "the educational opportunities of the Nation's children and adults by integrating early childhood education and adult education for parents into a unified program."
	The Head Start Program begins a family literacy initiative.
	Toyota gives the NCFL $2 million to launch the Families for Learning challenge grant program for five cities.
	The Family Literacy Commission is formed by the International Reading Association to study family literacy initiatives and issues.
1991	Even Start program is reauthorized by the Improving America's Schools Act as Part B of Title I of the ESEA.
	U.S. Department of Education funds Helping States Build Alliances for Family Literacy Project.
	Head Start is amended to include parent involvement requirements.
	The National Literacy Act of 1991 both renames Even Start as the Even Start Family Literacy Program and establishes the National Institute for Family Literacy.
1992	Even Start becomes state administered ($70 million budget, 340 projects, all 50 states, District of Columbia, and Puerto Rico).
1994	Even Start is reauthorized, requiring services to families most in need and extending services to teen parents. Projects were required to serve at least a 3-year age range of children.
	Head Start Act is included the federal definition of family literacy.
1995	Early Head Start is created by the Head Start Bureau, Administration for Children and Families.
	National Evaluation of the Even Start Family Literacy Program Final Report (report of first 4 years, 1989–1993) is published.
1996	Congress passes an amendment requiring Even Start instructional services to be intensive.
1998	America Reads program is modified to allow work-study students to participate in family literacy programs for their work assignment.
	Second National Evaluation of Even Start Family Literacy Programs (report of years 1994–1997) is published.
	Adult Education and Family Literacy Act (P.L. 105–220), part of the Workforce Investment Act of 1998, promotes family literacy.
	Reading Excellence Act amended Even Start by providing a definition for the term *family literacy services* to match other legislation with family literacy components. These included Head Start, the Adult Education and Family Literacy Act, and the Reading Excellence Act programs.
1999	The Omnibus Appropriations Act for PY2000 allowed Even Start programs to continue beyond 8 years.
2000	Even Start was reauthorized in the LIFT (Literacy Involves Families Together) Act, almost doubling its funding level to $250 million. Additional expectations were added including requiring projects to build on existing high-quality services to promote academic achievement of children and parents and to use instructional programs supported by scientifically based research.
2001	Even Start is reauthorized by the No Child Left Behind Act.
2002	Most states begin to implement the use of performance indicators to monitor and improve local projects.
2003	Third National Evaluation of Even Start Family Literacy Programs (report of years 1997–2001) is published.
	Classroom Literacy Interventions and Outcomes Study, an evaluation of 2 family literacy curriculum models in Even Start programs, is initiated.

comprehensive model from the start, identifying four program components: early childhood education, adult education, parenting support, and parent and child time together (Hayes, n.d.). More recent program initiatives of the National Center for Family Literacy are described by Darling in Section IX.

Even Start Family Literacy Program.   The federal government's Even Start Family Literacy Program is the best known intergenerational family literacy program. Building directly on the Kenan model, but also reflecting other efforts of the 1980s, Even Start provides direct literacy services for both adult and child, focusing on parents and children who are most in need. The program is geared toward parents and their children from birth through age 7, but other people serving in the parenting role can and do participate when a child's parents cannot. The program includes early childhood education, parenting education, and adult literacy and education. Programs generally take place in center settings supplemented by home-based instruction.

To enter Even Start, a family must have a parent who is eligible to participate in an adult education program under the Adult Education Act and one or more children of that parent must be under the age of 8 years. Even Start projects must provide participating families with an integrated program of early childhood education, adult literacy or basic education, and parenting education. The program's design is based on the belief that these components build on each other and that families need to receive all three services in order to effect lasting change and improve children's school success.

To achieve Even Start's goals, the U.S. Department of Education awards grants to state education agencies. Each state then makes competitive discretionary grants for demonstration programs to partnerships of local education agencies and other entities, such as community-based organizations. In addition to the state grant programs, funds are set aside for special discretionary grants to state education agencies for migrant programs and to Indian tribes and organizations (see Emberton, Section VII, this handbook, for a description of programs with Native American families.).

Since 1989, family literacy programs have experienced widespread interest and expansion. At the same time, interest in family literacy programs has been reflected in the growth of other programs across the country and in legislation that promotes family literacy, including the Reading Excellence Act, the Adult Education and Family Literacy Act, the Head Start Act, and the Community Services Block Grant Act.

The federal approach has four core components—early childhood education, adult education, parenting education, and parent–child literacy interactions—provided within an integrated framework. In the early childhood education component, children attend preschool classes or receive home-based instruction that focuses on literacy skills within a developmentally appropriate curriculum. The parenting education component addresses parent literacy needs through parenting classes that explore child development and other themes, parent support groups, and home-based instruction. Parent–child interactive literacy activities, a required part of these programs, offer a regularly scheduled time for parents and children to come together with the staff for learning about and engaging in positive parenting interactions, especially those focused on developing children's language and literacy. The adult education component offers opportunities for adults to develop and improve their literacy skills, complete high school diploma requirements or equivalents, and develop employment skills. Even Start also provides noninstructional support services such as transportation. Comprehensive literacy programs have grown dramatically since the late 1980s. For example, the federal Even Start program alone expanded from 76 projects serving approximately 2,500 families with a budget of $14.8 million in 1989 to 855 projects serving 32,000 families with a budget of $150 million in 2002. Other comprehensive programs are funded by local or private organizations and agencies, and some are supported by program development and research activities of the National Center for Family Literacy.

As these programs have grown, questions about their procedures and effectiveness have become more numerous, leading to debate about the best types of assessment instruments. These issues are considered next.

GENERAL PROGRAM ISSUES

Issues frequently raised in family literacy programs include those of culture and language, identified previously; quality of program components; and assessment both of program processes and of child, parent, and adult outcomes.

Program Characteristics

Family literacy programs following the federal definition include the four components identified earlier. As questions about program outcomes have become more prevalent over time, more attention has been focused on procedures within the program components. Writers are beginning to question whether simply providing the structure or framework for these programs is sufficient, or whether we need to provide considerably more help with curriculum and instructional procedures. Several authors describe family literacy program components in detail, including Fuligni and Brooks-Gunn; and Dickinson, St.Pierre, and Pettengill (early childhood programs); Powell (parenting education), Kelly (parent–child literacy interactions); and Comings and Alamprese (adult education). Potts discusses ways to integrate across all these components, whereas Harbin, Herrmann, Wasik, Dobbins, and Lam describe how family literacy programs can provide more integrated services by interacting with other agencies.

Assessment and Evaluation Procedures

A pervasive issue in discussions about the development of literacy skills and quality of family literacy programs is the adequacy of existing instruments for assessing child and adult literacy, parent–child literacy interactions, program processes, and program outcomes. In Section VIII, authors address each of these considerations, identifying existing instruments for some purposes but also noting the need to develop new ones. They discuss the uses of assessment data, with authors arguing that different kinds of information are needed to plan instruction for individual children or adults in comparison with standardized instruments used to measure program outcomes. Johnston and Yanoff, as well as Lonigan, Keller, and Phillips, tackle assessment of children from different perspectives. Powell, Okagaki, and Bojczyk consider issues in evaluating parent outcomes; and Van Horn addresses measures of adult literacy. Finally, St.Pierre, Ricciuti, and Tao look at evaluating programs as a whole. All authors observe that progress in program development depends on strong evaluation procedures and attention to how results can influence practice.

CONCLUSIONS

To discuss literacy and family literacy programs, we must first examine fundamental questions about literacy, asking how literacy is acquired; how culture, language, and family life interact with literacy acquisition; and how the home, school, and work environments relate to literacy development. In this chapter we have touched on some of these issues, which subsequent chapters also examine in depth. Other chapters explore debates about family literacy programs that range in subject matter from theory to effectiveness.

Among the debates the authors take on are whether to provide both parent and child direct services within the same program or to offer them in separate programs; whether each program component is equally valuable; and how well programs respond to diversity in culture and language. The appropriateness and quality of curriculum in each program component come under scrutiny, as do intervention services focused on literacy and concepts that guide intervention programs.

The authors raise questions about both short- and long-term outcomes for children and parents, in relation not only to literacy skills but also to other life-course events such as school success and employment. They ask how best to assess child, parent, and adult outcomes; they examine the role of different assessment procedures; and they explore the need to evaluate instructional practices in order to draw more valid conclusions about whether and how programs make a significant difference for families.

Other chapters cover curriculum and instructional strategies within the program components; discuss components specific to family literacy programs, such as parent–child literacy interactions; or address how to provide integration across all program components. Some authors look at adult–child relationships in both the classroom and the home, examining variables in both environments that influence literacy development. Others look outside the educational setting, asking how home visiting can advance program objectives and meet families' needs, and how the workplace and family literacy programs interact. Service integration with other organizations and agencies also receives attention.

Collectively, the authors of this handbook describe and illuminate the issues swirling around literacy, family literacy, and the implementation of family literacy programs. They make thoughtful recommendations for advancing research in the field and for improving services offered to children and parents.

REFERENCES

Allison, D. T., & Watson, J. A. (1994). The significance of adult storybook reading styles on the development of young children's emergent reading. *Reading Research and Instruction, 34*(1), 57–72.

Aram, D. M., & Hall, N. E. (1989). Longitudinal follow-up of children with preschool communication disorders: Treatment implications. *School Psychology Review, 18,* 487–501.

Auerbach, E. R. (1989). Toward a socio-contextual approach to family literacy. *Harvard Educational Review, 59,* 165–181.

Baker, A. J., Piotrkowski, C. S., & Brooks-Gunn, J. B. (1999). Home instruction program for preschool youngsters. *The Future of Children, 9*(1), 116–133.

Barbara Bush Foundation for Family Literacy. (1989). *First teachers.* Washington, DC: Author.

Barnett, W. S. (2001). Preschool education for economically disadvantaged children: Effects on reading achievement and related outcomes. In S. B. Neuman & D. K. Dickinson (Eds.), *Handbook of early literacy development* (pp. 421–443). New York: Guilford.

Benjamin, L. A., & Lord, J. (Eds.). (1996). *Family literacy: Directions in research and implications for practice.* Washington, DC: U.S. Department of Education-Office of Educational Research and Improvement, Office of Vocational and Adult Education, Office of Elementary and Secondary Education's Even Start Program.

Berk, L. E., & Winsler, A. (1995). *Scaffolding children's learning: Vygotsky and early childhood education.* Washington, DC: National Association for the Education of Young Children.

Britto, P. R., & Brooks-Gunn, J. (2001). Beyond shared book reading: Dimensions of home literacy and low-income African American preschoolers' skills. In P. Britto & J. Brooks-Gunn (Eds.), *The role of family literacy environments in promoting young children's emerging literacy skills,* pp. 39–52. San Francisco: Jossey-Bass.

Brizius, J., & Foster, S. (1993). *Generation to generation: Realizing the promise of family literacy.* Ypsilanti, MI: High/Scope Press.

Bronfenbrenner, U. (1974). Is early intervention effective? *Columbia Teachers College Record, 76,* 279–303.

Bronfenbrenner, U. (1979). *The ecology of human development: Experiments by nature and design.* Cambridge, MA: Harvard University Press.

Bronfenbrenner, U. (1986). Ecology of the family as a context for human development: Research perspectives. *Developmental Psychology, 22*(6), 723–742.

Bronfenbrenner, U. (1989). Ecological systems theory. *Annals of Child Development, 6,* 187–249.

Brooks-Gunn, J., Berlin, L. J., & Fuligni, A. S. (2000). Early childhood intervention programs: What about the family? In J. P. Shonkoff & S. J. Meisels (Eds.), *Handbook of early childhood intervention* (2nd ed.). New York: Cambridge University Press.

Bryant, D., & Maxwell, K. (1997). The effectiveness of early intervention for disadvantaged children. In M. Guralnick (Ed.), *The effectiveness of early intervention* (pp. 23–46). Baltimore, MD: Paul H. Brooks.

Chase-Lansdale, P. L., & Brooks-Gunn, J. (Eds.). (1995). *Escape from poverty: What makes a difference for children?* New York: Cambridge University Press.

Clay, M. M. (1993). *An observation study of early literacy achievement.* Portsmouth, NH: Heinemann.

Cunningham, A. E., & Stanovich, K. E. (1998). Early reading acquisition and its relation to reading experience and ability 10 years later. *Developmental Psychology, 33,* 934–945.

Daisey, P. (1991). Intergenerational literacy programs: Rationale, description, and effectiveness. *Journal of Clinical Child Psychology, 20,* 11–17.

Darling, S., & Hayes, A. E. (1989). *The William R. Kenan, Jr. Charitable Trust Family Literacy Project. Final Report 1998–1989.* Louisville, KY: National Center for Family Literacy.

Delgado-Gaitan, C. (1994). Sociocultural change through literacy: Towards empowerment of families. In B. Ferdman, R. M. Weber, & A. Ramirex (Eds.), *Literacy across languages and cultures* (pp. 143–170). Albany, NY: State University of New York Press.

Dickinson, D. K., & Sprague, K. (2001). The nature and impact of early childhood care environments on the language and early literacy development of children from low-income families. In S. B. Neuman & D. K. Dickinson (Eds.), *Handbook of early literacy development* (pp. 263–292). New York: Guilford.

Duncan, G. J., & Brooks-Gunn, J. (Eds.). (1997). *Consequences of growing up poor.* New York: Russel Sage Foundation.

Farran, D. C. (1990). Effects of intervention with disadvantages and disabled children: A decade review. In S. J. Meisels & J. P. Shonkoff (Eds.), *Handbook of early childhood intervention* (2nd ed., pp. 501–539). New York: Cambridge University Press.

Farran, D. C. (2001). Another decade of intervention for children who are low income or disabled: What do we know now? In J. P. Shonkoff & S. J. Meisels (Eds.), *Handbook of early childhood intervention* (2nd ed., pp. 510–548). New York: Cambridge University Press.

Gee, J. P. (2001). A sociocultural perspective on early literacy development. In S. B. Neuman & David K. Dickinson (Eds.), *Handbook of early literacy research* (pp. 30–42). New York: Guilford.

Gesell, A. L. (1925). *The mental growth of the pre-school child.* New York: Macmillan.

Goelman, H. (1984). The discussion: What was said. In H. Goelman, A. Oberg, & F. Smith (Eds.), *Awakening to literacy* (pp. 201–214). Portsmouth, NH: Heinemann.

Goodman, Y. M. (1980). The roots of literacy. In M. P. Douglas (Ed.), *Forty-fourth yearbook of the Claremont Reading Conference* (pp. 1–12). Claremont, CA: Claremont Reading Conference.

Handel, R. D., & Goldsmith, E. (1988). Intergenerational literacy: A community college program. *Journal of Reading, 32*(3), 25–256.

Hart, B., & Risley, T. T. (1995). *Meaningful differences in the everyday experiences of young American children.* Baltimore: Brooks.

Hayes, A. E. (n.d.) *A rationale for comprehensive family literacy services: Theoretical and philosophical foundations and a summary of findings from follow-up studies.* University of North Carolina at Wilmington, Wilmington, NC: Watson School of Education.

Heath, S. B. (1983). *Ways with words.* Cambridge, MA: Cambridge University Press.

Heath, S. B. (1989). Oral and literate traditions among Black Americans living in poverty. *American Psychologist, 44,* 367–373.

Infant Health and Development Program. (1990). Enhancing the outcomes of low-birth-weight, premature infants. *Journal of the American Medical Association, 263,* 3035–3042.

Juel, C. (1988). Learning to read and write: A longitudinal study of 54 children from first through fourth grades. *Journal of Educational Psychology, 78,* 243–255.

King, R., & Mc Master, J. (2000). *Pathways: A primer for family literacy program and development.* Louisville, KY: National Center for Family Literacy.

Kirsch, I. S., & Jungeblut, A. (1986). *Literacy: Profiles of America's young adults. Final report.* Princeton, NJ: National Assessment of Educational Progress. (ERIC Document Reproduction Service No. ED275 701).

Leichter, H. J. (Ed.). (1974). Some perspectives on the family as educator. Teachers College Record, 76 (2), 175–217.

Leichter, H. J. (Ed.). (1979). Families and communities as educators: Some concepts of relationships. Teachers College Record, 79 (4), 567–658.

Leichter, H. J. (1984). Families as environments for literacy. In H. Goelman, A. A. Oberg, & F. Smith (Eds.), *Awakening to literacy* (pp. 38–50). Portsmouth, NH: Heinemann.

Lombard, A. D. (1994). *Success begins at home: The past, present, and future of the Home Instruction Program for Preschool Youngsters.* Guilford, CT: Connelly-3-Publishing Group.

Lonigan, C. J., & Whitehurst, G. J. (2001). Emergent literacy and family literacy. In B. H. Wasik (Ed.), *A synthesis of research on family literacy*. Prepared for the U.S. Department of Education: University of North Carolina at Chapel Hill, Chapel Hill, NC.

Mathews, M. M. (1966). *Teaching to read: Historically considered*. Chicago: The University of Chicago Press.

Minuchin, P. (1985). Families and individual development: Provocations from the field of family therapy. *Child Development, 56,* 289–302.

Minuchin, P., Colapinto, J., & Minuchin, S. (1998). *Working with families of the poor*. New York: Guilford.

Moll, L. C. (Ed.). (1990). *Vygotsky and education: Instructional implications and applications of sociohistorical psychology*. New York: Cambridge University Press.

Monsour, M., & Talan, C. (1993). *Library-based family literacy projects*. Chicago, IL: American Library Association.

Morrow, L. M. (Ed.). (1995). *Family literacy: Connections in schools and communities*. New Brunswick, NJ: International Reading Association, Inc.

Motheread. (1999). *Fact sheet*. [Brochure]. Raleigh, NC: Author.

Motheread. (2000). *Motheread, Inc.* [Online]. Available at http://www.motheread.org/ National Center for Family Literacy (2003). www.famlit.org

National Center for Family Literacy. (NCFL). (2000). *Connecting families and work: Family literacy bridges the gap*. Louisville, KY: Author.

Neuman, S. B., & Dickinson, D. K. (2001). *Introduction*. In S. B. Neuman & D. K. Dickinson (Eds.), *Handbook of early literacy development* (pp. 3–29). New York: Guilford.

Nickse, R. S. (1990). Family literacy programs: Ideas for action. *Adult Learning, 1,* 9–13, 28–29.

Nickse, R. S., & Englander, N. (1985). At risk parents: Collaborations for literacy. *Equity and Choice, 1,* 11–18.

Nickse, R., Speicher, A. M., & Buchek, P. C. (1998). An intergenerational adult literacy project: A family intervention/prevention model. *Journal of Reading, 31,* 634–642.

Olds, D. L., & Kitzman, H. (1993). Review of research on home visiting for pregnant women and parents of young children. *The Future of Children, 3,* 53–92.

Parent-Child Program. (2003). www.parent-child.org

Pellegrini, A. D. (2001). Some theoretical and methodological considerations in studying literacy in social context. In S. B. Neuman & D. K. Dickinson (Eds.), *Handbook of early literacy research* (pp. 54–65). New York: Guilford.

Ramey, C. T., & Campbell, F. A. (1984). Preventive education for high-risk children: Cognitive consequences of the Carolina Abecedarian Project. *American Journal of Mental Deficiency, 89,* 515–523.

Reading is Fundamental. (2003). www.rif.org

Reese, L., & Gallimore, L. (2000). Immigrant Latinos cultural model of literacy development: An alternative perspective on home-school discontinuities. *American Journal of Education, 108*(2), 103–134.

Rescorla, L. (2000). Do late-talking toddlers turn out to have reading difficulties a decade later? *Annals of Dyslexia, 50,* 87–102.

Rescorla, L. (2002). Language and reading outcomes to age 9 in late-talking toddlers. *Journal of Speech, Language, and Hearing Research, 45,* 360–371.

Richards, R. T. (1998). When family literacy begins on the job. *Educational Leadership, 55*(8), 78–80.

Richardson, M. V., Sacks, K., & Ayers, M. N. (1995). Intergenerational literacy leads to empowerment of families and schools. *Reading Improvement, 32,* 85–91.

Rogers, R. (2002). Between contexts: A critical analysis of family literacy, discursive practices and literacy subjectivities. *Reading Research Quarterly, 37*(3), 248–277.

Scarborough, H. S. (1998). Early identification of children at risk for reading disabilities: Phonological awareness and some other promising predictors. In B. K. Shapiro, P. J. Accardo, & A. J. Capute (Eds.), *Specific reading disability: A view of the spectrum* (pp. 74–119). Timonium, MD: York Press.

Scarborough, H. S. (2001). Connecting early language and literacy to later reading (dis)abilities: Evidence, theory, and practice. In S. B. Neuman & D. K. Dickinson (Eds.), *Handbook of early literacy research* (pp. 97–110). New York: Guilford.

Smith, S. (Ed.). (1995). *Two generation programs for families in poverty: A new intervention strategy. Advances in applied developmental psychology, vol. 9*. Norwood, NJ: Ablex.

Snow, C. E., Barnes, W. S., Chandler, J., Goodman, I. F., & Hemphill, L. (1991). *Unfulfilled expectations: Home and school influences on literacy*. Cambridge, MA: Harvard University Press.

Snow, C., Burns, M., & Griffin, P. (1998). *Preventing reading difficulties in young children*. Washington, DC: National Academy Press.

Snow, C. E., & Tabors, P. (1996). Intergenerational transfers of literacy. *Family literacy: Directions in research and implications for practice*. In L. A. Benjamin & J. Lord (Eds.), Washington, DC: Office of Educational Research and Improvement, U.S. Department of Education.

Stone, A., Silliman, E., Ehram, B., & Apel, K. (Eds.). (in press). *Handbook of language and literacy development and disorder*. New York: Guilford.

Street, B. V. (1984). *Literacy in theory and practice*. Cambridge, UK: Cambridge University Press.

Sulzby, E., & Teale, W. (1991). Emergent Literacy. In R. Barr, M. L. Kamil, P. B. Mosenthal, & P. D. Pearson (Eds.), *Handbook of reading research* (Vol. II, pp. 727–757). New York, Longman.

Tabors, P. O. (1997). *One child: Two languages*. Baltimore: Paul H. Brookes.

Taylor, D. (1983). *Family literacy: Young children learning to read and write*. Portsmouth, NH: Heinemann.

Taylor, D. (Ed.) (1997). *Many families, many literacies: An international declaration of principles*. Portsmouth, NH: Heinemann.

Taylor, D., & Dorsey-Gaines, C. (1988). *Growing up literate: Learning from inner-city families*. Portsmouth, NH: Heinemann.

Taylor, D., & Strickland, D. S. (1986). *Family storybook reading*. Portsmouth, NH: Heinemann.

Teale, W. H., & Sulzby, E. (Eds.). (1986). *Emergent literacy: Writing and reading*. Norwood, NJ: Ablex.

Tharp, R. G., & Gallimore, R. (1998). *Rousing minds to life: Teaching, learning, and schooling in social context*. New York: Cambridge University.

Torgesen, J. K., Wagner, R. K., Rashotte, C. A., Rose, E., Lindamood, P., Conway, T., & Garvin, C. (1999). Preventing reading failure in young children with phonological processing disabilities: Group and individual responses to instruction. *Journal of Educational Psychology, 91*, 579–593.

Vygotsky, L. S. (1978). *Mind in society: The development of psychological processes*. Cambridge, MA: Harvard University.

Vygotsky, L. S. (1986). *Thought and language*. In A. Kozulin (Ed.), Cambridge, MA: MIT Press.

Wagner, M., & Clayton, S. (1999). *The Parents as Teachers Program: Results from two demonstrations*. Menlo Park, CA: SRI International.

Wasik, B. H., Dobbins, D. R., & Herrmann, S. (2001). Intergenerational family literacy: Concepts, research, and practice. In S. B. Neuman & D. K. Dickinson (Eds.), *Handbook of early literacy research* (pp. 444–458). New York: Guilford.

Wasik, B. H., & Hendrickson, J. S. (in press). Family literacy practices. In A. Stone, E. Silliman, B. Ehram, & K. Apel (Eds.), *Handbook of language and literacy development and disorder*. New York: Guilford.

Wasik, B. H., Ramey, C. T., Bryant, D. M., & Sparling, J. J. (1990). A longitudinal study of two early intervention strategies: Project CARE. *Child Development, 61*, 1682–1696.

Weikart, D. P., Bond, J. T., & McNeil, J. T. (1978). The Ypsilanti Preschool Project Preschool year and longitudinal results. *Monographs of the High Scope Educational Research Foundation* (No. 3). Ypsilanti, MI: High/Scope.

Whitehurst, G. J., & Lonigan, C. J. (1998). Child development and emergent literacy. *Child Development, 69*(3), 848–872.

Winter M., & Rouse, J. (1990). Fostering intergenerational literacy: The Missouri Parents as Teachers Program. *The Reading Teacher, 43*(6), 382–386.

Zigler, E., & Valentine, J. (1979). *Project Head Start: A legacy of the war on poverty*. New York: The Free Press.

2

Family Literacy in England: Theory, Practice, Research, and Policy

Peter Hannon
University of Sheffield, England

Viv Bird
National Literacy Trust, England

This chapter contributes to an international perspective on family literacy by providing an account of developments in one country—England—over the past 2 decades. We describe the theoretical context for family literacy in England and how practice has developed out of the linking of two strands of work: one in early childhood education and the other in adult literacy education. The research base for programs, particularly evaluations of effectiveness, is reviewed. We note U.S. influences on research and practice. To explain the current situation in England, we take an historical view of its development since the 1980s. The current attractiveness of family literacy for policymakers is highlighting some key issues such as the need for flexibility in programs and a progressive public policy that enables long-term planning of funding, program development, research, and professional development. It is possible that some of these issues will resonate with the experience of colleagues engaged in family literacy outside England.

Other chapters in this volume focus on U.S. work, as do other surveys, collections, and reviews published in the United States. For example, well over 90% of the citations from three key publications on family literacy (Morrow, 1995; Purcell-Gates, 2000; Wasik, Dobbins, & Herrmann, 2001) relate to the United States. It is undoubtedly true that international developments in theory, research, and practice have been greatly influenced by developments in the United States, but it would be a mistake to conclude that there is relatively little work of significance being undertaken elsewhere in the world. In the United Kingdom, for example, reviews by Hannon (1995) and Wolfendale and Topping (1996) indicate considerable activity and research. Cairney (2002) has reported on work in Australia. Reports from other countries, especially non-English-speaking ones, are not so readily accessible, but accounts included in Dombey and Meek Spencer (1994), Taylor (1997), and Auerbach (2002) indicate activity in Canada, France, Spain, Greece, New Zealand, Brazil, Mexico, and South Africa.

Theory

For the purposes of this chapter, we distinguish two basic meanings of the term *family literacy*. The first refers to interrelated *literacy practices within families*. This meaning, which can be traced back to a seminal study by Taylor (1983) in the United States, did gain limited currency in the 1980s among researchers and some practitioners in England. They were also influenced by related U.S. studies in the 1980s (Heath, 1983; Taylor & Dorsey-Gaines, 1988; Teale, 1986). But there was research in England that, even if it did not at first use the term family literacy, wholly or partly investigated literacy practices within families (Barton & Hamilton, 1998; Gregory, 1996; Hannon & James, 1990; Hirst, 1998; Weinberger, 1996). All of these studies described and analyzed existing family literacy practices, sometimes in relation to school literacy, but they did not research efforts to change family practices.

The second meaning of family literacy refers to certain kinds of *literacy programs involving families*. This meaning also reached England from the United States. The idea of programs or interventions to extend or change family literacy originated in the United States in the 1980s (e.g., Nash, 1987), but it was not until the 1990s that interest in interventions named as such became widespread in England. How that happened will be discussed later. There had, however, been family literacy programs in England, at least from the 1980s, even if they were not all called family literacy (Hannon, 1995). Hannon (2000) has pointed out that the second meaning of family literacy has effectively supplanted the first in England and suggests this occurrence is unfortunate insofar as it has deprived educators of a term that refers to literacy practices that occur independently of any program. This chapter is mainly concerned with family literacy programs in England, that is, the second meaning of family literacy. We define these as *programs to teach literacy that acknowledge and make use of learners' family relationships and engagement in family literacy practices*. This definition is fairly broad and it must be recognized that some in England (e.g., Adult Literacy and Basic Skills Unit [ALBSU], 1993a, 1993b) and some in the United States (e.g., Darling, 1993) promote a more restricted definition to include only those programs that *combine* literacy teaching for parents with literacy teaching for children from the same families. A restricted definition, however, leads to a restricted view of current activity and its historical roots.

There are several theoretical issues in family literacy that have implications for research, practice, and policy. Chief among these are understandings of the nature of the *family*, the concept of *literacy*, how *literacy inequalities* in society are understood, the kinds of *teaching* thought to be appropriate for adults and children in programs, and the *aims of programs*. How are these understood in England? Ideally, they would be clearly articulated in research, practice, and policy. Yet, as in many countries, apart from a handful of scholars, there is a generally atheoretical approach to family literacy in England.

The view taken of *family* is fairly pragmatic. There is widespread recognition in practice that families vary greatly in structure and that *parents* can be all kinds of care givers—including step-parents, grandparents, foster parents, other care givers—in a variety of different relationships and living arrangements. Nevertheless, it must be admitted that some programs, some of the time, revert to thinking in terms of conventional assumptions about family structure, for example, regarding what parents a child has at home.

Current theory of literacy tends to conceptualize it either as a set of cognitive skills or as a social practice or as some mix of the two (Hannon, 2000). In England, government policies are couched entirely in terms of skills. For example, the ministry concerned with education has recently been renamed the "Department for Education and *Skills*" (DfES) (the emphases in what follows are added.) It contains within it an Adult Basic *Skills* Strategy Unit. The most active quasi-independent government organization in the adult literacy field is called the Basic *Skills* Agency (BSA). A key government document in Adult Basic Education is titled *Skills for Life* (Department for Education and Employment [DfEE], 2000). At school level, literacy has been defined by government as something that "unites the important *skills* of reading and writing" (DfES, 2001, p. 3). Most practitioners in family literacy programs probably see their task as imparting skills and would not normally use the language of literacy practices. A few give primacy to strengthening and extending literacy practices in families. Most programs aim for

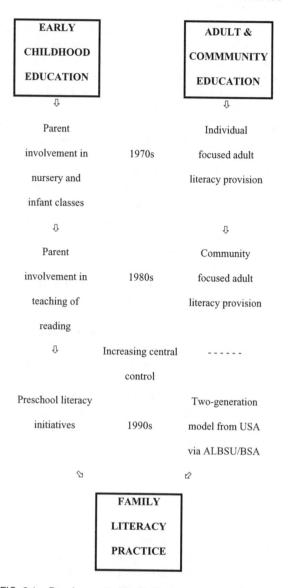

FIG. 2.1. Development of family literacy practice in England.

something more than imparting short-term skills. They hope for long-term changes in families, relating, for example, to support for children's school education, improvement of adults' basic skills, employability, or adults' attitudes to lifelong learning. Literacy inequalities are generally seen in terms of the unequal distribution of skills, particularly those thought to be in demand by employers, rather than unequal access to the social practices that involve written language.

Development of Practice and Research

The development of family literacy programs in England can best be understood in terms of two strands of development—one within early childhood education and one within adult literacy education. These developed separately through the 1970s and 1980s but began to link together in family literacy in the mid-1990s. Figure 2.1 summarizes what happened.

In the 1970s there was very little that could be counted as family literacy programs in England. Early childhood educators working in nursery (prekindergarten) and infant (kindergarten and grade 1) classes often had generally positive attitudes towards parental involvement, but these attitudes did not result in direct involvement in the teaching of literacy. Adult literacy education became a recognized field of activity in England in the 1970s, but teaching was generally focused on individual learners, often in one-on-one situations. Many adult learners were known to be parents but, although some tutors must have thought to link parents' literacy learning with that of their children, there were no systematic and well-documented approaches of that kind.

The development of family literacy practice in England has often been shaped, and sometimes driven, by research. The most influential research in the 1970s was that showing the importance of home (for which one can generally read family) factors in school achievement. Particularly influential, on account of its large nationally representative longitudinal sample and methodological rigor, was the National Child Development Study that showed the likelihood of children being *poor* readers or *nonreaders* at age 7 was very strongly related to social class (Davie, Butler, & Goldstein, 1972). There had also been an earlier influential study by Douglas (1964) and later one by Wedge and Prosser (1973) that linked educational measures (including reading test performance) to family and socioeconomic factors. Similar studies have been carried out in many countries but none more so over the years than in England where their effect throughout the 1970s was to encourage educational initiatives that linked home and school and involved parents. Toward the end of the decade, and into the next, there was research that focused more on literacy. It again confirmed the strong association with measures of school literacy attainment and socioeconomic factors (Hannon & McNally, 1986; Newson & Newson, 1977). One extremely influential study by Hewison and Tizard (1980) went further by identifying within a working class sample a specific family literacy practice (parents hearing children read) that was positively associated with children's reading test performance. Their findings were replicated by Hannon (1987). Other studies showed that the practice of actively promoting children's literacy development, although not universal, was more common in families than had been appreciated by schools (Hannon & James, 1990; Newson & Newson, 1977).

The 1980s

In the 1980s, some approaches that involved parents directly in the teaching of literacy developed to the point where they could be classed as family literacy programs in the broad sense outlined earlier. Development throughout the decade was research-led in that specific research studies received popular attention and in that new approaches, focused particularly on ways in which parents could be supported in hearing young children read at home, were designed and evaluated by researchers. A key initiative was the Haringey Reading Project (Tizard, Schofield, & Hewison, 1982) which, on the basis of the earlier findings by Hewison and Tizard (1980), cited previously, pioneered a 2-year program for children aged 6 to 8 in a disadvantaged area of London. Children took school-reading books home and parents were encouraged to help their children by talking about stories, listening to children's oral reading with minimal intervention, and ensuring that the shared reading experiences remained enjoyable. Tizard et al. found that the program produced significant reading test gains. The Belfield Reading Project (Hannon & Jackson, 1987), sought to follow the Haringey approach, was nationally influential in developing practice in parental involvement, but did not fully replicate findings regarding gains (Hannon, 1987).

These projects employed what Hannon (1995) has termed an "open approach" to parents hearing children read; that is, parents were given only very general guidance in what to do in assisting children's oral reading. The question arose as to whether parents—who lacked professional training and often had a low level of formal education—were competent in the role of hearing children read. To investigate this, Hannon, Jackson, and Weinberger (1986) carried out a detailed observational study of over fifty 6-year-old children in a disadvantaged area who were audiotaped reading at home to their parents and also reading in school to their class teachers. The adults' strategies were analyzed in terms of their preference for certain *moves* in reading sessions—for example, providing words or phrases, giving directions, invoking phonic rules, and encouraging reading for meaning or speculation. Although there were some interesting differences between the teachers' and parents' strategies (e.g., teachers were more active in making moves and displayed slightly more concern for meaning, whereas parents gave children more time), the overall findings clearly showed that the great majority of parents— even those with limited literacy—were a help, and could hardly ever be considered a hindrance in their children's learning (Hannon et al.). In the early 1980s, the idea of parents being so directly involved in a central part of the curriculum was a considerable challenge to educational orthodoxy in England, but by the end of that decade parents were widely accepted by schools as having an important role in the teaching of literacy.

The 1980s also saw the emergence of *prescriptive approaches* to parents hearing children read. The best known was *paired reading*, which involved parents simultaneously reading aloud with their children until the child indicated a desire to read independently and only joining in again if the child had difficulties (Topping & Lindsay, 1991; Topping & Wolfendale, 1985). These programs were generally short term (weeks rather than months or years) and targeted at children aged 7 or over who had reading difficulties. Programs were found to produce gains, mainly in terms of pretest/posttest comparisons of reading ages (Topping & Lindsay, 1992). Hannon (1995) describes some other prescriptive approaches, such as *shared reading*, developed in England in the period or, in the case of *Pause, Prompt and Praise* imported from New Zealand; but none of these were taken up as widely as paired reading. In addition to reading programs that emphasized parents hearing their children read, there were other kinds of family literacy programs such as *reading workshops* in which parents came into schools to work with their own children (e.g., Pearce, 1992; Weinberger, 1983). Another interesting development was *family reading groups* in which families' enjoyment of reading was encouraged through group discussion and book review sessions held in libraries, centers, and schools (Beverton, Hunter-Carsch, Obrist, & Stuart, 1993). These programs were evaluated in terms of process factors and families' views but not in terms of measured literacy outcomes for individuals.

Another line of research in the 1980s serving to justify family literacy programs was that showing the (previously overlooked) extent of young children's knowledge of literacy before formal schooling. Most work came from the United States, within the emergent literacy tradition (Goelman, Oberg, & Smith, 1984; Goodman, 1980; Hall, 1987; Teale & Sulzby, 1986). It showed that children's knowledge of literacy practices and skills valued by schools when they start formal education was a powerful advantage for later school literacy achievement (Harste, Woodward, & Burke, 1984; Heath, 1982, 1983). There was also significant research in England that pinpointed particular knowledge such as awareness of story (Wells, 1987), knowledge of letters (Tizard, Blatchford, Burke, Farquhar, & Plewis, 1988), and phonological awareness (Bryant & Bradley, 1985; Maclean, Bryant, & Bradley, 1987). Such research did not have an immediate impact on practice but created a climate favorable for the development of family literacy programs in subsequent years. If some children had significant literacy knowledge at school entry, it seemed reasonable to infer that they had acquired it from their families. If they did not have it (and if it was considered desirable that they should have it), there was a case for family literacy programs to help them acquire it.

Thus, family literacy programs in the broad sense were established in the 1980s in early childhood education to the extent that educators seriously involved parents in the teaching of reading to their children. Often, of course, grandparents, siblings, other family members, or caregivers took the parent role. However, programs remained somewhat limited in almost always focusing on reading to the neglect of writing, in being restricted to families with young children, and in rarely meeting adults' literacy learning needs.

Within adult literacy education in the 1980s, there was still very little that could be recognized as family literacy—in terms of either programs or research. Adult literacy tutors were rarely linked into early childhood parent involvement programs, although many tutors recognized that those of their students who were parents were often highly motivated to help their children avoid repeating their own educational experience. The early childhood parent involvement programs described previously tended to be implemented in communities where the issue of parents' literacy difficulties often arose. Anecdotal evidence in England, as in the United States, was not only that such parents could help their children, but also that, in some cases, parents' own literacy improved as a result of involvement (Jackson & Hannon, 1981; Parker, 1986; Raim, 1980). Unfortunately, these observations did not lead to family literacy programs deliberately focused on adults. There were, however, some developments in adult literacy education that paved the way for family literacy programs in the next decade. There was a shift away from one-on-one tutoring of adult learners to teaching them in groups and to initiatives engaging whole communities. Pioneering approaches by adult literacy tutors showed that parent literacy courses in community settings could, in a nonjudgemental way, help parents understand how to support their children's developing literacy (Bird & Pahl, 1994). On the other hand, changes in government funding systems in the late 1980s that reduced funding for outreach and development activity and switched adult basic education away from local authorities into further education colleges discouraged the development of community approaches including family literacy. It was not until the 1990s that adult literacy education was able to make a serious contribution to family literacy.

The Early 1990s

A new factor by the 1990s in England was concern about literacy *standards*. Concern was expressed by politicians, government agencies such as the national inspectorate for schools, employers, and a significant number of professional educators. For example, a government document asserted that "our performance in literacy is behind a number of comparable English-speaking countries" and "standards of literacy have not changed significantly between the end of the war and the early 1990s" (DFEE, 1997, p. 19). The effect was to quicken the pace of developments in both of the strands relevant to family literacy practice—early childhood education and adult basic education. The two strands began to link together in family literacy programs. Although there had been signs in the 1980s that educators in each field appreciated the importance of linking with those in the other, it was difficult to sustain and develop new practice in the absence of institutional and financial support. The situation changed dramatically in 1993 with an initiative taken by the ALBSU, a government-funded, quasi-independent agency that hitherto had been concerned only with adults.

ALBSU imported a model of family literacy from the United States. Though it only acknowledged origins in rather general terms, it is fairly clear that the inspiration was a model then being promoted vigorously in the United States by the National Center for Family Literacy (NCFL). NCFL and ALBSU defined family literacy programs almost identically in terms of required components: basic skills instruction for parents, early literacy education for young children, and parent–child activities; although ALBSU gave less emphasis to parenting education (ALBSU, 1993b; Darling, 1993). ALBSU secured government funding for its model.

The significance of the ALBSU initiative for England was that adult literacy education was for the first time firmly linked with early childhood literacy education. The effect, however, was that the term family literacy became, in the minds of some, only applicable to the ALBSU model. If one takes the broader definition of family literacy offered at the beginning of this chapter, then it should have also included the parent involvement programs in the 1980s described in the previous section.

ALBSU prepared the ground for its initiative by commissioning research from City University, London, into a sample of 1,761 families, with 2,617 children, drawn from the National Child Development Study sample (ALBSU, 1993c). Parents were asked in interviews whether, since leaving school, they had any problems with reading, writing, or spelling. Children's reading was tested by the Peabody Individual Achievement Test. The focus of the study was the link between parents' reported literacy difficulties and their children's literacy test attainment. Results showed that children of parents who reported having literacy difficulties were about twice as likely as others to be in the lowest quartile on reading test scores (ALBSU, 1993c). This result might be considered evidence that the low literacy attainment of children that was causing national concern was the result of parents' literacy difficulties. Hannon (2000), however, reinterpreted the ALBSU data and pointed out that the vast majority of children in the lowest quartile did *not* have such parents. Rather, their parents were in the great majority who did not report literacy difficulties. Nevertheless, findings from the ALBSU study helped persuade government that programs directed at families in which parents had literacy difficulties would have a significant impact on national literacy standards for children.

In 1993, ALBSU instituted four demonstration programs in "areas of deprivation" in England and Wales (a fifth, in a bilingual community, could not be successfully implemented). They were based in or near primary schools. Programs worked with both parents with poor basic skills, and few, if any, qualifications, and their children, aged 3 to 6. The programs involved courses lasting 96 hours over 12 weeks (6 hours a week for parents and children separately and 2 hours in joint sessions). They were less intensive than the Kenan model, promoted in the United States by the NCFL (see Wasik & Herrmann, this volume), but still substantial. Parents worked on their own literacy and on how to extend the help they gave to their children with reading and writing. Children were given intensive early years teaching, with a strong emphasis on writing and talking, as well as on reading. Evaluation findings—to which we return later—found that children and parents gained from programs (Brooks et al., 1997; Brooks, Gorman, Harman, & Wilkin, 1996; Brooks, Harman, Hutchison, Kendall, & Wilkin, 1999).

It is worth at this stage referring to another aspect of the ALBSU initiative that changed the national scene—a scheme of small grants to support local innovation in family literacy. The scheme enabled a wider range of organisations to become involved in family literacy and a variety of approaches were used. Research into the scheme did not address the issue of outcomes but did indicate the diversity of family literacy programs that had developed locally by 1995 (Poulson, Macleod, Bennett, & Wray, 1997). Some findings echoed those from the demonstration programs, for example, that joint parent–child sessions were believed to be particularly successful. But there were some programs that were very different from the demonstration program model, especially those working with bilingual families. One program, for example, targeted Muslim women and offered home-based provision by recruiting and training volunteers who were speakers of the main community languages and who then worked with the other women in their own homes. Another program involved parents using their creative and organizational skills to make *storysacks* (a decorated bag containing a book and soft toys, tapes, and other resources related to it). Most of the programs enabled early childhood and adult literacy educators to work together in ways that had not hitherto been possible.

The effect of the ALBSU initiative and its associated research was to establish a national prominence for family literacy—certainly, one model of it—that it had never had before. There were other developments in England in the 1990s. Reviews have been provided by Harrison

(1995) and Wolfendale and Topping (1996). In 1993, the National Literacy Trust, a charity, independent of government, was established. It aimed to work with others: to enhance literacy standards; to encourage more reading and writing for pleasure by children, young people, and adults; and to raise the profile of the importance of literacy in the context of social and technological change. It took the view that the involvement of the wider community—which included parents—would help in the creation of a culture that can more positively support literacy for all. Thus, the growth of family literacy projects, which increasingly involved local agencies, was seen by the National Literacy Trust as a valuable addition to the work of schools.

It was also in the 1990s that research from the previous decade into children's early literacy development began to influence practice (it being not unusual in England, as elsewhere, for there to be a lag of some years between research and its application). Family literacy programs began to recognize the importance of the studies, cited earlier, of emergent literacy and family literacy practices involving both children and parents. Other research that compared children's early language and learning experiences at home and in school (Tizard & Hughes, 1984; Wells, 1987) contributed to a reevaluation of the power of home learning. Building on this research, Hannon (1995, 1998) sought to develop a conceptual framework for family literacy programs, particularly those directed at children. He identified many ways in which home learning could be more powerful than school learning (e.g., in being shaped by immediate interest and need, in often seeming to be effortless, in spontaneity, in being a response to real rather than contrived problems, in being of flexible duration, in having a high adult–child ratio, in being influenced by adult models, and in allowing a "teaching" role for younger family members). In relation to literacy, he further suggested that families could provide children with four requirements—summarized as *ORIM*—for early learning.

O   *Opportunities* to read texts (including environmental print), to attempt writing, and to talk about literacy

R   *Recognition* of early literacy achievements, including the earliest signs of emergent literacy that can easily go unnoticed

I   *Interaction* with more proficient literacy users, usually through facilitation rather than instruction

M   *Models* of what it is to use written language in everyday family social practices, in the community, and at work

Family literacy programs can be understood—and designed—as attempts to extend what families provide for literacy learners in relation to the aforementioned. The ORIM framework has been shown by Nutbrown and Hannon (1997) and by Hannon and Nutbrown (1997) to provide a practicable basis—valued by practitioners—for the design of family literacy programs. A national review of early years' language and literacy parent involvement programs by the National Children's Bureau Early Childhood Unit found that the ORIM framework was employed by several programs (Pugh, 1996). Brooks et al. (1996) also reported that it had been used in ALBSU demonstration programs. ORIM is just as applicable to adults' literacy learning as it is to children's, but it has been taken up more widely within the early childhood education strand of family literacy work (in projects to be described in the next section) than it has in adult literacy education.

From the Late 1990s to the Present

In the late 1990s the model of family literacy developed by ALBSU was gradually main-streamed in England (by which time the organization's remit, interestingly, had been extended to learners of all ages and its name had been changed to the Basic Skills Agency, BSA). Some funding for family literacy was transferred into national education support grants for which local education authorities applied to government if they were prepared to provide co-funding. With the national literacy strategy rolled out into all schools in England, a short program (up to 12 hours) was introduced to help parents understand the new approaches to literacy in the primary classroom, notably the literacy and numeracy hours. The original family literacy model also continued, unchanged. The requirements continued to be somewhat inflexible in terms of parents having to attend classes and children having to be taught as a group. Thus, it continued to be only one form of family literacy program—often referred to as the *BSA model*—that was supported directly from central government funds. At the same time, a variety of other kinds of family literacy programs developed but on a smaller scale, funded by a variety of short-term sources (often local agencies focused on economic or social regeneration and also some independent charitable sources). Mainstream educational organizations such as schools or colleges rarely had funds of their own for family literacy work, but a complex pattern of partnerships meant they were often involved in provision.

The National Literacy Trust conducted several surveys in the late 1990s to identify literacy activity in England and other parts of the UK. Four main sectors were surveyed: local education authorities, including community education services; college adult basic education provision; libraries; and voluntary and local training organizations. The national picture revealed by surveys is of hundreds of family literacy initiatives, defined broadly as programs that aim to work through parents to improve the reading and writing of their children as well as those that have the improvement of the parent's literacy as an aim. Some initiatives are individual single-site programs; others involved whole sets of area-focused programs. Some programs were funded through the continuation of the ALBSU/BSA initiative and therefore conformed to the BSA model; but many have been funded by other local, national, or European sources such as the Further Education Funding Council, the Single Regeneration Budget, the Adult and Community Learning Fund or the European Social Fund. The latter sources, which take a wider focus on regeneration and social inclusion, have offered more flexibility in terms of how the program is delivered so that there are now significant alternative models of family literacy to the BSA model.

The program content, location, duration, and aims revealed by the surveys vary enormously. Most programs are conducted in English, but many are in other languages (Welsh, Bengali, Urdu, Punjabi, and Turkish). Many programs have been located in schools, but locations have included baby clinics, family centers, day nurseries, libraries, after-school support centers, travellers' sites, playgroups, churches, and housing schemes. Some programs involve parents in literacy-related activities such as making books or puppets. Some focus on the parents of very young children and babies, for example, through sharing books, storytelling, and nursery rhymes. Some provide resources for parents to use at home. Others seek to involve parents in school or center activities. Some are short fixed-term programs; others are open-ended. Where programs address parents' literacy, they usually offer some kind of accreditation for participants' learning—either through an established national scheme or through a range of local "open college" systems that accredit a wider range of courses. A great range of agencies have been involved, including schools relating to every age range, adult community colleges, further education colleges, voluntary organizations and education-business-training organizations, newspapers, community associations, ex-offender agencies, social services, and health care organizations. It seems that there have been several thousand families involved in programs. In summary, by the end of the 1990s, a great deal was happening and the term family literacy had become a familiar part of educational discourse across all sectors of education from the early years to adult and further education.

Some family literacy programs have made a national impact and have been reasonably well documented. In Sheffield, the REAL (Raising Early Achievement in Literacy) Project has been a research-led collaboration between the University of Sheffield, the local education authority, and schools in which a family literacy program—involving parents in children's preschool literacy development and meeting some of the parents' educational aspirations—was developed on the basis of ORIM framework (Nutbrown & Hannon, 1997). The REAL program was undertaken by preschool teachers who visited homes, provided books for loan, communicated with families by mail, and offered various group activities. Emerging findings from a qualitative and a randomized control trial (RCT) evaluation of the program indicate benefits for families, including significant literacy gains for children (Hannon & Nutbrown, 2001). Two other influential projects in England have used the ORIM framework. In Sefton, near Liverpool, the FAST (Families and Schools Together) program has had outreach workers who visit homes, talk with parents about the literacy opportunities that are already taking place in the home, and suggest ways in which these can be built on (Cook, 1994). Parents are also offered a series of workshops that could lead to accredited learning. Interestingly, parents have had a significant input into the running of the program and have shared some inservice courses with teachers. In the PEEP (Peers Early Education Partnership) in Oxford the ORIM framework has been extended beyond literacy to include also areas of child development, specifically numeracy, music, and self-esteem (Roberts, 2000). PEEP sought to develop an area-based program of group activities for the entire preschool age range from babies to school entrants at age 5.

Reading is Fundamental, UK (RIF, UK), based on the U.S. model and delivered by the National Literacy Trust across the UK, encourages families to enjoy stories and books together through a variety of promotional activities, which include providing books to children at no cost to them or their families. *Shared Beginnings*[1] is a program that is delivered in partnership with, for example, housing providers and early years organizations to provide an 11-week informal program for parents in their own communities. The program has been successful in getting parents to see in a practical way how they can develop their babies' and toddlers' language skills through play, sharing books, and in conversation, with the bonus of three new books to choose and keep, a feature of all RIF, UK programs (Hannon & Hirst, 2002).

A further impetus to the development of family literacy programs came in 1998 to 1999 with the National Year of Reading for England, a key part of the government's National Literacy Strategy and lifelong learning policy. The Year was run by a team based at the National Literacy Trust and included a high-profile media campaign with TV advertisements, monthly themes to encourage local activity, and a free booklet for parents, *A Little Reading Goes a Long Way*. The Year can claim some success in raising the profile for reading and increasing understanding of the different and imaginative ways parents can be supported in helping their children to read. During the Year, and since, the level of reader development work undertaken by libraries has greatly increased, very often with other partners. These include regular library sessions for parents and toddlers, *Books for Babies* initiatives (combining babies' health checks with a book gift event at the local library) and running, in partnership, a range of family literacy programs. The Year also brought to prominence the continuing need to help fathers to see their role in sharing books with their children. Many lessons were learned during the *Year of Reading* about how to reach parents, in particular fathers, in order to help them support their children's literacy development. Subsequently, the National Reading Campaign's Reading Champions initiative, also run by the National Literacy Trust, promotes the importance of male role models (particularly fathers and grandfathers) in encouraging boys to read.

As we bring the story up to the present, there has been an interesting shift in the focus of activity in family literacy in England. One example, reflecting recent concerns around social

---

[1]Copyright Reading Is Fundamental Inc. adapted and used by permission.

inclusion, is the change of emphasis in paired reading approaches away from an elite selected group of parents helping in schools to a greater attempt to involve all families in their own homes (Topping, 2001). There is another, more significant development. During the 1980s and early 1990s, most developments in family literacy originated from the early childhood education strand. During the 1990s, this strand linked with adult literacy education. Now, in the early years of another decade, it is noticeable that the source of new developments tends to be adult literacy education. Government policy and funding are focusing intensively on adult basic skills provision (DfEE, 2000), and it is in that context that opportunities have arisen for family literacy and family learning initiatives. Meanwhile, early childhood education has become more focused on school literacy rather than on family literacy, as a consequence of unrelenting pressure on schools to raise literacy standards as measured by national assessments and reported in widely published school performance tables. In the current political climate, there is some risk that family literacy programs will be seen only as a way of meeting adults' literacy needs rather than also meeting those of children.

Evaluation

There has been extensive evaluation of family literacy programs in England. Most of it has been conducted in relation to the early childhood education strand of family literacy. By the mid-1990s, over 30 studies were reviewed by Hannon (1995); as well as several earlier reviews of the literature, by other authors. Hannon concluded that there was substantial evidence of benefits, and no reports of negative consequences, of involving parents. Most evaluations concern programs that encouraged or supported parents in hearing children read—following either an open or a prescriptive approach. They have generally employed quasiexperimental designs or pretest/posttest comparisons using standardized tests (in effect using a test standardization sample as a quasiexperimental control group). There have been very few RCT evaluations. Nevertheless, given the overwhelmingly positive findings, it is probably safe to conclude that the parental involvement form of family literacy benefits children's literacy. What is harder to judge, given the limitations of research designs, is just how well it works. There is little evidence of programs having completely reliable, profound, and lasting effects for all families involved. Some programs in some circumstances appear to have considerable impact on some families but in other cases effects may be rather modest. The problem of take-up has often been overlooked in evaluations, even though, from a policy perspective, programs with low take-up cannot make much impact at community level. Apart from Hewison (1988) there is a lack of follow-up studies of early childhood literacy parental involvement programs. Neither are there good studies comparing the effectiveness of different kinds of programs. In practice, the conditions for direct comparison do not often arise, but research has helped identify factors to be kept in mind in choosing between programs. Hannon (1995) concluded that some programs are costly in professionals' time but may be helpful for older children who are having continued difficulties with reading (e.g., paired reading or pause, prompt, and praise); others might be suitable for all children at a younger age and may be integrated into ordinary school practice. Little is known about the effects of combining different forms of involvement. Another gap concerns involvement in writing, the predominant focus having been book reading. In summary, more needs to be researched, but enough has been done to conclude that in early childhood education parental involvement forms of family literacy programs are effective.

What about family literacy programs that aim to change parents' literacy too? Here, there are some interesting qualitative studies (e.g., in England, Finlay, 1999; in Scotland, Tett, 2000) that have illuminated important issues in program design, the nature of effects, and factors limiting effectiveness. The research with the greatest policy impact, however, has been a series of largely quantitative evaluations of the ALBSU demonstration programs carried out by Brooks and colleagues (1996, 1997, 1999). These researchers found that children in families who joined the demonstration programs made greater progress than those in the general population, and there were preprogram/postprogram gains for parents (Brooks et al., 1996). Further research found that children in the demonstration programs maintained their gains (Brooks et al., 1997) and that other programs developed for bilingual families also appeared to be effective (Brooks et al., 1999). However, there is as yet no convincing evidence in England (or, for that matter, in the United States) that intergenerational programs combining provision for adults with provision for children (including parent–child sessions) have greater effects, or are more cost effective, than separate child-focused or adult-focused programs (Hannon, 2000). Two linked issues that are seriously underresearched in those family literacy programs that require parents' participation as literacy learners are take-up and participation. If take-up by the parents in targeted groups is low (and Hannon, 2000, points to signs that this is often the case), the value of such programs is greatly diminished. Even if they do join programs, it matters whether they continue to participate—a factor rarely directly researched. Finally, it is unfortunate, and perhaps a little surprising, that no study has yet set out directly to test the strong claims made for the synergistic benefits of intergenerational programs as compared to stand-alone programs.

Current Key Policy Issues

Clearly, family literacy in England is popular with policymakers and has gained a certain momentum in the last few years, with largely positive benefits. On the plus side, there has been much more funding for family literacy programs. However, the pace of change has resulted in a distinct lack of clarity in what is now meant by the term family literacy. Very simply, family literacy needs to catch up with the rapidly changing policy climate and restate what it is for and where it fits. This view, we believe, is reflected in the four main issues currently facing family literacy in England: funding, flexibility in program design, professional development, and research and evaluation. The ways in which these issues are resolved will determine the future shape of developments.

First, the issue of *funding*. Recent years have seen increased government funding for family literacy programs, but it has often been of a short-term nature. Sometimes funding has been limited to supporting as little as a single 12-week program in one school with little prospect of continuation. This situation obviously inhibits recruitment and professional development of program staff as well as long-term planning of provision. It also makes it near impossible to sustain development work in communities. A further difficulty concerns the remit of agencies disbursing funds and their relation to the organizations providing family literacy programs. Until recently, most funding for family literacy was channelled through the Basic Skills Agency and local education authorities to *schools*. That funding has recently become the responsibility of the Learning and Skills Councils whose main remit nationally is to provide funds for further education and training in the postcompulsory sector, often to *colleges* providing vocational courses for younger or older adults. The effect of the new funding regime is likely to be that family literacy programs will be seen as a way of meeting the needs of adults rather than those of children or families. The Learning and Skills Council has yet to formulate a national strategy regarding family literacy. If it takes a narrow view, family literacy could become a minor component of adult basic skills provision. If it takes a broader view, and if it also supports local partnerships bringing together providers of early childhood as well as adult education, the Learning and Skills Council could lead family literacy into a new phase of development.

Second, and closely related to funding, is the issue of *flexibility* in program development. For many years the only form of program to have received steady government funding was the BSA model (the program described earlier that was adapted from the United States by ALBSU in 1993). Other forms of programs—for example, those originating from the early childhood education strand and focusing more on parental involvement in children's learning—did not qualify. Hannon (2000) has referred to the BSA model as a *restricted* form of family literacy program, in that its availability is restricted to those families where parents are interested, willing, and able to participate as learners themselves as well as to help their children's literacy. There are good grounds for believing that only a minority of the children who could benefit from family literacy programs have parents who, *at the time their children are in a program*, also want to be learners in adult literacy education or, for that matter, in any form of adult education. Other, more flexible programs are needed to complement the BSA model. The full potential of family literacy programs will only be realized when funding extends to more flexible programs that recognize its social as its well as educational benefits. For example, placing family literacy within a wider context of parenting would add value to current policy initiatives in England on crime reduction, tackling children's antisocial behavior in schools and in the wider community, as well as supporting health programs on teenage pregnancy and healthy living. There are signs of a willingness on the part of government at least to investigate potential link-ups through neighborhood renewal programs. Incorporating this approach nationally, however, would be a major challenge, not least in terms of the design and content of programs, and yet could produce even greater benefits for individual families and their communities.

From the perspective of educationalists, flexibility in program development is needed for other reasons. Often what is appropriate for some families in some communities is *stepped provision*. Many parents do not feel sufficiently confident to go on a family literacy course or see the need for it (even if program staff believe they would benefit). *Taster sessions* to attract new learners may be needed. After attending such sessions, parents often feel motivated and confident to take on a longer, more explicitly literacy-related, course. Though taster sessions— mostly of 3-hour duration—are increasingly recognized and funded, there is less appreciation of the need to fund taster courses of different lengths which would allow parents to progress at a pace that suits their individual circumstances and growing confidence. The challenge for funders is to recognize this kind of progression and allow providers sufficient flexibility to design appropriate programs. Another concern to many providers is *gender*. In practice the term family in family literacy programs means not only parent and child but also mother and child. In the ALBSU demonstration programs, for example, only 4% of the parents involved were fathers—an entirely typical finding. In recent years, there have been various attempts to increase the involvement of fathers but the point here is, again, that there is a need for flexibility in program design.

A third issue of great importance for the future is *professional development*. For both early childhood educators and adult educators, family literacy presents new professional challenges. For example, early childhood educators cannot plan teaching of adults without taking into consideration a number of factors that do not apply in the teaching of young children (e.g., adults' previous negative experiences of schooling; adults' self-awareness of their personal priorities, their learning needs, and their preferred learning strategies). Adult educators may not know much about preschool literacy development or school curricula. The answer is courses and other professional development opportunities to enable professionals to acquire new knowledge and skills. There have been some initiatives in England. The BSA has developed training materials and resources and provides training for family literacy practitioners as well as for those delivering programs in early years settings. It has also developed a 3-day basic skills awareness training program for early years professionals working in neighborhood nurseries, which is likely to be incorporated as an additional module into some national childcare qualifications. Higher level courses are being developed for adult basic skills teachers and these may eventually include family literacy. All these initiatives, however, are piecemeal, short term, and not linked up. The root cause is funding—unless and until professional development is seen as a national priority there will be little change.

The final issue that will determine future developments is the role of *research and evaluation*. There has been high-quality research in England and it has had an impact on policy, but the relationship between research and policy remains problematic. Policies are often devised and implemented—unsurprisingly—for political reasons. Sometimes the evidence is there; sometimes it is not. Policymakers often have much shorter time horizons than researchers (who, for example, may want to know the outcomes of a longitudinal study before reaching conclusions about "what works"). What is lacking in England is sustained research into basic issues. For example, there is still no direct evidence about the benefits to be gained by combining adult literacy and early childhood provision into unitary family literacy programs (as opposed to providing them separately in the conventional way). Is the whole really greater than the sum of the parts? Also, in England, we lack longitudinal studies of the effectiveness of programs, apart from the BSA model. Would the benefits of using other programs last longer? Would they work better for particular target groups, such as parents with low socioeconomic status, English speakers of other languages, fathers, or parents of children with special educational needs? Does using information and communication technology in family literacy programs add to the value of such programs? What effect does program content (including those determined by the participants themselves) have on success? There are many research questions that, if answered, would help support a more coherent and cost-effective approach to the range and funding of family literacy programs. But there is, as yet, no corresponding, long-term program of research.

CONCLUSIONS

In closing this account of family literacy in England—its development and the challenges it currently faces—it is interesting to venture comparisons with other countries, particularly with the United States. A distinctive feature of the English story is the vigor of the early childhood strand of family literacy. This strand is necessary for family literacy programs everywhere, but in England it has had a long history, has proliferated into many forms, and has had a particularly strong research and evaluation aspect. It was the adult education strand that, despite some preexisting commitment to outreach work and a few interesting initiatives, needed development and that was accelerated by England accepting ideas from the United States (a flow of ideas that does not seem to have occurred in the opposite direction). Other features are common to both countries. For example, the existence of clear funding streams (in the United States, Even Start; in England, the ALBSU/BSA schemes) has been vital for enabling practitioners to develop family literacy programs and to combine work from both relevant strands of education. In both countries, although there have been a variety of family literacy programs, influential organizations (in the United States, the NCFL; in England, the BSA) have promoted the primacy of one model. These countries—and others worldwide—continue to face the challenges of integrating theory and practice, of addressing literacy inequalities, and of preparing practitioners to work respectfully and effectively with parents and children. Some international exchange of ideas, experiences, and lessons learned could help all of us better serve families.

REFERENCES

Adult Literacy and Basic Skills Unit (ALBSU). (1993a). *Family Literacy News, No. 1*. London: Adult Literacy and Basic Skills Unit.
Adult Literacy and Basic Skills Unit (ALBSU). (1993b). *Framework for family literacy demonstration programs*. London: Adult Literacy and Basic Skills Unit.

Adult Literacy and Basic Skills Unit (ALBSU). (1993c). *Parents and their children: The intergenerational effect of poor basic skills.* London: Adult Literacy and Basic Skills Unit.

Auerbach, E. (Ed.). (2002). *Community partnerships.* Alexandria, VA: TESOL.

Barton, D., & Hamilton, M. (1998). *Local literacies: Reading and writing in one community.* London: Routledge.

Beverton, S., Hunter-Carsch, M., Obrist, C., & Stuart, A. (1993). *Running family reading groups: Guidelines on how to develop children's voluntary reading.* Widnes: United Kingdom Reading Association.

Bird, V., & Pahl, K. (1994). Parent literacy in a community setting. *RaPAL Bulletin, (24)* (Summer), 6–15.

Brooks, G., Gorman, T., Harman, J., Hutchison, D., Kinder, K., Moor, H., & Wilkin, A. (1997). *Family literacy lasts: The NFER follow-up study of the Basic Skills Agency's demonstration programs.* London: Basic Skills Agency.

Brooks, G., Gorman, T., Harman, D., & Wilkin, A. (1996). *Family literacy works: The NFER evaluation of the Basic Skills Agency's family literacy demonstration programs.* London: The Basic Skills Agency.

Brooks, G., Harman, J., Hutchison, D., Kendall, S., & Wilkin, A. (1999). *Family literacy for new groups: The NFER evaluation of family literacy with linguistic minorities, Year 4 and Year 7.* London: Basic Skills Agency.

Bryant, P., & Bradley, L. (1985). *Children's reading problems.* Oxford: Basil Blackwell.

Cairney, T. (2002). Bridging home and school literacy: In search of transformative approaches to curriculum. *Early Child Development and Care, 172*(2), 153–172.

Cook, M. (1994). Growing into literacy: An approach to home visiting. *Family Literacy News, 4* (November), 6–7.

Darling, S. (1993). Focus on family literacy: The national perspective. *NCFL Newsletter, 5*(1), 3.

Davie, R., Butler, N., & Goldstein, H. (1972). *From birth to seven: A report of the National Child Development Study.* London: Longman/National Children's Bureau.

Department for Education and Employment (DfEE). (1997). *Excellence in schools* (White Paper, Cm 3691). London: The Stationery Office.

Department for Education and Employment (DfEE). (2001). *Skills for life: The national strategy for improving adult literacy and numeracy skills.* London: Department for Education and Employment.

Department for Education and Skills (DfES). (2001). *The National Literacy Strategy: Framework for teaching* (3rd ed.). London: Department for Education and Skills.

Dombey, H., & Meek Spencer, M. (1994). *First steps together: Home-school early literacy in European contexts.* Stoke-on-Trent: Trentham Books.

Douglas, J. W. B. (1964). *The home and the school: A study of ability and attainment in the primary school.* London: MacGibbon and Kee.

Finlay, A. (1999). Exploring an alternative literacy curriculum for socially and economically disadvantaged parents in the UK. *Journal of Adolescent and Adult Literacy, 43*(1), 18–26.

Goelman, H., Oberg, A. A., & Smith, F. (Eds.) (1984). *Awakening to literacy.* Portsmouth, NH: Heinemann.

Goodman, Y. M. (1980). The roots of literacy. In M. P. Douglas (Ed.), *Claremont Reading Conference Forty-fourth Yearbook,* Claremont, CA: Claremont Reading Conference.

Gregory, E. (1996). *Making sense of a new world: Learning to read in a second language.* London: Paul Chapman Publishing.

Hall, N. (1987). *The emergence of literacy.* London: Hodder & Stoughton.

Hannon, P. (1987). A study of the effects of parental involvement in the teaching of reading on children's reading test performance. *British Journal of Educational Psychology, 57,* 56–72.

Hannon, P. (1995). *Literacy, home and school: Research and practice in teaching literacy with parents.* London and Bristol, PA: Falmer Press.

Hannon, P. (1995). The Sheffield REAL Project. *Literacy Today, (3),* 10–11.

Hannon, P. (1998). How can we foster children's early literacy development through parent involvement? In S. B. Neuman & K. A. Roskos (Eds.), *Children achieving: Best practices in early literacy.* Newark, DE: International Reading Association.

Hannon, P. (2000). Rhetoric and research in family literacy. *British Educational Research Journal, 26*(1), 121–138.

Hannon, P., & Hirst, K. (2002). *Report of an evaluation of Shared Beginnings.* London: National Literacy Trust.

Hannon, P., & Jackson, A. (1987). *The Belfield Reading Project Final Report.* London: National Children's Bureau.

Hannon, P., & James, S. (1990). Parents' and teachers' perspectives on preschool literacy development. *British Educational Research Journal, 16*(3), 259–272.

Hannon, P., & Jackson, A. (1987). *The Belfield Reading Project Final Report.* London: National Children's Bureau.

Hannon, P., Jackson, A., & Weinberger, J. (1986). Parents' and teachers' strategies in hearing young children read. *Research Papers in Education, 1*(1), 6–25.

Hannon, P., & McNally, J. (1986). Children's understanding and cultural factors in reading test performance. *Educational Review, 38*(3), 269–280.

Hannon, P., & Nutbrown, C. (1997). Teachers' use of a conceptual framework for early literacy education with parents. *Teacher Development, 1* (3), 405–420.

Hannon, P., & Nutbrown, C. (2001). *Outcomes for children and parents of an early literacy education parental involvement programme*. Paper presented at the Annual Conference of the British Educational Research Association, Leeds.

Harrison, C. (1995). Family literacy practices in the United Kingdom—An international perspective. In L. M. Morrow (Ed.), *Family literacy: Connections in schools and communities*. Newark, DE: International Reading Association.

Harste, J. C., Woodward, V. A., & Burke, C. L. (1984). *Language stories and literacy lessons*. Portsmouth, NH: Heinemann.

Heath, S. B. (1982). What no bedtime story means: Narrative skills at home and school. *Language in Society, 2,* 49–76.

Heath, S. B. (1983). *Ways with words: Language, life and work in communities and classrooms*. Cambridge: Cambridge University Press.

Hewison, J. (1988). The long term effectiveness of parental involvement in reading: A follow-up to the Haringey Reading Project. *British Journal of Educational Psychology, 58,* 184–190.

Hewison, J., & Tizard, J. (1980). Parental involvement and reading attainment. *British Journal of Educational Psychology, 50,* 209–215.

Hirst, K. (1998). Pre-school literacy experiences of children in Punjabi, Urdu and Gujerati speaking families in England. *British Educational Research Journal, 24*(4), 415–429.

Jackson, A., & Hannon, P. (1981). *The Belfield Reading Project*. Rochdale: Belfield Community Council.

Maclean, M., Bryant, P., & Bradley, L. (1987). Rhymes, nursery rhymes, and reading in early childhood. *Merrill-Palmer Quarterly, 33*(3), 255–281.

McGivney, V. (2000). *Recovering outreach: concepts, issues and practices*. Leicester: NIACE.

Morrow, L. M., Tracey, D. H., & Maxwell, C. M. (Eds.). (1995). *A survey of family literacy in the United States*. Newark, DE: International Reading Association.

Nash, A. (1987). *English Family Literacy: An annotated bibliography*. Boston: English Family Literacy Project, University of Massachusetts.

National Center for Family Literacy (NCFL). (1994). Communicating the power of family literacy. *NCFL Newsletter, 6*(1), 1.

Newson, J., & Newson, E. (1977). *Perspectives on school at seven years old*. London: Allen and Unwin.

Nutbrown, C., & Hannon, P. (Eds.). (1997). *Early literacy education with parents: A professional development manual*. Nottingham: NES-Arnold.

Parker, S. (1986). "I want to give them what I never had." Can parents who are barely literate teach their children to read? *Times Educational Supplement* (10 October), 23.

Pearce, L. (1992). Partners in literacy: Organising parents as tutors programmes in Cambridgeshire primary schools. *Links, 17*(1), 10–12.

Poulson, L., Macleod, F., Bennett, N., & Wray, D. (1997). *Family literacy: Practice in local programmes*. London: Basic Skills Agency.

Pugh, G. (1996). Language and literacy in the early years. *Literacy Today, 8,* 4.

Purcell-Gates, V. (2000). Family literacy. In M. L. Kamil, P. B. Mosenthal, P. D. Pearson, & R. Barr (Eds.), *Handbook of reading research, Volume III*. (pp. 853–870). Mahwah, NJ: Lawrence Erlbaum Associates.

Raim, J. (1980). Who learns when parents teach children? *The Reading Teacher, 33,* 152–155.

Roberts, R. (Ed.) (2000). *PEEP Voices: A five year diary*. Oxford: Peers Early Education Partnership.

Taylor, D. (1983). *Family literacy: Young children learning to read and write*. Exeter, NH: Heinemann.

Taylor, D. (Ed.). (1997). *Many families, many literacies: An international declaration of principles*. Portsmouth, NH: Heinemann.

Taylor, D., & Dorsey-Gaines, C. (1988). *Growing up literacy: Learning from inner-city families*. Portsmouth, NH: Heinemann.

Teale, W. H. (1986). Home background and young children's literacy development. In W. H. Teale, & E. Sulzby (Eds.) *Emergent literacy: Writing and reading* (pp. 173–206). Norwood, NJ: Ablex.

Tett, L. (2000). Excluded voices: Class, culture, and family literacy in Scotland. *Journal of Adolescent and Adult Literacy, 44*(2), 122–128.

Tizard, B., & Hughes, M. (1984). *Young children learning: Talking and thinking at home and in school*. London: Fontana.

Tizard, B., Blatchford, P., Burke, J., Farquhar, C., & Plewis, I. (1988). *Young children at school in the inner city*. London: Lawrence Erlbaum Associates.

Tizard, J., Schofield, W. N., & Hewison, J. (1982). Collaboration between teachers and parents in assisting children's reading. *British Journal of Educational Psychology, 52,* 1–15.

Topping, K. J. (2001). *Peer and parent assisted learning in reading, writing, spelling and thinking skills*. Spotlight No. 82. Edinburgh: Scottish Council for Research in Education.

Topping, K., & Lindsay, G. A. (1991). The structure and development of the paired reading technique. *Journal of Research in Reading, 15*(2), 120–136.

Topping, K., & Lindsay, G. A. (1992). Paired reading: a review of the literature. *Research Papers in Education, 7*(3), 199–246.

Topping, K., & Wolfendale, S. (Eds.). (1985). *Parental involvement in children's reading.* London: Croom Helm.

Wasik, B. H., Dobbins, D. R., & Herrmann, S. (2001). Intergenerational family literacy: Concepts, research, and practice. In S. B. Neuman, & D. K. Dickinson, (Eds.), *Handbook of early literacy research* (pp. 444–458). New York: Guilford.

Wedge, P., & Prosser, H. (1973). *Born to fail?* London: Arrow Books and National Children's Bureau.

Weinberger, J. (1983). *The Fox Hill Reading Workshop.* London: Family Service Units.

Weinberger, J. (1996). *Literacy goes to school: the parents' role in young children's literacy learning.* London: Paul Chapman Publishing.

Wells, G. (1987). *The meaning makers: Children learning language and using language to learn.* London: Hodder and Stoughton.

Wolfendale, S., & Topping, K. (Eds.). (1996). *Family involvement in literacy: Effective partnerships in education.* London: Cassell.

II

Children and Early Childhood Education Within Family Literacy Programs

This section expands on the role of adult–child interactions, child characteristics, literacy activities, and the need for quality settings and instruction in promoting early literacy development. It begins with Joseph Sparling's description of literacy interactions between the very young child and parents or caregivers, then moves on to Christopher Lonigan's more intensive examination of the components of emergent literacy and the relation between child characteristics and literacy development. Both authors note the early years' importance as a foundation for literacy and language development and the critical role that adults—both parents and teachers—play in this process. Next, chapters by Lesley Morrow and Jessica Temlock-Fields and Victoria Purcell-Gates take up the role of literature and storybook reading. The section concludes with Allison Fuligni and Jeanne Brooks-Gunn's review of early childhood interventions related to family literacy and a close examination of early childhood classrooms in family literacy programs by David Dickinson, Robert St.Pierre, and Julie Pettengill.

Sparling presents a broad-spectrum approach for facilitating literacy in young children. He sees the developing child's behavior as only gradually becoming uniquely identifiable as literacy and argues that their undifferentiated responses during the early years are in sync with a broad teaching strategy or curriculum. At the center of his approach is a curriculum based on Vygotsky's conceptual model, which suggests that a child's higher mental functions are formed through mediated activities with an adult or more competent peer—a process frequently called scaffolding. Oral language is a key component of his curriculum, a series of gamelike activities that can be used throughout the day in the home or early childhood care setting. Adults can introduce curriculum activities as part of natural, everyday events like eating, dressing, playing with toys, and book reading. Sparling describes his instructional model for the curriculum, which he organizes around three principles or strategies—notice, nudge, and narrate. This model helps adults become more sensitive observers of a child's behavior, learn ways to prompt and encourage the child, and then help the child understand the significance of his or her own actions. Sparling provides a valuable look at how very young children begin to develop the earliest literacy skills.

Lonigan presents emergent literacy as a developmental continuum, with its origins in a child's early life, and highlights areas of emergent literacy most linked to later reading. He then relates this information to family literacy programs. The model he describes includes two interdependent sets of skills and processes: outside-in and inside-out. The outside-in skills and processes represent children's understanding of the context of what they read, reflected in oral language and print motivation. The inside-out units represent knowledge of rules for translating writing into meaningful sounds, like letter knowledge, phonological processing skills, and vocabulary. With this conceptual framework as the background, he presents information on factors in the home environment, such as shared book reading, that can enhance oral language, an outside-in skill, and phonological processing, an inside-out skill. He concludes by identifying oral language skills as the most important ones for young children, because they provide the basis for phonological processing. He also makes recommendations for engaging parents more fully as partners in helping to promote children's literacy acquisition.

Morrow and Temlock-Fields closely examine the use of literature in both home and school settings. Consistent with the view that children's literacy skills develop within day-by-day authentic learning experiences, they discuss the importance of children's literature in literacy instruction. Noting the shift from the use of basal programs or reading instructional materials to the use of literature as an important part of the reading curriculum, they provide conceptual and empirical support for using literature to teach reading. They are guided by the principle that learning to read and write occurs in a book-rich context with an abundance of purposeful communication and where meaning is socially constructed. Other theoretical principles guiding the use of literature include Vygotsky's cultural–historical theory, in which children's social interactions with others, in the environments where reading, writing, and oral language occur, serve to promote literacy development. Morrow and Temlock-Fields offer many ways to incorporate literature into both home and school; to use literature to facilitate comprehension, print awareness, vocabulary, and fluency development; and to engage second-language learners. The overlap between this chapter and Sparling's will interest readers.

Purcell-Gates addresses the role of oral language versus written language in children's literacy development. She presents a case for the importance of written language, rather than oral language, in children's success at learning to read and write in school. She distinguishes between oral language used in conversation and written language produced when children pretend to read aloud, and she sees this written language coming from adults' reading to children. Noting that a basic assumption in the literacy community is that literacy development rests on an oral language base, she argues that, on the contrary, emergent literacy is based on knowledge of written language. Using evidence from studies of pretend reading, she illustrates her positions with data showing that one can distinguish children's written narrative registers from their oral narrative registers. Purcell-Gates thus challenges the belief that children who live in poverty often fail to achieve literacy tasks in school because of limitations in the oral language they learn in their homes. Children from poor backgrounds, she contends, can acquire written language by having storybooks read to them, not through changes in their families' oral language.

Early childhood education is central to family literacy programs. Though family literacy programs developed from an interest in combining adult education and early childhood education, it is possible to trace the development of early childhood intervention programs, noting how family literacy programs fit into the timeline of interventions for young children. In this section, Fuligni and Brooks-Gunn review early childhood interventions, one of the core components of family literacy programs. The authors first describe types of interventions for children from low-income families, the group that family literacy programs tend to target. They then review research on outcomes for these children, including cognitive, social, and emotional development, and discuss implications for family literacy programs. They conclude that the research offers strong support for early interventions that provide direct services to both children and their families, and they note that high-intensity, high-quality programs are the most likely to have positive outcomes. Next they review research on outcomes for children who are in family literacy programs. Evaluations of these programs tend to show that preschool children make moderate gains in language skills. But few experimental studies exist, making it difficult to offer conclusive statements about the programs' effects. Fuligni and Brooks-Gunn end with a strong set of recommendations for evaluation research essential to move the field forward, including not only rigorous experimental studies but also intensive studies of program processes and a much broader study of program outcomes.

Extending the discussion of early childhood programs, Dickinson, St.Pierre, and Pettengill examine the classroom, arguing strongly for changes of a magnitude that will alter children's developmental trajectories and parents' ways of supporting their children's language and literacy. They present findings from evaluations of family literacy programs that suggest such programs fall short of their goals. Though small effects are often seen, the authors believe that considerably more must be done to bring about large and significant changes. Presenting data that support Fuligni and Brooks-Gunn's conclusions about early childhood education, these authors note that quality early childhood interventions can bring about significant child outcomes. But interventions for the most needy children—those served in many family literacy programs—must offer more. The authors use classroom observational studies to show the need to improve programs that serve low-income children. One strategy to improve classroom quality—providing teachers and supervisors with additional information about early language and literacy and requiring them to apply what they learn to the classroom—has produced child outcomes that are positive but still only moderate. The authors identify other areas of potential change in the classrooms, including helping teachers engage parents more actively in their children's development, and gaining information from interviews with parents to help teachers individualize instruction.

These chapters on children and their home and classroom environments provide conceptual frameworks, empirical studies, and recommendations both for improving instructional and environmental settings and for conducting research on how best to provide effective early educational experiences that engage parents as well as children. Although all of these authors agree that variables like adult–child interactions and book reading are important for early literacy, the weight and justification they give to these variables differ.

3

Earliest Literacy: From Birth to Age 3

Joseph Sparling
University of North Carolina at Chapel Hill
and
Georgetown University

The emergent literacy perspective asserts that literacy development is taking place within the child, over time, and that the context for this development is decidedly social (Teale & Sulzby, 1986; Sulzby & Teale, 1991). To emerge, something needs to be there at the beginning (Hall, 1987). Indeed, the concept of emergent literacy implies that there is no definite separation or line between prereading and reading (National Research Council, 2001). Yet sometimes it *seems* as if a line has been crossed. At one time a child is not reading, and a few weeks later the child is beginning to recognize printed words and to read sentences from the page. But that moment of recognizing words on the page is no more the start of literacy than the start of a plant is the moment it breaks through the ground. A lot of unseen growth of roots and underground stems has gone on before, and the visible plant could not possibly survive and flourish if the underground parts were not a primary part of the plant and had not prepared the way.

Perhaps the difficulty in recognizing early literacy is that its *root work* is often invisible or unrecognized. Professionals and parents can easily fall into the pattern of thinking that there are no really early aspects of literacy or that these early aspects happen automatically and that we do not need to be concerned about literacy until later in the preschool years. Yet the earliest stages of literacy are not literally underground, like roots, so why do they typically go unrecognized? Perhaps because literacy moves from lesser to greater differentiation, like some other aspects of development (Sroufe, 1996). It is likely that the earliest literacy skills do not look much like reading or writing because they are not yet well differentiated from other cognitive and social behaviors. Our challenge, then, is to recognize and value the literacy components that are present in the very young child's broadly defined developmental behaviors.

BROAD-SPECTRUM APPROACH

The assumption that earliest literacy is embedded in broad and inclusive developmental strands, and only gradually becomes uniquely identifiable as literacy per se, leads to early intervention strategies that cast a broad net. The infant and young child's relatively undifferentiated responses during the first 3 to 5 years of life may be in better sync with the very general experiences offered by a broad-spectrum teaching strategy or curriculum. In fact, any practice that "puts too many eggs in one basket" and inhibits the widest possible experimentation and exploration could be counterproductive during infancy (Sparling, 1989). Specific teaching of behaviors that are recognizable as reading and writing become appropriate after the young child's behaviors and responses have reached greater differentiation.

A broad-spectrum approach has a track record as a winning strategy in areas of instruction where there is no clearly established roadmap. In 1972, Ramey and his colleagues began the Abecedarian intervention (Ramey et al., 1976) with the goal of improving later school success, especially in reading and math. We did not know for certain how to accomplish this goal, but because the program began in earliest infancy we used a broad-spectrum approach in the curriculum. We believed there was no theoretical or empirical basis for an approach that was narrowly targeted at reading and math performance at this early age. This broad approach in the first 5 years of life is validated by the significantly higher reading (and math) scores of the experimental group throughout elementary and secondary school (Campbell, Helms, Sparling, & Ramey, 1998) and later at age 21 (Campbell, Ramey, Pungello, Sparling, & Miller-Johnson, 2002).

If, in fact, early literacy behaviors are lumped with other behaviors, what does a broad-spectrum strategy for encouraging literacy in the earliest years look like? It looks like well-rounded life. It looks like enriched caregiving. All of the common events of living and caregiving are called into the service of this strategy.

FEATURES OF A BROAD-SPECTRUM CURRICULUM TO SUPPORT EARLY LITERACY

The early childhood curriculum implemented in the Abecedarian Project (Ramey et al., 1976), in Project CARE (Wasik, Ramey, Bryant, & Sparling, 1990), and in the Infant Health and Development Program (Ramey et al., 1992) is called Learningames, The Abecedarian Curriculum. It has five basic features: (a) *Game-like activities* are prescribed for individual children (Sparling & Lewis, 2000, 2001, 2002, 2003). Game activities, called Learningames, are easily understood and assimilated by day-care staff, home visitors, and parents. Each game is presented on a single, self-contained page. These bite-sized bits are not as daunting as other, book-length presentations of curriculum. A game might involve, for example, reading the story of *The Three Bears* and looking around for several sets of three objects to count. (b) *Periodic renewal* of activities allow the parent or teacher to use several games frequently for a while (2 weeks is the suggested period) but also to maintain the child's interest by soon moving on to something new. The period of use is long enough to allow for all aspects of good practice including observation, implementation, and assessment. (c) *Integration into daily life* makes the curriculum feel natural and comfortable in the home or child development center. The curriculum activities enrich care routines such as diapering, feeding, dressing, and special one-on-one times. (d) *Specific skills for children* in the curriculum activities provide for clarity and immediate utility. These skills are organized into several domains: social/emotional, oral language, early literacy, cognitive, and motor. (e) An *instructional model* for early education gives parents, caregivers, and teachers a pattern and approach for the teaching episodes in the curriculum. With this understanding, the adults can appreciate their own important contribution to the curriculum (Sparling et al., 1991).

Conceptual Model

The gamelike activities, the Learningames, are at the heart of our broad-spectrum approach. The conceptual rationale for the Learningames curriculum derives from Vygotskian theory

(Vygotsky, 1978). In this view, the fundamental way in which a child's higher mental functions are formed is through mediated activities shared with an adult or more competent peer. Each of the Learningames is one (actually a whole series) of these mediated activities. The adult serves a special role by surrounding the child's efforts with his or her own subtly supporting and enabling behaviors. This process is typically called scaffolding. Key among the adult's scaffolding behaviors is oral language, which provides the critical link between the social and the psychological planes of human mental functioning. For example, the adult's narration of the child's actions and decision making in a Learningames activity gives the child a template on which to build his or her own private speech, and, in the Vygotskian view, private speech is the primer mechanism of the child's self-regulation. This is but one example of the various psychological tools or processes that are nurtured within the child by the adult mediation that is characteristic of the Learningames interactions. *Learningames, The Abecedarian Curriculum* (Sparling & Lewis, 2000, 2001, 2002, 2003) places its emphasis squarely on the process and content of the adult–child interaction as the carrier of the educational intervention to promote literacy. In the next section the instructional model is described.

Instructional Model

The curriculum's instructional model takes into account the abilities of the preverbal child and is particularly suited for encouraging emergent literacy. The model is organized around three principles or strategies that are used sequentially:

- Notice
- Nudge
- Narrate

If these strategies are present in the adult's behavior, he or she typically finds it easy to implement a selected curriculum episode or to think of variations and to invent new educational activities throughout the day. In addition, these skills assist the teacher, parent, or caregiver in all aspects of the child's development and learning, even those aspects that may not be considered core parts of the curriculum. The use of these three techniques is discussed in the following sections.

Notice.   This strategy is something that adults responsible for young children are constantly using. It is easy to notice something that obviously demands attention, such as the child's distressed cry. However, in this instructional model the adult partner broadens his or her understanding of the term.

When educationally interacting with a child, noticing requires an active effort on the adult's part. It involves watching, listening, and waiting for clues about the child's readiness for an activity or response to an activity. With very small babies, it is especially important to notice little things they do. Watching the infant's eyes will help determine whether the infant is following the caregiver's movements or looking at the toy or book used in the game. Holding the child can provide clues to whether he or she is relaxed and responsive or tense and uncomfortable. Smiles and cooing are sure signs that things are going right, but other cues about how the child is feeling are not that obvious. A subtle message, for example, may be just the lowering of eyelids to break eye contact, or a slight turn of the head to show loss of interest.

Older children use many similar gestures and signals to communicate. As their language skills and vocabulary develop, their verbal responses will become an important part of their communication, but the child will continue to communicate in subtle, nonverbal ways. If a child moves closer or puts a hand on the adult's arm, the child may be indicating confusion. If the child starts messing up the toys or other play materials, he or she may be frustrated or bored. Noticing and interpreting these understated messages will help the adult to adapt the activity to suit the child's current status and thus will lead more smoothly and surely to the development of literacy skills.

Nudge.   Here the adult gently gets things going. The strategy involves both getting an activity started and prompting the child to take the activity a step further. The adult focuses the child's visual attention on an object or task by pointing, holding up toys or other materials, or handing an object to the child. Verbal nudging is particularly significant in literacy activities, and involves asking questions, suggesting possible manipulations of objects and materials, and imitating the sounds the child is making or the actions the child is taking. The adult will often act out a behavior for the child to imitate, or demonstrate a behavior by performing the activity first.

Like noticing, nudging requires attentive watching and waiting. The adult must provide the young child time to respond to prompts, to begin performing an activity, and to ask questions or make comments. Waiting provides time to observe how the child is reacting to the adult's nudge. The child may make several unsuccessful starts before settling in, or may respond in a way that differs from the caregiver's expectations. Allowing the child time to explore the task alone, without quickly redirecting his or her actions to predetermined goal behavior will promote the child's deeper involvement in learning activities.

When interacting with a child, nudging is a *two-way street*. On one hand, an adult may initiate a learning activity for a child, then guide the child to a particular outcome based on adult-determined goals. This is only one of several reasonable options. Often, the child will initiate activities, sometimes independently, and sometimes in the middle of an adult-initiated activity. The adult partner's natural tendency may be to immediately redirect the child to the original task; again, however, patient waiting and watching will allow the child to reveal the ways in which he or she is learning. Patience and watchfulness will help the caregiver modify and vary activities to best gain the child's pleasurable participation.

It is important to be flexible. Adhering too strictly to an activity's structure may prevent the child from following his or her own promptings and insights. The adult partner should encourage the child to explore activities independently, as active engagement is an essential feature of the learning process.

But the teacher, caregiver, or parent must also take an active role in modifying tasks to best suit the developmental needs of the child. The adult is careful to notice signs that the child is having difficulty with the task or activity. When the child seems to be floundering, the adult offers a nudge in the form of assistance to the child or a nudge that modifies the task. The adult's action can consist of reducing the number of choices, breaking a large task into several smaller ones, removing surrounding distractions, or assisting the child to complete the task. On the other hand, it is also important to pay attention to indications that the task may have become too easy for the child. The adult can keep the child engaged with a nudge that varies some of the aspects of the task, adds additional components, or substitutes new materials and objects. The goal of nudging is to keep the child challenged without being overburdened, to provide necessary assistance without taking over the task entirely, and to give the child the encouragement needed to feel pleasure and pride in developing skills.

Narrate.   In the third strategy, the parent, caregiver, or teacher narrates or describes the child's action or response to the adult's nudge. The narration tells the story, in real time, of what the child is doing. By describing current actions and events, the adult increases the child's cognitive awareness of the significance of his or her own actions. Through narration, actions that were intuitive or random are raised to a level of consciousness where the child can purposefully repeat or modify them.

FIG. 3.1.   Three-part instructional model of the broad-spectrum approach.

Another function of the adult's narration is to add new information about the objects and processes in the activity. Items may be labeled, choices described, and options enumerated. Simply narrating the choice, "You chose the red ball" adds color information, celebrates the choice, and affirms its significance. These techniques are used not only with play objects but also with print material, as in, "You turned two pages" or "Yes, you pointed to the picture of the monkey's hat."

Narration is not limited to descriptions and information but includes questions. Questions, some of them rhetorical, are interspersed among the adult's informational comments. Questions may range all the way from a raised eyebrow to sophisticated *why* and *how* questions. The child's responses to questions are sometimes actions and sometimes words. As the child's oral language ability increases, the adult seeks an increasing proportion of verbal responses. Adult narration that adds something to or builds on what the child has already said or done is particularly important to the child's growing literacy.

The final function of the adult's narration is to offer positive feedback. Like all of us, young children thrive on support and encouragement, and the caregiver's positive attention nurtures the child's learning behaviors. The adult may offer positive feedback for trying, doing one part, or successfully completing an entire activity. Much narration accomplishes more than one purpose, and descriptions of the child's actions, given in a positive tone, often double as praise, "You stacked two blocks!" The positive affect that colors the words of the narrator conveys the message that the child is competently doing a worthwhile activity. The adult's narration must be thought of as including all the nonverbal feedback expressed to the child. Natural responses such as clapping and showing facial delight are important and effective parts of the narration package.

The three parts of the instructional model are used in an ongoing cycle, as in Figure 3.1, with many iterations of the cycle during any single instructional episode.

Noticing what the child is doing is always the point of departure. What the adult observes guides the selection of an appropriate nudge to get things going. Once the child begins to respond, initiate, or talk, the adult takes on the role of narrator. Often the narration tracks what the child is doing, but at other times it guides the child's action in new directions. Whenever the adult notices a change in the child's behavior, the three-part cycle of the instructional model renews itself and begins again.

Enriched Caregiving

The instructional model is used in activities that are initiated specifically to accomplish a particular cognitive or social goal, that is, activities in a home or in a preschool setting that would be readily recognized as instructional episodes. But the model is used with equal frequency and effectiveness in interactions that occur in the homely and repeated events of daily caregiving. Caregiving events are of particular importance because they consume a significant portion of the very young child's waking hours, and because caregivers typically and intuitively invest these times with positive affect. The child *is* learning during caregiving, whether the caregiver intends it or not. So caregiving presents a ripe opportunity for accomplishing some of the goals of the curriculum. With the addition of selected curricular goals, routine care can become *enriched caregiving*. In enriched caregiving, each event is understood to have a care component and an educational component. The elevation of these caregiving routines to a level of educational significance is a basic tenet of the broad-spectrum curriculum approach. Caregiving routines that are especially ripe for enrichment include feeding, dressing/undressing, and bathing.

Feeding.   The educational component of feeding comprises actions such as speaking to the child while approaching from across the room, singing quietly to the child during bottle or breast feeding, talking about items such as the food/cup/spoon, encouraging an increasing degree of independence after age 1 year, making eye contact, and using the child's name. It also includes pointing to and reading aloud the print on the cereal box, pausing to write the name of a needed item on a grocery list while the child watches, and making up nonsense rhymes with the names of food.

Dressing/undressing.   The educational component of dressing and undressing for the youngest children includes encouraging a brief period of arm and leg play before the diaper is removed, gaining eye contact, and engaging in back-and-forth vocal play during the diaper change. Soon it includes naming some of the items of clothing, talking about the color of some items, encouraging the child to extend his or her arms or legs to assist in the dressing, allowing the child to hold one of the articles of clothing, making eye contact, and using the child's name. It includes pointing out the words on the child's T-shirt and finger-tracing the letters if they are large enough. As the child gets older, the caregiver points out smaller-print items such as clothing labels.

Bathing.   The educational component of bathing includes naming parts of the child's body, providing a floating bath toy (if the child is in a tub or sink), encouraging reaching or splashing, making eye contact, and using the child's name. The adult may trace soapy, letter-like forms on the child's tummy and may engage the child in a hunt for words that rhyme with or sound like body parts. The child will enjoy singing bath songs (such as *Rubber Ducky*) while acting out the words with the adult. Rhymes (such as *Rub-a-dub-dub*), alliterations (*ducky-ducky-dawdle*), and onomatopoeic words that the child can imitate (for example, *splish-splash*) are appropriate parts of the educational component of bath time.

Familiar or Ordinary Activities

In addition to the daily caregiving rituals, there are a number of ordinary activities of living that are so familiar and obvious that they may not usually be thought of as educational. Yet they have strong educational value. In the broad-spectrum approach these simple activities, and others like them, should be engaged in and repeated at every convenient occasion.

Naming Things Nearby.   The caregiver names objects and people in the child's immediate vicinity, often touching them or pointing to them while speaking. Ordinary things such as the window, the crib, or a specific toy are named frequently. When items have printed labels the adult points out the label as well as the item. New things and pictures are purposefully put in the room so that they may be pointed to and named. Print items such as phonebooks and newspapers are prominently included.

Going for a Walk. A walk (by an adult and two children) not only gives variety to the day's routine but also, in group care, provides an occasion for the caregiver or teacher to focus full attention on the two children who are accompanying him or her. Things that occur and events that are seen on the walk are used as educational resources. The walk may be indoors or outdoors. The adult points to things they see along the way, including advertising posters, house numbers, and street signs, and talks about these with the children.

Singing a Song. Caregivers sing songs to accompany many of the events of the day. Where appropriate, they include actions as a playful accompaniment to the songs. Adults encourage the children to join in on a word or two or a familiar action. Songs are used especially to calm or soothe children. The adult makes eye contact with nearby children as she sings. Songs with letter names (for example, e-i-e-i-o) or strong rhyming patterns are featured.

Back-and-Forth Verbal Play. For each very young child, the caregiver finds a variety of times during the day to talk (even though the child does not yet understand or say words). The emphasis is on the reciprocal quality of the vocalizations or words. That is, the experience takes the form of a conversation, with each party taking turns. The caregiver paces him- or herself to match the child's needs and style. In the first year of life the adult and child control and repeat sounds and imbue them with emotions. Later, as the child produces words, the conversation begins to take on real content, but the element of verbal play continues.

Reading a Book

The activity of reading a book is given a special place in the curriculum, even though, like singing a song, it could be thought of as one of the familiar or ordinary activities. Each day, at least two books with simple, clear pictures, are read to each child (preferably on an individual basis). Holding the child in his or her lap, the caregiver or parent goes through each book using techniques to draw responses from the child. The adults learn to draw responses from the child using *Conversation Books* (Lewis, 1987; Sparling, 1984; Sparling & Lewis, 1987), a set of 10 read-aloud books annotated with specific suggestions for the adult's behavior. The adult and child go through the book, engaging in a conversation as they go. From the book annotations the adult gets ideas on how to interact with the child as they talk and turn the pages. The interactions elicit responses from the child at three levels of difficulty or sophistication (Sparling, Lewis, & Ramey, 1995). The levels are the following:

- See
- Show
- Say

See. This is the simplest level of response and is available to even the youngest, preverbal children. At this level the adult points to, talks about, and names the pictures. The adult runs a finger under large words while reading them. Soon, the adult stops pointing to the pictures and watches the child's eyes to see if the child is looking at the picture that is being named.

Show. In the second level of response, the child gives or shows his response using some form of body language. At this level the adult does not point to the pictures but says something like, "Where's his hat?" or "Who's jumping?" and waits for the child to show which picture is correct. The child may pat, touch, or point to the item on the page. Sometimes the child can use other body language to show or act out the answer. For an advanced child, the adult may say, "Show me the word that says 'hat'" on a page that has only two or three words.

Say. The final level is used as soon as the child begins to gain some words. The adult tries to elicit this level of response by saying things like "What did the little boy find?" The child uses language to give his response. And, for an advanced child, the adult may point to a familiar word that the adult has read just a few moments earlier and may ask, "What does this word say?"

The adult tries to elicit these three levels of child response in a hierarchical fashion, moving up the scale when the child seems ready for a little more challenge and sliding back down when the child is puzzled or unable to respond. With all three levels available to the child, he or she will be able to give the most sophisticated response possible at the moment (Sparling et al., 1995). Adults who interact with very young children can use these books as templates and extend the patterns established in the *Conversation Books* to many other children's books. They can use the three levels of child response in other activities that are not directly book related.

The *Conversation Books* vary in difficulty from picture books with one word per page to stories and poetry books. They gain the young child's participation through many techniques in addition to those in the previous paragraphs. Reading a *Conversation Book* has several features (e.g., active engagement and questioning) in common with the technique called dialogic reading (Whitehurst & Lonigan, 2001). (See Lonigan, this volume, for an elaboration on dialogic reading.)

Script Awareness

Print awareness in reading is paralleled by script awareness in writing. The broad-spectrum curriculum approach systematically draws the children's attention to adult writing activities such as preparation of a grocery list or writing a letter. But even more central to the broad-spectrum approach is the utilization of the very young child's early spontaneous markings with a crayon to stimulate awareness of letter shapes and writing.

The adult begins by giving the beginner in art and in prewriting encouragement in the form of verbal approval and respect. The young child benefits also from language that increases awareness of the creative process and product, especially the elements of letters and script that, without adult remark, would go unnoticed by the child. The gaining of new names or labels for things gives the child a way of recalling and reusing an experience, including the experience of making a line that has a particular shape.

Because the young child does not have a high degree of control over his motions, the first drawings are usually little more than a few random marks. The physical process of scribbling is fascinating to the young child, though the marks themselves are of less interest to him. In talking about the very first scribbles, an adult can mention (a) the child's movements, (b) the way the scribble looks, and (c) the way the child probably felt as he made the drawing (Sparling & Sparling, 1973).

Movements. Commenting about movements emphasizes the actual physical process, the act of creating, and helps the child to be more aware of his or her own hand and arm movements. The development of motor coordination is a major task of the child during the scribbling period. Useful narration of motion includes, "Look how your hand moves up and down" and "Your crayon is making light little taps on the paper."

Looks.   Comments that center on the looks or visual features of their work help children to be more aware of the various kinds of things they spontaneously create. Appropriate comments here might be, "You've made some little dots and a long curvy line" and "These lines are way up in the corner of the paper."

Feelings.   An adult may comment on the children's feelings when these are apparent in facial and body expressions and noted in preference for certain shapes, colors, or ways of working. Comments such as, "You worked a long time, you must have enjoyed making those lines and shapes" help the children realize that their actions and feelings are understood and valued.

After many experiences, children gradually develop visual and fine motor control over their scribbles. They begin to be able to keep more of their marks on the paper and to repeat certain movements such as up and down and circular scribbles. Comments like "You made your hand go round and round—like a merry-go-round" can focus attention on this new ability to reliably repeat fine motor actions. Comments and labels can help children realize that they have made a certain mark many times or that they have created a great variety of lines and closed shapes. An adult might say, "You've drawn a small circle right inside this big one. That's hard to do." To call attention to the children's ability to control a writing/drawing instrument the adult can say, "You've made this shape three times" or "You can make the crayon do just what you want it to."

Most of the previous adult narrative remarks link scribbling to both art and writing. The last round of adult comments hone in more narrowly on features of the children's scribbling that have characteristics in common with script letters and writing. For instance, an adult might say: "These two lines cross just like an X." "Here's a straight line like the letter I." "This curve goes halfway around like the letter C." "These lovely marks are in a row, just like the letters in a word."

All of this adult narration and comment on the child's scribbling activities gives a social context to the early uses of a crayon or pencil that shape its meaning (Vygotsky, 1978) toward both art and writing. After marking with a crayon, young children sometimes spontaneously say, "Look at my writing." In the broad-spectrum curriculum approach we provide a social context that validates that youthful belief. Later, when the children begin to make letters and to write, it will feel like a comfortable and familiar line of work. They will be conscious of the fact that they have been at it for a long while.

THE MEMORY GAP

Many literate adults, perhaps most, have some early memories of the early moments when the words on a page began to make sense (i.e., when they were first aware that they could read) or, later, when they had a riveting early experience with a book. The author Michael Swanwick recounts how he stayed up all night to read Tolkien's *The Fellowship of the Ring*. It was a formative experience that assured his vocation as a writer (Swanwick, 2001). Personally, I can recall the time when my mother came into the first-grade classroom to listen to me read. The specific words she whispered to the teacher—"He can't have memorized all that"—are retained in memory 60 years later. Which is precisely to the point of why it is important for adults to know, celebrate, and communicate the significance of events in the young child's life. Adults cannot make every moment in the literacy journey an ah-ha! or a peak experience for the child, but we can acknowledge them as important waypoints on the trip. Our problem now is that important activities in the first 3 or 4 years of a child's life do not even register on the literacy radar of most professionals and parents. If these events do not register for the adults, it is highly unlikely that children will be able single-handedly to invest them with meaning and significance.

Why do we adults not use our own experiences and memories to recognize the earliest aspects of literacy? First, there is a limit to memories of early experiences. With the exception of a few emotionally charged events, we cannot recall most of our earliest growing-up experiences, an unfortunate phenomenon, because some of the most remarkable experiences of life occur in the first few years. For example, infants learn to trust, they begin to use their hands and eyes together in a coordinated way, and they take in all the sounds of human language and begin to sort them out and reproduce them for communication. In a literate environment, most young children also learn that certain marks on paper carry meaning and correspond to oral speech. Yet we reach adulthood without any conscious memories of how all these notable achievements took place or how our parents and environment helped us gain them. It is not surprising that many adults conclude that all these things are learned almost automatically.

So, although our memories can help us to be good parents to our elementary-school-age children and to our teenagers, they also may deceive us into underrating our role as parents to our youngest children. Parents need more than memories to spark ideas and games to help infants and toddlers grow in all early skills, including early literacy. The main thing they need is awareness. With greater awareness of the importance and interrelatedness of early literacy behaviors, parents may value these behaviors, may stimulate them more in children, and may communicate their significance as steps toward reading and writing.

TOWARD DEFINING A SPECIFIC EARLY LITERACY STRAND

To be able to help parents and caregivers, we need to raise our own professional awareness of the earliest steps toward literacy. Investigations that draw links between earlier and later literacy behaviors, and further define the path or various paths that young children take toward reading and writing, will enable future education and intervention efforts to add to the broad-spectrum curriculum approach for at-risk families and children. As described throughout this chapter, broad educational experiences are and will continue to be important for child development. But new knowledge could make it feasible to embed within the broad-spectrum base a focused sequence of experiences targeted more precisely on literacy outcomes.

I nominate three helpful lines of research and pose for each a question that would bring the knowledge base closer to enabling us to target interventions more precisely on the earliest levels of emergent literacy.

1. Written language knowledge is evidenced in 3- to 6-year-olds' pretend reading of storybooks (Sulzby, 1985). What behaviors in children younger than age 3 could give us a window on their awareness and knowledge of written language?

2. Young children show increased emergent literacy knowledge to the degree that they experience people reading and writing in the home (Purcell-Gates, 1996). What specifically are children capable of noticing about reading and writing in their environments at age 2, at age 1, and in the first year of life?

3. The dialogic reading (Whitehurst & Lonigan, 2001) strategy of giving the child a more active role during shared reading has been shown to enhance children's oral language development in the later preschool years (Whitehurst et al., 1994). Would a dialogic reading or other print-interaction intervention, begun with at-risk families and children in the first years of life and sustained over the preschool period, produce lasting effects on reading and writing? How could it smoothly be combined with other, broader intervention strategies?

We do not have to wait for these extensions of knowledge before successfully using the broad-spectrum approach to intervene with at-risk families and children. That is possible now. But with new and more specific knowledge about the earliest years, the literacy elements of the broad-spectrum approach will be sharpened and interventions of greater efficiency and efficacy will be designed.

REFERENCES

Campbell, F. A., Helms, R., Sparling, J. J., & Ramey, C. T. (1998). Early childhood programs and success in school. In S. Barnett & S. Boocock (Eds.), *Early Childhood care and education for children in poverty* (pp. 145–166). Albany, NY: State University of New York Press.

Campbell, F. A., Ramey, C. T., Pungello, E., Sparling, J., & Miller-Johnson, S. (2002). Early childhood education: Young adult outcomes from the Abecedarian Project. *Applied Developmental Science, 6*(1), 42–57.

Hall, N. R. (1987). *The emergence of literacy.* Portsmouth, New Hampshire: Heinemann Educational Books.

Lewis, I. (1987). *Conversation books* (4 titles). Lewisville, NC: Kaplan Press.

National Research Council. (2001). *Eager to learn: Educating our preschoolers.* Committee on Early Childhood Pedagogy. In B. T. Bowman, M. S. Donovan, & M. S. Burns (Eds.), *Commission on Behavioral and Social Sciences and Education.* Washington, DC: National Academy Press.

Purcell-Gates, V. (1996). Stories, coupons, and the *TV Guide*: Relationships between home literacy experiences and emergent literacy knowledge. *Reading Research Quarterly, 31,* 406–428.

Ramey, C. T., Bryant, D. M., Wasik, B. H., Sparling, J. J., Fendt, K. H., & LaVange, L. M. (1992). The Infant Health and Development Program for low birthweight, premature infants: Program elements, family participation, and child intelligence. *Pediatrics, 3,* 454–465.

Ramey, C. T., Collier, A. M., Sparling, J. J., Loda, F. A., Campbell, M. D., Ingram, M. D., Finkelstein, N. W. (1976). The Carolina Abecedarian Project: A longitudinal and multidisciplinary approach to the prevention of developmental retardation. In T. D. Tjossem (Ed.), *Intervention strategies for high risk infants and young children* (pp. 629–665). Baltimore, MD: University Park Press.

Sparling, J. (1980). The "memory gap" and early parenthood. *The newsletter of parenting* (published monthly by Highlights for Children, Inc., Columbus, OH), *3*(6), 2.

Sparling, J. (1984) *Conversation books* (5 titles). Lewisville, NC: Kaplan Press.

Sparling, J. (1989). Narrow- and broad-spectrum curricula: Two necessary parts of the special child's program. *Infants and Young Children, 1*(4), 1–8.

Sparling, J., & Lewis, I. (1987) *Conversation books* (1 title). Lewisville, NC: Kaplan Press.

Sparling, J., & Lewis, I. (2000). *Learningames: The Abecedarian curriculum, birth—12 months.* Chapel Hill, NC: Early Learning, Inc.

Sparling, J., & Lewis, I. (2001). *Learningames: The Abecedarian curriculum, 12–24 months.* Chapel Hill, NC: Early Learning, Inc.

Sparling, J., & Lewis, I. (2002). *Learningames: The Abecedarian curriculum, 24–36 months.* Chapel Hill, NC: Early Learning, Inc.

Sparling, J., & Lewis, I. (2003). *Learningames: The Abecedarian curriculum, 36–48 months, and 48–60 months* (2 vol.). Chapel Hill, NC: Early Learning, Inc.

Sparling, J., Lewis, I., & Ramey, C. (1995). *Partners for learning: Birth to 36 months.* Lewisville, NC: Kaplan Press.

Sparling, J., Lewis, I., Ramey, C. T., Wasik, B. H., Bryant, D. M., & LaVange, L. M. (1991). Partners, a curriculum to help premature, low-birth-weight infants get off to a good start. *Topics in Early Childhood Special Education, 11,* 36–55.

Sparling, J. J., & Sparling, M. C. (1973). How to talk to a scribbler. *Young Children, 28*(6), 333–341.

Sroufe, L. A. (1996). *Emotional development: The organization of emotional life in the early years.* New York: Cambridge University Press.

Sulzby, E. S. (1985). Children's emergent abilities to read favorite storybooks: A developmental study. *Reading Research Quarterly, 20,* 458–481.

Sulzby, E. S., & Teale, W. H. (1991). Emergent literacy. In R. Barr, M. L. Kamil, P. B. Mosenthal, & P. D. Pearson (Eds.), *Handbook of reading research* (Vol. II, pp. 752–758). New York: Longman.

Swanwick, M. (2001). A changeling returns. In K. Haber (Ed.), *Meditations on middle-earth* (pp. 35–46). New York: St. Martin's Press.

Teale, W. H., & Sulzby, E. (Eds.). (1986). *Emergent literacy: Writing and reading.* Norwood, NJ: Ablex.

Vygotsky, L. S. (1978). *Mind in society: The development of higher psychological processes.* Cambridge, MA: Harvard University Press.

Wasik, B. H., Ramey, C. T., Bryant, D. M., & Sparling, J. J. (1990). A longitudinal study of two early intervention strategies: Project CARE. *Child Development, 61*(6), 1682–1696.

Whitehurst, G. J., Epstein, J. N., Angell, A. C., Payne, A. C., Crone, D. A., & Fischel, J. E. (1994). Outcomes of an emergent literacy intervention in Head Start. *Journal of Educational Psychology, 86*, 542–555.

Whitehurst, G. J., & Lonigan, C. J. (2001). Emergent literacy: Development from prereaders to readers. In S. B. Neuman & D. K. Dickinson (Eds.), *Handbook of early literacy research* (pp. 11–29). New York: Guilford.

4

Emergent Literacy Skills
and Family Literacy

Christopher J. Lonigan
Florida State University

Family literacy programs are intergenerational interventions that aim to improve family functioning and family prospects by enhancing child and adult literacy. Interventions include teaching of literacy-related skills to parents and to children independently, as well as efforts to enhance children's literacy through involving parents as partners in their children's literacy development. An example of independent teaching of literacy-related skills would be enrollment of the parent in a high school equivalency degree program with simultaneous enrollment of the child in a center-based preschool program that included literacy-related curriculum components. An example of a literacy partnership between parents and children would be encouragement of a home-based program of family reading aloud of books and other print materials. Family literacy programs usually include both independent and family partnership approaches to enhancing family literacy. In addition, family literacy programs typically include a variety of components that aim to enhance the background functioning of the family in which literacy development might occur. For example, a family literacy program might try to help a family obtain food stamps or medical assistance, and it might deliver instruction on ways to discipline children, or methods of handling stress, and so forth.

An analysis of Even Start, the federal family literacy program, concluded that the relative emphasis in many local programs has shifted too far toward background issues of family functioning and too far away from focused efforts to enhance literacy skills (Haslam, 1998). Such shift in emphasis may partially explain why two controlled studies of Even Start have failed to find evidence of effectiveness in terms of children's literacy achievement (St.Pierre et al., 2002; St.Pierre, Swartz, et al. 1995). In keeping with this analysis, it appears that the time is right for a renewed emphasis on children's literacy within family literacy programs. The last decade has seen an explosion of research on the development of reading in children (Snow, Burns, & Griffin, 1998) and on the preschool precursors of learning to read and write (Whitehurst & Lonigan, 1998, 2001). This research has provided fundamental insights into the nature of reading and has given educational and family program specialists powerful new tools and approaches to deploy in the task of preventing reading difficulties in children. The goal of this chapter is to provide a brief survey of this knowledge base, with the particular aim of highlighting work that is relevant to family literacy programs.

BACKGROUND ON THE IMPORTANCE OF READING

Reading skills provide a critical foundation for children's academic success. Children who read well read more and, as a result, acquire more knowledge in numerous domains (Cunningham & Stanovich, 1998; Echols, West, Stanovich, & Zehr, 1996; Morrison, Smith, & Dow-Ehrensberger, 1995). Nagy and Anderson (1984, p. 328) estimated that the number of words read in a year by a middle-school child who is an avid reader might approaches 10,000,000 (about 1,000 times the number of words in this chapter), compared to 100,000 for the least motivated middle-school reader. By virtue of the sheer volume read, increased knowledge of the vocabulary and content domains (e.g., science or history) included in the texts would be expected. In contrast, children who lag behind in their reading skills receive less practice in reading than do other children (Allington, 1984), miss opportunities to develop reading comprehension strategies (Brown, Palincsar, & Purcell, 1986), often encounter reading material that is too advanced for their skills (Allington), and acquire negative attitudes about reading itself (Oka & Paris, 1986). Such processes may lead to what Stanovich (e.g., 1986) has termed a "Matthew effect" (i.e., the rich get richer while the poor get poorer), such that those children with poor reading skills fall further and further behind their more literate peers in reading as well as in other academic areas (Chall, Jacobs, & Baldwin, 1990), which become increasingly dependent on reading across the school years.

Although the development of skilled reading occurs without significant problems for the majority of children, an estimated one in three children experience significant difficulties in learning to read (Adams, 1990). There is strong continuity between the skills with which children enter school and their later academic performance. Children with limited reading-related skills rarely catch up to their peers (Baydar, Brooks-Gunn, & Furstenberg 1993; Stevenson & Newman 1986; Tramontana, Hooper, & Selzer 1988) and many continue to experience difficulties throughout their school years and into adulthood. Juel (1988), for instance, reported that the probability that children would remain poor readers at the end of the fourth grade if they were poor readers at the end of the first grade was .88. Children who are poor readers are frequently referred to special education classes (Lentz, 1988), and of those who experience the most serious reading problems, 10 to 15% drop out of high school, and only 2% complete a 4-year college program. Surveys of adolescents and young adults with criminal records and/or histories of substance abuse report that about 50% have reading difficulties (NICHD, 2000).

EMERGENT LITERACY

Whereas more traditional approaches to the study of reading often take as their starting point children's entry to the formal school environment, an emergent literacy approach conceptualizes the acquisition of literacy as a developmental continuum with its origins early in the life of a child, rather than an all-or-none phenomenon that begins when children start school. An emergent literacy approach departs from other perspectives on reading acquisition in suggesting there is no clear demarcation between reading and prereading. Current inquiry into emergent literacy represents a broad field with multiple perspectives and a wide range of research methodologies. The approach taken in this chapter is to highlight those areas of emergent literacy that research has shown to be linked with later reading and that might be most relevant for the design of family literacy programs.

Emergent Literacy: A Definition

The study of emergent literacy includes the skills, knowledge, and attitudes that are presumed to be developmental precursors to conventional forms of reading and writing (Sulzby, 1989; Sulzby & Teale, 1991; Teale & Sulzby, 1986; Whitehurst & Lonigan, 1998, 2001) and the environments that support these developments (e.g., shared book reading; Lonigan, 1994; Whitehurst et al., 1988). The conceptual model that is typical of research and intervention efforts within the emergent literacy domain is that individual differences in emergent literacy are causally and powerfully connected to individual differences in reading achievement.

Two Domains of Literacy and Emergent Literacy

Whitehurst and Lonigan (1998) proposed that emergent and conventional literacy consist of two interdependent sets of skills and processes: *outside-in* and *inside-out*, as represented in Figure 4.1. The outside-in units in the figure represent children's understanding of the context in which the writing they are trying to read occurs. The inside-out units represent children's knowledge of the rules for translating the particular writing they are trying to read into meaningful sounds (i.e., letter knowledge, phonological processing skills, and vocabulary).

For example, imagine a child trying to read the sentence, "She sent off to the very best seed house for five bushels of lupine seed" (p. 21 from *Miss Rumphius* by Barbara Cooney, New York:

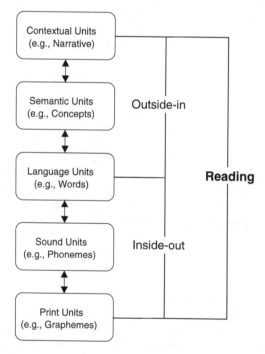

FIG. 4.1.   Fluent reading involves a number of component skills and processes. A reader must decode units of print (letters or graphemes) into units of sound (phonemes) and units of sound into units of language (words and sentences). This is an inside-out process. However, being able to say a written word or series of written words is only a part of reading. The fluent reader must understand those auditory derivations, which involves placing them in the correct conceptual and contextual framework. This is an outside-in process. The bidirectional arrows in the figure illustrate that there is cross-talk between different components of reading. For example, the sentence context affects the phonological rendering of the italicized letters in these two phases: "a lead balloon," "lead me there."

Puffin Books, 1982). The ability to decode the letters in this sentence into correct phonological representations (i.e., being able to say the sentence) depends on knowing letters, sounds, links between letters and sounds, punctuation, sentence grammar, and cognitive processes, such as being able to remember and organize these elements into a sequence. These are inside-out processes, which are based on and keyed to the elements of the sentence itself. However, a child could have the requisite inside-out skills to read the sentence aloud and still not read it successfully. What does the sentence mean? Meaningful comprehension of all but the simplest of writing depends on knowledge that cannot be found in the word or sentence itself. Who is the "she" referred to in the sentence? Why is she sending away for seed? Why does she need five bushels? What is lupine? In short, what is the narrative, conceptual, and semantic context in which this sentence is found, and how does the sentence make sense within that context? Answering these questions depends on outside-in processes, which require knowledge of the world, semantic knowledge, and knowledge of the written context in which this particular sentence occurred. Outside-in and inside-out processes ultimately are both essential to reading and work simultaneously in readers who are reading well.

Components of Emergent Literacy

Whitehurst and Lonigan (1998) reviewed research on emergent literacy with respect to each of the elements in Figure 4.1. This chapter will focus on two outside-in elements (oral language, print motivation) and two inside-out elements (phonological processing and letter knowledge) about which the evidence is strongest (see Table 4.1). Additional emergent literacy skills have been described, including understanding the conventions of print (e.g., left-to-right and top-to-bottom orientation of print, difference between pictures and print on a page; Clay, 1979) and the functions of print (e.g., that print tells a story or gives directions; Purcell-Gates, 1996; Purcell-Gates & Dahl, 1991), ability to "read" environmental print (e.g., recognizing product names from signs and logos), as well as emergent reading and emergent writing (i.e., pretending to read or write; Pappas & Brown, 1988; Purcell-Gates, 1988; Sulzby, 1986, 1988). However, evidence for the independence or predictive significance of these abilities is either negative or currently lacking. That is, although these abilities are sometimes associated with later reading when considered in isolation, research either has not generally supported a direct causal link between them and later decoding skills (Gough, 1993; Masonheimer, Drum, & Ehri, 1984) or has found that these behaviors appear to be better conceptualized as proxy measures for letter knowledge, phonological sensitivity, and oral language, as well as more exposure to print and other literacy-related activities (e.g., Lonigan, Burgess, & Anthony, 2000; Purcell-Gates, 1996).

Oral Language Skills

Reading is a process of translating visual codes into meaningful language. In the earliest stages, reading in an alphabetic system involves decoding letters into corresponding sounds and linking those sounds to single words. A substantial body of research has demonstrated positive correlations and longitudinal continuity between individual differences in oral language skills and later differences in reading (e.g., Bishop & Adams, 1990; Butler, Marsh, Sheppard, & Sheppard, 1985; Pikulski & Tobin, 1989; Scarborough, 1989; Share, Jorm, MacLean, & Mathews, 1984). In other words, children who have larger vocabularies and greater understanding of spoken language have an easier time with reading. The connection between oral language and reading is clear for outside-in skills that are measured with reading comprehension tasks (see the following section). Some studies also indicate that level of vocabulary has a significant impact on decoding skills very early in the process of learning to read but that its

TABLE 4.1
Key Components of Emergent Literacy

Outside-in skills

The knowledge and skills required to understand the context and meaning of text

📖 Oral language (vocabulary, syntactic, narrative understanding)

- Oral language provides the foundation for reading skills.
- Vocabulary development sets the stage for the emergence of phonological processing and early decoding skills.
- Oral language is crucial for reading comprehension after reading has moved beyond the initial learning to decode stage.

📖 Print motivation (interest in print)

- Early on, child interest facilitates interactions that provide opportunities for learning about print (e.g., shared reading, noticing, and asking about print in the environment)
- Later when the child is already reading, interest results in more reading practice and greater gains in reading achievement.

Inside-out skills

The knowledge and skills required to translate text into meaningful sounds (or sounds into text)

📖 Phonological Processing

- Alphabetic languages represent language at the phoneme level (i.e., letters correspond to phonemes in words).
- Almost all poor readers have a problem with phonological processing.
- Better *phonological sensitivity* (i.e., the ability to apprehend and/or manipulate smaller and smaller units of sound) facilitates the connection between letters and the sounds they represent in words.
- Better *phonological access* (i.e., retrieval of sound-based codes from memory) increases the ease of retrieval of phonological codes associated with letters, word segments, and whole words from memory, making it more likely that they can be used in decoding.
- Better *phonological memory* (i.e., ability to hold sound-based information in immediate memory) increases the likelihood that the phonemes associated with the letters of a word while decoding can be maintained in memory while decoding, freeing more cognitive resources for decoding and comprehension.

📖 Letter knowledge (i.e., letter identification and discrimination, letter-sound knowledge)

- Higher levels of letter knowledge facilitate the development of phonological sensitivity.
- Higher levels of letter knowledge facilitate the acquisition of decoding skills.

---

influence on decoding skills fades with development (e.g., Wagner et al., 1997). Recent studies provide strong support for a modular view of the components of reading and their linkages with preschool skills (Sénéchal & LeFevre, 2002; Storch & Whitehurst, 2002). Results of these studies indicate that the effects of oral language on early reading are indirect via their relationship with inside-out skills, which have a strong direct effect on decoding. Oral language does have a significant direct effect on reading comprehension.

A child's semantic and syntactic abilities assume great importance later in the sequence of learning to read, when the child is reading for meaning (e.g., see Gillon & Dodd, 1994; Mason, 1992; Sénéchal & LeFevre, 2002; Share & Silva, 1982; Snow, Barnes, Chandler, Hemphill, & Goodman, 1991; Storch & Whitehurst, 2002; Tunmer, Herriman, & Nesdale, 1988; Tunmer & Hoover, 1992; Vellutino, Scanlon, & Tanzman, 1991). In addition to the influence of vocabulary knowledge and the ability to understand and produce increasing complex syntactic constructions on children's literacy skills, Snow and colleagues (e.g., Dickinson & Snow, 1987; Dickinson & Tabors, 1991; Snow, 1983) have proposed that children's understanding of text and story narratives is facilitated by the acquisition of decontextualized language. Decontextualized language refers to language, such as that used in story narratives and other written forms of communication, that is used to convey novel information to audiences who may share only limited background knowledge with the speaker or who may be physically removed from the things or events described. In contrast, contextualized uses of language rely on shared physical context, knowledge, and immediate feedback. Children's decontextualized language skills are related to conventional literacy skills such as understanding story narratives, and print production (e.g., Dickinson & Snow).

Oral language also appears to have an influence on the acquisition of a key inside-out skill, phonological sensitivity, as defined in the following. Studies of both preschool (e.g., Burgess & Lonigan, 1998; Chaney, 1992; Lonigan et al., 2000; Lonigan, Burgess, Anthony, & Barker, 1998) and early elementary school children (e.g., Bowey, 1994; Wagner, Torgesen, Laughon, Simmons, & Rashotte, 1993; Wagner et al., 1997) have demonstrated significant concurrent and longitudinal associations between children's vocabulary skills and their phonological sensitivity skills. One potential explanation for this link is that children's memory for words in early childhood appears to progress from global (e.g., "homework" or "interesting") to segmented representations (e.g., "home" - "work" or /in/ /tar/ /ɛst/ /ing/) as a result of vocabulary growth (see Metsala & Walley, 1998, for review). As children learn more words, it becomes more efficient to remember words in terms of their constituent parts rather than as wholes. Children who have small vocabularies may be limited in their phonological sensitivity because their memory for words has not moved from global to segmented. These findings suggest that vocabulary development may set the stage for the emergence of phonological sensitivity (Fowler, 1991; Metsala & Walley, 1998).

Print Motivation

Because reading is a skill that improves the more it is practiced and because most of the opportunities to practice reading come in the form of reading for pleasure, children's motivation to interact with print materials would be expected to influence the rate of their literacy development. This might be as true of the development of emergent literacy as the development of formal literacy. Several studies have attempted to assess preschool children's interest in literacy, or print motivation, using a variety of methods such as parent-report of child interest, parent-report of the frequency of requests for shared reading (Lonigan, 1994), examining the proportion of time children spend in literacy-related activities relative to nonliteracy activities (e.g., Lomax, 1977; Thomas, 1984), or by examining the degree of children's engagement during shared reading (Crain-Thoresen & Dale, 1992). Some evidence suggests that these early manifestations of print motivation are associated with higher levels of emergent literacy skills and later reading achievement (e.g., Crain-Thoreson & Dale, 1992; Payne, Whitehurst, & Angell, 1994; Thomas, 1984; Scarborough & Dobrich, 1994). A child who is interested in literacy is more likely to facilitate shared-reading interactions, notice print in the environment, ask questions about the meaning of print, and spend more time reading once he or she is able. During the school years, higher levels of print motivation may lead children to do more reading on their own, resulting in greater growth in reading achievement (Cunningham & Stanovich, 1991, 1998; Stanovich & West, 1989; West, Stanovich, & Mitchell, 1993).

Phonological Processing Skills

Within the past 2 decades, a strong consensus has emerged concerning a key factor in the acquisition of reading and spelling in alphabetic languages. Research with a variety of populations and using diverse methods has converged on the finding that phonological processing skills play a critical role in the normal acquisition of reading (Adams, 1990; Wagner & Torgesen, 1987). Phonological processing refers to activities that require sensitivity to, or manipulation of, the sounds in words. Prior research has identified three interrelated clusters of phonological processing abilities: phonological sensitivity, phonological access to lexical store, and phonological memory (Wagner & Torgesen, 1987).

Phonological sensitivity refers to the ability to detect or manipulate the sound structure of oral language. Phonological sensitivity might be revealed by a child's ability to identify words that rhyme, blend spoken syllables or phonemes together to form a word, delete syllables or phonemes from spoken words to form a new word, or count the number of phonemes in a spoken word. For example, assessing sensitivity to phonemes might involve asking the child to count the number of phonemes in the word "donut," or to say what word results when the sounds /b/ . . . /a/ . . . /t/ are put together. Phonological sensitivity can be subdivided into two interrelated abilities: analysis and synthesis. Analysis skills reflect a child's ability to break words or syllables into smaller segments (i.e., deletion or counting tasks), and synthesis skills reflect a child's ability to blend smaller segments into syllables and words (i.e., blending tasks). The developing phonological sensitivity of young children progresses from sensitivity to large and concrete units of sound (i.e., words and syllables) to subsyllabic units of onset (i.e., the initial consonant or consonant cluster in a syllable) and rime (i.e., the vowel and final consonant or consonant cluster in a syllable) to small and abstract units of sound (i.e., phonemes; e.g., Adams, 1990; Anthony et al., 2002; Anthony, Lonigan, Driscoll, Phillips, & Burgess (2003); Fox & Routh, 1975; Lonigan et al., 1998, 2000). Well-developed phonological sensitivity likely promotes the development of decoding skills because graphemes in written language correspond to speech sounds at the level of phonemes.

Phonological memory refers to short-term memory for sound-based information. (Baddeley, 1986) and is typically measured by immediate recall of verbally presented material. For example, phonological memory might be assessed by having a child repeat nonwords of increasing length (e.g., "weem," "nokyisms"), repeat increasingly longer sentences (e.g., "The big dog," "The cat in the hat stood on the chair."), or repeat lists of digits that increase in length (e.g., "4 . . . 3," "5 . . . 2 . . . 8 . . . 4"). Efficient phonological memory might enable children to maintain an accurate representation of the phonemes associated with the letters of a word while decoding and, therefore, allow more cognitive resources to be devoted to decoding and comprehension processes.

Phonological access, or phonological naming, refers to the efficiency of retrieval of phonological information from permanent memory. Two measures of phonological naming have been used: isolated naming and serial naming. In isolated naming, the child is presented with a picture of a single object and the time to begin a pronunciation is measured. Performance on serial naming tasks for older children is typically measured as the time it takes for all individual elements in an array of letters, digits, or colors to be named. In younger children, performance on a serial naming task might be measured by asking the child to name a sequence of pictures of objects (e.g., rat, man, house, tree, snake) as fast as she or he can. Efficiency in phonological access might influence the ease with which a child can retrieve the phonological information associated with letters, word segments, and whole words, and increase the likelihood that he or she can use phonological information in decoding (Bowers & Wolf, 1993; Wolf, 1991).

These phonological processes are strongly related to subsequent decoding abilities (e.g., the ability to sound out words), and, in the absence of intervention, individual differences in these processes are highly stable from the late preschool period forward (Burgess & Lonigan, 1998; Lonigan et al., 1998, 2002; Storch & Whitehurst, 2002; Torgesen & Burgess, 1998; Wagner, Torgesen, & Rashotte, 1994; Wagner et al., 1993, 1997). For example, Wagner et al. (1997) reported that year-to-year stability coefficients for phonological sensitivity ranged from .83 (from kindergarten to first grade) to .95 (from second grade to third grade and from third grade to fourth grade). Lonigan et al. (2000) found that the 1-year stability of phonological sensitivity for a group of 4-year-olds approached 1.0.

Poor phonological processing is the hallmark of poor readers. There is a core phonological deficit (i.e., sensitivity or access) in nearly all poor readers, and there are deficits in other reading-related skills (e.g., vocabulary) in some poor readers depending on the degree to which their level of reading is discrepant from their level of general cognitive and academic functioning (Stanovich, 1988; Stanovich & Siegel, 1994). In other words, a poor reader may exhibit low levels of phonological processing skills compared to his or her same-age peers, but have oral language skills and general cognitive abilities that are consistent with age expectations (i.e., the condition typically referred to as *dyslexia*). In contrast, a poor reader may exhibit low levels of phonological processing skills, oral language, and general cognitive abilities compared to his or her same-age peers (i.e., a condition sometimes referred to as *garden-variety* poor reading). Both types of poor readers have deficient phonological processing. Children who have what is sometimes called a *double deficit* (i.e., poor performance on both phonological sensitivity and phonological access tasks relative to same-aged peers) tend to be at the very bottom of the distribution of reading ability (Bowers, 1995; Bowers & Wolf, 1993; McBride-Chang & Manis, 1996).

The majority of work concerning prereaders' phonological processing skills has examined phonological sensitivity. Individual differences in preschool and kindergarten children's phonological sensitivity are strongly related to early reading acquisition (e.g., Bradley & Bryant, 1983, 1985; Bryant, MacLean, Bradley, & Crossland, 1990; Lonigan et al., 2000; Stanovich, Cunningham, & Cramer, 1984). Children who are better at detecting rhymes, syllables, or phonemes are quicker to learn to read, and this relation is present even after variability due to factors such as IQ, vocabulary, memory, and social class are removed statistically (Bryant et al., 1990; MacLean, Bryant, & Bradley, 1987; Raz & Bryant, 1990; Wagner et al., 1994, 1997; Wagner & Torgesen, 1987). Moreover, experimental demonstrations that training children in phonological sensitivity positively affects reading support a causal relation between phonological sensitivity and early reading skills (e.g., Bradley & Bryant, 1985; Brady, Fowler, Stone, & Winbury, 1994; Byrne & Fielding-Barnsley, 1991a, 1993). For example, Byrne and Fielding-Barnsley (1991a) taught preschool children to identify a limited number of phonemes in the initial and final positions of words. These children scored higher on measures of phonological sensitivity than a control group and their abilities to decode words also was higher.

Letter Knowledge

Knowledge of the alphabet at school entry is one of the single best predictors of eventual reading achievement (Adams, 1990; Stevenson & Newman, 1986). In alphabetic writing systems, decoding text involves the translation of units of print (graphemes) to units of sound (phonemes), and writing involves translating units of sound into units of print. At the most basic level, this task requires the ability to distinguish letters. A beginning reader who cannot recognize and distinguish the individual letters of the alphabet will have difficulty learning the sounds those letters represent (Bond & Dykstra, 1967; Chall, 1967; Mason, 1980). In some cases, the task of learning letter-sound correspondence is facilitated by letter names that are the same as one of the phonemes that the letter represents. For example, the name of the letter "e" is the sound made by that letter in words like "be." In other cases letter names are different from the phonemes those letters map onto. For example, the word "not" would be pronounced as "en-ot" if the name of the letter "n" was the sound linked to that letter. The potentially confusing nature of letter name to sound correspondence has led developers of some curriculum materials to avoid letter names entirely when teaching children (e.g., Lindamood, 1995; McGuinness, 1997), preferring instead to teach directly that different letter shapes make different sounds; for example, the letter shape "a" makes two sounds (long-a and short-a).

To date, no research has evaluated the degree to which teaching the conventional names for letters is helpful or harmful to children compared to leaving out letter names and teaching the connection between letter shapes and sounds directly. Although teaching direct shape to sound correspondence is appealing from the perspective of simplifying the child's learning task, nearly all alphabet materials for prereaders focus on conventional letter names, and most children begin the formal task of learning to read with this background knowledge. Moreover, studies of early development of decoding and phonological sensitivity have generally found that letter-name knowledge is a stronger predictor of growth in these skills than is letter–sound knowledge (e.g., Burgess & Lonigan, 1998; Wagner et al., 1994). Letter names do provide relevant information about the sounds they represent (e.g., the /t/ in tee, /k/ in kay), and beginning readers appear to use this information in reading and writing (Ehri & Wilce, 1985; Read, 1971; Treiman, 1993).

In addition to its direct role in facilitating text decoding, letter knowledge appears to play an influential role in the development of phonological sensitivity, both prior to and after the initiation of formal reading instruction. Higher levels of letter knowledge are associated with children's abilities to detect and manipulate phonemes (e.g., Bowey, 1994; Johnston, Anderson, & Holligan, 1996; Stahl & Murray, 1994) but not rhyme and syllables (Naslund & Schneider, 1996). Wagner et al. (1994, 1997) reported the results of a longitudinal study that explicitly tested the influence of letter knowledge on subsequent phonological sensitivity development. They found that individual differences in kindergarten and first-grade letter knowledge were significantly related to measures of phonological sensitivity 1 and 2 years later. Similarly, Burgess and Lonigan (1998) found that preschool children's letter knowledge was a unique predictor of growth in phonological sensitivity across 1 year.

Despite these strong links between letter knowledge and later reading, interventions that teach children letter names alone do not seem to produce large effects on reading acquisition (Adams, 1990). As noted in the following section, interventions designed to promote emergent inside-out skills are most powerful when training in both phonological sensitivity and letter knowledge is included in the intervention (e.g., Bradley & Bryant, 1985). For example, combining training in phoneme identity by classifying words based on their initial sounds (e.g., bat, ball, beach, bell, and bill all start with the /b/ sound) with training to identify the initial letter of words (i.e., words that start with the /b/ sound like bat, ball, and beach, begin with the letter "b") appears to produce stronger effects on subsequent reading skills than the sound categorization training alone.

SOCIAL CLASS DIFFERENCES IN EMERGENT LITERACY

Because family literacy programs typically focus on families from low-income backgrounds, it is relevant to ask whether social class and reading difficulties are related as well as whether there are differences in environments that may support the development of emergent literacy skills. According to the 1991 Carnegie Foundation report, *Ready to Learn: A Mandate for the Nation*, 35% of children in the United States enter public schools with such low levels of the skills and motivation that are needed as starting points in our current educational system that they are at substantial risk of early academic difficulties. These data indicate that there is a significant mismatch between what many children bring to their first school experience and what schools expect of them if they are to succeed. This problem, often called school readiness, is strongly linked to family income. When schools are ranked by the median socioeconomic status (SES) of their students' families, SES correlates .68 with academic achievement (White, 1982). The National Assessment of Educational Progress (1991) and National Center for Education Statistics (2001) have documented substantial differences in the reading and writing ability of children as a function of the economic level of their parents. SES is also one of the strongest predictors of performance differences in children at the beginning of first grade (Entwisle & Alexander, cited in Alexander & Entwisle, 1988, p. 99). These performance differences have been reported in reading achievement and a number of the emergent literacy skills outlined previously.

Children from low-income families are at risk for reading difficulties (e.g., Dubrow & Ippolito, 1994; Juel, Griffith, & Gough, 1986; Smith & Dixon, 1995). These children are more likely to be slow in the development of oral language skills (e.g., Juel et al., 1986; Lonigan & Whitehurst, 1998; Whitehurst, 1996), letter knowledge, and phonological processing skills prior to school entry (Bowey, 1995; Lonigan et al., 1998; MacLean et al., 1987; Raz & Bryant, 1990). These differences in phonological processing skills relate to later differences in word decoding skills between children from higher and lower social economics status (SES) backgrounds (e.g., Raz & Bryant, 1990). There are large social class differences in children's exposure to experiences that might support the development of emergent literacy skills. Ninio (1980) found that mothers from lower SES groups engaged in fewer teaching behaviors during shared reading than mothers from middle-class groups. Numerous studies have documented differences in the pattern of book ownership and frequency of shared reading among lower versus higher SES families (e.g., Anderson & Stokes, 1984; Feitelson & Goldstein, 1986; Heath, 1982; McCormick & Mason, 1986; Raz & Bryant, 1990; Teale, 1986). Adams (1990, p. 85) estimated that a child from a typical middle-income family enters first grade with 1,000 to 1,700 hours of one-on-one picture-book reading, whereas a child from a low-income family averages just 25 hours.

ENVIRONMENTS THAT ENCOURAGE THE DEVELOPMENT OF EMERGENT LITERACY

Given the strong link between emergent literacy and later literacy, and the clear evidence that children from low-income homes have relatively low levels of emergent literacy compared to their peers from middle-income families, what can be done to improve the outside-in and inside-out skills of prereaders from low-income families (see Table 4.2)?

Oral Language Outcomes

Variations in Home Environments

Shared Reading.   The prototypical and iconic aspect of home literacy, shared book reading, provides an extremely rich source of information and opportunity for children to learn language in a developmentally sensitive context (e.g., DeLoache & DeMendoza, 1987; Ninio, 1980; Pellegrini, Brody, & Sigel, 1985; Sénéchal, Cornell, & Broda, 1995; Wheeler, 1983). For instance, Wells (1985) found that approximately 5% of the daily speech of 24-month-old children occurred in the context of storytime. Ninio and Bruner (1978) reported that the most frequent context for maternal labeling of objects was during shared reading. Shared reading and print exposure foster vocabulary development in preschool children (e.g., Cornell, Sénéchal, & Broda, 1988; Elley, 1989; Jenkins et al., 1984; Sénéchal & Cornell, 1993; Sénéchal, LeFevre, Hudson, & Lawson, 1996; Sénéchal, Thomas, & Monker, 1995), and print exposure has substantial effects on the development of reading skills at older ages when children are already reading (e.g., Allen, Cipielewski, & Stanovich, 1992; Anderson & Freebody, 1981; Cunningham & Stanovich, 1991, 1998; Echols et al., 1996; Nagy, Anderson, & Herman, 1987).

Other Home Activities.   Sénéchal et al. (1996) reported that other aspects of the home literacy environment (e.g., number of books in the home, library visits, parents' own print exposure) were related to children's vocabulary skills; however, only the frequency of library visits was related to children's vocabulary after controlling for the effects of children's print exposure. Payne, Whitehurst, and Angell (1994) found that adult literacy activities in low-income households (e.g., the amount of time a parent spends reading for pleasure) were not

TABLE 4.2
Promotion of Emergent Literacy Skills

📖 Many children from low-income families have less well-developed conventional and emergent literacy skills, including:

- Decoding
- Letter knowledge
- Phonological processing

📖 Home literacy environments in many low-income households are less developed, including:

- Less child-directed talk
- Less shared reading
- Fewer children's books and other literacy materials
- Fewer alphabet books and related materials

📖 Enhancing outside-in components

- Literacy-rich environments (e.g., children's books, library visits, writing materials) are associated with better oral language skills.
- Opportunities to engage in conversations with adults involving narrative and explanatory talk promotes decontextualized language skills.
- Shared reading provides opportunities for adults to model and teach vocabulary and other language skills.
- Dialogic reading, an interactive form of shared reading, has been proven to enhance substantially the oral language skills of preschool children.
- Creating links between material in school and the home environment can enhance children's interest in reading and writing.

📖 Enhancing inside-out components

- Literacy-rich home and school environments provide opportunities for children to interact with, talk about, and learn about print in meaningful contexts.
- Direct teaching of letters and print is associated with higher levels of letter knowledge.
- Alphabet books and games provide a means of increasing familiarity with letters.
- Phonological sensitivity training (both teacher-directed and computer-based programs) has been proven to enhance substantially children's phonological processing skills and their ability to decode text.
- Writing and invented spelling activities may promote the development of both letter knowledge and phonological sensitivity.
- Creating links between material in school and the home environment can enhance children's reading and writing abilities.

---

significantly related to children's oral language, which was best predicted by activities that directly involved the child (i.e., frequency of shared reading, number of children's books in the home, frequency of library visits with child). Other aspects of adult–child verbal interactions have also been implicated in the acquisition of some emergent literacy skills. For example, Dickinson and Tabors (1991; see also Beals, DeTemple, & Dickinson, 1994) reported that features of conversations among parents and children during meals and other conversational interactions (e.g., the proportion of narrative and explanatory talk) contributed to the development of children's decontextualized language skills.

Shared Reading Intervention

A number of interventions have been developed to enhance children's oral language skills through shared reading. The most widely researched and validated of these interventions is called dialogic reading (Whitehurst & Lonigan, 1998). Dialogic reading involves several changes in the way adults typically read books to children. Central to these changes is a shift in roles. During typical shared reading, the adult reads and the child listens, but in dialogic reading the child learns to become the storyteller. The adult assumes the role of an active listener, asking questions, adding information, and prompting the child to increase the sophistication of descriptions of the material in the picture book. A child's responses to the book are encouraged through praise and repetition, and more sophisticated responses are encouraged by expansions of the child's utterances and by more challenging questions from the adult reading partner. For 2- and 3-year-olds, questions from adults focus on individual pages in a book, asking the child to describe objects, actions, and events on the page (e.g., "What is this? What color is the duck? What is the duck doing?"). For 4- and 5-year-olds questions increasingly focus on the narrative as a whole or on relations between the book and the child's life (e.g., "Have you ever seen a duck swimming? What did it look like?"). Videotapes to train parents and teachers of preschoolers to engage in dialogic reading are available (Pearson Early Learning, 2003; Washington Research Institute, 1998; Whitehurst, 1992a, 1992b; Whitehurst, Lonigan, & Arnold, 1990).

Dialogic reading has been shown to produce larger effects on the oral language skills of children from middle- to upper-income families than a similar amount of typical picture-book reading (Arnold, Lonigan, Whitehurst, & Epstein, 1994; Whitehurst et al., 1988). Studies conducted with children from low-income families attending child care demonstrate that child care teachers, parents, or community volunteers using a 6-week small-group center-based or home dialogic reading intervention can produce substantial positive changes in the development of children's language as measured by standardized and naturalistic measures (Lonigan, Anthony, Bloomfield, Dyer, & Samwel, 1999; Lonigan & Whitehurst, 1998; Valdez-Menchaca & Whitehurst, 1992; Whitehurst et al., 1994a) that are maintained 6 months following the intervention (Whitehurst et al., 1994a). A large-scale longitudinal study of the use of dialogic reading over a year of a Head Start program for 4-year-olds showed large effects on emergent literacy skills at the end of Head Start that were maintained through the end of kindergarten; however, these positive effects did not generalize to reading scores at the end of second grade (Whitehurst et al., 1994b, 1999).

PHONOLOGICAL PROCESSING SKILLS

Variations in Home Environments

Most existing studies do not support a direct link between shared reading and growth in phonological skills (e.g., Lonigan, Dyer, & Anthony, 1996; Raz & Bryant, 1990; Whitehurst, 1996; but see Burgess, 1997). For example, Lonigan et al. found that growth in preschool phonological sensitivity was related to parental involvement in literacy activities in the home (i.e., frequency of parents' reading for pleasure, children observing parents reading), but growth in phonological sensitivity was not associated with shared reading frequency. Similarly, Sénéchal, LeFevre, Thomas, and Daley (1998; Sénéchal & LeFevre, 2002) reported that kindergarten and first-grade children's written language knowledge (i.e., print concepts, letter knowledge, invented spelling, word identification) was associated with parental attempts to teach their children about print but not exposure to storybooks. In contrast, children's oral language skills were associated with storybook exposure but not with parents' attempts to teach print. Some evidence suggests that exposure to alphabet books may increase children's letter knowledge and phonological processing skills (e.g., Baker, Fernandez-Fain, Scher, & Williams, 1998; Murray, Stahl, & Ivey, 1996). Some studies find a relation between experiences with word games in the home and the development of phonological processing (e.g., Fernandez-Fain & Baker, 1997), but other studies have not (e.g., Raz & Bryant, 1990).

Writing and Invented Spelling

Although it has received less attention, children's writing also may facilitate their development of letter knowledge and phonological sensitivity. Any form of phonetic writing requires knowledge of both letter sounds and phonological features of words. That is, although a child may spell the word "bike" as BK, this spelling reveals knowledge of the sounds coded by the letters *b* and *k* as well as two of the three phonemes in the word. Spelling words encourages children to analyze words into smaller units of sound and to link those sounds to letters. Clarke (1988) studied the effects of invented spellings in two first-grade classrooms. In these classrooms, children were encouraged to invent spellings of words for which they did not know the correct spelling. Compared to children in two classrooms where traditional spelling was emphasized, Clarke found that children in the invented spelling classrooms spent more time writing, wrote longer stories containing a greater variety of words, and scored higher on a standardized spelling test and a decoding task.

Phonological Skills Interventions

Teacher-Directed Interventions

Experimental studies of programs designed to teach children phonological sensitivity show positive effects on children's reading and spelling skills (e.g., Ball & Blackman, 1988; Bradley & Bryant, 1985; Lundberg, Frost, & Petersen, 1988; Torgesen, Morgan, & Davis, 1992; Uhry & Shepherd, 1992). Phonological sensitivity training programs that have included letter knowledge training (e.g., Ball & Blackman, 1988; Bradley & Bryant, 1985) produced larger gains than phonological sensitivity training alone (Wagner, 1996). The majority of these programs teach children how to categorize objects on the basis of certain sounds (e.g., initial phonemes). Other programs explicitly teach children phonological analysis and synthesis skills. For example, Torgesen et al. (1992) studied a 7-week group training program that taught children both analysis (e.g., identify initial, final, or middle sounds in words) and synthesis skills (e.g., say words after hearing their phonemes in isolation). Graduate students worked with groups of three children using a limited word list for all activities. Analysis training began by having children identify pictures that started with a specific sound (e.g., "What words for pictures begin with the /k/ sound, 'car,' 'cat,' 'hat,' 'bat?' ") or ended with a specific rime (e.g., "What words for pictures ended with the 'at' sound: 'hat,' 'bat,' 'hut,' 'map?' "). Training progressed until children could identify words with specific phonemes in initial, middle, and final positions (e.g., pick the pictures for hat, cat, and bat when asked for words that have the /a/ sound in the middle, say the /a/ in "bat" when asked for the middle sound, or say the /t/ in cat when asked for the last sound), and then required them to segment the words into the constituent phonemes (e.g., "Say all the sounds you hear in the word 'bat.' "). Synthesis training began by having children blend onset and rime to form a word (e.g., "What word is /b/ . . . 'at?' "), and progressed until children could say what a word was when said as its individual phonemes (e.g., blend the sounds, /t/ . . . /r/ . . . /u/ . . . /k/, spoken individually into the word "truck"). Training in both analysis and synthesis resulted in larger gains in both phonological sensitivity and a reading analog task than training in synthesis skills alone. Both training groups performed better than a group of control children who had listened to stories, engaged in discussions about the stories, and answered comprehension questions for an equivalent period.

Whereas most phonological sensitivity training studies have been conducted with children at the beginning stages of learning to read (i.e., kindergarten or first grade), Byrne and Fielding-Barnsley (1991a) found that preschool children (mean age = 55 months) exposed to 12 weeks of their *Sound Foundations* program (Byrne & Fielding-Barnsely, 1991b) demonstrated greater increases in phonological sensitivity than a group of control children exposed to storybook reading and a semantic categorization program, and some of these gains were maintained through the first and second grades (Byrne & Fielding-Barnsley, 1993, 1995). This intervention program consisted of teaching children six phonemes in the initial and final positions of words by drawing attention to the sound in words, discussing how the sound is made by the mouth, reciting rhymes with the phoneme in the appropriate position, and encouraging children to find objects in a poster that had the sound in the initial (or final) position. Worksheets in which children identified and colored items with the phoneme in the correct position were used, and the letter for the phoneme was displayed. A final stage of training introduced children to two card games that required matching objects on the basis of initial or final phonemes.

Lonigan and Torgesen (1999; see Lonigan, 2003) designed a comprehensive preschool pull-out program that included small-group phonological sensitivity training. Children participating in the small-group phonological sensitivity activities engaged in tasks designed to teach them how to blend and segment increasingly smaller units of words. For example, early in training, children were taught to blend or elide the components of compound words (e.g., "water" . . . "melon" = "watermelon," "hotdog" = "hot" . . . "dog"). Then, children were taught to blend and elide syllables (e.g., "mon" . . . "key" = "monkey," "el" . . . "e" . . . "phant" = "elephant") and ultimately onsets and rimes (e.g., /b/ . . . "at" = "bat," "cat" = /k/ . . . "at"). The abstract elements of parts of words were made more concrete by using puzzles of pictures of the words to correspond with putting sounds together or taking sounds apart. Children participated in these activities for four months for approximately 10 minutes per day. When compared to children who participated in small-group print activities or only the regular pre-K classroom activities, children exposed to the small-group phonological sensitivity intervention experienced significantly more growth in their phonological sensitivity skills.

Computer-Assisted Intervention (CAI)

Evidence also points to the effectiveness of software designed to teach phonological sensitivity skills to children (Barker & Torgesen, 1995; Foster, Erickson, Foster, Brinkman, & Torgesen, 1994; Lonigan, 2001; Lonigan et al., 2003; Olson, Wise, Ring, & Johnson, 1997; Wise, Olson, Ring, & Johnson, 1998). For instance, Foster, Erickson, Foster, Brinkman, and Torgesen (1994) conducted two experiments in which preschool and kindergarten children were randomly assigned to receive either their standard school curriculum or between 5 and 8 hours of exposure to *DaisyQuest* (Erickson, Foster, Foster, Torgesen, & Packer, 1992), a computer program designed to teach phonological sensitivity in the context of an interactive adventure game. Children in the experimental group in both studies demonstrated significant and large gains in phonological skills compared to the children in the no-treatment control group. The obtained effect sizes on tests of phonological sensitivity compared favorably to longer teacher-led programs with older children (e.g., Torgesen et al., 1992). Barker and Torgesen (1995) examined the effectiveness of the *DaisyQuest* program with a group of at-risk first-grade children who were randomly assigned to either an experimental or control group. Children in the experimental group received approximately 8 hours of exposure to the program, and children in the control group received an equal amount of exposure to computer programs designed to teach early math skills or other reading skills. Exposure to the *DaisyQuest* program produced significant and large improvements in children's phonological sensitivity and word identification skills compared to the control groups.

Lonigan et al. (2003) randomly assigned 41 children attending Head Start to either a CAI phonological sensitivity intervention group or a control group that received nothing in addition to the standard Head Start curriculum. Children assigned to the CAI group worked individually on a portable computer with *DaisyQuest* and *Daisy's Castle*. Trained research assistants worked on an individual basis with several children each day providing instruction as needed.

Intervention activities occurred for approximately 15 to 20 minutes, 4 to 5 days a week, for approximately 10 weeks. Children in the CAI group experienced significantly more growth in phonological sensitivity skills than did the children in the control group, but there were no differences between the groups in terms of growth in oral language or letter knowledge. In a second study, Lonigan (2001; described in Lonigan, 2003) randomly assigned 120 children from low-SES families attending either subsidized preschools or the local school district's pre-K program to one of four CAI groups: CAI training in (a) phonological sensitivity only (*DaisyQuest, Daisy's Castle*, and *Earobics*), (b) letter knowledge only (*Curious George ABC Adventure* and *Sesame Street ABC*), (c) combined phonological sensitivity and letter knowledge, or (d) math-control *Blues Clues Math*). CAI activities for all four groups occurred for approximately 15 to 20 minutes, 4 to 5 days a week, for approximately 10 weeks, and trained research assistants worked on an individual basis with several children each day providing additional instruction as needed. Children in the phonological sensitivity only and combined groups experienced significantly more growth in both phonological sensitivity skills and print knowledge than children in the letter-knowledge-only and math groups.

Results from the preschool studies indicate that CAI can be an effective means of promoting the phonological sensitivity skills of children from lower SES backgrounds who are at-risk of reading difficulties. CAI interventions provide one-on-one instructional activities, allow children to explore and learn at their own pace, and may be considered more developmentally appropriate practice than teacher-directed programs. However, although CAI was effective, it did not result in significant reductions in teacher time because children needed one-on-one attention to navigate the instructional activities or have the activities explained to them. Consequently, it is unlikely that CAI can be used as a primary means of promoting phonological sensitivity skills in preschool children who are at-risk of reading difficulties because many preschool children are likely to require a lot of attention from teachers to successfully interact with the program. However, CAI may be useful as an augmentative activity in the context of other interventions.

Creating Links Between Home and School

The potentially facilitative role of family involvement in children's literacy learning does not end with a child's school entry. In fact, the Even Start legislation provides for the provision of family literacy services up through age 7. Several interventions designed to promote parent's involvement in and coordination with their children's reading instruction have been developed. For instance, Morrow and colleagues have reported the results of a family involvement program for inner-city children and their families (Morrow, 1992; Morrow & Young, 1997). In this program, families were provided with materials similar to those in use at their children's schools and instructions for a variety of shared reading, writing, and story-telling activities that they could employ with their children. In a randomized evaluation of this program, Morrow and Young (1997) found significant effects on children's performances on a story-retelling and rewriting task, and on teachers' reports of children's reading and writing abilities and interest.

SUMMARY AND CONCLUSIONS

These data indicate that there are a number of interventions for preschool and early grade school children that make a significant impact on the key emergent literacy skills of children. Much of the early childhood and parenting interventions in family literacy programs are based on broad-based models such as High/Scope (e.g., Schweinhart, Barnes, & Weikart, 1993; Weikart, Deloria, Lawser, & Wiegerink, 1970), Parents as Teachers (Wagner & Clayton, 1998), or Home

TABLE 4.3

Emergent Literacy and Family Literacy Programs: Policy Implications

---

⊞ Incorporate focused emergent literacy modules into existing programs.
⊞ Integration of center-based and home-based components (e.g., dialogic reading)
⊞ Increase children's and parents' positive attitudes about literacy
⊞ Provide a sequenced approach to emergent literacy

- Oral language first (i.e., for 2- to 4-year-olds), followed by
- Letter knowledge and phonological sensitivity (i.e., late preschool and early grade school), followed by
- Coordination of home and school learning

⊞ Specific procedures for children (i.e., center-based modules)

- Frequent language interactions (staff, parents, volunteers)
- Multiple opportunities for interacting with literacy available by creating literacy-rich environment (i.e., books, letters, labels, and writing materials available)
- Include dialogic reading as preschool component.
- Include specific skills training components for letter knowledge and phonological sensitivity in preschool.
- Encouragement of writing activities (e.g., story writing with invented spelling)

⊞ Specific procedures for parents (i.e., parent training modules)

- Provide instruction and resources for creating literacy-rich home environments
- Provide training for using dialogic reading at home
- Provide training in promoting, identifying, and using incidental teaching opportunities involving print
- Provide training in use of scaffolded teaching interactions that build on children's knowledge and are sensitive to children's interests
- Provide programs that coordinate children's school-based activities and home activities with instruction and materials
- Provide training in use of a guided discovery strategy for read-aloud activities to promote children's accurate decoding (i.e., use of hints and prompts rather than just corrective feedback)
- Provide a motivational and supportive context for engaging in teaching interactions with children

---

Instruction Program for Preschool Youngsters (HIPPY) (Baker & Piotrkowski, 1996). Some of these programs have some evidence for efficacy (Barnett, 1995), whereas others do not (Baker & Piotrkowski; Wagner & Clayton, 1998). Many of the extant rigorous evaluations of preschool programs are for programs designed and delivered decades ago. Some center-based preschool curricula currently in use have no link to the programs that were evaluated, and some have changed substantially as they have evolved over the years. The research reviewed previously in this chapter indicates that early childhood and parental programs can be further optimized to improve emergent literacy skills. The addition of programs such as dialogic reading or phonological sensitivity interventions do not require a complete reengineering of the preschool curriculum. Instead, these programs can be integrated into existing curricula (see Table 4.3).

Research indicates that for some aspects of emergent literacy interventions, center-based and home-based approaches need to be integrated. For instance, in an evaluation of dialogic reading for low-income children attending subsidized child care, Whitehurst, Arnold et al. (1994) found that a combined home and school program was superior to a school program alone. Similarly, Lonigan and Whitehurst (1998) found that both a combined home and school program and a home-only program of dialogic reading were more effective than a school program alone, and Whitehurst et al. (1994b) found that higher levels of parent involvement with dialogic reading in the home produced larger effects on children's oral language skills.

Most evaluations of emergent literacy interventions have been of relatively short-term effects. Whitehurst's results show that even for interventions that produce significant improvement in children's skills, a catch-up or equalization effect reduces the tangible impact of the program over time (Whitehurst et al., 1999). Rather than conceptualizing these interventions as providing an inoculation against later reading difficulties, it is probably more reasonable to view these interventions as providing building blocks for additional educational experiences, reading acquisition, and academic success. Single-faceted interventions are unlikely to overcome the myriad of emergent literacy delays experienced by many children from low-income families.

Research with older children and experiences with preschool populations suggest that simply providing parents or teachers with materials to support emergent literacy will be insufficient. Training and the provision of a motivational context that supports a sustained focus on emergent literacy also are important. For instance, in the studies of Morrow and colleagues (e.g., Morrow & Weinstein, 1986), provisions of materials alone to parents were insufficient to produce substantial involvement with their children's literacy programs. As highlighted by Morrow and Young (1997) when parents were provided with the materials to use as well as instruction in how to use those materials with their children, parental involvement was higher and children's skills improved more. In evaluations of dialogic reading, it is clear that materials, instruction, and motivation are key elements to successfully sustaining involvement by parents and teachers.

POLICY IMPLICATIONS FOR FAMILY LITERACY PROGRAMS

Evidence concerning the development of emergent literacy skills suggests a sequenced approach to emergent literacy intervention. That is, oral language skills appear to provide the basis for the development of phonological processing skills. Similarly, letter knowledge is critical both for the development of decoding skills and for the development of phonological sensitivity. Consequently, it is likely that family literacy programs for young children (i.e., 2 to 4 years of age) should focus mainly on improving children's oral language skills. Inside-out skills such as letter knowledge and phonological sensitivity need to be taught explicitly in the late preschool and early grade school periods. Finally, developing and maintaining children's and parents' positive attitudes toward literacy should be a continuing focus across family literacy programs. This last step can best be accomplished by use of literacy materials and interaction techniques that are engaging and available to both children and parents (e.g., Tracey & Morrow, 1998).

High-quality and frequent one-on-one language interactions are needed to develop strong oral language skills (Huttenlocher, Haight, Bryk, Seltzer, & Lyons, 1991). Family literacy programs can incorporate these interactions using staff, parents, and volunteers. Interventions such as dialogic reading can provide a valuable and proven means of increasing children's oral language skills, particularly in the outside-in domain of emergent literacy (e.g., narrative skills) in the context of literacy materials.

The addition of components that target the inside-out skills of letter knowledge and phonological sensitivity to center-based intervention is both critical and relatively straightforward. As reviewed previously, there are a number of programs with demonstrated efficacy for children in late preschool to the first grade. Such programs include teacher-directed training programs (Adams, Foorman, Lundberg, & Beeler, 1998; Byrne & Fielding-Barnsley, 1991b) and computer programs like *DaisyQuest* (Erickson et al., 1992) or *Earobics*. Computer programs designed to teach phonological sensitivity, however, may be most beneficial as an adjunct to teacher-directed activities. Preschool environments rich with literacy-related materials and activities available to children provide the contexts in which children can explore reading and writing (Neuman & Roskos, 1993; Tracey & Morrow, 1998). This, in turn, provides a learning context for program staff to teach children letter knowledge, letter-sound correspondence, and other print concepts during children's self-directed activities.

Including program content for parent education components to target these inside-out skills is less straightforward. As noted earlier, evidence for a linkage between activities in the home and the development of inside-out skills indicate that direct efforts to teach these skills are required (e.g., Sénéchal et al., 1998; Sénéchal & LeFevre, 2002). However, research with middle-income families suggests that these parents of preschool children tend to make use of naturally occurring opportunities to teach their children about print (i.e., incidental learning; Baker et al., 1998). Because many of these children live in environments where text is prevalent and used frequently, the children have many opportunities to engage in literacy-related activities. In these contexts, parents can make use of incidental teaching opportunities to teach their children about the components and meaning of print.

Helping parents create these literacy-rich environments in the home should be a focus of family literacy programs. Helping parents utilize these literacy environments in a way that is maximally beneficial for children also needs to be a focus. That is, parents likely will require explicit instruction and practice in identifying, promoting, and using incidental teaching opportunities. Instruction and practice on providing scaffolding experiences around print and using a strategy of "guided discovery" rather than a more didactic approach should be provided. Among the materials that are likely to facilitate children's acquisition of inside-out emergent literacy skills are alphabet books. Such books tend to create more talk about print than do traditional storybooks (e.g., Bus & van IJzendoorn, 1988); however, these books are often not present in low-income households (McCormick & Mason, 1986) and infrequently afford opportunities for children to link alphabet shapes to sounds.

Programs that specifically coordinate children's literacy instruction in school and parent involvement at home can produce significant effects (Morrow & Young, 1997). Adaptations of the principles embedded in the shared-reading approach of dialogic reading program might usefully be extended to early text reading by children to link with the reading curriculum in early elementary school. As noted previously, in dialogic reading, the adult or parent serves as a coach to facilitate children's telling of the story. The type of help provided to the child is keyed to the skills already demonstrated by the child (i.e., scaffolded), builds on previous readings of the book, and follows the child's interest both within a book and in the choice of books. Extended from picture books to text-based books for older children, parents could provide children with guidance for decoding the text in the book, use repeated readings of the book across time to reinforce and build on prior success, and track and sustain children's interest in what is read.

Providing help for correct decoding might take the form of hints, clues, and strategies rather than corrective feedback. Parents in family literacy programs are likely to benefit from coaching and practice on how to participate in this type of guided-discovery read-aloud experience, how to provide hints and strategies (e.g., identifying individual letter sounds, sounding out words, varying vowel sounds, identifying similar words that the child can read, comprehension monitoring) that scaffold their children's current abilities, and how to focus on the multiple strands in the text (e.g., words, narrative, relations to child). This approach is likely to maintain children's interest in reading and be a more positive and rewarding experience than simply receiving corrective feedback.

CONCLUSIONS

Knowledge of an empirically supported emergent literacy model can be used to strengthen the impact of family literacy programs. Although evaluations of family literacy programs have demonstrated some positive effects (e.g., St.Pierre, Layzer, & Barnes, 1995; St.Pierre, Swartz et al., 1995), most evaluations have been focused on broader outcomes than the emergent literacy skills critical for children's reading success (i.e., oral language, letter knowledge, and phonological processing), and the effects have been quite modest. Most existing family literacy programs provide quality general early childhood education, parent education, and adult education (St.Pierre, Swartz et al.). The evidence reviewed in this chapter suggests a number of specific foci that should be incorporated into these programs to achieve maximal impact in breaking the cycle of illiteracy and poverty in the families served by family literacy programs.

ACKNOWLEDGMENTS

Preparation of this work was supported, in part, by grants from the National Institute of Child Health and Human Development (HD/MH38880, HD36067, HD36509, HD30988), the Administration for Children and Families (90YF0023), and the National Science Foundation (REC-0128970). An earlier version of this work was co-authored with Grover J. Whitehurst. Views expressed herein are solely those of the author and have not been cleared by the grantors or the previous co-author. Inquires concerning this work can be sent to Christopher J. Lonigan, Department of Psychology, Florida State University, Tallahassee FL 32306-1270 (e-mail: lonigan@psy.fsu.edu).

REFERENCES

Adams, M. J. (1990). *Learning to read: Thinking and learning about print*. Cambridge, MA: MIT Press.

Adams, M. J., Foorman, B. R., Lundberg, I., & Beeler, T. D. (1998). *Phonemic awareness in young children: A classroom curriculum*. Baltimore, MD: Brookes.

Alexander, K. L., & Entwisle, D. R. (1988). Achievement in the first 2 years of school: Patterns and processes. *Monographs of the Society for Research in Child Development, 53*(2, Serial No. 218).

Allen, L., Cipielewski, J., & Stanovich, K. E. (1992). Multiple indicators of children's reading habits and attitudes: Construct validity and cognitive correlates. *Journal of Educational Psychology, 84,* 489–503.

Allington, R. L. (1984). Content, coverage, and contextual reading in reading groups. *Journal of Reading Behavior, 16,* 85–96.

Anderson, A. B., & Stokes, S. J. (1984). Social and institutional influences on the development and practice of literacy. In H. Goelman, A. Oberg, & F. Smith (Eds.), *Awakening to literacy*. Exeter, NH: Heinemann.

Anderson, R. C., & Freebody, P. (1981). Vocabulary knowledge. In J. Guthrie (Ed.), *Comprehension and teaching: Research reviews* (pp. 77–117). Newark, DE: International Reading Association.

Anthony, J. L., Lonigan, C. J., Burgess, S. R., Driscoll, K., Phillips, B. M., & Bloomfield, B. G. (2002). Structure of preschool phonological sensitivity: Overlapping sensitivity to rhyme, words, syllables, and phonemes. *Journal of Experimental Child Psychology, 82,* 65–92.

Anthony, J. L., Lonigan, C. J., Driscoll, K., Phillips, B. M., & Burgess, S. R. (2003). Preschool phonological sensitivity: A quasi-parallel progression of word structure units and cognitive operations. *Reading Research Quarterly, 38,* 470–487.

Arnold, D. H., Lonigan, C. J., Whitehurst, G. J., & Epstein, J. N. (1994). Accelerating language development through picture book reading: Replication and extension to a videotape training format. *Journal of Educational Psychology, 86,* 235–243.

Baddeley, A. (1986). *Working memory*. New York: Oxford University Press.

Baker, A. J. L., & Piotrkowski, C. S. (August 1996). *Parents and children through the school years: The effects of the Home Instruction Program for Preschool Youngsters*. Final Report. New York: National Council of Jewish Women.

Baker, L., Fernandez-Fein, S., Scher, D., & Williams, H. (1998). Home experiences related to the development of word recognition. In J. L Metsala & L. C. Ehri (Eds.), *Word recognition in beginning literacy* (pp. 263–287). Mahwah, NJ: Lawrence Erlbaum Associates.

Ball, E. W., & Blachman, B. A. (1988). Phoneme segmentation training: Effect on reading readiness. *Annals of Dyslexia, 38,* 208–225.

Barker, T. A., & Torgesen, J. K. (1995). An evaluation of computer-assisted instruction in phonological awareness with below average readers. *Journal of Educational Computing Research, 13,* 89–103.

Barnett, W. S. (1995). Long-term effects of early childhood programs on cognitive and school outcomes. *The Future of Children, 5,* 25–50.

Baydar, N., Brooks-Gunn, J., & Furstenberg, F. F. (1993). Early warning signs of functional illiteracy: Predictors in childhood and adolescence. *Child Development, 64,* 815–829.

Beals, D. E., DeTemple, J. M., & Dickinson, D. K. (1994). Talking and listening that support early literacy development of children from low-income families. In D. K. Dickinson (Ed.), *Bridges to literacy: Children, families, and schools.* Cambridge, MA: Blackwell.

Bishop, D. V. M., & Adams, C. (1990). A prospective study of the relationship between specific language impairment, phonological disorders and reading retardation. *Journal of Child Psychology and Psychiatry and Allied Disciplines, 31,* 1027–1050.

Bond, G. L., & Dykstra, R. (1967). The cooperative research program in first-grade reading instruction. *Reading Research Quarterly, 2,* 5–142.

Bowers, P. G. (1995). Tracing symbol naming speed's unique contributions to reading disabilities over time. *Reading & Writing, 7,* 189–216

Bowers, P. G., & Wolf, M. (1993). Theoretical links among naming speed, precise timing mechanisms and orthographic skill in dyslexia. *Reading & Writing, 5,* 69–85.

Bowey, J. A. (1994). Phonological sensitivity in novice readers and nonreaders. *Journal of Experimental Child Psychology, 58,* 134–159.

Bowey, J. A. (1995). Socioeconomic status differences in preschool phonological sensitivity and first-grade reading achievement. *Journal of Educational Psychology, 87,* 476–487.

Bradley, L., & Bryant, P. E. (1983). Categorizing sounds and learning to read–A causal connection. *Nature, 301,* 419–421.

Bradley, L., & Bryant, P. (1985). *Rhyme and reason in reading and spelling.* Ann Arbor, MI: University of Michigan Press.

Brady, S., Fowler, A., Stone, B., & Winbury, N. (1994). Training phonological awareness: A study with inner-city kindergarten children. *Annals of Dyslexia, 44,* 26–59.

Brown, A. L., Palincsar, A. S., & Purcell, L. (1986). Poor readers: Teach, don't label. In U. Neisser (Ed.), *The school achievement of minority children: New perspectives* (pp. 105–143). Hillsdale, NJ: Lawrence Erlbaum Associates.

Bryant, P. E., MacLean, M., Bradley, L. L., & Crossland, J. (1990). Rhyme and alliteration, phoneme detection, and learning to read. *Developmental Psychology, 26,* 429–438.

Burgess, S. (1997). The role of shared reading in the development of phonological awareness: A longitudinal study of middle to upper class children. *Early Child Development and Care, 127–128,* 191–199.

Burgess, S. R., & Lonigan, C. J. (1998). Bidirectional relations of phonological sensitivity and prereading abilities: Evidence from a preschool sample. *Journal of Experimental Child Psychology, 70,* 117–141.

Bus, A. G., & van IJzendorn, M. H. (1988). Mother-child interaction, attachment, and emergent literacy: A cross-sectional study. *Child Development, 59,* 1262–1272.

Butler, S. R., Marsh, H. W., Sheppard, M. J., & Sheppard, J. L. (1985). Seven-year longitudinal study of the early prediction of reading achievement. *Journal of Educational Psychology, 77,* 349–361.

Byrne, B., & Fielding-Barnsley, R. F. (1991a). Evaluation of a program to teach phonemic awareness to young children. *Journal of Educational Psychology, 82,* 805–812.

Byrne, B., & Fielding-Barnsley, R. F. (1991b). *Sound foundations.* Artarmon, New South Wales, Australia: Leyden Educational Publishers.

Byrne, B., & Fielding-Barnsley, R. F. (1993). Evaluation of a program to teach phonemic awareness to young children: A one year follow-up. *Journal of Educational Psychology, 85,* 104–111.

Byrne, B., & Fielding-Barnsley, R. (1995). Evaluation of a program to teach phonemic awareness to young children: A 2- and 3-year follow-up and a new preschool trial. *Journal of Educational Psychology, 87,* 488–503.

Carnegie Foundation for the Advancement of Teaching. (1991). *Ready to learn: A mandate for the nation.* New York: Carnegie Foundation for the Advancement of Teaching.

Chall, J. S. (1967). *Learning to read: The great debate.* NY: McGraw-Hill.

Chall, J. S., Jacobs, V., & Baldwin, L. (1990). *The reading crisis: Why poor children fall behind.* Cambridge, MA: Harvard University Press.

Chaney, C. (1992). Language development, metalinguistic skills, and print awareness in 3-year-old children. *Applied Psycholinguistics, 13,* 485–514.

Clarke, L. K. (1988). Invented versus traditional spelling in first graders' writings: Effects on learning to spell and read. *Research in the Teaching of English, 22,* 281–309.

Clay, M. M. (1979). *Reading: The patterning of complex behavior.* Auckland, NZ: Heinemann.

Cornell, E. H., Sénéchal, M., & Broda, L. S. (1988). Recall of picture books by 3-year-old children: Testing and repetition effects in joint reading activities. *Journal of Educational Psychology, 80,* 537–542.

Crain-Thoreson, C., & Dale, P. S. (1992). Do early talkers become early readers? Linguistic precocity, preschool language, and emergent literacy. *Developmental Psychology, 28,* 421–429.

Cunningham, A. E., & Stanovich, K. E. (1991). Tracking the unique effects of print exposure in children: Associations with vocabulary, general knowledge, and spelling. *Journal of Educational Psychology, 83,* 264–274.

Cunningham, A. E., & Stanovich, K. E. (1998). Early reading acquisition and its relation to reading experience and ability 10 years later. *Developmental Psychology, 33,* 934–945.

DeLoache, J. S., & DeMendoza, O. A. P. (1987). Joint picturebook interactions of mothers and one-year-old children. *British Journal of Developmental Psychology, 5,* 111–123.

Dickinson, D. K., & Snow, C. E. (1987). Interrelationships among prereading and oral language skills in kindergartners from two social classes. *Early Childhood Research Quarterly, 2,* 1–25.

Dickinson, D. K., & Tabors, P. O. (1991). Early literacy: Linkages between home, school, and literacy achievement at age five. *Journal of Research in Childhood Education, 6,* 30–46.

Dubrow, E. F., & Ippolito, M. F. (1994). Effects of poverty and quality of the home environment on changes in the academic and behavioral adjustment of elementary school-age children. *Journal of Clinical Child Psychology, 23,* 401–412.

Echols, L. D., West, R. F., Stanovich, K. E., & Zehr, K. S. (1996). Using children's literacy activities to predict growth in verbal cognitive skills: A longitudinal investigation. *Journal of Educational Psychology, 88,* 296–304.

Ehri, L., & Wilce, L. (1985). Movement into reading: Is the first stage of printed word learning visual or phonetic? *Reading Research Quarterly, 20,* 163–179.

Elley, W. B. (1989). Vocabulary acquisition from listening to stories. *Reading Research Quarterly, 24,* 174–187.

Erickson, G. C., Foster, K. C., Foster, D. F., Torgesen, J. K., & Packer, S. (1992). *DaisyQuest.* Scotts Valley, CA: Great Wave Software.

Feitelson, D., & Goldstein, Z. (1986). Patterns of book ownership and reading to young children in Israeli school-oriented and nonschool-oriented families. *Reading Teacher, 39,* 924–930.

Fernandez-Fein, S., & Baker, L. (1997). Rhyme and alliteration sensitivity and relevant experiences in preschoolers from diverse backgrounds. *Journal of Literacy Research, 29,* 433–459.

Foster, K. C., Erickson, G. C., Foster, D. F., Brinkman, D., & Torgesen, J. K. (1994). Computer administered instruction in phonological awareness: Evaluation of the *DaisyQuest* program. *Journal of Research and Development in Education, 27,* 126–137.

Fowler, A. E. (1991). How early phonological development might set the stage for phoneme awareness. In S. A. Brady & D. P. Shankweiler (Eds.), *Phonological processes in literacy.* Hillsdale, NJ: Lawrence Erlbaum Associates.

Fox, B., & Routh, D. K. (1975). Analyzing spoken language into words, syllables, and phonemes: A developmental study. *Journal of Psycholinguistic Research, 4,* 331–342.

Gillon, G., & Dodd, B. J. (1994). A prospective study of the relationship between phonological, semantic and syntactic skills and specific reading disability. *Reading and Writing: An Interdisciplinary Journal, 6,* 321–345.

Gough, P. B. (1993). The beginning of decoding. *Reading and Writing: An Interdisciplinary Journal, 5,* 181–192.

Haslam, B. (1998). *Observational Study of Even Start Projects.* Washington, DC: Policy Studies Associates.

Heath, S. B. (1982). What no bedtime story means: Narrative skills at home and school. *Language in Society, 11,* 49–76.

Huttenlocher, J., Haight, W., Bryk, A., Seltzer, M., & Lyons, T. (1991). Early vocabulary growth: Relation to language input and gender. *Developmental Psychology, 27,* 236–248.

Jenkins, J. R., Stein, M. L., & Wysocki, K. (1984). Learning vocabulary through reading. *American Educational Research Journal, 21,* 767–787.

Johnston, R. S., Anderson, M., & Holligan, C. (1996). Knowledge of the alphabet and explicit awareness of phonemes in prereaders: The nature of the relationship. *Reading and Writing: An Interdisciplinary Journal, 8,* 217–234.

Juel, C. (1988). Learning to read and write: A longitudinal study of 54 children from first through fourth grades. *Journal of Educational Psychology, 80,* 437–447.

Juel, C., Griffith, P. L., & Gough, P. B. (1986). Acquisition of literacy: A longitudinal study of children in first and second grade. *Journal of Educational Psychology, 78,* 243–255.

Lentz, F. E. (1988). Effective reading interventions in the regular classroom. In J. L. Graden, J. E. Zins, & M. J. Curtis (Eds.), *Alternative educational delivery systems: Enhancing instructional options for all students.* Washington DC: National Association of School Psychologists.

Lindamood, P. (1995). Lindamood-Bell Learning Processes overview. In C. W. M. J. S. Pickering (Ed.), *Clinical studies of multisensory structured language education* (pp. 97–99). Salem, OR: International Multisensory Structured Language Education Council.

Lomax, C. M. (1977). Interest in books and stories at nursery school. *Educational Research, 19,* 100–112.

Lonigan, C. J. (1994). Reading to preschoolers exposed: Is the emperor really naked? *Developmental Review, 14,* 303–323.

Lonigan, C. J. (2001). *Outcomes of a computer assisted emergent literacy intervention with children at-risk for reading difficulties.* Unpublished data. Florida State University.

Lonigan, C. J. (2003). Development and promotion of emergent literacy skills in preschool children at-risk of reading difficulties. In B. Foorman (Ed.), *Preventing and remediating reading difficulties: Bringing science to scale* (pp. 23–50). Timonium, MD: York Press.

Lonigan, C. J., Anthony, J. L., Bloomfield, B. G., Dyer, S. M., & Samwel, C. S. (1999). Effects of two preschool shared reading interventions on the emergent literacy skills of children from low-income families. *Journal of Early Intervention, 22,* 306–322.

Lonigan, C. J., Burgess, S. R., & Anthony, J. L. (2000). Development of emergent literacy and early reading skills in preschool children: Evidence from a latent variable longitudinal study. *Developmental Psychology, 36,* 596–613.

Lonigan, C. J., Burgess, S. R., Anthony, J. L., & Barker, T. A. (1998). Development of phonological sensitivity in two- to five-year-old children. *Journal of Educational Psychology, 90,* 294–311.

Lonigan, C. J., Driscoll, K., Phillips, B. M., Cantor, B. G., Anthony, J. L., & Goldstein, H. (2003). Evaluation of a computer-assisted instruction phonological sensitivity program with preschool children at-risk for reading problems. *Journal of Early Intervention, 25,* 248–262.

Lonigan, C. J., Dyer, S. M., & Anthony, J. L. (1996, April). *The influence of the home literacy environment on the development of literacy skills in children from diverse racial and economic backgrounds.* Paper presented at the Annual Convention of the American Educational Research Association. New York, NY.

Lonigan, C. J., & Torgesen, J. K. (1999). *Preschool pre-literacy intervention for children at-risk of reading difficulties.* Unpublished grant proposal. Florida State University. Tallahassee.

Lonigan, C. J., & Whitehurst, G. J. (1998). Examination of the relative efficacy of parent and teacher involvement in a shared-reading intervention for preschool children from low-income backgrounds. *Early Childhood Research Quarterly, 17,* 265–292.

Lundberg, I., Frost, J., & Petersen, O. (1988). Effects of an extensive program for stimulating phonological awareness in preschool children. *Reading Research Quarterly, 23,* 263–284.

MacLean, M., Bryant, P., & Bradley, L. (1987). Rhymes, nursery rhymes, and reading in early childhood. *Merrill-Palmer Quarterly, 33,* 255–282.

Mason, J. M. (1980). When children do begin to read: An exploration of four year old children's letter and word reading competencies. *Reading Research Quarterly, 15,* 203–227.

Mason, J. M. (1992). Reading stories to preliterate children: A proposed connection to reading. In P. B. Gough, L. C. Ehri, & R. Treiman (Eds.), *Reading acquisition* (pp. 215–243). Hillsdale, NJ: Lawrence Erlbaum Associates.

Masonheimer, P. E., Drum, P. A., & Ehri, L. C. (1984). Does environmental print identification lead children into word reading? *Journal of Reading Behavior, 16,* 257–271.

McBride-Chang, C., & Manis, F. R. (1996). Structural invariance in the associations of naming speed, phonological awareness, and verbal reasoning in good and poor readers: A test of the double deficit hypothesis. *Reading and Writing, 8,* 323–339.

McCormick, C. E., & Mason, J. M. (1986). Intervention procedures for increasing preschool children's interest in and knowledge about reading. In W. H. Teale & E. Sulzby (Eds.), *Emergent literacy: Writing and reading* (pp. 90–115). Norwood, NJ: Ablex.

McGuinness, D. (1997). *Why our children can't read and what we can do about it: A scientific revolution in reading.* New York: The Free Press.

Metsala, J. L., & Walley, A. C. (1998). Spoken vocabulary growth and the segmental restructuring of lexical representations: Precursors to phonemic awareness and early reading ability. In J. L Metsala & L. C. Ehri (Eds.), *Word recognition in beginning literacy* (pp. 89–120). Mahwah, NJ: Lawrence Erlbaum Associates.

Morrison, F. J., Smith, L., & Dow-Ehrensberger, M. (1995). Education and cognitive development: A natural experiment. *Developmental Psychology, 31,* 789–799.

Morrow, L. M. (1992). The impact of a literature-based program on literacy achievement, use of literature, and attitudes of children from minority backgrounds. *Reading Research Quarterly, 27,* 250–275.

Morrow, L. M., & Weinstein, C. S. (1986). Increasing children's use of literature through program and physical design changes. *The Reading Teacher, 50,* 2–9.

Morrow, L. M., & Young, J. (1997). A family literacy program connecting school and home: Effects on attitude, motivation, and literacy achievement. *Journal of Educational Psychology, 89,* 736–742.

Murray, B. A., Stahl, S. A., & Ivey, M. G. (1996). Developing phoneme awareness through alphabet books. *Reading and Writing, 8,* 307–322.

Nagy, W. E., & Anderson, R. C. (1984). How many words are there in printed school English? *Reading Research Quarterly, 19,* 304–330.

Nagy, W. E., Anderson, R. C., & Herman, P. A. (1987). Learning word meanings from context during normal reading. *American Educational Research Journal, 24,* 237–270.

Naslund, J. C., & Schneider, W. (1996). Kindergarten letter knowledge, phonological skills, and memory processes: Relative effects on early literacy. *Journal of Experimental Child Psychology, 62,* 30–59.

National Assessment of Educational Progress. (1991). *The 1989-90 National assessment of reading and literature.* Denver: Author.

National Center for Education Statistics. (2001). *The nation's report card: Fourth-grade reading 2000.* Retrieved April 6, 2001, from http://nces.ed.gov/nationsreportcard/reading/results

Neuman, S. B., & Roskos, K. (1993). Access to print for children of poverty: Differential effects of adult mediation and literacy-enriched play settings on environmental and functional print tasks. *American Educational Research Journal, 30,* 95–122.

NICHD (2000). *Report of the National Reading Panel: Teaching children to read.* Washington, DC: U.S. Department of Health and Human Services.

Ninio, A. (1980). Picture book reading in mother-infant dyads belonging to two subgroups in Israel. *Child Development, 51,* 587–590.

Ninio, A., & Bruner, J. S. (1978). The achievement and antecedents of labeling. *Journal of Child Language, 5,* 1–15.

Oka, E., & Paris, S. (1986). Patterns of motivation and reading skills in underachieving children. In S. Ceci (Ed.), *Handbook of cognitive, social, and neuropsychological aspects of learning disabilities* (Vol 2). Hillsdale, NJ: Lawrence Erlbaum Associates.

Olson, R. K., Wise, B. W., Ring, J., & Johnson, M. (1997). Computer-based remedial training in phoneme awareness and phoneme decoding: Effects on post-training development of word recognition. *Scientific Studies of Reading, 1,* 235–253.

Pappas, C. C., & Brown, E. (1988). The development of children's sense of the written story language register: An analysis of the texture of "pretend reading." *Linguistics and Education, 1,* 45–79.

Payne, A. C., Whitehurst, G. J., & Angell, A. L. (1994). The role of literacy environment in the language development of children from low-income families. *Early Childhood Research Quarterly, 9,* 427–440.

Pearson Early Learning. (2003). *Read together, talk together.* New York: Author.

Pellegrini, A. D., Brody, G. H., & Sigel, I. (1985). Parent's book-reading habits with their children. *Journal of Educational Psychology, 77,* 332–340.

Pikulski, J. J., & Tobin, A. W. (1989). Factors associated with long-term reading achievement of early readers. In S. McCormick, J. Zutell, P. Scharer, & P. O'Keefe (Eds.), *Cognitive and social perspectives for literacy research and instruction.* Chicago: National Reading Conference.

Purcell-Gates, V. (1988). Lexical and syntactic knowledge of written narrative held by well-read-to kindergartners and second graders. *Research in the Teaching of English, 22,* 128–160.

Purcell-Gates, V. (1996). Stories, coupons, and the TV Guide: Relationships between home literacy experiences and emergent literacy knowledge. *Reading Research Quarterly, 31,* 406–428.

Purcell-Gates, V., & Dahl, K. L. (1991). Low-SES children's success and failure at early literacy learning in skills-based classrooms. *Journal of Reading Behavior, 23,* 1–34.

Raz, I. S., & Bryant, P. (1990). Social background, phonological awareness and children's reading. *British Journal of Developmental Psychology, 8,* 209–225.

Read, C. (1971). Pre-school children's knowledge of English phonology. *Harvard Educational Review, 41,* 1–34.

Scarborough, H. (1989). Prediction of reading dysfunction from familial and individual differences. *Journal of Educational Psychology, 81,* 101–108.

Scarborough, H. S., & Dobrich, W. (1994). On the efficacy of reading to preschoolers. *Developmental Review, 14,* 245–30.

Schweinhart, L. J., Barnes, H. V., & Weikart, D. P. (1993). *Significant benefits: The High/Scope Perry Preschool Study through age 27.* Ypsilanti, MI: High/Scope Press.

Sénéchal, M., & Cornell, E. H. (1993). Vocabulary acquisition through shared reading experiences. *Reading Research Quarterly, 28,* 360–375.

Sénéchal, M., Cornell, E. H., & Broda, L. S. (1995). Age-related differences in the organization of parent-infant interactions during picture-book reading. *Early Childhood Research Quarterly, 10,* 317–337.

Sénéchal, M., & LeFevre, J. (2002). Parental involvement in the development of children's reading skill: A five-year longitudinal study. *Child Development, 73,* 445–460.

Sénéchal, M., LeFevre, J., Hudson, E., & Lawson, E. P. (1996). Knowledge of storybooks as a predictor of young children's vocabulary. *Journal of Educational Psychology, 88,* 520–536.

Sénéchal, M., LeFevre, J., Thomas, E. M., & Daley, K. E. (1998). Differential effects of home literacy experiences on the development of oral and written language. *Reading Research Quarterly, 13,* 96–116.

Sénéchal, M., Thomas, E. H., & Monker, J. A. (1995). Individual differences in 4-year-old children's acquisition of vocabulary during storybook reading. *Journal of Educational Psychology, 87,* 218–229.

Share, D., & Silva, P. (1987). Language deficits and specific reading retardation: Cause or effect? *British Journal of Disorders of Communication, 22,* 219–226.

Share, D. L., Jorm, A. F., MacLean, R., & Mathews, R. (1984). Sources of individual differences in reading acquisition. *Journal of Educational Psychology, 76,* 1309–1324.

Smith, S. S., & Dixon, R. G. (1995). Literacy concepts of low- and middle-class four-year-olds entering preschool. *Journal of Educational Research, 88,* 243–253.

Snow, C. E. (1983). Literacy and language: Relationships during the preschool years. *Harvard Educational Review, 53,* 165–189.

Snow, C. E., Barnes, W. S., Chandler, J., Hemphill, L., & Goodman, I. F. (1991). *Unfulfilled expectations: Home and school influences on literacy.* Cambridge: Harvard University Press.

Snow, C. E., Burns, M. S., & Griffin, P. (Eds.). (1998). *Preventing reading difficulties in young children.* Washington, DC: National Academy Press.

Stahl, S. A., & Murray, B. A. (1994). Defining phonological awareness and its relationship to early reading. *Journal of Educational Psychology, 86,* 221–234.

Stanovich, K. E. (1986). Matthew effects in reading: Some consequences of individual differences in the acquisition of literacy. *Reading Research Quarterly, 21,* 360–407.

Stanovich, K. E. (1988). Explaining the differences between the dyslexic and the garden-variety poor reader: The phonological-core variable-difference model. *Journal of Learning Disabilities, 21,* 590–612.

Stanovich, K. E, Cunningham, A. E., & Cramer, B. B. (1984). Assessing phonological awareness in kindergarten children: Issues of task comparability. *Journal of Experimental Child Psychology, 38,* 175–190.

Stanovich, K. E., & Siegel, L. S. (1994). Phenotypic performance profile of children with reading disabilities: A regression-based test of the phonological-core variable-difference model. *Journal of Educational Psychology, 86,* 24–53.

Stanovich, K. E., & West, R. F. (1989). Exposure to print and orthographic processing. *Reading Research Quarterly, 24,* 402-433.

Stevenson, H. W., & Newman, R. S. (1986). Long-term prediction of achievement and attitudes in mathematics and reading. *Child Development, 57,* 646–659.

Storch, S. A., & Whitehurst, G. J. (2002). Oral language and code-related precursors to reading: Evidence from a longitudinal structural model. *Developmental Psychology, 38,* 934–947.

St.Pierre, R. G., Layzer, J. I., & Barnes, H. V. (1995). Two-generation programs: Design, cost, and short-term effectiveness. *The Future of Children, 5,* 76–93

St.Pierre, R., Ricciuti, A., Tao, F., Creps, C., Swartz, J., Lee, W., Parsad, A., & Rimdzius, T. (2002). *Third national Even Start evaluation: Report on program outcomes.* Cambridge, MA: Abt Associates Inc.

St.Pierre, R., Swartz, J., Gamse, B., Murray, S., Deck, D., & Nickel, P. (1995). *National evaluation of the Even Start Family Literacy Program: Final report.* Cambridge, MS: Abt Associates.

Sulzby, E. (1986). Writing and reading: Signs of oral and written language organization in the young child. In W. H. Teale & E. Sulzby (Eds.), *Emergent literacy: Reading and writing* (pp. 50–87). Norwood, NJ: Ablex.

Sulzby, E. (1988). A study of children's early reading development. In A. D. Pelligrini (Ed.), *Psychological bases for early education* (pp. 39–75). Chichester, England: Wiley.

Sulzby, E. (1989). Assessment of writing and of children's language while writing. In L. Morrow & J. Smith (Eds.), *The role of assessment and measurement in early literacy instruction* (pp. 83–109). Englewood Cliffs, NJ: Prentice-Hall.

Sulzby, E., & Teale, W. (1991). Emergent Literacy. In R. Barr, M. Kamil, P. Mosenthal, & P. D. Pearson (Eds.), *Handbook of reading research* (Vol. II, pp. 727–758). New York: Longman.

Teale, W. H. (1986). Home background and young children's literacy development. In W. H. Teale & E. Sulzby (Eds.), *Emergent literacy: Writing and reading.* Norwood, NJ: Ablex.

Teale, W. H., & Sulzby, E. (Eds.). (1986). *Emergent literacy: Writing and reading.* Norwood, NJ: Ablex.

Thomas, B. (1984). Early toy preferences of four-year-old readers and nonreaders. *Child Development, 55,* 424–430.

Torgesen, J. K., & Burgess, S. R. (1998). Consistency of reading-related phonological processes throughout early childhood: Evidence from longitudinal-correlational and instructional studies. In J. L. Metsala & L. C. Ehri (Eds.), *Word recognition in beginning literacy* (pp. 161–188). Mahwah, NJ: Lawrence Erlbaum Associates.

Torgesen, J. K., Morgan, S., & Davis, C. (1992). Effects of two types of phonological awareness training on word learning in kindergarten children. *Journal of Educational Psychology, 84,* 364–370.

Tracey, D. H., & Morrow, L. M. (1998). Motivating contexts for young children's literacy development: Implications for word recognition. In J. L Metsala & L. C. Ehri (Eds.), *Word recognition in beginning literacy* (pp. 341–356). Mahwah, NJ: Lawrence Erlbaum Associates.

Tramontana, M. G., Hooper, S., & Selzer, S. C. (1988). Research on preschool prediction of later academic achievement: A review. *Developmental Review, 8,* 89–146.

Treiman, R. (1993). *Beginning to spell.* NY: Oxford University Press.

Tunmer, W. E., Herriman, M. L., & Nesdale, A. R. (1988). Metalinguistic abilities and beginning reading. *Reading Research Quarterly, 23,* 134–158.

Tunmer, W. E., & Hoover, W. A. (1992). Cognitive and linguistic factors in learning to read. In P. B. Gough, L. C. Ehri, & R. Treiman (Eds.), *Reading acquisition.* Hillsdale, NJ: Lawrence Erlbaum Associates.

Uhry, J. K., & Shepherd, M. J. (1993). Segmentation/spelling instruction as part of a first-grade reading program: Effects on several measures of reading. *Reading Research Quarterly, 28,* 218–233.

Valdez-Menchaca, M. C., & Whitehurst, G. J. (1992). Accelerating language development through picture book reading: A systematic extension to Mexican day-care. *Developmental Psychology, 28,* 1106–1114.

Vellutino, F. R., Scanlon, D. M., & Tanzman, M. S. (1991). Bridging the gap between cognitive and neuropsychological conceptualizations of reading disability. *Learning and Individual Differences, 3,* 181–203.

Wagner, M., & Clayton, S. (1998). *The Parents as Teachers Program: Results from two demonstrations.* Menlo Park, CA: SRI International.

Wagner, R. K. (1996, April). *Meta-analysis of the effects of phonological awareness training with children.* Paper presented at the Annual Convention of the American Educational Research Association. New York, NY.

Wagner, R. K., & Torgesen, J. K. (1987). The natural of phonological processing and its causal role in the acquisition of reading skills. *Psychological Bulletin, 101,* 192–212.

Wagner, R. K., Torgesen, J. K., Laughon, P., Simmons, K., Rashotte, C. A. (1993). The development of young readers' phonological processing abilities. *Journal of Educational Psychology, 85,* 1–20.

Wagner, R. K., Torgesen, J. K., & Rashotte, C. A. (1994). Development of reading-related phonological processing abilities: New evidence of bidirectional causality from a latent variable longitudinal study. *Developmental Psychology, 30,* 73–87.

Wagner, R. K., Torgesen, J. K., Rashotte, C. A., Hecht, S. A., Barker, T. A., Burgess, S. R., Donahue, J., & Garon, T. (1997). Changing relations between phonological processing abilities and word-level reading as children develop from beginning to skilled readers: A 5-year longitudinal study. *Developmental Psychology, 33,* 468–479.

Washington Research Institute. (1998). *Talking and Books* [Video]. Seattle, WA: Author.

Weikart, D. P., Deloria, D. J., Lawser, S. A., & Wiegerink, R. (1970). *Longitudinal results of the Ypsilanti Perry Preschool Project.* Ypsilanti, MI: High/Scope Educational research Foundation.

Wells, G. (1985). *Language development in the preschool years.* NY: Cambridge University Press.

West, R. F., Stanovich, K. E., & Mitchell, H. R. (1993). Reading in the real world and its correlates. *Reading Research Quarterly, 28,* 34–51.

Wheeler, M. P. (1983). Context-related age changes in mother's speech: Joint book reading. *Journal of Child Language, 10,* 259–263.

White, K. (1982). The relation between socioeconomic status and academic achievement. *Psychological Bulletin, 91,* 461–481.

Whitehurst, G. J. (1992a). *Dialogic reading for Head Start, K, and pre-K for parents* [Video]. Stony Brook, NY: Author.

Whitehurst, G. J. (1992b). *Dialogic reading in Head Start, K, and pre-K for teachers* [Video]. Stony Brook, NY: Author.

Whitehurst, G. J. (1996). Language processes in context: Language learning in children reared in poverty. In L. B. Adamson & M. A. Romski (Eds.), *Research on communication and language disorders: Contribution to theories of language development.* Baltimore, MD: Brookes.

Whitehurst, G. J., Arnold, D. H., Epstein, J. N., Angell, A. L., Smith, M., & Fischel, J. E. (1994a). A picture book reading intervention in daycare and home for children from low-income families. *Developmental Psychology, 30,* 679–689.

Whitehurst, G. J., Epstein, J. N., Angell, A. C., Payne, A. C., Crone, D. A., & Fischel, J. E. (1994b). Outcomes of an emergent literacy intervention in Head Start. *Journal of Educational Psychology, 86,* 542–555.

Whitehurst, G. J., Falco, F., Lonigan, C. J., Fischel, J. E., DeBaryshe, B. D., Valdez-Menchaca, M. C., & Caulfield, M. (1988). Accelerating language development through picture-book reading. *Developmental Psychology, 24,* 552–558.

Whitehurst, G. J., & Lonigan, C. J. (1998). Child development and emergent literacy. *Child Development, 68,* 848–872.

Whitehurst, G. J., & Lonigan, C. J. (2001). Emergent literacy: Development from prereaders to readers. In S. B Neuman & D. K. Dickensen (Eds.), *Handbook of early literacy research* (pp. 11–29). New York: Guilford.

Whitehurst, G. J., Lonigan, C. J., & Arnold, D. S. (1991). *Dialogic reading: The hear-say method—A video workshop* [video]. Stony Brook, NY: Author.

Whitehurst, G. J., Zevenbergen, A. A., Crone, D. A., Schultz, M. D., Velting, O. N., & Fischel, J. E. (1999). Outcomes of an emergent literacy intervention from Head Start through second grade. *Journal of Educational Psychology, 91,* 261–272.

Wise, B. W., Olson, R. K., Ring, J., & Johnson, M. (1998). Interactive computer support for improving phonological skills. In J. L Metsala & L. C. Ehri (Eds.), *Word recognition in beginning literacy* (pp. 189–208). Mahwah, NJ: Lawrence Erlbaum Associates.

Wolf, M. (1991). Naming speed and reading: The contribution of the cognitive neurosciences. *Reading Research Quarterly, 26,* 123–141.

5

Use of Literature in the Home and at School

Lesley Mandel Morrow
Jessica Temlock-Fields
Rutgers University

Quality children's literature, both expository and narrative, needs to be an important part of literacy instruction at school and in the home (Scharer, 1992). The use of children's literature provides authentic learning experiences and activities to teach and foster literacy development. This chapter focuses on the importance of children's literature in literacy instruction at home and in the school. First, we will review research about literature-based instruction in general; second, we will concentrate on aspects of storybook reading in the classroom and at home. Third, we will draw conclusions concerning literature-based instruction and storybook reading at school and the implications for home.

BACKGROUND RATIONALE FOR USING LITERATURE IN LITERACY INSTRUCTION

The Value of Literature in Literacy Instruction

A guiding principle for the use of children's literature in literacy instruction is that learning to read and write occurs in a book-rich context—with an abundance of purposeful communication and where meaning is socially constructed (Cullinan, 1987). When using literature in literacy instruction the following occurs: (a) literature is used as an important vehicle for language arts instruction; it may be the sole or primary basis for reading instruction or it may be used to supplement a basal program; (b) opportunities exist for children to read books of their own choosing independently throughout the day; (c) children are provided with sustained time for both independent and collaborative reading and writing activities, and (d) adults and children are encouraged to interact and collaborate in activities that concern children's literature (Cullinan, 1990; Tompkins & McGee, 1993).

A strong read-aloud program, including daily read-aloud time, is also a crucial characteristic of literature-based instruction. In a study conducted by Lehman, Freeman, and Allen (1994), 85% of elementary teachers reported reading aloud to their students at least once a day. Storybook reading stretches the imagination, offers information, and exposes students to perspectives that they might not otherwise encounter. It enables them to reflect on events and ideas, both from their own lives and from the lives of others. By listening to and discussing stories, students become familiar with story language and story structure. They hear what fluent, expressive reading sounds like, and they can learn strategies to apply to their independent reading. Daily read-aloud time also has been an important component of research studies exploring the effects of literature-based reading instruction (Morrow, 1992; Smith, 1993).

To provide insights about operational definitions of literature-based instruction, Fisher and Hiebert (1990) conducted an observational study, examining the types of tasks engaged in by students in either literature-based or skills-based classrooms. The researchers used Doyle's (1983) task framework to contrast the learning opportunities provided to students in classrooms using the two approaches to reading instruction. Substantial differences in the kind and number of literacy tasks in the literature-based versus the skills-based classrooms were revealed by the study. Students in the literature-based classrooms spent significantly more time involved in literacy activities, especially in the production of connected text than students in skills-based classrooms. In literature-based classrooms, teachers had more control over the types of literature they read and their activities. The activities were also more cognitively complex, involving higher level thinking skills than the activities occurring in the skills-based classrooms. The students in the classrooms with literature-based instruction performed activities involving synthesis, integration, or generation of ideas as opposed to recognizing facts or recalling details.

Theoretical Framework

The nature of the learning that occurs as a result of adults reading stories to or with children is consistent in a number of literacy theories. Wittrock's (1974, 1986) model of generative learning supports the notion that the reader or listener understands prose by actively engaging in the construction of meaning and making connections with the textual information he or she hears or reads (Linden & Wittrock, 1981). According to Vygotsky's (1978) cultural–historical theory, literacy appears to develop from children's social interactions with others in specific environments of which reading, writing, and oral language are a part. The literacy activities and the interactions that are mediated by adults determine the ideas about and skills acquired for literacy development (Sulzby & Teale, 1987). Holdaway's (1979) model of developmental teaching, derived from observations of middle-class homes, asserted that children benefit most when their earliest experiences with storybooks are mediated by an adult who interacts with the child in a problem-solving situation. The child is asked to respond, and the adult offers information as needed to sustain the activity. In such situations, children and adults interact to integrate, construct, and develop understandings of the printed text.

The primary goal of storybook reading, then, is the construction of meaning from the interactive process between an adult and child. During story reading, the adult (parents, teachers, and others) should help the child understand and make sense of text by interpreting written language based on their experience, background, and beliefs. (Altwerger, Diehl-Faxon, & Dockstader-Anderson, 1985). According to Teale (1984), this process reflects Vygotsky's (1978) theory of learning because in story reading the interaction is interpsychological first, as it is negotiated between adult and child together, and intrapsychological next, when the child internalizes the interactions and can function independently.

The reader response theory has addressed issues about the reader of literature. The same types of issues seem to apply when we listen to stories. Reader response theory explains how readers, and those who listen to stories being read to them, interpret literature (McGee, 1992). Reader response theorists posit that literature is not an object to be studied, nor does it have one correct interpretation (Iser, 1978); rather, meaning in the text is constructed by the students' own interpretation of their experiences while they are reading and listening (Rosenblatt, 1978). Meaning, therefore, is a two-way process that resides in the transaction that occurs between the student and the text where the reader or listener constructs a personal environment guided by the text. The student uses prior experiences to select images and feelings that will enable him or her to shape the text, whereas the text shapes the reader by creating new experiences (McGee, 1992; Rosenblatt, 1978, 1991).

Rosenblatt (1978, 1991) identified two stances, aesthetic and efferent, that students can take, depending on their purposes for reading or listening to a piece of literature. When readers take an aesthetic stance when reading or listening to a story, poem, or play, their attention shifts inward to personal feelings, ideas, and attitudes. When taking an efferent stance in reading or listening to informational text, the readers' attention narrows in order to build up the meanings and ideas to be retained. Rosenblatt hypothesized that it is the student rather than the text that dictates the stance that is taken, and any text can be read in either way. She also suggested that, when reading any one text, readers shift along a continuum from the aesthetic to the efferent stance.

A BRIEF HISTORY OF LITERATURE-BASED INSTRUCTION

From the 1940s to the 1990s, basal programs (i.e., reading instructional materials) have been documented as the dominant reading materials used for instruction in American elementary classrooms (Shannon, 1989). However, in the 1990s, literature became an important part of the reading curriculum due to the availability of high-quality literature, the popularity of the whole language movement, and the prominence of reader response theory (Cullinan, 1990; Fisher & Hiebert, 1990; Goodman, 1989; Rosenblatt, 1978).

The first literature-based beginning reading programs were created in the late 1980s for selection in California, which mandated literature programs (California English/Language Arts Committee, 1987). By 1993, all the major textbook companies had begun producing materials for the changing reading curriculum in California (Hiebert, 1999). To support the implementation of literature in reading programs, the state textbook guidelines in California and Texas (California English/Language Arts Committee, 1987; Texas Education Agency, 1990) called for the elimination of contrived texts (those that controlled vocabularies, or shortened stories) and the use of text with literary merit.

The research on materials used for reading instruction documents the increasing significance of children's literature in the beginning of the 1990s. In a survey conducted in 1980, Gambrell (1992) explored the programs, approaches, and materials used in the reading curriculum. In this study, each of the 93 teachers who were observed reported using a basal program as the basis for reading instruction. Only 5% of the teachers, primarily at the kindergarten level, stated that they supplemented basal instruction with other materials or approaches. These results indicate almost sole reliance on the use of basal programs in the early 1980s. The study was replicated in 1990, and included 84 teachers from seven eastern states and the District of Columbia (Gambrell, 1992). Although 80% of the respondents reported using a basal program as the primary basis for reading instruction, more than 50% of these teachers indicated that they supplemented the basal program with children's literature—a significant increase from 1980. The most surprising finding was that the remaining 20% of the respondents reported using children's literature as the foundation for their reading program. In 1994, Strickland, Walmsley, Bronk, and Weiss interviewed teachers in eight states and found that 18% of the teachers reported using children's literature exclusively, whereas 80% used both basals and children's literature.

The most compelling evidence of widespread implementation of literature-based reading instruction in the United States comes from the findings of the 1992 National Assessment of Educational Progress (Mullis, Campbell, & Farstrup, 1993). This study revealed that teachers reported a "heavy" emphasis on literature-based instruction, and that the students of these teachers appeared to have higher levels of reading proficiency. With the increasing growth in the use of children's literature in the classroom, several concerns about the implementation of literature-based instruction began to emerge. Many teachers did not have current or appropriate course work for dealing with literature-based instruction and, therefore, many were not prepared to carry out instruction using this method (Cullinan, 1989). Policymakers and educators have questioned the sole use of literature-based instruction for beginning readers. They are concerned because some teachers focus most of their instructional time on story content, and not enough time on alphabetic principles. Consequently, students are not adequately acquiring essential reading skills.

Hiebert (1999) revisited the question of whether literature should be the sole material for reading instruction. She examined how young children best learn to dissect the written text and discovered that at the earliest stages of reading acquisition, especially when children are introduced to book reading in school rather than at home, careful attention must be paid to the texts they are using. She concluded that although authentic literature is vitally important, young children also need texts that are more systematic with skill development to learn how to read; skills must be explicitly taught. She considered several different types of texts and the tasks they pose for beginning readers. Hiebert concluded that literature is not the only source of materials for early literacy instruction. Consequently, researchers have noted that they need to continue to examine what type of materials are best for early childhood reading instruction.

SKILL DEVELOPMENT AND STORYBOOK READING

Storybook reading not only opens up new worlds to children but also influences children's achievement in various aspects of literacy development. During early childhood, reading to children has always been a vital experience in literature-based instruction (Purcell-Gates, 2001). In this section we review studies dealing with storybook reading that were carried out in both the home and the school and had positive effects on student achievement.

Correlational investigations and case studies demonstrate that young children, who have been read to habitually, know how to handle books and can identify the front of a book, the print to be read, and the appropriate direction for reading the print (Baghban, 1984; Morrow, 1983).

Several studies using experimental designs explore the effects of storybook reading as a regular classroom practice on children's achievement in various aspects of literacy development. In these investigations, the children in the experimental classrooms who were read to daily over long periods of time scored significantly better on measures of vocabulary, comprehension, and decoding ability than children in the control groups who were not read to by an adult (Bus, van IJzendoorn, & Pellegrini, 1995; Dickinson & Smith, 1994; Feitelson, Goldstein, Iraqi, & Share, 1993; Robbins & Ehri, 1994; Senechal, Thomas, & Monker, 1995).

Experimental investigations in school settings have tried to identify specific elements of storybook reading that enhance literacy skills. Each of the studies has involved children in some type of active participation before, during, and after storybook reading (Dickinson & Smith, 1994; Whitehurst & Lonigan, 1998). Other research has focused on the influence of the teacher when reading to a whole class in school (Teale, 1987). In the next section studies are reviewed that demonstrate skill development as a result of storybook reading.

COMPREHENSION, PRINT AWARENESS, VOCABULARY, AND FLUENCY DEVELOPMENT

The National Reading Panel (2000) identified elements in the teaching of reading that are necessary for learning to read. They include comprehension, phonemic awareness and phonics, vocabulary development, and fluency. The following studies about storybook reading demonstrate skill development in literacy instruction as a result of a particular storybook reading activity.

Comprehension

In experimental studies carried out in school settings where children participated with their teacher and peers in some part of the storybook reading experience, students' comprehension and sense of story structure improved in comparison to children in the control groups. The treatments involved activities implemented (a) before story reading, such as previewing the story through discussion and prediction and setting a purpose for listening; (b) during story reading, with a focus on ideas related to the story that were spontaneously discussed at appropriate times; and (c) after reading, such as discussing predictions and purposes set, role-playing stories, retelling stories, and reconstructing stories through pictures. These activities enabled children to relate various parts of a story to one another and to integrate information across the entire story (Morrow, 1985; Pellegrini & Galda, 1982).

Print Awareness

In studies that involved middle-income families reading to their children, growth was indicated in children's print awareness. Mothers were found to reference print more often while reading alphabet books to their children. It was also found that when parents were taught to use print-referencing strategies (i.e., pointing out elements of print that could be useful to children) when reading with young children, parental print referencing increased. This procedure led to an increase in their children's verbal interactions with print (Justice & Ezell, 2002; Justice, Weber, Ezell, & Bakeman, 2002).

Vocabulary Development

Social interaction is central to language development and thought (Vygotsky, 1978). Storybook reading investigations with preschool children have found that interactive storybook reading with open-ended discussion and questioning by the reader provided opportunities for extensive verbal expression resulting in vocabulary development (Dickinson & Smith, 1994; Wasik & Bond, 2001). The storybook reading provided a rich semantic context for new vocabulary. Children who had the opportunity to repeat new words from literature as it was being read to them increased in their vocabulary performance. Children whose parents and teachers used dialogic reading which involves interactive experiences between reader and listener increased their language skills more than students who worked only with one adult. Reading in an interactive manner gives children the occasion to hear and repeat rich language patterns, influencing their growth in vocabulary (Dickinson & Smith, 1994; Whitehurst & Lonigan, 1998).

Fluency

Storybook reading provides students with an authentic model for fluent reading. As the teacher reads at an appropriate rate with expression, proper punctuation, and pitch, he or she demonstrates how fluent readers sound. Although fluency was discussed as an important element for reading success in the National Reading Panel Report (2000), there is a need for more research on the topic. In a NAEP test (1992), 44% of students examined were deemed low in fluency when reading stories. Hoffman (1987) tested a fluency program in which students showed gains over those not involved in a fluency program, but data were not tested for statistical differences.

Fluent readers exhibit automaticity, which is the ability to read accurately and quickly by automatically decoding words. In addition, fluent readers demonstrate prosody, the use of appropriate pitch, inflection, and expression when reading, thus demonstrating understanding of text. Researchers have shown that automaticity and prosody improve with modeling (Stahl, Heubach, & Cramond, 1997). Studies by Rasinski (1991) and Ransinski, Padak, Linek, and Sturtevant (1994) indicate that automaticity and prosody also improved with strategies such as repeated reading and choral reading, which are linked to helping students comprehend the text. A pilot study examining the effect of partner reading and repeated reading on fluency showed a 1.8 grade level improvement in participants over a school year (Stahl et al.). The researchers have called for a theory-based model on how fluency develops to be utilized for the conception of a classroom model. Although more research is necessary, we can conclude that adult readers who engage young listeners in various activities before, during, and after sharing a book increase the potential to improve a child's overall oral fluency when reading. The different strategies suggested to build fluency that can be used with storybook reading include choral reading, echo reading, repeated reading, partner reading, and reader's theater.

STORYBOOK READING STRATEGIES THAT FOSTER POSITIVE EFFECTS ON ACHIEVEMENT

Interactive Behavior during Storybook Reading

Although the studies cited in this section highlight the positive effects of storybook reading, Meyer, Wardrop, Stahl, and Linn (1994) suggest that reading stories is not a magical activity for literacy development; it is the quality of the interaction that occurs during reading that results in positive effects rather than just storybook reading. They reported that storybook reading sessions in classrooms are often not of sufficient quality to engage students fully and to maximize literacy growth. Reading stories as an act in and of itself does not necessarily promote literacy; rather, certain methods, interactive behaviors, environmental influences, and attitudes enhance the potential of the read-aloud event for promoting literacy development (Bus & van IJzendoorn, 1997; Dickinson & Tabors, 1991).

As we know, the primary goal of the read-aloud event is the construction of meaning from the interactive process between adult and child (Vygotsky, 1978). During storybook reading, the adult helps the child understand the text by interpreting the written language based on experiences, background, and beliefs (Altwerger et al., 1985).

Studies focusing on teachers' interactive behaviors when reading to whole classes of children have documented the impact of teachers' reading styles on children's comprehension of stories (Green & Harker, 1982; Peterman, Dunning, & Mason, 1985). Teachers used different reading techniques as they read to children, spontaneously making decisions on how to engage the listeners as the story progressed. Teachers also employed conversation, questioning, and dramatization to involve children. Teachers who used a more analytic, cognitive approach furthered their students' growth more than those who simply asked for a basic retelling of facts (Bus & van IJzendoorn, 1997; Dickinson & Tabors, 1991).

A series of investigations were carried out in classrooms to determine children's comprehension of stories in whole-group, small-group, and one-to-one settings (Morrow, 1987, 1988; Morrow & Smith, 1990). The interactions that occurred within these different settings were also studied. On a test of comprehension, children who heard stories in small-group settings performed significantly better than children who heard stories read in a one-to-one setting, who in turn performed significantly better than children who heard stories read to the whole class. In addition, children who heard stories read in a small-group or a one-to-one setting generated significantly more comments and questions than did children in the whole-class setting. Thus, reading to children in small groups offers as much interaction as one-to-one readings, and it appears to lead to greater comprehension than whole-class or even one-to-one readings.

Children's responses to read-aloud experiences, both in questions and in comments, are a critical aspect of the interactive process. When questions are asked and then answered, children receive immediate feedback, which may aid their literacy development (Yaden, 1985). Holdaway's (1979) model for literacy instruction advocates that children have the opportunity to regulate their own learning by questioning adults in literacy situations such as storybook reading. Cochran-Smith (1984) found the types of questions and comments children make during story-reading events help us gain insights into the way young children attempt to construct meaning and make sense of text.

Repeated Readings

Children often request that favorite stories be read aloud, a practice that has attracted the attention of many scholars. Researchers have questioned whether lasting cognitive and affective benefits result from repeated readings of the same story. Roser and Martinez (1985) and Yaden (1985) suggest that children's comments and questions increase and become more interpretive and evaluative when they have listened to repeated readings of the same story. Children also elaborated more often and interpreted issues in the story following repeated readings. Case study investigations of repeated storybook readings found that in their comments and responses to the readings, children discussed more aspects of the text and discussed them in greater depth (Morrow, 2001; Snow, 1993; Snow & Goldfield, 1983). Sulzby (1985) reported that the familiarity that comes with repeated readings enables children to reenact stories or attempt to read them on their own.

In a study by Morrow (1987), when teachers repeated stories, the number and complexity of kindergarten children's responses increased. The youngsters offered many questions and comments that focused on meaning. Initially, they labeled illustrations. Later they gave increased attention to details, their comments and questions became interpretive and predictive, and they drew from their own experiences. They also began narrating—that is, reading or mouthing the story along with the teachers. Some children focused on structural elements, remarking on titles, settings, characters, and story events. After many readings, the children began to focus on print, questioning names of words, letters, or sounds. Some of the children began to recognize letters and words, and read them. These child activities occurred when the teacher behavior during the storybook reading included the following: managing, prompting responses, and supporting and informing. Examples of these teacher behaviors are given in the following:

1. **Managing**
   Introduce story.
   Provide background information about the book.
   Redirect irrelevant discussion back to the story.

2. **Prompt Responses**

Invite children to ask questions or comment throughout the story when there are natural places to stop.

Scaffold responses for children to model if no responses are forthcoming. ("Those animals aren't very nice. They won't help the little red hen.")

Relate responses to real-life experiences. ("I needed help when I was preparing a party, and my family shared the work. Did you ever ask for help and couldn't find anyone to give it to you? What happened?")

When children do not respond, ask questions that require answers other than yes or no. ("What would you have done if you were the little red hen and no one helped you bake the bread?")

3. **Supporting and Informing**

Answer questions as they are asked.

React to comments.

Relate your responses to real-life experiences.

Provide positive reinforcement for children's responses.

Repeated readings seem to be an important component in reading stories; the familiarity gained through the experience provides children with background information and allows them to discuss the story at a more sophisticated level of understanding.

Literature Discussion Groups

Reading to children is important, but what goes on before and after the reading is critical. Literature discussion groups are typically described as involving small groups of children (three to eight students) who read or listened to a story or novel over a period of time. Researchers who have explored the cognitive processes that are necessary for higher level thinking agree that deep-level understanding occurs for all ages through interactions with others (Almasi, 1995, 1996). Other researchers have reported that the collaborative nature of literature discussions appears to help students construct meaning and clarify confusions (Almasi, 1995; Eeds & Wells, 1989). Students in these studies were observed orchestrating turn taking, negotiating leadership, and drawing on various sources to clarify or agree on text interpretation.

Studies that have focused on discussion groups have used a variety of qualitative and quantitative methods to examine what happens when students engage in discussions about books they have listened to or read (Gambrell, 1996). There is evidence that prior to instruction or experience with literature discussion groups, students' responses tend to be unelaborated and their discussions involve limited interactions with peers and adults. For example, Eeds and Wells (1989) found that even without direct questioning by the teacher there was some evidence in students' discussions that they recalled text information, drew inferences, supported their inferences, and read critically. Students, however, did have difficulty making personal connections to text before the intervention of the discussion groups. Given opportunities to participate in discussions, these same students quickly learned to respond personally to their reading (Goatley, 1996).

The research on early elementary students' discussion of children's literature suggests that young children are capable of producing elaborate and sophisticated responses to literature, especially when supported with instruction. Across these studies, children were able to construct meaning, share personal reactions, and demonstrate strategic reading behaviors such as hypothesizing, interpreting, predicting, and evaluating. The research clearly indicates that reading and discussing children's literature offers students opportunities to explore interpretations of literature and respond at higher levels of abstract and critical thinking (McGee, 1992).

PROMOTING POSITIVE ATTITUDES AND INTEREST IN BOOKS

An important component of any literacy program is promoting positive attitudes toward reading to instill a lifelong reading habit. Early investigations on promoting interest in books and the use of literature in the classroom were mainly anecdotal and indicated that literature-based programs may enhance students' enthusiasm and foster positive attitudes toward books. When classrooms are filled with trade books and teachers encourage free reading, there is an improvement in children's reading achievement, gains in vocabulary and comprehension, increased reading, and better attitudes toward reading in comparison to children in schools who do not have the opportunity to do free reading with trade books (Fielding, Wilson, & Anderson, 1986). Morrow and Weinstein (1982, 1986) found that literature use increased dramatically when teachers incorporated enjoyable literature activities into the daily program, when library centers were created in the classrooms, and when recreational reading periods were scheduled on a regular basis.

Empirical research by Morrow (1992) and Morrow and Weinstein (1982, 1986) suggests specific activities in preschool through third grade that deal with use of literature to increase children's interest in books. The results of their studies indicate that one practice of utmost importance is to read to children daily. Storytelling by teachers and use of storytelling props, such as felt board stories, puppets, and taped stories, all were found to be valuable in creating interest in books. When teachers used storytelling props, the book represented was always present. Discussions that focused on interpretive and critical issues within the stories also served to heighten interest in books. In addition, using literature related to content-area topics, such as in social studies and science, correlated positively with children's increased use of literature, as did regular time set aside for independent reading.

Research findings concerning the effects of using literature in literacy instruction on children's attitudes toward reading have been mixed. Some studies have found that there is no difference between basal reading instruction and literature-based instruction on children's attitudes toward reading (McKenna, Kear, & Ellsworth, 1995; McKenna, Stratton, Grindler, & Jenkins, 1995). No studies were found demonstrating that basal reading instruction improved children's attitudes toward reading more than literature-based instruction. However, several studies using a range of quantitative and qualitative methodologies have revealed that literature-based programs positively affect children's attitude toward reading and frequency of reading (Dahl & Freppon, 1995; Goatley, Brock, & Raphael, 1995; Goatley & Raphael, 1992; Stewart, Paradis, Ross, & Lewis, 1996). Gambrell, Palmer, and Coding (1993) found that children want to read more when they are able to choose what they will read, have the opportunity to interact with others to discuss what they have read, and feel successful about reading.

The physical setting for storybook reading and use of literature by children can have a strong effect on motivation to read. Appropriate physical arrangement of furniture, material selection, and the aesthetic quality of different parts of a classroom, in this case the library corner, can provide a setting that contributes to teaching, learning, and promoting independent reading (Morrow 1982, 1983). Investigations have found that library corners were among the least popular areas in early childhood classrooms during free play periods. In most rooms, the library corners consisted of a bookshelf with books shelved in a disorderly manner. Frequently the library area was inaccessible or hard to find in a classroom. When found, these areas were unattractive and neglected. According to Morrow (2002), the work of creating an accessible library corner stocked with current selections of children's literature is worth the effort, because it is rewarded by children's increased interest in reading and reading achievement. It has been found that students in classrooms with extensive book collections use them 50% more when compared with classrooms where there were almost no books to be found (Morrow, 2001). Correlational and experimental studies have identified many positive relationships between the frequency with which young children use literature in the classroom and physical design characteristics of library corners. Studies also report increased use of literature during free choice periods in classrooms where library corners featured specific design characteristics (Anderson, Fielding, & Wilson, 1985; Morrow, 1982, 1983, 1987; Morrow & Weinstein, 1982, 1986). Library centers that promoted children's voluntary use of books were characterized by the following:

- They were partitioned off from the rest of the room.
- They had comfortable seating.
- They provided five to eight books per child.
- They had multiple genres of children's literature.
- They had a categorization system for storing the books.
- They employed a system for checking out books.
- They had open-faced bookshelves to feature books.
- They provided story props such as a felt board with felt characters, puppets, and a listening station with headsets and taped stories.

LITERATURE-BASED INSTRUCTION AND SECOND LANGUAGE LEARNERS

Today's classrooms are extremely diverse. Teachers are now faced with the necessity of reaching children whose first language is not English. How does literature-based instruction relate to these students? Roser, Hoffman, and Farest (1990) investigated the effect of literature-based instruction on second-language learners in kindergarten through second grade with an emphasis on oral language development. The study took place in a school district on the Texas/Mexico border. Research was in six elementary schools over a 10-month period. There were 78 teachers and 2,500 children in the study.

Preparation for the study involved the following: (a) supplying classrooms with large collections of children's literature, (b) creating literacy centers in the classrooms, (c) providing teachers with 70 literature units for the literature-based instruction along with professional development to help put this program into practice.

Treatment in the study included: (a) sharing books with children in multiple formats; (b) asking children to respond orally to books; (c) encouraging writing about stories read; (d) developing reading fluency to help children grow in language, reading, writing, and thinking; and (e) helping children to connect their lives to the literature.

To report the results of the literature-based instruction on the second-language students, teachers' reports of student progress included (a) students' fluency in reading and writing and (b) achievement on the California Test of Basic Skills. The results of the study indicated that a literature-based program could be successful in classrooms that served children with limited English who were from disadvantaged homes.

Research about second-language learners has found that these students need learning experiences that are meaningful and interesting for them (Cummins, 1989; Krashen & Terrell, 1983). Children's literature provides the opportunity to find something that is both meaningful and interesting for everyone. With folktales from their own countries, fairy tales, and other genres, it is possible to activate prior knowledge and raise interest.

The classroom with second-language learners that provides experiences with literature-based instruction is giving students the opportunities for choices; for interacting with peers; and for building self-confidence as they read aloud, carry out book talks, retell stories, and participate in literature circles. These activities all help with literacy and language acquisition.

There are idealogical differences when it comes to literature-based practices at home. Family literacy programs seek to make parents aware of the many things they can do with their children to help them with their academic achievement. Practices discussed in these sections would fall into this category. Some programs, for example, are concerned that parents are not doing these activities with their children and that it is the school's responsibility to teach them what they need to do (Nickse, 1991). Others express concern with this type of program, calling it a deficit model. The concern is with assuming that families do not know ways of sharing literacy with their children, and that teaching what to do may actually interfere and be an intrusion into the families' cultural ways of sharing literacy (Auerbach, 1995; Taylor, 1997). Both positions have some valid arguments and some supportive research (see Gadsden, this volume; Purcell-Gates, this volume, for further discussion of these debates).

ADAPTING STORYBOOK-READING TECHNIQUES FOR THE HOME

Parent involvement is critical to children's literacy development. It is the school's responsibility to draw parents into their literacy development program with information about how they can help at home. Although some family traditions do not emphasize the participation of school-like activities at home, it is evident that these practices are effective in enhancing children's concepts of reading. Schools must be sensitive to cultural differences and carefully suggest activities that complement family values. The following suggestions related to activities parents can do with their children can be encouraged by staff in family literacy programs.

One of the most important activities that can be done with children of all ages and from all backgrounds is the regular practice of storybook reading and storytelling. Storybook reading and storytelling at home are easy to do, do not take very long, are usually enjoyed by all, and have multiple benefits. In the previous literature review, we found research demonstrating that children developed skills from storybook reading and identified strategies that enhanced skill development. This information will be used to make suggestions for home involvement in storybook-reading activities for children.

As previously noted, children who are read to regularly show gains in the areas of vocabulary, comprehension, and decoding ability (Bus et al., 1995; Dickinson & Smith, 1994; Feitelson et al., 1993; Robbins & Ehri, 1994; Senechal et al., 1995). Parents can read to their children and enhance these skills with interactive experiences that allow children to predict, respond to, and retell stories. This can be done with children in early childhood and the elementary grades.

Comprehension

To enhance comprehension, parents can help build background knowledge before reading to children. For example, they can take a picture walk through the book one page at a time, using the illustrations to discuss what is happening throughout the story before reading the text. After the picture walk and before reading, the child can be asked by their parent to predict what they think the book will be about. Throughout the reading, the parent can ask open-ended questions about the story, such as "Why do you think that he or she did . . . " and "How do you think he or she felt when . . . ", thus encouraging the child to elaborate.

Once the reading has been completed, the child can retell the story in a variety of formats. Retelling can be a puppet show from behind the couch with stuffed animals. Sharing the story with a friend or sibling is another good home activity. These activities encourage children to construct meaning, thus increasing their comprehension of the story (Morrow, 1985; Pellegrini & Galda, 1982).

With older children, parents and children can look at chapter headings and subheadings to become acquainted with a book before reading. Often the book jacket will have a summary of the book.

Print Awareness.   The research described previously illustrated that adults who pointed out elements about print when reading to children found that children in turn remarked about print when reading themselves (Justice & Ezell, 2002; Justice, Weber, Ezell, & Bakeman, 2002). When reading to their children, parents can point out different print elements; for example, they can

- Point out similar letter patterns in words (e.g., plate, skate)
- Give the child their own sight words on index cards, when he or she encounters a new, unfamiliar word
- Point out punctuation, what it means, and how it helps with reading
- Point out a new prefix or suffix

The age of the child will determine which elements of text should be discussed.

Fluency.   Fluency is an important component that helps children decode and comprehend text. Storybook reading is perfect for helping children to become fluent. As parents read with their children, they should be aware of their own automaticity and prosody, as their reading serves as a model for their children to follow (Smith, 1978). If the adult reader is uncomfortable reading aloud new text, the adult can read it silently first. This initial reading will help the adult reader become more familiar with the text. This practice may improve inflection and rate when reading aloud. To enhance fluency, the parent and child can partner read. The more able reader should begin by reading one sentence, one paragraph, or a page. The partner then takes his or her turn to read a portion. Parents can also record the partner reading and then play it back. With guidance from the adult, the child may be able to pinpoint places in the story that need to be improved by discussing what caused a pause, or how more appropriate expression could be used.

After reading a story containing a few characters who use conversation, parent and child can do a reader's theater performance. Each one takes a character's part to read again with the proper inflection and rate. Fables are good reader's theater passages because they are short and involve talking characters.

Many activities can help less able readers. One activity, choral reading, helps the less able reader to be drawn into the rhythm of reading fluently. Another activity, echo reading, can be done at home. In echo reading, the more able reader reads a line first, and then it is repeated by the less able reader. These activities not only promote fluency at home but also, because comprehension and fluency are linked, may help with comprehension skills. Both the early childhood and the elementary grade children can participate in these fluency activities.

Interactive Reading

The research reviewed clearly supports reading with children as an interactive process. Research confirms that discussion, questioning, and sharing during the process of storybook reading fosters positive growth in children's self-monitoring and control of literacy acquisition (Holdaway, 1979; Yaden, 1985). The following prediction game is an interactive story-reading activity for parents and children to do together. The parent selects a piece of literature that is new for the child and reads the first few pages and then stops and closes the book. The parent asks the child to predict what will happen next and to tell why. Then, the parent resumes reading the next few pages and then asks the child to evaluate whether their prediction was accurate and to make a new prediction. Parents should continue this process through the end of the story. After the child learns this routine, the parent and child can switch roles so that the child is monitoring their parent's prediction.

According to Roser and Martinez (1985) and Yaden (1985), repeated readings with young children allow them to investigate a story in a more sophisticated manner by searching for answers to their own meaningful questions (Morrow, 2001; Snow, 1993; Snow & Goldfield, 1983). Teachers should let parents know the books that are read at school so parents can use them at home. Favorite books at home can be read over and over. Repeated readings at home help to develop word recognition, comprehension, and fluency. When rereading a familiar book, parents can tape-record the oral reading to check for fluency and use a child's retelling to note their comprehension. When children hear stories repeated, the rich language patterns from the literature become a part of their vocabulary (Dickinson & Smith, 1994; Whitehurst & Lonigan, 1998). These activities can be adjusted so they are appropriate for both early-childhood and elementary-school-age children.

Discussing Literature

We know that children make gains in comprehension, decoding ability, vocabulary, and motivation when given the opportunity to discuss what they have read. In school, students participate in literature study groups. In these groups they discuss a story or a book together that the group has read. This activity can be done at home with a parent as well. Once a story has been read by both parent and child, each can take a few of the following roles to discuss the text:

- *The Discussion Director*—develops a list of questions about the story for the parent and child.
- *The Literary Luminary*—selects a part of the book to read aloud.
- *The Illustrator*—draws a picture related to the reading. The representation could be a flow chart of the story or a roll story.
- *The Connector*—finds associations between the book and the outside world.
- *The Summarizer*—retells the main points of the story.
- *The Vocabulary Enricher*—looks for important words in the story and discusses their definitions.
- *The Travel Tracer*—tracks the action in the reading.
- *The Investigator*—shares background information about the topic of the story.

Not all of these roles need to be used, nor do the titles of the roles have to be as listed. Literature discussion groups can be used with children in early childhood and elementary school grades. The elements within the discussion need to be tailored, however, to the age of the child. Teachers need to introduce this technique to parents and send home books for discussing with their children.

MATERIALS AND MOTIVATION

When parents and children read together at home, ideally it should be a pleasant experience. The underlying purpose is to motivate a child's interest and foster a lifelong love of reading. It is important for parents to have a place to store books so they are accessible. In addition to this special location, parents may keep books in many areas throughout the home. Books can be on shelves, in play areas, in the bathroom, and in the kitchen. Parents should also establish a special place to read in the home. Places that are quiet, cozy, and comfortable, such as in the child's bed or in an easy chair, on the floor, or in a special room of the house, often encourage reading. Ideally, there would be good lighting in this space and distractions at a minimal to enhance comprehension. When ideal conditions do not exist, as may occur in a very small home with extended family members, discuss with parents how to arrange for storybook reading within the family's particular circumstances. In good weather, perhaps sitting outside is an option.

Parents should try to have a variety of genres of children's literature for a home library. The genres could include fiction and nonfiction books. Books from the library can be borrowed for the home library and books can be borrowed from school. When there is a special occasion parents should think about giving a book as a gift. Sharing books with friends can help to increase choices for reading at home.

Parents are a child's first teacher and the teacher a child will have for the longest period of time. Researchers have learned much about children's literacy development in the school and home. One of the most important things we have learned about literacy development is that early exposure to books and print is crucial. This early exposure enhances children's language development, a definitive predictor of reading success. It also exposes children to book concepts where they learn concepts such as the difference between the print and the pictures, the front of the book and the back of the book, and how to turn pages. They hear book language and how reading sounds. This knowledge will help their later success. We must enlist the help of parents so they recognize their importance in the literacy development of their children. Community and school programs need to reach out to parents to help them learn and understand about this important activity that bonds families.

ACKNOWLEDGMENT

I would like to acknowledge the help of Allison Porro and Heather Casey for retrieving the articles for the research review.

REFERENCES

Almasi, J. F. (1995). The nature of fourth grader's sociocognitive conflicts in peer-led and teacher-led discussions of literature. *Reading Research Quarterly, 30*, 314–351.

Almasi, J. F. (1996). A new view of discussion. In L. B. Gambrell & J. F. Almasi (Eds.), *Lively discussions! Fostering engaging reading* (pp. 2–24). Newark, DE: International Reading Association.

Altwerger, A., Diehl-Faxon, J., & Dockstader-Anderson, K. (1985). Read-aloud events as meaning construction. *Language Arts, 62,* 476–484.

Anderson, R. C., Fielding, L. G., & Wilson, P. T. (1985). Growth in reading and how children spend their time outside of school. *Reading Research Quarterly, 23,* 285–303.

Auerbach, E. (1995). Deconstructing the discourse of strengths in family literacy. *Journal of Reading Behavior, 27,* 643–660.

Baghban, M. J. M. (1984). *Our daughter learns to read and write: A case study from birth to three.* Newark, DE: International Reading Association.

Bus, A., van IJzendoorn, M. H., & Pelligrini, A. (1995). Joint book reading makes for success in learning to read: A meta-analysis on intergenerational transmission of literacy. *Review of Educational Research, 65,* 1–21.

Bus, A., & van IJzendoorn, M. H. (1997). Affective dimension of mother-infant picturebook reading. *Journal of School Psychology, 35,* 47–60.

California English/Language Arts Committee. (1987). *English-language arts framework for California public schools (kindergarten through grade twelve).* Sacramento, CA: California Department of Education.

Cochran-Smith, M. (1984).*The making of a reader.* Norwood, NJ: Ablex.

Cullinan, B. E. (1987). *Children's literature in the reading program.* Newark, DE: International Reading Association.

Cullinan, B. E. (1989). Latching on to literature: Reading initiatives take hold. *School Library Journal, 35,* 27–31.

Cullinan, B. E. (1990). Books, babies, and libraries: The librarian's role in literacy development. *Language Arts, 67,* 750–755.

Cummins, J. (1989). *Empowering minority students.* Sacramento: California Association for Bilingual Education.

Dahl, K. L., & Freppon, P. A. (1995). A comparison of inner city children's interpretations of reading and writing instruction in the early grades in skills-based and whole language classrooms. *Reading Research Quarterly, 30,* 50–74.

Dickinson, D. K., & Smith, M. W. (1994). Long-term effects of preschool teachers' book readings on low income children's vocabulary and story comprehension. *Reading Research Quarterly, 29,* 104–122.

Dickinson, D. K., & Tabors, P. O. (1991). Early literacy: Linkage between home, school, and literacy achievement at age five. *Journal of Research in Childhood Education, 6,* 30–46.

Doyle, W. (1983). Academic work. *Review of Educational Research, 53,* 159–199.

Eeds, M., & Wells, D. (1989). Grand conversations: An exploration of meaning construction in literature study groups. *Research in the Teaching of English, 23*(1), 4–29.

Elley, W. B. (1989). Vocabulary acquisition from listening to stories. *Reading Research Quarterly, 24,* 174–187.

Feitelson, D., Goldstein, Z., Iraqi, U., & Share, D. (1993). Effects of listening to story reading on aspects of literacy acquisition in a dialogic situation. *Reading Research Quarterly, 28,* 70–79.

Fielding, L. G., Wilson, P. T., & Anderson, R. C. (1986). A new focus on free reading: The role of trade books in reading instruction. In T. E. Raphael & R. Reynolds (Eds.), *Contexts of literacy* (pp. 149–160). New York: Longman.

Fisher, C. W., & Hiebert, E. H. (1990). Characteristics of tasks in two approaches to literacy instruction. *The Elementary School Journal, 91*(1), 3–18.

Gambrell, L. B. (1992). Elementary school literacy instruction: Changes and challenges. In M. J. Dreher & W. H. Slater (Eds.), *Elementary school literacy: Critical issues* (pp. 227–239). Norwood, MA: Christopher-Gordon.

Gambrell, L. B. (1996). What research reveals about discussion. In L. B. Gambrell & J. F. Almasi (Eds.), *Lively discussion! Fostering engaged reading* (pp. 25–38). Newark, DE: International Reading Association.

Gambrell, L. B., Palmer, B. M., & Coding, R. M. (1993).*Motivation to read.* Washington, DC: Office of Educational Research and Improvement.

Goatley, V. G. (1996). The participation of a student identified as learning disabled in a regular education book club: The case of Stark. *Reading and Writing Quarterly: Overcoming Learning Difficulties, 12*(2), 195–214.

Goatley, V. J., Brock, C. H., & Raphael, T. E. (1995). Diverse learners participating in regular education "Book Clubs." *Reading Research Quarterly, 30,* 352–380.

Goatley, V. J., & Raphael, T. E. (1992). Non-traditional learners' written and dialogic response to literature. *40th yearbook of the National Reading Conference* (pp. 313–322). Chicago: National Reading Conference.

Goodman, Y. M. (1989). Roots of the whole language movement. *The Elementary School Journal, 90,* 113–127.

Green, J. L., & Harker, J. O. (1982). Reading to children: A communicative process. In J. A. Langer & M. T. Smith-Burke (Eds.), *Reader meets author/Bridging the gap: A psycholinguistic and sociolinguistic perspective* (pp. 196–221). Newark, DE: International Reading Association.

Hiebert, E. H. (1999). Text matters in learning to read. *The Reading Teacher, 52,* 552–566.

Hoffman, J. (1987). Rethinking the role of oral reading. *Elementary School Journal, 87,* 367–373.

Holdaway, D. (1979). *The foundations of literacy.* Sydney: Ashton Scholastic.

Iser, W. (1978). *The act of reading.* Baltimore: John Hopkins University Press.

Justice, L. M., & Ezell, H. K. (2002). Use of storybook reading to increase print awareness in at-risk children. *American Journal of Speech-Language Pathology, 11,* 17–29.

Justice, L. M., Weber, S. E., Ezell, H. K., & Bakeman, R. (2002). A sequential analysis of children's responsiveness to parental print references during shared book-reading interactions. *American Journal of Speech-Language Pathology, 11,* 30–40.

Krashen, S. D., & Terrell, T. D. (1983). *The natural approach: Language acquisition in the classroom.* Englewood Cliffs, NJ: Alemany Press.

Lehman, B. A., Freeman, E. V., & Allen, V. G. (1994). Children's literature and literacy instruction: "Literature-based" elementary teachers' belief and practices. *Reading Horizons, 35,* 3–29.

Linden, M., & Wittrock, M. C. (1981). The teaching of reading comprehension according to the model of generative learning. *Reading Research Quarterly, 17,* 44–57.

McGee, L. M. (1992). Exploring the literature-based reading revolution (focus on research). *Language Arts, 69,* 529–537.

McKenna, M. C., Kear, D. J., & Ellsworth, R. A. (1995). Children's attitudes toward reading: A national survey. *Reading Research Quarterly, 30,* 934–955.

McKenna, M. C., Stratton, B. D., Grindler, M. C., & Jenkins, S. J. (1995). Differential effects of whole language and traditional instruction on reading attitudes. *Journal of Reading Behavior, 27*(1), 19–44.

Meyer, L., Wardrop, J., Stahl, S., & Linn, R. (1994). Effects of reading storybooks aloud to children. *Journal of Educational Research, 88,* 69–85.

Morrow, L. M. (1982). Relationships between literature programs, library corner designs and children's use of literature. *Journal of Educational Research, 75*, 339–344.

Morrow, L. M. (1983). Home and school correlates of early interest in literature. *Journal of Educational Research, 76*, 221–230.

Morrow, L. M. (1985). Retelling stories: A strategy for improving children's comprehension, concept of story structure and oral language complexity. *The Elementary School Journal, 85*, 647–661.

Morrow, L. M. (1987). The effect of small group story reading on children's questions and comments. In S. McCormick & J. Zutell (Eds.), Cognitive and social perspectives for literacy research and instruction. *37th yearbook of the National Reading Conference* (pp. 77–86). Chicago: National Reading Conference.

Morrow, L. M. (1988). Young children's responses to one-to-one story readings in school settings. *Reading Research Quarterly, 23*, 89–107.

Morrow, L. M. (1992). The impact of a literature-based program on literacy achievement, use of literature, and attitudes of children from minority backgrounds. *Reading Research Quarterly, 27*, 250–275.

Morrow, L. M. (2001). *Literacy development in the early years: Helping children read and write* (4th ed). Boston: Allyn & Bacon.

Morrow, L. M. (2002). *The literacy center: Contexts for reading and writing* (2nd ed). Portland, ME: Stenhouse Publishers.

Morrow, L. M., & Smith, J. K. (1990). The effects of group size on interactive storybook reading. *Reading Research Quarterly, 25*, 214–231.

Morrow, L. M., & Weinstein, C. S. (1982). Increasing children's use of literature through program and physical design changes. *The Elementary School Journal, 83*, 131–137.

Morrow, L. M., & Weinstein, C. S. (1986). Encouraging voluntary reading: The impact of a literature program on children's use of library centers. *Reading Research Quarterly, 21*, 330–346.

Mullis, I., Campbell, J., & Farstrup, A. (1993). *NAEP 1992 reading report card for the nation and the states: Data from the national and trial state assessments.* Washington, DC: U.S. Government Printing Office.

National Center on Education and the Economy. (1999). *Reading and writing grade by grade: Primary literacy standards for kindergarten through third grade.* Washington, DC.

National Reading Panel. (2000). *Teaching children to read: An evidenced based assessment of the scientific research literature on reading and its implications for reading instruction.* Washington, DC: National Institute of Child Health and Human Development.

Nickse, R. S. (1991). *A topology of family intergenerational literacy programs: Implications for evaluation.* Paper presented at the Annual Meeting of the American Educational Research Association, Chicago.

Pellegrini, A., & Galda, L. (1982). The effects of thematic-fantasy play training on the development of children's story comprehension. *American Educational Research Journal, 19*, 443–452.

Peterman, C. L., Dunning, D., & Mason, J. (1985). *A storybook reading event: How a teacher's presentation affects kindergarten children's subsequent attempts to read from the text.* Paper presented at the 35th annual meeting of the National Reading Conference, San Diego, CA.

Purcell-Gates, V. (2001). What we know about readers who struggle. Ch. 14: *Reading researchers in search of common ground.* Newark, DE: International Reading Association.

Rasinski, T. V. (1991). Fluency for everyone: Incorporating fluency instruction in the classroom. *The Reading Teacher, 43*, 690–692.

Rasinski, T. V. Padak, N., Linek, W., & Sturtevant, E. (1994). Effects of fluency development on urban second grade readers. *Journal of Educational research, 87*, 158–165.

Robbins, C., & Ehri, L. C. (1994). Reading storybooks to kindergartners helps them learn new vocabulary words. *Journal of Educational Psychology, 86*, 54–64.

Rosenblatt, L. M. (1978). *The reader, the text, the poem: The transactional theory of literary work.* Carbondale, IL: Southern Illinois Press.

Rosenblatt, L. M. (1991). Literature—S.O.S. *Language Arts, 68*, 444–448.

Roser, N., Hoffman, J. V., & Farest, C. (1990). Language, literature and at-risk children. *The Reading Teacher, 43*(8), 554–559.

Roser, N., & Martinez, M. (1985). Roles adults play in preschoolers' response to literature. *Language Arts, 62*, 485–490.

Scharer, P. L. (1992). Teachers in transition: An exploration of changes in teachers and classrooms during implementation of literature-based reading instruction. *Research in the Teaching of English, 26*(4), 408–445.

Senechal, M., Thomas, E., & Monker, J. (1995). Individual differences in four-year-old children's acquisition of vocabulary during storybook reading. *Journal of Educational Psychology, 87*, 218–229.

Shannon, P. (1989). *Broken promises: Reading instruction in twentieth century America.* Granby, MA: Bergin & Gavey.

Smith, F. (1978). *Understanding reading* (2nd ed). New York: Holt, Rinehart & Winston.

Smith, J. A. (1993). Content learning: A third reason for using literature in teaching reading. *Reading Research and Instruction, 32*(3), 64–71.

Snow, C. E. (1993). Families as social contexts for literacy development. *New Directions for Child Development, 61*, 11–24.

Snow, C. E., & Goldfield, B. A. (1983). Turn the page please: Situation-specific language acquisition. *Journal of Child Language, 10*, 551–569.

Stahl, S., Heubach, K., & Cramond, B. (1997). Fluency-oriented reading instruction. *National Reading Research Center Reading Research Report no. 79*, Athens, GA: National Reading Research Center.

Stewart, R. A., Paradis, E. E., Ross, B. D., & Lewis, M. J. (1996). Student voices: What works in literature-based developmental reading. *Journal of Adolescent & Adult Literacy, 39*, 468–478.

Strickland, D., Walmsley, S., Bronk, G., & Weiss, K. (1994). *School book clubs and literacy development: A descriptive study* (Report No. 2.22). Albany, NY: State University of New York, National Research Center on Literature Teaching and Learning.

Sulzby, E. (1985). Children's emergent reading of favorite books: A developmental study. *Reading Research Quarterly, 20*, 458–481.

Sulzby, E., & Teale, W. H. (1987). *Young children's storybook reading: Longitudinal study of parent-child interaction and children's independent functioning.* (Final Report to the Spencer Foundation), Ann Arbor, University of Michigan.

Taylor, D. (1997). Many families, many literacies: An international declaration of principles. Portsmouth, MA: Heinemann.

Teale, W. H. (1984). Reading to young children: Its significance for literacy development. In H. Goelman, A. A. Oberg, & F. Smith (Eds.), *Awakening to literacy* (pp. 110–121). London: Heinemann.

Teale, W. H. (1987). *Emergent literacy: Reading and writing development in early childhood.* Paper presented at the 36th annual meeting of the National Reading Conference. Austin, TX.

Texas Education Agency. (1990). *Proclamation of the State Board of Education advertising for bids on textbooks* (Proclamation 68). Austin, TX: Author.

Tompkins, G. E., & McGee, L. M. (1993). *Teaching reading with literature.* New York: Macmillan.

Vygotsky, L. S. (1978). *Mind in society: The development of psychological processes.* Cambridge, MA: Harvard University.

Wasik, B. A., & Bond, M. A. (2001). Beyond the pages of a book: Interactive book reading and language development in preschool classrooms. *Journal of Educational Psychology, 93*, 243–50.

Whitehurst, G. J., & Lonigan, C. J. (1998). Child development and emergent literacy. *Child Development, 69*, 848–872.

Wittrock, M. C. (1974). Learning as a generative process. *Educational Psychologist, 11*, 87–95.

Wittrock, M. C. (1986). Students' thought processes. In M. C. Wittrock (Ed.), *Handbook of research on teaching.* (pp. 297–314). New York: Macmillan.

Yaden, D. (1985). *Preschoolers' spontaneous inquiries about print and books.* Paper presented at the 34th annual meeting of the National Reading Conference, San Diego, CA.

6

Family Literacy as the Site for Emerging Knowledge of Written Language[1]

Victoria Purcell-Gates
Michigan State University

Much has been made of the construct of *family literacy* with, at times, the impression given that family literacy is primarily responsible for the academic success of children and the future of the country as a whole! The exact nature of the construct of family literacy, however, is currently a matter of varying beliefs, if not outright debate (Purcell-Gates, 2000). Many use the term *family literacy* to represent certain practices in which parents should engage with their children that will help them succeed in school. This lens on family literacy is instantiated in the many *programs* in place to teach parents these skills and practices (Darling & Hayes, 1996). Others argue that family literacy programs that take this stance fail to recognize the societal factors that are primarily responsible for children of poverty failing to succeed in school (Auerbach, 1995). These theorists remind us that the notion of family literacy came about through ethnographic research into the different ways that families weave literate practices throughout their daily activities (Taylor, 1997). Thus, family literacy is intended to be a descriptive construct, not a prescriptive one. My goal for this chapter is to contribute some specificity to the discussion by focusing on a crucial outcome of family literacy for the young children in the family: the emerging knowledge of the functions and forms of written language. This, I believe, will help us to understand the significance of the descriptive lens on family literacy and to make more valid recommendations for family literacy programs.

I intend to go into this topic in such a way as to clarify the relations among oral language development, written language development, and success at learning to read and write in school. This analysis, I believe, is necessary to counter the oft-made claim that children from homes of poverty, more often than not constituted of minority and marginalized people, fail to achieve in school literacy tasks proportionate to their middle-class peers because the oral language they learn in their homes is deficient in significant ways as it relates to reading and writing. The

---

[1]Several parts of this chapter have previously been published in Purcell-Gates, V. (2001). Emergent literacy is emerging knowledge of written language not oral. In P. B. Britto & J. Brooks-Gunn (Eds.), *Young children's emerging literacy skills in the context of family literacy environments.* San Francisco, CA: Jossely-Bass.

garden path down which this ill-informed claim leads us has significant implications for the nature of research into early literacy learning as well as for recommendations for literacy teaching.

CHALLENGING THE ORAL LANGUAGE BASE FOR LEARNING TO READ

There once was a brave knight and a beautiful lady. They went on a trip, a dangerous trip! They saw a little castle in the distance. They went to it. A mean, mean, mean hunter was following them, through the bushes at the entrance of the little castle. As he creeped out of the bushes, he thought what to do. As the drawbridge was opened, they could easily get in. . . .

This remarkable piece of language was produced by a 5-year-old kindergarten girl. She was not reading these sentences from a book; nor was she telling me a story. What she was doing was *pretending to read* orally from a wordless picture book. In the process, she was also revealing a type of language knowledge that she possessed—revealing linguistic competence through linguistic performance embedded in a congruent pragmatic context. (I had asked her to pretend to read to a doll; that is, she was the mommy and the doll was her little girl.)

This little girl did not *talk* like this, nor did any of the other 39 children in this one particular research sample (Purcell-Gates, 1988). I confirmed that they did not talk in this linguistic manner by comparing the way they used language when they pretended to read to the way they used language when they told me a personal narrative about an important event (like their birthday parties).

The language these children used when they pretended to read was, according to my linguistic analysis, the language of storybooks. The fact that it was rendered orally did not make it *oral language*. Rather, it was *written language*, produced by the children as they pretended to read aloud. As such, I contend, it is an important facet of the construct many refer to as *emergent literacy*. Because the construct of *literacy* implies written texts, or written language, then, according to the thesis I hope to advance in this chapter, *emerging literacy* needs to be concerned with the emerging conceptual and procedural knowledge of written language, including the reading and writing of that language. Any other concerns, such as home environments and preschool experiences, should be relevant to the study of emergent literacy only to the degree to which they contextualize, promote, or hinder the development of written language knowledge.

Further, concerns with oral language proficiency within the inquiry frame of emergent literacy should be approached from the written language proficiency perspective. Oral language, in and of itself, is not directly relevant to the study of emergent literacy, I contend. Rather, its appropriate inclusion as a piece of emergent literacy research is as an artifact of the ways in which emerging knowledge of written language has influenced oral language. This assertion makes sense only if one allows that *oral language*—including its vocabulary, syntax, and reference conventions—differs in significant ways from *written language* and its vocabulary, syntax, and reference conventions as well as from its pragmatic constraints.

EMERGENT LITERACY MODEL BASED ON EXPERIENCES WITH WRITTEN LANGUAGE USE

Emergent literacy is the development of the ability to read and write written texts. Written texts are constituted with written language. The model I have constructed for the emergent literacy process places at the center written language experience at different levels of specificity. This model posits that young children learn the underlying concepts of the reading and writing

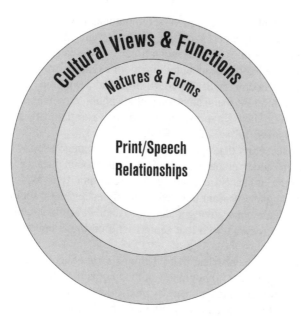

FIG. 6.1.   Children learn about written language within 3 dimensions, constrained by the uses, beliefs, and values accorded it by literate others in their lives.

processes as they experience written language in use in their lives (see Purcell-Gates, 1986 and 1995, for a full explication of this model based on the research into emergent literacy). Figure 6.1 displays the ways in which the different dimensions of written language knowledge relate to each other and highlights the constraints imposed by sociocultural contexts on uses of print. The part of this model relevant to the focus of this chapter is the middle dimension—the nature and forms of written language.

HISTORICAL ASSUMPTION OF ORAL LANGUAGE BASE FOR READING

Ever since Walter Loban published his 12-year developmental study showing a strong relationship between oral language ability and reading achievement (1963), the literacy community has held as one of its most basic assumptions that literacy development rests on an oral language base. Over the years, we have come to view reading and writing as *language* activities and, as such, we have essentially viewed the relationship between learners' oral language and their subsequent ability to read and write as facilitative and almost causal. Researchers and theorists have centered their efforts on examining this relationship, documenting it, and describing its development and social contexts (e.g., Cazden, 1972; Gee, 1989; Labov, 1972; Loban, 1963; Snow, 1991).

LANGUAGE VARIATION AND SOCIAL CONTEXT: THERE IS NO AVERAGE ORAL LANGUAGE

To begin my argument that emergent language knowledge is emergent knowledge of written language, not oral, I start with the deconstruction of the notion of *language*. Most of us now understand that any one language is composed of regional variations, or dialects, marked most significantly by pronunciation and vocabulary.

In addition to regional dialects, though, sociolinguists have been documenting for years the ways in which intralanguage, or dialect, variations are also related to social contexts. Thus, given experience with particular social contexts, we can predict, and recognize, the form of language we are likely to encounter when, for example, we attend a lecture, go to the grocery store, visit our doctor, testify in court, or attend a worship service. The identifying language features for different social contexts include phonology (the sounds of our words and sentences), word choice (lexis), syntax, topic, and such paralinguistic features as speed and rhythm of speech (Hymes, 1974; Stubbs, 1983).

The social context factors that appear to influence language use include power relations between speaker and listener; emotional, physical, and/or social distance between speaker and listener; function of the language used; and discourse community style. Thus, the same speaker will use a different language variant (termed variously as registers, sociolects, genres) when giving a lecture to a large class, giving a lecture to a small seminar, conversing with a close friend on the street, conversing with that same friend on the telephone, speaking to a bank teller, and so on.

Given the preceding, it seems clear that labeling a *form* of speech as *oral* is unnecessarily broad if we wish to point out, or highlight any of the linguistic features just listed. Of course, if we merely wish to distinguish the language by *mode*, then the use of the term *oral* works well to indicate that the mode is aural and not written. We could also simply use the term *speech* to indicate the same.

When the term *oral language* is used in most discussions of the relationships between oral language and emergent literacy development, what is being thought of are those very features that differ in use across social situation: phonology, word choice, topic, and syntax. The problem with this belief is that we now know, when it comes to actual speech, that no one of us speaks a form of language decontextualized from the social situation in which it is used. In other words, it is impossible to characterize one's speech, or oral language, without specifying its purpose, function, audience, and genre conventions (Bakhtin, 1981; Christie, 1987; Halliday & Hasan, 1985; Stubbs, 1983). There is no *average* (averaged across social contexts) speech for any of us that can be labeled and used to characterize, with any sort of linguistic specificity, *how we talk*.

Language variation in a literate society also extends to language that is written down. As with oral language, many variations exist within the broad category of written language, variations reflecting differing social situations mediated by print. These variations, as with oral language, reflect such factors as power and social relation between writer and reader, emotional, physical, and/or social distance between writer and reader, and function served by the written language. In the case of written language, written genres (socially determined written language variants) (Christie, 1987) are marked by such linguistic features as word choice, syntax, topic, and discourse community style. Thus, one can identify different patterns of these features across different text genres such as personal letters, mortgages, news stories, editorials, sports stories, encyclopedias, science reports, romance fiction, mystery fiction, and how-to manuals.

Oral/Written Language Differences

Although language variation, in response to changing social contexts, is the rule for all oral and written language use, it is also true that language varies in linguistically identifiable ways *by mode*. That is, it is possible to identify linguistic markers for language in use that would indicate whether the language was produced to serve primarily oral or primarily written functions. The types of linguistic features that distinguish oral from written language registers do not serve the primary purpose of allowing us to make this distinction. Rather, they function linguistically to allow the language user to accomplish different tasks for different purposes. These socially related constraints of task and purpose function always to shape language in significant ways.

Thus, we write language down if we need to communicate with someone who is not physically present at the moment—And the language produced reflects this purpose. We use writing to make a thought permanent because print continues to exist after we produce it, unlike oral speech. We write language down to serve legal and administrative functions because, in this literate society, print carries much more authority than speech. The linguistic markers that tend to distinguish oral from written language include word choice and variety, syntax, and reference conventions (Chafe & Danielewicz, 1986).

Vocabulary.   Vocabulary is a favorite language measure for emergent literacy researchers (Crain-Thoreson & Dale, 1992; Payne, Whitehurst, & Angell, 1994; Senechal, Thomas, & Monker, 1995; Snow, 1991). The preferred assessment is the Peabody Picture Vocabulary Test (PPVT), a norm-referenced test of receptive vocabulary (Dunn & Dunn, 1981). Repeatedly, correlation studies have shown a strong relationship between scores on the PPVT and scores on reading assessment measures. With this in mind, consider the findings of linguists who study oral and written language differences.

The vocabulary chosen for written language includes words that most users of the language would agree belong in books or other print contexts rather than in speech. These vocabulary items are identified as lexical choices between words with the same meaning, with the more common word (e.g., *use, show, pay attention to*) being rejected by the writer for a more literary one (e.g., *employ, state, heed*). Other linguists refer to these word types as "rare words" or "sophisticated words" (Weizman, 1996). These labels reflect the fact that these literary words are used less frequently overall than their more commonly used counterparts, and linguistic analyses document that, when they are used, they tend to appear in print rather than in speech.

Written texts also tend to reflect a greater variety of vocabulary, perhaps because of the greater time for choosing wording afforded by writing as compared to speaking (Chafe & Danielewicz, 1986). Variety of word use can be measured by type/token ratios, with the number of different words in a sample divided by the total number of words in the sample. Chafe and Danielewicz compared a formal speaking situation (formal lectures) with a formal writing situation (written essays). They found that the lectures had a type/token ratio of words of .19 as compared to essays with a ratio of .24. Even the more informal written texts of letters had a type/token ratio of words of .22, slightly higher than the formal spoken text of lectures.

Syntax.   Syntax is harder to reliably measure than vocabulary, but the assumption of a relation between speaking with an "elaborated" syntax and a "restricted" one and reading achievement has been with us since Bernstein's (1960) claim to this effect regarding working-class children in Britain. I suggest that much of the emergent literacy research that focuses on the oral language of parents and of parent–child interactions at least partially emanates from this assumption. With this possibility in mind, consider the linguistic differences in syntax between oral and written language.

The syntax found in written texts, as compared to that found in oral texts, is more embedded and often transformed. Embeddedness is accomplished with such constructions as dependent clauses, appositives, nominalizations, adjective and adverbial clauses, and attributive adjectives. Many more written sentences than oral ones are left-branching, in that the sentence does not begin with the subject to the verb but rather may begin with an adverbial clause, or other type of modifier clause, that the reader must hold in memory before encountering the subject (e.g., *Down through the forest in silent rushes, the river ran along its deadly course.*). Transformations more typical of written text than of oral language also appear within sentences at the clausal and lexical levels. For example, the preceding written example can be made even more "written" (i.e., more prototypically written as judged by "native readers") by inverting the subject and verb to *Down through the forest in silent rushes, ran the river along its deadly course*. These types of transformations are typically found in reported dialog, and even in text written for very young children. (e.g., *Begone! said the queen*. Here, are inverted not only the subject and verb but also the object; *"Begone"* of the verb *said* is also inverted.)

Due to the greater amount of composing time for writing, different processing demands for aural and written input, and stylistic differences, oral syntax is much more fragmented, with clauses and phrases more "strung together" than embedded (Chafe & Danielewicz, 1986). This results in what Bernstein (1960) referred to as the "elaborated" versus the "restricted" nature of speech. Not counting the typical disfluencies (false starts, repetitions, abandoned intonation units), speakers even in the most formal settings will not produce the type of syntactic constructions they would if they were writing. Those who have experienced public speakers who *read* their papers rather than *speak* their presentation know immediately that they are listening to a written text and not an oral one. Though intonation is one of the markers, the written syntactic constructions also significantly contribute to this recognition and make the presentation much more difficult to follow and comprehend by ear!

Reference Use.   Emergent literacy researchers have also focused on the use of decontextualized oral language (Snow, 1983, 1991). Because written language requires the use of decontexualized language, the reasoning goes, the ability to use oral language in a decontextualized way is a predictor of later reading achievement. However, the research on oral/written language differences can again provide a different lens on this seeming relation between oral language and reading achievement.

The use of decontextualized language—decontextualized from the immediate and shared physical context of the speaker/listener and/or writer/reader—is much more frequent in written than in oral language. In fact, by virtue of the physical and temporal space between writer and reader, written language is inherently characterized by decontextualized language (the exception being, perhaps, notes written between two friends in the same classroom commenting on an ongoing, present event). In oral language, topic and situation will dictate the degree to which decontextualized language is needed and is appropriate (Snow, 1983, 1991). Casual conversation will rely to a great degree on paralinguistic means and dialogic (speaker and listener) mediation of meaning. Gestures, facial expressions, and intonation are all paralinguistic factors that are appropriate to oral language. They are, however, rendered impossible for written language. Even when pictures are used to clarify written text, the meaning must remain within the linguistic (written) text.

The appropriate use of reference is central to making decontextualized language comprehensible to the reader. That which can be accomplished semantically through gestures, facial expressions, and intonation in oral communicative events must be accomplished in writing with explicit language and appropriate endorphoric referencing. *Exophoric references* are references to meaning outside of the text (Halliday & Hasan, 1976) and are not allowed in writing, which requires *endophoric referencing*, or within-text references (Rubin, 1978). One type of exophoric reference that is often misused by beginning writers are pointers, or deictics, such as "this," or "that," indicating that this nature of written language does not develop along with oral language competence but, rather, is specific to the nature of written text.

Differences Vary on Continuum of Social Constraints.   Linguistic markers of oral/written language differences occur most frequently when the social context for the language use is maximally different, such as oral conversations and written essays. When they are more alike—such as a formal speech and a written essay—the differences between literary and colloquial word choice would be smaller. However, using an example from the previous, unless a formal speech is actually a *reading* of a written essay, one is more likely to find fewer "rare words" in the speech than in the essay, less embedded syntax in the speech than in the essay, and more exophoric references reflecting the shared physical context of the speech than in the essay.

Sorting Out the Language/Literacy Relationships.   The previous discussion provides support for my thesis that although young children's developing, or emerging, language knowledge is central to emergent literacy, it is *not language knowledge writ large*. The incredible variation of language in response to sociocultural contexts, as well as to very basic oral/written language differences, render this latter theory overly general and loose to the point of inaccuracy.

At the very least, it is not helpful in the scientific sense given the resulting loss of specificity of operative linguistic factors like *vocabulary*, *syntax*, and the degree to which language is formed to account for needed degrees of *decontextualization*. No, the emerging language/literacy of young children must be the developing knowledge of the forms of written language, not oral language. Further, we are now increasingly acknowledging variation across written genres and beginning to demand that measures of young children's written language knowledge be made more specific than just *written language writ large* (Duke, 2000; Duke & Kays, 1998; Pappas, 1991; Purcell-Gates & Duke, 1999).

EVIDENCE OF DEVELOPING WRITTEN LANGUAGE KNOWLEDGE

In the last 2 decades several studies have documented the emergence of written language knowledge among young children. Sulzby (1985) mapped a developmental move made by 3- to 6-year-old children in the language they used to "read" favorite storybooks. They moved from the use of language more appropriate to *oral* language (i.e., language that assumed a shared physical context) to language more appropriate to *written* language (i.e., language that does not assume a shared physical context and thus is more explicit and decontextualized—see previous discussion). Note that their pretend readings were oral in the sense that they were produced aloud, aurally. However, the language used was not equally *oral* in the more pragmatic, sociocontextual sense of register or genre. Thus, for the first time in the emergent literacy field, researchers were differentiating sociocontextually determined registers within language produced aurally—and considered, therefore, as *oral*—and selecting out those registers tied experientially and pragmatically to print as *written* language knowledge and ability (Pappas & Brown, 1988).

Sulzby's task involved young children producing renderings (pretending to read) of written narrative text that had been repeatedly read to them. Pappas (1991) did the same with written exposition, recording the pretend readings young children did after hearing the text repeatedly read to them. Thus, both Sulzy and Pappas could begin to trace the development of this written language knowledge over time and experience with written text. However, with tasks such as these, the alternative explanation that children were simply getting better at repeating oft-heard sentences cannot be completely discounted. At that time, I began a series of studies utilizing a task designed to avoid this interpretation.

Desiring to explore the hypothesis that young children, through hearing written language read to them, *learn a linguistic register* that is specific to the social context in which it is used (i.e., storybooks and storybook reading), I designed a task that would require young children to compose this register without ever having heard a particular text. The theory and rationale for this research plan were well grounded in psycholinguistic and language acquisition research in which language production is taken as evidence of underlying rule-governed linguistic knowledge (Slobin & Welsh, 1971). I asked young preliterate kindergartners to apply their (hypothesized-by-me) knowledge of syntactic, lexical, and referential features identified (Chafe, 1982) as more typical of written than of oral language to a new textual situation, thus testing the actual existence of this knowledge. The language sample with which this chapter begins comes from this study.

I randomly selected well-read-to kindergarten children (see Purcell-Gates, 1988, for details of procedures) and asked them to perform two tasks: (a) to *tell* me about a recent birthday party, or other significant event (if the child's family did not celebrate birthdays or if the child could not remember the party); and (b) to pretend to *read* a story told by pictures in a wordless storybook and to make it *sound like a book story*. The first task was intended to elicit an oral narrative—decontextualized in the sense that its topic was about something not presently happening within the shared context of researcher and child (Snow, 1983, 1991); the second task was designed to elicit a written narrative (albeit delivered orally)—also decontextualized but assumed, or pretended, to be *written*. Thus, in addition to testing the hypothesis that these well-read-to children *possessed* knowledge of a written narrative register, I could also test the counter hypothesis that they could produce this language orally because they normally *spoke* this way when recounting narratives. I could eliminate one of these counter claims by looking for real differences in the frequency of occurrences of those features considered as markers of written text, as compared to oral, between the two samples produced by each child. I was looking for linguistic evidence that these young children spoke narratives differently from how they "read" them.

The data from this study, with its within-subject analysis, strongly confirmed that these children differentiated oral and written narrative language within their overall language knowledge and could produce each different register, given the appropriate social context (i.e., a request to tell about a past event and a request to pretend read a story from a book to a doll/child). My analysis of the data for this study (Purcell-Gates, 1988, 1991, 1992) revealed that these children did not speak their oral narratives in the same linguistic register with which they pretended to read.

Their written narrative registers were distinguished from their oral narrative registers in the following ways: (a) They were syntactically more integrated; (b) they were lexically more literary and varied; (c) they were lexically and syntactically more involving through the use of high-image verbs, image-producing adverbials, and attributive adjectives; and (d) they were more decontextualized through appropriate endophoric reference use. In other words, these 5-year-olds, when placed in a typically oral language social context of *telling* someone about a past event, did not talk in the same way as they did when they were placed in a typical written language social context of *reading* aloud from a book. The language used for each differed in its vocabulary, syntax, and degree of decontexualization—all linguistic factors deemed relevant to emerging literacy and early reading success.

HOME ENVIRONMENT AND LEARNING THE FEATURES
OF WRITTEN LANGUAGE

It makes sense to believe that this knowledge of written language comes from being read to, and parents have been told to read to their children for years. Unfortunately, there has been little research that shows a causal relationship between reading to young children and their written language knowledge. It would be unethical to design a good experiment with random assignment to condition to test this theory that children learn the linguistic register of written stories by being read to! However, support for this thesis does come from data collected over the years with the same "pretend-read" task. This task has been used in three other studies involving exclusively low-socioeconomic-status (low-SES) children (Dahl & Freppon, 1995; Purcell-Gates, 1996; Purcell-Gates & Dahl, 1991). The results of all of these studies show clearly that the written register knowledge of the children, most of whom had not been read to extensively prior to kindergarten, is almost nonexistent as compared with that of the well-read-to children at the start of kindergarten.

Further support for this theoretical linking of written storybook register knowledge and being read to came from a participant-observation study of 24 low-SES children in their homes. For this study, all uses of print were documented and the 4- to 6-year-old children in the homes were given the pretend-reading task, among others, designed to measure emergent literacy knowledge (Purcell-Gates, 1996). Within this group of children, a significant correlation was found between being read to and scores on this task.

A significant implication, or outcome, of this cluster of studies is that socioeconomic status and language ability have been disentangled. By pulling out the specific language knowledge of written storybook register, we can see that children from homes of poverty have this knowledge to the extent to which they have experienced it in use, that is, hearing it read aloud.

This implication comes first from the 1988 well-read-to study, for which the children were randomly selected from a pool, or population, of children who had all been deemed "well read to." To create this pool of young children, I sent home a questionnaire to all kindergarten and second-grade children in each of the three elementary schools in a midsize town in northern California. The items on the questionnaire were constructed to reveal (a) which families read to their children, (b) the length of time they had been reading to their children, and (c) the frequency with which they read to their children. The final well-read-to pool consisted of children who for the most part had been read to from birth to 6 months of age, at least 5 times a day. As a group they had heard an incredible amount of written storybook language in their young lives.

Relevant to the current discussion, though, is the fact that the socioeconomic status of the children who were deemed well read to included families on welfare, one-parent families, families headed by grandparents or guardians, parents who were blue-collar laborers, white-collar workers, professionals, and university professors. Thus, though the entire pool from which the subjects for the study could be deemed well read to, they could not be characterized as fully middle class.

The remaining studies that used the pretend-read task were composed of all low-SES children. By restricting the subject pool in this way, we could also disentangle SES status and language knowledge. Recall that a widely accepted premise is that low-SES children cannot produce decontextualized language orally, one of the supposed factors explaining their relative low literacy achievement. Because the pretend-read task calls for the elicitation of *both* oral and written language samples ("Tell me about your last birthday party [or other significant event]."), we could examine the oral ability of the children as well as their knowledge of written registers. Purcell-Gates, McIntyre, and Freppon (1995) reanalyzed the pretend-read data from the three previous studies using the pretend-read task (Dahl & Freppon, 1995; Purcell-Gates, 1988; Purcell-Gates & Dahl, 1991). The reanalysis of these data revealed several interesting insights regarding this issue of SES and language ability.

Is it true that these randomly selected, low-SES (total N of 37 used for the reanalysis) children cannot produce decontextualized language orally? It is not true that these children cannot talk about a past event in perfectly appropriate language. Their oral narratives were coherent and unambiguous, both to the researcher during the telling (thus, sharing the physical context with the speaker) and to readers of the transcripts for whom paralinguistic factors, such as facial expression and gesturing) were unavailable. However, it is true that they cannot, for the most part, produce appropriate decontextualized *written* language before formal literacy

TABLE 6.1

Means and Standard Deviations on Measures of Written Language Features Use by Well-Read-To
and Two Low-SES Samples from Reanalysis of Pretend-Read Task Used in 3 Studies

Group	Occurrences		Breadth	
	Beginning K	End First Grade	Beginning K	End First Grade
Oral register scores				
Well read to	25.25	—	39.60	—
(n = 20)	(7.91)		(8.22)	
Low SES	24.21	24.16	25.63	27.37
Sample 1[a]	(20.10)	(19.87)	(14.67)	(11.92)
(n = 19)				
Low SES	19.33	18.67	24.11	30.45
Sample 2[b]	(9.85)	(9.63)	(11.23)	(13.78)
(n = 18)				
Written register scores				
Well read to	52.83	—	61.70	—
(n = 20)	(24.17)		(19.90)	
Low SES	28.05	56.11	36.47	52.26
Sample 1[a]	(24.06)	(24.47)	(16.36)	(12.29)
(n = 19)				
Low SES	21.28	60.16	30.72	63.56
Sample 2[b]	(22.77)	(20.08)	(21.04)	(13.63)
(n = 18)				

[a]Purcell-Gates, V., & Dahl, K. (1991). Low-SES children's success and failure at early literacy learning in skills-based classrooms. *JRB: A Journal of Literacy, 23*, 1–334.

[b]Dahl, K., & Freppon, P. A. (1995). A comparison of inner-city children's interpretation of reading and writing instruction in the early grades in skills-based and whole language classrooms. *Reading Research Quarterly, 31*, 50–74.

instruction commences, as the more middle-class, well-read-to children could. Thus, these data suggest the operative difference between the well-read-to and low-SES children lies in the written language sphere and not in the oral one.

In Table 6.1, data for the frequencies of use of written language linguistic features in both the children's oral narratives and their pretend-read (written) narratives are presented for the three samples: the well-read-to kindergartners (Purcell-Gates, 1988), the Purcell-Gates and Dahl (1991) low-SES kindergartners and first-graders, and the Dahl and Freppon (1995) low-SES kindergartners and first-graders. The column marked Breadth contains the means and standard deviations for the uses of different types of linguistic features that mark written language as different from oral language (e.g., direct quotes, attributive adjectives, literary language; see previous discussion). The column marked Occurrences contains the means and standard deviations for the number of times the children employed each feature.

Looking more closely (see Table 6.1) at the oral and written narrative register scores of the well-read-to and the low-SES children, we can see that the well-read-to children use a broader range (i.e., a greater variety) of linguistic features that make their language more explicit and decontextualized, both when speaking (oral) and when pretending to read (written). These scores appear in the column marked Breadth. In terms of breadth, the well-read-to children scored significantly higher than each of the low-SES samples for both oral and written registers. However, when counting overall frequency of linguistic features that mark oral/written language differences (i.e., fewer types but more of each), there is no significant difference among the three groups for the oral register. These scores appear in the column marked Occurrences. In other words, when speaking with the purpose of telling a listener about a past event, children in both randomly selected low-SES groups used certain language features that make language more explicit and decontextualized as many times as did the well-read-to children.

I hypothesize that this mixed picture could reflect two sources of influence: (a) the facilitative effect of written language knowledge on oral (for the well read to) and (b) the commonality of oral language ability to use decontextualized language for recounting past events. The children who have heard many instances of written narrative language have learned a broader variety of written language markers that they can call on when asked to "sound like a book." All children, though, have had experience by kindergarten in telling stories or accounts of past events. The language needed to do this includes some of the same linguistic features, because the pragmatic function of these features is to relate an event that is not occurring at the time of the telling.

This scenario becomes a firmer possibility when we look at the *change* in the oral and written registers for the low-SES children by the end of their first-grade years (the well-read-to sample was not followed over time). The children in the low-SES groups repeated the task at the end of first grade, and their scores were examined for evidence that they had learned a written register over these 2 years by virtue of being read to in school (see Table 6.1). By the end of the first grade, the children as a group had increased the number of features marking explicit and decontextualized language in their oral samples (Breadth column in Table 6.1), maintaining their scores in the frequency with which they used each feature (Occurrences column in Table 6.1), the area in which they did not differ at the beginning of kindergarten from the more middle class, well-read-to group. Their written register scores, though, show dramatic changes, rising to a "no difference" status with the scores of the well-read-to children (see Purcell-Gates et al., 1995, for details of significance testing).

So we can see the oral language of the low-SES children, as it is formed by an oral decontextualized language task, becoming somewhat more explicit and decontextualized after 2 years of schooling that included exposure to written text read orally. We also see their written decontextualized language register taking real and visible form after 2 years of schooling.

Oral Language to Written Language or Written to Oral?   Many researchers point to the ability to use more "elaborated" language in oral settings as an important precursor of reading achievement. They cite the use of rare words, complex syntax, and decontextalized language in the speech of successful children. How does this relate to the thesis being developed here and to the evidence for that thesis? It is true, in the data just presented, that the oral personal narratives of the well-read-to children were also highly effective as examples of oral decontextualized language ability (Snow, 1983, 1991). Following is a sample of the oral personal narrative language used by the same child whose pretend reading language is presented early in this chapter.

> . . . I got a rainbow heart. And so did my friend, my best friend at the party. My friend Kee, who's actually the same birthday. And then I know another person with a June 1st birthday, but he's a boy. And his name is Brandon. And he's just down the street. And then after my party, we had like a little family party, and we went to the San Francisco Zoo.

There can be no argument that oral language skill is related to written language knowledge. However, I argue that the direction of the effect is *from written to oral*, rather than the other way around. Many parents of young children will report anecdotally their amusement with the words and phrases that appear in the speech of their children from the books the parents have read to them.

Carol Chomsky (1972) conducted one of the few empirical studies to document evidence in support of this theory that written language knowledge influences oral language performance. In a study designed to investigate acquisition of complex syntactic structures in children ages 6 to 16, she documented that exposure to written text, with its more complex syntactic structures, played a role, independent of IQ, in influencing linguistic (oral) stage.

More support for this thesis of a written-to-oral effect comes from the Purcell-Gates et al. (1995) reanalysis data presented earlier. As suggested, viewing these data through this written-to-oral influence lens suggests that exposure to written language will not only lead to increased facility with it but also to some boosting of oral use of features that typically mark written language, especially those that facilitate decontextualized language use.

Finally, I offer a more speculative argument for the written-to-oral directional effect. I suspect that a systematic analysis of the PPVT items would reveal that those items/words that allow for the maximum variation in scores at the top end would be considered more "written," that is, rare or infrequent in use. This possibility suggests that children who score in the upper ranges of this test have learned these words, through the influence on their own oral vocabulary as well as that of their parents, of written text from which those rare words come. In other words, children and adults will appropriate vocabulary and syntax from written text to use in their speech when the sociolinguistic context seems appropriate. Those persons who are exposed to more written text written at increasingly more complex levels will have more opportunities to appropriate such vocabulary. My suggested analysis of PPVT items help to explain the high correlation, and ultimate confound, of SES (highly determined by parental education level) and score on the PPVT.

THE LANGUAGE IN EMERGENT LITERACY IS WRITTEN

The argument just presented is not meant to be taken as a claim that oral and written language exist in separate spheres or that they are *different* languages. Nor is it meant to deny the primary status of oral language. Clearly an underlying language disability stemming from neurological compromise or severe environmental deprivation would affect the ultimate development of written language knowledge—as described herein—as well as oral language knowledge. Rather, my desire is to develop an argument for asserting the primacy of written language experience and exposure as explanatory for emergent literacy development prior to formal instruction. I believe that the evidence strongly suggests that it is exposure to print and to print use that allows children to construct critical emergent literacy concepts from which they can develop as effective readers and writers. The heavy focus on oral language development and on the quality of children's oral language exposure is leading us off track when considering the relationships between language and literacy.

IMPLICATIONS FOR FAMILY LITERACY PRACTICE

Recognizing written language knowledge as the important variable of emergent literacy knowledge suggests that family literacy policy and programs understand that the goal must be to increase young children's experience with and exposure to written language texts in their homes. The current popularity of recommending storybook reading does work toward this goal, and this practice should be continued. However, the vast majority of family literacy providers do not have a full understanding of *why* reading to young children is so helpful to their future academic success in the sense of increasing the written language knowledge of children. Rather, there seems to be the troubling belief that activities to change the ways in which parents talk to their children are equally facilitative. There is no evidence that changing the ways in which parents talk to their children will increase their achievement in school. If one accepts my thesis of the primacy of written language knowledge to emergent literacy knowledge, there is no logic to the labor-intensive efforts to change the speech patterns and events in homes. Language and culture are intractably intertwined (Gee, 1989). Attempts to change primary discourse such as home oral language are attempts to change home cultures, and this is probably not possible nor desirable, given the colonialist and imperialist connotations of such attempts. Rather, emergent literacy development can be more effectively facilitated by working to increase written language use and exposure in the home.

There are many additional ways to increase written language exposure beyond that of storybook reading. Studies of home literacy practice and emergent literacy studies have shown increased emergent literacy knowledge to the degree to which children experience people reading and writing *anything* (such as coupons, magazines, newspapers, flyers, food product text, or the Bible). Further, this emergent literacy knowledge increases the more that people in the home read and write a wide variety of texts that also include texts with more complex language such as newspapers, novels, or encyclopedias as compared to coupon or flyer text (Purcell-Gates, 1996). The written language environment in the home affects young children's conceptual grasp of the symbolic nature of print, their growing understanding of the alphabetic principle, and their knowledge of crucial concepts of print, in addition to their linguistic knowledge of written registers (Purcell-Gates, 1996).

Parents can be encouraged to read and write more for their own purposes, in addition to reading to their children. They can be urged to point out the print that they, themselves, use as they negotiate their way through life's activities and requirements. As part of this effort, they can be educated as to the facilitative effect this will have on their children's success in school so that they no longer believe that the only way to help their children is to perform school-like tasks with them in the home (e.g., alphabet games, printing practice, and so on). Although these school-type activities are helpful, they do not fully explain the relative success of children from homes of high literacy use as compared to children from homes of relatively low literacy use. With the focus on *written language experiences*, suggestions for parents can be more specific and less amorphous (for example, "Talk to your kids more.") and incidental ("Use rare words when you eat dinner with your kids.") to the operative factors in emergent literacy growth.

IMPLICATIONS FOR EMERGENT LITERACY AND FAMILY LITERACY RESEARCH

Making this move to a focus on developing written language knowledge will allow emergent literacy and family literacy researchers to more carefully specify, assess, and confirm operative cognitive and linguistic factors that make learning to read and write easy or more difficult for individual children. It will allow us to explain the differential effects that various types of knowledge have on the stages of developing literacy abilities. For example, developing knowledge of print-related concepts such as letter and sound relationships and sight word reading and spelling appear to have more of an effect on learning to read at the early stages. Lexical and syntactic knowledges of written language, on the other hand, do not show up as predictors of beginning reading but appear to play significant roles in developing literacy abilities with more complex text than is used with beginning readers—a stage of literacy development that occurs around the third and fourth grades (Chall, Jacobs, & Baldwin, 1990; Purcell-Gates et al., 1995).

Focusing on emerging written, and not oral, language knowledge will also help emergent literacy researchers avoid confusing confounds in their measures and analyses. These confounds and confusions result when children's language is evaluated in mixed contexts like 'telling' stories, 'dictating' stories (to be written), 'conversing' at the dinner table with families, 'recalling' a story heard (oral or written), and so on. Each of these synonyms for talking, marked with single quotes, actually indicate different sociolinguistic contexts for language use.

By maintaining a focus on written language environments, activities, and experiences, researchers of family literacy programs will be better able to identify dependent and independent variables for their studies. They will also be able to construct more valid and reliable measures of impact that are not confounded with oral language and cultural variables that are so hard to sort out and control. Researchers may also begin to sort out the relative impacts of such factors as written language exposure, parenting styles, and interactional strategies on children's cognitive and linguistic development—all of which appear entangled in policy and outcome measures currently.

Finally, I wish to make the argument again for increased sophistication in our treatment of language issues in relation to learning and literacy. Language in use is language that varies according to social context. It is not nearly accurate enough to use the term *language* or *oral language* to indicate any particular linguistic form. Language variation within the language repertoire of a single-language user and across people is real in both speech and writing. It varies along dimensions that are significant to reading, writing, and, thus, learning from text. Let us acknowledge this variation and build this knowledge into our research, theorizing, and practice.

REFERENCES

Auerbach, E. (1995). Deconstructing the discourse of strengths in family literacy. *Journal of Reading Behavior, 27,* 643–660.

Bakhtin, M. M. (1981). *The dialogic imagination: Four essays.* Austin, TX: The University of Texas Press.

Bernstein, B. (1960). Language and social class. *British Journal of Sociology, 12,* 271–276.

Cazden, C. (1972). *Child language and education.* New York: Holt, Rinehart and Winston.

Chafe, W. (1982). Integration and involvement in speaking, writing, and oral literature. In D. Tannen (Ed.), *Spoken and written language: Exploring orality and literacy* (Vol. IX of *Advances in discourse processes*). Norwood, NJ: Ablex.

Chafe, W., & Danielewicz, J. (1986). Properties of spoken and written language. In R. Horowitz & S. J. Samuels (Eds.), *Comprehending oral and written language* (pp. 83–113). New York: Academic Press.

Chall, J., Jacobs, V., & Baldwin, L. E. (1990). *The reading crisis: Why poor children fall behind.* Cambridge, MA: Harvard University Press.

Chomsky, C. (1972). Stages in language development and reading exposure. *Harvard Educational Review, 42,* 1–33.

Christie, F. (1987). Genres as choice. In I. Reid (Ed.), *The place of genre in learning: Current debates.* Geelong, Australia: Deakin University Press.

Crain-Thoreson, C., & Dale, P. S. (1992). Do early talkers become early readers? Linguistic precocity, preschool language, and emergent literacy. *Developmental Psychology, 28,* 421–429.

Dahl, K., & Freppon, P. A. (1995). A comparison of inner-city children's interpretation of reading and writing instruction in the early grades in skills-based and whole language classrooms. *Reading Research Quarterly, 31,* 50–74.

Darling, S., & Hayes, A. E. (1996). *The power of family literacy.* Louisville, KY: National Center for Family Literacy.

Duke, N. K. (2000). 3.6 minutes per day: The scarcity of informational texts in first grade. *Reading Research Quarterly, 35,* 202–224.

Duke, N. K., & Kays, J. (1998). "Can I say 'once upon a time'?": Kindergarten children developing knowledge of information book language. *Early Childhood Research Quarterly, 13,* 295–318.

Dunn, L. M., & Dunn, L. (1981). *Peabody Picture Vocabulary Test.* Circle Pines, MN: American Guidance Service.

Gee, J. P. (1989). Literacy, discourse, and linguistics: Introduction. *Journal of Education, 171*, 5–17.

Halliday, M. A. K., & Hasan, R. (1976). *Cohesion in English*. London: Longman Group Limited.

Halliday, M. A. K., & Hasan, R. (1985). *Language, context, and text: A social semiotic perspective*. Geelong, Australia: Deakin University Press.

Hymes, D. (1974). *Foundations in sociolinguistics: An ethnographic approach*. Philadelphia, PA: University of Pennsylvania Press.

Labov, W. (1972). *Language in the inner city: Studies in Black English vernacular*. Philadelphia, PA: University of Pennsylvania Press.

Loban, W. (1963). *The language of elementary school children*. Research Report No. 1. Urbana, IL: National Council of Teachers of English.

Pappas, C. C. (1991). Young children's strategies in learning the "book language" of information books. *Discourse Processes, 14*, 203–225.

Pappas, C. C., & Brown, E. (1988). The development of children's sense of the written story register: An analysis of the texture of kindergartners' 'pretend reading' texts. *Linguistics and Education, 1*, 45–79.

Payne, A. C., Whitehurst, G. J., & Angell, A. L. (1994). The role of home literacy environment in the development of language ability in preschool children from low-income families. *Early Childhood Research Quarterly, 9*, 427–440.

Purcell-Gates, V. (1986). Three levels of understanding about written language acquired by young children prior to formal instruction. In J. Niles & R. Lalik (Eds.), *Solving problems in literacy: Learners, teachers & researchers* (pp. 259–265). Rochester, NY: National Reading Conference.

Purcell-Gates, V. (1988). Lexical and syntactic knowledge of written narrative held by well-read-to kindergartners and second graders. *Research in the Teaching of English, 22*, 128–160.

Purcell-Gates, V. (1991). Ability of well-read-to kindergartners to decontextualize/recontextualize experience into a written-narrative register. *Language and Education, 5*, 177–188.

Purcell-Gates, V. (1992). Roots of response. *Journal of Narrative and Life History, 2*, 151–161.

Purcell-Gates, V. (1995). *Other people's words: The cycle of low literacy*. Cambridge, MA: Harvard University Press.

Purcell-Gates, V. (1996). Stories, coupons, and the *TV Guide*: Relationships between home literacy experiences and emergent literacy knowledge. *Reading Research Quarterly, 31*, 406–428.

Purcell-Gates, V. (2000). Family literacy: A research review. *Handbook of Reading Research* (Vol. 3, pp. 853–870). New York: Lawrence Erlbaum Associates.

Purcell-Gates, V., & Dahl, K. (1991). Low-SES children's success and failure at early literacy learning in skills-based classrooms. *JRB: A Journal of Literacy, 23*, 1–334.

Purcell-Gates, V., & Duke, N. K. (1999). *Explicit explanation of genre within authentic literacy activities in science: Does it facilitate development and achievement?* (Grant 9979904). Washington, DC: National Science Foundation.

Purcell-Gates, V., McIntyre, E., & Freppon, P. (1995). Learning written storybook language in school: A comparison of low-SES children in skill-based and whole language classrooms. *American Educational Research Journal, 30*, 659–685.

Rubin, A. D. (1978). *A theoretical taxonomy of the differences between oral and written language* (Technical Report No. 35). University of Illinois at Urbana Champaign: Center for the Study of Reading.

Senechal, M., Thomas, E., & Monker, J. (1995). Individual differences in 4-year-old children's acquisition of vocabulary during storybook reading. *Journal of Educational Psychology, 87*, 218–229.

Slobin, D., & Welsh, C. A. (1991). Elicited imitation as a research tool in developmental psycholinguistics. In C. S. Lavatelli (Ed.), *Language training in early childhood education* (pp. 170–185). Urbana, IL: University of Illinois Press.

Snow, C. (1983). Literacy and language: Relationships during the preschool years. *Harvard Educational Review, 3*, 165–189.

Snow, C. (1991). The theoretical basis for relationships between language and literacy in development. *Journal of Research in Childhood Education, 6*, 5–10.

Snow, C., Barnes, W. S., Chandler, J., Goodman, I. F., & Hemphill, L. (1991). *Unfulfilled expectations: Home and school influences on literacy*. Cambridge, MA: Harvard University Press.

Stubbs, M. (1983). *Discourse analysis: The sociolinguistic analysis of natural language*. Chicago, IL: University of Chicago Press.

Sulzby, E. (1985). Children's emergent abilities to read favorite storybooks: A developmental study. *Reading Research Quarterly, 20*, 458–481.

Taylor, D. (Ed.). (1997). *Many families, many literacies: An international declaration of principles*. Exeter, NH: Heinemann.

Weizman, Z. O. (1996). *Sophistication in maternal vocabulary input at home: Does it affect low-income children's vocabulary, literacy, and language success at school?* Unpublished doctoral dissertation, Harvard Graduate School of Education, Cambridge, MA.

7

Early Childhood Intervention in Family Literacy Programs[1]

Allison Sidle Fuligni and Jeanne Brooks-Gunn
Columbia University

One of the core goals of family literacy programs is to serve young children through the provision of early childhood education services. According to the mandate given by the Even Start Family Literacy legislation, Even Start programs are to provide an age-appropriate education to prepare children for success in school and life experiences. The empirical basis for providing early childhood education services comes from decades of research showing that early education helps improve the cognitive and academic functioning of children, particularly those who come from economically disadvantaged families and communities (e.g., Campbell & Ramey, 1994; Lazar, Darlington, Murray, Royce, & Snipper, 1982; Schweinhart, Barnes, & Weikart, 1993). An emerging set of studies goes beyond the simple question of effectiveness to explore actual program processes and mechanisms of program effects (Berlin, O'Neal, & Brooks-Gunn, 1998; Hauser-Cram, 1990; Schorr & Booth, 1991).

In this chapter, we summarize the major findings in the field of early education intervention for economically disadvantaged children and highlight important lessons from this research for the early education services within family literacy programs. We focus primarily on programs designed for low-income children, because family literacy programs tend to target this population. Although early childhood intervention programs often address the home environment and/or family functioning, our review will highlight programs that include a specific educational component for the target child. Because Even Start Family Literacy programs serve children from birth through age 7, we will discuss programs serving children in this age range, including programs for infants and toddlers, preschoolers, and programs supporting the transition to schooling. The chapter begins with an overview of early childhood intervention research by describing (a) types of intervention for disadvantaged children; (b) research evidence for intervention impacts on children's cognitive, social, and emotional development;

[1]Portions of this chapter are modified from a previous paper by the authors: A. S. Fuligni and J. Brooks-Gunn (2000). The healthy development of young children: SES disparities, prevention strategies, and policy opportunities. In B. D. Smedley and S. L. Syme (Eds.), *Promoting Health: Intervention Strategies from Social and Behavioral Research*. Washington, DC: National Academy Press.

and (c) implications of the research findings for family literacy programs. Second, research on outcomes for children in family literacy programs themselves is summarized, and finally, we synthesize the findings from both streams of research, offering recommendations for the future implementation and evaluation of family literacy programs.

OVERVIEW OF EARLY CHILDHOOD INTERVENTION IN FAMILY LITERACY PROGRAMS

Early Intervention Services for Disadvantaged Children

Recent media and public policy attention has focused on the early years of life as a crucial period of development warranting attention and specialized input. New research on brain development has illustrated the ill effects of early deprivation and neglect on children's later cognitive and emotional functioning (Shore, 1997). Studies of the quality of child care environments for children cared for outside the home have brought attention to the dangers of poor child care environments, as well as the potential benefits of supportive, stimulating child care (Cost, Quality and Child Outcomes Study Team, 1995, 1999; National Institute of Child Health and Human Development [NICHD] Early Child Care Research Network, 2000; Whitebook, Howes, & Phillips, 1990). However, the increasing emphasis on providing positive and developmentally appropriate experiences to economically disadvantaged young children to enhance the likelihood of their optimal development is not a novel area of interest.

During the 1960s, President Johnson's War on Poverty spurred the creation of many programs attempting to help end the generational spread of poverty and dependence by giving young children enhanced learning experiences and other forms of support. These experiences were intended to prepare them to enter school with the skills and motivation necessary to promote later academic success. Model preschool programs, such as the High/Scope Perry Preschool (Weikart, 1989), and large-scale public programs, such as Head Start, illustrate the early focus on providing children at environmental risk with compensatory experiences before school entry. Since that time, numerous types of intervention services have been designed for young children considered to be at risk for poor school outcomes because of biological risk (such as premature birth or low birth weight), established disabilities (such as Down syndrome or autism), or environmental risk (such as poverty and low maternal education) (Guralnick, 1997).

Early childhood educational intervention for children from economically disadvantaged families has taken many forms. Programs can be classified according to the location of service delivery, with the most common forms being home-visiting programs, center-based programs, and programs that offer combinations of home- and center-based services. Home-visiting programs are often parent focused, with a professional or paraprofessional visiting the home on a weekly, biweekly, or monthly basis to help improve some aspect of parental functioning. Home-visiting programs with an educational component often strive to teach parents intellectually stimulating ways of interacting with their young children, such as by bringing books, toys, or other materials to the family and demonstrating how to use them with the child. Home visits may or may not be combined with other family-support services, such as counseling or referrals to any needed community social services. Many home-based programs are designed to begin before or shortly after the birth of the child and serve the family during the child's infancy and toddlerhood. (See Bryant and Wasik, Section V, this volume, for an elaboration on home visiting and literacy interventions.)

Two large-scale examples of educationally oriented home-visiting programs are the Parents as Teachers (PAT) Program for parents of diverse socioeconomic backgrounds with children from birth to age 3 (Wagner & Clayton, 1999; Winter & Rouse, 1990), and the Home Instruction for Parents of Preschool Youngsters (HIPPY) which is designed to teach low-income parents of preschoolers to engage in specific academically oriented activities with their children (Baker, Piotrkowski, & Brooks-Gunn, 1998).

Center-based early childhood programs for economically disadvantaged children bring children together in a more formal, school-like setting to provide developmentally appropriate learning and socialization experiences to children in a group. Although such centers typically serve 3- and 4-year-olds, many programs have center-based components that begin much earlier in the child's life.

Many programs combine center-based and home-visiting services, often in conjunction with other family support services, to provide a comprehensive program to the family similar to Even Start. Well-known examples of these are the High/Scope Perry Preschool, which combined weekly home visits with a five 1/2-day per week preschool program for 3- and 4-year-olds; the Houston Parent Child Development Center (PCDC; Johnson & Walker, 1987), which provided a year of biweekly home visits followed by a year of center-based educational care; and the more recent Infant Health and Development Program (IHDP, 1990), which provided weekly home visits during the first year of life, then twice a month between the ages of 1 and 3 when the children were also attending day care. More recently, the Early Head Start program has been implemented to provide family support and early childhood services, with individual programs offering either home-visiting services, center-based services, or a combination of both approaches to low-income families with children aged zero to 3 years (Love et al., 2001).

Research on Early Childhood Intervention Effects

In over 30 years of early childhood educational intervention for disadvantaged children, a large body of research evaluating program effects has been amassed. Several recent reviews are helpful in summarizing these findings (Barnett, 1995; Bryant & Maxwell, 1997; Farran, 2000; Yoshikawa, 1995). In this section, we review research findings for home-visiting and center-based programs, including both small model programs and large-scale public programs (such as Head Start). First, program effects on cognitive and linguistic functioning are discussed, including short-term effects, long-term follow-up effects, school transition services designed to prolong program effects, and effects on school performance. Next, we present research findings on outcomes for children's social and emotional functioning. Third, we discuss the following important factors mediating program effects: (a) characteristics of programs and participants, (b) interactions between programs and participants, and (c) effects on parents.

Cognitive Outcomes for Children in Early Intervention Programs

Short-Term Gains. Short-term effects of early intervention are those effects that are evident at or soon after the completion of program participation. Historically, the key indicator of the success of an early intervention program has been increases in IQ scores, or other assessments of intellectual functioning. Many programs have shown cognitive gains for participating children immediately following program participation compared with children who did not receive the intervention. Center-based programs starting in infancy have documented the largest effects on IQ. For example, children participating in the Abecedarian Project preschool program since age 4 months or younger exhibited higher IQ scores than control group children by 18 months of age (Campbell & Ramey, 1994), and children who participated in the Infant Health and Development Program showed significantly higher IQ scores and receptive language scores than the control group at age 3, when intervention was completed (Brooks-Gunn et al., 1994; IHDP, 1990).

Other center-based preschool programs report smaller but significant effects on children's IQ scores. The Consortium for Longitudinal Studies conducted a sophisticated analysis across 11 different early intervention programs that served children in the 1960s and 1970s. Based on an intensive analysis of these programs, the authors concluded that the finding that "a well-run, cognitively oriented early education program will increase IQ scores of low-income children by the end of the program is one of the least disputed results in education and evaluation" (Royce, Darlington, & Murray, 1983; p. 426). Across the studies, immediate posttest IQ gains averaged 7.42 points higher for program than for control group children. More recently, Barnett (1995) reviewed both small, model programs (such as the Abecedarian Project and the Perry Preschool Program) and large-scale public interventions (such as Head Start and public prekindergarten programs). This analysis revealed significant program effects on children's IQ scores at school entry for 11 of 12 model programs. The smallest effects are found in large-scale programs, and in Barnett's review only 1 out of 5 large-scale programs that included such measurements showed positive program effects.

Programs providing home-visiting services without a center-based early education component report the fewest effects on child IQ. A review of 19 home-visiting programs for low-income families conducted by Olds and Kitzman (1993) found that although 15 of the programs placed specific emphasis on the promotion of young children's cognitive and linguistic development, results for children were mixed. Only six of the studies found significant benefits for children's intellectual outcomes. Among these were the Ypsilanti-Carnegie infant stimulation project (Epstein & Weikart, 1979) and the Gordon Parent Education Infant and Toddler Program (Jester & Guinagh, 1983). Similarly, of 16 home-based programs reviewed by Benasich, Brooks-Gunn, and Clewell (1992), 14 assessed child cognitive outcomes, and 9 found immediate positive gains. The effective programs included the Family Development Research Programs (Lally, Mangione, & Honig, 1988) and the Florida Parent Education Project (Gordon, Guinagh, & Jester, 1977).

Long-Term Gains.   Perhaps as well known as the findings of the initial success of early intervention for cognitive outcomes of low-income children is the *fade-out* effect—Initial program-related advantages in IQ and achievement test scores begin to diminish as control children obtain school experience. For instance, the initial IQ differences for preschool children in the Consortium studies began to diminish by 3 or 4 years after children had completed the intervention, and most IQ differences were gone by 7 to 10 years after program completion (Royce et al., 1983). However, some early childhood experts prefer not to focus on the finding of a diminution of effects, but rather on the question of how we can expect 1 year of high-quality intervention (sometimes occurring for only 4 hours a day) to completely offset the effects of poverty, low parental education, poor housing, parental unemployment, and the many other experiences that combine to affect the functioning of economically disadvantaged children (Zigler, 1998). The so-called fade-out of intervention effects seems inevitable in many cases, given that many attendees of preschool programs for low-income children (such as Head Start) go on to attend schools of substantially lower quality than children from higher income families (Lee & Loeb, 1995). However, some early interventions do report lasting effects. Here we report long-term intervention effects on intellectual functioning and then discuss efforts to maintain intervention effects through the school years.

Center-based programs beginning in infancy report continued IQ effects years after the intervention is concluded. Of the interventions reviewed by Barnett (1995), the two model programs that provided intensive center-based programs for infants (Abecedarian Project, Campbell & Ramey, 1994; Milwaukee Project, Garber, 1988) reported IQ effects that maintained significance into the adolescent years. The Infant Health and Development Program reported smaller, but still significant effects on IQ for the heavier group of low-birth-weight infants at age 8 (McCarton et al., 1997).

Less information is available on the long-term cognitive effects of large-scale programs like Head Start. Although there have been relatively few experimental studies to estimate the effects of Head Start, those that have been conducted have reported small positive effects on children. Barnett (1995) reports that effects for Head Start programs tend to be smaller than those for public school preschools. However, Head Start children tend to be more economically disadvantaged, so direct comparisons with public preschool students may be inappropriate because of the other factors that might influence outcomes for these children. A meta-analysis by McKey and colleagues (1985) concluded that any meaningful Head Start effects dissipate by the end of the second year of school. In a study in which children were randomly assigned either to a small model program through first grade or to Head Start, both interventions produced gains, but there was a larger effect on long-term achievement among children in the model program (Sprigle & Schaefer, 1985, in Barnett, 1995). On the other hand, when Lee, Brooks-Gunn, Schnur, and Liaw (1990) compared Head Start children with children from the same neighborhood who attended another preschool program or who received no early intervention, they found that although there was a diminution of effects over time, the Head Start children did continue to have higher cognitive scores into the first-grade year. These effects held when initial family characteristics were controlled, so even though the group of children in Head Start was initially more disadvantaged, they received greater benefits from attending Head Start. Although some home-visiting programs have been followed to assess their long-term effects, there have been no long-term IQ effects documented (Olds et al., 1999; Olds & Kitzman, 1993).

School Transition Services.   As a response to the fade-out of early intervention effects, some programs have offered follow-up services to support children as they enter formal schooling. School-age supports may include home visits, a home-school coordinator to help with the transition and improve communication between family and school, after-school care programs, and tutoring services. The Head Start Transition program, begun in 1992, provided ongoing services to children and families who formerly participated in Head Start programs as the children entered kindergarten and through the child's third-grade year. The Transition project included a comprehensive set of services to enhance children's and families' experiences in the school setting. An early evaluation of this program suggested that the children adjusted well to kindergarten, enjoyed school, and were motivated to achieve academic success (Head Start Bureau, 1996). Over the first few years of elementary school, these former Head Start children achieved significant gains in math and reading scores, moving from kindergarten scores well below the national average to scores at the national average in third grade. The transition intervention program did not show meaningful improvements for children's outcomes relative to comparison children, however. Wide variation in implementation, as well as similar supports offered by many comparison schools, may have contributed to the lack of program effects (Ramey et al., 2000).

Some model programs have instituted school-age follow-on services as well. Both the Abecedarian Project and Project CARE (Wasik, Ramey, Bryant, & Sparling, 1990) included random assignment of children into a school-aged intervention that included provision of home-school resource services during the first 3 years of school after children had participated in intensive home- and center-based interventions in the years before school (Burchinal, Campbell, Bryant, Wasik, & Ramey, 1997; Campbell & Ramey, 1994, 1995). Children who participated in the preschool child care intervention had the highest IQ and achievement scores at age 8 and were less likely to be retained in the first 3 years of school. These effects were maintained through age 15. Although no additional positive effect was found with the school-age intervention for children who participated in the preschool program (Burchinal, Campbell, Bryant, Wasik, & Ramey, 1997), children who received the school-age services without the preschool intervention had higher achievement scores than children who received no intervention at all (Campbell & Ramey, 1995).

The Chicago Child-Parent Center (CPC) Program offered up to 6 years of early intervention for Chicago children aged 3 to 9 years from low-income families. Follow-up research found that participation in the preschool and kindergarten years was associated with enhanced achievement scores and reduced placement in special education. Participation in the school-age program in grades 1 through 3 was more closely associated with lower rates of grade retention and delinquent behaviors (Reynolds, 1997; Reynolds, Temple, Robertson, & Mann, 2001).

School Performance.   In addition to the traditional IQ assessments, standardized reading and mathematics tests have been used to determine the effectiveness of early childhood programs on children's academic abilities at school entry and during the school years. The Consortium studies found that early intervention was related to math and reading achievement test scores at grade 3 (Royce et al., 1983), and Barnett's review (Barnett, 1995) reported 5 of 11 model programs with positive effects on elementary achievement scores.

Similar to the long-term findings for IQ scores, program effects on children's achievement test scores are not consistently sustained throughout the school years. In the Consortium studies, program effects ceased to be significant for reading test scores after third grade, and effects on math test scores diminished after third grade, becoming nonsignificant by grade 6 (Royce et al., 1983). Among the large-scale public programs reviewed by Barnett (1995), long-term achievement test effects were quite variable. Four programs reported no effects on achievement scores at all, 5 found early effects that faded after third grade, and 12 others found varying patterns of positive program effects after third grade. Some programs documented higher achievement scores for intervention groups as late as eighth grade, whereas others found positive effects in some grades but not in others. None of these large-scale programs used randomized methodology and most did not include pretests (Barnett, 1995). Several studies that have followed early intervention children through the school years indicate that even when test scores become similar for program and control children, children who experienced early childhood intervention are less likely to be retained in grade, are referred to special education less often, and graduate from high school at higher rates (Lazar et al., 1982; Royce et al., 1983, Schweinhart et al., 1993).

Social and Emotional Well-Being Outcomes

In the first decades of early childhood intervention, goals were clearly cognitive in nature. The cycle of poverty would be broken, it was hypothesized, if poor children could succeed in school. Therefore, early childhood programs were expected to have effects on intellectual outcomes as measured by standardized tests of intelligence and achievement in reading and math. At that time, less attention was paid to program effects on children's social and emotional development, as these outcomes were considered unrelated to children's school success. As a result, measures of noncognitive outcomes, such as behavior problems or emotional development, tended not to be addressed in the early studies. However, some home-visiting programs showed short-term positive effects on infant and child behavior (Olds & Kitzman, 1993). Types of behavior positively influenced by early intervention included reduced night-waking at 1 year, improved self-confidence and social skills at 3 years, and fewer problem behaviors at 6 years (Guteilus, Kirsch, MacDonald, Brooks, & McErlean, 1977); improved mother–child interactions and less gaze aversion (Field, Widmayer, Greenberg, & Stoller, 1982); more cooperation (Thompson et al., 1982); more positive mood at 6 months (Olds, Henderson, Chamberlin, & Tatelbaum, 1986); and increased infant reciprocity during a feeding situation (Dawson, van Doorninck, & Robinson, 1989). IHDP found significantly fewer mother-reported behavior problems among intervention children at 3 years, particularly when the mother had lower levels of education (IHDP, 1990), but the effects were only marginally significant by the time the children were 5 years old (Brooks-Gunn et al., 1994).

Longer term follow-up studies of children who participated in the early model intervention programs have documented differences between program and control children in the areas of problem behavior and delinquency. For instance, the Perry Preschool Program, a small-scale early intervention program that has received much attention because of the quality of its longitudinal investigation, has now followed the participating children through age 27. The program has documented positive effects of program participation for both cognitive and social/emotional outcomes. In addition to program effects on cognitive scores, grade retention, and special education, program children engaged in fewer delinquent behaviors at age 14 and were less involved with the criminal justice system at ages 19 and 27 (Schweinhart et al., 1993).

Factors Influencing Program Success

Based on evidence that some programs can make a difference in long-term outcomes for the children who participate, we must ask what makes them successful. In order to more thoroughly understand how early intervention works, key aspects of interventions—such as program characteristics, characteristics of the participants, and the interaction between programs and participants—must be considered (Berlin et al., 1998; Bryant & Maxwell, 1997). In terms of program characteristics, we discuss the types and intensity of program services, as well as the program's theoretical approach. Important participant characteristics include family and individual levels of risk, such as low birth weight and low maternal education or IQ. Finally, we consider the importance of a good match between the participants and program staff as well as pathways by which program effects may operate.

Yoshikawa (1995) has summarized findings across 40 early intervention studies and has identified four programs that had high rates of success in producing long-term effects on antisocial and delinquent behavior. These include the Perry Preschool findings described earlier, the Syracuse University Family Development Research Project (Lally et al., 1988), the Yale Child Welfare Project (Seitz & Apfel, 1994), and the Houston Parent Child Development Centers (PCDC) (Johnson & Walker, 1987). Yoshikawa notes that these programs initially had effects on children's cognitive and verbal abilities, and on their parents' parenting skills prior to their long-term social outcomes. In addition, successful programs combined early education and family support components; provided intensive levels of services (frequent home visits, high number of hours of early childhood education); began during the child's first 5 years of life; targeted low-income populations; and provided quality early childhood programs with theoretically based curricula and low participant-to-staff ratios (Yoshikawa, 1995).

The particular theoretical approach, staff, and cultural relevance of a program partially determine the effects on participants (Berlin et al., 1998). Consequently, researchers should attend to these theoretical factors when measuring program effects. For example, evaluation research should be guided by discussions with program staff regarding their particular theories about how change will take place as well as documentation of actual program activities. Using such an approach, researchers can attempt to measure the same processes and outcomes that program staff believes they are addressing through their services.

The type of services delivered by a program (e.g., home-visiting versus center-based interventions) may play a role in the domain of functioning they will affect. For instance, home-based services tend to target parental well-being and mental health and improved parent–child relationships. These types of programs may have stronger effects on parents while providing an indirect influence on children (Berlin et al., 1998; Yoshikawa, 1995). The Hawaii Healthy Start program is an example of an intervention that provided intensive home visiting to parents at risk for abusing their newborn infants. This initiative resulted in more positive parenting attitudes and child-parent interactions at 6 and 12 months, but no program effects on the children's scores on cognitive measures (McCurdy, 1996). On the other hand, center-based programs, by providing educational services directly to children, are more likely to have direct effects on children's cognitive and linguistic development. A review of 27 intervention programs found that 90% of center-based versus 64% of the home-based programs resulted in immediate intervention effects on children's cognitive developmental outcomes; 1 year after the program had ended, the effects were maintained in 67% of center-based versus 44% of the home-based programs (Benasich, Brooks-Gunn, & Clewell, 1992).

The issue of method of service delivery has been explicitly tested in one study using random assignment techniques and highlighted by Berlin and her colleagues (Berlin et al., 1998). Project CARE contrasted home-visiting services with home-visiting plus center-based services (Wasik, Ramey, Bryant, & Sparling, 1990). The children receiving the combined home and center-based services consistently scored higher on the Bayley developmental scales and on IQ and achievement tests than the children receiving only home visits. However, no differences were found between the two groups in either home environment or parents' childrearing attitudes. These findings held through middle childhood and early adolescence (Burchinal et al., 1997), supporting the positive influence of the center-based plus home visiting program.

Berlin and her colleagues also provide examples of how the quantity of services can make a difference in how early interventions work. Studies generally report a positive relationship between the amount of intervention (frequency and duration of program participation), and program benefits. In the IHDP program, a greater quantity of services received was associated with higher 36-month IQ scores, the number of home visits received was associated with improved maternal assistance in a mother–child problem-solving activity at 30 months (Liaw, Brooks-Gunn, & Spiker, 1997), and overall program participation was positively related to the families' home environment at 12 months and to child IQ scores at 36 months (Liaw et al., 1997; Ramey et al., 1992; Sparling et al., 1991). Length of participation in the Chicago Child-Parent Centers was associated with higher reading achievement, lower rates of grade retention, lower rates of delinquency, and higher passing rates on a life-skills competence test, with benefits extending into the adolescent years (Reynolds, 1997).

The program and its characteristics do not operate in isolation. Characteristics of program participants also make a difference in program effectiveness. Vulnerable families appear to reap greater benefits from early intervention programs than do families with fewer risk factors, although families with extreme, multiple-risk factors are less likely to benefit than families with moderate levels of risk. For example, the IHDP program for low-birth-weight infants had greater effects on cognitive development and reduction of behavior problems in children of less educated mothers (Brooks-Gunn, Gross, Kraemer, Spiker, & Shapiro, 1992; Liaw & Brooks-Gunn, 1993), but children in this sample who were at the extremely low end of the birth-weight spectrum (under 2,001 grams) had lower rates of program effectiveness than the heavier low-birth-weight (2,001 to 2,500 grams) group (Brooks-Gunn et al., 1992; Brooks-Gunn, Klebanov, Liaw, & Spiker, 1993). The intervention was most effective for children with more environmental disadvantage (low maternal education and income) but less biological disadvantage (i.e., the heavier children in the low-birth-weight sample).

Initial intellectual disadvantage is also associated with greater benefits of intervention. Bryant and Maxwell (1997) report that some of the largest program effects have been found in the Milwaukee project, which served mothers with IQs below 75 (Garber, 1988), and greater effects of Head Start have been found for children who began with below-average intellectual abilities (Lee, Brooks-Gunn, Schnur, & Liaw, 1990).

Berlin and her colleagues (1998) have argued that although program and participant characteristics are of extreme importance, the interactions between the program and participants are most critical. Participants must be fully engaged in the program to benefit, and this engagement requires successful relationships between the participants and the program staff. IHDP analyses showed higher child IQ scores and higher home environment ratings among participating families in which both mother and child were rated as having "high" active participation in the program (Liaw, Meisels, & Brooks-Gunn, 1995). In addition, a match between participants' needs and program services is needed in order for the program to be relevant and actively engage the participants. (Both Comings and Alamprese discuss adult participation in Section IV.)

When considering how early intervention programs work to improve child outcomes, we must also consider the pathways through which such effects may take place. The hypothesis that children will benefit from program effects on their parents is reflected in the fact that many family literacy programs include parenting and adult education components. Although both of these components and their effects on parents are discussed in other chapters of this volume, here we briefly discuss the indirect effects of parent-directed services on child outcomes.

Program developers typically assume the child can be influenced indirectly through the mother (Benasich et al., 1992). Therefore they seek to improve mother–child interactions and teaching skills, raise mothers' self-esteem and emotional functioning, promote her return to school or employment, and increase her knowledge about child development. Among the 27 programs reviewed by Benasich et al., the most commonly assessed maternal outcomes were education and employment, mother–infant interaction, and maternal knowledge and attitudes. Ten of the 11 programs assessing maternal education and employment found positive effects, and the same rate of positive findings existed for programs measuring mother–infant interactions. Seven of the 10 programs assessing maternal knowledge and attitudes found positive effects.

Although programs may expect their parent-focused services to have indirect effects on child outcomes, few studies have explicitly tested this pathway (Brooks-Gunn, Berlin, & Fuligni, 2000). Burchinal and her colleagues (1997) used the Abecedarian Project and Project CARE data to test whether the effect of the home-visiting intervention component on children's cognitive outcomes was mediated by its effects on parental authoritarian attitudes and the quality of the home environment. The analysis did not support the parenting variables as mediators of program effects, as some of the necessary pathways were not significant. Possible explanations for the lack of findings here may be the specific parenting measures used (no actual parent–child observations), or the fact that with three different treatment groups, sample size in each group may have been too small to detect such effects (Brooks-Gunn et al., 2000).

Data from the IHDP are more supportive of parent-mediated intervention effects. Linver and Brooks-Gunn (2001) found evidence that the IHDP effect on the home environment mediated treatment effects on children's cognitive scores at ages 3 and 5 years, and behavior problems at age 3 years. A second analysis of IHDP effects found a parental pathway through maternal depressive symptoms and life events (Lee & Brooks-Gunn, 1998). The family-oriented, parent intervention that included a focus on problem-solving and coping skills had direct effects on the emotional health outcomes of only those mothers who had a large number of stressful life events. In turn, it was the intervention group children of mothers with high depressive scores and high numbers of stressful life events who showed higher cognitive test scores and lower depressive/anxious symptoms than children with similar mothers in the follow-up group.

These results give some support for the notion that one pathway for intervention effects on child outcomes is through program effects on parents.

Summary and Implications

In summary, the research reviewed here suggests positive effects for children from low-income backgrounds, including initial gains in intellectual and achievement scores and longer term outcomes reflecting more successful school experiences (less special education placement, less grade retention, and higher graduation rates). The reduction of behavior problems and delinquency has also been reported.

In terms of program characteristics, researchers note that in order to maximize the likelihood of improving children's intellectual and academic outcomes, services should be provided directly to the child; home-visiting services alone are more likely to affect parenting and home environment than child outcomes, though they may add to the effectiveness of center-based interventions (Barnett, 1995; Berlin et al., 1998; Bryant & Maxwell, 1997; Yoshikawa, 1995). Although there have not been extensive comparisons of different curriculum approaches, the content of the child-focused intervention is important. The current thinking is that *child-initiated* or *child-focused* models are most beneficial (Bredekamp, 1987; Bryant & Maxwell, 1997). Additional studies comparing curriculum models are underway.

Other important factors for early intervention are nicely captured in the following principles of effective early intervention. These are (a) timing, programs that begin earlier in the child's life and last longer; (b) intensity, programs providing more hours per day, or days per week of services; (c) delivery, direct (versus indirect) provision of learning experiences; (d) breadth, programs with more comprehensive services and using multiple routes to affect child development; (e) individual differences, attention to children's initial risk status and program-participant match; (f) environmental maintenance of development, adequate ongoing supports to sustain program effects are crucial to prevent them from diminishing over time; and (g) cultural relevance, programs must be culturally relevant and appropriate for participants of diverse cultural backgrounds (Ramey, Ramey, Gaines, & Blair, 1995).

The implications of this body of research for family literacy programs are positive; research supports the effectiveness of early intervention programs that provide direct services to both children and their families, and this is exactly what family literacy programs do. The importance of providing intensive, high-quality programs to young children and continuing their support across the preschool and early elementary years is highlighted by this research. The finding of stronger effects from model programs than large-scale programs such as Head Start is important, because some family literacy programs (including Even Start) use Head Start and other large public programs for their early childhood component. The following section outlines research findings for children participating specifically in family literacy programs.

EARLY CHILDHOOD EDUCATION IN FAMILY LITERACY PROGRAMS

In this section, we focus our discussion on early childhood education within the context of family literacy programs. First, we describe the types of early education services children receive in family literacy programs, and we review evaluation research on family literacy programs to address specifically the question of effects and outcomes for participating children.

Early Childhood Services in Family Literacy Programs

In Even Start as well as other family literacy programs, the early childhood services may be implemented by the family literacy program, or the program may collaborate with another agency in the community to provide early childhood education. It is common for individual projects to have several collaborative partners in early childhood education. Many family literacy programs, including Even Start sites, employ Head Start as their primary early childhood component. The first national evaluation of Even Start (St.Pierre et al., 1995b) reported that Head Start services were available in 67% of Even Start projects, Chapter 1 prekindergarten programs were available at 50% of projects, and 87% offered some other type of preschool program. Even Start projects also collaborated with public schools to provide services to school-age children: 78% of projects have children enrolled in kindergarten; and 70% of programs with school-age children under age 8 are receiving other early childhood education services through the public schools. The second national Even Start evaluation (Tao, Gamse, & Tarr, 1998) reported that although 70% of projects provided their own early childhood services for infants and toddlers, a majority of sites collaborated with outside agencies to provide services to older children: 33% used public schools, 25% used Head Start, and 18% used other preschool and child-care programs.

Many Even Start Programs focus their early childhood services on the preschool years. From 1994 to 1997, children aged 3 to 5 years constituted 42 to 47% of participating Even Start children. The number of children aged birth through 2 years has increased in recent years to 30% of participating children. School-age children represent the smallest group of children served (Tao et al., 1998).

A study of Even Start program services to support the transition to kindergarten identified five programs that incorporated particularly promising transition services. Parents and staff reported that the following services are helpful to families with children entering elementary school: accompanying Even Start families to school-related transition activities, such as orientation; educating parents about the transition; empowering parents to act as children's advocates in the school setting; meeting with school staff to discuss entering children's needs and strengths; and supporting parents' involvement in the school setting (Riedinger, 1997).

Research on Family Literacy Program Effects on Children

The primary sources of evaluation research on family literacy programs are three national evaluations of the federal Even Start program. The first national evaluation, conducted on the first round of Even Start programs funded from 1989 to 1992, included a small sample of randomly assigned control groups for comparison purposes in addition to collecting entry and follow-up data from all Even Start sites (St.Pierre et al., 1995b). The second national evaluation, including programs funded from 1993 to 1996, concluded in 1998. Although there is no control group, it includes outcome data for a moderate-sized subset of programs (Tao et al., 1998; Tao, Swartz, St.Pierre, & Tarr, 1997). The third national evaluation began collecting data in the 1997 to 1998 program year, including annual data from all Even Start programs and an experimentally controlled study evaluating the program's effectiveness in 18 programs (St.Pierre et al., 2000b). The main findings from these evaluations vis-à-vis impacts of the programs on children are summarized in the following sections.

The First National Even Start Evaluation

The methods and uses of the Even Start National evaluation are reported in more depth by St.Pierre, Ricciuti, and Tao in Section VIII. Here we examine outcomes for young children. The first Even Start evaluation (St.Pierre et al., 1995b) measured cognitive effects on children using standardized achievement tests—the PreSchool Inventory (PSI; a measure of school readiness), Peabody Picture Vocabulary Test (PPVT) and Child's Emergent Literacy Test. This evaluation had two components: (a) a national component collecting preprogram and follow-up data on all families participating in Even Start nationally, and (b) an in-depth study of 10 Even Start sites with randomly assigned control groups for five of these sites. The in-depth study focused on children who were 3 or 4 years old.

In the national sample, children's PSI and PPVT scores increased over the program year at a rate that was larger than that expected based on normal development. In the in-depth study, Even Start children gained more than control group children on the PSI, but control group children caught up at the 18-month posttest, a finding that was likely due to 80% of them having enrolled in preschool or kindergarten programs by that time. Furthermore, the in-depth study revealed no significant program group-control group differences in PPVT gains and no significant program effects on the emergent literacy measure (St.Pierre et al., 1995b).

Regression analyses on 614 families with valid data for family background, participation, and child outcomes revealed significant associations among these variables. The amount of time children spent in early childhood education was significantly positively related to PPVT posttest scores, and the amount of time parents spent in parenting education through Even Start positively contributed to PPVT scores beyond the effects of early childhood education. These participation variables were stronger predictors of PPVT posttest scores than other family variables such as family income or the number of children's books in the home.

The Second National Even Start Evaluation

The second national evaluation covered the 1993 to 1994 program year through the 1996 to 1997 program year. This evaluation also included two components: (a) the Universe Study, designed to obtain participation and program implementation data on all local projects, and (b) the Sample Study, which included educational outcome measures at program entry, at the end of the program year, and the end of the following year for a sample of 57 projects (Tao et al., 1998).

Children's cognitive skills were assessed using the PreSchool Inventory (PSI) and the Preschool Language Scales (PLS-3). Comparisons of pretest and posttest scores showed significant gains on both measures, with length of time in the program associated with steeper growth curves. Because the PLS is an age-standardized measure, scores are not expected to change with development alone. Therefore, the evaluators inferred that the improvement was related to children's participation in Even Start. However, this conclusion was not empirically tested by comparison with a nontreatment group. Furthermore, the authors note that although most families remained in the program long enough to provide pretest data (collected within 30 days of program entry), some did not stay through the end of the year, and only about 10% were still enrolled in the program by the end of the second year. The group of families that stayed through the second year had higher levels of education, income, and employment, and were more likely to speak languages other than English at home. Therefore, the sample of families with 2 years of longitudinal outcome data are not representative of the sample with pretest data only, or data from pretest and one posttest (Tao et al., 1998).

The researchers conducting this second national evaluation were not able to document support for the consistent link between service intensity, program characteristics, or participant characteristics and participant outcomes that was documented in the earlier national evaluation. They note that the quality of some of the data varied over the years of this evaluation, possibly contributing to the lack of a clear connection (Tao et al., 1998).

The Third National Even Start Evaluation

The third national evaluation of the Even Start program was conducted by Abt Associates and Fu Associates and covered the 4 years of program implementation from 1997 to 1998 through 2000 to 2001. This evaluation incorporated outcome data from the revised national reporting system (Even Start Performance Information Reporting System; ESPIRS) and a randomized controlled study of 18 Even Start projects (the Experimental Design Study; EDS). Inclusion of the EDS component in this evaluation helped to address criticisms of the prior two national evaluations that either did not include randomly assigned control groups (the second evaluation) or included only a small sample of randomly assigned participants from a small number of programs (the first evaluation). The EDS included over 400 participants from 18 different Even Start programs (St.Pierre et al., 2003). Findings from this evaluation are based on comparisons of pretest–posttest improvement in children's assessment scores for

Even Start participants, control group participants, and participants in the Head Start FACES study. Children's language and cognitive skills were assessed using the PPVT-III and several subtests of the Woodcock-Johnson Psycho-Educational Battery—Revised. Though Even Start children showed some improvement on both cognitive and language measures from the pretest to the posttest, gains were similar for both the Even Start group and the non-Even Start control group, and also similar to gains made by children in the Head Start FACES study (St.Pierre et al., 2003). The absence of a greater gain among the Even Start children suggests that their participation in Even Start did not have a stronger impact on their literacy development than they would have experienced in Head Start or even in other community early childhood services available to the control group members.

An important finding from this third national evaluation was that Even Start families are significantly more disadvantaged than the low-income population served by Head Start. Even Start is meeting its mandate to serve the most needy families. Thus, Even Start programs are facing the challenge of serving a very low-income and low-literacy population. Although low-income children have been shown in many studies to make larger gains than middle-income children in early childhood education programs, there may be a curvilinear relationship between risk and program impact such that the highest risk participants experience less growth on the cognitive and linguistic outcomes measured here. Programs also struggle with keeping families involved in the program long enough to make significant educational gains.

Finally, the requirement that Even Start programs utilize services available in the community rather than duplicate services may have an impact on the quality of the instruction provided to children and parents. Quality ratings of the classrooms in the EDS identified some areas, including language and reasoning, that may need to be emphasized more in the early childhood instruction component of the Even Start programs (St.Pierre et al., 2003)

Other Evaluations

In addition to the national Even Start evaluations, several individual family literacy programs have published evaluations of their programs, often with the support of the National Center for Family Literacy (NCFL) (e.g., Mikulecky, Lloyd, & Brannon, 1994). Even Start programs are also required to conduct local evaluation activities, though the content of local evaluations is not mandated; consequently, many projects focus these evaluation efforts on topics of most importance to their site (St.Pierre et al., 2000).

Individual evaluations of family literacy programs have also reported program effects on preschool cognitive measures, although these rely almost exclusively on pretest–posttest designs. For instance, evaluations of the PACE program in the late 1980s found positive gains for children (average gain—28%) on the Child Observation Record (COR) (Heberle, 1992). A study of 32 Toyota Families for Learning programs in 10 cities also found positive program effects on the COR and compared those gains with gains reported by the High/Scope Educational Research Foundation on a sample of children with similar backgrounds attending other early childhood programs. The comparison children also made significant gains on the COR, but children in the Toyota family literacy programs had gains that were significantly higher (Philliber, Spillman, & King, 1996). These researchers also reported improvements in children's PPVT scores from the 11th percentile at the beginning of program participation, to the 19th percentile at the end of the school year. Although there was no comparison group for this finding, the authors noted that percentile rankings would not be predicted to change over time given normal development for children not in an intervention (Philliber et al., 1996).

One model Even Start program, the Family Intergenerational Literacy Model (FILM), reported preschool cognitive gains that were larger than those found in the National Even Start Evaluation for the same program year (Richardson & Brown, 1997). This program was validated in 1994 by the Program Effectiveness Panel and became one of the first family literacy programs in the U.S. Department of Education's National Diffusion Network. FILM includes five components: (a) adult education, (b) parent discussion groups, (c) home visits, (d) parent–child interaction playgroups, and (e) an early learning center. In the 1993 to 1994 program year, the average gain on children's PreSchool Inventory (PSI) scores was 11.94, compared to a 5.8 point average gain for the same year in the first National Even Start Evaluation. Similarly, Preschool Language Scale-3 (PLS-3) scores increased in 1994 to 1995 by an average of 12.9 points, compared to a 5.2 point gain reported in the first National Evaluation.

Summary and Conclusions

The evaluations reported previously provide a generally positive picture of children's outcomes from family literacy programs. Preschool children appear to make moderate but significant gains in language skills following program participation. However, few measures of the characteristics of the early childhood programs themselves are in existence. For example, for very young children, there are virtually no reports of day-care quality measures, such as staffing ratios, turnover rates, or safety measures.

The lack of control groups is another concern. With few exceptions, studies rely almost exclusively on pretest–posttest models, making estimation of program effects difficult.

Finally, most studies are limited to studying preschool cognitive outcomes. As stated previously, findings in this area have been generally positive, but evaluators may be missing other important program outcomes by failing to measure social, emotional, and behavioral outcomes. Similarly, the research focus on the preschool years has left open the question of how programs affect children of other ages—infants, toddlers, and school-age children. These concerns, and others, are reflected in the recommendations for practice and evaluation of family literacy programs articulated in the following section.

RECOMMENDATIONS

Recommendations for Practice and Implementation

1. A primary goal of any early childhood education program, including those in family literacy programs, must be ensuring that the setting where young children receive care is of the highest possible quality. Issues of promoting staff development, reducing child/staff ratios, providing developmentally appropriate curriculum and continuity of care for the child, and adhering to safety regulations are all important for child well-being (Cost, Quality and Child Outcomes Study Team, 1995, 1999; Howes, Smith & Galinsky, 1995; Whitebook et al., 1990). Recent longitudinal data from over 800 children who had attended 170 different child-care centers suggest that early child-care quality is related to math and language skills as well as to peer relations and behavior problems in second grade (Cost, Quality and Child Outcomes Study Team, 1999). However, the quality of early childhood settings varies dramatically. Research assessing child-care environments using an extensive observational measure of quality (the Early Childhood Environment Rating Scale [ECERS]; Harms & Clifford, 1990; Harms, Clifford, & Cryer, 1998) has found that across a diverse sample of child-care centers, quality is generally in the medium range (3 to 5 points on a scale from 1 to 7), with over 11% scoring below the minimal quality rating of 3 points (Cost, Quality and Child Outcomes Study Team, 1999). The ECERS instrument can also be used as an internal self-assessment, and family literacy programs would benefit from using such a tool to guide quality improvement efforts.

2. In addition to ensuring the overall quality of the early childhood setting, family literacy programs need to pay special attention to the quality of the literacy environment they provide for young children. One current study of family literacy programs has developed a measure that can be used to assess the literacy environment of the preschool classroom (Wasik, personal communcation). This observation code assesses a variety of teacher, child, and classroom variables in order to gain information on the classroom resources that support literacy and language development (i.e., books, drawing/writing materials, reading space, and book-reading interactions).

3. The research findings presented previously highlight the benefits of providing comprehensive services to multiple family members. These results are encouraging for family literacy programs that provide parent services such as parenting education and interactive literacy activities between parents and children as well as age-appropriate early childhood education services. Programs may want to consider enhancing home-visiting, case management, or other one-on-one services to parents and families in addition to center-based child components. Such approaches will help ensure that individual family strengths and needs are addressed, and will enhance program-participant relationships, all of which may lead to stronger program effects.

4. Programs should focus on developing a working definition of "full implementation." Benchmarks should be created regarding the percentage of families provided with particular services, the intensity of services, staff training, the percentage of families served only temporarily, and links to other service agencies in the community. Often, evaluations are conducted on programs that are not being fully implemented, thus reducing the likelihood of obtaining positive results. The Early Head Start Research and Evaluation Project employed detailed definitions of program implementation across a variety of dimensions and found that these were related to program impacts on children and families (Love et al., 2001).

5. If programs want to have positive effects on child cognitive, literacy, and school outcomes, they need to provide intensive programs directly to the child. Even Start and other family literacy programs should aim to offer high-quality, center-based care to children on a consistent basis, not just by providing care while the parents attend meetings and parenting classes, but for a substantial amount of time each week.

6. Although early education research has found benefits from intensive intervention during infancy and long-term intervention (e.g., 3 years or more), the focus in family literacy programs is often on the preschool years. Support for expanding services for infants, school transition services, and ongoing services for school-age children is needed. However, if these services are expanded, efforts would also have to be made to retain families for longer periods of time. For instance, the primary reason families join Even Start programs is to pursue adult literacy and education goals (Tao et al., 1998), and the completion of adult education goals is a common reason for leaving family literacy programs. Additional efforts may be needed to retain families for longer term services. Even Start has begun to address this issue by allowing families to remain in the program for the early childhood education, parenting education, and support components even when adult education services have been completed.

7. Programs should spend some time outlining their theories of change—their beliefs about how their program helps children and how it may exert differential effects for different types of child outcomes (i.e., emotional, cognitive, or school success). Programs may need to hire a facilitator to guide this process.

8. Programs should realistically consider the intensity of the services they offer to families. There is a trade-off between the amount of intervention that can be provided and the number of families that can be served. Programs should determine how many families could be served with a program that is intense enough to make a difference.

9. More programs should consider how they could facilitate continuity of services for families as children progress through preschool and elementary school. Again, programs must

be realistic about the number of families they can keep in the program through the transition to elementary school. Are pieces of the program, such as literacy activities in the home, more tailored to preschoolers than to school-age children? Do different techniques need to be used to help parents with children of different ages? What types of links are programs forging with elementary schools and existing preschools? Attention to all of these issues will be important for continuing to serve children throughout these early years of schooling.

10. Welfare reform will affect a parent's ability to participate in all components of family literacy programs. Projects will need to tailor both core and support services to be responsive (and relevant) to the needs of working parents, by scheduling them on off-hours, providing more home-based services, and continuing to provide supports such as transportation, child care, and meals to help remove barriers to participation. Because working parents have less time, coordination of services will be important, so that more services such as child-care and parenting education are offered at the same site.

11. Consistent with the previous recommendation, programs need to consider the changing needs of poor parents, especially in light of welfare reform. If more parents are required to work, then literacy and GED programs may become less useful, at least in the short term. Family literacy programs should work on forming links with work programs. (Askov elaborates on the links between literacy and the workplace in Section IV.) Family literacy programs should continue to consider the balance between literacy needs and vocational needs for the populations they serve.

Recommendations for Evaluation Studies

1. A big gap in the evaluation research exists in the measurement and description of specific early childhood education services. In response to *black box* criticisms (Berlin et al., 1998), new studies should assess program processes and base outcome comparisons on levels of participation and services received. Understanding the processes and procedures of the early childhood components of family literacy programs as well as obtaining valid and reliable measures of effectiveness are essential for new research efforts. Such approaches will help to answer the questions of how intervention programs affect their participants, and why some participants benefit more than others.

2. Studies of child outcomes including nontreatment comparison groups are needed. Random assignment to experimental and control groups would be the ideal methodological approach. However, ethical concerns often prevent such designs from being used in intervention research because of the requirement that services be denied to some families and children. Alternatively, comparison groups with similar ethnic, cultural, and socioeconomic backgrounds could be employed to estimate the effects of program participation.

3. Although the lack of rigorous, controlled experimental evaluations is a concern, we also recommend the continuation of rich descriptive studies, such as those being conducted on a local level at many Even Start sites (St.Pierre et al., 2000a; Wasik, Herrmann, Dobbins, & Roberts, 2000) and the individual evaluations of model programs such as FILM (Richardson & Brown, 1997). Carefully controlled experimental studies and rich, descriptive studies both add to the body of knowledge about how family literacy programs are working.

4. Evaluations must carefully select the outcome measures most appropriate to the specific project being assessed. Evaluators should work with project directors to design outcome studies appropriate to the goals of the particular programs. In addition, programs need to indicate where they expect to have an effect, and evaluations should measure those outcomes, rather than test a multitude of outcomes and then find only one or two significant effects. In other words, programs should first prioritize their goals, and then researchers should assess the same things programs are trying to affect in participants.

5. The field of family literacy studies needs an expanded focus on the entire age range of children served, not just the 3- and 4-year-olds. Again, working in conjunction with program administrators, researchers should determine what are the program goals for infants, toddlers, preschoolers, and school-age children and devise studies to determine program effectiveness in these areas.

6. As discussed earlier in this chapter, few studies have explicitly tested the indirect effect of programs on child outcomes through their effects on parents. When studies measure effects on parents and children, this mediating pathway should also be evaluated. The examples described previously, in which program influences on mothers mediated program effects on child outcomes (Burchinal et al., 1997; Linver & Brooks-Gunn, 2001), came from programs that offered both home-visiting and center-based child care, so they had both direct and indirect effects on children. Such models should be set up and explicitly tested in evaluations of family literacy programs.

7. Finally, the field of early intervention needs to see maternal outcomes and parenting outcomes as important in their own right, even if there are not comparable effects for children. We should not expect every program to result in enhanced child outcomes. For instance, when programs target reading activities in the home but offer only a few home visits, they should not expect to make a lasting effect on child cognitive ability. Improved parent outcomes will undoubtedly improve the home experiences of children even if they do not have a measurable effect on cognitive tests.

REFERENCES

Baker, A., Piotrkowski, C. S., & Brooks-Gunn, J. (1998). The effects of the Home Instruction Program for Preschool Youngsters (HIPPY) on children's school performance at the end of the program and one year later. *Early Childhood Research Quarterly, 13,* 571–588.

Barnett, W. S. (1995). Long-term effects of early childhood programs on cognitive and school outcomes. *The Future of Children, 5,* 25–50.

Benasich, A. A., Brooks-Gunn, J., & Clewell, B. C. (1992). How do mothers benefit from early intervention programs? *Journal of Applied Developmental Psychology, 13,* 311–362.

Berlin, L. J., O'Neal, C. R., & Brooks-Gunn, J. (1998). What makes early intervention programs work?: The program, its participants, and their interaction. In L. J. Berlin (Ed.), Opening the black box: What makes early child and family development programs work? [Special Issue]. *Zero to Three, 18,* 4–15.

Bredekamp, S. (Ed.) (1987). *Developmentally appropriate practice in early childhood programs serving children from birth through age 8.* Washington, DC: National Association for the Education of Young Children.

Brooks-Gunn, J., Berlin, L. J., & Fuligni, A. S. (2000). Early childhood intervention programs: What about the family? In J. P. Shonkoff & S. J. Meisels (Eds.), *Handbook of early childhood intervention* (2nd ed., pp. 549–588). New York: Cambridge University Press.

Brooks-Gunn, J., Gross, R., Kraemer, H., Spiker, D., & Shapiro, S. (1992). Enhancing the cognitive outcomes of low birth weight, premature infants: For whom is the intervention most effective? *Pediatrics, 89,* 1209–1215.

Brooks-Gunn, J., Klebanov, P. K., Liaw, F., & Spiker, D. (1993). Enhancing the development of low birth weight, premature infants: Changes in cognition and behavior over the first three years. *Child Development, 64,* 736–753.

Brooks-Gunn, J., McCarton, C., Casey, P., McCormick, M., Bauer, C., Bernbaum, J., Tyson, J., Swanson, M., Bennett, F., Scott, D., Tonascia, J., & Meinert, C. (1994). Early intervention in low birth weight, premature infants: Results through age 5 years from the Infant Health and Development Program. *Journal of the American Medical Association, 272,* 1257–1262.

Bryant, D., & Maxwell, K. (1997). The effectiveness of early intervention for disadvantaged children. In M. J. Guralnick (Ed.), *The effectiveness of early intervention* (pp. 23–46). Baltimore: Brookes.

Burchinal, M. R., Campbell, F. A., Bryant, D. M., Wasik, B. H., & Ramey, C. T. (1997). Early intervention and mediating processes in cognitive performance of children of low-income African-American families. *Child Development, 68,* 935–954

Campbell, F., & Ramey, C. (1994). Effects of early intervention on intellectual and academic achievement: A follow-up study from low-income families. *Child Development, 65,* 684–698.

Campbell, F., & Ramey, C. (1995). Cognitive and school outcomes for high risk African-American students at middle adolescence: Positive effects of early intervention. *American Educational Research Journal, 32,* 743–772.

Cost, Quality and Child Outcomes Study Team. (1995). *Cost, quality, and child outcomes in child care centers.* Denver: Economics Department, University of Colorado at Denver.

Cost, Quality and Child Outcomes Study Team. (1999). *The children of the Cost, Quality, and Outcomes Study go to school: Executive summary.* Chapel Hill, NC: Frank Porter Graham Child Development Center, University of North Carolina at Chapel Hill.

Dawson, P., van Doorninck, W. J., & Robinson, J. L. (1989). Effects of home-based, informal social support on child health. *Developmental and Behavior Pediatrics, 10,* 63–67.

Epstein, A. S., & Weikart, D. P. (1979). *The Ypsilanti-Carnegie infant education project: Longitudinal follow-up.* Ypsilanti: MI: The High/Scope Educational Research Foundation.

Farran, D. C. (2000). Another decade of intervention for children who are low income or disabled: What do we know now? In J. P. Shonkoff & S. J. Meisels (Eds.), *Handbook of early childhood intervention,* (2nd ed., pp. 510–548). New York: Cambridge University Press.

Field, T., Widmayer, S., Greenberg, M. A., & Stoller, S. (1982). Effects of parent training on teen-age mothers and their infants. *Pediatrics, 69,* 703–707.

Garber, H. L. (1988).*The Milwaukee Project: Preventing mental retardation in children at risk.* Washington, DC: American Association on Mental Retardation.

Gordon, I. J., Guinagh, B. J., & Jester, R. E. (1977). The Florida Parent Education Infant and Toddler Programs. In M. C. Day & R. K. Parker (Eds.), *The preschool in action: Exploring early childhood programs* (pp. 95–127). Boston: Allyn & Bacon.

Guralnick, M. J. (1997). Second-generation research in the field of early intervention. In M. J. Guralnick (Ed.), *The effectiveness of early intervention* (pp. 3–20). Baltimore: Brookes.

Guteilus, M. F., Kirsch, A. D., MacDonald, S., Brooks, M. R., & McErlean, T. (1977). Controlled study of child health supervision: Behavioral results. *Pediatrics, 60,* 294–304.

Harms, T., & Clifford, R. M. (1990). *The Early Childhood Environment Rating Scale.* New York: Teachers College Press.

Harms, T., Clifford, R. M., & Cryer, D. (1998). *Early Childhood Environment Rating Scale: Revised edition.* New York: Teachers College Press.

Hauser-Cram, P. (1990). Designing meaningful evaluations of early intervention services. In S. J. Meisels & J. P. Shonkoff (Eds.), *Handbook of early childhood intervention* (pp. 583–602). Cambridge, MA: Cambridge University Press.

Head Start Bureau. (1996). *Head Start children's entry into public school: An interim report on the National Head Start-Public School Early Childhood Demonstration Study.* Washington, DC: Department of Health and Human Services.

Heberle, J. (1992). PACE: Parent and child education in Kentucky. In T. G. Sticht, M. J. Beeler, & B. A. McDonald (Eds.), *The intergenerational transfer of cognitive skills. Volume I: Programs, policy, and research issues* (pp. 136–148). Norwood, NJ: Ablex.

Howes, C., Smith, E., & Galinsky, E. (1995). *The Florida child care quality improvement study: Interim report.* New York: Families and Work Institute.

Infant Health and Development Program (IHDP). (1990). Enhancing the outcomes of low birthweight, premature infants. *Journal of the American Medical Association, 263,* 3035–3042.

Jester, R. E., & Guinagh, B. J. (1983). The Gordon Parent Education Infant and Toddler Program. In *As the twig is bent . . . Lasting effects of preschool programs* (pp. 103–132). Hillsdale, NJ: Lawrence Erlbaum Associates.

Johnson, D. L., & Walker, T. (1987). Primary prevention of behavior problems in Mexican-American children. *American Journal of Community Psychology, 15*(4), 375–385.

Lally, R. J., Mangione, P. L., & Honig, A. S. (1988). The Syracuse University Family Development Research Program: Long-range impact of an early intervention with low-income children and their families. In D. R. Powell (Ed.), *Advances in applied developmental psychology: Vol. 3. Parent education as early childhood intervention: Emerging directions in theory, research, and practice* (pp. 79–104). Norwood, NJ: Ablex.

Lazar, I., Darlington, R., Murray, H., Royce, J., & Snipper, A. (1982). Lasting effects of early education: A report from the Consortium for Longitudinal Studies. *Monographs of the Society for Research in Child Development, 47*(2-3, Serial No. 195).

Lee, K., & Brooks-Gunn, J. (1998). *Effects of early intervention upon maternal behavior: Consequences for 3 year old's outcomes.* Unpublished manuscript. Teachers College, Columbia University.

Lee, V. E., Brooks-Gunn, J., Schnur, E., & Liaw, F. (1990). Are Head Start effects sustained? A longitudinal follow-up comparison of disadvantaged children attending Head Start, no preschool, and other preschool programs. *Child Development, 61,* 495–507.

Lee, V. E., & Loeb, S. (1995). Where do Head Start enrollees end up? One reason why preschool effects fade out. *Educational Evaluation and Policy Analysis, 17,* 62–82.

Liaw, F., & Brooks-Gunn, J. (1993). Patterns of low birth weight children's cognitive development and their determinants. *Developmental Psychology, 29*, 1024–1035.

Liaw, F., Brooks-Gunn, J., & Spiker, D. (1997). *Effects of early intervention services on 3-year-old children's social competence and parents' interactions with children.* Unpublished manuscript.

Liaw, F., Meisels, S., & Brooks-Gunn, J. (1995). The effects of experience of early intervention on low birth weight, premature children: The Infant Health and Development Program. *Early Childhood Research Quarterly, 10*, 405–431.

Linver, M., & Brooks-Gunn, J. (2001). *Parenting as mediating early intervention effects upon young children.* Unpublished manuscript.

Love, J. M., Kisker, E. E., Ross, C. M., Schochet, P. Z., Brooks-Gunn, J., Boller, K., Paulsell, D., Fuligni, A. S., & Berlin, L. J. (2001). *Building their futures: How Early Head Start programs are enhancing the lives of infants and toddlers in low-income families.* Washington, DC: U.S. Department of Health and Human Services.

McCarton, C. M., Brooks-Gunn, J., Wallace, I. F., Bauer, C. R., Bennett, F. C., Bernbaum, J. C., Broyles, R. S., Casey, P. H., McCormick, M. C., Scott, D. T., Tyson, J., Tonascia, J., & Meinert, C. L. (1997). Results at age 8 years of early intervention for low-birth-weight premature infants: The Infant Health and Development Program. *Journal of the American Medical Association, 277*, 126–132.

McCurdy, K. (1996). *Intensive home visitation: A randomized trial, follow-up and risk assessment study of Hawaii's Healthy Start Program: Executive Summary.* Report submitted to Administration for Children, Youth and Families, U.S. Department of Health and Human Services.

McKey, R. H., Condelli, L., Granson, H., Barrett, B., McConkey, C., & Plantz, M. (1985). *The impact of Head Start on children, families, and communities.* (Final report of the Head Start Evaluation, Synthesis, and Utilization Project). Washington, DC: CSR.

Mikulecky, L., Lloyd, P., & Brannon, D. (1994). *Evaluating parent/child interactions in family literacy programs.* Paper presented at the National Conference on Family Literacy, Louisville, KY.

National Institute of Child Health and Human Development (NICHD) Early Child Care Research Network. (2000). The relation of child care to cognitive and language development. *Child Development, 71*, 960–980.

Olds, D. L., Henderson, C. R., Chamberlin, R., & Tatelbaum, R. (1986). Preventing child abuse and neglect: A randomized trial of nurse home visitation. *Pediatrics, 78*, 65–78.

Olds, D. L., & Kitzman, H. (1993). Review of research on home visiting for pregnant women and parents of young children. *The Future of Children, 3*, 53–92.

Olds, D. L., Henderson, C. R., Kitzman, H. J., Eckenrode, J. J., Cole, R. E., & Tatelbaum, R. C. (1999). Prenatal and infancy home visitation by nurses: Recent findings. *The Future of Children, 9*, 44–64.

Philliber, W. W., Spillman, R. E., & King, R. (1996). Consequences of family literacy for adults and children: Some preliminary findings. *Journal of Adolescent and Adult Literacy, 39*(7), 558–565.

Ramey, C. T., Bryant, D. M., Wasik, B. H., Sparling, J. J., Fendt, K. H., & LaVange, L. M. (1992). Infant Health and Development Program for low birth weight, premature infants: Program elements, family participation, and child intelligence. *Pediatrics, 89*(3), 454–465.

Ramey, C. T., Ramey, S. L., Gaines, K. R., & Blair, C. (1995). Two-generation early intervention programs: A child development perspective. In S. Smith (Ed.), Two generation programs for families in poverty: A new intervention strategy. *Advances in Applied Developmental Psychology* (Vol. 9, pp. 199–228). Norwood, NJ: Ablex.

Ramey, S. L., Ramey, C. T., Phillips, M. M., Lanzi, R. G., Brezausek, C., Katholi, C. R., Snyder, S., & Lawrence, F. (2000). *Head Start children's entry into public school: A report on the National Head Start/Public School Early Childhood Transition Demonstration study.* Washington, DC: U.S. Department of Health and Human Services.

Reynolds, A. J. (1997). *Long-term effects of the Chicago Child-Parent Center Program through age 15.* Paper presented at the biennial meeting of the Society for Research on Child Development, Washington, DC.

Reynolds, A. J., Temple, J. A., Robertson, D. L., & Mann, E. A. (2001). Long-term effects of an early childhood intervention on educational achievement and juvenile arrest. *Journal of the American Medical Association, 285*(18), 2339–2346.

Richardson, D. C., & Brown, M. (1997). *Family Intergenerational Literacy Model. Fact sheet and impact statements.* Oklahoma City, OK: National Diffusion Network.

Riedinger, S. A. (1997). *Even Start: Facilitating transitions to kindergarten.* Washington, DC: U.S. Department of Education.

Royce, J. M., Darlington, R. B., & Murray, H. W. (1983). Pooled analyses: Findings across studies. In *As the twig is bent... Lasting effects of preschool programs.* Hillsdale, NJ: Lawrence Erlbaum Associates.

Schorr, L. B., & Booth, D. (1991). Attributes of effective services for young children: A brief survey of current knowledge and its implications for program and policy development. In L. B. Schorr, D. Booth, & C. Copple (Eds.), *Effective services for young children* (pp. 23–45). Washington, DC: National Academy Press.

Schweinhart, L. J., Barnes, H. V., & Weikart, D. P. (1993). *Significant benefits: The High/Scope Perry Preschool Study through age 27.* Ypsilanti, MI: High/Scope Press.

Seitz, V., & Apfel, N. (1994). Parent-focused intervention: Diffusion effects on siblings. *Child Development, 65*, 677–683.

Shore, R. (1997). *Rethinking the brain: New insights into early development.* New York: Families and Work Institute.

Sparling, J., Lewis, I., Ramey, C. T., Wasik, B. H., Bryant, D. M., & LaVange, L. M. (1991). Partners, a curriculum to help premature, low birth weight infants get off to a good start. *Topics in Early Childhood Special Education, 11,* 36–55.

Sprigle, J. E., & Schaefer, L. (1985). Longitudinal evaluation of the effects of two compensatory preschool programs on fourth- through sixth-grade students. *Developmental Psychology, 21,* 702–708.

St.Pierre, R. G., Layzer, J. I., & Barnes, H. V. (1995a). Two-generation programs: Design, cost, and short-term effectiveness. *The Future of Children, 5,* 76–93.

St.Pierre, R., Swartz, J., Gamse, B., Murray, S., Deck, D., & Nickel, P. (1995b). *National evaluation of the Even Start Family Literacy Program: Final Report.* Washington, DC: U.S. Department of Education, Planning and Evaluation Service.

St.Pierre, R., Ricciuti, A., & Creps, C. (2000a). *Synthesis of local and state Even Start evaluations.* Washington, DC: U.S. Department of Education, Planning and Evaluation Service.

St.Pierre, R., Ricciuti, A., Tao, F., Creps, C., Kumagawa, T., & Ross, W. (2000b). *Third national Even Start evaluation: Interim report on 1997-98 and 1998-99 data.* Washington, DC: U.S. Department of Education.

St.Pierre, R, Ricciuti, A., Tao, F., Creps, D., Swartz, J., Wang, L., Parsad, A., & Rimdzius, T. (2003). *Third national Even Start evaluation: Program impacts and implications for improvement.* Washington, DC: U.S. Department of Education.

Tao, F., Gamse, B., & Tarr, H. (1998). *National evaluation of the Even Start Family Literacy Program:* 1994-1997 final report. Washington, DC: U.S. Department of Education.

Tao, F., Swartz, J., St.Pierre, R., & Tarr, H. (1997). *National evaluation of the Even Start Family Literacy Program: 1995 interim report.* Washington, DC: U.S. Department of Education, Planning and Evaluation Service.

Thompson, R. J., Cappleman, M. W., Conrad, H. H., et al. (1982). Early intervention program for adolescent mothers and their infants. *Developmental and Behavioral Pediatrics, 3,* 18–21.

Wagner, M. M., & Clayton, S. L. (1999). The Parents as Teachers program: Results from two demonstrations. *The Future of Children, 9,* 91–115.

Wasik, B. H., Herrmann, S., Dobbins, D. R., & Roberts, J. (Fall, 2000). Family literacy: A promising practice for the twenty-first century. In B. Day (Ed.), *North Carolina Association for Supervision in Curriculum and Development,* 7–19.

Wasik, B., Ramey, C., Bryant, D., & Sparling, J. (1990). A longitudinal study of two early intervention strategies: Project CARE. *Child Development, 61,* 1682–1696.

Weikart, D. P. (1989). Early childhood education and primary prevention. *Prevention in Human Services, 6*(2), 285–306.

Whitebook, M., Howes, C., & Phillips, D. A. (1990). *Who cares? Child care teachers and the quality of care in America.* Final report, National Child Care Staffing Study. Oakland, CA: Child Care Employee Project.

Winter, M., & Rouse, J. (1990). Fostering intergenerational literacy: The Missouri Parents as Teachers Program. *The Reading Teacher, 43*(6), 382–386.

Yoshikawa, H. (1995). Long-term effects of early childhood programs on social outcomes and delinquency. *The Future of Children, 5*(3), 51–75.

Zigler, E. (1998). By what goals should Head Start be assessed? *Children's Services: Social Policy, Research, and Practice, 1*(1), 5–17.

8

High-Quality Classrooms: A Key Ingredient to Family Literacy Programs' Support for Children's Literacy

David K. Dickinson
Boston College

Robert G. St.Pierre
Abt Associates

Julia Pettengill
Education Development Center

The need for early childhood programs that foster literacy by supporting both the family and the child is clear and compelling, especially when we consider those families who are most at risk due to poverty, immigrant status, language spoken, or racial background. If we are to prepare children for success in Western technological societies, we must help them obtain the literacy skills required to function in such societies. If children born into families on the economic margins of our society are to find their way into the economic mainstream, we need to provide them effective added support during the preschool years for literacy development. Further, growing evidence suggests that the most potent way to provide the needed support must include both center-based child care and support to families that build parents' understanding of their role in supporting their child's long-term academic development and help them to adopt home practices that effectively foster children's current and future literacy development. Despite evidence that child-care programs that serve at-risk populations can bolster children's growth, it is not clear that they are able to make changes that are of the magnitude required if we are to bring about required changes in children's developmental trajectories or in parents' ways of supporting their children's language and literacy development.

We argue that early childhood and family literacy programs must be prepared to aim for very substantial improvements in the literacy development of participating children and families. Of course, small effects are helpful. But researchers, program developers, and policymakers are fooling themselves if they believe that the problems can be solved with interventions that make marginal improvements. The magnitude of the changes that are required on the part of the children and families on the economic margins of society are much larger than has been recognized in the past.

Consider families that participate in Head Start and Even Start, two flagship federal programs for low-income families. Data from the Head Start FACES study (U.S. Department of Health and Human Services, 2001) and the national Even Start evaluation (St.Pierre, Ricciuti, et al., 2002) show that Even Start and Head Start families are poor, undereducated, and underemployed by any standards. In 1997, 41% of Even Start families and 13% of Head Start families had annual incomes under $6,000; only 26% of Even Start families and 53% of Head Start families had an employed parent; and only 15% of Even Start parents and 72% of Head Start parents had a high school diploma or GED. At pretest, the average Even Start child scored 72.5 on the Peabody Picture Vocabulary Test (PPVT) (Dunn & Dunn, 1997), compared with an average pretest score of 84.6 for Head Start children. Thus, Head Start children scored a full standard deviation below the national norm, and Even Start children scored almost another full standard deviation below Head Start children.

The most successful child development intervention programs have been able to make short-term changes in child IQ scores of between 0.5 and 1.0 SD (Barnett, 1995; Infant Health and Development Program, IHDP, 1990). Because the average Head Start child scores about 1.0 SD below national norms, we might expect that the very best interventions developed to date could just about erase this deficit, at least in the short run. But what about children served by Even Start? Even if it were possible to improve their PPVT scores by a full standard deviation, they still would lag behind national norms by a full standard deviation.

The family literacy approach of engaging parents as teachers of their children is an appealing avenue to possibly enhancing the effectiveness of stand-alone early childhood education programs. But, similar to their children, parents in Head Start and Even Start families are in very difficult circumstances. The national Even Start evaluation reports that, in spite of making significant gains while in the program, Even Start parents scored very low on literacy instruments when compared with national norms. After about a school year in Even Start, the average parent scored at the 5th percentile on the Woodcock-Johnson Letter-Word Identification subtest, the 2nd percentile on Passage Comprehension, the 14th percentile on Word Attack, the 1st percentile on Reading Vocabulary, the 2nd percentile on the Reading Comprehension cluster, and the 8th percentile on the Basic Reading Skills cluster (Woodcock, McGrew, & Mather, 2001). It is hard to imagine that parents who are having this degree of difficulty with their own literacy skills will find it easy or natural to read and discuss books with their child or to talk to their child about the world using varied vocabulary—two activities most strongly associated with family support for language and early literacy development (Bus, van IJzendoorn, & Pellegrini, 1995; Dickinson & Tabors, 2001; Hart & Risley, 1995).

In this chapter we will support the argument that we just laid out and then examine some of the challenges that currently limit the effectiveness of existing programs. Using early results and insights drawn from ongoing studies we then suggest promising directions for family literacy programs in the coming years. In our discussion, we adopt Wasik's definition of "family literacy" as "... a concept that includes naturally occurring literacy practices within the home, family, and community and as a formal activity, exemplified by organized instruction usually linked with educational settings" (Wasik, Dobbins, & Herrmann, 2001, p. 445). Although we will focus on the formal structural dimension, we will draw on research that has illuminated the important role of family practices.

WE NEED TO START EARLY AND INCLUDE THE FAMILY

For most of the past century, literacy was conceived of as an issue that we should begin to worry about once children enter the public schools. It was widely believed that the preschool years were the purview of the family, and for children in child care, it was their social and emotional growth that should be the primary, if not sole, concern of providers. Though the importance of the early years for social and emotional health is still strongly supported (Shonkoff & Phillips, 2000), there have been developments in literacy research that have had a profound impact on how we conceive of literacy. Over the past 20 years, researchers first discovered *emergent literacy* (Sulzby & Teale, 1991), and more recently have accorded children's literacy-related development in the preschool years the status of *early literacy* (e.g., Neuman & Dickinson, 2001).

Long-Term Stability of Literacy-Related Abilities

The importance of development during the preschool years has been highlighted by *Preventing Reading Difficulties* (Snow, Burns, & Griffin, 1998), *Eager to Learn* (Bowman, Donovan, & Burns, 2001), *and From Neurons to Networks* (Shonkoff & Phillips, 2000), reports issued by three distinct expert panels. These reports draw on the many studies that have demonstrated powerful long-term linkages among literacy abilities as children are beginning school and their later school success (e.g., Baydar, Brooks-Gunn, & Furstenberg, 1993; Hanson & Farrell, 1995, Sameroff, Seifer, Baldwin, & Baldwin, 1993; Whitehurst & Lonigan, 2001). One particularly noteworthy study is the work of Cunningham and Stanovich (1997), who found that first-grade reading ability was a strong predictor of a variety of 11th grade measures of reading ability, even when measures of cognitive ability were partialled out. Similarly, the Home-School Study recently reported first-order correlations between kindergarten measures of receptive vocabulary, decoding, and print knowledge with seventh-grade reading comprehension and decoding in the range of .50 to .68 (Snow, Tabors, & Dickinson, 2001).

The remarkable stability of performance in language skills, phonemic awareness, and print-related knowledge now has been traced back to the preschool years (McCardle, Scarborough, & Catts, 2001; Scarborough, 2001). Even though there is some difference of opinion regarding the long-term interrelationships among these three systems of knowledge (Dickinson & McCabe, 2001; Dickinson, McCabe, Anastasopoulos, Peisner-Feinberg & Poe, in press), there is unanimity of opinion that the preschool years provide an optimal time to build children's language, phonemic awareness, and knowledge of print and how it functions.

The Important Role of the Family

Many important recent studies have examined the development of language and literacy-related skills in the preschool by examining children in home and out-of-home care settings and found significant evidence of the impact of home factors on children's development during the preschool years (NICHD, 1999, 2000, 2001, 2002; Sameroff et al., 1993). For example, the NICHD study of child-care reported analyses of the impact of home and child care on children's development at ages 15, 24, and 36 months that provide evidence of the growing impact of home characteristics on children over this age period. Measures of children's school readiness and expressive and receptive language were found to be moderately affected by the quality of the home environment. Small to modest effects on these abilities were found for the quality of mother's stimulation and receptive vocabularies (NICHD, 2000; Snow, Tabors, & Dickinson, 2001). As children move from the preschool years into school, home effects persist (Leseman & de Jong, 1998; Peisner-Feinberg et al., 2001; Snow, Tabors, & Dickinson, 2001).

Clearly, if we wish to have optimal impact on children's long-term language and literacy development, we need to strive to enhance the ability of families to support their child's development. Though it can be extremely difficult to reach families, the potential for having a lasting effect is considerable. There is some indication that patterns of family interactions are relatively stable over time (Hart & Risley, 1995; Leseman & de Jong, 1998), whereas the quality of classrooms children experience varies from preschool to the school years and from 1 year to the next (Peisner-Feinberg et al., 2001). Unfortunately, evaluations of the effectiveness of family literacy programs that seek to raise the performance of children by working with families have been mixed and somewhat disappointing (Wasik et al., 2001). In particular, evaluations of federal programs designed for low-income populations have found only limited evidence as to their effectiveness at enhancing the school readiness and cognitive development of preschool-age children and their parents.

The research base on family-focused programs is small but growing. Smith (1995) provides a discussion of the characteristics and implementation of several national two-generation programs, and Blank (1997) reports on six small-scale two-generation service projects and draws conclusions about implementation problems with associated implications for a two-generation theory. Recently, evaluations of some of the largest and most visible family-focused programmatic efforts have been published. These include national studies of the Comprehensive Child Development Program (Goodson, Layzer, St.Pierre, Bernstein, & Lopez, 2000), the New Chance Program (Quint, Bos, & Polit, 1997), and the Even Start Family Literacy Program (St.Pierre et al., 1995). Evidence from these studies supports the following conclusions.

Family-focused programs initially increase the rate of participation of children and their parents in relevant social and educational services. However, these differences in service use diminish or disappear over time. Because participation in educational services often does not differ greatly for intervention versus control groups, it is not surprising that these studies find that family-focused programs have small or no short-term effects on a wide set of measures of child development. The same studies show that family-focused programs do have scattered short-term effects on measures of parenting including time spent with child, parent teaching skills, expectations for child's success, attitudes about child-rearing, and parent–child interactions. Though some of these programs have large short-term effects on attainment of a GED, these accomplishments are not accompanied by effects on tests of adult literacy. There are few effects on income or employment and no evidence of effects on the psychological status of participating mothers as measured by level of depression, self-esteem, or use of social supports. Finally, correlational analyses generally show that amount of participation is positively related to test gains and GED attainment.

This assessment indicates that family-focused programs, as currently designed, have quite limited effects over a 2- to 5-year period. It says little about anticipated long-term effects, but many researchers believe that it is not reasonable to expect long-term effects in the absence of substantially large short-term effects.

Given the importance of families to children's long-term development, we must continue the search for more effective ways to enhance their ability to foster children's growth. However, we must also take full advantage of classrooms, the other dominant means of intervening to help children. Later we consider the extent to which center-based programs currently employ effective strategies for helping parents foster their child's literacy development.

THE IMPORTANCE OF HIGH-QUALITY CLASSROOMS

If our primary goal is to ensure that children enter school with the language skills, attitudes toward books and literacy, and knowledge about print that are needed for success in the early grades, then there is considerable evidence that we need to provide children high-quality center-based early childhood experiences. For decades researchers have sought to determine the impact of center-based preschool experiences on children's development. Barnett (1995, 2001) has summarized the results of studies of the long-term effects of child care on children's development and concludes that there is convincing evidence of both short- and long-term benefits from receiving high-quality care (see also, Bowman, Donovan, & Burns, 2001). The enduring effects of high-quality interventions now have been found to extend into the adult years (Burchinal et al., 2000; Burchinal, Lee, & Ramey, 1989; Campbell & Ramey, 1994; Schweinhart, Barnes, Weikart, Barnett, & Epstein, 1993; Wasik, Ramey, Bryant, & Sparling, 1990).

More recently, a number of studies have examined the impact of variations in the quality of standard community-based classrooms on children's growth. Studies of the impact of programs during the preschool era have found evidence of the impact of classroom quality. The NICHD study (2000, 2002) of child care found clear evidence of the impact of classroom quality on language and cognitive performance during the preschool years after the effects of homes were controlled. Center-based programs were found to offer the most support and to have modest effects on children's growth. Significantly, this study found the strongest effect sizes when they contrasted the top-quartile with bottom-quartile measures of quality of care. Such a comparison revealed a large effect size of .48 on language comprehension at age 36 months. Another study of development during the preschool years was conducted by Burchinal and her colleagues (2000), who analyzed the development of a sample of African American children and found a relationship between higher levels of child care quality in the first 3 years of life and better performance on child outcomes (including cognitive, language, and communication measures) after controlling for the impact of individual and family characteristics.

Two recently released studies have linked the quality of children's experiences during the preschool years to subsequent schooling success. The Cost Quality and Outcomes study (Peisner-Feinberg et al., 2001) followed a large group of children into second grade. Using two measures of classroom quality, a composite measure of quality and a measure of teacher–child closeness, this team found evidence of small to modest effects on vocabulary, math, and reading at grade 2. Using extensive data on the nature of language experiences in the classrooms and homes of a sample of low-income children, researchers of the Home-School Study of Language and Literacy found evidence of sizable effects of classroom experiences at the end of kindergarten after controlling for home experiences (Dickinson, 2001b, 2001c). An analysis of the growth trajectories of these children up to grade four revealed the lasting impact of the preschool years, as the variance in children's kindergarten levels of performance associated with variations in the quality of their classroom experiences continued to account for significant variance at the end of the fourth grade (Roach & Snow, 2000).

Thus, the evidence is clear that children's growth during the preschool years is implicated in their long-term literacy success, that variations in quality in community-based programs can have measurable effects that linger at least into the middle grades on children's literacy, and that carefully designed interventions can have effects that are still evident in the early adult years.

CURRENT APPROACHES TO DESCRIBING CLASSROOM PRACTICES

Although researchers have provided evidence that variability in the quality of care can make a difference, the size of the effects associated with variation in the quality of community-based classrooms has tended to be small to modest. Taken together, these results suggest that, if we are to have sizable effects on children, we must substantially enhance the extent to which classrooms support children's literacy development. The need for such improvement comes as no surprise given the changes in how literacy has been viewed in early childhood circles. In the final 2 decades of the 20th century there was a major shift in our understanding of the origins of literacy, a shift that resulted in major changes in notions of what is appropriate practice in early childhood classrooms (Dickinson, 2002). Changes of such magnitude take time to implement, as is evidenced by the confusion of many front-line staff about the appropriateness of different literacy-related practices and by a lag in the content of standards related to literacy that are employed for accreditation of programs.

If we are to attempt to construct classrooms that provide optimal support for language and literacy development, it is critical that we have a clear conception of the dimensions that are key. Therefore, we now discuss some of the dimensions likely to be important, starting with approaches commonly seen in research in the early childhood field and then shifting to discuss a dimensional approach that grows from a language and literacy perspective.

Traditional Early Childhood Approach

The studies reviewed earlier as well as others have generally described classroom quality in terms of two broad sets of variables, structural and process. Structural features of classrooms include variables such as teacher–child ratio and teacher education. Such variables have repeatedly been found to be important predictors of children's development, though it is not certain the exact means by which essentially static descriptions of classrooms are translated into the dynamics that affect children. Of the many possible mechanisms that may be identified, it seems probable that one dominant pathway must be through the manner in which teacher–child conversations are affected by factors such as class size and educational background. These pathways may not be as direct as one would expect.

Let us consider educational background briefly. A mechanism by which education may result in changed practices may be through shifts that are engendered in teacher's beliefs about development. A recent study of variables that describe different dimensions of classroom quality concluded that the effects of education are mediated by teachers' beliefs (Abbott-Shim, Lambert, & McCarty, 2000; McCarty, Lambert, & Abbott-Shim, 2001). This finding still does not take us to the point of understanding how beliefs translate into actions, but it may well be that more child-centered belief systems lead teachers to engage in conversations that are more sensitively attuned to children, the type of semantically contingent talk that has been found to foster growth in classrooms (Dickinson, 2001c). Because educational level is associated with how mothers converse with children as they read books and converse in informal settings (Heath, 1984; Leseman & de Jong, 1998), it may be that teachers' conversational strategies also change as a result of taking courses on early childhood education.

Classroom Process Variables

Typically classroom processes have been assessed using the *Early Childhood Environment Rating Scale* (ECERS) (Harms, Clifford, & Cryer, 1998). This comprehensive measure captures many aspects of classrooms that have long been recognized as being important to supporting development. These dimensions include the nature of teacher–child conversations, the quality of activities provided children, and the emotional climate of the classroom. Because most studies use total ECERS scores, it is hard to be certain which scales carry the most weight, but there is some indication that the Language and Reasoning subscale, when used alone, can have predictive power (Dickinson, 2001c; Zill, Resnick, & McKey, 1999). The importance of this scale is significant because it provides a relatively straightforward way of seeing links between the variable and classroom dynamics.

The importance of the quality and frequency of teacher–child conversations also has been examined using coding systems designed to assess the quality of interactions. For example, Howes and Smith (1995) employed a system developed by Howes and found that scores reflecting more intense and effective interactions were related to more high-level cognitive activity by children. The NICHD research team also devised a measure of teacher–child interaction that it created specifically to assess the quality of interactions and found that it helped predict children's development (NICHD, 2000, 2001).

Classroom quality measures also have included consideration of the nature of the materials available, reflecting the value placed on child-initiated activities. For example, the *Classroom Profile* (Abbot-Shim & Sibley, 1998), another well-established measure of classroom quality, has a scale that describes the amount of variety of learning materials available. Scores on this scale have been found to help predict the language and literacy of children in Head Start (Dickinson & Sprague, 2001).

The importance of the emotional climate of classrooms, an aspect of classrooms long valued by early childhood teachers, also has recently been supported by the finding of the Cost Quality and Outcomes study that the quality of the teacher–child relationship, as rated by the teacher, has effects on children's development that can still be detected in second grade (Peisner-Feinberg et al., 2001). The importance of the relationship between the teacher and the child has been documented in a second study conducted in Head Start, lending further support to the importance of this dimension of classrooms (Peisner-Feinberg & Burchinal, 1997; Peisner-Feinberg et al., 2001). We can only speculate about the mechanisms by which the closer relationship between the teacher and the child comes to have enduring effects on children. Once again, one possible pathway is through the nature of teacher–child conversations. When teachers feel closer to children, they may talk with children more, and their conversations may more often touch on topics of importance to the child. Also, it may be that teachers feel free to challenge such children's thinking more because they feel confident about the quality of their relationship.

Thus, established approaches to describing classroom quality have repeatedly revealed the importance of a variety of features of classrooms, including structural variables (especially teacher–child ratio and teacher education) and process variables that include warm, engaged teacher–child interactions, close teacher–child relationships, and varied materials that are accessible and clearly organized.

A Language and Literacy Perspective: Dimensions of Classroom Quality

Though early childhood researchers have been devising one approach to examining classrooms, researchers from a language and literacy orientation have viewed classrooms through different lenses. This perspective is relatively new in early childhood settings and there is far less consensus regarding which variables to consider and how to examine them. We now briefly discuss dimensions of classrooms that this perspective deems to be important.

The language and literacy perspective, like the traditional early childhood approach, places primary emphasis on the quality of teacher–child conversations. It is distinctive in that specific aspects of conversations are highlighted. These features include responding to children in ways that build on and extend what children are saying, engaging in extended interactions during unstructured times but not in group conversations, challenging children's intellectual capacities, and using varied vocabulary. In a study that examined the fine-grained details of teacher–child conversations, these conversational features were combined into composite variables. Regression analyses that controlled for home demographics found these classroom variables added sizable variance to prediction of the language and early literacy scores of children from low-income homes (Dickinson, 2001c; Tabors, Snow, & Dickinson, 2001).

The dimension of early childhood classrooms that has received the most attention by those working from a language and literacy perspective is book reading. Dickinson, McCabe, and Anastasopoulos (2003) recently noted that these studies have examined varied aspects of the use of books in classrooms. They suggest that, to fully understand the impact of book use, researchers should examine book reading along the following five dimensions: (a) the nature of the book area, (b) the amount of time provided for adult–child book reading, (c) the extent to which available books are linked to the curriculum of the classroom, (d) the quality of full-group book-reading events, and (e) the extent to which teachers support parents' abilities to effectively read books with their children.

Each of these proposed dimensions has been considered to one degree or another in different studies, but we are far from knowing if all of these variables play important roles to supporting children's growth. Though the picture is unclear for some of these dimensions, there is strong evidence that the nature of teacher–child interactions during book reading can have measurable effects on children's language learning (Dickinson, 2001a; Dickinson & Smith, 1994). In addition, intervention research has shown that increased access to books and improvements in the quality of interactions as books are read can have at least short-term beneficial effects on children's language development (Arnold & Whitehurst, 1994; Duke, 2000; Karweit, 1989, 1994; Whitehurst & Lonigan, 1998, 2001). Of course, a massive literature on home book-reading practices (see reviews by Bus, van IJzendoorn, & Pellegrini, 1995; Scarborough & Dobrich, 1994) as well as work involving home interventions using books (Whitehurst & Longian, 1998, 2001) provides support for the dimension related to classroom support for book reading in the home (also see Morrow, this volume).

Even though there have been extensive efforts to link children's learning to book-reading practices, we know relatively little about the impact of other literacy-related classroom practices on children's development. The Home-School Study of Language and Literacy (Dickinson, 2001b) provides one source of information. When children were 3 and 4 years old, classrooms were observed and teachers and children were simultaneously audiotaped throughout the day. Conversational variables were by far the strongest predictors of children's growth; however, measures of the quality of curriculum and of support for writing also were related to children's literacy development.

Summary

So far we have established that classroom quality can support children's language and literacy development, but that the amount of impact of classrooms is limited. To better understand why this might be, we have reviewed briefly dimensions of classrooms that are considered when quality has been measured. We have noted that traditional and language- and literacy-oriented approaches both highlight the importance of teacher–child interaction, with the language and literacy perspective placing special emphasis on the extent to which conversations are sustained and intellectually engaging and on the variety of vocabulary used. Both approaches also value the availability of learning materials, but the literacy approach highlights literacy-related materials and practices. Finally, the traditional approach has emphasized the emotional dimensions of teacher–child relationships whereas the literacy-oriented approach typically has not, although there is some evidence that more positive affect is found among those teachers who provide stronger support for language (Densmore, Dickinson, & Smith, 1995) (see Pianta, this volume). We now will employ this framework for considering classroom quality as we review studies of classrooms.

WHAT LEVEL OF QUALITY IS TYPICAL IN STANDARD EARLY CHILDHOOD CLASSROOMS?

We now will draw upon the two traditions for studying quality in early childhood classrooms that we just described, concentrating on those aspects of classrooms that research and theory indicate are the strongest candidates for supporting children's language and literacy development. Our review is not exhaustive; rather it is intended to provide a sense of the broader picture. As will become apparent, when specific dimensions of quality are examined in this fashion, we find many areas where significant improvements over current practice could occur. We first will briefly review patterns found in a range of Head Start and other classrooms serving low-income families. We then consider the nature of support found in Even Start classrooms, classrooms that are part of this important federally funded family literacy program.

Head Start and Other Programs for Low-Income Families

Over that past decade we have carried out studies in roughly 150 classrooms throughout New England. One of these studies, the Home-School Study of Language and Literacy Development (Dickinson & Smith, 1994; Dickinson & Tabors, 2001) provides extensive details about the importance of certain kinds of language interactions. It is not feasible to detail the range of language behaviors identified; suffice it to say that those dimensions of classroom conversation that were most predictive of children's growth (e.g., cognitively challenging extended conversations, varied vocabulary) were among the least common kinds of conversation seen. A subsequent examination of teacher–child conversation using a time-sampling methodology with a different sample again revealed that teachers rarely (15% or less) engage in conversations that extend and deepen topics and rarely discuss or explain the meanings of new words. This study also found that the vast majority (79% at 3 years, 72% at 4) of teacher talk during book reading is devoted to issues that make few cognitive demands of the children. Mostly, teachers focus on organization of the task, simple feedback, and naming activities. Relatively little talk makes higher cognitive demands of children (17% at three, 26.6% at 4). Thus, the features of conversations most predictive of later growth are those least commonly observed.

We also have extensive data on book-reading practices from 166 observations in 100 classrooms (in 69 cases classrooms were visited twice). We found that the time allocated for book reading is limited. In 66 cases no book reading at all was observed and in 100 observations where book reading did occur, the average amount of time spent reading books was 9.56 minutes ($SD = 4.17$). In only 36% of the observations did adults ever read to children in small groups or individually. We also found disappointing results related to the provision of books linked to a theme, an indication of the extent to which books are integral to the curricular life of classrooms. In only 19% of the classrooms were there three or more books related to a current curricular theme. Also, in roughly two-thirds of all classrooms, no books were to be found in varied activity areas (e.g., science, dramatic play, blocks).

Finally, we have some data on the extent to which teachers support parental efforts to use books with their children. One item on the classroom observation tool, Early Language and Literacy Classroom Observation (Smith, Dickinson, Sangeorge, & Anastasopoulos, 2002), assesses this aspect of book use. For the 91 classrooms for which we have data, the mean rating on a scale of 1 (minimal evidence of home support) to 5 (strong evidence) was 2.78 ($SD = 1.39$). This rating indicates that, in most classrooms observed, there was only some evidence that home support for children's literacy was considered integral to classroom-based programs and goals. That is, interactions between home and school included some information about ways to support children's language, literacy, and learning, and the families were provided materials that supported children's literacy skills that could be understood and used by families. However, much was missing. There was not strong evidence of regular conversation about children's first- and second-language learning or literacy acquisition, no evidence of helping parent's facilitation of their children's learning by building on families' social/cultural experiences, and no evidence that teachers encouraged families to seek out and use community resources.

Thus, although broad-gauged examinations of classroom quality find that variability in quality supports development, when we examine classroom practices through the magnifying lens of the language and literacy perspective, we find considerable room for improvement in classrooms that serve low-income children. We now turn to consider the early childhood classrooms associated with Even Start.

Family Literacy Programs

Family literacy programs represent an important model for improving the literacy skills, cognitive development, and school readiness of young children. Unfortunately, large-scale studies of the effectiveness of family literacy programs have found only limited impacts on children when compared to children in randomly assigned control groups (St.Pierre et al., 1995; St.Pierre, Ricciuti et al., 2002; Wagner & Clayton, 1998). One hypothesis that would at least partially account for these findings is that the early childhood classroom experience provided through family literacy programs may be relatively weak. This contention is supported by data from the recently completed national evaluation of the Even Start program, the nation's largest family literacy initiative. This study compared Head Start and Even Start classrooms to control group classrooms. Each cohort was found to show modest gains in vocabulary, with gains associated with classroom quality, and the second cohort showed growth on a measure of early literacy (Zill, Resnick, & McKey, 1999; Zill, McKey, & Tarullo, 2002). Thus, if Even Start classrooms achieve parity with Head Start, it is possible that they are providing some support for improved growth of language and literacy skills.

There is little difference between the daily classroom activities offered to children in Even Start, Head Start, and control classrooms. The national Even Start evaluation (St.Pierre, Ricciuti, et al., 2002) surveyed teachers of children who were randomly assigned to be in Even Start or in a control group in 18 different Even Start projects. Teachers were asked to report on the kinds of classroom activities that were available to children on a daily or almost daily basis. Almost all Even Start children in center-based classrooms have many different kinds of literacy-related activities available to them on a daily or almost daily basis including the number concepts or counting (95%), letters of the alphabet or words (94%), and reading stories (90%). Though we do not have systematic research evidence about the kinds of teacher–child interactions that occur in family literacy classrooms, the data cited here show that roughly the same percentage of children who were randomly assigned to a control group found their way into preschool classrooms that offered the same kinds of broad literacy-related activities on a daily or almost daily basis.

Data also are available on the daily activities conducted in Head Start classrooms (U.S. Department of Health and Human Services, 2001). On the whole, teachers of children in Even Start and Head Start classrooms reported much the same frequency of literacy-related activities. The one exception is that Even Start classrooms work on letters of the alphabet and words more often than Head Start classrooms (94 versus 69%). On the other hand, Head Start classrooms are more likely than Even Start classrooms to do nonliteracy activities such as indoor physical activities (90 versus 70%), outdoor physical activities (93 versus 74%), health (93 versus 63%) and science (83 versus 58%).

The Overall Environment of Even Start and Head Start Classrooms Looks Quite Similar

As part of the national Even Start evaluation, one early childhood classroom in each of 18 Even Start projects was observed for approximately 3 hours in order to complete the *Early Childhood Environment Rating Scale* revised edition (Harms, Clifford, & Cryer, 1998). The average ECERS score for 18 Even Start projects is 4.9, indicating an overall rating of good quality. Subscale scores vary somewhat across Even Start classrooms. Three subscales (space/furnishings, personal care, and interaction) have average scores of 5.0 or greater, indicating good or better quality. Of particular relevance to family literacy programs, the language-reasoning subscale is a measure of the books available for children and how those books are used, as well as the communication and language skills that are used and encouraged in the classroom. The average score on this subscale is 4.8, indicating that about half of the classrooms were rated as good quality or better on this subscale, and half were rated below good. Classrooms that had ratings below 5.0 generally do not have a wide variety of books and other language materials available to children for a large portion of the day. Furthermore, reasoning and communication skills are not frequently encouraged by the staff.

The national Even Start evaluation also investigated the extent to which early childhood classrooms had books and areas for book reading, as well as writing areas and tools for writing or displays of children's written work. By using the *Literacy Checklist* (Smith et al., 2002) we found that all of the early childhood education classrooms that were observed have a large number of books displayed and available for children to use. In all of the classrooms, there is a specific area set aside only for book reading, and the books are appropriate for a range of reading levels. However, books are available in at least one other part of the classroom such as in a dramatic play or blocks area in only 47% of the classrooms.

Eighty-seven percent of the rooms have a distinct area set up for writing, stocked with paper and writing tools (93%). However, only 47% of the classrooms have templates or other tools to help children form letters, and evidence of writing around the room is rare. Only 26% of the rooms have examples of children's writing or dictations on display, and few rooms (less than 20%) have writing tools or props in multiple areas (e.g., note pads in dramatic play area). When subscale scores are computed for the *Literacy Checklist* we see that Even Start classrooms lag behind Head Start classrooms on the Books subscale (means of 9.7 versus 11.1, respectively), the Writing subscale (means of 8.8 versus 10.4, respectively), and the Total score (means of 18.5 versus 21.6, respectively) for the Literacy Checklist. The differences in scores between Even Start and Head Start classrooms are consistent, but not very large, on the order of 1/3 to 1/2 Standard Deviation (or SD) in size. This means that, compared with Head Start, Even Start classrooms have somewhat fewer books available to children and are less likely to have writing areas and tools for writing or displays of children's written work.

Taken as a whole, these data show that the early childhood education classrooms run by family literacy projects are not much different from the classrooms attended by children assigned to a control group or from Head Start classrooms. To the extent that the observed projects provide good examples of family literacy practices, it will be difficult to find improved child performance in family literacy programs solely on the basis of the early childhood experience offered to participating children.

Family literacy program theory hypothesizes that positive impacts on children will result not only from participation in early childhood education but also from a family's full participation in cross-generational services including adult education and parenting education for parents and parent–child activities for parents and children together. However, unless the quality of those services is exemplary, we should not expect to see significantly improved child performance.

IMPROVING THE QUALITY OF SUPPORT FOR LANGUAGE AND LITERACY

The data we have reviewed on programs that serve low-income children make clear the need for significant improvements in the quality of support for early literacy development. Over the past 6 years Dickinson has been engaged in a program of research designed to achieve this goal. These efforts provide some promising directions for improving classroom quality while simultaneously revealing some challenges that must be met if we are to enhance substantially program quality and the impact of preschool on the language and literacy of children from low-income homes.

Improving Classroom Quality

Dickinson and a team from the Center for Children and Families at Education Development Center (EDC) have been striving to improve the quality of literacy support in Head Start and community child-care agencies through a credit-bearing academic course. Many early childhood teachers have very limited higher education and those with college-level coursework often did not have courses that dealt with recent research on early literacy. Therefore, we have developed a course called the Literacy Environment Enrichment Program (LEEP), which teachers and their supervisors take as a team. The course provides basic information about early language and literacy development and the assignments require teachers to apply the material being learned to classroom practice. Supervisors support teachers on their coursework and engage in many of the same assignments as teachers, while also learning techniques of effective supervision. At several points during the year supervisors use tools provided by LEEP to conduct observations and engage in follow-up conversation with their partner teachers.

Researchers from EDC have been studying the impact of LEEP on teaching practices for 3 years using instruments designed to capture differences in support for language and literacy development. Forty teachers who completed the course were recently compared to 62 comparison group teachers who were drawn from comparable programs using selection criteria similar to those employed to identify teachers to take the course. Regression analyses that controlled for teacher demographic characteristics (e.g., years of experience, college courses, racial background) and fall scores on our assessment tools, found highly significant effects ($p < .001$) for course participation, with changes of more than a standard deviation on some measures. Analysis of the size of these effects indicates that they can be classified as "large" to "very large." Changes of this magnitude have been seen for three waves of teachers, leading us to feel reasonably confident that classroom quality can be enhanced through effective in-service coursework. Furthermore, an ongoing qualitative study of teachers and supervisors indicates that changes set in motion during this course persist for up to 2 years (Kloosterman, 2001, 2002).

Of course the ultimate test of the effectiveness of an intervention is its ability to raise the achievement levels of children. Evaluations of LEEP to date have examined children only during the year when their teachers are taking the course. Children are pretested in the fall (October, November) and posttested in the spring (April, May). The course runs from early November through late March; thus, teachers are only beginning to learn about and adopt effective practices during the year. In spite of the fact that children do not receive a full school year of enhanced instruction, we have found significant effects on receptive vocabulary (PPVT-III, Dunn & Dunn, 1997) and weaker but still significant effects on print knowledge and phonemic awareness. These effect sizes are determined to fall in the "small" effect range. These findings are a cause for hope as they demonstrate that enhanced classroom quality can translate into much-needed acceleration of children's growth. However, the fact that children from low-income families have so far to go, and, to date, only a modest impact has been found on measures of literacy, points to the need for further effort to boost children's growth. One way that children's growth might be further accelerated is if their child's classroom teacher helps parents adopt more effective practices.

Teachers as Agents of Change in Literacy Practices of Families

The classroom teacher is potentially a very powerful force of improvement of literacy. As we have noted, skilled teachers can provide classroom experiences of great significance while also helping parents adopt more effective practices. If teachers are to support parents, they need to engage parents in conversations about aspects of family life that are central to supporting children's literacy development and teach parents basic information about literacy. Unfortunately, responses we have received from students enrolled in LEEP have led us to realize that many classroom teachers may need considerable support if they are to be effective in fostering home literacy practices. Recently we have asked teachers to develop a profile of one child throughout the course. One facet of this project is to interview a family member on three occasions to learn about the child's home experiences and learn of possible implications of home practices for her work with the child in the classroom.

The first assignment, given early in the course, asked teachers to develop an interview for parents about aspects of the child's home experiences that relate to the nature of support for language and literacy provided in the home. Initially we asked teachers to consider a broad range of topics about family culture and did not tell them what to ask about in particular. Teachers' responses provide some insight into the extent of the manner in which many preschool teachers who work with low-income families may communicate with families when they attempt to discuss literacy-related practices.

One common response was for the teachers to focus on the social and emotional climate of the home, sometimes to the exclusion of considering any issues more directly linked to literacy development. For example, one teacher wrote, " What is important for this family is to stay together, love each other, and be there for each other." Another commented, "This family stresses being obedient and that being respectful and obedient leads to being a good student." And another summary analysis was, "From the conversation it was confirmed that the parents spend quality time with the child." Such failures to deal with issues related to language and literacy were surprisingly common. The extent to which some teachers did not understand the nature of relevant information is starkly indicated by the summary comment of a teacher when asked to reflect on what she learned that was different from what she anticipated from the family. She said, "Something different was that the entire family never buys clothes without pockets. It's almost like a tradition. Even the child looks for pockets in clothes she likes!" When teachers did address language and literacy, their comments typically were vague. One teacher wrote, "Very single-worded mother. Loves her child and wants to see him go places. Got the impression that literacy is strong at home." In these responses we again see the centrality of the social environment, now combined with global characterization of the general quality of home support for literacy. Statements about families having "strong" language and literacy practices were common, whereas details about issues such as the frequency of the book reading, who read these books, which books were read, where the family obtained their reading materials, and the language used to read were rarely to be found.

For the second assignment related to writing a portrait of the child's development and home experiences, we gave teachers a set of questions from a form we developed in collaboration with a Head Start program (Dickinson & Lewkowicz, 1997). The form includes a set of introductory questions about the child's home environment (number of adults, size of the home, safety) and then has a number of queries about what the child does alone and with parents (e.g., book reading, TV viewing, favorite toys and games). In spite of our effort to focus teachers on specific home practices linked to language and literacy, when they wrote their profile of the family, some teachers still were primarily interested in the introductory questions about the home environment and did not focus on issues related more directly to literacy. For example, one teacher stated, "What I noticed from the interview is that Daniel does not get to go outside much. Children this age need lots of play or running time. Daniel lives in a very tough neighborhood with drug dealers and people hanging around. With this information, now I understand why Daniel has so much energy and wants to run and play. He also has a hard time playing with other children—maybe because he is isolated." Another teacher commented,

"I learned about how many people Shawn and his mother live with. We were not aware of this at the center. Since it appears that it is crowded, this is a child that may need quiet spaces for a while until he is ready to join in!"

On the other hand, with concrete data in hand, a number of teachers' responses did manage to provide the broad picture of the child's situation with also addressing dimensions of the home that included specific practices linked to literacy. The following is an example:

> This child lives in an extended family setting and is not experiencing a lot of child/adult interactions due to mom's frequent absence from the home due to her work schedule. The child also spends a lot of time watching television after school and in the evening. As a teacher, I will now plan more one on one child/teacher interactions. I will plan to provide books from the classroom lending library and encourage the mother to encourage other family members to read to the child. I will also encourage the mother to spend quality time with her child on her days off and to visit the public library (several blocks away from her home). I will send picture books and writing materials home at intervals.

Certainly literacy is grounded in the social fabric of families' lives (Barton & Hamilton, 1998; Street, 1984), but when the traditional concern of early childhood teachers for the social and emotional welfare of the child is combined with limited understanding of language and literacy, the result can be a failure to think clearly about those aspects of the home that are most directly linked to supporting language, intellectual, and literacy growth. The tendency of teachers to lose focus on language and literacy when thinking about families highlights a major challenge. In order for teachers to provide high-quality classrooms and help families support their child's language and literacy development, teachers need to be able to articulate their own pedagogy. For this to occur teachers need professional development about language and early literacy development to help in gaining information from families, to analyze this information to learn what families might do to better support their child, and to understand lessons it may hold for improvements in classroom practice. When such professional development is not possible, developers of family literacy interventions need to be aware of potential limitations in the capacities of many preschool teachers to engage in effective conversations with families about literacy.

In closing, we are heartened by the fact that the nation has realized the need to bolster the language, literacy, and intellectual development of young children. As we turn our attention to the needs of children from populations that historically have struggled with the academic demands of public schools, the magnitude of the gap between those with and those without economic, linguistic, and social advantages has become increasingly apparent. Honest recognition of this gap and of our current limited ability to bridge it is a first step. Now the challenge is to identify the settings and strategies that provide the most leverage for efforts to bolster children's growth. Certainly early childhood classrooms are one such location. We believe that we desperately need to find ways to create classrooms in which children's language, literacy, and intellectual growth are stimulated in ways that enable rapid and sustained growth along multiple dimensions. Though this challenge might seem to be stating the obvious, the fact is that our nation has not taken seriously the importance of the preschool years. And, by in large, early childhood educators have been ambivalent about the extent to which early childhood programs for children from low-income families should bolster children's intellectual and academic growth while also encouraging play and fostering social and emotional growth. If policymakers, researchers, family educators, and early childhood educators can acknowledge the distance we have to travel and can agree on common goals, we can at least start working on this ambitious and critically important endeavor.

ACKNOWLEDGMENTS

The research reported in this paper includes data collected by the New England Quality Research Center, based at Education Development Center, which was supported by grants 90YD0094 and 90-YD-0015 by the Agency for Children and Families. Data reported also were collected with support from the Office of Education Research and Improvement, R305T990312-00, the Interagency Educational Research Initiative, REC-9979948, and the Spencer Foundation. All of this work was carried out at the Center for Children & Families at Education Development Center. We especially thank the teachers and children in the Head Start Programs where we worked for their patience and support of our research.

REFERENCES

Abbott-Shim, M., Lambert, R., & McCarty, F. (2000). Structural model of Head Start classroom quality. *Early Childhood Research Quarterly, 15*(1), 115–134.

Abbott-Shim, M., & Sibley, A. (1987, 1998). *Assessment profile for early childhood programs.* Atlanta, GA: Quality Assist.

Arnold, D. S., & Whitehurst, G. J. (1994). Accelerating language development through picture book reading: A summary of dialogic reading and its effects. In D. K. Dickinson (Ed.), *Bridges to literacy: Approaches to supporting child and family literacy* (pp. 103–128). Cambridge, MA: Blackwell.

Barnett, W. S. (1995). Long-term effects of early childhood programs on cognitive and school outcomes. *The future of children: Long-term outcomes of early childhood programs* (Vol. 5, No. 3, pp. 25–50). Los Altos, CA: Center for the Future of Children, the David and Lucile Packard Foundation.

Barnett, W. S. (2001). Preschool education for economically disadvantged children: Effects on reading achievement and related outcomes. In S. Neuman & D. K. Dickinson (Eds.), *Handbook of early literacy development.* New York: Guilford Press.

Barton, D., & Hamilton, M. (1998). Local literacies: Reading and writing in one community. New York: Routledge.

Baydar, N., Brooks-Gunn, J., & Furstenberg, F. F. (1993). Early warning signs of functional illiteracy: Predictors in childhood and adolescence. *Child Development, 64,* 815–829.

Blank, H. (1997). *Theory meets practice: A report on six small-scale two-generation service projects.* New York: Foundation for Child Development.

Bowman, B. T., Donovan, M. S., & Burns, M. S. (Eds.). (2001). *Eager to learn: Educating our preschoolers.* Washington, DC: National Academy Press.

Burchinal, M. R., Lee, M. W., & Ramey, C. T. (1989). Type of day-care and preschool intellectual development in disadvantaged children. *Child Development, 60,* 128–137.

Burchinal, M. R., Roberts, J. E., Riggins, Jr., R., Zeisel, S. A., Neebe, E., & Bryant, D. (2000). Relating quality of center-based child care to early cognitive and language development longitudinally. *Child Development, 71,* 339–357.

Bus, A. G., van IJzendoorn, M. H., & Pellegrini, A. D. (1995). Joint book reading makes for success in learning to read: A meta-analysis on intergenerational transmission of literacy. *Review of Educational Research, 65*(1), 1–21.

Campbell, F. A., & Ramey, C. T. (1994). Effects of early intervention on intellectual and academic achievement: A follow-up study of children from low-income families. *Child Development, 65,* 684–698.

Cunningham, A. E., & Stanovich, K. E. (1997). Early reading acquisition and its relation to reading experience and ability 10 years later. *Developmental Psychology, 33*(6), 934–945.

Densmore, A., Dickinson, D. K., & Smith, M. W. (April, 1995). *The socio-emotional content of teacher-child interaction in preschool settings serving low-income children.* Paper presented at the annual meeting of the American Educational Research Association, San Francisco, CA.

Dickinson, D. K. (2002). Shifting images of developmentally appropriate practice as seen through different lenses. *Educational Researcher, 31*(1).

Dickinson, D. K. (2001a). Book reading in preschool classrooms: Is recommended practice common? In D. K. Dickinson & P. O. Tabors (Eds.), *Beginning literacy with language: Young children learning at home and school* (pp. 175–203). Baltimore, MD: Brookes.

Dickinson, D. K. (2001b). Large-group and free-play times: Conversational settings supporting language and literacy development. In D. K. Dickinson & P. O. Tabors (Eds.), *Beginning literacy with language: Young children learning at home and school* (pp. 223–255). Baltimore, MD: Brookes.

Dickinson, D. K. (2001c). Putting the pieces together: The impact of preschool on children's language and literacy development in kindergarten. In D. K. Dickinson & P. O. Tabors (Eds.), *Beginning literacy with language: Young children learning at home and school* (pp. 257–287). Baltimore, MD: Brookes.

Dickinson, D. K., & Lewkowicz, C. (1997). *The child's educational opportunities.* Newton, MA: EDC, Inc.

Dickinson, D. K., & McCabe, A. (2001). Bringing it all together: The multiple origins, skills and environmental supports of early literacy. *Learning Disabilities Research and Practice, 16*(4), 186–202.

Dickinson, D. K., McCabe, A., & Anastasopoulos, L. (2003). A framework for examining book reading in early childhood classrooms. In A. van Kleeck, S. A. Stahl, & E. B. Bauer (Eds.), *On reading books to children: Parents and teachers* (pp. 95–113). Hillsdale, NJ: Lawrence Erlbaum Associates.

Dickinson, D. K., McCabe, A., Anastasopoulos, L., Peisner-Feinberg, E., & Poe, M. (2003). The comprehensive language approach to early literacy: The interrelationships among vocabulary, phonological sensitivity, and print knowledge among preschool-aged children. *Journal of Educational Psychology, 95*, 465–481.

Dickinson, D. K., & Smith, M. W. (1994). Long-term effects of preschool teachers' book readings on low-income children's vocabulary and story comprehension. *Reading Research Quarterly, 29*, 104–122.

Dickinson, D. K, & Sprague, K. (2001). The nature and impact of early childhood care environments on the language and early literacy development of children from low-income families. In S. Neuman and D. K. Dickinson (Eds.), *Handbook of early literacy development* (pp. 263–292). New York: Guilford Press.

Dickinson, D. K., & Tabors, P. O. (Eds.). (2001). *Beginning literacy with language: Young children learning at home and in school.* Baltimore, MD: Brookes Publishing Company.

Duke, N. K. (2000). Print environments and experiences offered to first-grade students in very low- and very high-SES school districts. *Reading Research Quarterly, 35,* 456–457.

Dunn, L. M., & Dunn, L. M. (1997). *Peabody Picture Voacabulary Test-Third Edition.* Circle Pines, MN: American Guidance Service, Inc.

Goodson, B. D., Layzer, J. I., St.Pierre, R. G., Bernstein, L. S., & Lopez, M. (2000). Effectiveness of a comprehensive five-year family support program on low-income children and their families: Findings from the Comprehensive Child Development Program. *Early Childhood Research Quarterly, 15*(1), 5–39.

Goodson, B. D., Layzer, J. I., St.Pierre, R. G., Bernstein, L. S., & Lopez, M. (2000). Effectiveness of a comprehensive five-year family support program on low-income children and their families: Findings from the Comprehensive Child Development Program. *Early Childhood Research Quarterly, 15*(1), 5–39.

Hanson, R. A., & Farrell, D. (1995). The long-term effects on high school seniors of learning to read in kindergarten. *Reading Research Quarterly, 30,* 908–933.

Harms, T., Clifford, R. M., & Cryer, D. (1998). *Early Childhood Environment Rating Scale: Revised Edition.* New York: Teachers College Press.

Hart, B., & Risley, T. (1995). *Meaningful differences in the everyday lives of American children.* Baltimore, MD: Brookes.

Heath, S. B. (1984). *Way with words: Language, life and work in communities and classrooms.* Cambridge: Cambridge University Press.

Howes, C., & Smith, E. W. (1995). Relations among child care quality, teacher behavior, children's play activities, emotional security, and cognitive activity in child care. *Early Childhood Research Quarterly, 10*, 381–404.

Infant Health and Development Program (IHDP). (1990). Enhancing the outcomes of low-birth-weight, premature infants. *Journal of the American Medical Association, 263*(22), 3035–3042.

Karweit, N. (1989). The effects of a story-reading program on the vocabulary and story comprehension skills of disadvantaged prekindergarten and kindergarten students. *Early Education and Development, 1*, 105–114.

Karweit, N. (1994). The effect of story reading on the language development of disadvantaged prekindergarten and kindergarten students. In D. K. Dickinson (Ed.), *Bridges to literacy: Approaches to supporting child and family literacy* (pp. 43–65). Cambridge, MA: Basil Blackwell.

Kloosterman, V. I. (2001, June). *A qualitative examination of the impact of the literacy environment enrichment project on preschool teachers' and supervisors' practices.* Paper presented at the 13th Annual Conference on Ethnographic and Qualitative Research in Education, Albany, NY.

Kloosterman, V. I. (2002, April). *Supervision in preschool education and the impact of the literacy environment enrichment project.* Paper session, Annual Conference of the American Education Research Association (AERA), New Orleans, LA.

Leseman, P. M., & de Jong, P. F. (1998). Home literacy: Opportunity, instruction, cooperation and social-emotional quality predicting early reading achievement. *Reading Research Quarterly, 33,* 294–318.

McCardle, P., Scarborough, H. S., & Catts, H. W. (2001). Predicting, explaining, and preventing children's reading difficulties. *Learning Disabilities Research & Practice, 16*(4), 230–239.

McCarty, F., Lambert, R., & Abbott-Shim, M. (2001). The relationship between teacher beliefs and practices and Head Start classroom quality. *Early Education and Development, 12*(2), 225–238.

NICHD Early Child Care Research Network. (1999). Child outcomes when child care center classes meet recommended standards for quality. *American Journal of Public Health, 89*, 1072–1077.

NICHD Early Child Care Research Network. (2000). The relation of child care to cognitive and language development. *Child Development, 71*, 960–980.

NICHD Early Child Care Research Network. (2001). Child care and children's peer interactions at 24 and 36 months: The NICHD study of early child care. *Child Development, 72*, 1478–1500.

NICHD Early Child Care Research Network. (2002). Early child care and children's development prior to school entry: Results form the NICHD Study of early child care. *American Educational Research Journal, 39*(1), 133–165.

Neuman, S. B., & Dickinson, D. K. (Eds.). (2001). *Handbook of early literacy research.* New York: Guilford.

Peisner-Feinberg, E., & Burchinal, M. (1997). Concurrent relations between child care quality and child outcomes: The study of cost, quality, and outcomes in child care center. *Merrill-Palmer Quarterly, 43*, 451–477.

Peisner-Feinberg, E. S., Burchinal, M. R., Clifford, R. M., Culkin, M. L., Howes, C., Kagan, S. L., & Yazejian, N. (2001). The relation of preschool quality to children's cognitive and social developmental trajectories through second grade. *Child Development, 72*(5), 1534–1553.

Quint, J. C., Bos, J. M., & Polit, D. F. (1997, July). *New Chance: Final report on a comprehensive program for disadvantaged young mothers and their children.* New York: Manpower Demonstration Research Corporation.

Roach, K. A., & Snow, C. E. (2000, April). *What predicts 4th grade reading comprehension?* Paper presented at the annual conference of the American Education Research Association, New Orleans, LA.

Sameroff, A. J., Seifer, R., Baldwin, A., & Baldwin, C. (1993). Stability of intelligence from preschool to adolescence: The influence of social and family risk factors. *Child Development, 64*, 80–97.

Scarborough, H. (2001). Connecting early language and literacy to later reading (dis)abilities: Evidence, theory, and practice. In S. B. Neuman & D. K. Dickinson (Eds.). *Handbook of early literacy research* (pp. 97–110). New York: Guilford.

Scarborough, H. S., & Dobrich, W. (1994). On the efficacy of reading to preschoolers. *Developmental Review, 14*, 245–302.

Schweinhart, L. J., Barnes, H. V., Weikart, D. P., Barnett, W. S., & Epstein, A. S. (1993). *Significant benefits: The High/Scope Perry preschool study through age 27* [Monographs of the High/Scope Educational Research foundation No. 10]. Ypsilanti, MI: High/Scope Press.

Shonkoff, J. P., & Phillips, D. A. (Eds.). (2000). From neurons to neighborhoods: The science of early childhood development. National Research Council and Institute of Medicine. Washington, DC, National Academy Press.

Smith, M. W., Dickinson, D. K., Sangeorge, A., & Anastasopoulos, L. (2002). *The early language and literacy classroom observation (ELLCO).* Baltimore, MD: Brookes Publishing Company.

Smith, S. (Ed.). (1995). Two-generation programs for families in poverty: A new intervention strategy. *Advances in Applied Developmental Psychology* (Vol. 9). Norwood, NJ: Ablex.

Snow, C. E., Burns, M. S., & Griffin, P. (Eds.). (1998). *Preventing reading difficulties in young children.* Washington, DC: National Research Council, National Academy Press.

Snow, C. E., Tabors, P. O., & Dickinson, D. K. (2001). Language development in the preschool years. In D. K. Dickinson & P. O. Tabors (Eds.), *Beginning literacy with language* (pp. 1–26). Baltimore: Brookes.

St.Pierre, R. G., Ricciuti, et al. (in press). *Third national Even Start evaluation: Program outcomes.* Cambridge, MA: Abt Associates Inc. for the U.S. Department of Education, Planning and Evaluation Service (contract EA97049001).

St.Pierre, R. G., Swartz, J. P, Gamse, B., Murray, S., Deck, D., & Nickel, P. (1995, January). *National evaluation of the Even Start Family Literacy Program: Final report.* Cambridge, MA: Abt Associates Inc. for the U.S. Department of Education, Planning and Evaluation Service (contract LC90062001).

Street, B. V. (1984). *Literacy in theory and practice.* Cambridge, UK: Cambridge University Press.

Sulzby, E., & Teale, W. (1991) Emergent literacy. In R. Barr, M. L. Kamil, P. B. Mosenthal, & P. D. Pearson (Eds.), *Handbook of Reading Research* (Vol. II). New York: Longman.

Tabors, P. O, Snow, C. E., & Dickinson, D. K. (2001). Homes and schools together: Supporting language and literacy development. In D. K. Dickinson & P. O. Tabors (Eds.), *Beginning Literacy with Langauge: Young children learning at home and school* (pp. 313–338). Baltimore, MD: Brookes.

U.S. Department of Health and Human Services. (2001). *Head Start FACES: Longitudinal findings on program performance. Third progress report.* Washington, DC: Author.

Wagner, M., & Clayton, S. (1998). *The Parents as Teachers Program: Results from two demonstrations.* Menlo Park, CA: SRI International.

Wasik, B. H., Dobbins, D. R., & Herrmann, S. (2001). Intergenerational family literacy: Concepts, research, and practice. In S. B. Neuman & D. K. Dickinson (Eds.), *Handbook of early literacy research* (pp. 444–458), New York: Guilford Press.

Wasik, B. H., Ramey, C. T., Bryant, D., & Sparling, J. (1990). A longitudinal study of two early intervention strategies: Project CARE. *Child Development, 61*, 1682–1696.

Whitehurst, G. J., & Lonigan, C. J. (1998). Child development and emergent literacy. *Child Development, 69*(3), 848–872.

Whitehurst, G. J., & Lonigan, C. J. (2001). Emergent literacy: Development from pre-readers to readers. In S. B. Neuman & D. K. Dickinson (Eds.), *Handbook of early literacy research* (pp. 11–29). New York: Guilford.

Woodcock, R. W., McGrew, K. S., & Mather, N. (2001). *Woodcock-Johnson III Tests of Achievement.* Itasca, IL: Riverside Publishing.

Zill, N., McKey, R. H., & Tarullo, L. (May, 2002). *FACES: An assessment battery to track children's cognitive development in Head Start and early elementary school.* Presentation at the NICHD/Columbia University meeting on cognitive measurement for large-scale studies, Washington, DC.

Zill, N., Resnick, G., & McKey, R. H. (April, 1999). *What children know and can do at the end of Head Start and what it tells us about the program's performance.* Paper presented at the Biannual Convention of the Society for Research In Child Development, Albuquerque, NM.

III

Parenting and Parent Education

A focus on parenting education distinguishes family literacy programs from those that provide only early childhood or adult education. The view that parenting education can maximize program benefits finds support from many sources, including theories about the role parents play in children's lives as well as empirical studies documenting the importance of family and parent practices for children's emerging language and literacy and for their social and emotional growth.

Douglas Powell describes promising strategies for parenting education in family literacy programs. To illustrate how parental beliefs affect parent behaviors, he describes four relevant dimensions, including family–verbal environment; supports for early literacy; parents' expectations for children's learning and development; and active engagement of the parenting role. He also discusses indirect influences, such as the family's ecological context. Next, he presents a set of strategies for working with parents, including guidelines to incorporate family perspectives, use focused discussions and interactive strategies, and provide specific information and explicit feedback to parents regarding their child's literacy development. He makes practical suggestions about how to implement these strategies. He then presents a summary of what we know about parenting education within family literacy programs, reporting data from the national evaluations of Even Start. He compares promising approaches to current practices and offers a set of ideas for strengthening approaches that have the potential to be effective. He concludes with a discussion of issues that need attention.

At the center of children's literacy development are the interactions and relationships between children and adults. Robert Pianta takes an in-depth look at theory and evidence to show the importance of these relationships for all areas of development, paying special attention to literacy. He provides support for the hypothesis that learning to read is a developmental process involving social and cultural mechanisms as well as cognitive and linguistic skills. Parent attitudes and beliefs about literacy are also essential aspects in this developmental process. He notes that the adult–child relationships important for the development of literacy begin in infancy and that secure parent–child relationships are predictors of children's interest in reading, vocabulary, and print awareness. Such supportive relationships, however, may be necessary but not sufficient for literacy competence. Pianta writes that adult–child interactions also need an instructional component focused on specific skills. He then analyzes these adult–child relationships in more detail using a systems perspective and identifies major implications for family literacy programs. He notes, for example, that relationships between children and adults are multifaceted and offer many opportunities to affect literacy growth.

The next two chapters describe different ways to provide parent education within family literacy programs. Kim Kelly discusses parent–child literacy interactions, often referred to as PACT Time; Flora Rodriguez-Brown paints a picture of Project FLAME, a stand-alone parent education program provided through group meetings.

PACT (parent and child together) Time has been part of family literacy programs since the beginning and, in its initial design, is unique to comprehensive family literacy programs. Kelly covers PACT Time's conceptual framework and the research base that supports meaningful parent–child interactions in children's development. Building on the concepts of adult–child relationships identified by Pianta, she illustrates how PACT Time can foster parent–child relationships, with examples from Even Start, Head Start, and school-age programs. A typical preschool PACT Time experience occurs in the familiar environment of the child's classroom. PACT Time is a structured opportunity for parents and children to increase meaningful interactions focused on language and literacy development in a high-quality learning environment. The goal is for parents to generalize skills learned in this setting to the home environment and their daily interactions with their children. Kelly concludes with information on PACT Time outcomes and a recommendation for instruments to assess them.

Even Start data show that over 40% of participating families are Hispanic. Within the United States, the number of Hispanic families continues to grow significantly. Although statistics differ across Latino groups (e.g., Cubans have a higher high school graduation rate than do Mexicans). Hispanics are more likely than the general population to have lower literacy rates, to be underemployed, and to have children who lag behind their mainstream peers in reading and writing. These concerns led Flora Rodriguez-Brown to develop Project FLAME, a parent support family literacy model program, which she describes in her chapter. Building on the belief that literacy learning is more culturally bound than are other areas of knowledge, she developed the program to address parental and home factors. FLAME's four goals are to help parents provide literacy opportunities and act as positive literacy models for their children, to improve parents' literacy skills so they can more effectively support their children's learning, and to improve relationships between parents and schools. Instructional components are designed to advance these goals.

These chapters, then, give us information on parental characteristics that contribute to children's learning; underscore the importance of parent–child relationships for all domains of development, including literacy; and show us two different ways to provide parent education.

9

Parenting Education in Family Literacy Programs

Douglas R. Powell
Purdue University

Parenting education holds significant potential for maximizing the benefits of family literacy programs. A growing body of research points to the powerful influences of parents on the development of children's literacy and school-related competence. Two recent major reports include guidelines for family support of children's literacy development. The National Research Council, in its report titled *Preventing Reading Difficulties in Young Children,* recommends that home and preschool activities include adult–child shared book reading (Snow, Burns, & Griffin, 1998). Shared book reading stimulates verbal interaction to enhance language development and knowledge about print concepts. The report also recommends activities that direct young children's attention to the phonological structure of spoken words and that highlight the relations between print and speech. A position statement on children's learning to read and write, developed by the International Reading Association and the National Association for the Education of Young Children (1998), includes illustrative practices for parents and family members to support children's development in early reading and writing from preschool through third grade. Appropriately, parenting education is viewed as a key ingredient for facilitating children's early literacy development in family literacy programs, including the Even Start Family Literacy Program (Powell & D'Angelo, 2000).

This chapter describes promising strategies of parenting education in family literacy programs. It identifies pertinent content and summarizes current thinking about appropriate practices in working with parents, reviews available research on the current state of parenting education in family literacy programs, and offers recommendations on needed directions in advancing the role and efficacy of parenting education in family literacy interventions. The paper also identifies needed directions in research on parenting education focused on literacy outcomes.

PROMISING APPROACHES TO PARENTING EDUCATION

Content: Important Dimensions of Parenting

Decisions about the curriculum or content of parenting education focused on children's literacy and school-related outcomes can be informed by studies of parenting contributions to children's literacy development and other school-related outcomes. This section identifies parenting behaviors and beliefs associated with children's literacy and school-related competence, including transitions to school.

A wide range of family variables in longitudinal studies predicts subsequent school-related performance. For example, the *Home Observation for Measurement of the Environment* (HOME) scale includes six subscales tapping various aspects of parental support of early cognitive and social–emotional development (Bradley & Caldwell, 1984). It has been found to correlate with school achievement in first grade and with children's academic achievement test scores at 11 years old (Bradley, Caldwell, & Rock, 1988). The subscales include emotional and verbal responsiveness of the mother, provision of appropriate play materials, and opportunities for variety in daily stimulation. In another longitudinal study, maternal variables such as teaching style, communication efficiency and style, and affective tone of interaction between mother and child in the preschool period predicted children's school readiness at 5 and 6 years of age and school achievement at 12 years (Hess, Holloway, Dickson, & Price, 1984). Yet another longitudinal study found that family provision of literacy experiences for children (e.g., buying and reading books) was the strongest long-term predictor of children's achievement in word recognition, vocabulary, and reading comprehension (Snow, Barnes, Chandler, Goodman, & Hemphill, 1991). Other recent longitudinal studies have found that a range of variables related to the home literacy environment and family characteristics are highly predictive of children's early literacy skills (e.g., Storch & Whitehurst, 2001; Tabors, Roach, & Snow, 2001).

The influences of parental behaviors and beliefs are inextricably interwoven into daily parent–child exchanges. No single parent or family variable has been found to dominate others in predicting school readiness and achievement (Hess et al., 1984) and children's developmental outcomes (Bee et al., 1982). Nevertheless, four major dimensions of parental behaviors and beliefs are related to children's literacy outcomes and early school success: (a) family verbal environment, including joint book reading and emotional affect and control in the parent–child relationship; (b) supports for early literacy, including the provision of reading and writing materials in the home; (c) parents' expectations of the child's learning and development; and (d) active engagement of the parenting role. Parents' abilities to function effectively in each of these areas are influenced by a number of factors, especially a parent's connections with community and other resources for supporting basic individual and family needs. Each of these areas is described in the following sections (see also Powell & D'Angelo, 2000).

Family Verbal Environment.   The quality of adult–child verbal exchanges within families has long been associated with children's school-related outcomes (e.g., Hess & Shipman, 1965). Research in the past 2 decades has added depth to our understanding of the types of adult–child interactions that promote children's language competence.

A longitudinal study by Hart and Risley (1995) found that children's everyday family experiences with language and interaction in the first 3 years of life accounted for 60% of the variance in measures of accomplishment (vocabulary growth, vocabulary use, Stanford–Binet IQ score) at age 3 years and in receptive vocabulary (Peabody Picture Vocabulary Test) and language development at ages 9 and 10 (third grade). These linkages existed regardless of the child's race.

Observations from more than 1,300 hours of casual interactions between parents and their children were organized into five areas of language and interaction: language diversity (nouns, modifiers, verbs), feedback tone (affirmatives and prohibitions), symbolic emphasis (sentences: clauses, verb tenses), guidance style (how often the child is asked rather than told what to do), and responsiveness (child's experience with controlling the course of interaction). All five of the derived variables predicted child accomplishment at age 3 years and in third grade.

There were striking socioeconomic differences in family experiences with words. Estimates indicate that the average child in a family on welfare heard 616 words per hour, the average child in a working-class family heard 1,251 words per hour, and the average child in a professional family heard 2,153 words per hour. Extrapolations of these data to a 5,200-hour year are as follows: 11 million words in a professional family, 6 million words in a working-class family, and 3 million words in a family on welfare.

Other research shows that everyday family conversations provide children with opportunities to learn about narratives (e.g., De Temple & Beals, 1991; Heath, 1983). For example, Beals (2001) found strong positive relationships between narrative and explanatory talk during family mealtimes in the preschool years and children's scores on literacy-related measures when children were 5 years of age. Narrative talk includes extended discourse about an event that has happened or will happen and usually takes several turns in a conversation. Explanatory talk provides logical connections among objects, events, concepts, or conclusions. Also, mothers' use of rare words with her preschooler has been found to be related to language and literacy skills at kindergarten age (Tabors, Beals, & Weizman, 2001).

Parent–child book reading is another important verbal exchange that contributes to children's literacy skills. The ways in which parents manage the book reading interaction, especially asking and responding to questions about text (e.g., DeTemple, 2001; Pellegrini, Brody, & Sigel, 1985), predict children's literacy outcomes.

Two reviews of research on effects of the quantity and quality of joint parent–child book reading concluded that book reading between parent and preschooler moderately correlates with children's development of language and literacy skills, including later reading achievement (Bus, van IJzendoorn, & Pellegrini, 1995; Scarborough & Dobrich, 1994). Scarborough and Dobrich found that other variables such as socioeconomic status and parent's attitude toward reading accounted for more of the variability in children's language and literacy competence than did parent–preschooler book-reading experiences.

The quality of family verbal environments reflects two child-rearing dimensions—level of affect or warmth and level of restrictiveness versus permissiveness—that are important predictors of children's school-related competence. Attentive, warm, and flexible maternal behaviors during infancy and preschool years have been associated with young children's intellectual development. For example, the affective quality of the mother–child relationship (e.g., responsiveness, warm concern, acceptance, emotional displays of affect) when children were 4 years of age was strongly correlated with school readiness at ages 5 and 6 years and with school achievement at 12 years of age (Estrada, Arsenio, Hess, & Holloway, 1987). Mother–child attachment security has been related to the quality of mother–child interactions, such as the mother's level of paying attention to the child during activities related to written language (Bus & van IJzendoorn, 1988). Further, mothers' use of direct control tactics (e.g., commands without explanations) in teaching and disciplinary situations with 4-year-old children has been negatively related to children's school-related abilities at 4 to 6 years of age and at 12 years of age (Hess & McDevitt, 1984).

The ease of children's adjustment to school also is associated with affect and control dimensions of the parent–child relationship. Parent–child interactions characterized by a controlling parent and a resisting child, or by a directing child, have been negatively associated with a child's social adjustment to school. In contrast, the length of parent–child time engaged in physical play was favorably related to social adjustment to school (Barth & Parke, 1993). The researchers speculate that the ability of a parent and child to initiate and maintain rough-and-tumble play provides opportunities for a child to develop skills in self-regulation of behavior and "reading" another's emotional cues that promote sensitive and responsive interactions with others outside the family. A controlling parent at home may offer few opportunities for children to practice initiating and organizing play or other social interactions; these interactions in turn enhance children's skills for coping with a new social setting. In parent–child situations where the child is directive, the child's dominance over a passive parent may promote an abrasive interaction style with peers, resulting in peer rejection early in the school year.

Extrapolations of data in the Hart and Risley (1995) study indicate that, in a 5,200-hour year, the average child would hear 166,000 encouragements to 26,000 discouragements in a professional family, 62,000 encouragements to 36,000 discouragements in a working-class family, and 26,000 encouragements to 57,000 discouragements in a low-income family (Hart & Risley, 1995). (In the following chapter, Pianta provides an elaborate discussion on parent–child relationships and literacy development.)

Supports for Literacy.   Parent–child interactions do not occur in a vacuum. Everyday exchanges in families are embedded in a context of literacy provisions and parental beliefs that support or limit the development of children's language and literacy competence.

Literacy provisions in the home include access to reading and writing materials such as picture dictionaries and alphabet books (Sulzby & Teale, 1991). Parents' own reading habits and uses of literacy for problem solving, such as initiating a search for assistance with a telephone directory, are models for children (Goodman, 1986).

Children of parents who view reading as entertainment have a more positive view of reading than do children of parents who emphasize the skills aspect of reading development (Baker, Scher, & Mackler, 1997). Parental enthusiasm about literacy activities, including a view of reading as fun, contributes to children's reading skills and attitudes (Baker, Serpell, & Sonnenschein, 1995; Sonnenschein, Baker, Serpell, & Schmidt, 2000). DeBaryshe (1995) found that both the degree to which mothers exposed their children to joint book reading and the quality of mothers' book-reading interactions were associated with maternal attitudes about what and how children learn from reading (i.e., emphasis on the enjoyment, knowledge, and oral language growth from reading) as well as with a mother's self-efficacy as a teacher of her child (Self-efficacy pertains to expectations about the degree to which he or she is able to perform competently and effectively as a parent. See Teti & Gelfand, 1991.)

Expectations of Child's Learning and Development.   What parents think about the processes of children's development, including understandings of parental roles in fostering children's development and learning, contributes in an important way to children's literacy and school-related outcomes. Constructivist views on child development (i.e., a view of development as a complex process that involves the child as an active contributor to his or her own development) have been positively associated with children's cognitive abilities at 3 to 4 years of age (McGillicuddy-DeLisi, 1985) and with children's reading and arithmetic test scores at 5 to 6 years of age (Johnson & Martin, 1985). Parental assessment and expectations of their children's abilities are also correlated with children's school-related outcomes. For example, mothers' expectations of their children's level of educational attainment have been associated with children's vocabulary, reading comprehension, and writing production 4 years later (Snow et al., 1991).

Active Engagement of Parenting Role.   With regard to parents' understandings of their roles in fostering children's learning, a recent review of research literature on parental beliefs proposed three factors as central to parents' decision to become involved in their children's formal education: (a) construction of the parent role (What am I supposed to do in relation to my child's education and educational progress?); (b) sense of efficacy for helping their child succeed in school (Can I exert a positive influence on my child's educational outcomes?); and (c) invitations, demands, and opportunities for parent involvement (Do my child and school want me to be involved?) (Hoover-Dempsey & Sandler, 1997).

Parents' self-efficacy beliefs are associated with numerous indices of parental functioning (for a review, see Coleman & Karraker, 1997). Self-efficacy may enable parents to act on the knowledge of child development. One study found that among less confident mothers no variation existed in the quality of mother–toddler interaction based on differences in the maternal level of child development knowledge. However, increased knowledge was associated with more effective interactions with the child among the more confident mothers (Conrad, Gross, Fogg, & Ruchala, 1992). Another study found that maternal self-efficacy beliefs mediated the relation between the child's difficult temperament and the extent of family involvement in home learning activities in Head Start families (Machida, Taylor, & Kim, 2002).

Indirect Parent Influences.   In addition to the aforementioned four direct parental influences on children's literacy development and school-related outcomes, one area of indirect parent influence is very important. Parents' ability to function effectively in supporting their child's literacy development (e.g., interacting in affirmative ways with the child) is connected to the strength of linkages with community and other resources (e.g., extended family and friends) for meeting basic individual and family needs. The ecological contexts in which parents and families carry out their daily lives enable or hinder families' abilities to promote their members' growth and development (Bronfenbrenner & Morris, 1998). Resources that help parents maintain good physical and mental health and to use effective coping strategies in responding to environmental influences are important conditions for parenting. For example, effective coping strategies enable parents to buffer children from debilitating stress factors in the environment. When coping strategies are weak, a parent's capacity to be active and goal-directed in managing the environment is compromised (Bradley, 2002).

In summary, parents' contributions to children's literacy development and school-related outcomes embrace a wide set of behaviors and beliefs. Consider the parent–child language and interaction variables found to be influential in the Hart and Risley (1995) longitudinal study of children's language development and accomplishment. The uses of language, such as the number and diversity of words and the complexity of sentence structure, were key contributors to children's language development. The way in which parent–child interactions took place also was important. Hearing affirmations versus prohibitions, being asked versus being told what to do, and having some influence on the course of interaction significantly shaped children's language outcomes. Verbal interactions between parent and child are part and parcel of the quality of the relationship between parent and child. What is more, children's language-rich experiences in families are connected to enabling factors, including the availability of language materials, parents' approaches to reading and writing, and parents' views of their parenting role and competence.

Methods: Strategies for Working with Parents

A thin empirical base exists for formulating recommendations on appropriate methods in parenting education. A paucity of well-designed and pertinent studies inform approaches to parenting education. Many promising methods are based on prevailing theoretical orientations in the field. Seven methods are described in the following sections.

Incorporate Family Perspectives.   The long-standing social work principle of "begin where the client is" is a preferred approach in many parenting interventions (Provence, Naylor, & Patterson, 1977). Theoretical perspectives in the adult-education literature also support a learner-centered approach to education (Brookfield, 1989). An analysis of the evaluation efforts of five family literacy programs in Illinois suggests that program content relevant to a participant's life is critical to recruitment and retention (Ryan, Geissler, & Knell, 1994). Gathering information about parents' goals for their child is a strategy for tailoring a curriculum to a parent's interests (Segal, 1985). A family's information can be incorporated into suggested parenting approaches and activities that are part of daily interactions in a family (Bernheimer & Keogh, 1995). Low-income parents' reports of their preschool child's literacy development have been good predictors of their child's language and literacy performance in kindergarten and first grade (Dickinson & DeTemple, 1998). Appropriate practices in parenting education respectfully build on parents' views and intentions.

Use Focused Discussion and Interactive Strategies.   Guided discussion is a tool for building on parents' views of their situations. Some evidence indicates that group-based discussions flowing from parents' interests and guided by a professional have greater positive effects on parents' child-rearing attitudes (especially openness and flexibility) than does a structured and predetermined curriculum used in a home-visit approach (Slaughter, 1983). Focused discussion among parents allows individuals to rework their existing beliefs in order to accommodate new ideas from peers or program staff. For instance, guided dialogs between a mother and a home visitor have helped socially isolated, low-income mothers living in a rural setting to become more actively engaged in conceptualizing and interacting with their children in ways that would promote cognitive development and a sense of self-competence (Bond, Belenky, & Weinstock, 1992).

Provide Instructional Guidance on Activities That Support Children's Literacy Development.   Providing specific information and explicit feedback to parents regarding their child's literacy development is beneficial. Telling a parent to read to his or her child is insufficient guidance for many parents (Mikulecky, 1996). Programs need to provide concrete instruction on how to support literacy development through joint book reading and other provisions outlined earlier in this paper. Interventions that systematically provide instruction on literacy activities have been effective with lower income parents (Neuman, Hagedorn, Celano, & Daly, 1995). One example is coaching parents on how to orally label objects, hold a child's attention, ask questions, interact with text-specific comments, and provide feedback to the child (Edwards, 1994; Neuman & Gallagher, 1994). A second example is teaching parents how to expand on the child's telling of a story from a book. This approach has been successfully taught to parents in the Dialogic Reading program wherein the adult assumes the role of an active listener and the child is the storyteller. A child's engagement of a book is encouraged through the adult's seeking questions, adding information, and expanding on the child's descriptions (Whitehurst et al., 1994). (See chapters by Morrow and Temlock-Fields and Purcell-Gates for more on parent storybook reading.)

Tailor Program Guidance to Individual Parent–Child Relationships.   Specific information given to a parent–child dyad probably is more useful than information offered in a group setting. Structured parent–child activity is a good opportunity to individualize program messages. Especially in home visits, the staff person can relate to the parent–child dyad within the family's home environment. Parents may disclose new information or function in the home differently than in a center, providing staff with a fuller understanding of a family's beliefs and practices. A richer portrait of the parent and child also can be developed by simply observing the nature of family interactions at home. This information can help inform the home visitor of how to best help the family. (Additional suggestions for home visitors are provided in Section V by Bryant and Wasik.)

Extend the Lessons of Parenting Experiences.   The experiences of parenting are connected to other adult roles, especially parents' jobs (Parcel & Menaghan, 1994). A demonstration program has used Head Start parent involvement activities as the first rungs of a ladder aimed at moving individuals toward self-sufficiency. The program designers link parental activities supporting children's development to parents' career plans. For example, punctuality (e.g., getting a child to school on time) may be a general competency that could be transferred to job training and work settings (Herr, Halpern, & Majeske, 1995).

Provide Multiple Supports and Flexibility for Program Participation.   A study of 17 family education programs aimed at helping lower income parents support young children's learning found that programs maintained flexibility in their operations to respond to a variety of family circumstances. This flexibility included meeting parents at different locations and times and employing home visits for connecting and individualizing work with parents (Goodson, Swartz, & Millsap, 1991). A study of two levels of support for participation in an eight-session educational workshop aimed at first-grade parents found that the higher level of support (e.g., providing child care and transportation) attracted 10% more of the invited parents than the lower support arrangement (Dolan & Haxby, 1995).

Maintain Frequent and Sustained Interaction With Parents.   Parenting beliefs and practices are deeply rooted phenomena that require long-term and intense attention for meaningful change and support to occur. New information about the development of children interacts with parents' existing constructs; ideas that seem discrepant or irrelevant are likely to be rejected (Goodnow & Collins, 1990; for implications for parenting education, see Powell, 1996). Meaningful change comes slowly. Analyses of outcome studies of 10 early intervention programs targeted at family functioning indicate that pervasive and sustained effects are more likely to be realized when the intervention includes 11 or more contacts over at least a 3-month period (Heinicke, Beckwith, & Thompson, 1988). This finding has important implications for setting intensity levels for parenting education in family literacy programs.

APPROACHES TO PARENTING EDUCATION IN FAMILY LITERACY PROGRAMS

Family literacy programs typically provide parenting education services that include group discussions, sometimes with presentations by invited speakers, hands-on activities, and home visits. The Even Start Family Literacy Program also requires that programs provide interactive literacy activities for parents and their children. These activities generally occur in early childhood classrooms or home visits and occasionally during field trips. The most detailed information available on approaches to parenting education in family literacy programs comes from three national evaluations of the Even Start Family Literacy Program (St.Pierre et al., 1995; St.Pierre et al., 2003; Tao, Gamse, & Tarr, 1998).

National evaluations of Even Start have gathered data on the most frequently addressed topics in parenting education activities. Topics included in the third evaluation (2000–2001) may be organized by the parenting domains discussed previously in this chapter:

- *Family Verbal Environment.* More than two thirds of Even Start projects reported that the following topics were among the 10 most frequently addressed: promoting parent–child reading together and other literacy activities (93%); understanding how talking with a child promotes child literacy (73%); and how to manage child behavior (77%), a topic which presumably includes attention to guidance style, responsiveness, and affective quality of the parent–child relationship. A relatively small number of Even Start projects frequently addressed the topic of how to ask good (meaningful, open-ended) questions of children (18%). Two other topics conducive to language and literacy opportunities—how to promote a child's social skills development and how to help children with homework—were addressed frequently by fewer than one half of projects (47% and 25%, respectively).

- *Supports for Literacy.* One topic included in the third Even Start evaluation pertains to this domain of parenting. Forty percent of projects indicated that their parenting education activities frequently addressed how to provide a child with easy access to reading and writing materials.

- *Expectations of Child's Learning and Development.* About three fourths of projects reported that the following two topics were among the most frequently addressed: general understanding of how children develop (81%) and helping parents understand what to expect of their children (74%) (St.Pierre et al., 2003).

In terms of indirect parent influences, one half or more of Even Start projects indicated that the following topics were among the 10 most frequently addressed in parenting education: building parents' self-esteem (60%), building parents' life skills (59%), and building parents' awareness of community and social services (50%). A similar percentage of projects frequently addressed parents' understanding of good health and nutrition (48%) and awareness of vocational/education opportunities (36%) (St.Pierre et al., 2003). An observational study of 12 Even Start programs discovered that programs generally found it difficult to focus on literacy-related content with parents in the context of family crises and other stressful circumstances that serve to preoccupy parents' interests and energies (Haslam & Stief, 1998).

In a separate study of five Even Start projects with promising transition-to-kindergarten strategies, program time was devoted to teaching parents how to work with school staff, ways of volunteering at their child's school, and what kind of kindergarten experience parents should expect for their child (Riedinger, 1997). Some projects in this study also used the adult education component to address school relationship issues. For example, in one project's adult literacy class, participants learned how to write a letter to the school about a child's absence.

The third national evaluation of Even Start also provides information on the content focus of parent–child interactive literacy activities. In 2000 to 2001, more than one half of projects indicated that reading aloud (64% in centers, 74% in home visits) and working on cognitive skills such as shapes and colors (51% in centers, 54% in home visits) were among the five most frequently pursued activities. Other literacy activities frequently undertaken by programs included story telling (33% in centers, 31% in home visits), working with letters and writing (25% in centers, 30% in home visits), working with numbers such as counting and number games (25% in centers, 30% in home visits), and literacy-related social activities such as library nights (36% in centers, 24% in home visits).

Although overall there were few differences in activities offered in centers and home visits, some programs appear to have pursued the opportunity to individualize work with parents and children in home visits. For example, in 2000 to 2001, more programs offered instruction and coaching of specific parenting skills (40% in home visits, 20% in centers) and modeling/practicing positing parenting behaviors (56% in home visits, 46% in centers) in home visits rather than in centers. On the other hand, more programs offered activities to promote sharing/working with others in a center (46%) rather than in home visits (16%) (St.Pierre et al., 2003).

Data from the third national evaluation (2000–2001) indicate that, on average, Even Start programs provided about 173 hours of parenting education per year. Although most Even Start parents (89%) participated in parenting education in 2000 to 2001, the amount of participation was far less than the amount of hours of parenting education offered by a program. Parents participated on average in 42 hours of parenting education annually in 2000 to 2001 and 1999 to 2000. In both 1999 to 2000 and 2000 to 2001, parents received an average of 5.8 hours of parenting education per month for a period of 7.1 months. Programs provided an average of about 13 hours a month of parent–child interactive literacy activities, and parents participated in about 5.2 hours per month for an average of 7.1 months (St.Pierre et al., 2003). The number of hours in which parents participated in parenting education has fluctuated over time in Even Start programs. On average, parents participated in 58 hours of parenting education in 1992 to 1993, 32 hours in 1994 to 1995, 27 hours in 1995 to 1996, 28 hours in 1996 to 1997, 52 hours in 1997 to 1998, and 53 hours in 1998 to 1999 (St.Pierre et al., 1995, 2003; Tao et al., 1998).

There is wide variation across Even Start programs nationally in the intensity of parenting education services offered. In 2000 to 2001, 23% of programs offered 20 or more hours of parenting education per month, 31% offered between 10 and 20 hours of parenting education per month, 32% offered between 4 and 10 hours a month, and 14% offered 4 or fewer hours of parenting education each month. Not surprisingly, the number of hours of parenting education offered per month is linked to the level of parent participation in parenting education services. Parents in projects offering fewer than 5 hours of parenting education per month participated for an average of 24 hours per year, whereas parents in projects offering 18 or more hours of parenting education each month participated in an average of 65 hours of parenting education per year. Similarly, families receiving between 5 and 9 types of support services participated in an average of 57 hours of parenting education per year, compared to 23 hours for families that received no support services (St.Pierre et al., 2003). Findings from the second national evaluation of Even Start also indicate that the number of hours of participation in parenting education varies greatly across parents and is positively related to the number of support services received by a family and hours of parenting education offered by a program (Tao et al., 1998).

In terms of method of parenting education, a majority of programs (55%) indicated in the second national evaluation that the approach to instruction was "mostly individualized"; slightly more than one third of programs reported the instruction in parenting education was a combination of standardized and individualized approaches. Even Start projects used a mostly locally developed curriculum (38%) or a combination of commercially available and locally developed curricula (41%) for parenting education (Tao et al., 1998). This information is not included in the third national evaluation of Even Start.

Little systematic information is available on the structured parent–child activity time in Even Start. One tradition within this time period, based on the National Center for Family Literacy model, calls for a parent to follow his or her child's lead in the activity; the child is to select the joint activity. Questions have been raised about the merits of this approach when it conflicts with culturally based norms about the parent being *in charge* of learning. Another piece of anecdotal information about the Even Start parent–child activity time is that parents often are reluctant to leave an adult-focused session for the parent–child time (Powell & D'Angelo, 2000) (see Jacobs, ch. 11, this handbook, for a description of parent–child activity time in family literacy programs).

Parenting education was more likely to be integrated with the Even Start early childhood education component than with the basic adult education services. The second national evaluation found that the same or parallel activities occurred "usually or always" between parenting education and early childhood education in 54% of the projects, and 78% of projects reported joint activities "usually or always" occurred between parenting and early childhood education. The same or parallel activities occurred "usually or always" between parenting and adult basic education in 42% of projects, and joint activities between these two components occurred "always or usually" in 72% of projects. The second national evaluation also found that level of integration across program components (e.g., components taught by same instructors or using same or similar activities) was positively related to number of hours of participation in parenting education (Tao et al., 1998).

Examples of integrating parenting education with other Even Start components were identified in a recent study of promising practices in nine Even Start programs serving infants and toddlers and their families (Nathanson, Stief, Marzke, & O'Brien, 1998). For instance, programs encourage parents to observe infants and toddlers in early childhood classrooms, and many projects decorate their early childhood classrooms with parents in mind (e.g., posting developmental charts and learning objectives). One project created a *curriculum action plan* across all components (adult education, parenting education, early childhood education) that ensured content continuity across the Even Start program. This project staff generally believed that teaching parents about their children's learning and development is more effective when program components purposefully integrate lessons and when the lessons involve the children themselves. Additional examples of intergrating across program components is provided by Potts in Section VII.

NEEDED DIRECTIONS IN PARENTING EDUCATION IN FAMILY LITERACY PROGRAMS

Promising Versus Current Practices

When the promising approaches to parenting education described previously are compared to our current understanding of the scope of parenting education practices in the nation's largest family literacy program (Even Start), the following conclusions emerge:

1. The range of parenting education content covered in most Even Start programs is consistent with the finding that many family factors are associated with children's school-related outcomes.

2. Program attention to family verbal environments, children's language development, and supports for literacy experiences is well targeted in terms of research findings on the importance of these family variables. However, it appears that some key components of a stimulating family verbal environment—asking meaningful, open-ended questions of children that can prompt extended conversations—receive insufficient attention in Even Start programs.

3. Programs that expend a significant amount of energy in helping parents meet basic family needs run the risk of becoming generic social service programs. As a result, parent and child literacy outcomes may not be affected by the program. One way for programs to meet this challenge is to connect literacy instruction to topics of immediate concern to the parent (e.g., employment, housing, safety, immigration) (Auerbach, 1995). Support for this approach comes from Boudin (1993), who has written a detailed description of the pedagogical process of incorporating critical literacy teaching practices into a skills-based literacy curriculum, using the topic of AIDS in prison as a means of connecting women's experiences to the acquisition of literacy skills.

4. Most programs seem to recognize and use the learner-centered principle of incorporating parent perspectives into program content and method. For example, programs often have parents participate in the selection of instructional activities.

5. Of particular note is the conclusion that the average number of hours of participation in parenting education is *less intense* than probably needed for significant change in parenting beliefs and practices. This conclusion suggests there is not an adequate and uniform *floor* of systematic attention to parenting in Even Start programs.

6. The parent–child interactive literacy time is a promising opportunity to strengthen the parent–child relationship as well as the parents' understanding of their child. More needs to be known about how this time is used in Even Start programs and what its potential might be to influence parent–child interaction.

7. Parents' beliefs about child development processes and their role in supporting their children's learning appear critical to active parent engagement of learning opportunities for their child. Research is unclear, however, in indicating whether or not Even Start programs give sufficient attention to discussing with parents beliefs about their role in supporting children's literacy development.

8. The generally limited attention to combining parenting education and adult education suggests more could be done to maximize the connections between parenting experiences and other life skills as well as parenting and adult learning.

Strategies for Strengthening the Use of Promising Approaches

In this section several strategies are proposed for strengthening the use of approaches that have been shown to have potential.

Clarity on Goals and Outcomes.   Broad definitions of the role of parenting education in family literacy programs may lead to loosely focused work and varying levels of program commitment to parenting. Statements of mission and vision for parenting education could provide an overarching framework to guide content and method decisions as well as connections with other program services. A clear focus on desired children's outcomes might help program designers identify core content.

Guides to Curriculum Development.   There are many advantages to locally developed curricula, especially when the characteristics and interests of the target population are central to local programming directions. Many existing family literacy programs seem to have limited access to what is known. Consequently, knowledge of research and lessons from other programs need to be made available to local program staff in a systematic and concrete way. Curricula for children need to be organized by children's developmental periods.

Training and Technical Assistance.   Even Start programs devote more in-service staff development time to parenting education than to other components. This situation is most likely due to the fact that the Even Start staff rather than other agencies more frequently provides the parenting component, a consequence of the generally limited number of agency resources for parenting education in most communities (Tao et al., 1998). Little is known about the technical resources available to Even Start programs in carrying out in-service training on parenting education, and tools such as the one proposed in the following section may be useful. A stronger training and technical assistance system for Even Start at regional and national levels may be needed to implement these suggestions.

Recently, the U.S. Department of Education has taken steps in the directions suggested previously. Specifically, a framework for parenting education in Even Start has been developed and training tools for implementing the framework in local programs are being generated (Powell & D'Angelo, 2000). The framework offers guidance on the goals of the parenting education component stating, for example, that the goal of parenting education in Even Start is to strengthen parents' support of their young children's literacy development and early school success.

NEEDED DIRECTIONS IN RESEARCH ON PARENTING EDUCATION
IN FAMILY LITERACY PROGRAMS

Four types of research can inform decisions about promising approaches to parenting education in family literacy programs. First, studies of parental effects on children's literacy and school-related outcomes previously can be used to formulate guidelines on the content of parenting education (type 1). This type of research, however, cannot provide information on appropriate methods of parenting education and typically leaves unanswered the question of whether the parenting variable(s) associated with children's school-related outcomes is amenable to change or support through parenting education. For example, is it possible for joint book reading, found to be beneficial to children in naturalistic studies (e.g., Bus, van IJzendoorn, & Pellegrini, 1995), to be fostered among parents who do not read to their children?

To answer questions about whether and how key parenting practices can be influenced via a parenting education program, we need studies of parenting education approaches that provide parents with information and skills informed by research on parenting contributions to children's school-related outcomes. Three additional types of program research are useful to consider in this regard.

Ideas about what parents should do to promote their children's emergent literacy are best tested initially in a stand-alone parenting education program that evaluates a single approach to parenting knowledge and/or skills (type 2). The primary advantage of a stand-alone program for testing the effects of a parenting education strategy is the elimination of other influences via program services. An example of this type of program evaluation is the Whitehurst et al. (1994) study of a language development approach to picture book reading. The chief limitation of research on a single approach in stand-alone parenting education programs is the absence of data on the relative efficacy of a particular approach in comparison to another approach to parenting education.

One can also go beyond a single approach to evaluate planned variations in stand-alone parenting education programs (type 3). Evaluations of planned variation in the content and/or methods in stand-alone programs provide useful comparison information on the merits of different approaches to parenting education. Examples include an investigation of two different approaches to parenting education and support—a home visiting and group discussion—in a Chicago housing project (Slaughter, 1983) and a randomized trial of home visiting that varied the type and length of work with pregnant women to prevent preterm delivery and low birth weight (Olds et al., 1986). Evaluations of either a single approach or a planned variation in approaches to parenting education in stand-alone programs do not yield information on the implementation and impact of a prescribed parenting education approach with other services (e.g., adult education). This limitation can be addressed through planned variation in parenting education within comprehensive programs.

Another research approach to answer *whether or how questions* is to compare planned variation in approaches to parenting education in comprehensive programs (type 4). This is the strongest set of studies to determine best practices in parenting education. These studies systematically vary elements of the parenting education component while holding constant the other components of the comprehensive program. The parenting education component could be varied across identical comprehensive programs by content, method, or intensity. For example, a high-intensity model of parenting education could be compared to a less intense model of parenting education (Smith, 1995).

The availability of useful studies is uneven across the type of study previously described and the three types of research described in this section. There are a growing number of longitudinal studies that examine links between children's school-related outcomes and parenting knowledge, attitudes, and behaviors (type 1). There are a small number of relevant investigations of a single approach (type 2) or planned variation (type 3) in stand-alone parenting education programs. A major limitation of research in this area is that most investigations typically involve White, middle-class populations. For example, studies have been conducted with middle-class parents to compare the effects of different group-based parenting education curricula (for a review, see Dembo, Sweitzer, & Lauritzen, 1985). Findings of these studies with middle-class parents cannot be generalized to parenting education approaches in family literacy programs that focus on low-income families with low literacy skills.

The extant literature contains no research on planned variation in approaches to parenting education in comprehensive programs (type 4). A number of comprehensive interventions with a significant focus on parenting have been evaluated in the past 2 decades, including Even Start (St.Pierre & Swartz, 1995; Tao et al., 1998), the Comprehensive Child Development Program (St.Pierre, Layzer, Goodson, & Bernstein, 1997), Avance (Johnson & Walker, 1991), the Parent Child Development Centers (Andrews et al., 1982), and the Yale Child Welfare Project (Seitz & Apfel, 1994; Seitz, Rosenbaum, & Apfel, 1985). However, these evaluations were not designed to yield systematic data on the efficacy of different approaches to parenting education or on the unique contribution of the parenting education component to program outcomes.

Much more research activity is needed on planned variation in stand-alone programs and comprehensive programs (types 3 and 4). Quite simply, different approaches to parenting education need to be compared in a systematic manner. Although planned variation studies proved to be difficult on a large-scale basis (Rivlin & Timpane, 1975), research and program development work with a small set of local programs may be feasible at this stage of Even Start's development. There is great potential in identifying and supporting a small segment of programs for research and development purposes.

Even Start can contribute to methodological advances in the challenging enterprise of research on parenting and parenting interventions (Powell, 1994). Measurement is among the areas where further work is needed. Investigators typically measure parenting beliefs, including attitudes, as program outcomes. Often in these investigations there is a theoretical assumption that beliefs serve as guides of actual parenting behavior. The belief–behavior connection is poorly understood. Furthermore, it is common to find a weak or no correlation between conceptually linked beliefs and behaviors, and for the directionality of links between belief and behavior to be unclear (Sigel, 1992). Further, commonly used measures of parenting attitudes have been criticized for confounding a mixture of statements about attitudes, beliefs, behavioral intentions, and self-perceptions; and for focusing on global, decontextualized child-rearing attitudes (Holden & Edwards, 1989). Because parental beliefs about literacy have been associated with parental behaviors and children's literacy development, as noted earlier, research on Even Start offers an opportunity to refine measurement strategies and contribute to our understandings of belief–behavior relationships.

CONCLUSIONS

Children's literacy development begins very early in life and occurs over time through innumerable interactions with a range of environments (Whitehurst & Lonigan, 1998). The quality of literacy experiences in the home environment is a major contributor to children's literacy outcomes and early school success, and family literacy programs are on solid ground in the inclusion of parenting education as a means of enhancing family support of children's emergent literacy. There is a credible and growing body of empirical knowledge for informing decisions about the content or curriculum of parenting education focused on children's literacy development and early school success. There also is a fledgling set of studies and theoretical perspectives for informing decisions about the methods of teaching and supporting parents.

Existing approaches to parenting education in Even Start are consistent with some, but certainly not all, of the promising practices in parenting education recommended in the extant literature. The intensity of parents' participation in the Even Start parenting education component is especially questionable. Well-designed studies are needed regarding the nature and effects of a number of specific program practices. Research on the relative effects of contrasting strategies of parenting education in family literacy programs also is needed. Even Start holds considerable promise as a research setting for examination of program strategies as well as advances in parenting research methodology, including measurement of parenting behaviors and beliefs.

REFERENCES

Andrews, S. R., Blumenthal, J. B., Johnson, D. L., Kahn, A. J., Ferguson, C. J., Lasater, R. M., Malone, P. E., & Wallace, D. B. (1982). The skills of mothering: A study of Parent Child Development Centers. *Monographs of the Society for Research in Child Development, 47*(6, Serial No. 198).

Auerbach, E. R. (1995). Which way for family literacy: Intervention or empowerment. In L. Morrow (Ed.), *Family literacy: Connections in schools and communities* (pp. 11–28). Newark, DE: International Reading Association.

Baker, L., Scher, D., & Mackler, K. (1997). Home and family influences on motivations for reading. *Educational Psychologist, 32,* 69–82.

Baker, L., Serpell, R., & Sonnenschein, S. (1995). Opportunities for learning in the homes of urban preschoolers. In L. M. Morrow (Ed.), *Family literacy: Connections in schools and communities* (pp. 236–252). Newark, DE: International Reading Association.

Barth, J. M., & Parke, R. D. (1993). Parent-child relationship influences on children's transitions to school. *Merrill-Palmer Quarterly, 39,* 173–195.

Beals, D. E. (2001). Eating and reading: Links between family conversations with preschoolers and later language and literacy. In D. K. Dickinson & P. O. Tabors (Eds.), *Beginning literacy with language: Young children learning at home and school* (pp. 75–92). Baltimore: Brookes.

Bee, H. L., Barnard, K. E., Eyres, S. J., Gray, C. A., Hammond, M. A., Spietz, L. A., Snyder, C., & Clark, B. (1982). Prediction of IQ and language skills from perinatal status, child performance, family characteristics, and mother-infant interaction. *Child Development, 53,* 1334–1356.

Bernheimer, L. P., & Keogh, B. K. (1995). Weaving interventions into the fabric of everyday life: An approach to family assessment. *Topics in Early Childhood Special Education, 15,* 415–433.

Bond, L. A., Belenky, M. F., & Weinstock, J. S. (1992). Listening partners: Helping rural mothers find a voice. *Family Resource Coalition Report, 11,* 18–19.

Boudin, K. (1993). Participatory literacy education behind bars: AIDS opens the door. *Harvard Educational Review, 63,* 207–232.

Bradley, R. H. (2002). Environment and parenting. In M. H. Bornstein (Ed.), *Handbook of parenting, 2nd edition: Vol. 2. Biology and ecology of parenting* (pp. 281–314). Mahwah, NJ: Lawrence Erlbaum Associates.

Bradley, R. H., & Caldwell, B. M. (1984). The relation of infants' home environments to achievement test performance in first grade: A follow-up study. *Child Development, 55,* 803–809.

Bradley, R. H., Caldwell, B. M., & Rock, S. L. (1988). Home environment and school performance: A ten-year follow-up and examination of three models of environmental action. *Child Development, 59,* 852–867.

Bronfenbrenner, U., & Morris, P. (1998). The ecology of developmental processes. In W. Damon (Ed.) & R. M. Lerner (Vol. Ed.), *Handbook of child psychology, fifth edition. Vol. 1: Theoretical models of human development* (pp. 993–1028). New York: Wiley.

Brookfield, S. D. (1989). Facilitating adult learning. In S. B. Merriam & P. M. Cunningham (Eds.), *Handbook of adult and continuing education* (pp. 201–220). San Francisco: Jossey-Bass.

Bus, A. G., & van IJzendoorn, M. H. (1988). Mother-child interactions, attachment and emergent literacy: A cross-sectional study. *Child Development, 59,* 1262–1272.

Bus, A. G., van IJzendoorn, M. H., & Pellegrini, A. D. (1995). Joint book reading makes success in learning to read: A meta-analysis on intergenerational transmission of literacy. *Review of Educational Research, 65,* 1–21.

Coleman, P. K., & Karraker, K. H. (1997). Self-efficacy and parenting quality: Findings and future applications. *Developmental Review, 18,* 47–85.

Conrad, B., Gross, D., Fogg, L., & Ruchala, P. (1992). Maternal confidence, knowledge, and quality of mother-toddler interactions: A preliminary study. *Infant Mental Health Journal, 13,* 353–362.

DeBaryshe, B. D. (1995). Maternal belief systems: Linchpin in the home reading process. *Journal of Applied Developmental Psychology, 16,* 1–20.

DeTemple, J. M. (2001). Parents and children reading books together. In D. K. Dickinson & P. O. Tabors (Eds.), *Beginning literacy with language: Young children learning at home and school* (pp. 31–51). Baltimore: Brookes.

DeTemple, J. M., & Beals, D. E. (1991). Family talk: Sources of support for the development of decontextualized language skills. *Journal of Research in Childhood Education, 6,* 11–19.

Dembo, M. H., Swietzer, M., & Lauritzen, P. (1985). An evaluation of group parent education: Behavioral, PET, and Adlerian programs. *Review of Educational Research, 55,* 155–200.

Dickinson, D. K., & DeTemple, J. (1998). Putting parents in the picture: Maternal reports of preschoolers' literacy as a predictor of early reading. *Early Childhood Research Quarterly, 13,* 241–261.

Dolan, L., & Haxby, B. (1995). *Removing barriers to learning: Factors that affect participation and dropout in parent interventions. Report No. 27.* Baltimore: Center on Families, Communities, Schools, and Children's Learning, Johns Hopkins University.

Edwards, P. A. (1994). Responses of teachers and African-American mothers to a book-reading intervention program. In D. K. Dickinson (Ed.), *Bridges to literacy: Children, families, and schools* (pp. 175–208). Cambridge, MA: Blackwell.

Estrada, P., Arsenio, W. F., Hess, R. D., & Holloway, S. D. (1987). Affective quality of the mother-child relationship: Longitudinal consequences for children's school-relevant cognitive functioning. *Developmental Psychology, 23,* 210–215.

Goodman, Y. M. (1986). Children coming to know literacy. In W. H. Teale & E. Sulzby (Eds.), *Emergent literacy: Writing and reading.* Norwood, NJ: Ablex.

Goodnow, J. J., & Collins, W. A. (1990). *Development according to parents: The nature, sources, and consequences of parents' ideas.* Hillsdale, NJ: Lawrence Erlbaum Associates.

Goodson, B. D., Swartz, J. P., & Millsap, M. A. (1991). *Working with families: Promising programs to help parents support young children's learning.* Prepared for the U.S. Department of Education, Office of Planning, Budget and Evaluation.

Hart, B., & Risley, T. R. (1995). *Meaningful differences in the everyday experience of young American children.* Baltimore: Brookes.

Haslam, B., & Stief, E. (1998, November). *Observational study of Even Start Family Literacy Projects: Preliminary findings.* Washington, DC: Policy Studies Associates. Also, Haslam, B. (1998, October). Presentation at the U.S. Department of Education State Even Start Coordinators' meeting, San Diego.

Heath, S. B. (1983). *Ways with words.* Cambridge: Cambridge University Press.

Heinicke, C. M., Beckwith, L., & Thompson, A. (1988). Early intervention in the family system: A framework and review. *Infant Mental Health Journal, 9,* 111–141.

Herr, T., Halpern, R., & Majeske, R. (1995). Bridging the worlds of Head Start and welfare-to-work: Building a two-generation self-sufficiency program from the ground up. In I. Sigel (Series Ed.) & S. Smith (Vol. Ed.), *Advances in applied developmental psychology, Vol. 9: Two generation programs for families in poverty: A new intervention strategy* (pp. 161–197). Norwood, NJ: Ablex.

Hess, R. D., Holloway, S. D., Dickson, W. P., & Price, G. G. (1984). Maternal variables as predictors of children's school readiness and later achievement in vocabulary and mathematics in sixth grade. *Child Development, 55,* 1902–1912.

Hess, R. D., & McDevitt, T. M. (1984). Some cognitive consequences of maternal intervention techniques: A longitudinal study. *Child Development, 55,* 2017–2030.

Hess, R. D., & Shipman, V. C. (1965). Early experience and the socialization of cognitive modes in children. *Child Development, 36,* 869–886.

Holden, G. W., & Edwards, L. A. (1989). Parental attitudes toward child rearing: Instruments, issues, and implications. *Psychological Bulletin, 106,* 29–58.

Hoover-Dempsey, K. B., & Sandler, H. M. (1997). Why do parents become involved in their children's education? *Review of Educational Research, 67,* 3–42.

International Reading Association and National Association for the Education of Young Children. (1998). Learning to read and write: Developmentally appropriate practices for young children. *Young Children, 53,* 30–46.

Johnson, D. L., & Walker, T. B. (1991). *Final report of an evaluation of the Avance Parent Education and Family Support Program.* Report submitted to the Carnegie Corporation. San Antonio, TX: Avance.

Johnson, J. E., & Martin, C. (1985). Parents' beliefs and home learning environments: Effects on cognitive development. In I. E. Sigel (Ed.), *Parental belief systems* (pp. 25–50). Hillsdale, NJ: Lawrence Erlbaum Associates.

Machida, S., Taylor, A. R., & Kim, J. (2002). The role of maternal beliefs in predicting home learning activities in Head Start families. *Family Relations, 51,* 176–184.

McGillicuddy-DeLisi, A. V. (1985). The relationship between parental beliefs and children's cognitive level. In I. E. Sigel (Ed.), *Parental belief systems* (pp. 7–24). Hillsdale, NJ: Lawrence Erlbaum Associates.

Mikulecky, L. (1996). Family literacy: Parent and child interactions. In L. A. Benjamin & J. Lord (Eds.), *Family literacy: Directions in research and implications for practice* (pp. 55–63). Washington, DC: U.S. Department of Education.

Nathanson, S., Stief, E., Marzke, C., & O'Brien, E. (1998). *First steps toward school success: Promising practices in Even Start Family Literacy projects serving infants and toddlers and their families.* Report prepared for the U.S. Department of Education. Washington, DC: Policy Studies Associates.

Neuman, S. B., Hagedorn, T., Celano, D., & Daly, P. (1995). Toward a collaborative approach to parent involvement in early education: A study of teenage mothers in an African-American community. *American Educational Research Journal, 32*(4), 801–827.

Neuman, S. B., & Gallagher, P. (1994). Joining together in literacy learning: Teenage mothers and children. *Reading Research Quarterly, 29,* 382–401.

Olds, D. L., Henderson, C. R., Tatelbaum, R., & Chamberlin, R. (1986). Improving the delivery of prenatal care and outcomes of pregnancy: A randomized trial of nurse home visitation. *Pediatrics, 77,* 16–28.

Parcel, T. L., & Menaghan, E. G. (1994). *Parents' jobs and children's lives.* New York: Aldine de Gruyter.

Pellegrini, A. D., Brody, G. H., & Sigel, I. E. (1985). Parents' book-reading habits with their children. *Journal of Educational Psychology, 77,* 332–340.

Powell, D. R. (1994). Evaluating family support programs: Are we making progress? In S. L. Kagan & B. Weissbourd (Eds.), *Putting families first: America's family support movement and the challenge of change* (pp. 441–470). San Francisco: Jossey-Bass.

Powell, D. R. (1996). Teaching parenting and basic skills to parents: What we know. In L. A. Benjamin & J. Lord (Eds.), *Family literacy: Directions in research and implications for practice* (pp. 65–71). Washington, DC: U.S. Department of Education.

Powell, D. R., & D'Angelo, D. (2000). *Framework for Parenting Education in Even Start Family Literacy Programs.* Washington, DC: U.S. Department of Education.

Provence, S., Naylor, A., & Patterson, J. (1977). *The challenge of daycare.* New Haven, CT: Yale University Press.

Riedinger, S. A. (1997). *Even Start: Facilitating transitions to kindergarten.* Prepared for the U.S. Department of Education. Washington, DC: Mathematica Policy Research, Inc.

Rivlin, A. M., & Timpane, P. M. (1975). Planned variation in education: An assessment. In A. M. Rivlin & P. M. Timpane (Eds.), *Planned variation in education: Should we give up or try harder?* (pp. 1–21). Washington, DC: Brookings Institution.

Ryan, K. E., Geissler, B., & Knell, S. (1994). Evaluating family literacy programs: Tales from the field. In D. K. Dickinson (Ed.), *Bridges to literacy: Children, families, and schools* (pp. 236–264). Cambridge, MA: Blackwell.

Scarborough, H. S., & Dobrich, W. (1994). On the efficacy of reading to preschoolers. *Developmental Review, 14,* 245–302.

Segal, M. (1985). A study of maternal beliefs and values within the context of an intervention program. In I. E. Sigel (Ed.), *Parental belief systems: The psychological consequences for children* (pp. 271–286). Hillsdale, NJ: Lawrence Erlbaum Associates.

Seitz, V., & Apfel, N. (1994). Parent-focused intervention: Diffusion effects on siblings. *Child Development, 65,* 677–683.

Seitz, V., Rosenbaum, L. D., & Apfel, N. H. (1985). Effects of family support intervention: A ten-year follow-up. *Child Development, 56,* 376–391.

Sigel, I. E. (1992). The belief-behavior connection: A resolvable dilemma? In I. E. Sigel, A. V. McGillicuddy-DeLisi, & J. J. Goodnow (Eds.), *Parental belief systems: The psychological consequences for children* (2nd ed., pp. 433–456). Hillsdale, NJ: Lawrence Erlbaum Associates.

Slaughter, D. T. (1983). Early intervention and its effects on maternal and child development. *Monographs of the Society for Research in Child Development, 48*(4, Serial No. 202).

Smith, S. (1995). Evaluating two-generation interventions: Current efforts and directions for future research. In I. Sigel (Series Ed.) & S. Smith (Vol. Ed.), *Advances in Applied Developmental Psychology, Vol. 9: Two generation programs for families in poverty: A new intervention strategy* (pp. 251–270). Norwood, NJ: Ablex.

Snow, C. E., Barnes, W. S., Chandler, J., Goodman, I. F., & Hemphill, L. (1991). *Unfulfilled expectations: Home and school influences on literacy.* Cambridge, MA: Harvard University Press.

Snow, C. E., Burns, M. S., & Griffin, P. (Eds.). (1998). *Preventing reading difficulties in young children.* Washington, DC: National Academy Press.

Sonnenschein, S., Baker, L., Serpell, R., & Schmidt, D. (2000). Reading is a source of entertainment: The importance of the home perspective for children's literacy development. In K. A. Roskos & J. F. Christie (Eds.), *Play and literacy in early childhood: Research from multiple perspectives* (pp. 107–124). Mahwah, NJ: Lawrence Erlbaum Associates.

St.Pierre, R., Layzer, J., Goodson, B., & Bernstein, L. (1997). *The effectiveness of comprehensive case management interventions: Findings from the National Evaluation of the Comprehensive Child Development Program.* Technical report. Cambridge, MA: Abt Associates, Inc.

St.Pierre, R. G., & Swartz, J. (1995). The Even Start Family Literacy Program. In I. Sigel (Series Ed.) & S. Smith (Vol. Ed.), *Advances in Applied Developmental Psychology, Vol. 9: Two generation programs for families in poverty: A new intervention strategy* (pp. 37–66). Norwood, NJ: Ablex.

St.Pierre, R., Swartz, J., Gamse, B., Murray, S., Deck, D., & Nickel, P. (1995). *National evaluation of the Even Start family literacy program: Final report.* Cambridge, MA: Abt Associates, Inc.

St.Pierre, R., Ricciuti, A., Tao, F., Creps, C., Swartz, J. Lee, W., Parsad, A., & Rimdzius, T. (2003). Third national Even Start evaluation: Program impacts and implications for improvement. Washington, DC: U.S. Department of Education.

Storch, S. A., & Whitehurst, G. J. (2001). The role of family and home in the literacy development of children from low-income backgrounds. In P. R. Britto & J. Brooks-Gunn (Eds.), *The role of family literacy environments in promoting young children's emerging literacy skills* (pp. 53–71). San Francisco: Jossey-Bass.

Sulzby, E., & Teale, W. H. (1991). Emergent literacy. In R. Barr, M. L. Kamil, B. Mostenthal, & P. D. Pearson (Eds.), *Handbook of reading research* (pp. 173–206). Norwood, NJ: Ablex.

Tabors, P. O., Beals, D. E., & Weizman, Z. O. (2001). "Young know what oxygen is?" Learning new words at home. In D. K. Dickinson & P. O. Tabors (Eds.), *Beginning literacy with language: Young children learning at home and school* (pp. 93–110). Baltimore: Brookes.

Tabors, P. O., Roach, K. A., & Snow, C. E. (2001). Home language and literacy environment: Final results. In D. K. Dickinson & P. O. Tabors (Eds.), *Beginning literacy with language: Young children learning at home and school* (pp. 111–138). Baltimore: Brookes.

Tao, F., Gamse, B., & Tarr, H. (1998). *National evaluation of the Even Start Family Literacy Program. Final report.* Washington, DC: U.S. Department of Education, Planning and Evaluation Service.

Teti, D. M., & Gelfand, D. M. (1991). Behavioral competence among mothers of infants in the first year: The mediational role of maternal self-efficacy. *Child Development, 62,* 918–929.

Whitehurst, G. J., & Lonigan, C. J. (1998). Child development and emergent literacy. *Child Development, 69,* 848–872.

Whitehurst, G. J., Arnold, D. H., Epstein, J. N., Angell, A. L., Smith, M., & Fischel, J. E. (1994). A picture book reading intervention in daycare and home for children from low-income families. *Developmental Psychology, 30,* 679–689.

10

Relationships Among Children and Adults and Family Literacy

Robert C. Pianta
University of Virginia

For as long as literacy has been studied, interactions and relationships between children and adults have been recognized as the primary medium through which literacy is acquired. From birth, children engage in increasingly elaborated and symbolically mediated interactions with caregivers in which emotion, cognition, and communication are intertwined and organized. The capacity, skill, and interest to read, understand, and produce written language emerge out of this complex, dynamic, multisystem process (Snow, Burns, & Griffin, 1998). In this sense, literacy, both broadly conceived and narrowly viewed, is only one marker point along a broad and long developmental progression in which children's capacities and skills emerge from child–adult relationships.

Learning to read is more than just acquiring cognitive or linguistic skills—It is also a developmental process involving social and cultural mechanisms (Benjamin & Lord, 1996; Heath, 1982; Teale, 1986). Although one way a focus on relationships appears in research on early literacy has been in studies of joint storybook reading by mothers and children (deJong & Leseman, 2001; Juel, 1998), it is abundantly clear that caregivers play a much broader and long-standing role in these developmental mechanisms in terms of providing language stimulation and conversation; co-regulation of attention, arousal, interest, and emotional experience; and direct transmission of phonological information and content (e.g., Baker, Mackler, Sonnenschein, & Serpell, 2001; Benjamin & Lord, 1996; Hart & Risley, 1992; Morrow, Rand, & Smith, 1995; Whitehurst & Lonigan, 1998). In interactions between children and adults, the transmission of literacy-relevant information occurs at multiple levels and across multiple domains—including encouraging the belief that the printed word is interesting and that it conveys culturally relevant information and involving the ways in which phonemes and graphemes map onto one another. Family literacy programs deal with this phenomenon in all its complexity.

A developmental systems perspective can be helpful in considering the role that adult–child relationships play in the complexity of acquiring proficiency in literacy. This perspective provides some conceptual tools that can be helpful to researchers and practitioners (Lyon, 2002; Snow et al., 1998). In this view, the child is viewed as a dynamic system developing in multilayered contexts with emphasis placed on the linkages between and among capacities within the child (e.g., among social, language, and cognitive development) and between the child and the external world (e.g., how social relationships and interactions with adults and peers function in relation to the child's emerging skills). Interactions and transactions are a primary focus of inquiry and theory in a systems-informed perspective (Sameroff, 1995).

DEVELOPMENTAL SYSTEMS THEORY

As has been described, literacy behavior emerges from a multitude of component processes and transactions with the environment. General systems theory (GST) has a long history in the understanding of biological, ecological, and other complex living systems (e.g., Ford & Ford, 1987; Ford & Lerner, 1992) and has been applied to child development by numerous investigators (e.g., Ford & Lerner, 1992; Sameroff, 1995). Several key principles used by this perspective can be helpful in advancing our understanding of the role of adult-child relationships in the development of literacy. These principles include a focus on multiple levels of analysis and the concept of distributed capacity.

Units of Analysis Across Multiple Levels

Systems link with other systems within and across many levels of analysis or abstraction. Understanding the function of a given system or unit (such as a child's self-regulation or phonological awareness) requires attention not only to that unit's actions but also to how it functions in a broader context or hierarchy of systems (such as child–adult relationships, families, or classrooms). The consequence of this perspective is that efforts to study, assess, or change complex developmental processes such as literacy are incomplete and fundamentally unproductive unless they take into consideration how the unit of focus at a given time or situation (e.g., whether a child knows letters) functions within the multiple systems in which it is embedded. The area of family literacy is strongly identified with this principle of multilayered systems by virtue of its emphasis on understanding and improving the child's developing competence in literacy in the context of family values and practices, culture, and parents' own literacy skills and interests (e.g., Benjamin & Lord, 1996).

This principle of interacting systems is apparent in literacy acquisition in other ways as well. Recent views of literacy development posit two related but distinct components of literacy behaviors—one involving meaning, language, interest, and understanding and the other involving phonological processing, metalinguistic, and cognitive skills (e.g., Lyon, 2002; Senechal, LeFevre, Smith-Chant, & Colton, 2001). Similarly, Snow and Tabors (1996) discuss the components of literacy as organized within enjoyment/engagement and linguistic/cognitive mechanisms. The fact that there is lively debate about the distinctness of these two domains of processing, their relation to one another (e.g., sequential or co-acting), and whether instructional approaches should focus more strongly on one relative to the other (Foorman, Francis, Fletcher, Schatschneider, & Mehta, 1998; Whitehurst & Lonigan, 1998; Yaden, Rowe, & MacGillivray, 1999) is testimony to the challenge of forming integrative and comprehensive theory and applications in a multisystem world. Theories of literacy acquisition must address in some fashion this multisystem, multidomain phenomenon and so require conceptual tools that correspond to this complexity.

Distributed Capacity

As just noted, developmental capacity and behavior in one domain or functional unit cannot be understood without reference to other domains or units. A young child's capacity to engage in a book-reading task is dependent on a host of skills, many of which involve or are embedded in the child's experiences and interactions with personal and material resources in a variety of settings. Children are in dynamic interactions with these settings, constantly exchanging information, material, and energy (Ford & Ford, 1987). In this view, the developing child has somewhat permeable boundaries and properties that appear to *reside* in the child but are actually distributed across *both* the child and the resources they engage within these settings (Hofer, 1994; Resnick, 1994). For the young child, skills related to attention, problem solving, literacy, general knowledge, social cognition, and self-control—that are typical foci of assessment or instruction—are distributed across the child and settings via interactions and relationships. Literacy behaviors displayed by children, even those at the level of skills involved in processing phoneme–grapheme associations, are in part embedded in these interactions and, in this view, not properties of the child per se (Whitehurst et al., 1994). In this view, relationships between children and adults are a conduit for energy and information that fuel developmental change.

Any comprehensive view of the development of literacy must therefore take into account the nature and function of child–adult relationships (Mikulecky, 1996). There is little doubt that the field recognizes this, as evidenced by the scores of articles on parent–child storybook reading (e.g., Bus, van IJzendoorn, & Pellegrini, 1995), child–teacher interactions, and instructional practices in child-care preschool and elementary school settings (e.g., NICHD Early Child Care Research Network, 2002), and intervention approaches that specifically target parent–child interactions (e.g., Whitehurst et al., 1994), as well as by several chapters in this handbook, especially those in Section II. This body of work suggests that becoming a facile independent reader involves multilevel developmental processes that are activated and regulated by interactions with more competent readers. For most young children, these more competent readers are adults. Yet despite a long-standing and growing recognition of the importance of child–adult relationships in work on literacy development and family literacy in particular, certain key features of these relationships, as systems, need greater emphasis as work in this area moves ahead.

First and foremost, if one acknowledges the value of adult–child relationships for literacy development, then it is necessary to recognize that such relationships do not simply appear when the child enters preschool and early elementary school, but their contributions to literacy development extend back into infancy and involve competencies and functions that bear little resemblance to book reading. Second, as the field of family literacy continues to work to support the ways in which adult–child relationships enhance literacy growth and development, a model of relationship components and processes can be an important tool for advancing research and theory.

RELATIONSHIP THEMES IN INFANCY AND EARLY CHILDHOOD

It is no surprise to most researchers and practitioners in early literacy that any attempt to understand or enhance literacy acquisition must address the function of child–adult (largely child–parent) relationships. However, to the extent that there has been a focus on these relationships, the focus to some degree has been constrained by age and by domain. That is, most considerations of adult–child relationships and early literacy (with notable exceptions) have their primary focus on literacy and language as the sole developmental domains of interest and/or limit the timeframe of consideration to the toddler or preschool age and older. Yet, to the extent that these domain- and time-constrained studies have validated the need to place increasing emphasis on adult–child relationships, then it is necessary to take a more comprehensive view of how these relationships function to support literacy competence. A starting point for this effort is a discussion of broad, integrative relationship themes starting in early infancy and moving into and through the preschool and early elementary period.

Sroufe (1989, 1996) describes the developmental themes around which interactions between children and caregiving adults (parents, child-care providers, teachers) are organized over time. The interactions and transactions that take place around these themes could be considered core conditions that support development for many outcomes, including literacy. These early adult–child relational themes include (a) regulation and modulation of physiological arousal; (b) formation of an effective attachment relationship; and (c) self-reliance, organization, and coordination of environmental and personal resources. These themes are fairly global in terms of level of analysis—They describe relational processes and mechanisms within which are organized those processes and mechanisms we typically associate with literacy acquisition, for example, dialogic reading, playing rhyming games, or learning language and vocabulary. As such, it can be easy to dismiss their importance for outcomes such as literacy. But one reason for attending to these relational-level themes is that, functionally, these relational processes can undermine developmental progress in processes that are more specifically literacy related. For example, as will be seen, mother–child dyads in which the mother fails to respond sensitively and responsively to the infants' interactive cues are often the same dyads in which problems with interaction get in the way of competent storybook reading or interactive rhyming games (e.g., Bus et al., 1995).

The first relationship theme involves *regulation and modulation of physiological arousal and joint attention*. In the first months and year of life, the infant (and caregiver) must tolerate increasingly complex physical and social stimulation and maintain an organized state in the face of this increasing complexity. This organized state leads to periods of joint attention and mutuality—the basis of exploration of the object and interpersonal world. Cycles of sleep and alertness, feeding, interest, and arousal all begin to become organized very early on within this period. The immature status of the newborn predisposes the child to require caregiver interactions to help maintain organization in the face of cyclic physiologic, arousal, and state variations (Hofer, 1994; Sander, 1975).

In competent forms of adaptation, the infant responds to routines set by caregivers and, with caregivers, establishes regular rhythms of feeding, activity/alertness, and sleep. Competence-supporting contexts ensure the maintenance of smooth, regular, predictable routines and practices that are contingent on infant cues. The infant and caregiver coordinate their interactive behaviors to establish routines that, in turn, form the basis of self and relationships (Sroufe, 1989). Interactive patterns generally broaden to include interactive play (e.g., peek-a-boo games); form a relational matrix that organizes the infant in the face of increasingly complex stimulation; and lay the foundation for processes related to communicative intent, function, and skill.

In less competent forms of adaptation at this stage there may be a tendency toward over- and underarousal. The infant may show little or no predictability in terms of routines, little interest in interactions, or is so difficult to settle and soothe that caregivers become increasingly stressed and unpredictable. These maladaptive patterns of behavior are linked with patterns of incompetent adaptation later in development: insecure attachment, poor exploration, and inadequate self-regulation (Sroufe, 1996). These patterns of infant maladaptation are often embedded in interactions with highly stressful environments in terms of financial or psychosocial stress, intrusive caregiving interactions, over- and understimulating households, maternal depression, and child maltreatment. These environments contribute to infant and relational maladaptation via disordered child–caregiver interactions (e.g., Cohn, Campbell, Matias, & Hopkins, 1990; Egeland, Pianta, & O'Brien, 1993) that disrupt the ways that these interactions transmit knowledge and skill, which ultimately may affect literacy-specific interactions.

This early phase of development has marked consequences for literacy outcomes. Difficulties in establishing shared attention and engagement predict problems in behavioral and emotional regulation that have consequences for the level of enjoyment and information conveyed in joint book-reading interactions that take place later in toddlerhood and the preschool years (Bus et al., 1995). Problems in the caregiving regulatory system (Hofer, 1994) early in infancy strongly influence the emergent self-regulatory capacities of the preschool child and undermine the extent to which child–adult interactions function effectively to transmit information and experiences to the child in an efficient and effective way. The quality of these early child–adult interactions affect whether the child will be a willing or skilled partner in activities in which language and communication (either oral or print based) is involved. Thus, family-based or home-based early intervention approaches that focus on enhancing the quality of very early child–caregiver interactions; that reduce risk factors such as parental (maternal) depression; and that provide emotional, informational, and instrumental support to parents can be among the most foundational aspects of communities' efforts related to child and family literacy (Fuligni & Brooks-Gunn, 2000). The importance of these early interactional patterns for later literacy development cannot be underestimated. To the extent that the vast majority of language development supporting later literacy occurs within the home setting and is predicated on these early interactive rhythms and communicative styles and skills (e.g., Snow, Barnes, Chandler, Goodman, & Hemphill, 1991), attempts to enhance literacy for underachieving children can only be strengthened by attention to the earliest patterns of dyadic regulation.

Building on the establishment of interactive rhythms that effectively regulate physiological variation and produce bouts of joint dyadic cooperation and turn taking, the next relational theme emerges during the latter months of the first year of life and continues on through childhood: the formation and maintenance of an effective attachment relationship. An effective attachment develops as a consequence of early patterns of interaction, affords the child a sense of emotional security in the context of a relationship, and provides a basis for exploration of the object and interpersonal world. Adult responsiveness, emotional availability, and an effective signaling system all play important roles in attachment processes (Ainsworth, Blehar, Waters, & Wall, 1978), as does the caregiver's previous attachment experiences and own self-regulation of attention and emotion (Fonagy, Steele, & Steele, 1991; Main & Hesse, 1990; Zeanah et al., 1993).

Fundamentally, attachment processes are a relationship-level mechanism for regulating emotion and behavior related to security and threat, which has important consequences for an immature organism beginning to move around on its own (Sroufe, 1996). Attachment mechanisms involve attention, motor behavior, fear and wariness, and signaling systems between the caregiver and the child. Critically, to the extent that these systems function effectively, the child is free to move about and explore the social and material world in the presence of the caregiver (or a surrogate). When threat is perceived or experienced by the child or caregiver, attachment processes are activated, the child and caregiver seek proximity to each other, the caregiver provides comfort and assurance, attachment is deactivated, and the child is free to move away again and explore (Ainsworth et al., 1978). This link between attachment and exploration involves an integration of social and cognitive processes by which social and emotional development play key roles in advancing cognitive skill through enabling efficient and active exploration of, and attention to, information in the environment. This exploration-supporting function of attachment is often called the *secure-base* function, a term that recognizes this idea of an adult–child relationship serving as a conduit to information. The extent to which a relationship serves this secure base function is related to the child's sense of emotional (and physical) safety and security; the effectiveness, depth, and complexity of communication and emotional expression between adult and child; and the adult's skilled integration of new information into ongoing interactive sequences. From the standpoint of families' roles in literacy development, it is important to emphasize the central role that emotion plays in the attachment relationship (Sroufe, 1996).

Not surprisingly, secure attachment has been shown to be predictive of language development, emergent literacy and reading, cognitive development and play, and social interaction
with peers and other adults (Bus & van IJzendoorn, 1988; Erickson, Sroufe, & Egeland, 1985;
Sroufe, 1989). Attachment, in particular secure base behavior, functions prominently in the
joint book-reading interactions of parents and children that are considered so essential for
enhancing the child's interest in reading, vocabulary, emerging awareness of print–sound relationships, and conventions associated with literate behaviors (Bus et al., 1995). Securely
attached children display more positive emotions during joint storybook-reading interactions
and engage in more extended discussions of the book (Bus, Belsky, van IJzendoorn, & Crnic,
1997; Bus et al., 1995). For example, in one study of 44 to 63-week-old infants, insecurely
attached children were less attentive and engaged during book-reading interactions with their
mothers (Bus & van IJzendoorn, 1997).

Starting in the toddler period, coming full form in the preschool years, and continuing
throughout childhood, functional self-reliance, organization, and coordination of personal and
environmental resources through the establishment of an ever-widening zone of secure-base
behavior becomes an increasingly important theme of parent–child interactions. The concept
of self-reliance recognizes the relational base of the child's efforts to meet social and task-
related demands and focuses on the child's use of his or her own and others' resources to
engage information and tasks available to the child. Effective self-reliance is observed when
the child enthusiastically engages problems in the world and persists in using his or her own
efforts to address the problem, and before giving up or getting too frustrated, signals for and
uses resources from others to solve the problem. This capacity for exploring the world is built
on the relationship foundations of attachment and is supported by the relationships currently
available to the child and how those relationships tolerate and support the child's emerging
autonomy. There is little question that early literacy, usually in the forms of listening to and
telling stories, engaging in conversations, participating in and attending to joint storybook
reading, playing games with words and songs, and even starting to learn letters, is a major
component of child–adult interactions in this period (e.g., Snow et al., 1991).

Storybook reading in the preschool years has been researched extensively, and a number
of positive outcomes are the result of children being read to from an early age. As Juel (1998)
articulated in a book chapter on emergent literacy, children learn about the values and beliefs
shared by cultures and they gain knowledge of how stories are put together and how characters
are portrayed. Children who are frequently read to have been exposed to interesting vocabulary
and they will enter school likely to understand the types of questions about books that teachers
will ask of them (Juel, 1998). Joint storybook reading has been demonstrated to be a source of
knowledge about print (Snow & Tabors, 1996), an introduction to written language concepts,
and has both a socioemotional component and an instructional component. (See chapters by
Purcell-Gates and Morrow and Temlock-Fields, Section II.)

Juel (1998) argues that the two skills that best predict success in reading in the first grade
(phonemic segmentation and alphabet knowledge) are more than likely partly developed from
having been read to before entering school. There seem to be direct and indirect effects associated with joint storybook reading and children's emerging literacy skills. Scarborough and
Dobrich (1994) found evidence for indirect effects of joint storybook reading on the development of oral language skills and emergent literacy. One of the most influential and powerful
skills children learn from being read to is that books and other forms of print are to be appreciated because the written word conveys meaning in a variety of ways. Children's motivation for
investing in reading-related pursuits is cultivated through joint storybook reading, because they
begin to learn that understanding the written word is a tool for enjoyment and for learning how
the world works. Yet these storybook interactions also convey rich information about language,

how oral and more abstract printed forms of communication are integrated and connected to one another (Juel, 1998; Snow et al., 1991), and the ways in which parents call attention to those connections provide the child with key skills as they move on in their exposure to print (Whitehurst et al., 1994). The child's willingness to explore these new, more abstract forms of language, and to thus engage in the kind of more instructionally focused interactions that they require, in large part emerges from the prior relational themes of attachment and secure-base functioning.

Building on the effective attachment relationship developed within infancy, the caregiver–child dyad organizes the child's advancing motor, cognitive, and communicative skills to support exploratory forays with the caregiver providing regulation (comfort, information) at a distance while the child practices autonomy and emerging skills. (The Notice-Nudge-Narrate model described in chapter 4 by Sparling is germane to this description of caregiver–child interactions.) This period creates new challenges and rewards to child–caregiver interaction—on the one hand they afford some relief from some physical aspects of caregiving, whereas on the other they elicit new feelings in the parent (e.g., anxiety over control, pride) and child limit testing as a challenge to the relationship. Thus the child–caregiver relationship reorganizes in this period—it must tolerate the child's autonomy strivings while at the same time provide substantial support. The relationship is more complex than it was in infancy, especially as experienced by the caregiver, when predictable routines were by and large the primary challenge.

Kopp and Wyer (1994) suggest that nonverbal communication involving gestures and social/emotional behaviors (body posture, intentional movements, facial expressions) are a core process in the regulation of child–adult interactions and children's emotions during this developmental period. Mastering basic functions of emotional and behavioral regulation are fundamental aspects of competence that are undertaken in the preschool period by the parent–child (and the teacher–child) dyad that are ultimately transferred to the child and become basic foundations for learning in school. Maintaining balanced interest and arousal while exploring the world builds on gestural functioning while integrating more symbolic and abstract verbal forms. A key issue in the preschool period, according to Kopp and Wyer, is this integration of gestural and verbal forms of regulation.

Adult–child dyads that competently regulate preschoolers' emotional experience tend to also support the development of skills in domains such as literacy. As noted earlier, mother–preschooler dyads characterized by secure attachment and cooperative, responsive interactions read together more frequently (Bus & van IJzendoorn, 1995), find reading together more enjoyable and rewarding (Bus et al., 1995); and children in these dyads receive more literacy-related information and instruction (Bus & van IJzendoorn, 1988). Thus, how the mother–child dyad functionally regulates the child's emotional experience through the toddler's preschool years can have important consequences for literacy development. Efforts to promote literacy development in family literacy programs must take seriously this emotion-regulation function of the relationship between child and parent at this age.

The child–parent relationship regulates several aspects of emotional development according to Thompson (1994)—the production of emotion, relief of emotional distress, reinforcement of certain emotional experiences, interpretation of emotion and emotion cues, and strategies for self-regulation. Increased organization, intentionality, functionality, and complexity of emotion regulation processes often are used as markers of the difference between *early* and *middle childhood*, whereas deficits in these skills are viewed as central to the most common behavior problems in children and are related to difficulty using instructional resources in home, preschool, and classroom settings. Difficulties in emotion regulation and related functions often interfere with the social interactions and instructional interactions that are designed to increase growth in academic skills and may also be correlated with basic psychological mechanisms related to attention and executive function that are implicated in literacy-related competencies (Thompson, 1994).

Thompson (1994) suggests that neurophysiological processes, attention, interpretation of emotion-related events, encoding of internal emotion cues, access to coping resources, regulating emotional demands of certain settings, and selecting adaptive response alternatives are all part of emotion regulation, and each of these is influenced by interactions with adults. Language and symbols become an increasingly functional component of emotion regulation in this period. Greenberg and colleagues (Greenberg, Kusche, & Speltz, 1991; Greenberg, Speltz, & DeKlyen, 1993) describe the adult as intertwined in emotion regulation (providing comfort for arousing experiences and labels for the child's affective states) to such an extent that regulation occurs in the context of the child–adult relationship. Affective labels, first nonsymbolic, then symbolic, form the basis for emerging links among cognition, language, and emotion that are then enacted in various forms between child and adult. These symbols for emotional experience, acquired in the context of the child–adult relationship, have consequences for self-reliance as related to mastery of increasingly challenging preacademic skills.

However, emotional security and sensitive responsiveness during this preschool period, although perhaps necessary for establishing relationship-level functioning that supports ongoing enjoyment of reading and engagement in language-focused activities, may not be a sufficient condition for competence as an independent reader (Baker et al., 2001; de Jong & Leseman, 2001). During the later preschool years and continuing for several years into elementary school, a more intentionally instructional component of adult–child interaction, in which the adult provides cues to phone–grapheme relations and elicits the child's performance and practicing of these skills, becomes a key determinant of the child's capacity to actually read text independently (Haden, Reese, & Fivush, 1996; Hochenberger, Goldstein, & Haas, 1999; Pellegrini, Perlmutter, Galda, & Brody, 1990). It is at this phase of literacy development—when language and interest-focused interactions that once had primarily a social and emotional goal become integrated with instructional interactions that have a skill-based goal—that the capacity of adult–child relationships to support literacy growth and development are most heavily taxed and stressed.

The introduction of a skill-focused, instructional component to adult–child literacy interactions (such as storybook reading) appears to be the single-most challenging aspect of parents' (and early childhood teachers') helping children to learn to read. This instructional capacity and function of the adult–child relationship appears directly linked to the child's success in decoding phoneme–grapheme relations (Mikulecky, 1996) and is therefore fundamental to the child's emerging competence as an independent reader. From this point onward, how adult–child relationships introduce and accommodate this instructional form of interaction and ultimately balance skill-focused intentions with enjoyment/meaning-focused interactions is a challenge that can determine whether or not the child will competently read (Mikulecky, 1996; Snow & Tabors, 1996).

Available data suggest that this challenge emerges in the preschool years and continues onward throughout early childhood and into the elementary school years (Baker et al., 2001; Haden et al., 1996; Hockenberger et al., 1999; Whitehurst et al., 1994). That parents, child-care providers, and elementary school teachers show such enormous variation in the instructional component of literacy-related interactions with children in the preschool and early elementary school years, in the presence of, on average, quite positive social and emotional interactions, is evidence of the degree to which the integration of instructional interactions in literacy is an enormous challenge facing these adults and about which we simply do not yet know enough (e.g., NICHD, 2002; Whitehurst et al., 1994). This challenge is compounded in family literacy programs in which parents are often challenged by life circumstances, and the social and emotional foundations of relationships can be compromised (Mikulecky, 1996; Powell, 1996).

Summary

Clearly, relationships between children and adults play a prominent role in the development of literacy-related competencies starting as early as infancy and extending into the preschool and elementary school years. With regard to literacy development, adult–child relationships serve two primary functions. They support the development of basic task-related skills such as attention, conceptual development, communication skills, and reasoning as well as the motivation and interest to approach tasks in an organized, confident manner, to seek help when needed, and to use help appropriately. This cluster of skills establishes the communicative and motivational infrastructure for literacy growth—enhancing the child's sense that reading can be a means of accessing meaningful information and enjoyment. For example, parent–child dialog is ideal for maximizing language growth in young children and for facilitating the acquisition of reading skills (Allison & Watson, 1994; Pressley, 1998; Snow, Burns, & Griffin, 1998). The other function served by adult–child relationships is instructional—through which intentional efforts by the adult call increasingly explicit attention to the grapheme–phoneme code in all its forms. In joint literacy interactions such as storybook reading parents offer cues and clues to decoding that provide the child with essential skills promoting independence as a reader (Juel, 1998; Whitehurst et al., 1994). The motivational/communicative function of the relationship supports the instructional function but cannot replace its unique importance for literacy growth. This situation may be particularly true for children who are likely to have difficulty learning to read, as evidence suggests that explicit instruction in phonological skills appear a necessary condition for poor readers to attain proficiency (Blachman, 1997). Thus, adult–child relationships serve two interdependent functional goals with regard to literacy— motivation/communication and instruction/skill acquisition.

To this point relationships have been discussed primarily in terms of interactions between the child and the adult, noting constructs such as sensitivity, instruction, attention, and communication. Yet relationships are composed of components that extend beyond interactions, components that often can determine the value of those interactions for development. The next section presents a model for understanding, and ultimately researching, these components and their functioning within a relationship, consideration of which could have implications for further addressing the role of adult–child relationships in facilitating growth and development in literacy.

A Model of Adult-Child Relationship Processes

Up to this point, adult–child relationships have been identified as important factors in literacy development, yet little has been discussed in terms of the actual aspects of these relationships themselves: their key components and how they function. However, as adult–child relationships gain prominence in the work of family literacy researchers and practitioners, a more elaborated understanding of these relationships is key for capturing and enhancing their potential influences on literacy. In Fig. 10.1, the child–adult relationship is depicted as a system composed of several components and processes. The model is intended as a guide for identifying and understanding these features and how they interrelate.

Consistent with Hinde (1987) and others (Sameroff & Emde, 1989) the model views relationships as dyadic systems, and therefore the principles of systems that were described earlier apply to these relationships. From a systems perspective a relationship between a parent (or teacher) and a child is not equivalent to only their interactions with each other, or to their characteristics as individuals. The relationship, as a system, is composed of subordinate units and subsystems, but is not reducible to a certain unit or subsystem. A relationship between a teacher and an adult is not wholly determined by that child's temperament, intelligence, or

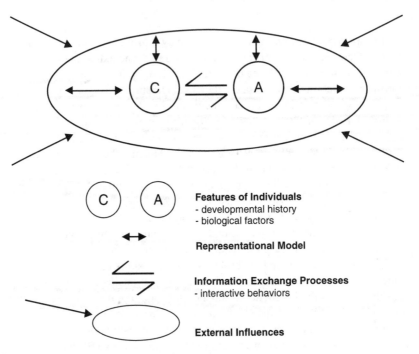

FIG. 10.1.   A conceptual model of adult–child relationships.

communication skills. Nor can their relationship be reduced to the pattern of reinforcement between them. Relationships are the organization of these features of interactions or individuals into a coherent whole (Sroufe, 1989), and so efforts to describe or modify relationships must often address both the parts and the whole (Pianta, 1999).

The model of relationship systems depicts several components that can each be the focus of assessment and intervention. First, relationships embody features of the individuals involved. These features include biologically predisposed characteristics (e.g., temperament), personality factors, the individuals' developmental history, as well as features closely connected to the quality of the relationship itself—what Bowlby (1969) called the members' "representation" of the relationship. Next, relationships include feedback processes, the purpose of which is to exchange information between the two individuals. These processes include behavioral interactions, language and communication, perceptions of self and other—that serve as feedback mechanisms in the context of this dyadic system. This feedback, or information exchange processes, is critical to the smooth functioning of the relationship. These feedback mechanisms serve the function of regulating the two individuals' behavior with regard to certain functional goals, which in the case of literacy could be the functions described in the previous section—motivation/communication and instruction/skill acquisition. Finally, adult–child relationships are affected by the settings and conditions in which they are embedded.

Features of Individuals in Relationships.   At the most basic level, relationships incorporate features of individuals. These include biological facts (such as gender) or biological processes (such as temperament, genetics, stress reactivity) as well as developed features such as personality, self-esteem, or intelligence. One's developmental history affects interactions with others, and in turn, relationships (Zeanah et al., 1993; Fonagy et al., 1991). For example, an adult's history of being cared for can be related to how they understand the goals of teaching and in turn relate to the way she interprets and attends to a child's emotional behavior and cues (Zeanah et al.). Powell (1996) describes the ways in which parents' attitudes and beliefs about literacy can shape their behaviors toward facilitating their children's acquisition of literacy skills, an aspect of how a product of a parent's development becomes a feature of that individual that plays a major role in how the relationship system supports literacy development for the child. Features of parents and other adults such as education, occupation, interests, and attitudes will all be organized within the adult–child relationship and potentially play an active role in shaping its functional significance.

Representations.   One thing that individuals bring to relationships is what is termed an *internal working model* or *representational model* of relationships (Bowlby, 1969; Stern, 1989). In layman's terms, this model is like a map, a guide, or a template that the individual carries with him or her that contains a set of rules or guides for behavior in relationships, based on previous and current experience in relationships. It can be fairly specific, like a model for relationships with children (in your own family or in your own classroom), or general, like a model for all relationships. From an adult's perspective, these models encompass the adult's (parent, teacher) accumulated feelings and beliefs about their behaviors with children (what works and does not work in getting children to comply), their goals for interaction with children (how they relate to 5-year-olds), and their goals for interacting with a specific child in a specific situation, such as reading a book together (Juel, 1988). Powell's (1996) argument that family literacy interventions must start with parents' beliefs about parenting and the goals of parents for their interactions with their children is consistent with this view of how representations constrain behavior.

There are several key points about representation models. First, they are systems. They are feelings, beliefs, memories, and experiences that have been encoded and stored in some abstracted, but organized form. This organization is a system—feelings that have been stored about one relationship have the potential to affect feelings about another relationship. Second, they are open systems. That is, the content of representational models (e.g., the information stored in them), though fairly stable, is open to being changed based on new experience. This assumption is a critical feature of representational models with respect to intervention and in fact forms the basis for many efforts within family literacy programs to enhance the quality of parenting. Third, representational models reflect two sides of a relationship (Sroufe & Fleeson, 1988) and so a parent struggling to do a good job teaching a child to read approaches this task both with views of how to teach but also how he or she was taught—again an argument for approaching family literacy interventions from the perspective of the parent.

Representational models can have an effect on the formation and quality of a relationship through brief, often subtle qualities of moment-to-moment interaction with children such as the adult's tone of voice, eye contact, or emotional cues (Katz, Cohn, & Moore, 1996), and in terms of the tolerances that individuals have for certain kinds of interactive behaviors. Thus, adults with a history of avoidant attachment, who tend to dismiss or diminish the negative emotional aspects of interactions, will behave differently in a situation that calls for a response to the emotional needs of a child than will adults whose history of secure attachment provides support for perceiving such needs as legitimate and responding to them sensitively. Recall the findings that indicate that children classified as having an insecure, particularly avoidant, attachment toward their mothers are exposed to less literacy information and less enjoyment in joint storybook-reading situations (Bus et al., 1995). These findings are consistent with the premise that the child's need for support during a storybook-reading situation activates representations of the mother that lead her to respond to her child's cues in ways that deflect those bids and reduce the emotional and informational value of the storybook-reading situation.

Working with parents (and other adults) in assisting them to form and maintain relationships with children that support key developmental functions such as self-reliance, emotion regulation, and literacy requires attention to those parents' representations of adult–child relationships. This work involves attention to how these adults represent relationships with their own child in the present and is also likely to involve how they experienced relationships with adults as a child, perhaps specifically involving literacy but not exclusively. The child also represents this relationship and has views about how supportive or demanding or helpful or punitive they can expect the parent to be in a given situation (Kerns, 1994). To the extent that such views are activated by a situation such as reading together, one could expect them to interfere with, or facilitate, the interaction between adult and child in that situation. Thus, it is important, in the context of thinking about family literacy interventions, to recognize that the representational components of adult–child relationships can constrain the function of the relationship to support literacy, through either motivational/communicative processes or instruction skill acquisition (e.g., Baker et al., 2001; Bus et al., 1995; Powell, 1996).

Information Exchange and Feedback Processes. Relationships can also be understood in terms of feedback processes that involve exchanges of information and behavior between the two individuals (adult and child). These processes are absolutely critical to how a relationship functions to regulate the behavior of the individuals involved. Feedback processes are most easily observed in interactive behaviors, but also include other means by which information is conveyed from one person to another. More specifically, what people do with, say or gesture to, and perceive about one another are major components of feedback mechanisms. Furthermore, the qualities of or *how* information is exchanged (via tone of voice, posture/proximity, timing of behavior, contingency or reciprocity of behavior) may be even more important than what is actually performed behaviorally (Kopp & Wyer, 1994).

Feedback processes serve a critical function in relationships, because it is through these processes that behavior and activity between the two individuals can be co-regulated (Ford & Ford, 1987). Bowlby (1969) refers to parent–child relationship systems as functioning as "goal corrected partnerships" in which the interactive behaviors of the parent and the child are coordinated and articulated to perform a particular function. This function can have developmental significance for the child. Thus, for example, the child's proximity-seeking behavior and the mother's protective comforting behavior together serve to promote attachment security. In this respect, the parent–child dyad is a control system in which feedback loops between parent and child, through which information is exchanged, provide a means of accomplishing a particular goal.

This concept of feedback mechanisms and goal-corrected functioning may be particularly relevant for family literacy interventions and theories of the role of parent–child relationships in the development of literacy more generally. As has been argued earlier, the literature suggests that adult–child relationships serve two key functions with regard to literacy (in a broad developmental sense)—they provide the child with interest in and enjoyment of literacy as a means of communication and understanding, and they provide the child with instructional input and opportunities to become facile in the decoding of grapheme–phoneme relations and metalinguistic skills. *Both* of these functions, or goals, of adult–child interactions around literacy-related activities appear critical; dysfunction with regard to either undermines the child's facility as an independent young reader. These two relational goals, at times, may be exclusive of one another such that too much attention to one at the expense of the other, or developmentally inappropriate sequencing, could undermine the relationship's support for literacy development. Thus, integration and balancing of these relationship goals are important for successful literacy development.

However, an alternative view is that at *all* ages and phases of literacy acquisition, the goal of motivation/interest/communication is primary and it is the criterion function by which the components of a relationship should be measured. In this sense, if the child does not experience the relationship as a functional and supportive secure base for exploration (regardless of age or need for instruction), then it will not function to support the instructional function. In either case, unless adult–child relationships (with either parents or teachers) intentionally focus on the instructional function or goal of decoding grapheme–phoneme relations, then the child is not likely to become a facile reader. Attention to how feedback mechanisms serve these two functional goals is a clear objective of family literacy interventions.

For family literacy practitioners, observing adult–child interactions is a common practice. When observing interactions to gauge the relative balance of motivational and instructional functions, it is particularly important to note the following:

- The degree of cooperative involvement and responsivity (Are interactions mutual, coordinated, and interdependent, or more unidirectional?)
- The emotional tones exchanged verbally and nonverbally (Is the primary emotional experience one of warmth, negativity, or dismissal?)
- The spontaneity of behavior (Does the child spontaneously and readily engage with the adult?)
- Physical proximity (How do the individuals organize themselves physically in relation to one another?)
- Caregiving (In situations of need on the part of the child, is this expressed by the child; are these cues responded to by the adult; and how well timed are these responses?)

These dimensions of interaction, or feedback, between adults and children have importance as indicators of the quality of this dyadic system for accomplishing functional goals. Signs of negativity, disengagement, and poor timing are good indicators that the value of interactions for the child is being undermined.

External Influences.   Systems external to the child–adult relationship also exert influence on it. For example cultures can prescribe timetables for learning to read that interact with the qualities of the developing adult–child relationship. In Sweden where children are not taught to read until they are 7, pressures on the instructional goal of parent–child relationships with respect to literacy acquisition are not nearly as great as they are in the United States, in which parents and teachers increasingly expect a solid base of literacy skills in 5- and 6-year-olds (Rimm-Kaufman, Pianta, & Cox, 2000). The role of parent–child relationships in promoting literacy becomes increasingly emphasized and is the subject of advertising and cultural interventions. Poorly communicated messages to parents to enhance and increase their instructional interactions with children (many of whom read poorly themselves and may be struggling even at the secure-base functions of reading) may in fact inadvertently undermine the ways in which the parent–child relationship supports the motivational and communicative function of the relationship. Thus, care must be taken to recognize the dual functions of adult–child relationships when creating policies and programs intended to raise children's skills.

Family literacy programs are themselves external influences on the parent–child relationship (Fuligni & Brooks-Gunn, 2001; Powell, 1996) (see Powell, this volume) and must be examined for the degree to which they support a balanced, integrated approach to facilitating the two functions these relationships serve in the acquisition of literacy. Differential emphasis on these functions, through either assessment or training, can have consequences for the relationship's functional value for developmental gain in literacy. Family literacy programs are also usually embedded in wider social support or early intervention service systems that can have multiple agendas and functions (such as health services, job training, and child care); may lack sufficient well-trained or knowledgeable staff; and often have little control over funding, resources, or direction and can therefore be somewhat unstable (Farran, 2000; St.Pierre et al., 1995;

Whitebook, Howes, & Phillips, 1990). These features of social service and early intervention programs can impede or interfere with the capacities of even well-designed family literacy interventions because they tend to overload intervention staff, reduce the intensity of the intervention, and create an imbalance in the emphasis of the intervention (Powell, 1996), all of which can have consequences for the extent to which the intervention will support the adult–child relationship. (See Jacobs, Ch. 11, this handbook, for a discussion of parent–child literacy interactions in family literacy programs.)

Summary

In summary, relationships between two individuals are multifaceted, complex systems. Child–adult relationships regulate development through a set of processes characteristic of dyadic systems. Applications of systems theory to adult–child relationships recognize a number of parameters of importance: representations, feedback mechanisms, timing and contingency of interaction, and the role that external influences can play in shaping these component processes. Importantly, these components form a system—They all are connected to one another in mutually influencing linkages. Representations guide behavior but behavior also affects representations. Feedback processes structure interactions but are also influenced by the kind of interactions that take place. This emphasis on the multidirectional connections among the components of a relationship system is important for intervention practices designed to change relationships because it suggests that relationships can be accessed through many possible points and changed as a function of creating pressure at any of these points (Pianta, 1999). For family literacy practitioners this means attending to the ways in which beliefs and interactions and abilities all interact within a given relationship. Starting from the parents' perspective (Powell, 1996), it means focusing on that component of the relationship the parent identifies as a goal of change, while at the same time (from the child's perspective) keeping in mind the need for this relationship to provide the child a secure base from which to explore the world of print.

CONCLUSIONS AND IMPLICATIONS

Relationships between children and adults play a prominent role in children's learning to read and are a central focus of family literacy activities intended to promote literacy in a range of circumstances. For family literacy programs to adequately harness the potential of adult–child relationships for developmental gain, several major points from this review stand out as having implications for family literacy efforts.

1. *Relationships between children and adults have developmental histories that trace back to early infancy.* Although adult–child relationships are a central focus of literacy research in work on joint storybook reading and oral language development, observed qualities of relationships in these circumstances are predicted by patterns of interaction that can be observed as early as the first few months of life and involve feeding, play, physiological, and arousal mechanisms. Thus, comprehensive approaches to family literacy will deploy resources not only toward reading to toddlers and preschoolers but also toward learning how to read an infant's cues and having fun playing peek-a-boo.

2. *Relationships between children and adults affect literacy growth and development by serving two functional goals: (a) providing a base in motivation, interest, communication, and general knowledge; and (b) instructing the child explicitly in the link between written and spoken language, particularly at the phonemic level.* It is important, as research and theory

move ahead, to recognize these two functions as separate as well as interrelated. Further understanding of their sequencing and interpretation in a wide range of populations and settings, in both naturalistic and intervention studies, is critical to efforts that productively and efficiently help children learn to read.

3. *Relationships between children and adults are multifaceted systems that offer many potential points of entry or foci of inquiry to practitioners and researchers.* It would be short-sighted to see adult–child relationships only in terms of behavioral interactions between two individuals. Such a focus often results in unsuccessful efforts to intervene to change inter-actions and can lead to unproductive and devaluing experiences for the parent (or teacher) and practitioner. Comprehensive views of adult–child relationships as dyadic systems com-posed of multiple, interrelated components require family literacy efforts to address all of these components and their interrelations.

ACKNOWLEDGEMENTS

The work reported herein was completed under the Educational Research and Development Centers Program, PR/Award Number R307A60004, as administered by the Office of Educa-tional Research and Improvement, U.S. Department of Education. However, the contents do not necessarily represent the positions or policies of the National Institute on Early Childhood Development and Education, the Office of Educational Research and Improvement, or the U.S. Department of Education, and readers should not assume endorsement by the federal government.

REFERENCES

Ainsworth, M. D., Blehar, M. C., Waters, E., & Wall, D. (1978). *Patterns of attachment: A psychological study of the strange situation.* Hillsdale, NJ: Lawrence Erlbaum Associates.

Allison, D. T., & Watson, J. A. (1994). The significance of adult storybook reading styles on the development of young children's emergent reading. *Reading Research and Instruction, 34,* 57–72.

Baker, L., Mackler, K., Sonnenschein, S., & Serpell, R. (2001). Parents' interactions with their first-grade children during storybook reading and relations with subsequent home reading activity and reading achievement. *Journal of School Psychology, 39*(5), 415–438.

Benjamin, L. A., & Lord, J. (Eds.). (1996). *Family literacy: Directions in research and implications for practice. Sum-mary and papers of a national symposium* (Washington, DC, September 7–8, 1995). Washington, DC: Department of Education.

Blachman, B. (Ed.). (1997). *Foundations of reading acquisition and dyslexia.* Mahwah, NJ: Lawrence Erlbaum Associates.

Bowlby, J. (1969). *Attachment and loss, vol. 1: Attachment.* New York: Basic Books.

Bus, A. G, Belsky, J., van IJzendoorn, M. H., & Crnic, K. (1997). Attachment and bookreading patterns: A study of mothers, fathers, and their toddlers. *Early Childhood Research Quarterly, 12*(1), 81–98.

Bus, A. G., & van IJzendoorn, M. H. (1988). Mother-child interactions, attachment, and emergent literacy: A cross-sectional study. *Child Development, 59,* 1262–1273.

Bus, A. G., & van IJzendoorn, M. H. (1995). Mothers reading to their 3-year-olds: The role of mother-child attachment security in becoming literate. *Reading Research Quarterly, 30*(4), 998–1015.

Bus, A. G., & van IJzendoorn, M. H. (1997). Affective dimension of mother-infant picturebook reading. *Journal of School Psychology, 35*(1), 47–60.

Bus, A. G., van IJzendoorn, M. H., & Pellegrini, A. D. (1995). Joint book reading makes for success in learning to read: A meta-analysis of intergenerational literacy. *Review of Educational Research, 65,* 1–21.

Cohn, J., Campbell, S., Matias, R., & Hopkins, J. (1990). Face-to-face interactions of pastpartum depressed and non-depressed mother-infant pairs. *Developmental Psychology, 26,* 15–23.

deJong, P. F., & Leseman, P. P. M. (2001). Lasting effects of home literacy on reading achievement in school. *Journal of School Psychology, 39*(5), 389–414.

Egeland, B., Pianta, R. C., & O'Brien, M. (1993). Maternal intrusiveness in infancy and child maladaptation in early school years. *Development and Psychopathology, 5,* 359–370.

Erickson, M. F., Sroufe, L. A., & Egeland, B. (1985). The relationship between quality of attachment and behavior problems in preschool in a high-risk sample. In I. Bretherton & E. Waters (Eds.), *Growing points of attachment: Theory and research. Monographs for the Society of Research in Child Development, 50* (1–2, Serial No. 209). Chicago: University of Chicago.

Farran, D. C. (2000). Another decade of intervention for children who are low income or disabled: What do we know now? In J. P. Shonkoff & S. J. Meisels (Eds.), *Handbook of early childhood intervention* (2nd ed., pp. 510–548). New York: Cambridge University Press.

Fonagy, P., Steele, H., & Steele, M. (1991). Maternal representations of attachment during pregnancy predict the organization of mother-infant attachment at one year of age. *Child Development, 62,* 891–905.

Foorman, B. R., Francis, D. J., Fletcher, J. M., Schatschneider, C., & Mehta, P. (1998). The role of instruction in learning to read: Preventing reading failure in at-risk children. *Educational Psychology, 90*(1), 37–55.

Ford, D. H., & Ford, M. E. (1987). *Humans as self-constructing living systems.* Hillsdale, NJ: Lawrence Erlbaum Associates.

Ford, D. H., & Lerner, R. M. (1992). *Developmental systems theory: An integrative approach.* Newbury Park, CA: Sage.

Fuligni, A. S., & Brooks-Gunn, J. (2000). Early childhood intervention programs: What about the family? In J. P. Shankoff & S. J. Meisels (Eds.), *Handbook on early childhood intervention.* (2nd ed., pp. 549–588). New York: Cambridge University Press.

Greenberg, M. T., Kusche, C. A., & Speltz, M. (1991). Emotional regulation, self-control, and psychopathology: The role of relationships in early childhood. In D. Cicchetti & S. Toth (Eds.), *Rochester symposium on developmental psychopathology* (pp. 21–55). Hillsdale, NJ: Lawrence Erlbaum Associates.

Greenberg, M. T., Speltz, M. L., and DeKlyen, M. (1993). The role of attachment in the early development of disruptive behavior disorders. *Development and Psychopathology, 5,* 191–213.

Haden, C. A., Reese, E., & Fivush, R. (1996). Mothers' extratextural comments during storybook reading: Stylistic differences over time and across texts. *Discourse Processes, 21,* 135–169.

Hart, B., & Risley, T. R. (1992). American parenting of language-learning children: Persisting differences in family-child interactions observed in natural home environments. *Developmental Psychology, 26*(6), 1096–1105.

Heath, S. B. (1982). What no bedtime story means: Narrative skills at home and school. *Language in Society, 11,* 49–76.

Hinde, R. (1987). *Individuals, relationships, and culture.* New York: Cambridge University.

Hochenberger, E. H., Goldstein, H., & Haas, L. S. (1999). Effects of commenting during joint book reading by mothers with low-SES. *Topics in Early Childhood Special Education, 19,* 15–27.

Hofer, M. A. (1994). Hidden regulators in attachment, separation, and loss. In N. A. Fox (Ed.), *The development of emotion regulation: Biological and behavioral considerations. Monographs of the Society for Research in Child Development, 59* (Serial No. 240, pp. 192–207).

Juel, C. (1998). What kind of one-on-one tutoring helps a poor reader? In C. Hulme & R. M. Joshi (Eds.), *Reading and spelling: Development and disorders* (pp. 449–471). Mahwah, NJ: Lawrence Erlbaum Associates.

Katz, G. S., Cohn, J. F., & Moore, C. (1996). A combination of vocal, dynamic and summary features discriminates between three pragmatic categories of infant-directed speech. *Child Development, 67,* 205–217.

Kerns, K. A. (1994). A longitudinal examination of links between mother-child attachment and children's friendships in early childhood. *Journal of Social & Personal Relationships, 11,* 379–381.

Kopp, C., & Wyer, N. (1994). Self-regulation in normal and atypical development. In D. Cicchetti & S. Toth (Eds.), *Disorders and dysfunctions of the self: Rochester Symposium on Developmental Psychopathology, Vol 5* (pp. 31–56). Rochester: University of Rochester Press.

Lyon, G. R. (2002). Reading development, reading difficulties, and reading instruction: Educational and public health issues. *Journal of School Psychology, 40*(1), 3–6.

Main, M., & Hesse, E. (1990). Is fear the link between infant disorganized attachment status and maternal unresolved loss? In M. Greenberg, D. Cicchetti, & M. Cummings (Eds), *Attachment in the preschool years* (pp. 161–182). Chicago: University of Chicago Press.

Mikulecky, L. (1996). Family literacy: Parent and child interactions. In L. A. Benjamin & J. Lord (Eds.), *Family literacy: Directions in research and implications for practice. Summary and papers of a national symposium* (Washington, DC, September 7–8, 1995). Washington, DC: Department of Education.

Morrow, L. M., Rand, M. K., & Smith, J. K. (1995). Reading aloud to children: Characteristics and relationships between teachers' and student behaviors. *Reading Research & Instruction, 35*(1), 85–101.

NICHD Early Childhood Research Network. (2002). The relation of kindergarten classroom environment to teacher, family, and school characteristics and child outcomes. *The Elementary School Journal, 102*(3), 225–238.

Pellegrini, A. D., Perlmutter, J., Galda, L., & Brody, G. H. (1990). Joint reading between black Head Start children and their mothers. *Child Development, 61,* 443–453.

Pianta, R. C. (1999). *Enhancing relationships between children and teachers.* Washington, DC: American Psychological Association.

Powell, D. (1996). Teaching parenting and basic skills to parents: What we know. In L. A. Benjamin & J. Lord (Eds.), *Family literacy: Directions in research and implications for practice. Summary and papers of a national symposium* (Washington, DC, September 7–8, 1995). Washington, DC: Department of Education.

Pressley, M. (1998). *Reading instruction that works: The case for balanced teaching.* New York: Guilford.

Resnick, L. B. (1994). Situated rationalism: Biological and social preparation for learning. In L. Hirschfield & S. Gelman (Eds.), *Mapping the mind: Domain specificity in cognition and culture* (pp. 474–493). Cambridge, England: Cambridge University Press.

Rimm-Kaufman, S. E., Pianta, R. C., & Cox, M. J. (2000). Teachers' judgments of problems in the transition to kindergarten. *Early Childhood Research Quarterly, 15*(2), 147–166.

Sameroff, A. J. (1995). General systems theories and psychopathology. In D. Cicchetti & D. J. Cohen (Eds.), *Developmental psychology, Volume 1: Theory and methods* (Wiley Series on Personality Processes) (pp. 659–695). New York: Wiley.

Sameroff, A. J., & Emde, R. N. (1989). *Relationship disturbances in early childhood: A developmental approach.* New York: Basic.

Sander, L. (1975). Infant and caretaking environment: Investigation and conceptualization of adaptive behavior in a system of increasing complexity. In E. J. Anthony (Ed.), *Explorations in child psychiatry* (pp. 129–166). New York: Plenum.

Scarborough, H., & Dobrich, W. (1994). On the efficacy of reading to preschoolers. *Developmental Review, 14,* 245–302.

Senechal, M., LeFevre, J., Smith-Chant, B. L., Colton, K. V. (2001). On refining theoretical models of emergent literacy: The role of empirical evidence. *Journal of School Psychology, 39*(5), 439–460.

Snow, C. E., Burns, M. S., & Griffin, P. (Eds.). (1998). *Preventing reading difficulties in young children.* Washington, DC: National Academy Press.

Snow, C. E., Barnes, W. S., Chandler, J., Goodman, I. F., & Hemphill, L. (1991). *Unfulfilled expectations: Home and school influences on literacy.* Cambridge, MA: Harvard University Press.

Snow, C., & Tabors, P. (1996). Intergenerational transfer of literacy. In L. A. Benjamin & J. Lord (Eds.), *Family literacy: Directions in research and implications for practice. Summary and papers of a national symposium* (Washington, DC, September 7–8, 1995). Washington, DC: Department of Education.

Sroufe, L. A. (1989). Relationships and relationship disturbances. In A. Sameroff & R. Emde (Eds.), *Relationship disturbances in early childhood* (pp. 97–124). New York: Basic.

Sroufe, L. A. (1996). *Emotional development: The organization of emotional life in the early years.* New York: Cambridge University Press.

Sroufe, L. A., & Fleeson, J. (1988). Attachment and the construction of relationships. In W. Hartup, & Z. Rubin (Eds.), *Relationships and development.* Hillsdale, NJ: Erlbaum.

Stern, D. (1989). The representation of relationship patterns: Developmental considerations. In A. J. Sameroff & R. Emde, (Eds). *Relationship disturbances in early childhood* (pp. 52–69). New York: Basic.

St.Pierre, R., Swartz, J., Gamse, B., Murray, S., Deck, D., & Nickel, P. (1995). *National evaluation of the Even Start Family Literacy Program: Final report.* Washington, DC: U.S. Department of Education, Planning and Evaluation Service.

Teale, W. H. (1986). Home background and young children's literacy development. In W. H. Teale & E. Sulzby (Eds.), *Emergent literacy: Writing and reading* (pp. 173–206). Norwood, NJ: Ablex.

Thompson, R. A. (1994). Emotion regulation: A theme in search of definition. In N. A. Fox (Ed.), The development of emotion regulation: Biological and behavioral considerations. *Monographs of the Society for Research in Child Development, 59* (Serial No. 240, pp. 25–52).

Whitebook, M., Howes, C., & Phillips, D. A. (1990). *Who cares? Child care teachers and the quality of care in America.* Final report, National Child Care Staffing Study. Oakland, CA: Child Care Employee Project.

Whitehurst, G. J., Arnold, D. S., Epstein, J. N., Angell, A. L., Smith, M., & Fischel, J. E. (1994). A picture book reading intervention in day care and home for children from low-income families. *Developmental Psychology, 30,* 679–689.

Whitehurst, G. J., & Lonigan, C. J. (1998). Child development and emergent literacy. *Child Development, 69,* 848–872.

Yaden, Jr., D. B., Rowe, D. W., & MacGillivray, L. (1999). *Emergent literacy: A polyphony of perspectives* (CIERA Report #1-005). Ann Arbor, MI: University of Michigan, School of Education.

Zeanah, C. H., Benoit, D., Barton, M., Regan, C., Hirschberg, L., & Lipsitt, L. (1993). Representations of attachment in mothers and their one-year-old infants. *Journal of the American Academy of Child and Adolescent Psychiatry, 32,* 278–286.

11

Parent and Child Together Time

Kim Jacobs
National Center for Family Literacy

Parent–child interactions are the heart of family literacy services. Whether at home, in the classroom, or in the community, meaningful parent–child interactions can lead to enhanced language, literacy, emotional, and cognitive development. Parents benefit as well. Parents who are learning to support their children's language and literacy development have the opportunity to enhance their own literacy skills when reading to their children. This chapter discusses those family literacy programs in which parents learn new ways to interact with their children by attending parent education sessions and by engaging in parent–child literacy interactions. These parent–child interactions around literacy are described in many programs as Parent and Child Together (PACT) Time, based on the model developed by the National Center for Family Literacy. These interactions bring parents and children together to work, play, read, and learn.

This chapter discusses the conceptual framework of how and why PACT Time was developed. The research base that supports the value of meaningful parent–child interactions in children's development is presented with emphasis on children's language, early literacy, and cognitive development. A discussion follows of the comprehensive preschool model of PACT Time and a look at PACT Time in Even Start, Head Start, and school-age programs. Challenges for implementation of PACT Time as well as variations in design and delivery are also addressed. The chapter concludes with a discussion of the outcomes of PACT Time experiences and the importance of measuring those outcomes for programs and families.

THE CONCEPTUAL FRAMEWORK OF PACT TIME

The conceptual framework of PACT Time originated with the development of the Parent and Child Education (PACE) program in Kentucky and the Kenan Trust Family Literacy programs implemented in Kentucky and North Carolina in the late 1980s (Brizius & Foster, 1993). The original broad goals of PACT Time were to improve speaking, listening, reading, and writing skills of parents and children and to guide parents in understanding the value of positive interactions with their children through play. The acronym PACT Time represents a promise, or a pact between parents and children, one that symbolizes a lifetime commitment to learning.

In an effort to break the intergenerational cycle of low literacy, the transference of literate behaviors within families became a focal point of PACT Time experiences, a unique characteristic of the family literacy approach. Often, parents attending these early family literacy programs did not perceive themselves as educators or feel knowledgeable about how to help their children learn. By providing high-quality early childhood education, adult education, and prevocational training, along with parent discussion groups and time for parents and children to interact, these programs strived to empower parents to think of themselves as their child's first teacher.

In these early programs, parents and children arrived at school together and spent portions of their day both together and apart as they participated in educational and interactive experiences. Children benefited from quality care and education while parents concentrated on the pursuit of a General Educational Development (GED) equivalency or other training on site. Meal times, as well as regularly scheduled PACT Time experiences, provided opportunities for parents and children to come together socially, as well as to work and learn together.

A basic, underlying element of early PACT Time models was to provide a setting in which parents could practice new skills learned during parent education sessions in a risk-free environment. This setting provided support for parents as they interacted, played with, and learned about their children. Early programs focused on what teachers thought parents needed to know to work with their children. Soon, programs realized a more effective approach was for parents to share their goals, needs, and wishes for their children with teachers and to work together to build on their children's strengths, as well as on their own strengths as parents, to guide children's development. As PACT Time further developed, the concepts of child-initiated play, plan-do-review, and transfer-home were explored and implemented.

Building on these early efforts of the PACE and Kenan programs, the National Center for Family Literacy (NCFL) model of PACT Time emerged. NCFL has further refined practices to develop a common structure for PACT Time with concrete goals, which will be discussed later in this chapter. Typically, this model focuses on preschool-aged children and their parents, although programs such as Even Start, the Family and Child Education (FACE) program (see Emberton, chap. 25, this volume), and Toyota Families in Schools (TFS) (see Darling, chap. 31, this volume) have broadened the model to include services for families with infants through elementary-school-age children.

MEANINGFUL PARENT–CHILD INTERACTIONS

Meaningful parent–child interactions build on parents' increasing knowledge of children's needs, interests, and development and help parents transfer that knowledge into quality interactions with their children to foster development and promote school success. The value of meaningful parent–child interactions is central to the implementation of quality PACT Time experiences within family literacy services, regardless of the setting or age of the child.

The importance of children's first years of life and the role parents play in children's development have a strong empirical base. Studies in neuroscience indicate the importance of attachment and parent–child interaction to stimulate a child's growing development (Bowman, Donovan, & Burns, 2001; Egeland & Erickson, 1999; Gopnick, Meltzoff, & Kuhl, 1999; Shore, 1997). Studies on the emotional–social development of children address the significance of attachment, resilience, and protective factors on child development (Werner, 1996). Children who build strong attachments with their parents, having their cues responded to and needs met, are building an important foundation for later development, findings reinforced in the chapter by Powell and Pianta in Section III. In addition, recent early literacy and reading research points to the central role adults play in children's developing language and literacy (Dickinson & Tabors, 2001; Hart & Risley, 1995, 1999). Furthermore, studies on adult–child and parent–child relationships also make clear the significant role adults play in children's cognitive development and school success (Pianta, 1999; Snow, Barnes, Chandler, Goodman, & Hemphill, 2000).

For years, experts have debated the importance of nature versus nurture theories of child development. More recently, researchers note the significance of both in promoting development. According to Shore (1997), how humans develop and learn depends critically and continually on the interplay between an individual's genetics and an individual's environment, including nutrition, surroundings, care, stimulation, and teaching. Roskos and Twardorz, in chapter 16 of this handbook, expand on this interplay between genetics and the environment.

Parents and children build unique relationships that contribute to a child's emotional and cognitive development. Responsive and involved parents show respect for children's needs and provide a variety of quality experiences for their children. Quality shared activities between parents and children often come from involvement in playful interactions during families' and children's everyday routines. Conversations during meal or bath times, reading together, baking cookies, or going camping can all represent meaningful parent–child interactions. Such incidental teaching is discussed further by Sparling in Section II.

There are two important considerations regarding how parents and children interact. The first is that natural interactions, rather than artificial interventions, are the preferred provision for meaningful experiences. Second, the most important support parents need in order to facilitate meaningful parent–child interactions is the provision of time (Gopnick et al., 1999). These considerations have imperative implications for PACT Time. Not all parents instinctively know what constitutes meaningful parent–child interactions or take the time to provide them. Furthermore, some parents lack models of meaningful parent–child relationships. These factors are particularly influential when discussing the value of PACT Time in family literacy programming, when planning for these experiences in a meaningful way, and when demonstrating to parents how they can transfer these supportive skills into the home. How well children learn to cope while their parents find it difficult to manage the stressors of daily life, let alone find the time to engage in meaningful parent–child interactions, is an added factor.

So, if nurture is important for children's healthy development, what does this mean for PACT Time experiences? What does this say about the quality of interactions parents and children experience together?

What it means is that this dance between nature and nurture, these environmental influences, experiences, teachings, and relationships that exist between parents and children, is important. It further demonstrates that parents, teachers, and caregivers who interact with children on a day-to-day basis directly affect children's emotional and cognitive growth. It is no different for children's language and literacy development.

Hart and Risley (1995, 1999) discuss the quality of parent-child interactions and parent-child talk in everyday parenting that can lead to basic language competence. Their work indicates that the way parents talk to children affects children's language use, vocabulary growth, and learning. They also found that the amount of talk parents share with their children generally correlates with parents' socioeconomic status (SES). Hart and Risley (1995) conclude that what parents say and do with their children in the first 3 years of language learning has an enormous impact on how much language children learn and use. Their data show, however, that no matter what the family SES, the more time parents spend talking with their children everyday, the more rapidly children's vocabulary is likely to grow, and the higher the child's score in an IQ test is likely to be at age 3 (Hart & Risley, 1999). To further emphasize the significance of rich interactive experiences, Mikulecky (1996) states that

> Parent-child interactions are important to a child's developing literacy abilities. It is becoming increasingly clear that these interactions involve a good deal more than simply reading to children and providing them with books...(A) growing body of research indicates that the way in which a parent speaks with a child may have as much or more to do with later reading achievement of the child than actual time spent reading to the child. (p. 1)

HOME–SCHOOL CONNECTION

Another study of preschool- and kindergarten-aged children addresses the home–school connection in children's language and literacy development. Dickinson and Tabors (2001) look at the correlation between what parents do at home and what teachers do at school that affects children's literacy and language development. Observations made in both the home and school focused on the quantity and quality of interactions parents and teachers have with children involving literacy and language development. At home, the study focused on parent–child interactions such as reading books together, playing together, mealtime conversations, how parents talk with their children, and the home support and environment provided for children. An analysis of the home environment section of the study indicates that children who demonstrated higher level skills in language and literacy development in kindergarten were, on the whole, those children who had experienced interesting talk with lots of new words and literacy activities such as frequent and varied book readings with adults.

It is clear, then, that adults play a significant role in guiding children's language and literacy development. The literacy-related interactions children experience at home with a significant adult influence not only early language and literacy development, but also literate behaviors modeled and practiced at home carry over to the school setting.

QUALITY OF PARENT–CHILD RELATIONSHIPS

There is evidence that the quality of parent–child relationships provides an infrastructure on which children can build relationships with other adults, particularly teachers; and that quality teacher–child relationships contribute to both the emotional and the academic skill development of children (Pianta, 1999). Children's learning, whether through play or in the framework of a well-structured lesson plan, increases when presented within the context of a quality relationship. According to Pianta (1999),

> Adult-child relationships are critical regulators of development; they form and shape it. In the early years, relationships with adults, primarily parents (usually mothers) but often child-care providers or other family members, form the infrastructure of development that supports nearly all of what a child is asked to do in school: relate to other people, be persistent and focused, stay motivated to perform, be compliant-assertive, communicate, and explore the world. (p. 17)

It stands to reason then, that the absence of meaningful parent–child interactions may have an inhibiting effect on a child's growth and development. Experienced practitioners in the field of family literacy draw attention to the fact that many parents need guidance and support in understanding just how much these interactions matter and in knowing how to engage in meaningful parent–child interactive experiences.

Within the context of comprehensive family literacy services, this guidance and support comes in the form of the adult education and parent education components. According to the National Adult Literacy Survey (U.S. Department of Education, 1993), 21 to 23% of adults, or some 40 to 44 million of the 191 million adults in this country, demonstrate skills in the lowest level of literacy. Often these adults live in poverty, attempt to cope with welfare reform mandates, and are often unemployed. All struggle with basic reading, writing, and quantitative tasks. Consequently, as many of these adults manage difficulties with their own low literacy or educational skills, they find it hard to relate to those same developing skills of their children. They struggle with parental responsibilities such as reading to their children, helping with homework, or reading a note from their child's teacher. Typically, these are the same characteristics observed of parents involved in family literacy programs.

Significantly, however, studies consistently show that as a parent's educational level increases, particularly the mother's, so does the likelihood that children's literacy skills will increase (Sticht & Armstrong, 1994), that children's educational attainment will be greater (U.S. Department of Education, 2000), and that parents are more likely to exert a positive influence on their children's academic achievement (Benjamin, 1993).

An added benefit of PACT Time experiences for adult learners is the opportunity for parents to address some of the gaps they may have had in their own early education experiences. By interacting with their children and learning more about how to support their children's learning, parents often discover or rediscover missing keys to their own understanding of basic concepts (King & McMaster, 2000) and seek to fill those gaps by pursuing or completing their education.

Given this review of the value of meaningful parent–child interactions and the provision of those experiences for both parents and children within family literacy services, a number of conclusions may be drawn.

1. Children benefit from meaningful interactions with their parents (and other adults) in order to grow and develop in a variety of ways.
2. Many parents lack the skills and support from others in order to meaningfully interact with their children.
3. Parents are better equipped when they have time to practice interaction skills and can learn how to recognize and make time for meaningful interactions daily.
4. Some parents lack information and knowledge about children's cognitive, language, and literacy development and have difficulty helping their children achieve desired outcomes and attain school success.
5. Parents need guidance and support to be intentional about their interactions with children, not only within a school setting but also at home.
6. High-quality parent–child relationships help children build relationships with other adults later in life and lead to increased emotional and academic skills.
7. As parents' educational levels and literacy skills rise, so does the likelihood of children's educational success.

PACT Time offers parents and children structured opportunities deliberately designed to increase and facilitate meaningful parent–child interactions focused primarily on language and literacy development in a high-quality learning environment, where they can learn and play and grow together. Ideally, parents then transfer those skills and abilities into their home environments and into their everyday interactions with their children, in turn fostering lifelong learning behaviors.

THE CORE ELEMENTS OF PACT TIME

In 1998, Congress passed legislation that created a consistent definition of family literacy services. This federal definition states that government programs utilizing federal funds to provide family literacy services should integrate four areas of education including "interactive literacy activities between parents and their children" or PACT Time. This definition also states that intensity and duration of services should be sufficient enough to make sustainable changes in families. Essentially, well-implemented, comprehensive family literacy programs provide frequent opportunities (intensity) for parents and children to play and work together in a learning environment that supports all areas of child development and provide those services over time (duration) so families can consistently work toward making positive changes in behaviors.

A number of goals have been developed for PACT Time by the National Center for Family Literacy. Although these goals may vary from program to program, according to the strengths, needs, and cultures of the families in each community, they provide guidance for developing PACT Time experiences. The foundational goals of PACT Time are listed in the following section.

- To aid parents in discovering, reaffirming, and expanding their roles as parents to build on their strengths as leaders of their families and teachers of their children
- To enhance parents' awareness of how children learn and develop language and literacy and specifically how their own children learn best
- To give parents tools, techniques, and strategies to support their children's learning, language, and literacy development
- To provide an opportunity for parents to practice these new strategies in a supportive environment, where teachers can model learning techniques and offer suggestions and support
- To help parents feel comfortable using these new strategies while interacting with their children daily at home and in the community (National Center for Family Literacy [NCFL], 2002).

The fundamental principles of PACT Time are based on research and practical experience. The structure includes (a) the intergenerational aspect of parents and children learning together; (b) parent education; (c) the learning environment; (d) the sequence of PACT Time activities; (e) a balance of child- and adult-initiated experiences; (f) preparing, guiding, and reflecting PACT Time experiences; (g) staff working in a supportive role; (h) transferring PACT Time into the home; (i) and integration of all four family literacy components.

1. The *intergenerational transfer between parent and child* is a significant and powerful factor to consider for the provision of PACT Time. Culture, language, knowledge, family stories, literate and social behaviors, poverty, and more, are passed from generation to generation, from parent to child. As discussed, the parent–child relationship is pivotal in the child's learning process, whether that learning is positive or negative. PACT Time is an attempt to focus on the beneficial development of that parent–child relationship in order to increase the skills parents have, to enhance the learning of the children, and in the process, to help break intergenerational cycles such as poverty and low literacy.

2. *Parent education (Parent Time)* and PACT Time build on each other. Like PACT Time, Parent Time is a regularly scheduled session that provides an opportunity for parents to share concerns and strategies for dealing with home issues and day-to-day challenges. Understanding that parents come to family literacy with certain strengths, the primary focus is to reinforce and enhance parenting skills, particularly parents' understanding of child development, and

language and literacy development. Through parent education, parents increase their self-esteem and confidence in their ability to provide a stable home and learning environment for their children. They learn how to access local resources, discuss issues related to parenting and family support, and learn ways to improve interpersonal and communication skills.

The ongoing support of children's language and literacy development is, of course, central to PACT Time experiences. Parent Time is prime time for parents to learn how children develop language and literacy skills, and how they, as their children's first teachers, can support that development on a daily basis. The information and skills learned in Parent Time can then be transferred into PACT Time settings and practiced under the guidance of supportive staff. The reverse is also true. Parents' regular interactions with their children fuel their desire to know and understand more about their children's development. Parent Time provides the opportunity for them to explore developmental information in depth. Building on the strengths of parents, parent education is an important component for many parents striving to experience successful interactions with their children. Helping parents to help themselves is essential to this process and is a common theme in family literacy programs.

3. The *learning environment* for a typical preschool PACT Time experience is the child's classroom, where children are comfortable and familiar with their environment and the expectations for behavior. As with any high-quality preschool classroom, the setting should be an appropriate learning environment conducive to preschool education and designed to facilitate child-initiated center-based play. The setting should also provide a daily routine, a balance of small and large group activities, appropriate adult–child interactions, and a variety of materials available for active learning. To foster parent–child interaction, it is important that the PACT Time setting also accommodate adult learners, providing adequate arrangements for parents to comfortably play and interact with their children. Parents will feel more welcome in the environment if adult-size furniture is available. Classrooms should be both culturally and literate rich, considering the needs, cultures, and languages of the children and families in the program. Learning environments for infants and toddlers or school-age children will be structured a bit differently according to individual needs and developmental ages/stages of the children but maintain the same basic concepts. All environments strive to provide optimal learning experiences for both children and parents.

4. Well-planned PACT Time takes advantage of a *sequence of events* that is both typical and practical. In a center-based preschool program, this sequence conveniently fits into the child's daily routine, considering also the routines of parents as they attend their adult education and Parent Time classes. PACT Time can be flexibly scheduled for any time of the day, but there are advantages to certain scheduling provisions. Because young children often have a difficult time separating from their parents, it may be appropriate to schedule PACT Time around those times when parents and children come together naturally. Arrival and departure times, and before lunch, are typically good times to schedule PACT Time. This eliminates the frequent "comings and goings" of parents and minimizes the number of transitions children experience throughout the day. Sequencing PACT Time for school-age children may require additional planning to tie into a child's regular school-day schedule; a description of school-age PACT Time can be found later in this chapter. PACT Time is often more effective when scheduled during the times children are more active and alert. The typical center-based sequence of PACT Time has evolved into a routine that is both familiar and comfortable for children, parents, and teachers alike. (See Table 11.1 for a description of a typical PACT Time sequence.)

5. This sequence allows for a *balance of child- and adult-initiated experiences*, child-centered activities, and intentional teaching. Times are allocated for children to plan for and choose experiences according to their interests, and times are provided for parents and/or teachers to plan for and lead small group or Circle Time activities. Often, parents will include their children in the planning and carrying out of the activities. Both teachers and parents learn to

TABLE 11.1
Typical PACT Time Center-Based Sequence (Preschool Model)[a]

Staff and parents prepare	Staff and parents discuss a number of different ideas for interactions and decide on one that reflects the child's interests, developmental goals, and the parents' needs and interests in learning about their child's language and literacy development. Staff often provide a focus for parents for observation.
Parents and children plan together 5 minutes	Parents and children consider where to play, what they will do, what materials they may use, and what they might talk about.
Parents and children work and play together 30–45 minutes	Parents engage with their children and respond to their child's lead. They act as models for their children, utilizing new strategies developed from Parent Time or previous parent-child interactions. Staff act as participant observers, providing materials when necessary, watching for the strengths of the interaction, and considering the connections to other family literacy components that may benefit the parent and child. When appropriate, staff also joins in the play and act as literacy models for parent and child. This is an opportunity for joint interaction between staff, parents and children—an open and relaxed chance for interaction and fun.
Parents and children review 5 minutes	Parents and children have a simple discussion about their work and play as they clean up, encouraging a habit of review and reflection.
Staff model a literacy experience (Circle Time) 5–10 minutes	This time is an opportunity for parents and children to come together in a large group to experience a literacy activity. Often this will be a Circle Time experience that involves reading a storybook, participating in a game, song or finger play, and concluding with an idea for a transfer-home activity to reinforce the learning that occurred in the classroom. This activity is intentionally planned and designed to meet children's goals for language and literacy development, as well as to model strategies for parents they may have learned in Parent Time, and may want to try with their children.
Transfer home ideas	At the conclusion of PACT Circle Time, staff shares an idea or activity with parents and children to transfer the activity home—reinforcing the learning that occurred in the classroom.
Parents review and reflect 10–15 minutes	Reflection time is most effective when it happens as soon as possible after PACT Time. Parents may discuss with teachers and peers, or write in a journal or learning log their reflections of their children's learning and their time together, often internalizing new understandings and strategies for working with their children. The setting for the reflection varies depending on program design but is often done before adult education or Parent Time. Some review opportunities may be brief, while others may be detailed and lengthy. This time should be a natural opportunity to discuss children and their growth, and build connections to other components of family literacy services. This review and reflection time guides parents in thinking about the next interactive experience they will have with their child

[a] (National Center for Family Literacy, 2003).

enhance and scaffold experiences for children. Throughout the day, teachers will intentionally plan experiences to help children meet certain outcomes in language and literacy development. In time, parents can also learn to actively plan and lead these kinds of experiences.

6. The process of *preparing, guiding, and reflecting PACT Time experiences* is based on High/Scope Educational Research Foundation's plan-do-review process (Hohmann & Weikart, 1995) practiced in many early childhood programs and adapted for adults in many adult education programs. Family literacy programs also utilize and benefit from the use of plan-do-review.

PACT Time experiences usually follow the simple process of *preparing for the interaction* (planning), *guiding* and supporting the interaction (doing), and *reflecting* on the interaction (reviewing) when it is finished. This process can be applied in infant/toddler, preschool, and school-age programs in appropriate ways.

7. *Staff play a critical role* in the successful implementation of the plan-do-review process. When preparing for parent–child interactions, both staff and parents make plans for the interaction, thinking about environment and materials, extending and enhancing the experience, and providing language and literacy connections, whether the experience will take place in the classroom or at home. Children, with help from adults, plan and prepare for the experience as well. When guiding parent–child interactions, staff support new ideas parents have about interacting and playing with their children and serve as guides or role models in the classroom or during Parent Time. Parents support and guide children throughout the experience by using a variety of strategies learned in Parent Time. And, when reflecting on parent–child interactions, staff listen as parents reflect on their interactions with their children and offer guidance and support for ways to enhance experiences in the future. Parents evaluate the effectiveness of their strategies and work to identify new strategies that will help them further support future learning experiences.

8. The ultimate goal of PACT Time is for parents to *transfer the PACT Time experience*— their new knowledge and skills learned and their expanded understanding of the value of meaningful parent–child interactions—into their everyday interactions with their children. By providing parents with a transfer-home activity at the end of each PACT Time session, staff can model for parents appropriate interactions, guide them in their activities at home, and help them reflect on their experiences. As parents become increasingly comfortable in their roles of planning and guiding experiences with their children on their own, they may need less guidance from staff.

9. *Integration* speaks to the demonstration of the connectedness of all four components of comprehensive family literacy services. In many ways, this connectedness is most evident in PACT Time. Parents learn about child, language, and literacy development in Parent Time, they practice new skills or strategies learned for working with their children during PACT Time, they interact in children's classrooms and participate in the children's daily routine, and they prepare for and reflect this experience in Parent Time or adult education. Often, the children's and adults' curricula, or current themes or subjects of learning, come together during the PACT Time experience to enhance learning for both children and parents (see Potts, chap.19, this volume).

PACT Time is a time for parents and children to come together to read, play, learn, and practice new skills in a neutral setting with the guidance of knowledgeable family literacy staff. The specific goals and the framework of PACT Time vary from program to program, but are often designed with similar elements, as described. When parents feel successful in the classroom and understand the value of meaningful parent–child interactions in general, they begin to initiate PACT Time experiences beyond the classroom setting, actively seeking opportunities to increase and improve their own daily learning interactions with their children.

PACT TIME IN DIFFERENT PROGRAMS

A wide variety of interactive parent–child experiences are built into many types of literacy programs in countless settings. Libraries frequently offer story hours or family nights where parents and children interact around literacy experiences. The primary purpose of library service to early childhood is to introduce parents to the library as a parenting information center and to demonstrate ways of sharing books and nonbook materials with very young children (Greene, 1991). Many correctional institutions offer interactive literacy experiences for prisoners with their children, allowing incarcerated parents and their children to continue to develop relationships (V. Tardaewether, personal communication, January 25, 2002). Public high school programs that offer services such as parenting education and in-school child care for teen parents often require interactive experiences within the school day. Community education, public before- and after-school and early child care programs, family day care, and early intervention programs are all avenues for offering meaningful parent-child experiences.

Family literacy programs are encouraged to reach out into the community to connect with agencies that can assist with providing quality parent–child experiences that meet the unique needs and cultures of the families in their programs. Any of the previously mentioned agencies or programs could provide systems for the successful delivery of PACT Time. Established programs know the value of collaboration for the delivery of services, particularly when striving to provide services with increased intensity and duration.

PACT Time within comprehensive family literacy services is intended to be integrated with the other three components of family literacy services: adult education, children's education, and parenting education, and is offered with intensity and duration as indicated in the federal definition of family literacy services.

Over the years, PACT Time has been successfully implemented with intensity and duration in many center-based family literacy programs. One such example is the Family and Child Education (FACE) program. Since 1992, FACE, a collaboration between Parents as Teachers, the High/Scope Educational Foundation, and the National Center for Family Literacy, has provided a continuum of family literacy services for American Indian children, ages birth through third grade, and their families. (Emberton, Section VII, provides a detailed description of the FACE program.) These services include PACT Time offered in the traditional center-based model, as well as through home visits. Adaptations of this model have been implemented in the Toyota Families in Schools (TFS) project, which works with the families of elementary-school-age children in the public school setting, and in the United Parcel Service (UPS) Careers for Families project, where the PACT Time experience is expanded to introduce children to the world of work that their parents are experiencing.

With the original authorization of the federal Even Start program in 1988, PACT Time and Parent Time components were blended into one component called parenting education (U.S. Department of Education, 1998). Today, Even Start family literacy programs strive to model the mandated federal definition of family literacy services and support the integration of all four components of comprehensive family literacy services. The following example of an Even Start program in Oregon illustrates the typical PACT Time model and the core elements of PACT Time previously discussed. It also demonstrates how one program addressed challenges that erupted over an 8-year span of funding. This example represents the integration of PACT Time into all four components of family literacy in a typical preschool model. Following this example, a discussion of how PACT Time is approached differently in Head Start and elementary school-age programs is presented. Because programs exist in communities with diverse and specific needs, interests, and challenges, the last section will address variations in program design.

Even Start—Oregon Example

Designed after early family literacy models, an Oregon program served parents with preschool children and met 3 full days a week. The program was located on-site at a local elementary school with adult education classrooms in the same building. Staff included early childhood teachers and adult educators. PACT Time and Parent Time were daily events and part of the regular routine for parents and children. Information on this program comes from an interview with a former staff member (C. Nelson, personal communication, January 10, 2002).

Parents and children met separately during the morning, then came back together at lunchtime. Prior to parents arriving at the children's classroom, teachers would talk with children and plan for the PACT Time experience. A teacher would ask each child individually what he or she would like to do with the child's parent for PACT Time. The child would dictate, point, or gesture while the teacher wrote down the response on a sticky note with the child's name or symbol. As time progressed, older children wanted to write or draw their own plans. Teachers then delivered these plans to parents in the adult education classroom, where they could discuss the plans and prepare for PACT Time. Over the course of the year, these sticky notes, which parents kept in their journals, were a wonderful record of children's interests as well as their growth in planning, oral communication, and writing over time, and were incorporated into portfolios. This process represents one way children can plan and parents and staff can document children's progress.

The PACT Time routine consisted of child-initiated choice time, as parents and children played and worked together according to the children's plans. Both early childhood and adult education staff participated each day in PACT Time, which staff believed was valuable and essential in order to model the importance of PACT Time for parents. Once each week, parents and children visited the school library together to check out books. A favorite experience for both parents and children was engaging in story writing on the computer. Parents and children regularly participated in joint story writing, often with children dictating and parents writing the story. Staff encouraged conversations between parents and children while using the computers and saw advantages to both parents and children engaged in a learning activity that was new for both.

At the conclusion of PACT time, parents quietly read stories to their children as they prepared for a nap. Once children were resting, parents returned to their adult education classrooms for Parent Time to reflect/debrief PACT Time for that day, discuss other parent education issues, and delve further into parent education topics.

At the end of the day, parents returned to the children's classroom where the day would close with a group Circle Time activity and good-bye song. A transfer-home activity was introduced and reviewed and sent home with each parent and child. Once parents and children left, staff debriefed the day's activities.

During the second wave of Even Start funding, due to school administration and policy changes, the program's site was moved from the elementary school campus to a local community college. This change posed some initial and ongoing challenges for staff and parents. Children (now infants, toddlers, and preschoolers) attended classes in the early childhood center on campus and were located in three separate rooms. Adults attended adult education classes on campus, a 5-minute walk from their children's classrooms. A portable unit assigned to the Even Start program was available for Parent Time and other uses. Essentially, parents and children now had to relocate often during the day to participate in some activities.

Although the initial challenge was compensating for the physical distance between children and parents and the subsequent scheduling conflicts, staff strived to maintain the PACT Time structure developed during the first years of the project. A new challenge for both parents and staff was the blending of both Even Start and non-Even-Start children in the classroom. Some teachers, not working in Even Start previously, found it difficult to be flexible and were somewhat uncomfortable with parents in their classrooms. Staff addressed how to best work with all children in the classroom, particularly those whose parents were not involved during PACT Time. A third challenge was introducing infants and toddlers to the program and learning to adjust PACT Time to meet the needs of very young children. (See the section Variations in Program Design: Infant and Toddler Programs later in this chapter.)

An additional concern was that adult education teachers who had participated in PACT Time in the past now found it difficult to attend due to class-scheduling conflicts and the inability to get to the early childhood classroom on time. Adult educator participation in PACT Time slacked off. The end-of-the-day closure with Circle Time and a transfer-home activity was maintained but took place in the Parent Time classroom for all parents and children. Moving children from their comfortable environments and into another setting at the end of the day often presented some difficulty in transition.

Although staff felt successful during the second 4 years of their project and both parents and children progressed in their achievements, some felt the family literacy model used the previous 4 years had been diluted and that the present model was not as cohesive. Although the change in physical setting presented a number of challenges, the staff believed they were successful in getting parents and children together regularly for PACT Time. Following ongoing professional development and the provision of more specific guidelines that better defined their roles, all teachers came to recognize the value of family literacy and PACT Time.

Head Start

With the reauthorization of Head Start in 1998, family literacy in Head Start and Early Head Start programs came under the mandate of the federal definition of family literacy services. Supporting early literacy development in children and supporting parents in their role as their child's first teacher, however, have always been central to the goals of Head Start. This concept is also central to family literacy. There are some noteworthy differences between Even Start and Head Start programs, though, which bring about a differentiation in the delivery of PACT Time. Even Start is a family literacy program that first qualifies the adult, then the child, for services. Adults are required to participate if they desire services for their children. Head Start is a comprehensive child development program that provides many services to Head Start children and families, of which family literacy is an option. Adults are not required to participate. Head Start qualifies the child for services first, then that child's parent may volunteer to become a part of family literacy services if desired.

These differences influence how PACT Time is designed and delivered in Head Start programs. Early literacy development and school readiness of children are of prime concern to Head Start staff, and critical to the attainment of child outcomes. Head Start recognizes the parent as a key figure in this process of helping children learn language and develop literacy skills in preparation for kindergarten. There are challenges within Head Start programs for the delivery of PACT Time utilizing a center-based approach. These challenges are not unlike the challenges of other family literacy programs (e.g., welfare reform issues, adequate facilities, consistent parent involvement, funding, and staffing) and produce similar results— many Head Start parents simply cannot get to the classroom for scheduled, center-based PACT Time experiences. Therefore, a large number of Head Start programs strive to focus on the strengths of parents as their child's primary teacher and guide them through parent training/education and home visiting to understand the importance and facilitation of meaningful parent–child interactions. Staff model how parents can initiate these interactions on their own, in their own homes, during daily routines, and in the family's natural environment and community.

Though Head Start programs value helping parents recognize the importance of meaningful interactions with their children in settings other than the classroom, it is possible for center-based PACT Time experiences to exist in Head Start classrooms. Given children's and families' needs and interests, many Head Start programs offer a variety of parent–child interactive experiences, of which regularly scheduled, center-based PACT Time is an option, by adapting appropriate program designs and building on effective collaborations with community partners (such as Even Start).

School-Age Programs

Family literacy builds on the inextricable link between parents' education and children's academic achievement. Title I and other school reform efforts have increasingly recognized the value of parent involvement in promoting high standards of children's academic achievement (NCFL, 2001a). PACT Time can play a powerful role in increasing meaningful parent involvement in elementary school programs.

Launched in 1998 by the National Center for Family Literacy with funding from the Toyota Motor Corporation, the TFS program set out to increase the achievement of at-risk children, ages 5 to 12, by implementing strong family literacy services in elementary schools. Title I, the federal program aimed at disadvantaged schools, encourages the use of funds for family literacy services if a substantial number of children being served have parents with low literacy skills. Furthermore, family literacy is an acceptable parental involvement strategy for Title I schools. Fifteen school districts and 45 elementary schools, all of which operate with Title I funding, have established the TFS program. As with all family literacy programs, TFS emphasizes the parents' role as learners and as supporters of their children's education.

School administrators recognize that a parent's lack of basic skills is a barrier to supporting children's learning (Title I Monitor, 2000). They also realize that parent involvement, which may initially be high during preschool and early primary years, generally dwindles as children move through elementary school. The TFS approach to family literacy brings at-risk elementary school children and their parents together to learn in the elementary school setting. The primary goal of this reform initiative is to improve children's academic success; the venue to achieve this goal is increasing meaningful parent involvement by raising the educational attainment of parents (NCFL, 2001a).

PACT Time in school-age programs increases communication between parents and teachers. It assists parents in understanding the academic needs of their children, allows them to observe appropriate strategies to use, and, through reflection and Parent Time, helps them acquire the necessary tools and skills to support their children (Sledd & Yero, 2001). According to Yero (2001), PACT Time within schools provides:

> A framework for true parent involvement in learning. Parents who are acclimated to the school culture and prepared to enter their children's classrooms through adult education classes participate in their children's learning process and observe their children's learning behavior in the classroom. Parents also have the opportunity to see firsthand how their children interact with other classmates and with the teacher. Classroom teachers work with parents to assist them in helping their children meet state standards, modeling instructional strategies that are scientifically based on reading research and sound educational practices that carry over to the home. Additionally, parents apply the academic skills gained in adult education sessions and identify future personal goals as they participate in classroom activities with their child. (pp. 39–40)

PACT Time in elementary school programs embraces the same basic tenets and goals of PACT Time in birth-to-five programs and is structured similarly. An intentional plan-do-review process is implemented. Preparing both staff (elementary teachers and adult education instructors) and parents for the experience is necessary for all to understand the purposes and benefits of PACT Time. The *do* part of the process involves the content of PACT Time, the experiences or activities in which parents and children will participate together. This content is based on children's classroom objectives and parents' academic goals; activities are designed to meet the goals for both. Review, or reflection, occurs immediately after the PACT Time session, allowing parents time to reflect on and internalize not only the learning experience shared with their child but also their own new learning as they progress toward their academic goals.

Organizing PACT Time in an elementary school can be especially challenging because it may occur in several classrooms and periodically throughout the day. Also, not all children in a classroom will have parents who participate. Scheduling, facilities, the integration of all four components of family literacy, and teamwork all contribute to the design of PACT Time in the elementary school. Some key considerations for making PACT Time work in this setting are listed in the following.

- All staff need a clear understanding of how PACT Time works with school-age children.
- All staff support the concept of the parent as a learning partner with the child.
- Parents understand the goals of PACT Time and how to work with their children at school and at home.
- Planning with all staff, including adult education instructors, classroom teachers and others, occurs regularly.
- Classroom teachers create warm, accepting environments for parents and welcome them into the classroom, provide space for parent and child to work together, and treat the adult as a learner in the classroom (Logan, 1999).

PACT Time and family literacy in the elementary school setting lend themselves to a continuum for the provision of services to at-risk children and their low-literacy parents. As stated earlier in this chapter, research provides the evidence that the early years of learning are critical to children's overall successes, and that parents contribute greatly to this process through the development of their interactions and relationships with children. We also know that for many reasons, countless parents feel that their jobs are done as their children grow older. They may feel intimidated or inadequate and might lack the confidence needed to help their children in elementary school and beyond. They also may not have the skills or time to be involved as they would like. With that lack of involvement, children's achievement will often lag behind. PACT Time in the elementary school setting, within the context of a quality family literacy program, can help bridge the gap between student achievement and parent involvement. As Title I schools continue to seek out improved avenues to foster both academic achievement and meaningful parent involvement, PACT Time in the elementary school setting can help bridge that gap.

Variations in Program Design

Infant and Toddler Programs.   Programs such as Even Start and Early Head Start that serve infants and toddlers recognize that the typical preschool sequence of PACT Time is not practical for these age groups. Interaction between parents and their infant and toddler children typically revolves around care and routines and is individualized to children's needs. Parents may need additional guidance to help them realize how caregiving times are also learning opportunities for both child and parent, even in terms of early language and literacy development, as well as opportunities for strengthening attachment.

In family literacy programs serving infants and toddlers, parents may be encouraged to spend a few extra minutes with their children after they arrive at school in the morning. During this time, teachers can have books and comfortable chairs available for parents to share a quick story with their children before leaving for their own classroom. Encouraging parents to spend mealtimes with their children is also important. Generating discussions and conversations around daily routines provides many opportunities for increased language and vocabulary development. Diapering and preparing for nap time are other opportunities for positive interaction and talk time, as is down-on-the-floor play time. Importantly, all of these activities are easily transferred to the home environment.

Older toddlers might enjoy small group activities and Circle Times, particularly if parents are available to interact with them one to one. It is important to remember, however, that attention spans of toddlers are short, and it is unrealistic to expect them to sit for long periods of time. Best practice suggests that only if the toddler is ready and desires to participate, should he or she do so. Parents of infants and toddlers may require a lot of support from teachers in order to fully understand how to support their child's early learning and may need a daily focus for PACT Time. This need can be particularly true for teen parents. Encouraging consistent participation in PACT Time and learning to facilitate meaningful parent–child interactions at home help parents and children establish literacy routines early in the child's life.

Welfare Reform/Working Parents.   When welfare reform legislation was passed in 1996, it presented a major challenge for family literacy programs, specifically for PACT Time. With more parents working, going to school, or participating in community service, programs have found it difficult to get parents into the classroom, especially programs offering only half-day services. Although many family literacy practitioners successfully manage center-based PACT Time with a handful of parents and a room full of children, some programs choose additional options.

Some of the most successful options allow for flexibility in the design and scheduling of PACT Time. Some parents may choose to arrive and depart from school when it is convenient for their job or personal schedules. This situation may or may not happen on a daily basis. Programs may allow parents to join their children in their work, play, or meal times throughout the day, rather than at a designated time in the daily routine. In order for this approach to be successful, parents need to be fully aware of their role and need to have gained some knowledge about the purpose of PACT Time, particularly in order to stay focused on language and literacy development experiences. Parent Time is a good time to discuss the meaning and purpose of interactive experiences and allows for more individualization of those experiences for both child and parent. Parents need guidance and preparation to understand the value of PACT Time and how they, and their child, can get the most from the experience. Teachers also need to plan and be prepared for the possibilities of having parents in their classrooms intermittently throughout the day.

Programs also may want to consider flexibility in their hours of operation and in the scheduling of staff. Where feasible, some programs extend hours beyond the school day, for 1 or more days per week, and provide group PACT Time experiences for families. Often, meals or snacks are provided. Parents and children may spend the entire evening together or may work as independent groups before coming together as a family later in the evening. Many programs offer similar services on Saturdays. These arrangements call for flexibility in scheduling, providing release time for staff, and possibly the securing of funds to pay for additional staff and facilities to provide these kinds of services. As mentioned earlier in this chapter, collaboration of services with other community agencies can also help meet families needs and schedules and provide services with the desired intensity and duration.

Home Visiting.   Many programs make use of their home-visiting requirements to provide time for parents and children to interact and for staff to introduce and model meaningful interactions. Even Start, Early Head Start and Head Start, and FACE programs, for example, all utilize home visiting as part of their offered services. Some programs increase the number of required home visits in order to enhance the intensity of services. During home visits, staff provide assistance for parents about how to successfully guide their children in their language and literacy development and offer them ideas and activities for meaningful experiences. For programs that are entirely home based, such as some Head Start and Early Head Start programs, parent–child experiences are provided in the home more frequently and are supplemented with regularly scheduled group socializations (or PACT Time) experiences.

Although programs vary in design and delivery, a family literacy home visit typically includes experiences that address all four components. One advantage to parent–child interaction during home visits is that the entire family can participate. Fathers, siblings, grandparents, elders, extended family members, and other significant adults in the child's life can benefit from this group interaction time. Flexibility is key when working with families in a home-visiting situation, so typical schedules may need to be modified.

In summary, a combination of many or all of these options and variations for the successful delivery of PACT Time make it possible for Even Start, Head Start, school-age programs, and for many other models of family literacy programming to provide opportunities for meaningful parent–child interactive experiences. Furthermore, programs that collaborate with each other to provide quality family literacy programming may find it less challenging to provide comprehensive, four-component family literacy services with the intensity the federal definition requires. In whatever ways PACT Time interactions are offered, it is important for staff and parents to understand the basic tenets of meaningful parent–child interactions and to work within these options to provide families adequate opportunities to improve language and literacy skills.

GOALS FOR PACT TIME EXPERIENCES

Measuring the effectiveness of family literacy programs requires a clear statement of the intended effects on participants (NCFL, 2001b). As a rule, programs should consider their own anticipated outcomes for the participants in their programs, depending on the families served, their goals, cultures, and the communities in which they live. Some programs have both suggested and mandated outcomes. These guidelines also pertain to PACT Time. Several participant outcomes for parent–child interaction are listed here. They include a range of abilities, behaviors, and accomplishments appropriate for native English speakers and/or second-language learners. This list can be used as a sample for program staff as they work through their own processes of defining short-term outcomes and lasting impacts for parents.

1. Short-term outcomes of PACT Time for parents
   - Increase quality and quantity of time spent reading, writing, talking, playing with children, and listening to children
   - Display positive attitudes toward children
   - Communicate positively and effectively with children
   - Apply knowledge of children's development and behavior management techniques
   - Use routine interactions with children in school and home to encourage learning and language development
   - Use observations of children's abilities to plan appropriate activities with children
2. Long-term impacts of PACT Time for parents
   - Maintain positive, supportive interactions with children
   - Apply knowledge of stages of children's development by refining communication and behavior management techniques appropriately over time
   - Support/assist children with homework and school-related activities as needed. (NCFL, 2001b)

These anticipated outcomes for parents also signify expectations for participating children's language and literacy development. Mikulecky, Lloyd, and Brannon (1995) report that family literacy programs are successful in making positive changes in many of the areas of parent–child interaction important to children's future literacy success. They showed that parents from family literacy programs engaged in a wider range of reading and writing activities with their children at home, drawing and writing with their children and using educational materials and games. Parents also displayed more children's drawings and writing. Parents and children played together more often and parents became more aware that children learn through play. The level of parent–child talk also provided more explanation, rather than direct instruction.

Evaluations of the FACE program, according to the *Bureau of Indian Affairs Family and Child Education Program Evaluation Report* (Yarnell, Pfannenstiel, Lambson, Treffeisen, 1997, 1998) conclude significant impacts in the areas of student achievement, home literacy, and parent involvement. Nearly 96% of children demonstrated gains in personal and social development, almost all 3-year-olds (96%) and most 4-year-olds (90%) demonstrated improved language and literacy skills, and almost all 4-year-olds (96%) demonstrated improvement in mathematical thinking and social studies domains. Parents read to and told stories to their child, played with their child, and continued to interact with their child throughout elementary school significantly and more frequently than parents who did not participate in FACE programs. FACE parents talked about their child's progress with teachers, participated in school and classroom events, attended parent–teacher conferences, observed and assisted in their child's classroom, and served on school committees or boards significantly and more frequently than parents who had never participated in FACE programs.

Both of these studies and a recent Even Start study (U.S. Department of Education, 1998) indicate that intensity and duration of services produce greater results. Parents who participated in FACE programs (including participation in regularly scheduled PACT Time and Parent Time and frequent home visits by parent educators) reported high frequencies of home literacy activities and significant long-term impacts on parent support of learning in the home. Families in Even Start programs that provided large amounts of time for parents and children together had more supportive home environments (e.g., more materials in the home, parent–child learning activities, positive approaches to discipline) than did families in projects that offered smaller amounts of parent–child time together. Powell (1996) also speaks to the importance of providing long-term, intensive work with parents, especially those living in high-risk circumstances, to achieve sustained effects in parenting behaviors. (see Powell, chap. 9, this volume).

A look at the analysis of the year 3 data compiled on NCFL's Toyota Families in Schools programs shows that children's involvement in TFS programs led to positive changes in attendance, classroom behavior, and other performance-related variables. Also, by exposing parents to what children are learning in their classrooms, as well as by guiding parents to work and learn together, the programs helped both parents and children enhance the development of mutually beneficial learning relationships. Specific to the interactions and behaviors of parents and children, the analysis reports increased family trips to the library, decreased television viewing, increased adult reading of a daily newspaper, and increased the variety of reading materials in the home (Tucker & Hill, 2002).

At the writing of this chapter, data on both TFS children and comparison children are currently being collected in five TFS school districts. This longitudinal database will include standardized test scores, teacher grades, attendance data, and other variables that will provide some preliminary assessments about the impact of TFS on children's performance in school (Tucker & Hill, 2002).

CONCLUSION

Parent–child interactions are central to children's achievement. PACT Time experiences provided in the context of comprehensive family literacy programming provide parents and children the opportunities to work, play, and learn together in a model setting with guidance from supportive staff. The development of children's language and literacy skills, as well as cognitive development and school readiness, is emphasized. The primary goal of the PACT Time experience is for parents to practice and reflect on their interactions with children, to become comfortable in their role as teachers of their children, and then ultimately to transfer those skills into positive, ongoing interactions with their children.

PACT Time happens at home, at school, or in the community, and builds on the integration of all four components of family literacy services. Programs design and deliver PACT Time according to the needs and cultures of their families and often develop their outcomes by which to measure achievement. Although challenges, issues, and variations of design and delivery are not specific to any one family literacy program, universal concerns are addressed in many ways to meet a variety of needs. Family literacy programming strives to address the language and literacy learning goals of both children and parents served and to move families closer to the attainment of those goals through the use of meaningful parent–child interactive experiences.

REFERENCES

Benjamin, L. A. (1993). *Parents' literacy and their children's success in school: Recent research, promising practices, and research implications.* Washington, DC: Office of Educational Research and Improvement.

Bowman, B. T., Donovan, M. S., & Burns, M. S. (Eds.). (2001). *Eager to learn: Educating our preschoolers.* Washington, DC: National Academy Press.

Brizius, J., & Foster, S. (1993). *Generation to generation: Realizing the promise of family literacy.* Ypsilanti, MI: High/Scope Press.

Dickinson, D. K., & Tabors, P. O. (2001). *Beginning literacy with language: Young children learning at home and school.* Baltimore: Brookes.

Egeland, B., & Erickson, M. F. (1999, October/November). Findings from the parent-child project and implications for early intervention. *Zero to Three,* 3–10.

Gopnick, A., Meltzoff, A. N., & Kuhl, P. K. (1999). *The scientist in the crib.* New York: William Morrow.

Greene, E. (1991). *Books, babies and libraries: Serving infants, toddlers, their parents and caregivers.* Chicago: American Library Association.

Hart, B., & Risley, T. R. (1995). *Meaningful differences in the everyday experiences of young American children.* Baltimore: Brookes.

Hart, B., & Risely, T. R. (1999). *The social world of children learning to talk.* Baltimore: Brookes.

Hohmann, M. H., & Weikart, D. P. (1995). *Educating young children.* Ypsilanti, MI: High/Scope Press.

King, R., & McMaster, J. (2000). *Pathways: A primer for family literacy program design and development.* Louisville, KY: National Center for Family Literacy.

Logan, B. (1999, November). Parent and child together (PACT) time in elementary schools: Implementation practices from Toyota families in schools. *Momentum.*

Mikulecky, L. (1996). *Family literacy: Parent and child interactions. In Family Literacy: Directions in research and implications for practice* (OERI Publication No. EC 95-9006). Washington, DC: US Government Printing Office.

Mikulecky, L., Lloyd, P., & Brannon, D. (1995). *Evaluating parent/child interactions in family literacy programs.* Louisville, KY: National Center for Family Literacy.

National Center for Family Literacy. (2000). *Training and staff development for family literacy practitioners, participant manual.* Louisville, KY: Author.

National Center for Family Literacy. (2001a). *Creating partnerships for learning.* Louisville, KY: Author.

National Center for Family Literacy. (2001b). *Outcomes and measures for family literacy programs* (2nd ed.). Louisville, KY: Author.

National Center for Family Literacy (NCFL). (2003). *Foundations in family literacy: Participants' manual.* Louisville, KY: Author.

Pianta, R. C. (1999). *Enhancing relationships between teachers and children.* Washington, DC: American Psychological Association.

Powell, D. (1996). Teaching parenting and basic skills to parents: What we know. In *Family Literacy: Directions in research and implications for practice* (OERI Publication No. EC 95-9006). Washington, DC: US Government Printing Office.

Shore, R. (1997). *Rethinking the brain, new insights into early development.* Executive Summary. New York: Families and Work Institute.

Sledd, N., & Yero, S. (2001, August). Families in schools: Milestones and more. *Momentum, 1.*

Snow, C. E., Barnes, W. S., Chandler, J., Goodman, I. F., & Hemphill, L. (1991, 2000). *Unfulfilled expectations: Home and school influences on literacy.* London, England: Harvard University.

Sticht, T. G., & Armstrong, W. B. (1994) *Adult literacy in the United States: A compendium of quantitative data and interpretive comments.* Washington, DC: National Institute for Literacy.

Title I Monitor. (2000, January). *Barriers to parent involvement in high- and low-poverty Title I schools identified by principals.* Special Report.

Tucker, J., & Hill, H. (2002, February). An analysis of families in schools research. *Momentum, 3.*

U.S. Department of Education. (1998). *Even Start: Evidence from the past and a look to the future. Planning and evaluation service analysis and highlights.* Washington, DC: Author.

U.S. Department of Education. National Center for Education Statistics. (1993). *Adult literacy in America: A first look at the results of the national adult literacy survey.* Washington, DC: Author.

U.S. Department of Education. National Center for Education Statistics. (2000). *America's Kindergartners.* Washington, DC: Author.

Werner, E. (1996, Winter). How children become resilient: Observations and cautions. *Resilience in Action,* 18–28.

Yarnell, V., Pfannenstiel, J., Lambson, T. & Treffeisen, S. (1997, 1998). *Bureau of Indian Affairs Family and Child Education Program: 1997 and 1998 Evaluation Reports.* Overland Park, KS: Research & Training Associates, Inc., for the Office of Indian Education Programs, Bureau of Indian Affairs, U.S. Department of the Interior.

Yero, S. (2001, Summer). Family literacy: Pathways to success. *The State Education Standard.* 38–41.

12

Project FLAME: A Parent Support Family Literacy Model

Flora V. Rodríguez-Brown
University of Illinois at Chicago

Hispanics have a long history in the United States, predating many later immigrants, and, as such, they have been part of the fabric of our country for centuries. Today, however, we are seeing a large increase in the Hispanic immigrant population. According to a recent U.S. Census Bureau report, approximately one out of eight people in the United States is Hispanic (Terrien & Ramírez, 2000). Moreover, Americans of Hispanic origin are the fastest growing ethnic group in public schools (Sable & Stennett, 1998). In Chicago alone, one third of the school population is Hispanic.

The Hispanic population is hardly homogeneous. Nevertheless, significant differences separate Hispanics as a whole from non-Hispanic Whites. For example, Hispanics are more likely to be less than 18 years old and to live in central cities in metropolitan areas. In terms of education achievement, three out of five Hispanics have graduated from high school, a statistic that varies across Latino groups (e.g., Cuban and other Hispanics show a graduation rate of 73 and 71%, respectively, whereas Mexicans show a 51% graduation rate). Furthermore, as a group, Hispanics are much more likely than non-Hispanic Whites to be unemployed and living in poverty. Hispanic children represent 16.2% of all children in the United States but 29% of all children in poverty.

Population growth and educational trends for Hispanics have held steady for some time. Twelve years ago, the National Council of La Raza (1990) reported that the population of Hispanics was growing five times as fast as that of non-Hispanics. Three years earlier, Applebee, Langer, and Mullis (1987) reported that Hispanics at all grade levels were lagging behind their mainstream peers in reading and writing achievement. Recently, Sable and Stennett (1998) reported that although the achievement gap had narrowed, significant literacy and achievement gaps continue to exist between the Hispanic population and the non-Hispanic Whites.

The problem of low achievement is complex, and efforts at home or at school alone most likely will not be sufficient to solve it. Schools frequently do not recognize the knowledge that children bring with them unless it is consistent with mainstream models of learning, placing children from linguistically and culturally diverse homes at a disadvantage. Heath

(1987) describes how home and school can differ in communication styles, views of literacy, and the nature of literacy interactions, thus limiting literacy learning. Others point to home–school differences in cultural models of learning (Reese & Gallimore, 2000; Rogers, 2002), discourses, and understandings of literacy itself (Gee, 1999; The New London Group, 1996).

One way to address the problem is to develop partnerships between school and home. Such partnerships get parents involved in their children's home literacy learning and school achievement (Epstein, 1990, 1991). Furthermore, instruction that takes families' social, cultural, and linguistic strengths into account enhances both school and home literacy learning (Delgado-Gaitan, 1992; Gallimore & Reese, 1999; Goldenberg, 1987; Moll, 1998; Reese & Gallimore, 2000; Rogers, 2001, 2002; and Serna & Huddelson, 1993). According to Moll, Amanti, Neff, and González (1992) and Moll and Greenberg (1990), increasing and recognizing opportunities to learn outside of school, particularly at home, can decrease the incongruency in literacy learning.

Reese and Gallimore (2000) have found that new immigrant families' cultural learning models, although important to their everyday life, are not static. Through interaction with teachers and other school personnel, parents learn to adapt to beliefs and practices supported by the schools, except when they see change as a threat to traditional morals. For example, explicit requests from teachers that Hispanic parents read to their children at home produced the desired effect. Reese and Gallimore recommend that teachers make concrete requests to Hispanic parents in support of their children's literacy learning at home. This approach is more effective than offering "one-shot" workshops on reading at home or simply telling parents that reading with their children is a good idea.

Family literacy programs offer families a long-term commitment toward parents' understanding of their role as their children's first and most important teachers. Also, some family literacy programs support school personnel's efforts to learn about the cultural models of learning, discourses, and understandings of literacy that children bring from home (Paratore, 2001; Rodríguez-Brown, 2001a). Thus, these programs strengthen the connection between learning at home and at school and enhance opportunities for children to succeed.

PARENT INVOLVEMENT IN THE HISPANIC COMMUNITY

Because literacy learning is social and cultural in nature (Heath, 1983; Rogers, 2001, 2002), it seems natural for literacy to develop best within the context of the family. But Latino parents, citing their own lack of English proficiency and low levels of schooling, tend to believe that they cannot support their children's literacy learning. They tend to view teachers as experts and do not want to interfere with the teacher's role (Flores, Cousin, & Díaz, 1991). From their own cultural framework, relatively new immigrant parents see their role as teachers differently than does the mainstream population. In Spanish, there are two words related to teaching, *educar* (to educate) and *enseñar* (to teach), with distinct and specific meanings. Hispanic parents generally believe that their role is expressed by *educar*: to educate their children, that is, to help their children to become good people by learning morals, manners, and values. In contrast, they believe that the school's role is *enseñar*: to teach subjects such as math, science, reading, and writing (Goldenberg, 1987; Reese, Balzano, Gallimore, & Goldenberg, 1995; Rodríguez-Brown, 2001b; Valdes, 1996). The parents' ambivalence toward the teacher role and their high regard for teachers' expertise lead them to question whether teachers or schools expect or even want them to support their children's learning at home. These sociocultural factors further validate Reese and Gallimore's (2000) observation that it is best to ask Hispanic parents explicitly to get involved in their children's learning.

The following pages describe and discuss the components, implementation, and effectiveness of Project FLAME. FLAME is an acronym for Family Literacy: *aprendiendo, mejorando, educando* (learning, improving, educating). The program was developed to help Hispanic parents become more involved in their children's learning at home and to reduce discontinuities between home and school (Rodríguez-Brown & Shanahan, 1989). It focuses directly on parents and only indirectly on their children. Parents attend family literacy workshops twice a month and also participate in other activities.

A COMPREHENSIVE FAMILY LITERACY MODEL

The FLAME program was originally designed to enhance literacy learning in a population composed mostly of recent Hispanic immigrants (Rodríguez-Brown & Shanahan, 1989). It was based on the belief that literacy learning is more culturally bound than other aspects of school learning and, as such, it is more influenced by parents and the home. As developers of the FLAME model, we believed that the literacy culture of the home was more likely to diverge from that of the school in classrooms whose children came from homes where English was a second language or was not used at all. We also believed that communication styles, views of literacy, and the nature of literacy interactions would be different at home and at school, and that this difference would affect Hispanic children's literacy development. Recent research by Gee (1999), The New London Group (1996), Goldenberg, (1989), Reese and Gallimore (2000), and Rogers (2002) supports our beliefs.

Based on these early beliefs and assumptions, we proposed to train parents to become good literacy models and to support their children's literacy development in the language the parents knew best. Our planning took into account the context of the family. The concept of *familia* (Abi-Nader, 1991) is central to cultural descriptions of Hispanics, and meeting the family's needs is one of the greatest motivations for Hispanic parents to support their children's learning and school success (Delgado-Gaitan, 1992; Quintero & Huerta-Macías, 1990). Family literacy was the vehicle we used to help families learn and use literacy at home in order to reduce the discontinuities between home and school.

FLAME was developed as a community program, based in the schools and run by the Center for Literacy, and more recently by the Bilingual/ESL Program, at University of Illinois at Chicago. It was designed for Hispanic families who have children between 3 and 9 years old. With funding from the U.S. Department of Education, the program began in 3 Chicago public schools in 1989. We served approximately 20 families per school during the first 3 years. Since then, FLAME has expanded to serve 10 schools, and by 2002 we served about 200 families annually. The program model has been disseminated nationally to about 40 other sites.

THEORETICAL ASSUMPTIONS, OBJECTIVES, AND COMPONENTS

Four basic assumptions underlie Project FLAME's design. We believe that a supportive home environment is essential to literacy development; that parents can have a positive effect on their children's learning; that parents who are confident and successful learners themselves will be the most effective teachers for their children; and, finally, that literacy is the school subject most likely to be influenced by the family's social and cultural contexts.

The program has four objectives:

- To increase parents' ability to provide literacy opportunities for their children
- To increase parents' ability to act as positive literacy models for their children

- To improve parents' literacy skills so they can more efficiently initiate, encourage, support, and extend their children's learning
- To increase and improve the relationship between the parents and the schools.

To fulfill these objectives, the program has four components supported by literacy-learning research: literacy opportunity, literacy modeling, literacy interaction, and home–school connection. Our program activities address one or more of these components, each of which is described in the following sections.

Literacy Opportunity

A supportive home environment provides children with opportunities to use literacy. Children with such opportunities are more successful in school. According to Wheeler (1971), the provision of such opportunities alone is a powerful stimulus to literacy learning in young children. To perform well in school literacy learning, children need to be familiar with a culture of literacy. Thus, the availability of literacy materials at home allows children the opportunity to see literacy in action and to experiment with literacy.

This program component helps us reach our first objective: to increase parents' ability to provide literacy opportunities for their children. Project FLAME teaches parents to find and choose appropriate books, magazines, and other literacy materials. Parents learn how to use public libraries to make more literacy materials available to their children. Parents also learn to develop a literacy corner at home, where children can use pencils, scissors, and other materials to support their early literacy learning.

Literacy Modeling

For our purposes, a literacy model is defined as a significant person in the child's environment who uses literacy in an open and obvious manner. Children who see their parents reading and writing do better at school reading than children who do not see their parents engage in these activities (Metritech, 1987). Furthermore, several studies report that changing mothers' strategies for reading to their children can improve literacy learning for both Hispanic children (Gallimore & Goldenberg, 1989) and other children of low socioeconomic status (Edwards, 1988). However, Gallimore and Goldenberg found that Hispanic parents who are only learning English tend not to share literacy with their children, possibly because of the parents' limited literacy skills or their lack of English proficiency. Also, Heath (1987) found that parents at times, in their zeal to expose their children to English, fail to provide a rich, active language environment at home. Several studies have shown that parents are more likely to serve as effective literacy models and to participate in their children's literacy learning when they see themselves as effective learners (Nickse, Speicher, & Buchek, 1988; Van Fossen & Sticht, 1991).

This component helps us reach our second objective, namely, to increase parents' ability to act as positive literacy models for their children. In order to become positive literacy models, we encourage parents to increase their own literacy and language use, to use reading and writing in the company of children, and to draw the children's attention to this behavior. The primary vehicle for helping parents become positive literacy models is English as a second language and/or basic skills classes offered through the program.

Literacy Interaction

Direct interaction between parents and children has a positive influence on children's learning (Paratore, 1994; Paratore, Melzi, & Krol-Sinclair, 1999; Tobin, 1981). For example, children who are read to often are more successful at school than those who do not have such experiences (Feiltelson & Goldstein, 1986). (See Purcell-Gates, this volume, for additional information on storybook reading.) Literacy interactions, which include formal direct instruction as well as reading to children or encouraging them to pretend to read, acquaint children with story structures and literacy conventions (Teale, 1984).

This component helps us reach our third objective: to increase parent's literacy skills so they can better initiate, encourage, support, and extend their children's learning. Through Project FLAME, parents participate in activities that prepare them to read to their children more effectively. They learn how to talk with their children about books and how to build children's phonemic awareness through songs, games, and other interactive activities. They also learn about community resources they can share with their children to support literacy learning.

Home–School Connection

According to Goldenberg (1987), Hispanic children's literacy knowledge is highest when teachers and parents maintain frequent contact with each other. Similarly, Silvern (1988) found that social and cultural discontinuities between the home and the school interfere with literacy learning. In this program component, we strive toward our fourth objective: to increase and improve the relationships between parents and schools. FLAME's home–school connection component helps parents understand what happens in the classroom and what the school expects of their children. Conversely, teachers learn about parents' concerns and aspirations.

Through Project FLAME, parents learn about the teachers' classroom role. They visit classrooms to observe teachers, an activity that helps parents develop and practice ways to communicate with teachers about literacy learning. The visits also increase home–school collaboration. Through classroom visits and informal talks with teachers, good relations and mutual respect develop between parents and schools. For all these activities the focus of the program is not only on reading but also on writing and other literacy-related skills that prepare children for schooling.

INSTRUCTIONAL PROGRAM

FLAME activities are designed so that each one contributes to more than one of the program's four objectives or components. Thus, an activity might simultaneously facilitate literacy modeling and literacy interaction, or it might promote the home literacy environment while also facilitating home–school relations. This approach helps us address the complexity of creating a home literacy culture. The program activities recognize and reflect the interactions among the objectives and components.

Training Activities

The program's instructional design includes two integrated sets of training activities: *Parents as Teachers* and *Parents as Learners*.

Parents as Teachers is the family literacy program's core. These semimonthly workshops (held from October to May) focus on the four components of our model. They cover literacy opportunity (increasing the range of literacy materials and experiences at home), literacy modeling (encouraging parents to model literacy uses to their children), literacy interaction (demonstrating ways to engage in literacy activities with children), and home–school connection (providing opportunities for teacher–parent discussions and classroom observation). The sessions take place in the language that the parents know best. Table 12.1 lists the topics of the workshops and describes the content of each.

Parents as Learners includes twice-weekly, 2-hour sessions on basic skills, General Educational Development (GED), or English as a Second Language (ESL), according to participants'

TABLE 12.1
Project FLAME—Parents as Teachers Sessions

Creating home literacy centers
This session demonstrates creating and using a home literacy activity center in a box that includes items such as pencils, crayons, paper, scissors, paste, magazines, and pictures.

Book sharing
This session discusses and demonstrates the most effective ways to share books with children. Parents discuss how to talk about books and share books when your own literacy is limited.

Book selection
This session highlights quality criteria for selecting books appropriate for children's needs and interests.

Library visit
This session includes a public library tour, complete with applications for library cards.

Book fair
In this session, parents purchase (with coupons provided by the program) English- or Spanish-language books for their children.

Teaching the ABCs
This session explores simple ways to teach letters and sounds, with an emphasis on language games, songs, and language experience activities.

Children's writing
This session explores how young children write and demonstrates ways to encourage writing at home.

Community literacy
This session highlights ways parents can share their own literacy uses with their children while at the market, in the community, and during other daily activities outside the home and at home.

Classroom observations
In this session, parents visit classrooms to gain a sense of how their children are taught in schools.

Parent–Teacher get-togethers
In this session, parents, teachers and principals gather for guided discussion about children's education.

Math at home
This session demonstrates games and activities for helping children understand numbers and arithmetic.

Parents and homework
This session discusses and demonstrates ways in which parents can monitor and help with children's homework even when they cannot do the homework themselves.

Songs, games, and language: A family celebration
This lesson serves as the culminating event for the Project FLAME Literacy Curriculum. The lesson is designed as an event that the entire family can attend.

needs. The sessions' purpose is to support the parents' role as learners and as models of literacy learning. In practice, this activity has also served to attract or recruit parents to the program.

The Parents as Learners sessions focus on the specific literacy learning needs of parents at each site. They are usually connected to Parents as Teachers. For example, parents may create books for their children during the ESL class, an activity that increases home literacy opportunities.

Other FLAME Activities

Parents as Leaders. FLAME's basic family literacy program has been described previously. Once we began working with parents, however, we developed other activities to complement the original program and to make it more relevant to the community it serves.

When we started to offer the literacy workshops, parents consistently raised issues that were relevant to their families' daily lives. In order to keep the focus of the program on literacy, we developed a *beyond literacy* activity, Parents as Leaders, a summer leadership institute. Typically, parents choose issues that interest the family and/or the community and that they would like to learn more about and understand better. We then arrange for speakers to address their concerns. The summer institutes have covered topics such as discipline at home, parents' rights, immigration, banks and their role in the community, and the use of hospital services. These topics shaped the content and procedures of other program activities.

Trainers of Trainers. Another instructional activity developed to answer participants' needs is Training of Trainers, which addresses the issue of capacity building in the community. Its objective is to train people in the community to offer the FLAME program when the sponsoring university cannot do so. Training of Trainers allows parents who have graduated from FLAME to develop their literacy leadership activities in the community. Participants are parents who have completed 2 years in the basic program and show promise as literacy leaders. We train them to plan FLAME workshops that are relevant to parents in the community.

Trainees and university staff meet every other Friday to plan and develop materials and activities for the next literacy session. In the first year, the trainees serve more as assistants to university staff. In the second year, they are in charge of the workshops, with the university staff's assistance. After 2 years, they receive a diploma recognizing that they have completed the training to become FLAME trainers themselves. These parents are paid a fee for preparation and workshops during training. Several graduates have been hired to provide family literacy training in schools in Chicago.

Parents as Volunteers. Because FLAME parents want to volunteer in their children's schools, but some teachers are uneasy about such parents' leading their classrooms, we introduced a Parents as Volunteers component, which we have instituted successfully at one school. Parents sign up in the principal's office to volunteer in classrooms. Then the principal asks teachers if they need trained parent volunteers. Teachers who say yes give the FLAME program staff information, books, or other guidance about what a parent volunteer should do. Thus, parents are prepared to teach before they enter the classroom.

We also hire FLAME graduates to provide childcare for the program. These parents are trained to do educational activities with the children and are paid for their services.

A SOCIOCULTURAL FRAMEWORK IN SUPPORT OF PROJECT FLAME

All the aforementioned activities are now part of the FLAME program. The original program design (content and activities) was developed to supply what we believed the parents needed in order to support their children's literacy learning at home (Rodríguez-Brown & Shanahan, 1989). Working with families in a community context, however, made us aware of the need to listen to their voices and concerns. This close contact is a necessary element of keeping the program relevant to its participants and has helped us respond to the needs they identify by adding new activities to the original framework.

We also recognized how much knowledge families bring to the program. It became important to recognize this knowledge and use it in our planning. In order to do so, I saw a need to develop a sociocultural framework that could undergird all program activities. The work of Gee (1999), Reese and Gallimore (2000), Rogers (2001, 2002), and The New London Group (1996) provides the basis of this framework. These authors have emphasized the need to recognize that culturally and linguistically different parents have a lot of knowledge that they share with their children, and that they may use cultural models of learning different from those of the mainstream. Parents may not only use a language other than English but also bring their own primary discourses and understandings of literacy into programs such as FLAME. These differences need to be recognized and used as starting points for what is taught or shared through the program. Sociocultural research-based programs *add to* and *build on* what the parents bring to the program, giving them new linguistic and cultural repertoires and knowledge, rather than trying to change their cultural practices. From this approach it follows that family literacy programs that function within a sociocultural framework should (a) accept and validate parents' native language and the knowledge they bring into the program; (b) welcome and embrace differences in cultural learning models, discourse, and understandings of literacy; (c) tell program participants that the knowledge they acquire is to be added to their existing knowledge and repertoires; (d) recognize that not all knowledge is acquired in English; and (e) recognize that parents should share literacy with their children in the language they know best. In Project FLAME, we believe that following these principles is one of the reasons for our success.

PARTICIPANT CHARACTERISTICS, EVALUATION PROCEDURES, AND OUTCOMES

Characteristics of FLAME Participants

The demographic picture of parents involved in FLAME varies little from year to year. For this chapter, we take the characteristics of the FLAME population for the school year 1998 to 1999 to represent our participants. In that year, most of the participating parents were natives of Mexico, and most primarily used Spanish at home. The average parent came to the United States slightly more than 10 years ago, and most were in their 30s. Both mothers and fathers had finished about 8 years of schooling. The average family had 1.65 children between 3 and 9 years of age (the target population for Project FLAME). Many also had older or younger children. Parents were asked to describe their proficiency in both English and Spanish. Most parents called their writing and reading proficiency in Spanish good or very good. In English, however, almost all of the mothers and two thirds of the fathers reported little or no reading and writing proficiency. This self-reported language proficiency information served as a justification to provide family literacy workshops in Spanish, the language the parents knew best.

Each year, families are recruited for the program through the schools that the FLAME program serves. Prospective participants must have a child or children attending the school as well as a preschool age child (3 to 4 years old). They sign an informed consent for themselves (to allow us to collect demographic and home literacy uses information and language proficiency data) and another consent to allow their 3- to 6-year-old children to be tested. The few families in our observational studies sign a separate consent. Once the consents are signed and the parents agree to participate in Project FLAME, they are interviewed to check their eligibility for the program.

Parent Self-Report Data

Participants fill out a questionnaire each year between September and early October, and again in May. It includes a section reporting home literacy activities and availability of literacy related materials, as well as a section on home–school relations. The questionnaire's purpose is to learn about the parents' prior interest in and knowledge of the family literacy program's components and to examine changes over the school year.

Parents respond to the questions about literacy activities using a 3-point scale, where a 1 means that they never do an activity at home or with their children and a 3 means that they do the activity all the time. We have found that parents in Project FLAME believe they must report some literacy uses at home in order to be admitted to the program and thus tend to provide an initial rating of 2. This can cause problems in assessing the program's impact. Nevertheless, the data show small but significant postprogram differences in uses of literacy related to three Project FLAME components, namely, literacy opportunity, literacy modeling, and literacy interaction. A comparison of pre- and postprogram responses shows that parents made significant improvements in such activities as showing children signs and words in the street, using the library as a literacy resource, checking books out of the library, reading more books and magazines for themselves, reading and writing with their children, and teaching their children the alphabet (Rodríguez-Brown, Li, & Albom, 1999).

The Home–School Connection

Because Project FLAME seeks to enhance relations between home and school, the questionnaire asks about the parents' role in supporting their children's schoolwork, using a 3-point scale with questions such as "How much do you know about what your child learns in school?" and "Do you talk to your child's teacher?" Though postprogram gains were small (just as with the other components, parents tended to report some activity before they started the program), they were statistically significant for six of seven items. Significant differences occurred in parent's self-reported knowledge about what their children learn in school, their willingness to talk to their children's teachers, and their ability to support their children's literacy learning at home. The only item that showed no significant change from fall to spring was one that asked whether the children bring home homework every day: Parents consistently reported that their children did so.

In summary, we can conclude that participation in Project FLAME activities increased parents' understanding of the home–school relationship and the uses of literacy at home. The reports also show that parents seem to better understand their role as teachers of their children, as well as the need to interact with teachers and the school to support their children's learning (Rodríguez-Brown et al., 1999).

Parents' Improvement in English Literacy

As explained previously, FLAME parents participate in ESL classes in order to learn or improve English proficiency and skills. These twice-weekly classes, which help parents become literacy models for their children, use a participatory communicative approach for instruction. The classes focus mostly on topics of interest to the parents and on oral communication skills. Topics covered in past years' classes include using the phone to call the school, the teacher, or the doctor's office; shopping for food or cosmetics; and applying for a job.

Parents who realize they are able to use the English they practice in class start inquiring about the proper way to say things, which ties in with grammar lessons and again is immediately relevant to their everyday life. Parents also become interested in the role of written language and learn to value journal keeping and creative writing. Every year, FLAME parents publish an anthology of their writings. They can contribute in Spanish, English, or both. Parents have written about their homes, keeping up a house, their children, their families in Mexico and in Chicago, and their experiences in coming to the United States. They compare their life in Mexico to their life in the United States. Many of them write poetry; others write essays. Some highly literate parents enjoy editing their own writings.

Each year, parents are tested in September or in early October and again in May on their English-proficiency skills, using the Adult-LAS (De Avila & Duncan, 1993). Their tests scores are used to place them in the appropriate level of ESL instruction at the beginning of the school year and to assess their English proficiency at the end. The Oral Proficiency LAS measures parents' listening comprehension and oral language ability. The parents must use nouns, verbs, and adjectives while looking at pictures. They also answer questions after listening to a recorded conversation and produce oral sentences while looking at pictures. The Reading Proficiency-LAS Test measures fluency, mechanics, reading for information, and vocabulary. A comparison of pre- and posttest scores in the Adult-LAS Oral and Reading Tests for the school year 1998 to 1999 showed significant gains in every subtest related to oral language and reading. Although FLAME's ESL lessons do not emphasize formal instruction in grammar and academic English, these results suggest parents are learning language skills through the participatory approach. Because the approach is relevant to their lives, they also enjoy themselves.

Observational Studies

Over the years, we have collected qualitative information, mostly from observations and field notes, about a small sample of FLAME families. We use these data to validate and complement our findings from analysis of parents' self-reports and of testing data. In a year-long project, a FLAME staff member (Mulhern, 1991) studied the literacy behaviors of three Project FLAME families in order to find out whether family literacy behaviors changed when they attended the program. These three families gave written consent to allow FLAME staff to visit their home and to collect observational data.

The Fernández, Díaz, and Morela families had low incomes. Their school-age children participated in the free lunch program. The fathers had temporary jobs and frequently were unemployed. Each family in this study included a child enrolled in a state preschool program for low-income families, and these children were chosen for the observations. One of the three mothers in the study had much more education than did the others; she had been a kindergarten teacher aide in Mexico before moving to Chicago.

Each family was visited six times during the year. The observations took place in each family's home. The researcher focused mostly on the preschool child and the mother, although the homes' general literacy environment also received some attention. Field notes taken during the observations were analyzed for recurrent events within families and across families related to Project FLAME's four components (literacy opportunity, literacy modeling, literacy interaction, and home–school connections). Focusing on activities related to the FLAME components allowed the researcher to identify literacy activities that were common in each household. Then parents (usually the mother) were interviewed in order to clarify the purpose of some of the activities and to validate the information collected through field notes. Literacy interactions between mothers and their children, interviews, and book-sharing sessions were tape-recorded and transcribed. Their content was also categorized according to the four FLAME components. Artifacts of children's writings and observations at FLAME sessions were collected to complement the observation data. During one of the last visits, parents were asked to select a book and read it with their children, and they were interviewed further about their literacy practices. The patterns that emerged from the collected data corresponded mainly with three of Project FLAME's four theoretical components. The findings by component follow.

Literacy Opportunity

Mrs. Morela's placement of a literacy box (developed through FLAME) and books on a table in the living room resulted in frequent use of those materials by the children. A similar situation occurred in the Fernández home. In both of these homes, children read and wrote frequently during visits. In contrast, the Diaz family kept books in a bedroom, and the target child never used them during the observations.

In general, FLAME staff reported that once parents understood that children could learn from books before they are able to read independently, parents' attitudes about allowing children to handle books changed. While enrolled in the program, parents also learned to use the library and borrow books to increase the availability of books at home.

Literacy Modeling

With regard to literacy modeling, the three families showed a great range of literacy modeling and availability of literacy materials. The Fernández family, who had the highest level of education, also had the broadest range of literacy materials and used literacy for various purposes, including reading for pleasure. The Díaz and Morela families used literacy primarily to fulfill daily living routines (e.g., paying bills) and school-related functions (e.g., doing homework, reading school notices). These families had only a few books at home. The case studies reinforced the FLAME program's emphasis on making writing materials and books easily available to children, showing that children use accessible materials more frequently.

Literacy Interaction

FLAME workshops emphasize techniques that better enable the parents to engage in literacy activities with their children. An examination of two major aspects of literacy, shared book reading and emergent writing, revealed varied patterns of parent–child interaction among the families studied.

Nevertheless, all the children were read to at home. Furthermore, it was also clear that the children were familiar with the books at home and were accustomed to having books read to them. The widespread understanding that being read to allows children to learn about writing (Teale, 1984, 1986; see Purcell-Gates, this volume; Wells, 1986) makes this finding a significant one.

Early Literacy Development

Parents read materials to children that were appropriate for the children's ability level. They read with expression and seemed to enjoy the books as much as their children did. In addition, two of the three parents used a variety of strategies to get the children involved in the reading. They asked questions, checked for understanding, asked labeling questions, and related the books to the children's lives. Two of the target children also engaged in reading-like behaviors, which are considered learning-to-read strategies (Doake, 1985). Also, all children engaged in pretend reading, which allows children to reconstruct written text (Pappas & Brown, 1988).

A significant revelation was that parents bought books in English rather than in Spanish at the FLAME book fair. This occurred in spite of the fact that parents, in order to be good reading models for their children, were encouraged to read to their children in the language they knew best. The parents then translated the books into Spanish as they read to their children. Parents could not point to words in the book because the written English words did not correspond with what they said. Thus, the children could not relate the oral language to the written language as they listened to a favorite book. A further problem was that parents were not proficient in English and sometimes had to check the dictionary or ask someone else for an equivalent word in Spanish. This led us to emphasize to FLAME parents that they should read to their children in the language they know best. Not only could most parents read more fluently in Spanish, but also the children would have the opportunity to match oral and written language (Teale, 1986). We recognize, however, that parents wanted books in English in order to develop their own skills in English.

With regard to emergent writing, we encouraged parents to include children in their writing activities and to recognize children's written approximations as meaningful. However, encouraging writing was a hard concept for parents to understand, as they retained traditional beliefs about writing. They believed that children need to learn to write letters correctly before they can write text. This belief was more evident in the Díaz family, although it appeared to a lesser extent in the other two. Mrs. Díaz explained that her son wrote letters but no words. She believed that her child would learn to read more easily if he knew how to write the letters well.

Parents in the other two families eventually accepted their children's emergent writing as meaningful. Mrs. Morela specifically explained that she had learned this belief from FLAME. Of the three children observed, Mrs. Morela's daughter engaged in writing more frequently than the other two children. The mother usually recognized her daughter's intention to write as meaningful and praised her literacy approximations. Although all the parents received the same training from FLAME, a wide range of parents' understanding about emergent writing was evident in the observations.

The data collected from these case studies demonstrate the impact FLAME had on the availability and use of reading materials in the homes. Parents knew the importance of reading to children, and children enjoyed reading together with their parents. Two of the three families better recognized the value of getting the children interested in books as a way to support their learning to read.

Second Observation Study

During the academic year 2001 to 2002, we again studied literacy use in FLAME families, using the same observational methodology as before. Families were visited three times a year, and field notes of the observations were analyzed to learn how they used literacy at home. One family, the Castillos, gave us some insight into the literacy life of FLAME families who have both school-age and preschool children. In the Castillo family, the school-age children who know English quite well have taken on the role of reading in English to the younger child. By contrast, the mother tends to use the community (e.g., acknowledging literacy found in the neighborhood, pointing to signs in the street, pointing to sight words in the store, visiting the public library) to enhance the preschool child's literacy skills. Although the family does not have many books at home, except for school textbooks and some books acquired through FLAME, they purchased a computer. The computer is used for games, but it is also where the father, who was a dentist in Mexico, teaches science to his school-age children while he practices English with them. In this family, literacy learning is important for everyone, but there are well-defined supporting roles for the different members. Mrs. Castillo is so involved in family literacy that she asked to be accepted in the Training of Trainers program. She is becoming a family literacy leader in the community. The positive influence of the father's job-related knowledge on literacy learning in this family seems to confirm and support previous research findings on the father's role by Reese, Gallimore, and Goldenberg (1999).

Child Outcomes

Because we want to know whether the parents' participation in Project FLAME workshops has an effect on their children's literacy learning at home, children from participant families who are 3 to 6 years old are administered a battery of tests. We use the following instruments for this assessment:

- *Letter Recognition Tests.* One test consists of recognition of uppercase letters and the other of recognition of lowercase letters. The raw scores reflect the number of upper- and lowercase letters recognized by the children. The tests are given in Spanish.
- *The Boehm Test of Basic Concepts* (Boehm, 1986). This test measures concept development (e.g., time, quantity) as a reflection of cognitive development. The test is administrated in both Spanish and English (different versions) in order to avoid confounding lack of English or Spanish proficiency with concept development. Children in kindergarten or first grade are given the school-age version of the test, whereas younger children are given the preschool version.
- *Print Awareness Test* (the Stones/Piedras Test developed by Marie Clay, 1979). This test is given in Spanish and measures children's knowledge of print conventions, such as the left-to-right reading orientation in Spanish and English.
- *LAS-English Language Proficiency Tests and the Pre-LAS* (De Avila & Duncan, 1987; Duncan & De Avila, 1986). The Pre-LAS is given to children aged 4 to 6 years old. It measures children's oral/aural language ability. Children in kindergarten and first grade are also administered the LAS-Oral Language proficiency test that measures oral language proficiency in English.

FLAME Effectiveness in Children From Participant Families

We compared pre- and postprogram scores in the battery of tests described previously for children whose parents attended the FLAME program during the academic year 1998 to 1999. These data—reported previously as part of a Biennial Evaluation Report submitted to the U.S. Department of Education (OBEMLA), as required by the funding agency (Li, 2000)— showed that 3- to 6-year-old children whose parents participated in Project FLAME achieved statistically significant gains in uppercase-letter recognition, lowercase-letter recognition, and the Clay Print Awareness test. Furthermore, 3- and 4-year-olds achieved significant gains at posttesting on the Spanish Pre-Boehm Test and the Pre-LAS, while 5- and 6-year-olds gained significantly in the English Boehm test and the LAS. No significant gains were found in the Pre-Boehm Test administered in English, most likely reflecting a lack of English proficiency among the 3- and 4-year-olds. Nor were significant gains found in the Boehm Test administered in Spanish, possibly because the kindergarteners and first graders who took it were learning many of the tested concepts at school in English.

Although pretest–posttest comparisons are not the most rigorous way to show program effectiveness, the results suggest that parents in Project FLAME are making a difference in preparing their children for schooling in the United States. The findings are noteworthy in that the majority of the children tested were not participating in any other school- or community-based intervention or program.

During the 1991 to 1992 school year, one of the Project FLAME schools allowed us to give the same battery of tests to a group of 4-year-old children attending their State of Illinois preschool program. The preschool program is offered to a limited number of 4-year-old low-income children who are at risk of failing at school. Their parents did not participate in FLAME or in other interventions at the school. This arrangement allowed us to have a comparison group of children who were enrolled in a preschool program. Thus, we were able to use a quasi-experimental design and compare 18 FLAME children, who were not enrolled in a formal preschool program, to a group of 21 children attending the state-funded preschool program.

The two groups were paired according to age (4), ethnicity (Mexican), home language (Spanish), and neighborhood (the same for both groups). The comparison group children came from families with a somewhat higher SES, in that the parents reported more stable employment and income. The parents were also more successful in finding community resources, such as the preschool program, for their children.

The parents of both groups signed informed consents to allow us to test their children. The children were administered the Letter Recognition Tests (uppercase and lowercase), the Boehm Test, and the Clay Print Awareness Test (Piedras) in October 1991 and May 1992. All the tests were administered in Spanish. (These data were presented in a report made to the Illinois State Board of Education's Offices of Community Programs, Early Childhood Education, and Bilingual/ESL Education in 1993 [Rodríguez-Brown, 1993], and were described in Rodríguez-Brown and Meehan, 1998).

We first examined differences in the groups' pretest scores. The FLAME children's scores were significantly lower for all three measures: uppercase-letter recognition, lowercase-letter recognition, and print awareness. The difference between the two groups on the Boehm Test was not significant. After adjusting for the pretest scores, we found no statistically significant differences between the two groups' posttest gains on all measures. In other words, each group achieved equal amounts of gain across time. Although the FLAME children lagged behind the comparison group at pretest in several areas related to early literacy learning, they were gaining knowledge at the same rate as the children attending a formal preschool program.

Clearly, according to this small study, children can acquire literacy skills while their families are involved in Project FLAME. This learning occurs even though the children do not experience any direct FLAME program intervention. The intervention is directed instead at their immigrant parents, who typically have limited literacy skills themselves, limited experience with school, and limited English proficiency. Having a comparison group allowed us to gather more information about whether the increases in children's performance were the result of the FLAME program, rather than of the normal development, maturation, learning, or exposure that all children experience. The results support the notion that creating a rich home literacy environment can increase children's achievement.

NETWORKING, SELF-EFFICACY, AND PROJECT FLAME PARTICIPANTS

In my work with recent Hispanic immigrants in Chicago, I have learned how isolated the new families are, even in communities that share their language and culture. This isolation was not foreseen in planning our family literacy program. However, as the program grew, we saw how important it is that families network with each other. Networking activities go beyond interactions in the family literacy workshops and the ESL classes to developing friendships that are sustaining, supportive, and lasting.

As explained earlier, FLAME validates the parents' native language and knowledge as it encourages them to share literacy with their children at home. During program activities, we encourage parents to share their cultural models of learning, discourses, and understandings of literacy with other parents; at the same time, we provide them with new information that they can add to their existing repertoires. By heightening parents' awareness of their own knowledge, we enhance the parents' self-efficacy in their role as teachers. But this self-efficacy also extends to their life in the community and society.

Before enrolling in FLAME, many of the mothers in our program never went out of their houses without their husbands. Through Project FLAME, they have made friends, gone to the library, and taken public transportation. FLAME has affected families in positive ways that go beyond literacy.

I believe that learning English alone was not sufficient to attain the project's goals. Rather, the networking they began while participating in FLAME, and the self-efficacy they gained while supporting their young children's literacy development, helped these parents move beyond their immediate community, look for jobs, and achieve a sense of fulfillment they had never imagined.

CONCLUSION

Family literacy programs offer learning and opportunities for everyone. When programs are developed within the context of the family, they validate parents' knowledge and enhance parents' image as models of learning. Validation of knowledge is particularly relevant to new immigrant parents who find themselves isolated. Through family literacy, parents learn the importance of continuing to share literacy with their children in the language they know best (Cummins, 1986; Rodríguez-Brown & Mulhern, 1993), thereby validating their native language while both parents and children learn English. The FLAME family literacy program allows families to develop networks in the community and gives parents an enhanced sense of self-efficacy. This, in turn, allows participants to be successful as parents and as members of society. For these reasons, family literacy programs can be feasible alternatives to adult education and generic parent involvement programs.

REFERENCES

Abi-Nader, J. (1991, April). *Family values and the motivation of Hispanic youth.* Paper presented at the annual meeting of the American Educational Research Association, Chicago, IL.

Applebee, A., Langer, J. A., & Mullis, I. (1987). *Learning to be literate in America.* Princeton, NJ: Educational Testing Service.

Boehm A. E. (1986). *Boehm Test of Basic Concepts-Revised.* San Antonio, TX: The Psychological Corporation/Harcourt, Brace & Jovanovich, Inc.

Clay, M. M. (1979). *Stones—The concepts about print test.* Auckland: Heinemann.

Cummins, J. (1986). Empowering minority students: A framework for intervention. *Harvard Educational Review, 55,* 18–36.

De Avila, E. A., & Duncan, S. E. (1987). *The Language Assessment Scales (LAS).* Monterrey, CA: CTB/McGraw-Hill.

De Avila, E. A., & Duncan, S. E. (1993). *The Adult-Language Assessment Scales (A-LAS)* Monterrey, CA: CTB/McGraw-Hill.

Delgado-Gaitan, C. (1992). School matters in the Mexican-American home: Socializing children to education. *American Educational Research Journal, 29,* 495–513.

Doake, D. (1985). Reading-like behavior: Its role in learning to read. In A. Jagger & M.T. Smith (Eds.), *Observing the language learner* (pp. 82–98). Newark, DE: International Reading Association.

Duncan, S. E., & De Avila, E. A. (1986). *Pre-Language Assessment Scales (LAS).* Monterey, CA: CTB/McGraw-Hill.

Edwards, P. A. (1988, December). *Lower SES mothers learning of book reading strategies.* Paper presented at the annual meeting of the National Reading Conference, Tucson, AZ.

Epstein, J. (1990). School and family connections: Theories, research and implications for integrating sociologies of education and family. In D. Unger & M. Sussman (Eds.), *Families in community settings: Interdisciplinary perspectives* (pp. 99–126). Binghamton, NY: Haworth.

Epstein, J. (1991). Effects on student achievement of teachers' practices of parent involvement. In S. Silvern (Ed.), *Literacy through family, community and school interaction* (pp. 261–276). Greenwich: CT: JAI Press.

Feiltelson, D., & Goldstein, Z. (1986). Patterns of book ownership and reading to young children in Israeli school-oriented and non-school-oriented families. *Reading Teacher, 39,* 924–930.

Flores, B., Cousin, P. T., & Díaz, E. (1991). Transforming the deficit myths about learning, language and culture. *Language Arts, 68,* 369–379.

Gallimore, R., & Goldenberg, C. N. (1989, April). *Social effects on emergent literacy experiences in families of Spanish-speaking children.* Paper presented at the annual meeting of the American Educational Research Association, San Francisco, CA.

Gallimore, R., & Reese, L. J. (1999). Mexican immigrants in urban California: Forging adaptations from familiar and new cultural resources. In M. C. Foblets & C. I. Pang (Eds.), *Culture, ethnicity and immigration* (pp. 245–263). Leuven, Belgium: ACCO.

Gee, J. P. (1999). *An introduction to discourse analysis: Theory and method.* New York: Routledge.

Goldenberg, C. (1987). Low income Hispanic parents' contributions to their first grade children's word recognition skills. *Anthropology of Education Quarterly, 18,* 149–179.

Goldenberg, C. N. (1989). Parents' effects on academic grouping for reading: Three case studies. *American Educational Research Journal, 26,* 329–352.

Goldenberg, C. N., & Gallimore, R. (1991). Local knowledge, research knowledge, and educational change: A case study of early reading improvement. *Educational Researcher, 20*(November), 2–14.

Heath, S. B. (1983). *Ways with words.* Cambridge: Cambridge University Press.

Heath, S. B. (1987). Sociocultural context of language development. In California Department of Education (Ed.), *Beyond language: Social and cultural factors in schooling language minority students* (pp. 143–186). Los Angeles, CA: Evaluation Dissemination and Assessment Center.

Li, R. F. (2000). *Project FLAME Academic Excellence. Biennial Evaluation Report (1998-2000).* Unpublished manuscript.

Metritech. (1987). *The Illinois Reading Assessment Project: Literacy survey.* Champaign, IL: Metritech.

Moll, L. C. (1998). Turning to the world: Bilingual schooling, literacy, and the cultural mediation of thinking. *National Reading Conference Yearbook, 47,* 59–75.

Moll, L. C., Amanti, C., Neff, D., & González, N. (1992). Funds of knowledge for teaching: Using a qualitative approach to connect homes and classrooms. *Theory Into Practice, 31*(1), 132–141.

Moll, L. C., & Greenberg, J. B. (1990). Creating zones of possibilities: Combining social contexts for instruction. In L. C. Moll (Ed.), *Vygotzky and Education* (pp. 319–348). New York: Cambridge University Press.

Mulhern, M. M. (1991). *The impact of a family literacy project on three Mexican-immigrant families.* Unpublished manuscript, University of Illinois at chicago.

National Council of La Raza. (1990). *Hispanic education: A statistical portrait.* Washington, DC: Author.

Nickse, R., Speicher, A. M., & Buchek, P. C. (1988). An intergenerational adult literacy project: A family intervention/prevention model. *Journal of Reading, 31,* 634–642.

Pappas, C., & Brown., E. (1988) The development of children's sense of the written story register: Analysis of the texture of kindergarteners' "pretend reading" texts. *Linguistics and Education, 1,* 45–79.

Paratore, J. R. (1994). Parents and children sharing literacy. In D. Lancy (Ed.), *Emergent literacy: From research to practice* (pp.193–216). New York: Praeger.

Paratore, J. R. (2001). *Opening doors, opening opportunities. Family literacy in an urban Community.* Needham Heights, MA: Allyn & Bacon.

Paratore, J. R., Melzi, G., & Krol-Sinclair, B. (1999). *What should we expect from family literacy?: Experiences of Latino children whose parents participate in an intergenerational literacy project.* Newark, DE: IRA/NRC.

Quintero, E., & Huertas-Macías, A. (1990). Learning together: Issues for language minority parent and their children. *Journal of Educational Issues of Language Minority Students, 10,* 41–56.

Reese, L., Balzano, S., Gallimore, R., & Goldenberg, C. (1995). The concept of educatión: Latino family values and American schooling. *International Journal of Educational Research, 23*(1) 57–81.

Reese, L., & Gallimore, L. (2000). Immigrant Latinos Cultural Model of Literacy Development: An alternative perspective on home-school discontinuities. *American Journal of Education, 108*(2) 103–134.

Reese, L., Gallimore, R., & Goldenberg, C. N. (1999). Job-required literacy, home literacy environments, and school reading: Early literacy experiences of immigrant Latino Children. In J. G. Lipson & L. A. McSpadden (Eds.), *Negotiating power and place at the margins: Selected papers on refugees and immigrants* (Vol. VII, pp. 232–269). Washington, DC: American Anthropological Association.

Rodríguez-Brown, F. V. (1993, November). *Exemplary program and practice: A request for nomination as an academic excellence program model for Project FLAME.* Unpublished manuscript. University of Illinois at Chicago.

Rodríguez-Brown, F. V. (2001a). Home-school collaboration: Successful models in the Hispanic community. In P. Mosenthal & P. Schmitt (Eds), *Reconceptualizing literacy in the new age of pluralism and multiculturalism, Advances in reading & language research* (pp. 273–288). Greenwich, CT: Information Age Publishing (IAP), Inc.

Rodríguez-Brown, F. V. (2001b). Home-school connections in a community where English is the second language. In V. Risko & K. Bromley (Eds.), *Collaboration for diverse learners: Viewpoints and practices* (pp. 273–288). Newark, DE: International Reading Association.

Rodríguez-Brown, F. V., Li, R. F., & Albom, J. A. (1999). Hispanic parents' awareness and use of literacy-rich environments at home and in the community. *Education and Urban Society, 32,* 41–57.

Rodríguez-Brown, F. V., & Meehan, M. A. (1998) Family literacy and adult education: Project FLAME. In C. Smith (Ed.), *Literacy for the twentieth-first century* (pp.176–193). Westport, CT: Praeger.

Rodríguez-Brown, F. V., & Mulhern, M. M. (1993). Fostering critical literacy through family literacy: A study of families in a Mexican-immigrant community. *Bilingual Research Journal, 17*(3/4), 1–16

Rodríguez-Brown, F. V., & Shanahan, T. (1989). *Literacy for the limited English proficient child: A family approach.* Proposal submitted to OBEMLA/USDE, under the Title VII ESEA Family Literacy Program. Unpublished Manuscript. University of Illinois at Chicago.

Rogers, R. (2001). Family literacy and cultural models. *National Reading Conference Yearbook, 50,* 96–114.

Rogers, R. (2002). Between contexts: A critical analysis of family literacy, discursive practices and literacy subjectivities. *Reading Research Quarterly, 37*(3), 248–277.

Sable, J., & Stennett, J. (1998). The educational progress of Hispanic students. In National Center for Educational Statistics, *The condition of education 1998* (pp. 11–19). Washington, DC: U.S. Department of Education.

Serna, I., & Huddelson, S. (1993). Becoming a writer of Spanish and English. *Quarterly of the National Writing Project and the Center for the Study of Writing and Literacy, 15*(1), 1–5.

Silvern, S. (1988). Continuity/discontinuity between home and early childhood education environments. *Elementary School Journal, 89,* 147–160.

Teale, W. H. (1984). Reading to young children: Its significance for literacy development. In H. Goelman, A. Oberg, & F. Smith (Eds.), *Awakening to literacy* (pp. 110–121) Portsmouth, NH: Heinemann.

Teale, W. (1986). Home background and young children's development. In W. Teale & E. Sulsby (Eds.), *Emergent literacy: Writing and reading* (pp. 173–206). Norwood, NJ: Ablex.

Terrien, M., & Ramírez, R. R. (2000). The Hispanic population in the United States. In U.S. Department of Commerce, Economics and Statistics Administration. *Current Population Reports. Issued March 2001.* Washington, DC: U.S. Census Bureau.

The New London Group. (1996). A pedagogy of multiliteracies: Designing social futures. *Harvard Educational Review, 66*(1), 60–62.

Tobin, A. W. (1981). *A multiple discriminant cross validation of the factors associated with the development of precocious reading development.* Unpublished doctoral dissertation, University of Delaware Newark.

Valdes, G. (1996). *Con respeto: Bridging the differences between culturally diverse families and schools.* New York: Teachers College Press.

Van Fossen, S., & Stitch, T. G. (1991). *Teach the mother and reach the child: Results of the intergenerational literacy action research project.* Washington, DC: Wider Opportunities for Women.

Wells, G. (1986). *The meaning makers.* Portsmouth, NH: Heinemann.

Wheeler, M. E. (1971). *Untutored acquisition of writing skill.* Unpublished dissertation. Cornell University, Ithaca, NY.

IV

Adult Education

Adult education has been described as the critical factor in comprehensive family literacy programs. Though past interventions that focused on young children also included parent education, few interventions have included a strong focus on adult education and literacy skills. In this section, we see a rationale for the important role of adult education in family literacy programs. Positive adult outcomes in literacy and education can potentially lead to employment and to a stronger economic base for the family. They can also lead to a recognition of the importance of literacy opportunities in the life of their child. Such changes could then produce a synergistic effect on family members that would go beyond outcomes that might be produced by early childhood education or adult-education-only programs. Though such beliefs about the value of adult education were fundamental to early family literacy program initiatives, their influence on both adult education and on other family outcomes is still a matter of debate. The question of whether adults show as much progress in family literacy education programs as they would in stand-alone adult education programs is, for example, still open to debate.

Among the issues facing adult education is the need to assure high-quality instruction. As John Comings observes in his chapter on its processes and content, adult education is distinct from K–12 education. Adults have a different set of motivators, which must be taken into account when designing educational programs. For example, adults choose to participate in educational programs and often face considerable obstacles to doing so. As a result, adult education programs must develop plans to help adults persist in reaching their educational goals. Comings identifies several strategies to support persistence, including the use of authentic curriculum that builds on adults' life experiences and addresses their motivation to learn. He also points to the need to look at appropriate instructional groups and to consider a wider, more useful definition of program participation that goes beyond classroom learning.

In another look at adult education within family literacy programs, Judith Alamprese provides a detailed look at the adult education and literacy system in the United States, describing funding sources, target populations and participants, and the service delivery system. She also addresses persistence in adult education services, issues in learner assessment, instructional services, and evidence of program effectiveness. Drawing much of her data from the federal Even Start Family Literacy Program, including its three national evaluations, she reports on significant changes in the programs' adult population over the past 15 years. She notes in particular how program enrollment and family structure have changed over time, and how the economic status of families has changed. Of particular interest are her reviews of outcomes data on adult basic skills. Agreeing with Comings on the importance of adult persistence in these programs, she presents data on some of the factors that influence adult participation and ways to overcome obstacles. She also articulates future directions for practice and policy as well as for research and evaluation.

Eunice Askov, in her chapter on workforce literacy and technology, elaborates on the importance of these two factors for employment in contemporary society and, because of their objectives for adult employment, for family literacy programs. Noting adults' need to support themselves and their families, she discusses trends that affect family literacy programs. These include emphasis on a work-first approach in federal funding, in contrast to an emphasis on long-term education. She raises the concern that people in family literacy programs often need a considerable amount of time to prepare for today's workplace. She also observes changes in priorities among adults enrolled in family literacy programs. Many more adults are now interested in employment-related goals than they were a decade ago, and she illustrates a positive approach to integrating workforce literacy into family literacy developed by the National Center for Family Literacy in partnership with Jobs for the Future. She also discusses the assumption that adult education is an important component of comprehensive family literacy programs, with potential benefits to children when their parents work opportunities change. When parents are gainfully employed and have sufficient income to support their families, families are often less stressed, creating the possibility that parents will be more aware of the need to promote children's language and literacy skills. Moreover, parents' ability to use technology can translate into an ability to help children develop the same skills.

From this section we can see that adults enrolled in comprehensive family literacy programs have opportunities to foster their own education, employment, and economic conditions. In so doing, they can better support their families and bring more experience to helping their own children. Yet we also see that they face numerous challenges and struggle with personal obstacles to participation. Programs are encouraged to provide appropriate adult learning opportunities and to respond to adults' workplace literacy needs. We also see that numerous questions remain about the role of adult education offered in combination with the other components of family literacy programs and about how to make these programs more effective.

13

The Process and Content of Adult Education in Family Literacy Programs

John P. Comings
*National Center for the Study of Adult Learning and Literacy,
Harvard Graduate School of Education*

When compared to K–12 education, the body of research on adult education is quite small. As a result, adult educators often look to the K–12 research for guidance on decisions about both the process and the content of instruction. However, this guidance can only be useful if it is tempered by an understanding of the fundamental differences between the system of adult education and the system of child schooling. This chapter explores four essential differences between the adult education and child schooling systems and provides advice to practitioners in family literacy programs on how to address the issues raised by these differences.

The first of these differences is that adults choose to participate in educational programs, whereas children participate because of legal mandates and strong social and cultural forces that identify schooling as the proper work of childhood. Adults must make an active decision to participate in each class session and often must overcome significant barriers in order to attend classes. Consequently, family literacy programs need to meet the challenge of encouraging persistence on the part of their adult learners. Supporting adults' persistence in attending family literacy programs serves the same purpose that compulsory attendance serves in K–12 schooling.

A second difference is that though academic learning occupies only a small part of the life of most adults and is usually a temporary activity, schooling is a significant part of a child's life and continues for many years. Children live in environments that support a long-term, full-time commitment to schooling; thus, the academic content is more relevant to their lives. Adults, by contrast, organize their lives around work, family, and community, and these life roles are the source of content that is relevant and interesting to them. Family literacy programs are challenged to bring authentic content from adult life into the classroom so that their students can put the skills and knowledge learned in class into practice in their lives. Authentic content in family literacy programs can increase the motivation to learn and the opportunity to practice skills that the progression from one grade to another provides in K–12 schooling.

Another difference in K–12 schooling and adult education is that though adults who achieve at the same level on a standardized test have a much more diverse sets of skills, knowledge, and abilities, most children who are in the same grade and have the same achievement level have similar sets of skills, knowledge, and abilities. Consequently, family literacy programs have to focus on assessing each adult student's strengths and needs in order to develop curriculum that meets his or her learning needs. Identification of these strengths and needs in family literacy programs produces instructional groups that K–12 schooling forms in part by grades and classes designed for students with different abilities.

A fourth distinction is that adults use episodes of program participation and self-study to build their skills and knowledge in order to meet goals that are important to them, whereas children engage in continuous participation in order to meet the goals that are set by schools. The organization of most family literacy programs is like that of a school, with classes that meet at specific times and in specific places. As a result to address adult needs, family literacy programs will need to consider learning opportunities organized in ways that make it convenient for adults to participate. The provision of a range of services can maximize the opportunity for continuous learning for adults in family literacy programs that the K–12 system provides through schools that have set meeting places and schedules. For example, a program that provides classes that meet 2 hours per day, 3 days a week might change to provide only one 2-hour class per week and provide the other 4 hours through activities that take place at a more convenient place on a schedule arranged by the student. Those other activities might include self-study on a computer at work, an open-entry, open-exit tutoring session held at a local library, and a videotape lesson watched at home.

SUPPORTS FOR PERSISTENCE

Teachers in family literacy programs hope that their adult students will persist in learning until they reach their educational goals. However, the average time that an adult spends in a program is less than 70 hours in a 12-month period (U.S. Department of Education, 2001). These figures do not include adults who drop out before they complete 12 hours of instruction, lowering the average significantly. Recognizing that 70 hours of instruction is less than 1/10 of the time that a K–12 student spends in class during a year, the need to engage adults for longer periods of participation is clear.

Several studies have observed that approximately 100 hours of instruction may be the minimum needed by adults to achieve an increase of one grade-level equivalent on a standardized test of reading comprehension (Darkenwald, 1986; Perin & Greenberg, 1993; Sticht, 1982). Although some adults who enter a family literacy program may have specific goals that require only a few hours of instruction, for example, to complete diploma requirements, most adult students have instructional needs that require much more participation in instruction long-term effort. Program participation of even 100 hours will not enable most adult students to reach their learning goals.

The 1992 National Evaluation of Adult Education Programs (NEAEP) (Young, Fleischman, Fizgerald, & Morgan, 1994) found that more than 50% of adult students left their programs within the first 3 months of instruction. Almost half of the students who dropped out did so during the first 6 weeks. These findings from NEAEP support the contention of some experts that the first 3 to 6 weeks of program participation are key to persistence (Quigley, 1997).

Though NEAEP found that 44% of participants left their programs satisfied, only 5% left having achieved their goals. The goals that students mentioned were passing the General Educational Development (GED) test; attaining a better job; and improving reading, writing, and math skills. Because most adults are leaving programs before completing the 100 hours needed to make measurable progress and are reporting that their goals have not been achieved, improving persistence rates is critical for any effort to increase program impact. The importance of persistence has been noted by a number of researchers (Beder, 1991; Comings, Parrella,

& Soricone, 1999; Quigley, 1997; Tracy-Mumford, 1994). Though they have taken different perspectives, collectively their findings inform the field. These findings are summarized in the following sections.

Perspectives on Persistence

Beder (1991) provides a comprehensive and thorough review of essential factors that play into an adult's decision to participate and persist in adult education. He first explores personal motivation as the force that helps adults overcome barriers to participation imposed by their lives. He then focuses more closely on those specific barriers. Beder suggests that adult education programs must change their recruitment and instruction practices to be congruent with the motivations and life contexts of adult learners. He contends that if programs do so more adults will enter them, and their students will persist longer.

Two studies that looked at the barriers to persistence from the point of view of participants and potential participants were examined in Beder's review (Beder, 1990; Hayes, 1988). Both these studies point to perceptions by some adults that they may not (a) benefit from participation in education programs, (b) be able to learn, (c) enjoy participation in formal learning programs, or (d) be able to overcome the many barriers to participation. Together, these beliefs compromise a powerful set of negative forces that keep adults from entering or persisting in adult education programs.

Beder concludes by suggesting that programs that seek to provide educational services to adults must acknowledge the validity of these perceptions related to participation. Although engaging participants in adult education is never easy, Beder suggests that the effort could be more productive if programs had the resources to match instruction to the needs and learning styles of their adult students.

Tracy-Mumford (1994), in reviewing the findings of a large number of studies, focuses on offering advice to programs on improving persistence. She calls for programs to develop a commitment to and a plan for increasing persistence. A program commitment to persistence sends a strong message to students that the program is there to help them reach their goals, but because students' goals can change, the program must be flexible and accommodate new goals that arise. For a commitment to student persistence to be meaningful, programs should have a set of criteria for measuring persistence as well as defined strategies that reduce dropout, increase student hours of attendance, improve achievement, increase attainment of personal goals, and improve completion rates.

The effective persistence plan that Tracy-Mumford (1994) describes is one that provides support to students and improves instruction. She summarizes her findings with a list of recommendations for a persistence plan that weaves support strategies into all aspects of the program structure.

- Recruitment should provide enough information that potential students can make an informed decision about enrolling.
- Intake and orientation should help students understand the program, set realistic expectations, build a working relationship with program staff, and establish learning goals.
- Initial assessment should provide students and teachers with information on both cognitive and affective needs, be integrated into instruction, and form the foundation for measuring progress.
- Programs and teachers should recognize student achievement.
- Counseling should identify students at risk of dropping out early.
- Referral services should coordinate with other agencies to ensure that all students become connected to the support services they need.

- A system for student contact and follow-up with dropouts should help students return to the program and provide information on ways to improve service.
- Noninstructional activities should help form a bond between the program and its students and their families.
- Program evaluation should involve students in assessing and offering advice on each aspect of the program.
- Child care and transportation assistance should be provided.
- Instruction and instructional staff should be of sufficient quality to support effective learning.

Tracy-Mumford's (1994) list of recommendations is comprehensive and functional because it translates theory into practical advice. Finding the resources to address all the aforementioned suggestions will not be possible for most family literacy programs, but following some of these suggestions should contribute to increased student persistence. As a strategy to help with persistence, Tracy-Mumford suggests that programs form a student persistence team (made up of teachers and students) that coordinates dropout prevention activities and collects data on student persistence. A team such as this could review the list of support strategies and decide those that best serve their needs and are within the program's resources.

Quigley (1997) notes that most dropouts occur in the first few weeks of program participation and, therefore, programs should pay attention to factors that affect early dropout. He sees three major constellations of factors that contribute to dropout, referring to them as *situational* (influences of the adult's circumstances), *institutional* (influences of systems), and *dispositional* (influences of the adult's previous experience in school). He believes that adults have overcome situational barriers, such as the need for day care or transportation, before they arrive at a program. Although such arrangements may fall apart later, they have little effect in the first few weeks of instruction. Institutional barriers, such as an inflexible schedule of classes, have also been overcome at initial enrollment, though they may have an effect later. Quigley focuses his attention on the dispositional influences, believing these cause adult students to dropout in the first few weeks of program participation.

In considering dispositional influences, Quigley suggests that the intake and orientation processes of the first 3 weeks are critical to improving student persistence. He suggests that a student's history of negative school experiences should be discussed during intake and orientation as a way to ensure that early negative school experiences are addressed. He also recommends that intake begin with goal setting and planning for success, and he advises that students be matched to teachers and classes that can meet their goals and learning needs. Quigley suggests that because students are adults, they can take charge of this process, but they may need help formulating their learning goals and may need useful information to be provided for making learning decisions.

Quigley (1997) also reports findings from a pilot effort he undertook with incoming students. He implemented three interventions: (a) intensive support by a team of teachers and counselors, (b) small-group instruction, and (c) one-on-one tutoring. The objective was to match students with teachers and classes that would meet their goals and learning needs, thus promoting persistence. The small-group approach produced the highest persistence, followed by the team approach, and then the one-on-one tutoring. The three intervention groups had higher persistence rates than a comparison group who attended regular program classes. His results suggest that putting students into classes that met their needs appears to have increased persistence.

Persistence among pre-GED students was examined by Comings et al. (1999). They found that immigrants, adults over the age of 30, and parents of teenage or grown children were more likely to persist than were other adult students. The greater likelihood of persistence by immigrant students in ESOL classes is well documented in other studies (e.g., Young et al., 1994). Comings and colleagues also found that this higher persistence level continues as immigrants learn English and move on to pre-GED programs.

Adults who are over 30 are more likely to have teenage or grown children than those under 30, thus freeing up time for adult education, and contributing to higher persistence. It may also be that grown children of adult students are encouraging their parents to join and persist in a program. These findings might suggest that older students persist longer because they benefit from the maturity that comes with age and they no longer have the responsibilities of caring for young children.

This study also interviewed students about the supports and barriers to persistence in their own lives. The adult students identified a wide range of supports and barriers to their persistence. Four clear trends were evident when the research team analyzed their responses. The study team recorded these trends and considered them in the context of the literature reviewed to develop advice for programs. This advice was organized into four supports for promoting persistence and each is discussed in the next section.

SUPPORTS FOR PROMOTING PERSISTENCE

1. The first support to persistence is management of the positive and negative forces that influence persistence. In searching for a framework for analyzing data, the research team sought a theoretical model that would place the adult learner in a central position and be useful to program managers who are seeking practical advice on how to increase persistence. The study team chose to employ a force-field analysis as developed by sociologist Lewin (1999). Lewin's theory places an individual in a field of forces that are supporting or inhibiting action along a particular path. Understanding the forces, identifying which are strongest, and deciding which are most amenable to manipulation provides an indication of how to help someone move in a desired direction, in this case reaching an educational goal.

Adult students in this study emphasized positive forces, with most mentioning at least three positive forces. The strongest positive force mentioned by adult students was the support of other people, particularly that of their families, friends, teachers, and fellow students. Other positive forces included self-efficacy and personal goals. In contrast, many students mentioned either no negative forces or just one, usually one specific to the individual's life situation, such as a need for child care or transportation.

The force-field analysis views these barriers and supports as having various levels of importance, ranging from those that have no significant effect on persistence to those that have a very strong influence. The analysis also suggests that improvement in one force might offset the effects of another force that cannot be directly influenced. Thus, an adult with a very strong desire to be educated in order to help his or her children might put aside the embarrassment of participating in a program, whereas strong embarrassment might keep a less strongly motivated student from participating.

For adult students, positive forces (such as the desire to help their children succeed in school) help support persistence in a family literacy program. On the other hand, negative forces (such as the lack of free time to study) push adults to drop out. From the time adults enter a program to the time when they exit because they achieve their goals or drop out, both positive and negative forces are acting on them. Any intervention meant to increase persistence must help adults strengthen the positive forces and lessen the negative forces.

Family literacy programs should help students develop an understanding of the negative and positive forces that affect their persistence. Building on that understanding, each student can then make plans to manage these forces so that persistence is more likely. Adult students should first identify all the forces that are acting on them. They should then decide which of these forces are strong enough to have a significant effect on their persistence. Finally, each student should make a determination as to which of these strong forces he or she can change; that is, which positive forces can be made stronger and which negative forces can be made weaker.

The force-field theory itself offers a tool for understanding and planning to manage the forces that affect persistence. Students can be encouraged to discuss their persistence in terms of the force-field theory and to base their plans on that discussion. A classroom force-field activity can begin with students identifying all the supports and barriers to their persistence. They can then categorize the forces into those that are most likely to help or hinder their persistence. Once students identify crucial forces, they can plan to strengthen their supports and weaken the barriers. The analysis and management of the forces that affect persistence may be an individual responsibility or may be something that a group of students can do together. For example, most students in a class are likely to have transportation needs, and a group force-field activity might lead to ride sharing or a request to a public agency for transportation support. In some cases, of course, the outcome of this activity may be the early dropout of students who are not able to make changes that can facilitate their involvement. If this situation occurs, staff should help students make a plan to return to the program if possible, when they can participate.

2. The second support to persistence is building self-efficacy around learning. Although the term *self-confidence* is more common in the adult education literature, it is a general term that describes a global feeling of being able to accomplish most tasks. Self-efficacy focuses on a specific task and describes the feeling of being able to accomplish that task, in this case successful learning in family literacy programs. This study drew from the theory of social scientist Bandura (1986) for advice on building self-efficacy. Bandura's theory of self-efficacy can act as a powerful framework within which programs can help students learn that they can be successful in a family literacy program. We have drawn on his theory for suggestions on building self-efficacy. The following kinds of experiences can be used by family literacy programs to help participants build self-efficacy.

Mastery experiences allow an adult to be successful in learning and to have evidence of that success. Instruction should not be designed, however, to produce only easy and constant success. Adults also need experience in overcoming failure and eventually achieving success through a sustained effort; instruction can help with this objective. Family literacy programs can provide regular recognition of student progress and celebrate student achievement. Instruction should provide opportunities for success early in program participation to give students the opportunity to experience success, but teachers also need to help students deal with and learn from failure.

Vicarious experiences are provided by social models. Adult learners should be exposed to adults who have similar backgrounds and life experiences and who have succeeded in a family literacy program. These role models, both through the knowledge they share directly and through the indirect teaching of their behavior, help adult students acquire the skills needed to manage the many demands of learning. Programs should involve successful present or former students as speakers during enrollment and orientation activities and recruit former participants to be counselors, teachers, and directors.

Social persuasion reinforces self-efficacy through support from teachers, staff, counselors, fellow students, family, and friends. Adult students need verbal assurances, in part to overcome their negative experiences with learning during K–12 schooling. Family literacy practitioners can give verbal assurances and encourage students' family members to provide positive reinforcement, as well. Teachers can also develop a culture of support among students in their classes.

Opportunities to address physiological and emotional states help students to cope with the tension, stress, and other negative emotions that can both result from and lead to poor self-efficacy. Family literacy programs should help their adult students to perceive and interpret their emotional states in ways that do not affect their self-efficacy. Family literacy practitioners can use life histories and dialog journals to help students identify the physical and emotional issues that can affect their learning. Simply acknowledging that these feelings can affect learning can help diminish their negative effects on students.

3. The third support to persistence is the establishment of clear student goals. The process of goal setting begins even before an adult enters a family literacy program. A potential student experiences an event that causes him or her to begin thinking about entering a family literacy program. The event for a young mother might be when her first child begins school. She might believe that she does not have the skills to help her child succeed in school, or she might feel she needs a higher income to provide more opportunities to her child. These events provide potential adult students with goals that they hope to accomplish by entering a family literacy program. The staff of the program must help potential adult students define their goals and understand the many instructional objectives on the road to achieving them. Teachers can then use those student goals as the context for instruction. Because goals may change, students and teachers need to reassess goals periodically.

In the portion of the study that asked specifically about why each adult entered a program (Comings et al., 1999), adults tended to list a sequential and common string of goals. The full string of goals included these four: "get a GED, go to college, get a better job, and help my children." Some people mentioned all of these, and some mentioned just a few. Those who only said, "get a GED," might have added some of the other goals had they been prompted by a simple "Why?" To have a better understanding of the student's goals, the teacher and each student should enter a continuous dialog about goals. With this understanding, the teacher can structure learning activities and choose instructional materials that support the goals of the student.

The Equipped for the Future (EFF) initiative (Stein, 2000) offers an approach to understanding and defining the educational objectives needed to reach the most common goals expressed by adults in this study. Other goal-setting approaches might work as well, but one powerful factor in favor of EFF is that it focuses on the broader purposes of education, which includes the adult roles of worker, family member, and citizen. Goals related to both work and family were certainly the most common in the Comings et al. (1999) study, but other goals such as EFF's category of citizenship are especially important to some students. The EFF initiative includes a set of standards that outline what a student should know and be able to do to effectively play each of the important adult roles.

4. The fourth support to persistence is student progress toward reaching their goals. Because progress toward goals is an important support to persistence, it is important to help adult students make progress toward reaching their goals and help them assess their progress. To accomplish these objectives, program services need to be of sufficient quality that students can make progress, and assessment procedures need to be in place to allow students to determine their progress. Much of the recent interest in assessing student progress has arisen from the need to build systems of program accountability. However, helping students assess their own progress may entail tools and methods that are not appropriate for accountability purposes. On the one hand, accountability systems need instruments that are easy to collect and quantify, although such instruments may not be useful to students and may be difficult to integrate into instruction. On the other hand, portfolio and authentic assessment approaches might be very useful in helping adults determine their own progress and can be an integral part of an instructional approach, although they may have weaknesses as the basis for an accountability system (see Van Horn, chap. 29, this volume).

Further research should produce a hybrid assessment system that can serve both needs identified previously and can lead to certification of progress. At present, most adults who enter family literacy programs will gain certification only if they pass the GED test or acquire a high school diploma. Program-level certification (in smaller increments) may be helpful to student morale, but state-level or even national certification of achievement assessed in smaller increments of student progress may be more meaningful by providing a range of goal steps. These certificates of achievement might provide the same mark of progress that occurs when a child moves from one grade to the next.

The greatest focus of literature in the area of adult education is on the issue of persistence. This literature exists because of the recognition that increasing the time that adult students spend in programs is key to achieving the goals of family literacy or any other kind of adult education programs. Persistence is a good measure of program quality. When a program makes improvements in its services, an increase in its overall persistence rate is a vote by students that those changes are having a positive effect. The term *persistence* is used here, even though the terms *participation, retention*, and *engagement* are more common in adult education literature. Participation often refers to the decision on whether or not to enroll in a family literacy program, whereas the term persistence is used to focus attention on helping students who are enrolled to stay longer in a program. The word retention places attention on a program's efforts to keep students longer, but persistence is a student's own effort to continue learning, even though it is supported by program efforts. Engagement can mean both participation and the level of attention a student pays to instruction. Persistence is meant to denote students staying in their programs for as long as they can, continuing to stay engaged with learning when they cannot attend, and then returning to a program as soon as they can.

AUTHENTIC CONTENT FOR THE CURRICULUM

As adults learn the skills of English, literacy, and math, they use educational materials and engage in activities that have a content focus. Academic content includes the subjects taught in schools such as history, science, and literature. Authentic content includes activities from everyday life that require the use of English, literacy, and math skills, such as raising children, earning a living, and participating in cultural and religious activities. Adult education theory and recent research support the need for authentic content.

Most adult education theory builds on the work of Knowles (1970), who proposed the following five assumptions about adult learners (Merriam & Caffarella, 1999, p. 272):

- As a person matures, his or her self-concept moves from that of a dependent personality toward that of a self-directed human being.
- An adult accumulates a growing reservoir of experience, which is a rich resource for learning.
- The readiness of an adult to learn is closely related to the developmental tasks of his or her social role.
- There is a change in time perspective as people mature—from future application of knowledge to immediacy of application, and, therefore, an adult is more problem centered than subject centered in learning.
- Adults are motivated to learn by internal factors rather than by external ones.

These theoretical assumptions argue for authentic curriculum content. Such content interests adults, and they will choose to focus on it when it is available. Authentic curriculum also builds on the reservoir of life experience that adults have accumulated, because the authentic curriculum is integral to that experience. Authentic content grows out of the social roles of adults and builds abilities that are of immediate use in those roles. Authentic content addresses the internal factors that motivate adults to learn.

Sticht, Armstrong, Hickey, and Caylor (1987) provide an example of how Knowles' theory works in practice with what they call the *functional context education* approach. This approach builds on the principle that adults usually want to understand the functional utility of the content they are learning. Functional context education includes three propositions that provide a framework within which to use the content derived from students' lives. These propositions include (a) increasing motivation by making explicit the relationship between the content and its specific application in the adult student's life after the educational program; (b) learning by ensuring that instruction builds on the adult student's prior knowledge; and (c) increasing the likelihood that the abilities developed in the educational program will be put into practice by deriving instructional content, as much as possible, from the future context in which the adult student will apply the abilities being acquired.

To examine the value of different reading programs, Sticht et al. (1987) analyzed the reading gains made by 12,000 adult students, some of whom were in general reading programs and some of whom were in reading programs that were focused on reading needed in specific jobs. The latter programs were examples of functional context education. The study found that the adult students in *job-related* reading programs made gains in *general* reading that were as great or greater than those in the general reading programs. More importantly, the gains made in job-related reading by those in the job-related reading programs were three to four times greater than for those in the general reading program.

Purcell-Gates (2001) looked at the application of the theoretical construct of authentic content in adult literacy programs to see if it had an impact on learning. She examined how adults in literacy programs use literacy skills in their everyday lives and the type of instruction that best increased the degree of everyday literacy activity. More specifically, she focused on whether the degree of authenticity of the texts and activities employed in the classroom has a positive effect on change in literacy practices outside the program.

Data were collected on out-of-program literacy practices from 173 adults attending 83 different classes across the country. The adult literacy students were both native born and foreign born and ranged in age from 18 to 68 years. They were currently learning in a range of classes or in tutorial arrangements in adult basic education (ABE), GED, and English for speakers of other languages (ESOL) programs. When study participants began attending the classes, they ranged from preliterate (19%) to a grade level of 11 or higher (7.5%), but most were reading in the fourth- to seventh-grade range. Each class was assigned a score that reflected their class location along a continuum of the use of authentic content.

In order to document the use of literacy outside the classroom, researchers interviewed students in their homes at the beginning and at the end of participation in the literacy class. Participants were asked if their reading or writing practices had changed since they started attending the literacy class. The structured questionnaire asked about 50 different literacy practices such as reading bedtime stories with their children, using reading and writing on the job, reading the newspaper, writing letters, or reading labels on medicine bottles.

In order to document the type of literacy program the learner was attending, researchers asked the teachers of participating students to fill out an extensive questionnaire on the literacy program's content, activities, and materials. In addition, researchers observed classes and interviewed teachers to understand further how class materials were used and how the class was structured. From these three sources of qualitative data (the questionnaire, class observation, and teacher interview), researchers identified the particular program according to the degree of authenticity.

Analysis of the data revealed that the degree of authenticity of class literacy activities and text had a moderate effect on change in student literacy practices. This outcome was true after controlling for the other factors that also showed independent significant effects on literacy practice change. These factors include literacy level of the student when beginning the program, number of days the student had attended the program, and the non-ESOL status of the student. The strongest independent effect was a student's literacy level at the beginning of the class. The lower their literacy levels, the greater the change in literacy practices reported by students. Complementing this effect was the finding that the longer students attended classes, the more change in literacy practices they reported. ESOL students were less likely to report changes in English literacy practices than were other students. This result may be because many students were engaging in literacy practices in their native language (Purcell-Gates, 2000).

Literacy Practices in the Home

The increase in reading in everyday life by parents is very important for the impact that family literacy programs attempt to have on children. The recent report of the National Research Council, *Preventing Reading Difficulties in Young Children* (Snow, Burns, & Griffin, 1998), points out that success in learning to read in school is related to the preparation and support provided by parents before children enter school and while children are students in the first three grades. Purcell-Gates (1995) provides a case study of a family of four in which a school-age child is struggling to learn to read. Neither the child's mother nor his father use reading and writing in their daily lives, and the boy never sees these skills used in his home. Both parents are intelligent, but they never developed good reading skills. The father was interested in history and nature and watched TV and videotapes on these two topics, but he never read about them. The child in this family was living in a home that included very little written language and when he entered school, he was unfamiliar with reading.

At the opposite end of the spectrum, Taylor (1985) studied children in families where literacy was an important and pervasive element in their homes. The children who grew up in these highly literate homes developed complex linguistic skills and extensive vocabularies early in life. Their parents demanded more detail from them when they answered questions, and these children heard complex vocabulary in their everyday lives. Children in these families learned to read and write as a natural part of their lives, and they viewed literacy as important and interesting. Reading and writing, for them, was another way of communicating and school was a familiar and friendly environment.

Focusing family literacy programs on content that is interesting and important to adult students can support motivation and achievement, particularly increased reading skills related to the content. For family literacy programs, content related to parenting should have this quality of authenticity. If participants do not find parenting information interesting, other content that does interest them can improve skills that will also be helpful in the role of parent. The needs and interests of the participants should dictate the content of instruction.

IDENTIFYING STRENGTHS AND NEEDS: APPROPRIATE INSTRUCTIONAL GROUPS

Adults come to family literacy programs with a set of strengths and limitations built up over their lifetime. Two adults with the same background may appear to have the same skills, knowledge, and abilities, particularly if they have similar scores on a standardized test. Although they appear to be similar, one may benefit from a specific approach to instruction whereas the other does not. This difference in performance can sometimes be explained by differences in the specific skills, knowledge, and abilities that each adult brings to the classroom. If teachers are not aware of these differences, they may provide instruction that is effective for some and not for others.

One example of critical differences is the reading skills of adult students. Most family literacy programs assess reading ability with a reading comprehension test. Reading, though, is made up of a set of component skills, one of which is comprehension. Two adults with the same comprehension score may need to improve different component skills to increase their comprehension test score. The components of reading include print skills such as phonics (the ability to pronounce the sounds that correspond to written letters and syllables) and decoding (the ability to read words), but also include oral vocabulary, background knowledge, and reading fluency (the speed and ease of reading).

Strucker and Davidson (2002) administered reading component tests to nearly 1,000 adult students in over 30 learning centers in seven states (Connecticut, Massachusetts, New Hampshire, New York, Rhode Island, Tennessee, and Texas). Their sample reflects the range of the adult learner population across lines of gender, ethnicity, age, educational level, and region of the country. They gave comprehensive reading tests to 600 ABE and 400 ESOL students in English. Because of limited resources for translation into other languages, participants in the study were limited to (a) Spanish speakers, (b) immigrants who spoke English well enough to be interviewed and understand test directions in English, and (c) native English speakers.

Adults at all levels of ABE and ESOL skill levels were tested in English-reading skills using the *Diagnostic Assessments of Reading* (DARTTS) (Roswell & Chall, 1992), *the Woodcock–Johnson Word Attack* (Woodcock & Johnson, 1997), and the *Peabody Picture Vocabulary Test III* (PPVT) (Dunn & Dunn, 1997). Spanish speakers were tested in Spanish reading using parts of the latter two tests previously adapted in Spanish. The purpose of these tests was to further determine if a problem in English-reading fluency is also present in the reader's native language and if this problem inhibits the acquisition of new reading skills in English. Additional tests (listening skills, short-term memory, naming, and phonological awareness) were given to different groups of ESOL students based on their primary language.

Scores from the series of reading tests were used to make up a student's individual reading profile. The ABE and ESOL individual profiles were entered into a database and subjected to cluster analysis, a procedure that groups students with similar profiles in reading strengths and weaknesses. These clusters revealed different types of readers who were currently enrolled in family literacy programs. The study found that:

- Approximately 30% of ABE students had limited print skills.
- Approximately 45% of ABE students had basic print skills but still needed to develop higher level print skills.
- Approximately 15% of ABE students had adequate print skills but needed to develop stronger vocabulary, background knowledge, and reading fluency.
- Approximately 10% of ABE students had reading skills sufficient to pass the GED.
- Approximately 95% of Spanish speakers had adequate print skills in Spanish.

Overall, the data indicate that most of the native English speakers had scores that would place them in special education if they were children. In fact, many of these students had been in special education or received other forms of extra help when they were in school. Analysis of the data revealed 10 different clusters of readers, discussed in the following sections.

A strong GED cluster accounted for approximately 10% of the sample and was comprised of individuals who have strong skills in all reading components. This group should have no trouble passing the GED test after a few months of preparation and would probably be able to succeed in postsecondary education. The differences in component skills among this group were negligible.

Two clusters were at the pre-GED level and constituted 25% of the sample. The first group demonstrated strong print skills but weak vocabulary, whereas the second group had somewhat stronger vocabulary and much weaker print skills. Most adults in these two clusters could pass the GED, though without concentrated effort, their scores would probably be low. Both groups would probably have difficulty with the kind of reading demanded by postsecondary education and training programs. Instruction that focused on building vocabulary and background knowledge would work best with the cluster that had strong print skills but might not work well for those students who had weak print skills. An instructional focus on print skills would likely be of little help to the group with weak vocabulary. Although these two groups might have had similar scores on a test of reading comprehension, they require very different teaching strategies.

Four clusters were comprised of intermediate readers for a total of 47%. One group, constituting 17% of the sample, had good print skills but weaker vocabulary than the first pre-GED group noted previously. Another intermediate group, which constituted 7% of the sample, needed help on both print skills and vocabulary. Two additional low intermediate groups comprised 16% of the sample. One group had slightly weaker print skills. It is not clear whether the groups were different enough to merit separate placement or teaching approaches, but the group with weaker print skills had a reading rate that would impede comprehension and require additional instructional support. These four clusters might also have had similar comprehension scores, but they require four different curricula, each emphasizing a different set of component skills.

The three remaining clusters include reading-disabled beginners and ESOL students. One group (10% of the sample) of nonnative English speakers was conversationally fluent in English but had very little literate vocabulary, and though they seemed misplaced in ABE, their fluency kept them out of ESOL. A second group (7% of the sample) was comprised of roughly half ESOL students and half native English speakers who were reading disabled beginners. All in this cluster had low vocabulary and low scores on a variety of reading tests. A third group (2% of the sample) consisted of very reading-disabled beginners. Three quarters of this group were English speakers. This is a group where reading comprehension scores might be similar, but some students score low because they are reading disabled and others score low because they are non-English speakers. Again, the same instructional approach would not work with both of these groups.

To address the reading problems of adult students effectively, practitioners need to know the actual strengths and weaknesses of their adult students. Knowledge of these component skills provides the information needed to design effective curriculum.

Kegan et al. (2001) looked beyond the acquisition of literacy, language, and increased content knowledge to ways in which students in adult learning programs make meaning of their experience of the world, their way of knowing. This study was based on the hypothesis that coping with the demands of adult life requires a qualitative transformation of mind, analogous to the change from magical thinking to concrete thinking required of the school-age child or the development from concrete to abstract thinking required of the adolescent.

The Adult Development Study (Kegan et al., 2001) built on Kegan's theory of adult development. Kegan and his team of researchers were interested in the deep changes or transformational learning adult students undergo in adult learning settings. In this developmental perspective, an adult's beliefs amount to an interpretive lens through which he or she makes meaning. This lens filters the way a person takes in, organizes, understands, and analyzes experiences. Adults gradually evolve from a simpler way of knowing to a more complex way of knowing at their own pace depending on the available supports, scaffolding, appropriate developmental challenges, and encouragement for growth.

Kegan's theory identifies three qualitatively distinct ways of knowing most prevalent in adulthood: (a) instrumental, (b) socializing, and (c) self-authoring.

Instrumental.   Someone making meaning with an instrumental way of knowing understands and organizes his or her experience of self, others, and the world by concrete attributes, events, and sequences, by observable actions and behaviors, and by his or her own vantage point, interests, and preferences.

Socializing.   Someone making meaning with a socializing way of knowing has a more abstract and internal orientation to the world. The self, others, and the world participate in a swirl of values, loyalties, and longer term purposes that are seen to underlie events, attributes, and immediate preferences. Other people are experienced not merely as resources or supplies to the self but as sources of internal validation, orientation, or authority.

Self-Authoring.   Someone with a self-authoring way of knowing has the capacity to take responsibility for and ownership of their own internal authority, to be the maker of their own system of belief. These people have the capacity not only to identify abstract values, ideals, and longer term purposes but also to prioritize and integrate competing values, to appeal to the expectations and demands of others in comparison to one's own internal judgments, and to author an overall system of belief or personal ideology of their own.

Although development is a gradual process and the complete evolution from one comprehensive way of knowing to another may take years, identifiable and significantly different steps exist along the way. Each step creates a new framework for adults to think about themselves as parents, students, and workers.

Kegan and his researchers were particularly interested in how participants made sense of their instruction, their own motives and goals for learning, their expectations for themselves and their teachers, and their definitions of and sense of themselves in their social roles as students, workers, and parents. Additionally, they sought to understand how students described program supports and challenges to their general learning and improvement of competence in the worker, parent, and student roles. For their work, the researchers identified three exemplary programs. They looked for programs that were longer term (9 to 14 months) and that intentionally incorporated a variety of supports to facilitate adult learning (i.e., tutoring, advising, and technology). Moreover, they sought programs that included practices and curriculum aimed at supporting the enhancement of a specific competency in one of three adult social roles: student, parent, and worker. The sites chosen included a pre-enrollment program at a community college, a family literacy site, and a high school diploma program oriented to the worker role.

Students included men and women ranging in age from their early 20s to midlife. Most were immigrants, non-White, nonnative English speakers from lower socioeconomic backgrounds. A total of 41 students participated in the study. Data were collected by a variety of methods, including open-ended qualitative interviews, structured exercises, classroom observations, focus groups, and quantitative survey measures.

The study identified significant changes in the developmental level for some adults in these programs, even during a period as short as a year. The new information, skills, and ideas gained in their program led to changes in their way of making meaning. Students made gains in what they knew but also modified how they knew. They grew to demonstrate new and more complex ways of knowing.

In each setting, the researchers discovered a diversity of students' ways of knowing—an intriguing and less visible new form of pluralism, or diversity. Students demonstrated a range of ways of knowing that was virtually identical to the range found in previous studies with samples of native-English-speaking adults. The profile of adult students was not skewed toward the lower end of a developmental continuum and, therefore, adult students should not be presumed to construct experience less complexly than anyone else does. Some students with limited formal education demonstrated developmentally complex meaning systems, and people of similar ages or cultural backgrounds were sometimes distinguished by very different ways of knowing. As many of the study participants were undergoing a process of acculturation, students with different ways of knowing demonstrated notable differences in their descriptions of the changes related to the process of gaining fluency in English and the American culture. Students with the same way of knowing, on the other hand, gave descriptions of changes that had striking similarities.

Students with an instrumental way of knowing might prefer instruction that puts the teacher at the center, that has measurable increments of success, and that follows a specific set of procedures. Students with a socializing way of knowing might prefer learning in groups, peer teaching, and personalized forms of assessment. Those with a self-authoring way of knowing might prefer a self-directed approach to learning in which the teacher is just one of several sources of knowledge. The study found that adults with all three ways of knowing could learn together in groups. In fact, working together as a group helps students make developmental gains. Each student, though, may tend to participate in the group process in ways that work best with his or her way of knowing.

The Adult Development Study suggests that differences in developmental ways of knowing are important variables and represent a new form of pluralism that adult educators need to take into account in their work. Familiarity with students' different meaning-making systems can help explain why the very same curriculum, classroom activities, or teaching behaviors can leave some students excited while others feel lost or deserted. Adult educators need to develop a variety of instructional designs, encompassing a range of adult students' ways of knowing. This new form of pluralism also expands the understanding of the possible outcomes of family literacy programs. Qualitative transformation in an adult's way of knowing is a possibility, even in the brief period of a program year. Greater transformation may occur over longer periods.

Another distinction among adult students is their different abilities in nonacademic activities, such as music, art, conversation, auto repair, or counseling. Teachers are often impressed by the nonacademic abilities of their students and wonder how this potential can be used to enhance learning in family literacy programs. Gardner's theory of Multiple Intelligences (MI) provides another way at looking at adult students' strengths and abilities (Gardner, 1993). Gardner's theory defines intelligence as the ability to solve problems or create products that are valued in one or more cultures or communities. MI theory counters the view that a single measure of intelligence, such as an IQ test, is adequate and contends that all humans are made up of varying kinds and degrees of intelligences. Currently, eight forms of intelligence have been recognized: linguistic, logical–mathematical, spatial–visual, bodily–kinesthetic, musical, interpersonal, intrapersonal, and naturalist.

MI theory, which emphasizes the positive ways that people acquire knowledge and interact with the world, may be especially valuable to teachers working with adult students who have experienced repeated difficulties in learning. Adults have years of experience developing their strongest types of intelligence, and this strength may form a foundation for success in academic subjects. MI is not a theory of education, but it can inform good practice and expand the capacity of teachers to bring out the best in their students.

Although a large literature describes how MI theory influences the learning of children and young adults, its exploration in adult learning is new. Kallenbach and Viens (2002) helped a group of adult education teachers explore the application of MI theory to their practice. Each teacher developed a specific MI theory research question to frame her qualitative study. Teachers were required to rigorously observe and document the educational activities they designed and all interactions with students, as well as their own reflections and perceptions. Teachers recorded these observations in journals that served as a source of project data. In addition, teachers devised a set of data collection strategies related to their specific research question, such as field notes, videos, or interviews between students and teachers. Each teacher analyzed her data and presented her findings in monthly progress reports.

In this situation, MI theory served as a tool for developing the adult students' knowledge about their own learning. The theory gave the students a positive framework within which to discuss and reflect on their past successes and failures at learning. This self-reflection was an important, preliminary step to identifying individual learning strategies. The teachers found themselves relinquishing some control over instruction by giving their students choices among learning and assessment activities and respecting their individual ways of learning and knowing. The teachers perceived a noticeable shift in the teacher-to-student power relationship in the course of the Adult Multiple Intelligences study (Kallenbach & Viens, 2002) that they attributed to their MI-based practices. Over time, students began taking more initiative and control over the content or direction of the activities.

Family literacy practitioners can use MI theory as a framework to explore the abilities of their students in ways that can inform instruction. This application might lead to instruction that uses the student's strongest intelligence to learn academic content, such as teaching reading with the lyrics of songs. An exploration of MI theory might lead to a teacher offering several different ways to learn the same thing, each employing a different intelligence. The most important contribution, though, might be a change in instruction that helps students start learning with their strengths rather than with their weaknesses.

In summary, students may appear to have similar strengths and weaknesses when they arrive at a literacy program. A reading comprehension test will do little to inform a teacher or student about the best content or process of learning. A larger range of knowledge about students' skills, knowledge, and abilities can lead to instruction that is more effective.

ORGANIZATION AND STRUCTURE OF LEARNING ACTIVITIES

Most family literacy programs employ a classroom model in which adult students come to a defined place to study at specific times. Though teachers encourage further learning and practice outside the classroom, the resources of the program are focused on time in class. For most programs, participation in services is equivalent to time in class. The high dropout rate and low persistence rate of students in adult education programs are indications that attending classes on a set schedule and at a specific place can be difficult.

Wikelund, Reder, and Hart-Landsberg (1992) call for broadening the definition of participation to acknowledge that adults engage in education in many ways other than by attending formal classes. They also explore the ways in which existing research and theory fail to provide programs with useful models for defining participation. The Wikelund et al. review concludes that research and theory, as well as practice, should break out of the framework of K–12 schooling. A new definition of participation would acknowledge that adult learning, even improvements in literacy skills, could take place outside formal programs. With this expanded definition, programs would attempt to support learning at times when adults are not able to attend classes. Classes can serve as part of an instructional process that also involves other aspects of a student's life.

National statistics of adult student participation leave an impression that all students attend just one class during a 12-month period, but students sometimes have a different view of participation. Sticht, McDonald, and Erickson (1998) found that 25% of the ESOL students in programs in the San Diego, California area had actually transferred to other classes. A student in one class might decide to attend a different class or even join a different program because of life changes. For example, if a fellow student who is providing a ride to the class changes to another program, then the rider may go with him. Although students are moving from one learning experience to another, their program often is unaware that they continued in another program.

Students are also involved in study outside of classes. Two studies have found that self-study may be an important part of an adult's instructional process. In the Comings et al. (1999) study on persistence, one aspect of students' previous educational experience was associated with student persistence. Adults who had been involved in previous efforts at basic skills education, self-study, or vocational skill training were more likely to persist than those who had not. This relationship was particularly strong for adults who had undertaken self-study. In a second study Reder and Strawn (2001) examined how adults improve literacy skills. This longitudinal study in Portland, Oregon, is following 1,000 adults, all of whom are high school dropouts. Thirty-four percent of the high school dropouts who have never been in an adult education program were involved in self-study to improve their basic skills or prepare for the GED. Of those who had been in programs, 46% had been involved in similar self-study. Of the group of dropouts who acquired a GED during the first 2 years of the study, 74% had been involved in self-study.

These findings suggest family literacy programs should help students plan how they can use both formal program participation and self-study to build a pattern of learning. These different ways of learning can become a plan that allows an adult the opportunity to move in and out of formal participation in a family literacy program without the stigma or loss of learning that dropping out entails. Rather than dropping out, the student could be helped to continue learning through self-study.

Program directors and teachers reading this chapter might point to the low level of resources they have as the reason why they cannot address the issues raised here. Although these issues are complex, and programs with substantial resources could address them easier than could those with few resources, every program can realign their efforts in a way that builds on the theory and research presented in this chapter. An underutilized resource in every program is its adult students. Adult students can be involved in decision making and active partners, but evidence suggests such involvement is not common.

Purcell-Gates, Degener, and Jacobson (1998) found that very few of the 416 programs in their study involved students in making decisions around curriculum and other program components. Even though most teachers think of themselves as learner centered, many do not involve their students as active partners in instruction (Beder, 2001). Teachers see positive interpersonal relationships as learner centered, such as caring about their students, treating them with respect, and learning a lot about their personal lives. Teachers and program directors also know that their adult students are a resource, but they seem to rarely use their adult students to improve instruction.

CONCLUSIONS

In each of the four differences between child schooling and adult education discussed in this chapter, adult students are the source of the information needed to address the issue raised. There are several ways this can be done. Program directors and teachers can involve their students in identifying (a) supports to persistence, (b) relevant content for curriculum, (c) appropriate instructional groups, and (d) a wider and more useful definition of program participation. Programs can work with students in this way without additional resources and can integrate these discussions into activities that build skills and knowledge.

To support persistence, family literacy programs can use their intake and orientation process along with the first few weeks of class as a time to focus on persistence. The goal of this effort should be to help students identify all of the supports and barriers to their own persistence.

Students will find that they share many of these in common, and these shared supports and barriers can lead to a discussion of how they can build on their supports and address the barriers to persistence. This discussion will also give their teacher information on how to help his or her students to persist in their studies. This discussion can include reading and writing exercises that will provide the teacher with a better understanding of the students' strengths and weaknesses and can lead to additional exercises that focus on specific skills. This approach requires no additional resources, but these discussions may identify a need for a program to develop a specific support for their students (e.g., day care, counseling, or transportation assistance).

To identify relevant content, teachers in family literacy programs can use class discussion to identify common content of interest to students. Of course, adults in family literacy programs are concerned about their children's success in school, but this concern may be only one of many situations that can motivate them to use their literacy skills. The class discussion can also focus on ways that students use literacy in their lives, both on ways they enjoy using literacy skills and on ways in which their low literacy skills create barriers. Students can then bring in the types of materials they are using in their lives, and these materials can be the focus of their attention.

To build appropriate instructional groups, family literacy programs can ask students to describe the reading problems they have or that they remember from school and the ways in which they have been successful with any kind of learning. Self-report on reading skills and learning styles may be difficult for students at first, but if they are provided with opportunities to talk about prior successes, they can develop more and more self-awareness. Teachers can help build this self-awareness by providing different types of learning experiences, both on content (such as phonics, spelling, or vocabulary) and on process (learning on a computer, in a discussion group, with a workbook, or by direct teacher instruction). If students are provided an opportunity to reflect on what they have just experienced, they can build a better understanding for themselves and be able to share it with their teacher.

To develop an expanded approach to participation, family literacy programs can provide students with opportunities to learn that are connected to their classroom. Most libraries provide internet access and offer audio, video, print, and software self-learning materials that students can use to augment their time in class. Libraries and community-based organizations can provide volunteer tutors who might work one on one or in small groups with students from a program. Students can form discussion groups that meet outside of class but focus their discussion on the materials covered in the program. All of these approaches can help extend learning, as well as be a way for students to stay connected to learning and to the program when, for whatever reason, they cannot attend class. If students feel connected to a program, they may be more likely to come back when their circumstances change and they have time to attend class again.

The suggestions in the last four paragraphs provide program directors and teachers with ways to address the four differences described in this chapter even without additional resources. Family literacy program staff can discuss these suggestions and also come up with many ways to build on these suggestions. If they continue this dialog they will learn from their own experience and develop effective ways to help their students learn.

Additional resources would, however, open up many more possibilities. With more resources, programs could employ a counselor who would help students think about their persistence and their learning. Program staff could develop curriculum that incorporates student interests. The program could provide professional testing to develop student profiles and purchase computers and other self-learning materials that would offer a wider approach to participation. Family literacy program staff, as well as their students and supporters, should advocate for the increased resources that will make this expanded level of effort possible.

REFERENCES

Bandura, A. (1986). *Social foundations of thought and action: A social cognitive theory.* Englewood Cliffs, NJ: Prentice-Hall.

Beder, H. (1990). Reasons for nonparticipation in adult basic education. *Adult Education Quarterly, 40*(4).

Beder, H. (1991). *Adult literacy: Issues for policy and practice.* Malabar, FL: Krieger.

Beder, H. (2001). *Classroom dynamics in adult literacy education* (NCSALL Rep. No. 18). Cambridge, MA: National Center for the Study of Adult Learning and Literacy.

Comings, J., Parrella, A., & Soricone, L. (1999). *Persistence among adult basic education students in pre-GED classes* (NCSALL Report No. 12). Cambridge, MA: National Center for the Study of Adult Learning and Literacy.

Darkenwald, G. (1986). *Adult literacy education: A review of the research and priorities for future inquiry.* New York: Literacy Assistance Center.

Dunn, L., Dunn, L., Robertson, G., & Eisenberg, J. (1997). *Peabody Picture Vocabulary Test-Revised (PPVT-R).* Circle Pines, MN: American Guidance Service.

Gardner, H. (1993). *Frames of mind: The theory of multiple intelligences.* New York: Basic Books.

Hayes, E. (1988). A typology of low-literate adults based on perception of deterrents to participation in adult basic education. *Adult Education Quarterly, 39*(1).

Kallenbach, S., & Viens, J. (2002). *Open to interpretation: Multiple intelligences theory in adult literacy education* (NCSALL Rep. No. 21). Cambridge, MA: National Center for the Study of Adult Learning and Literacy.

Kegan, R., Broderick, M., Drago-Severson, E., Helsing, D., Popp, N., & Portnow, K. (2001). *Toward a new pluralism in ABE/ESOL classrooms: Teaching to multiple "cultures of mind"* (NCSALL Rep. No. 19). Cambridge, MA: National Center for the Study of Adult Learning and Literacy.

Knowles, M. (1970). *The modern practice of adult education: Andragogy versus pedagogy.* New York: Association Press.

Lewin, K. (1999). *The complete social scientist: A Kurt Lewin reader.* In Martin Gold (Ed.). Washington, DC: American Psychological Association.

Merriam, S., & Caffarella, R. (1999). *Learning in adulthood: A comprehensive guide.* San Francisco: Jossey-Bass.

Perin, D., & Greenberg, D. (1993). Relationship between literacy gains and length of stay in a basic education program for health care workers. *Adult Basic Education, 3*(3).

Purcell-Gates, V. (1995) *Other people's words: The cycle of low literacy.* Cambridge, MA: Harvard University Press.

Purcell-Gates, V., Degener, S., & Jacobson, E. (1998). *U.S. adult literacy program practice: A typology across dimensions of life-contextualized/decontextualized and dialogic/monologic* (NCSALL Rep. No. 2). Cambridge, MA: National Center for the Study of Adult Learning and Literacy.

Purcell-Gates, V., Degener, S., Jacobson, E., & Soler, M. (2000). *Affecting change in the literacy practice of adult learners: Impact of two dimensions of instruction* (NCSALL Rep. No. 17). Cambridge, MA: National Center for the Study of Adult Learning and Literacy.

Quigley, B. (1997). *Rethinking literacy education: The critical need for practice-based change.* San Francisco, CA: Jossey-Bass.

Reder, S., & Strawn, C. (2001). Program participation and self-directed learning to improve basic skills. *Focus on Basics* (Vol. 4, Issue D). Cambridge, MA: National Center for the Study of Adult Learning and Literacy.

Roswell, R. G., & Chall, J. (1992). *DARTTS: Diagnostic assessment of reading and trial teaching strategies.* Chicago: Riverside.2

Snow, C., Burns, M. S., & Griffin, P. (Eds.). (1998). *Preventing reading difficulties in young children.* Washington, DC: National Academy Press.

Stein, S. (2000). *Equipped for the Future standards: what adults need to know and be able to do in the 21st century.* Washington, DC: National Institute for Literacy, U.S. Department of Education.

Sticht, T. (1982). *Evaluation of the reading potential concept for marginally illiterate adults.* Alexandria, VA: Human Resources Research Organization.

Sticht, T., McDonald, B., & Erickson, P. (1998). *Passports to paradise: The struggle to teach and to learn on the margins of adult education.* San Diego, CA: Consortium for Workforce Education and Lifelong Learning.

Sticht, T., Armstrong, W., Hickey, D., & Caylor, J. (1987). *Cast-off youth: Policy and training methods from the military experience.* New York: Praeger.

Strucker, J., & Davidson, R. (2002). Adult reading components study. In *The First Five Years* (NCSALL Rep. No. 23). Cambridge, MA: National Center for the Study of Adult Learning and Literacy.

Taylor, D. (1985). *Family literacy: Children learning to read and write.* Exeter, NY: Heinemann.

Tracy-Mumford, F. (1994). *Student retention: Creating student success.* (NAEPDC Monograph Number 2). Washington, DC: National Adult Education Professional Development Consortium.

U.S. Department of Education. (2001). *1999-2000 report on adult education*. Washington, DC: U.S. Department of Education.

Wikelund, K., Reder, S., & Hart-Landsberg, S. (1992). *Expanding theories of adult literacy participation: A literature review* (Technical Rep. No. TR 92-1). Philadelphia, PA: National Center on Adult Literacy.

Woodcock, R. W., & Johnson, M. B. (1997). *Woodcock-Johnson Diagnostic Reading Battery*. Itasca, IL: Riverside.

Young, M., Fleischman, H., Fizgerald, N., & Morgan, M. (1994). *National evaluation of adult education programs*. Arlington, VA: Development Associates.

14

Understanding Adult Education in the Context of Family Literacy

Judith A. Alamprese
Abt Associates Inc.

Adult education and literacy services play a pivotal role in family literacy programs. As one of the core components of the main federal program supporting family literacy—the Even Start Family Literacy Program—these instructional services promote adult basic education (ABE), adult secondary education (ASE), English as a second language (ESL), and preparation for the General Educational Development (GED) certificate or the high school diploma. The assumption guiding Even Start and other multicomponent, comprehensive family literacy programs is that adults who participate in basic education services will develop the skills and knowledge they need to enhance their children's education, their own literacy, and their families' economic outcomes. As the critical link with parenting education, early childhood education, and parent and child interactive literacy services, adult education enables adults to change the intergenerational cycle of poverty by advancing both their own and their children's education.

Recent legislation and funding initiatives have emphasized delivery of adult education services in the context of family literacy. With the passage of the Adult Education and Family Literacy Act (AEFLA), Title II of the Workforce Investment Act of 1998 (P.L. 105-220), federally funded state adult education programs have an explicit goal of supporting family services as part of their adult education system. Eleven states have enacted legislation to expand family literacy services administered through their adult education offices. Additional funding provided by state legislatures has enabled state adult education offices both to increase family literacy services within existing Even Start programs and to support the development of new family literacy services. Furthermore, foundations have invested in family literacy (e.g., the John S. and James L. Knight Foundation's support of the National Center for Family Literacy's Family Independence Initiative) in part because they view this service as a way to help current and former welfare clients become economically independent and strengthen their parenting skills. Because the adult education component of family literacy is seen as key to adults' success in supporting their families educationally and economically, we need a better understanding of the types of adult education services delivered in family literacy programs and the impact these services have on adult participants' outcomes.

This chapter examines the role of adult basic education and adult secondary education services in comprehensive family literacy programs, particularly those provided under Even Start, the program for which the most comprehensive evaluation data are available. As a context for understanding the adult education component of family literacy programs, I review the operation and outcomes of federal- and state-supported adult basic education services offered in local communities, which include Even Start and constitute the majority of adult basic education services nationally. Finally, I discuss future directions for research on the implementation and outcomes of adult education in family literacy, as well as for organizing and delivering family literacy services.

OVERVIEW OF THE ADULT EDUCATION AND LITERACY SYSTEM

Funding Sources

Adult education and literacy in the United States is often described as a mosaic of services rather than a cohesive system intended to support adults' learning in and out of the classroom. These services include adult basic education for learners with skills below the eighth-grade level, adult secondary education for learners earning a high school diploma or the GED, and English literacy instruction for non-native-born adults who desire to improve their English language skills (in this paper, the terms *English literacy* and *English as a second language* are used interchangeably). Funding for these services comes primarily from federal and state government sources. According to the most recent comprehensive study of federal funding for adult education, there were 84 programs within 11 federal agencies in fiscal year 1989 that authorized or supported some type of adult education activities. Of these, 27 programs had adult education as a priority in their authorizing legislation (Alamprese & Sivilli, 1992). Although a number of programs authorize adult education activities, the major discrete federal funding for adult education and literacy comes from the Adult Education State-Administered Basic Grants Program under the Adult Education and Family Literacy Act. This federal adult education money is matched by state appropriations for adult education and often supplemented with local funding. In fiscal year 2002, the Basic Grants Program received $565,000,000. Approximately $70,000,000 of the Basic Grants Program was reserved for English Literacy/Civics Education. These federal adult education funds are leveraged by more than 1 billion dollars in state and local funding (U.S. Department of Education, 2002a). By comparison, the Even Start Family Literacy Program is a modest funding source for adult education. In the most recent data available, the U.S. Department of Education's Division of Adult Education and Literacy estimated that approximately $18,600,000 from Even Start went to direct adult basic education and literacy services in family literacy programs in fiscal year 1998 (U.S. Department of Education, 1998).

Target Population and Participants

Services provided under the Adult Education and Family Literacy Act are targeted to adults 16 and older who are not enrolled or are not required to be enrolled in secondary school; who lack sufficient mastery of basic skills to function in society; who lack a high school diploma; or who lack basic English skills. Unlike Even Start, AEFLA-supported services do not have an income criterion for participation and cannot be provided to teen parents under 16 or teen parents over 16 who are attending school. Nonetheless, these services are intended to serve adults who are most in need of educational services in order to improve their quality of life and economic well-being.

Estimates of the target population of adults who could benefit from basic education have been derived based on adults' levels of education and skill proficiency. According to 2000 Census data, approximately 35 million adults age 25 and older have not attained a high school diploma or an equivalent. Estimates of the target population for basic skills instruction are even greater. As indicated in the results of the National Adult Literacy Survey, which measured adults' skill proficiencies in prose, document, and quantitative literacy, approximately 90 million adults lack adequate information processing skills—that is, the skills they need to function successfully in contemporary society (Kirsch, Jungeblut, Jenkins, & Kolstad, 1993).

The number of adults served by federally funded projects is small in comparison with the need. For program year 2001 to 2002, the U.S. Department of Education reported that 2.8 million people were enrolled in adult education programs supported by the State-Administered Basic Grants Funds of AEFLA. Almost half (1.2 million) received ESL instruction, 38% (1 million) were enrolled in adult basic education instruction, and 20% (546,000) participated in adult secondary education services (U.S. Department of Education, 2003). The majority (85%) of enrollees during this period were under the age of 44, and, of those under the age of 44, 48% were between 16 and 24 years of age. Slightly more than half (53%) of participants were female. For the first time, Hispanic or Latino participants were the dominant group, making up 40% of those enrolled (U.S. Department of Education, 2002b). In addition to adults served in programs funded under AEFLA, two national adult literacy volunteer organizations—Laubach Literacy Action and Literacy Volunteers of America—sponsor tutoring and small classes in literacy instruction for adults. During 2000 to 2001, 235,000 adults received literacy services offered by these organizations, which recently joined together to form ProLiteracy America (Laubach Literacy Action, 2002; Literacy Volunteers of America, 2002). Information from AEFLA and the volunteer literacy organizations indicates that the potential beneficiaries of literacy services far exceed the number who currently participate in their services.

Service Delivery System

Adults in local communities can access basic education and literacy services through a variety of organizations and agencies. During the 2000 to 2001 program year, approximately 147,000 personnel provided services under AEFLA Basic Grants-funded programs. Almost half (47%) were part-time workers, and the rest were full-time staff (14%) or volunteers (39%). These individuals were associated with about 5,000 grant recipients, of which slightly less than half (45%) were local educational agencies. Other types of providers were postsecondary institutions (primarily community colleges, 12%), community-based organizations (24%), and correctional institutions (9%). A variety of organizations, including libraries, literacy councils, private industry councils, and sheltered workshops, constituted the remaining 10% (U.S. Department of Education, 2002a, 2002b). Another 129,000 volunteers provided literacy services during 2000 to 2001 through services offered by Laubach Literacy Action and Literacy Volunteers of America (Laubach Literacy Action, 2002; Literacy Volunteers of America, 2002).

Persistence in Adult Education Services

The descriptive literature on learner persistence in adult education is among the most substantial in the field (Beder, 1991; Comings, Parrella, & Soricone, 1999; Quigley, 1997; Tracy-Mumford, 1994; Wikelund, Reder, & Hart-Landsberg, 1992.). The focus of such studies has moved from discussions of why adults decide to participate and what inhibits their participation or prompts them to leave to an exploration of strategies that can motivate adults to persist. The definition of persistence is being broadened to include adults' activities in self-directed learning when they leave programs for a period of time, as well as their participation upon returning to formal programs (Comings et al.).

Research on adults' motivation to participate in basic education programs has reported four primary reasons: educational advancement, self-improvement, literacy development, and economic advancement (e.g., Beder & Valentine, 1990). Although these four reasons are often cited, the data regarding employability as a goal for enrollment in basic education has not been consistent (Moore & Stavrianos, 1995). While most studies have shown that 15 to 20% of ABE participants cite economic reasons for enrollment, a longitudinal study of ABE participants in Tennessee found that over half did so (Merrifield, Smith, Rea, & Crosse, 1994). The difference in results may be explained by the methodologies used in the studies.

In their summary of studies on barriers to participation, Comings et al. (1999) cite four types of perceptions that could influence adults' decision to enroll in basic education. Adults may believe that they will not benefit from participation, will not be able to learn, will not like participating in formal learning settings, and will not be able to overcome the various barriers to participation. Comings et al. support the conclusion reached by a number of researchers that the prevailing theories and descriptive studies do not adequately account for all of the interrelated forces that influence adults' decisions to participate in adult education. Rather, the forces affecting adults' participation in adult education are complex and are too difficult to analyze through descriptive studies.

A number of studies have discussed actions that programs can take to increase adults' participation and persistence. Tracy-Mumford (1994) suggested that programs can infuse retention strategies into their operational components, such as intake, orientation, assessment, and counseling. This approach assumes that learners are motivated by a variety of experiences and that programs should enhance their services to ensure that learners' perceptions about themselves and the program reinforce their participation. Quigley (1997) examined the challenge of retaining learners during their initial weeks of participation and the dispositional factors that he believes cause adults to drop out during this period. He suggested that programs pay particular attention to learners' prior history of negative experiences with school and focus their intake and orientation activities on matching learners to appropriate instruction to maximize their likelihood of achieving their goals.

Comings et al. (1999) have used research as a tool to develop advice for practitioners on how to keep adults engaged. They employed a force-field analysis to examine the barriers adults face and the supports that are available to them, as well as the relative importance of barriers and supports to adults' involvement. The study's respondents identified support from others, particularly from their families, friends, teachers, and fellow learners, as the most important factor affecting their persistence. Two other supports that learners identified were being able to build their self-efficacy and being successful in establishing a goal. The authors' analysis of study participants' persistence data found that one of the supports that learners had identified—their establishment of a goal—was related statistically to learners' attendance. The study suggests a number of actions that adult education programs can take to assist learners by creating a human support network, building their self-efficacy, and helping them set meaningful goals.

Adult education program staff view learner persistence as a critical challenge to delivering quality services. Although descriptive studies provide insights into learners' motivation to participate and the types of activities that can assist them, more rigorous research is needed to test strategies that can facilitate learners' persistence.

Learner Assessment

The learner assessment process has been a continual challenge to adult education programs supported with federal and state funds. Prior to the development of the National Reporting

System for Adult Education and the implementation of accountability requirements mandated by the Workforce Investment Act of 1998, there were no federal guidelines regarding the processes for learner assessment in adult education programs. Staff had the flexibility to use a variety of standardized and nonstandardized instruments, including instructor-developed tests and curriculum-related assessments. Data from these assessments often were not reliable or consistent. As a result of the federal accountability requirements, adult education programs have moved toward a more systematic process for monitoring learners' progress and providing feedback and reinforcement to learners.

Several aspects of adult education services have made it difficult for staff to conduct standardized learner assessments and collect high-quality data. These include the structure of "open-entry/open-exit" services, limited staff training in the administration of standardized assessments, and the perception among some adult education program staff that the available instruments are not adequate measures of learner outcomes. The General Accounting Office's (1995) report on measuring results in adult education discusses these challenges and their implications. For example, open enrollment—allowing learners to begin instruction at any time during the program year—poses obstacles for pre- and posttesting. When learners are able to enter at any point in the instructional cycle, it is difficult for programs to implement a consistent pretest schedule and for learners to benefit from sufficient instruction to show measurable gains on a posttest.

A related issue is the administration of assessment instruments, which affects the quality of data that are collected. When the staff carrying out a national evaluation of adult education programs analyzed assessment data that local programs had collected, they found inconsistent results because instruments had not been administered properly (Young, Hipps, Hanberry, Hopstoch, & Golsmat, 1994). State efforts to set performance standards have also been hampered by the variable quality of programs' assessment practices. As states analyzed their assessment data to set learners' performance goals, they found inaccuracies that prompted new efforts to train staff on learner assessment administration procedures (Alamprese & Stickney, 1999). These state training activities, as well as the U.S. Department of Education's development of guidelines for assessment and data collection have helped programs to document learners' skill gains more reliably (Condelli, 2000).

Although the administration of existing assessment instruments has improved, adult education program staff have questioned whether these instruments adequately document adult learner outcomes. Instructors have challenged the types of information assessed on general literacy tests and suggested a need to replace multiple-choice tests with applied performance assessments (Alamprese & Stickney, 2001). The challenge in designing alternative assessments is to develop reliable and valid processes that are both time efficient and financially feasible. The National Research Council (Mislevy & Knowles, 2002) has raised awareness among practitioners and policymakers about the complexity of developing performance assessments while providing useful information about the limitations of existing learner assessment and steps to take in designing new assessments. One effort to expand assessment options is the National Institute for Literacy's work in creating an applied performance assessment system for Equipped for the Future.

As a linchpin of adult education, learner assessment provides information that directs learners' placement, guides the types of instruction to be delivered, and documents learning results. Given assessment's role in adult education, continued efforts must be made to improve the quality of assessment data and expand the types of available assessments.

Instructional Services

Instruction is one of the least documented areas in adult basic education. Beder and Medina (2001) discuss the lack of empirical studies on instruction and the dominance of prescriptive literature. Only a few studies of adult education have included systematic class observation or examined the relationship between instructional type and learner outcomes.

According to Beder and Medina (2001), one of the first national studies using class observations was that of Mezirow, Darkenwald, and Knox (1975), in which descriptive data on 59 basic literacy and ESOL classes in five cities were collected. This study found that learners' diversity impeded the formation of social groups, the sharing of experience, and peer teaching. The teaching strategies in these classes emphasized communication of factual information, and question-and-answer routines were often used. Instructors also engaged in activities to reduce learners' failure rates, such as breaking tasks into their simplest components and rewarding successes with praise.

Beder and Medina's (2001) own qualitative study of instruction sought to describe its delivery and content. They observed 20 adult literacy classes in eight states and interviewed their instructors. The study found two types of instruction: discrete skills instruction (in 80% of the observed classes) and making meaning instruction (in 20%). In classes teaching discrete skills, instructors prepared and delivered lessons conveying factual information and obtained literal recall from learners. In these classes, commercially published materials were used; lessons had a distinct beginning and ending; and there was a focus on reading, writing, math, and GED test preparation. The making meaning classes were characterized by a focus on developing learners' higher level abilities and basic skills, and by an emphasis on instructor–learner collaboration, the use of authentic materials, and the role of the instructor as a facilitator. The authors identified seven classroom processes that are important for understanding the activities in an adult literacy classroom: sanctioning, engagement, directing, correcting, helping, expressing values and opinions, and community. They also found that classroom dynamics were shaped by the classroom's composition, turbulence caused by continuous enrollment, and pressures from the need to engage in fund-raising.

In one of the first studies to examine the relationship between instruction and learner outcomes, Alamprese, Tao, and Price (2004) studied reading instruction in 130 classes for first-level learners in 16 states. In this correlational study, reading content and instructional strategies were documented through class observations and in-depth interviews with instructors. The authors found that the type of reading instruction was associated with low-level learners' skill gains as measured by reading decoding tests. Classes that were organized, sequential, and emphasized the teaching of structured phonics were more likely to have low-level learners who demonstrated gains on decoding tests. These classes were primarily instructor directed, used a combination of commercially published and instructor-developed materials, and encouraged high learner engagement.

The limited research on instruction in adult education points to the need for more systematic examination of teaching and learning, particularly for experimental studies that examine the types of instruction that predict learners' knowledge and skill gains. Given the diversity of the adult education learner population, such studies would need to consider learners' skill levels, learning goals, and type of instruction.

Evidence of Program Effectiveness

Research on the effectiveness of adult education programs has been slow to develop. Beder's (1999) review of the outcomes and effects of adult education programs discussed factors that he believes account for the dearth of quality evaluation studies. One is that adult education outcome assessments have received low priority and little federal funding. Only three national evaluations of the adult education delivery system have been commissioned in the past 30 years (Kent, 1973; Young et al., 1980; Young, Morgan, Fitzgerald, & Fleischman, 1994), and these non-experimental studies were not able to collect outcome data adequate for drawing inferences about the effectiveness of adult basic education services. Three experimental studies—the evaluations of the Even Start Family Literacy Program and the National Workplace Literacy program—were limited in that they did not assess the range of services provided by adult basic education programs. A number of states have conducted evaluations of their own adult education services, but these have been primarily descriptive studies with limited outcome data.

The methodological limitations of past studies, including the lack of controlled program evaluations, have made it difficult to determine whether observed outcomes of adult basic education services are the result of learners' participation in the program, or whether similar outcomes would have been observed in the program's absence (Moore & Stavrianos, 1995). A related problem has been the use of information reported by instructors and learners regarding the progress and consequences of program participation. Although such observations provide helpful information, they lack objectivity. Finally, the limitations of standardized tests (such as the Tests of Adult Basic Education and the Comprehensive Adult Student Assessment System) and their lack of validity in the eyes of many adult educators have posed obstacles for assessing program outcomes.

Although past evaluations have not provided a clear understanding of adult basic education programs' effectiveness, they have produced information about learner characteristics that may affect learning outcomes. Most studies have documented learners' varied goals, their patterns of participation, and their education and employment history. These data are important variables in any prediction model of adult learner outcomes. Furthermore, emerging research on instruction and the operational components of adult basic education programs provides new instruments that can be used to measure the extent to which the type of instruction and services affects learner outcomes. With these advancements in measurement, the adult education field is better prepared to conduct experimental studies that address critical questions: whether adults who participate in basic education services increase their knowledge and skills; and the extent to which learners' personal characteristics, the instruction they receive, and the services provided by adult basic education programs predict their learning outcomes.

ADULT EDUCATION IN THE CONTEXT OF FAMILY LITERACY

Both the Adult Education and Family Literacy Act and the Even Start Family Literacy Program are intended to serve individuals who need further skill development in order to be successful family, workplace, and community members. Information about these programs is of interest to policymakers, but comparisons between participants in local adult education programs and those receiving services provided by Even Start are difficult because the types of data collected about program enrollees and the ways in which these data are analyzed and reported are not comparable.

Information about participants in federally funded adult education and literacy programs has come from national evaluations. The last study of participants in programs supported with funds from the Adult Education Act (which preceded the AEFLA) was conducted during the 1991 to 1992 program year. These data present the most detailed picture available for comparative purposes (Young et al., 1994).

The Even Start program, in its national evaluation, collected annual individual-level data through the Even Start Performance Information Reporting System (ESPIRS) through program year 2000 to 2001. The U.S. Department of Education published periodic reports based on its analyses of the ESPIRS data, which were a useful source of information about the demographic, background, and participation characteristics of Even Start enrollees. The Department of Education has also funded in-depth studies of Even Start participants as part of its first and third national evaluations, which provide participant and program data.

Even Start Participants

Since Even Start's inception in 1989, the program has changed not only in terms of the numbers of projects funded and families served but also with regard to the characteristics of participants. Although results from the third national evaluation of Even Start for the program years of 1997 to 1998, 1998 to 1999, 1999 to 2000, and 2000 to 2001 are the most current published data about the characteristics of participants (St.Pierre et al., 2002), information from the first and second national evaluations also are helpful in understanding the program's evolution (St.Pierre, Layzer, & Barnes, 1995; Tao, Gamse, & Tarr, 1998).

Program Enrollment and Family Structure.   During the 2000 to 2001 program year, 31,859 families participated in Even Start across 855 projects, an increase of 11% in the number of projects over the previous year and a slight decrease in the number of families. Since Even Start began in 1989 to 1990, the number of adult participants has increased ninefold. Meanwhile, the percentage of Even Start participants living in extended families has more than doubled over the past 10 years. Approximately half of the families served during 2000 to 2001 had two parents with children, 25% were headed by single parents, and 26% were extended families (St.Pierre et al., 2002).

Economic Status.   One of Even Start's objectives is to serve economically disadvantaged families, and the data from the third national evaluation indicate that the projects are reaching their target population. More than 80% of families enrolling in Even Start in the program years 1998 to 2001 had annual incomes below the federal poverty level, and 39% had incomes of less than $9,000 per year. Although the majority of Even Start participants had low incomes, the percentage of families receiving government assistance has decreased by 20% since 1989 to 1990. Of the participants enrolled in Even Start during 2000 to 2001, twenty-seven percent reported that their primary source of income was government assistance, while employment wages constituted the main source of income for 66% of families. These statistics point to the serious economic challenges that Even Start participants face in trying to earn a living wage above the poverty level, the effects that welfare reform has had on families' receipt of benefits, and the role that the adult education component of family literacy may be expected to play in helping families address their economic needs.

Family Diversity and Prior Educational Experience.   Two areas in which the picture of Even Start participants has shifted over time are diversity and adult participants' educational level at the time of enrollment. For example, the proportion of Hispanic families in Even Start has more than doubled since the beginning of the program, from approximately 17% of enrollees in 1989 to 1990 to 46% in 2000 to 2001. As the number of Hispanic families has increased, the representation of Caucasian families has declined from 38% in 1989 to 1990 to 30% in 2000 to 2001; the percentage of African American families fell from 36 to 19% over the same period. In 2000 to 2001, nonnative English speakers made up 45% of all newly enrolled parents, and about 75% of such parents reported difficulty in understanding, speaking, and/or reading English. Of parents who spoke a language other than English at home when they entered Even Start in 2000 to 2001, 16% reported difficulty reading in their native language, 10% had difficulty speaking in their native language, and 19% had difficulty writing in their native language (St.Pierre et al., 2002).

The number of adults entering Even Start with less than a high school diploma has increased over time. Eighty-four percent of adults who enrolled during program year 2000 to 2001 had not received a high school diploma or GED, compared to 77% of new enrollees during 1989 to 1990. There has been a gradual increase in the percentage of participants with very low levels of education; 13% of Even Start enrollees during 2000 to 2001 had not progressed beyond primary school.

The increase in the number of Even Start participants with limited English proficiency and lower levels of formal education has influenced the types of adult education services offered. Projects had to increase the amount of English-language instruction they provide as well as develop multiple levels of language instruction.

Reasons for Participating in Even Start

Adult participants' main reason for enrolling in Even Start is to improve their own education. Almost half (47%) of new parents enrolling in 2000 to 2001 cited educational advancement through Even Start as their primary goal for enrolling. Participants also identified a number of goals related to their children's success, including improving their parenting skills (38%), becoming a better teacher of their children (29%), and improving their children's chances of future school success (31%). Almost a quarter of parents said that they enrolled to improve their chances of obtaining a job (St.Pierre et al., 2002). By contrast, in the second national Even Start evaluation (1996–1997), only 5% of parents identified job attainment as a reason for participation (Tao et al., 1998).

Parents' increased focus on gaining employment reflects the changing needs of adults participating in Even Start and has affected the content of adult education services. In the third national evaluation, project directors were asked about the extent to which they provided various services to help parents prepare for employment. In 2000 to 2001, almost 90% of Even Start projects prepared parents for employment by using adult education class time to discuss vocational topics and job retention and to show adults how to access community services and vocational information. Similarly, about 80% of the projects used time in parenting classes to administer career interest/exploration surveys and to practice job skills (St.Pierre et al., 2002).

An example of an intensive approach to integrating adult education and employment preparation services was the Family Independence Initiative (FII), a demonstration project of the National Center for Family Literacy. In the FII family literacy programs, staff expanded the adult education component to include career awareness and job readiness training, so that welfare recipients in these programs could meet the requirements under Temporary Assistance for Needy Families (TANF) concerning job participation and work experience. Family literacy parents participated in job shadowing, mentoring, and job experience activities. Although family literacy program participants complied with the work-first policy under TANF, they also advanced their education and developed job skills (Alamprese & Tao, 2001; Alamprese & Voight, 1998).

Participation in Adult Education Services

Although almost all of the participants in Even Start programs receive adult education services, the extent to which they access the full range of services has varied. In program year 2000 to 2001, Even Start grantees reported offering 487 hours of instruction for GED preparation, 504 hours for adult secondary, 476 hours for intermediate adult basic education (5–8), and 473 hours for beginning adult basic education. Each of these figures represented an increase over the second national evaluation, but the greatest change was in the hours offered for beginning adult basic education, which expanded by 21% between 1996 to 1997 and 2000 to 2001 (St.Pierre et al., 2002; Tao et al., 1998.).

The third national Even Start evaluation defined the services offered by projects in terms of intensity. A high-intensity project was defined as one that offers 60 or more hours of instruction each month, and a low-intensity project as one offering 8 or fewer hours per month. Some of the Even Start projects delivered all of the aforementioned adult education instructional services, whereas others offered only one type of service. A project was considered to have medium-intensity services if it offered moderate intensity (between 8 and 60 hours per month) in at least one area of instruction but did not deliver any high-intensity services. According to these definitions, about one fourth of all Even Start projects provided high-intensity adult education services in 2000 to 2001. Only 14% of projects offered high-intensity ESL services, with about two thirds providing either high-moderate (between 30 and 60 hours per month) and/or low-moderate (between 8 and 30 hours per month) intensity of services.

The number of hours of adult education services that Even Start participants actually accessed stands in sharp contrast, however, to the amount of services that were available. During 2000 to 2001, parents received an average of 19.6 hours of adult education services per month for an average of 7 months, or approximately 30% of the hours that were available to them. The average of about 141 hours per year is greater than that reported in previous evaluations (St.Pierre et al., 2002). In contrast, adults participating in basic education programs funded under the Adult Education and Family Literacy Act in 2000 to 2001 accessed 87 hours of services (M. Dean, personal communication, June 12, 2003). In Abt Associates' study of reading instruction for first-level learners in adult basic education programs, participants averaged 124 hours of attendance in a year, and, on average, study participants accessed 63% of the reading class hours available to them (Alamprese et al., 2004).

Factors Affecting Participation

The comprehensive family literacy model exemplified by Even Start is predicated on parents' ability to access more hours of services than adults in basic education generally do. Data from the third national evaluation of Even Start showed that projects had expanded the number of hours that adult education services are available and that parents in adult basic education services, on average, accessed 1.5 times more hours. However, parents' patterns of participation varied. To explain this variation, the evaluation examined the relationship between parents' participation and project and family characteristics. Adults in families who received between five and nine support services attended an average of 181 hours of adult education per year, compared to 81 hours per year for families who received no support services (St.Pierre et al., 2002). Other adult education studies have also shown that support services facilitate adults' participation. The study of reading instruction for low-level learners found that receipt of support services had a positive association with program participants' attendance (Alamprese et al., 2004). In an investigation of the factors affecting adult learner persistence in basic education, participants identified their receipt of support services as a critical factor in their attendance (Comings, Parrella, & Soricone, 1999).

Other factors related to Even Start parents' participation in adult education were their education level, their age, and the number of hours of adult education that projects offered. Parents who enrolled in Even Start with a formal education of grades 0 to 6 spent less time in adult education (an average of 130 hours per year) than parents who entered with a higher education level. Parents' age was also a factor, with teen parents accessing a greater number of hours than older parents. Teen parents participated an average of 214 hours per year compared with about 140 hours for older parents. Project structure was also related to participation patterns. Projects that offered more hours of adult education services had more hours of participation when compared to projects with lower service intensity. Parents in projects that offered 54 or more hours of adult education per month accessed an average of 201 hours annually, compared to an average of 94 hours per year in projects that offered less than 20 hours per month of adult education services (St.Pierre et al., 2002).

These findings point to the structure of adult education program services as an important factor affecting adults' participation. Measurement of the quality of program services is a new area in adult education research, and programs differ in the extent to which they offer quality services (Alamprese et al., 2004). The types and quality of adult education services, particularly in a multicomponent service such as family literacy, may also be a key factor affecting participants' success.

Curricular Content of Adult Education Services in Family Literacy

The results from the second national Even Start evaluation provide the most current information about curricular content in the universe of Even Start projects. In this evaluation, project directors were asked to describe the extent to which their adult education curricula incorporated functional literacy approaches (defined as the application of literacy-related skills to real-life situations and practical activities). They also were asked whether the context of lessons involved life skills, vocational skills, or parenting practices. The evaluation results showed that most Even Start project sites in 1996 to 1997 included at least some functional literacy in their adult basic education curricula, and that its use had increased over previous program years. These data may be compared to information from the most recent national evaluation of the adult education system, in which less than half the programs reported were using functional life skills curricula (Young et al., 1994). It may be that, in order to meet the needs of its clients, Even Start must offer adult education services that are more oriented toward using functional context materials. This practice is likely influenced by the training that the National Center for Family Literacy provides to Even Start and other family literacy providers, which emphasizes the delivery of adult education services in the context of family-related issues (National Center for Family Literacy, 1996). The recent Equipped for the Future (EFF) project for developing content standards in adult education also emphasizes the teaching of basic skills in the contexts of contemporary life roles, including the family (Stein, 1997). And given that the data from the national evaluation of adult education programs are dated, it may be the case that the adult education system's use of life skills materials has increased as well.

A recent development in Even Start projects' adult education curricula that has not been documented by a national evaluation is an emphasis on reading instruction. The Equipped for the Future Reading Project piloted the integration of evidence-based reading instruction into a number of programs, and NCFL training has also stressed reading instruction. This emphasis on reading should address the needs of the large percentage of family literacy parents who have limited formal education.

OUTCOMES FOR ADULT EDUCATION PARTICIPANTS IN FAMILY LITERACY

A key goal underlying the comprehensive family literacy model is that adults will improve their basic skills after 1 year's participation, and that this improvement will lead to later effects on their children. Other likely outcomes of adults' participation in family literacy services include attaining a GED or high school diploma or obtaining employment. The three national Even Start evaluations provide the most comprehensive data about adults' basic skill outcomes, but other studies also supply useful findings.

Basic Skills Outcomes

The second national Even Start evaluation collected data on participants as a whole, as well as on a sample of about 2,200 families from up to 57 selected projects for the 1994 to 1995,

1995 to 1996, and 1996 to 1997 program years. For this group of participants, known as the Sample Study, project staff were trained to administer either the Test of Adult Basic Education (TABE) or the Comprehensive Adult Student Assessment System (CASAS), including a pretest, posttest, and second posttest where possible (Tao et al., 1998). In Even Start's third national evaluation, 18 projects participated in the Experimental Design Study (EDS); they voluntarily agreed to assign incoming families randomly to be in Even Start or a control group, in order to assess Even Start's impacts. Pretests, posttests, and 1-year follow-up data were collected from EDS families during 2000 to 2001 and 2001 to 2002. Measurements in the EDS focused more on adults' language skills than on the functional literacy or general skills assessed in the CASAS and TABE, respectively. The EDS used four subtests of the Woodcock–Johnson Psycho-Educational Battery—Revised: Letter–Word Identification, Word Attack, Passage Comprehension, and Reading Vocabulary (St.Pierre et al., 2003).

TABE Outcomes.   The TABE is a norm-referenced assessment designed to measure achievement in reading, mathematics, language, and spelling. The test items are written to reflect language and content appropriate for adults and to measure understanding and application of conventions and principles commonly taught in adult basic education curricula (CTB/McGraw-Hill, 1987). In the second evaluation's Sample Study of Even Start participants, projects administered the TABE reading and mathematics tests to 277 adults. The TABE reading results indicated that adults in Even Start for a year gained an average of 23 points, a statistically significant gain. Similar growth was seen in the math test. In general, for the reading and math tests, Even Start participants at the median gained between 1 to 1 $\frac{1}{2}$ grade levels in the 6 months from pretest to posttest, whereas participants at the 75th percentile gained 2 or more grade levels over the same period. Evidence from other studies suggests that adults gain, on average, 1 grade level after about 80 to 100 hours of instruction (approximately one program year) (Tao et al., 1998). The results for the Even Start participants on the TABE would suggest that these adults progressed more quickly than the average adult education participant.

CASAS Outcomes.   The CASAS was administered not only to participants in the Sample Study but also to those in the In-Depth Study during the first national evaluation (St.Pierre et al., 1995). This instrument is an adult-oriented functional assessment that measures a broad range of adult literacy skills and their application in real-life domains such as consumer economics, government and law, occupational knowledge, consumer resources, and health (Rickard, Stiles, & Martois, 1990).

Adults in the Sample Study who took the CASAS reading test at both pretest and posttest gained an average of 4.2 scale score points, equivalent to a gain of .22 *SD* units. Additionally, adults gained an average of 5.9 points on the math test from the pretest to the posttest approximately 6 months later. This gain is nearly $\frac{1}{2}$ *SD* larger than the gain seen for reading. It should be noted that the pretest scores for math were lower than those for reading, thereby allowing more room for growth.

In comparing these data to those in the first national Even Start evaluation, the gain of 4.2 in reading is nearly four times larger than the 1.2 gain observed in the control group in the In-Depth Study. When translated into *SD* units, .22 in reading for the Sample Study is comparable to the .26 observed in the experimental group in the first evaluation (Tao, Gamse, & Tarr, 1998).

The adults tested with the CASAS differed somewhat from those assessed with the TABE. On average, the CASAS group had completed more years of schooling, were less needy than Even Start participants as determined by their scores on the need index used in the study, and were more likely to be African American than those tested with the TABE.

Half of the Sample Study participants received fewer than 126 hours of adult education between the pre- and posttest over the course of the program year. The bottom 25% received fewer than 52 hours and the top 25% received more than 188 hours. But the amount of instruction was a significant predictor of gains only for the TABE math test. Furthermore, adults whose pretest scores were low had greater estimated gain scores than did adults with higher pretest scores. These findings are consistent with the research reported by Mikulecky and Lloyd (1993) that gains in academic performance for adults come slowly, and that even after 100 to 120 hours of instruction in a program year, adults in TABE programs advance only about one grade level (Tao, Gamse, & Tarr, 1998).

Another source of participant outcome data is the evaluations prepared by local Even Start projects (St.Pierre, Ricciuti, & Tao, ch. 30, this volume). In a recent synthesis of these evaluations conducted by St.Pierre, Ricciuti, and Creps (2000), the authors noted that while few local evaluations had pretest and posttest data (and none had control or comparison groups), almost all projects that reported such data showed statistically significant gains for adults as measured by the TABE or CASAS.

Even Start participant outcome data in reading and math, then, show growth in basic skills taking place among adult participants. But the extent to which participation in adult basic education services was the cause of this growth is not clear and requires further investigation.

Outcomes From the Woodcock–Johnson-Revised.   The majority of adults who participated in the third national Even Start evaluation's EDS identified themselves as Hispanic or Latino and lived in urban areas. This group represents a different sample from the two previous evaluations and reflects the changing face of Even Start families.

After participating in Even Start, adults scored significantly higher on two of the four subtests of the Woodcock–Johnson-R, including Letter–Word Identification (.21 *SD*) and Word Attack (.40 *SD*), as well as on the Woodcock–Johnson Basic Reading Skills cluster (.33 *SD*). However, researchers also noted that the EDS adults had very low scores when compared with national norms based on the general population. Overall, the adults participating in EDS had very low skills at entry into the program and were able to increase those skills, but their progress was no better than that of the control group (St.Pierre et al., 2003).

Other Outcomes.   In addition to examining growth in basic skills, the second Even Start evaluation collected information on a number of other outcomes. For example, although the majority of participants in the Universe Study (61.7%) and the Sample Study (64.7%) were not employed either at the beginning or at the end of the program year, approximately one fifth of each of these groups of adults was employed at both points in time. In the first Even Start evaluation, nearly 10% of those unemployed at intake had found a job by the end of the program year. In the second evaluation, 18% overall and 16% of those in the Sample Study had found work by the end of the program year (Tao, Swartz, St.Pierre, & Tarr, 1997). This outcome is interesting in light of the fact that only 4% of the parents said that finding employment was a goal for participation in the program.

Research on work-focused family literacy programs provides some encouraging results about employment-related outcomes. An evaluation of the National Center for Family Literacy's Family Independence Initiative showed that participants who attended well-structured family literacy programs with robust work-readiness services were significantly more likely to find employment during the follow-up year (44%) than participants who attended less structured programs (25%, $p < .05$ by a χ^2) (Tao & Alamprese, 2003). These data show that quality of services offered by family literacy services may play an important role in the outcomes achieved by participants.

Approximately half the adults in both the Universe Study and the Sample Study in the second national evaluation said that attaining a high school diploma or a GED certificate was the main reason they enrolled in Even Start. About the same proportion (10%) in both the Universe and Sample Studies attained the GED during the 1995 to 1996 program year. In the first Even Start evaluation, it was reported that 7.1% of all participants without a high school diploma at intake attained the certificate over the program year. In the first evaluation's In-Depth Study, 14.3% of adults in the program and 3.6% of the control group attained a GED over a 9-month period. The percentage of adults in the Sample Study who attained the GED certificate was less than that of the In-Depth Study but still higher than the proportion in the In-Depth Study control group (Tao et al., 1997).

The National Center for Family Literacy (1996) has reported outcomes for 200 families who participated in comprehensive family literacy programs trained by the Center's staff. Among these families, 51% of adult participants had received the GED or another high school equivalency certificate; 43% of the participants had jobs at the end of the program year compared to 14% who were employed before enrolling. The differences in these results from the Even Start evaluation may be that the programs with which the National Center works receive more technical assistance from the National Center's staff.

Although reported GED outcomes are positive, more data are needed to understand the extent to which adult education services in family literacy programs cause these outcomes. As an interim step, it would be desirable to compare the results of all types of outcomes to those achieved by general adult education programs, but the data provided by the most recent national evaluation of those programs are limited (Young et al., 1994). Another data source for comparison is state evaluations. In two statewide programs that used CASAS for assessing learner performance (Alamprese, 1993; Alamprese et al., 1987), the gains achieved by learners were comparable to or greater than those reported in the two Even Start evaluations.

NEEDED DIRECTIONS IN RESEARCH AND EVALUATION

The limitations of the national Even Start evaluations and evaluations of federally and state supported adult education programs point to the need for more rigorous studies that can produce better outcome data and information about the relationship between adult education program services and learner outcomes. This information is critical to our understanding of the role adult education plays in family literacy, as well as to the formulation of state policy and the improvement of program practice.

The Even Start evaluations provide a limited understanding of the types of services that projects offer in the adult education component of family literacy. Generally, information has been collected about hours of instruction, the extent to which instruction is taught in context, the provision of staff training, the mode of instruction (whole group, individualized), and the time of the day in which instruction is delivered. However, these data do not provide an in-depth understanding of how programs operate or of the content and strategies that are used in instruction. Measures that have been developed to assess reading instruction and adult basic education program operations provide new resources that can be used to enhance the quality of evaluations in family literacy as well as adult education (Alamprese et al., 2004).

A second area for further attention is the need for more controlled studies that can address the question of whether adults learn as a result of participating in family literacy programs. Conducting such studies is indeed challenging, and more efforts are needed to motivate program or project staff to support and participate in such efforts. Without controlled studies, we will not be able to address the policy question of whether the public investment in family literacy is well spent.

Finally, instruments that measure outcomes other than skill gains need to be developed. Family literacy program staff often report that participants have grown personally and socially as a result of their participation in services. These outcomes are important to document. With better measures of family literacy programs, policymakers would be better equipped to describe the ultimate effects that such programs have on adult participants and on their relationships with their families.

DIRECTIONS FOR PRACTICE AND POLICY

Directions for Practice

Information from descriptive studies of family literacy programs provides guidance that program administrators and staff should consider in designing and implementing adult education and other components of family literacy services. In their study of family literacy programs serving welfare recipients, Alamprese and Tao (2001) found three factors that are important to address in the early design and implementation of services. The first is the capacity of the program's administrator. Programs that had a knowledgeable administrator who understood the complexity of organizing and managing a multicomponent family literacy program were more likely to have integrated services within the first year of operation. The administrator plays a critical role in organizing the varied components of service, in identifying staff with the capabilities to carry out services, and in working across agencies to access the types of services that are needed to offer a comprehensive family literacy program. The design of a family literacy program needs to include an administrator who can identify and hire skilled staff and who has experience in developing multicomponent services.

Another important issue that affects the early operation of a program is the recruitment plan. The National Even Start evaluations show that the type of families participating in family literacy services is changing. Therefore it is critical for programs to assess the target population for family literacy and to develop a multimethod recruitment plan to identify participants for service. As studies of persistence in adult education have shown, participants who have a clear understanding of a program's services and can set specific goals are more likely to attend the services. The development of a recruitment plan and comprehensive intake services will help to ensure successful participation.

A third factor to address is instruction in the adult education component of family literacy. The delivery of multilevel instruction is common in family literacy programs, and more attention is needed in the design of teaching strategies and content that can address a variety of learners' backgrounds. The recent emphasis on reading instruction also points to the need for better alignment between the instruction provided to children and that provided to their parents, and to the potential of using a common approach to reading in both components of service. For parents who are low-level adult learners, structured reading instruction can help them to develop their own decoding skills while facilitating their work with their children in supporting early literacy and language development.

Directions for Policy

The delivery of robust family literacy services requires training and technical assistance. State family literacy offices play a critical role in providing resources to support program staff's development of basic skills and in helping them learn how to conduct appropriate learner assessment. States' provision of ongoing training and technical assistance that incorporates the emerging evidence about effective adult education instruction can assist family literacy program staff in delivering quality services. Furthermore, as the results from more rigorous research become available, state offices will have data about the amount of instructional time required for adult skill development that they can use in setting policies for the intensity and duration of services based on demonstrated learner outcomes. Family literacy policies that take into account the findings from research and evaluation can help to ensure the delivery of services that is based on the best available knowledge and experience.

REFERENCES

Alamprese, J. (1993). *Systematizing adult education: Final evaluation report of the Connecticut Adult Performance Program (CAPP).* Washington, DC: COSMOS Corporation.

Alamprese, J., Hemphill, D., Ramirez, S., Rickard, P., Tibbetts, J., & Wise, J. (1987). CBAE Evaluation Study Report. *Investing in change: Competency-based adult education in California.* San Diego, CA: Comprehensive Adult Student Assessment System.

Alamprese, J., & Sivilli, J. (1992). *Study of federal funding sources for improving coordination in adult education programs.* Washington, DC: COSMOS Corporation.

Alamprese, J., & Stickney, E. (1999). *Improving programs through policy and professional development: Lessons learned from Project Quality in Adult Literacy (EQuAL).* Bethesda, MD: Abt Associates Inc.

Alamprese, J., & Stickney, E. (2001). *View from teachers: Report on the national forum on adult education and literacy.* Bethesda, MD: Abt Associates Inc.

Alamprese, J., & Tao, F. (2001). *Family independence initiative (FII): Lessons learned about developing and delivering family literacy services to welfare recipients.* Bethesda, MD: Abt Associates Inc.

Alamprese, J., Tao, F., & Price, C. (2004). *Study of reading instruction for low-level learners in adult basic education programs.* Bethesda, MD: Abt Associates Inc.

Alamprese, J., & Voight, J. (1998). *Delivering family literacy in the context of welfare reform: Lessons learned.* Bethesda, MD: Abt Associates Inc.

Beder, H. (1991). *Adult literacy: Issues for policy and practice.* Malabar, FL: Krieger.

Beder, H. (1999). *The outcomes and impacts of adult literacy education in the United States.* Cambridge, MA: The National Center for the Study of Adult Learning and Literacy.

Beder, H., & Medina, P. (2001). *Classroom dynamics in adult literacy education.* Cambridge, MA: The National Center for the Study of Adult Learning and Literacy.

Beder, H., & Valentine, T. (1990). Motivational profiles of adult basic education students. *Adult Education Quarterly, 40*(2), 78–94.

Comings, J., Parrella, A., & Soricone, L. (1999). *Persistence among adult basic education students in pre-GED classes* (NCSALL Rep. No. 12). Cambridge, MA: The National Center for the Study of Adult Learning and Literacy, Harvard Graduate School of Education.

Condelli, L. (2000). *Measures and methods for the national reporting system for adult education.* Washington, DC: U.S. Department of Education.

CTB/McGraw-Hill. (1987). *Tests of adult basic education: Examiner's manual.* Monterey, CA: CTB/McGraw-Hill.

Kent, W. (1973). *A longitudinal evaluation of the Adult Basic Education Program.* Falls Church, VA: System Development Corporation.

Kirsch, I. S., Jungeblut, A., Jenkins, L., & Kolstad, A. (1993). *Adult literacy in America: A first look at the results of the National Adult Literacy Survey.* Princeton, NJ: Educational Testing Service.

Laubach Literacy Action. (2002). *2001 annual report.* Syracuse, NY: Author.

Literacy Volunteers of America. (2002). *2001 annual report.* Syracuse, NY: Author.

Merrifield, J., Smith, M., Rea, K., & Crosse, D. (1994). *Longitudinal study of adult literacy participants in Tennessee: Year two report.* Knoxville, TN: Center for Literacy Studies, University of Tennessee.

Mezirow, J., Darkenwald, G., & Knox, A. (1975). *Last gamble on education.* Washington, DC: Adult Education Association of the U.S.A.

Mikulecky, L., & Lloyd, P. (1993). The impact of workplace literacy programs: A new model for evaluating the impact of workplace literacy programs. Philadelphia, PA: The National Center of Adult Literacy.

Mislevy, R., & Knowles, K. (Ed). (2002). *Performance assessments for adult education.* Washington, DC: National Academy Press.

Moore, M. T., & Stavrianos, M. (1995). *Review of adult education programs and their effectiveness: A background paper for the reauthorization of the Adult Education Act.* Washington, DC: Mathematica Policy Research, Inc.

National Center for Family Literacy. (1996). *Outcomes and measures in family literacy programs.* Louisville, KY: Author.

Quigley, B. (1997). *Rethinking literacy education: The critical need for practice-based change.* San Francisco, CA: Jossey-Bass.

Rickard, P., Stiles, R., & Martois, J. (1989). *Psychometric background and measurement issues related to the development of the CASAS.* San Diego, CA: CASAS.

Stein, S. (1997). *Equipped for the future: A reform agenda for adult literacy and lifelong learning.* Washington, DC: The National Institute for Literacy.

St.Pierre, R. G., Layzer, J. I., & Barnes, H. V. (1995). Two-generation programs: Design, cost, and short-term effectiveness. *The Future of Children, 5,* 76–93.

St.Pierre, R., Ricciuti, A., & Creps, C. (2000). *Synthesis of local and state Even Start evaluations.* Washington, DC: U. S. Department of Education, Office of the Under Secretary, Planning and Evaluation Service.

St.Pierre, R., Ricciuti, A., Tao, F., Creps, C., Swartz, J., Lee, W., & Parsad, A. (2002). *The third national Even Start evaluation: Report on program outcomes.* Washington, DC: U.S. Department of Education, Planning and Evaluation Service.

St.Pierre, R., Ricciuti, A., Tao, F., Creps, C., Swartz, J., Lee, W., & Parsad, A. (2003). *Third national Even Start evaluation: Program impacts and implications for improvement.* Washington, DC: U.S. Department of Education, Planning and Evaluation Service.

Tao, F., & Alamprese, J. (2003). *Family independence initiative (FII): Follow-up study report.* Bethesda, MD: Abt Associates, Inc.

Tao, F., Gamse, B., & Tar, H. (1998). *National Evaluation of the Even Start Family Literacy Program: 1994-1997 final report.* Washington, DC: U. S. Department of Education, Office of the Under Secretary, Planning and Evaluation Service.

Tao, F., Ricciuti, A., St.Pierre, R., & Mackin, K. (2003). *State administration of the Even Start Family Literacy Program: Structure, process, and practices.* Washington, DC: U.S. Department of Education.

Tao, F., Swartz, J., St.Pierre, R., & Tarr, H. (1997). *National evaluation of the Even Start Family Literacy Program: 1995 interim report.* Washington, DC: U. S. Department of Education, Office of the Under Secretary, Planning and Evaluation Service.

Tracy-Mumford, F. (1994). *Student retention: Creating student success* (NAEPDC Monograph No. 2). Washington, DC: NAEPDC.

U. S. Department of Education, Office of Vocational and Adult Education. (1998). *Data fact sheet: Adult education.* Washington, DC.

U. S. Department of Education, Office of Vocational and Adult Education (2002a). *Adult education and literacy: Data fact sheet.* Washington, DC.

U.S. Department of Education, Office of Vocational and Adult Education (2002b). State-administered adult education program: Total enrollment by age. Washington, DC: Author.

U.S. Department of Education, Office of Vocational and Adult Education (2002c). State-administered adult education program: Enrollment by educational functioning level, ethnicity, & age. Washington, DC: Author.

U. S. Department of Education, Office of Vocational and Adult Education (2003). *State-administered adult education program: 2002 enrollment.* Washington, DC: Author.

U. S. General Accounting Office. (September, 1995). *Adult education: Measuring program results has been challenging.* Washington, DC: Author.

Wikelund, K., Reder, S., & Hart-Landsberg, S. (1992). *Expanding theories of adult literacy participation: A literature review* (NCAL Technical Rep. No. TR 92-1). Philadelphia, PA: National Center on Adult Literacy.

Young, M., Hipps, J., Hanberry, G., Hopstoch, P., & Golsmat, R. (1980). An assessment of the state-administered program of the Adult Education Act: Final report. Arlington, VA: Development Associates.

Young, M. B., Morgan, M., Fitzgerald, N., & Fleischman, H. (1994). *National evaluation of adult education programs: Draft final report.* Arlington, VA: Development Associates.

15

Workforce Literacy and Technology in Family Literacy Programs

Eunice N. Askov
Goodling Institute for Research in Family Literacy,
The Pennsylvania State University

Programs on workforce literacy and on family literacy seem to be far apart, yet both programs may be found in the same adult education agency. Workforce literacy instruction focuses on the role of the adult as worker and helps the client find employment or improve job prospects. On the other hand, family literacy programs that include the adult education component emphasize the parenting role of the adult in nurturing their child's literacy and language development. Little coordination seems to occur among these programs (with autonomous operations and separate funding streams), although adults who are served in both programs have overlapping needs.

In this chapter, I will discuss workforce literacy and technology and relate these to family literacy programs. My purpose is to explore the advantages of integrating workforce literacy and technology into family literacy programs and to suggest some creative ways that this might be accomplished. On a broader level, the purpose of this chapter is to suggest that adult education agencies might begin to view themselves as comprehensive educational organizations that meet the various educational needs of adults in their communities. Instead of looking to the funding sources that exist, these agencies might instead look first at the needs of their communities more globally. From that point of view, they might then seek various sources of funding to match the needs in the community. If both workforce literacy and family literacy are needed, then agency leaders might begin to think creatively about how to put these two needs together programmatically in their communities.

Because work is a prime consideration for adults in their attempts to support themselves and their families, it makes sense to incorporate workforce literacy into family literacy programs. The 1997 National Study of the Changing Workforce (Families and Work Institute, 2001) provides some interesting insight into the current status of families and work. The 1997 study also provides comparisons to the 1977 and 1992 studies of the workforce. Of the wage and salaried workers included in the 1997 representative sample, 46% are parents. Nearly one in five of the employed parents is single. More than three out of four married employees have spouses or partners who are also employed. Sixty-seven percent of the married male employees with children under 18 had employed partners in contrast to 49% in 1977. These national trends show increasing numbers of parents, both men and women, are in the workforce to support their families.

In spite of the growing trend of employment of both parents, unemployment rates among people with very low literacy skills (about 23%, or 44 million adults) were four to seven times higher than for people in the labor force with very high literacy skills as assessed by the National Adult Literacy Survey (Kirsch, Jungeblut, Jenkins, & Kolstad, 1993; Sum, 1999). Underemployment is also a common problem among adults with low literacy skills. Significant differences in wages between those with low and those with high literacy skills exist. The National Even Start Association (NESA, 2002) reports that the population served under the Even Start Act (authorizing family literacy programs) includes 80% of the families having an income below $15,000, with over 40% having incomes below $6,000. NESA also reports that participants have low levels of education (86% have not completed high school, as compared to 27% of Head Start parents). Dependence on public assistance, which supports families of unemployed adults, has now become time limited, as described in the next section.

IMPACT OF THE WELFARE-TO-WORK LEGISLATION

The Personal Responsibility and Work Opportunity Reconciliation Act or PRWORA (U.S. Congress, 1996) has emphasized a "work-first" approach, rather than long-term education. Consequently, the law encourages short-term training programs for welfare recipients. Although the states have been given considerable latitude in how they implement the law, education has not been a priority in the effort to get people off welfare rolls (Hayes, 1999). Many former welfare recipients have been placed in entry-level positions at low wages (Grubb, Badway, Bell, & Castellano, 1999). Such jobs do not usually have career paths that lead people to true self-sufficiency, thus tending to keep people in the same marginal status of those on welfare (Ehrenreich, 2001; Sheared, McCabe, & Umeki, 2000; Ripke & Crosby, 2002). (The reader may want to consult other books [e.g., D'Amico, 1999; General Accounting Office, 1999; Knell, 1998; Martin & Fisher, 1999; Ripke & Crosby, 2002] that explore this topic in depth.)

With the passage of PRWORA in 1996, the National Center for Family Literacy (NCFL) became concerned about the difficulty for parents in attending family literacy programs that were typically operated during the day. Because a large number of parents attending these programs were welfare recipients, it was deemed important to incorporate work-related activities as part of the adult education component of family literacy programs. In fact, NCFL reported in *Momentum* (November 2000) that the number of parents expressing employment-related goals at the time of entry into family literacy programs dramatically increased with the passage of PRWORA (1996) from 1% in 1991 to 37% in 1999. NCFL (2002) also reported that the percentage of families receiving public assistance at entry ranged from 81% in 1991 to 45% in 1999, showing that parents have moved into the workforce during that time period. If a family literacy program is providing workforce development as part of the adult education curriculum, this assistance in helping adults find employment, or improve employment status, can act as a positive force in program retention, as described by Comings in this volume.

To provide technical assistance in incorporating workforce development into family literacy programs, NCFL partnered with Jobs for the Future, a nonprofit organization dedicated to educational and economic opportunity for those most in need (http://www.jff.org/jff). Through this partnership, Jobs for the Future (1999) created a comprehensive guide for how workforce literacy might be incorporated into family literacy programs. This attempt to bring the world of workforce literacy into the world of family literacy has been successful in specially funded family literacy programs. These NCFL programs have indeed integrated workforce literacy into their family literacy programs (NCFL, 2000), concluding that family literacy can be a "...welfare-to-work strategy that focuses on strengthening the family unit while helping the parents become economically stable" (p. 19). Family literacy programs that can partner with other organizations to offer job training to parents that will result in skilled labor positions are doing more than simply removing people from the welfare rolls. In the next section we explore the general need for workforce literacy programs.

NATIONAL NEED FOR WORKFORCE LITERACY PROGRAMS

A pressing need for skilled workers exists nationally. Recent estimates for the year 1997 report 60% of the jobs in the country were skilled, whereas 20% were unskilled; however, in 1959 those percentages were reversed (U.S. Department of Commerce et al., 1999). Among the skilled labor positions technical skills are still important, but they are not sufficient (Askov & Gordon, 1999; Murnane & Levy, 1996). The so-called *soft skills*, such as analyzing work situations, performing problem solving, communicating with supervisors and coworkers, and working in teams, have risen in importance as workers are expected to be self-directed and accountable in their jobs (Murnane & Levy).

Two national studies conducted during the 1990s were influential in recognizing the importance and broad conception of employability skills (the skills needed for work) and workforce literacy. A study by the American Society for Training and Development or ASTD (Carnevale, Gainer, & Meltzer, 1990) identified 16 skill groups across all job families. These skills (paraphrased) included literacy skills (reading, writing, computation), communication (speaking and listening), problem solving, career development (self-esteem, motivation and goal setting, and career planning), teamwork, and leadership. Subsequently, the U.S. Department of Labor, which had funded the ASTD study, established the Secretary's Commission on Achieving Necessary Skills (SCANS) (1991). SCANS identified 36 important employability skills, including the ability to use resources, interpersonal skills, information, systems, and technology. The SCANS skills have formed the basis for curriculum development for preparation and functioning in the workplace. More recently, the Institute for the Study of Adult Literacy at Penn State (2000) developed the Foundation Skills Framework, an interagency project to develop a common definition and conceptual model of the basic skills and knowledge that adults need to obtain or maintain employment and advance to higher paying jobs. The framework consists of 21 foundation skills and knowledge areas, with corresponding lists of competencies that are used to develop curriculum and assessment procedures.

The National Association of Manufacturers (2001) conducted its third survey of manufacturing industries in the United States. Survey respondents said that the greatest skills gap exists in production workers (skilled hourly workers), rather than in computer or information technology workers as found in previous studies. The deficits currently reported are basic employability skills, such as attendance and work ethic, and literacy skills (reading, communication, and math). In other words, the skills identified by SCANS and the ASTD study are those most in need in the modern workforce.

Furthermore, production workers are expected to be flexible, able to learn new tasks and technology demands quickly. They must be self-directed in their jobs because the assembly line now frequently uses machine robots instead of people for routine jobs. Decision making has been passed down to the production floor where the product is being made (Resnick & Wirt, 1996). In the next section, we explore how workforce literacy can benefit the adults and children who are served by family literacy programs.

ABILITIES DEVELOPED BY WORKFORCE LITERACY PROGRAMS

This section explores the advantages of integrating workforce literacy into family literacy programs. First is a discussion of the empowerment that can occur as adults acquire literacy skills that enable them to participate in the workplace.

Snow and Tabors (1996) argue that adult education classes need to "develop their students' self-images as 'readers' and 'writers'...to convey a sense of both the functional and entertainment value of reading and writing" (p. 5). Adults who feel good about themselves as readers and writers engage in literacy practices, such as reading for their own information and enjoyment as well as reading storybooks with their children. Adults who use their literacy skills in the workplace feel better about themselves as readers and convey that to their children.

McDonald and Scollay (2002) make a similar point: Improvement of parental literacy does not have a direct effect on children's literacy as assumed in the concept of an intergenerational transfer of literacy skills. Instead, the relationship is more complex and indirect, requiring an identity change on the part of parents. According to the authors' study of family literacy participants, parents who incorporate literacy into their lives have an impact on their children's literacy development by using literacy skills at home.

Equipped for the Future (Stein, 2000) identifies role maps for adults as both parents and workers (see also Comings, this volume). Some of the key activities under the worker role map could also be applied to the family, especially under the broad area of responsibility of "Plan and Direct Personal and Professional Growth." For example, one key activity is "Balance and support work, career, and personal needs," which includes the family as a consideration in the workplace. Another key activity is "Plan, renew, and pursue personal and career goals," which also acknowledges the importance of the family in planning career development. Likewise, key activities in the parent/family role map are suggestive of those in the worker role map, such as "Balance priorities to meet multiple needs and responsibilities" which is similar to "Balance individual roles and needs with those of the organization" in the worker role map (see www.nifl.gov/lincs/collections/eff/eff.html). The overlap in responsibilities and abilities for parents and workers suggests that success in the workplace will have a positive effect on the functioning of the adult as a parent.

Van Fossen and Sticht (1991) describe a workforce development program offered by the Wider Opportunities for Women (WOW) that trains women in nontraditional jobs. Women enrolled in the WOW program report that as a result of their education and training they spend more time with their children talking about school, helping with their homework, reading with them, and participating in school activities. The women's experiences in nontraditional occupations, such as construction and transportation, that require the use of literacy skills apparently lead to a realization of the importance of literacy skills for their children.

How do workforce literacy programs encourage positive self-images in adult students, many of whom have had negative experiences with literacy skills in K–12 schooling? Drawing on the work of Bandura (1977), a person's beliefs and expectations (self-efficacy) about his or her capability to accomplish tasks successfully determine whether or not the person attempts the tasks, the amount of effort expended, and perseverance in the tasks when difficulties occur (see Comings, this volume, for additional information on self-efficacy). In other words, success in one task tends to give people confidence to tackle new related tasks. Conversely, if adults had difficulties in school, they might have low expectations of their ability to accomplish academic tasks. Setting the academic tasks in the context of work (rather than in the general education context where they may have previously failed) may give adults a new opportunity to learn. If they experience some measure of success, their self-confidence may be improved and they may be willing to attempt new work-related academic tasks.

Now that we have established the abilities that can be developed by workforce literacy programs, we will consider the criteria for an effective workforce development program that not only prepares an adult for the workplace but also enhances his or her role as a parent.

CHARACTERISTICS OF EFFECTIVE WORKFORCE DEVELOPMENT

Literacy programs in which both the teacher and students learn collaboratively are effective in creating positive self-images in learners, in contrast to those that rely on rote learning assigned by the teacher (Askov, 2000). These programs are built on the assumption that knowledge is socially constructed and influenced by prior knowledge and experiences. Literacy content and skills are not taught in isolation from the learners' knowledge and experiences. Instruction is situated in a meaningful (authentic) context (Bruner, 1990) in project-oriented and problem-based learning. In this approach, literacy instruction includes learners' application of literacy skills and active learning that incorporates uses of literacy. Literacy is contextual; it is not *a one size fits all* curriculum or list of skills. Individuals also vary in their need for literacy skills at any point in time in their lives. Learners construct new knowledge and skills through interacting with others in doing real-world projects. Learning that closely resembles the participants' real world occurs as a social process involving others.

The teacher's role in this type of program changes substantially from being a transmitter of knowledge to a facilitator of learning and resource person (Brophy, 1998; Giddens & Stasz, 1999). Teachers, along with learners, design instruction to meet the learners' needs, interests, background knowledge, and skills within a particular context. This approach fits well in learning workforce literacy skills as well as the so-called soft skills and attitudes. (See Berns & Erickson, 2001, and Brown, 1998, for examples of instruction using this approach. See Windschitl, 2002, for a discussion of the research related to constructivism in practice.)

Workers must be able to apply academic skills to the workplace (Bailey, 1997). In other words, they must be able not only to know the academic skills but also to relate learning to work applications. An instructional approach that encourages application and practice of literacy skills is important so that the adult can immediately use the skills that are taught. In the workplace, adults need to use integrated skills (e.g., reading, writing, and math) that cross disciplines and can be transferred across jobs. The approach to teaching and learning that is described in this section encourages the integration of skills in solving real-world problems.

How does an adult education teacher know the basic educational skills that will be needed for adult students who find jobs in the local community? Which literacy skills seem to be important across many entry-level jobs? Askov (1996), based on a survey of the skills taught in the National Workplace Literacy Program projects, identified frequently occurring skills in entry-level jobs, including recognizing technical vocabulary, following written directions, locating information, scanning materials for specific facts, and reading for details. Such skills, presented in a context that is appropriate for the local workplaces, represent a starting point for curriculum development. Customization to the context of the workplace, however, is essential to ensure that transfer occurs between learning in the classroom and learning on the job (Askov & Van Horn, 1993).

Adult education teachers, however, should determine the workforce literacy skills that are needed in their communities. Often the greatest employment opportunities exist in small businesses—those that are least likely to be able to sustain a workplace literacy program onsite. Linkages need to be built between the adult education providers and the local businesses and business organizations. These linkages may already be established if the provider agency has a workforce development outreach program. In addition to these efforts, teachers also need to ask parents about their career aspirations so that the jobs they choose are meaningful to them.

An annotated bibliography on workforce education (Imel, 1999b) provides a helpful list of readings as well as a discussion of workforce education. Furthermore, another annotated bibliography (Imel, 2000) on the Workforce Investment Act (WIA), which was passed in 1998 and is similar in the work-first objectives of PRWORA, provides a discussion of the act and an annotated list of readings.

WORKFORCE LITERACY IN THE ADULT COMPONENT OF FAMILY LITERACY PROGRAMS

In this section, we discuss how workforce literacy may be integrated into the adult component of a comprehensive family literacy program through various program models. Jobs for the Future (1999) provides excellent suggestions for incorporating career exploration and work-based learning into family literacy programs through field trips, field investigations, job shadowing, rotations with different employers and departments, mentoring, community service learning, and internships (p. 6). The report provides detailed guidelines for these experiences and suggestions for setting them up in the local community. It also stresses the need to establish a network of local employers that are willing to provide a variety of work-related learning experiences to the adults in family literacy programs. Useful tools are provided in the appendices of the report to help family literacy programs incorporate work-based learning. The report acknowledges that this type of programming in family literacy represents a *paradigm shift* for both teachers and learners from viewing the adult only in the parent role to also considering the adult as worker (p. 51). Furthermore, Peyton, Wheeler, and Dalton (1998) advocate for states to incorporate family literacy into welfare reform programs, as well as to provide examples of programs and descriptions of how family literacy instructors can link with community social service agencies and employers.

Strawn (1998) discusses various program models for practitioners serving welfare recipients. She categorizes program models into (a) work-related basic education; (b) work-related basic education and job training combined; (c) work-related basic education, job training, and unpaid work combined; and (d) work-related basic education, job training, and paid work combined. Although these are not within the context of family literacy, the examples of programs provided in the report reveal possibilities for the adult education component.

Furthermore, Ripke and Crosby (2002) point out that mixed models of basic education combined with employment training that include an emphasis on work have led to more positive and longer lasting effects on earnings than education and job training offered separately. Intuitively, this combination makes sense, as adults have the opportunity to apply basic skills in the real-world tasks of work.

Although not writing specifically about adults with limited literacy skills, Billett (2002) describes "workplace pedagogic practices" that represent three interdependent types of guided engagement with work activities (p. 33). He calls the first type "Participation in work activities," consisting of learning through everyday work activities, sequencing of tasks, opportunities to participate, and opportunities to access goals required for performance. The second type called "Guided learning at work" consists of guidance from experienced employees, modeling and coaching, use of techniques to engage workers in independent learning, and development of understanding. The third type is "Guided learning for transfer," which uses questioning, problem solving, and scenario building to extend learners' knowledge to novel situations (p. 34). These components are important in transitioning adult learners into the workplace. The movement from workplace education in the family literacy program to job training to placement in a job with "guided engagement with work activities" should be coordinated through the network of community agencies and companies that work with the family literacy program.

ROLE OF TECHNOLOGY IN INSTRUCTION

Technology has become pervasive in our society. Furthermore, the jobs that are growing in number are those that involve the use of technology while unskilled labor jobs are decreasing. This trend is predicted to continue (Kemske, 1998). Job security is also increasingly being tied to technological proficiency even in nontechnical workplaces (Ginsburg & Elmore, 1998). Use of technology is listed as one of the common activities in Equipped for the Future as described previously (Stein, 2000), which recognizes the importance of technology across the various demands on adults in today's society (see www.nifl.gov/lincs/collections/eff/eff.html).

The adult students who are served, however, are the least likely to have access to computers, the Internet, and the knowledge to use either one (National Telecommunications and Information Administration, 1999). Furthermore, as Levesque (2000) comments, "Many parents believe that their families' economic plight further disadvantages their children in school because they could not afford a home computer or Internet access" (p. 4).

This so-called *digital divide*, or the gap between the *haves* and *have nots* of technology, has captured media attention (www.digitaldividenetwork.org). Those who are educated and have access to technology are benefiting from the current economic prosperity and availability of jobs. Undereducated adults tend not to have access to technology either at home or in the workplace. Without access to and knowledge of computers and the Internet, low-literate adults appear to have little chance to successfully bridge that divide.

Adult literacy programs might be a place where low-literate adults can be helped across the digital divide through access to technology for instruction. (See Imel and Wagner, 1998, for a discussion of several models of technology instruction. See Berger, 2001, for an evaluation of research findings related to the effectiveness of using computers for instruction.) Askov and Means (1993), however, reported that adult literacy programs not only lacked access to technology, but also many states lacked a technology plan for adult basic education. Furthermore, online technologies are not widely available in adult education programs (Hopey, Harvey-Morgan, & Rethemeyer, 1996). Although a growing number of programs have access to technology for instruction compared to earlier studies, access to appropriate hardware, software, and professional development are still problems for many programs (Sabatini & Ginsburg, 1998). Other problems frequently cited are cost, training, and inappropriate instruction as well as access to technology and integration of technology into instruction (Millar, 1996). As a result, adult literacy programs tend to be behind K–12 education in the adoption and use of technology in instruction (Elmore, 1997).

Although Elmore (1997) attributes part of the reluctance to use technology in adult literacy programs to software lacking in creativity and being geared to children, Askov and Bixler (1998) point to the possibilities of using computer simulations for instruction. Simulations allow the adult learner to apply literacy skills to real-world problem-solving situations in a safe environment. Computer simulations, such as *A Day in the Life...* (1993), a workforce literacy software program that poses real-life work problems requiring application of literacy skills in their solutions, offer a bridge between the classroom and the workplace. Computer simulations give adults the opportunity to apply academic skills in a workplace environment without the worry of making mistakes on the job.

Another problem preventing the widespread use of technology that Elmore (1997) identifies is the lack of staff development and preparedness to use technology. It is now evident that investing in technologies for the classroom has little educational impact *unless* teachers know how to use these powerful tools effectively to enhance teaching and learning and are supported in their efforts (U.S. Congress, Office of Technology Assessment, 1993). An essential component often missing from technology implementation efforts is professional development that helps teachers think about how technology can support learner's educational goals and learn how to manage a class that is learner centered with ongoing learner feedback.

Several professional development projects relating to technology have recently been funded. Tech21, a professional development project supported by the U.S. Department of Education at the National Center on Adult Literacy, University of Pennsylvania (www.tech21.org), aims to help adult educators learn how to use technology to improve instruction. Similarly, Project IDEAL (Improving Distance Education for Adult Learners) at the University of Michigan, funded by a combination of state and federal sources, provides assistance to staff in a growing number of states to implement distance education in adult literacy programs (www.rcgd.isr.umich.edu/ideal/). A monograph, funded by the U.S. Department of Education, Office of Vocational and Adult Education, discusses the issues of expanding access to adult literacy services by implementing online distance education in adult literacy programs in the United States and by contrast in Australia (Askov, Johnston, Petty, & Young, 2003).

As described in Coming's chapter, Reder and Strawn's longitudinal study (2001) reports that adults do engage in self-directed study to improve their literacy skills. This finding suggests that various forms of technology as well as distance education may be appropriate for improving workforce literacy skills. Technology and distance education seem particularly appropriate for family literacy programs in which adults need to improve not only their literacy skills for support of their children's literacy development but also their literacy skills for employability.

Distance education offers the promise of access for students who may be fully employed during the day, or who are home-bound with disabilities, small children or elders to care for, or otherwise unable to attend traditional classes. It may also be useful to supplement instruction provided in the adult education component of family literacy programs. More broadly, learning at a distance through technology promises different approaches to literacy instruction that may appeal to undereducated adults who want to be part of modern society. Electronically mediated instruction offers the promise of access for adults unable to attend traditional classes by extending learning opportunities to the home, community center, and workplace (Askov & Bixler, 1998). Access to technology, however, remains a problem for those in poverty, often with the least access to publicly supported facilities. An annotated bibliography on technology (Imel, 1999a) provides a helpful list of readings as well as a discussion of the necessity of technological proficiency.

Askov, Johnston, Petty, and Young (2003) report on the national field test of an online distance education program, Workplace Essential Skills, and provide a case study of Pennsylvania. The findings from the case study (Johnston & Petty, 2001) indicate that professional development is crucial for instructors as they take on new roles in online distance education. They suggest that accountability procedures required for state funding may need to be relaxed initially. For example, Pennsylvania programs were not required to report learners' pre- and posttest scores during the experimental period. Another finding is that students appear to be more successful if they are employed and functioning at higher literacy levels (i.e., different from the traditional student who enters a family literacy program).

Many of the capabilities of computer technology, such as interactivity and potential for immediate feedback, support the constructivist theories of learning discussed previously (Dimock, 2000). In fact, the constructivist learning theory has recently become entwined with distance learning, although early attempts at distance education in higher education were built on the transmission model of correspondence study in which knowledge is imparted from the professor to the students who are at a distance (Burge, 1988). For example, Relan and Gillani (1997) define Web-based instruction as the application of "... cognitively oriented instructional strategies within a constructivist and collaborative learning environment, utilizing the attributes and resources of the World Wide Web" (p. 43). Internet technology now makes learning possible in a social environment because learners can be linked in a virtual classroom with an instructor. The Internet has opened up opportunities for social learning leading to the development of higher order thinking and learning.

Although interactivity is essential in a constructivist learning environment, and Internet technology can promote this interactivity, effective instruction does not automatically result (Daley et al., 2001). In fact, technology strongly influences learning, making students' attitudes toward and perceptions of technology important. Daley et al. (2001) recommend that instructors take the time to develop the online learning climate to promote learning. For example, early activities might involve establishing work groups among the students, encouraging e-mail use, and posting frequently to a class bulletin board. In fact, a key role for an online instructor is to act as a facilitator to carefully monitor and support online interactions (Burge, 1994). A skilled instructor is necessary to ensure that the online groups work together collaboratively as intended (Gunawardena & Zittle, 1997).

This section has explored the benefits of using technology in adult literacy programs. In the next section we discuss the integration of workforce literacy and technology in family literacy programs.

BENEFITS TO CHILDREN

The focus in this chapter has been on the benefits of workforce development and technology to the adults participating in comprehensive family literacy programs. In family literacy programs the assumption is that the four components of adult education, early childhood education, parenting education, and parent–child interactive literacy activities complement each other. In other words, what occurs in the adult component should benefit not only the adult but also the child. It also seems intuitive that children will also benefit from their parents' involvement in workforce development and technology use. This section explores how children may potentially benefit, both directly and indirectly.

Ripke and Crosby (2002) point out that children from low-income families experience less success in school than those from higher income families. The impact of poverty is particularly great in children ages 0 to 5. The National Center for Children in Poverty (1999) reports that children from low-income families are less ready for school and are held back in school at least twice as often. If workforce education can provide the requisite education and training to enable parents to improve their job prospects and income, children as well as adults will benefit. Using technology for instruction further prepares adults for the modern workplace. In this section, we explore the implications of workforce development in the adult component of family literacy programs on children's literacy development.

As discussed earlier in this chapter, parents who are empowered by entering the workplace and being able to support their families report feeling good about themselves. This engagement in fulfilling work by parents may lead to better relationships with their children. Parents' expectations of their children may be increased; thus, they lead to greater achievement by the children (Parsons, Adler, & Kaczala, 1982). This engagement may also lead parents to greater awareness of the literacy abilities that their children need for school success as well as the eventual workplace; hence, they have more interest in helping their children in school (Van Fossen & Sticht, 1991). Furthermore, adults who feel better about themselves are likely to encourage literacy development in their children (McDonald & Scollay, 2002). In fact, Ripke, Huston, and Mistry (2001) have demonstrated that parents' job characteristics (e.g., wages) are associated with parents' educational expectations for their children; these expectations correlate positively with the children's own aspirations and expectations.

On the other hand, being employed in low-level, dead-end jobs may not have the same effect as employment in more rewarding jobs. Often these low-level jobs are the first to be cut in an economic downturn, returning a family to welfare dependence. Some research has shown that this cyclical effect of on and off work/welfare can be damaging to children (Ripke & Crosby,

2002). Low-income jobs can also lead to stress and depression, both of which can negatively affect parenting and children's welfare and achievement in school. However, because most studies relating parental employment to children's development are correlational, not causal, it is difficult to make definitive statements about the effects of a parent's employment on children. The one experimental study conducted in this area (Magnuson & McGroder, 2001), cited in Ripke and Crosby (2002), did show that increases in the mother's education were significantly positively related to children's academic school readiness and negatively related to academic problems. Furthermore, Shields and Behrman (2002), as described in Ripke and Crosby (2002), point out that providing a child with a role model of a parent in an educational program may be even more important than providing a role model of a working parent.

If adults are functioning at the low literacy levels that are typically found in family literacy programs, then education is a long, slow process until a person can reach the level of obtaining a high school equivalency certificate (hence, an opportunity for a job that can support a family). Unfortunately, most states, operating with the "work first" model, do not allow that much time for education before welfare benefits are cut off (Sparks, 2001). Thus, the potential of influencing child outcomes by having parents achieve a higher education level will usually not come about under the current welfare-to-work system. Nevertheless, adults who are looking for work may engage in certain literacy practices that would be beneficial for children to witness because parents are role models for their children. For example, adults may read the newspaper to identify jobs in the community. Adults may also engage in writing at home in the preparation of a resume. They may go to the library to use a computer for typing their resumes. They may use a telephone book to schedule an appointment for an interview. They may prepare a budget to determine how pay can be allocated against expenses. Children who see their parents engaged in these types of literacy activities may realize the importance of literacy skills in their lives through their parents' example.

Adults in family literacy programs who are not working can also positively influence their children's literacy development in other ways. For example, they may engage in work experience in their child's school. Often family literacy programs ask the parents to volunteer time in the school to provide them with responsible work experience as well as to help the teachers with the many tasks of preparing instructional materials and managing groups of children. Children whose parents work in the school may benefit from seeing their parents in an assisting role. Participation in a child's school gives the parent a better understanding of the school and better access to communication with teachers (Hoover-Dempsey & Sandler, 1995, 1997).

CONCLUSION

Offering workforce development with an emphasis on using technology is appropriate in a family literacy program. Not only are the parents learning skills that may enhance the economic security of the family, but also the children may benefit by seeing their parents employed and by the stability that may come to the family from regular income. Furthermore, the component of family literacy programs designed to enhance parent–child interactivity to promote children's literacy development may also be an opportunity during which parents and children can work together on work-related literacy tasks, such as reading a newspaper with children in the lower elementary grades.

Mixed models, in which the parents engage in education and work experience, seem to make the most sense both in terms of increasing the parents' ability to support the family and in terms of impacting the children. Parents benefit from further education and training by improving their chances to find fulfilling work that will enable them to support their families. Children benefit from the positive role models of seeing their parents as both students and workers. Furthermore, adults who learn to use computer technology as part of an instructional program can also positively influence their children's education. As their children learn to use computers in school, parents can work with their children on the computer perhaps in a library or community technology center.

However, a number of research questions exist. We do not know the differential impact of the transition to the workplace on very young children in family literacy programs as opposed to older children who are in preschool or in the early elementary grades. Furthermore, we need to implement random assignment experiments to study the effects of various models rather than rely solely on data from correlational studies. Also, more research is needed to demonstrate the impact of a constructivist approach to instruction in the adult education component of family literacy programs in preparing parents to become workers. In fact, many research questions exist about family literacy programs that require researchers, policymakers, and practitioners to work together to find the answers. Interdisciplinary approaches hold the most promise in exploring this complex approach for giving "value added" to adult and early childhood education (see Askov, 2002, for an elaboration of research directions).

In spite of the many unanswered questions about best practices in family literacy programs, providers need to bring the two programs, family literacy and workforce development, together so that both programs can benefit from each other. As a result, both programs will be strengthened with positive outcomes for the parents and children who are served by these programs.

REFERENCES

Askov, E. N. (1996). *Framework for developing skill standards for workplace literacy*. Washington, DC: National Institute for Literacy. (ERIC Document Reproduction Service No. ED400426)

Askov, E. N. (2000). Adult literacy. In A. L. Wilson & E. Hayes (Eds.), *Handbook of adult education* (pp. 247–262). San Francisco: Jossey-Bass.

Askov, E. N. (2002). *Family literacy: A research agenda to build the future*. University Park, PA: The Pennsylvania State University, Goodling Institute for Research in Family Literacy.

Askov, E. N., & Bixler, B. (1998). Transforming adult literacy instruction through computer-assisted instruction. In D. Reinking, M. C. McKenna, L. D. Labbo, & R. D. Kieffer (Eds.), *Literacy & technology for the 21st century* (pp. 167–184). Mahwah, NJ: Lawrence Erlbaum Associates.

Askov, E. N., & Gordon, E. E. (1999). The brave new world of workforce education. In L. G. Martin & J. C. Fisher (Eds.), *The welfare-to-work challenge for adult literacy educators*. New Directions for Adult and Continuing Education (No. 83, pp. 59–68). San Francisco, CA: Jossey-Bass.

Askov, E. N., Johnston, J., Petty, L. I., & Young, S. J. (2003). *Expanding access to adult literacy with online distance education*. Cambridge, MA: Harvard University, National Center for the Study of Adult Learning and Literacy.

Askov, E. N., & Means, T. S. B. (1993). A state survey of computer usage in adult literacy programs. *Journal of Reading, 36*(8), 658–659.

Askov, E. N., & Van Horn, B. H. (1993). Adult educators & workplace literacy: Designing customized basic skills instruction. *Adult Basic Education, 3*(2), 115–125.

Bailey, T. R. (1997). *Integrating academic and industry skill standards*. Berkeley, CA: National Center for Research in Vocational Education, University of California. (ERIC Document Reproduction Service No. ED413472)

Bandura, A. (1977). Self-efficacy: Toward a unifying theory of behavioral change. *Psychological Review, 84*, 191–215.

Berger, J. I. (2001). Effectiveness of computers in ALBE classrooms: An analytical review of the literature. *Adult Basic Education, 11*(3), 162–183.

Berns, R. G., & Erickson, P. M. (2001). Contextual teaching and learning: Preparing students for the new economy. *The highlight zone: Research @ work* (no. 5). Columbus, Ohio: National Dissemination Center for Career and Technical Education.

Billett, S. (2002). Toward a workplace pedagogy: Guidance, participation, and engagement. *Adult Education Quarterly, 53*(1), 27–43.

Brophy, J. (1998). *Failure syndrome students*. ERIC Digest. Champaign, IL: University of Illinois, Clearinghouse on Elementary and Early Childhood Education. (ERIC Document Reproduction Service No. ED419625)

Brown, B. L. (1998). *Applying constructivism in vocational and career education* (Information Series No. 378). Columbus, Ohio: ERIC Clearinghouse on Adult, Career, and Vocational Education, Center on Education and Training for Employment, College of Education, The Ohio State University. (ERIC Document Reproduction Service No. ED428298)

Bruner, J. (1990). *Acts of meaning*. Cambridge, MA: Harvard University Press.

Burge, E. J. (1994). Learning in computer conferenced contexts: The learners' perspective. *Journal of Distance Education, 9*(1), 19–43.

Burge, L. (1988). Beyond andragogy: Some explorations for distance learning design. *Journal of Distance Education, 3*(1), 5–23.

Carnevale, A. P., Gainer, L. J., & Meltzer, A. S. (1990). *Workplace basics: The essential skills employers want*. San Francisco, CA: Jossey-Bass.

Daley, B. J., Watkins, K., Williams, S. W., Courtenay, B., Davis, M., & Dymock, D. (2001). Exploring learning in a technology-enhanced environment. *Educational Technology and Society, 4*(3) (ifets.ieee.org/periodical/vol 3 2001/daley.pdf).

D'Amico, D. (1999). Politics, policy, practice, and personal responsibility: Adult education in an era of welfare reform (NCSALL Rep. No. 10A). Boston, MA: National Center for the Study of Adult Learning and Literacy, Harvard University.

A Day in the Life... (1993). [Computer Software] Billerica, MA: Curriculum Associates.

Dimock, V. (2000). *Applying technology to restructuring and learning*. Austin, TX: Southwest Educational Development Laboratory.

Ehrenreich, B. (2001). *Nickel and dimed; on (not) getting by in America*. New York: Metropolitan Books.

Elmore, J. (1997). *Adult literacy, technology and public policy: An analysis of the southeastern United States region*. Philadelphia, PA: National Center on Adult Literacy.

Families and Work Institute. (2001). *Feeling overworked: When work becomes too much; executive summary*. New York: Author. Retrieved on December 17, 2002, from http://www.familiesandwork.org/summary/nscw.pdf

General Accounting Office. (1999). *Welfare reform: Assessing the effectiveness of various welfare-to-work approaches*. Washington, DC: Author. (ERIC Document Reproduction Service No. ED432699)

Giddens, B., & Stasz, C. (1999). Context matters: Teaching and learning skills for work. Berkeley, CA: University of California, National Center for Research in Vocational Education. (ERIC Document Reproduction Service No. ED434270)

Ginsburg, L., & Elmore, J. (1998). *Technology in the workplace: Issues of workers' skills* (Technical Report). Philadelphia, PA: Consortium for Advanced Education and Training Technologies, National Center on Adult Literacy. (ERIC Document Reproduction Service No. ED417302)

Grubb, W. N., Badway, N., Bell, D., & Castellano, M. (1999). Community colleges welfare reform: Emerging practices, enduring problems. *Community College Journal, 69*(6), 31–36.

Gunawardena, C. N., and Zittle, F. J. (1997). Social presence as a predictor of satisfaction within a computer–mediated conferencing environment. *American Journal of Distance Education, 11*(3), 8–26.

Hayes, E. (1999). Policy issues that drive the transformation of adult literacy. In L. G. Martin & J. C. Fisher (Eds.), *The welfare-to-work challenge for adult literacy educators*. New Directions for Adult and Continuing Education (No. 83, pp. 3–14). San Francisco, CA: Jossey-Bass.

Hoover-Dempsey, K., & Sandler, H. M. (1995). Parental involvement in education: Why does it make a difference? *Teachers College Record, 97*(2), 310–331.

Hoover-Dempsey, K., & Sandler, H. M. (1997). Why do parents become involved in their children's education? *Review of Educational Research, 67*(1), 3–42.

Hopey, C., Harvey-Morgan, J., & Rethemeyer, R. (1996). *Technology and adult literacy: Findings from a survey on technology use in adult literacy programs*. Philadelphia, PA: National Center on Adult Literacy.

Imel, S. (1999a). *Technological proficiency as a key to job security*. Trends and Issues Alert No. 6. Columbus, Ohio: ERIC Clearinghouse on Adult, Career, and Vocational Education.

Imel, S. (1999b). *Work force education: Beyond technical skills*. Trends and Issues Alert No. 1. Columbus, Ohio: ERIC Clearinghouse on Adult, Career, and Vocational Education.

Imel, S. (2000). *The Workforce Investment Act: Some implications for adult and vocational education*. Trends and Issues Alert No. 11. Columbus, Ohio: ERIC Clearinghouse on Adult, Career, and Vocational Education.

Imel, S., & Wagner, J. (1998). *The Internet as an instructional tool in family literacy programs*. (ERIC Document No. ED425005)

Institute for the Study of Adult Literacy. (2000). *Work-based foundation skills framework resource guide*. University Park, PA: Author.

Jobs for the Future. (1999). *Work-related learning guide for family literacy and adult education organizations*. Boston, MA: Author. Retrieved on October 7, 2002, from http://www.jff.org

Johnston, J., & Petty, L. I. (2001). *Adult education in non-classroom settings: A pilot test in Pennsylvania using Workplace Essential Skills.* Harrisburg, PA: Pennsylvania Department of Education, Bureau of Adult Basic and Literacy Education. Available at http://www.able.pde.gov/distance.htm

Kemske, F. (1998). HR 2008: A forecast based on our exclusive study. *Workforce, 77*(1), 46–60.

Kirsch, I. S., Jungeblut, A., Jenkins, L., & Kolstad, A. (1993). *Adult literacy in America: A first look at the results of the National Adult Literacy Survey.* Washington, DC: National Center for Education Statistics, U.S. Department of Education.

Knell, S. (1998). *Learn to earn: Issues raised by welfare reform for adult education, training and work.* Literacy Leader Fellowship Program Reports, *III*(3), B. Washington, DC: National Institute for Literacy.

Levesque, J. (2000). Across the great divide. *Focus on Basics, 4(C)*, 1, 3–5.

Magnuson, K., & McGroder, S. (2001). *The effect of increasing welfare mothers' education on their young children's academic problems and school readiness.* Chicago: Northwestern University and University of Chicago, Joint Center for Poverty Research.

Martin, L. G., & Fisher, J. C. (Eds.). (1999). *The welfare-to-work challenge for adult literacy educators.* New Directions for Adult and Continuing Education, No. 83. San Francisco, CA: Jossey-Bass.

McDonald, B. A., & Scollay, P. A. (2002, April). *The focus on family in adult literacy improvement.* Paper presented at the annual meeting of the American Educational Research Association, New Orleans, LA.

Millar, D. (1996). *Executive summary of the use of educational software in adult literacy programs: A comparison of integrated learning systems and stand-alone software.* Ottawa: National Literacy Secretariat.

Murnane, R. J., & Levy, F. (1996). *Teaching the new basic skills. Principles for educating children to thrive in a changing economy.* New York: Free Press.

National Association of Manufacturers. (2001). The skills gap 2001. Washington, DC: Author. Retrieved December 17, 2002, from http://www.nam.org/

National Center for Children in Poverty. (1999). *Young children in poverty: A statistical update.* New York: Author.

National Center for Family Literacy. (2000, November). *Connecting families and work: Family literacy bridges the gap.* Louisville, KY: Author.

National Center for Family Literacy. (2000, November). *Momentum.* Louisville, KY: Author.

National Center for Family Literacy. (2002). Trend analysis of primary family literacy research database. Unpublished raw data. Louisville, KY: Author.

National Even Start Association. (2002). *Even Start Family Literacy Program. Fact sheet distributed at the annual conference.* San Diego, CA: Author.

National Telecommunications and Information Administration. (1999). *Falling through the net: Defining the digital divide. A report on the telecommunications and information technology gap in America.* Washington, DC: National Telecommunications and Information Administration, U.S. Department of Commerce.

Parsons, J. E., Adler, T., & Kaczala, C. M. (1982). Socialization of achievement attitudes and beliefs: Parental influences. *Child Development, 53,* 322–329.

Peyton, T., Wheeler, M. G., & Dalton, D. (1998). *States can use family literacy programs to support welfare reform goals.* Washington, DC: National Governor's Association, Center for Best Practices. (ED 463 420).

Reder, S., & Strawn, C. (2001). Program participation and self-directed learning to improve basic skills. *Focus on Basics, 4*(D), 14–17.

Relan, A., & Gillani, B. (1997). Web-based instruction and the traditional classroom: Similarities and differences. In B. Khan (Ed.), *Web-based instruction.* Englewood Cliffs, NJ: Educational Technology Publications.

Resnick, L. B., & Wirt, J. G. (Eds.). (1996). *Linking school and work: Roles for standards and assessment.* San Francisco, CA: Jossey-Bass. (ERIC Document Reproduction Service No. ED389915)

Ripke, M. N., & Crosby, D. A. (2002). The effects of welfare reform on the educational outcomes of parents and children. *Review of Research in Education, 26,* 181–261.

Ripke, M., Huston, A., & Mistry, R. (2001). *Parents' job characteristics and children's occupational aspirations and expectations in low-income families.* Poster session presented at the biannual conference of the Society for Research in Child Development, Minneapolis, MN.

Sabatini, J., & Ginsburg, L. (1998). *Instructional technology utilization survey of mid-western adult literacy programs.* Philadelphia, PA: University of Pennsylvania, National Center on Adult Literacy. Retrieved December 17, 2002, from http://literacyonline.org/NCRTECSVY/ncrel1.html

Secretary's Commission on Achieving Necessary Skills. (1991). *What work requires of schools: A SCANS report for America 2000.* Washington, DC: U.S. Department of Labor. (ERIC Document Reproduction Service No. ED332054)

Sheared, V., McCabe, J., & Umeki, D. (2000). Adult literacy and welfare reform: Marginalization, voice, and control. *Education and Urban Society, 32*(2), 176–187.

Shields, M. K., & Behrman, R. E. (2002). Children and welfare reform: Analysis and recommendations. *Future of Children, 12*(1). Retrieved from http://www.futureofchildren.org

Snow, C., & Tabors, P. (1996, January). *Intergenerational transfer of literacy*. Paper presented at the symposium for Family Literacy: Directions in Research and Implications for Practice, Washington, DC. Retrieved September 12, 2002, from http://www.ed.gov/pubs/FamLit/integ.html

Sparks, B. (2001). Adult basic education, social policy, and educator's concerns: The influence of welfare reform on practice. *Adult Basic Education, 11*(3), 135–149.

Stein, S. (2000). *Equipped for the future content standards: What adults need to know and be able to do in the 21st century*. Washington, DC: National Institute for Literacy.

Strawn, J. (1998). *Beyond job search or basic education: Rethinking the role of skills in welfare reform*. Washington, DC: Center for Law and Social Policy.

Sum, A. (1999). *Literacy in the labor force: Results from the National Adult Literacy Survey*. Washington, DC: National Center for Education Statistics, U.S. Department of Education.

U.S. Congress, Office of Technology Assessment (1995). *Adult literacy and new technologies: Tools for a lifetime* (OTA-SET-550). Washington, DC: Government Printing Office.

U.S. Congress, Personal Responsibility and Work Opportunity Reconciliation Act. (1996). Public Law 104–193. Washington, DC.

U.S. Department of Commerce, U.S. Department of Education, U.S. Department of Labor, National Institute for Literacy, and Small Business Administration. (1999, January). *Summit on 21st century skills for 21st century jobs*. Washington, DC: U.S. Office of Personnel Management. Retreived December 17, 2002, from http://www.opm.gov/events/1999/jan12-99.htm

Van Fossen, S., & Sticht, T. (1991, July). *Teach the mother and reach the child: Results of the intergenerational literacy action research project of Wider Opportunities for Women*. Washington, DC: Wider Opportunities for Women.

Windschitl, M. (2002). Framing constructivism in practice as the negotiation of dilemmas: An analysis of the conceptual, pedagogical, cultural, and political challenges facing teachers. *Review of Educational Research, 72*(2), 131–175.

V

The Home Environment
and Home Services

This section addresses the home environment specifically. First, Kathleen Roskos and Sandra Twardosz offer a detailed review of processes and resources in the home that relate to literacy development. Next, Carol Hammer and Adele Miccio provide a description of the home literacy environment for Hispanic families. Then Donna Bryant and Barbara Wasik identify the rationale for home visiting services and discuss how to enhance them.

Many authors have discussed features of the home environment that promote literacy, especially storybook reading by parents. Several writers have provided a model that helps to frame our thinking about resources in the home, including Leichter (1984), Britto and Brooks-Gunn (2001), and Powell (chap. 28, this handbook). Throughout these writings, two important dimensions are evident—on the one hand, processes or activities, including interpersonal interactions and relationships; on the other, the physical environment. In this section, Roskos and Twardosz examine the home environment from a bioecological perspective. In so doing, they distinguish three categories of resources in the home: physical resources (time, space, and materials), social resources (people, knowledge, and emotional relationships), and symbolic resources (routines, as well as community, social, and cultural resources, such as libraries). Reviewing the research on storybook reading, they examine what has been learned about these resources. To their surprise, they discover that many have received scant attention. For example, although researchers frequently address the availability of books and other print materials in the home, few studies have attended to resources of time and space. Similarly, many studies discuss the person who reads to children (though information is reported mainly about the mother), but few consider the knowledge base that adults in the home possess, or their emotional relationships. Nor do we learn much about routines or influences from outside the home. Consequently, Roskos and Twardosz call for more attention to resources that researchers have neglected in order to obtain a more complete picture of reading to children in the home.

Hammer and Miccio discuss the home environment for nonmainstream cultures, noting that few studies have focused on book reading interactions for parents and children in these families. Even fewer address Hispanic mothers and their children. Drawing on their work with Puerto Rican families, the authors provide rich descriptions to illustrate parents' beliefs, home literacy practices, use of literacy resources in the home, and parental storybook reading styles. They identify three different reading styles: textbook, labeling, and child-centered. They also examine frequency of children's literacy activities, mother–child literacy activities, and the presence of literacy materials in the homes. They report findings for both sequential and simultaneous learners of English, seeing few differences between the two groups of children. Other findings are revealing, however. For example, children scored lower on standardized instruments in their second year of Head Start than they did in their first. The authors conclude that these children need additional support both in preschool and at home.

There are many reasons to provide services for families in their homes, especially services that help them further their own literacy goals. Bryant and Wasik identify numerous advantages of visiting families in the home, including the fact that early literacy has been strongly linked to the literacy artifacts and activities in the home environment. Thus, providing services in the home makes it possible to respond more fully to family needs and strengths. Home visiting is also family focused and flexible, and it offers the opportunity to individualize services. Being in the home lends itself to addressing how parents can support their children's literacy skills. Bryant and Wasik describe two different approaches to home visiting, looking at two different intervention programs: Parents as Teachers, in which home visiting is the main component; and Even Start, in which home visiting is used in combination with other services. They also discuss influences on program quality and outcomes, program integrity, educational credentials, training and supervision, and intensity of services, among other considerations. They conclude with a set of recommendations for improving services to families and for advancing research.

In combination, these two chapters give us a look inside the home. They help us see the need to examine the many resources that can help enhance literacy skills, going considerably beyond our current state of knowledge, and they show us how we can help families use the resources they possess to provide a richer setting for their children's learning.

16

Resources, Family Literacy, and Children Learning to Read

Kathleen A. Roskos
John Carroll University

Sandra Twardosz
University of Tennessee

Toward the end of the 20th century, the role of family in children's literacy development and acquisition took on a new identity, referred to as *family literacy*. Although home and hearth have long been linked to nurturing literacy (e.g., reading to children), the concept of family literacy widened the lens on family life to include the many "ways parents, children and extended family members use literacy at home and in the community" (Morrow, 1995, p. 7). Simultaneously, the concept exploded the possibilities for research. Considerable interest developed in understanding the family's contribution to its own reading and writing practices (adults and children) and in understanding the potential of programs designed to help families in improving their literacy education effectiveness.

Two broad streams of research ensued from this new view of family literacy. One of these focused on the literacy habits indigenous to the family, such as book reading, correspondence with relatives, children's homework, and the reading and writing embedded in everyday routines (see, for example, Schieffelin & Cochran-Smith, 1984; Snow, 1987; Taylor & Dorsey-Gaines, 1988). Another stream examined the influences of interventions on family literacy practices (Auerbach, 1995; Gadsden, 1995; Potts & Paull, 1995), including such interventions as organization-sponsored programs (e.g., Even Start Family Literacy) and health care initiatives (e.g., literacy promotion in pediatric settings) (Needlman, Klass, & Zuckerman, 2002). A strong undercurrent in much of this research involves the interface between literacy education within the family and that of formal schooling and the family's role at this juncture. Here also resides the complex issue of the family environment and its influences on children's literacy acquisition and achievement, relative to broader social contexts.

The environment of the family is densely layered, consisting of physical features and arrangements, interpersonal interactions, and emotional and motivational climates that combine and recombine synergistically into patterns of thinking and doing (Leichter, 1984). To study literacy in the family, therefore, is to study the environment of the family and its adaptive uses of literacy as a social tool. Either deliberately or through implication, environmental factors come under the investigative lens in search of the presence and use of literacy both within the family system and imposed from outside the family. The degree of *academic pressure* in school and community, for example, influences and is influenced by the literacy practices and expectations of families and community members (Serpell, 1997). Family literacy research is inherently environmental; it examines not only the physical surroundings of child and family, but also the sociocultural habits, patterns, and pressures that shape family literacy practices.

However, conceptualizing everything that occurs around and in the family as environment makes this variable too unwieldy and lacking in focus. Discerning where environment begins and ends in the dynamics of family literacy experience is very difficult. One solution to this problem is to make better use of the construct *proximal process*, which is the central feature of the bioecological model of human development (Bronfenbrenner & Ceci, 1994; Bronfenbrenner & Morris, 1998; Ceci & Hembrooke, 1995). Viewing the environment of family literacy in conjunction with this construct of proximal process may help us to specify the term *environment*, yet preserve its centrality in the constitution of family literacy practices.

Taking up this challenge, we begin our chapter with a brief description of the proximal process construct as a central idea in a bioecological view of development and change. This view helps us to distinguish *processes* in the environment (*patterns of activation*) from *resources* of the environment (*affordances*), which combine to create family literacy practices and adaptations. We then turn to family literacy research with an eye to the resources of environment that support or constrain proximal processes, and that, in turn, support children's literacy development and acquisition. In discussing resources, we focus particularly on book-reading studies, because access to books in the home and parent–child interactions around books are the hallmarks of family literacy and are the most heavily researched. We then discuss the role that resources of the home environment play in the literacy experiences and education for children. Finally, we make suggestions for new research questions about which environmental resources matter, how they matter, and under what circumstances, for family literacy.

PROXIMAL PROCESSES IN THE ENVIRONMENT AND RESOURCES OF THE ENVIRONMENT

Processes in the Environment

The central focus of the bioecological view of human development (Bronfenbrenner & Ceci, 1994; Bronfenbrenner & Morris, 1998; Ceci & Hembrooke, 1995) is process: the means by which genes and experience interact over time to produce competent human beings. Effective psychological functioning (directing and controlling one's own behavior, coping with stress, acquiring knowledge, and establishing and maintaining rewarding relationships) is influenced by genes, but not directly produced by them. Taking a bioecological view, the central question becomes: How do genetic material and experience interact in everyday environments to produce individuals with varying levels of competence? The basic answer, from a bioecological view, may be found in proximal processes (Bronfenbrenner & Ceci, 1994).

Proximal processes—those closest to the individual—are patterns of activation wherein experience interacts with the individual's genetic component. Such processes are the engines of development, or the drivers, that produce stability and change throughout the life span. To qualify as a full-blown proximal process, an interaction must have the following characteristics:

- Be stable over extended periods of time
- Occur often
- Allow for the active participation of the individual
- Become progressively more complex

Not all of an individual's experiences fit the definition of proximal processes. Losing a tooth, for example, is not a proximal process, because it does not become progressively more complex. Occasional participation in a sport or accomplishing routine tasks might not be considered proximal processes either. Parent–child interaction, playing alone or with others, reading and writing, problem solving, acquiring new skills, and caring for others in distress, on the other hand, are common examples of proximal processes.

Several other important features characterize proximal processes as interaction mechanisms. Similar to Vygotsky's (1934) zone of proximal development concept, they serve to mobilize and sustain attention, accumulate knowledge, and encourage the individual to reach slightly beyond current functioning (Bronfenbrenner & Ceci, 1994; see chapter 3 of this volume). They frequently occur in the context of emotional relationships (Bronfenbrenner & Morris, 1998). These processes are situated within immediate and more distal environments, which help determine, along with the biopsychological characteristics of the person, the effectiveness of processes in developing genetic potential. Proximal processes, therefore, are not of the environment, but rather they are in it. They serve as patterns of activity that help organize everyday experience; they are the who, what, where, when, and why of daily life (Tharp & Gallimore, 1988).

By contrast, resources are part of the environment—what is out there. They are the affordances or resources of the immediate environment (e.g., time, space, people, objects, or knowledge), which can either promote or hinder the occurrence of proximal processes (Gibson, 1979). They are what the environment offers or furnishes its inhabitants, for good or ill. Resources available in the more distal environment of the neighborhood or community simultaneously impact those in the immediate environment. In studying resources of the community, Neuman and Celano (2001), for example, documented the presence of books in stores, classrooms, and libraries; the presence and condition of signs in business areas; and the physical characteristics of public places that could invite reading in low- and middle-income communities. These researchers concluded that middle-income children were likely to be deluged with print, but that lower income children would need to persistently seek print opportunities. Thus, the environment of family literacy is that which surrounds and affords resources for those proximal processes most relevant to family literacy practices and literacy development of all family members.

To look more closely at these concepts, we take up the familiar activity of reading to children. This activity can be considered a proximal process that is related to many aspects of human competence in literate societies. It occurs within *microsystems*, one of which is the family. The family microsystem includes the family setting, which has particular physical, social, and symbolic resources that invite, permit, or inhibit engagement in proximal processes (Bronfenbrenner & Morris, 1998). If reading to children is going to drive development as a high-level proximal process, then it must fit the criteria identified earlier: be stable, occur often, allow for active child participation, and become progressively more complex. Whether or not these activities occur depends, in part, on the support or lack of support provided by the physical, social, and symbolic resources present in the family setting. Resources that come to mind include blocks of uninterrupted time with few distractions, the availability of a variety of reading materials, people in the home who can read, and comfortable places to sit. Thus, the physical, social, and symbolic resources of the family setting comprise the environment within which the proximal process of reading to children is located. The presence or absence of these resources, and the extent to which they are accessed and used, can support or hinder the occurrence of storybook reading and the extent to which an individual's genetic potential in particular areas is developed.

Similarly, children's independent exploration of books and print in the home can be viewed as a reciprocal interaction between the child and materials that can promote exploration and creativity, and that becomes progressively more complex—a proximal process, in other words. Such processes also depend upon the physical, social, and symbolic resources of the family setting.

One crucial point, from this perspective, is that high levels of proximal processes can also buffer individuals from the effects of disorganized or otherwise unfavorable environments. If reading in the home is a high-level proximal process (stable, frequent, active, challenging), it might buffer the child from the effects of a child care environment where the only exposure to books is in a large group context with little opportunity for child participation. Alternatively, a child care classroom, in which resources are mobilized to promote proximal processes related to early literacy development might mitigate the effects of a family setting with a weak literacy environment. Making the process–resource distinction, and thus demarcating the boundaries of environment along these lines, opens up new possibilities for examining family literacy influences.

Another equally critical point is that all of the participants in a proximal process are viewed as developing individuals who can be changed by high levels of the proximal process in a setting (Bronfenbrenner & Morris, 1998). From this perspective, the parent or other family member who reads to a child as part of a frequently occurring stable routine may develop greater skill as a reader, heightened sensitivity to the communication attempts of very young children, and elaborated knowledge about the genres of children's literature. In short, the proximal process itself contributes to the capacity of the overall system, enhancing the literacy potential of its physical, social, and symbolic resources.

In this section, we have distinguished family literacy processes (stable patterns of increasingly complex reciprocal interaction that help to produce development) from the resources of the immediate and more distal family environment that promote or hinder their occurrence. Separating the processes from the resources, and defining physical, social, and symbolic resources precisely allows for a more accurate assessment of what may be available to families and how these resources can be used. These environmental resources are discussed next.

Resources of Environment and Family Literacy

Our main inquiry in this chapter focuses on the role of environment in family literacy practices, and in particular, how its features help families prepare children for the schooling and society that they will inevitably encounter. We define the environment as those literacy resources at hand in the family niche, including (a) physical, (b) social, and (c) symbolic resources.

Physical Resources. Physical resources include *space, time,* and *materials.* Spatial arrangements and their furnishings provide a physical resource that can foster or inhibit engagement in reading and writing. A functional area for shared reading, for example, most likely would be located away from distractions and traffic (to the extent possible in a home), might be somewhat enclosed, would have comfortable seating and adequate lighting, would be relatively quiet, and would have a place for storage of books currently being read. There could be several such spaces in a home, offering *activity pockets* (Johnson, 1987) specially designed for reading and writing.

Time as a resource is critical for the existence of high-level proximal processes related to literacy development. Shared book reading, for example, requires frequent, relatively uninterrupted periods of time when both participants are ready to devote their attention to the book and to each other. Furthermore, it is helpful if the duration of the session can depend on the interest of the participants, rather than upon external pressure to do something else, and if preceding events do not leave participants too distracted or upset to enjoy the book and each other. Thus, a consideration of time as a resource includes the issue of when literacy events occur in the flow of everyday activities and issues related to the deliberate scheduling of those events. Blocks of time for shared reading can be spontaneously carved out of the day, as when a child brings a book to a parent and the parent discontinues another activity to read, or they can occur as part of a planned routine, such as bedtime storybook reading. However, they can occur only when both of the participants are together. In today's society, time together can be a scarce resource in families in which all adults work outside of the home and have only brief hours together. Thus, whether time is a resource for literacy development will depend on how it is managed.

Finally, physical resources include the familiar hands-on materials of literacy, such as books (quantity and quality), printed matter (newspapers, magazines, brochures), writing tools and supplies (paper, address books, lists), technologies (TV, computer) and print-bearing objects (e.g., games, toys, clothes) (see chapter 5 of this volume, for materials in the home).

Social Resources.   The human potential, or the social resources, are the persons present in the home, their willingness to share responsibilities for family tasks and activities, their knowledge, and the quality of the emotional relationships they have with one another. Shared book reading, as a typical example, can benefit younger children when more than one reader resides in the home (adult or older sibling), increasing opportunity for shared reading and also exposure to different reading styles and discussion topics. The general presence of another adult can relieve daily responsibilities for parents or older siblings, thus creating greater willingness (in the sense of less pressure) to sit down and share a book with a younger child or to help with a child's homework. Adults' funds of knowledge also tremendously influence the nature and tenor of literacy practices that occur in the home. Storybook reading, for example, is shaped by adults' knowledge of child development and children's books, and their sensitivity to children's queries. Furthermore, the overall emotional relationship of the adult and the young participant is an important variable in the value of reading to a child (Bus & van IJzendoorn, 1988; see also chapter 10 of this volume, for a discussion of adult–child relationships and literacy).

Symbolic Resources.   These resources move us to a layer of environment that Wartofsky (1979) terms *secondary artifacts*, or representations of real objects, and to ways of using them (cited in Cole, 1996). We describe these as *literacy routines* that may occur in the home setting, such as the bedtime story routine or the grocery-shopping routine. Taken as a whole, routines preserve and transmit patterns of action and beliefs about literacy. As resources of the environment, they are the objectifications of family needs and intentions already invested with literacy content, that is, concepts, attitudes, feelings, and beliefs about literacy (Wartofsky, 1973). Said another way, routines are the symbolic planks of the family's literacy practices— what literacy means or signifies for its members. Some households may contain more literacy routines than others, or more elaborated routines than others, and may thus imbue reading and writing with greater symbolic meaning and significance.

We describe physical, social, and symbolic resources separately, so that their possible contributions to proximal processes do not remain hidden. Ultimately, all three forms of resources work together and influence one another, as well as the process. In turn, the continued occurrence and development of the process may influence the resources of the family environment. For example, the presence of plentiful physical resources, in the form of quality children's books and a comfortable, well-lit, protected area, may prompt children to approach adults with requests to read and may motivate a parent to make periods of uninterrupted time available, by asking another family member to take responsibility for competing tasks. Once parent and child are involved in routine occurrences of shared reading, and books are read over and over again, then more books may be desired to carry on the routine. Interest in an increasing variety and complexity of reading material may prompt visits to libraries and bookstores, the perusal of book catalogues, and requests for books as gifts. However, obtaining more reading material depends on resources in the more distal environment, such as accessible libraries and bookstores, and relatives or other adults able to purchase gifts. If reading material continues to be available, increasing parental and child knowledge about books and commitment to literacy routines may set the stage for further investigation into children's literature, integration of computer-based activities into shared reading episodes, and the search for information to answer questions that have arisen as books are shared. Family members' funds of knowledge are thus increased and can be used during future shared reading episodes. Finally, the literacy-related physical resources of the home, with which we began this example, are themselves a product of the parents' knowledge, routines remembered from childhood or visible in the homes of friends, and literacy demands of the work setting.

Family members may not continue to invest resources in literacy activities, such as reading to children, unless the interaction itself is enjoyable and seems to be promoting the child's education. The quality of the emotional relationship between child and adult, what the adult and eventually the child know about the book-sharing process, and the availability of books that continue to be challenging, help make this routine a high-level proximal process. In turn, the fact that it is a high-level process can influence the family to continue making resources, such as time, available for it.

ANALYSIS OF RESOURCES IN STUDIES OF FAMILY BOOK READING

Using the descriptions of physical, social, and symbolic resources just provided, we applied the resource lens to the treatment of the family environment in a collection of storybook-reading studies. Several criteria guided our selection of studies for this analysis. First, the articles needed to be reports of research that involved the systematic collection and analysis of data, using quantitative and/or qualitative methodologies in ways that met the criteria of scientific evidence. Second, the studies needed to focus on reading to children as it occurred in real time and space, rather than on retrospective reports of this activity. Resources of the environment, we reasoned, would more likely be described when the process of book reading was immediately visible to investigators. Studies that occurred partly or entirely in the laboratory were considered for inclusion if there was a clear connection to reading within a family context. Additionally, studies were considered that focused only on reading to children, as well as those that focused more broadly on literacy within the family, which could include reading to children. Third, the studies needed to be strong representatives of the field of family literacy as a topic of inquiry, a concept of literacy acquisition and education, and a research agenda for understanding the role of families in children's literacy development.

With these criteria in mind, we assembled a collection of 12 studies, spanning the 18-year period from 1980 to 1998 (see Table 16.1.) The selection process involved searching peer-reviewed journals (e.g., *Reading Research Quarterly);* reviewing the content and reference lists of books and review chapters on family literacy, family literacy programs, early literacy development, and storybook reading; examining the cumulative work of specific researchers who have conducted research programs on reading to children; and searching personal collections of articles for representative examples. Articles from conference proceedings were excluded, because page constraints may have caused authors to omit information on resources of the environment; conference presentations and unpublished work also were not considered for inclusion. Although we did not conduct an exhaustive search of the literature, we did continue the search until it became abundantly clear that additional effort was not yielding studies that were different in purpose, scope, or methodology from those already found.[1]

---

[1]The following additional journals were consulted during the process of assembling the 12 studies that were included in the analysis: *Developmental Psychology, Discourse Processes, Early Childhood Research Quarterly, Early Education and Development, Journal of Genetic Psychology, Journal of Literacy Research, Journal of Research in Childhood Education, New Directions for Child and Adolescent Development.*

TABLE 16.1
Description of Book-Reading and Family Literacy Studies

Study	Description
Ninio (1980)	Forty mother-infant dyads (20 high socioeconomic status, European origin; 20 low socioeconomic status, Asian and North African origin) were observed once at home in a book-reading context. The relationship between mothers' teaching strategies and infants vocabulary acquisition was the focus. Readings were recorded by audiotape and written notes.
Heath & Thomas (1984)	One year ethnographic case study/intervention with a young, unemployed high school dropout and her two children involved the introduction of a literacy artifact (children's books) and a literacy event (reading to her 2-year-old). Readings were audiotaped by the mother.
Teale (1986)	Naturalistic longitudinal study (3–18 months duration) of the home literacy experiences of 24 low-income preschool children (Anglo, Black, Mexican) focused on the physical literacy environment (written language) and the social literacy environment (what was done with the written language). Field notes, audiotaping, and interviews were used.
Bus & van IJzendoorn (1988)	Cross-sectional study with 45 children (18–66 months) and their mothers was conducted during one visit to a laboratory playroom, using situations common in homes. The purpose was to describe relations in motherchild interactions as they relate to written language, attachment security, and performance on emergent literacy measures.
Yaden, Smolkin, & Conlon (1989)	Longitudinal studies (1 and 2 years duration) of preschoolers' questions during book-reading were conducted in the homes of nine children and their parents. Readings were audiotaped.
Pellegrini, Perlmutter, Galda, & Brody (1990)	Experimental study was conducted during 10 home visits with 13 low-income families. Specific texts (narrative and expository, familiar and traditional) were provided by researchers to determine if teaching strategies would vary by text and would prompt child participation. Reading sessions were videotaped.
Phillips & McNaughton (1990)	Two descriptive studies were conducted of 10 middle-class families with established reading routines. Parents kept records of reading to children for 1 month; investigators then supplied books, and readings were audiotaped for 4–6 weeks. Interactions were analyzed.
Dickinson, De Temple, Hirschler & Smith (1992)	Descriptive study of reading to preschool children at home and at school was conducted with 25 mothers and children from low-income families, to examine models of the relationship between the two settings. Audiotaping and interviews occurred during two home visits when children were 3 and 4 years old.
Arnold, Lonigan, Whitehurst, & Epstein (1994)	Experimental intervention study involved 64 children and mothers (middle and upper SES) divided into videotape, direct training, and control groups. Dialogic reading training occurred in the laboratory with audiotaping of mothers reading to children at home. Duration of study was 5 weeks.
Taylor (1995)	Descriptive study of family literacy was conducted with 12 families, each with a 6-year-old child. There were four groups composed of urban/rural and more/less educated mothers. Journals were kept by parents for the week between two interviews, and extensive lists of literacy materials and family activities were compiled.
Purcell-Gates (1996)	Descriptive study of 20 low-income families' uses of print, and its relationship with the emergent literacy knowledge of the children, was conducted for 1 year. Field notes from home observations and a variety of emergent literacy assessments were used.
Leseman & de Jong (1998)	Longitudinal study of 89 children and families from three ethnic groups involved three observations of book reading over 3 years. Numerous measures of literacy opportunity, instruction, cooperation, and emotional quality were used in an effort to predict language/literacy development.

The final 12 studies selected for the collection offer a robust sample of investigations on book reading to children in families. The collection features a variety of researchers, disciplines, perspectives, methodologies, journals, and edited books; well-articulated methodologies and evidence; and classic studies cited repeatedly in the field. Not many studies on reading to children met the criteria described. We had expected to be inundated with descriptions of how the reading process operates within various types of families. We had also expected to find many more studies in which the effectiveness of interventions to enhance reading to children was evaluated with observational data collected within the home and by self-report. But our

TABLE 16.2
Definitions of Physical, Social, and Symbolic Resources

Resource	Definition
Physical	
Space	Places in the home where reading to children occurs; furnishings, lighting, seating, storage for books and other print materials; privacy yet visibility of the space; location relative to noisy/distracting activities, such as TV, computer, music, games, visitors, phone, heavily trafficked areas; location relative to literacy-enhancing activities/materials, such as computer, drawing/writing supplies; crowding within the space.
Time	Amount of time family members are together in the home; use or organization of time; amount of uninterrupted leisure time parent and child share; presence or lack of a predictable schedule; placement of reading to children in the sequence of household events; events preceding the reading that might influence the quality of the interaction.
Materials	Quantity, quality, and variety of print materials that are or could be used in reading to children; the condition, genres, developmental appropriateness, and physical characteristics of those materials; accessibility of print materials to children; presence of equipment or materials that could enrich or hinder reading to children, such as TVs, computers, and software, drawing/writing materials, information about children's literature; print materials relevant for household functions or family members' employment.
Social	
People	Number and types of people who reside in the home or who are frequent visitors and potential readers for children; additional person(s) present during shared reading, who could enrich the conversation; ways in which people share household responsibilities, so that someone can read to children; presence of people who may hinder the reading process.
Knowledge	What people in the family know that can contribute to the reading interaction, including literacy level, languages spoken in the home, skill at managing household responsibilities, so that there is time to read; knowledge about children's literature, child development, community resources for obtaining books, book-related media and events; vocabulary and background knowledge.
Emotional Relationships	Affective quality of the interaction during reading sessions; information about the parent–child relationship in general; reference to enjoyment, pleasure, and/or positive or negative emotional expression or relationships with books.
Symbolic	
Routines	Reading to children occurs as a regular, planned activity, rather than occasionally, and has distinctive features; family members can describe it, or know why they are doing it, or would mention it to describe what their family is like.
Community, society, culture	Outside influences on the process of reading to children within the family: libraries, schools, type of parental employment, churches, adult education programs, community and cultural traditions.

search proved otherwise, indicating that there are far fewer scientifically based book-reading studies in family settings than popularly thought.

We then conducted an analysis of these studies to examine their treatment of resources as facilitators or inhibitors of reading to children in the family setting. We applied a two-part analytic procedure that consisted of identifying and coding the resources described in each research report.

Drawing on theory and research (Evans, Maxwell & Hart, 1999; Johnson, 1987; Risley, 1977; Roskos & Neuman, 2001; Twardosz, 1984; Wachs, 1989), we first developed formal definitions of physical, social, and symbolic resources. As indicated in Table 16.2, space, time, and materials are included in the major category of physical resources. The category of social resources includes people, their knowledge, and emotional relationships. Symbolic resources are subdivided into routines within the family and the outside influences of community, society, and culture. Each of these subcategories was defined. For example, the definition of the physical resource of space includes details such as its location and how it is furnished, as well as its relationship to other spaces, noise, traffic, and potential literacy resources.

To test the definitions, we applied them to two articles and made adjustments before agreeing to their final form. Through joint discussion and negotiation, we also established a coding system (rubric) for assessing the quality of information about resources supplied in a research report (see Table 16.3). We then each used these analytic tools to inventory the resources described in each of the 12 studies and to rate the quality of the information according to the rubric. Information about the resources took a variety of forms within the studies, ranging from being the focus of the study to receiving a brief mention with little development, to not being mentioned at all. For example, Bus and van IJzendoorn (1988) investigated the contribution of attachment between mother and child to aspects of the reading process, so that, in this case, the social resource itself (the emotional relationship) was the focus of the study. In contrast, Dickinson, De Temple, Hirschler, and Smith (1992) mentioned in their discussion that the children enjoyed books with their mothers, thus deepening their bonds with mothers and books. However, this social resource was not a focus of their study and was not measured in any way. The wide range in the type of information provided about each resource was captured by assigning a number from 0 to 3 to code the treatment of each resource in each study, as described in Table 16.3.

TABLE 16.3
Coding System for Information Provided About Resources

Code	Explanation
0	The resource was not mentioned.
1	The resource was mentioned briefly in some part of the article. It could be a characteristic of the participants, a feature of the setting, or a casual observation the authors made during the study and mentioned in the results or discussion. It may have been measured, but was clearly a peripheral part of the study, and its relationship to the process of reading to children was not discussed.
2	More information was provided about the resource than is described in code 1, but the resource was clearly not an integral part of the study. There was some discussion about how the resource supported or hindered the process of reading to children.
3	The investigation of the resource was an integral part of the study. It could be a dependent or independent variable in an experimental study, or could be described and discussed extensively in a descriptive or ethnographic study. Its relationship to the process of reading to children was clear.

TABLE 16.4
Analysis of Resources in the Collection of Studies

	Resources							
	Physical			Social			Symbolic	
Study	Space	Time	Materials	People	Knowledge	Emotional Relationships	Routines	Community Society Culture
Ninio (1980)	0	0	0	0	1	0	0	1
Heath & Thomas (1984)	2	2	2	2	1	0	1	0
Teale (1986)	0	0	3	3	3	0	1	3
Bus & van IJzendoorn (1988)	0	0	0	0	3	3	0	0
Yaden et al. (1989)	0	1	2	1	1	0	1	1
Pellegrini et al. (1990)	0	0	3	0	1	0	0	0
Phillips & McNaughton (1990)	0	3	3	1	1	0	1	1
Dickinson et al. (1992)	0	1	3	1	1	1	1	1
Arnold et al. (1994)	0	0	1	1	1	0	1	0
Taylor (1995)	0	1	3	1	1	0	1	1
Purcell-Gates (1996)	0	0	3	3	1	0	0	3
Leseman & de Jong (1998)	0	0	0	0	2	3	1	1

Note: Scores range from 0 (*no mention of resource*) to 3 (*resource is integral part of study*).

RESULTS OF THE ANALYSIS

Results from our ad hoc analysis are visually displayed in Table 16.4. In the following section, we briefly summarize these results to foreground the evidence and role of environmental resources in the examination of book reading within the family setting.

Physical Resources

Space. Clearly, among the research studies, space is the most neglected resource variable, with only two of the studies including any information at all. Heath and Thomas (1984) described the distraction and noise from TV, radio, and people passing through, which characterized the living room where the young mother sometimes read to her child. Purcell-Gates (1996) also briefly mentioned the background noise from TV that occurred in a home where reading to children never occurred. These characteristics of the space are presented as hindrances or the absence of resources that would support reading to children. Clearly, the vast majority of the researchers did not locate the process of reading to children, even in the most basic sense of describing the room and its furnishings, whether reading took place in a variety of spaces or one particular space, or if books and other print materials were conveniently arranged within an area or were scattered around the house. This information was missing regardless of whether researchers were investigating established family routines or brought the books with them and set up a reading situation for the study.

Time.   Time as a resource was mentioned in about half of the studies, but most instances consisted only of a brief reference to the time at which reading occurred (e.g., bedtime). Phillips and McNaughton (1990) specifically asked parents to note the time when recording details of all storybook-reading events. Again, Heath and Thomas (1984) provided more in-depth information, briefly discussing the fact that the child and his mother had little time alone together, given her household responsibilities and the number of people living in the home. None of the researchers provided information about whether families had predictable schedules and how they managed numerous family responsibilities to have time to read to their children.

Materials.   In contrast to the resources of space and time, books and other print materials received a great deal of attention. Only 25% of the studies did not mention materials in the home, and in those the researchers provided their own books (Bus & van IJzendoorn, 1988; Leseman & de Jong, 1998; Ninio, 1980). The types of books and other print materials typically formed an integral part of the studies, and elaborate classification systems were developed to describe them. Pellegrini et al. (1990) focused on the effect of genre and format of reading materials on teaching interactions. Purcell-Gates (1996) developed a system for coding the text level (size of linguistic unit and features associated with written as compared with oral language) of every material read or written within observed literacy events. Some types of information are not provided about materials, however, such as those easily accessible to young children and whether the children's books contain quality literature and are undamaged. Also, only Taylor (1995) described related materials that could support or hinder reading to children, such as TV and computer software (see chapter 5 of this volume for additional discussion on storybook reading in the home and the use of resources).

Social Resources

People.   The description of persons (e.g., mothers, fathers, grandparents, siblings, relatives, or friends) regularly in the environment as potential readers and supporters of book reading with young children shows an interesting breakdown in this collection of studies. Aside from the mother, a quarter of the studies make no mention of other persons in the home environment who might engage in book reading with young children. Rather, the focus is on the mother–child dyad as the primary source of book-reading experience. Half of the studies do, however, mention the presence of others who occasionally may contribute to book reading in the home. Yaden et al. (1989), for example, report that, along with mothers, several fathers and a grandmother joined in book-reading episodes. Likewise, Dickinson et al. (1992) and Phillips and McNaughton (1990) state that other readers were available to children. Taylor (1995) mentions that a coping strategy for mothers with lower levels of education was to use siblings as surrogate parents for reading activities. Another fourth of the studies do provide more detail about the number and types of people available in the environment as potential readers. The Purcell-Gates (1996) study is especially descriptive, creating family trees that show the range of participants in literacy events. Similarly, Teale (1986) coded participant structures for each literacy event, but not with enough specificity to determine the possible readers per household. In addition to the lack of information on potential or actual readers, no information was provided about the division of responsibilities among family members.

Knowledge.   All of the authors remark, at some level, that family members' knowledge can contribute to the reading interaction. Although the majority of studies refer to basic facts, such as the educational level of parents, extent of adults' reading in the household, home language, socioeconomic status, job status, and literacy level of children, typically, only the mother's educational level is cited. Going beyond reference to one or two facts, Teale (1986), Bus and van IJzendoorn (1988), and Leseman and de Jong (1998) provide more detail that speaks to the knowledge resource. Teale (1986) includes the literacy ability of people around, and interacting with the focal child in the analysis. Bus and van IJzendoorn (1988) measure the child's emergent literacy knowledge and make the point that children with more emergent literacy competence make greater demands on the mother's knowledge and also acquire more knowledge in instructional interactions with the mother. Taking another approach, Leseman and de Jong (1998) use multiple measures to provide an indicator of the knowledge available for use in reading interactions. Omitted across all studies is any reference to people's knowledge about child development and children's literature.

Emotional Relationships.   Emotion and emotional relationships are rarely described as resources in this set of studies. Only 2 of the 12 studies discuss affective qualities and their influences in any depth. Dickinson et al. (1992) note that a beneficial factor of the home reading experiences was children's enjoying books with their mothers, thus deepening their relationships with their mothers and with books, but this reference is more of a descriptive aside. On the other hand, for Bus and van IJzendoorn (1988), the emotional relationship is a focal point of their research, and they describe in considerable detail how emotion serves as an interpersonal resource in reading interactions between mother and child. The emotional atmosphere surrounding the interaction of securely attached dyads is more robust and positive, allowing mothers to demand more from their young ones, yet maintain a motivating and pleasurable book-reading experience. Leseman and de Jong (1998) also observed that the more friction in parent–child book-reading interactions, the lower the reading comprehension scores (see chapter 10 of this volume for additional information on relationships between parents and children).

Symbolic Resources

Routines.   Beyond the mere presence or absence of a book-reading routine in the home, we do not learn much about the distinctive features of this routine as a regular, planned activity of family life from this collection of studies. With the exception of Taylor (1995), most authors cite whether the routine is established or not, but they do not inventory its features (e.g., when, how often, where, and with whom) nor describe its investments (e.g., time, arrangements, materials, priority, and value). Teale (1986), for example, points out that storybook reading was not a regular routine in many of the low-income homes of the preschoolers he studied. Although 3 of 22 households did include a storybook-reading routine, Teale (1986) does not provide a description. By contrast, tracing the literary and oral reading traditions of Iceland, going back several centuries, Taylor (1995) embellishes on the book-reading routine, revealing the details of its significance for Icelandic families in their daily life.

Community, Society, Culture.   Similar to literacy routines, most authors give brief mention to outside influences on family literacy practices. Several refer to library use and bookstore shopping, but without much discussion as to the impact of these experiences on family literacy interactions. School involvement is cited as a positive influence for family literacy and book reading. Workplace literacy, however, is rarely mentioned as having any spillover into family life. Two authors from the group do devote considerable attention to resources outside the family setting as variables integral to their studies. Teale (1986) identifies school, work, religious, and information network domains as influencing home literacy experiences of low-income preschool children. Along these same lines, Purcell-Gates (1996) describes two domains of literacy events: home and school. Although the domain of work did not contribute to home literacy, when children began school parents increased their involvement in literacy interactions with their children.

Returning to Table 16.4 and reviewing the summary information for the eight categories, that equivalent amounts of information related to storybook reading are not available for each type of family resource is clear. Spatial characteristics, one of the most immediate and concrete features of a home, are mentioned in only 1 of the 12 studies. Time is typically treated only in the most cursory manner, as are routines and outside influences. Emotional relationships are either a central feature of a study or not addressed. More information is available about people and their knowledge, but the richest information exists for print materials.

DISCUSSION

Our analytic inventory of resources in these 12 studies took us where we did not expect to go and led us to several realizations. At the start of our inquiry, we applied a bioecological lens to the family literacy environment, separating proximal processes within the home from resources at hand. We then set out to examine reading to children as a proximal process surrounded by resources of the family—physical, social, and symbolic—that may support or constrain this pattern of activity. From a bioecological perspective, if reading to children is truly a proximal process, that is, a stable interaction that occurs often, allows for active participation, and becomes increasingly more complex, then this activity has the power to combine with genetic potential in ways that build the capacity of the child (and adult) to learn literacy.

We gathered together a collection of family literacy studies with two goals in mind: first, to discover the role resources play in the family storybook-reading process and second, to generate new research questions about what resources matter most and under what conditions specific resources are most crucial in facilitating this process. Then the unexpected findings emerged. We found that we do not have sufficient information about family book reading to address these two goals.

Very needed is a fuller "descriptive" picture of book reading to children as a proximal process naturally occurring within real family settings. Prevailing research methods tend to generate fragmentary knowledge about the extent to which this process actually happens in real life. For example, in some studies, reading to children is observed once or only occasionally across a lengthy period of time. In others, investigators bring the books and reading routine with them into homes where it may not typically occur, or studies are done partially or entirely in a laboratory. From these slices, we cannot always confirm that reading to children was actually entrenched as a proximal process (and thus was powerful enough to impact literacy development) within the family settings of the studies' participants, even though the findings generated by such studies may be singularly illuminating. Studies with repeated, systematic observations over time of intact book reading to children are necessary. Such studies can capture the activation of the process, as well as the increasing complexity that might occur if reading to children is frequent and allows for active participation.

Also needed is information involving the role of family resources in helping or hindering book reading within the home environment. We simply do not have a good descriptive inventory of these resources, even when looking at the broad agenda of studies. Understandably, when research is conducted in the laboratory or when investigators provision the study with routines and books themselves, we do not readily acquire knowledge about the immediate resources of the family environment. Yet, even observational studies conducted in the home setting rarely describe how book reading fits into family life or how resources, such as time together in the home, willingness of family members to share household responsibilities, or places that are conducive to shared book reading, contribute to the existence of this practice or of other family literacy practices. The sole exception is the category of print materials, a physical resource that has received considerable attention while the resources of time and space have been virtually neglected.

Resource information, however, is critical, because the argument could be made that book reading varies across families more often because of resource coordination within the family environment than because of individual preferences, styles, and dispositions of family members (Diamond, 1999). The evolution of book reading as a family literacy practice, in other words, may have as much to do with the family's capacity to make use of its resources as with its access to them. That environmental resources influence human behavior is an old idea, but one not easily explained. Analysis of proximate resources (of the environment) that give rise to book-reading processes (in the environment) requires observations related to the orchestration of multiple resources (physical, social, symbolic), if inquiry is to fully explain the role of environment in constituting family literacy practices such as book reading. Resources, in sum, and how they are used in families, demand fuller attention if we are to accurately determine the family environment effects on book reading and subsequently on children learning to read (Cohen, Raudenbush, & Ball, 2000; Diamond, 1999). Variations in resource allocation and a family's capacity to maximize its resources may have more to do with the emergence and efficacy of book-reading patterns than is traditionally thought.

Although our review did not yield much information about either book reading as a proximal process or the role of family resources in this process, it did provide information that indicates directions for future research. We now discuss these briefly in relation to descriptive research on literacy within the family unit and the development and evaluation of interventions that focus specifically on reading to children as a new or adapted practice for families.

As mentioned previously, descriptive studies that use repeated measures of family literacy practices over time, such as that of Purcell-Gates (1996), can provide a more complete picture of reading to children as a proximal process within families. However, describing the process more thoroughly is not enough. We need to capture the scope and variety of resources that surround these events, as depicted in Table 16.2. These resources can support, hinder, or prevent the process, depending on their abundance and how they are used. The same resource, such as the presence of a TV or of multiple persons in a household, can work for or against reading to children. Furthermore, as the studies by Heath and Thomas (1984) and Bus and van IJzendoorn (1988) indicate, we cannot take for granted such basic resources as enough time and a positive emotional relationship between parent and child as a backdrop for shared reading. Information about the plethora of family resources in the immediate environment should be recorded, thus going beyond the reading event and basic descriptive information. Potentially critical pieces of information that will assist us in determining the range of family conditions that allow book reading to exist, and even to flourish, include the following: (a) whether or not there is space with seating and accessible books; (b) the occurrence of interruptions from phone calls or requests from other family members; (c) the emotional tone of interactions; (d) how long the reading continues, if it appears to be rushed, and why it ends; and (e) roles of other family members in protecting the reading routine from interruption.

To obtain descriptive data, skilled interviewing of family members may be required for informing observation. Family members can be queried about the amount of time they are at home together; how predictable the family schedule is; whether or not a parent is at home at the children's bedtime; the demands that extracurricular activities, such as sports, place on the family; the value that is placed on reading to children; and the planning that keeps a supply of books in the home. Interviewing families that lack shared reading would be just as important as interviewing families in which it is a frequent occurrence. Even in studies designed only to document aspects of the shared reading process, such as types of parent–child interaction or use of specific language forms, it should be possible for investigators to incorporate basic information about family resources into descriptions of the participants and settings. Rather than simply stating that reading to children was a regular family routine, investigators could provide a richer description that included attention to physical, social, and symbolic resources. In other words, we can learn from parents in a wide variety of circumstances about the resources they have and how they manage them so that reading to children is supported or not.

One possible outcome of an agenda of descriptive research on family resources is that a threshold on resources may be identified. Below this threshold, one would not expect family storybook reading to exist, and efforts to inform and persuade parents to begin this routine would be fruitless. Instead, efforts might need to focus on basic issues of family stability and survival. For families who fall above the resource threshold, but who do not have a well-developed storybook-reading routine in place, the implications are different. These parents may benefit from discussion and support geared to establishing and maintaining the routine of reading to their children within their particular family circumstances. Thus, in addition to addressing the topic of how to read to children (a strong focus of family literacy programs [e.g., Handel, 1999]), educators would provide or solicit specific information about physical, social, and symbolic resources and how these could be used to begin and maintain a storybook-reading or other family literacy routine. Information about how to choose a time for reading, arrange the space and display books, limit TV viewing, or recruit family members as readers may need to be communicated in a manner that builds on the family's current knowledge and resources. The effects of including knowledge and assistance in the use of family resources on the maintenance of a routine of storybook reading could then be evaluated experimentally.

In closing this chapter, we observe that our examination of a familiar activity—family storybook reading—from a bioecological perspective expanded our view well beyond what occurs during the interaction or process itself to the resources of the family environment that surround it and contribute to its very existence. Doing so also forced us to conclude that we do not know much about the ways in which physical, social, and symbolic resources support or hinder storybook reading. This realization, in turn, led to ideas for both descriptive and intervention research which go beyond the interaction and teaching that occur during storybook reading to focus on the accessibility and management of family resources. Thus, although difficult to pull apart at the explanatory roots, the conceptual separation of literacy processes from literacy resources as a way of bringing focus to the unwieldy variable of environment may ultimately result in more comprehensive approaches to issues in family literacy.

REFERENCES

Included in the collection of studies reviewed.

Arnold, D. H., Lonigan, C. J., Whitehurst, G. J., & Epstein, J. N. (1994). Accelerating language development through picture book reading: Replication and extension to a videotape training format. *Journal of Educational Psychology, 86*, 235–243.

Auerbach, E. R. (1995). Which way for family literacy: Intervention or empowerment. In L. M. Morrow (Ed.), *Family literacy: Connections in schools and communities* (pp. 11–28). Newark, DE: International Reading Association.

Bronfenbrenner, U., & Ceci, S. J. (1994). Nature–nurture reconceptualized in developmental perspective: A bioecological model. *Psychological Review, 101*, 568–586.

Bronfenbrenner, U., & Morris, P. A. (1998). The ecology of developmental processes. In W. Damon & R. M. Lerner (Eds.), *Handbook of child psychology,* Vol. 1 (5th ed.), *Theoretical models of human development* (pp. 993–1028). New York: Wiley.

Bus, A. G., & van IJzendoorn, M. H. (1988). Mother–child interactions, attachment, and emergent literacy: A cross-sectional study. *Child Development, 59*, 1262–1272.

Ceci, S. J., & Hembrooke, H. A. (1995). A bioecological model of intellectual development. In P. Moen, G. H.

Elder, Jr., & K. Luscher (Eds.), *Examining lives in context: Perspectives on the ecology of human development* (pp. 303–345). Washington, DC: American Psychological Association.

Cohen, D. K., Radenbausch, S. W., & Ball, D. L. (2002). *Resources, instruction and research.* In F. Mosteller & R. Boruch (Eds.). *Evidence matters: Randomized trials in education research* (pp. 80–119). Washington D.C.: Brookings Institution Press.

Cole, M. (1996). *Cultural psychology: a once and future discipline.* Cambridge, M.A.: The Belknap Press of Harvard University Press.

Diamond, J. (1999). *Guns, germs and steel: The fates of human societies.* New York: Norton.

Dickinson, D. K., De Temple, J. M., Hirschler, J. A., & Smith, M. W. (1992). Book reading with preschoolers: Coconstruction of text at home and at school. *Early Childhood Research Quarterly, 7,* 323–346.

Evans, G. W., Maxwell, L. E., & Hart, B. (1999). Parental language and verbal responsiveness to children in crowded homes. *Developmental Psychology, 35,* 1020–1023.

Gadsden, V. L. (1995). Representations of literacy: Parents' images in two cultural communities. In L. M. Morrow (Ed.), *Family literacy: Connections in schools and communities* (pp. 287–304). Newark, DE: International Reading Association.

Gibson, J. J. (1979). *The ecological approach to visual perception.* Boston: Houghton Mifflin.

Handel, R. D. (1999). *Building family literacy in an urban community.* New York: Teachers College Press.

Heath, S. B., & Thomas, C. (1984). The achievement of preschool literacy for mother and child. In H. Goelman, A. Oberg, & F. Smith (Eds.), *Awakening to literacy* (pp. 51–72). Portsmouth, NH: Heinemann.

Johnson, L. C. (1987). The developmental implications of home environments. In C. S. Weinstein & T. G. David (Eds.), *Spaces for children: The built environment and child development* (pp. 139–157). New York: Plenum.

Leichter, H. (1984). Families as environments for literacy. In H. Goelman, A. Oberg, & F. Smith (Eds.), *Awakening to literacy* (pp. 38–50). Portsmouth, NH: Heinemann.

Leseman, P. P. M., & de Jong, P. F. (1998). Home literacy: Opportunity, instruction, cooperation and social-emotional quality predicting early reading achievement. *Reading Research Quarterly, 33,* 294–318.

Morrow, L. M. (Ed.) (1995). *Family literacy: Connections in schools and communities.* Newark, DE: International Reading Association.

Needlman, R., Klass, P., & Zuckerman, B. (2002, January). Reach out and get your patients to read. *Contemporary Pediatrics, 19*(1), 51–69.

Neuman, S. B., & Celano, D. (2001). Access to print in low-income and middle-income communities. *Reading Research Quarterly, 36,* 8–26.

Ninio, A. (1980). Picture-book reading in mother–infant dyads belonging to two subgroups in Israel. *Child Development, 51,* 587–590.

Pellegrini, A. D., Perlmutter, J. C., Galda, L., & Brody, G. H. (1990). Joint reading between Black Head Start children and their mothers. *Child Development, 61,* 443–453.

Phillips, G., & McNaughton, S. (1990). The practice of storybook reading to preschool children in mainstream New Zealand families. *Reading Research Quarterly, 25,* 196–212.

Potts, M. W., & Paull, S. (1995). A comprehensive approach to family-focused services. In L. M. Morrow (Ed.), *Family literacy: Connections in schools and communities* (pp. 167–183). Newark DE: International Reading Association.

Purcell-Gates, V. (1996). Stories, coupons, and the *TV Guide*: Relationships between home literacy experiences and emergent literacy knowledge. *Reading Research Quarterly, 31,* 406–428.

Risley, T. R. (1977). The ecology of applied behavior analysis. In A. Rogers-Warren & S. F. Warren (Eds.), *Ecological perspectives in behavior analysis* (pp. 149–163). Baltimore, MD: University Park.

Roskos, K., & Neuman, S. B. (2001). Environment and its influences for early literacy teaching and learning. In S. B. Neuman & D. K. Dickinson (Eds.), *Handbook of early literacy research* (pp. 281–292). New York: Guilford.

Schieffelin, B., & Cochran-Smith, M. (1984). Learning to read culturally: Literacy before schooling. In H. Goelman, A. Oberg, & F. Smith (Eds.), *Awakening to literacy* (pp. 3–23). Portsmouth, NH: Heinemann.

Serpell, R. (1997). Critical issues: Literacy connections between school and home: How should we evaluate them? *Journal of Literacy Research, 29*(4), 587–616.

Snow, C. E. (1987). Factors influencing vocabulary and reading achievement in low income children. In R. Apple (Ed.), *Toegepaste Taalwetenschap in Artikekn,* Special 2 (pp. 122–148), Amsterdam: ANELA.

Taylor, D., & Dorsey-Gaines, C. (1988). *Growing up literate: Learning from inner-city families.* Portsmouth, NH: Heinemann.

Taylor, R. L. (1995). Functional uses of reading and shared literacy activities in Icelandic homes: A monograph in family literacy. *Reading Research Quarterly, 30,* 194–219.

Teale, W. H. (1986). Home background and young children's literacy development. In W. H. Teale & E. Sulzby (Eds.), *Emergent literacy: Writing and reading* (pp. 173–206). Norwood, NJ: Ablex.

Tharp, R., & Gallimore, R. (1988). *Rousing minds to life.* Cambridge, England: Cambridge University Press.

Twardosz, S. (1984). Environmental organization: The physical, social, and programmatic context of behavior. In M. Hersen, R. M. Eisler, & P. M. Miller (Eds.), *Progress in behavior modification,* Vol. 18 (pp. 123–161). Orlando, FL: Academic Press.

Vygotsky, L. (1934). Thought and language, Translated by Alex Kozulin (1986). Cambridge, MA: MIT.

Vygotsky, L. (1978). *Mind in society: The development of higher mental processes.* M. Cole, V. John-Steiner, S. Scribner, & E. Souberman (Eds. & Trans.). Cambridge, MA: Harvard University Press. (Original work published 1934).

Wachs, T. D. (1989). The nature of the physical microenvironment: An expanded classification system. *Merrill-Palmer Quarterly, 35,* 399–419.

Wartofsky, M. (1979). *Models: Representations and the scientific understanding.* Dordrecht, Holland: D. Reidel.

Yaden, D. B., Jr., Smolkin, L. B., & Conlon, A. (1989). Preschoolers' questions about pictures, print conventions, and story text during reading aloud at home. *Reading Research Quarterly, 24,* 188–214.

17

Home Literacy Experiences
of Latino Families

Carol Scheffner Hammer
and Adele W. Miccio
The Pennsylvania State University

Many factors affect children's ability to learn to read and write. Because literacy development is influenced by the attitudes of the family, the school, the community, and the society at large, one must understand the sociocultural context in which literacy development takes place. Although many characteristics of Latino families will overlap with those of the dominant middle-class White community, the beliefs that form the attitudes and values of minority communities may differ from the mainstream in important ways (Garcia Coll, Meyer, & Brillon, 1995). When working with ethnic minority families to support children's literacy development, professionals must be sensitive to the beliefs and values of the community, and also be knowledgeable about the language and literacy development of bilingual children.

This chapter begins with a brief discussion of the Latino population in the United States. The section that follows addresses factors that may impact children's literacy development. The remainder of the chapter discusses the results of two investigations of the home literacy practices of Puerto Rican families living in poverty in central Pennsylvania. The first study investigated mothers' beliefs about their children's literacy development and mothers' book-reading styles. The second examined the relationship between children's home literacy experiences and their literacy outcomes. Because individual differences exist within all populations, the results of these studies may not be representative of all Puerto Rican families, nor of all poor families. These findings do, however, call attention to factors that professionals should consider when working with families from similar backgrounds and communities.

THE LATINO POPULATION IN THE UNITED STATES

The Latino population is rooted in Spain's colonization of the New World, and, consequently, Spanish speakers encompass the largest single language minority in the United States (Therrien & Ramirez, 2001). Spanish speakers in this country represent many different dialect regions of Spain and the Americas and identify with their country or region of origin (Harrison, Wilson, Pine, Chan, & Buriel, 1990). The three largest groups living in the United States are

Mexican, Cuban, and Puerto Rican (Therrien & Ramirez, 2001). Although various immigrant groups are spread throughout the United States, the largest concentrations of Spanish speakers of Mexican descent reside in New Mexico and southern Colorado and the border states of California, Arizona, and Texas. The largest community of Cuban Americans occupies the Florida peninsula; New York City and other large cities in the Northeast and Midwest are home to large Puerto Rican communities (Canfield, 1981; Hammond, 2001). Thousands of Puerto Ricans comprise the most dominant Latino group in New York City. In addition, many have moved to upstate New York and other areas of New Jersey and Pennsylvania.

Latino communities in the United States share many linguistic and sociocultural experiences. Differences in linguistic and cultural traditions and practices exist between the various groups, as a result of socioeconomic factors, diverse political histories, immigration experiences, cultural sensibilities, and social dilemmas (Suarez-Orozco & Paez, 2002; Zentella, 2002). Additionally, Latino individuals face the same challenges of acculturation and coping with discrimination and prejudice that come with being a member of a minority group in this country (McAdoo, 1983).

FACTORS IMPACTING CHILDREN'S LITERACY DEVELOPMENT

Information shared in this section highlights key factors that impact children's literacy development, with most of the discussion addressing the Latino population in general. These factors include parenting practices, cultural beliefs about education, language proficiency, and the educational environment in which children learn to read.

Parenting Practices

Before discussing Latino families' parenting practices, it is necessary to briefly discuss the importance of culture to all facets of life. Anthropologists agree that culture is learned, consists of interrelated beliefs and practices, is shared by its members, and serves to define the boundaries of a group (Hall, 1976). Language is inextricably linked to culture and is a vehicle through which cultural beliefs and practices are conveyed (Schieffelin & Ochs, 1983; Schwartz, 1981). Additionally, it has been well documented that cultural values and beliefs are reflected in child-rearing practices of the adults of a given community who teach children how to become competent members of the group (Ochs & Schieffelin, 1984; Ogbu, 1988; Rogoff, 1981).

All members of a culture, however, do not universally agree on the values of that culture (Rogoff, 1990), and variations will occur "because of differences in their genes, their family's position in the community, their material resources and the chance circumstances in life" (Rogoff, 1990, p. 118). Cultural differences exist among Latino families, depending on their country of origin, and, like other cultural groups, individual variations are found within each group.

Traditional Hispanic values include a deep sense of the importance of the family and loyalty to the family. Latino families are often large and extend across generations, which also include godparents and close friends. Nearly one third of U.S. Latino families consist of five or more people (Therrien & Ramirez, 2001). The extended family forms a social support network and emphasizes interpersonal relationships and mutual respect among members (Vega, Hough, & Romero, 1983).

Because Latino culture emphasizes community and, most important, the family (Zuniga, 1998), families support each other by offering emotional and monetary support and by sharing resources across the extended family. Homes often include multiple generations, and families tend to live in the same neighborhood as other relatives, often having daily contact with one another. Consequently, families are closeknit and interdependent. Decisions take into account the family as well as the individual (Zuniga, 1998).

This familial orientation accentuates the importance of children to Latino families and the need to provide a positive nurturing environment free of negative emotions, such as anger and aggression (Roseberry-McKibben, 2002). Traditional parenting practices teach respect for authority and adherence to conventions that serve to maintain family identity (Zuniga, 1998). Close personal distances are maintained, and embraces and physical contact between individuals are common. Negative behaviors are deemphasized in circumstances involving conflict (Roseberry-McKibben, 2002). In general, Latino parents strive to establish warm and nurturing relationships with their children: "Emphasis is typically placed on close mother–child relationships, interpersonal responsiveness and development of proper demeanor and sense of dignity" (Garcia Coll et al., 1995, p. 198).

Because children are to be respectful of their parents and elders, they are not expected to take part in adult conversations, to interrupt adults, or to express their preferences or opinions. Teaching interactions in which parents ask children direct questions, of which the answers are known, or in which children talk about what they are doing, are not emphasized. Therefore, talk about books and academic subjects may differ from those employed by families who are White and middle class. Rather than stressing question and answer interactions, Latino families focus on modeling respect and politeness (Roseberry-McKibben, 2002). Children are taught to engage in harmonious relationships with others and to interact with adults in a respectful manner (Zuniga, 1988). Thus, a well-educated child is one who recognizes the "inner importance, dignity, and respect of an individual" (Garcia Coll et al., 1995, p. 197), compared to an individual's relative social and economic status.

Although there are many traditional Latino cultural practices, differences occur in the extent to which individual families maintain these practices for reasons including parental education and social class, region of the country, generational status, and acculturation stage (Zuniga, 1998). Although traditional male and female roles, for example, have been characterized by male dominance and female submissiveness, gender roles have been relaxed, as a result of women's employment outside the home. As a result, more families have joint parental decision making than was seen in earlier generations (Zuniga, 1998). Families who have lived in the United States for a longer period of time are more likely to have integrated practices of the mainstream culture into their behaviors.

Cultural Beliefs About Education

Parents' views on literacy are related to their beliefs about a child's education (Neuman, Hagedorn, Celano, & Daly, 1995). Their attitudes toward a child's education will be reflected in the caregiving environment, as well as in their relationships with professionals in the educational system and in decisions that are made regarding school experiences.

Relatively little research has been conducted on Latino parents' beliefs about education. The research that has been conducted reveals that the views of many Latino parents may differ from those of White, middle-class parents. For example, Latino parents typically do not emphasize the attainment of academic and developmental milestones at an early age (Garcia Coll et al., 1995). More specifically, Mexican mothers are more likely to view their mothering role as their primary responsibility and do not assume the responsibility for teaching academics (Garcia, Mendez Perez, & Ortiz, 2000). Mexican American mothers often hold beliefs that are more traditional and authoritarian than those of Euro-American mothers (Rodriguez & Olswang, in press).

Once the child enters the educational system, Latino parents demonstrate support for their children's education, by ensuring that children attend school and complete their homework

(Delgado-Gaitan, 2001). Furthermore, they may spend hours assisting their children with homework, but may not ask teachers questions for fear that they may be viewed as being critical of the children's teachers.

Latino parents typically believe that the teacher should be respected and that the teacher's authority should be not challenged. The teacher, and not the parents, has the knowledge to support children's learning. Because of their respect for the teacher and desire not to interfere with the teacher's work, some parents may not participate in classroom activities or school functions. This statement is supported by the work of Peña (2000), which demonstrated that traditional Mexican American families believe they are being helpful when they maintain a respectful distance from the educational system (Peña, 2000). Often, these differences between parents' and teachers' cultural views of education may result in parents being viewed as uninvolved or uncaring (August & Hakuta, 1997, Chavkin & Gonzalez, 1995; Delgado-Gaitan, 2001).

Parents may also refrain from being involved in school activities and meetings, because they do not understand the U.S. educational system and/or because of a lack of confidence in their own abilities (Delgado-Gaitan, 2001). This situation is particularly true of parents who were educated outside of the United States or who stopped their own education at a young age for financial or familial reasons (Delgado-Gaitan, 2001). In addition, misunderstandings between the home and school can occur when teachers schedule a meeting with the parents. Many Latino parents may believe their child has misbehaved (sometimes punishing their children before the meeting has occurred) and do not understand that meetings can also be used to share positive information.

Individual differences in parents' beliefs about education exist, with the level of parental education and income level being related to the extent to which parents actively participate in their children's educational experiences. Moreno and Lopez (1999) found that the higher the educational achievements of the mothers, the more the mothers viewed their direct involvement in education as important. Working-class parents, on the other hand, believed their role was to teach manners and rudimentary skills, so that their children were ready to learn when it was time to go to school (Casanova, 1987; Lareau, 1989). However, when parents with low incomes perceived themselves as influential in helping their children learn to read, they became directly involved in their children's educations and had a direct impact on the outcomes (Goldenberg; 1987). Thus, parents who are more knowledgeable about and/or comfortable interacting with the U.S. school system typically will be more involved in their children's education.

The degree of involvement in school-related activities is also related to parents' proficiency in English (Delgado-Gaitan, 1990). Some parents have limited abilities in English that greatly reduce their ability to participate in their children's education. Parents, for example, may be unable to read announcements/invitations that are written in English, and as a result, they may miss a meeting/conference or a school event. Additionally, parents may be unable to assist their children because the children's homework is in English and instructions are not provided in the parents' language. Thus, although parents are concerned about their children's ability to do well academically, their participation in school events may appear limited. A parent's lack of direct involvement with the school is not an indicator of a lack of interest in their children's education; rather, it may indicate a respect for the school's authority or a lack of confidence in one's own abilities to communicate well with school personnel (Delgado-Gaitan, 2001).

Language Proficiency in Two Languages and Literacy

In addition to parental characteristics, children's proficiency in Spanish and English is another factor to consider, because the language abilities of bilingual children can differ greatly. These differences are related to varying degrees of contact with Spanish speakers and English speakers. Latino children may be raised in homes where only Spanish is spoken and may begin to learn English when they enter preschool or elementary school. These children are often referred to as *sequential learners* of Spanish and English (Bhatia & Ritchie, 1999; McLaughlin, 1984; Meisel, 1994). Others may learn Spanish and English from birth and may be referred to as *simultaneous* learners of language (Bhatia & Ritchie, 1999).

Children who are simultaneous learners of Spanish and English may have very different experiences from one another. Some children may develop strong language abilities in both languages; others may have strong receptive and expressive language abilities in one language, but only receptive ability in the second language. Additionally, children exposed to English at home and in their communities may be learning a nonstandard dialect of English. Although nonstandard dialects of English are rule-governed systems (Wolfram, 1991), use of a nonstandard dialect places a child at risk, because it differs from the dialect used in educational settings (Snow, Burns, & Griffin, 1998). The patterns of exposure children have to Spanish and English may affect their literacy outcomes.

Hispanic children who are learning to speak both English and Spanish may be at an advantage in some areas, but may have added challenges in other areas, when learning to read. For example, children who are simultaneous learners of Spanish and English have been shown to develop superior phonological awareness abilities because of their experience attending to two different phonological (i.e., speech sound) systems (Bialystok, 1986, 1997). Exposure to two languages assists children in attending to the phonological features of language and in extracting information from abstract linguistic structures (such as sounds in words).

On the other hand, children who have minimal exposure to English prior to attending school (i.e., sequential learners) may be at a disadvantage, because the phonological system of Spanish differs from the phonological system of English. Therefore, these children may experience difficulty performing phonological awareness tasks, such as analyzing English words into their component sounds, particularly when the sounds involved do not occur in Spanish or are sounds that may not be combined into particular syllable structures in Spanish (Edelsky, 1986). For example, the consonants /s/ and /t/ occur in both languages. In Spanish, however, these consonants may not occur together in the onset of a syllable, as in the English word *star* (Hammond, 2001). This situation makes it difficult for a child to separate the blend into its component sounds. As a result, children learning to read in English and who have had minimal exposure to English, may have difficulty with phonemic awareness, letter–sound correspondences, and decoding tasks simply because of their lack of familiarity with the language.

Another cause of difficulty for children learning English is their limited knowledge of the vocabulary. Research has consistently shown that oral language competency is related to reading competency in a given language (National Reading Panel, 2000; Snow et al., 1998). If children have a limited vocabulary in English, they may not be able to make sense of what they read. It is unclear, however, whether or not a minimal proficiency in the vocabulary of the second language is necessary to successfully learn to read (see Fitzgerald, 1995, for a review).

Additionally, children with superficial skills in English may also have more difficulty exploiting the grammatical system to assist their comprehension when learning to read. Decoding accurately and fluently involves knowledge of vocabulary and grammar, as well as a secure phonological base, as discussed previously. Evidence suggests that carryover from the oral language skills of Spanish to English only occurs if both languages are used in the educational setting (Snow, 1990; Velasco, 1989).

The Educational Environment

Many Latino children in the United States attend public educational systems or participate in programs that promote acquisition of English. In many cases, schools have limited or no resources for support of a child's home language despite research indicating that advantaged bilingual children with no English skills prior to school require 5–7 years to achieve a level of proficiency in English that supports academic learning (Collier & Thomas, 1989; Garcia, 2000). Academic instruction in English without adequate opportunity to learn English leads to difficulties because of an inadequate foundation for learning new material and difficulties learning to read in English.

A lack of support for bilingualism also has important consequences for the family. Maintenance of the home language enables identification with members of the community who share the same histories and provide the support system for the child. On the other hand, the ability to speak English smoothes integration into the larger community and especially the school (Zentella, 2002). Latino children who have a command of English may have a brighter view toward socioeconomic mobility, but also may be alienated from some family members and their cultural community. Ideally, bilingual children who have regular contact with both monolingual Spanish and English speakers learn to switch rapidly from one language to the other. In addition, it has been documented that bilingual children experience cognitive benefits that enhance one's ability to be literate, including greater awareness of semantic relationships and grammatical rules and, especially, better phonological awareness abilities (Bialystok, 1986, 1988, 1992, 1997).

In summary, educators who work with children from a variety of cultural backgrounds face many challenges related to literacy. They must be sensitive to different cultural beliefs about educational support and to the implications of differing levels of English reading ability among parents. Educators must make the effort to communicate with monolingual Spanish-speaking parents and to explain aspects of the mainstream educational system that may differ from the family's traditions. When doing so, educators must be careful to respect a family's traditions so that children may thrive in their home environments rather than place the school and home environments at odds with each other.

As children grow older and exposure to the mainstream culture increases, families learn more about the dominant culture's values and behaviors and are often expected to adapt to these cultural norms (Garcia Coll et al., 1995). How families respond to these challenges will have major consequences for interpersonal relationships and language proficiency and literacy development in English.

HOME LITERACY EXPERIENCES OF PUERTO RICAN CHILDREN

In order to understand children's home literacy experiences, knowledge is needed about the home literacy experiences of children from specific Latino cultures, and more specifically, how parents from these communities use books with their children and the types and frequency of literacy activities that occur in the home. Two studies that address this need are discussed in the remainder of the chapter. The first investigated the book-reading styles and parental beliefs of Puerto Rican mothers of Head Start children. The second examined the relationship between the home literacy experience of Puerto Rican Head Start children and their early literacy outcomes. These studies address the key factors discussed in the previous section through the investigation of parents' beliefs about literacy, as well as of the literacy experiences they provide their children, and the consideration of children's exposure to Spanish and English.

A Puerto Rican Community in Pennsylvania

As reported earlier in the chapter, the majority of Puerto Ricans families living in the mainland United States have settled in the northeast portion of the country, including New York,

New Jersey, and Pennsylvania. Many Puerto Rican families in Pennsylvania have resided in their communities for over 50 years, and some are more recent immigrants who have come to join family members on the U.S. mainland or to seek employment.

Families discussed in the studies that follow lived in central Pennsylvania and were of low income, making their children eligible for Head Start services. Although many of the parents in these studies were born in the United States, their level of acculturation to the dominant community is affected by their socioeconomic status (Rauh, Wasserman, & Brunelli, 1990). Many of these families had their education stopped early for various personal and familial reasons. The pressures of meeting expectations of other family members as well as the expectations from the schools have also influenced the degree of acculturation. Furthermore, they must also cope with the stresses of unemployment, unsafe neighborhoods, and limited health care (McAdoo, 1983).

Mothers' Beliefs and Book-Reading Styles With Their Head Start Children

Research on children's book-reading experiences has focused primarily on families who are White and from middle-class backgrounds. This research has demonstrated that White, middle-class mothers guide their children's participation by establishing joint action routines (Ninio & Bruner, 1978). As part of their verbal routines during these interactions, parents frequently ask *wh*-questions (i.e., what, where, when) (Anderson-Yockel & Haynes, 1994), change the level of difficulty of their utterances as their children's language develops and their ability to participate increases (Ninio & Bruner, 1978; van Kleeck, Gillam, Hamilton, & McGrath, 1997), and progress from producing questions that ask the children for basic information to asking more abstract questions that require their children to predict what will happen (van Kleek et al., 1997).

Relatively few studies have focused on book-reading interactions between mothers and children from nonmainstream cultures. A review of the literature identified five investigations that have examined book-reading interactions between African American mothers and their children (Anderson-Yockel & Haynes, 1994; Hammer, 2000; Hammer, Nimmo, Cohen, Clemons, & Achenbach, 2002; Heath, 1983; Pelligrini, Perlmutter, Galda, & Brody, 1990).

Even fewer studies have been located that specifically examined the book-reading experiences of Latino mothers and their children. Teale (1986) studied the book-reading experiences of Latino, White, and African American children from low-income backgrounds. She found that children from all three cultural groups were exposed to literacy events although the types and amount of literacy activities varied within each of the groups. Like Teale (1986), Delgado-Gaitan (1990) demonstrated that a range of literacy opportunities was provided to Mexican American children.

Similarly, minimal research has explored Latino parents' views about children's early literacy development. Only a handful of studies have been conducted on the home literacy environment of Latino families (cf. Delegado-Gaitan, 1990; Teale, 1986). Given the differences in cultural views about education, differences may exist between Latino parents' views of literacy and children's literacy development and how mothers look at books with their children.

Although the works of Teale (1986) and Delgado-Gaitan (1990) provide the field with valuable information, the need for more specific information on maternal beliefs and book-reading styles of Latino mothers and their children led to a study conducted by Hammer and her colleagues (Hammer, 2002; Hammer et al., 2002). The study involved 10 Puerto Rican mothers and their children. In order to participate, the mothers and children had to qualify financially for Head Start services. In addition, the children needed to be typically developing, as demonstrated by there being no parent or teacher concerns about the children's abilities.

The mothers averaged 27 years of age and slightly less than 12 years of education. Thirty percent were employed outside the home, and 40% were married or had a steady partner. All mothers lived under difficult financial conditions. Most experienced a tragic event during their early years and had dropped out of school; in several instances, there was a relationship between the traumatic event and the mother dropping out of school. The children averaged 53 months of age, with equal numbers of males and females in the group. Based on the mothers' reports and observations of the first author, only one of the children from the group was fluent in Spanish. All were proficient in English.

The mothers and their children were seen for three sessions. During the first two sessions, semi-structured interviews were conducted with the mothers, in order to obtain information about their beliefs about children's literacy development. All the mothers were fluent in Spanish and English, and interviews were conducted in the language of the mothers' choice. All mothers chose to be interviewed in English. During the audiotaped interviews, guide questions were used to discuss the mothers' views about literacy development and their role in facilitating their children's emerging ability to read. After the interviews were completed, the audiotaped interviews were transcribed word for word and were coded using procedures commonly used to code qualitative interview data (Miles & Huberman, 1994; Patton, 2002).

During the second and third sessions, the mothers and their children were provided with four books. The mothers were asked to look at the books as they normally would when reading books to their children. Once completed, the sessions were transcribed verbatim. The communicative acts produced by the mothers and children were coded using a system that was based on Fey's (1986) system for coding communicative acts (e.g., labels/comments, reading of text, and questions, etc.) and were adapted to a book-reading interaction, so that behaviors displayed by the participants were captured by the system. After the book-reading sessions were coded, the percentage of utterances in each of the communicative acts categories was determined. Information about the communicative acts produced by each dyad, through a careful review of the videotapes, was used to perform a qualitative analysis, through which the book-reading styles of the dyads were determined.

The results of the semi-structured interviews demonstrated that the mothers held a wide range of beliefs about literacy development, and observations of the mother–child interactions revealed four book-reading styles within the group of 10 Head Start mothers and children: text reading, labeling, child-centered, and combinational. Examples of the differing maternal beliefs and the four book-reading styles are described next through four case studies. Note that the mothers and children were given pseudonyms (individuals with more traditionally Latino names were given Latino pseudonyms, and individuals with names typically used by the mainstream population were given more traditionally mainstream names).

Textbook-Reading Style: Liz.   At the time of the study, Liz was married and had three children. Her youngest child attended Head Start and had lived with her grandmother until the age of 3 years, which is a relatively common practice in Puerto Rican families. Liz dropped out of school because of a traumatic experience with a male student. Liz was fluent in both Spanish and English, but talked primarily to her children in English, because her husband did not speak Spanish.

During the interview, Liz shared much information about her child's early literacy development. When she was asked how children learned to read, Liz indicated that children learned by their parents reading to them and pointing to the words as they read. She added that having children repeat the words was important. Liz admitted that she did not read frequently to her child, and that she read only when her child brought her a book to read. Liz credited her husband with helping her child learn to read, by reading books to her everyday. She continued by stating that she and her husband "promised each other anything that we could not have for us or we didn't learn, we'll try to teach our girls the best way." Liz had a limited number of literacy materials available for her child such as scissors, markers, crayons, and a mat with the alphabet on it. She also subscribed to a magazine that was appropriate for children. Her daughter had 6 books at home and 24 at her grandmother's home. Because Liz valued books and wanted to make certain they were well maintained, the children's books were kept out of reach from her child. Liz and her husband allowed their child to interact with the books when either one of the parents read to their daughter. When asked what she was doing to help her child get ready for kindergarten in the following year, Liz indicated that she was teaching her daughter her full name, numbers, and shapes. She was uncertain whether or not she should be working on other abilities, "because [she didn't] know what she's [her daughter] lacking." Liz hoped to send her children to a private school, because they lived in a "rough" area. Her ultimate goal was for her child to complete college. In order to meet this goal, she and her husband were saving money from her husband's earnings.

Liz employed a text-reading style when reading books to her children. A text-reading style was defined as 60% or more of the mothers' utterances consisting of text read directly from books. Specifically, 68% of Liz's utterances consisted of lines of text. She occasionally paused to label a picture or make a comment (13% of her utterances), and asked few questions about the book (3% of her utterances). In the following excerpt, Liz's style is exhibited, (lines labeled "M" represent utterances spoken by the mother, and "C" represents utterances produced by her child; utterances consisting of text read from the book are italicized, reading errors of the mother are included).

M: *By the big red barn, in the great green field, there was a pink pig, who was learning to squeak. There was a great big horse and a very little horse.*
(Mother shows her child the book). You see the big horse? And the little calf. These are called a calf.

C: Mommy, they hiding.

M: Okay, second page. *And on a very barn is a weather vane, of course, a golden flying horse. There was a big pile of hay and a little pile of hay, and that is where the children play.*

C: Mommy, that's a little pig (C points to the picture).

M: *But in this story, the children are always only the animals are here today.*

C: There bugs (Child points to the picture). Bugs.

M: *In a field of corn.* Do you know how to say this? Let's do this. Cockadoodledoo.

C: Cockadoodledoo.

M: *In the barn, there was a rooster (pause) and a peacock, too.* That's a peacock. Ain't that pretty ?

This text-reading style differs greatly from the labeling style used by Sharon, as described in the following section.

Labeling Book-Reading Style: Sharon.   Sharon had two children who were under 4 years of age and was expecting her third. She lived with her boyfriend in a housing project in a well-kept apartment, and was employed full-time. She communicated to her children in Spanish and English, and her boyfriend spoke English to them. Her children talked primarily in English, although they knew some Spanish words and phrases. Sharon worked the third shift in an unskilled position and was hoping to obtain a daytime position. She did not graduate from high school, and remembered that she liked reading when she was younger, but found it boring as an adult.

As demonstrated, Sharon's beliefs about children's literacy development complemented her book-reading style, because she believed that children learned to read by looking at pictures and by people talking about them. Sharon reported that her work schedule limited the time to read to her two children. She read to them when they brought her a book to look at together. Concerning literacy materials in the home, Sharon's children had several literacy toys available to them. Sharon reported they had four books, magnetic letters, child-sized chairs with their names on them, paper, and pencils. When asked what she was doing to help her son get ready to read, she stated she had her son repeat the names of the letters after her. According to Sharon, she was not actively teaching her child anything in particular to help him prepare for kindergarten. At the time of the study, she had not thought about specific goals for her children when they became adults.

Sharon employed a labeling style when looking at books with her son, which differed greatly from the text-reading style of Liz. A *book-reading style* was defined as one in which minimal reading of text occurred and in which the majority of utterances were labels/comments. Unlike Liz, only 2% of Sharon's utterances consisted of lines of text. Forty-one percent of her utterances were labels or comments about the books. These utterances contained basic information about the pictures. Sharon complemented her labeling/commenting with a high percentage of *wh*-questions (27%), which elicited basic information from her child such as the name of the picture, as opposed to requesting information about the story or predicting what would happen in the story. The following is an excerpt that illustrates her style. Utterances produced in Spanish are translated into English within parentheses.

M:	Mira. ¿Que es eso?	(Look. What's that?)
C:	Apple.	
M:	Apple.	
M:	*On Monday he ate an apple.* Mira. (Look.)	What is that?
C:	A gallo.	(A rooster.)
M:	Yeah. ¿Y eso?	(And that?)
C:	Sheep.	
M:	Uhhuh.	
C:	A quackquack.	
M:	Un quackquack.	(A quackquack.)
M:	And what's the name? Un duck.	(A duck.)
C:	Duck.	
M:	Es un goose de esos.	(It's one of those goose.)

Thus Sharon's style resembled a vocabulary lesson during which the names of items were provided to the child. Additional information about the various vocabulary items was not provided by the mother during this labeling exercise.

Child-Centered Book-Reading Style: Leticia.   Leticia was a single mother of three children, ranging in age from 9 months to 5 years of age. Leticia did not complete high school and was not working outside the home at the time of the study. Throughout her life, Leticia had encountered numerous emotional, medical, and financial challenges. Her primary support came from her grandparents and her daughter's godmother with whom she was very close.

Leticia's beliefs about how children learned to read matched her book-reading style. Leticia thought children learned to read by looking at the pictures and determining what was happening in the story based on their own experiences. She stated that children learned to read

by pictures, really. Just to think how they doing their things and how would they do their movements and how she would react. Because for her to recognize what's going on, she has to learn that by herself and then ask me questions. I really don't know how to start off a story with her, unless she uses her own imagination to think about it. She was taught to use her imagination.

Leticia looked at books in English with her child several times a week. Leticia's grandmother also read books to her child in Spanish, in an effort to teach her Spanish. In addition, her child's godmother took her to the library every week. The godmother also gave the child most of the 40 children's books that were in the home. Approximately 20 of the books were available for the child to look at; the other 20 were stored away, so that they would not be damaged when children of friends and relatives came to visit. Leticia's daughter had a number of literacy-related toys in her home. In addition to books, she had a memory game, alphabet flash cards, markers with letters on them, paper, pens, pencils, and scissors. Unlike Liz and Sharon, Leticia had an active agenda for helping her child get ready to read and get ready for kindergarten. Leticia was teaching her daughter how to identify and write letters of the alphabet and to write her name. She also was working on teaching her daughter rhyming words, opposites, and the names of body parts. When asked what her goal was for her children when they became adults, Leticia replied, "To have a better life than I did."

When Leticia looked at books with Josephine, her 5-year-old daughter, Leticia employed a *child-centered style* that was defined as the mother allowing and encouraging her child to be the primary storyteller. During the book-reading interactions, Leticia's daughter told a story that contained several components of a narrative. Leticia only interrupted her daughter when she made a factual mistake, such as mislabeling a vocabulary item. Leticia occasionally read the text from the book (25% of her utterances) and asked a small number of questions (12% of her utterances). The following excerpt illustrates Leticia's individual style:

C: Okay. I'll read this one. It's called by Friend Lee. It was Friend's name, a dog with a duck and a rabbit. They was trying to climb up a lot of ladder. They couldn't reach high. Then they tried to get away. It wasn't too high. Tried to build that. It wasn't too high. They was trying to build that. They was jumping and jumping. The rabbit was hopping and they was jumping.

M: On the bed.

M: What's he doing?

C: Climbing up the bed to jump. That's what I do. And when they're tired they lay down and go to sleep. What's these two doing? Them two?

M: They're talking, I guess.

C: Yup, they're talking.

It should be pointed out that other mothers who used a child-centered style differed slightly from Leticia's style. Some would encourage their child to look through the book before reading the story to them, and during this time some mothers asked questions about the pictures to help their child develop an understanding of the plot of the story. Others read the book to their children after the child told the story by looking at the pictures in the book.

Combinational Book-Reading Style: Maria.   At the time of the study, Maria was married and had five children, with the youngest being 18 months of age. Maria dropped out of school when her oldest child, who had multiple disabilities, was born. Maria's current goal was to obtain a GED and take computer classes. Although Maria did not work at the beginning of the project, she acquired a job at a local fast-food restaurant by the end of the study. Maria and her husband were fluent in Spanish and English. Her children, however, spoke primarily in English and understood some Spanish. Spanish was the only language spoken by the children's grandparents.

Maria believed that children learn to read by first looking at the books and predicting what would happen in the story then reading the story to determine the actual plot. Gradually, the child becomes familiar with small words (e.g., she, the) that build up the child's confidence in learning to read. Maria read to her child several times a week, but did not enjoy reading herself. She indicated that reading to her children was a priority, because it was important to her husband. Her husband read frequently, but did not read to the children on a regular basis. In addition to reading to her children, Maria described how she and her girls often jointly constructed stories apart from books. During these times, Maria picked the theme (e.g., the Spice Girls coming to their house) and told the story, pausing for her daughters to contribute to the events in the story.

When reading books with her child, Maria reported that her child had many books, but they were packed away, because she and her husband were hoping to move out of his parents' home. She did not know, however, when that would happen. She indicated that her daughter had various writing instruments available to her and a toy computer with letters on it. Maria did not appear to have an active agenda in terms of what she was doing to help her child get ready to read or to get ready for kindergarten. She indicated that she helped her older daughter with her homework.

Maria's goal for her children was for them to complete high school and obtain an education. She stated that she wanted her "children to be somebody." After they established themselves, she would be happy if they married someone with whom they had a good relationship. She also hoped that her children would be bilingual.

Maria demonstrated a *combinational book-reading style*, which is the fourth style that was observed within this population. This style was characterized by the mother assuming the lead in reading the books and using a combination of labels/comments, questions, and utterances read from the text. For example, 42% of Maria's utterances were from the text, 9% were labels/comments, 15% were *wh*-questions, and 14% were responses to her daughter's statements and questions. Like the child-centered style, the combinational style was employed by several of the mothers. Maria's style differed slightly, in that she occasionally encouraged her daughter to personalize the story by naming the characters after family members, as illustrated by the following, when looking at a storybook about farm animals.

M: *There was a great big horse and a very little horse.*

C: That's you and me.

M: Uhhuh.

C: That's you.

M: OK.

M: *And on every barn is a weather vane, of course, a golden flying horse.* What's this?

C: A horse.

M: A horse. *There was a big pile of hay and a little pile of hay, and that is where the childrens play.* See. This is the hay. This is where they play at. Who's this?

C: Mommy and me.

M: And who's this?

C: Celia.

M: Celia? Okay. *But in this story, the children are away. Only the animals are here today. The geese and the goats were making funny noise down in their throat. An old scarecrow was leaning on his hoe. And a field mouse was born.*

C: I want that one.

M: See. *In a field of corn.* What is that?

C: A mouse.

M: And what's this?

C: A big big butterfly. And that's a little butterfly.

M: That's a big butterfly and a little butterfly?

C: Yeah.

M: Okay.

From these varied examples, one can see that a range of book-reading styles, literacy beliefs, and literacy practices existed within this Puerto Rican community. Mothers displayed styles that included (a) encouraging their children to be the story tellers by using the pictures and imagination to guide their "reading"; (b) providing their children with a vocabulary lesson; (c) reading directly from the text, possibly in an attempt to preserve the authors' words and story (Heath, 1982); and (d) providing a book-reading experience that focused on the text of the book, while vocabulary items were named, comments were made about the pictures, and questions were asked of the child. We assumed that these styles are not unique to the Puerto Rican cultures. Therefore, we encourage practitioners to determine the book-reading styles of the mothers with whom they work and to base their interventions on the mothers' particular style of book reading, as is discussed in the final section of this chapter.

The home literacy environment, however, provides children with more than joint book-reading experiences. The following section provides the results of a related study that investigated the broader home literacy environment of Head Start children.

HOME LITERACY EXPERIENCES OF HEAD START CHILDREN OF PUERTO RICAN DESCENT

Research has established a link between language skills and literacy development (Snow et al., 1998). Children with a strong foundation in their native language and with support for early literacy development, through home activities such as book reading, are presumed to develop skills that will transfer to English language and literacy in later childhood. Many bilingual children in the United States, however, are at risk for not having the environmental support for acquiring two languages and for acquiring English literacy. In addition, the ways that parents and communities encourage language and literacy learning differ across cultures.

As noted, a small knowledge base about Latino children's home literacy experiences has begun to be developed; however, we do not have enough information to adequately understand the literacy practices of this cultural group, nor their relationship to later literacy outcomes of children. Two considerations must be made when studying Latino children's literacy experiences: First, it is important to consider the language status of the children (children may be developing Spanish and English sequentially or simultaneously); second, it is important to consider the specific Hispanic culture of the families. Although there are commonalities in cultural beliefs and practices among Hispanic cultures (e.g., family loyalty, collective orientation, emphasis on relationships, and mutual respect), differences exist because of variability in economic, political, and regional factors (Garcia Coll et al., 1995).

Overview of the Study

As part of a larger longitudinal investigation to identify risk and protective factors for children's English literacy outcomes, Hammer, Miccio, and Wagstaff (2003) addressed these concerns by investigating the home literacy experiences of bilingual Head Start children of Puerto Rican descent. Forty-three Puerto Rican mother–child dyads were recruited through local Head Start programs in two counties in central Pennsylvania. The participating children were all typically developing (i.e., had no parent or teacher concerns about their development) and were enrolled in their first year of Head Start. The average age of the children at the beginning of the study was 3 years 8 months.

At the beginning of the study, mothers provided information on their children's language status. Based on this information, children were divided into two groups: simultaneous and sequential language learners. Simultaneous language learners were defined as children who were spoken to by family members in both English and Spanish prior to 3 years of age ($n = 28$). Sequential learners were children who were spoken to in Spanish in the home and who were then first spoken to in English by teachers in Head Start or other significant members of their community after the age of 3 years ($n = 15$) (Goodz, 1994; McLaughlin, 1984).

Participating mothers were of Puerto Rican descent and spoke a Puerto Rican dialect of Spanish. The mothers in the two groups were similar in age, years of education, current employment, and income level. Mothers of the sequential learners averaged 27 years of age and 10.4 years of education. Forty percent worked outside the home. The mothers of the simultaneous learners averaged 25.5 years of age and 11.3 years of education. Half of the mothers of this group worked outside the home, and all had low annual incomes, making their children eligible for Head Start services. The mothers in the two groups differed in place of birth: Nearly all of the mothers of the sequential learners were born in Puerto Rico and less than 10% were born on the U.S. mainland; in contrast, half of the mothers of the simultaneous learners were born in Puerto Rico.

Home Language Use Among Adults

Over 90% of the mothers of the sequential learners and 28% of the mothers of the simultaneous learners reported that Spanish was spoken among adults in the home or that more Spanish than English was spoken in the home. On the other hand, only 8% of the mothers of the sequential learners indicated that adults in their home used equal amounts of Spanish and English, compared to 37% of the mothers of the simultaneous learners. Thirty-eight percent of the simultaneous learners' mothers reported that more English than Spanish or all English was spoken among adults in their homes. Thus, communication between adults in the homes of sequential learners typically was in Spanish; communication in the homes of simultaneous learners was in English in the majority of homes.

Home Language Use With Children

Language use with children varied greatly across a continuum of Spanish and English usage. Seventy percent of the sequential learners' mothers indicated that the adults in their home used only Spanish when speaking to their children; 30% used equal amounts of Spanish and English. On the other hand, only 16% of the mothers of the simultaneous learners spoke Spanish or more Spanish than English to their children. Twenty-eight percent of the mothers used equal amounts of Spanish and English with their children. Forty percent of the mothers of the simultaneous learners indicated that they spoke more English than Spanish with their children, and 16% spoke only English when talking to their children. All children in the simultaneous group, however, were exposed to Spanish in their home environment and community. Thus, sequential learners typically were spoken to in Spanish by their parents, and simultaneous learners were talked to primarily in English when communicating to their parents.

Learning About Home Literacy Experiences

As part of a larger investigation, trained home visitors from the families' community conducted home visits with the mothers. During the visits, the home visitors administered the Home Activities Questionnaire developed by Hammer and Miccio (2000). The questionnaire was administered in the language of the mothers' choosing. When administering the questionnaire, the home visitors asked the mothers a series of questions about the activities that the mothers and children did at home and carefully explained that the mothers and children were not expected to do all of the activities listed. To account for varying levels of maternal reading abilities, the home visitors read the questions to the mothers and recorded the mothers' responses on the questionnaire.

The Home Activities Questionnaire contained 71 questions that focused on home literacy events. Questions targeted the frequency of (a) children's literacy activities (e.g., reading a book, coloring, pretending to write), (b) mother–child literacy activities (e.g., looking at books together, teaching the child the alphabet, telling stories to the child), and mothers' literacy activities (e.g., reading a book, reading the *Bible*, paying bills). In addition, mothers were asked about the presence of literacy materials in their homes, their enjoyment and their children's enjoyment of reading, and their goals for their children's education.

Using a framework proposed by Hess and Holloway (1984) and Snow et al. (1998), responses of the two groups about their home experiences were compared, as they related to the following factors: (a) value placed on literacy; (b) press for achievement; (c) availability of reading materials; and (d) reading with children. The first three factors were addressed through the creation of scales.

Value Placed on Literacy.   The first scale, the value placed on literacy, included items that reflected the frequency with which mothers engaged in various literacy activities. Examples of items that reflected the frequency with which the mother valued literacy in daily life included reading items such as a book, the *Bible*, a church newsletter, a newspaper, sales advertisements, or magazines. Checking out books from the library or using a dictionary or encyclopedia also demonstrated value placed on reading. Other household tasks such as using recipes, making a grocery list, or paying bills, as well as sending cards or letters, were also included in the scale.

The value placed on literacy did not differ between the homes of sequential and simultaneous learners ($p = .89$). Mothers in both groups reported that they engaged in adult literacy activities infrequently or, on average, slightly over one time per month.

Press for Achievement.   The second scale, the mothers' press for achievement, investigated how frequently mothers responded to their children's reading interest by taking them to the library, and how frequently they taught their children early academic skills (e.g., the alphabet and numbers, letter sounds, colors, shapes, and counting). Coloring with children and teaching them to write also provided evidence of a press for achievement.

A significant difference ($p = .01$) was found between the two groups of mothers, regarding the press for achievement. Mothers of the simultaneous learners participated in these activities (e.g., teaching the alphabet and letter sounds) more frequently than did the mothers of the sequential learners. On average, mothers of the simultaneous learners engaged in teaching activities or took their children to the library on a weekly basis. Mothers of the sequential learners participated in these activities approximately two to three times per month.

Availability of Reading Materials.   The third scale, the availability of reading materials, combined items that involved the number of children's and adult books in the home. No differences were found between the two groups concerning to the number of books for adults and the number of books for children in the families' homes. Both groups of mothers had few books in their homes. The mothers reported having an average of 1–10 adult and children's books in their homes.

Reading to Children.   Finally, the frequency of reading with children was examined. The mothers of the two groups did not differ significantly in the frequency at which they read to their children. On average, the mothers in both groups read to their children 2–4 days a week.

Relationships Among the Four Scales

Hammer et al. (2003) calculated correlations among the four factors: value placed on literacy, press for achievement, availability of reading materials, and reading to children. The value placed on literacy correlated significantly with the press for achievement for both groups combined ($r = .36$, $p = .02$) and for the group of simultaneous learners ($r = .42$, $p = .03$). This relationship did not hold for the mothers of the sequential learners. In addition, a significant relationship was found ($r = .51$, $p = .05$) for the entire group between the mothers' press for achievement (e.g., as demonstrated by teaching children) and reading to children. No other statistically significant relationships were observed among these four factors.

Thus, Hammer et al.'s (2003) findings revealed only one key difference between the home literacy experiences of the sequential and simultaneous learners. Specifically, the two groups differed regarding the press for achievement found in the home as measured by maternal teaching activities. The mothers of the simultaneous learners engaged more frequently in teaching preacademic and early literacy abilities, such as colors, shapes, letters, and numbers. A possible explanation for this difference may relate to potential differences in the mothers' educational experiences: 50% of the mothers of the simultaneous learners were born in the United States, compared to 7% of the sequential learners. Mothers born on the U.S. mainland may be more familiar with the culture of mainland schools and with skills that children are expected to have already acquired by the time they enter school. The current emphasis on teaching children preacademic concepts, such as letters and numbers, is reflected in the teaching activities of the mothers of the simultaneous learners. Some mothers from Puerto Rico may follow more traditional parenting behaviors, which reflect the values of nurturing children and supporting the parent–child relationship, as well as networking among community members and extended families (Zentella, 1998). These mothers value education and literacy, but children may be encouraged to learn independently through observation. Formal academic work may be reserved for teachers and the school system (Kayser, 1998; Langdon, 1992).

Differences between the two groups regarding to the value placed on literacy as measured by maternal literacy activities, the availability of reading materials, and the frequency with which mothers read to their children were not observed (Hammer et al., 2003). The lack of differences between the two groups is somewhat expected, given the similarity in the educational and economic backgrounds of the mothers in the two groups. Average academic achievement for both groups of mothers was less than a high school diploma. Previous research has documented a relationship between maternal education and home literacy activities (Federal Interagency Forum on Child and Family Statistics [FIFCFS], 2002; Snow et al., 1998). However, a larger percentage of the mothers in this investigation (44%) reported reading to their children on a daily basis than the percentage of mothers from the nationwide sample (31%) collected by the FIFCFS (2002). A primary difference between our study and the FIFCFS investigation is that FIFCFS is based on a national sample, which included families whose children attended an educational program as well as those that did not. Attendance in an educational program such as Head Start, which encourages reading to children, may impact the mothers' behavior. Another reason for the lack of differences between the two groups may be the fact that all participating families had low incomes. Economic disadvantage limits families' ability to purchase literacy materials and, in turn, may reduce the number of different literacy activities in the home along with the range and number of literacy materials in the home. Economic disadvantage also causes stress in families (August & Hakuta, 1997), potentially reducing their ability to engage in leisure activities such as reading for pleasure or for information.

Early Literacy Outcomes

In addition to collecting data on children's home literacy experiences, trained research assistants from the children's community administered the Test of Early Reading Ability–2 (TERA–2; Reid, Hresko, & Hammill, 1991) twice to all children. The TERA–2 was first administered during the sixth month of the children's first year in Head Start, then was administered a second time during the second month of their second year in Head Start. The test was administered in English, because the ultimate aim of the larger investigation was to examine the effects of different modes of bilingual language acquisition on emerging English literacy.

T tests were conducted to determine if significant differences existed between the two groups of children in relation to their home literacy experiences and their performances on the TERA–2. In addition, correlations were calculated to determine if significant relationships existed between the four factors discussed previously and the children's performance on the TERA–2.

The standard scores of the two groups of children did not differ at the time of the initial administration of the TERA–2: The sequential learners had a standard score of 88, and the simultaneous learners had a standard score of 90. Although below the mean for the test, these scores were within one standard deviation of the test mean. A significant difference was observed between the two groups when the TERA–2 was given the second time. The simultaneous learners scored significantly better than the sequential learners ($p = .05$). The standard scores for both groups of children, however, were lower at the second administration than of the first. When tested during the second year of Head Start, the simultaneous learners averaged a standard score of 85 and the sequential learners a standard score of 77. Thus, the entire group scored significantly lower ($p = .0009$) the second time the TERA–2 was administered. Both groups of children scored at least 1.5 standard deviations below the mean the second time. This is of concern, because the children will be expected to have emergent literacy abilities comparable to those of monolingual children entering kindergarten, when they move into the elementary school system. Fortunately, the children in this study had another year in Head Start. Perhaps, gains in their literacy abilities will occur during that time.

Relationships Between the Four Scales and the TERA–2

Correlations were calculted between the four scales (value placed on literacy, press for achievement, availability of reading materials, and reading to children) and the children's performance on the TERA–2. No significant relationships were observed between the four factors and the children's performance on the standardized measure. This finding suggests no observable differences in the emerging literacy abilities of the sequential and simultaneous learners during their first year in Head Start. All children performed at the lower end of the average range. Differences were observed during the first half of the children's second year in Head Start, when sequential learners performed significantly lower than simultaneous learners, but this result may relate to the children's language-learning status. Sequential learners may need to continue to focus their efforts on learning English rather than on acquiring even more academic abilities, such as knowledge about literacy. Possibly, the sequential learners may not have acquired the English language abilities necessary to advance their early literacy abilities in English.

Children's developing literacy abilities in Spanish are equally as important as their literacy abilities in English. As part of the larger study, Hammer and Miccio are collecting data on children's Spanish language abilities through the use of informal measures. A preliminary review of the children's performance on letter identification tasks, phonological awareness tasks, and Clay's (1979) Concepts about Print (translated into Spanish) suggested no differences in these children's early literacy abilities in Spanish and English. To supplement this preliminary evidence, conversations with parents from the community, as well as with Head Start teachers and administrators, indicated that most families in these particular communities emphasize their children's English literacy abilities. In addition, there is anecdotal evidence that many individuals in this community of second-generation status are unable to read and write in Spanish with proficiency.

Discussion of Results

A surprising result of this study was that the early English language abilities of participating children were lower in the second year of Head Start and that the children no longer scored within one standard deviation of the test mean on the standardized measure (TERA–2). The amount and extent of literacy activities that occurred in the homes and in the Head Start classrooms may have been sufficient to establish an early foundation for literacy during the children's first year. In the second year of Head Start, however, the frequency of literacy activities and availability of literacy materials in the homes may not have been sufficient to support the acquisition of additional literacy abilities. Although the Head Start programs include literacy activities in the children's classroom experiences on a daily basis, the children may need additional support both at Head Start and at home. The low occurrence of literacy activities in the homes of the families participating in this study suggests that Head Start programs may need to place even more emphasis on literacy learning activities in the classroom, or they may need to enhance their work with parents by encouraging more literacy activities in the home.

As noted earlier, relationships were not found between the children's performance on a standardized measure of early English literacy and the four factors of the home environment proposed in Snow et al.'s (1998) model. There are a number of possible reasons. First, the scales (value placed on literacy, press for achievement, availability of reading materials, and reading to children) may not have completely captured the essential aspects of the home literacy environment. The activities examined in this study, however, are supported by research on children's early literacy development (cf. Dickinson & DeTemple, 1998; Dickinson & Tabors, 2001; Hess & Holloway, 1984; Snow et al., 1998).

Second, the model may not fully apply to the population that participated in this investigation, or the model may need to be expanded. More direct teaching about literacy rather than modeling of literacy activities may be necessary to promote children's literacy development in a second language. One might expect, for example, that mother–child book reading contributes to children's literacy outcomes. Although mothers from this community were observed reading books to their children, the mothers restricted their talk to the pictures in the books or the story line of the book, and rarely engaged in talk about components of the book, letter identification, the process of reading, or print awareness. Such talk around books is a common phenomenon in schools, and children may be at a disadvantage when the home styles of interaction do not match those employed at school (cf. Heath, 1983).

A third reason why relationships may not have occurred between the four factors and children's scores on the TERA-3 is that there may be a critical level of literacy activities in the home that must be achieved before home literacy activities impact literacy outcomes. Possibly more frequent engagement in literacy activities and the availability of more literacy materials in the home may have resulted in a significant relationship between home literacy activities and a standardized measure of early reading ability.

A final explanation is that the TERA–2 (Reid et al., 1991) is not measuring literacy-related abilities that are affected by the four factors (Snow et al., 1998) discussed in this study. Most of the factors involved children observing their mothers engaging in literacy events, being exposed to various literacy materials, and experiencing literacy when their mothers read to them. Scarborough and Dobrich (1994) argued that early book reading does not have long-ranging effects on children's literacy development, rather more frequent direct teaching may be needed. The items on the TERA–2 involve recognition of environmental print (e.g., identification of product logos) and recognition or identification of letters. These skills may be more difficult to learn through observation. Although one of the factors discussed by Hess and Holloway (1984) involves parental teaching of literacy and academic abilities, the mothers apparently did not engage in these activities often enough for their efforts to have an impact.

What is clearly illuminated in these findings is that we need to know more about how young children acquire two languages and the effect bilingualism has on emerging literacy (see chapter 24 in this volume). More research on the process of literacy acquisition in bilingual children is necessary so that well-informed recommendations may be provided to parents for literacy support in the home. In addition, further research should lead to expanded options and improved practices in preschool programs so that the most advantageous learning environment is available in both settings.

CONSIDERATIONS FOR WORKING WITH PUERTO RICAN FAMILIES

English fluency and literacy alone do not necessarily result in second-language students' academic success in the United States. Rather, the quality of teacher–student interactions and peer interactions may be more important to minority student success (Cummins, 1996). The teacher–family relationship is more difficult if cultural conflicts occur, because teachers and families do not share the same expectations regarding the responsibilities of the school and the parents with regard to the children's education (Delgado-Gaitan, 1990; Valdez, 1996). Thus, it is important that teachers and families work together to create a positive learning environment.

Involve Parents in Educational Activities

Involving parents in the educational activities of their preschool-aged children is particularly crucial (Hammer et al., 2003). Cummins (1989) argued that the students' languages and cultures should be incorporated into the school culture and that parents and communities should be involved in the students' school experiences. This is difficult if communication occurs only in English. Because language and culture are closely intertwined, ignoring the home language may limit the parents' participation in school activities and may make them feel their language and culture are not valued. In addition, parent–teacher associations may support parent involvement by including parents in the educational experiences of their children (Delgado-Gaitan, 2001).

Communicate in Parents' Language of Choice

In order for educators and parents to work together, educators need to determine parents' English and Spanish language abilities and the parents' preferred language of communication both orally and in writing (Hornberger, 1992). Although some parents prefer to speak in Spanish, other parents, particularly those educated in the United States, may not know how to read and write in Spanish and may prefer to communicate in Spanish orally and in English during written communication.

In order to successfully communicate with parents and children, educational programs must have access to both interpreters and translators. By communicating to parents in Spanish as well as in English, educators not only assure that important meeting/activity notices are understood, but they also demonstrate that they value the home language and bilingualism.

Provide the Child Time to Learn English

Children who are learning a second language, such as English, need time to learn the new language. Research has shown that children require 2–3 years to engage in interpersonal interactions fluently and 5–7 years to achieve a level of proficiency in English that will allow them to learn academically (Cummins, 1981). Therefore, when a child enters an English-speaking or bilingual academic program, it is important to give the child time to adjust to the classroom (Tabors, 1997). Additionally, educators can support the children's language development by placing the language to which children are exposed into the immediate context. This can be accomplished by talking about events currently happening and by repeating the sentences that they produce, which helps the children link the language with the event. Educators can also place their language in context by setting up and following routines, including daily routines, routines for performing various activities, and verbal routines that accompany the events and activities of the day. As the children become more proficient in speaking English, teachers may vary the routine and increase the length or complexity of their sentences (Tabors, 1997).

Instruct in Both English and Spanish

If children have been raised in a home in which Spanish is spoken or if the children have not acquired proficiency in English, it is critical that children are talked to and taught in their first language (Garcia, 2000). It is very difficult for children to learn new concepts or how to read in English if they are instructed only in a language (i.e., English) that they do not fully comprehend. Research has shown that reading instruction in the children's first language does carry over to reading instruction in the second language (Snow et al., 1998). This situation does not mean that instruction cannot occur in both languages. Based on our experiences, we suggest that children be taught in both Spanish and English, so that they can acquire new concepts in their primary language while they are learning to speak and read in English.

Respect Parent Beliefs

As discussed, Puerto Rican parents may have beliefs about their children's literacy development that differ from those of the dominant language community. Hammer (1998) argued that educators develop an understanding of parents' beliefs and practices by conducting semi-structured interviews, during which the practitioner places emphasis on eliciting the family's views and experiences about literacy. Rather than asking a preset list of questions, a set of questions are developed that foster faster conversation between the professional and the family. After establishing a rapport with the family, the practitioner uses the questions to elicit the family's views. The professional is careful not to dominate the conversation, but instead listens to the family, allowing the family to share information that is most important to them. Through this process, information is gradually obtained about family members' educational and literacy experiences, about beliefs of how children learn to read, and about literacy practices. The information gained can be used to tailor interventions to an individual family by providing suggestions and activities that build on family beliefs and practices.

Provide a Rich Literacy Environment in the Home

By valuing the home language and culture, parents are encouraged to participate more fully in their children's education. Parents should be encouraged to provide a rich literacy environment in the home language and in the ways in which parents are most comfortable (Hammer et al., 2002). Programs must support children's English literacy development by building on children's home language experiences and on the first language abilities that children possess when they enter school.

Be Sensitive to Challenges of Poverty

Additionally, educators need to understand the special needs of bilingual children from low-income backgrounds who come to early childhood and elementary school programs with a broad range of home literacy experiences and English literacy abilities. Schools can assist parents in providing a literacy-rich environment by assuring that literacy materials are available in the home. More important, schools can support parents by understanding the additional stresses and circumstances that low-income families experience, assisting families in obtaining needed resources, and recognizing that basic survival needs may take precedence over literacy activities.

Successful relationships can be fostered between school personnel and Latino communities. To do so, professionals need to acquire knowledge about Latino cultures so that they may maximize the benefits of their interactions with Latino families. Successful communication between teachers and parents can help eliminate cultural misunderstandings between families and professionals.

Although this chapter primarily discussed preschool-aged bilingual children, successful alliances between parents and children at this age will foster positive relationships at school age that benefit older children's continued literacy development. More research on the process of literacy development in bilingual children will lead to a better understanding of the critical factors of the process and to more explicit recommendations for parents for providing literacy support in the home.

ACKNOWLEDGMENTS

This research was supported under grant 1R01HD39496–02, as part of the Biliteracy Research Network, funded by the National Institute of Child Health and Human Development and the Institute of Education Sciences, and by a grant from the American Speech Language Hearing Association. The authors wish to express thanks to the parents and children who participated in these investigations. In addition, the authors are grateful to the staff of the Head Start programs in central Pennsylvania who participated in the studies, to the home visitors for their assistance with data collection, to Sandy Rosario for her coordination of the project, and to Jill Detwiler for her assistance with data analysis.

REFERENCES

Anderson-Yockel, J., & Haynes, W. (1994). Joint picture-book reading strategies in working-class African American and White mother–toddler dyads. *Journal of Speech, Language and Hearing Research, 37,* 583–593.

August, D., & Hakuta, K. (Eds.). (1997). *Improving schooling for language-minority children: A research agenda.* Washington, DC: National Academy Press.

Bhatia, T. K., & Ritchie, W. C. (1999). The bilingual child: Some issues and perspectives. In W. Ritchie & T. Bhatia (Eds.), *Handbook of child language acquisition* (pp. 569–646). San Diego, CA: Academic Press.

Bialystok, E. (1986). Factors in the growth of linguistic awareness. *Child Development, 57*(1), 398–510.

Bialystok, E. (1988). Levels of bilingualism and levels of linguistic awareness. *Developmental Psychology, 24*(4), 560–567.

Bialystok, E. (1992). Attentional control in children's metalinguistic performance and measures of field independence. *Developmental Psychology, 28,* 654–664.

Bialystok, E. (1997). Metalinguistic awareness: The development of children's representations of language. In C. Pratt & A. Garton (Eds.), *Systems of representation in children: Development and use* (pp. 211–233). London: Wiley.

Canfield, D. L. (1981). *Spanish pronunciation in the Americas.* Chicago: University of Chicago Press.

Casanova, U. (1987). Ethnic and cultural differences. In V. Richardson-Koehler (Ed.), *Educator's handbook* (pp. 379–393). New York: Longman.

Chavkin, N., & Gonzalez, D. L. (1995). *Forging partnerships between Mexican American parents and the schools.* Washington, DC: Office of Educational Research and Improvement (ERIC Document Reproduction Service No. 388 489).

Clay, M. M. (1979). *The early detection of reading difficulties* (2nd ed.). Auckland, NZ: Heineman.

Collier, V. P., & Thomas, W. P. (1989). How quickly can immigrants become proficient in school English? *Journal of Education Issues of Language Minority Students, 16,* 187–212.

Cummins, J. (Ed.) (1981). The role of primary language development in promoting educational success for language minority students. In California State Department of Education, *Schooling and language minority students: A theoretical framework* (pp. 3–49). Los Angeles: Evaluation, Dissemination, and Assessment Center.

Cummins, J. (1989). *Empowering minority students.* Sacramento, CA: California Association for Bilingual Education.

Cummins, J. (1996). *Negotiating identities: Education for empowerment in a diverse society.* Ontario, CA: California Association for Bilingual Education.

Delgado-Gaitan, C. (1990). *Literacy for empowerment: The role of parents in children's education.* New York: Falmer.

Delgado-Gaitan, C. (2001). *The power of community.* Lanham, MD: Rowman & Littlefield.

Dickinson, D., & DeTemple, J. (1998). Putting parents in the picture: Maternal reports of preschoolers' literacy as a predictor of early reading. *Early Childhood Research Quarterly, 13,* 241–261.

Dickinson, D., & Tabors, P. (2001). *Building literacy with language: Young children learning at home and school.* Baltimore: Brookes.

Edelsky, C. (1986). Habia una vez: Writing in a bilingual program. Norwood, NJ: Ablex.

Federal Interagency Forum on Child and Family Statistics (2002). *America's children: Key national indicators of well-being.* Washington, DC: U.S. Government Printing Office.

Fey, M. (1986). *Language intervention for young children.* Austin: PRO-ED.

Fitzgerald, J. (1995). English-as-a-second language learners' cognitive reading processes: A reviews of research in the United States. *Review of Educational Research, 65,* 145–190.

Garcia, B., Mendez Perez, A., & Ortiz, A. A. (2000). Mexican American mothers' beliefs about disabilities: Implications for early childhood intervention. *Remedial & Special Education, 21,* 90–102.

Garcia, G. (2000). Bilingual children's reading. In M. Kamil, P. Mosenthal, P. Pearson, & R. Barr (Eds.), *Handbook of reading research,* Vol. III (pp. 813–834). Mahwah, NJ: Lawrence Erlbaum Associates, Inc.

Garcia Coll, C., Meyer, E., & Brillon, L. (1995). Ethnic and minority parenting. In M. Bornstein (Ed.), *Handbook of parenting: Biology and ecology of parenting* (pp. 189–209). Mahwah, NJ: Lawrence Erlbaum Associates, Inc.

Goldenberg, C. N. (1987). Low-income Hispanic parents: Contributions to their first-grade children's word-recognition skills. *Anthropology & Education Quarterly, 18,* 149–179.

Goodz, N. S. (1994). Interactions between parents and children in bilingual families. In F. Genesee (Ed.), *Educating second language children: The whole child, the whole curriculum, the whole community* (pp. 61–81). Cambridge, England: Cambridge University Press.

Hall, E. T. (1976). *Beyond culture.* New York: Doubleday.

Hammer, C. S. (1998). Toward a 'Thick Description' of families: Using ethnography to overcome the obstacles to providing family-centered services. *American Journal of Speech–Language Pathology, 9,* 5–22.

Hammer, C. S. (2000). "Come sit down and let mama read": Book reading interactions between African American mothers and their infants. In J. Harris, A. Kamhi, & K. Pollock (Eds.), *Literacy in African American communities* (pp. 21–43). Hillsdale, NJ: Lawrence Erlbaum Associates, Inc.

Hammer, C. S. (2002). *African American and Hispanic mothers' views of their children's literacy development.* Unpublished manuscript.

Hammer, C. S., & Miccio, A. W. (2000). *Home Activities Questionnaire.* Unpublished manuscript.

Hammer, C. S., Miccio, A. W., & Wagstaff, D. (2003). Home literacy experiences and their relationship to bilingual preschoolers' developing English literacy abilities. *Language, Speech and Hearing Services in Schools, 34,* 20–30.

Hammer, C. S., Nimmo, D., Cohen, R., Clemons, H., & Achenbach, A. (2002). *Book reading interactions between African American and Puerto Rican Head Start children and their mothers.* Manuscript submitted for publication.

Hammond, R. M. (2001). *The sounds of Spanish: Analysis and application.* Somerville, MA: Cascadilla.

Harrison, A. O., Wilson, M. N., Pine, C. J., Chan, S. Q., & Buriel, R. (1990). Family ecologies of ethnic minority children. *Child Development, 61,* 347–362.

Heath, S. B. (1982). What no bedtime story means: Narrative skills at home and school. *Language and Society, 11,* 49–76.

Heath, S. B. (1983). *Ways with words.* New York: Cambridge University Press.

Hess, R. D., & Holloway, S. (1984). Family and school as educational institutions. In R. D. Parke (Ed.), *Review of Child Development Research, 7: The Family* (pp. 179–222). Chicago: University of Chicago Press.

Hornberger, N. H. (1992). Biliteracy contexts, continua, and contrasts: Policy and curriculum for Cambodian and Puerto Rican students in Philadelphia. *Education and Urban Society, 24,* 196–211.

Kayser, H. (1998). *Assessment and intervention resource for Hispanic children.* San Diego, CA: Singular.

Langdon, H. W. (1992). Language communication and sociocultural patterns in Hispanic families. In H. W. Langdon, & L-R. L. Cheng (Eds.), *Hispanic children and adults with communication disorders* (pp. 99–131). Gaithersburg, MD: Aspen.

Lareau, A. (1989). *Home advantage: Social class and parental intervention in elementary education.* New York: Falmer.

McAdoo, H. P. (1983). Societal stress: The Black family. In H. McCubbin & C. Figley (Eds.), *Stress and the family.* New York: Brunner/Mazel.

McLaughlin, B. (1984). *Second-language acquisition in childhood, Vol. 1: Preschool children* (2nd ed.). Hillsdale, NJ: Lawrence Erlbaum Associates, Inc.

Meisel, J. (1994). Code-switching in young bilingual children: The acquisition of grammatical constraints. *Studies in Second Language Acquisition, 16,* 413–439.

Miles, M. B., & Huberman, A. M. (1994). *Qualitative data analysis: An expanded sourcebook,* (2nd ed.) Thousand Oaks, CA: Sage.

Moreno, R. P., & Lopez, J. A., (1999). Latina mothers' involvement in their children's schooling: The role of maternal education and acculturation. *JSRI Working Paper Series, 44,* 1–18.

National Reading Panel (2000). *Report of the National Reading Panel.* Washington, DC: U.S. Government Printing Office.

Neuman, S. B., Hagedorn, T., Celano, D., & Daly, P. (1995). Toward a collaborative approach to parent involvement in early education: A study of teenage mothers in an African-American community. *American Educational Research Journal, 32,* 801–827.

Ninio, A., & Bruner, J. (1978). The antecedents of labelling. *Journal of Child Language, 5,* 1–15.

Ochs, E., & Schieffelin, B. B. (1984). Language acquisition and socialization: Three developmental stories and their implications. In R. Schweder & R. Levine (Eds.), *Culture theory* (pp. 276–320). New York: Cambridge University Press.

Ogbu, J. U. (1988). Diversity and equity in public education: Community forces and minority school adjustment and performance. In R. Haskins & D. MacRae (Eds.), *Policies for America's public schools: Teachers, equity, and indicators* (pp. 11–28). Norwood, NJ: Ablex.

Patton, M. (2002). *Qualitative evaluation and research methods.* Thousand Oaks, CA: Sage.

Pelligrini, A., Perlmutter, J., Galda, L., & Brody, G. (1990). Joint reading between Black Head Start children and their mothers. *Child Development, 61,* 443–453.

Peña, D. C. (2000). Parent involvement: Influencing factors and implications. *The Journal of Educational Research, 94,* 42–54.

Rauh, V. A., Wasserman, G. A., & Brunelli, S. A. (1990). Determinants of maternal child-rearing attitudes. *Journal of the American Academy of Child and Adolescent Psychiatry, 29,* 375–381.

Reid, D. K., Hresko, W., & Hammill, D. (1991). *Test of Early Reading Ability–2.* Austin, TX: PRO-ED.

Rodriguez, B., & Olswang, L. B. (in press). *Mexican-American and Anglo-American mothers' beliefs about child rearing, education, and language impairment. Journal of speech Language Pathology.*

Rogoff, B. (1981). Schooling and the development of cognitive skills. In H. C. Triandis & A. Heron (Eds.), *Handbook of cross cultural psychology: Developmental psychology,* Vol. 4 (pp. 33–85). Boston: Allyn & Bacon.

Rogoff, B. (1990). *Apprenticeship in thinking: Cognitive development in social context.* New York: Oxford University Press.

Roseberry-McKibben, C. (2002). *Multicultural students with special language needs* (2nd ed.). Oceanside, CA: Academic Communication Associates.

Scarborough, H. S., & Dobrich, W. (1994). On the efficacy of reading to preschoolers. *Developmental Review, 14,* 245–302.

Schieffelin, B., & Ochs, E. (1983). *A cultural perspective on the transition from prelinguistic to linguistic communication.* Hillsdale, NJ: Lawrence Erlbaum Associates, Inc.

Schwartz, T. (1981). The acquisition of culture. *Ethos, 9,* 4–17.

Snow, C. (1990). The development of definitional skill. *Journal of Child Language, 17,* 697–710.

Snow, C., Burns, M. S., & Griffin, P. (Eds.). (1998). *Preventing reading difficulties in young children.* Washington, DC: National Academy Press.

Suarez-Orozco, M. M., & Paez, M. M. (2002). Introduction: The research agenda. In M. M. Suarez-Orozco & M. M. Paez (Eds.), *Latinos: Remaking America* (pp. 1–38). Berkeley: University of California Press.

Tabors, P. O. (1997). *One child, two languages.* Baltimore, MD: Brookes.

Teale, W. (1986). Home background and young children's literacy development. In W. Teale & E. Sulzby (Eds.), *Emergent literacy: Writing and research* (pp. 173–206). Norwood, NJ: Albex.

Therrien, M., & Ramirez, R. (2001). *The Hispanic population in the United States* (U.S. Census Bureau Report P20–535). Washington, DC: U.S. Census Bureau.

Valdez, G. (1996). *Con Respeto: Bridging the distances between culturally diverse families and schools.* New York: Teachers College Press.

van Kleeck, A., Gilliam, R., Hamilton, L., & McGrath, C. (1997). The relationship between middle-class parents' book-sharing discussion and their preschoolers' abstract language development. *Journal of Speech Language Hearing Research, 40,* 1261–1271.

Vega, W., Hough, R., & Romero, A. (1983). Family life patterns of Mexican Americans. In G. Powell, J. Yamamoto, A. Romero, & A. Morales (Eds.), *The psychosocial development of minority group children* (pp. 194–215). New York: Brunner/Mazel.

Velasco, P. (1989). *The relationship of oral decontextualized language and reading comprehension in bilingual children.* Unpublished doctoral thesis, Harvard University Graduate School of Education, Cambridge, MA.

Wolfram, W. (1991). *Dialects and American English.* Englewood Cliffs, NJ: Prentice Hall.

Zentella, A. C. (2002). Latina languages and identities. In M. Suarez-Orozco & M. A. Paez, (Eds.). *Latinos: Remaking America* (pp. 321–338). Berkeley: University of California Press.

Zuniga, M. (1988). Chicano self-concept: A proactive stance. In C. Jacobs & D. Bowles (Eds.), *Ethnicity and race: Critical concepts in social work* (pp. 71–83). Silver Spring, MD: National Association of Social Workers.

Zuniga, M. (1998). Families with Latino roots. In E. Lynch & M. Hanson (Eds.), *Developing cross-cultural competence* (pp. 209–250). Baltimore.

18

Home Visiting and Family Literacy Programs

Donna Bryant and
Barbara Hanna Wasik
University of North Carolina at Chapel Hill

Home visiting as a way of providing services to families in need has a long history in health, social services, and education. Many services in use today have their roots in the advances made in social services during the late 1800s and early 1900s. Early services were often designed for mothers and children, the sick, and the poor. Home visiting for educational purposes was also prevalent in the early 1900s, with visiting teachers serving as a link between home and school.

In the 1980s and 1990s, home visiting programs for families with young children multiplied throughout the United States. Their development and expansion was supported by research showing the importance of the earliest years in children's lives and by a belief that offering services in the home has advantages, compared to seeing families in an office, school, or clinic. Thousands of home visiting programs exist for families with young children, with a wide range of goals, target populations, and procedures (Wasik & Roberts, 1994). Although most of them share a belief that building a good relationship with the family is important, the home visitor's role, the content of the visits, and the intensity and duration of the program can be quite variable.

Home visits are conducted in many types of educational programs, some of which are strongly related to literacy, others less so. For example, home visits are an integral (and sometimes mandated) part of comprehensive family literacy programs. Even for programs that would not necessarily consider literacy to be their primary mission (e.g., Early Head Start, Home Instruction for Parents of Preschool Youngsters, Healthy Families America, Parents As Teachers [PAT]), promoting children's literacy is an important objective. Both types of home visiting programs are the focus of this chapter.

We first consider home visiting's advantages as an approach for helping families enhance their children's language and literacy development, then we describe home visiting's role in two major home visiting programs. Next, we discuss some of the challenges for both home visitors and programs involved in delivering services to families and children through home visiting. Finally, we recommend directions for improving the efficacy of home visiting as a service delivery system for family literacy.

329

WHY VISIT IN THE HOME?

Home visiting offers several advantages as a strategy for reaching and supporting families. It is family-focused and flexible, meeting parents on their own terms in their own homes, signifying respect for their time and for them as individuals. These characteristics should help build trust between visitor and parent. Home visiting occurs in the natural setting of the home. Parents discuss information with an educator in the home that they might not discuss in an office or center, giving home visitors better information with which to tailor the help provided or the materials brought to the family. Through learning about family routines, expectations, and beliefs, the home visitor can become more culturally sensitive to families' backgrounds and traditions. The home visitor can build on existing family strengths and practices and, if a family needs additional help, can make referrals that are sensitive to the family's values and that fit within the type of help-seeking they are likely to accept. This section elaborates on several factors related to being in the home that might facilitate a home visitor's work with a family vis-à-vis literacy.

The first and most obvious reason for focusing on family literacy through home visiting is that emergent literacy has been strongly linked to the literacy artifacts and activities in the natural environment (Heath, 1983; Taylor, 1983; and see chapter 5 in this volume). Several writers have named factors in the home environment that influence literacy development, including Leichter (1984), Britto and Brooks-Gunn (2001), Wasik and Hendrickson (in press), and chapter 16 in this volume. Although their frameworks differ, they all recognize that interactions among family members, especially parents and children, and physical resources, including literacy materials, both influence early literacy development.

Numerous research studies have also supported the importance of activities and resources in the home for children's literacy development. The focus of these studies ranges from parent–child storybook reading and parent–child relationships to the home environment. This volume contains detailed presentations of this research in chapters 4 and 5.

Even if young children attend day care or preschool, they spend the majority of their waking hours in the home, and the home is where most of their early literacy skills develop. The activities of daily life help many children develop the foundation to become proficient readers and communicators. Such everyday activities include watching a parent write a shopping list, seeing older siblings do schoolwork, or watching grandparents read the newspaper.

Resources in the home, including books and other literacy artifacts, can also promote literacy learning. Seeing the home environment firsthand provides the home visitor with knowledge about resources and processes that the visitor can use in discussions with parents, to help them recognize ways they can incorporate literacy activities into everyday life.

Interpersonal interactions among children, parents, and others in the house are best and most naturally observed in the home. Evidence shows that the nature of parents' language with their young children can strongly support or undermine children's early language and literacy learning; home visitors observing families in the natural environment can make recommendations for modifying parent–child interactions. In everyday language interactions between parent and child, the visitor can listen for a match between the child's level of understanding and the parent's verbalizations; for level of language use; for whether or not a respectful tone is present; and for whether or not the parent's language is too controlling, negative, or threatening.

With knowledge of typical parent–child interactions, the home visitor can help the parent think of alternatives. The visitor can suggest or provide activities that build on and enhance the parents' strengths and that help build competencies in activities that are new for the parents. For example, if a parent seems to ignore the child's pointing to and labeling an object, the visitor can discuss how such child behaviors can be used as opportunities to expand on the child's knowledge and to improve oral language. The visitor can mention how important it is to observe children and to become more aware of what they know. Parents can learn strategies to help expand their children's vocabulary and understanding of things around them.

Home visits make possible individualized intervention for the parent. Even if the parent attends parent education groups, as in most family literacy programs, he or she may need help in incorporating certain practices into the daily routine. Home visitors, by focusing on the particular circumstances of each parent and child in the home, can draw on the family's unique strengths as a foundation for building literacy skills.

Another reason to visit the home is to observe parent–child shared storybook reading, providing a home visitor the opportunity to encourage and build on these interactions. Parent–child storybook reading will probably not occur during a home visit, unless requested by the visitor, but it can become an integral part of visits. For example, a typical visit in the PAT program includes a short time in which a parent reads a book aloud with the child. Shared reading is an optimal time to learn words and sounds and to strengthen the socioemotional bond between parent and child. Of course, reading with a child may not be helpful or fun, if the interpersonal interaction is not positive (Dickinson & Tabors, 1991; see chapter 10 of this volume). Visitors who observe parents reading with their children can tell whether or not they read with enthusiasm and elaboration or with disinterest and impatience.

Even if shared book reading is not, or cannot be, an explicit part of visits, the home visitor can use the time in the home to engage the parent and child in activities related to literacy development. For example, the visitor and mother, father, or other primary caregiver might talk about how to establish routines of storybook reading, ways to engage the child during reading, and how to have the child become a more active participant in the book-reading activity. Through conversation, the visitor can assess whether or not, and how frequently, the parent engages in shared book reading and can reinforce or encourage such activities.

In comprehensive family literacy programs with both center-based and home-based components, the home visitor, parent educator, or family specialist who visits the parent can strengthen the tie between the center-based program and the home. Epstein (1991) found that good partnerships between school and home were related to parents' involvement in their children's home literacy learning. Home visitors can reinforce information presented at a recent parent group meeting. They can assess parents' understanding of a topic and can answer questions parents may have after trying out the ideas presented at the parent group. Home visitors can tell parents about classroom literacy activities that seem especially interesting to the child and can encourage the parents to provide similar activities at home. In addition, if attendance at the center-based program is a problem, the visitor can help parents think through issues that might be preventing them or their child from attending regularly. As these examples show, there are many ways that home visitors can reinforce the partnership between the center and the home.

Another advantage of visiting in homes is that it takes home visitors into communities, which differ in the opportunities they offer to encourage literacy. Home visitors learn what resources or activities are available in different neighborhoods, for example, parks, libraries, and community centers, or the visitor will find out the quality of the public transportation system. This kind of information can help the home visitor encourage parents to get involved in community activities that would be good for the family and for the child.

Practical reasons also exist for providing help to families in their own homes. Families with no or limited transportation may more likely participate in a program that brings services to them, rather than expecting the family to come to the program's office. Families in poverty are especially likely to have difficulties with transportation, yet are the very families we want to reach with literacy interventions. Poverty is a major factor in children's literacy. Poor children suffer more language delays and reading difficulties than others (Snow, Burns, & Griffin, 1998). Engaging poor families and families under stress in any type of intervention, is challenging. Visiting the home increases the likelihood that families receive the intervention.

Visiting families in their homes to promote adult and child literacy offers many advantages. It provides an understanding of the family's everyday life and the types of materials and routines in the natural environment that serve as the basis for children's literacy. The observation of interpersonal interactions, from greetings to behavior management to storybook reading, provides an interventionist a good sense of the family's interpersonal communication. A skilled visitor can use all of this knowledge to better help the family promote children's literacy skills.

THE ROLE OF HOME VISITING WITHIN TWO PROGRAMS THAT PROMOTE FAMILY LITERACY

This section summarizes the role of home visiting in two different family literacy program models. The PAT program delivers services primarily through individual home visits, and the Even Start Family Literacy Program uses home visiting as but one aspect of an approach that also includes center-based intervention for children, parent education groups, parent–child literacy interactions, and adult education. Both programs are described here.

Parents as Teachers

The PAT model began as a pilot project in Missouri in 1981 and has become one of the largest home visiting programs for infants and toddlers in the country, currently serving about 300,000 children in over 3,000 programs (PAT, 2003). Since 1993, 4- and 5-year-olds have been included in PAT and now make up 33% of children in the program. The program's major goals are to enhance child development and school achievement through parent education that is accessible to all families. The four PAT components are personal visits, group meetings, screening, and a resource network. One-hour home visits are scheduled monthly, biweekly, or weekly, depending on family needs and the sponsoring program's budget. Parent group meetings offer another opportunity for families to acquire information about child development. Parent educators conduct screening and assessment to help parents understand their children's development and areas of strengths and concern. Programs also link families with other community agencies, if needed.

The PAT National Center in St. Louis supports local programs by providing training for home visitors (called *parent educators*). PAT strongly recommends that parent educators have professional education and experience in education or social work with young children and families, although local programs make the hiring decisions. One week of preservice training by certified PAT trainers is required before parent educators begin work. Programs themselves undergo annual recertification and must document that they have provided 10–20 hr of in-service training. PAT also provides a complete curriculum (Born to Learn) that parent educators can use with families during home visits.

PAT is not strictly a literacy program and does not promote itself as such. Yet many of the activities that PAT parent educators use with parents and children encourage literacy development. For example, among activities for 8- to 14-month-old babies and their parents, the Born to Learn curriculum includes listening to songs and nursery rhymes, reading simple books, pointing to pictures and naming them, and naming the things the baby points to (PAT, 1999). PAT provides activities, videotapes, and handouts to use during home visits with parent and child. The parent educator's role is to explain, model, and encourage the parents to become involved in these activities with their children and to engage in them frequently.

The PAT program has been the focus of several evaluation studies (e.g., Pfannenstiel, Seitz, & Zigler, 2002; Wagner, Spiker, & Linn, 2002). A recent study showed that how the PAT program is implemented is as important as the planned activities. In a study of PAT in California, in which families were to have one visit a month, the average number of visits was 20 visits over 3 years. In addition, only 15% of families attended any group meeting, so that the majority of the intervention was delivered via home visits (Wagner & Clayton, 1999). For literacy interventions being delivered via home visits, these findings illustrate the importance of ensuring an adequate frequency of contact between parents and visitors, especially when home visiting is the only avenue of service. The PAT National Center uses research results such as these to decide what program areas need strengthening or modification.

Even Start Family Literacy Program

Even Start is a two-generation educational program, integrating early childhood education for children under age 8 years and adult and parenting education for eligible low-income parents. Its goals are to improve educational outcomes for children and educational and employment outcomes for parents, through increasing literacy behaviors and improving parenting skills. From a small demonstration program authorized by Congress in 1989, Even Start has become a large national program focused on parents' and children's literacy. In 2000–2001, approximately 32,000 families participated in 855 Even Start projects in all 50 states, with funding totaling $150 million (U.S. Department of Education [DOE], 2003). In the following year, the number of projects increased to 1,125, and the budget increased to $250 million.

In the past few years, total national enrollment in Even Start has decreased, even though the total number of programs has increased. Also, the average number of families served by each program has dropped from 62 families per program in 1991 to 37 families in 2001. This reduction resulted from a conscious decision at the DOE to focus resources most intensively on the neediest families, in order to achieve the best results. The first national Even Start evaluation (St.Pierre et al., 1995) showed that families in programs offering more hours of services participated more and that such families had better learning gains than those who participated less frequently (see chapters 13 and 14, this volume, for a discussion of parent participation).

The first chapter in this book described the four main components of Even Start programs: early childhood education, parenting education, adult education (literacy or basic skills training), and parent–child joint literacy activities. Home visiting, or home-based instruction, is considered part of the parent education component. It is also linked with all of the other program components. Although the goals of Even Start are defined in the federal legislation and the component services are specified, Congress prohibits the DOE from specifying curriculum. Thus, unlike PAT programs, Even Start programs have a common name, but do not share a common curriculum.

The components of Even Start programs support literacy through formal, organized instruction of children and parents and through home visiting—a more informal, individualized approach to promoting literacy development. The Even Start statute requires local programs to provide integrated instructional services, with an educational focus on their families through home-based services. The objective is to advance the educational goals of the program, including strengthening the literacy skills of parents and children. These home-based services are seen as increasing the intensity and individualization of the program and the access of some families to services (U.S. DOE, 2001). Even Start programs are the primary providers of the early childhood education component and adult educational services, although many projects form collaborations with local service providers to serve some or all of their families (U.S. DOE, 2003). In the most recent national evaluation, the average Even Start program offered 173 hours of parenting education per year, including home visits and parent group meetings, as well as 157 hours of joint parent–child activity time. Because participation is reported by component, home visits and parent group attendance were not reported separately, but 89% of families participated in parent education. A slightly higher percentage (93%) of parents with limited English proficiency participated in parenting education. However, parents participated in only about 25% of the parent education activities offered to them, and half the families left the program within 10 months.

Even Start staff generally delivers the program's parenting education component, because of the paucity of existing community programs with which to contract. The staff provides home visits and parent group meetings, using a variety of curriculum resources to increase parents' understanding of their role in the education of their children and providing information about child development. Home visitors take toys and books into the home and often model an activity or technique to use with the child. Parenting education is also included in the parent–child literacy interaction time, often referred to as Parents and Children Together Time. This time is regularly scheduled for parents and children to interact (with staff guidance) in games or activities focused on development of children's language and literacy. Some Even Start home visitors integrate these Parents and Children Together activities into their visits with families, although this is not done systematically. The parent education component is not what generally draws parents into Even Start, but, rather, it is most often the adult education component. But once enrolled, parents report learning how to play with their children, having more patience, and using less physical punishment (St.Pierre & Swartz, 1995).

Not only do Even Start home visitors provide and encourage home-based literacy activities between parent and child, but they also have the opportunity to support adult literacy by helping parents set goals and develop strategies for achieving them. The adult education component of Even Start usually consists of services to prepare the parent for attaining a GED, English instruction, adult basic education, computer instruction in reading and math, and a variety of other adult education services. Local community colleges often provide the adult education. The average amount of adult education instruction offered to parents across programs is 30–40 hr per month.

Even Start families tend to be even more disadvantaged than families in the national Head Start evaluation. They have a much lower annual household income, and the parents are much less likely to have a high school diploma. Even Start parents scored at the first percentile on reading comprehension skills when they entered the program. Even Start meets the Congressional mandate to serve families that are "most in need of" educational services.

The most recent Even Start national evaluation included 18 programs that participated in a randomized study, each assigning 20 families to Even Start and 10 families to a control, nontreatment group (U.S. DOE, 2003). The results of that study showed that Even Start children and parents made gains in literacy and other measures, but so did those in the control group. For example, both groups of children gained 4 standard score points on the Peabody Picture Vocabulary Test (Dunn & Dunn, 1997), a measure of receptive language.

The study found that Even Start offers an extensive set of services for a number of hours a month and that the amount of early childhood education and adult education has increased since the previous national evaluation. However, Even Start families do not participate in these services at levels that would be needed to achieve the desired outcomes. Those who do participate more often are more likely to have a child who makes greater gains. Obtaining higher levels of parent and child participation is a challenge for Even Start, as in all home visiting and family literacy programs.

The home visitors in both the PAT and Even Start programs support parents and families in their roles as the child's first and most important teacher. The parent educators in both programs focus on language and literacy as one of the major domains of development. The visitors provide information and literacy materials to parents, demonstrate and model activities that stimulate children's language and literacy development, and support and encourage parents to be frequently engaged with their children in telling stories, reading, and many other activities that support literacy.

A number of quality considerations for Even Start home-based instruction have been identified. Some of these overlap with considerations listed previously. Other activities noted as important are to keep literacy as a primary focus; to maintain regularly scheduled visits; to balance attention to parent–child relationship building, child development, and parents' needs and interests; and to help parents have an active role in shaping the visit (a complete listing of these quality considerations is reported in U.S. DOE, 2001). Although the Even Start staff is trained to address a number of family issues that may arise in the home, they are also to link with other agencies, as appropriate (see chapter 20 of this handbook for ways to foster service coordination with other agencies).

The PAT program and the Even Start program are well-known home visiting programs that promote family literacy throughout the United States and other countries (see chapter 2 of this volume). Many early childhood education programs, however, also include home visiting or home-based instruction as part of their literacy services. In the following section, we discuss some of the issues faced by home visitors when providing these services.

STRATEGIES FOR PROMOTING FAMILY LITERACY

This section describes practical issues faced by home visitors in family literacy programs. Both content and interpersonal interactions are important factors in the success of their work. Hannon (1995) suggests that interventionists should be wary of promoting literacy as an end in itself. Rather, he suggests that parents are more motivated to promote literacy, and to engage in literacy-related activities, if they see such activities as a means to reach goals that they value for themselves or for their children.

Earlier in this book, Powell (chapter 9) summarized the four major dimensions of parental behaviors and beliefs that are related to children's literacy outcomes and early school success: (a) the family verbal environment, (b) supports for early literacy, (c) parents' expectations of children's learning and development, and (d) active engagement of the parenting role. As noted earlier, an advantage of home visiting is that a home visitor can assess all these important dimensions on every visit, which is something that would be impossible to do in an office or classroom setting. Knowledge of these dimensions of parenting allows the home visitor to better select, prepare, and introduce the literacy-enhancing activities that are part of the literacy program.

A number of authors recommend practices for working with parents. After evaluating five family literacy programs, Ryan, Geissler, and Knell (1994) suggested that programs should include content relevant to a participant's life. This suggestion is one area in which the home visitor's knowledge of everyday activities and availability of materials becomes helpful. Perhaps the environment is rich in print materials, but they are not often used with children, or perhaps the environment is basically lacking in print materials of any kind. The visitor can support positive activities that parents already engage in with their children and can suggest additional activities that fit the family's situation, encouraging the use of materials already in the home or possibly providing new materials for playing with and teaching the child.

Bernheimer and Keogh (1995) suggested that new approaches and activities should be built into families' existing daily interactions. They call this approach to intervention *ecocultural*. In the home, visitors obtain knowledge about other adults or older siblings who might also be encouraged to play literacy-promoting games with the young child. Given the hectic schedule of most modern families, just finding time to play with a child is sometimes challenging.

Visitors get a sense of daily life and can help parents develop literacy activities that fit into specific times of day or that take advantage of the presence of a friend or relative. For example, the parent might care for a school-age niece or nephew every afternoon after school, and this older child could be given special activities and an important role in helping the younger child with language and literacy.

With the current national debates concerning the most appropriate ways to teach language and literacy, home visitors might be unsure about the best ways to help parents promote early literacy and language development. The research literature provides some direction. For example, research links three components of early literacy most strongly to later conventional literacy and reading: phonological processing, print awareness, and oral language (Whitehurst & Lonigan, 2001). How can home visitors help parents teach their children in these three domains in a way that promotes mutual enjoyment of preliteracy and reading activities without being too academic?

Luckily, home visitors generally do not start from scratch. Most parents are already involved in enhancing their children's early literacy development, through the variety of activities they engage in every day. Parents may not think of everyday activities as learning activities or label them as such, but, without any special help, many parents rear children who are ready to learn to read when they go to school, and some even before. Other parents may not have the resources to do so, including time and energy. Still others may believe that children do not need to be read to or do not need to play with pencils and paper until they enter school. Home visitors in family literacy programs interact with a range of families—some with few literacy resources and others with many—so that home visitors need to develop an approach to their work that is flexible, individualized, and based on each family's strengths.

Latino families are a case in point. They often worry that their lack of English proficiency and low levels of education prevent them from supporting their children's literacy learning. They are also more likely to view teachers as experts in teaching their children and to see their parental role as teaching life skills and values, rather than academic knowledge (Rodriguez-Brown, 2001). For these reasons, programs such as Project FLAME have been developed to increase Latino families' involvement in their children's learning at home (see chapter 12 in this volume).

Many home visitors are also parents and possess a range of experiences in encouraging language and literacy development with their own young children. They have a base of ideas and skills from their own lives, which have been supplemented with sufficient training from their program and materials, to use with families as they make home visits. Thus, both visitors and parents bring experiences and resources into the relationship.

Parents may think that there are special ways of teaching reading and that they are not experts. Our technical language regarding literacy and reading (e.g., phonemic awareness, morphemes) actually promotes this idea, so visitors should guard against unwittingly giving the impression that promoting literacy can only be done by experts. In homes, parents generally teach their children one-on-one in a variety of real-life activities, although they might not call this teaching. Such teaching can be very different from the way literacy is sometimes taught in preschool classrooms, which have structured activities such as morning sign-in, reading circle, and alphabet time. Home visitors who have come from a preschool classroom background will certainly notice many differences between classroom and home literacy support activities.

Although some parents may want to use, or already use, the more formal practices of an educational setting, helping parents use the informal events of everyday family life as the primary way to promote children's literacy often works best and seems less like an assignment from school. This approach does not, however, preclude occasional explicit suggestions or guidance from the home visitor about activities or behaviors that would help the child's literacy development.

Home visitors are sometimes challenged by families who accept and comply with visits, but who do not seem invested in the literacy process or who have personal obstacles that prevent spending time with their child in literacy-related activities. In such situations, home visitors who have been trained to use problem-solving skills can help parents develop solutions to these challenges (Wasik & Bryant, 2001). Rather than simply making suggestions about ways that parents can help their children in areas such as oral language or recognizing letters, home visitors can take the next step by helping parents see how these objectives can fit into their family life. For example, visitors can engage parents in discussions about how to carry out these objectives. A visitor might say: "We have been talking about how much your child likes for you to read to her, but you said you had trouble finding time in your busy day to do this. Would you like to see if together we can figure out some ways this could be done?" or "In the past, when you wanted to really do something but didn't seem to have time, were there some things you were able to do that helped you find the time?" Guiding parents through a problem-solving process might increase opportunities for literacy learning by helping parents identify obstacles and generate solutions. Visitors can use a step-by-step procedure to help parents think through solutions to their objectives. Such a procedure is especially valuable in family literacy programs, because it incorporates one of the goals of adult education, namely, promoting adult problem-solving skills.

Taking advantage of incidental learning opportunities is a good literacy-enhancing strategy that home visitors often try to teach their families. As noted, children learn from all kinds of everyday events. Incidental teaching takes advantage of the unplanned, natural interactions of children's everyday life, to increase the use of language. Good incidental teaching begins with an activity or interaction initiated by the child, then is built on by the adult, using language that is age-appropriate. The interaction should be brief, positive, and focused on the child's selected activity. The adult can expand on the child's language, describe or ask questions about what is happening, and encourage the child to use language (Lutzker & Bigelow, 2002; see chapter 3 of this volume for additional ways to use everyday activities to promote language and literacy.)

Home visitors also practice incidental teaching, as they find opportunities in their interactions with families to encourage literacy-enhancing activities as a part of daily life. By doing so, visitors model incidental teaching by sharing impromptu ideas or reinforcement with parents, when the opportunity arises. For example, the visitor could support a positive parent–child communication that the visitor notices.

Promoting shared book reading is another frequent emphasis of home visitors who are trying to encourage literacy skill development in preschoolers. Many preschool children encounter books at home, but not as often as might be optimal. A British study observed 165 children, aged 3 and 4 years old, in their homes, for six 1-hr periods over several days (Davie, Hutt, Vincent, & Mason, 1984). Nearly all the children (94%) looked at books at some point, and adults often did so with them. However, the total amount of time engaged with books was quite small—only 3% of the children's day, compared to 9% spent watching television. Encouragement and support of shared book reading by the home visitor seems warranted for all families.

In the United States, research has shown that parents in low-income families and in African American families read to their children less frequently than do middle-class White families (Anderson-Yockel & Haynes, 1994; Hammer, 2001). Another study found that 41% of low-income families reported reading to their preschooler every day, compared to 61% of families above the poverty line. The percentage of families reporting daily reading was 64% for Whites, 44% for African Americans, and 39% for Hispanics (Federal Interagency Forum on Child and Family Statistics, 1999).

These results suggest the need for home visitors to have a variety of ways of encouraging parents to read more frequently with their children, including talking about the value of reading, providing books, asking that parents read to their child throughout the week, providing logs for recording book-related activities, and following up with questions about reading experiences. The goal is to foster a positive attitude toward books and literacy and many experiences with books and literacy materials. Knowing the activities that children and their parents typically engage in during the day and evening can help the home visitor make suggestions regarding shared book reading that fit better into the family's lifestyle and that are more likely to be used by parents. Asking direct questions, such as "Do these seem like activities you might want to do?" can help the visitor understand the parents' objectives or the obstacles that prevent them from engaging in more literacy-enhancing activities.

Home visitors in family literacy programs provide a range of suggestions to parents, including reading to children frequently, sitting close to children when reading, and encouraging children to talk about a story by asking a variety of questions. They also suggest that parents turn the television off while reading and limit television time in general, make the activity enjoyable, and encourage other readers in the house to read with the child. Many of these suggestions can be modeled by the home visitor or with the home visitor and parent joining together. To address the limited number of books in some homes, programs may have children's books in a lending library that the home visitor can check out to families. Purcell-Gates, in chapter 6, suggests additional ways parents can acquire storybooks for their children.

Like all early educators these days, home visitors are paying attention to the debates in the field regarding the tension between emphasizing meaning and enjoyment of reading versus phonemic awareness and preacademic skills. Of course, these goals are not mutually exclusive, and many activities promote both. Parents teach phonemic awareness to their children through enjoyable activities, such as singing and reciting nursery rhymes, playing word games, and by having fun with sounds and songs. Parents teach print awareness by being readers themselves and by acting as models for their children, labeling street and store signs for children, and, of course, by reading books. Parents teach oral language by telling stories, singing songs, having frequent conversations with children, asking and answering questions about words, and elaborating on children's talk. All of these are enjoyable activities that also teach children early literacy skills.

ISSUES FOR PROGRAMS USING HOME VISITING FOR FAMILY LITERACY

The previous section dealt with issues that face home visitors as they interact with families and try to encourage literacy activities. This section notes four broad issues that programs employing home visitors as literacy interventionists must consider: (a) staff credentials and education, (b) training and supervision of home visitors, (c) intensity of services, and (d) identification of service population. All home visiting programs face these issues, not just those whose goal is literacy promotion.

Educational Credentials

Many factors influence decisions about staffing, including philosophy, budget, and language context. Some home visiting programs want interventionists who share the social characteristics and values of the clients, thinking they might be more effective than outsiders, however well educated. A modest program budget can cause programs to hire less educated home visitors than they might prefer. In communities with high proportions of families whose native language is not English, the need for bilingual home visitors sometimes drives programs to hire paraprofessionals from within the community.

Wasik and Roberts (1994) found that 60% of home visiting programs for children do not require visitors to have bachelor's degrees. Of those that did not require a bachelor's degree, some required a Child Development Associate (CDA) credential, which is especially helpful for home visitors and is frequently obtained by Head Start staff. Decisions about home visitors' qualifications are critical to a program's overall success, yet research provides little evidence about the merits of requiring a bachelor's degree. A review of 15 home visiting programs, focused on cognitive and language development of young children in low-income families, showed that only 6 programs had significant benefits for children and that 5 of the 6 programs employed home visitors with bachelor's degrees (Olds & Kitzman, 1993).

A recent randomized study compared families of infants visited by nurse home visitors (with at least a B.A. degree and nursing credentials), families visited by paraprofessional home visitors, and a control group of families who received no home visiting (Olds et al., 2002). That study showed only one significant difference in 30 measured outcomes for the group visited by paraprofessionals, compared to the control group, but 12 significant differences for the mothers and children visited by nurses, compared to the control group. For both groups of families, more effects were seen among mothers who had low psychological resources. Although the study could not directly compare nurse to paraprofessional visits, for most outcomes the effects in families visited by paraprofessionals were about half as large.

These results were obtained even though the paraprofessionals made as many attempts to visit as did the nurses. Olds et al. (2002) attribute the difference to the natural legitimacy that nurses have: the public thinks nurses have the highest ethical standards and are the most honest of all professionals. This perception gives nurses power to engage parents and to bring about adaptive behavior changes and probably accounts for the lower number of no-shows. This situation alone could account for the observed outcome differences, rather than the visitors' educational levels per se. Olds et al. (2002) also thought that paraprofessional home visitors in the Nurse Family Partnership had a hard time making good use of the visit guidelines and supervision. Of course, that study pertains to home visitors of families of pregnant women and newborns, which is a younger group than is typically served by family literacy programs. Similar studies within family literacy programs would help supervisors know whether higher educational standards for home visitors are warranted.

Training and Supervision of Home Visitors

Home visitors in family literacy programs must know child development broadly and language and literacy development specifically. Three areas of additional training seem warranted and are sometimes overlooked in training protocols: (a) relationship-building skills, (b) working effectively with a parent as an adult learner, and (c) problem solving.

Relationship-Building Skills.   Home visiting is such a relationship-based intervention that home visitors need to be very well trained in relationship-building skills. Established over a period of time, the relationship serves as the foundation for the help that is offered. It must begin with the development of trust between the home visitor and the parent and, in positive situations, evolves into a working alliance in which both have a commitment to work together to help the parent become more effective in reaching goals. Although certain personal characteristics may give some home visitors an edge in communicating with families, many interpersonal skills and techniques can indeed be learned. The fundamental helping skills of listening, observing, reflecting, supporting, questioning appropriately, and prompting are examples of skills that should be included in home visitor training to help them forge strong relationships with families (Wasik & Bryant, 2001). The ability to establish a working relationship, to convey empathy and respect, and to interact with genuineness, are all essential skills for the home visitor.

Adult Learner Considerations.   Home visitors' training frequently neglects essential knowledge and skills required to interact effectively with a parent of a young child. The early childhood education career track often takes effective teachers of young children out of the classroom and assumes that they are able to use their knowledge of young children to help parents. In fact, quite different learning styles and approaches to teaching are usually needed, and these are sometimes shortchanged in training. Becoming familiar with assumptions about adult learners should lead to more effective home visiting practices (see chapter 13 of this volume).

One concern noted in the literature is that visitors tend to shy away from directly teaching parents better interaction skills. This phenomenon probably occurs for many reasons, one of which may be insufficient training. Programs need to provide training that addresses adult behavioral change, along with child development. Many visitors in family literacy home visiting programs are trained in child development or are more experienced with teaching children. Visitors may be afraid that any explicit coaching or teaching would be culturally disrespectful or viewed as not supportive of parents. Thus, they may avoid learning coaching and teaching skills. When home visitors have been taught ways to interact more effectively with parents, stronger parent outcomes have been obtained (Lutzker & Bigelow, 2002). In addition, visitors' recommendations must be sufficiently precise so that parents will understand the desired behaviors; for example, visitors might make a specific suggestion, such as having 10 min of adult–child shared book reading every day. Specific suggestions like this allow both parent and visitor to discuss whether the suggestion can be implemented and, later, to see whether it was implemented.

Problem-Solving Skills.   In two interventions, we have trained home visitors in problem-solving techniques; our results show that problem solving is a helpful approach for home visitors to incorporate in their work (Wasik, Ramey, Bryant, & Sparling, 1990; Wasik, Bryant, Lyons, Sparling, & Ramey, 1997). The rationale, training program, and processes of our problem-solving model are more thoroughly described in our book (Wasik & Bryant, 2001). In general, home visitors who recognize that problem solving is important for coping effectively with day-to-day difficulties, and who understand the problem-solving process, can help families learn to use a problem-solving approach to address barriers to literacy development. Many parents adopt the problem-solving process as a way of addressing both personal and parenting concerns.

Intensity of Services to Families

What should be the intensity of home visiting family literacy services? Different programs offer visits ranging from once per week to once per month. In a study that compared three different schedules of home visiting to low-income parents of young children, weekly home visits seemed effective, but outcomes did not differ for children visited bimonthly or monthly (Powell & Grantham-McGregor, 1989). Results from the multisite study of the PAT program showed more positive outcomes for children and families who participated in more visits, although the differences were not consistent across outcomes and were quite modest (Wagner, Spiker, Hernandez, Song, & Gerlach-Downie, 2001). A review of 10 programs that focused on family functioning showed that sustained effects were more likely when the intervention included 11 or more contacts over at least 3 months (Heinicke, Beckwith, & Thompson, 1988).

These three studies lead to two conclusions: First, there is likely to be a dosage effect in home visiting programs, that is, greater participation of families and children will lead to better outcomes; second, there may be some intensity threshold below which a few services are not effective. Home visitors sometimes wonder whether their extensive and persistent efforts to visit families who are hard to schedule and reach might be better spent serving families who are more regular participants. Determined home visitors generally go to great lengths to reach the hard-to-engage family, hoping that a few contacts will be better than none and that a little participation might eventually lead to more. Unfortunately, there is little research evidence to help them make these decisions. Future studies of intensity must also take into account the fact that, in general, only about half the scheduled home visits in some programs are actually completed (Hebbeler & Gerlach-Downie, 2002).

Identification of Service Population

An important issue for family literacy programs is to characterize families that home visiting could benefit. The ways in which Even Start programs recruit families illustrates the dilemma of whom to serve. Some Even Start programs have tried to recruit families who are *ready to learn*, defined by Even Start as low-income families who are headed by adults who need further education, but are not experiencing major family crises (St.Pierre & Swartz, 1995). These programs have relatively high participation rates for the core services. Other Even Start programs have tried to enroll the most *difficult to reach* families, meaning those with the lowest skill levels, facing the most severe educational and social problems. Such families are often hard to engage in the core services, and the programs must spend significant energy trying to support their participation. Which is the better strategy? If scarce resources should be spent on those likely to benefit from them, it seems intuitive that those who are ready to learn should be the first served, but we do not actually have evidence supporting this strategy. In addition, state and federal funding for programs often includes regulatory language requiring the service of those most in need, without defining clearly what this means.

RECOMMENDATIONS FOR IMPROVING HOME VISITING AS A STRATEGY FOR FAMILY LITERACY

Based upon our knowledge of home visiting services in general and their potential for enhancing children's literacy development, either through child-focused programs or through more comprehensive family literacy programs, we conclude this chapter with our thoughts about present tactics and future research, which, we believe, can improve home visiting as a strategy for family literacy.

Assure Fidelity to the Model of Home Visiting

Family literacy programs that use home visiting as a strategy need to have a well-articulated model of behavioral change that is understood by the home visitors and that's reflected in their practices in the homes. A qualitative study used videotapes and interviews of home visitors in a California program using the PAT model and explored why the program was not more effective (Hebbeler & Gerlach-Downie, 2002). The study found that visitors emphasized their social support role and placed little emphasis on changing parenting behavior. Although they believed strongly that what they were doing with parents would improve developmental outcomes for children, the home visitors operated from various assumptions about how that was going to happen. For example, they provided parents with a great deal of information, but did less to promote changes in parent–child interaction that could influence child outcomes.

Implementing this recommendation first requires that a program specify the components and procedures it wants home visitors to implement and describes how those procedures should lead to the desired outcome. A program following a national model of home visiting needs to thoroughly understand the goals, processes, and activities of the national model. A home visiting program that has been developed at a local level also needs to think through and spell out its own goals and standards. Once it is established and understood, both types of programs—national and local—need to ensure fidelity to the model. Hiring excellent home visitors, then training and supervising them well, are the best ways to accomplish this objective.

Provide Appropriate Training and Supervision

A responsible program provides for continual professional development for its visitors. Pre-service and in-service training are important, because few educational institutions provide training in home visiting (Weissbourd, 1987). In our book on home visiting, we discussed a number of competencies we believe home visitors should have: the fundamental helping skills of observation, listening, and questioning; and specific techniques for home visiting, including modeling, role playing, using personal examples, and homework (Wasik & Bryant, 2001).

Given the need for home visitors who can directly address issues of changing parents' behaviors, we also need to begin asking ourselves how well we train home visitors in behavioral change procedures. Home visitors use behavioral change strategies most when helping parents use less punitive behavior management strategies with their children (e.g., Lutzker's Project SafeCare). Are home visitors trained to use those same behavioral change strategies when interacting with parents? Do they, for example, discriminate when they provide parents with positive feedback? In a study that involved videotaping of home visits, researchers discovered that home visitors almost indiscriminately rewarded any positive parental behavior toward the child to try to make parents feel supported (Hebbeler & Gerlach-Downie, 2002). Parents may interpret such support as encouragement to continue all the behaviors they were engaged in, even though the home visitor might not have intended this. Project SafeCare in Los Angeles, a home visiting program for families at risk for child maltreatment, uses direct instruction, modeling by the home visitor, parental practice with feedback from the home visitor, and homework assignments as ways of helping parents to distinguish among child behaviors and to select the appropriate response to the child (Lutzker & Bigelow, 2002). At times, positive responses might be called for; at other times, redirecting the child to a more appropriate activity may be necessary.

Even Start programs devote more time to in-service staff training in the area of parenting education than to other components, probably because almost half of Even Start programs provide this service with their own staff (Tao, Gamse, & Tarr, 1998). Recently, the U.S. DOE developed a framework for parenting education, and training tools for using the framework in local programs are being generated (Powell & D'Angelo, 2000). Powell, in chapter 9, on parenting education, notes that parenting education is a key ingredient for facilitating children's literacy development in Even Start and other family literacy programs and provides helpful suggestions for parent education strategies in these programs.

Once trained, home visitors need ongoing guidance and support. However, supervisors rarely accompany visitors on their home visits, which is unfortunate, because new home visitors need opportunities to discuss their work, improve their skills, and receive feedback and reassurance. Wasik and Sparling have developed a supervisor rating scale to help supervisors be more systematic in what they look for and comment upon when they accompany a home visitor

(Wasik & Sparling, 1998). Group supervision can be helpful, too, giving visitors an opportunity to discuss their challenges and successes. Because home visitor pay is often low, turnover is high. Supporting home visitors in their role through good supervision and professional development can reduce turnover and burnout.

Increase the Engagement of Families

As noted earlier, many home visiting programs report widely varying levels of family participation in home visits, with often less than half the intended number of contacts. Given that dosage is probably related to child and family outcomes, we must pay more attention to increasing family engagement in family literacy home visiting programs. Hiring skilled home visitors, and training and supervising them well, are essential to achieving more participation, but additional strategies must be investigated. Some suggest that parent participation would rise if parents were involved in the planning process, setting goals for themselves and the program. Maximizing family input into the content and procedures, as well as into the time and place of home visits, should increase families' level of interest and involvement. Providing families with attractive and easy-to-use materials, whether in written or videotaped format, might also increase participation. With modern printing technology, new curriculum materials produced by long-term programs look remarkably more attractive than such materials from 10 years ago. Being sensitive and responsive to cultural differences is also likely to increase a family's comfort with the visitor and interest in the materials.

Another way some programs try to increase engagement is to enroll families they think might be more open to the intervention, such as first-time mothers (Olds et al., 2002). Parents of older children may more likely think they know enough and/or do not need help, so enrolling primiparous women is thought to enhance interest and participation.

Embed Home Visiting in More Comprehensive Programs

Home visiting provides an avenue for helping families promote children's literacy development, but home visiting alone is probably not enough to achieve most of the gains that our programs attempt to achieve. Weiss (1993) writes that home visiting is "necessary but not sufficient" (p. 113). She and others (Gomby, 2003) recommend embedding home visiting programs in more comprehensive community programs that include multiple services to meet families' needs. Child care is one service that is widely needed by families. A quality center-based experience can be beneficial for young children, as well as a necessity for families, and is also a venue in which parents can be reached. For example, home visitors in programs with both a child care and home visiting component can meet with teachers and parents together, to share information about children's progress and to support parents' engagement in activities with children at home. The package of center-based child care plus home visiting, used in the Infant Health and Development Program (IHDP, 1990), made significant differences in the lives of young children, with large effects in major outcomes at age 3. Because of IHDP's design, we cannot disentangle the effects of child care from those of home visiting. But we do know that, by age 3, the intervention had made a difference. Even Start is another example of an intervention (for adult and child literacy) that includes a center-based component for children and one for parents, as well as parent group meetings and home visits.

Embedding literacy-focused home visiting in more comprehensive programs also may help provide the family with other services that are needed in times of crisis. An observational study of 12 Even Start programs discovered that parent educators had difficulty focusing on literacy content when parents were in the midst of stressful family events (Haslam & Stief, 1998). Home visits may need to focus on other topics besides literacy, until a crisis is resolved. If the home visitor is not trained to provide the needed help—and many are not—the comprehensive program's other resources could be brought to bear.

Conduct More Research

The lack of strong empirical support for the efficacy of home visiting for promoting school readiness is a major issue for programs that rely solely on home visiting as an intervention strategy, as well as for programs that include home visiting as one of many strategies. As noted earlier, a review of 15 home visiting programs, using random assignment to treatment and control conditions, showed that only 6 programs had significant benefits for children (Olds & Kitzman, 1993). An even more recent review of six evaluations of programs following national home visiting models (e.g., PAT, Home Instruction Program for Preschool Youngsters) confirmed that few benefits were demonstrated, and, when there were benefits, they usually applied only to a subset of families on a limited number of outcomes (Gomby, Culross, & Behrman, 1999). The results are disappointing, especially given the great efforts that programs put forth to contact families. Nevertheless, weak effects seem to occur. Reviews of programs that have gone beyond home visiting for the sole purpose of child development, to those that have also included adult education, job training, and parenting education, show that these programs, too, have yielded modest results, at best (Berrey & Lennon, 1998; St.Pierre & Layzer, 1998).

The unanswered question is, What does it take to change parenting behaviors in ways that are strong enough and lasting enough to affect children's cognitive and language outcomes? Family dynamics are complex. Many families in the programs profiled in this chapter, and others in this book, face additional family stresses, such as poverty, unemployment, teen parenting, and abusive relationships. Such families are likely to require help that goes beyond what the typical home visiting program or family literacy program can provide. Families may need referral to programs that are qualified to address serious life issues. Strategies that family literacy programs can use to coordinate and integrate their services with other agencies are described in chapter 20 of this volume.

Most studies of the effects of home visiting programs that include literacy as a focus have used a quasi-experimental design, comparing families and children participating in a program to a group of families not participating in the program, because of parent choice, program availability, or other factors. Because many such studies also lack baseline or preprogram data, it is not certain that the families in the two groups were comparable on important characteristics. Such quasi-experimental designs do not allow conclusions as strong as those designs involving random assignment of some families to a home visiting group and other families to a control group. A study that uses random assignment has the potential to more clearly answer the causal question, although conducting randomized studies in real-world service delivery programs is challenging.

In addition to randomized studies, we also need longitudinal studies and descriptive and qualitative studies, to understand the process of home visiting. For example, what actions of home visitors affect parental engagement? What program processes or parent characteristics relate to low attrition rates? Such questions can be answered with longitudinal studies of participants in individual programs. We also need to know if some materials or curricula are better suited than others to helping parents help their child become literate. Several early childhood education curriculum comparison studies are under way with funding from the federal Institute of Education Sciences, but the curricula being studied are all center-based. The fourth evaluation of the Even Start Family Literacy Programs will also be examining two different early childhood education curricula. Studies of literacy curricula provided only through home-based services are needed as well.

For the future, we believe that home visiting will continue to be recognized as an important component of literacy interventions for families with young children. For some families, it can provide a sufficient intervention for positive outcomes. For other families, it will not have major effects on its own. In these situations, home visitors provide families with information, support, and encouragement for literacy, and they also link parents and children into a more comprehensive set of community programs.

REFERENCES

Anderson-Yockel, J., & Haynes, W. (1994). Joint picture-book reading strategies in working-class African American and White mother-toddler dyads. *Journal of Speech, Language, and Hearing Research, 37*, 583–593.

Bernheimer, L. P., & Keogh, B. K. (1995). Weaving interventions into the fabric of everyday life: An approach to family assessment. *Topics in Early Childhood Special Education, 15*(4), 415–433.

Berrey, E. C., & Lennon, M. C. (1998). Teen parent program evaluations yield no simple answers. *The Forum: Research forum on children, families, and the new federalism, 1*(4), 1–4.

Britto, P. R., & Brooks-Gunn, J. (2001). Beyond shared book reading: Dimensions of home literacy and low-income African American preschoolers' skills. In P. Britto & J. Brooks-Gunn (Eds.), *The role of family literacy environments in promoting young children's emerging literacy skills* (Vol. 92, pp. 39–52). San Francisco: Jossey-Bass/Pfeiffer.

Davie, C. E., Hutt, S. J., Vincent, E., & Mason, M. (1984). *The young child at home*. Windsor, England: NFER-Nelson.

Dickinson, D. K., & Tabors, P. O. (1991). Early literacy: Linkages between home, school, and literacy achievement at age five. *Journal of Research in Childhood Education, 6*, 30–46.

Dunn, L., & Dunn, L. (1997). *The Peabody Picture Vocabulary Test (3rd ed.)*. Circle Pines, MN: American Guidance Service.

Epstein, J. (1991). Effects on student achievement of teachers' practices of parent involvement. In S. Silvern (Ed.), *Literacy through family, community and school interaction* (pp. 261–276). Greenwich, CT: JAI.

Federal Interagency Forum on Child and Family Statistics. (1999). *America's children: Key national indicators of well-being, 1999*. Washington, DC: U.S. Government Printing Office.

Gomby, D. S. (2003). Building school readiness through home visitation. Report to the first 5 California Children and Families Commission. Available at www.ccfc.ca.gov/School/Ready.htm

Gomby, D. S., Culross, P. L., & Behrman, R. E. (1999). Home visiting: Recent program evaluations—Analysis and recommendations. *The Future of Children: Recent Program Evaluations, 9*(1), 4–26.

Hammer, C. S. (2001). Come sit down and let mama read: Book reading interactions between African American mothers and their infants. In J. Harris, A. Kamhi, & K. Pollock (Eds.), *Literacy in African American communities* (pp. 21–44). Hillsdale, NJ: Lawrence Erlbaum, Associates, Inc.

Hannon, P. (1995). *Literacy, home and school: Research and practice in teaching literacy with parents*. London: Falmer.

Haslam, B. (1998, October). Presentation at the U.S. Department of Education State Even Start Coordinators' Meeting, San Diego, CA.

Haslam, B., & Stief, E. (1998, November). *Observational study of Even Start Family Literacy Projects: Preliminary findings*. Washington, DC: Policy Studies Associates.

Heath, S. B. (1983). *Ways with words: Language, life and work in communities and classrooms*. Cambridge, England: Cambridge University Press.

Hebbeler, K. M., & Gerlach-Downie, S. G. (2002). Inside the black box of home visiting: A qualitative analysis of why intended outcomes were not achieved. *Early Childhood Research Quarterly, 17*, 28–51.

Heinicke, C. M., Beckwith, L., & Thompson, A. (1988). Early intervention in the family system: A framework and review. *Infant Mental Health Journal, 9*(2), 111–141.

Infant Health and Development Program Consortium. (1990). Enhancing the outcomes of low birth weight, premature infants: A multi-site randomized trial. *Journal of the American Medical Association, 263*, 3035–3042.

Leichter, H. J. (1984). Families as environments for literacy. In H. Goelman, A. A. Oberg, & F. Smith (Eds.), *Awakening to literacy* (pp. 38–50). Portsmouth, NH: Heinemann.

Lutzker, J. R., & Bigelow, K. M. (2002). *Reducing child maltreatment: A guidebook for parent services*. New York: Guilford.

Olds, D. L., & Kitzman, H. (1993). Review of research on home visiting for pregnant women and parents of young children. *The Future of Children, 3*(3), 53–92.

Olds, D. L., Robinson, J., O'Brien, R., Luckey, D. W., Pettitt, L. M., Henderson, C. R., et al. (2002). Home visiting by paraprofessionals and by nurses: A randomized, controlled trial. *Pediatrics, 110*(3), 486–496.

Parents as Teachers. (1999). *Born to Learn Curriculum*. St. Louis, MO: Parents As Teachers National Center.

Parents as Teachers (2003). Retrieved March 2003 from www.patnc.org

Pfannenstiel, J. C., Seitz, V., & Zigler, E. (2002). Promoting school readiness: The role of the Parents as Teachers program. *NHSA Dialog, 6*(1), 71–96.

Powell, C., & Grantham-McGregor, S. (1989). Home visiting of varying frequency and child development. *Pediatrics, 84*(1), 157–164.

Powell, D. R., & D'Angelo, D. (2000). *Guide to improving parenting education in Even Start family literacy programs.* Washington, DC: Office of Educational Research and Improvement.

Rodriguez-Brown, F. V. (2001). Home-school connections in a community where English is the second language. In V. Risko & K. Bromley (Eds.), *Collaboration for diverse learners: Viewpoints and practices* (pp. 273–288). Newark, DE: International Reading Association.

Ryan, K. E., Geissler, B., & Knell, S. (1994). Evaluating family literacy programs: Tales from the field. In D. K. Dickinson (Ed.), *Bridges to literacy: Children, families, and schools* (pp. 236–264). Malden, MA: Blackwell.

Snow, C. E., Burns, M. S., & Griffin, P. (Eds.). (1998). *Preventing reading difficulties in young children.* Washington, DC: National Academy Press.

St.Pierre, R. G., & Layzer, J. I. (1998). Improving the life chances of children in poverty: Assumptions and what we have learned. *SRCD Social Policy Report, 12*(4), 1–28.

St.Pierre, R., Swartz, J., Gamse, B., Murray, S., Deck, D., & Nickel, P. (1995). *National evaluation of the Even Start Family Literacy Program: Final report.* Washington, DC: U.S. Department of Education, Office of the Under Secretary, Planning and Evaluation Service.

St.Pierre, R. G., & Swartz, J. P. (1995). The Even Start Family Literacy Program. In S. Smith (Ed.), *Two generation programs for families in poverty: A new intervention strategy* (pp. 37–66). Norwood, NJ: Ablex.

Tao, F., Gamse, B., & Tarr, H. (1998). *National evaluation of the Even Start Family Literacy Program: 1994–1997 final report.* Washington, DC: U.S. Department of Education.

Taylor, D. (1983). *Young children learning to read and write.* Exeter, NH: Heinemann.

U.S. Department of Education. (2001). *Guide to quality: Even Start Family Literacy Program implementation and continuous improvement, Vol. 1* (Rev. ed.). Washington, DC: Author. Office of Compensatory Education, Even Start Family Literacy programs.

U.S. Department of Education. (2003). *Third national Even Start evaluation: Program impacts and implications for improvement.* Retrieved 2003, from www.ed.gov/pubs/evenstart_third

Wagner, M. M., & Clayton, S. L. (1999). The Parents as Teachers program: Results from two demonstrations. *The Future of Children: Recent Program Evaluations, 9*(1), 91–115.

Wagner, M., Spiker, D., Hernandez, F., Song, J., & Gerlach-Downie, S. (2001). *Multisite Parents as Teachers evaluation. Experiences and outcomes for children and families.* Menlo Park, CA: SRI International.

Wagner, M., Spiker, D., & Linn, M. I. (2002). The effectiveness of the Parents as Teachers program with low-income parents and children. *Topics in Early Childhood Special Education, 22*(2), 67–81.

Wasik, B. H., & Bryant, D. M. (2001). *Home visiting, Procedures for helping families.* Thousand Oaks, CA: Sage.

Wasik, B. H., Bryant, D. M., Lyons, C., Sparling, J. J., & Ramey, C. T. (1997). Home visiting. In R. T. Gross, D. Spiker, & C. W. Haynes (Eds.), *Helping low birth weight, premature babies: The Infant Health and Development Program* (pp. 27–41). Stanford, CA: Stanford University Press.

Wasik, B. H., & Hendrickson, J. S. (in press). Family literacy practices. In A. Stone, E. Silliman, B. Ehrem, & K. Apel (Eds.), *Handbook of language and literacy development and disorder.* New York: Guilford.

Wasik, B. H., Ramey, C. T., Bryant, D. M., & Sparling, J. J. (1990). A longitudinal study of two early intervention strategies: Project CARE. *Child Development, 61,* 1682–1696.

Wasik, B. H., & Roberts, R. N. (1994). Home visitor characteristics, training, and supervision: Results of a national survey. *Family Relations, 43,* 336–341.

Wasik, B. H., & Sparling, J. J. (1998). *Home visit assessment instrument.* Chapel Hill: The Center for Home Visiting, University of North Carolina at Chapel Hill.

Weiss, H. B. (1993). Home visits: Necessary but not sufficient. *The Future of Children, 3,* 113, 128.

Weissbourd, B. (1987). Design, staffing, and funding of family support programs. In S. L. Kagan, D. R. Powell, B. Weissbourd, & E. F. Zigler (Eds.), *America's family support programs* (pp. 245–268). New Haven, CT: Yale University Press.

Whitehurst, G. J., & Lonigan, C. J. (2001). Emergent literacy: Development from prereaders to readers). In S. B. Neuman & D. K. Dickinson (Eds.), *Handbook of early literacy research* (pp. 11–29). New York: Guilford.

VI

Coordination and Integration Issues in Family Literacy

Several concepts and practices associated with program coordination and integration are pertinent for family literacy programs. The one most often discussed is the need for integration across the four required components of family literacy programs: early childhood, parent, and adult education, and parent–child literacy interactions, discussed in the first chapter in this section. Indeed, federal guidelines call for projects to integrate the components into a unified family literacy program. Coordination and integration efforts can benefit family literacy programs in many other ways. In the second chapter, the authors take a broad view of many service integration opportunities, with a focus on those with other organizations.

Meta Potts provides us with a detailed look at how programs can integrate across components. She discusses how program integration distinguishes family literacy programs from other literacy approaches, and she describes how the shift from individual to family in human services has influenced family literacy. She notes the importance of planned and purposeful component integration that takes families' goals and needs into account. Observing that such integration is complex, she provides a set of staff approaches that can make it work, such as defining literacy broadly and using similar educational theories across components. She describes complementary philosophies of education that also contribute to component integration, drawing on a constructivist theory to illustrate how concepts related to early childhood and adult education overlap. She identifies administrative factors that influence integration, drawing attention to the need for staff development. Potts then describes in detail how to implement component integration. She offers a sample planning document, and she gives practical examples that link one component's goals and content with those of another.

When we look at programs' relations with other organizations and agencies, coordination and integration take on a very different meaning. Gloria Harbin and her colleagues, Barbara Hanna Wasik, Suzannah Herrmann, Dionne Dobbins, and Wendy K. K. Lam, address the topic of service integration and family literacy programs. These authors define service integration as connectedness among providers, making services to families more coordinated and responsive. They describe five levels at which child service integration can occur: with clients, within programs, between programs, in policy, and in organization. They observe that integration efforts frequently address only one of these five levels; failure to address all five, they argue, means fragmented services and lost opportunities for families and children. They use a systems model to illustrate relations and interactions among the elements of a service system, including such functions as public awareness and support and individual planning and service delivery.

The model includes the need for an integrated infrastructure, with complementary policies and standards among cooperating agencies. The authors name barriers and facilitators of service integration and offer ways to overcome the former. Finally, they give examples of how family literacy programs use service integration strategies and recommend ways to make such efforts more successful.

These two chapters provide a foundation to consider coordination and integration in family literacy programs, providing models, concepts, and strategies for integrating across program components and across agencies and organizations.

19

Integration of Components in Family Literacy Services

Meta Potts
National Center for Family Literacy

Family literacy services, as defined by federal legislation and the National Center for Family Literacy (NCFL, 2001), include four interdependent components: children's education, adult education, interactive literacy activities for parents and children, and parenting education. Although other literacy approaches may offer one or more of these components, comprehensive family literacy services offer these components as an intentional system of educational influence and intervention.

In comprehensive family literacy services, these components are not viewed as isolated occurrences; rather, each component is systematically designed to be an essential element of a greater whole, which addresses and facilitates goals for families more broadly than any single component. This comprehensive approach deliberately engages parents and children in an array of educational experiences, separately and together, to strengthen the learning bond and foster lifelong learning behaviors within a family unit.

As the concept of family literacy began to develop in the 1980s, it was immediately clear that educational agencies and organizations would need to collaborate. Thus, one level of integration evident in family literacy services is cross-agency collaboration that allows programs to strategically combine the services they offer, meeting the multiple needs and goals of disadvantaged families, but still maintaining a deliberate focus and preventing a duplication of services within a community.

Another level of integration—and the one that is the focus of this chapter—is the intention of family literacy providers to combine educational experiences for parents and children, in order to bring about greater, more sustained outcomes for both. Integration of the four primary components is a key factor to the effectiveness of comprehensive family literacy services. *Component integration* refers to an intentional system of delivery that works to maximize effectiveness of quality adult and child education, by coordinating strategies for greater impact on individuals and on the family unit as a whole. Family literacy is based in part on the correlations between the educational and socioeconomic status of parents and the academic achievement of their children. Likewise, component integration seeks to build on these correlations, in order to positively influence those factors likely to affect them, and to help educators and parents become more aware of the correlations. Knowledge of these relationships can lead parents and teachers toward activities that promote educational gains for both parents and children.

Component integration can be described as integrated activities that support the development of literacy of both parents and children. Some examples of component integration activities include:

- In adult education class, parents can select reading materials from children's literature to share with their children during Parent and Child Together (PACT) time and/or at home, preparing for this time by discussing, writing about, and dramatizing the story and extending literature choices.
- Parents can bring inexpensive household items from home to make learning toys for children, tying these toys to developmentally appropriate learning experiences for children and to the learning experiences implicit in the adult education curriculum. These toys can then be used in the children's classroom and during PACT time.
- Parents can read, write about, and discuss such topics as children's cognitive development, school readiness skills, and the role of play in children's learning, as part of the adult education curriculum. They can then try techniques at home and discuss them at the next parent education session.

This level of component integration may seem deceptively simple on the surface. To implement component integration and maximize its effectiveness, however, requires significant commitment, planning, and teamwork on the part of program staff, and support from program leaders. Efforts must be intentional, grounded in educational and developmental theories, and understood by staff and parents alike.

This chapter explores some of the research and practical field experiences that both justify and clarify the use of component integration as a system for delivery of family literacy services. Programmatic, staff, and administrative approaches are discussed, using theoretical and actual examples of successful integration. Attention to systems thinking, team planning, and quality implementation is emphasized. In conclusion, some consideration to effective evaluation of component integration is given.

INTEGRATION OF COMPONENTS: THE DEFINING
CHARACTERISTIC OF DELIVERY

In writing about the family literacy model, Popp (1992, 2001a) describes perhaps the most significant difference between family literacy services and other literacy approaches:

> Prior to the development of the family literacy model, three types of programs were addressing the problem of intergenerational cycles of poverty: adult education, early childhood education, and parenting programs. These programs focused on individual adults or children from undereducated families and attempted to intervene in the cycle of school failure and poverty.

The family literacy model shifted the focus from the individual to the family. (Popp, 2001a, p. 1)

The philosophical and pedagogical shift from individual to family, which characterizes family literacy programs, precipitated a new approach to service delivery, known as *integration*. Integration has become a critical, defining characteristic of family literacy services, working to create a system for delivery of curriculum, instruction, and assessment. Rather than providing stand-alone, isolated services, such as early childhood education or adult basic skills education, family literacy programs bring parents and children together to learn, weaving key strategies and messages throughout the four primary components: adult education, age-appropriate children's education, interactive parent–child literacy activities (PACT time), and parenting education (parent time). Integration of these components is intentionally used as a cohesive system to promote learning within the family unit.

Integration is sometimes referred to as the fifth component in comprehensive family literacy services. When implemented effectively, integration strengthens the learning experience for both adults and children, by reinforcing skills acquisition through a variety of learning activities. According to Hayes (1996):

> In a model family literacy program, the system of influences on the family—and ultimately on the future of the child—is greater than that of all the parts acting independently. Each part of the model program and its intended effects is necessary for program effectiveness, but acting separately they do not comprise sufficient conditions for causing many important changes in capabilities, attitudes, values, expectations, patterns of behavior, and in the system of meaning within a family unit. (p. 23)

Throughout the development and implementation of family literacy services over the last decade, practitioners have observed how common learning takes place in mutually beneficial ways, when integration of the components is deliberate and facilitated as part of the overall delivery design. There are many ways this intentional integration is accomplished. Literacy instruction is connected to parents' topics of concern and is extended into parenting education sessions; parental behaviors and beliefs related to children's education are addressed as part of adult instruction; parent education is linked to facilitating children's literacy development; and PACT time offers key experiences for parents and children to exchange concepts and information, particularly as these experiences enhance literacy development.

In the following program example, note how literacy instruction is integrated among the components, through an array of activities, and also note the impact that this ultimately has on the students' comprehension of that instruction.

> We knew that what we were seeing in "Beth's" Parent Time session in North Carolina was not what we had seen in other family literacy programs. We listened as parents talked about their own Christmas pasts and compared them to Truman Capote's story, *A Christmas Memory*, which they had read in their adult education classroom that morning.
>
> "We never hunted no pecans or made fruitcakes for the neighborhood," said one mother. "My dad just drank and cussed and ruined Christmas for us every year."
>
> "Let's stop here and write in our journals," urged "Beth." "What kind of holiday do you want for your children?"
>
> We followed the group as they left this discussion and writing assignment and joined their children in PACT Time, where the conversations, laughter and excitement were already in progress. As the moms and kids stuck evergreen into Styrofoam and glued sparkles on their centerpieces, I asked them what they were making.
>
> "We're building Christmas memories," they said. (Potts & Freeman, 1990, pp. 1–2)

Even though literacy-centered events occur within the practices of each component, the desired literacy development and academic achievement for participating family members takes place especially when those parent and child practices intersect. Adult and child learners use literacy to accomplish various tasks, to communicate, and to teach each other. Bronfenbrenner (1977) calls this phenomenon "reciprocal teaching and learning." Not only does specific learning take place in a comprehensive family literacy program, but interaction also provides opportunities to expand understanding about the learning process itself, which can strengthen the family unit and build behaviors for lifelong learning for both adults and children. An example of this reciprocal learning occurred when this author observed a 4-year-old boy who had been studying and playing with shapes, while his mother studied geometry in the room next door—a planned integrative event. When parents and children gathered for PACT time, the early childhood teacher shared the book *Shapes, Shapes, Shapes*, a photo journal by Tana Hoban, to which the children had already been exposed in small-group time. When the book reading ended, the children and their parents took a room walk to identify shapes in the classroom. "Look, mommy," said the young boy, "I can see through that rectangle." With confirmation from the mother, lessons on geometry were reinforced for both parent and child.

Planned integration of the components in family literacy is a powerful strategy and provides the intensity of instruction advocated by Hayes (1996) and others (Dwyer, 2000; NCFL 2001; Popp, 1992, 2001b; Warren, 2001). It epitomizes the adage, "The whole is greater than the sum of its parts." Conversely, a component that does not contribute to the whole, either because of inherent constraints in the program design or through a lack of planning to purposefully integrate the components, may weaken the effectiveness of both the individual component and overall family literacy services as they are intended.

RECOGNIZING INTEGRATION AS A VALUE-ADDED ELEMENT

In their earliest efforts to design family literacy staff professional development, the NCFL recognized the vital role integration would play in the delivery of family literacy services (Potts & Freeman, 1989). NCFL's description of component integration has remained constant over the years:

> The power of family literacy comes from the integration of the interdependent components: Children's Education, Adult Education, Parent and Child Together (PACT) Time, and Parent Time. When the components are woven together by a team of family literacy instructors, the result is a comprehensive, unique service to individuals and families. (NCFL, 2001, p. 9).

The federal definition of family literacy, which is now found in several pieces of legislation, including the Elementary and Secondary Education Act (reauthorized in 2002) and the Adult Education and Family Literacy Act (part of the Workforce Investment Act), also specifies the integration of the four components as a key ingredient of family literacy services. The legislation governing the William F. Goodling Even Start Family Literacy Program (Title I, Part B, of the Elementary and Secondary Education Act) describes the intent and depth of component integration in its Statement of Purpose, which states:

> It is the purpose of this subpart to help break the cycle of poverty and illiteracy by . . . improving the educational opportunities of the Nation's low-income families by integrating early childhood education, adult literacy or adult basic education, and parenting education into a unified family literacy program.

The *Guide to Quality: Even Start Family Literacy Programs* (Dwyer, 2000) challenges programs to "connect instruction within and across components through meaningful and consistent program messages and planning, thereby providing an intensive experience intended to change intergenerational patterns associated with low literacy" (p. 15). This document further clarifies the intent of component integration:

> The purpose of integrating components is to ensure that families receive consistent messages about the value of education and learning from all staff. Integration of instruction within and

across components ensures that, for each family member, the interrelatedness of learning in a variety of situations and mastery of new information and skills is thorough and complete. (p. 15)

The consistent legislative support for component integration indicates a belief that integration is an essential strategy for ensuring that comprehensive services are offered to families. The success of component integration implementation, however, is difficult to evaluate. First, many variables come into play when implementing a family literacy program, such as quality of instruction in the four components, adequacy of physical facilities to foster integration, and the complex challenges that enrolled families often face. Second, there are few, if any, standardized systems of measurement of component integration. We can, however, point to several studies of high-quality family literacy programs that provide support for component integration, particularly as a contributing factor to both academic and nonacademic gains made by families (program outcomes) and as a contributing factor that strengthens program delivery (program processes). Philliber, Spillman, and King (1996) report that high-quality family literacy programs can result in greater gains in literacy for adults and children than can stand-alone programs. In addition, Hayes (2001a) points out that many families who enroll in family literacy programs report that they would not participate in other, less integrated programs, to a point of completion.

A study (Yarnell, Pfannenstiel, Lambson, & Treffeisen, 1998) on the long-standing Family and Child Education program shows that 80% of participants report that the program helps them to better understand child development, to interact more effectively and frequently with their children, and to become more involved in their children's education. These findings were true for participants who received home services, center-based services, or both. Considered in addition to the academic gains that both adults and children made during the program year, these findings further attest to the value-added benefits that can result from integration of the family literacy components (see chapter 25 in this volume).

Warren (2001) reported on a 3-year statewide study of Even Start programs in Massachusetts, which followed 300 families for at least 2 years and 28 of those families for 3 years. Although the intent was not to focus on integration, the study showed that the most successful Even Start programs were those that purposefully included integration of components in their plan for delivery. The results suggest that family outcomes are closely linked to the degree to which programs engage in formal planning, goal setting, and monitoring, and to the extent to which program components are integrated.

RESEARCH-BASED APPROACHES TO FOSTERING AND SUSTAINING COMPONENT INTEGRATION

Systems Thinking: A Philosophy for Staff and Family Development

Many comprehensive family literacy programs, in which integration of the components is a planned and purposeful activity facilitated by staff and which take into account the goals and needs of enrolled families, utilize systems thinking. Senge (1990) writes that systems thinking provides a framework that prevents the breakdown of organizations, because those who practice such thinking move beyond individual brilliance and innovation, "pulling their diverse functions and talents into a productive whole. . . . By seeing wholes, we learn how to foster organizational health" (p. 69).

Systems thinking is advantageous on two levels: It encourages practitioners to shift their view of a family literacy program from separate components to a whole of interrelationships, and it also alters the views on family beyond parental influences on children, to a more in-depth perspective on the ways total families interact and influence other family members.

Furthermore, without systems thinking, there is little incentive or means to integrate the parts (components) into a whole, or a cohesive system of influence and instruction. Successful integration requires "shared vision," which, according to Senge (1990), "is not an idea...not even an important idea...but rather a force in people's hearts...a force which focuses the energies of groups and creates a common identity" (pp. 206–207).

Fostering organizational health, or the stability and consistency of family literacy services, also fosters the health of the families enrolled (as evidenced by their continued participation and progress toward achieving goals). Family systems are complex and incorporate biological, environmental, educational, economic, and social factors. Further, family literacy programs have traditionally targeted services toward low-income, low-literate families who face a multitude of both educational and noneducational obstacles. It is therefore crucial that program staff be able to recognize and celebrate the structure, relationships, and functions of individuals within the entire family and to rely upon the whole family as resources within the process of integration.

The acknowledgment of the family as an entire entity is critical because structure in any system resists change. Changes in participants often affect other members in the family, and these changes may threaten relationships and the comfort level of the status quo. Such consequences need to be recognized by staff, and programs should be prepared to support new, emerging family structures. Staff working in family literacy has repeatedly observed that, without family involvement, change in one member of the family will likely be temporary. Further, they are aware that whatever the reaction of the family to the changes in the individual, the effects are not likely to be neutral (Hayes, 1989; Potts, 1992).

Wasik, Dobbins, and Herrmann (2000) recommend that, "in family literacy programs, assumptions about what parents may be able to do with their child need to take into consideration the home environment and the resources and needs of other family members" (p. 449). Systems thinking, and the subsequent teamwork that accompanies it, will help family literacy program staff move away from focusing on separate, individually centered practice, into family-centered practice, which in turn supports and strengthens family functioning on the whole. To do this effectively, and to incorporate integration strategically, individuals on the staff are well served if they understand how and why each component of family literacy operates.

This understanding of family literacy program dynamics comes from an appreciation of mental models and the determination to create new ones (Senge, 1990). Most teachers have mental models of what should happen in their classrooms. Often, adult educators focus on adult outcomes, such as obtaining a GED, acquiring job skills, or improving English language skills. Children's educators may be primarily interested in encouraging language and literacy development, while also attending to the emotional, social, and physical development of children. In providing family literacy services, staff are encouraged to not only address individual achievement, but also to attend to the family as a system for enhancing learning overall.

Quality and Integration Within the Four Components

There are three primary conditions that appear to enable the successful integration of the four components of comprehensive family literacy services: (a) compatible component design, with corresponding educational philosophies; (b) complementary standards for learning; and (c) integrated approaches to teaching. Hayes (1996, 2001b), in setting out conditions for the success of this combination, proposed the following general principles for quality family literacy program design, in which integration is the hallmark:

> The components of high-quality family literacy programs should meet the design standards for the best single-service programs serving the same single-service goals and similar clients. That is, the

programs for the adults should be as high in quality, intensity, and duration as the best programs serving only adults, and the programs for the children should be as high in quality, intensity, and duration as the best programs serving only children.

All program components should be linked to intensify the total program experience by using the experiences in each component as content for learning and reflection in other components. Learnings are generalized across contexts by having them used in any appropriate program component. (Hayes, 1996, p. 33)

According to Alamprese (2000), "The adult education component is a key link" (p. 63). Focusing on teaching adult literacy and lifelong learning skills, within the context of family-related issues, provides educators a pathway for intentionally planning for integration across the components. Influenced by the Equipped for the Future (EFF) project (Stein, 1997), which provides one framework that is readily accessible to integration across the components, many adult education teachers in family literacy settings are using the four categories of EFF standards to connect what adults need to know and be able to do with what children need to learn for success in school and in life (see chapters 13 and 14 in this volume).

These four categories—communication skills, decision-making skills, interpersonal skills, and lifelong learning skills—provide a structure that is not limited to functional literacy for adults, but that also helps identify practical goals for both teaching and learning for adults. Proficiency in each category is defined by a set of specific active-learning functions, such as "Read with understanding" or "Use math to solve problems and communicate," which are then described more explicitly through a series of performance indicators. These indicators provide learners with concrete definitions of what it means to accomplish or master a particular skill, and they provide teachers with a clear picture of why and how mastery is attained.

In family literacy programs, mastery is accomplished as capabilities are transferred to other settings and learning is generalized across the components. Later in this chapter, four sample planning documents (the tables) lead the reader through the integration process that makes this transference possible and, more important, likely. Tables 19.2–19.4 utilize categories from the EFF framework, to demonstrate an intentional approach to component integration. These examples further clarify how standards and teaching approaches can be woven throughout the family literacy experience, to strengthen integration and overall program effectiveness.

Family literacy services have been adapted to serve children of varying ages, from infant and toddler to elementary school. Each program will obviously adopt a model of children's education that is appropriate to the ages of children served. However, within the context of family literacy, the children's education component is part of a larger system of influence. To be the most effective in an integrated model, children's curriculum, instruction, and assessment should work together in a framework that coincides with the philosophy and framework of the adult education component. Often, this objective translates into a deliberate effort to consider children's education as a continuum of knowledge, skills, and thinking processes.

One model, the High/Scope framework for educating young children (Weikart & Holmann, 1995), based on the concepts of Jean Piaget, practices delivery with a fundamental premise in mind: Children are active learners who learn best from activities they plan and carry out themselves. Key experiences serve as guideposts for planning and evaluating programs for young children.

Another model implemented in many Even Start programs is the Work Sampling System (Jablon, 1996), an active-learning approach that identifies seven areas of child learning and further defines these domains through specific skills acquisition. Tables 19.2–19.4 use these domains to illustrate how the children's education component may be integrated with the other components of family literacy, while maintaining the integrity and accountability of the educational experience for children.

The other two components in family literacy services—parenting education (Parent Time) and interactive literacy activities between parents and children (PACT Time)—also have specific sets of learning goals and performance indicators, and these too are most effective when approached with philosophies and practicalities similar to those applied when designing the adult education and children's education components.

For the Parent Time component, the EFF Project again provides one framework that might be considered when developing performance indicators for the Parent/Family Member Role (one of three roles of adult learners identified by EFF), which are easily integrated with elements from the other components. The suggested indicators for the Parent/Family Member Role are broken down into three sets of key activities: Promote family members' growth and development, meet family needs and responsibilities, and strengthen the family system. The performance indicators for the Worker Role established by EFF may also be used in Parent Time, or may serve as guidance in integrating an additional component sometimes offered by family literacy programs, often referred to as Community Service or Volunteering. The Worker Role, which can be used to develop workplace skills and promote volunteerism, is mapped into four sets of key activities: Do the work, work with others, work within the big picture, and plan and direct personal and professional growth.

Anticipated outcomes for PACT Time have been outlined by the NCFL and primarily focus on parents' increased skills and knowledge of how children learn and how parents can support and influence that learning. These outcomes were clearly defined, with the integration of the other components in mind. Tables 19.2–19.4 use these outcomes for PACT Time and the EFF performance indicators, for both Parent Time and Community Service, to demonstrate how not only curriculum, but also how assessment, may be blended to provide an encompassing approach to instruction.

Staff Approaches That Can Foster Component Integration

The examples of frameworks just described, and used in the tables in this chapter, begin to indicate the complexity of component integration within family literacy services. Component integration is not necessarily a naturally occurring phenomena within the complex and directed system of well-implemented family literacy services. Rather, it is a distinctive and intentional strategy that relies on the commitment of staff to team planning and working with members of families, both as individual students and as a part of a larger family unit. To be most effective, it requires coordination inside and outside the classroom, and a blending of traditional disciplines of adult education and children's education, as well as elements of social services.

There are four approaches that staff can adopt, which can help to facilitate teamwork and integration within a family literacy setting: (a) the adaptation of a broad definition of literacy; (b) the utilization of similar educational theories across the components; (c) a commitment to the use of play, stimulation, and challenge as a means of acquiring knowledge; (d) and the use of a strengths model approach. These approaches are especially effective when considering the target population of family literacy services—a population that often faces multiple barriers to achieving educational and self-sustaining goals.

A Broad Definition of Literacy.   Family literacy has traditionally embraced a broad view of literacy, which takes into account the skills that both children and adults need to find success in school and life. Family literacy programs focus on language and literacy development for both parents and children, but particularly with the intent that effective learning behaviors will be established that will influence ongoing success. In addition to believing that individual component curriculum goals are strengthened by connections to overall program curriculum goals, staff in family literacy programs usually view literacy as a total package made up of complementary skills.

Although this broader definition of literacy certainly includes the essential skills of reading and writing, for adults, it acknowledges that a high literacy is required to carry out roles and responsibilities in the 21st century:

> In the early part of the twentieth century, education focused on the acquisition of literacy skills: simple reading, writing and calculating. It was not the general rule for educational systems to train people to think and read critically, to express themselves clearly and persuasively, to solve complex problems in science and mathematics. Now at the end of the century, these aspects of high literacy are required of almost everyone in order to negotiate successfully the complexities of contemporary life. (Bransford, Brown, & Cocking, 1999, p. 4)

For children, the definition of literacy has also expanded to include a complex set of skills and activities, described by Snow, Burns, and Griffen (1998) as reading together, listening and conversing, drawing, writing and sharing, analyzing, problem solving, and playing in complex processes.

With the recognition that literacy is expansive comes the reassurance that substantial links exist between the two components of adult education and early childhood education in family literacy services, as well as opportunities to use literacy as an avenue for integration with the other components. For example, when parents value their own academic preparation in the use of communication technology and view it as a lifelong learning skill, they are more likely to sit at computers with their children, in classrooms or libraries, and work through problems together. When parents view observation as an obtainable skill, they may actively transfer knowledge gained during PACT Time to discussions in Parent Time that objectively assess their children's literacy development, compared to prior experiences. When children see their parents writing in journals and creating essays and poems, they are likely to appreciate their own attempts to convey ideas in writing.

Just as the adult education and children's education components are linked through a broad view of literacy, so too are the Parent Time and PACT Time components. Reading, writing, speaking, listening, planning, problem solving, and other literacy skills are critical in both Parent Time and PACT Time, and these activities can also serve to bridge the two components. Skills can be learned, modeled, practiced, reviewed, and reinforced, when the staff is attentive to the literacy linkages between these components. As an example of the dynamic between Parent Time and PACT Time, consider the intentional integration strategies in the following scenario.

In a family literacy program, a parent may raise the topic of family health, as a result of reading an article in a parenting magazine about the possible hazards of immunization. Because of the information she gathered from the article, the parent now questions whether or not she should get her child vaccinated. Perhaps the rest of the class agrees, once the topic has been raised, that there is some concern about the safety of immunizations. To address these concerns, the teacher may turn to the EFF standard, Learn Through Research, asking the class to research the topic, and share the information they gain with the rest of the class.

To integrate the children's education component, the children's teachers may incorporate a health and safety center into their classroom, which includes a first-aid station and supplies. In the dress-up area, for example, the teachers may provide uniforms of health care professionals, such as a nurse's tunic and a doctor's lab coat, and may provide children's literature about safety and health in the special topics bookrack.

During PACT Time, parents might be invited to play in the health and safety center and might be encouraged to participate in all the domains of learning with their children: reading the topic books and talking to the children about safety and wellness (language and literacy), reassuring the children of their parents' presence and care (social/emotional development), building a hospital with blocks (mathematical thinking), and measuring their height and weight and recording changes over time (scientific thinking).

A broad definition of literacy helps staff develop a rich content framework for parent education that lends itself easily to integration among the other components as well. By keeping literacy at the core of instruction within each component, both staff and families are able to make connections among all of their educational experiences.

Complementary Educational Philosophies.   One premise used in children's education is that children learn by engaging in natural problem-solving situations. This approach, referred to as *constructivism*, can also have applications to adult education principles, and may be a particularly effective strategy in working with parents who are facing a myriad of complex challenges in their daily lives. When utilized in conjunction with component integration, constructivism becomes another system of guidance for intergenerational learning. The constructivist view of early childhood education is marked by:

- Attention to a child's level of development
- Attention to the environments in which learning takes place
- Emphasis on learning, rather than on teaching
- Awareness of the learner's need for social interaction
- Focus on real experience
- Awareness that learners must participate in their own learning

The constructivist view of adult learning, defined by Lambert and Walker (1995), describes how people construct their reality and make sense of their world. Its application to the field of education suggests that students make their own meaning and is based in part on Plato's contention that knowledge is formed within the learner and is brought to the surface by a skilled teacher through processes of inquiry and dialogue. Very similar to the constructivist view of early childhood education, the constructivist view of adult education asserts that:

- Knowledge and beliefs are formed with the learners who assimilate new information into what they already know.
- Learning is a social activity that is enhanced by shared inquiry.
- Reflection and metacognition are essential aspects of constructing knowledge and meaning.
- Learners play a critical role in assessing their own learning.
- The outcomes of the learning process are varied and often unpredictable.

The constructivist approach allows students to direct the learning, sharing responsibility for the implementation and success of projects.

The constructivist approach is not new, but, until the late 1980s and early 1990s, it was more apparent in early childhood programs than in older children's classrooms, and was notably absent as a philosophical view in most adult education classrooms. However, as more adult education teachers began to adopt the tenets of cognitive learning theory, they also adopted the perspective that teaching and learning are best served when the student's goal is primary, and that prior learning nurtures new learning (Lambert & Walker, 1995). These same educators began to adapt classroom practices to include the science of thinking and learning, by including constructivist strategies in their teaching.

Expert teachers also include the intended literacy focus that provides for phonemic awareness and phonics instruction and for adequate and appropriate attention to fluency, vocabulary, and text comprehension. At the same time, teachers are able to provide opportunities for students to solve problems that reflect the needs for mathematical and scientific thinking, as their lives become more complex and varied. These practices are complementary, not antithetical, to the constructivist approach.

When family literacy staff members share a similar philosophical stance, such as the application of constructivist theory in children's and adult education, the components of their programs are easier to integrate. They are more likely to arrive at compatible strategies in planning sessions and will be able to carry out their plans with similar approaches. For example, consider a program in which the core team of educators uses similar or complementary monitoring, observation, and listening strategies, as both adults and children work independently and together. The adult education teachers can work with the parents on how to monitor their children's learning, ask appropriate questions, and guide their progress. During PACT Time, both early childhood teachers and adult education teachers may watch for application of these skills, and can discuss the results of this strategy in a debriefing session during Parent Time. Using a consistent teaching approach throughout all of the components helps define expectations for both students and educators.

Play, Stimulation, and Challenge as Means of Acquiring Knowledge. Perhaps moreso than in stand-alone education programs (particularly those that target adult learners), family literacy practitioners recognize the value of play as an educational activity that has benefits for both adults and children. Further, family literacy has long recognized that active learning, and providing a variety of learning experiences, is often an effective approach to working with families with diverse strengths and skills. Significantly, in PACT Time, structured play is seen as a key strategy for bringing together the knowledge gathered in the other components and as a culmination of learning experiences expressed through interactive literacy activities.

Among the benefits of playing and learning in the children's classroom are that children:

- Test theories and adapt them as they go along
- Work through emotional conflicts in creative ways
- Investigate social roles in preparation for family and community activities
- Continue to develop language and focus their attention (NCFL, 2001a, p. 19)

Most educators can agree that children need opportunities for exploration, pretense, and play as ways to acquire knowledge. Fewer may be inclined to recognize that play and challenge are also legitimate methods to employ in the adult classroom. Von Oech (2001) invites adults to play with ideas and problems, in order to have mastery over a situation, which is an attitude similar to a child playing a game that "allows one to push and move the various pieces, so as to find out what works and what doesn't" (p. 112).

A belief in the value of play also encourages the learner to recognize that language itself is a kind of playing with words, shaping abstract thoughts and fragments of ideas into clearer forms of communication. Children craft representations with crayons and blocks, imitating people and places; adults do the same with words, forming rich descriptions and broad analyses. Children try to make sense of the world by asking Why? How? and When? Adults do the same with pictures, numbers, and equations, marking and comparing to solve problems. When teachers in individual components within family literacy make these kinds of connections, integration can be enhanced by intentionally incorporating play throughout instruction, using play as a concrete strategy to reinforce concepts for both adults and children.

In addition to supporting literacy development, play can also impact emotional or social behavior. According to Goleman (1995), people who overcome hardships, who demonstrate a resiliency to adverse circumstances such as drug abuse or other dangerous lifestyles, have acquired "a sociability that draws people to them, self-confidence, an optimistic persistence in the face of failure and frustration, the ability to recover quickly from upsets, and an easygoing nature" (p. 256). This kind of sociability can be learned in the process of complex play.

Further, Ackerman (1999) draws a distinction between simple play and deep play, noting that deep play is characterized by challenge, discovery, and creativity—three elements that certainly can contribute to the learning experiences of both adults and children. According to Ackerman, "deep play is central to the life of each person and to society, inspiring the visual, musical, and verbal arts; exploration and discovery. . . . Swept up by the deepest states of play, one feels balanced, creative and focused" (p. 17).

A Strengths Model Approach.   From its inception, the comprehensive family literacy design has striven to employ a strengths model approach to program implementation, both within individual components and as it applies to component integration. A deficit model has been defined as one that focuses on school-like academic activities, implying that such a focus indicates that parents lack the abilities to prepare their children for success in school (Auerbach, 1989; Taylor, 1997). In contrast, a strengths model encourages programs to focus on the family as a source of information for constructing literacy learning, and assumes that parents are capable of, and potentially enthusiastic toward, supporting the acquisition and application of language and literacy skills.

It is perhaps more relevant not to view a strengths model approach as dependent on content (school-like academic activities vs. family construction of learning), but rather on a context that is respectful of parents' goals, that values their ideas, and that includes them in intervention strategies. Either approach can be considered a strengths model, if parents determine the objectives, defining for themselves what they want to be able to do and the skills they need to carry out that construct. Warren (2001) calls this an "empowerment model," because the responsibility for change is transferred from the staff to the family members.

An approach that utilizes a strengths or empowerment model for the implementation of services can define staff thinking and the ways they intentionally design the integration of components. Recognizing that parents are usually the leaders and decision makers within their families, staff value the knowledge and experience parents bring to a program setting. Staff familiar with family systems theory, which recognizes the importance of family structure and functions, are able to align content and context according to the principles of learning and quality design standards.

Using a strengths model approach, staff can work with parents to clarify their goals for themselves and for their children, in each of the components, and events can be designed to recognize the progress made toward achieving those goals, while encouraging further practice. Staff members can plan for reinforcement of skills and knowledge, repeating the application across time and across the components. A strengths model approach is supported when time is allowed for self-reflection and review, so that participants can observe and evaluate how their own learning is transferred from one component to another and from one experience to another.

Using a concrete example of how the strengths model can inform component integration, Popp (2001c) describes a teacher-led conversation with families, which centers on a core set of program messages.

In this process, all of the teachers in the family literacy program engage in dialogue with family members. They reinforce program messages as opportunities arise during normal program activities. The teachers meet regularly to update one another on how families are progressing in the program and to identify messages that need to be addressed.

An example of the use of dialogue could work like this. A parent is frustrated with lack of progress on an algebra lesson in the adult education class. It brings back memories of failure in school and is affecting her participation in the other components of the program. When she visits the early childhood room for parent–child interaction time, the early childhood teacher might engage the parent in a dialogue about how children are using blocks to make patterns. She points out that the patterns might center around colors, shapes, sizes, or combinations of these variables.

The parent says, "Variables. That is what I am doing in math right now. Using variables in algebra." The teacher says, "Yes, your daughter is studying variables, too." (p. 1)

In the above example, even simple affirmation, expressed through component integration, connects the parent to her own learning experience and that of her child's. Here, too, combination of a strengths model approach and staff team planning clearly can have a powerful and succinct effect on the family learning system.

ADMINISTRATIVE FACTORS THAT IMPACT COMPONENT INTEGRATION

As discussed throughout this chapter, component integration in family literacy programs is an intentional and structured strategy designed to maximize the effectiveness of individual components offered in tandem. To facilitate integration, there are three administrative areas that can enhance (or inhibit) implementation: facilities, planning, and staff development.

Facilities

Providing and designing appropriate facilities for comprehensive family literacy services is an often overlooked factor that can have a tremendous impact on service delivery. Not only do family literacy programs need to accommodate children and adult learners separately, but they must also provide space conducive to parent–child interaction.

Successful integration of the components is aided by a setting that allows easy access by participants to classrooms and learning labs that are used on a regular basis and that also encourages movement between these locations, physically and visibly connecting the four components. The room where PACT Time is held is especially important. It should be large enough and contain adequate equipment, so that staff can interact with families as they work and play together. To honor parents and to encourage their participation, the room should be designed in a way that welcomes adult learners, in addition to children.

For a variety of reasons, which may include funding and scheduling restrictions, not all family literacy programs are able to colocate adult and child classrooms. Although some programs successfully offer services utilizing creative solutions to space issues, it is recommended that programs make every effort to colocate classrooms, as a way to foster integration. I have observed a program in which the adult education and early education classrooms were literally miles apart. Subsequently, efforts to plan for integration were disjointed, PACT Time was implemented only superficially, the outcomes for families did not meet expectations, and the program closed. On the other hand, I have also observed services offered in Louisville, Kentucky, in which adjoining classrooms for parents, 3 to 5-year-olds, and infants and toddlers were designated. In this environment, parents and children moved freely among the desks and computers in the adult education classroom and among various areas and baby cribs in the children's rooms, interacting and learning together throughout their day-to-day activities. These programs are still intact after 12 years of operation.

Planning

If outcomes for families correlate with the quality of planning time, as Warren (2001) indicates, it follows that such time should be incorporated into the regular routine for educators. Because of the complexity of component integration, team planning that involves all staff is essential to maximizing integration potential. Dedicated planning sessions can allow staff members to devote time and attention to intentional teaching strategies that build on students' goals, strengths, and expectations. Hayes (1989, 1996) recommends that a program management structure use the strategies of cooperative planning, decision making, and reflection, in the design of quality services.

This conviction that planning is essential to providing effective family literacy services is reflected in the beliefs and actions of Jacquelyn Power, principal of the Blackwater Community School on the Gila River Reservation. She believes that integration of the components is so critical for success in providing family literacy services that she attends the Family and Child Education planning meetings with the staff every Friday, to discuss how, when, and where the enrolled parents and children will interact. Further, she helps staff evaluate the current transference of learning across the components and monitors how strategies do and do not help families make continual progress toward goals. To emphasize the importance of planning to integration, Power often holds these team planning meetings in her office (personal communication, January 14, 2002).

The innovative change process described by Hayes (1996) leads to continuous improvement, if all parties involved agree to planned and deliberate action, then implement that action with the full support of the institution. Demonstrated support for team planning, as exemplified by the Blackwater program, is a key element to successful component integration.

Staff Development

The benefits of providing comprehensive services to multiple family members are compounded by efforts to give staff, themselves, an extensive educational experience, expanding their perspectives and broadening the opportunities for integration of the program components. Based on interviews with administrators in a variety of programs, team learning across the components, and training specifically in component integration, are priorities for well-established family literacy programs. Further, Cathy McTighe, training coordinator at the NCFL, confirms that the demand for staff development, focusing on component integration, is steady: "The requestor usually mentions that their folks [teachers of individual components] are having a tough time seeing the whole picture, and they need reinforcement of the concept and the need for integration of those components, once the program is up and running" (personal communication, November 2, 2001).

State departments of education also offer in-service sessions for teachers, on component integration. In Arizona, a supplemental grant was awarded to two high-quality family literacy programs, The Family Tree in Mesa and Pima College in Tucson, and charged each to serve as models for best practices. Both programs also provide all of the family literacy training for the state programs (state-funded and Even Start), in connection with the NCFL. In addition to generalized family literacy implementation training, they offer other specific training opportunities in integration, PACT Time, team building, and other topics, when requested. Program administrators and trainers Linda Mead and Marilyn Box write that:

> Always, integration is on the minds of all staff and we have many requests for technical assistance around integrating the components. Here are our findings that we speak about in our trainings:
> • Integration in family literacy evolves. The efforts to integrate are ongoing; it takes a while to really understand the importance of integrating the components.

- We concentrate on integrating the "big messages" of family literacy, more than the integration of themes. For example, we always ask, "What big messages do you want families to remember 5 years after they have left the program?" Then it becomes clear that we are not talking about Halloween themes or bunny rabbit themes, or even science themes. It is about messages that families need to know.

With these big messages in mind, we try to show family literacy teams how they can incorporate these into the curriculum in all components (personal communication, November 20, 2001)

In Hawaii, the state Even Start office appointed a specialist who coordinates training and staff development and who offers technical assistance to programs. The specialist, Sandra Ishikawa, reports that training in component integration is perhaps the most sought-after category, following initial family literacy training. "It is not easy to grasp at first," she says, "and staff members are not used to this kind of coordination. Sometimes it takes several opportunities to hear the integration messages and several months of operating programs together to make it work" (personal communication, October 23, 2001).

Sara Mansbach, the director of Family Literacy Programs in Greenville, South Carolina, reports that:

In my work with comprehensive family literacy programs, the Family Learning GED Programs in Greenville, SC, I view my role as administrator as that of a coach/team player. In Greenville, each program's team consists of the Adult/Parent Education teacher and several Early Childhood Infant/Toddler staff members. With my teams I plan for, help deliver, and continuously evaluate the integration of the four components. As coach, I have to be thoroughly familiar with each of the components, stressing to the staff and the parents that it is through participation in the four combined elements that the greatest progress can be made. (personal communication, November 17, 2001)

Professional development that stresses team learning and coordination, along with allowing for adequate team planning time and providing facilities that intentionally foster parent–child–teacher interaction, can be combined to ensure the more likely success of component integration. Attention to these factors also sends an important message to parents enrolled in family literacy programs—that their participation is valued and integral to the success of the learning experience.

WHAT DOES COMPONENT INTEGRATION LOOK LIKE?

The tables that follow illustrate what is meant by the integration of messages, concepts, and goals in a family literacy program. Table 19.1 is a sample planning document, which may be used as a tool during team sessions to facilitate integration across all of the components. The strength of this document lies in tying together common frames of reference to content, by mapping out themes across standards, domains of learning, areas of responsibility, and concepts used across adult, child, and parent education. To be useful for actually implementing integration across the components, this document obviously will require input from all teaching staff.

Table 19.2 builds from the planning table and provides an overarching framework for the four primary components of family literacy services. It also includes the additional component of Community Service Time, which some programs offer. Each column in the table addresses learning goals or standards of performance for one of these components. It is especially crucial that staff members understand and agree upon achievement goals for each component; when staff agrees upon an approach that will lead to integration, the likelihood of achieving program goals increases.

TABLE 19.1

Family Literacy Component Integration—Planning Document

Focus on component:	With integration into other components			Primary goal: (taken from framework)	
Adult Education	*Early Childhood Education*	*Parent Time*	*PACT Time*	*Community Service Time*	
Content standard: Desired outcomes/ components of performance:	**Domain of learning:** Desired outcomes/ areas of learning:	**Area of responsibility:** Desired outcomes/ key activities:	**Area of responsibility:** Desired outcomes/ performance indicators:	**Area of responsibility:** Desired outcomes/ key activities:	
Methods: Materials:	Methods: Materials:	Methods: Materials:	Methods: Materials:	Methods: Materials:	

Planning document for integration of the components. Effective integration requires significant team planning; see the section on planning under Administrative Factors that Impact Component Integration. Community Service Time is sometimes offered as a separate component in family literacy programs.

TABLE 19.2

Family Literacy Component Integration—Overview of Standards, Domains of Learning, and Areas of Responsibility

Adult Education	Early Childhood Education	Parent Time	PACT Time	Community Service Time
EFF STANDARDS **Communication skills** Read with understanding. Convey ideas in writing. Speak so others can understand. Listen actively. Observe critically. **Decision-making skills** Use math to solve problems and to communicate. Solve problems and make decisions. Plan. **Interpersonal skills** Guide others. Resolve conflict and negotiate. Advocate and influence. Cooperate with others. **Lifelong learning skills** Use information and communications technology. Learn through research. Reflect and evaluate. Take responsibility for learning.	**DOMAINS OF LEARNING** **Language and Literacy** *Areas of learning:* listening; speaking; literature and reading; writing; spelling **Personal and social development** *Areas of learning:* Self-concept; self-control; interaction with others; conflict resolution; approach to learning **Mathematical thinking** *Areas of learning:* Patterns and relationships; number concept; geometry and spatial relations; measurement **Scientific thinking** *Areas of Learning:* Observing; questioning and predicting; explaining and forming conclusions **The arts** *Areas of learning:* Expression and representation; artistic appreciation **Physical development** *Areas of learning:* Gross motor development; fine motor development; personal health and safety	**AREAS OF RESPONSIBILITY** **Promote family members' growth and development** Make and pursue plans for self-improvement. Guide and mentor other family members. Foster informal education of children. Support children's formal education. Direct and discipline children. **Meet family needs and responsibilities** Provide for safety and physical needs. Manage family resources. Balance priorities to meet multiple needs and responsibilities, Give and receive support outside the immediate family. **Strengthen the family system** Create a vision for the family and work to achieve it. Promote values, ethics, and cultural heritage within family. Form and maintain supportive family relationships.	**AREAS OF RESPONSIBILITY** **Performance indicators (parents)** Improved communication skills Increased knowledge of children's literature and importance of sharing books with children Increased confidence in their own ability to extend their children's experiences and to actively plan ways to do so Increased knowledge of age-appropriate behaviors and activities Increased ability to identify children's needs and interests Increased ability to demonstrate mature parental behaviors Increased ability to set realistic goals	**WORKER ROLE: AREAS OF RESPONSIBILITY** **Volunteer** Acquire a sense of service. **Do the work** Organize, plan, and prioritize work. Respond to and meet new work challenges. Take responsibility for assuring work quality and results. **Work with others** Communicate with others. Give assistance. Seek and receive assistance, support motivation, and direction Value people different from oneself **Work within the big picture** Work within organizational norms. Use organizational goals, performance, and structure to guide work activities. **Plan and direct personal and professional growth** Learn new skills. Pursue work activities that provide satisfaction.

This table illustrates corresponding standards, domains of learning, and performance indicators for the components of a family literacy program. Staff may choose a learning goal from any column, to enter the system and begin planning for integration of the components.

The EFF standards provide clear content goals for adult education. For an early childhood education component, there are Domains of Learning, which may be linked easily with the adult education standards. Likewise, the Areas of Responsibility in the three components of Parent Time, PACT Time, and Community Service Time provide contextual links to the application of the adult education standards. As they plan for integration, staff may enter the system at any component. Clearly, however, adult education can provide a key link for accomplishing the overall objective of component integration: to strengthen the total program.

Table 19.3 illustrates a plan that enters the system in the adult education component and seeks to integrate the EFF standard, Convey Ideas in Writing, into the other components. Let us assume that adult students have recognized a need to write effectively for a variety of purposes. Referring to Table 19.2, their goal may be identified under the category Communication Skills in the adult education column. Once the driving goal is selected in one component—in this case, Convey Ideas in Writing—we can select compatible goals for the other components. But first, it is important to work through one component, deciding upon the desired outcomes and performance indicators, before moving to the other components for the purpose of integration. Having a clear objective defined in one component will help in selecting and working through objectives and strategies for the remaining components.

Starting with the adult education component, each EFF standard has two parts: a title, such as Convey Ideas in Writing, and Components of Performance, which will indicate when the standard has been mastered. Working down the adult education column in Table 19.3, we select a variety of methods that will help adults accomplish their goal. Finally, we identify the materials that we must have on hand to carry out the methodology.

Our next step is to integrate the adult education component and the early childhood education component. We examine the Domains of Learning listed in column 2 of Table 19.2, and select the Domain, Language and Literacy, as a compatible goal area to work from in Table 19.3. We further define the desired outcomes as "Using Writing to Express Ideas," described in the Work Sampling System as an area of learning and in the High/Scope System as a key experience. Next, we identify appropriate methods, depending on the target age group, and list materials that children will use to achieve the goals.

In column 3 of Table 19.2, we select the Area of Responsibility, Promote Family Members' Growth and Development, as the goal for integrating Parent Time. Desired outcomes are identified as "Foster informal education of children" and "Support children's formal education." To bring about these outcomes, methods are selected that will expose parents to their children's current literacy development and engage them in that development. We forecast the materials that parents will need to carry out the plan. We move to the Parent Time component, located in column 3 in Table 19.2 and select the Area of Responsibility, Promote Family Members Growth and Development, as our goal. We identify the outcomes we seek as "Foster informal education of children" and "Support children's formal education." We ask ourselves, How can we accomplish the goal? and decide that we must spend time on the concepts of emergent literacy, as part of our Parent Time curriculum. We forecast the materials that we will need to carry out the plan.

What do we hope to see in PACT Time as a result of the core learning in Adult Education, Early Childhood Education and Parent Time components? Because this integrative experience is focusing on writing and communication, we select from column 4 of Table 19.2 the desired outcomes "Improved communication skills" and "Increased confidence in their own ability (as parents) to extend their children's experiences and to actively plan ways to do so." From there, we again identify appropriate methods and materials. If our program has a separate community service component, we work through the final column of our planning document in a similar manner.

The selection of methods and materials should be congruent across the components, and, when carefully selected to work together, these can help to further integrate the components.

TABLE 19.3

Family Literacy Component Integration—Project Focus on Adult Education Goals

	Focus on component: Adult Education	With integration into other components		Primary goal: Convey ideas in writing
Adult Education	*Early Childhood Education*	*Parent Time*	*PACT Time*	*Community Service Time*
Content standard: Convey ideas in writing.	**Domain of learning:** Language and literacy	**Area of responsibility:** Promote family members' growth and development.	**Area of responsibility:** Parents—strengthening literacy development	**Area of responsibility:** Do the work.
Desired outcomes/components of performance: Determine the purpose for communication. Organize and present information to serve the purpose. Pay attention to conventions of English language usage. Seek feedback and revise.	**Desired outcomes/areas of learning:** Using writing to express ideas	**Desired outcomes/ key activities:** Foster informal education of children. Support children's formal education.	**Desired outcomes/ performance indicators:** Improved communication skills Increased confidence in their own ability to extend their children's experiences and actively plan ways to do so	**Desired outcomes/ key activities:** Organize plant, and prioritize work. Respond to and meet new work challenges.
Methods: Parents will learn concepts of essay writing and practice writing to a variety of audiences. They will write in journals and reading logs at least twice a week.	**Methods:** Children will dictate or write stories, poems, titles, and explanations of their pictures. Appropriate writing for age groups will include scribble writing, stamping, and drawing in reading logs and journals.	**Methods:** Introduce parents to concepts of emergent literacy and tools of literacy. Show collections of children's attempts to write. Make reading log by sewing cover and paper with heavy twine.	**Methods:** Complete cover for reading log, with child in art area. After parents read to their children, they will log their children's and their own responses in a reading log. They will label children's drawings with titles and children's ideas about their work.	**Methods:** Provide examples of writing needs in the workplace, such as listing, record keeping, reporting. Practice with samples from various work sites.
Materials: Reading logs Journals Writing tools	**Materials:** Reading logs Journals Writing tools	**Materials:** Tools of Literacy poster Directions for sewing reading logs together Tack board, paper, twine Scissors	**Materials:** Art supplies	**Materials:** Examples of workplace writing

This table illustrates a plan that is intended to improve the writing skills of adult students and to integrate this primary goal across all components. The plan is a result of student goal setting in the adult education classroom.

These tables are meant to be planning documents, and other methods will emerge as a particular project takes shape.

Table 19.4 illustrates a plan that enters the system with a focus on the Parent Time component. In this case, parents in the program have expressed a concern about using appropriate discipline with their children. In column 3 of Table 19.2, we identify the Area of Responsibility, Promote Family Members' Growth and Development, as the goal for Parent Time. The parents have already identified the outcome they seek: "Direct and discipline children," which we expand on our planning document to reflect the parents' concerns. From there, we select methods and materials that will help parents accomplish their goal.

Next, we work through the other components, identifying the standards, indicators, and desired outcomes, as well as the methodologies and materials. Note, too, that the adult education EFF content standard, Observe Critically, has been selected to guide the methodology used in the Parent Time component.

EVALUATING COMPONENT INTEGRATION

Although component integration is a major strategy that family literacy programs employ to meet the goals of families, there is a need for evaluation (a) to determine when and how component integration is being used (i.e., program processes) and (b) to determine integration's influence on staff and participants (i.e., program outcomes). Within programs, staff often struggle with ways to document the results of their efforts to implement component integration. Further, staff want to know how the complexities of integration make a difference in the success of the program.

The first need is for program evaluation. Program directors and staff need to determine if they are meeting their own goals of component integration. Staff anecdotal records and parents' own observations and anecdotal records have been used to determine if and how component integration is being implemented. However, additional methods and procedures need to be used.

Popp (1992) suggests the use of the family portfolio is one assessment procedure that has potential for evaluating component integration. Parents and children can contribute to both the content and evaluation of the portfolio, by "collaborating with teachers in the development of criteria for selecting what goes into portfolios and the criteria by which those contents will be judged" (p. 2). Portfolios are generally considered to be informal assessments, and Popp's suggestion that teachers and parents collaborate to develop criteria for assessing progress is in keeping with this chapter's earlier mention that few, if any, standardized assessments of component integration exist. Nevertheless, family portfolio, as described by Popp, can be an appropriate assessment tool for helping programs evaluate both outcomes and processes.

Eventually, regular use of the family portfolio as a means of recording PACT Time interaction can encourage parents and children to reflect on their activities. Teachers also gain valuable information about a parent's "level of engagement with the child, expectations of child performance, knowledge of child development, and values and beliefs about literacy" (Popp, 1992, p. 11). For example, staff can note how parents' journal entries in the portfolio change over time, moving from an activity focus to a focus on personal skills to a focus on how a functional skill will transfer to real life in family interaction, workplace performance, and community participation. The following excerpts from a parent's journal entries show this progression:

(a) Completed the test on long division and passed! Never thought I could do math.
(b) Getting ready to take the GED. When I pass, I'll finish the application that I got from the speaker in Parent Time last week.

TABLE 19.4

Family Literacy Component Integration—Entering System in the Parent Time Component

Primary Goals: Promote family members'
growth and development—
Using appropriate discipline)

Focus on component: Parent Time	With integration into other components			
Adult Education	Early Childhood Education	Parent Time	PACT Time	Community Service Time
Content standard: Listen actively. **Desired outcomes/ components of performance:** Attend to oral information. Clarify purpose for listening and use appropriate listening strategies. **Methods:** Invite school psychologist to present information about child development and age-appropriate discipline. Parents will use a listening guide. Dr. Jean will follow up with discussion during Parent Time. Parents will write in their journals, addressing questions raised by Dr. Jean. Introduce books. **Materials:** Books, journals	**Domain of learning:** Personal and social development **Desired outcomes/areas of learning:** Self concept, growth of Self-confidence self control, increased ability to express self in healthy ways **Methods:** In small-group time, children will construct body outline, color and label, put magnets on back for hanging display. Add books to literacy area: *I Like Me* and *On the Day You Were Born.* **Materials:** Books Butcher paper, markers, magnets	**Area of responsibility:** Promote family members' growth and development. **Desired outcomes/key activities:** Direct and discipline children— provide consistent and loving adult supervision with appropriate discipline. **Methods:** Focus on EFF standard: Observe critically. Using a viewing guide, parents will watch the videotape *Appropriate Discipline at the Right Time.* Discussion will follow with school psychologist, Dr. Jean. Schedule conferences. **Materials:** Videotape and player Viewing guide for each parent Discussion guide for each parent Conference sign-up sheet	**Area of responsibility:** Parents—actively embracing the parenting role. **Desired outcomes/performance indicators:** Increase knowledge of age-appropriate behaviors and activities. **Methods:** Observe parent–child interaction as they complete the body oulines; offer support as needed; provide alternative materials if conflicts occur. Read book, *I Like Me,* in Circle Time. Send home children's pictures with directions on how to construct a frame. **Materials:** Book Camera, film Directions for frame for each family	**Area of responsibility:** Plan and direct personal and professional growth **Desired outcomes/ key activities:** Learn new skills. **Methods:** Parents will observe parent–child interaction while shopping, visiting, working, attending religious services. Note various actions and reactions of both adults and children, as well as concerns and positive thoughts. **Materials:** None

This table illustrates a staff plan to help parents with appropriate disciplinary methods. The plan is a result of staff observations and conversations with parents regarding their concerns about physical discipline.

(c) Learning the things I need to know for when my child has math homework. It will feel good to be able to help her.

(d) Learned how to budget, so we can start saving for a house. Never realized how basic math skills would help me do this. I asked Bruce how big his room will be. He said, "seventy-eight miles," and I said, "I don't think so!"

(e) We played math games at Tessie's birthday party. I made the cards myself.

(R. Popp, personal communication, August 24, 2002)

Other methods of evaluating the program's use of component integration could involve systematic staff evaluation of their efforts on a weekly basis, summarizing and reviewing ways component integration has been used in the preceding week. A program might also have an evaluator make observations and conduct interviews, to obtain information about integration implementation that could be used for program improvement purposes.

A more difficult question is how to document the impact of component integration on efforts to create an environment in which positive changes occur. Outcomes of participating parents and children can be compared to outcomes of nonparticipating families, but these outcomes will not necessarily be conclusive regarding the impact of component integration, because participant outcomes are influenced by a variety of program elements. Identifying or developing ways to assess how component integration specifically impacts not only participant outcomes, but also program processes, would be a useful pursuit. For example, does the intentional implementation of component integration influence how team planning is accomplished? How does component integration influence methods of instruction or professional development for staff? Does component integration inform decisions about facility design?

Unlike the four primary components of family literacy, component integration does not have easily identifiable desired outcomes, independently. Rather, its effectiveness is determined by the effectiveness of the other components, as they work together to create a system of positive educational influence.

REFERENCES

Ackerman, D. (1999). *Deep play*. New York: Random House.

Alamprese, J. (2000). Understanding adult education in the context of family literacy. In Wasik, B. H. (Ed.), *Synthesis of research on family literacy programs*. Chapel Hill: University of North Carolina.

Auerbach, E. R. (1989). Toward a sociocontextual approach to family literacy. *Harvard Educational Review, 59*, 165–181.

Bransford, J., Brown, A. L., & Cocking, R. R. (Eds.). (1999). *How people learn: Brain, mind, experience, and school*. Washington, DC: National Academy Press.

Bronfenbrenner, U. (1977). Toward an experimental ecology of human development. *American Psychologist, 32*, 513–531.

Dwyer, C. M. (2000). *Guide to quality: Even Start family literacy programs*. Portsmouth, NH: RMC Research.

Goleman, D. (1995). *Emotional intelligence: Why it can matter more than IQ*. New York: Bantam.

Hayes, A. E. (1989). *William R. Kenan Charitable Trust: Family literacy project, Final project report*. Wilmington: University of North Carolina at Wilmington.

Hayes, A. E. (1996). *Breaking the cycle of undereducation and poverty: Family literacy programs as a system of influence—A summary of research findings*. Louisville, KY: National Center for Family Literacy.

Hayes, A. E. (2001a). *High-quality family literacy programs: Child outcomes and impacts*. Wilmington: University of North Carolina at Wilmington, Watson School of Education.

Hayes, A. E. (2001b). *Making the case for family literacy*. Goodling Institute for Research in Family Literacy, College of Education, The Pennsylvania State University.

Jablon, J. (1996). *Work Sampling System* (3rd ed.). New York: Rebus Planning Associates.

Lambert, L., Walker, D., Zimmerman, D. P., Cooper, J. E., Lambert, M. D., Gardner, M. E., et al. (1995). *The constructivist leader*. New York: Teacher's College Press.

National Center for Family Literacy (NCFL). (2001). *Training and staff development for family literacy practioners: Participants' manual.* Louisville, KY: Author.

Philliber, W. W., Spillman, R. E., & King, R. E. (1996). Consequences of family literacy for adults and children: Some preliminary findings. *Journal of Adolescent & Adult Literacy, 39,* 558–565.

Popp, R. J. (1992). *Family portfolios: Documenting change in parent–child relationships.* Louisville, KY: National Center for Family Literacy.

Popp, R. J. (2001a). *Progressive pediatrics: Emphasis on early childhood literacy.* Louisville, KY: Children and Youth Project, University of Louisville School of Medicine.

Popp, R. J. (2001b). *Component integration in family literacy programs.* Retrieved November 1, 2001, from the Partnership for Family Education and Support (PFES) Web site: http://www.bobpopp.com/html/ no__110.html

Popp, R. J. (2001c). Using dialogue to promote component integration in family literacy programs. Retrieved November 1, 2001, from the Partnership for Family Education and Support (PFES) Web site: http://www.bobpopp.com/html/no__111.html

Potts, M. (1992). *A strengths model for learning in a family literacy program.* Louisville, KY: National Center for Family Literacy.

Potts, M., & Freeman, B. L. (1990). *Kenan family literacy program site visit reports.* Unpublished manuscript.

Senge, P. (1990). *The fifth discipline: The art and practice of the learning organization.* New York: Doubleday/Currency.

Snow, C. E., Burns, M. S., & Griffin, P. (Eds.). (1998). *Preventing reading difficulties in young children.* Washington, DC: National Academy Press.

Stein, S. (1997). *Equipped for the future: A reform agenda for adult literacy and learning.* Washington, DC: The National Institute for Literacy.

Taylor, D. (Ed.). (1997). *Many families, many literacies: An international declaration of principles.* Portsmouth, NH: Heinemann.

Von Oech, R. (2001). *Expect the unexpected: A creativity tool based on the ancient wisdom of Heraclitus.* New York: Time Warner.

Warren, L. (2001, April 7). Report on statewide study of Even Start programs in Massachusetts. Message posted to nifl-family@literacy.nifl.gov.

Wasik, B. H., Dobbins, D. R., & Herrmann, S. (2001). Intergenerational family literacy: Concepts, research, and practice. In S. B. Neuman & D. K. Dickinson (Eds.), *Handbook of early literacy research* (pp. 444–458). New York: Guilford.

Weikart, D., & Holmann, M. (1995). *Educating young children: Active learning practices for preschool and childcare programs.* Ypsilanti, MI: High/Scope Educational Research Foundation.

Yarnell, V., Pfannenstiel, J., Lambson, T., & Treffeisen, S. (1998). *Bureau of Indian Affairs Family and Child Education Program: 1998 Evaluation Report.* Overland Park, KS: Research & Training Associates, for the Office of Indian Education Programs, Bureau of Indian Affairs, U.S. Department of the Interior.

20

Integrating Services for Family Literacy

Gloria L. Harbin, Suzannah Herrmann, Barbara Hanna
Wasik, Dionne R. Dobbins, and Wendy K. Lam
University of North Carolina at Chapel Hill

Service integration refers to the amount of connectedness among providers that makes services to families more coordinated and responsive. Professionals in education and human services have recently become more aware of the numerous, complicated needs of children and their families—needs that often go beyond a single program, agency, or organization. Yet, the services various agencies or organizations provide for the same child and family often tend to be fragmented and at times inaccessible. Recognition of this problem has encouraged various endeavors to coordinate or integrate services provided to individual children and families (Richardson, 1973). Dating back over three decades, programs have engaged in a variety of interagency initiatives (Agranoff, 1991; Hassett & Austin, 1997; Kagan, 1993; Konrad, 1996; Lawson & Sailor, 2000; Waldfogel, 1997). Most of these initiatives have sought to create, in the phrasing of the General Accounting Office, "methods to unite or link the services provided by different agencies to serve the same population" (1992, p. 2).

In the effort to remedy fragmentation, policymakers have mandated the coordination of services for many human service programs funded by the federal government. Some of these include literacy programs (Even Start); programs for children in poverty (Head Start, Early Head Start); programs for infants, toddlers, and preschool children with disabilities (The Individuals with Disabilities Education Act, 1991, and children's mental health programs); programs for children in need of health care (Early Periodic Screening Diagnosis and Treatment, Children with Special Health Care Needs); and, of course, welfare reform.

Historically, a variety of terms have described efforts to alleviate this fragmentation among both individuals and systems (Hassett & Austin, 1997; Konrad, 1996). In fact, different types of services often use their own idiosyncratic sets of terms. For example, public administration researchers describe the relationship between or among organizations with terms such as *networks* (Agranoff & McGuire, 2001) or *coupling of organizations* (Wieck, 1976). In examining intervention and prevention services for young children with or at risk for disabilities, practitioners have used such terms as *cooperation, coordination, collaboration* (Bruner, 1993; Intrilligator, 1986; Melaville & Blank, 1991) and, more recently, *service integration* (Hassett & Austin, 1997; Kagan, 1993; Konrad, 1996). In linking educational services with other health services, schools use terms like *school-linked services* (Behrman, 1992), *partnerships* (Cordiero, 1996), *full-service schools* (Dryfoos, 1994), and *community schools* (Lawson & Sailor, 2000).

Other terms associated with the concept of service integration include *comprehensive services, coherent services, broad spectrum of services*, and *community integration* (Agranoff, 1991). Lawson and Sailor (2000) identified such additional terms as *interprofessional collaboration, interdisciplinary case management, interagency coordination, policy decategorization, systems change, cross-systems change*, and *comprehensive systems of care*. All these terms allude, more or less, to overcoming categorical barriers and reducing existing divisions in providing families and children with services, but these various terms and their nuances also indicate different processes, intensities, or foci. Consequently, a great deal of confusion surrounds their precise meanings. Recently, we find increasing agreement about the meaning of the term *service integration*, as a point on a continuum of increasingly cohesive relationships among agencies or programs (Harbin, McWilliam, & Gallagher, 2000; Kagan, 1993; Konrad, 1996). We discuss this idea of a continuum of closeness and connectedness between agencies in more detail later in this chapter.

Evidence from studies of other human service programs suggests the value of collaboration and service integration. In their studies of children in poverty, and children with disabilities (Harbin et al., 2000; Kagan, 1993; Knitzer, 1982), researchers discovered at least five organizational benefits resulting from collaboration: (a) an ability to serve more children, (b) an increase in funding for program operation attributable to sharing resources, (c) a tendency to identify and serve children earlier, (d) a tendency to provide services to children and families quicker, and (e) an ability to provide a broader array of services. Examples of benefits to individuals included enhanced child development, enhanced family capacity, and reduced confusion and frustration about how to access services. In a qualitative study of nine diverse communities, Harbin et al. (2000) found that children and families tended to obtain more positive outcomes in those communities, with more comprehensive and coordinated service delivery than in communities with less collaboration.

Some evidence also attests to the benefits of service integration in family literacy, as well (Padak, Sapin, & Ackerman, 2001; St.Pierre and Layzer, 1996; St.Pierre et al., 2001; Tao, Gamse, & Tarr, 1998; Tice, 2000). Consequently, regarding family literacy interventions, strong beliefs have developed about the importance of integrating services. Integrated literacy services are believed to produce a synergistic effect, culminating in benefits beyond what might occur if the services are offered in a fragmented manner (Alamprese, 1996; National Center for Family Literacy [NCFL], 1997).

Drawing upon the evidence from its family literacy work, the NCFL (1997) suggested that family literacy programs can serve as a "single point of contact or referral for families and a vehicle for the integration of services" (p. 14). The *Guidebook* produced by NCFL also suggests a number of benefits associated with collaboration in family literacy. Table 20.1 includes the benefits that the *Guidebook* presents.

Integrating social support services with family literacy services also appears to provide families with access to a wider array of services to meet their needs (Alamprese, 1996; Dwyer, 1995; Haslam & Suh, 2000; NCFL, 1997; Quezada & Nickse, 1993; St.Pierre & Layzer, 1996). Even Start family literacy programs rely heavily on services from collaborating agencies, particularly in the provision of early childhood and adult education services (St.Pierre et al., 2001). In a study of 10 Even Start projects by Haslam and Suh (2000), almost all project directors, partners, and collaborators believed their working relationships made possible a more comprehensive set of services. In Even Start, in addition to education services, the human services that parents most commonly received included child care, meals, family support, social services, and transportation. Services the children most commonly received included child care, meals, and transportation (St.Pierre et al., 2001).

TABLE 20.1
Examples of Benefits of Collaborative Efforts in Family Literacy

- Integration of early childhood, adult education, and parent education into a comprehensive family-focused curriculum
- Shared facilities serving both children and adults
- Provision of transportation for both children and their parents, through agreements with public schools
- Provision of meals for both children and parents, through the school lunch program or through funds provided by local sources
- Shared cost of teacher salaries, using a variety of funding sources
- Child care services for younger children of the parents in the program
- Improved public relations, through local media and the networks of the collaborating agencies
- More effective recruitment and increased retention of families, because of higher visibility and the proactive approach of collaborating agencies
- More effective use of volunteers with both children and parents
- Better access to counseling and support services for the family, not just individual members of the family
- Additional sources of books and materials through public and school libraries
- Access to computer training through public schools, area technical centers, community colleges, or universities
- Assistance in making transitions, as children enter kindergarten and parents move on to further education, job training, and employment
- Increased funding to enhance and expand family literacy in the community

Note: Adapted from *The Family Literacy Answer Book* (pp. 14–15), by the National Center for Family Literacy, 1997, Louisville, KY: Author. Copyright 1997 by National Center for Family Literacy. Adapted by permission.

Despite its importance, however, service integration remains a complex and difficult principle to implement successfully (Elder, 1979; Gans & Horton, 1975; Martinson, 1982; Richardson, 1973; Rogers & Farrow, 1983; Weiss, 1981). Consequently, this chapter synthesizes the lessons learned from family literacy initiatives (Alamprese, 1996; Dwyer, 1995; St.Pierre et al., 2001), then it supplements these important lessons with those lessons learned from early care and education (Kagan, 1993). Finally, it incorporates lessons learned from programs for children with disabilities and their families (Flynn & Harbin, 1987; Harbin & McNulty, 1990; Harbin et al., 2000; Knitzer, 1982).

One can, of course, integrate services across agencies for different aspects of family literacy, but the main focus of many family literacy programs has been to integrate family literacy educational services, and many guidelines provided to programs suggest ways of meeting this objective. Integrating human services for families is, however, also important to consider. Human services refers to assisting families with such concerns as child care and protection, basic needs, mental and physical health, family support, financial information, and transportation (Trivette, Dunst, & Deal, 1996). If one considers the human service needs of both children and families, in the integration of family literacy programs, then one can enhance the access to and use of educational services (Maslow, 1962). Service integration for family literacy, in this chapter, denotes the integration of both human and educational services.

The synthesis of service integration lessons across several professional fields allowed us to draw conclusions and make recommendations to more adequately address the difficulties in successfully implementing service integration in family literacy. This chapter begins with an empirically grounded *conceptual framework*, to clarify the concept of service integration. This framework is followed by a section that presents ways family literacy programs can integrate services into a comprehensive family literacy system that includes both educational and human service components, and that suggests a group of strategies to integrate family literacy services systematically. The chapter concludes with recommendations for addressing additional issues, in order to promote service integration in family literacy.

CONCEPTUAL FRAMEWORK OF SERVICE INTEGRATION

Service integration would be a much easier task if one could focus on a single variable to ensure effectiveness, but service integration includes many partners operating within many dimensions and elements (Flynn & Harbin, 1987; Konrad, 1996). Therefore, program administrators need to recognize and understand all the elements and factors that influence the effectiveness of service integration. To help explain these elements and factors, we present a framework that synthesizes and integrates the knowledge gained empirically from studies in a variety of human services initiatives. This framework includes six dimensions: (a) an *ecological vision* (Maslow, 1962; Trivette et al., 1996); (b) the *levels of service delivery* and organization at which integration occurs (Kagan, 1993; Bruner, 1993); (c) the amount of coordination as measured by points along a *continuum of integration* (Harbin et al., 2000; Konrad, 1996); (d) *systems knowledge* and thinking; (e) dimensions of the *agency culture* of service (Harbin, 1996); and (f) *barriers and facilitators* that influence the effectiveness of integration (Flynn & Harbin, 1987; Harbin & McNulty, 1990).

The Ecological Vision

The ecological and transactional models of development suggest the importance of addressing the child's development, in addition to increasing the family's well-being and capacity to facilitate and support the development of their child (Bronfenbrenner, 1979; Garbarino, 1990; Maslow, 1962; Sameroff & Chandler, 1975). These broad areas include child education; child care; child protection; medical and dental care; food and clothing; housing; adult education and information; cultural, social, and religious development; transportation; economic security; legal services; and recreation (McKnight, 1987; Trivette et al., 1996). These broad categories of resources, offered together, would constitute a comprehensive array of services to meet child and family needs that span the public and private sectors. Table 20.2 presents the resource categories delineated by Trivette et al. (1996), along with a list of programs in most communities that one can use for serving diverse individuals in family literacy programs. To create one of the more comprehensive models to integrate education and human services, family literacy initiatives should include all resource categories listed in Table 20.2. Providers should cooperatively identify all the relevant community resources in each category and employ an ecological vision of service delivery at all levels listed in the next section.

Levels of Service Delivery

One useful way to understand service integration is to focus on the level at which it occurs (Bruner, 1993s; Kagan, 1993). The first level delineated is at the *client* level, which refers to the integration of services for individual children and families across providers and agencies (Bruner, 1993; Kagan, (1993). Strategies that promote the identification and integration of a broad array of services needed at this client level include the creation of an ecomap (McWilliam, 1992), needs assessment interviews and checklists (Bailey & Simeonsson, 1990), the use of a transdisciplinary approach (McGonigel, Woodruff, & Roszmann-Millican, 1994), and the employment of a skilled case manager or service coordinator (Bruder & Bologna, 1993; Zipper, Hinton, Weil, & Rounds, 1993).

The second level is the *within-program* level, which encompasses the coordination of components within a single program. At this level, practitioners and administrators within the program reach an agreement on ways of carrying out such program activities as screening, diagnostic assessment, individual plan development, and service delivery.

TABLE 20.2

Comprehensive Services for Children and Families

Child Education	Child Care	Child Protection	Adult Education/ Information	Medical/Dental	Emotional	Cultural/Social/ Religious
State at-risk programs for 3- and 4-year-olds	Child care centers	Child Protective Services	Even Start	Early, periodic screening, diagnosis and treatment (EPSDT)	Mental health centers	Churches
Head Start	Family child care homes	Department of social services	GED and literacy programs	Health department	Parent-to-parent groups	Synagogues
Early Start	Resource and referral networks	Foster homes	Parenting classes and centers	• Well-baby clinic	Alcohol and substance abuse groups (AA)	Mosques
Even Start	State child care initiatives	Safety promotion program sponsored by various agencies	Employment training	• Special health care program	Support groups	Cultural organizations
Part C (formerly H)	Babysitting cooperatives	Domestic violence prevention	Resource, information, and referral services	• Specialized clinics	Clergy (counseling)	Civic organizations
Preschool special education	Mother's Morning Out		Job Training Program	• Nutrition programs		Neighborhood groups
Evaluation team and agency	Play groups			Hospitals and clinics		
Service coordination	Social security insurance (SSI) child care subsidies			MDs and private providers		
Developmental disabilities	Respite care			Medical and health programs (Passport; Yale health model)		
Specialized centers (blind, deaf, autism)				Sickle cell program		
Private clinics (therapy)				Hospice programs		
University programs						
Hospital programs						
Private programs and centers						
Private preschools						
Private nursery schools						
Library story hour						

Transportation	Food/Clothing	Economic	Physical	Legal	Recreation	Other
Public transportation	Food banks	Family support programs (Developmental Disabilities)	Habitat for Humanity	Advocacy groups	Library	Technical assistance programs
State or locally funded transportation programs	WIC	Social services and public welfare	Housing (HUD)	Legal services	YMCA	Civic groups
Taxi	Social services and public welfare	Medical insurance	Social services and public welfare		Zoo	Businesses
Volunteer organizations	Civic Organizations	Medicaid	Shelters		Museum	Volunteers
		Civic Organizations			Gyms	
					Horseback riding	
					Art classes	
					Mother's Morning Out	
					Park and recreation programs	
					Tumbling	

The third level is the *between-program* level, which relates to the links between programs, whether the programs are within the same agency (intra-agency programs), or whether programs are located in different agencies, or a combination of both. At this level, administrators and direct providers cultivate knowledge of the programs and services that other programs provide, then they use this knowledge to link individual clients with an array of services and to integrate these services.

The fourth level is the *policy* level, at which administrators and stakeholders come together to create complementary and coordinated policies to define and support a comprehensive and integrated service system. One typically reaches this level through interagency, intergovernmental, or inter-sector boards or councils. Rules and regulations imposed by federal and state governments affect the work done at the community level. For example, those who work to coordinate services for families in literacy programs, who are also eligible for the Work First program, confront federal rules and regulations governing Work First, which emphasize finding work for a client. Although the Work First program appreciates literate clients, literacy is far from its primary focus. For a person who coordinates family literacy services, this difference in goals can pose a problem in getting referrals from Work First caseworkers, because ensuring adult literacy often receives little emphasis in Work First, but dialogue can bring the mission and policies of the two programs together.

The fifth level, the *organization* level, creates government structures to support and facilitate the other four levels. For example, many states have created family literacy consortiums as part of statewide initiatives.

All too frequently, service integration efforts address only one of these five levels, but, unless they address all five levels and use an ecological vision, their services remain fragmented, resulting in service gaps and overlaps, as well as in lost opportunities for families and children.

Continuum of Integration

As we have seen, the terms for the concept of service integration have evolved through time (Harbin & West, 1998; Intrilligator, 1986; Kagan, 1993; Konrad, 1996). Practitioners commonly suppose that differing amounts of integration can occur at each of the five service delivery levels just described. However, Intrilligator (1986) distinguished between three increasing amounts of connectedness—cooperation, coordination, and collaboration—a distinction that has been adopted in family literacy, as well (NCFL, 1997; Padak & Sapin, 2001).

The NCFL (1997) distinguished collaboration from cooperation and coordination and placed these three concepts on a continuum. *Cooperation* entails having the family literacy program acknowledge the other programs in the community serving the same target population, although relationships between programs tend to remain informal. *Coordination* suggests a more formal relationship with other programs in the community, and agreed-upon relationships between administrators of programs may exist. *Collaboration* means sharing intended goals, results, resources, and responsibilities among community organizations, in order to serve those in family literacy programs better.

Konrad (1996) delineated five amounts of integration, which she placed along her own continuum: (a) information sharing and communication, (b) cooperation and coordination, (c) collaboration, (d) consolidation, and (e) integration. In a qualitative study of nine diverse communities, Harbin and West (1998) identified six qualitatively different amounts of integration, ranging from a program-centered approach to a system for all children. In the program-centered approach, little coordination exists with other programs. The program may have contracts or agreements with other programs, but each program operates more or less autonomously. At the highest end of the continuum comes the sixth level, which is the most comprehensive and integrated system of education and human services for all young children and their families. Harbin and West (1998) described integration, using the following four

TABLE 20.3
Service System Models: Infant and Toddler

Single-Program-Dominated

- Lead agency dominates decision making
- Coordinates with other agencies only when necessary
- Informal agreements; an interagency council may exist, but is used primarily to inform one another about each agency's activities
- Focus of system on education of special population

Network of Programs Beginning to Coordinate

- Lead agency dominates decision making, but other agencies provide input or reactions
- Interagency council is recently established or recently began to plan cooperatively
- Focus of system on education of special population
- Meetings focus primarily on representatives providing information about their programs and activities

Loosely Coupled With Primary Coordination Focused on Educational Intervention

- Multiple intervention programs provide leadership for decisions
- Interagency council is instrumental in cooperative design of procedures to be used across all intervention providers; coordination with other agencies (e.g., health and social services) is secondary
- Primary focus of system on education of special population and secondary focus on human service needs

Moderately Coupled Multiagency System

- Agencies contribute fairly equally to decision making, but leadership comes from lead agency
- A formal interagency council has developed formal interagency procedures for service delivery
- Focus of system on educational and human service needs of special population, and potentially their families' needs as well

Strongly Coupled Multiagency System

- Strong cooperative interagency council is the vehicle for all participants to have say, and private programs and providers also are integrated into decision making
- Many or most intervention activities are cooperative endeavors
- Focus of system on meeting educational and human service needs of multiple special populations

LICC Is Lead Agency for Comprehensive and Cohesive System for Children

- Cooperative, equal decision making
- All programs and providers (public and private) share common values and have participated in planning equally
- Comprehensive array for young children and their families, including specialized and natural community programs and resources

elements: (a) the overall organizational structure that guides service delivery, (b) the amount and nature of interagency decision making, (c) the scope of the target population, and (d) the scope and nature of service resources utilized. This last element refers to the number of resource categories identified in Table 20.2.

Table 20.3 depicts the continuum of models. The darkened circle in each model indicates the lead agency—in this case, the Even Start program. The lines show the strengths of the relationships or linkages between and among the agencies or programs. Dotted lines indicate a weaker linkage than a solid line. The models in Table 20.3 indicate a continuum of relationships between the Even Start program and other programs in the community. At the top of Table 20.3 (which is actually the lowest end of the continuum), the Even Start program functions fairly autonomously. Although they are evolving in complexity, the first three models focus primarily on the education component of family literacy. The fourth model also includes human services. In the fifth model, the system moves beyond the issue of family literacy to focus, in addition, on meeting the needs of such special populations as children in poverty and children with disabilities. The sixth and most complex model indicates that family literacy is embedded in a comprehensive system designed to meet the needs of all young children and their families. Harbin et al. (2000) have provided a more in-depth description of each of the levels of integration.

In a qualitative study of 75 children and their families, across three states, Harbin et al. (2000) found that the most positive child and family outcomes occurred in those communities using the three most coordinated and integrated models (models 4, 5, and 6). Model 3 on the continuum (Loosely Coupled Service System) focused primarily on integrating education services. Consequently, that large-scale qualitative study detected the value in integrating both education and human services and the available resources.

In a national survey of state early intervention coordinators in the 50 states and the District of Columbia, using the six models previously described, Harbin et al. (2002) asked the states to rate the amount of their service integration. As mentioned before, the continuum ranged from (1) *a program focus* to (6) *an integrated system focus*. Only 2 states reported using a program-only focus (model 1); 15 states reported using a networking approach (model 2), and 18 reported a group of agencies coordinating educational services across agencies (model 3). Ten states had begun to integrate education and human services (model 4). Only 4 states indicated using a strongly integrated approach (model 5), and 1 state had developed a collaborative system for all young children and their families. Harbin, Kameny, Pelosi, Kitsul, and Fox (2002) found similar results in 42 communities within a single state. These results indicate that, despite federal and state legislation, profound variance exists in the amount of service integration achieved by states and communities for services to young children with disabilities.

Systems Knowledge

A *system* is a set of interconnected elements forming an organizational whole (Hoy & Miskel, 1987). In order to understand a particular phenomenon like child performance, we often take it apart to study its individual constituents. In systems theory, however, the interrelationships among these constituents are as important as each of the individual elements. For example, the essence of a symphony orchestra cannot be fully understood and appreciated by merely examining the individual instruments and players. The set of relationships and interactions among these instruments and players, along with the printed music, the conductor, and the acoustics, produce beautiful music. Systems theory has been used extensively to understand such phenomena as organizations, schools, economics, and families. Envisioning and integrating a system of services requires knowledge of, and attention to, all components of the system (Harbin, 1988). All too frequently, individuals attend to only portions of the system, such as direct services to children and families. Successful integration initiatives, however, address all of the system elements, recognizing that a change in one element will probably require changes in other elements.

To reach major family literacy goals, one must integrate the activities of the many programs and agencies for each of the system elements. Figure 20.1 displays the elements of a comprehensive system: The elements in the outer ring of the figure address the functions of

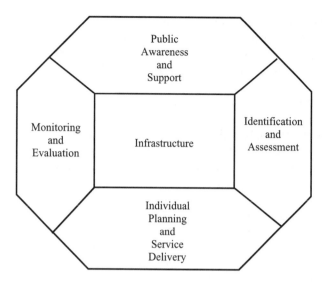

FIG. 20.1.   Elements of a service system.

the system; the inner part of the figure contains the infrastructure, which must be designed to support the functional components located in the outer ring.

Public Awareness and Support.   The purposes of this component include informing the general public and policymakers about the importance of literacy services, informing the public about the availability of the services, and obtaining support for services. Families in need of literacy services always form a diverse group; therefore, one needs a variety of materials, methods, techniques, and strategies to make everyone aware of the existence of family literacy services. Disjointed public awareness and support activities, carried out by numerous programs, result in confusion for the families. To accomplish the goals of finding families in need of literacy services as early as possible, and to provide easy access to the system, requires all relevant agencies to exercise a collaborative approach to public awareness.

The general public and policymakers must also become aware of the need for family literacy services. Service programs and systems develop within the sociopolitical environment of the state and community, and the attitudes and values of policymakers and citizens, greatly affect which programs get funded, the extent of funding, and the nature of the programs themselves (Marshall, Mitchell, & Wirt, 1985). When key community members misunderstand or disparage a particular program, chances for its success diminish. By contrast, gaining the support of key local politicians and administrators promotes access to such important resources as facilities, space, and staff necessary to provide family literacy services in an optimal manner.

Creating and nurturing an environment that understands and supports the concept of comprehensive literary services is a critical first step, and a good reputation is essential. Therefore, to accomplish the goals of this component, administrators must learn how to advertise and promote family literacy among the general public, policymakers, and other agencies. If the right climate does not exist, family literacy collaborators ought to consider strategies and tactics to improve it (Mattessich, Murray-Close, & Monsey, 2002). For example, administrators can make presentations to civic and governmental groups, to encourage support for literacy services. Chances for this support increase, when, instead of competing for resources from county and state funders, agencies present an integrated request for funds. This collaborative request demonstrates cost-effective requests without duplications. The political and social climate is dynamic and can change, and one must continually monitor that climate, to keep the collaborative family literacy system and its activities as consistent as possible with the values of the community (Mattessich, Murray-Close, & Monsey, 2002).

Identification and Assessment. Sooner or later, decisions concerning who receives services raise controversy and disagreement among policymakers and consumers. The definitions, eligibility criteria, and family needs assessment procedures, along with the tools and procedures used for screening and diagnostic assessment, all affect the number and types of children and families who receive services. The extent to which agencies can coordinate their policies and assessment activities also affects the success of this initiative. The participation of agencies and individuals in the private sector (e.g., physicians and child care providers) directly influences who gains access to the service system.

All too frequently, each program has its own assessment procedures. As a result, families must endure time-consuming, often redundant assessments from several programs. Families benefit when programs integrate assessments and collaboratively determine eligibility for their programs. A coordinated database, shared across agencies, can help the agencies identify families and use existing assessments, thus reducing duplication. This kind of integration leads to timely service access for families and savings for the whole system.

Individual Planning and Service Delivery. The diverse needs of children and their families can require the attention of many disciplines and agencies, and the configuration of the services provided can be determined in part by the coordination among agencies and in part by the qualifications of those providing the services. The focus of such a comprehensive service system must be to ensure that a broad array of quality education and human services remains available to all eligible children and families in their community. In planning this array of services, individuals should include the 14 types of education, care, and human services in Table 20.2 (Trivette et al., 1996).

All providers should know about and use recommended practices from diverse disciplines. The National Association for the Education of Young Children has developed a set of recommended practices to be used in programs for young children. The Division of Early Childhood, which is part of the Council for Exceptional Children, developed a handbook of recommended practices for programs to use with young children with disabilities, and also recommended practices for working with families. Similarly, *The Family Literacy Answer Book* (NCFL, 1997) sets forth a list of recommended practices to be used in family literacy initiatives. Examples of practices that should be used across agencies and providers include (a) family-centered practices that respect and empower families, (b) practical interventions based on daily routines, (c) interventions that recognize and build on the strengths of children and families, and (d) interventions that respect and honor diverse cultural values.

The values that guide the service system invariably affect which services are included, how they are provided, and who provides them. Including the private sector (e.g., child care centers and homes and other private programs) also influences the nature of the service provision. Because of the diverse needs of children and their families, services must be selected within an individualized planning process that includes all relevant service providers and the family. The use of a single intervention plan, common to all agencies and providers, reduces confusion and frustration for families and better integrates services to individuals (Salisbury et al., 1993).

Monitoring and Evaluation. Systematic evaluation serves to appraise a program's effectiveness and success. If services are to be improved, one must know what works, for whom, and under what conditions. The use of both formative and summative evaluations, for both individual service programs and the total service system, is critical to the development and provision of quality services.

Because effective programs and systems are outcome-driven, the ultimate child and family outcomes of service delivery must be identified and must form the basis for the evaluation. The evaluation should also focus on key system operation outcomes, including, for example, easy, early, and timely entry into services; easy access to a broad array of services; a good deal of coordination; family involvement; and of course, family satisfaction.

Integrated Infrastructure.   To build comprehensive services statewide, the many agencies involved must construct complementary policies and standards, which prevent duplication of effort by alerting each agency to the responsibilities of the others and, thereby, ensuring a coordinated array of services. This infrastructure includes the policies to guide service delivery; an administrative structure for service delivery; a supply of qualified personnel, along with policies and procedures to hire them; personnel development activities; the funding necessary for service provision; a coordinated data system; and such mechanisms and arrangements as an interagency or inter-sector council, to ensure the coordination of services.

These cohesive service system components interact to affect the nature and quality of the services individual children and families receive. Autonomous programs find it difficult to integrate their activities and procedures into a single system for each of the five system components described earlier. Nevertheless, their ability to integrate their activities and procedures influences the extent of service integration on the continuum of models also described earlier. Figure 20.2 presents some of the tasks to be achieved in each of the five system components, if service integration is to take place.

Program or Agency Culture

One feature influencing any attempt to develop a coordinated system of services is that each agency has its own way of doing things. When they have separate and different missions, different target populations, different philosophies, and different administrative structures, agencies often find a common approach difficult to agree on. Organizational literature suggests that one key operating principle of an organization is to maintain itself by protecting its boundaries (View & Amos, 1994). The resulting rigidity complicates what should ideally be a common mission among agencies to provide the best possible services, through a coordinated system. Harbin (1996) described some of the forces contributing to these agency boundaries. For example, the health department seeks to protect and promote good health for all individuals from birth through old age, and the public schools seek to provide for the educational needs of school-aged children. This example also demonstrates a difference in target populations: Although overlap in the individuals receiving services from both agencies does occur, the target groups are far from identical.

Harbin (1996) also identified several different dimensions on which agencies often differ, and one should recognize and address these dimensions and their differences, in order to produce an integrated service system. Together, these dimensions form the agency's culture, or the staff's view of "the way things are done." All too often, differences in the way things are done produce conflicts during efforts to coordinate or integrate services. We often hear these differences called "turf issues," which then get incorrectly interpreted as a power struggle between agencies. This simplistic deduction further polarizes participants, complicating an already difficult collaborative task. If, instead, providers would try to recognize and understand the differences and how to approach them, efforts at collaboration and integration might succeed. The following paragraphs describe the dimensions that most affect and create agency culture.

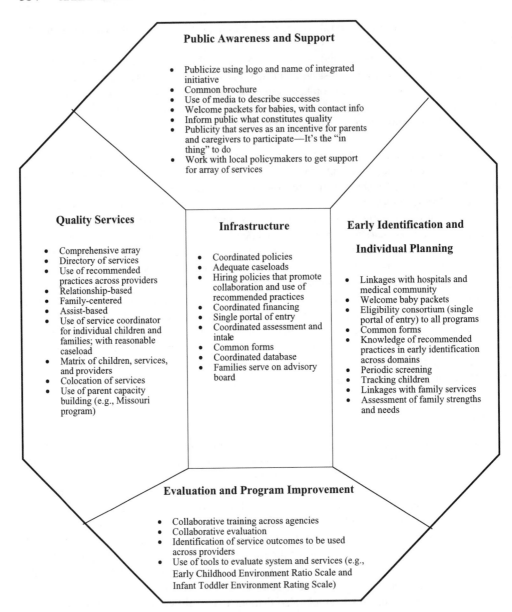

Public Awareness and Support

- Publicize using logo and name of integrated initiative
- Common brochure
- Use of media to describe successes
- Welcome packets for babies, with contact info
- Inform public what constitutes quality
- Publicity that serves as an incentive for parents and caregivers to participate—It's the "in thing" to do
- Work with local policymakers to get support for array of services

Quality Services

- Comprehensive array
- Directory of services
- Use of recommended practices across providers
- Relationship-based
- Family-centered
- Assist-based
- Use of service coordinator for individual children and families; with reasonable caseload
- Matrix of children, services, and providers
- Colocation of services
- Use of parent capacity building (e.g., Missouri program)

Infrastructure

- Coordinated policies
- Adequate caseloads
- Hiring policies that promote collaboration and use of recommended practices
- Coordinated financing
- Single portal of entry
- Coordinated assessment and intake
- Common forms
- Coordinated database
- Families serve on advisory board

Early Identification and Individual Planning

- Linkages with hospitals and medical community
- Welcome baby packets
- Eligibility consortium (single portal of entry) to all programs
- Common forms
- Knowledge of recommended practices in early identification across domains
- Periodic screening
- Tracking children
- Linkages with family services
- Assessment of family strengths and needs

Evaluation and Program Improvement

- Collaborative training across agencies
- Collaborative evaluation
- Identification of service outcomes to be used across providers
- Use of tools to evaluate system and services (e.g., Early Childhood Environment Ratio Scale and Infant Toddler Environment Rating Scale)

FIG. 20.2.   Comprehensive, integrated service system.

Differences can emerge between agencies in their philosophies and goals regarding intervention strategies, how services are coordinated, and the type and degree of family involvement in service delivery (Dunst, Trivette, Starnes, Hamby, & Gordon, 1993; Marshall et al., 1985). An agency may have little knowledge or understanding of another agency's programs or of whom to contact in that agency (Bronheim, Cohen, & Magrab, 1985; Harbin, 1996). Another factor to understand about the relationship between agencies is the extent to which a climate of trust exists between them and whether the agency staff members are open to new ideas and change, when it is needed (Bronheim et al., 1985; McLaughlin, 1982; Murphy, 1973).

Whether or not an agency's administration supports interagency coordination, and whether or not staff work cooperatively with the staff from other agencies, is another important dimension of relationships between agencies (Flynn & Harbin, 1987). How an agency communicates with other agencies helps to define its relationship with them (Bronheim et al., 1985). Ease of contact, type of contact (formal vs. informal), how contact is initiated, and the level of trust among staff members from different agencies, all constitute important aspects of communication. Another important dimension is that of planning and policy development (Harbin, 1996; Harbin & McNulty, 1990). The policies of one agency regarding service delivery may differ from others, or even conflict with them (Sabatier & Mazmanian, 1979; Van Horn & Van Meter, 1977). Planning procedures may also differ, including the role of stakeholders (e.g., the actual families) in the planning process (Harbin, 1996; Harbin & McNulty, 1990). All these differences can limit or discourage efforts to plan cooperatively.

The structure and mechanisms of agencies may differ with respect to size, complexity, geographic areas served, and services provided (Flynn & Harbin, 1987; Van Horn & Van Meter, 1977). Agencies may decline to share referral systems and informational databases about children and their families. Personnel from different agencies may or may not enjoy similar training and expertise, or may lack experience working together on committees concerned with service delivery (Bronheim et al., 1985). Agencies may use the same terms, but imbrue them with different meanings. Agencies may differ in terms of management style or decision-making approaches and quality of the resources (Greenberg, 1981). Similarities or differences may exist in the populations that various agencies serve (Bronheim et al., 1985). Where similarities exist, competition among agencies for funding, staff members, and clients may take place. The personal affinities and social relationships among personnel from different agencies can also affect the relationships among the agencies themselves (Bronheim et al., 1985). Many practitioners assume that close social and working relationships among staff members from different agencies naturally promote closeness between the agencies. Finally, the physical location of one agency in relation to another has an effect on the ease of coordination or integration between them (Bronheim et al., 1985).

The literature indicates that each of these dimensions influences, in some way, successful service integration, but, based upon case studies of six diverse states and nine diverse communities, as well as her consultation experience in numerous other states and communities, Harbin (1996) concluded that it is less one of these factors in isolation, than the combination of factors, that is most liable to raise barriers to cooperative and collaborative development of an integrated service system. She hypothesized, moreover, that the closer the similarities of these agencies in these key dimensions, the easier, and hence the more successful, the efforts at integration of activities and services are likely to be.

Harbin, Kameny, Pelosi, Kitsul, and Fox (2002) recently confirmed this theory, when statistically significant differences emerged among six key agencies regarding the level of closeness on the key dimensions just described. In North Carolina, three of the six agencies are mandated to collaboratively determine eligibility, and study results indicated that these three agencies rated themselves as more similar to one another than to the other three agencies not required to collaboratively determine eligibility. An examination of data collected before the mandate indicated that the relationship among the three agencies had been less collaborative then. Therefore, a well-crafted mandate appears to provide an impetus for agencies to increase their similarities on such key dimensions as the philosophy and the values guiding service delivery.

Barriers and Facilitators

Although now accepted as a logical strategy for improving services, coordination has been difficult to operationalize successfully (Brewer & Kakalik, 1979; Gans & Horton, 1975; Weiss, 1981). Professionals have encountered a variety of barriers as they try to coordinate the functions of the service system described earlier—namely, public awareness, identification, service provision, and evaluation—as well as in developing and implementing the infrastructure (i.e., policies, training and funding).

Instead of conducting studies that address multiple barriers simultaneously, most researchers have designed their studies to address a targeted aspect of service coordination or integration (Flynn & Harbin, 1987). The array of individual or targeted variables includes administrative linkages (Gans & Horton, 1975; Schmidt & Kochan, 1977; Litwak & Hylton, 1962; Lynn, 1976; Pollard, Hall, & Keeran, 1979), or the interpersonal behaviors of those involved in the process (Bronheim et al., 1985). We have seen few attempts to address the multidimensional nature of interagency coordination. Flynn and Harbin (1987) developed a framework, useful as a guide for addressing coordination and integration, which contains five broad interactive dimensions: climate, people, process, resources, and policies. Harbin and McNulty (1990) modified this framework by adding the *structure* dimension. In a recent review of the literature, Mattessich, Murray-Close, & Monsey (2001) identified such similar factors as environment, membership characteristics, process, structure, communication, purpose, and resources.

Researchers across several fields of study have identified barriers to, and facilitators of, service integration (Elder, 1979; Flynn & Harbin, 1987; Kagan, 1993.) The researchers who specifically addressed family literacy include Dwyer (1995), NCFL (1997), Padak et al. (2001). The framework Harbin developed in 1990 still serves as a useful tool for organizing these facilitators and barriers. Those engaging in service integration can use this framework to anticipate the pitfalls, as they seek to institute a higher level of integration (models 4, 5, and 6) and to work collaboratively to develop the education and human resources components of the family literacy system. In turn, this understanding can help participants avoid the many barriers and, in fact, turn them into features that can promote service integration. The following paragraphs list and discuss the elements, identified across many fields, that influence the effectiveness of service integration (Harbin, 1990).

Climate and History.   In this contextual dimension, key decision makers view collaboration as important (NCFL, 1997). One finds here a level of mutual trust among players (Tice, 2000). Administrators value collaboration (Hayes, 1982), and they develop a climate of cooperation, instead of competition (Dwyer, 1995). All the relevant stakeholders feel a sense of ownership (Dwyer, 1995; Quezada & Nickse, 1992). Previous approaches to services have produced positive associations with coordination (Weatherly, 1979). Political leaders who control resources publicly support the mission of the collaborative group, or at least tolerate it (Mattesich, Murray-Close, & Monsey, 2002). Family literacy collaborators need to spend time selling the collaborative system to key leaders (Mattesich et al., 2002). A positive political and social climate motivates collaborators to engage in difficult tasks (Mattesich et al., 2002). These interactions tend to maximize people's strengths, to minimize weaknesses, and to build community (Tice, 2000).

People.   In this important human dimension, one finds involvement of key people from the relevant stakeholder groups (Dwyer, 1995; Quezada & Nickse, 1992); a shared vision among these stakeholders (Harbin et al., 1990; Tice, 2000); a low turnover rate among collaborators (Dwyer, 1995); typically, a key individual with strategic planning leadership skills (Harbin et al., 2000; Kagan & Bowman, 1997); and members with skills in interpersonal relations, negotiation, and conflict resolution (Alamprese, 1996; Christensen, 1982). Effective collaborators have the ability to view situations from perspectives other than their own and can influence people beyond their own agencies (Rogers & Farrow, 1983).

Process.   In establishing an effective process in which successful integration can occur, one finds regular communication among members (Rogers & Farrow, 1983), members avoiding professional jargon (Martinson, 1982), the use of a collaborative strategic planning process (Quezada & Nickse, 1992; Tice, 2000), and sufficient time allocated for members to work together (Rogers & Farrow, 1983).

Resources.   In this crucial dimension, one finds resources available to support the work of the interagency group (Garland & Linder, 1994); interagency members with the authority to commit the resources of their agencies (Rogers & Farrow, 1983); all the fiscal, human, and facilities resources of the collaborators clearly identified (Edwards, 1994; Van Horn & Van Meter, 1977); and the agencies developing collaborative requests for funds for all agencies, rather than competing for financial resources (Colby, 1987).

Policies.   The policies of each of the agencies, as well as the nature of their formal agreements, are also important. In exemplary integration initiatives, one finds that the agencies' policies have been reviewed, so that they are complementary (Bronheim et al., 1985; Harbin & McNulty, 1990; Steiner, 1976); so that meaningful state and local interagency agreements exist (Rogers & Farrow, 1983); and so that the agencies' policies contain common procedures and definitions (Dwyer, 1995).

Structure.   The organizational structure of the agencies and the interagency group affect its success. The flexibility of the agency can facilitate its ability to coordinate with other agencies (Bronheim et al., 1985), a productive and well-functioning interagency planning group is essential for successful coordination (Flynn & Harbin, 1987), a group of agency administrators that meets to coordinate policies is in place (Harbin & McNulty, 1990), state and local roles and responsibilities are clearly delineated (Albritton & Brown, 1986), and the interagency organizational structure uses forthright communication mechanisms and coordination strategies (Alamprese, 1996; Kagan, 1993).

Data supporting the importance of these key facilitators and barriers indicated that localities in North Carolina had made gains in all six categories between 1994 and 2000 (Harbin, Kameny, Pelosi, Kitsul, & Fox, 2003). These gains were accompanied by gains in the amount of coordination and collaboration. Although gains occurred in all six dimensions, the largest increase came in the area of policies. The state had undertaken many initiatives to make state and local policies complementary across agencies. In addition, North Carolina has one of the most comprehensive interagency agreements in the country. The results that Harbin et al. (2003) presented indicate that the efforts to make policies more complementary enable localities to improve their ability to integrate services.

INTEGRATING FAMILY LITERACY SERVICES WITH OTHER ORGANIZATIONS IN THE COMMUNITY

This section addresses the application of the dimensions of the previously described framework for service integration. We begin by suggesting the amount of integration that appears to promote the effectiveness of the family literacy services, then we provide an example of an array of resources that constitutes an ecological approach to designing a family literacy system, containing both education and human resources. The section ends with a discussion of a variety of strategies designed to follow a systems-oriented approach, and to increase the integration at all levels of service delivery and for all service system components.

An Ideal Amount of Integration

The NCFL (1997) suggested that services offered by only one agency probably fall short in effectively meeting the varied needs of families. The NCFL acknowledged the need to focus on the family unit, to address the social (human) service needs of the family, in order to develop its educational or literacy skills. The NCFL (1997) program can serve as a "single point of contact or referral for families" (p. 14) to a wide array of services in the broader family literacy system. The Even Start Family Literacy Program allocates block grants to states wherein localities compete for funding. Funding is designed to build on local community resources, and it gradually decreases over time. These collaborative arrangements with the family literacy programs provide educational services critical to the core components. Even Start dollars amount to seed money. Family literacy programs using Even Start dollars must actively seek out other resources to underwrite their services, rather than seeing the family literacy program as a separate entity with minimal coordination with few organizations in the community, as exemplified by models 1 and 2 in Table 20.3. An integrated system of family literacy, on the other hand, would most likely approximate models 4 and 5 described in Table 20.3, with each organization making many kinds of contributions.

Array of Resources

Thorough information about an integrated family literacy system can demonstrate how extensive the contributions of the various organizations can be. For example, Herrmann (2003) collected information on a program in a rural county in a southeastern state, from 1999 to 2001, through two lengthy, open-ended interviews with the project coordinator, concerning the Even Start program's array of services and collaborative arrangements. During that time, the program served 35 families in 1999–2000 and 34 in 2000–2001. Table 20.4 sets forth the various community organizations and the nature of their contributions. The family literacy service system in that community contains services from nine of the resource categories described earlier in the chapter (Trivette et al., 1996). To construct the broad array of education and human resources, 15 representatives from 10 organizations in the community served on the family literacy program's advisory board, which addressed issues related to making these resources work collaboratively for the benefit of the families served.

Strategies to Facilitate Integration

The effective integration of family literacy services requires knowledge and use of a combination of strategies, some to facilitate service integration at the child and family direct service level, and others to facilitate integration among programs at the service, policy, and organizational levels (Garland & Linder, 1994; Harbin, 1996; Kagan, 1993). Some strategies are used with a single component, such as public awareness; other strategies can be used to improve several components. The common practice of using one or two strategies is, however, inadequate for effective service integration. Therefore, this section presents a comprehensive array of strategies required by the complexities of service integration. The next paragraphs identify the most useful strategies for facilitating service integration. The more comprehensive and integrated family literacy service systems will require use of most of these strategies.

Public Awareness.   As mentioned earlier, the first component of the family literacy system is public awareness. This system component requires strategies designed to inform the public about the importance and availability of services. One of the most important strategies is a single brochure or flier for all the relevant agencies together, rather than for each individual

TABLE 20.4
Example of Family Literacy Program: List of Organizations and Contributions

Organization	*Contribution*
Community college	Salaries for teachers
	Materials
	Staff development
	Assist in participant recruitment
	Help with public image (PR)
	Facilities (single-ride mobile unit)
School System	Facilities
Exceptional children's program	Access to school resources
County food services	Salaries for teachers
Primary school faculty and staff	Help with public image (PR)
Junior high	Meals and snacks
Senior high school	Workshops for parents on transitions to K
	Provide volunteer setting for parents
	Donations from student clubs
Head Start	Provide preschool area
Health department	Workshops for parents on health issues
	Health screenings for children
	Meet the needs of participant health issues
Department of social services (Work First)	Referrals
	Day care
	Transportation
	Assists in recruitment
Evaluation clinic	Referrals
	Evaluations
Literacy council	Help with public image (PR)
	Provides tutors
	Book drive donations
Smart Start	Transportation
	Child care
	Salaries for parent educators
Local businesses	Provide classroom equipment
	Provide volunteers
	Assist with employment placement
	Funding for staff development
	Donate to program paper amenities
Library	Provides reading activities for early childhood and parent classes
	Offers activities at the library
County family resource center	Provides activities for families
	Recruitment
	Donations to families
	Provides summer activities for families
County interagency transportation	Coordinate transportation for families
Community support center	Referrals
	Provides information to families on services available to them
Mental health	Provide mental health services
	Provide parenting sessions

(Continued)

TABLE 20.4
(Continued)

Organization	Contribution
Job Training Partnership Act (JTPA) (council of governments)	Recruitment Assists with employment placement
Cooperative extension agency	Provide parenting sessions Provides and funds summer activities for families
Local churches	Donations to families for personal needs Recruitment
Law enforcement	Parenting workshops (self-defense, drug abuse, seat belt safety) Provided child ID cards for families Donated maps and driver's manuals to parents
Fire department	Parenting workshops: fire prevention, home safety, CPR Donations: free smoke detectors
Hospitals	Shared information with families on hospitals Provide activities for children that are medically related Donations: first aid kits
Women's support organization	Counseling Parenting workshops on domestic violence and sexual assault
Employment security commission	Provides information about services Assists with job placement
Regional library	Provides literacy activities for families
Even Start	Salaries Staff development related to family literacy Materials and supplies

program. The brochure should contain the telephone number for the agency that serves as the point of entry; publicizing only one telephone number reduces confusion. In addition, a single public awareness announcement in the media also gets broader recognition and support from the media. Finally, collaborative presentations to local and county businesses and governmental offices tend to build the case for support for, and increase the visibility of, all relevant programs.

Collaborative Eligibility Determination.   Some evidence indicates that, when a multi-agency team collaboratively determines eligibility, children and their families benefit by the identification of, and referral to, a wider range of resources than when a single program determines eligibility (Harbin et al., 2000). A routines-based interview and the development of an ecomap similar to that outlined by McWilliam (1992), facilitate the systematic identification of those agencies with which families are involved and those additional agencies that can deliver useful services and to which referrals should be made.

Common Forms.   When families receive services from more than one agency, they must often provide the same demographic information to each agency or program, which is a time-consuming, frustrating, and redundant requirement. Moreover, agencies often mistakenly think that confidentiality requirements prevent them from sharing information with other agencies. In many instances, of course, all an agency needs is family consent to share the information.

Most families willingly provide this consent, if it means they need to provide demographic information only once. Therefore, the collaborative development and use of a common family information form can facilitate service integration.

Shared Data System.   In fact, sharing information, with the consent of the family, is essential to service integration, but an ability to share data across agencies requires them to use compatible computer hardware and software, including similar data fields (e.g., age, name, address, telephone number, and program entry date), contained on the common data form. Although a shared or collaborative data system can be difficult to accomplish, some communities have accomplished this for young children with disabilities (Garland, personal communication, 2003; Salisbury, Palombaro, & Hollowood, 1993). Sharing data becomes easier at the local level, if state agencies agree and lay the foundation. A state interagency group, which also includes families, can provide leadership in developing an integrated state data system. The North Carolina legislature, for example, understanding the importance of data that are consistent across agencies, funded a pilot project to develop an integrated data system (N.C. House Bill 1840, 1999).

Single Individual Service Plan.   All too frequently, each agency or program with which the family is involved creates a separate service plan. Without a single service plan, service integration can be difficult and often elusive. In the use of the transdisciplinary approach, McGonigel et al. (1994) suggested developing a single, integrated service plan (McWilliam, 1992; Salisbury et al., 1993). A group of representatives across agencies often find it useful to develop a single format with agreed-upon content for the cross-agency individual service plan.

Service Coordinator.   Once again, families frequently have more than one service coordinator, including one from each program, but rarely do these coordinators communicate with one another; in fact, they are often unaware of the others' existence. Therefore, the agencies collaborating with a family should select a single coordinator to facilitate the integration of services listed on the individual plan. This strategy reliably enhances service integration.

Colocation.   *Colocation* refers to the practice of providing services to children and adults in the same location (Alamprese, 1996; Dwyer, 1995). Family literacy programs often colocate educational services, to improve access to services and to increase participation. Colocation has been found to improve family accessibility and, especially when transportation is an obstacle, to provide opportunities for parents and their children to spend time together (St.Pierre, Layzer, Goodson, & Bernstein, 1997).

An examination of two family literacy systems demonstrates the benefits of colocating human services with the educational services. Tice (2000) studied a family literacy system in Ohio, with adult basic education, parenting education, and early childhood education colocated in a public housing project. Other collaborators located on-site included the department of human service's Woman, Infants, and Children program and mental health services, both of which contributed to the family literacy system. By colocating these important family services, the programs were successful in developing their clients' literacy, self-sufficiency, and work readiness. In fact, Tice (2000) found 5 of the 14 resource categories, listed earlier in the chapter, colocated in one place.

In Florida, Roth, Myers-Jennings, and Stowell (1997) found one family literacy program operating in partnership with the local school district and the department of health and rehabilitative services, all colocated at the family services center on a local school campus. Additional collaborating programs housed in this family services center provided educational and supplemental services, including economic assistance, adult education, state-supported early intervention, mental health care, parenting education, employment training, child care, and primary health care screening.

Adult participants in the Florida study attributed four specific benefits to the provision of services in one location: (a) increased communication among professionals from different agencies; (b) increased accessibility of resources; (c) clients' "increased sense of family"; and (d) increased ability of parents to serve as positive role models for their children in their literacy and academic efforts and for coping with daily challenges. In addition to positive steps toward family reading and writing literacy, the authors observed increased self-respect, self-efficacy, and political and social empowerment among the participants (Roth et al., 1997).

Integrated Staff Training.   As mentioned previously, many of the families and their children who participate in Even Start receive services from other programs as well, and it can be frustrating and confusing when professionals from one program suggest one approach but professionals from another program recommend a different approach. This situation can lead to families with conflicted allegiances and loyalties. Consequently, families benefit substantially if all of the professionals with whom they work agree about what constitutes the best or recommended practice. Therefore, training that is provided to service providers from multiple agencies fosters the use of recommended practices across service providers and agencies. Collaborative training facilitates communication and development of collaborative working relationships, as well.

Joint Planning and Programming.   Collaborative partnerships can range in intensity and formality, from an informal relationship with a key liaison person at another organization, who can assist in obtaining additional services for an individual family, to meeting regularly with many other representatives of early childhood and adult services. Herrmann (2003) found that Even Start coordinators recognize the importance of social networks for facilitating the integration of services. The Even Start national evaluation found that communities used joint administrative boards to integrate services (St.Pierre et al., 2001). Flynn and Harbin (1987) delineated four stages of coordinating council development with the tasks to be accomplished at each stage. In a study of local interagency coordinating councils (LICCs) in North Carolina, Harbin et al. (2003) found LICCs likelier to complete tasks related to process, but often failing to complete action tasks. Harbin et al. (2003) theorized that the development of the LICC at one stage qualitatively affected the functioning and development at the next stage: That is, the more tasks completed at a lower stage, the higher the number of tasks accomplished at the next stage. If an interagency group addresses all of the tasks to be completed at each stage and collaboratively addresses all components of the service system (e.g., public awareness and child identification), the group will be able to design a successfully integrated system. But, if the interagency group omits some of the tasks or fails to address some of the service system components, a less-than-effective planning group and a fragmented system result. Participatory decision making and the inclusion of all the relevant stakeholders, including families, are crucial to a successful planning process. Research confirms the importance of developing trust, implementing a consensus approach to conflict resolution, and valuing the contributions of all members (Flynn & Harbin, 1987; Harbin & McNulty, 1990; Tice, 2000). Some communities sponsor many collaborative initiatives, each with its own focus and its own board or council, and it is important for family literacy to be represented on each. Because these many councils can waste time, however, some communities now assign a single board or council to integrate all the initiatives.

Shared Funding.   Federal requirements usually prohibit the mingling of funds from categorical programs—a restriction ensuring that funds are spent to provide services for the children and families for whom they were originally intended. To address this barrier, integrated family literacy systems that require such similar activities as public awareness, finding eligible participants, and assessment, need to find ways to share funding. Agency members from a community-integrated family literacy system can collaboratively plan a particular component, such as public awareness, then each can decide what type of resources to contribute. These contributions can be, for example, funds for printing the brochure, or they can take the form of staff contributions, such as contributing personnel to conduct assessments. Table 20.4 shows examples of how public and private organizations both contributed resources for such various system functions as parent training and facilities.

Interagency Agreements.   Interagency agreements often lack the specificity to be meaningful and workable (Harbin & McNulty, 1990; Rogers & Farrow, 1983). The interagency agreement is the primary policy that guides and supports integrated service planning and provision. Therefore, the more detailed the agreement, the more guidance it provides and the higher the likelihood that all concerned individuals follow common procedures, definitions, and regulations. Building on the literature, notably Mayer and Ford (1980) and Eckland (1989), Harbin and Van Horn (1990) identified 26 elements to ensure that state and local interagency agreements were meaningful.

Agreements including these 26 elements articulate what the agency decision makers hoped to achieve by collaborative service delivery, as well as which services will be coordinated and how the coordinated service delivery will occur. Equally important is the specificity of the contributions (e.g., funding, human resources, and facilities) each agency provides. This level of specificity helps bridge the differences and build a shared vision among the agencies.

To meet the wide array of educational and human resource needs of individuals participating in family literacy programs, administrators should create a comprehensive, ecological system of services. The creation of a family literacy service system can be both complex and challenging, requiring numerous strategies. Finally, for these strategies to be effective, the participating organizations will almost certainly need to revise their policies and the way they organize their services.

CONCLUSIONS AND RECOMMENDATIONS

Service integration has been widely accepted as the logical solution to a categorical and fragmented service system in many fields, and service integration is now so fundamental to the construction of family literacy programs that it has been described as "a natural" (Padak, Sapin, & Ackerman, 2001) and "defining characteristic" (Dwyer, 1995), distinguishing family literacy programs from many other early intervention programs. Despite the promise, integrating services in family literacy shows that barriers remain to accomplishing this important goal. The complexity of the concept, coupled with the lack of effective models, has led to implementation difficulties. In this chapter, we offered a framework of interrelated factors to be addressed systematically, for service integration to be effective. Local family literacy program leaders can use Table 20.3 to determine the amount of service integration currently in place. Similarly, community leaders can examine the breadth of education and human resources in their system of services, using Tables 20.2 and 20.4 to assist them. As local leaders strive to create a more comprehensive and integrated system, they can use Figure 20.2 to help them integrate all elements of their system, including public awareness and support, client identification and assessments, individual service plans and direct services, and evaluation and infrastructure. Finally, to implement this framework effectively, we provide strategies to facilitate the development of a comprehensive and integrated family literacy service system. The strategies we have described (e.g., colocation of services, a single intervention plan, and joint planning) provide starting points for the administration and implementation of family literacy service systems. As research and evaluation efforts expand in this area, other strategies specific to family literacy systems may emerge, but we must address four additional challenges if we are to make significant progress in service integration.

The first challenge is to stop creating separate systems for different target groups and to create a cohesive service system for all of the families and their children in the community. A single service system would alleviate the stigma often associated with programs for at-risk populations and would attract wider community acceptance for supporting services. The second challenge is to develop an adequate cadre of leaders with skills in systems development, strategic planning, participatory planning, systems change, and conflict resolution (Garland & Linder, 1994; Harbin et al., 2000; Kagan & Bowman, 1997). Service integration needs an infusion of knowledgeable and skilled leaders with an ecological mission. The third challenge is to develop reliable tools to guide the creation and direction of the service system, as well as to guide in the complex task of service integration. We also need tools to evaluate the level and nature of service integration and the quality of our service systems. The fourth challenge is to design and conduct sound research that addresses the complexities of comprehensive and collaborative service systems (Knapp, 1995). It is critical to conduct further studies of the components of successful service integration and to examine the link between service integration and positive outcomes for children and families. We also need more studies to determine if service integration efforts help to make services more accessible, appropriate, responsive, and useful.

As we address these important challenges, local family literacy leaders can obtain their own data, using it to detect areas of a system in need of improvement. Local evaluation data provide information useful locally and information that can contribute to our growing knowledge of the value and challenges of integrating family literacy services across the country.

REFERENCES

Agranoff, R. (1991). Human services integration: Past and present challenges in public administration. *Public Administration Review, 51*(6), 533–542.

Agranoff, R., & McGuire, M. (2001). Big questions in public network management research. *Journal of Public Administration Research and Theory, 11*(3), 295–329.

Alamprese, J. (1996). Integrated services, cross-agency collaboration, and family literacy. In L. Benjamin and J. Lord (Eds.), *Family literacy: Directions in research and implications for practice* (pp. 17–23). Washington, DC: U.S. Department of Education.

Albritton, R., & Brown, R. (1986). Intergovernmental impacts on policy variations within states: Effects of local discretion on general assistance programs. *Policy Studies Review, 5*(3), 529–35.

Bailey, D., & Simeonsson, R. (1990). *The family needs survey.* Chapel Hill: Frank Porter Graham Child Development Center, University of North Carolina at Chapel Hill.

Behrman, R. E. (1992). School linked services. *The Future of Children, 2*(1).

Brewer, G., and Kakalik, J. (1979). *Handicapped children: Strategies for improving services.* New York: McGraw-Hill.

Bronfenbrenner, U. (1979). *The ecology of human development: Experiments by nature and design.* Cambridge, MA: Harvard University Press.

Bronheim, S., Cohen, P. D., & Magrab, P. R. (1985). Evaluating community collaboration: A guide to self-study. In S. Bronheim, P. D. Cohen, & P. R. Magrab (Eds.), *The inter-unit relationship scale.* Washington DC: Georgetown University Child Development Center.

Bruder, M. B., & Bologna, T. M. (1993). Collaboration and service coordination for effective early intervention. In W. Brown, S. K. Thurman, & L. F. Pearl (Eds.), *Family-centered early intervention with infants and toddlers: Innovative cross-disciplinary approaches* (pp. 103–127). Baltimore, MD: Brookes.

Bruner, C. (1993). *Co-location, common intake, and single point of entry: Are they the best answers to service fragmentation?* Des Moines, IA: Child and Family Policy Center.

Christensen, M. (1982). Interagency collaboration in Virginia: Services for the handicapped learner. *Dissertation Abstracts International, 43*(4), 1111.

Colby, C. R. (1987). Cooperation among agencies serving individuals with disabilities. (Texas A&M University, 1986), *Dissertation Abstracts International, 47*(12), 4369.

Cordiero, P. A. (Ed.). (1996). *Boundary crossings: Educational partnerships and school leadership.* San Francisco: Jossey-Bass.

Dryfoos, J. (1994). *Full-service schools: A revolution in health and social services for children, youth, and families.* San Francisco: Jossey-Bass.

Dunst, C. J., Trivette, C. M., Starnes, A. L., Hamby, D. W., & Gordon, N. J. (1993). *Building and evaluating family support initiatives: A national study of programs for persons with developmental disabilities.* Baltimore, MD: Brookes.

Dwyer, C. (1995). *Guide to quality: Even Start family literacy programs.* Portsmouth, NH: RMC Research.

Eckland, J. *State interagency agreements: Analysis of elements and characteristics.* Unpublished manuscript. University of North Carolina at Chapel Hill.

Edwards, P. (1994). Responses of teachers and African-American mothers to a book-reading intervention program. In D. Dickinson (Ed.), *Bridges to literacy: Children, families, and schools* (pp. 175–208). Cambridge, MA: Blackwell.

Elder, J. O. (1979). Coordination of service delivery systems. In P. R. Magrab & J. O. Elder (Eds.), *Planning for service to handicapped persons.* Baltimore, MD: Brookes.

Flynn, C., & Harbin, G. L. (1987). Evaluating interagency coordination efforts using a multidimensional, interactional, developmental paradigm. *Remedial and Special Education, 8*(3), 35–44.

Gans, S. P., & Horton, G. T. (1975). *Integration of human services: The state and municipal level.* New York: Praeger.

Garbarino, J. (1990). The human ecology of early risk. In S. Meisels & J. Shonkoff (Eds.), *Handbook of early childhood intervention* (pp. 78–96). Cambridge, England: Cambridge University.

Garland, C. W., & Linder, T. W. (1994). Administrative challenges in early intervention. In L. J. Johnson, R. J. Gallagher, J. B. LaMontagne, J. J. Gallagher, P. L. Hutinger, & M. B. Karnes (Eds.), *Meeting early intervention challenges: Issues from birth to three* (pp. 133–163). Baltimore, MD: Brookes.

Greenberg, G. (1981). Block grants and state discretion: A study of the implementation of the Partnership for Health Act in three states. *Policy Sciences, 13*, 155–181.

Harbin, G. (1988). Implementation of P.L. 99-457: State technical assistance needs. *Topics in Early Childhood Special Education, 8*(1), 24–36.

Harbin, G. (1990). *Interagency agreement rating scale.* Chapel Hill, NC: FPG Child Development Institute, The University of North Carolina at Chapel Hill.

Harbin, G. L. (1996). The challenge of coordination. *Infants and Young Children, 8*(3), 68–76.

Harbin, G., Bruder, M. B., Reynolds, C., Mazzarella, C., Gabbard, G., & Staff, I. (2002). *Service coordination policies and models: National status.* Chapel Hill, NC: FPG Child Development Institute, The University of North Carolina at Chapel Hill.

Harbin, G. L., Clifford, R., Gallagher, J., Eckland, J., & Place, P. (1990). *Implementation of P.L. 99–457, Part H: A cross-state analysis of factors influencing policy development.* Chapel Hill, NC: Frank Porter Graham Child Development Center, The University of North Carolina at Chapel Hill.

Harbin, G., Kameny, R., Pelosi, J., Kitsul, Y., & Fox. E. (2002). *Identifying desired outcomes of early intervention: Executive summary.* Chapel Hill, NC: FPG Child Development Institute, The University of North Carolina at Chapel Hill.

Harbin, G., Pelosi, J., Kameny, R., Kitsul, Y., & Fox. E. (2003). *LICCs in North Carolina: How well are they working? An Executive Summary.* Chapel Hill, NC: FPG Child Development Institute, The University of North Carolina at Chapel Hill.

Harbin, G., Pelosi, J., Kameny, R., McWilliam, R., & Kitsul, Y. (1993). *Barriers and facilitators to coordination scale.* Chapel Hill: The University of North Carolina at Chapel Hill.

Harbin, G. L., & McNulty, B. A. (1990). Policy implementation: Prescriptives on service coordination and interagency cooperation. In S. J. Meisels & J. P. Shonkoff (Eds.), *Handbook of early childhood intervention.* Cambridge, England: Cambridge University Press.

Harbin, G. L., McWilliam, R. A., & Gallagher, J. J. (2000). Services for young children with disabilities and their families. In J. P. Shonkoff, & J. P. Meisels (Eds.), *Handbook of early childhood intervention* (2nd ed.). New York: Cambridge University Press.

Harbin, G. L., & Van Horn, J. (1990). *Interagency Coordinating Council Roles and Responsibilities.* Chapel Hill, NC: Carolina Policy Studies Program, FPG Child Development Institute, The University of North Carolina at Chapel Hill.

Harbin, G., & West, T. (1998). *Early intervention service delivery models and their impact on children and families.* Chapel Hill: Early Childhood Research Institute on Service Utilization, Frank Porter Graham Child Development Center, The University of North Carolina at Chapel Hill.

Haslam, B., & Suh, J. (2000). *Report on the observational study of even start family literacy projects.* Policy Studies Associates, Inc.: Washington, DC.

Hassett, S., & Austin, M. J. (1997). Service integration: Something old something new. *Administration in Social Work, 21*(3-4), 9–30.

Hayes, C. D. (Ed.). (1982). *Making policies for children: A study of the federal process.* Washington, DC: National Academy Press.

Herrmann, S. (2003). *Perceptions of power structures in integrating services for family literacy.* Unpublished doctoral dissertation, University of North Carolina at Chapel Hill.

Hoy, W., & Miskel, C. (1987). *Educational administration: Theory, research, and practice.* New York: Random House.

Individuals with Disabilities Education Act. (1991). *P. L. 102-119 (20 U.S.C.) Sections 1400–1485.* Washington, DC.

Intrilligator, B. A. (1986, April). *Collaboration with schools: A strategy for school improvement.* San Francisco, CA: Paper presented at the annual meeting of the American Educational Research Association.

Kagan, S. L. (1993). *Integrating services for children and families: Understanding the past to shape the future.* New Haven, CT: Yale University Press.

Kagan, S. L., & Bowman, B. T. (Eds.). (1997). *Leadership in early care and education.* Washington, DC: National Association for the Education of Young Children.

Knapp, M. S. (1995). How shall we study comprehensive, collaborative services for children and families? *Educational Researcher, 24*(4), 5–16.

Knitzer, J. (1982). *Unclaimed children: The failure of public responsibility to children and adolescents in need of mental health services.* Washington, DC: Children's Defense Fund.

Konrad, E. L. (1996). A multidimensional framework for conceptualizing human services integration initiatives. *New Dimensions for Evaluation, 69,* 5–20.

Lawson, H., & Sailor, W. (2000). Integrating services, collaborating, and developing connections with schools. *Focus on Exceptional Children, 33*(2), 1–22.

Litwak, E., & Hylton, C. F. (1962). Interorganizational analysis: A hypothesis on coordinating agencies. *Adminstrative Science Quarterly, 6*(4), 395–420.

Lynn, L. E. (1976). Organizing human services in Florida: A study of the public policy process. *Evaluation, 3*(1/2), 58–78.

Marshall, C., Mitchell, D. E., and Wirt, F. (1985). Assumptive worlds of education policy makers. *Peabody Journal of Education, 62*(4), 90–115.

Martinson, M. C. (1982). Interagency services: A new era for an old idea. *Exceptional Children, 48*(5), 389–394.

Maslow, A. (1962). *Toward a psychology of being.* Princeton, NJ: Van Nostrand.

Mattessich, P. W., Murray-Close, M., Monsey, B. R. (2001). *Collaboration: What makes it work.* Saint Paul, MN: Wilder Foundation.

Mayer, C., & Ford, M. *Child find document.* State of Alaska, Department of Education, and Easter Seal Society for Alaska's Crippled Children and Adults.

McGonigel, M. J., Woodruff, G., & Roszmann-Millican, M. (1994). The transdisciplinary team: A model for family-centered early intervention. In L. J. Johnson, R. J. Gallagher, M. J. Montagne, J. B. Jordan, J. J. Gallagher, P. L. Hutinger, et al. (Eds.), *Meeting early intervention challenges: Issues from birth to three* (2nd ed., pp. 95–131). Baltimore: Brookes.

McKnight, J. (1987). Regenerating community. *Social Policy.* (Winter Issue), 54–8.

McLaughlin, M. (1982). State involvement in education quality issues. In J. Sherman, M. Kutner, & K. Small (Eds.), *New dimensions of the federal–state partnership in education.* Washington, DC: Institute for Educational Leadership.

McWilliam, R. A. (1992). *Family-centered intervention planning: A routines-based approach.* Tucson, AZ: Communication Skill Builders.

Melaville, A. I., & Blank, M. J. (1991). *What it takes: Structuring interagency partnerships to connect children and families with comprehensive services.* Washington, DC: Education and Human Service Consortium.

Murphy, J. (1973). Title V of ESEA: The impact of discretionary funds on state education bureaucracies. *Harvard Educational Review, 43*(3), 362–385.

National Center for Family Literacy. (1997). *The family literacy answer book: A guidebook for teachers and administrators of family literacy programs.* Louisville, KY: Author.

North Carolina House Bill 1840. (1999). *S.L. 1999-237 Section 11.42.* Raleigh, NC.

Padak, N., & Sapin, C. (2001). *Collaboration: Working together to support families.* Columbus, OH: Ohio Literacy Resource Center.

Padak, N., Sapin, C., & Ackerman, C. (2001). "Title I bought that coffee pot!" Family literacy professionals learn to collaborate. In V. Risko & K. Bromley (Eds.), *Collaboration for diverse learners: Viewpoints and practices* (pp. 87–101). Newark, DE: International Reading Association.

Pollard, A., Hall, H., & Keeran, C. (1979). Community service planning. In P. R. Magrab & J. O. Elder (Eds.), *Planning for service to handicapped persons.* Baltimore: Brookes.

Quezada, S., & Nickse, R. (1993). *Community collaborations for family literacy handbook.* New York: Neal-Schumann.

Richardson, E. (1973). *Responsibility and responsiveness (II): A report on the H.E.W. potential for the seventies.* Washington DC: U.S. Department of Health, Education, and Welfare.

Rogers, C., & Farrow, F. (1983). *Effective state strategies to promote interagency collaboration: A report of the handicapped public policy analysis project.* Washington DC: Center for the Study of Social Policy.

Roth, J., Myers-Jennings, C., & Stowell, D. (1997). How integration of services facilitates family literacy: Testimony from Even Start participants. *Journal for a Just and Caring Education, 3*(4), 418–32.

Sabatier, P., & Mazmanian, D. (1979). The conditions of effective implementation: A guide to accomplishing policy objectives. *Policy Analysis, 5*(4), 481–504.

Salisbury, C., Palombaro, M., & Hollowood, T. (1993). On the nature and change of inclusive schools. *Journal of the Association for Persons With Severe Handicaps, 18*(2), 75–84.

Sameroff, A. J., & Chandler, M. J. (1975). Prenatal risk and the continuum of care taking causality. In F. Horowitz, M. Hetherington, S. Scarr-Salapatek, & G. Siegel (Eds.), *Review of child development research,* Vol. 4 (pp. 187–244). Chicago: University of Chicago Press.

Schmidt, S. M., & Kochan, T. A. (1977). Interorganizational relationships: Patterns and motivations. *Administrative Science Quarterly, 22,* 220–234.

Steiner, G. (1976). *The children's cause.* Washington, D.C.: The Brookings Institute.

St.Pierre, R., & Layzer, J. (1996). Informing approaches to serving families in family literacy programs: Lessons from other family intervention programs. In L. Benjamin & J. Lord (Eds.), *Family literacy: Directions in research and implications for practice* (pp. 81–88). Washington, DC: U.S. Department of Education.

St.Pierre, R., Layzer, J., Goodson, B., Bernstein, L. (1997). *The effectiveness of comprehensive, case management interventions: Findings from the National Evaluation of the Comprehensive Child Development Program.* Washington, D.C.: Abt Associates, Inc.

St.Pierre, R., Ricciuti, A., Tao, F., Creps, C., Kumagawa, T., & Ross, W. (2001). *Third national Even Start evaluation: Description of projects and participants.* Washington, DC: U.S. Department of Education.

Tao, F., Gamse, B., & Tarr, H. (1998). *National evaluation of the Even Start family literacy program: 1994–1997 Final report.* Washington, DC: U.S. Department of Education Planning and Evaluation Service.

Tice, C. (2000). Enhancing family literacy programs through collaboration: Program consideration. *Journal of Adolescent and Adult Literacy, 44*(2), 138–145.

Trivette, C. M., Dunst, C. J., & Deal, A. G. (1996). Resource-based early intervention practices. In S. K. Thurman, J. R. Cornwell, & S. R. Gottwald (Eds.), *The contexts of early intervention: Systems and settings* (pp. 73–92). Baltimore: Brookes.

U.S. General Accounting Office, D. o. H. R. (1992). (GAO/HRD-92-108). *Integrating human services: Linking at-risk families with services more successful than system reform efforts. Report to the Chairman, Subcommittee on Children, Family Drugs, and Alcoholism, Committee on Labor and Human Resources, U.S. Senate.* Gaithersburg, MD: U.S. General Accounting Office.

Van Horn, C., & Van Meter, D. (1977). The implementation of intergovernmental policy. In S. Nagel (Ed.), *Policy Studies Review Annual,* Vol. 1 (pp. 97–120). Beverly Hills, CA: Sage.

View, V. A., & Amos, K. J. (1994). *Living and testing the collborative process: A case study of community-based services integration.* Arlington, VA: Zero to Three, National Center for Clinical Infant Programs.

Waldfogel, J. (1997). The new wave of service integration. *Social Service Review, 71*(3), 463–484.

Weatherly, R. A. (1979). *Reforming special education: Policy implementation from state level to street level.* Cambridge, MA: MIT Press.

Weiss, J. A. (1981). Substance vs. symbol in administrative reform: The case of human services coordination. *Policy Analysis, 7*(1), 21–45.

Wieck, K. (1976). Educational organizations as loosely coupled systems. *Administrative Science Quarterly,* (21), 1–19.

Zipper, I. N., Hinton, C., Weil, M., & Rounds, K. (1993). *Service coordination for early intervention: Parents and professionals.* Cambridge, MA: Brooklin.

VII

Diversity and Culture

To discuss literacy in our pluralistic society, we must carefully consider the diversity in beliefs, practices, and languages across families. We no longer view literacy and language as independent of these family characteristics.

Vivian L. Gadsden's chapter opens this section with a broad look at the intersections of literacy and culture as essential for understanding, studying, and working with diverse families. She develops brief, provocative images of four families and uses them to illustrate her points about issues of diversity and race. She examines reading research as the backdrop for a discussion of how family literacy is linked to cultural identity and practice, reminding us that the term *culture* is often used in a general manner, when we should be addressing issues of race and ethnicity. She then describes two family literacy programs. She looks at the procedures they use to inform discussion of diversity and culture, and she reports on each program's successes in building on family strengths. Yet much is lacking in these programs. She notes the importance of exploring program participant's cultural history, evaluating outcomes, improving practices, and addressing deeper issues of values, beliefs, and folklore in families. She provides an agenda for practice and research.

Using an ecocultural perspective of early literacy, Lynne Vernon-Feagans, Darlene Head, and Kristen Kainz examine the macrosystem as it influences literacy, language, and school success in young children. They focus on the community and on professionals within institutions that provide the teaching of literacy. Their model of early literacy combines an ecological view of child development with a cultural view of the myths that lead to erroneous ideas about children. They examine myths—including those of individual competition and hard work, disadvantage and differences, dysfunctional parenting and families, lack of ability and skill, and poor motivation—that appear most relevant in the development of literacy interventions for nonmainstream families and their children. They next examine the consequences of false beliefs and the degree to which family literacy programs accept or reject such beliefs. Agreeing with Gadsden, they see little critical discourse about diversity. Although they commend research demonstrating that literacy practices and characteristics of the home explain academic and literacy achievement better than does family status, the authors nevertheless note that little research within culture or ethnicity has been conducted. They emphasize the need to view families as they are and not through the lens of societal myths.

Building on the strong connections among literacy, language, and culture, the next three chapters probe a number of issues related to serving English-language learners within family literacy programs. Heide Spruck Wrigley provides a very broad view of the characteristics and needs of families who speak a language other than English at home, addressing the challenges and opportunities they present. As background, she first paints a picture of demographic shifts in the United States since the 1980s, which have brought us large numbers of people who do not speak English. She then discusses the need for a philosophical approach to English as a second language and literacy that can bring together curriculum and teaching and that can inspire teachers and students. She identifies five orientations used in adult English-language learner education, such as helping adults fit into society or (the most popular approach) making English as a second-language learning socially and culturally relevant (although Gadsden and Vernon-Feagans et al. note that these approaches do not explore family beliefs and practices deeply enough). Wrigley's discussion of these approaches may help programs reflect on their own practices in relation to their goals.

John Strucker, Barbara Pan, and Catherine Snow tackle the challenges that non-English-speaking students pose for family literacy programs. They present demographic data on those who speak a language other than English in the home, with a focus on the changing face of family literacy programs. Next, they review research on second language acquisition and on literacy development. Examining adults with limited English proficiency in Even Start, they report that many had limited education in their native language. Furthermore, participants' English proficiency varies widely. Several factors must be considered in planning for these individuals, including their age (which influences rate of acquisition), how easily they acquire phonological awareness, and their previous educational experience. The authors also discuss early childhood programs for children learning English as a second language, as well as five types of programs identified as models for serving these children, such as immersion and bilingual programs. They identify three elements that family literacy programs can employ to serve English-language learners, and they conclude with a set of recommendations for research and for providing more effective services.

Although diversity has received much attention in studies of culture and language in family literacy programs, few writers have discussed Native American families. Yet a unique partnership has been in effect since 1991, to provide family literacy services for parents and children in these families. Sharyl Emberton describes the development of this program, Family and Child Education (FACE) and the role of its partners, the Office of Indian Education Programs within the Bureau of Indian Affairs, the Parents as Teachers Programs, the National Center for Family Literacy, and the High/Scope Educational Research Foundation. She presents data on educational needs, such as high school dropout levels, that make family literacy programs particularly advantageous for providing services to Native American families. Then she enumerates the goals that guide FACE programs' design, including, for example, increasing the number of parents who can promote their children's development and establishing home–school partnerships. The FACE programs emphasize cultural identity, exploration, and connection; Emberton draws examples from several programs, to illustrate how they foster parent and child outcomes.

Collectively, these chapters provide a rich set of issues and data that must be considered in making programs respond better to families with different backgrounds, languages, practices, and beliefs. The authors' recommendations will help programs and researchers address critical issues.

21

Family Literacy and Culture

Vivian L. Gadsden
University of Pennsylvania

Fundamental to any discussion of family literacy and culture are two interpretive issues. The first concerns what we mean by family literacy. Are we referring to parent–child learning, with a specific focus on the development of reading and writing abilities and the transfer of knowledge from parent to child? Are we referring to reciprocal relationships in which a first-generation immigrant child assumes the responsibility of responding to family matters requiring reading and writing and serves as an interpreter for the parents? Are we referring to adults who are learning to read and write at the same time that their children are learning to read and write? Are we referring to literacy as a core of reading, writing, and problem-solving activities and abilities that draw from the social, cultural, and contextual experiences, knowledge, and histories of learners? These are questions with which the field continues to grapple. The second issue questions what we mean by culture and builds on descriptions and understandings of culture and cultural difference in relation to race and as a more encompassing concept. Discussions about culture, in both private and public spaces, can evoke either deep interest or profound discomfort, or, in some cases, both reactions. This chapter considers these two interpretative issues within the context of family literacy and cultural studies research, practice, and the broader notion of inquiry.

The following images are intended to provide lenses onto some of the issues that constitute such inquiry and considerations for practice and research.

Image 1. Andrew describes himself as an African American father. For the past year, he has been attending a family literacy program. His parents were born and raised in the French-speaking Carribean, and came to the United States as young adults, when Andrew was 3 years old. Although he identifies as an African American, he celebrates and embraces what he considers his Caribbean culture. In working with Andrew, the teacher in the program, Joanna, who is of Polish and Italian descent, assumed that his family origins were in the United States. Andrew is a quiet man who shares information about himself only after he feels a sense of mutual trust. Only during a storytelling session did Joanna learn of Andrew's cultural background and the significance he attaches to it—significance that he considers in relation to language difference, cultural/racial difference, and the acts and experiences associated with immigration and immigrant status in the United States.

Image 2. A young mother of Irish descent, Elaine, sits at the kitchen table reading through an assignment for her adult literacy class. Sitting next to her is her 6-year-old daughter, Jessica, who is feverishly flipping through a children's book of folktales from different countries. Elaine takes a break from her literacy assignment and tries to help Jessica read a story. In the course of reading the story, Elaine remembers different customs and stories that were shared at family gatherings by her grandparents and other family members. She describes them to Jessica. If asked what her cultural background is, Elaine immediately says "American"; she notes that since she has only lived in America, she can only know American culture. Yet, at the moment that she interacts with her daughter around the folktale, she identifies strongly as a woman of Irish ancestry whose family's culture reflects certain values, beliefs, expectations, and practices.

Image 3. A Puerto Rican grandfather and his grandchildren read *Bible* stories in preparation for Sunday church services at a local Evangelical church. The grandfather notices that his young, preschool grandson, Miguel, is attempting to write out the story, drawing scribbles that he "reads" out loud. As Miguel reads, his English is punctuated lightly with several Spanish words and expressions, to catch his grandfather's attention, whose smile indicates that he is pleased not only that Miguel is trying to read, but also that he uses Spanish words that are a part of his linguistic, cultural, and family history.

Image 4. An extended family meets for an annual family event, celebrating their Jewish ancestry. An uncle helps a young boy, Sam, read from the *Torah.* Later, Sam returns to school, where there is a discussion about family roots and generating family trees. Sam decides that he wants to trace his family's roots and asks his parents for help. His parents assist him, but suggest that he also talk with his uncle. Jane, Sam's mother, teaches in a family literacy program. A child of a Holocaust survivor, she often utilizes stories in her class to focus on the common themes of social consciousness, historical events, and contemporary problems. Her upper-middle-class status separates her from her students; her family history of oppression connects her.

In each of these vignettes, literacy is the visible element of learning. People are reading and using a range of written and oral materials to understand something new or to enhance their knowledge of something learned earlier. Less visible but equally poignant are the familial and cultural histories, experiences, and expectations that help learners frame, consider, and revise their goals, plans, and approaches to learning literacy. As these vignettes suggest, both literacy and culture are inherently cognitive acts, as well as social interactions that occur between and among different entities: the text and the reader, the learner and other learners, the learner and the teacher, and the individual learner in a family and family members.

In each of the images, family members interpret family practices, and the cultural meanings attached to them, in ways that help to achieve their literacy and learning goals. In each, as well, the significance of family, literacy, and culture are firmly and intricately intertwined. Two or more family members are engaged in literacy learning and literacy interchanges: Intergenerational learning is occurring, between an adult who teaches and a child who learns, although in some cases, the learning may be bidirectional. Family members enact behaviors and participate in family-sanctioned rituals. In short, each image represents both an interpersonal interaction within families and a valuing of culture and literacy that falls under the rubric of family literacy.

Although these images are not all occurring in family literacy programs, they represent some of the home, familial, and cultural issues that learners bring to programs and the kinds of issues that get raised, ignored, minimized, or misunderstood within classrooms. In this way, family literacy programs are no different than many K–12 classrooms, which focus on what are called the celebratory features of cultures (e.g., costumes, foods, and dances), rather than on intellectually inviting discussions about traditions, beliefs, and practices; on people who share a common culture; or on the complexity of changes that eventually occur among traditions, beliefs, and practices. Classrooms that focus on the latter also consider culture as being more than national heritage (e.g., Korean or American). They try to address the ways in which culture is constructed as part of individuals' ethnic, racial, or national identity, as well as their other identities (e.g., poor or gay) that are formed out of a shared perspective, life circumstances, or societal response and institutional barriers.

These issues of culture have always been a part of discussions in family literacy, both in the written work of researchers and in the talk of practitioners about their efforts to address the needs of diverse families. Within the concept of family literacy, the root term *literacy* represents a body of work in reading that, for almost two decades, has centered mostly on the ways that readers derive meaning from texts and on how the processes of making meaning are linked to the cultural, historical, and social contexts in which literacy is learned and used. When the term *family* is attached to literacy, the combination creates a particular significance for the role of these cultural and social contexts in literacy learning. That is, it presupposes a relationship among family members, between family members and the larger community, and to the cultural contexts in which families are situated (Gadsden, 1998). This relationship contributes to and sustains family members' literacy development and is influenced by the traditions and histories of learners who themselves are diverse and are part of a diverse cultural and family legacy (Duran, Revlin, & Havill, 1995; Gadsden, 2002).

Family literacy is associated with thousands of varied programs and projects, from Head Start to Even Start to other privately and publicly funded early childhood efforts which are designed to enhance reading, writing, and other literate acts in the home. A common description of the programs is that their mission is to address the needs of low-literate parents, to eradicate low literacy, and to increase the literacy options and opportunities for these parents' children. Particularly noteworthy is that the adults in these families (and hence in these programs) not only have low levels of reading and writing, but also typically represent low-income and minority parents who live in urban areas (although large numbers of low-income White families in rural and urban areas participate in these programs). Some researchers (e.g., Strickland, 1995; Taylor, 1997) have argued that the emphasis of family literacy programs on eradicating illiteracy within these poor families has been too narrow and misdirected, not focusing enough on research about how different families use cultural knowledge to promote literacy. These researchers suggest that the field has drawn too heavily from models (often called *deficit models*), in which poor and minority families are seen as deficient—in their cognitive abilities, valuing of literacy and learning, and knowledge of the world—and as being to blame for their own conditions of poverty and limited access to opportunity (Klassen-Endrizzi, 2000). Thus, a mismatch often exists between the findings of research on literacy within families (Gadsden, 1998; Moll, 2000; Moll & Greenberg, 1990; Willett & Bloome, 1992) and the emphasis of family literacy programs.

This view of literacy, as being embedded in social and cultural meanings and contexts, is not new. From the 1980s to the present, researchers and practitioners alike have focused on the social processes in literacy learning and have highlighted the significance of culture and context in understanding and supporting children's literacy development. Two seminal works in literacy and family literacy (Heath, 1983; Taylor & Dorsey-Gaines, 1988) both argue that the study of family literacy is more than the study of individual learners within a family or within programs, alone. Learners typically do not leave family influences or cultural markers at home upon entering literacy instruction.

In the early 1990s, Purcell-Gates (1993) referred to the increasing significance of studying culture in family literacy—not simply what is taught or what is studied, but also who teaches and who conducts research on groups such as minorities. She suggests, and I agree, that family literacy research is by its very nature research into cultural practice and requires that researchers and practitioners seek to understand culture from the perspective of the cultural insider. Recent writings on family literacy and family literacy programs (e.g., Osterling, 2001; Quintero, 1999; Whitehouse & Colvin, 2001) remind us that, in family literacy, as in K–12 reading research, we have been far more successful highlighting the importance of sociocultural perspectives than in determining what constitutes either a culturally centered framework or approaches that do not rely upon one-size-fits-all instructional packages.

This chapter focuses on the intersections of family literacy and culture as real and potential sources for understanding, studying, and working with diverse families. This focus is interspersed with related issues of diversity and race and draws heavily upon the tacit assumptions about literacy, families, and culture in the four images in the introduction of this chapter. The next section describes the role of reading research as an historical backdrop for current efforts that link family literacy to issues of cultural identity and practice. After that, I examine definitions of culture and their relationship to family literacy, and then I focus on programs, exploring the ways in which they understand and build upon issues of difference, diversity, and culture, as well as on the approaches they use to address these issues with learners and practitioners. Later in the chapter, I identify literacy and educational research that can inform discussions of culture and diversity. Finally I suggest ways of crafting a research and practice agenda that can lead to a broadened framework which integrates social, cultural, and intergenerational contexts within the study of family literacy.

This chapter is limited in its capacity to provide a single, simple, sure approach to, or explanation of, the cultural domains of literacy. Rather, it is intended to examine, and to encourage practitioners to examine, what the issues are, how people have tried to make sense out of these issues, and what might be needed to move forward in developing a compelling and useful work that contributes to an empirical body of knowledge. Such examination requires that family literacy educators take what Cochran-Smith and Lytle call an "inquiry approach" (see Cochran-Smith & Lytle, 1999, 2001), which, as they suggest, implies more than the practitioner peering into the lives of learners. The private and public images associated with literacy—particularly for those with low levels of formal literacy—necessitates that the learner and the teacher engage in the reciprocal processes of learning and teaching in order to understand the cultural and social experiences that shape the learners' lives.

In addition, this chapter is developed around two perspectives commonly discussed in the study of families and family literacy. First, parents are children's first socializers; they introduce young children to the world—to ways of behaving, learning, and interacting with others and their social environments. Second, families constitute a significant social context in which cultural practices, beliefs, meanings, and values around literacy are shared, understood, and transferred from one generation to another. The family is seen as representing the ethnic, racial, and national identity and history of its members. Culture encompasses the changing definitions of the family itself and the role that each family member, from birth through old age, plays in the life-course of the family.

The present is a particularly significant time in the field of family literacy. Increasing emphasis on the need for scientifically based approaches and analyses in literacy and education will require more intensive focus on empirical approaches to the study of family literacy, greater clarity on what is meant by family literacy, and critical reviews of models designed to support families learning literacy. Reports such as Snow, Burns, and Griffin's *Preventing Reading Difficulties in Young Children* (1998), prepared for the National Research Council, have heightened the attention to these issues and have reinforced the need for children to develop abilities that enable them to make meaning of written texts. Meaning making, from the perspective presented in this chapter, is an essentially cognitive and social task that calls upon reader's prior knowledge, as well as on their current understandings and uses of language. Families and literacy learning settings that serve families are ideal sites to examine these issues.

HISTORICAL CONTEXTS FOR READING AS A SOCIAL AND CULTURAL PROCESS

Reading and literacy studies are appropriate contexts in which to begin a discussion of the intersections between family literacy and culture. Families have long been the site of inquiry for the study of reading and literacy, as far back as the 18th and 19th centuries (Demos, 1970). However, not until the 1960s and 1970s did these studies directly address the cultural dimensions of literacy within families or the importance of exploring culture in designing and implementing instructional approaches. In the late 19th and early 20th centuries, family literacy studies centered on the lives of children and families of European ancestry who were from upper-income homes, who were literate, and who were exposed to high levels of literacy within the home (Demos, 1970; Monaghan, 1991). Because these families shared a common social status and land of origin, researchers probably found little reason to examine the intragroup differences and the relationship between these differences and the cultural histories that divided or connected the families.

Current family literacy research and practice are the recipients of this work and of reading research that, by necessity in the 1960s, began to grapple with issues of culture and race. By that time, the political and social landscape in America was changing, and African Americans and other groups, considered ethnically and culturally different from mainstream Whites, were seeking equal access to education. Discussions emanating from historical events, such as court-ordered desegregation and the civil rights movement, and from publications such as the Moynihan (1965) and Coleman (1966) reports, thrust reading and literacy to center stage in the debate surrounding African American children's cognitive ability, that is, whether African American children were intellectually inferior to White children and what African American children needed in order to achieve in school and society.

Despite a growing emphasis on the cultural and familial backgrounds of children, the resulting educational and social science research did not necessarily, or primarily, focus on culture as a means for understanding the needs of African American children, nor did it draw upon cultural frameworks. For example, studies of African American children focused on the ways in which Black culture itself constrained the cognitive development of children, that is, on the ways in which cultural traditions, practices, and linguistic codes set Black children apart from White children or interfered with or reduced their reading development. Much of this work focused on the racial label *Black* as a single, categorical variable that helped to distinguish the problems of Black children from those of White children and families, and tended to ignore the culture around which African American children and their families defined their lives.

On the other hand, the reading and linguistics research of the time focused on children within families, across diverse cultural, social, and community contexts. This work includes Goodman's studies (1965, 1968) on the language-experience approach; Labov's study (1968) of African American dialects, with children and families in New York City; Durkin's research (1966) on parent–child interactions around reading in poor, urban communities; and other studies with a similar focus. All of these researchers suggested that the cultural and social settings in which children learn and develop language and literacy were important sources of information and were useful tools of instruction and support—not simply for poor Black children and families, but also for other children of color, poor White children, and children, across ethnic and social lines, who were experiencing difficulty in learning to read and write in traditional school settings. The idea had surfaced that culture, family, and contexts were important to understanding literacy learning. This body of work was complemented by studies in fields such as sociology, psychology, and anthropology that were focused on poor families, Black families, and families representing diverse minority groups (e.g., Billingsley, 1968; Stack, 1974).

The shifts in reading research that occurred in the 1960s and 1970s helped scholars to move past the boundaries of direct genetic relationships (between parents and children) and to expand narrow frameworks of reading and writing as discrete areas of knowledge, developed primarily or only in school contexts. As a result, reading research, focusing more widely on literacy, produced several identifiable and practical results for literacy research and programs concerned with children and families (Gadsden, 2003).

First, this shift enhanced the focus on parents and families, in both the number of studies and depth of analysis. In a search conducted for this chapter, my students and I identified numerous articles, reports, and book chapters that focus on literacy and families (e.g., parents and children, children and families, and families), from the 1960s and early 1970s to the present. Second, this shift led to increased attention to literacy development within different ethnic groups, although low-income African American and Latino families are still the dominant focus of most cultural studies in literacy. Third, it promoted a serious consideration of, and response to, issues affecting immigrant families; children and parents who do not speak English as a first language are studied alongside of, and in tandem with, other families who seek to create opportunities for their children. In short, the work opened up discussions about the ways in which learners representing diverse cultural, ethnic, and class backgrounds approached, used, and valued literacy. It encouraged teachers and researchers alike to examine more carefully the role of parents and other adults in children's learning, the nature of these interactions, and the reciprocal relationships between learning within the home and learning within classrooms.

By focusing on the contexts for learning and the ways in which these contexts affect cultural and ethnic groups and the individuals in them, researchers who study K–12 and family literacy can explore assumptions that "there are more similarities between the ways in which people use print than there are differences" (Taylor, 1997, p. 551). These assumptions help us deconstruct what have been called *deficit models*, which, as Strickland (1995) argues, inadvertently, but effectively, put the burden and blame on parents and communities for the low performance of poor and minority children (Taylor, 1997). In other words, these assumptions help us examine critically and challenge notions that poor and minority children and their families lack something important, whether it is cognitive, social, cultural, or some combination of these dimensions.

Like reading and other areas of inquiry focused on the cultural domains of learning, family literacy has only recently begun to explore the options and possibilities for constructing an integrative framework that addresses and responds to the issues of culture, race, and difference. These issues are germane to both research and practice.

CULTURE WITHIN FAMILIES AND FAMILY LITERACY

Defining Culture

Culture is often an enchanting and exotic concept in both research and public discourses, within and outside discussions of families and literacy. It connotes traditions associated with the past and involving the transfer of knowledge from one generation to another. It may be transmitted through oral histories within families and communities or through written social accounts. Taylor (1871) described culture as "that complex whole which includes knowledge, belief, art, morals, law, custom, and any other capabilities and habits acquired by man [or woman] as a member of society" (p. 2). In Taylor's definition of culture, and in the definitions by contemporary anthropologists and ethnographers, culture is not seen as a fixed core of traditions or as a predetermined set of restrictive or descriptive features. Although culture includes history and tradition, it also involves fluid, changing practices affected by context, time, and individual choice.

This analysis of culture challenges our tendency to equate it with ethnic background or race and to minimize the subcultural identities within ethnic categories of people (Zuberi, 2001). Examples include references and attributions to a uniform *Black culture* or *Black community* and use of the term *African American* to refer to African Carribeans, Carribean Americans, and Africans. Although these groups may share a common historical background in Africa, they often differ in the way they have translated their African heritage within Western societies. In much the same way, *Asian culture* is used to refer to diverse groups who differ dramatically in history and practices and who sometimes have had contentious relationships, because of war and conquest, prior to their arrival in the United States. In other instances, Cambodian immigrants and other Southeast Asians are compared with Chinese from mainland China, Japanese Americans, or Chinese Americans whose families have lived in America for four generations. This tendency to link culture with minority group status has at least two implications: (a) It ignores intracultural differences, that is, the diversity within groups; and (b) it ignores the cultural contexts, artifacts, and memories within a range of immigrant groups, a large number of whose members entered the United States from Europe and other parts of the world as indentured servants, with non-White status, or with histories of oppression.

Culture and Family Literacy

According to Kris Gutierrez, Professor of Education, University of California:

> *Fluency in Spanish allowed me to serve, at the age of 3 and 4, as translator—cultural broker, as it were—for my grandmother, who spoke no English. My language also created a special place and role in my grandparents' home and gave me access to conversations my parents had. . . . There was something wonderful about third- and fourth-generation Chicano children who could move so easily across these fluid linguistic and cultural borders. Our rich linguistic resources and literacy skills, however, were neither valued nor utilized in school. Fluency in two languages was invaluable in our community, and we were praised for it—as long as we used our special knowledge outside of school.*
> (Gwen, 1996, in *Language Arts*, pp. 308–314)

This section begins with this quotation from Gutierrez to reinforce the intergenerational nature of literacy and the different roles that children of non-English-speaking immigrants play in translating tasks requiring reading and writing. The issues of cultural and linguistic exclusion arise in otherwise seemingly innocuous learning environments, and the nature of such exclusion may be difficult for educators to understand or prepare for, irrespective of the programs or focus of work. Family literacy educators, such as those in K–12 schools, often have limited knowledge of the experiences of minority groups and have vastly different definitions of culture and of the approaches that should be used to integrate culture within research or practice, as Gutierrez's account suggests. However, the term *culture*, and the study of culture, share with the concept of *family* an emphasis on cohesiveness and solidarity, that is, traditions, expectations, and practices that ostensibly serve a common purpose. This purpose typically includes the healthy development of children and the welfare of the family itself.

In most cases, cultural and familial connectedness protects learners and can be used in proactive ways by practitioners to engage, embellish, and enrich literacy instruction and learning. This approach entails more than selecting a few facts about the learner's cultural or ethnic group. Rather, it requires understanding what the role of these facts—and the traditions and practices associated with them—has been in a group's history, how they are understood within the learner's family, and how they might be used by programs and practitioners to build a knowledge base for all learners within a program. Instruction can center on a range of issues, situations, and dilemmas that encourage critical thinking and analysis and that require learners to participate in increasingly complex literacy tasks, some of which are discussed in subsequent sections of this chapter.

In other cases, however, family cohesiveness may debilitate a learner, when the expectations of the family and of the school context either conflict or are at odds (see Roberts, Richards, & Bengston, 1991). Consider, for example, the learner in a family literacy program in Philadelphia who remembers being told that "it [was] silly to want to be anything other than a good wife and mother." Upon the urging of her family to marry, and based upon her sense of Puerto Rican culture, as expressed in her home and immediate environment, she came to think that in fact her options and potential were limited and that women in the family should not aspire to high intellectual and professional goals.

Family literacy should attempt to capture the transformative value of literacy that occurs within both familial and cultural contexts. For nondominant power groups, this focus is particularly important, but is sometimes difficult to capture. Au (1995) suggests, for example, that literacy learning places conflicting demands upon students. In one instance, "students must understand the history and culture of their own immediate environment," and in another, "they must appropriate the culture and code of the dominant group in order to transcend their environment" (p. 88). Family literacy programs are a special context in which these demands are enacted and, as a result, may facilitate or thwart learning. They either represent a comfortable space for learners who accept most or all of the family culture, or they become a locus of conflict. When the experiences and values assigned to information, learning, and uses for learning within a family literacy setting contradict the family culture, the significance of learning may be reduced. When they agree, cohere, or are understood, they offer a place for discussion and a context for learning. Most analyses of research and programs indicate that family literacy does result in learning, although determining the nature, quantity, and sustainability of that learning has been elusive.

Family Cultures

My interest in family literacy and culture has been sustained by my work with individual learners and has been sparked by observations of these learners within and outside their family contexts. This interest has also been reinforced by research, such as the studies cited in this chapter, which points to the significance of culture as an encompassing concept to locate and understand the static and changing life choices of learners as participants in programs and as family members. My own work (Gadsden, 1994, 1995, 1998; Gadsden & Ray, 2002) attempts to connect cultural messages and meanings, which families attach to literacy and identity formation, to how literacy and learning are understood and used by the individual learner. Based on research on family development and literacy within multiple generations of African American, Latino, Native American, and White families, the work is centered on a theoretical construct that I call *family cultures*. In research with African American and other families over more than 10 years, the families themselves have created these cultural frameworks, or family cultures, within and across different generations.

One example of the uses of such a framework emerged from a study conducted with second and third graders in an urban school, in which teachers worked with parents to engage their children in literacy that was culturally based. Using their own family stories as a potential source of knowledge, the children and parents whom I observed conducted a series of investigations into their family history, locating events and changes in family constellations over time, identifying transitions in geographic location, and examining their own history within the context of the social history of the United States. Parents and children participated in reciprocal activities in which the parents' knowledge and resources as adult family members were negotiated with the child's interest in discovering information that linked their experience with the family, as well as sharing such information with other family members, peers, and the teacher. The assignments were given weekly and required that the students and their parents pursue a new piece of their familial and cultural puzzle, unpacking something unexpected about the way in which the family practices, over time, contributed to a family culture.

Family cultures are developed through political, cultural, and social histories that affect family members and eventually contribute to a core of meanings, beliefs, and practices that family members use to approach learning and to guide life activities. They revolve around family-defined premises that family members hold as central to their purpose and to the life trajectory of their children. Family cultures often influence—if not dictate, in many instances—the ways that individual family members think about, use, and pursue literacy and how they persist in educational programs. The presence of these family cultures or frameworks provides information about family expectations, family members' beliefs and attitudes about literacy, and the nature and role of social practices within different family contexts. Thus, in conceptualizing a framework for family literacy programs, program goals should weigh family expectations and the social and cultural practices in which the family currently engages.

In family cultures, individual family members and the collective family unit assess their identities within the context of known and imagined possibilities, constantly reconciling the limitations of their immediate contexts with a view of the future. For historically oppressed individuals and groups, these cultures are developed and given credibility through memories and legacies often associated with historical successes and real and contrived explanations for apparent failures and shortcomings within families. School, community, and society are perceived as complicit in offering and denying opportunity. This perception is implied in the common statement, "I would have gotten more grades if times hadn't been so hard," mapped against the expectations for children in the family, "That's why I made sure that I worked, so that my children could have a better time of it," or "The opportunities were there, I just didn't use them." These perceptions are found in the identities that are formed, the sense of family and community caring, and the idea of education as a cultural and community tradition, as well as in issues of race and kin networks.

ADDRESSING CULTURE AND DIVERSITY: ISSUES FROM PROGRAMS

Programs can't deal with literacy alone. Every community has issues, and every culture has strengths. Programs must be [deliberate] in responding to both.
    (*Bilingual Family Literacy Teacher in Metropolitan Midwestern City, Personal Interview*)

What does it mean for a family literacy program to address issues of culture and diversity? Does a family literacy program revise all of its instructional approaches? Does it aim to diversify the population it serves? Does it attend to issues of class and race? Does it make an effort to explore with learners their cultural history? How do family literacy programs think about and address these issues? How can they improve their work in this area? My study of and work in family literacy programs suggest that these questions represent only a subset of issues that programs face in developing the structural and philosophical bases of their work. However, these issues are worth exploring in relationship to the ideologies around teaching, culture, and diversity that family literacy educators bring to the design of programs and their day-to-day practice. This section describes general features of family literacy program content and the populations served; then commentaries are presented from interviews with three practitioners in two family literacy programs, in order to examine the ways in which they define, explore, grapple with, and integrate issues of culture and diversity.

Programs and Populations: Overview

Family literacy programs are diverse in structure, focus, and curricula, as well as in the way they respond to differences among learners, instructors, and instruction. They aim to respond to the legislative mandate for family literacy programs, which includes three categories, described in other chapters of this volume: (a) early childhood, (b) parenting, and (c) adult education. Within these three categories, programs define themselves differently: as intergenerational literacy programs, parent education programs, family education programs, early literacy programs, and parent–child reading programs. Some programs are affiliated with larger efforts (e.g., Parents as Teachers, Central Intermediate Unit, Family Services), and other programs are targeted for particular populations (e.g., Migrant Education programs).

Literacy programs face a range of problems regarding how they operate, how they invite participation, and how they define their missions. Some of these problems involve the public perception of literacy programs as meeting the needs of illiterate people, a comment that our research team heard on several occasions, while working with Head Start parents and staff participating in our family literacy study. Thus, some programs choose to use the term *learning,* instead of literacy, in their titles—for example, Parents and Children Learning Together[1]—or to refer more generally to their programs as parent workshops (e.g., Ermis, 1996; Klassen-Endrizzi, 2000).

Programs vary by focus and location (Wasik, 1997) and differ in the primary adult populations they serve. For example, in addition to getting parents involved, some programs recruit grandparents as a way to engage children in literacy learning and to help children learn more about their heritage. Others, including many Even Start programs, are located in schools, and still others, which complement Even Start activities, are administered through outreach efforts and are operated by churches and faith communities. A final variation is offered in community centers or in prisons, and may encourage the use of computers or prepare parents to reconnect with their children.

The National Evaluation of Even Start Reports (St.Pierre & Layzer, 1998) indicated that most Even Start parents had not obtained a high school diploma or its equivalent, with almost 50% having reached no higher than ninth grade. At that point, teen parents accounted for 13% of participants. Approximately 50% of the families relied on government assistance as their primary source of income. Hispanics were described as the largest minority group served, followed by African Americans, then Asian/Pacific Islanders and Native Americans. However, Caribbean Americans and Asian Americans such as Cambodians and Khmer were also likely to be found in adult literacy English as a second language programs.

Although the families in family literacy programs often resemble each other in terms of income level, they may differ in the ways they acquire and use this income or define themselves socially. For example, a family may be classified as being low-income, but hold expectations and values that typically are associated with different segments of the middle class. Not uncommonly, successful adults say that not until they entered college did they learn that they had

[1] This study was part of a families and literacy project conducted by graduate students and myself at a Head Start program in Philadelphia, Pennsylvania.

been poor or disadvantaged as children. In other words, their parents and other families in their communities were members of a cultural subgroup that maintained expectations and ways of seeing the world that often set them apart from other families of similar income. Families in literacy programs differ in race, cultural traditions, ethnic heritage, religion, gender, class, and life experiences. However, they also differ in the literacies that they bring to the program, the ways in which they learn literacy, the purposes and everyday uses they have or will have for literacy, the value they assign to literacy as well as the reasons they assign it, and the family cultures that they bring to the literacy learning experience.

There are several neglected issues in the study of family literacy programs, but two are of particular interest. The first addresses the question, Who are the members of the unit *family* served by family literacy programs or considered by family literacy programs in developing missions and curricula? The second follows from the first: How are the issues of father involvement addressed in family literacy programs (see Gadsden, 2003). There are few fathers who participate in family literacy programs and little information about those who do attend (see Gadsden, 2003; Gadsden, Brooks, & Jackson, 1997). Although there is evidence that some researchers and programs are addressing this issue (e.g., Edwards, 1995; Gadsden, 2003; Klassen-Endrizzi, 2000), most programs serve mothers, because mothers have traditionally been children's primary or sole caregivers. Some of the problems associated with engaging fathers stem from the unavailability of some fathers who serve as the family's primary breadwinners; in other cases, fathers live outside of the home and are not considered as important by program staff, are difficult to reach, or are not accessible. The issue of father involvement raises questions about how gender is discussed and approached in programs. The questions include how boys and girls learn literacy, the instructional materials that are most useful for boys versus girls, and the nature of interactions between parent and child. It also raises questions about how prepared programs are to involve fathers, an increasing number of whom are children's primary caregivers or want to be involved more actively in their children's development.

Culture and Diversity: How Programs are Responding to the Challenge and Possibility

There are both long-standing and emerging efforts within programs throughout the country to address the issues of culture and diversity within the context of family literacy. Many are programs that have a large population of one specific minority group, for example, Mexican Americans; others serve urban areas with a diverse population of different minorities. There are fewer discussions of family literacy program efforts focused on populations of low-income Whites. In studies that describe family programs and summaries of the programs themselves, I continue to be struck by two themes. The first is the reported impact on parents' expectations. Program staff and parents typically speak of how program participation raised their expectations of themselves and their children. However, few parents speak specifically about the impact of their participation, or other parents' participation, on children's school performance, based on any identifiable or measurable achievement data. The second theme is the relatively limited staff diversity within programs. Despite programs serving large numbers of minority populations— e.g., African American and Latino parents and children—or immigrant groups, programs often do not employ staff from the ethnic groups served by the program, in instructional or administrative capacities.

For me, the slowly emerging good news is that program staff and practitioners are raising issues and posing questions about how programs, practitioners, and researchers build upon or address culture and diversity and, to some degree gender. These programs understand the need to learn about and draw upon cultural knowledge and experience, not only as a way to engage and invite learners into the literacy classroom, but also as an essential element of understanding the best ways to engage diverse learners (mothers and fathers; men and women), identify and monitor the implementation of the best materials and resources, and use cultural knowledge to increase learning gains and learning opportunities.

How would research and practice begin to reimagine this work? Many programs are doing much of this work, and indeed the discourse in the field has changed. First, they would have to move past the notion that there is a single package or set of packages that holds all of the answers. Second, they would have to spend more time focused on preparing teachers to understand the issues evident within families themselves, beginning with their own family, literacy, cultural experiences, and personal/literacy autobiographies. The best way to engage teachers about other people's histories is to ask them to learn more about their own and to use what they learn as a way to begin a discussion with students about their family backgrounds.

Third, they would help teachers identify, read, and use literature that explains culture and its differences from and similarities to race or ethnicity. Often, teachers and others use the three terms (*culture, ethnicity*, and *race*) interchangeably. The advantages of focusing on culture is that the teacher can come to distinguish the specific issues of race and ethnicity and to understand how the term can be applied to a range of accepted practices and traditions, in addition to how those practices and traditions eventually change over time to create new cultures.

Fourth, teachers would begin to face their own prejudices, stereotypes, and beliefs, exploring the sources of these beliefs and determining how to unpack their assumptions with knowledge from texts and the stated experiences of the learners whom they teach. Fifth, they would begin to relate to and teach students differently. By observing students, teachers could determine students' interests and work, in order to build upon them. They could choose provocative work that allows learners to question difficult realities of our history (such as the migration of Native Americans and the Trail of Tears) and negative stereotypes and myths (such as that African Americans are lazy and Irish Americans are alcohol abusers), mapping the experiences of others onto their own. They would become acquainted with children's and adult literature about different groups, in fiction and nonfiction, historical, and literary.

Finally, they would provide opportunities for family literacy teachers to learn from one another and from specialists from the separate areas of families, literacy, and culture, to explore emerging issues and develop appropriate approaches. These opportunities could range from engaging the experts from local school districts and local universities in writing projects, for example, to utilizing interactive video technology to create peer and expert–teacher interchanges that encourage linkages with family literacy specialists in other geographic locations.

The programs described in the next three sections are struggling with some of these issues and have experienced many successes, primarily because their staffs have accepted the notion that the programs can serve all families. They have also recognized that family literacy programs must draw on multiple textual and human resources, in order to succeed, and that staff themselves must confront their own misperceptions, fears, and prejudgments of those who differ from them. However, these issues continue to confound the field, along with questions of how to address culture, diversity, and race within learning and teaching and what emphasis to place on them. We are still only on the cusp of initiating and engaging in a critical discourse about these concerns in K–12 settings or in the larger society.

The Even Start Family Literacy Program in Cityville.[2]   Located in a midsize southern state, the Cityville program was established in 1990 and serves more than 120 low-income families, mostly mothers and children. The program is structured around the three areas required

---

[2]Pseudonyms have been used to identify the names and locations of the programs and to honor promises of confidentiality.

by the legislative mandate. Families represent a variety of groups: approximately 65% of the families are African American, 30% are European-American, and 5% are Latino and Asian. In serving this diverse population and recognizing the limitations of staff in understanding and identifying the full gamut of need, issues, and interests, the program surveys the participants upon entering the program. Staff members work with parents to help them set goals for their participation in the program. They ask parents to share information about their community and to bring in pictures from home that tell something about the family. In addition, each parent is encouraged to bring in items or artifacts that children value. Staff members then are able to use this information to guide their work with parents and children and to ensure that the program responds to parents' goals and interests.

The Cityville program has charged its staff to make issues of culture and diversity a part of their primary work. Staff members focus on parents' self-esteem, conflict resolution, and personal management (i.e., decision making and problem solving). The program specifically addresses the balancing act in which parents find themselves—e.g., simultaneously handling home, children, and the transition from welfare to work—and challenges staff members to help parents combine issues of child development, nutritional needs, and children's school performance and achievement.

The program director states that the staff makes every effort to ensure that the curriculum identifies and collects information that responds to the diversity, cultural histories, and immediate needs and interests of the families who are learning literacy. The books used in the program are described as representing a broad range of cultural issues, topics, and characters. Programs are driven by parents' needs and the curriculum that staff members think is important. They are developed around cooperative learning, peer tutoring, and the premise that these approaches are important to sharing information about issues that affect families and family life.

When asked to identify the greatest challenge in developing a program that responds to issues of culture, the director stated that programs must learn about the families themselves: "Putting [parents and children] in books is not enough," she said. The director indicated that her program serves parents, children, and families who have many literacy needs, multiple personal and familial demands, and few financial resources. At the same time, they are members of groups whose histories have been poorly studied in the past. For this program, the idea of "just making books available and accessible responds to an important part of the problem, but only a fraction of the problem that [family literacy learners, programs, and practitioners] face." Literacy programs such as the one in Cityville must rely on parents as sources of information and must develop frameworks that enable family literacy learners to build on family and cultural strengths.

The Hometown Even Start Program.   The Hometown Even Start program was established in the spring of 1991. Hometown, a suburb of a large metropolitan area in the midwest, has a diverse ethnic population. Many of the current residents are African Americans, who, over the past 25 years, have moved to Hometown from surrounding cities and southern states. In Hometown and the bordering suburban neighborhoods, there is also a growing Chaldean/Arabic-speaking population, primarily of immigrants from Iraq. Because of the population shifts, the program emphasizes training in English as a second language. A large, White, middle-class population still resides in Hometown, but these families either have adult children or enroll their children in schools other than the local public schools.

The objective of Hometown's Even Start program is to enable parents to become conventionally literate and able to participate as full partners in their children's education and school readiness development. At the time of the interview, the program served 60 families, 58 of whom were Chaldean. Participants were primarily young mothers with low levels of education, who had not yet obtained their high school diplomas. Two fathers participated regularly, and other fathers attended special activities. The director indicates that the two African American parents usually chose to participate in the adult basic education component, because they demonstrated higher levels of reading ability. Most of the program participants come from low-income families and receive some form of government assistance.

Members of the Hometown program's staff have many opportunities and resources upon which to draw for addressing culture and literacy. The staff is ethnically and culturally diverse. The program offers one or two in-service sessions each month, and the staff meets weekly to share information. Three parents have been hired to assist in the day-to-day activities of the program, staff, and participating families. The program's curriculum combines appropriate parts of the Kenan model (described in chapter 1 of this volume), with program units developed internally. It integrates issues that respond to the specific needs of the population served and of the staff who provide those services. According to the director and the bilingual teacher, the staff members aim to establish mutual trust between themselves and the families.

The staff is encouraged to pay attention to, and to address, issues of language diversity and differences in values, which the director described as including topics such as promptness, the status and role of women, and attitudes toward work. The differences between staff and family values are one source of frustration, however. Staff members deal with issues ranging from parents' disciplining of children to problems such as alcoholism in families. One of the largest areas of concern for the program is women's health and support. To increase women's knowledge of, and access to, health facilities, the staff works with the local health department.

In addition to the director, the bilingual education teacher provides a rich perspective on cultural and diversity issues in both the Even Start family literacy and the Hometown programs. The bilingual education teacher is of Chaldean ancestry and is assisted by a bilingual education aide who is a Chaldean emigre to the United States. Both are speakers of Arabic. The bilingual education teacher highlighted the need to establish trust between the staff and the families. She spoke in thoughtful terms about what family literacy programs such as Even Start mean, not only to Chaldean families who are faced with choosing between the cultural values and folklore associated with their countries of origin and the dominant values in the United States, but also to African American and other families who are American-born. For her, the cultural and diversity issues for all Even Start programs, including her own, are to consider the implications for the family literacy workplace, that is, the ways that cultural values are understood and explored by and within programs; who is served; who is providing instruction and support; what the quality and nature of the curriculum are; and what the two main constituencies, teachers and families, understand about each other, for purposes of helping children and adults learn.

Parecki, Paris, and Siedenberg (1996, 1997) found that programs such as Hometown's focused on cultural issues in several contexts and for several reasons. In one case, the program worked collaboratively with efforts funded under the former Job Training Partnership Act (JTPA). In addition to being concerned with the economic and educational well-being of families who attended their program, JTPA had realized the need to address cultural issues. Because the majority of participants in Even Start were Chaldean- and Arabic-speaking, JTPA was sensitive to any cultural lapses that could have arisen. The bilingual aide worked in both JTPA and Even Start, to help foster communication among staff, participants, and their families. JTPA recognized that participants are literate in their own cultures and utilized these natural literacy abilities through the use of computer programs that accommodate the Arabic language. This program was used to create newsletters that were distributed, in both English and Arabic, to students, their families, and other community members.

As both the director and the bilingual education teacher noted, the core of their effort centered on the interaction between learning and values and on the ways that families cope with expectations of the staff and society. However, the process by which staff members became more knowledgeable was not easy. For example, in their efforts to help the mothers make the transition from welfare to work or from school to work, staff sometimes (mis)interpreted the behavior of the Chaldean mothers as demonstrating disinterest or resistance. Upon closer scrutiny, it became clear that the mothers' seeming lack of school-to-work goals could be explained by understanding the intensity of their relationships with their families and their belief that, in the absence of public support, family members' support would make up for the lost income or help with financial burdens. The bilingual education teacher stated that these mothers' expectations are typically accurate, at least in the short-term. The challenge to the staff, the bilingual education teacher suggested, is to prepare the families for the range of challenges they will face over the short-term and long-term. Both the director and the bilingual education teacher agree that literacy is a fundamental tool for addressing the challenges that these mothers will face. However, they also think that the range of literacy and life issues is such that the staff "can't deal with literacy alone."

Other Culturally Focused Programs.   Over the past 5 years, several other programs and approaches have been described in literacy and early childhood education publications. Some programs are less formal than others; nevertheless, they use innovative strategies. To date, there is no empirical evidence on the efficacy of these approaches and almost no critical observations by researchers. However, the programs have been able to sustain themselves and the participation of learners. The approaches themselves also indicate the efforts of the programs to explore new territories, in order to ensure the deepest engagement and most active learning of the parents, children, and family members served.

Among the strategies that have been described is the use of family stories. In my own work, we have developed entire scripts with parents and children, as well as extended family members, about their family histories. The written texts that emerge from the interviews and research of the children and their families become a part of the reading texts of the family as a biological and literate unit. These scripts are developed initially around photographs. The strategies are reported in other programs.

For example, family stories are increasingly used as a way to engage both children and parents. Family stories are just that, and those who have used them as an engagement strategy learn about the family and their cultural histories. Meoli (2001), in her work with families, encouraged them to share their stories in their native language, which allows them to fuse the cultural and linguistic features of their lives and to understand both features within the context of the English-language literacy that they are learning.

Photography has also emerged as a useful approach and has been used with a range of learners in K–12 settings, as well (Ewald, 2000). Spielman (2001) describes the project's purpose as collecting evidence about "learning in the life . . . of the families" (p. 764). The program engaged parents in much the same way that other programs have engaged parents and children in learning, that is, the parents and/or children bring in artifacts and tell stories. Perhaps the most unique feature of the program—the photowalk—allows the teacher, parents, and children to uncover a range of literacies or, as Street (2001) would suggest, multiple literacies. In this program, the photowalk was intended to familiarize the parents and children with cameras, but also to make them observers and recorders of their communities, community life, and community language and social interactions. Several other features of the approach are noteworthy, including the teacher and program participants (co)editing and drawing out themes from the collected work. The interactional approach between the families and the teacher, which this strategy encourages—engaging teachers as learners and consumers of the cultural knowledge of others and giving teachers alternative ways of thinking about achieving the goals of teaching and learning—is particularly important.

Family literacy programs often must consider the issue of cultural difference or convergence, as they consider language and linguistic differences. Osterling (2001) and Quintero (1999) both address the needs of nonnative speakers within literacy programs. They highlight an issue that is often unexamined in programs: the potential for a program to address the language difference of an émigré, without exploring the cultural transition and transformations that occur during the process of immigration and resulting in a new identity.

Last, several researchers and practitioners, myself included, have been focusing on father involvement in early childhood programs. Literacy and family literacy are increasingly examined in this discussion. A 2002 issue of *Young Children*, for example, addresses these and other issues around how to get fathers involved, what sensitivities should be considered to engage fathers and staff in such programs, and how to respond to the complexities of gender and culture within these efforts.

Summary.   Several questions were posed at the beginning of this chapter. One critical issue questions what it means for a program to address issues of culture and diversity. Can it do so without sacrificing a focus on reading, writing, and other problem-solving literacies? The premise of this chapter is that it can, but that the full breadth of approaches and options requires a level of investment around curricula content and the literature sources used, teacher preparation, and articulated expectations about outcomes and the measurement of change and improvement.

The message from the Cityville and Hometown programs, from the other programs described, and from Even Start Family Literacy evaluations and reports is that practitioners and other staff members can and do focus on ethnic heritage and cultural artifacts in developing programs. Programs appear to try to build on these familial and cultural artifacts in ways that make families feel comfortable and ready to learn. It also appears that traditional approaches are not enough to identify or address issues of culture and diversity. Most programs are unable to articulate a clear approach or vision around culture, as a part of their programmatic framework or instructional approach. Yet, these cases provide examples of the fundamental elements necessary for creating strong programs that move past simplistic notions of addressing cultural diversity, for example, developing a way of teaching that leads to family literacy learners defining and using literacy to enhance their personal development and knowledge of different histories—both their own and those of other groups.

The Hometown and Cityville Even Start programs indicated that they focus on family strengths, and both identify a range of activities that enable practitioners to serve families. However, several items are missing from these reports. For example, the Cityville program did not provide much information about the values or beliefs of the families served. On the other hand, the Hometown program focused more heavily on the cultural values of the Chaldean families, perhaps because of their relatively young history in the United States, than on the values of other families. Neither in reports from the two programs nor in the literature on family literacy programs are there rich accounts of the folklore that has been developed in families and communities, the ways in which programs access such information, the uses of assessments or interviews to obtain these data, or the possibilities for constructing programs that reflect the diversity in beliefs and practices. What is shared in several summaries is the need to help families value education. The implicit, but not-so-subtle, presumption here is that, when family members have low levels of literacy, they also devalue literacy. In some programs, this presumption may be coupled with an assumption that seeking information about families, their histories, beliefs, and practices is unnecessary.

Many programs provide abstract images of their programs, suggesting that issues around culture, diversity, and race are add-ons to the regular intake, instruction, and curriculum planning. As Parecki et al. (1996) state, curricula and instruction are difficult areas for programs, in general. Programs draw upon a range of resources to develop and sustain their activities. Some program models use approaches that reflect a combination of recent instructional innovations in the field of reading; others provide little or no instructional or assessment framework(s). Programs, according to the Parecki et al. (1996) study, tend to pick and choose from existing models,[3] to develop curricula that respond to the specific needs of the families that they serve.

Because family literacy programs and curricula are still in the formative stages of development and because the field offers such possibility for (re)conceptualizing, understanding, and exploring issues of diverse groups of children and families, now is an appropriate time to build systematic approaches to teaching literacy to family members, in which culture, diversity, race, and difference are at the core of a framework, rather than an appendage to it. This effort requires that researchers and practitioners work together in field studies that address specific issues of how programs prepare teachers to work with culturally diverse populations. Together, they also must identify what literature is used within programs, what the features of a culturally responsive curriculum would include, how texts focused on different cultural and ethnic groups are chosen and discussed, and what opportunities programs provide for students to examine the practices, beliefs, and behaviors of groups other than their own. However, to focus in greater depth, the field should also consider several questions that persist: Do family literacy programs make an effort to explore with learners their cultural history? How do programs set outcome indicators or evaluate outcomes in this area? How can they improve their work in this area? How do programs address deeper issues of values, beliefs, and folklore in families which cohere with, or diverge from, those of the programs and the practitioners who run them? Family literacy research and research on schooling offer some insights and models for supporting child and adult learners in families, but also wrestle with the conceptual limitations in relationship to cultural and contextual issues.

STRANDS OF RESEARCH

Research on culture and family literacy may be divided into four different strands. One strand focuses on diverse populations, but does not specifically address issues of culture. Most studies refer simply to the need for programs to provide services to minorities or to address the experiences of a specific minority group. In general, these studies provide descriptions rather than rigorously examine the cultural domains of learning and teaching or their implications for families. An example is a 1997 study by Kermani and Janes, which reports several interesting findings from their observations of a tutorial program for low-income Latino families. The authors identify several challenges around serving the families and conclude that family literacy entails a complex set of issues. However, they provide only minimal analysis of the cultural relationships among the learners or between learners and staff. They also do not provide detailed descriptions of the materials used or of the program's understanding of its mission.

A few other studies provide images of parents and children engaging in culturally sensitive and appropriate literacy activities within and outside of traditional school settings. They describe different populations of ethnic learners, most of whom have low levels of income. For example, Elish-Piper (1997) focuses on the purposes and types of literacy uses by low-income families participating in a summer program. Neuman, Hagedorn, Celano, and Daly

---

[3]Four family literacy models are often identified by practitioners. The practitioners are familiar with these because of their involvement in the programs, marketing, or references; they report, based on Parecki et al. (1996) study, that they have the greatest success when parts of the models are combined with their own approaches. The models are (a) the *Kenan model* developed by the National Center for Family Literacy, (b) the *Parents as Partners* program, developed by Edwards and published by Children's Press, (c) the Missouri *Parents as Teachers* program, developed by Winter and her colleagues (see Winter and Rouse, 1990), and (d) the Home Instruction Program for Preschool Youngsters.

(1995), through a literacy chronology of a year-long program with adolescent African American mothers, provide information on the young mothers' beliefs about learning and literacy and the uses of peer discussions to uncover these beliefs. Gadsden (2003), Gadsden et al. (1997), and Ortiz, Stile, and Brown (1999) provide a synthesis of issues confronting fathers who are engaged in literacy programs and who are seeking to improve both their parenting skills and their literacy. Morrow and Young (1997) use literature-based approaches that are culturally relevant with African American and Latino children and parents, to increase children's achievement and interest in literacy.

A second strand of studies makes the point that family literacy efforts, more often than not, develop programs and expectations for mainstream, White, middle-class families, rather than for the diverse populations in family literacy programs. Puchner (1997) observed the problems stemming from mismatches between program approaches and the cultural practices of the populations served (these mismatches were also mentioned by the Hometown program). Using case studies from a U.S. program serving Southeast Asian immigrants, who are primarily of Cambodian descent and from rural villages in Mali, Puchner suggests that European-dominant approaches were applied to teaching other cultural and ethnic groups. The approaches proved to be incongruent with the needs of non-Europeans in both sites. From her review of multiple studies, including her own research, she concludes that family literacy efforts should address directly what constitutes a strengths model and how to implement it (Puchner, 1997).

A third strand responds to the issues of culture by focusing on diversity and the need for multiple models that address diverse needs. As is true in other fields, literacy specialists may assume that the issues of culture are incidental to the provision of services. In other words, they may believe that cultural sensitivity is a nice thing to do or is politically correct, but does not add much to learning. As a consequence of this thinking and in the case of minorities, for example, they may assume that, if "you work with one minority, you have the knowledge to work with all." Service providers may also assume that there are few differences in the way that information is received by different groups and that there may be differences between groups, but few differences within groups, whether working with White or non-White populations. Work in this strand extends arguments of studies in the second strand, by challenging researchers and practitioners to rethink and to eliminate concepts and approaches that assume such uniformity of approach.

Yamauchi and Tharpe provide a poignant example of this tendency to misunderstand and misapply expectations, based on their work with Native American children. Although not focused specifically on family literacy, the study highlights the problem of subtle assumptions that undermine teaching and learning in diverse cultural and ethnic groups. The authors discussed the ways in which researchers and practitioners often generalize their experiences with one group to others with which they are not familiar. Referring to their own good intentions in working with Native Americans, Yamauchi and Tharpe initially generalized their experiences with Hawaiian children to the Native American students in their study, only to find an unresponsive and disengaged class of students. Not until they met with, spoke with, and learned about and from the Native American children and their families, were they able to establish a program agenda that complemented and opened up discussion about cultural values and folklore. This exchange helped the researchers understand how to engage the students.

A fourth strand attempts to look critically at the intersection between family and culture and the ways in which culture is implied or embedded in the practices of individual family members who are learning literacy in programs. Most of these studies use cultural frames of reference to study family literacy and to acknowledge their importance in accessing and engaging families, as well as to determine what learners know, what they want to know, and what they are willing to invest. For example, in *Other People's Words: The Cycle of Low Literacy,* Purcell-Gates (1995a) documents parent–child literacy within a low-income, White, Appalachian family.

As she notes, sociocultural theories of learning allow all learners to be seen as members of a defined culture, highlight the role that their identity plays in determining what they will understand about the world, and indicate the ways in which they will interpret information. The protagonists in her account, Jenny and her son, Donny, represented a specific cultural subgroup among White, low-income families; they manipulated literacy and personal events in relationship to the cultural markers that were influenced by their social class, geography, and family folklore and values about learning, schooling, and societal options. In order to move forward, to develop as readers and writers, Purcell-Gates (1995a) states:

> Donny and Jenny needed to see and experience the connectedness of literacy and life. They needed to bring print into their world. Jenny needed to read real text in order to learn to read. The texts given to her to read earlier were not 'real' to her. Donny needed instruction that could bring print into his world for the first time. (pp. 176–177)

In one of the few studies that focuses specifically on culture, Bhola (1996) proposes a model of family literacy in which the family is at the center of the model. The family is located in a network of mutual relationships with multiple institutions, such as schools and workplaces. Stating that family literacy should balance a view of the home, family, and individual members, Bhola designs a curriculum in which the whole family is considered. The model also builds on the family's cultural capital and makes visible who has power in the family and how this power is negotiated in the family and with surrounding institutions.

My own work on family cultures aims to provide a framework for thinking about the ways culture is examined within family functioning and literacy learning and for charting the ways in which families develop their own cultures as a subset of large and complex cultural traditions, beliefs, histories, and folklore. A popular activity is using family portraits as the primary instrument to examine family cultures. Family portraits are interpreted as intergenerational artifacts that have uses in identifying familial themes and literacy categories. The family portrait or photograph offers one venue for examining family members' roles in the culture of family.

In one second-grade classroom, we asked the teacher and students to paint their own family portraits, with the help of a parent or other family member, or to bring in a family picture. We used these family pictures as a way to begin talking about the family cultures of the teacher, the students, and the research team, and connecting these to images of literacy uses within the family. Children were assigned literacy tasks of labeling family members and of making connections between and among family members. They narrated the process by which they drew the picture and shared problem solving around who was included and who was left out. This activity led to a series of other tasks during the course of the year, and children engaged their parents and the teacher in a variety of reading and writing episodes that enlightened them about their family culture and ethnic heritage, while developing the literacies of reading, writing, and problem solving.

Parents and children in the project participated in several activities within and outside of school. Children conducted investigative tasks about family cultures and, along with their teacher and parents, developed their own family history frameworks. With parents, community members, siblings, and peers, they developed stories and compared these stories with those of other groups. They used these stories as a source of knowledge. They read unfamiliar, standard school texts, and they were able to bring their prior knowledge to the text, in critical ways. In other words, they did not sacrifice the cognitive part of schooling. Rather, it was an essential part of the social process of learning.

Several of the themes that run through the four strands are a part of ongoing K–12 studies and analyses and focus on a variety of areas from which family literacy can draw. For example, multicultural education offers several different perspectives, ranging from celebration of cultural tradition models to more critical analyses of the role of teachers. Multicultural education specialists, appropriately and increasingly, are questioning issues of access and equity within classrooms and schools (Grant & Sleeter, 1988; Nieto, 1999). A second area centers on cultural congruence, which students experience when their teachers share an understanding of the cultures, and dissonance, which students experience when their cultures are alien to their teachers (Irvine, 1990). A third is drawn from reading, linguistic, and anthropological studies that focus on culture, difference, and pedagogy (Au, 1995; Delpit, 1995; Dyson, 2002; Ladson-Billings, 1997; Moll, 2000). The concept of *funds of knowledge* is a particularly useful framework, which suggests that students draw upon a repertoire of cultural capital built up over time and found within families and communities.

The research cited here, as a collective body of work, begins to tease out some of the issues of culture, by focusing on beliefs. However, as is true for the models, none provides a comprehensive portrait. Furthermore, each could be enhanced through a more intensive analysis of how, inclusive of class issues, the roles of social setting and culture interact with approaches to instruction, participation in activities, literacy outcomes, and uses of knowledge within and outside of classroom learning.

FUTURE DIRECTIONS

Production technology has advanced enough that we can customize almost anything—computers, kitchens, etc. But we still haven't figured out how to customize education. In areas such as literacy, we can and should attend to the cultural features of contexts, of individuals, and of families.
(Rethemeyer, 2000, Commentary on Education and Literacy)

Although culture is the focus of this chapter, issues of culture, race, and ethnicity, along with those around class and gender, cut across all of the chapters in this volume. In these chapters, authors have addressed the ways in which family literacy programs and research attempt to achieve the goals of improving literacy among, and for, parents and children in Even Start family literacy efforts. The analyses reveal that considerable success within research and practice has occurred, from early childhood to English as a second language activities, and often has required enormous investments by staff, who have had little access to research and tools for instruction and assessment. Not unlike the findings within these chapters, the analysis for this chapter suggests that family literacy models and frameworks attempt to respond to cultural and social issues, but that they may need to reconfigure the priority issues and the processes by which they seek information. We know that family literacy practice and research have attempted to address the issue of culture, but, as is true in other educational contexts, questions around culture and issues of diversity lie at the margins of the field.

A perennial problem in the field is also worth noting. Because so many family literacy practitioners talk about the difficult everyday life problems faced by many of the poor families served, observers of family literacy programs often see issues such as culture, difference, and the life needs of families as one and the same, or they question whether mention of, or efforts to address, these issues interfere with the real mission of family literacy programs—to teach reading and writing. I suggest that family literacy and culture are linked by nature: culture, like literacy, concerns both the lived and written experiences and accounts of learners, as members of families and society. Literacy is more than reading and writing; it involves a range of problem-solving abilities that children and adults need and possess and that are acted out daily within a cultural context. Once programs venture to understand issues of culture and of families' interpretations of their own cultures, they will be exposed to a wider range of texts and sources of information, not only for teaching, but also for learning how to use literacy and for helping learners use literacy to challenge the barriers that obstruct their access to opportunities.

The present is a particularly important time for the future of family literacy. Compared to other areas of literacy, there are few empirical studies. At the same time, there is considerable wisdom that can be drawn from the experiences of teachers. Possibly, however, as efforts are developed to enhance the scientific rigor of the field, the salience of issues around culture and context may be lost. To reduce this possibility, existing, as well as new, conceptual frameworks, which consider the broad expanse of relationships, social interactions, and cognitive strengths, will need to be created, tested, and refined.

Future directions in family literacy research and practice should help to:

• Make issues of culture and diversity a priority, not only for developing mutual trust, which is critical to establishing and sustaining participation, but also for the development and examination of innovative curricula and materials. The development of such curricula will need to be predicated upon the belief, however, that issues of culture, family knowledge, and social and familial context are critical to any instructional effort including families, not only at the edges or margins, as so often is the case.

• Identify learner and program indicators that reflect the importance of culture and cultural knowledge. The process of developing such indicators could be implemented as a collaborative activity with specialists in the field, helping to chart changes in the participants and the program.

• Explore in greater depth the meaning and applications of strengths models, in which practitioners systematically set out to learn about the knowledge and skills that learners and their families bring to the teaching and learning of literacy. These may range from cognitive abilities to social skills to community resources. Many of the discussions about family literacy and family literacy models encourage researchers and practitioners to focus on family strengths and to develop models that enable families to access and utilize resources effectively. From what is known, these strengths refer to learners' resources, which enable them, and ultimately the program, to build and support social connections between the family and others in the community, as well as to promote relationships between children and parents (Stanton, 1991).

• Increase the recognition in family literacy of the lifelong nature of learning and the multiple strengths that children, parents, and other family members bring to the prospect of learning. Increasingly, family literacy programs are based upon an expanding set of assumptions about teaching and learning. Inherent in these assumptions is the belief that the family is an educative community in which shared learning experiences occur and that "providing educational support to any family, particularly to families who lack... resources, is an awesome challenge... that combines the need to establish a basis of support services with particular skills and strategies for dealing with a family's learning needs" (U.S. Department of Education, 1996, p. 1). Researchers and programs need to identify the specific strengths and to operationalize the concept of lifelong learning in order to measure growth and its relationship to literacy acquisition and achievement, for children in school and adults over the life-course.

• Decide whether issues of culture and cultural contexts are important for the conduct of studies and the implementation of programs. A research design symposium, sponsored by the Office of Educational Research and Improvement, in 1995 (see LeGrand, 1996), was developed around five themes: assumptions and perceptions about family literacy (i.e., conceptions about families, literacy, and clients served), what we know from research and practice and how we know it; defining features of family literacy programs (e.g., strategies, program content, and structure), priorities for the future (e.g., fundamental areas, issues, and questions), and priorities in a research and practice agenda. What is absent from this list is how the research and practice agenda are related to policy initiatives within the larger context of family support and what the cultural imperatives are in the study of family literacy and the provision of family literacy programs.

• Confront difficult issues that influence the cultural histories of learners. As talk about family support increases and states struggle with welfare reform, questions around literacy, within and outside of families, and its role in the transition to work will be a critical part of public discourse. Welfare reform and family support initiatives are tied to the ability of individuals to utilize existing literacies and to develop new ones. Social policies that structure opportunities for people to use, and that value such learning and support their families, are fundamental to any national or local agenda of family support, as are policy investments in a developmental approach to strengthening families. Evolved from previous work in reading, the current and future focus encompasses a much wider set of populations and goals—from intergenerational learning to life-span development.

• Encourage programs to prepare staff members, through readings, visits, focus groups, and an examination of curricular materials, to become familiar with a large body of work that discusses culture in its broadest sense and the particular issues within selected groups. The rhetoric of culture typically is represented in references to race, low-income status, and low levels of participant literacy, but rarely reflects the acquisition and use of a sound body of knowledge by the family literacy educators themselves.

• Build upon what we know, and conduct intensive analyses to determine what we need to learn. We know more about family literacy than we did a decade ago, but we are faced with how much more there is to learn and with how to disentangle the complexities that arise from problems that interfere with learning, such as poverty and poorly funded schools. Still, we are in the early stages of conducting research, understanding the broad scope of issues or achieving modest coherence—of what we know or do not know—among research studies, and providing responses that can improve assessment, learning, and teaching.

We know a little about the kinds of studies that may need to be pursued and the ways that family literacy as intervention is, or is not, effective. Longitudinal studies, as Hayes (1996) argues, offer us the most important information to understand the nature of outcomes. Such research, he suggests, should focus on problems, not symptoms. In other words, we should examine the stated and known barriers to an individual's learning literacy, not simply the behaviors and practices that appear to be barriers or that are inconsistent with our own perceptions of the world. Such appearances are often fraught with cultural misunderstanding. In their analysis of family literacy intervention, St.Pierre and Layzer (1999) tell us that, although some small positive effects are evident among some participating mothers and children in family literacy programs, there are no large effects. However, as they indicate, research on family interventions reveals that high-quality, high-intensity programs do produce large effects.

Two basic questions persist in planning for family literacy research efforts: Who are the families? and How do they describe literacy within their own family trajectories or family futures? Research might assist programs and practitioners in responding to these questions and others, by conducting studies that do not simply examine what happens to children at school, but also before and after school, as well as also what happens to adult learners in programs, before a session or after a session. In addition, researchers and practitioners need to form reciprocal and respectful relationships, in which a critical discourse can lead to positive action and can inform policy.

REFERENCES

Au, K. (1995). Multicultural perspectives on literacy research. *Journal of Reading Behavior, 27,* 85–100.

Bhola, H. S. (1996). Family, literacy, development and culture: Interconnections, reconstructions. *Convergence, 29,* 34–45.

Billingsley, A. (1968). *Black families in White America.* Englewood Cliffs, NJ: Prentice-Hall.

Cochran-Smith, M., & Lytle, S. (1999). Relationships of knowledge and practice: Teacher learning in communities. In A. Iran-Nejad & P. D. Pearson (Eds.), *Review of research in education* (Vol. 24, pp. 251–307). Washington, DC: American Educational Research Association.

Cochran-Smith, M., & Lytle, S. L. (2001). Beyond certainty: Taking an inquiry stance on practice. In A. Lieberman and L. Miller (Eds.), *Teachers caught in the action: Professional development in practice* (pp. 45–60). New York: Teachers College Press.

Coleman, J. S. (1966). *Equality of educational opportunity.* Washington, DC: Government Printing Office.

Delpit, L. (1995). *Other people's children: Cultural conflict in the classroom.* New York: New Press.

Demos, J. (1970). *A little commonwealth: Family life in Plymouth Colony.* New York: Oxford University Press.

Duran, R., Revlin, R., & Havill, D. (1995). *Verbal comprehension and reasoning skills of Latino High School students* (Research Report 13). Santa Cruz, CA: National Center for Research on Cultural Diversity and Second Language Learning.

Durkin, D. (1966). *Teaching young children to read.* Boston: Allyn & Bacon.

Dyson, A. H. (2002). *The brothers and sisters learn to write: Popular literacies in childhood and school cultures.* New York: Teachers College Press.

Edwards, P. A. (1995). Empowering low-income mothers and fathers to share books with young children. *Reading Teacher, 48*(7), 558–564.

Elish-Piper, L. (1997). Literacy and their lives: Four low-income families enrolled in a summer family literacy program. *Journal of Adolescent & Adult Literacy, 40,* 256–268.

Ermis, S. (1996). Once upon a time . . . families reading together: Promoting early literacy through parental workshops. *State of Reading, 3,* 11–16.

Ewald, W. (2000). *Secret games: Collaborative works with children, 1969–1999.* New York: Scalo.

Gadsden, V. L. (1994). Understanding family literacy: Conceptual issues. *Teachers College Record, 96,* 58–86.

Gadsden, V. L. (1995). Representations of literacy: Parents' images in two cultural communities. In L. M. Morrow (Ed.), *Family literacy: Connections in schools and communities* (pp. 287–303). New Brunswick, NJ: Rutgers University Press.

Gadsden, V. L. (1998). Family cultures and literacy learning. In J. Osborn & F. Lehr (Eds.), *Literacy for all: Issues in teaching and learning* (pp. 32–50). New York: Guilford.

Gadsden, V. L. (2002). Current areas of interest in family literacy. In J. Comings, B. Garner, & C. Smith (Eds.), *Annual Review of Adult Learning and Literacy.* Thousand Oaks, CA: Jossey-Bass.

Gadsden, V. L. (2003). Expanding the concept of "family" in family literacy: Integrating a focus on fathers. In A. DeBruin-Parecki & B. Krol-Sinclair (Eds.), *Family literacy: From theory to practice.* Newark, DE: International Reading Association.

Gadsden, V. L., Brooks, W., & Jackson, J. (1997, March). *African American fathers, poverty, and learning: Issues in supporting children in and out of school.* Paper presented at the annual meeting of the American Educational Research Association, Chicago, IL.

Gadsden, V., & Ray, A. (2002). Engaging fathers: Issues and considerations for early childhood educators. *Young Children, 57*(6), 32–42.

Goodman, K. S. (1965). *A linguistic study of cues and miscues in reading.* (Clearing House No. RE000029). Detroit, MI: ERIC Resources in Education. (ERIC Document Reproduction Service No. ED020864)

Goodman, K. S. (1968). *Words and morphemes in reading.* (Clearing House No. RE000029). Detroit, MI: ERIC Resources in Education. (ERIC Document Reproduction Service No. ED011482)

Grant, C. A., & Sleeter, C. E. (1988). Race, class, and gender and abandoned dreams. *Teachers College Record, 90,* 19–40.

Gwen, M. (1996). Literacy and culture in the classroom: An interview with Kris Gutierrez. *Issues in Applied Linguistics, 7*(2), 308–314.

Hayes, A. (1996). Longitudinal study of family literacy program outcome. In L. Benjamin & J. Lord (Eds.), *Family literacy: Directions in research and implications for practice.* Washington, DC: U.S. Department of Education.

Heath, S. B. (1983). *Ways with words: Language, life, and work in communities and classrooms.* Cambridge, MA: Cambridge University Press.

Irvine, J. J. (1990). *Black students and school failure: Policies, practices, and prescriptions.* New York: Praeger.

Kermani, H., & Janes, H. A. (1997). *Problematizing family literacy: Lessons learned from a community based tutorial program for low-income Latino families*. Paper presented at the Annual Meeting of the American Educational Research Association. (ERIC Document Reproduction Service No. ED408380)

Klassen-Endrizzi, C. (2000). Exploring our literacy beliefs with families. *Language Arts, 78*(1), 62–69.

Labov, W. (1968). *A study of the non-standard English of Negro and Puerto Rican speakers in New York City, Vol. 1: Phonological and grammatical analysis*. Washington, DC: Office of Education, Bureau of Research.

Ladson-Billings, G. (1997). *The Dreamkeepers: Successful teachers of African-American children*. New York: Wiley.

LeGrand, R. (1996). *Family literacy: Directions in research and implications for practice*. Washington, DC: U.S. Department of Education, Office of Educational Research and Improvement.

Men in the lives of children: Special issue. (2000). *Young Children, 57*(6).

Meoli, P. L. (2001). Family stories night: Celebrating culture and community. *The Reading Teacher, 54*(8), 746–747.

Moll, L. C. (2000). Inspired by Vygotsky: Ethnographic experiments in education. In C. D. Lee & P. Smagorinsky (Eds.), *Vygotskian perspectives on literacy research: Constructing meaning through collaborative inquiry* (pp. 256–268). New York: Cambridge University Press.

Moll, L. C., & Greenberg, J. (1990). Creating zones of possibilities: Combining social contexts for instruction. In L. C. Moll (Ed.), *Vygotsky and education* (pp. 319–348). Cambridge, MA: Cambridge University Press.

Monaghan, E. J. (1991). Family literacy in early 18th-century Boston: Cotton Mather and his children. *Reading Research Quarterly, 26*, 342–370.

Morrow, L. M., & Young, J. (1997). A family literacy program connecting school and home: Effects on attitude, motivation, and literacy achievement. *Journal of Educational Psychology, 89*, 736–742.

Moynihan, D. P. (1965). *The Negro family: The case for national action*. Washington, DC: Department of Labor, Office of Policy, Planning, and Research.

Neuman, S. B., Hagedorn, T., Celano, D., & Daly, P. (1995). Toward a collaborative approach to parent involvement in early education: A study of teenage mothers in an African-American community. *American Educational Research Journal, 32*(4), 801–827.

Nieto, S. (1999). *The light in their eyes: Creating multicultural learning communities*. New York: Teachers College Press.

Ortiz, R. W., Stile, S., & Brown, C. (1999, September). Early literacy activities of fathers: Reading and writing with young children. *Young Children, 54*(5), 16–18.

Osterling, J. P. (2001). Waking the sleeping giant: Engaging and capitalizing on the sociocultural strengths of the Latino community. Bilingual *Research Journal, 25*(1–2), 59–88.

Parecki, A., Paris, G., & Siedenburg, J. (1997). Family literacy: Examining practice and issues of effectiveness. *Journal of Adolescent and Adult Literacy, 40*(8), 596–605.

Parecki, A. D., Paris, S. G., & Seidenburg, J. L. (1996). *Characteristics of effective family literacy programs in Michigan* (Tech. Rep. No. TR96-07). Philadelphia: University of Pennsylvania, National Center on Adult Literacy.

Puchner, L. D. (1997). *Family literacy in cultural context: Lessons from two case studies*. Philadelphia: National Center on Adult Literacy.

Purcell-Gates, V. (1993). Issues for family literacy research: Voices from the trenches. *Language Arts, 70*, 670–677.

Purcell-Gates, V. (1995a). *Other people's words: The cycle of low literacy*. Cambridge, MA: Harvard University Press.

Purcell-Gates, V. (1995b). Research for the 21st century: A diversity of perspectives among researchers. *Language Arts, 72*, 56–60.

Quintero, E. (1999). The new faces of Head Start: Learning from culturally diverse families. *Early Education & Development, 10*(4), 475–497.

Roberts, R. E., Richards, L. N., & Bengston, V. L. (1991). Intergenerational solidarity in families: Untangling the ties that bind. *Marriage and Family Review, 16*, 11–46.

St.Pierre, R. G., & Layzer, J. I. (1999). Using home visits for multiple purposes: The Comprehensive Child Development Program. *Future of Children, 9*, 134–151.

Snow, C. E., Burns, S., & Griffin, P. (1998). *Preventing reading difficulties in young children*. Washington, DC: National Academy Press.

Spielman, J. (2001). The family photography project: "We will just read what the pictures tell us." *The Reading Teacher, 54*(8), 762–770.

Stack, C. B. (1974). *All our kin: Strategies for survival in a Black community*. New York: Harper & Row.

Stanton, J. (1991). *Family resource, support, and parent education programs: The power of a preventive approach*. Family Impact Seminar. Meeting Highlights and Background Briefing Report, Washington, DC.

Street, B. V. (Ed.). (2001). *Literacy and development: Ethnographic perspectives*. New York: Routledge.

Strickland, K. (1995). *Literacy, not labels: Celebrating students' strengths through whole language*. Portsmouth, NH: Heinemann.

Taylor, D., & Dorsey-Gaines, C. (1988). *Growing up literate: Learning from inner city families*. Portsmouth, NH: Heinemann.

Taylor, D. (Ed.). (1997). *Many families, many literacies: An International declaration of principles.* Portsmouth, NH: Heinemann.

Taylor, E. B. (1871). *Primitive cultutre.* London: John Murray.

Wasik, B. A. (1997). Volunteer tutoring programs: Do we know what works? *Phi Delta Kappan, 79,* 282–287.

Whitehouse, M., & Colvin, C. (2001). "Reading" families: Deficit discourse and family literacy. *Theory Into Practice, 40*(3), 212–219.

Willett, J., & Bloome, D. (1992). Literacy, language, school and community: A community-centered perspective. In C. Hedley & A. Carrasquillo (Eds.), *Whole language and the bilingual learner* (pp. 35–57). Norwood, NJ: Ablex.

Winter, M., & Rouse, J. (1990). Fostering intergenerational literacy: The Missouri parents as teachers program. *The Reading Teacher, 43,* 382–386.

Yamauchi, L. A., & Tharp, R. G. (1995). Culturally compatible conversations in Native American classrooms. *Linguistics and Education, 7,* 349–367.

Zuberi, T. (2001). *Thicker than blood: An essay on how racial statistics lie.* Minneapolis, MN: University of Minnesota Press.

22

An Ecocultural Perspective on Early Literacy: Avoiding the Perils of School for NonMainstream Children

Lynne Vernon-Feagans,
Darlene Head-Reeves, and
Kirsten Kainz
University of North Carolina at Chapel Hill

The terms *emergent literacy* and *family literacy* denote approaches to literacy research, as well as approaches to literacy intervention programs for families and children. These terms encompass many different theoretical orientations, from Taylor's (1983) landmark book about young children learning to read and write to the influential work of the National Center for Family Literacy directed by Darling; to the oral language basis of literacy advanced by Heath (1983), Dickinson (1994), and Vernon-Feagans (1996), among others; to Fletcher and Lyon's (1998) emphasis on phonological awareness/processing.

These diverse perspectives on literacy and its acquisition have in common the passionate energy of their proponents, the certainty of their purpose, and their desire to improve the lives and life trajectories of children and families through literacy. Yet these perspectives often disagree fundamentally with respect to their basic assumptions, theoretical orientations, and intervention strategies. Some literacy proponents argue that, for young children, phonology is the most important code to crack in learning to read (Fletcher & Lyon, 1998), but others champion the importance of both oral language and phonological processing (Snow, Burns, & Griffin, 1998). Still others consider home and preschool literacy practices most important (Dickinson & Tabors, 2001). All of these professionals and their perspectives have gained legitimacy through the interpretation of research findings and by their own theoretical perspectives on children's development. Each has made some contribution to an understanding of the literacy skills of children and families. Heretofore, absent from these literacy controversies, we intend here to suggest a way of thinking about emergent and family literacy that can clarify some of the underlying philosophies of these perspectives, as well as the importance of accepting a perspective that embraces a more ecological and cultural approach to literacy acquisition.

This chapter lays out an ecocultural model of literacy, with a particular emphasis on some of the false premises that have influenced the family and emergent literacy approaches to literacy acquisition. Unlike many other models that examine literacy and early learning, with the child and/or family as the central target(s) of intervention, our model focuses on the community and the professionals within our institutions who provide the leadership in the teaching of literacy. The target for competence and readiness is not conceptualized as residing within the child or family, but rather in the capability of the institutions where children and families are engaged. As the professionals within these institutions, we are the ones who need to develop strategies for teaching literacy skills, regardless of prevalent beliefs about social class and culture as impediments to literacy. By placing the onus on professionals and communities for teaching all children, we transfer responsibility for children's learning from the family to the institutions and professionals who serve them. The failure of children and families to acquire literacy is really ours, not the failure of the children and the families. This perspective may seem to be only a modest shift in thinking, but it does shift the focus of intervention from the children and families to the professionals and their institutions. Although most professional educators would agree that teaching all children is their responsibility, subtle ways of framing the issues can shift the blame to families and their children, in ways that can actually hurt the learning process. We have become convinced that our ecocultural approach to teaching and learning, whether it is a literacy program delivered in the home to children and families or a program delivered in schools, can help us better recognize the diverse needs of families and their children and thus can lead to better programs. We discuss our perspective on early literacy by presenting a model that emphasizes the cultural and contextual factors important to an understanding of early literacy skills.

AN ECOCULTURAL MODEL OF EARLY LITERACY

Our model of early literacy combines Bronfenbrenner's (1979) ecological view of child development with a cultural view of the myths that lead us astray in our thinking about early development (Heath, 1983; Ogbu, 1982, 1991; Rogoff, 1990, 2003; and Vernon-Feagans, 1996). Readiness for school and learning in our model does not reside within the child or family, but is squarely situated in our institutions and in the powerful players within our societal institutions. As the heads of social service agencies, principals of schools, teachers, professors at universities, or policymakers, we have the power to develop literacy competence in children. Often, however, we lack the knowledge base about children and families, even as we develop programs to promote children's literacy development. Families with varied cultural and economic backgrounds can be challenging to serve, but an emphasis on a reflective approach to families can help us serve all children appropriately and effectively.

We have organized our model to represent three major spheres of influence on the readiness of communities and schools to teach our children. We use Bronfenbrenner's framework (1979) to describe these areas of influence. At the most proximal sphere of influence on children, Bronfenbrenner described microsystems and mesosystems. The *microsystems* are the daily settings in which the child participates, and can include the home, the child care center, an extended family home, the church, or the public school. Each of these settings imposes different demands for behavior and generally includes different adults and peers. The better the connections among these settings, the better the child can make the transition from one setting to another. These connections are called *mesosystems* and include a variety of elements, including belief systems, attitudes about children, the relationships among the people themselves, and between the settings. Thus, when the attitudes and beliefs of the adults in the two settings are similar and the adults in the two settings have strong interpersonal relationships, the child adapts better in both settings. Lacking these similarities, children may find the transition difficult from one microsetting to another. These microsystems have been the ones most targeted for intervention. Family literacy programs have often targeted the home as the microsystem that can benefit from intervention (Darling & Paull, 1994).

The next level in Bronfenbrenner's model is the exosystem. The *exosystem* contains settings in which the child does not participate; nevertheless, these settings influence the child's life and development. Some of these settings might include the parents' workplace or schoolboard meetings. Although these have been shown to be important in the lives of young children, they do not compel us to address them in this part of the model.

For most of the chapter, we concentrate on a third important sphere of influence: the macrosystem. We do this because it appears to be the system that has received the least attention among the important influences on children's lives. The *macrosystem* constitutes the beliefs and policies in the larger environment that can influence child outcomes. For instance, welfare policies that require more mothers to enter the workforce may indirectly affect young children's development, as their mothers' attitudes about work change and as the need for child care outside the home increases. Beliefs about individual freedom and responsibility, rooted in our Constitution, can also influence the ways in which families view themselves and the ways in which professionals intervene with families. We believe that these macrosystem beliefs, including many myths in our larger society, influence the readiness of communities and schools to receive children. These myths, or false beliefs, often go unquestioned by many of us and yet exert a powerful force on society's thinking. In addition, they may be impervious to change, because we have yet to confront their deleterious influence on children and families. Many scholars have described these myths in different ways (Auerbach, 1989, 1995a, 1995b; Taylor, 1997; Taylor & Dorsey-Gaines, 1988). We extend their comments by placing these myths in a larger framework that helps reshape emergent and family literacy research. Our review of the literature reinterprets some of the research, from a more ecocultural perspective.

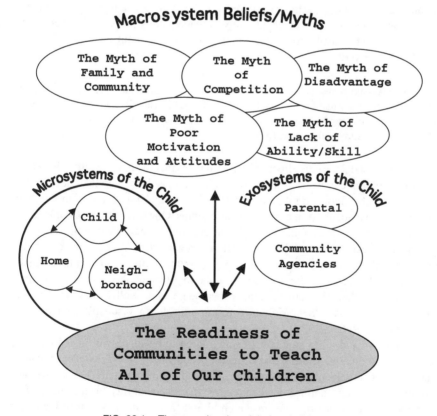

FIG. 22.1. The ecocultural model of early literacy.

THE MACROSYSTEM: SOCIETAL MYTHS AND BELIEFS
THAT INFLUENCE CHILD LITERACY

In Bronfenbrenner's model (1979), the macrosystem includes the beliefs and policies in the larger society that affect children's lives and development. This area often goes unexplored in studies of literacy acquisition, especially with respect to the belief systems that underlie many of our approaches and attitudes about children, which in turn influence our teaching of children. Important to understand is the larger society's beliefs about families living in poverty and families from oppressed ethnic groups—families that are out of the mainstream of the American middle class. Many of these beliefs have helped shape policies and programs for these children and their families, including the family literacy programs, over the last decade. Many of these beliefs about the importance of the family in the child's life, and the importance of education, have been beneficial, even critical, to the success of programs. But some of the beliefs in the larger society have been harmful in shaping our programs for families and children because they have been based on false assumptions about families. We plan to help dispel some of the myths that keep us from developing effective programs for nonmainstream American families and their children.

No matter what their backgrounds, almost all children come to school ready and eager to learn. Several studies of poor and minority families confirm that almost all poor children come to school with high hopes for success, from families that value education and have great aspirations for their children's educational future (Fitzgerald, Spiegel, & Cunningham, 1991; Vernon-Feagans, 1996). Yet many children outside the mainstream of the middle class culture do poorly in school, particularly in reading. We generally attribute the failures of most children to their poor environments and rarely to inadequately prepared teachers, schools, or other institutions. This attribution reflects underlying myths about poverty and ethnicity. As Taylor (1997) observed:

> Sex, race, economic status, and setting cannot be used as significant correlates of literacy. The myths and stereotypes that create images of specific groups (families who are poor, inner-city families, teenage mothers and their children) have no relevance when we stop counting and start observing and working with people. (p. 117)

Perhaps the most deleterious effects of these myths is that the mainstream beliefs about poor and minority children can be transmitted to children themselves, who then develop the belief that failure inevitably looms on the horizon (Steele, 1992). This result is, in fact, the single most insidious consequence of maintaining these myths. One can find an example of this early self-doubt in nonmainstream children in the description of the transition to school among a group of poor African American children (Vernon-Feagans, 1996). Their conversations among friends and family were audiotaped as they played outside after school in their kindergarten year. One of the kindergarten boys, Melvin, spoke to a teenage boy of his excitement about entering school and then his realization that he would never do well, even in kindergarten. The teenager was heard to say, "See, Melvin, you stop likin' to go to school when you get there" (Vernon-Feagans, 1996, p. 122).

Helping Melvin and other nonmainstream children to be successful in school, by, for example, promoting positive learning experiences, becomes easier when we as educators reject the prevalent myths in the mainstream culture. By challenging the beliefs about the values and skills of nonmainstream families, we can remove the responsibility for the successful acquisition of literacy and other skills from the child and family and place it on the community and its schools. We now describe five of these false beliefs or myths that have helped shape the way we develop school and other intervention programs for nonmainstream children and their families: (a) the myth of individual competition and hard work, (b) the myth of disadvantage and difference, (c) the myth of dysfunctional parenting and families, (d) the myth of lack of ability or skill, and (e) the myth of low motivation. Debunking these myths helped us reinterpret the failure of the nonmainstream children in school and other programs as a failure of these programs, rather than as a failure of the children in them. We have chosen the myths we consider to have the most detrimental influence on the development of early family intervention and literacy programs for nonmainstream families and their children.

The Myth of Individual Competition and Hard Work

Our society promulgates a general belief that individuals and families are responsible for their own destinies and that the failure of families to get and to hold good jobs, and to take advantage of opportunities in the larger community, bespeaks a lack of moral character of those individuals and families (Auerbach, 1989, 1995a; Purcell-Gates, 1998, 2000). Furthermore, American society applauds individual achievement and personal competition. Almost all of our schools, and even our community institutions, foster this individualistic belief system, but it rarely underlies the belief systems of the families and children being served (Heath, 1983; Vernon-Feagans, 1996).

The idea that home life transmits the value of hard work, and that this transmission translates into achievement at school, is rooted in a work ethic that permeates Western capitalist societies. In *The Protestant Ethic and the Spirit of Capitalism,* Max Weber (1905/1958) outlined the role of Western religions and a corresponding work ethic as the foundation for modern capitalist societies. Formally defined, the *Protestant work ethic* is a "set of values embodied in early Protestantism, which has controversially been linked to the development of modern capitalism" (Marshall, 1998). Weber found Protestantism providing a rationale for hard work and discipline as a form of religious asceticism or self-denial. Then the church and home transmitted these values to children as they grew. Moreover, hard work and the success of individuals and families provided outward signs that members of the community were predestined to be among the elect, or God's chosen ones. Eventually, a cultural axiom became established: Hard work, through competition in the workplace and at home, leads to success—a sign of moral rectitude. Unfortunately, the converse principle also appeared: Lack of success means lack of hard work, which is a sign of moral weakness attributable to the individual and to their family. This myth underlies the new welfare reform in the last 5 years and explains our attitudes about many of the children and families whose lack of economic success we in the larger society link to a belief that this signals some form of moral weakness.

Katz (1989) reiterated the moral tones of hard work in his history of poverty in the latter half of the 20th century. According to Katz, since the early 1800s, U.S. social and educational policy has distinguished between the deserving poor and the undeserving poor, so designated according to their ability and willingness to work. Early in the country's history, the deserving poor were understood as unable to participate in hard work because of illness, age, or disability. The undeserving poor belonged to a class of paupers whose supposed vice and insolence explained their poverty. Although the terminology has changed through time, the notion of the undeserving poor has persisted. In the 1960s, as academicians rediscovered poverty, the notion of the undeserving became intermingled with theories of a culture of poverty and cultural deprivation. Consequently, we often understand poverty as intergenerational and resulting from patterns of behavior and interactions specific to the poor.

Thus, cultural myths regarding the morality of hard work and concomitant success underlie modern interpretations of family literacy. More specifically, the current understanding of family literacy emphasizes the value of parental effort in a child's literacy development. We expect parents to work on behalf of their children, to provide appropriate contexts, materials, and activities that promote school-related learning in the home. We understand children's abilities, measured at school entry, to be the fruits of parents' hard work. Alternatively, we blame the family context when children begin school with skills that differ from, or lag behind, their peers. Such limited understanding of family literacy and parental efforts fails to accommodate the diversity of home life and family arrangements in the United States. Further, by refusing to expand our understanding of readiness for literacy, we may relegate some students to almost certain failure during the early school years, when reading is so important for success, thereby establishing and maintaining a cycle of low literacy.

Highly related to the concept of hard work is the belief that competition and individual responsibility for hard work are highly desirable. Yet, for those out of the mainstream and for those the mainstream culture persecutes, competition and individual responsibility may actually be disadvantageous. Among oppressed groups, collective will and sharing of responsibility often lead to protection from the mainstream culture and survival (Ogbu, 1982, 1985; Sutton-Smith & Roberts, 1981). One can observe various beliefs of nonmainstream America about competition in the games children play. Sutton-Smith and Roberts (1981) found the differences in these games arising from the sociocultural perspectives of their communities. The two main perspectives are *playing to win* and *playing to play*. These two opposing philosophies arise both from different worldviews and from the economic circumstances of the cultural group. Western mainstream culture certainly stresses playing to win; thus, it is no surprise that more competitive games are played in the mainstream culture than in minority and nonmainstream cultures of poverty (Sutton-Smith & Roberts, 1981; Vernon-Feagans, 1996). These nonmainstream groups of families, who often find themselves economically and racially discriminated against by the mainstream culture, need their mutual support to survive both materially and culturally, and this need naturally appears in the games their children play. An extension of this concept can also be seen in the way adults guide children. In nonmainstream and African American families, several adults may oversee the welfare of a child, so that success is seen as a joint effort extending beyond the child's nuclear family. In this way, oppressed cultures have forged alliances across people of different ages and from different families to protect themselves from the more powerful mainstream community.

The noncompetitive games Sutton-Smith and Roberts (1981) described were prevalent in the historical frontier culture of mainstream America, when survival was an issue for everyone. Games like jump rope and limbo were observed frequently in this early period because of the need for children to learn solidarity and commitment to one another across age and skill levels. These games, unlike many competitive games, included children of widely different ages and abilities, and they provided for children of different ages a chance to work together for a common purpose and to enjoy one another, no matter what the skill level of the individual participant. There were no real winners or losers in these games, and older children helped the younger children perform their best. Rogoff (1990, 2003) suggests that this apprenticeship model of learning, with higher skilled players helping beginners accomplish the goals of a task or game, can have great benefits even among mainstream children.

Vernon-Feagans's (1996) study of children's play after school in kindergarten revealed differences in the play between mainstream and poor African American children, which supported Sutton-Smith's observations about play as a reflection of cultural needs. Overall, mainstream middle-class children played almost exclusively with children their own age, or a year or two younger, and played more competitive games (20% of the time vs. 8% of the time), compared to the African American children. On the other hand, the African American children engaged in more noncompetitive games and sang songs much more often than the mainstream children (24 vs. 11%). These noncompetitive games allowed for children of many varying ages to play because winners and losers were less important to the execution of the goals of the games. For instance, limbo was observed to include children as young as 1 year and as old as 18.

Furthermore, 34% of the talk of African American girls centered on rhyming games and songs like "Little Sally Walker," which required these children to dance and to add a new rhyming word before each refrain. This particular song had been sung almost word for word 200 years ago in colonial America, when cooperative games were important even in the mainstream culture (Courlander, 1963).

Vernon-Feagans also suggested that poor African American boys talked more than either African American girls or mainstream boys and girls. Their ability to engage in joint storytelling, which included complex sequences of events and complex language, was superior in most ways to the mainstream children's talk in their neighborhoods (Feagans & Haskins, 1986; Vernon-Feagans, 1996). Still, this sophisticated talk failed somehow to translate into superior language performance in school. In fact, a negative correlation appeared between the quantity and quality of neighborhood talk and a teacher's ratings of language sophistication for the African American children, even as a positive correlation emerged for mainstream children.

Unfortunately, few teachers capitalize on these storytelling skills and games, which include rhyming and other aspects of sophisticated emergent literacy, for developing literacy partnerships between nonmainstream families and literacy programs. In addition, the tradition of older children teaching younger children, which is so prevalent in many African American communities, has yet to become a central strategy for learning in mainstream schools and family programs.

The Myth of Disadvantage and Difference

The word *disadvantaged* became a popular way to characterize the environments of children living in poverty, no doubt because of the 1966 book *The Disadvantaged Child*, by Frost and Hawkes. Children in poverty certainly are disadvantaged in that they have fewer resources than other children. But the term has come to connote disadvantage in almost every aspect of the biology and environments of poor children and their families. The gradual reaction to the overuse of *disadvantaged* has been to substitute the milder word *difference*. Unfortunately, this term has the same problem as *disadvantaged*. Even though the term was meant to signify only differences between poor and/or minority families and their mainstream counterparts, it soon came to mean differences related to disadvantage, as well as something less desirable. We still hear the term *difference* used in our teacher training institutions, and it still contains within it the belief that children who have different experiences from more mainstream children do not have as many good experiences for schooling as mainstream children.

The book entitled *Schooling Disadvantaged Children*, by Natriello, McDill, and Pallas (1990), provides a good example of right motives, but false beliefs, in the application of the word *disadvantage* to poor and minority children. The authors reviewed the dispute about using the word, but persisted in using it anyway. They presented two reasons not to use this term when talking about poor or ethnically diverse populations. First, defining a group of children as disadvantaged misdirects the intervention efforts away from the institutions responsible for educating children and toward the problems of the children themselves. The onus falls on the wrong people. Second, identifying children as disadvantaged can also lead to a self-fulfilling prophecy that hinders learning. That is, the children begin to believe they are disadvantaged and to see themselves as unable to succeed. Both of these points are strong reasons to avoid using the term *disadvantaged*.

Even after acknowledging the credibility of their own criticisms, Natriello et al. (1990) decided to use the word, but broadened the definition so that disadvantage could occur in three places: the home, the community, and the school. This expansion improved the construct somewhat, but it still invited an educational institution to blame the victim (the family) for learning failures. The authors used the following example in their working definition *disadvantage*, which indicted the families and communities they purported to help:

> There are several implications of this definition that deserve special comment. First, families and communities may be viewed as educationally deficient without necessarily being socially deficient. For example, a strong, loving family may simply be unequipped to provide an educationally stimulating environment for its children. This may stem from cultural differences that make experiences in the family incompatible with those in U.S. schools or from economic limitations that leave families without sufficient resources beyond those necessary for survival. (p. 13)

This kind of argument typifies those that lead many benevolent educators to create a paternalistic system that devalues the experiences of children out of the mainstream. Most families out of this mainstream culture provide stimulating and valuable learning experiences for their children, but these experiences may not be the ones mainstream schools value (Heath, 1983; Taylor, 1997; Taylor & Dorsey-Gaines, 1988). Trying to understand and use the experiences of nonmainstream children may challenge professionals, but it can help dispel the harmful myths in the larger society.

These subtle attitudes and beliefs, which professionals apply to poor and ethnically diverse children and their families, reach children in the classroom through such practices as ability group formation and the segregation of those possessing or lacking certain skills. These attitudes convey to children a belief about their ability to learn, reinforced by the actual practices the teachers employ. First, no matter what their potential, children in poverty, and especially minority children in poverty, tend to be placed in lower ability groups in early elementary school than do other children (Vernon-Feagans, 1996). This practice reflects teachers' assumptions that children reared in poverty need compensatory programs, are unlikely to progress at a rapid rate, and rarely function at the same level as children from more privileged backgrounds. Although all teachers in Vernon-Feagans's 1996 study said that they believed children could progress to higher ability groups and that placement in the groups did not mean less complex material was being presented, the data clearly suggests otherwise. The teachers all seemed well prepared and handled the groups well. The attention and work behavior of the children in all the ability groups was observed to be high. Yet, the complexity of the lessons in the higher ability groups was higher than in the lower ability groups, and the teachers seemed to be more comfortable and effective with these higher groups. In the time between kindergarten and second grade, few children shifted into a higher ability group. In fact, the African American children, who in kindergarten were found to be in low-ability groups 35% of the time, occupied the lowest ability groups 60% of the time in second grade. Only 6% of the mainstream group appeared in the lowest ability groups by second grade. Other studies have found that the early performance of children in the first few years of life lays the foundation for later school performance because academic trajectories are difficult to alter after the first few years of formal schooling (Alexander & Entwisle, 1988).

Second, Vernon-Feagans (1996) reported that poor African American children received less effective guidance from teachers than mainstream children, even at the individual level. In a book-reading task, teachers asked concrete and abstract questions about the book. The results revealed that mainstream and African American children were able to correctly answer the same number of questions about the story, but that teachers offered less useful responses to the incorrect answers from African American children.

Overall, the results of this study suggest that poor African American children are at risk for failing in school, despite a desire to succeed and an adequate level of competence. The teachers appeared to act on an impression of disadvantage by placing children in low-ability groups to compensate for their lack of readiness and by being less able to teach them, despite a competence commensurate with that of their more advantaged peers in answering questions.

Several other studies of poor white children and their families show that they often get labeled "disadvantaged," when evaluated in the preschool or school by their teachers and by their interactions with adults in the school setting, but when observed at home these same children often appeared to be receiving rich experiences in their families (Feagans & Haskins, 1986; Snow, Barnes, Chandler, Goodman, & Hemphill, 1991; Tizard, Blatchford, Burke, Farquhar, & Plewis, 1988; Tizard & Hughes, 1984). Tizard and Hughes concluded that, "in our opinion, it is time to shift the emphasis away from what parents should learn from professionals, and towards what professionals can learn from studying parents and children at home" (p. 267).

A number of studies have shown the importance of the early years in school, especially for poor and ethnically diverse children: Early success leads them toward more success later on, but early failure is difficult to overcome later (Alexander & Entwisle, 1988; Snow et al., 1991). As Donaldson (1978) observed, these small gaps between children at school entry get wider, if they are not soon closed. The myth of disadvantage widens these gaps, even when accompanied by earnest intentions of remediation and compensatory programs.

The Myth of Dysfunctional Parenting and Families

Closely related to the disadvantage difference myth is the constellation of myths about the families and communities of these children. Children who come from single-parent, mother-headed households tend to be categorized as disadvantaged. This fact, coupled with poverty, has been shown to be a negative predictor of school success (Huston, 1991), but, within these families, one finds many strengths that compensate for an absent father and the lack of economic resources. Unfortunately, these "social address" variables, as Bronfenbrenner (1979) called them, such as single parenthood, poverty, and social class, are laden with social values that mark children from these kinds of backgrounds as coming from dysfunctional family environments. Phrases like "single parent," and the often-accompanying "poverty" or "low income," evoke images of an impoverished family life for these children. Social address variables like these hardly describe the processes that occur in families, processes that may be different from mainstream families, but that are complex and rich, nevertheless.

A number of studies have documented the rich environment available in families whose structure and functioning differs from those of mainstream families (Heath, 1983; Stack, 1974, 1996). These accounts often describe a rich extended network of family members to whom children talk and learn from. As one can see from the interviews Vernon-Feagans (1996) conducted with both mainstream and African American families, all the families valued education and saw it as the avenue toward ultimate success for their children. Beliefs about families and communities, and even about what was "best for our children," proved to be remarkably similar for both the mainstream and African American families. Both groups of families saved money for their children's future college education. Fitzgerald et al. (1991) found similar results when they asked African American and mainstream families to discuss their educational beliefs and values. One must be alert to the many similarities between mainstream and nonmainstream families when it comes to family values and attitudes toward education.

Some differences between mainstream and nonmainstream families have led, however, to myths about these differences, including the following two illustrative examples. One difference centers on family structure and poverty and on the supposition that more nonmainstream children, in nonnuclear families with fewer economic resources, find it more difficult to cope with the stresses in life. The second difference involves discipline, and the assumption that

African American families hold more authoritarian views of parenting and use more physical punishment.

Many studies show African American families and families living in poverty to be more liable to have bad jobs, to have less education, and to be headed by a single female than are mainstream families (see Duncan & Brooks-Gunn, 1997; Huston, 1991). Families out of the mainstream, with fewer economic resources, have also been found to have poorer mental health, more health problems, and a host of associated problems related to both income and education. Although these factors can, of course, have real negative consequences for children and families, most poor families have strengths and devise strategies that address their economic and family realities. In the research and policy work, one finds an apparent compulsion to portray families in need by generalizing across the data. In reading recent work on poverty, a reader must marshal a careful analysis of the results to gain a differentiated picture of families living in poverty. There is a myth that many of these families are dysfunctional because a lack of resources creates stress that prevents them from supporting their children's learning in school.

The mainstream culture has always valued the self-sufficient nuclear family, while ignoring the important benefits in other kinds of family structures that can promote child development. For example, many children in nonmainstream families live in extended family networks (Stack, 1974). These often complex arrangements can expose a child to a variety of influential people who go ignored by our intervention programs. For instance, in a single month, the average African American child in the Vernon-Feagans study (1996) saw 37 different relatives outside the nuclear family: the mainstream children saw on average only two different relatives. This startling statistic suggests a different, but rich environment, which includes multiple-generation child care, sibling and cousin care, and a host of complicated arrangements that maximize economic resources for the benefit of a family and its children. Understanding how these families manage to share resources, rear children, and prepare them for life has yet to be fully understood by the mainstream culture and has yet to be incorporated into most family programs that target the mother or the household for intervention.

Another example of a documented difference between mainstream and African American families involves discipline practices (Nightingale, 1993; Vernon-Feagans, 1996). Poor African American families have been found to rely on physical punishment for children, and mainstream families have been found to use this form of punishment much less frequently. This difference in disciplining may explain at least some of the alienation of African American families from mainstream schools and from other social institutions in their communities. Much appears in the middle-class research literature about the evils of physical punishment, and the myth has taken hold that physical punishment equates to child abuse. No doubt, physical punishment can lead to abuse, and, coupled with the poverty and stress of family life, this form of punishment may at times be dysfunctional. But one should hesitate to consider the judicious use of physical punishment to be a bad parenting practice without understanding its roots and its effect on the children. Recent work by Deater-Deckard, Dodge, Bates, & Pettit (1998) found physical punishment to be related to negative outcomes for mainstream children, but not, in general, for African American children, which suggests a difference in meaning of physical punishment within these two family groups.

In interviews with African American families, Vernon-Feagans (1996) found physical punishment generally to be used with forethought, in response to purposeful disobedience or cruelty to others by children. The families believed in the appropriateness of this discipline approach and even allowed those outside the family, with authority in the community, to apply physical punishment to their children. This form of punishment had been used within the culture for as long as they knew and had produced good and kind adults. Yet, mainstream professionals, who misunderstand the meaning of many of the different behaviors in nonmainstream families, often dismiss or ignore benign effects from judicious use of physical punishment.

In a book about inner-city youth, *On the Edge: A History of Poor Black Children and Their American Dreams*, Nightingale (1993) attributes some of the violence and suffering of inner-city children to physical punishment. Nightingale, in short, blamed the victims. He certainly made a strong argument for a decrease in the excessive use of force on children, but he failed to understand the historical roots of judicious physical punishment in the Black community that had led to positive outcomes for children. This passage shows Nightingale failing to acknowledge the African American values that allow for physical discipline:

> The particular enthusiasm for American traditions of forceful child rearing among inner-city parents—and their rejection of "progressive" philosophies—also reflects their own experiences of indignities and powerless feelings brought on by poverty, troubles with employment, and racism. However, for both parents and children, the tradition itself, the respectability of its Christian and mainstream origins, and the official sanction it receives from the law-and-order policies of American's police, courts, and prisons all help to make the forceful child-rearing approach an important source of legitimacy for values of violence in the inner city. Also, the tradition can be used all too often to legitimate parental behavior that leaves children with hurtful and even traumatic memories. (p. 81)

This myth of bad childrearing practices receives support in the schools, which uniformly reject the legitimacy of physical punishment in certain settings. A mother in the Vernon-Feagans study (1996) described a typical incident, which reflected this conflict in values between the mainstream discipline practices and African American discipline traditions. The mother described how she had "popped" her child (a quick, loud spank on the backside) for talking back to an adult at a Sunday picnic. The child, only 8 years old at the time, turned around and threatened the mother: "I'm gonna tell my teacher on you. You'll see, you're not supposed to hit children. You can go to jail." Although this back talk resulted in another quick pop, the mother admitted she was a bit worried about her child saying anything about the incident to a teacher in the mainstream school. But mostly she was angry that the schools would probably reject her discipline practices. She considered the public schools too lenient, allowing children to misbehave without adequate punishment. Clearly, schools may not want to sanction the physical punishment of children, but, if the schools had been able to recognize the legitimacy of judicious physical punishment, they could have helped to prevent the further alienation of African American families. The message from education about proper disciplinary values is yet another way the system devalues the families of the African American children.

All professionals who work with children from poor and minority families should acknowledge and respect different views on childrearing practices and guard against this myth of dysfunctional parenting. Programs that even implicitly devalue parents invariably encounter difficulty helping families help their children succeed.

The Myth of a Lack of Ability or Skill

The fourth myth, and the first related directly to the child, centers on a child's lack of ability or skill. Although the stronger version of this myth lost currency by the late 1960s, it remains today, in a more subtle, but often insidious, form. Particularly within the educational community, educators generally consider lack of ability to be a false premise. But a remnant accepts the supposition that poor and minority children disproportionately lack the skills to do well in school and need some form of remediation to catch up with children from more enriched environments. The stronger form of this myth recently resurfaced in more subtle scholarship in books like *The Bell Curve* (Herrnstein & Murray, 1994), suggesting that racial IQ differences reflect real genetic differences and implying that early intervention efforts to decrease this difference are futile.

Studies of poor and minority children rarely find these children's skills to be reliably less developed than those of other children. Heath (1983), for example, found elaborate and sophisticated storytelling among very young African American boys. Feagans and Haskins (1986) and Vernon-Feagans (1996) found poor African American boys talking more than middle-income White children and found the quality of their talk to be superior to that of middle-income children. Tizard and Hughes (1994) found elaborate and complex talk between poor mothers and their 4-year-old daughters at home, but this kind of talk among these same girls failed to emerge at preschool. A theme that runs through these studies suggests that language skills in the homes of poor children seem to be far superior to their language skills in school. Clearly, these children could display language abilities at home, but the schools apparently lacked a context that fostered this competence. But school is, of course, where children are evaluated for their abilities and skills, and displaying less competence at school naturally leads to an inference of a lack of ability.

Even in cases in which African Americans have succeeded within the system, they continually confront expectations of failure. In his autobiographical book about growing up African American in the United States, Staples (1994) recalled one of his first academic experiences in graduate school at the University of Chicago. As he talked to a faculty member about one of her classes, she said to him, "We have been horrible to the Black people, we have treated them so badly! We have to make it up. It may take you a little longer to get the degree, but you will get it" (p. 26). This benevolent but paternalistic attitude had its impact. Staples' reaction to this statement almost certainly reflects the thought processes of much younger children in their early school years, when they are too young to articulate this myth. Staples wrote about his reaction to the well-intentioned psychology professor:

> I was numb. It seemed Erika [the professor] had told me that I was a dull child, to be treated with pity and patience, that I should accept her condolences in advance for the difficulty I would have. The best I could do was nod until I got my senses back. Back at the hotel, I went over my documents. The transcript said dean's list, dean's list, dean's list. It said Alpha Chi National Scholarship Honor Society. It said cum laude graduate, and I cursed myself for falling six one-hundredths of a percentage point short of magna cum laude. I read again the wilted clipping from *The Delaware County Daily Times*—"Brent A. Staples . . . has won a Danforth Fellowship for advanced study for the Ph.D. degree. . . . Nowhere did the story say that I was a foundling who'd gotten into college by accident. (pp. 26, 36)

Steele (1992) suggested a compelling argument for why so many Black students fail in the school system, when other poor children do not fail at the same high rate. He concluded that the devaluation of their ability and skill is almost inescapable:

> Sooner or later it forces on its victims two painful realizations. The first is that society is preconditioned to see the worst in them. Black students quickly learn that acceptance, if it is to be won at all, will be hard-won. The second is that even if a Black student achieves exoneration in one setting—with the teacher and fellow students in one classroom, or at one level of schooling, for example—this approval will have to be rewon in the next classroom, at the next level of schooling. Of course, individual characteristics that enhance one's value in society—skills, class status, appearance, and success—can diminish the racial devaluation one faces. And sometimes the effort to prove oneself fuels achievement. But few from any group could hope to sustain so daunting

and everlasting a struggle. Thus, I am afraid, too many Black students are left hopeless and deeply vulnerable in America's classrooms. (p. 74)

Thus, the devastating myth of poor ability and skill persists. The continual barrage of information about the achievement gap raises so many issues over poor and minority children's abilities because the gap between minority and majority achievement and between White and, especially, African American achievement remains large, even after the desegregation of schools in the 1970s and 1980s. A number of national panels and policy analysts have offered a host of reasons and a set of different solutions for this gap in achievement (see Jencks & Phillips, 1998; Lieberman & Hoody, 1998). Yet, even after decades of trying to eradicate this gap, the United States remains unsuccessful and some recent data suggests that the gap is growing (Lee, 2002). Young children who are poor or from minority families clearly hear about the achievement gap in their families and schools and can easily interpret these data as suggesting that they face enormous obstacles to success in the current system. Thus, the debate can serve poor and minority children only if they see institutions changing now in order to help them succeed. This myth of inadequate abilities and skills must be fought, and children must understand that they come to school with the experiences they need to acquire the skills that spell success. We professionals often underestimate the effect of our beliefs on others, and especially on children. It may be difficult to celebrate the experiences and abilities of all children, but it is nonetheless crucial for poor and minority children who have known discrimination from early childhood and who need to feel their unique abilities, skills, and experiences affirmed.

The Myth of Poor Motivation

Children from poor and minority families are often characterized as having poor attitudes and lacking the motivation to learn. This belief—the myth of poor motivation—is often directly attributed to the children themselves, and their teachers too often invoke it as a way to understand such undesirable school behavior as overactivity or a high absentee record. This perceived lack of motivation is often seen as a reflection of the lack of ambition in the children; the children do not want to better themselves; or they do not value formal schooling. Nothing could, of course, be further from the truth.

Steele (1992) discussed this persistent mythology as applied to Black Americans and its tragic effects on children's belief systems during the schooling process. He argued that the mainstream beliefs about Black educational achievement caused what he called "disidentifying with school." During this process of disidentification, children, who have come to school ready to learn, quickly sense their home and community experiences devalued by the educational system. Their schools discount the value of their community, their experiences at home, their parent's childrearing strategies, and their own abilities. Just when these children need to accept school as a setting for the development of self-worth, they realize that, for them, this development is unlikely to occur. The result is children who lose interest in school, so that they can make themselves less vulnerable to the failure they see coming there.

Steele suggested that this disidentification can spread quickly in schools and that defectors from this disidentification often find themselves ostracized by other disaffected Black children. Steele described this process in college, but it can happen at every level of the schooling process:

She disidentifies with achievement; she changes her self-conception, her outlook and values, so that achievement is no longer so important to her self-esteem. She may continue to feel pressure to stay in school—from her parents, even from the potential advantages of a college degree. But now she is psychologically insulated from her academic life, like a disinterested visitor. Cool, unperturbed. But, like a painkilling drug, disidentification undoes her future as it relieves her vulnerability. (p. 74)

Another example of a macrolevel myth, which can lead to the misattribution of poor motivation, is the way in which teachers misinterpret a child's intent during lessons. In the teacher–child tutorial session described earlier in this chapter, teachers asked the children a series of questions about a wordless picture book. Although the mainstream children and poor African American children answered the same number of questions correctly, the two groups made different kinds of errors in their responses. African American children more than twice as often supplied answers irrelevant to the form of the question. Even when they did not know the answer to the question, they would try to say something. By contrast, the mainstream children more often said, "I don't know" or remained silent. Teachers appeared to be effective in helping mainstream children get the right answer when they said, "I don't know" or were silent, but they were ineffective in helping the African American children when they gave irrelevant answers. More than twice as often, the teachers ignored the irrelevant answers given more by the African American children and moved on to the next question; yet, with the mainstream children, who more often did not try to answer questions they didn't know the answer to, the teachers often rephrased the question and helped them try to find the right answer. Why was this the case? In part, it was probably because teachers did not know how to deal effectively with the kinds of answers the African American children gave, so they simply ignored the wrong answer. But one can infer other reasons, too.

Asked why they ignored the irrelevant answers more often than other kinds of errors and did not stop to help the child get the right answer, the teachers tended to fall back upon a misattribution about the motivation of the child. Most of the teachers said that the irrelevant answers showed that children were not taking the story seriously or had not listened carefully to the question. The teachers believed that the African American children, who more often supplied irrelevant responses, lacked motivation and were less serious about the task at hand. They did not associate this conclusion with the answer "I don't know," which the mainstream children made more often. Others have described this tendency among poor children to try to answer a question when they do not know the answer and in so doing make a category mistake or an irrelevant response. Blank (1975) and Blank, Rose, and Berlin (1978) coined the phrase "unteachable responses" to describe these irrelevant answers, because they, too, found teachers lacking the strategies to help children who made these responses.

A different way in which teachers perpetuate misattributions about motivation relate to how the children handle narrative material. From observations in the neighborhood, Feagans and Haskins (1986) and Vernon-Feagans (1996) observed oral storytelling to be a highly valued activity in the African American communities (see also Heath, 1983). But this storytelling differed in some important ways from the way mainstream children told stories. In their home settings, the African American children were encouraged to embellish upon stories, so that if they retold the same story, they incorporated some new elements to make the story more interesting, especially if the audience had already heard the story once. But the mainstream culture and its schools expect children to retell stories accurately and without embellishment. In fact, teachers strongly encourage verbatim recall and praise children who can perfectly retell stories read to them earlier. Poor African American children, when asked to retell a story read at school, would embellish it and reconstruct the story, even after direct instructions to tell the story as it had been told to them (Feagans & Farran, 1982). In the Feagans and Farran study, they behaved as though it was ridiculous to retell a story they knew the adult had heard and understood. But because they had not yet learned the school's expectations, they produced more interesting, but less accurate retelling. The teachers, and even some of the researchers, interpreted this behavior as defiant or at least as a lack of motivation when listening to the story in the first place. Thus, the mainstream culture interpreted differences in performance between children from different backgrounds as lack of motivation, therefore, ever so subtly devaluing inventive children.

THE ECOCULTURAL MODEL AND FAMILY AND EMERGENT LITERACY

Having described five myths that illustrate some of the false beliefs about nonmainstream children and their families, we turn to a specific examination of the extent to which literacy programs either accept or reject these myths. Mostly through constraining both our theoretical discourse and research methodologies, these myths serve as filters in interpreting and understanding the mesosystems and microsystems that are important spheres of influence in children's literacy development, leaving us with a distorted image of how these microsystems actually mediate literacy development in children.

In describing the field of intergenerational literacy, Gadsden (1998) found a "relative absence of a critical discourse about diversity and culture, above and beyond the recognition of differences alone" (p. 33). Traditional discourses in the field emphasize middle-class definitions of knowledge and what constitutes literacy-enriching experiences, while giving short shrift to issues of diversity. To the extent that diversity is incorporated in traditional discourses, it serves to compare mainstream, middle-class families to low-income and minority families and to highlight the ways in which the latter two groups fail to measure up to middle-class standards. One salient characteristic of many family literacy initiatives is the use of a language that demonstrates a fundamental lack of regard for the cultural backgrounds and experiences of diverse families. Such programs use a language that implies disease and pathology in families, for example, "Illiteracy breeds illiteracy" and "the intergenerational disease of illiteracy" (Taylor, 1997). Gadsden (2000) proposed the development of an integrative framework of intergenerational literacy, in which formerly unexamined and marginalized issues move to the foreground, particularly diversity in its broadest sense, and including diversity in terms of family form, class, and age, as well as ethnicity, race, and culture (p. 874).

In terms of theoretical perspectives on family literacy policy and interventions, family literacy programs often embody some or most of the societal myths described earlier. Researchers and educators who take a nontraditional approach to family literacy argue that mainstream models espouse and perpetuate myths of community, family, and individual dysfunction and inadequacy and, as such, represent a deficit approach to family literacy. Such an approach appears in many forms, from the use of disparaging rhetoric about families, to the tendency to favor school-like practices in the home, but eschewing naturally occurring literacy activities that may be inconsistent with practices seen in schools, to the use of correlational research to imply causal connections between low literacy and unemployment, poverty, and low educational attainment, to the widespread practice of offering prefabricated literacy programs uninformed by local issues or the expressed needs of the participants (Auerbach, 1989, 1995a, 1995b, 1997; Taylor, 1997).

One can find a model for a new perspective in the emergent literacy research that takes a comparatively broad view of what it means to be literate. Even though it is a limited theoretical perspective because it fails explicitly to address racism and classism, it does present a reasonable framework within which to study literacy acquisition and embraces a more ecologically valid approach.

An emergent literacy paradigm articulates a view of literacy acquisition as a developmental process that begins essentially at birth (Teale & Sulzby, 1986). This theory contradicts a reading readiness model of reading, that is, the idea that children learn to read when they enter kindergarten or first grade. Instead, children begin acquiring literacy from the very beginning of life through the active engagement with their environment. Literacy acquisition is also viewed as a social process. Children develop language patterns and acquire literacy concepts, skills, and knowledge, by interacting with others, by observing people in their environment engaging in literate behaviors, and by exploring their environment independently. Because we treat literacy acquisition as a developmental process that begins long before children enter school and is mediated by social interactions, the family, and home environment, it is by definition vitally important within the emergent literacy framework.

Proposing a broader view of literacy development, Sulzby and Teale (1991) delineated the features of an emergent literacy perspective. Unlike the reading readiness model, literacy development, they proposed, begins long before children experience formal instruction. Emergent literacy is a developmental process with all aspects of literacy—including oral language, reading, writing, and spelling—developing concurrently and interrelatedly, as children experience literacy events through social interactions with adults. In sum, the emergent literacy perspective takes a broad view of literacy, emphasizing the developmental nature of literacy learning and the importance of the first few years of a child's life in later literacy acquisition.

Thus, emergent literacy research focuses on a variety of human and environmental characteristics within the family that mediate literacy development. The initial research on the role of family and the home environment in literacy development and later academic achievement often focused on such family status and demographic characteristics as socioeconomic status and parental educational achievement (Baker, 1999; Gadsden, 1994; Metsala, 1996; Purcell-Gates, 2000). But this line of research frequently revealed only a modest predictive relation between demographic factors and later academic achievement. Researchers soon realized that socioeconomic status is not particularly predictive of academic success when analyzed independent of home environment variables (Purcell-Gates, 2000; Scarborough & Dobrich, 1994; see also chapter 5 in this volume).

Researchers began to consider the role of the contextual environment of the home on literacy development—examining such specific characteristics of the home environment as the number of books and other reading materials on hand, as well as specific learning practices and activities in the home—to be better predictors of later academic achievement (Baker, 1999; Metsala, 1996; Purcell-Gates, 2000; see also chapter 16 in this volume). Findings from this later strand of research suggested that many of the home characteristics predictive of later academic achievement included such literacy-related characteristics as availability of children's books, space and opportunities for reading, abundant reading materials for adults, and positive parental attitudes about reading (Baker, Serpell, & Sonnenschein, 1995). Furthermore, this research now suggests that the kinds of specific activities and practices in the home that predict later academic success are also literacy-related, for example, modeling of reading behaviors by parents, regular visits to the library, and shared storybook reading between children and their parents (Enz & Searfoss, 1996; Griffin & Morrison, 1997; Morrow, Paratore, Gaber, Harrison, & Tracey, 1993; Saracho, 1997a, 1997b). Thus, researchers began to narrow their focus of inquiry to literacy practices and characteristics in the home, as potentially more explanatory of later academic and literacy achievement than family status characteristics per se (Adams, 1999; Purcell-Gates, 2000). Unfortunately, little of this research has so far focused on the individual differences within a cultural or ethnic group that are also predictive of literacy; rather, it has focused only on describing mainstream families or on comparing mainstream families with low-income or minority groups.

A similar line of research has focused on the microsystem of the child care environment outside the home. Although recent work from the NICHD Early-Childcare Research Network (2000), for example, posits the home as a much more powerful influence on development than the child care setting, the quality of the child care setting, and the characteristics associated with particular preschool practices, make a definite difference for some groups of children (Dickinson & Smith, 1994; Whitehurst et al., 1994a, 1994b; Whitehurst & Lonigan, 1998). In these studies and reviews of research, storybook reading and dialogic reading appear to promote emergent reading abilities (see Chapter 4 in this volume). Recent studies by Dickinson and Tabors (2001) and Dickinson and Sprague (2001) identified three composite variables closely related to later early reading skills: classroom vocabulary environment, the quality of a teacher's talk, and curriculum quality. They also found that high classroom quality can compensate for a less optimal home environment.

The research has focused with much less emphasis on the mesosystems or the connections between the home and child care or preschool settings, although we know that teachers and parents may see the children differently, but often have little substantive interaction (Feagans & Manlove, 1994). Dickinson and Tabors (2001) found mothers' reports of contact with teachers and teachers' reports of contact with families to be moderate predictors of children's literacy success in school, suggesting that strong mesosystem connections may indeed help children make a successful adaptation between settings (chapter 8, in this volume, provides an elaboration on the effect of teachers' interactions with parents).

Although this emergent literacy framework has expanded our view of literacy acquisition and places its acquisition in context, Yaden, Rowe, and MacGillivray (2000) found an explanatory theoretical model of early literacy acquisition to be absent from the field, particularly as the field relates to diverse cultural groups and social contexts. Previous theoretical work in emergent literacy posited models of early literacy acquisition that considered the cognitive aspects of literacy development separately from its sociocultural aspects. But future research in emergent literacy should explicate the interrelationship of the sociocultural and sociocognitive aspects of literacy development and should expand our knowledge and understanding of the various protective or resilience factors that help children of diverse cultural backgrounds become successful (Yaden et al., 2000).

Circumscribed theoretical perspectives have their counterpart in much of the research examining home and family influences on children's literacy development. Here, too, societal beliefs and myths about children and their families have constrained the kinds of research questions and methods that literacy researchers use. In general, researchers have taken an etic, or transcultural, approach to early literacy research, to the extent that a well-articulated model of literacy development in White, mainstream, middle-class families was developed, then superimposed on diverse groups of children, despite the possibility that a generalized model of literacy might not adequately explain literacy development for all children (Garcia, Pearson, & Jimenez, 1994). The implications of an etic approach included a failure to seriously consider alternative family dynamics and different ways of using literacy in families.

Although we can see an increasing trend toward conducting research with diverse groups, much of the early research in emergent literacy centered on White middle-class families. The models of literacy development that evolved out of this early research reflected traditional and culturally mainstream families (Gadsden, 2000). As researchers set out to extend their research to different populations, many continued to use these early models of literacy development with families of varying race and ethnicity, gender, class, and family form. As noted earlier, Gadsden (2000), has argued persuasively for an integrative framework in which traditional discourses within the field broaden to include critical analyses of race and class: "The most critical of these is a focus on diverse families, diverse not only in ethnicity, race, and culture, but also in family form, class, age, and stage within the life course" (p. 874). For example, when examining parental and familial influences on young children's literacy development, the literacy research has focused primarily on interactions between the mother and child. In some families, however, members of the extended family unit, and even members of the neighborhood or community, share the caregiving roles (Vernon-Feagans, 1996). Thus, research that emphasized literacy interactions between mother and child, to the exclusion of other important relationships, tended to ignore facilitative literacy interactions that children may have experienced with other important adults and older children.

We often present storybook reading as one of the most effective ways of promoting children's literacy acquisition. Researchers have hypothesized that storybook reading facilitates literacy development by promoting print awareness, vocabulary, metalinguistic awareness, and comprehension in children by familiarizing them with story grammars and decontextualized language (Snow et al., 1998). Yet some debate persists about the actual importance of this bookreading activity for literacy development. Scarborough and Dobrich (1994) conducted a review of the literature over the past 30 years to discover what seems to be certain about the influence of parental reading to preschoolers on children's literacy. As they began to review this body of literature, they found inconsistent support for the widely accepted contention that reading to preschoolers makes an important contribution to literacy development. They found, in fact, that the amount of joint storybook reading accounts for only 8% of the variation in later reading achievement. In addition, they also examined the small number of studies that reported data on the relation between the quality of parent joint bookreading and later literacy, and found even less evidence for a relation between the quality of bookreading and later literacy. Scarborough and Dobrich (1994) ultimately concluded that, although this literature provided evidence of some connection between storybook reading and literacy acquisition, the relation was more modest than one would expect, given that reading to preschoolers has been routinely touted as one of the most effective ways parents can help their children become readers.

An even more quantitative meta-analysis of empirical articles, by Bus, van IJzendoorn, and Pellegrini (1995), found again that joint bookreading between parent and child accounted for only about 8% of the variance in early literacy, but those authors interpreted their finding as evidence for the importance of bookreading. In addition, this meta-analysis also examined the effect of bookreading on oral language, and this relation emerged as stronger than the one between bookreading and literacy, suggesting that oral language may mediate the relation between bookreading and early literacy. They also found that the relation was the same for both low-income and middle-income families. Other researchers, such as Whitehurst and Lonigan (1998), have presented a model of early literacy in which the environment for literacy, including joint bookreading, plays a role in literacy, but is just one of several factors important in early literacy development. Lonigan, in chapter 4 of this volume, makes this very point.

Given all this information and such modest effect sizes in recent research, one can argue an excessive emphasis on storybook reading as the principal vehicle in the home for promoting children's literacy development. By clear implication, other elements of the child's environment also contribute to literacy skill. Furthermore, some research indicates that low-income families engage in a variety of literacy activities in the home, beyond storybook reading, for example, reading newspapers, reading the television program guide, playing games, and using written directions for home improvement activities (Garcia et al., 1994). When low-income and African American families do read to their children, we have evidence that they adjust their language to the skills of their children, as other families do, but they also use a different style of interaction with print, which needs to be studied much more extensively (Hammer, 1999, 2001; Vernon-Feagans, Hammer, Miccio, & Manlove, 2001). Thus, instead of simply superimposing a model of literacy development on all groups, it behooves literacy theorists and researchers to identify the strengths of various types of families that facilitate children's success with literacy, regardless of ethnic background, class, or family culture.

One final methodological limitation of research on early literacy development bears mentioning. As a relatively new area of inquiry, much of emergent literacy research has been descriptive and correlational in design. Early work exploring literacy practices within the family and the literacy environment of the home used self-reporting techniques, including parent surveys, questionnaires, and interviews. Over the past decade, researchers have begun to incorporate other methodologies, such as naturalistic observations in the home and longitudinal studies. More recent studies also employ mixed designs with both quantitative and qualitative methodologies (Gunn, Simmons, & Kameenui, n.d.).

CONCLUSION

Societal myths and preconceptions about children and their families pervade our thinking, as we consider the most effective ways to promote children's literacy development. Our beliefs about the nature of low-income and minority families influence the kinds of programs we create. If we believe these families to be dysfunctional, our program goals will reflect the desire to make them functional. If we believe poor children and their parents to be unmotivated to succeed, our program design, as well as our interactions with program participants, will reflect that belief. In developing an ecocultural model of early literacy, we intend to encourage reflective introspection about the nature and content of our own belief system and the role these beliefs play in our understanding and interpretation of the contexts that influence children's literacy development. Those truly interested in helping all children experience success with literacy consider it imperative to remove the filters of societal myths from their eyes in order to comprehend clearly the issues important in promoting children's literacy.

Almost all children come to school ready to learn, and we need only to be ready for them. The challenge in this century for educators is to be ready to teach all children, especially when most will be non-White and many will be living below the poverty line. Education remains the last great hope for children living in poverty and for oppressed groups. Family literacy programs can kindle the hopes in these children, with a determined emphasis on understanding their families, without accepting the subtly disruptive myths still so pervasive in American culture.

REFERENCES

Adams, M. J. (1999). *Beginning to read: Thinking and learning about print.* Cambridge, MA: MIT Press.

Alexander, K., & Entwisle, D. (1988). Achievement in the first 2 years of school: Patterns and processes. *Monographs of the Society for Research in Child Development, 53*(2, Serial No. 218).

Auerbach, E. R. (1989). Toward a social-contextual approach to family literacy. *Harvard Educational Review, 59*(2), 165–181.

Auerbach, E. R. (1995a). Deconstructing the discourse of strengths in family literacy. *Journal of Reading Behavior, 27*(4), 643–661.

Auerbach, E. R. (1995b). Which way for family literacy: Intervention or empowerment? In L. M. Morrow (Ed.), *Family literacy connections in schools and communities* (pp. 11–27). Newark, DE: International Reading Association.

Auerbach, E. R. (1997). Reading between the lines. In D. Taylor (Ed.), *Many families, many literacies: An international declaration of principles* (pp. 71–81). Portsmouth, NH: Heinemann.

Baker, L. (1999). Opportunities at home and in the community that foster reading engagement. In J. T. Guthrie & D. E. Alvermann (Eds.), *Engaged reading: Processes, practices, and policy implications* (pp. 105–133). New York: Teachers College Press.

Baker, L., Serpell, R., & Sonneschein, S. (1995). Opportunities for literacy learning in the homes of preschoolers. In L. M. Morrow (Ed.), *Family literacy connections in schools and communities* (pp. 236–252). Newark, DE: International Reading Association.

Blank, M. (1975). Mastering the intangible through language. In D. Aaronson & R. W. Rieber (Eds.), *Developmental psycholinguistics and communication disorders* (pp. 46–57). New York: The New York Academy of Sciences.

Blank, M., Rose, S. A., & Berlin, L. J. (1978). *The language of learning: The preschool years.* New York: Grune & Stratton.

Bronfenbrenner, U. (1979). *The ecology of human development.* Cambridge, MA: Harvard University Press.

Bus, A. G., van IJzendoorn, M., & Pellegrini, A. D. (1995). Joint bookreading for success in learning to read: A meta-analysis on intergenerational transmission of literacy. *Review of Educational Research, 65,* 1–21.

Courlander, H. (1963). *Negro folk music, USA.* New York: Columbia University Press.

Darling, S., & Paull, S. (1994). Implications for family literacy programs. In D. K. Dickinson (Ed.), *Bridges to literacy* (pp. 273–284). Cambridge, MA: Blackwell.

Deater-Deckard, K., Dodge, K. A., Bates, J. E., & Pettit, G. S. (1996). Physical discipline among African-American and European-American mothers: Links to children's externalizing behaviors. *Developmental Psychology, 32,* 1065–1072.

Dickinson, D. K. (Ed.). (1994). *Bridges to literacy.* Cambridge, MA: Blackwell.

Dickinson, D. K., & Smith, M. W. (1994). Long-term effects of preschool teachers' book readings on low-income children's vocabulary and story comprehension. *Reading Research Quarterly, 29,* 105–122.

Dickinson, D. K., & Sprague, K. (2001). The nature and impact of early childhood care environments on the language and literacy development of children from low-income families. In S. B. Neuman & D. K. Dickinson (Eds.), *Handbook of early literacy research* (pp. 263–280). New York: Guilford.

Dickinson, D. K., & Tabors, P. O. (2001). *Beginning literacy with language.* Baltimore: Paul H. Brookes.

Donaldson, M. (1978). *Children's minds.* London: Fontana.

Duncan, G. J., & Brooks-Gunn, J. (1997). *Consequences of growing up poor.* New York: Russell Sage Foundation.

Enz, B. J., & Searfoss, L. W. (1996). Expanding our views of family involvement. *Elementary School Journal, 86,* 277–294.

Feagans, L., & Farran, D. (Eds.). (1982). *The language of children reared in poverty: Implications for evaluation and intervention.* New York: Academic.

Feagans, L. V., & Haskins, R. (1986). Neighborhood dialogues of Black and White 5-year-olds. *Journal of Applied Developmental Psychology, 7,* 181–200.

Feagans, L. V., & Manlove, E. E. (1994). Parents, infants, and day-care teachers: Interrelationships and implications for better child care. *Journal of Applied Developmental Psychology, 15,* 585–602.

Fitzgerald, J., Spiegel, D. L., & Cunningham, J. W. (1991). The relationship between parental literacy level and perceptions of emergent literacy. *Journal of Reading Behavior, 23*(2), 191–213.

Fletcher, J. M., & Lyon, R. G. (1998). Reading: A research based approach. In W. M. Evers (Ed.), *What's gone wrong in America's classrooms.* Washington, DC: Hoover Institution.

Frost, J. L., & Hawkes, G. R. (Eds.) (1966). *The disadvantaged child: Issues and innovations.* Boston: Houghton Mifflin.

Gadsden, V. L. (1994). Understanding family literacy: Conceptual issues facing the field. *Teachers College Record, 96*(1), 58–86.

Gadsden, V. L. (1998). Family cultures and literacy learning. In J. Osborn & F. Lehr (Eds.), *Literacy for all: Issues in teaching and learning* (pp. 32–50). New York: Guilford.

Gadsden, V. L. (2000). Intergenerational literacy within families. In M. L. Kamil, P. B. Mosenthal, P. D. Pearson, & R. Barr (Eds.), *Handbook of reading research, Vol. 3* (pp. 871–887). Mahwah, NJ: Lawrence Erlbaum Associates Inc.

Garcia, G. E., Pearson, P. D., & Jimenez, R. T. (1994). *The at-risk situation: A synthesis of reading research.* Urbana-Champaign: Center for the Study of Reading, University of Illinois at Urbana-Champaign.

Griffin, E. A., & Morrison, F. J. (1997). The unique contribution of home literacy environment to differences in early literacy skills. *Early Child Development and Care, 127–128,* 233–243.

Gunn, B. K., Simmons, D. C., & Kameenui, E. J. (n.d.). *Emergent literacy: Synthesis of the research.* Retrieved on July 26, 2002, from http://idea.uoregon.edu/~ncite/documents/techrep/tech19.html

Hammer, C. S. (1999). Guiding language development: How African American mothers and their infants structure play. *Journal of Speech and Hearing Research, 42,* 1219–1233.

Hammer, C. S. (2001). Come sit down and let mama read: book reading interactions between African American mothers and their infants. In J. Harris, A. Kamhi, & K. Pollock (Eds.), *Literacy in African American communities* (pp 21–44) Hillsdale, NJ: Lawrence Erlbaum Associates Inc.

Heath, S. B. (1983). *Ways with words.* Cambridge, England: Cambridge University Press.

Herrnstein, R. J., & Murray, C. (1994). *The bell curve: Intelligence and class structure in American life.* New York: Free Press.

Huston, A. C. (1991). *Children in poverty: Child development and public policy.* New York: Cambridge University Press.

Jencks, C., & Phillips, M. (Eds.). (1998). *The Back–White achievement gap.* Washington, DC: Brookings Institution.

Katz, M. B. (1989). *The undeserving poor: From the war on poverty to the war on welfare.* New York: Pantheon.

Lee, J. (2002). Racial and ethnic achievement gap trends: Reversing the progress toward equity? *Educational Researcher, 31,* 3–12.

Lieberman, G. A., & Hoody, L. L. (1998) *Closing the achievement gap: Using the environment as an integrating context for learning*. Poway, CA: Science Wizards.

Marshall, G. (Ed.). (1998). *The Oxford dictionary of sociology*. Oxford, England: Oxford University Press.

Metsala, J. L. (1996). Early literacy at home: Children's experiences and parents' perspectives. *The Reading Teacher, 50*(1), 70–72.

Morrow, L. M., Paratore, J., Gaber, D., Harrison, C., & Tracey, D. (1993). Family literacy: Perspectives and practices. *The Reading Teacher, 47*(3), 194–200.

NICHD Early Childcare Research Network (2000). The relation of child care to cognitive and language development. *Child Development, 71,* 960–980.

Natriello, G., McDill, E. L., & Pallas, A. M. (1990). *Schooling disadvantaged children: Racing against catastrophe*. New York: Teachers College Press.

Nightingale, C. H. (1993). *On the edge: A history of poor Black children and their American dreams*. New York: Basic Books.

Ogbu, J. (1982). Societal forces as a context of ghetto children's school failure. In L. Feagans & D. C. Farran (Eds.). *The language of children reared in poverty* (pp. 117–138). New York: Academic Press.

Ogbu, J. U. (1985). A cultural ecology of competence among inner-city Blacks. In M. B. Spencer, G. K. Brookins, & W. R. Allen (Eds.), *Beginnings: The social and affective development of Black children* (pp. 45–66). Hillsdale, NJ: Lawrence Erlbaum Associates Inc.

Ogbu, J. U. (1991). Minority status and literacy in comparative perspective. In S. R. Graubord (Ed.), *Literacy* (pp. 141–168). New York: Hill & Wang.

Purcell-Gates, V. (1998). Growing successful readers: Homes, communities, and schools. In J. Osborn & F. Lehr (Eds.), *Literacy for all: Issues in teaching and learning* (pp. 51-72). New York: Guilford.

Purcell-Gates, V. (2000). Family literacy. In M. L. Kamil, P. B. Mosenthal, P. D. Pearson, & R. Barr (Eds.), *Handbook of reading research, Vol. 3* (pp. 853–870). Mahwah, NJ: Lawrence Erlbaum Associates Inc.

Rogoff, B. (1990). *Apprenticeship in thinking: Cognitive development in social context*. New York: Oxford University Press.

Rogoff, B. (2003). *The cultural nature of human development*. Oxford, England: Oxford University Press.

Saracho, O. N. (1997a). Perspectives on family literacy. *Early Child Development and Care, 127–128,* 3–11.

Saracho, O. N. (1997b). Using the home environment to support emergent literacy. *Early Child Development and Care, 127–128,* 201–216.

Scarborough, H. S., & Dobrich, W. (1994). On the efficacy of reading to preschoolers. *Developmental Review, 14,* 245–302.

Snow, C. E., Barnes, W. S., Chandler, J., Goodman, I. F., & Hemphill, L. (1991). *Unfulfilled expectations: Home and school influences on literacy*. New York: Cambridge University Press.

Snow, C. E., Burns, M. S., & Griffin, P. (Eds). (1998). *Preventing reading difficulties in children*. Washington, DC: National Academy Press.

Stack, C. B. (1974). *All our kin: Stategies for survival in a Black community*. New York: Harper & Row.

Stack, C. B. (1996). *Call to home: African-Americans reclaim the rural south*. New York: Basic Books.

Staples, B. (1994, February 6). Into the white ivory tower. *The New York Times Magazine*, pp. 22–36.

Steele, C. M. (1992, April). Race and the schooling of Black Americans. *The Atlantic Monthly,* April, 68–78.

Sulzby, E. S., & Teale, W. H. (1991). Emergent literacy. In R. Barr, M. Kamil, P. Mosenthal, & P. D. Pearson (Eds.), *Handbook of Reading Research, Vol. 2* (pp. 727–757). New York: Longman.

Sutton-Smith, B., & Roberts, J. M. (1981). Play games and sports. In H. C. Triandis & A. Heran (Eds.), *Handbook of cross-cultural psychology, Vol. 4*. Boston, MA: Allyn & Bacon.

Taylor, D. (1983). *Family Literacy: Young children learning to read and write*. Por-smouth, NH: Heinemann

Taylor, D. (Ed.). (1997). *Many families, many literacies: An international declaration of principles*. Portsmouth, NH: Heinemann.

Taylor, D., & Dorsey-Gaines, C. (1988). *Growing up literate: Learning from inner-city families*. Portsmouth, NH: Heinemann.

Teale, W. H., & Sulzby, E. (Eds.). (1986). *Emergent literacy: Writing and reading*. Norwood, NJ: Ablex.

Tizard, B., Blatchford, P., Burke, J., Farquhar, C., & Plewis, I. (1988). *Young children at school in the inner city*. Hillsdale, NJ: Lawrence Erlbaum Associates, Inc.

Tizard, B., & Hughes, M. (1984). *Young children learning*. Cambridge, MA: Harvard University Press.

Vernon-Feagans, L. (1996). *Children's talk in communities and classrooms*. Cambridge, MA: Blackwell.

Vernon-Feagans, L., Hammer, C. S., Miccio, A., & Manlove, E. (2001) Early language and literacy skills in low-income African American and Hispanic children. In S. B. Neuman & D. K. Dickinson (Eds.), *Handbook or early literacy research* (pp. 192–210). New York: Guilford.

Weber, M. (1958). *The Protestant ethic and the spirit of capitalism* (T. Parsons, Trans.). New York: Scribner and Sons. (Original work published in 1905)

Whitehurst, G. J., Arnold, D., Epstein, J., Angell, A., Smith, M., & Fischel, J. (1994a). A picture book reading intervention in daycare and home for children from low-income families. *Developmental Psychology, 30,* 679–689.

Whitehurst, G., Epstein, J., Angell, A., Payne, A., Crone, D., & Fischel, J. (1994b). Outcomes of an emergent literacy intervention in Head Start. *Journal of Educational Psychology, 86,* 542–555.

Whitehurst, G. J., & Lonigan, C. J. (1998). Child development and emergent literacy. *Child Development, 69*(3), 848–872.

Yaden, D. B., Rowe, D. W., & MacGillivray, L. (2000). Emergent literacy: A matter (polyphony) of perspectives. In M. L. Kamil, P. B. Mosenthal, P. D. Pearson, & R. Barr (Eds.), *Handbook of reading research, Vol. 3* (pp. 425–454). Mahwah, NJ: Lawrence Erlbaum Associates, Inc.

23

We Are the World: Serving Language-Minority Adults in Family Literacy Programs

Heide Spruck Wrigley
Aguirre International

Language-minority families—families that speak a language other than English at home—often face tremendous challenges in making a life for themselves and in supporting their children's education. Many live under difficult circumstances, because family members are scattered in different countries. Financial resources are often scarce, especially if they are shared with relatives still living across borders or overseas. Economic opportunities are often limited as well, particularly for those who had to leave school in the primary grades. Lack of English and differences in culture pose significant obstacles, because parents must navigate systems that are complex and confusing, while trying to learn a language that is no less so.

Family literacy programs have great potential for addressing these issues. They can offer parents opportunities to learn English and to improve their education while helping them to sort out the challenges of living in the United States. They can help parents who live in two cultures and negotiate between two languages, explore the role of language in their lives. They can engage families in shared literacy experiences that draw on family strengths and values. But they can also provide assistance and comfort to families that are disintegrating under the pressures of resettlement. With adult education, these programs can further strengthen parents' competence, so that they are prepared to access higher education, get a job that pays a living wage, challenge inequities, and participate in building strong communities. Also, by collaborating with other agencies, such programs can help parents address problems that affect the family's well-being, such as those related to health care, legal rights, work, and education.

Given all these options, how then are programs to decide where to focus? Working with communities and parents to determine priorities and to choose a guiding philosophy can be a good starting point. Examining demographic trends can help programs get a better sense of new immigrants' educational needs and can help plan for the future. Finally, exploring what has worked for other programs, reviewing the literature, and discovering new ideas can breathe new life into a program and energize teachers and students to move in new directions.

This chapter addresses some of the challenges and opportunities inherent in working with language-minority families. The first part describes demographic changes related to linguistic diversity and discusses some of the educational orientations available to programs seeking a coherent philosophy for immigrant education. The second part lays out promising practices from the field, including projects and processes that programs have created to offer rich, meaningful educational experiences that make a difference in families' lives.

SHIFTS IN DEMOGRAPHICS[1]

More people came to the United States in the 1990s than in any other decade in the nation's history. As a result, all across the country, schools are seeing more and more children whose parents speak a language other than English at home. Many of these families are recent arrivals, and a significant number are settling in different states than did earlier immigrants. In Iowa, Georgia, Kentucky, and North Carolina, for example, 40% of all immigrants have come to this country within the last 10 years. Some states, such as Arkansas and Idaho, have seen their immigrant populations increase by over 150% in that time frame, a trend that presents new challenges for communities and schools (Passel & Zimmermann, 2001).

New immigrants tend to have poorer English skills than earlier arrivals. In fact, the 1990 census showed that almost half the immigrants who entered the country during the previous 3 years did not speak English well (compared with one fourth of all foreign-born residents). This trend will require family literacy programs to design services for parents and children who are new to both English and to the United States. Meeting this challenge will demand significant investment in literacy services that help newcomers understand both language and culture, so they can navigate services and systems and advocate for themselves, their children, and their communities.

Family literacy programs operate within a larger demographic picture that shows increasing numbers of language-minority adults and their children making their home in the United States. Currently, the foreign-born population in the U.S. is over 30 million, constituting about 11% of the population overall, and the numbers are likely to increase (U.S. Census Bureau, 2002). New immigrant adults may come from English-speaking countries or may have studied English abroad, but a significant number are new English learners. Indeed, the United States Census reports that among those who speak a language other than English at home, 5.7 million adults report not speaking English well. An additional 2.6 million adults say they do not speak English at all. These data add up to over 8 million adults—nearly 5% of the adult population— who have limited proficiency in English and could benefit from English-language and literacy services. Family literacy programs provide one such option, at least for parents of young children.

Nearly half of all immigrants (about 43%) come from Spanish-speaking countries. The majority of those are from Mexico (30% of the overall immigrant population). According to the 2002 census, 19,594,395 people in the United States are Spanish speakers, and half of them report speaking English less than very well, making up a significant group of adults and families who could benefit from language and literacy services. A smaller group (26%) speaks languages associated with Asia and the Pacific Islands, and they report similar proficiency

---

[1] Some of the information in the demographic section has been adapted from an earlier paper by Wrigley, Richter, Martinson, Kubo, and Strawn (2003), *The language of opportunity: Expanding employment opportunities for adults with limited English proficiency*. Washington, DC: Center for Law and Social Policy.

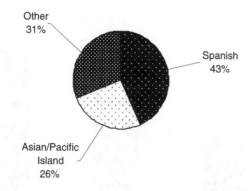

FIG. 23.1.   The foreign-born population by language spoken.

levels; that is, only half report speaking English very well. Figure 23.1 illustrates language distribution among the U.S. foreign-born population.

Where Do Language-Minority Populations Settle?

Language-minority families tend to be clustered in certain states. As a result, the share of the adult population that does not speak English well is much greater in some states and cities than in others. For example, the metropolitan areas of Los Angeles and New York City are home to one third of all immigrants in the United States (Schmidley, 2001). In these cities, large majorities (from two thirds to three fourths) of immigrant adults report not speaking English well (Capps et al., 2002).

Education Levels and Poverty Rates

Educational levels among the foreign-born show a bimodal distribution: One third lack a high school education, which is a proportion twice as large as among native-born adults. (Educational needs are even greater for immigrants from Mexico, two thirds of whom have not completed high school.) At the same time, however, the immigrant population has the same proportion of college-educated adults as their native-born counterparts: Roughly one fourth of the foreign-born have a bachelor's degree or higher (Schmidley, 2001, Figure 14-1).

Immigrants constitute a high percentage of the working poor. They have higher rates of employment than their U.S.-born counterparts, but at the same time, they earn lower wages than native-born workers. As a result, over 20% of immigrant families live below the poverty line—a proportion twice as high as that of the native-born population, as illustrated in Figure 23.2 (U.S. Census Bureau, n.d.). That means that many clients who come to family literacy programs need support services to help them deal with the burdens of poverty, for example limited access to quality child care, limited transportation options, and inadequate health care. They also need advice on how to negotiate the social service system.

Low wages are also common for many adults whose certificates and degrees do not transfer from their native country to the United States. As a result, immigrants who had good jobs at home often find themselves underemployed and struggling in their new surroundings— circumstances that can lead to bitterness or depression. As one older man from Russia told me "In my country, I was a truck driver; here I am nobody." When serving uprooted participants whose lives are now much sadder than before, many family literacy programs try to find ways to bring joy into clients' lives and provide emotional support along with language and literacy services.

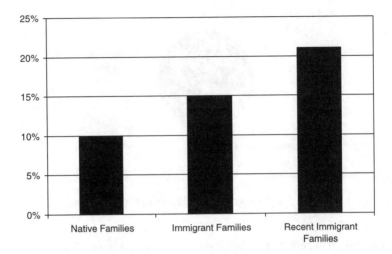

FIG. 23.2.   Poverty rates among immigrants, 1999.

Education, English Proficiency, and Literacy

The vast majority of language-minority parents who participate in family literacy programs are not yet fully proficient in English and come with the goal of improving these skills. Some are able to develop literacy in English quite easily, but others struggle a great deal learning to read and write in English.

What influences the acquisition of English-literacy skills the most? First and foremost, it is the parents' level of schooling and the level of literacy they have attained in their native language. Some immigrant groups tend to have less schooling and lower literacy skills than others. For example, Russian and Chinese parents who completed high school in their home country often pick up English literacy quite easily, whereas Mexican and Hmong parents, who often have not attended school beyond the elementary level, may find it extremely difficult to read and write in English.

Lack of experience with school-based skills, including such seemingly simple tasks as holding a pencil and forming letters, makes it hard work to write and read. The process, however, becomes easier over time. Once parents have "cracked the code" of literacy and see the relationship between the language encoded in print and the thoughts and ideas expressed in oral language, progress can happen quickly, as long as the text makes sense and is accessible in terms of both language and content. Given these differences among immigrants, programs are well advised to try to respond to the needs of parents who lack schooling. Such parents need opportunities to become familiar with print in a variety of ways, including developing literacy in their native language, to build the underlying skills necessary to process print.

One Size Does Not Fit All: Approaches to the Adult ESL Curriculum

Many family literacy programs struggle to find a philosophical approach to English as a second language (ESL) and literacy that ties together curriculum and teaching, provides a common framework for discussing program goals, and inspires both students and staff to work hard around a common goal. In my experience, program staff who share a common perspective have an easier time making decisions about teaching and learning, and are less likely to chase new funding that does not match the program focus. A program with a clear focus has direct benefits for children and parent participants as well; they can see why the program has selected a certain approach and how individual pieces fit within the model. Conversely, parents are often confused and frustrated when classes merely present a series of activities (fun though they may be) and fail to engage them in literacy work that is important and worthwhile.

What to teach and why? These have long been important questions for educators (Bruner, 1996; Freire, 1985; Eisner, 1994; Pinar, 1995; Wrigley, 1992). And debates about the merits of various ideologies have a long history (Eisner, 1974). Among the different ideas about curriculum, five orientations frequently manifest themselves in adult immigrant education. Each is rooted in history and offers the possibility of serving as a guiding philosophy for family literacy programs.

Fitting In: Social and Economic Adaptation.   The fitting in orientation sees education's function as helping to meet the critical economic and social needs of learners, their community, and society at large. Programs that follow this model are designed to help families acquire the skills and knowledge needed to be self-sufficient, to function effectively in society, to access services, and to integrate into mainstream society. This model is probably the most common currently in use. It has its roots in the Applied Performance Level study of the 1970s (Crandall & Imel, 1991) and in the early refugee resettlement curricula developed in Europe in the early 1980s (Sheils, 1988).

Family literacy programs that have adopted this model tend to focus on survival skills and competencies. They help parents become familiar with the school system and understand teachers' expectations. Key competencies are often established, at least as a guide for teachers to follow, and assessments are matched to the curriculum. When the goal is to prepare parents for the workplace, programs often select standards and competencies that focus on employment-related communication and literacy skills, variously known as *necessary* or *essential skills*. These standards include national skill sets, such as those developed by the Secretary's Commission on Achieving Necessary Skills in the United States (http://wdr.doleta.gov/SCANS, 2003) or the framework for essential skills developed by Human Resources Development of Canada (http://www15.hrdc-drhc.gc.ca/english/es.asp).

Critics of the approach (Auerbach, 1986; Collins, Balmuth, & Jean, 1989; Tollefson, 1989, 1995, 2001) point out that programs that emphasize fitting immigrants into the existing society silently accept the status quo and teach students to do the same. As a result, inequities in the system remain unchallenged, immigrants are taught to know "their place," and children learn to not question authority.

Critics also see the fitting-in orientation as a legacy of earlier Americanization movements that supported forced assimilation. They point to the efforts of the government to remove Native American children from their families and to put them into boarding schools so that they could more easily learn English and accept the White culture's values.

Learning How to Learn: Developing Cognitive Skills Related to Literacy.   The learning-how-to-learn orientation is based on models of cognitive processing, which in turn are extrapolated from brain research (Bransford, Brown, & Cocking, 1999; Cromley, 2000; Hartman, 2001). This approach tends to stress process over content, strategies over skills, and understanding over memorization. It is linked to a social constructivist perspective, which holds that there are no objective interpretations of texts; instead, all meaning is constructed by a reader who interprets what is read, bringing to bear perceptions, experiences, and prior knowledge. Such interpretation is also influenced by the social contexts in which literacy occurs (Hudelson, 1994; Jonassen, 2000; Taylor, 1999).

The cognitive approach to learning, although widely discussed in the literature (Kucer, 2001; Rumelhart, 1994; Smith, 1994a), is not often encountered in the practice of immigrant education, at least not on the adult level. Both national studies that I have been involved with (Wrigley & Guth, 1992; Condelli & Wrigley, 2003) found almost a total absence of approaches that stress strategies for metacognition, or for developing language awareness as a way to understand how English works or how literacy is used to convey meaning. The reason for this absence probably lies less in a rejection of the model by teachers and programs and more in the fact that strategy-based learning, apparent in methods such as *inquiry grammar* (trying to discover grammar rules, rather than merely memorizing them) or *comparative analysis* (discussing how one's native language differs from the language to be learned), is generally not part of the staff development that ESL instructors and family literacy teachers receive.

Learning how to learn has its detractors, as well. Critics say that cognitive models merely acknowledge issues of social context, generally avoiding the realities in which literacy occurs. They see supporters of the model as focusing on the individual's interaction with print and, in the process, failing to recognize that requirements for English literacy are often used to limit access for language minorities. From this perspective, although the model may be appropriate for young children who are learning to read, it is too limiting for adults trying to cope with literacy in an often unjust world.

Basic Skills: A Common Educational Core Experience.   The basic skills orientation has its roots in academic rationalism (Hirst & Peters, 1974) and reflects the notions of a core curriculum designed to provide a common set of educational experiences for all students. These experiences include development of basic literacy skills, acquisition of standard English, and an understanding of key concepts associated with various fields, such as American culture and history. In terms of literacy, it might mean a great deal of emphasis on acquisition of decoding skills, along with practice in proper pronunciation. In terms of English language, the focus is likely to be on standard grammar.

Advocates of this perspective emphasize that the country can only survive if newcomers are taught the values that Americans share. They maintain that failing to teach proper skills and accepted standards means cheating students and limiting their opportunities (see also Delpit, 1995). They also point to newcomers' needs to develop the skills to pass the GED and the Test of English as a Foreign Language (TOEFL), so they can succeed in postsecondary programs. Proponents also point out that unless language-minority parents learn to speak standard English and write without major errors in grammar and spelling, they will not be able to help their children with homework.

In the field of family literacy, the basic skills manifests itself most commonly in programs that stress a grammar-based approach to English or that prepare parents for the GED (in English or in Spanish). But the emphasis on decoding continues in the reading field; more and more ESL literacy programs are adopting a basic skills model to teaching initial literacy.

Critics of this approach are many. They argue that the basic skills approach merely asks students to practice and study pieces of the language (e.g., pronunciation, sentence structure, paragraph reading, writing an essay) without addressing the underlying cognitive processes that help or hinder students' understanding or production of a text. Linguists and literacy educators who challenge this approach stress that language and literacy are developmental processes and that making errors is a necessary part of the process (Kucer, 2001; Lightbown & Spada, 1993). They hold that learning a language and learning to read require hypothesis testing and a process of trial and error (Brown, 1994; Ellis, 2002). Opponents also argue that a "just do it" approach that focuses on surface skills fails to teach students that meaning-making and comprehension are cognitive processes that rely on active involvement with ideas and texts. They further maintain that ignoring the social aspects of learning robs adult students of the opportunity to engage in inquiry and collaboration (Auerbach, 1989; Lambert & Walker, 1995). As a result, students may actually be ill-prepared to take on the challenges of the world beyond the classroom, where language and literacy are not neatly laid out, but appear in tasks that tend to be fuzzy and ill-defined.

Celebrating Our Differences: Personal and Cultural Relevance. The personal relevance orientation emphasizes the primacy of personal experience and sees language and literacy as means of expressing feelings and thoughts. Grounded in the humanism of Rogers (1969) and Maslow (1954), this philosophy supports individual educational development and the psychological freedom that results from experiencing a personally relevant curriculum in a noncoercive environment. Proponents of the approach maintain that adults can assess their own learning needs and goals and, given the right tools, can then decide what works for them and assess their own progress. Self-actualization is one of the major goals.

In family literacy programs, this orientation manifests itself through students writing personal accounts and short autobiographies, working in groups to create language experience stories, or engaging in collaborative projects that place their experiences within a cultural framework. In some programs that support personal relevance, learners' lives become the curriculum (Weinstein, 1999). An emphasis on personal and cultural relevance also supports learner projects, particularly those that focus on common cultural experiences and self-directed learning. Several family literacy programs in the field are implementing this approach (Wrigley, 1998).

In our research on ESL literacy programs, we found the personal and cultural relevance orientation to be quite common. The *language experience approach*, in which students work as a group to write about a common experience, is perhaps the most popular method for connecting oral language and print—for both children and parents. The creation of stories, poems, and pictures that depict culture is an integral part of most family literacy programs.

Critics of this orientation highlight a number of shortcomings. They argue that personal relevance might be a good starting point for literacy development but might not be sufficient to prepare students for higher education or for the workplace (Delpit, 1995). They also hold that focusing primarily on students' experiences fails to stretch students in new directions and keeps them from taking on more challenging reading tasks (Adams, 1990). Critics also claim that a focus on the kind of multiculturalism that celebrates differences and invites us to all "get along," fails to address hard issues, such as racism or other social inequities that are part of immigrant life. In terms of assessment, most funding sources are skeptical if learner progress is mostly self-defined. They point to the need to capture progress in language and literacy in more objective forms, such as those mandated by Even Start and the National Reporting System (for further discussion of this question, see Wrigley, 1998).

Making a Difference: The Social Change Orientation. Issues of power lie at the heart of the social change orientation, which looks toward social reconstruction and liberation movements. Some theorists see schools as sites not just for learning, but for culture and politics as well (Apple, 1993; Aronowitz & Giroux, 1993). They see the educational system as a place where certain forms of literacy are legitimated and others are devalued. Proponents stress that, although literacy can be used as a tool for empowerment, being literate does not itself confer power and control. From this perspective, limited literacy and education are the result of inequitable social conditions. If literacy is to make a difference in immigrant families' lives, then individual literacy development must be linked to community change and social action. In ESL literacy programs, this orientation finds its strongest reflection in program designs that follow a model laid out by Brazil's Paolo Freire, who linked literacy teaching with community issues and explained that reading the word is reading the world (Freire & Macedo, 1987).

The social change perspective has given rise to Freire-inspired participatory ESL literacy programs. These programs use issues in learners' lives to explore social realities and to develop literacy. Many of these programs focus on helping parents understand how the school system works. They try to "unpack" school expectations, while exploring strategies for advocacy and change. Such programs may take on community issues, such as a lack of safe places for children to play, or they may question policies that place disproportionate numbers of bilingual children in special education classes.

Truly participatory programs with a strong emphasis on social justice and community action are rare, however, particularly in family literacy programs in which parents speak different languages and still struggle with English. In our work, we found very few programs that were committed to participatory practices and not just to learner-centered teaching with a sociocultural emphasis. Participatory programs that we did find were run by community-based organizations in which students and teachers shared a common language, so that discussions of hot issues and community concerns were possible (see also Auerbach, 1996, 2002; Rivera, 1999).

The social change orientation has been criticized on various grounds: political, educational, and practical. On the political side, opponents maintain that the role of immigrant education should be integration into society and acceptance of a common set of values and beliefs. Some fear that a focus on societal problems could result in alienation, pessimism, and cynicism, and could lead immigrants to feel their powerlessness even more acutely. From an educational perspective, others argue that participatory teaching is an abdication of the teachers' responsibility to teach the skills that students want to acquire (English and literacy) and that politics should remain outside the classroom. In this view, any time taken up with discussion of social ills and politics detracts from the study of basic skills.

Even those who sympathize with the participatory approach sometimes raise objections on practical grounds. They emphasize that most ESL teachers are not from the learners' community and know very little about the problems that students face. They may know even less about the systems that students will need to navigate in order to, for example, fight an eviction notice, respond to a summons after a shooting in the neighborhood, or deal with the stress of being without "papers." Some critics maintain that, because teachers have little experience with community development, they sometimes provide the wrong information and may end up trivializing important issues.

Toward a Synthesis

The literature makes clear distinctions between various orientations and ideologies. Program practice, however, often looks quite different. The educational experience that children and parents receive in family literacy programs tends to depend much more on the teacher's preference or the materials available than on the philosophy the program has chosen.

In the final analysis, programs and teachers often end up mixing and matching approaches as teachers come and go and funding mandates shift with the wind. In our work, when we ask teachers what their philosophies are, "eclectic" is by far the most common answer. Eclecticism, however, may not be the best choice if the goal is to build a quality program. Although exposure to a variety of approaches might serve students well at times, trying to be all things to all people can result in a smorgasbord of literacy activities that are overwhelming to the teacher, confusing to students, and, in the end, less effective than a more focused approach.

Great benefits come from choosing, if not a single philosophy, then at least complementary approaches that adhere to the principles of adventurous teaching and engaged learning. The result can be an educational orientation flexible enough to encompass both teacher preferences and student goals.

The following section offers practical examples of programs doing literacy work with language-minority adults in a family literacy context.

PROMISING PRACTICES

Language-minority families are far from a homogeneous group. They differ in their languages and cultural backgrounds, their purposes for participating in programs, and the goals they have set for themselves and for their families. Programs differ as well, in philosophy, focus, and their commitment to providing the best possible program for all parents. How, then, do different kinds of literacy programs respond to the needs and goals of parents who speak a language other than English? How do they connect literacy to the daily lives of learners and connect classrooms to the community? Some practices are discussed next, organized by the educational orientations discussed earlier. Several of the examples highlighted come from Project IDEA (Institute for the Development of Education for Adults), a statewide staff development project in Texas with which I was involved for 6 years; others are examples from site visits for two national studies on adult ESL literacy, one in the early 1990s and another from 1998 to 2003. Examples from Chicago and Socorro, Texas, come from research and technical assistance work with local projects in these areas.

Fitting In

The goal of many immigrant families is to find a place for themselves in U.S. society—a place where they can feel safe and comfortable to raise their children to be happy and productive adults. For many, fitting in requires the essential skills necessary to find and keep a job that pays a living wage. Increasingly, ESL literacy programs are offering opportunities for parents to develop work-related communication and literacy skills, along with other employability skills, such as finding a job that matches their preferences, identifying work in the hidden job market, and negotiating interviews. The more successful programs involve parents in discussing workplace issues, brainstorming ideas, and solving problems related to child care, transportation, and the conflicting demands of work and family.

In one project in Texas, parents decided to create videos that illustrated interactions in a job interview, focusing on what to do and what not to do. As one can imagine, the negative examples were both funnier and more effective than the serious presentations. In one video, the women went all-out to drive home "how to make sure you don't get a job"—they dressed in high heels, black stockings, and low-cut dresses. The job applicant chewed gum, slouched in her chair, and took out a mirror to fix her lipstick while the interviewer was talking on the phone. She responded to statements about the job's responsibilities with "Whatever" and asked how long she had to work before she could take her first vacation.

The women in the program spent a great deal of time identifying what counts in a job interview, then presenting the opposite, internalizing important issues in the process. Those who watched benefited as well, as they discussed which questions to ask and how to present themselves in a professional manner. As one student told me: "We learned what 'wear your best clothes to the interview' means—Sunday going-to-church clothes, not Saturday night party clothes." By taking a serious situation and making it ridiculous, the women presented the important issues and received credit for doing creative work. In the process, these women not only developed their language and literacy skills, but also acquired some of the essential skills associated with success in life and at work, such as working with a team to create a product under a deadline.

In another Texas project, a group of students created a bilingual phrasebook to help other students just beginning to learn English. In doing so, they brainstormed situations in which English was needed, then generated English words, phrases, and sentences to use in those environments. Situational contexts included the post office, the store, and the beauty parlor, where phrases such as "I think you overcharged me" or "I would like my hair layered with highlights" might come in handy. Along with the phrases and their Spanish translations, the students included a pronunciation guide. Calling the final product *Pocket English*, they made sure the phrasebook would easily fit into a bag or pocket.

Learning How to Learn

Learning how to learn, marshalling cognitive and metacognitive abilities, is a challenge for anyone taking on unfamiliar learning tasks. Adults who went to school for only a few years and who have little experience organizing learning materials and making meaning of unfamiliar texts face serious difficulties. Many parents are aware that, for themselves and for their children, how much English they learn and how well they learn it is closely tied to both educational progress and economic success—and that learning to read with understanding is an essential component of that process.

A number of family literacy programs involve immigrant parents in the reading and writing process, modeling strategies for meaning-making and for discussing books with their children. Two projects I'm familiar with were particularly successful because they involved parents in writing books for their children.

In Long Beach, California, a group of Khmer-speaking parents from Cambodia wanted their children to see and read books that reflected their culture. Although the local community center had copies of traditional folk tales written in both Khmer and English, the children were much more drawn to the books they saw their peers read, which included more modern illustrations and funnier stories. The mothers decided to write a book of their own for the children, adapting one of the kids' favorites and giving it a Cambodian twist. The book they selected was Judith Viorst's *Alexander and the Terrible, Horrible, No Good, Very Bad Day:* the story of a little boy for whom everything goes wrong all day, and who, to top it all off, has to eat spinach for dinner. In the Khmer version, the young child faces similar misadventures, but the illustrations show a Cambodian home, and the food he hates is a traditional Cambodian dish. Not surprisingly, the book project was a solid success. The children took it to school, the teacher read it to the whole class, and the Cambodian kids excitedly reported that their American friends were very impressed and kept asking, "Your mom wrote a book just for you?"

In creating their story, the mothers used a writing process model designed to create cognitive engagement and build metacognitive awareness in new writers. As the women thought about their audience, or struggled with what they wanted to say and how they wanted to say it, and wrote and rewrote various sections, they used many of the strategies that are integral to learning how to write. In the end, they spent much more time engaged with language and literacy than they would have in a program with a more conventional literacy component.

An Even Start family literacy class in San Antonio went through a similar process. The women in the program decided to create books to read together with their children as part of a celebration of family literacy. They very much wanted to demonstrate the reading strategies that they had learned as part of the program, such as stopping at the end of a page, asking children to predict what might come next, inviting them to talk about the pictures, and encouraging them to connect their own experiences with the story.

A Word of Caution.   These projects were successful, in large part, because the parents involved were excited about books and had sufficient English proficiency to tackle writing a story. There is need for a bit of caution, however. For parents new to English and new to literacy, the admonishment "Read to your children" not only might be *not* useful, but it might even be counterproductive. Children and parents tend to feel uncomfortable when the parent still struggles to read, and stories of children correcting their parents' English are not uncommon. It is easy to see how this practice undermines the parent's authority, causing confusion and frustration. Furthermore, children learn a great deal from talking about stories they hear and about their own experiences in similar situations. If parents are encouraged to talk about books with children in English, and their English is not yet strong, the conversation is likely to be shallow, focusing on surface facts, rather than on deeper understanding. Although some parents enjoy reading books to children in the home language, others may lack the literacy skills in the native language to do so comfortably. Some parents may not see reading books together as a very important part of their parenting repertoire, preferring other activities instead. In working with parents, we need to remember that there are many ways for parents to *support their children's education*, and that reading aloud is only one strategy to accomplish that goal. Asking parents to discuss the different ways in which they interact with their children and validating these experiences can bracken overview of literacy and thesis.

Basic Skills: Word Power

Learning to speak English well is the primary goal of most immigrant parents who participate in family literacy programs. Many of these parents come to the learning table with very traditional notions of what it means to "do school." They may enjoy carrying out projects and writing stories, but they also want to develop their English skills from the bottom up, getting rid of accents that interfere with communication, understanding how English works (grammar and structure), and learning scores of new words.

These adult learners know that an ever-increasing vocabulary will allow them to get ideas across, even with limited control over the language, and will help them pick up basic information from newspaper headlines, from notices that schools send home, and in conversations. Helping these adults increase their English vocabulary may be one of the best ways of responding to their need for basic skills instruction, while fostering language and literacy development. The following strategies, observed in classrooms with beginning ESL students, help serve that goal.

Personal Dictionaries.   Personal dictionaries, or collections of words that students want to remember, are an effective way to help students focus on words that have meaning for them, instead of trying to remember all the words introduced as part of a learning unit. As words and phrases are introduced in conversations and in readings, students select those they want to remember and build their own dictionaries, using personal address books or by putting the letters of the alphabet at the top of the pages of a notebook. Teachers may print up pages for students to fill in and keep in a three-ring binder, although pages created this way are not as portable as smaller books that allow students to study their words on the bus or as they wait in line during errands. In some family literacy programs, parents show their children how to create these dictionaries for themselves, encouraging them to add pictures and drawings for key concepts they need in school.

What's Your Favorite?   Asking students to focus their learning on a few favorite words they want to remember and teach to others helps students who are new to English take charge of their own learning. As part of vocabulary study, each student identifies a word to focus on. The vocabulary item may be a word that strikes them as unusual, gives them trouble, or represents a familiar feeling. At set times during the week, selected students present their special word to the class, using a large poster board, overhead projectors, or a computer screen. In teaching their vocabularies to the class, they highlight meaning, pronunciation, and use, while other students repeat the word and take notes. Beginning students, in particular, can benefit from this activity, because it offers them a measure of control, while gently pushing them into new directions, such as having to present information in front of a group. I once watched a class in

Chicago, in which the students had jobs in factories around town, when one worker taught his favorite word, explaining the meaning and modeling pronunciation and word stress everyone had great fun saying the word and remembering it: *re-im-burse-ment*.

You Can Take It With You.   A teacher at Portland Community College devised a clever way to help her students remember basic information that schools, clinics, and social service agencies kept asking for. She helped her students create index cards with their address, phone number, and social security number; punched holes in the cards; and showed her students how to put them on key rings. Students were thrilled to have a handy reminder of important data and kept adding information to the cards.

Remembering in a Flash.   Flashcards have long been a mainstay of language teaching. Students write words that they want or need to know on one side of the card, then write a sentence with a blank space where the new word might fit on the backside. Students can look at the word and generate the sentence on the back, helping them to understand the environment in which the word is used. They can then start with the sentence containing the blank and try to think of the word that fits, helping them to remember key vocabulary. Other ways to use flashcards include putting a drawing on the back of the card, which helps visual learners to make associations between pictures and print. Flashcards lend themselves easily to use in family literacy programs, because the method works well for all language learners, whether they are children or adults. We have used this approach with elderly immigrants in Chicago, who kept complaining that they were too old to remember anything. To show solidarity with her students, the teacher wrote words she wanted to remember in Serbo-Croatian and encouraged the students to test her on her knowledge of their language. Intrigued by this method, some of the grandparents created flashcards to teach their grandchildren key Bosnian words, such as *bombone* (candy).

Social and Cultural Relevance

The social and cultural relevance orientation to literacy is perhaps the most popular approach found in programs that serve language-minority families. It encompasses activities ranging from setting up a multicultural potluck dinner, so that students from different countries can get to know each other, to discussions of differences and commonalities across cultures, societies, and political systems.

Artifacts and Cultural Memories.   Several of the teachers in the Socorro Even Start program, all part of the El Civics on the Border project, have asked students to bring in an item that reminds them of home and discuss what it means to them. Several students brought in *bibles* that had been in their family for several generations; others displayed items that their mothers and grandmothers had used, for example, a handmade shawl, a tortilla press, a large *mocajete* (a lava basalt mortar for grinding corn or spices). As a follow-up project, the women decided to teach students elsewhere how to make homemade tortillas from scratch, creating an illustrated guide in the process. They used the technique of creating storyboards, which had been introduced as part of the civics curriculum, and developed a sequence of pictures and texts, using photographs taken with digital cameras to illustrate the process.

I first saw the artifact activity demonstrated in the El Barrio Popular Education Program in East Harlem in New York City. The teacher brought in a musical instrument, a food item, and a religious icon, and asked students to talk and write about three questions: What is it? What do you know about it? and What do you want your children to remember? By starting with physical items that have meaning in students' lives, teachers are able to highlight cultural traditions and connect the generations in ways that are much more immediate than what written texts alone can accomplish.

Women's Stories. Many successful family literacy programs exist in areas where parents speak the same language and are grounded in the community. Examples include Hmong families in Fresno, California; Vietnamese in Arlington, Virginia; or Latinos in El Paso, Texas. Because students and teachers can use the native language to explain, clarify, and discuss, possibilities for rich literacy work exist. These possibilities are more difficult to realize where students do not share a common language and have to struggle with English to get a point across.

Although more difficult initially, sharing stories and forging ties across cultures is possible in classes where language groups come together. A highly successful project in that respect is the Refugee Women's Alliance in Seattle, Washington, which developed an ESL curriculum called Family Talk Time. When I visited the program, the women who participated came from countries as diverse as Ukraine, Laos, and Eritrea. All were new to English, and several were learning to write for the first time. As the theme for the month, the teacher had chosen "key events in our lives." She asked the students to share with one another what happens in their country when a baby is born, when a couple is married, or when family members get too old to take care of themselves. The women strived to explain and understand, while translators went from table to table to help clarify. Talk was slow, but the women were highly engaged and fascinated by the events described. Each person used several means to tell the story—drawing pictures, sharing photographs, or writing down key words to be translated. This lesson worked because the women were genuinely interested in what one another had to say, which is often not the case when parents see literacy activities as mere language practice.

Visual Information. Using pictures, photographs, and videos is one of the most successful ways of introducing English and literacy to parents whose English skills still need a great deal of development. The Coalition for the Limited English Speaking Elderly in Chicago (one of the English Language and Civics demonstration projects that I have been involved with) uses visual information as the core of a curriculum used with elderly immigrants and refugees from Bosnia, China, Iraq, Syria, Korea, India, and Vietnam. With funding from the U.S. Department of Education, the State of Illinois, and the Retirement Foundation (which pays for field trips), the coalition purchased overhead projectors, digital cameras, and a video camera for teacher use. Pictures (still and moving) serve to introduce ideas, to show people and places, and to document students' experiences as they go on field trips to farms, supermarkets, and various ethnic neighborhoods. We asked the participants to tell us a little bit about their lives and explain how and why they came to the United States, then we captured their stories on video. Other ethnic groups then watched the videos, which became a basis for conversation and further stories as each group contributed thoughts and feelings about themselves. Because decreasing social isolation and building a positive sense of personal identity are goals of the project, the program organizes visits among the different language groups several times a year. Pictures and letters are exchanged after each visit between immigrants who come from different countries and who live in linguistically isolated neighborhoods. They serve as reminders that they are acknowledged and appreciated and provide opportunities for authentic communication with other newcomers.

An intergenerational component of the project involves U.S.-born students from a local high school who wanted to know more about immigrants and to contribute to the community. The young students watched a video called *Immigrant Elderly Tell Their Stories*, in which elderly refugees talk about their lives before and after coming to the United States. Through hearing real people talk about the trauma of war, the sorrow of being uprooted, and the difficulties of

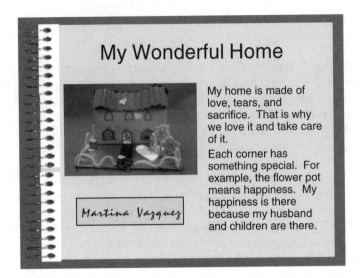

FIG. 23.3.   Picture of page in a student project showing a model and description of their dream house.

adjusting to a new country, the students gained a much better sense of the lives and backgrounds of groups they knew little about. As *service learning*, these students participated in a Valentine's Day party the project had organized and got to know the people whom they had watched on the video that was part of the project webpage and showed individual refugees from Bosnia telling the story of how they had come to the United States.

Family Projects.   Designing cookbooks, family albums, and memory books has long been a hallmark of family literacy programs. Several projects stand out in my mind: A group of learners along the Texas–Mexico border created a family quilt, using icons similar to family crests to communicate the values that they hold dear. One family chose a house to illustrate the dream that kept them working; another quilted a big smiley face on a square to illustrate to themselves and others that, although they were poor and struggling, they lived together in one place (in this area, many families are divided by the border). The quilt was given a place of honor on a wall in the children's school.

An Ideal Neighborhood.   For many poorer families, the dream of a house plays a big role. One parent–child group in the Even Start program in Socorro used construction paper and a lot of imagination to create their dream houses and write a few sentences about them. From each window, a picture of the family peers out. An El Civics class took the project one step further. Students used the construction paper project to create an ideal community that included churches, clinics, schools, recreation centers, and parks—the latter two of which were missing in their real neighborhoods (Fig. 23.3).

In other places, students have participated in culture fairs: exhibiting food, wooden toys, or books of songs and stories that they remember from back home. In some programs, women spend a great deal of time making Christmas cards and decorating them with beads and glitter, in order to share them with others. Families have taken their cards to children's hospitals or nursing homes. In several communities, parents and children visited a local fire station, bringing along cookies and cakes to express their appreciation to the fire fighters in memory of September 11. Parents and children still talk about their surprise at seeing that one of the fire*men* was in fact a fire*woman*, prompting discussions about gender and jobs.

Limitations of Cultural Celebrations.   As popular as cultural projects are in family literacy programs, they have their detractors. Some parents detest working with scissors, paper, and glue. I remember one Chinese parent begging the teacher, "Please don't make me do glitter." She wondered, perhaps, how cutting and pasting with her children would help them get into Berkeley or Harvard. In the focus groups and interviews we conducted, many parents, particularly those who have strong literacy skills in their native language, told us that they preferred academic topics, such as learning about the geography, history, and government of the United States, to the life skills and parenting curriculum they encountered in the family literacy program they attended.

Participatory Education

As mentioned earlier, taking on issues of power and social justice is often difficult in family literacy programs. Most funding sources expect objectives to be predefined, outcomes to be prespecified, and tests to be standardized. Opportunities to challenge the existing economic and political system are very much limited by the bureaucratic structures in which family literacy programs operate. In fact, I have only seen one case in which participants served on the board of directors and effectively ran the program.

The community-based program, El Barrio Popular Education Program in East Harlem, New York City, served women from Puerto Rico and the Dominican Republic. The women set full bilingualism as one of the program's goals, and it offered Spanish classes from beginning to advanced (from Spanish literacy to the Spanish GED), as well as ESL classes. As part of the program, the women also ran a food co-op, including a catering business; staged benefits (a fashion show); and created a *foto-novela* about sexual harassment. Art work became an important part of the curriculum, as well—the art the women produced was later exhibited in New York's Museum of Modern Art. The program thrived under the guidance of a director who had experience in popular education and who was talented at raising funds. As a result, it became an example in which students and staff "walked the walk" of participatory education (see also Rivera, 1999).

In some cases, participatory education can evolve when students feel strongly about an issue and when opportunities for political participation present themselves. One such case involved a legislative proposal to allow all immigrants to obtain drivers' licenses, regardless of their status. As discussions about legislative changes got under way, students in Sacramento, California, met with lawmakers to discuss what a change in the law meant for them, in a state where it is very difficult to get to work or to a hospital without driving a car. Other issues that students in different communities have taken on include trash strewn around a neighborhood, raw sewage in a ditch near a residential neighborhood, and lack of job training opportunities for parents who speak little English.

In other instances, a program might integrate aspects of empowerment education into its curriculum. The Even Start Family Literacy and Adult ESL Program in Socorro is a case in point. The program, which has a 3-year grant from the Texas Educational Agency, is integrating English-Language and Civics, through a model that combines project-based learning with engaged learning through technology. Focusing on culturally and historically relevant projects, students visited local painters and muralists, interviewed bakers who had been serving the local community for over 50 years, and created an inquiry project on the history of the 400-year-old missions still in use in the area. To document visits and present their findings, students created videos, brochures, and PowerPoint presentations, later showcasing their work at a citywide conference for teachers in El Paso and a school-wide exhibit for other parents in the community.

In 2003, students took on social, economic, and political issues as well: They listened to a Woody Guthrie song about a group of Mexican farm workers who, about to be sent back to Mexico, died in a plane crash in Los Gatos, New Mexico. The song, called "Deportees," provided opportunities to discuss the nature of work in Mexico and the United States and to learn more about the farm labor movements through Web searches on the Bracero program, Cesar Chavez, and the farm labor movements in the American South. The war with Iraq offered opportunities to look at the U.N. Declaration on Human Rights and to discuss the role that individuals throughout history have played in peace and war. After reading a series of quotes by people who were active in working for peace and justice, students selected a quote and a person to research further, using print encyclopedias as well as the Internet. They then commented on the thoughts expressed by figures as distinct as Emilio Zapata ("It is better to die on your feet than live on your knees"), Martin Luther King ("We should never forget that everything Adolf Hitler did in Germany was legal and everything the Hungarian freedom fighters did was illegal"), and Gandhi ("Be the change you want to see in the world"). Linking history, current events, and personal insights allowed the students to form a broader perspective on world events, while inviting them to grapple with the larger issues of peace and war, including issues related to personal ethics and social morality.

What About the Men?   Although the vast majority of parents in family literacy programs are women, men participate as well. Teachers often struggle to find topics and activities that engage men and that help them acquire the skills they want to learn. Inviting men to come together and discuss what interests them might help identify subjects to include in the literacy curriculum. Here is an example: In an ESL literacy program in Chapel Hill, North Carolina, run by AmeriCorps volunteers, the men suggested that motorcycles would make a good subject for discussion and inquiry. In their world (all were young, unmarried Latinos in blue collar jobs), much of the social talk revolved around comparison of the relative merits of a Harley versus a BMW or comments regarding the new Yamaha that was on display at a local dealer. The young men, from small villages in Mazatlan, very much wanted to be part of these discussions. They were eager to learn the language associated with "guy stuff"—machines, motors, tools, and gear.

Some teachers respond to these requests to include a broader set of topics in family literacy by asking students (men and women) to bring in their favorite tools and to demonstrate to the children how to use them. Some bring catalogues from Sears and other stores to the class and invite the group to create plans for a home repair business. As they do so, they also select tools and other materials to buy, comparing prices and creating budgets as they go.

Making sure that we connect with the boys, as well as with the girls, in family literacy programs also deserves consideration. One teacher in El Paso, working in a middle-class neighborhood where parents often did professional work, wanted to make sure that all of the kids could see their parents' strengths and feel proud of them. She invited parents to visit her third-grade class to demonstrate a skill. The star turned out to be a Mr. Acosta, a recent immigrant from Mexico, who showed the kids how he changed the oil in his 1989 Chevy truck. In the children's eyes, parents who spend their days doing paperwork, or using computers, clearly could not compete with the talents of this dad. His son walked tall that day.

CONCLUSION

As programs hear more and more about the benefits of direct instruction and explicit teaching of reading, it might appear that the practices just discussed, although successful in the field, are not supported by research. This is not so. The latest national study, *What Works for Adult ESL Literacy Learners* (Condelli & Wrigley, 2003), strongly supports the kind of rich teaching that links classrooms to communities (while also stressing the need to spend time on language and literacy practice). Other research (Parcell, 1998) shows similar results, demonstrating that the use of authentic materials that reflect real life literacy tasks has a positive effect on the literacy behaviors of adults. In the end, we must acknowledge that adult immigrants bring a wealth of knowledge and experience to the learning process, and that, in trying to negotiate life in the United States, they need much more than reading and writing skills. Being aware of both the opportunities and challenges that language-minority families face will allow us to match approaches and curricular to what matters in learners' lives.

REFERENCES

Adams, M. J. (1990). *Beginning to read: Thinking and learning about print.* Cambridge, MA: MIT Press.

Apple, M. (1993). *Official knowledge: Democratic education in a conservative age.* New York: Routledge.

Aronowitz, S., & Giroux, H. (1993). *Education still under siege.* Westport, CT: Bergin & Garvey.

Auerbach, E. (Ed.) (2002). *Community Partnerships.* Alexandria, VA: TESOL.

Auerbach, E. (1996). *Adult ESL literacy: From the community to the community.* Mahwah, NJ: Lawrence Erlbaum Associates.

Auerbach, E. R. (1989). Toward a social-contextual approach to family literacy. *Harvard Educational Review, 59,* no. 2 (May 1989), 165–181.

Bransford, J. D., Brown, A. L., & Cocking, R. R. (Eds.). (1999). *How people learn: Brain, mind, experience, and school.* Washington, DC: National Academy Press.

Brown, D. (1994). *Teaching by principles.* Englewood Cliffs, NJ: Prentice Hall.

Capps, R., Ku, L., Fix, M., Furgiuele, C., Passel, J. S., Ramchand, R., et al. (2002, March). *How are immigrants faring after welfare reform? Preliminary evidence from Los Angeles and New York City.* Washington, DC: The Urban Institute.

Condelli, L., & Wrigley, H. S. (2003). *What works for adult ESL literacy students?* Findings from a Naional Study. Washington, D.C. American Institutes for Research.

Crandall, J., & Imel, S. (1991). Issues in adult literacy education. *The ERIC Review, 1*(2), 2–8.

Delpit, L. (1995). The silenced dialogue: Power and pedagogy in educating other people's children. In L. Delpit, *Other people's children: Cultural conflict in the classroom* (pp. 21–47). New York: New Press.

Ellis, R. (2002). *The study of second language acquisition.* Oxford, England: Oxford University Press.

Freire, P., & Macedo, D. (1987). *Literacy: Reading the word and the world.* South Hadley, MA: Bergin-Garvey.

Hartman, H. J. (2001). *Metacognition in learning and instruction: Theory, research, and practice.* Boston: Kluwer.

Hirst, P. H., & Peters, R. S. (1974). The curriculum. In Eisner, E. W., & Vallance, E. (Eds.), *Conflicting conceptions of curriculum.* Berkeley, CA: McCutchan Publishing.

Kucer, S. B. (2001). *Dimensions of literacy: A conceptual base for teaching reading and writing in school settings.* Mahwah, NJ: Lawrence Erlbaum Associates, Inc.

Lambert, L., & Walker, D. (1995). Learning and leading theory: A century in the making. In L. Lambert, D. Walker, D. Zimmerman, M. Gardner, & P. Slack (Eds.), *The constructivist leader* (pp. 1–27). New York: Teachers College Press.

Lightbown, P., & Spada, N. (1993). *How languages are learned.* Oxford, England: Oxford University Press.

Maslow, A. H. (1954). *Motivation and personality.* New York: Harper and Row.

Passel, J. S., & Zimmermann, W. (2001, April). *Are immigrants leaving California? Settlement patterns of immigrants in the late 1990s.* Washington, DC: The Urban Institute.

Purcell-Gates, V., Degener, S., & Jacobson, E. (1998). U.S. adult literacy program practice: A typology across dimensions of life contextualized/decontextualized and dialogic/monologic. *NCSALL Reports #2.* Cambridge, MA: The National Center for the Study of Adult Learning and Literacy/World Education.

Rivera, K. (1999). *Native language literacy and adult ESL instruction.* Washington, D.C. Center for Applied Linguistics.

Rogers, C. (1969). *Freedom to learn.* Columbus, OH: Merrill.

Schmidley, A. D. (2001, December). *Profile of the foreign-born population in the United States: 2000.* Washington, DC: U.S. Census Bureau.

Sheils, J. (1988). *Communication in the modern languages classroom.* Strasbourg: Council of Europe, Council for Cultural Cooperation.

U.S. Census Bureau (2002). *The foreign-born population in the United States: March 2002.* Current Population Survey (CPS) March 2002 (P20-539). Washington, D.C. U.S. Census Bureau.

U.S. Census Bureau. (n.d.). *Profile of the Foreign-Born Population in the United States, 2000.* Retrieved September 23, 2002, from http://www.census.gov/population/www/socdemo/foreign/ppl-145.html

Viorst, J., & Cruz, R. (1972). *Alexander and the terrible, horrible, no good, very bad day.* New York: McMillan.

Weinstein, G. (1999). *Learners' lives as curriculum: Six journeys to immigrant literacy.* Washington, DC and McHenry, IL: Center for Applied Linguistics and Delta Systems.

Wrigley, H. S. (1998). Assessment and accountability: A modest proposal. In *Adventures in assessment: Learner-centered approaches to assessment and evaluation in adult literacy,* Vol. 11, Winter, pp. 47–54. Boston, MA. World Education.

Wrigley, H. S., & Guth, G. (1992). *Bringing literacy to life: Issues and options in adult ESL literacy.* San Mateo, CA: Aguirre International.

24

Family Literacy for ESOL Families: Challenges and Design Principles

John Strucker, Catherine Snow,
and Barbara Alexander Pan
Harvard University

This chapter addresses the particular challenges faced by family literacy programs serving students who are non-English-speaking. Most adult literacy and early childhood programs in the United States have taken native English speakers as the norm, and the programs were not prepared to address the enormous demographic changes over the last 30 years. These demographic changes have resulted in almost all these programs now enrolling at least a few families with low proficiency in English, and many programs include a majority of non-English speakers. The difficulties faced by programs in adapting to these new participants' needs have, unfortunately, not been alleviated by directly relevant contributions from program evaluation studies, and, consequently, information to help design programs to serve immigrant and limited-English-proficiency groups is needed.

As a first step toward conceptualizing family literacy programs for non-English speakers, we begin by discussing demographic trends affecting family literacy programs serving English-language learners. We cover society's assessment of the needs of these families and also the reports by these families of their own proficiency levels, goals, and reasons for participation. Second, we summarize some insights from basic research on second-language acquisition and on literacy development and provide some recommendations for program design and procedures. Next, we discuss issues related to family literacy programs serving learners with limited English proficiency (LEP) and those who are English-language learners. Finally, we identify and discuss three principles that can be useful to guide research and evaluation in the area of English for speakers of other languages (ESOL) family literacy.

DEMOGRAPHIC TRENDS AFFECTING ESOL FAMILY LITERACY

This section addresses demographic trends that affect practice in family literacy programs.

Society's Needs Assessment in ESOL Family Literacy

As most of us are aware, the number of people in the United States who speak native languages other than English has been rising steadily in recent years. In the 1990 U.S. census, 13.8% of the population reported speaking a language other than English at home (U.S. Census Bureau, 1990). By the 2000 census, that percentage had risen to 17.9%, more than 23% of whom reported that they spoke English not well or not at all (U.S. Census Bureau, 2000). Regarding English literacy, the National Household Education Survey (NHES; 1997), conducted in 1995, found that only 37% of the nonnative speakers of English reported that they read English well. These self-reports are consistent with results of the National Adult Literacy Survey (NALS; Kirsch, Jungeblut, Jenkins, & Kolstad, 1993), in which respondents were tested on a variety of real-world English literacy and numeracy tasks.

Five levels are used for classifying individuals based upon their performance, with Level 1 being the lowest level and Level 5 being the highest level. The following information helps to illustrate Levels 1 and 2:

- Prose literacy tasks at Level 1 involved reading "relatively short text to locate a single piece of information."
- Quantitative tasks at Level 1 involved "relatively simple arithmetic operations, such as addition."
- Prose literacy tasks at Level 2 involved "plausible but incorrect information" and the integration of "two or more pieces of information."
- Quantitative tasks at Level 2 required readers "to perform a single operation . . . stated or easily determined from . . . the material (e.g., an order form)." (Kirsch et al., 1993, p. 10)

People reporting native languages other than English made up 20% of those in the two lowest levels of the NALS (Levels 1 and 2) and 25% of those in Level 1 (the lowest level) (Kirsch et al., 1993). According to the NALS, adults in Levels 1 and 2 generally earn less income, are more likely to be unemployed, are more likely to be receiving welfare, and are less likely to participate in voting and other civic activities, than are adults in NALS Levels 3, 4, and 5 (Kirsch et al., 1993). Moreover, their capacity for lifelong learning is severely constrained by their low literacy skills. Further, most adults in Level 1 and some at Level 2 are probably less able to support the literacy development and school success of their children. Adults in Levels 1 and 2 who also have LEP probably face additional obstacles to supporting their children's English literacy.

LEP adults appear to have a substantial interest in improving their English speaking and literacy. The NHES (1997) found that, of the 63% of nonnative speakers of English who did not report reading English well, 11% said they had actually taken an ESOL class within the last 12 months, and 16% reported that they were strongly interested in taking such classes, with an additional 9% reporting they were moderately interested. Further, increasing numbers of LEP adults are enrolling in classes to improve their English speaking and reading skills. The national percentage of adult learners enrolling in ESOL classes has doubled in less than two decades, from 19% of all learners in 1980 (Office of Vocational and Adult Education, [OVAE], 1991) to 39% in 1996 (OVAE, 1998). In California, two out of every three adult education students are now enrolled in ESOL classes (OVAE, 1998). Increased ESOL enrollments are not limited to border states or areas that are traditional centers of immigration. States such as Maine (7%) and North Carolina (15%) now report significant numbers of ESOL enrollees (OVAE, 1998).

This rise in LEP enrollees has been reflected in Even Start Family Literacy programs. The percentage of Even Start adults reporting primary languages other than English has risen markedly, from 21% in 1989–1990 to 39% in 1996–1997 (Tao, Gamse, & Tarr, 1998) and to 42% by 1998–1999 (St.Pierre, Riccuiti, Tao, & Creps, 2001). Of the 42% of Even Start parents who reported speaking languages other than English at home, 35% speak Spanish, and 7% speak other languages (St.Pierre et al., 2001). These data reflect broader trends in the adult basic education population. NALS researcher Andrew Kolstad (personal communication, July 6, 1998) reported that, in NALS Levels 1 and 2, Spanish speakers (accounting for 13.8% of all U.S. adults) were the most numerous language group, after English speakers. However, the linguistic picture quickly becomes very diverse after English and Spanish. Thirty other languages account for the remaining 6.1% of the Level 1 and Level 2 population, with no single language accounting for more than 0.6% of the total, and with 21 languages accounting for 0.1% or less (A. Kolstad, personal communication, July 7, 1998). Coping with this language diversity presents a serious challenge to state and local K–12 educators in many areas of the United States, and it poses a similar challenge to Even Start programs.

Needs Assessment From the Standpoint of ESOL Families

Tao et al. (1998) found that learning English was the second most frequently cited reason given by all parents for enrolling in a family literacy program. They also noted that 27% of the Even Start sites reported that many families needed translation and interpretation services, and 4% of the sites reported that all families needed such services. In an earlier Even Start report, Tao, Swartz, St.Pierre, and Tarr (1997) documented that many Even Start ESOL parents are relative newcomers to the United States: 32% of the Hispanic families and 44% of the Asian families had been in the country for 5 years or less.

Tao et al. (1998) also summarized ESOL Even Start parents' evaluations of their English proficiency: 26% reported that they spoke English not at all, and 50% reported that they spoke English not well. English literacy self-reports were similar: 30% said they read English not at all, and 47% said they read English not well. These figures on time of residence in the United States and self-reported English speaking and reading reveal the need for improved English skills that is felt by many Even Start parents.

What about the native-language educational backgrounds of these LEP adults? Most LEP adults in Even Start had limited native-language educational backgrounds: 60% of the LEP adults participating in Even Start reported completion of nine or fewer years of schooling, with many reporting substantially fewer (St.Pierre et al., 2001). Years of schooling do not necessarily correlate with higher levels of skills, if the schooling took place in rural areas in developing countries, especially in areas that have been disrupted by war and famine. Moreover, not all immigrants' formal schooling occurred in their native languages. For example, Haitian Creole speakers, indigenous Mexicans speaking Native American languages, and speakers of many West African languages, all began school as *second-language learners*. Adults with limited native-language education levels have fewer literacy skills and less school-based background knowledge available for transfer to English. They are often faced with learning a concept, in math, social studies, or science, for the first time in English. In addition, those with few years of primary education may not have had the chance to learn basic study skills that can be applied to their ESOL learning. Finally, even if these adults with LEP learn to *speak* English fluently, their low levels of formal education may make it difficult for them to support their children's school success beyond the primary literacy levels.

CONTRIBUTIONS FROM RESEARCH ON SECOND-LANGUAGE AND LITERACY LEARNING

Differences Among Participants in English Proficiency

Language proficiency, either in a first or second language, is not a unitary phenomenon (Snow, 1991). An individual's language proficiency or skill varies across linguistic tasks, each of which presents slightly different performance demands. For example, different skills are used in conversing face to face, with an active and collaborative interlocutor, than are necessary for conveying the same information to a distant or unspecified audience. Although adult native speakers display some unevenness of skill level across tasks, such discrepancies are even more pronounced in young children and second-language learners, whose range of language experiences in the target language are often more constricted. Furthermore, when individuals who are bilingual enter new settings where the opportunities for interaction in one of their languages are reduced, they often suffer attrition of skills in that language (Grosjean, 1982). Both these phenomena—wide variability in contexts of English use and vulnerability to attrition—mean that English-language skills among nonnative speakers enrolled in family literacy programs may vary enormously, in ways that are not easily predictable on the basis of length of residence. Such differences in English-language skills are relevant for family literacy programs targeting or including ESOL participants, because level of proficiency in English has been found to relate to English-reading fluency and comprehension (for review, see Devine, 1988), as well as to reading strategies (Cziko, 1980).

Age Differences Among Participants Learning English

Because family members participating in family literacy programs range widely in age, individuals can be expected to learn and acquire English at different rates and achieve different competence levels. Reviews of the research literature, by Krashen, Long, and Scarcella (1979), Krashen, Scarcella, and Long (1982), and, later, by Long (1990, 1993), suggest that adults proceed through the early stages of second-language acquisition faster than do children. Furthermore, older children appear to have an advantage over younger children in the early stages of acquisition. The age advantage for older learners is particularly apparent in morphological and syntactic development (Snow & Hoefnagel-Höhle, 1978), but is also observable in phonology during the earliest stage of acquisition. In terms of rate of acquisition, adults and adolescents seem to learn a second language faster than young children, particularly during the first months or years of learning. Many of these studies included people with relatively high levels of literacy and formal schooling in their native languages, so caution needs to be taken in interpreting these results for Even Start ESOL parents. More research among low-literacy adults is needed to refine our understanding of how they acquire foreign languages.

Although older individuals enjoy an initial advantage in rate of acquisition, they are less likely to ultimately achieve native-like competence. Particularly in pronunciation (Oyama, 1976), but also in grammatical (morphosyntactic) skills (Johnson & Newport, 1989; Patkowski, 1982, 1990), individuals who begin learning a second language early in childhood tend to ultimately achieve levels of competence closer to those of native speakers. Age-related differences in second-language pronunciation abilities are unlikely to affect literacy acquisition directly, but they may have an effect if pronunciation difficulties occur for forms that signal important grammatical differences. Failure to perceive or produce those forms can affect reading comprehension, writing, and comprehensibility in one's spoken language (Berman, 1984). For example, a learner who does not distinguish *walk* from *walked* might well miss crucial information in reading a relatively simple text. Of course, in classrooms, these age-related differences in rate and ultimate achievement in second-language acquisition are not easily observable, because age and length of exposure are often confounded. For example, in a given family literacy program, one might have adults and young children who are just beginning to acquire English, as well as adults who have been exposed to English for a number of years.

Differences Across Languages

In addition to differences in rate of acquisition of a second language related to learner characteristics, there are also differences in rate of acquisition and patterns of errors related to the learner's native language. Languages more closely related to English are generally acquired by native English speakers more quickly than are languages less closely related. One rather gross measure of the time required to attain proficiency in different languages is the duration of intensive courses offered by the Foreign Service Institute for federal foreign service staff. Odlin (1989) reports, for example, that native speakers of English who are learning Spanish or French can be expected, after 20 weeks of intensive full-time training, to reach levels that would require 44 weeks of similarly intense training in Serbo-Croatian or Mandarin Chinese. By the same token, students of ESOL, who are native speakers of languages less closely related to English, can be expected to require longer periods of training to achieve given levels of English proficiency than native speakers of languages more closely related to English. These differences probably reflect both lexical and grammatical similarities across the native and target languages. However, it is worth noting that descriptions based on typological similarity across languages have focused on second-language learners who are already literate in their first language. It is possible that learners with poor literacy skills in their native language may be less able to capitalize on those lexical similarities between their native language and English that are more transparent in written than in spoken form.

Other differences across languages are specific to the orthographies involved (Koda, 1989), that is, the representation of the sounds of a language by written or printed symbols. Phonological awareness at the level of individual sounds (phonemic awareness) is important for decoding text in alphabetic languages, but not in nonalphabetic languages, such as Chinese. Adults and children who read Chinese characters or Japanese kanji scripts do not demonstrate the same kinds of phonemic awareness as individuals already literate in an alphabetic script (Bialystok, 1997; Mann, 1986; Read, Yun-fei, Hong-Yin, & Bao-Qing, 1986). Even among alphabetic languages, there is wide variation in the predictability of phoneme–grapheme correspondence, with English being much less predictable than Spanish, for example. Literate native Spanish speakers may bring very different expectations to the English-literacy acquisition task. Although some research (e.g., Feitelson, 1987) suggests that orthographic similarity between first and second languages may promote transfer of reading skills or strategies, other researchers have suggested that such effects may be short-lived (Carlo, 1994). The implications of native-language literacy for English-literacy acquisition depend on characteristics of the orthography in the learner's native language and on their oral and literacy levels in English. For example, a well-educated Spanish speaker may start acquiring English literacy with an advantage over an equally well-educated Chinese speaker, but, once the Chinese speaker has learned and practiced English decoding sufficiently, differences between the learners will be minimized.

Differences in Adult Learners' Previous Educational Experiences

Although many immigrants to the United States arrive with strong educational backgrounds, others come from countries whose educational systems have been disrupted by political or social unrest, and still others come from countries in which no more than a few years of education are obligatory or customary, especially in rural areas. Individuals from all these situations may find themselves in ESOL literacy classes or family literacy programs. Although literate in their first language to a level considered functional in their home countries, many may find that the background knowledge they have acquired may not be sufficient or relevant to second-language texts that they must read, either in or outside the classroom. Conversely, the background knowledge that they bring may not be tapped by literacy activities in the new cultural context. Because insufficient familiarity with content has adverse consequences for reading comprehension in second- as well as first-language literacy (Carrell, 1987), these adults face particular challenges.

Low levels of native-language education among Even Start parents can also have implications for staffing. Teachers working with some adults with low levels of native-language literacy may need to be prepared to teach both ESOL and reading pedagogy. If adults' reading skills are very low in their first language (e.g., below grade equivalent 5) and they have not had opportunities to read very much in their native language, then they may not have achieved levels of orthographic processing and fluency that will automatically facilitate English decoding. As a result, teaching reading in English may involve more than simply presenting a cursory review of English sounds and spelling, then counting on students' native-language orthographic processing to carry them through. These adults may need an approach to reading instruction that is similar to what research and practice have found to be effective with children: direct, systematic, sequential teaching of English phonics, combined with ample opportunities to read meaningful, connected text, both orally and silently (Adams, 1994; Snow, Burns, & Griffin, 1998). ESOL adults may learn these second-language orthographic processing skills somewhat faster than do children, and teachers would certainly want to use adult materials; nevertheless, a careful, systematic approach to instruction may be appropriate.

Part of participating in any school is understanding the roles and expectations of being a student. Different cultures construct the student–teacher relationship, and the responsibilities of students and teachers, differently. The degrees to which students engage in rote memorization versus analysis, to which teacher-centered versus student-originated instruction occurs, and to which peer interaction is incorporated into instruction, vary across cultures and educational systems. Indeed, some of these same dimensions differentiate adult literacy programs in the United States (Purcell-Gates, Degener, & Jacobson, 1998). For those arriving from other countries, it is necessary for family literacy programs to be aware of, and responsive to, the student roles and expectations previously held by family members.

Differences in First- and Second-Language Literacy Experiences and Instruction

As Hornberger (1994) points out, educational programs for linguistic-minority children range from those that completely ignore native-language literacy instruction, or that provide minimal, short-term instruction as a transition to English literacy, to those that actively strive to develop and maintain both native-language and English-literacy skills. Preschool, kindergarten, and school-aged children may enter family literacy programs having had diverse literacy and emergent literacy classroom experiences in their native language. Similarly, adult ESOL learners bring with them varying experiences with literacy instruction in their native language, not only with respect to the amount of explicit instruction, but also with the nature of that instruction (McKay & Weinstein-Shr, 1993). These experiences influence the participants' expectations of what constitutes instruction, and will also shape their notions about the uses of print (Cochran-Smith, 1984). Furthermore, the functions of first-language literacy and types of first-language texts with which participants have interacted may differ from the functions and texts necessary in their second language, English (Ramirez, 1994).

Adults and children who have achieved some proficiency in native-language literacy may apply what they know about first-language reading and writing to reading and writing in English (Cummins, 1980; Edelsky, 1982). Such transfer can occur at many different levels. *Conceptual transfer*, for example, involves experience with the functions of print, or the nature of literacy forms. *Linguistic transfer* would include, for example, access to word knowledge based on cognates or understanding that tense or number need to be marked. *Metacognitive transfer* refers to the use in a second language of strategies for reading comprehension, such as previewing the text, using context to guess at word meanings, and self-monitoring (Hudelson, 1987; Jimenez, Garcia, & Pearson, 1996). What can be transferred from first-language reading depends to some extent on the level of native-language literacy the individual has achieved.

Although supporting students' transfer of literacy skills from any specific native language to English may be a desirable instructional strategy, we must recognize that very little information exists about the normal course of literacy development for most languages and orthographies. Fluent readers of Turkish can be presumed to have achieved sophisticated levels of phoneme segmentation, but fluent readers of Arabic may well be operating with the syllable, rather than the phoneme, as the smallest meaningful unit. Many Spanish readers may have learned to read consonant–vowel units, for example, *ba, da, la,* and *ma*. Initially, this may help to direct them to focus on individual sounds, which are especially useful in English reading, with its multiplicity of syllable types and frequent consonant clusters (Adams, 1994). Bernhardt (1987) has shown that, in German, a language in which much syntactic and semantic information is carried by the article, fluent readers focus much longer on articles than do fluent readers of English. German speakers learning English ultimately discover that transferring this strategy is not helpful. At first, some readers of Arabic may experience difficulty with spelling English vowels, because vowels are not represented in most Arabic writing. The way vowels are written in English can also present initial problems for students from the East African nation of Eritrea, because, in Amharic, vowels are written as small marks that can appear at different points all around a consonant letter, in effect combining consonant and vowel symbols in one annotated character.

Such orthographic differences between written English and other languages are not insurmountable; they are routinely overcome by ESOL learners, for example, by Amharic speakers who learn that English vowel sounds are represented by letters. However, more research in this area is needed, so that ESOL teachers can anticipate difficulties and ensure that transitions from the first to the second language occur more easily for adult learners.

DESIGN PRINCIPLES FOR FAMILY LITERACY PROGRAMS SERVING ESOL FAMILIES

Many factors can make an ESOL adult literacy program more challenging than similar programs designed for the English-speaking adult basic education population. In this section, we raise issues related to the special status of family literacy programs specifically designed for learners with limited proficiency in English, as well as for those that include a high percentage of ESOL learners.

Range of Levels Represented

For both the adults and the children in ESOL family literacy programs, a wide range of levels of proficiency in English may be represented. Focusing on the parents first, these levels include four groups: (a) adults who have just arrived in the United States with essentially no knowledge of English; (b) adults who have lived here for some time, but who have had limited opportunities to use or to hear English; (c) adults who have never previously lived in an English-speaking country, but who have studied English as a foreign language; and (d) adults who have a fair level of speaking and oral comprehension ability in English, but who have limited literacy skills, and perhaps limited capacities in more formal oral settings. When adults representing these different levels are together in one classroom, perhaps even with a few native speakers in an adult basic education curriculum who are seeking literacy support, the challenge to the teacher is enormous, and selecting instructional goals becomes difficult. In a heterogeneous group, the pedagogical decision to focus on oral versus literate skills, or on basic versus more advanced literacy skills, can limit the value and utility of instruction, for some participants.

Issues of different language backgrounds provide challenges for the parenting component of family literacy programs. Challenges arise from cultural differences in parental beliefs, problems in understanding the unwritten rules of parental versus school responsibility, parental roles in supporting educational achievement and communicating with the school, and appropriate discipline. These challenges may be particularly difficult to address in ways that are clear to beginning English-language learners. Strategies for addressing these matters are relatively straightforward, when the immigrant group is numerous or when program personnel speak the immigrant language; programs must work harder when an isolated family, from an unfamiliar background, arrives. Fortunately, resources such as the Center for Applied Linguistics (www.cal.org) provide handbooks for immigrants in a variety of languages, as well as brief guides to the culture and language of immigrant groups for program personnel. They also provide referrals to other resources. However, more research and more usable resources are needed in this area.

Children of immigrant parents may display limited proficiency in English, similar to their parents, or may have acquired considerable real or partly illusory proficiency from television, playmates, and older siblings. Assessing the language skills of young children is much harder, however, as is determining precisely what aspects of language should be emphasized in educational programs designed for them. Furthermore, given the wide age range of children included in family literacy programs, and the enormous developmental differences and corresponding differences in appropriate literacy and language activities for younger and older children, the design of an educational program is extremely difficult. Detailed, context-specific research is needed, not just for family literacy programs, but for Head Start and primary school education, as well.

Early Childhood Education for Children Learning English as a Second Language

Language-teaching programs for children can be placed on a continuum determined by the degree to which the first language is used in instruction or for noninstructional support, and the degree to which teaching of content (in this case, literacy skills) occurs in the first or the second language. We identify five different types here.

First, programs in which English is used all the time, and in which the second-language speaker is integrated into a classroom of primarily native speakers, are called *submersion programs*, some of which provide some ESOL support, or structured teaching of English-language skills. Second, programs that serve only or primarily second-language speakers, but use only English, are typically *sheltered English programs*—that is, an explicit attempt is made to use simple, comprehensible English as a mechanism for teaching English skills. Third, programs that use simplified English with a class full of children who have the same first language (and thus can use that language for peer interaction) are called *immersion programs*. Fourth, programs that use the native language for some instructional purposes are *bilingual programs*; fully bilingual programs teach subject matter in the native language, sometimes reviewing that same material in English as a mechanism for learning English. A more frequently encountered (but not necessarily better) model is one in which a single teacher alternates between the use of the native language and English, based on what is considered optimal. Finally, *two-way bilingual programs* incorporate children who are native speakers of English and provide instruction in both English and the other language. The presence of English-speaking children increases the amount of input from native speakers and expands the kinds of communicative activity that go on in English.

A family literacy program needs to decide—given local demographics, available teaching skills, and participant preference—which model will work best for the early childhood education component of that specific program. The decision is made more difficult by the greater vulnerability of native-language skills among young children, and the possibility that early exposure to English-only educational settings will threaten the continued development of native-language skills.

An additional factor that needs to be considered in designing the early childhood component of a family literacy program is the array of programs available in the local school system. If bilingual or two-way bilingual programs are provided, hurrying young children into English in their preschool years is not necessary. Children will be better served by acquiring solid skills in their native language and by making use of the educational programs available from kindergarten to develop English competence (Snow et al., 1998). If the local schools provide only submersion, with or without ESOL for non-English speakers, or for speakers of particular languages represented in the family literacy program, then some exposure to English for preschool-aged children may be beneficial.

The presence of children who do not share a language with the majority creates enormous challenges in early childhood settings. Such children often display their frustration at their difficulties in communicating by withdrawing, having tantrums, or becoming aggressive. The social communication that enables children to learn English is difficult to establish, because their peers are often insensitive to their difficulties, ignoring or rejecting the nonnative speaker (Tabors, 1997). The classroom teacher needs enormous skill and understanding to deal with the special demands of children with low proficiency in English, and professional development directed to this end should be provided.

Time on Task

Young children take about 5 years to acquire a vocabulary of about 5000 words in their first language (Adams, 1994). Normally developing first-language speakers of English spend a year or two noticing and learning about the alphabet and about the phonological structure of words that they know, before they ever receive formal instruction in reading. Once they enter kindergarten, they spend a year practicing preliteracy skills, followed by a year and a half or so mastering the letter–sound relationships in English orthography, followed by another 2 years of practice in reading skills and comprehension strategies, before they become independent readers at about age 9 (Adams, 1994; Snow et al., 1998). Given that adults are somewhat more efficient than children in acquiring oral second-language skills, adults are probably more efficient than children in acquiring literacy, as well, under ideal circumstances. Unfortunately, ideal circumstances are rarely obtained in the United States. Countries providing adequate settings, such as The Netherlands and Israel, typically create full-time language programs, which last several months and which provide financial support, so that newcomers can take advantage of these programs (Verhallen, 1996).

Adult literacy and ESOL programs in general, including family literacy programs, are subject to what Sticht, McDonald, and Erickson (1998) call "turbulence." They describe how some students may enroll, attend for a few weeks, then drop out for good; others spend a few weeks in class, then disappear, to return later in the semester for the last few weeks; others keep plugging along, but manage to miss every other class; others (because of open-entry–open-exit policies) join a class at various points in the semester (up to and including the final weeks); and only a small fraction of students (fewer than 10% in some classrooms) start a class at the beginning, attend regularly, and miss a minimum number of classes throughout the semester. This turbulence makes planning lessons difficult, undermines instruction, and disrupts the strong network of peer support that can help adults learn. Currently, programs are funded on the basis of the number of students enrolled, not student attendance and persistence. This funding criterion gives programs disincentives to maximize attendance and persistence. Changing the incentives might well lead to strategies such as providing transportation, child care, outreach to the students' employers, and counseling, to promote regular attendance (Comings, Parrella, & Soricone, 1999).

In addition to the difficulties posed by attendance, many adult ESOL learners have few opportunities outside formal instructional settings for practicing their literacy, English-speaking, and listening skills. Teachers could use assignments and support networks for practice opportunities outside of class. For example, the Dutch second-language programs for newcomers provide contacts with host families and internships with employers as supports to the in-class learning (Verhallen, personal communication, 2001). Without these kinds of opportunities, the goals of the educational programs must be realistic regarding the limited in-class time available to students for learning.

RESEARCH AND EVALUATION PRINCIPLES

Design of a Family Literacy Program to Serve ESOL Families

A family literacy program that served ESOL families effectively would be characterized by the following elements:

1. A mechanism for ensuring appropriate placement of families in programs, based on parents' English proficiency, first-language literacy skills, educational history, and needs for language and literacy skills in English, as well as on their goals for their children and their children's educational options.

2. Teachers who are appropriately prepared to deal with the needs of ESOL families and children. Such teachers would be knowledgeable about the course of literacy acquisition in a second language and about the cultural differences they might encounter.

3. A research-based curriculum that takes into account the realities of how much time families can spend in family literacy programs. Given welfare reform and other constraints on the weekly schedules of immigrant families, programs cannot typically expect more than a few hours a week of participation, and adult literacy programs in general must deal with frequent absenteeism and adjustments to the life circumstances of their students. Curricular designs that presuppose several hours a week of class time and considerable out-of-class study time simply will not work.

These three elements are relatively easy to define, but extremely difficult to implement. Each of the three raises a number of research questions and presupposes adequate resources. For example, we know little about how best to evaluate ESOL family needs, how to design and deliver professional development about English-language learning efficiently and effectively, or how to adapt curricula for the ESOL family literacy population. We sketch here an array of questions that need to be addressed and an array of resources that need to be available to allow family literacy programs serving ESOL families to incorporate all of these elements.

Complexity of Evaluating and Improving Family Literacy Programs

Regarding family literacy programs, Hayes (1996) argued that they "may . . . be less efficient in producing direct, short-term effects [such as] General Educational Development (GED) production, job placements, or other *direct* adult education goals" (p. 1) than pure adult education programs, which focus on these single outcomes exclusively. Hayes also pointed out that family literacy programs have multiple and complex goals for parents and their children: Some goals are narrowly academic, such as improving a parent's reading or English speaking and listening; but other goals are inherently more complex and harder to achieve, involving a range of issues pertaining to family culture and basic parent–child interactions. We believe that researchers and policymakers should be cautious when comparing results in family literacy programs with those in regular adult education programs.

Program implementation can be difficult and inefficient because parents and children in family literacy programs range in levels in English speaking, listening, and literacy. This situation most often happens in Even Start programs with large and diverse recruitment areas. A one-room schoolhouse is created in the classroom, in which teachers must divide the limited available instructional time among students on different levels. This situation results in less time on-task for some learners than they would receive in a regular ESOL program with multiple levels of homogeneous classes. The lack of responsiveness for the range of levels of ESOL families should not be accepted as the inevitable result of the multiple and complex goals of family literacy programs.

Researchers and evaluators should be careful to identify shortcomings, such as poor organization or assessment and the absence of staff training that can impact program effectiveness. Moreover, higher expectations are in order for ESOL family literacy. For example, some ESOL family literacy programs could be expected to produce faster gains in English speaking and listening than regular adult ESOL classes, if these parents participate in the real-world context of their children's school and language development, which facilitates their own English skills. The task facing researchers and evaluators of ESOL Even Start programs is to find ways of documenting, measuring, and evaluating what are inherently complex teaching and learning environments.

Proposed Research Agenda to Guide Program Improvement

Relating to the three major design principles articulated earlier, we propose areas for research that will directly improve ESOL family literacy programs.

Appropriate Placement. We know little about which families benefit optimally from family literacy programs. It would also be desirable to know for which families the parenting component carries added value. For example, adults struggling with the first stages of acquiring oral or literacy skills in English may not benefit from parenting activities or, alternately, parenting activities may constitute ideal circumstances for acquiring basic English. We propose systematic research focused on the question, Which families benefit most from which types of programs?

Even before questions of appropriate placement can be seriously posed, however, we also need tools to categorize and characterize families' needs. Much better assessment tools are needed for making decisions about native-language literacy skills and about the

English-language and literacy skills of ESOL speakers. The assessments currently utilized have not solved the dilemma of choosing between contextually rich, but often unreliable, measures versus more objective, but less informative measures, particularly for oral language proficiency. Native-language literacy assessments are available only for a few languages, and even then are often of limited utility to monolingual English teachers. Developing comprehensive but usable assessment tools constitutes a major research agenda that is prerequisite to making placement decisions for parents, for children, and for families.

In addition to assessments of language and literacy skills, we need tools for determining family goals and desires. Programs will always function better if they meet the needs and the personally formulated goals of participants, yet too often curriculum is designed without input from the students. Family goals are shaped by family configuration (e.g., whether the children are infants or of school age and needing help with homework, or whether issues of interface with health providers and school practitioners arise or not). Family goals for their children's language skills also need consideration. Some immigrant families value the rapid acquisition of English by their children over the maintenance of the home language; others might seek help with the challenge of maintaining bilingualism in the home. Families often do not realize that their children's school success is not necessarily dependent on having achieved English proficiency during the preschool period, nor are they always aware of the fragility of the first language in young children. If programs obtained information from the families about their goals and preferences, parenting education could help immigrant families address these kinds of issues.

Mechanisms and Resources for Professional Development.   Family literacy programs serving ESOL learners work well if practitioners understand the complexities of literacy learning in a second language and the potential enormity of cultural differences between immigrants and the traditional adult basic education learners. This implies mastering considerable technical information about language and literacy development, in addition to considerable specific information about the linguistic and cultural groups the teachers encounter in their classrooms. Empathy toward members of other cultures is a prerequisite, but is insufficient to solve the issues of communicative breakdown and to determine what specific kinds of information about American society and cultural practices are necessary for learners.

Professional development is a major challenge in the adult literacy field, because qualifications to teach in adult programs vary greatly across states, and most teachers work part-time. Furthermore, opportunities for ongoing professional development are limited by fiscal considerations, are typically of short duration (brief workshops), and are of uneven quality (Florez, 1997). Considerable expansion and improvement of the professional development opportunities for family literacy practitioners is needed.

Information about the immigrant groups encountered by teachers could be disseminated more widely, using electronic media, but, in addition, networks of informants should be established to provide targeted information. For example, a network could be developed of college and university researchers, drawn from education, anthropology, and linguistics, to cover many of the languages and cultures of students in ESOL programs. So, via the Internet, an ESOL family literacy teacher in Vermont might contact a scholar at a university in California for information about the language and culture of Eritreans.

The considerations noted here for adult literacy instructors also apply to early childhood practitioners. Professional qualifications are often not a prerequisite for employment, and opportunities are limited for participation in well-structured or well-designed professional development networks. Even professionally trained early childhood educators typically have had limited instruction in critical topics, such as language development, bilingualism, and cultural differences. Traditionally, training has emphasized the importance of unstructured play and social development—curricula that may not in themselves provide the rich input needed to ensure optimal English-language acquisition for non-native-speaking children.

Well-Designed Curricula.   Content of adult ESOL instruction, of parenting education, and of early childhood programs is well established. Two directions are appropriate for building on these content areas: adapting Even Start curricula for ESOL learners, and determining the important focus for ESOL families, given limited instructional time.

An initial issue in adult ESOL literacy instruction is to determine the goals of the learners. Do they need English and English literacy primarily for purposes of survival in this society (conversational English, reading signs, product labels, and other limited print skills)? Or are they seeking the skills that would offer access to advanced job training and professional advancement (requiring much more focus on reading comprehension and writing skills, for example)? The need to focus instruction on the more advanced skills depends in part on the native-language accomplishments of the learners; highly literate and educated immigrants may well be able to apply instruction in conversational English and basic English orthography to broader, more challenging literacy contexts. Those arriving with little formal education in the first language, however, will need to acquire for the first time in their English-literacy classes, the skills that are needed for job interviews, for reading complex texts, and for writing formal letters because they do not have these skills in the native language. Good curricular design would take these various factors into consideration, and would allocate the limited resources of time and instructional focus accordingly.

In addition, current curriculum design often does not account for the limited time ESOL Even Start participants can spend in class, or outside of class, on literacy skills. Adults can be relatively fast and efficient language learners, but they do need to devote time to the task. Yet, many adult learners live and work in contexts in which they hear or read little English outside of their literacy classes. One goal of the curriculum should be to assess the language-learning resources of the learners (Can they use independent reading as a basis for learning English? Can they engage in casual conversation with native speakers, effectively? Do they have the study skills that would enable them to use vocabulary lists or grammar books?) and to adjust the teaching to those resources.

Last, technology may have an important role to play in the curriculum of adult ESOL learners and their children in Even Start. In addition to learning to use computers and Internet resources, technology could play a direct role in second-language speech and reading acquisition for adults and children. Computer speech-recognition software could enable busy adults to use an interactive language lab in their homes. Children and adults could explore interactive children's books and vocabulary-building activities in their native language or in English. Adults could learn to use the Internet to maintain contact with native-language literacy and cultural activities.

Finally, we recommend the following undertakings:

- Developing better assessment tools for characterizing native-language and English-literacy skills
- Developing assessment tools for determining families' parenting goals and desires
- Assessing which families benefit most from which kinds of programs
- Compiling information about linguistic and cultural needs of various groups
- Training for staff on working with multilanguage learners
- Evaluating procedures for disseminating information about linguistic and cultural differences to program staff
- Adapting Even Start curricula for ESOL learners
- Developing tools to reflect adult learners' literacy goals
- Designing and evaluating technology-based learning aids.

CONCLUSION

Although many important questions remain to be answered, researchers and experienced practitioners in the fields of language acquisition, reading, and early childhood development know a great deal about best practices, for example, how to create effective language and literacy environments for children and how to help adults learn new languages and become more literate. The challenge is to implement best practices in the space occupied by Even Start and other family literacy programs, given the low salaries and limited professional preparation typical of adult literacy and early childhood settings. With the introduction of better procedures for placing families in programs, of more substantive professional development for family literacy practitioners, and of better-structured curricula, these challenges can be addressed.

REFERENCES

Adams, M. J. (1994). *Beginning to read.* Cambridge, MA: MIT Press.

Berman, R. (1984). Syntactic components of the foreign language reading process. In J. C. Alderson & A. H. Urquhart (Eds.), *Reading in a foreign language.* New York: Longman.

Bernhardt, E. B. (1987). Cognitive processes in L2: An examination of reading behaviors. In J. Lantolf & A. Labarca (Eds.), *Research in second language learning: Focus on the classroom.* Norwood, NJ: Ablex.

Bialystok, E. (1997). Effect of bilingualism and biliteracy on children's emerging concepts of print. *Developmental Psychology, 33,* 429–440.

Carlo, M. (1994). *Does orthographic structure similarity affect visual word recognition in English–Spanish bilinguals?* Unpublished doctoral thesis, University of Massachusetts at Amherst.

Carrell, P. L. (1987). Content and formal schemata in ESL reading. *TESOL Quarterly, 18,* 441–469.

Cochran-Smith, M. (1984). *The making of a reader.* Norwood, NJ: Ablex.

Comings, J., Parrella, A., & Soricone, L. (1999). *Persistence among adult basic education students in pre-GED classes* (NCSALL Reports No. 12). Cambridge, MA: National Center for the Study of Adult Learning and Literacy.

Cummins, J. (1980). The cross-lingual dimensions of language proficiency: Implications for bilingual education and the optimal age issue. *TESOL Quarterly, 14,* 175–187.

Cziko, G. A. (1980). Language competence and reading strategies: A comparison of first- and second-language oral reading errors. *Language Learning, 30,* 101–116.

Devine, J. (1988). The relationship between general language competence and second language reading proficiency: Implications for teaching. In P. Carrell, J. Devine, & D. Eskey (Eds.), *Interactive approaches to second language reading* (pp. 260–277). Cambridge, England: Cambridge University Press.

Edelsky, C. (1982). Writing in a bilingual program: The relation of L1 and L2 texts. *TESOL Quarterly, 16,* 211–228.

Feitelson, D. (1987). Reconsidering the effects of school and home for literacy in a multicultural cross-language context: The case of Israel. In D. Wagner (Ed.), *The future of literacy in a changing world.* Oxford, England: Pergamon.

Florez, M. C. (1997). *The adult ESL teaching professional.* Washington, DC: National Clearinghouse for ESL Literacy Education. (ERIC Document Reproduction Service No. EDO-LE-98–02.)

Grosjean, J. (1982). *Life with two languages.* Cambridge, MA: Harvard University Press.

Hayes, A. (1996). *Longitudinal study of family literacy program outcomes.* Retrieved August 15, 2000, from <http://www.ed.gov/pubs/FamLit/long.html>

Hornberger, N. H. (1994). Continua of biliteracy. In B. M. Ferdman, R. Weber & A. G. Ramirez (Eds.), *Literacy across languages and cultures.* Albany, NY: State University of New York Press.

Hudelson, S. (1987). The role of native language literacy in the education of language minority children. *Language Arts, 64,* 827–841.

Jimenez, R. T., Garcia, G. E., & Pearson, P. D. (1996). The reading strategies of bilingual Latina/o students who are successful English readers: Opportunities and obstacles. *Reading Research Quarterly, 31,* 90–112.

Johnson, J. S., & Newport, E. L. (1989). Critical period effects in second language learning: The influence of maturational state on the acquisition of English as a second language. *Cognitive Psychology, 21,* 60–99.

Kirsch, I. S., Jungeblut, A., Jenkins, L., & Kolstad, A. (1993). *Adult literacy in America: A first look at the results of the National Adult Literacy Survey.* Princeton, NJ: Educational Testing Service.

Koda, K. (1989). Effects of L1 orthographic representation on L2 phonological coding strategies. *Journal of Psycholinguistic Research, 18,* 201–222.

Krashen, S. D., Long, M. H., and Scarcella, R. C. (1979). Age, rate, and eventual attainment in second language acquisition. *TESOL Quarterly, 13,* 573–582.

Krashen, S. D., Scarcella, R. C., & Long, M. H. (Eds.). (1982). Child–adult differences in second language acquisition. Rowley, MA: Newbury House.

Long, M. H. (1990). Maturational constraints on language development. *Studies in Second Language Acquisition, 12*(3), 251–285.

Long, M. H. (1993). Second language acquisition as a function of age. In K. Hyltenstam & A. Viberg (Eds.), *Progression and regression in language.* Cambridge, England: Cambridge University Press.

Mann, V. A. (1986). Phonological awareness: The role of reading experience. *Cognition, 24,* 65–92.

McKay, S. L., & Weinstein-Shr, G. (1993). English literacy in the U.S.: National policies, personal consequences. *TESOL Quarterly, 27,* 399–419.

National Household Education Survey (NHES) (1997). Washington, DC: U.S. Department of Education, National Center for Educational Statistics.

Odlin, T. (1989). *Language transfer: Cross-linguistic influence in language learning.* Cambridge, England: Cambridge University Press.

Office of Vocational and Adult Education. (1991). *Enrollment of participants by instructional programs, 1990.* Washington, DC: U.S. Department of Education.

Office of Vocational and Adult Education. (1998). *Enrollment of participants by instructional programs, 1996.* Washington, DC: U.S. Department of Education.

Oyama, S. C. (1976). A sensitive period for the acquisition of a nonnative phonological system. *Journal of Psycholinguistic Research, 5*(3), 261–283.

Patkowski, M. (1982). The sensitive period for the acquisition of syntax in a second language. *Language Learning, 30*(2), 449–472.

Patkowski, M. (1990). Age and accent in a second language: A reply to James Emil Flege. *Applied Linguistics, 11,* 73–89.

Purcell-Gates, V., Degener, S., & Jacobson, E. (1998). *U.S. adult literacy program practice: A typology across dimensions of life-contextualized/decontextualized and dialogic/monologic* (NCSALL Report No. 2). Boston, MA: World Education.

Ramirez, A. G. (1994). Literacy acquisition among second language learners. In B. M. Ferdman, R. Weber, & A. G. Ramirez (Eds.), *Literacy across languages and cultures.* Albany, NY: State University of New York Press.

Read, C., Yun-Fei, Z., Hong-Yin, N., & Bao-Qing, D. (1986). The ability to manipulate speech sounds depends on knowing alphabetic spelling. *Cognition, 24,* 31–44.

Snow, C. E. (1991). Language proficiency: Towards a definition. In G. Appel & H. W. Dechert (Eds.), *A case for psycholinguistic cases* (pp. 63–89). Amsterdam: John Benjamins.

Snow, C. E., Burns, S. M., & Griffin, P. (Eds.). (1998). *Preventing reading difficulties in young children.* Washington, DC: Academy Press.

Snow, C. E., & Hoefnagel-Höhle, M. (1978). Critical period for language acquisition: Evidence from second language learning. *Child Development, 49,* 1263–1279.

Sticht, T., McDonald, B., & Erickson, P. (1998). *Passports to paradise: The struggle to teach and learn on the margins of adult education.* San Diego, CA: Consortium for Workforce Education and Lifelong Learning.

St.Pierre, R., Riccuifi, A., Tao, F., & Creps, D. (2001). National evaluation of the Even Start family literacy program: 1998–2000. Washington, DC: U.S. Department of Education, Planning and Evaluation Service.

Tabors, P. (1997). *One child, two languages: A guide for early childhood educators of children learning English as a second language.* Baltimore, MD: Paul H. Brookes Publishing.

Tao, F., Gamse, B., & Tarr, H. (1998). *National evaluation of the Even Start family literacy program: 1994–97 final report.* Washington, DC: US Department of Education, Planning and Evaluation Service.

Tao, F., Swartz, J., St.Pierre, R., & Tarr, H. (1997). *National evaluation of the Even Start family literacy program, 1995 interim report.* Washington, DC: U.S. Department of Education, Planning, and Evalution Service.

U.S. Census Bureau. (1990). *U.S. Abstracts.* Washington, DC: Author.

U.S. Census Bureau. (2000). *U.S. Abstracts.* Washington, DC: Author.

Verhallen, S. (1996). *Taalstages op de werkvloer (Language lessons in the workplace).* Amsterdam: Institute for Language Research and Language Education, University of Amsterdam.

25

Family and Child Education (FACE): Family Literacy Services for American Indians

Sharyl Emberton
National Center for Family Literacy

The Family and Child Education (FACE) program is a unique collaborative partnership designed to provide comprehensive family literacy services for American Indian families. For more than a decade, the FACE program has drawn from the expertise of the Bureau of Indian Affairs (BIA) at the federal level, three national educational organizations (Parents as Teachers [PAT] National Center, High/Scope Educational Research Foundation, and the National Center for Family Literacy [NCFL]), and local educators. This collaboration serves a remarkably diverse population, representing more than 25 American Indian tribes, and subsequently emphasizes the value of culturally rich instruction and practice.

FACE PROGRAM DESCRIPTION

Conceived in 1989 and instituted in 1991, the FACE program has been ambitious from the start, providing services for families with children ranging from birth to third grade. Because staff are trained in the PAT home-based model, the NCFL four-component family literacy model, and the High/Scope curriculum, FACE programs are able to offer a continuum of services to families that includes early literacy experiences for children and that help children successfully make the transition to elementary school. FACE also works to increase the educational level of participating adults, about half of whom have completed less than the equivalent of a high school education (Yarnell, Pfannenstiel, Lambson, & Treffeisen, 2000). FACE programs also emphasize, through both home-based and center-based services, the crucial role that parents play in their child's success.

Training for staff has been a hallmark of the FACE program from its inception. A rigorous training schedule is maintained with all program sites, from group training to on-site technical assistance to specialized seminars on specific topics, such as assessment and special education. All three national organizations provide ongoing training in their area of expertise. In addition to this intensive training delivery system, the Office of Indian Education Programs (OIEP), which oversees the FACE program, fully supports and encourages regular team planning at the local level. This commitment to professional development and local coordination has certainly contributed to the program's continued success.

Another unique aspect of the FACE program is its targeted approach to infusing Native language and culture into programming. By integrating curriculum and culture, the FACE program ensures its relevance to individual program participants and to their communities. Not only does this integration enhance the learning experience for both adults and children, but it helps to propagate the cultures of a population that historically has been oppressed. By fostering intergenerational learning in families, the FACE program encourages the transference of culturally important information from adults (parents, teachers, and community elders) to children.

This chapter describes the FACE program, the social environment in which it was created, and the needs it addresses. The main focus of the chapter explores program examples that demonstrate how FACE educators have rewoven the threads of culture and language to strengthen the wholeness of the family and the overall well-being of each American Indian culture.

A LOOK AT THE PRESENT

My children are mirrors with which I may see myself; mirrors not only of the present, but of the past and, most importantly, the future of my family. A family not even yet born, a family three generations from mine.

Kymberlie, 1995, Chief Leschi
(cited in NCFL, 2001, p. 13)

Although most readers probably are familiar with the history of the American Indian population in the United States, some population characteristics are worth reviewing as they relate to education, economic stability, and the delivery of family literacy services. Some of these characteristics illustrate the ongoing strife that has impacted American Indians across multiple generations. Nevertheless, there are many strengths within this population, upon which family literacy services build. Also, remember, throughout the following review, that the American Indian population encompasses many different cultures: There are more than 500 federally recognized tribes and Alaska Native groups. In this chapter, culture is viewed as much broader than ethnic background; rather, culture is seen as including variables such as family dynamics, religion, profession, childrearing practices, educational background, gender concepts, geography, and diet.

According to the Census 2000 brief, *The American Indian and Alaska Native Population 2000* (Ogunwole, 2002), 4.1 million people identify themselves as American Indians or Alaska Natives, which is approximately 1.5% of the total United States population. Although comparing previous numbers accurately is difficult, because of changes in the definitions of racial categories, the census reports that the American Indian/Alaska Native population grew more quickly between 1990 and 2000 than did the overall U.S. population. A large portion of the American Indian population resides in the western region of the country (43%), but also are well represented in the South (31%) and Midwest (17%).

Goodluck and Willeto (2001) highlight 10 indicators of well-being for American Indian children, comparing them to benchmarks for the general U.S. child population identified in the Annie E. Casey Foundation's *Kids Count Data Book 2001*. Specifically, they found that teen birth rates are considerably higher among the American Indian/Alaska Native population than the birth rates of White teens, and that the percentage of teens who are high school dropouts is almost double the national rate. They further recognize that American Indian and Alaska Native children experience poverty at a much higher rate than all children living in the United States, that American Indian children are more likely to live in single-parent families, and that many American Indian communities offer few employment opportunities for parents. Significantly, Brown et al. (2001) report that American Indian welfare caseloads have not declined as quickly as for other populations, following the 1996 passage of welfare reform, stating that "anecdotal reports from TANF [Temporary Assistance for Needy Families] program staff are that clients have deeper and more multi-faceted needs than were ever anticipated" (p. 16).

In addition to these general living characteristics of a traditionally impoverished and isolated population, the history of American Indian education in the United States documents the decline of Native culture and language. Through government-operated schools designed to assimilate American Indians, students were not allowed to speak their Native languages or to engage in cultural activities. Many children were physically separated from their parents and extended family members. Although these policies were outlawed in the 1930s, their influence did not substantially dissipate until the 1970s, when schools were allowed to begin exercising some local control.

The Swinomish Tribal Mental Health Project (1994) describes the social disruption and cultural degradation that still resound in American communities today, as a result of these intrusive policies. Many American Indian parents and grandparents who are now middle-aged have been deeply affected by a forced disconnect with their culture. This disconnect has manifested itself in numerous areas, including the loss of Native languages, an inability of children to fit into either Native or non-Native society, a lack of family structure, a higher rate of depression and violence, and the loss of American Indian role models.

St. Germaine (2000) sums up how external factors have—and have not—affected American Indians' perception of the educational system.

> Universally defined, education is the means by which a society transmits its culture unto its young. However, for the past two centuries, AI/AN [American Indian/Alaskan Native] communities, as quasi-sovereign nations, were prevented from imparting their own values, heritage, and customs to their children. It was only in the late 20th century that tribes were authorized by the federal government to share in the role of education. Considering the educational maltreatment of native people and de-Indianizing experiences disguised as school curriculum, it is actually surprising that so many Indian parents today do view the institution of the school as a trusted ally in the rearing of their children. (p. 5)

Comprehensive family literacy services are designed to help families most in need—families who face similar barriers, like high rates of teen births, high school dropout levels, and unemployment. FACE family literacy programs further focus on honoring, preserving, and integrating culture, through education, to increase short- and long-term gains.

DEVELOPMENT OF THE FACE PROGRAM

> *The program has given me a chance to learn about my culture. Learning about my culture gave me an awareness, understanding and appreciation of who I really am as a mother, as a friend to my classmates, as a learner, and as a woman.*
>
> Adrienne, 1995, Chi Chi'l Tah
(cited in NCFL, 2001, p. 13)

In the 1980s, amid a landscape of unmet family needs and children performing far behind their nonminority counterparts in school, the OIEP within the BIA began exploring intervention strategies that focused on families. Dixie Owen, then an education specialist with the OIEP, presented a concept paper to OIEP leadership, for a program combining services to children and families (NCFL, 2001). The program would provide early intervention for children, while offering educational services to families, and also would strengthen activities in the elementary school classrooms.

This concept led Owen and others to pursue national models for working with disadvantaged families, with an emphasis on educational strategies. In 1989, Owen and William Mehojah, Jr., of the OIEP, approached the PAT National Center, Inc., NCFL, and the High/Scope Educational Research Foundation, about the possibility of forming a collaborative partnership to meet the needs of American Indian families. The BIA identified six schools, representing various tribes, to pilot the program, originally called the Early Childhood/Parental Involvement Pilot Program.

From the start, professional development was an anchor for the program. In 1991, the three collaborating national partners provided implementation training, technical assistance visits, follow-up training, and training in the High/Scope curriculum, to the six selected sites. Additionally, Research and Training Associates were brought on board to start an evaluation at each of the sites, immediately, and have continued to collect data on the program in subsequent years.

The program was renamed the Family and Child Education (FACE) program in 1992, and has since grown to 32 sites (one site closed in 1995) in a total of 11 states (see Figure 25.1). FACE services are currently available in about one fourth of the eligible BIA schools. Seventeen of the sites provide family literacy services to American Indian families on the Navajo reservation in Arizona and New Mexico, the largest reservation in the country. These programs are in rural, remote areas. In many of these communities, the school and the tribal chapter house are focal points.

Twelve of the additional programs in the nine other states are located in isolated, rural areas, where the school is the major employer in the community. Most of these communities are hampered by a lack of resources, including limited job training and employment opportunities, no public transportation services, limited health care and no preventive health resources, no higher education opportunities, insufficient housing, limited sanitation services, and inadequate

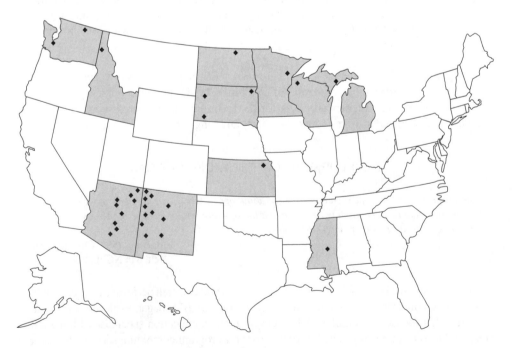

FIG. 25.1.   FACE program map.

TABLE 25.1
FACE Sites

State	Site	Tribe
Arizona	Little Singer	Navajo
	Chinle	Navajo
	Rough Rock	Navajo
	T'iis Nazbas	Navajo
	Cottonwood	Navajo
	Jeehdeez'a (Low Mountain)	Navajo
	Blackwater	Pima (Akimel O'odham)
	Gila Crossing	Pima (Akimel O'odham)
	Salt River	Pima (Akimel O'odham)/Maricopa (Pee Posh)
Idaho	Coeur d'Alene	Coeur d'Alene
Kansas	Kickapoo	Kickapoo
Michigan	Hannahville	Powtawatomi
Minnesota	Fond du Lac	Ojibwe
Mississippi	Conehatta	Choctaw
New Mexico	Ta'Hajiilee-He (Canoncito)	Navajo
	Nenahnezad	Navajo
	Na'Neelzhiin Ji Olta' (Torreon)	Navajo
	Chi Chi'l Tah	Navajo
	Ch'oosghai (Chuska)	Navajo
	Wingate	Navajo
	Alamo Navajo	Navajo
	Crownpoint	Navajo
	Atsa Biyaazh (Shiprock)	Navajo
	Tohaali	Navajo
	Ramah Navajo	Navajo
North Dakota	Dunseith	Chippewa/Cree
South Dakota	Enemy Swim	Sisseton-Wahpeton Sioux
	Takini	Lakota
	Little Wound	Oglala Sioux
Washington	Paschal Sherman	Colville Federated Tribes
	Chief Leschi	Puyallup (serving 54 tribes)
Wisconsin	Lac Courte Oreilles	Ojibwe

utility services. From the listing in Table 25.1, only four programs (Tohajiilee-He, Chief Leschi, Salt River, and Gila Crossing) are located close to urban areas, where educational, economic, social, and health resources are more readily accessible to families.

Despite these challenges, the FACE program has flourished, and, given its strong, positive evaluations, continued expansion will probably continue in the future. Additionally, FACE has celebrated many achievements over the years, both locally and nationally. In 1997, Little Singer Community School and Blackwater Community School were selected as 2 of the 25 pilot sites for the National Institute for Literacy's Equipped for the Future (EFF) project, a standards-based reform initiative for adult education. In 2002–2003, five FACE programs served as a pilot group for the EFF reading project. PAT piloted their Born to Learn curriculum in 1998, with 60 families from five FACE sites.

FACE STUDENTS AND OUTCOMES

In the 2000 study of the FACE program, Yarnell et al. (2000) describe how the FACE program has increased over its tenure. In 1990, FACE served 466 adults and children at six sites. In 2000, when the program was operating in 22 sites, 3,139 individuals (adults and children) participated, representing about 1,190 families. Over its first 10 years, the program served approximately 13,400 individuals, representing 4,500 families.

Approximately two thirds of FACE adult students are female, most of whom are mothers of the children with whom they attend (others may be grandmothers, aunts, or older siblings). The average age of participating FACE adult students is 29 years, but about 10% are under the age of 20. About half of adults participating in adult education completed less than the equivalent of a high school education, and nearly three fourths are unemployed. Fewer than two thirds of FACE children reside with both parents, and between 40% and 50% of FACE children live in households that receive public assistance. Approximately two thirds of participating children reside in homes where a second language other than English is spoken (Yarnell et al., 2000).

The evaluations of FACE have been consistently encouraging, and reflect significant impacts in all four components of comprehensive family literacy services (children's education, interactive literacy activities between parents and children, parenting education, and adult education). According to Yarnell et al. (2000), using Meisel's *Work Sampling System* development checklist, virtually all FACE preschool children who were assessed (95%) demonstrate improved proficiency in personal and social development during preschool participation. Almost all 3-year-olds (94%) and most 4-year-olds (81%) demonstrate improved language and literacy skills, and most preschoolers (84%) also demonstrate improvement in mathematical skills.

Yarnell et al. (2000) found that reports provided by parents indicate that most FACE parents (about 85%) experience the following impacts as a result of FACE participation: increased understanding of child development, increased involvement in their child's education, more effective interaction with their child, and more time spent with their child. Parents also report that they help their child with schoolwork (97%), communicate with the teacher about their child (82%), attend classroom or school events and visit their child's classroom (75%), and volunteer their time to provide instructional or other assistance in their child's classroom (60%).

Since the program's inception, more than 400 FACE adult students have obtained their GED or high school diploma, and at least 1,400 have obtained employment (Yarnell et al., 2000). Taken in the context of total program participants over the past 10 years (6,500 adults), these gains, although positive, may not seem overwhelmingly impressive. However, measured within the context of the significant barriers many of these adult students face, the gains have more meaning. Perhaps equally important is that 75% of adults report that they became more self-directed and self-disciplined as a result of participating in FACE (Yarnell et al., 2000).

STRUCTURE AND SCOPE OF FACE PROGRAM SERVICES

Each FACE program site operates through a BIA-funded American Indian school and offers a three-tiered approach to family education services. Families receive services in the home, in a center or school, or both. FACE staffing at each site typically consists of a coordinator, an adult education teacher, an early childhood teacher, an early childhood coteacher, and at least one parent educator.

This staff works together to implement the educational frameworks designed and adapted by the three collaborating national partners. The PAT program focuses on home-based services for families and their young children, who range in age from birth through 3 years. PAT-trained parent educators visit participants' homes on a weekly or biweekly basis, to provide learning experiences for the children and opportunities for parent–child interaction. The home-based services also include screening of the children's development and, when appropriate, referrals to other community resources. Monthly group meetings are held to bring parents together to provide a forum for discussion and sharing. Sometimes, adult education services are also offered as part of the home-based services.

NCFL provides training in the four-component approach to family literacy, offered in schools to families with preschool-aged children. Families attend classes 4 days per week, participating in all four components every day. Adults receive at least 2.5 hours of adult education and 1 hour of parenting education (called Parent Time) daily. Children receive at least 4 hours of early childhood education, using the High/Scope curriculum, with a particular emphasis on language and literacy development. Parents and their children participate together in interactive literacy activities (also known as Parent and Child Together Time, or PACT Time) for 1 hour each day.

To help teachers provide a smooth transition for children from preschool into elementary school, the High/Scope Educational Research Foundation trains teachers of grades K–3 in the High/Scope curriculum. This training includes instruction on active learning concepts, classroom arrangement, daily schedules, content, teacher–child interaction, and assessment. As children enter elementary school, FACE services often continue to provide PACT Time experiences, giving parents who remain in the program a daily opportunity to work with their children.

In addition to collaborating with PAT, NCFL, and High/Scope, many FACE sites also partner with other programs, such as Head Start and Even Start, to round out services for families. Community collaboration is also highly valued throughout the FACE program, to help extend opportunities, especially for adults, and to enhance the cultural richness of the programs.

When the BIA established the FACE program, they identified six goals, building from the National Education Goals and the Indian America 2000 Goals, to serve as guidelines for the overall program design (NCFL, 1996):

1. To help parents gain motivation, skills, and knowledge needed to become employed or to pursue further education
2. To increase the number of parents prepared to promote their children's development
3. To establish home–school partnerships
4. To provide a means for early detection of potential learning problems
5. To increase the developmental skills of children, to prepare them for academic and social success in school
6. To reduce family problems that interfere with constructive growth and development (p. 1)

None of these specifically identifies the roles of culture and language as either a strategy to achieve these goals or as a stand-alone goal of the program. However, in 1994, FACE staff, representing the 23 sites participating at that time, worked together to develop a shared vision for the program, which perhaps better describes the commitment to designing and implementing a program that meets the specific needs of its target population. Among the objectives they list are the following:

- The FACE program will continue to grow and eventually include sites at each BIA-supported school.
- FACE will prosper as a national and intertribal program, containing both center- and home-based components with the essential attributes of each component in place and functioning.

- Flexibility will exist within the communities, while maintaining the integrity of the program model.
- FACE will purposefully integrate both the Native culture and language into the program.
- FACE will educate families on their community responsibilities, and prepare them to assume their role as community leaders. ("Revisiting Our Vision," 1995)

The emphasis on cultural identity, exploration, and connection is evidenced by the fact that 95% of the parent educators who provide home-based services are American Indian, and about two thirds of the center-based staff members are American Indian (Yarnell et al., 2000). This emphasis also is interwoven throughout the numerous training opportunities for FACE staff, through instruction, methodologies, and materials. FACE staff also is required to participate in cultural and language instruction classes. Even Navajo staff who are fluent speakers of the language attend classes to continue improving their proficiencies in the language. Often, staff attends these classes with the families they teach through FACE. Examples of how culture and Native language are infused into the day-to-day practice of FACE sites is discussed later in this chapter.

The value of ongoing training and staff development cannot be overstated. In addition to encouraging a philosophy of continuous program improvement, training and planning opportunities help staff work toward intentionally incorporating relevant cultural experiences throughout all the services offered through the FACE program. The OIEP has mandated that staff dedicate 1 day per week for team planning. In addition to working through specific curriculum or instructional strategies, this time also offers staff the opportunity to plan for recruitment, community collaboration, and connecting with other school-wide and tribal initiatives.

In her testimony before the Subcommittee on Early Childhood, Youth and Families, Committee on Education and the Workforce, Hannahville Indian Community Program Coordinator Rose Potvin (1999) explained the value of training and planning at the local level:

> FACE staff members meet weekly to coordinate their efforts to ensure that comprehensive services are provided for families. Joint planning sessions help team members focus on a common vision for the program that includes support of families' language and culture. . . . By requiring all FACE staff and a school administrator to attend trainings, the integration of the services is strengthened and the program receives administrative support. (pp. 6–7)

Yarnell, Pfannenstiel, Lambson, & Treffeisen (1998) also state that the commitment to training, as exemplified by the FACE program, contributes greatly to the success of the program in meeting the needs of its clientele. They note the following:

> The training program serves not only to provide professional development and guidance in program implementation, but also to provide support to program staff in addressing local challenges. The comprehensive training supports the integration of program components and the emergence of the FACE model for American Indian family education. The focus on integrating tribal culture and language in the program ensures that services are relevant for the intended population. (p. 2)

Justifying the intentional bridging of culture and classroom is often easier than the actual planning and implementation. The following section describes program activities and strategies that have successfully integrated culture and education, strengthening the family system in the process.

FACE PROGRAM EXAMPLES: CULTURE IN THE CLASSROOM AND BEYOND

Weaving culture and Native language throughout the family literacy services provided by FACE programs is essential, but not simple. Planning, creativity, and ingenuity, as well as ongoing communication with, and feedback from, families, keep this kind of curriculum fresh, meaningful, and productive.

To work effectively and to keep students involved, curriculum built around culture and Native language must be connected to students' goals and must be relevant to their lives. The relevance of learning activities, accomplished at least partly through incorporating culture into curriculum, will help students move toward their goals and stay motivated to achieve them.

The examples described in the following pages are from FACE programs serving various tribes in which family literacy services have been strengthened by giving explicit attention to the meaningful inclusion of culture and language into curriculum for families. Many of the examples that follow began with culture as the impetus, but some examples started with a particular interest or educational goal that savvy staff members were able to capitalize on, molding a generic learning experience into one of individual and cultural relevance. Often, culturally based curriculum is developed in one component of a program (adult education, early childhood, PACT Time, Parent Time, or home-based), then expands to other components as interest builds and commitment grows (see chapter 19 in this volume). Occasionally, those efforts in FACE programs that focus on culture impact an entire school or a whole community.

The nine program examples that follow were chosen because they demonstrate ingenuity and team planning, and also because they represent the wide range of services that FACE programs provide. In these examples, culture is woven through the following topics: home-based parent education, EFF, building curricula around parent interests, linking curricula and culture, early literacy development, preserving Native language, integrating curriculum across the four components, community impact, and fostering cultural pride.

Building the Foundation of Family Culture and Language Through Home-Based Parent Education

Parent educators often provide the first link between families and the schools, through the FACE program. Because 97% of the parent educators are community members, they know the families, are fluent in the language, and are able to build positive connections between home and school.

The PAT Born to Learn curriculum is used in the home-based component, through weekly or biweekly visits to families by a parent educator. The parent educator will often work with the child, parent, and several members of the family, including grandparents, aunts, uncles, or other relatives. These sessions utilize all of the required components of the PAT model: rapport building, observation, parent–child activity, and summary.

The Little Singer FACE program, in operation since 1992, is located at the Little Singer Community School of about 120 students, ranging from preschool to eighth grade. The community is in a remote area of the Navajo Reservation, accessible by dirt road, about 60 miles east of Flagstaff, Arizona. In this FACE program, parent educators Luann Johnson and Rosabelle Nelson use the PAT curriculum as a basis for their visits, and make adjustments, as needed, to address culture and language. Most home visits are conducted in Navajo, the first language of most of their families. Cultural teachings and parenting lessons are interwoven with Born to Learn information and handouts. Johnson and Nelson have had extensive coursework, through Dine College, on Navajo culture and language. Their personal connections and professional development help them to authentically honor and encourage Navajo traditions and values through their visits.

The following example illustrates the blending of a learning experience with respect for families' concerns and traditions. Some mothers at the Little Singer FACE program inquired about using the traditional Navajo cradleboard for their babies, because they had heard that it would retard their child's physical development. Many tribal peoples have used cradleboards for centuries to carry and protect their babies. Babies are laced onto the board area of the Navajo cradleboard and a wooden "rainbow" above the head protects the baby from injury in case of an accidental fall. Keeping the baby in the cradleboard is meant to provide a secure emotional environment and to promote a baby's straight and strong back (National Indian Telecommunications Institutes, n.d.). The parent educators went to work researching the mothers' questions and found that using the cradleboard for young babies is appropriate and does not adversely affect development. They also were able to reassure parents that many families carry their infants in commercial carriers that serve a similar purpose, but that lack the cultural significance of the Navajo cradleboard.

Connecting Cultural Values Through EFF

In 1994, the National Institute for Literacy in Washington, DC was charged with responding to the National Education Goal 6 (U.S. Department of Education, 1994): "Every American adult will be literate and possess the knowledge and skills necessary to compete in a global economy and exercise the rights and responsibilities of citizenship."

Building on research conducted in 1990 by the Secretary's Commission on Necessary Skills, the National Institute for Literacy began a 10-year initiative, called Equipped for the Future (EFF), to develop a framework (Stein, 2000) that would bring a common language and process to adult education nationwide. Through grassroots input from adult students, four purposes for learning were identified: *learning for access and orientation, learning for voice, learning for independent action,* and *learning as a bridge to the future.* With these purposes in mind, EFF mapped out broad areas of responsibility for adults to effectively embody their roles as citizen/community member, worker, and parent/family member. A framework of 16 standards was then developed, to define the core knowledge and skills adults need to carry out these roles.

Teachers in the Little Singer and Blackwater FACE programs participated in the field development phase of EFF, to explore whether cultural values and traditions could be effectively woven into the EFF framework. Both programs found that EFF concepts were consistent with the spirit of FACE and with the complex tribal philosophies that are mirrored in each community's tribal symbols, values, and traditions. In both programs, the adult educators determined that for EFF to work effectively within FACE programs, it should be interpreted from an American Indian perspective.

The Blackwater FACE program, established in 1993, is located an hour south of Phoenix, Arizona, at Blackwater Community School on the Gila River Community, which serves the Akimel O'odham and Pee Posh tribes. The small preschool-to-third-grade school has about 200 students. Jacquelyn Power, adult educator, made connections to EFF, using the Man in the Maze, the tribal symbol of the community. In the maze, man moves through four areas, representing the four directions and depicting the human figure as he searches for entry, moves toward knowing and understanding, begins to teach others, and explores the future.

Power's adult students made the connection between these four culturally significant areas and the four purposes outlined in the EFF framework: access to information, voice, independent action, and bridge to the future. They then applied this perspective to their educational relationship with their children, and recognized four intergenerational goals that were in keeping with the framework:

- Introduce new information to children
- Provide children with opportunities to make choices and make decisions

- Encourage independence and problem solving among children
- Support children's curiosity and delight in learning

The influence of EFF continued to filter into the other components at the Blackwater program. Activities in Parent Time and PACT Time focused on how emotional support and encouragement fosters children's development. Parents made *I Love You Because* . . . books to share with their children. Through adult education, the parents investigated and discussed current issues that challenge their community and tribe, such as the high rate of diabetes, the lack of a dependable water supply, and the continuing loss of Native language and culture. They looked at each project and lesson as part of a larger purpose, a framework that connected them to their ancestors, as well as to the contemporary world and the future of their children.

In the Little Singer FACE program, Etta Shirley, adult educator, and the adult students, connected EFF to the Navajo philosophy of learning. This philosophy, adopted by the school and tribe, forms the foundation for a harmonious Navajo life, and describes a holistic view of life that strives for beauty, peace, joy, and harmony. Benally (as cited in Navajo Division of Education, 1990) describes this philosophy, stating that "understanding and practicing the essence of the principles placed in each of the Four Directions will give us a strong foundation to make wise decisions for ourselves, our families and our communities" (p. 1). The Little Singer program was able to link the elements of this philosophy to the four EFF purposes for adult education:

- Seek ways to improve your immediate surrounding, so that your teaching will reflect your knowledge from within. (Access to information)
- Be aware of what you say to others in a way that does not hurt anyone. Speak so that others can understand you, and always be confident in your talk to all people. (Voice)
- Do not wait to be told what to do and how to do it; use your thinking abilities to make valuable decisions on how to do things on your own. (Independent action)
- Watch your thoughts, your attitude, your existence, for they are the essence of what you are molding—your child. (Bridge to the future)

Once adult learners connected to these four major purposes, they were more receptive to the EFF standards. They further linked the four EFF skill clusters (communication, decision making, interpersonal, and lifelong learning) to the four Navajo houses of North, South, East, and West. By establishing a foundation that was culturally meaningful to them, students were able to use the EFF standards as they worked toward their own personal goals. Shirley and her students captured their new interpretation of the EFF framework in a drawing that ties EFF to Navajo rug weaving, further deepening the cultural relevance of the framework. This representation hangs in the adult education classroom as a daily reminder of the students' commitment to weave together culture and education. (see Figure 25.2)

Building Curriculum Around Parent Interests

At the Alamo Navajo FACE program, located 30 miles north of the small community of Magdalena, New Mexico, the adult education component became a hub for building cottage industry opportunities for the families. The area is very isolated, job opportunities are scarce, and the chance to learn about developing a business is rare. Like many Navajo communities, many of the parents express their artistic skills through jewelry making and drawing, but there was no organized effort to build on these talents.

In 1998, Mary Mank, adult educator, organized a Parent Time session on cake decorating, because of parent interest. Training was provided by an agent from the county extension office, which provides various training and resources on homemaking, agriculture, family topics, 4–H, and so on. The six parents who attended this session experienced success in decorating

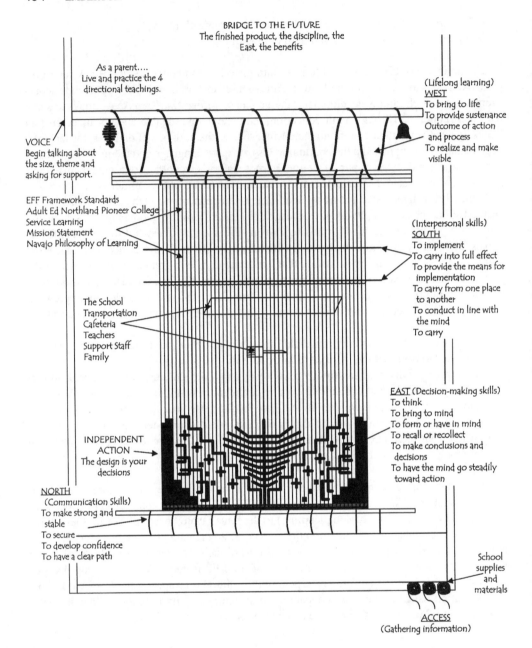

BRIDGE TO THE FUTURE
The finished product, the discipline, the
East, the benefits

As a parent....
Live and practice the 4
directional teachings.

(Lifelong learning)
WEST
To bring to life
To provide sustenance
Outcome of action
and process
To realize and make
visible

VOICE
Begin talking about
the size, theme and
asking for support.

EFF Framework Standards
Adult Ed Northland Pioneer College
Service Learning
Mission Statement
Navajo Philosophy of Learning

(Interpersonal skills)
SOUTH
To implement
To carry into full effect
To provide the means for
implementation
To carry from one place
to another
To conduct in line with
the mind
To carry

The School
Transportation
Cafeteria
Teachers
Support Staff
Family

EAST (Decision-making skills)
To think
To bring to mind
To form or have in mind
To recall or recollect
To make conclusions and
decisions
To have the mind go steadily
toward action

INDEPENDENT
ACTION
The design is your
decisions

NORTH
(Communication Skills)
To make strong and
stable
To secure
To develop confidence
To have a clear path

School
supplies
and
materials

ACCESS
(Gathering information)

FIG. 25.2. Weaving Equipped for the Future into Navajo Life.

their cakes and wanted to learn more. With Mank's leadership, these parents began to pursue obtaining cake pans, decorating tubes, recipes, and other necessary materials. The FACE program set aside a small fund for exploration and, because their classroom was in the former home economics area, there was access to ovens, sinks, and worktables.

The class obtained a few pans and some groceries and began to make cakes. Within a short time, the school faculty began ordering cakes for parties and holidays, and when the community heard about their endeavor and word spread about the quality of the goods, orders began pouring in for wedding, birthday, and other specialty cakes.

Mank and the parents realized they would need a strategy to make the burgeoning business a meaningful learning opportunity. They developed a business plan that included a budget, definitions of responsibilities for the students, and ideas for marketing their products. As the first Valentine's Day approached, the class was inundated with orders for 25 cakes.

Now the parents make cakes, suckers, and other confections, for many holidays, special occasions, and tribal events, producing about 500 cakes per year. They made a special cake representing the "Keeping the Circle Strong" FACE logo, for display at the Department of the Interior in Washington, DC, in celebration of the 10th anniversary of the FACE program. One parent has begun her own successful in-home cake-making business. The parents report that they have been able to apply the lessons learned from this experience to other aspects of their lives. They know more about budgeting, the value of their time, how important planning is to success, and how challenging it is to meet deadlines.

Linking Curriculum and Culture

At the Ramah Navajo/Pine Hill FACE program, situated about 75 miles from Gallup, in central New Mexico, as adult students worked diligently toward improving their math skills to pass the GED, it became clear that some of the concepts were difficult for the students to master. Every morning, Bob Hymer, the adult educator, began class with a brain teaser problem, to connect the math skills the students were learning to real-life situations. But Hymer was dissatisfied with the progress the students were making and with their inability to apply the skills, when an opportunity arose that would use math to find the solution to a Navajo-based lesson.

With leftover building materials from another on-campus project, Hymer and the students made plans to build a hogan, the traditional Navajo home, within the confines of their classroom. Hymer realized that the students would need to utilize many math skills to plan and complete their building project. At first, the students were anxious to begin building the hogan, but Hymer posed some important questions that needed to be answered before they could begin: How big a hogan could they build in the given space? What materials would they need? Did they have enough leftover materials or would they need to purchase more? What would any new materials cost? Who would do the work? How much time would it take? How would they use the hogan once it was completed?

Several of the students had previous experience in construction, and a few had built hogans for their families, but this situation posed at least one unusual challenge—building the hogan within the dimensions of the classroom. Measuring and planning were the next steps, then students worked to develop a blueprint, to scale, of their proposed hogan. After several attempts, they had a plan and were ready to start construction. With minimal purchases of extra materials, assigning work responsibilities, setting daily goals, and following their plan, they were able to complete the hogan in about a month. They now use their hogan for special gatherings, as a quiet reading area, and to conduct Parent Time sessions. To complete their project, the students reflected on how their newly acquired math skills could apply to real-life situations. The parents reported that the math and problem-solving skills that they used to build the hogan helped them on the GED test, especially in the math area.

Creating Cultural Content for Early Literacy Development

The Alamo Navajo early childhood and FACE teams build cultural literacy in both English and Navajo, through book writing and book sharing. Parents and children have become expert book producers and have produced more than 100 books, which they read together during daily PACT Time sessions and also take home to add to their own libraries. They have also distributed many of the books throughout the community.

The technique of producing these digital books, called *webbes*, was introduced to the staff by Michael McGuffee, an educational consultant and author. These small books are printed using a template on the computer and cost approximately 35 cents per book to produce. According to Condon and McGuffee (2001), "Webbes are, by definition, relevant to those who write and read them. . . . The content is their very own lives. The pictures are their very own pictures, and the text is in their very own language" (p. 6).

Books of interest to Navajo families, and especially to young children, are scarce, and books about topics specific to the Alamo Navajo community do not exist. So the parents, armed with digital cameras and their own interests, began producing individualized books, often providing both Navajo and English text. Books have been produced about special events, such as *Going to the Zoo* and *Alamo Days*. Others teach concepts, such as *Shapes*, *Colors*, and *My Farm Animal Counting Book*. Some books were written specifically to take home, with titles like *This is My Family*, *This is Me!* and *Friends*. Many books describe cultural information and events, including *Carding the Wool*, *The Hike to Alamo Mountain*, *Navajo Squash Pie*, and *How to Make Blue Corn Tamales*. Still other books are written just for fun, like *That Crazy Sheep*, *Chidi (Vehicles)*, and *Wheels on the Bus*. For a parent meeting on good health, the parents produced enough books titled *This Is the Way We Wash Our Hands* to give one to every family to take home. These *webbes* books have become very popular choices for parents to read to their children at PACT Time and while settling down at rest time. Families also report that their at-home libraries have grown, and time spent reading with children has greatly increased, since they began publishing their own books.

Teachers have reported that parents have also improved their writing skills and have become adept at organizing their ideas into books that have child appeal. Another benefit of producing these books has been the increased computer know-how that parents have developed. FACE parents who were afraid of this technology now use the digital camera, printers, the Internet, and the book templates with ease, even solving related computer problems.

Preserving Native Language Through Family Literacy

On the Gila River Indian Community, which includes the Gila Crossing and Blackwater FACE programs, located just south of Phoenix, the numbers of fluent speakers of the Native language have dwindled at an alarming rate. The dominance of the English language has been fueled by the encroachment of metropolitan Phoenix on these Native communities. Looking to preserve the Pima (Akimel O'odham) language, educators from the community traveled to model programs in Hawaii, where language and cultural preservation efforts were experiencing success. As a result, the River Children Project has been implemented on Gila River, to strengthen and rebuild language skills and cultural knowledge for the tribal members.

The FACE program at Blackwater Community School works to involve parents in activities to assist their own families and others in revitalizing the culture and language. Families engage in specific writing, reading, speaking, listening, and art activities each week. Parents and children together write Pima concept books about counting, animals, people, and food, during PACT Time. Parents also read and interpret Native stories through story maps, group research, and discussion during their adult education class.

The River Children Project has sparked great enthusiasm among participants, and, in March 2002, at the National Conference on Family Literacy, five parents presented a session titled "Native American Literature: Preserving Language through a Grassroots Effort," at which they shared the project objectives and materials that they had developed for their children and the community. Through the project, families also have opportunities to hear the stories of the elders told in the Pima language and then to repeat these stories for their children and other students. In addition to this focus on Native language, families are learning traditional dances, such as the basket dance, and traditional skills, such as uses for traditional plants. As one parent remarked about the experience, "I had no idea how much I didn't know about my people. This makes me proud."

Integrating Culturally Relevant Curriculum Throughout the Components

The Gila Crossing FACE program was established in 2001 at the Gila Crossing School, where the preschool-through-eighth-grade school has more than 400 students. Throughout the community, as in many American Indian tribes, diabetes is a major health problem and is at epidemic proportions. Now tribes are seeing Type II diabetes in their young students, sometimes at a rate more than 10 times the average among the general population (Bradley, n.d.). In order to combat this problem, the Gila River Community has instituted a diabetes prevention program, called *Asugha*. Gila Crossing School has implemented a no-sugar policy, each class has a plot in the school's large garden area, school menus are carefully planned, diabetes education is part of each class curriculum, and students in each class must exercise every day.

The FACE program has built on these school mandates by creating a curriculum that is integrated across the four components of their family literacy program. Parents learn about good health and nutrition, in Parent Time, and similar information is shared with the children through early childhood education. The parents put their learning to use by planning no-sugar parties for their children. They also have developed no-candy holiday treats that they sell for fund-raising. In their large area of garden, the students plant lots of edibles, including broccoli, lettuce, and several varieties of peppers. They also share the bounty of the hydroponics garden inside the greenhouse, where there are tomatoes, spinach, and other vegetables that are served in the school cafeteria. Every day, students participate in a 1-mile walk around the school campus, and, once a week, PACT Time is devoted to gardening, when parents and children work side by side to tend their growing produce and harvest their healthy foods. During adult education, parents journal about their experiences with good health, explore topics on the Internet, and map what to grow in their garden. Through these integrated and active learning experiences, parents and children not only work toward improving their health, but also practice their reading, writing, communication, math, and problem-solving skills.

Changing a Community Through Parent–Child Literacy Interactions

Family literacy often brings the issue of literacy to the attention of not only families in need, but of the entire community as well. Since its inception, a primary thrust of FACE has been focused on strengthening the literacy development of children, both at school and through lap time at home, when parents read to their children.

The Alamo Navajo FACE program recognized a broader challenge to increasing literacy in the enrolled children. A community assessment established that the average reading level of community members was third grade, showing that reading to and with children was not valued by the community as a whole. So the team set out to focus their efforts on fostering the importance of reading with children throughout the community—a laudable task.

At Alamo Navajo, FACE operates within the school system, which also administers Head Start, Early Head Start, family services, and early intervention. These programs generally work side by side, but chose to collaborate on a project that would raise overall awareness of the importance of literacy. With the help of their local school board and a number of volunteers, this broadly based team developed a short video for families titled *Shich'i'iinilta'* *(Read with Me)* in Navajo (McGuffee & Alamo Navajo School Board, 2001). The video footage includes only families from the Alamo Navajo community, and shows adults and children reading together, telling stories, and enjoying literacy experiences in a variety of typical and atypical settings, from the classroom to the home to outdoor activities. The video has limited narrative, which is in both Navajo and English. Positive images of elders, infants, preschoolers, fathers, mothers, school-age children, and other family members, all enjoying literacy experiences, entertain the viewer, and building a literacy environment in the home, school, and community is emphasized. The Alamo Navajo staff launched their campaign to increase literacy development, at a community gathering early in 2002. Everyone in the small community was either a star in the video or knew family members who were featured. Together, they watched the video, discussed the ideas presented, talked about what families could do to encourage literacy development, and shared a meal. Afterwards, families went home with a copy of the video and free children's books.

Although it is too soon to measure the long-term results of these efforts at Alamo Navajo, the teachers report more interest from both parents and children in borrowing books to take home. Anecdotally, the teachers report that parents have told them that they used to keep their books on a high shelf, so that nothing would happen to them. Now they are reading them to the children and even establishing their own home libraries.

Fostering Cultural Pride and a Sense of Giving to Others

A national tragedy and an opportunity for students to share their feelings about peace and patriotism inspired FACE students at the Kickapoo program in Powhatan, Kansas. Historically, American Indians have the highest per capita record of military service of any ethnic group. Their commitment is complex, drawing from the tribal warrior tradition and other valued cultural qualities of strength, honor, pride, devotion, and wisdom, which fit well with military tradition (Naval Historical Center, 1997).

Following the September 11, 2001, terrorist attacks, many discussions occurred among the students, with their teacher, Malissa Richey-Hill, about the event and the effects it was having, even on their small tribal community. Families were fearful for their safety and distrustful of those who looked different. They also felt helpless to improve the world, and they worried about the future of the nation. At the same time, they felt great pride in the contributions that Native people had made to the strength of the United States.

An article in *Midwestern Living* magazine provided the impetus for this small group of adults to make a lasting and unique contribution for peace. Each adult student made a quilt square to donate to the "Living Peace Quilts Project," which then would be assembled into quilts to be auctioned to raise funds for relief efforts. During the 3 weeks of work on the quilts, the students concluded that unselfishly working together for a purpose, beyond the boundaries of one's own community, had incredible rewards for them. They used their quilt designs to express their feelings of patriotism and their commitment to freedom and to their families.

The students also examined their own cultural pride in the contributions that American Indians have made historically, and continue to make, toward maintaining the strength and safety of the nation. In the process of designing and creating the quilt squares, and in the discussions and research that resulted, the adult students integrated academic skills in math, language, problem solving, design, and exploring current events.

There are literally hundreds of other examples of how FACE programs across the country have enhanced the culture and Native language opportunities for the families they serve. Programs develop and share lists of the best Native books that they have identified for parents and children. At Takini, in South Dakota, families celebrate every morning with an opening circle of drumming led by a father and son, and families have participated in a traditional buffalo slaughter. T'iis Nazbas staff and parents in Northern Arizona plan and lead several events during Native American week at the school. The Coeur d'Alene program in Idaho has developed *The Alphabet Coloring Book* in the Coeur d'Alene language. Torreon parents in New Mexico were instrumental in beginning a Meals on Wheels program for their community's senior citizens. At Tohajiilee-He, also in New Mexico, the program started a child care center, so that families with infants could be involved in their center-based program, and trained the home-based parents to staff the center. The Chinle (Arizona), Wingate (New Mexico) and Lac Courte Oreilles (Wisconsin) programs participate in the Foster Grandparent program, which places elders in FACE classrooms, to provide cultural education and language models for children and parents. Cottonwood (Arizona) parents spend time job-shadowing other school staff for job experience opportunities, and, at Nenahnezad in New Mexico, parents developed curriculum based on a theme of interest to the entire school population. Chi Chi'l Tah in New Mexico and Enemy Swim in South Dakota have developed regular school newsletters to inform families about family literacy.

CONCLUSION

The FACE project began over a decade ago as a small family literacy program serving American Indian families. The program model was designed by melding the best attributes of three nationally known educational entities into program services for families with children, from birth through third grade. The ambitious mission of FACE—to make a difference in the lives of families, by incorporating their culture and language specifically and directly into the program design—has been realized. Culture has pervaded, not as an add-on layer to the full complement of services for families, but rather as a crucial aspect of solid and meaningful curriculum. The positive impacts of FACE on the families and communities involved have been far-reaching. They have been documented by yearly evaluations and testimony from the individuals who have benefited from the program services.

This chapter has provided selected program examples of how culture and Native language can enrich learning while engaging and enlightening both young and older learners. Many more examples of creatively developed curricula, rich with cultural underpinnings, are evident in each of the 32 FACE programs. FACE programs have provided an effective vehicle for increasing student outcomes, while also fostering community and cultural knowledge and pride.

With the expectation of future expansion of the FACE program to more communities, many more American Indian people can benefit from these carefully designed and well-implemented family literacy services. FACE also serves as a model for any family literacy program seeking to improve the delivery of services, through team planning, staff development, collaboration, and making the educational experience relevant to learners' lives.

REFERENCES

Bradley, J. (n.d.) *Type 2 diabetes: What's next? NARTC conference looks at impact on minority youth.* Retrieved May 9, 2002, from University of Arizona, Native American Research and Training Center Web site: http://www. ahsc.arizona.edu/nartc/newsletters.htm

Brown, E. F., Whitaker, L. S., Springwater, M., Cornell, S., Jorgensen, M., Hale, M., et al. (2001). *Welfare, work, and American Indians: The impact of welfare reform. A report to the National Congress of American Indians.* St. Louis, MO: Kathryn M. Buder Center for American Studies, Washington University, and Tucson, AZ: Native Nations Institute for Leadership, Management and Policy, The University of Arizona.

Condon, M. W. F., & McGuffee, M. (2001). *Real epublishing, really publishing! How to create digital books by and for all ages.* Portsmouth, NH: Heinemann.

Goodluck, C. T., & Willeto, A. A. A. (2001). *Native American Kids 2001: Indian children's well-being indicators data book.* Seattle, WA: Casey Family Programs and Flagstaff, AZ: Northern Arizona University.

McGuffee, M. (Executive Producer) & Alamo Navajo School Board (Producer). (2001). *Shich'i'iinilta* [Motion picture]. (Available from Alamo Navajo Early Childhood Center, PO Box 907, Magdalena, NM 87825)

National Center for Family Literacy. (1996). *Family and Child Education: Keeping the circle strong.* (Available from the National Center for Family Literacy, 325 West Main St., Suite 300, Louisville, KY 40202.)

National Center for Family Literacy. (2001). *FACE 1991–2001: A Journey Through 10 Years of FACE.* Louisville, KY: Author.

National Indian Telecommunications Institute. (n.d.) *Navajo cradleboard.* Retrieved May 6, 2002, from http://www. niti.org/users/tushka/windowrock/cboyd/cradleboardweb.htm

Navajo Division of Education. (1990). *T'áá diné bo-óhoo'aah Bindii'a': Navajo Philosophy of Learning* [Brochure]. Window Rock, AZ: Author.

Naval Historical Center. (1997, August 15). *20th century warriors: Native American participation in the United States military.* Retrieved May 9, 2002, from http://www.history.mil/faqs/faq61-1.htm

Ogunwole, S. V. (2002). *The American Indian and Alaska Native population: 2000* (U.S. Census Bureau Brief 2000, No. C2KBR/01-15). Washington, DC: U.S. Census Bureau.

Potvin, R. (1999, July 20). *Testimony before the Subcommittee on Early Childhood, Youth and Families, Committee on Education and the Workforce. Hearing on examining education programs benefiting Native American children.* Retrieved April 19, 2002, from U.S. House of Representatives Web site: http://edworkforce.house. gov/hearings/106th/ecyf/indian72099/potvin.htm

Revisiting our vision. (1995, August). *Face to Face, 1*(6), 2.

St. Germaine, R. D. (2000, May 30–June 1). *A chance to go full circle: Building on reforms to create effective learning.* Paper presented for the National American Indian and Alaska Native Education Research Agenda Conference. Albuquerque, NM. Retrieved April 19, 2002, from http://www.indianeduresearch.net/ed451970.htm

Stein, S. (2000). *Equipped for the Future content standards: What adults need to know and be able to do in the 21st century.* Washington, DC: National Institute for Literacy.

Swinomish Tribal Mental Health Project. (1994). *A gathering of wisdoms, tribal mental health: A cultural perspective.* LaConner, WA: Swinomish Tribal Community.

U.S. Department of Education. (1994). H.R. 1804 Goals 2000: Educate America Act. Retrieved October 7, 2003, from: http://www.ed.gov/legislation/GOALS2000/TheAct/index.html

Yarnell, V., Pfannenstiel, J., Lambson, T., & Treffeisen, S. (1998). *Bureau of Indian Affairs Family and Child Education Program: 1998 Evaluation Report.* Overland Park, KS: Research & Training Associates, for the Office of Indian Education Programs, Bureau of Indian Affairs, U.S. Department of the Interior.

Yarnell, V., Pfannenstiel, J., Lambson, T., & Treffeisen, S. (2000). *Bureau of Indian Affairs Family and Child Education Program: 2000 Study.* Overland Park, KS: Research & Training Associates, for the Office of Indian Education Programs, Bureau of Indian Affairs, U.S. Department of the Interior.

VIII

Assessment and Evaluation

In earlier chapters, authors have called for better ways of assessing program processes, evaluating child and parent outcomes, and improving program services. The authors in this section take on difficult issues in assessment, addressing goals, procedures, instruments, cultural relevance, and problems with interpreting data.

The first two chapters tackle assessment of young children's emergent literacy skills. A central debate focuses on whether to use instruments that are standardized and quantitative or individualized and qualitative. Peter Johnston and Liz Yanoff argue for qualitative, informative evaluations, Christopher J. Lonigan, Kimberly D. Keller, and Beth M. Phillips contend that standardized assessments of children's language and literacy are important.

Johnston and Yanoff review developments of the past 20 years to illustrate the changing objectives and values associated with early childhood assessment. The pendulum moves back and forth between an emphasis on accountability testing for young children and a belief that such testing is inappropriate. They discuss the political and educational forces that drive these shifts. Although they view assessment as noticing, documenting, interpreting, and representing children's literacy behaviors, they observe that assessment has other functions, including accountability, screening, and diagnosis. Johnston and Yanoff's central theme is that assessments are only successful when they lead to improved instruction and learning environments for children. They see the teacher as the primary agent of assessment, and they identify what teachers need to observe about children and what instructional significance to assign to particular observations. The authors then describe assessment instruments that approach early literacy from different perspectives, noting the advantages of each in connecting assessment and instruction. They conclude by discussing broader views of reliability and validity, and they argue for multiple perspectives and sources of data in assessing children's literacy, including parent involvement.

The advantages of determining children's strengths and weaknesses in specific areas of early literacy lead Lonigan, Keller, and Phillips to stress accurate assessments of children's emergent literacy skills, specifically basic concepts, oral language, phonological processing skills, and print awareness. They argue that standardized instruments serve this purpose well, because such instruments have clear and consistent administration and scoring criteria, typically good reliability and validity, and test scores that can be converted into data showing a child's performance in relation to that of a normative group. Lonigan et al. note that standardized tests are not intended to identify specific instructional goals. They describe research showing each skill area's relevance for children's later school achievement, then present detailed information about the purpose, characteristics, and qualities of instruments designed to assess that skill. Their chapter concludes with recommendations for how to select appropriate instruments.

Douglas R. Powell, Lynn Okagaki, and Kathryn Boyczyk tackle assessment for determining parent participation and outcomes. They argue that such efforts must begin by recognizing that family literacy programs serve culturally diverse, minority, and low-income parents. Most of the literature on parenting education is based on middle-income majority families, and generalizations from this literature to participants in family literacy programs can be misleading. They discuss three dimensions of parenting beliefs and behaviors that vary by social class and cultural background: parental goals and expectations, approaches to literacy, and family roles and relationships. Then they address topics that must be considered when assessing parent participation and parent outcomes. For example, determining the frequency with which parents participate is not sufficient without obtaining information on the quality of their participation. The authors note that assessing parent outcomes can be difficult, because parent education does not address some characteristics that are known to be predictors of child outcomes, such as parental warmth. They stress the importance of considering whether desired program outcomes go against parents' cultural norms. And they conclude by observing that understanding parent participation and outcomes can inform the pathways of influence of children's development.

Barbara Van Horn takes on issues of assessing adult education. She first identifies the broader definitions used to define adult education. She notes that considerable funding for adult education within family literacy programs comes from state or federal governments or private foundations, and that these funding sources often specify the expected outcomes. For example, Even Start Family Literacy programs align their outcomes for adults with those established in the Adult Education and Family Literacy Act. Van Horn summarizes federal accountability requirements, discusses different types of assessments and their advantages and limitations, analyzes the purposes of assessment (screening and placement, guiding instruction, and setting goals), and describes selection criteria and assessment planning. She covers both formal and informal assessments, including strategies for developing and using the latter instruments, and makes recommendations for effectively assessing English language learners. Noting the anxiety that can arise in a testing situation, she suggests how to provide a supportive test environment and ends her chapter with the observation that assessment practices should provide information on what is taught and should document both the program's effectiveness and the individual learner's progress.

A focus on program evaluation and continuous program improvement brings this section to closure. Robert St.Pierre, Anne Riccuiti, and Fumiyo Tao, building on considerable experience with the Even Start Family Literacy programs, examine how three national Even Start evaluations have led to program improvement. They trace the outcomes of each evaluation and identify how each contributed to new program directions. For example, the first national evaluation provided data on program implementation, helping to determine areas in which technical assistance was needed. Next, they discuss potential uses of state-level studies or evaluations. These efforts are intended to help states foster program improvement by, for example, identifying concerns at the local level and providing technical assistance or identifying high-performing projects and sharing effective practices. They then describe evaluation studies conducted by local Even Start programs and conclude with a set of recommendations for using data to continuously improve family literacy programs.

26

Early Childhood Assessment
and Family Literacy

Peter Johnston and ElizabethYanoff
University at Albany, State University of New York

The literacy assessment of young children is in a state of upheaval. Political forces have set the pendulum swinging wildly. Consider, for example, the use of early literacy assessment for accountability purposes. The 1980s saw an increase in states' efforts to implement high-stakes accountability testing in earlier grades in school. However, the pendulum slowed in the 1990s, at least for the assessment of young children, and reversed course. Writing in 1996, Shepard, Taylor, and Kagan concluded that states had virtually eliminated accountability testing in grades K–3. They considered this shift a positive move away from an era, characterized earlier by Shepard (1994), as involving . . . "testing of 4-, 5-, and 6-year-olds [that] has been excessive and inappropriate" (p. 212). They considered it inappropriate, because, among other things, it distorted the curriculum, leading, for example, to "the teaching of decontextualized skills" (p. 212).

Between 1996 and 2003, we have seen a renewed focus on testing, as federal and state governments proceed to establish extensive testing of literacy at earlier ages than Shepard et al. had even considered. For example, new legislation, attached to Head Start funding, requires the assessment of the language, literacy, and numeracy development of all enrolled 3- to 5-year-old children three times per year, beginning in the fall of 2003 (Bush, 2002). Guidelines for literacy assessment in these early childhood years are simultaneously becoming more restrictive, focusing attention centrally on tests classified as "scientifically based" and views of literacy that emphasize children's knowledge of words and their components (National Reading Panel, 2000; U.S. Department of Education [U.S. DOE] 2002a, 2002b, 2002c, 2002d).

The stakes associated with early childhood literacy assessments are also rising rapidly. Head Start programs will be evaluated based on the results of their students' test scores (Bush, 2002). States will be barred from receiving federal funds for certain early literacy programs, unless the testing regimen is maintained (National Association for the Education of Young Children [NAEYC], 2002). The current administration's position, as articulated by U.S. Secretary of Education Rod Paige, is that "anyone who opposes annual testing of children is an apologist for a broken system of education that dismisses certain children and classes of children as unteachable" (U.S. DOE, 2002d, paragraph 14). This testing is justified, the press release notes, because,

> Life is full of exams, judgment calls and forms.... All can be stressful, but they are all part of a life that we accept. In order to provide a quality education for every child in America, we must first test them to find out which children are not learning at the level or pace necessary to keep up. (U.S. DOE, 2002d)

Speaking here of the No Child Left Behind legislation, Secretary Paige and the Bush administration express the "testing-for-results" view that is currently permeating the legislation surrounding preschool and elementary education (Bush, 2002; U.S. DOE, 2002a, 2002c). The United States is not alone in this trend toward greater testing pressure. Five-year-olds in England and Japan face standardized tests involving literacy—in England for accountability and grouping purposes (Fletcher & Lyon, 1998), and in Japan for admission to private schools (Tolbert, 1999).

This reversal in views regarding the assessment of young children is in the face of considerable agreement among professional organizations and child advocates that the use of standardized, norm-referenced tests with young children, particularly for high-stakes purposes, has no place in early childhood (Clay, 1993a; FairTest, 1995, n.d.; International Reading Association and National Council of Teachers of English Joint Task Force on Assessment [International Reading], 1994; International Reading Association, 1999; Johnston, 1992; NAEYC, 1991). Indeed, the National Education Goals Panel (1998) asserted that "high-stakes assessments intended for accountability purposes should be delayed until the end of third grade (or preferably fourth grade" p. 21). There appears to be no evidence that accountability testing is effective in improving education, and some evidence that it is not effective at all (Johnston, 1998; McNeil, 2000; Sacks, 1999; Smith, 1991; Smith & Rottenberg, 1991).

These tensions concerning accountability testing are far from trivial in their potential impact on children and on families, and they reflect deep differences in ways of thinking about children, literacy, learning, and assessment. In what follows, we examine these differences and argue for informed documentary assessments that include the context of literacy learning as much as individual development.

EARLY LITERACY AND LEARNING

At home, children come to know the "ways with words" (Heath, 1983) and the "funds of knowledge" (Moll, Amanti, Neff, & Gonzalez, 1992) of their communities, and they acquire the practices, values, beliefs, relationships, and feelings associated with literacy in those communities. Consider what a child learns about the nature of literacy when they share a storybook or a family story on a parent's knee, or observe a parent send and receive mail (electronic or otherwise), sort coupons for shopping, or use a TV guide (on or off screen). When children enter school, a new community shapes their literate practices and defines what counts as literacy. Although children are learning about the conventional organization of texts (e.g., books, advertisements, computer screens) and about the relationships between speech and print and the strategic uses of print, they are also learning about the significance of their own experience and the nature of the social world in which they and the texts operate. They learn who can do what with print, who can ask questions of whom under what circumstances, who gets to produce and consume texts, and what it means to be competent in literacy. As Hicks (2002) suggests, "Child learners come to *be* and *know* with others as they engage in discourse practices fully saturated with cultural meanings" (p. 23), that is, they are constructing literate identities (Bean, 1997; Gee, 1996).

Consider the first grader who said, when asked what someone needs to be a writer, "Eraser, pencil" (focusing on materials—the order is probably not incidental), and when asked what kind of writer he was, said, "A printer." This child lives in a different schooled, literate world than other first graders, who responded with terms like *poet* or *scary writer*, suggesting the adoption of *writer* as part of their identity (Johnston & Rogers, 2001, p. 378).

Thus, children do not simply acquire literacy. They acquire particular kinds of literacy that may or may not serve them well in particular situations. For example, if children acquire an uncritical literacy—a literacy in which they have no sense of agency—they merely become better prepared to be managed by societal literacy practices. We raise this point, particularly, because even quite young children can learn a critical literacy (Vasquez, 2001). For example, the first grader who observed, after a shared reading of a book, "The authors left me with a question in my head and they need to clarify their words" (Bahrmann, 2000), is becoming critically literate.

To say that children are acquiring complex personal and social knowledge is not to neglect other aspects of literacy acquisition, such as what children are learning about the organization of words, letters, speech, and so forth. Rather, it is to emphasize that these are only part of a complex set of understandings and processes that might become objects of assessment. It is easy to become overly concerned with particular dimensions of literate practice to the neglect of others. As Taylor and Dorsey-Gaines (1988) point out in their study of family literacy,

> Literacy is not a discrete event, nor is it a package of predetermined skills. The complex, yet oversimplified, boundaries that we have established so that we can count, weigh, and measure literacy do not exist. They are of our own making. (p. 201)

In reality, literacy is complicated and intertwined with our ways of living, a fact not missed by family literacy participants. In a study of family literacy programs, Neuman, Caperelli, and Kee (1998) found that, "for most participants, family literacy was not a narrowly defined concept consisting of basic reading skills.... [It] was viewed more broadly as a cultural concept, a way for thinking, behaving, and responding to one's environment" (p. 246).

Yet, the tendency to oversimplify—the desire to count and contain literacy—continues to divide educators. For example, there is currently considerable debate in the research community regarding the significance of phonemic awareness for literacy learning. Some argue that phonemic awareness has been documented through research as a prerequisite to acquiring literacy and that reading is primarily a matter of decoding (Fletcher & Lyon, 1998; Grossen, 1996). This position is currently also favored by lawmakers and is becoming enforced through controls on both assessments and instructional programs (National Reading Panel, 2000; U.S. DOE, 2002b). Others, however, have raised questions about the nature and interpretation of the supporting research (Allington & Woodside-Jiron, 1999; Dressman, 1999). In particular, there remain questions regarding the degree to which the phonological awareness tests (a) accurately reflect the construct of literacy, or even of phonological awareness (i.e., construct validity); (b) accurately reflect the relationship between the norms and the range of phonological systems children bring to the tests; and (c) accurately reflect the relationship between nonmainstream children's phonemic and phonological awareness and their achievement (Dressman, 1999; see chapter 27 in this volume, for a different perspective).

Early childhood literacy assessment is influenced not only by views of early literacy, but also by more general views of learning and development. Following from Gesell's (1925) view that maturational development precedes learning, reading readiness tests attempt to decide who is developmentally ready for learning to read. This belief, and the procedures that follow from it, continue, despite researchers arguing against readiness testing beginning with Gates (1937). Further, readiness principles contradict the reality lived by educators, who find that their students come to school with very different kinds of literacy experiences. In a position statement, the National Association of Early Childhood Specialists in State Departments of Education (2000) argues,

> Children entering school come from markedly different backgrounds. Assessment procedures must not penalize children at school entry for responses that have heretofore been appropriate for them or which they have not yet had a chance to develop. Screening and assessment does not substitute for an observant, competent, caring teacher and a responsive curriculum. (Discussion of Principle 5, para. 8)

For these reasons, readiness should be viewed as a characteristic of teachers and classroom environments. Teachers and schools need to be ready for children who enter school with a diversity of experiences and skills. As Clay (1993a) suggests, *"They are all ready to learn something*, but are starting from different places" (p. 6, emphasis in original). This position follows from a sociocultural model of learning and development which recognizes that children learn the skills of literacy through scaffolded experiences with others (Vygotsky, 1934/1978). Meisels (1998) acknowledges this position, by reframing the Clinton era call for "every child ready to learn by 2000" as,

> By the year 2000 all children will have an opportunity to enhance their skills, knowledge, and abilities by participating in classrooms that are sensitive to community values, recognize individual differences, reinforce and extend children's strengths, and assist them in overcoming their difficulties. (p. 25)

There is, however, a sense in which children are or are not ready to learn a particular concept or skill. For example, when a child has no insight into the phonological structure of the English language, or knows no letters of the alphabet, they are unlikely to be able to learn to self-correct from print while reading. In Vygotsky's terms, this type of self-correction would be beyond the child's zone of proximal development and could not be done even with assistance, such as that provided by an adult (Vygotsky, 1934/1978). This concept of what can only be accomplished with assistance is an important aspect of assessment, and it provides the necessary information for organizing productive instruction. Locating this zone of development for children is possible only through interaction and is one reason why we argue that on-the-spot assessment, in classroom or home, by informed adults, is the most important form of assessment.

Different definitions of literacy and learning have serious implications for what is assessed (and consequently, what is taught) in early literacy programs. In a similar way, different views of assessment, its qualities and its functions, influence what is assessed and how it is assessed.

ASSESSMENT: DEFINITIONS AND RELATIONSHIPS

We view *assessment* as the practices of noticing, documenting, interpreting, and representing children's literate behaviors. This view might, but mostly need not, involve *testing*—a subset of assessment in which the behaviors are elicited and documented under standardized conditions. The primary function of any literacy assessment is to guide optimal instruction for each child. Position statements by the major relevant organizations make this function very clear (International Reading, 1994; NAEYC, 1991; Phye, 1997). Numerous other assessment functions are commonly described, such as accountability, screening, and diagnosis, but ultimately these are only successful if they lead to improved instruction and learning environments for children.

Engel (1990) distinguished three levels of assessment: (a) Moment-to-moment assessment that teachers do as they interact with children around their reading and writing (much of this assessment will not be recorded); (b) documentation of children's literacy development, which allows teachers, students, and family members to take stock of development and plan future practice; and (c) assessment with more aggregation across students and time, so that teachers, in dialogue with their educational community, can look at classroom practice with an eye to development. Each level requires that a larger group of individuals enter a common conversation and use common constructs, data, and criteria. Without collective agreement, there will be constant misunderstanding and conflict (Chester, Maraschiello, & Salinger, 2000). On the other hand, the process of generating that collective agreement, albeit incomplete, pays dividends in learning for all parties.

Like literacy, assessment practices are discursive cultural practices bound up with ways of knowing, valuing, behaving, believing, relating, and, most important, representing (Johnston, 1997; McDermott & Varenne, 1995; Taylor, 1993). Assessments, like other social texts, are fundamentally interpretive and socially consequential, at once reflecting and imposing sets of values and beliefs, and shaping identities (Fairclough, 1992; Gee, 1996). Each assessment community has different emphases, different ways of gathering data, different interpretive practices, and different language for representing students' performance.

Parents are introduced to expected literacy practices and values, in part, through the assessments that frame their children's literacy development, and parents' own schooling histories further reinforce these expectations. Consequently, assessment practices play a role in organizing the discourse around young children, even in their homes. The cultural models (Gee, 2000) of assessment insinuate themselves into home discourse, so that parents' ways of representing their children's academic development are institutionalized. Parents learn to expect normative performance indicators and medical-style diagnoses—descriptors that commonly establish limiting positions for students, their families, and even teachers. These diagnoses provide a means of institutional, symbolic domination and intimidation (Bourdieu, 1991; Fennimore, 2000; Rogers, 2002). Not incidentally, reports of child abuse peak when report cards go home (Valentine, 1990). Even when parents eschew these models in their language at home, when they arrive at school to advocate for their children, the discourse of school literacy assessment readily overpowers even the most committed (Rogers, 2002).

The Internet enforces and extends this relationship. Increasingly, we see scientific literacy assessment at home encouraged on the Internet, partly, it seems, to cultivate a market for home literacy instruction products. An example (perhaps symptom) of these issues is provided by the arrival of tests, such as Reading Edge, which are available and advertised on the Web with all the trappings of science, to parents of young children. Such tests offer to diagnose potential problems with reading development and remediate them with products available from the same company, in this case, the FastForWord family of programs, "Computer-based training using the latest brain research, for rapid gains in language and reading" (Scientific Learning, 2002a). On the FastForWord investor information site, the company notes an annual increase rate of nearly 100% in the number of students signed up for its testing and language/reading programs since 1997 (Scientific Learning, 2002c) and an annual revenue growth of 100% (Scientific Learning, 2003). The company expects

> educators' awareness about how well our programs fit with the goals of the new No Child Left Behind federal education legislation . . . coupled with the new emphasis on scientifically validated and proven products, to contribute significantly to our continuing growth. (Scientific Learning, 2002b)

The popularity of such products is likely to be fueled by, and to fuel, the ongoing presence of national and local test scores, as well as stories in the public media of widespread literacy failure.

Understanding the source of these developments requires understanding the lingering rhetoric of traditional assessment in early childhood education. Assessment is part of a process in which children and their families are schooled to talk and think about themselves, each other, and literacy. Children learn a language (including the relevant social relationships) through which they come to understand who they are and how parents/caregivers can view themselves in relation to their child's developing literacy. When a child is *identified* as needing particular resources, by being out of the norm, there is a great deal that happens along with the identification of *need*. Normative assessments, particularly those used to winnow out students who are out of step in their development, commonly invoke the language of deficits and disabilities (Johnston, 1993; McDermott, 1993; Mehan, 1993). Even a language of strengths brings right behind it the language of weakness (Auerbach, 1995); this language is very different from describing what the child knows and can do independently or with some (defined) support, what the child can almost do (although not yet conventionally), or what the child is working to acquire.

Consider further the assessment function of identifying children requiring additional support or special services, which may seem to concerned parents like a good idea, particularly because we know that early intervention can make a big difference for children who somehow get off on the wrong foot in literacy development (Clay, 1993b, 2001; Vellutino & Scanlon, 1998). In practice, however, such assessments can have a negative effect. For example, a school psychologist, who commonly has less background in literacy learning than the classroom teacher, can carry out the assessments, leading to the child being pulled out of class to receive instruction from a special education teacher who also often has less background in literacy learning than the classroom teacher (Allington & McGill-Franzen, 1989). Another problem is the continued use of intelligence tests to identify children with reading disabilities, tests that have been shown to be un- or misinformative in this context (Fletcher et al., 2001; Hallahan & Mercer, 2001; Stanovich, 2000; Stuebing et al., 2002; Vellutino et al., 1996).

Like identification procedures, accountability pressures also shift teachers' and other educators' language and descriptions of children's development in unproductive directions (Deci, Siegel, Ryan, Koestner, & Kauffman, 1982; Johnston, 1993). The structure of the assessments changes the way teachers represent students. For example, a teacher discussing the test that third graders had to take made observations in which children were referred to by their test scores, "One of our definite 'fours' misunderstood Part 3 [of the test] and wrote a perfectly beautiful essay on the wrong subject.... He's a two, borderline three, right now and we hope that this enrichment program will put him over the edge" (Baudanza, 2001, p. 8). This categorical language is common in descriptions of children who do not fit the cultural model (Gee, 1996) and is often accompanied by judgmental words like *should* and *needs*.

If accountability assessment practices result in an overly restricted literacy curriculum, as they often do (Crooks, 1988; Paris, Turner, & Lawton, 1991; Smith, 1991; Smith & Rottenberg, 1991), they defeat the purpose of the assessment and thus lose validity. Further, under the pressures of accountability systems, children considered likely to struggle with literacy can be screened out of school as *not ready*, can be side-tracked into *special services* or can be given "the gift of time" (Graue, DiPerna, 2000) by being retained or placed in transition rooms, thus ensuring these predictions. Despite good intentions, these practices can lead to as many as two thirds of a cohort being separated from their peers by the end of early childhood (McGill-Franzen & Allington, 1993). Not only have none of these practices demonstrated any value in relation to improving the quality of literacy instruction or children's school experience, but, also, the reverse is often the case (Allington & McGill-Franzen, 1995; Bredekamp, 1987; Shepard & Smith, 1986; Smith, 1991; Smith & Rottenberg, 1991; Stallman & Pearson, 1991). In any case, the tests used lack, commonly by a substantial margin, the technical adequacy required for such weighty decisions (National Education Goals Panel, 1998; Shepard, 1994; Shepard & Smith, 1986).

Effective assessment should productively restructure the learning environment and focus teaching, so that the primary goal of optimizing instruction will be achieved. Instead of working "to identify children who may be in need of specialized services or intervention" (NAEYC,

1991, p. 32), we might identify what children know and can accomplish independently or with support (Johnston & Rogers, 2001).

TEACHERS AND ENVIRONMENTS FOR LEARNING

There is considerable professional agreement that the teacher is the primary agent of assessment (Brozo & Brozo, 1994; International Reading, 1994; Johnston, 1997; NAEYC, 1991; Phye, 1997). The corollary to this belief is that improving assessment necessarily entails building teachers' professional knowledge about children's literacy development and the context of this development. They must know what to observe and what instructional significance to assign to particular observations (Johnston, 1987; Lyons, Pinnell, & Deford, 1993; Pressley, Allington, Wharton-MacDonald, Collins-Block, & Morrow, 2001). Teachers who cannot describe a student's literacy development in some detail are more likely to refer students to a committee on special education for classification and services (Broikou, 1992). A teacher needs to know the following (Athey, 1990; Johnston, 1993):

- How the child manages print and literacy interactions
- How the child inquires into language in different settings
- What languages and funds of knowledge (Moll et al. 1992) the child brings to the classroom
- How home language patterns relate to classroom language practices
- What literacy knowledge and practices the child controls, partially understands, and can do with some assistance
- The logic of the child's errors
- How to recognize and build on knowledge about literacy systems evidenced in children's behavior
- How to communicate with children and families about literacy learning progress (NAEYC, 2001)

Understanding what children know often requires imagining, with sensitivity to culture and context, the logic of the behavior, from the student's perspective, and recognizing what must be known in order to accomplish a particular behavior. For example, Cirino (2001), teaching children in a prekindergarten day care class, recorded the following:

> "The pig is getting married. The husband is giving a Valentine's card." Four-year-old Anne smiled as she "read" her picture to June, James, and me. . . .
> "I'm making a pig, too," piped James, drawing. "Oops! I guess it looks more like a turtle." Five-year-old James then wrote "TAEL" (turtle) directly underneath his rendition.
> "What is your turtle doing?" I asked casually.
> "I guess it's walking on the letters," was James's literal response. He wrote next to "TAEL" "WCE LD" (James did not leave spaces between these words) and read aloud, "A turtle is walking on the letters."
> "That's funny!" giggled June, who was writing beside her illustration of a cat. She had written, "this Is MI MAT AND BKSITH IT HASa caT IS BKSITH The SIB AV MY MTA Is caT" and then rhythmically chanted, "This is my mat and because it has a cat is because the symbol of my mat is cat!" (p. 79)

From observing and participating in the literacy practices of these children, Cirino has learned a great deal about what these students know and can do. For example, Cirino uncovered Anne's use of a literacy register (i.e., booklike language) and sense of literacy functions, James's and June's grasp of the phonological structure of speech and of the relationships between speech and print, James's ability to adjust his topic to meet new needs, and June's use of rhyme and explanation. Cirino also uncovered each child's different concepts of word and understandings of literacy conventions, as well as the children's confidence and approach to literacy, the ways they interact in their learning, and much more—all are evident without interrupting learning for testing. Some further interactions with the children could lead to even more detail and a sense of what they might be able to do with some support.

This assessment has essentially taken no instructional time and, because it was directly observed, is more memorable and can be responded to more effectively than if it were a test. The conversational and relational context allows the teacher to turn attention to the significant aspects of a particular student's learning, in a timely way that helps the student achieve their own goals. For example, at reading time, James would profit from some attention to his understanding of what constitutes a word, such as helping him read books with three or four words per page, pointing to each as he reads it. Such instruction would not be useful for June.

If teachers are unaware of these aspects of literacy, however, they will not be noticed. Lack of awareness of the significance of context would also be problematic. For example, children commonly find themselves assigned to read materials based on an expected competence rather than on their actual competence, resulting in their being asked to read texts beyond or below their ability. Performance on such materials often has all the hallmarks commonly used to describe children assigned to remedial programs or to special education—lack of independence, failure to self-correct, and lack of fluency (Clay, 1991). Failure to attend to these indicators can have long-term consequences. However, attending to them and viewing them as indicators of negative traits of learners, rather than as indicators of an unsatisfactory situation, would be equally problematic. Essentially teachers must be knowledgeable about, and understand, the intersections of literacy, literacy behaviors, and literacy contexts.

Documentary forms of assessment explicitly depend on the expertise of a human "sensitive observer" (Clay, 1993a) or "kidwatcher" (Goodman, 1978). They also rely on the discursive currents of the classroom to enable and encourage children to talk about and examine their literacy practices in interaction with teachers and peers, particularly in collaborative work and play (Helm, Beneke, & Steinheimer, 1998; Himley & Carini, 2000; NAEYC, 2001), to "make learning visible" (Project Zero & Reggio Children, 2001). Indeed, especially for young children, play is a particularly rich source of information about children's grasp of the structures and functions of literacy practice (Roskos & Neuman, 1993; Teale, 1991; Whitmore & Goodman, 1995). A contextualized case study is the basis for this approach to assessment, and good published examples can be found of children from as young as 3 years old (e.g., Scrivens, 1998). For a teacher, it is not enough to know what a child can and cannot do; it is helpful also to know what a child can almost do, or can do with some support. This information arises principally in interactions with children, as they strive to accomplish projects that are just beyond their independent reach (Feuerstein, 1979; Rogoff, 1995; Vygotsky, 1962/1934).

Indeed, analysis of these interactions informs us not only about children's development, but also about the nature of instruction, which contextualizes children's learning. Because the learning environment must change, early literacy assessment should involve an examination of the instructional environment, as much as an examination of a child's acquisition of skills and practices (Johnston, 1997; Meisels, 1998). For example, we will want to know the following about the instructional environment:

- Whether appropriate materials are accessible
- Whether reading and writing are presented as social, purposeful, and meaningful

- Whether the processes of reading and writing are made visible through modeling or coproduction
- Whether students' experience and literate performances are visibly valued
- Whether there is sufficient time and reason to read and write
- Whether classroom talk supports independence, values problem solving, and is positive, focused, reflective, and nonjudgmental (Allington & Johnston, 2002; Clay, 1991; Johnston, 1997; Pressley et al., 2001)

For the teacher, context is as critical as cognition for instruction, and, in assessment, context should be considered as possible grounds for problematic performance (Gregory, 1997; Johnston, 1997). Outside the classroom, however, the cultural model persuades people that science involves stripping away context and making simple numerical or categorical comparisons concerning cognition (Johnston, 1989). This distinction gives us the notion of *formal* and *informal* assessments, privileging the unmarked[1] term *formal assessments,* and leaving teachers—the pivotal agents in the process—with the inferior informal assessment, readily trumped in a meeting by formal measures.

Impending federal policy assumes that increased formal testing will optimize literacy instruction in preschool and early schooling (U.S. DOE, 2002a, 2002c). However, in spite of its possible auditing function, formal assessment is not particularly helpful for designing instructional improvement. A more productive model for improving literacy instruction in preschool and early elementary classrooms would be to help teachers become active researchers of their own practice (Cochran-Smith & Lytle, 1993; Hubbard & Power, 1993), with action research as the norm (Huber, 1994; Kemmis & Wilkinson, 1998; Noffke, 1995)—a model in which teachers are researching their own teaching and their students' learning, thus integrating teaching, learning, assessment, and professional development. We could then reclassify assessments as *traditional* and *documentary* or *informed* (Johnston & Rogers, 2001).

DISPARATE ASSUMPTIONS, DISPARATE PRACTICES

Consider the ways three different assessment instruments approach early literacy assessment: The Phonological Awareness Literacy Screening (PALS; Invernizzi & Meier, 2000; Invernizzi, Meier, Juel, & Swank, 1997), the Observation Survey (OS; Clay, 1993a), and the Primary Language Record (PLR; Barrs, Ellis, Hester, & Thomas, 1989). Each assessment has a substantial and positive history and has found favor in the state of New York in the past 5 years, or has been used as the basis for the local development of other assessments. Each achieves some of the recommendations for early literacy assessments suggested by Meisels and Piker (2001), who address standardization and psychometric principles, although they accomplish this objective in different ways. The assessment instruments also provide information on what should be observed and how to interpret the observations. The PLR and, to a substantially lesser extent, the OS allow for students' generation of personal meanings, acknowledgement and acceptance of multiple primary languages, examination of writing as well as reading, accommodation of cooperative group work, and multiple means of knowledge demonstration. Most important, however, in the context of this chapter, these instruments represent different views of literacy, assessment, and learning.

---

[1] The unmarked term is the default, as in male (unmarked) and female (marked).

The Phonological Awareness Literacy Screening (PALS).[2]

The PALS was designed for measuring "the fundamental components of the learning-to-read process" and "identifying" those children who are relatively behind in their acquisition of these fundamental literacy skills" (Invernizzi et al., 1997, p. 1). It currently is a mandated screening instrument in Virginia, at grade levels K–3—a grade extension of the original, which was developed only for K–1 use. Conceptually, the PALS test draws on a model of reading represented by a simple Venn diagram showing reading as the overlap between sound awareness and print awareness. From this model, the authors argue that "word recognition in isolation is the most accurate indicator of reading achievement" (p. 2). Further, they note that the number of phonemes represented in the spelling of five high-frequency consonant–vowel–consonant (CVC) words was the best predictor of "children in need of additional instruction in phonological awareness and early literacy skills in both kindergarten and first grade" (Invernizzi & Meier, 2000, p. 67).

The subtests at the kindergarten level are rhyme, beginning sound, lowercase letter recognition, letter sounds (most recent version includes vowels, uppercase letters except X, but including SH and QU), spelling (five CVC words), concept of word (pointing), and concept of word (word identification). At the first grade level, word lists representing preprimer, primer, and first grade levels are added. The test originally included a "sense of story" assessment that "has shown a strong relationship . . . [with] reading comprehension" (p. 44). This test was dropped for a while, because it "was far too time consuming relative to its contribution to the overall purpose of PALS" (p. 44), but has been reinstated in the most recent version. The construct *literacy*, as represented in PALS, focuses on children's understanding of the alphabetic principle and word recognition. The manuals emphasize the reliability of the subtests.

Concerning communicating with parents, the PALS manuals suggest that a parent–teacher conference should be held that begins with the teacher explaining the purpose of the PALS and the nature of what is assessed, avoiding jargon, and showing the kinds of items used. The teacher should also explain how parents can help at home and what additional instruction the student will receive at school. There is no suggestion that the teacher should inquire into family literacy or language practices, and communication is only from teacher to parent. The manuals present concise explanations of the logic and specific remedial actions to be taken for students performing below expectation in particular areas.

The Observation Survey (OS)

Developed by Clay (1993a), the OS has a screening function similar to that of the PALS. However, the OS manual also emphasizes the ongoing documentation of progress. Like the PALS, the OS manual places some emphasis on standardization, reliability, and noninteractive administration. It also documents some similar aspects of literacy and provides normative information on some components. The OS documents children's conceptual knowledge of words (read and written) and letters, concepts about print, hearing and recording sounds in words, and the qualities of written language. Its focus is entirely on initial literacy acquisition (through second grade at most) except for the running records of reading (i.e., written records of children's oral reading strategies), which extend further into the child's school career.

The OS's theoretical frame of reference and assumptions are quite different from the PALS. The OS focuses attention on the child's strategic control of literate processes while actually reading and writing. For example, the OS turns attention to children's efforts to monitor their reading and writing, to search for cues, and to figure out or cross-check and confirm attempts.

---

[2] One recent version of the PALS II is titled *The Phonological Awareness and Literacy Screening.*

Rather than being based on a theory of word learning, it is based on a theory of problem solving for meaning. Similarly, whereas the PALS is only somewhat concerned with whether the child understands what is read, the OS is concerned with the extent to which the child's processing system is meaning-directed, self-correcting, and self-extending. Attention to such features places a greater demand on the teacher's skill and understanding of literate learning.

The Primary Language Record (PLR)

The PLR approaches literacy assessment in a very different way from either the PALS or the OS. Although it shares some theoretical orientation with the OS—indeed, it relies on some of the same components, such as running records and writing samples—it takes a more expansive, social view of literacy, and a different, more complex view of assessment functions and the relationship between home and school and the participants. As the PLR authors write:

> Developments in language and literacy do not take place in isolation from one another. This record provides a basis for making connections between different aspects of development in all the major language modes—talking and listening, reading, and writing—and for observing children using language for learning across the whole curriculum (Barrs et al., 1989, p. 8).

The PLR also emphasizes a collaborative research view of documenting development over time.

The PLR is considered integral in the teaching and learning environment. The criteria used for designing it included that it must inform and support the daily classroom practice of teachers; inform and support the students; inform and support the family environment and family literacies; and provide clear and useful information to parents, students, administrators, and other interested community members. Fundamentally interactive and requiring interviews with children and their parents, the PLR does not eliminate dimensions of literacy in the interests of time.

The PLR consists of three major sections and records data collected at intervals throughout the school year. The first section is a record of conferences between the teacher and the child and between the teacher and the child's parents. For example, parents are asked in interviews to describe their child's at-home literacy. The interview provides prompts that help parents to understand what is significant about home literacy practices and that also open the possibility of initiating new literacy practices. For example, suggested discussion topics include "the child's knowledge and enjoyment of story and opportunities that might be possible for story telling and story listening" and "opportunities that might be possible for writing at home and whether the child chooses to write" (p. 13). Teachers and parents must agree on what is recorded in the PLR. In the second section of the PLR, teachers record information about the "child as a language user" (p. 16). The form guides teachers to record the child's development, along with any teaching or experiences that "have helped/would help development" in talking and listening, reading, and writing (pp. 16–17). The final section of the PLR includes comments by the parents and child, as well as information for the next year's teacher. The manual describes in detail how observations can be made and described through the PLR.

This approach to assessment takes more seriously than do the PALS or OS the child's literate life and culture outside of school, in the family, and the communicative and educative function of assessment systems. In this regard, it accommodates well the concept of *ongoing assessment,* which is a central concern of participants in family literacy programs, and such assessment provides concrete evidence for teachers, parents, and children of the growth and new skills developed in the program (Neuman et al., 1998). Recognizing the centrality of teacher expertise, the manual also provides ample description and demonstration of how reading and writing develop, emphasizing conceptual, skill, and process learning, and the context necessary for productive literate performance. In doing so, the authors make clear the values and assumptions sustaining, and supported by, the assessment.

The PLR manual focuses assessment attention on both the child's development and the context in which it occurs, insisting that "progress or lack of progress should always be seen in relation to the adequacy of the context" (Barrs et al., 1989, p. 18). Indeed, the manual provides a range of contexts to consider, in the form of a grid of learning contexts (e.g., collaborative reading and writing activities, play, dramatic play, drama, and storytelling) and social contexts (e.g., pair, small group, child with adult) (Barrs et al., 1989). In this way, unlike the other two assessments, the PLR addresses what a child can do independently and with various kinds of support.

The PLR also reports on children's learning in multiple ways. For example, to summarize and quantify development *as a reader* (not the same as development *in reading*), two 5-point scales are used, one representing the extent of independence and the other representing extent of experience (see Table 26.1 for examples). These constructs are defined with accompanying exemplars, including aspects such as "pleasure and involvement in story and reading, alone

TABLE 26.1

Examples of Primary Language Record Reading Scales
(Points 2 and 4 from 1–5 Scales)

Becoming a Reader: reading scale 1	
Dependence	
Non-fluent reader	Tackling known and predictable texts with growing confidence but still needing support with new and unfamiliar ones. Growing ability to predict meanings and develop strategies to check predictions against other cues such as the illustrations and the print itself.
2	
Fluent reader	A capable reader who now approaches familiar texts with confidence but still needs support with unfamiliar materials. Beginning to draw inferences from books and stories read independently. Chooses to read silently.
4	
Independence	
Inexperienced	
Less experienced reader	Developing fluency as a reader and reading certain kinds of material with confidence. Usually chooses short books with simple narrative shapes and with illustrations and may read these silently; often re-reads favorite books. Reading for pleasure often includes comics and magazines. Needs help with the reading demands of the classroom and especially with using reference and information books.
2	
Experienced reader	A self-motivated, confident and experienced reader who may be pursuing particular interests through reading. Capable of tackling some demanding texts and can cope well with the reading of the curriculum. Reads thoughtfully and appreciates shades of meaning. Capable of locating and drawing on a variety of sources in order to research a topic independently.
4	
Experienced	

Note. From Primary Language Record: Handbook for Teachers (pp. 26–27), by M. Barrs, S. Ellis, H. Hester, and A. Thomas, 1989, London: Inner London Education Authority/Centre for Language in Primary Education. Copyright 1989 by Inner London Education Authority/Center for Language in Primary Education. Adapted with permission.

and with others" and "the range, quantity and variety of reading in all areas of the curriculum" (Barrs et al., 1989, p. 28). Writing development is also considered multidimensional and is divided into the dimensions of composition and transcription. Development in compositional dimensions should include increases in, among other things, control of a range of genres, collaborative practices, sustained engagement, attention to audience, the development of a voice (i.e., an author's unique style), and the child's use of experience. Development in transcriptional dimensions should include increases in control of spelling, punctuation and format, and handwriting.

Emphasis on what the child can do is deliberate, stressing its importance for framing the work of parents and other teachers. For example, in a sample reading report for a 6-year-old boy, we find

> A. is becoming far more confident in tackling known and some unknown texts. He is progressing toward being a moderately fluent reader and is making steady progress. He is developing strategies such as checking guesses, initial sounds, picture cues, and is beginning to read in phrases. Although still below the class average, A. is highly motivated and shows a sound interest and pleasure in reading. He attempts a wide variety of books in terms of subject matter and complexity. (Barrs et al., 1989, p. 23)

This brief sample details information that will help A and his parents and teachers plan the next steps in his reading at home and at school.

Additional Assessment Tools

Expanding to even broader assessment systems, we have assessments such as the Work Sampling System, a system of developmental guidelines and checklists, portfolios, and written summary reports designed by Meisels and his colleagues (Dichtelmiller, Jablon, Dorfman, Marsden, & Meisels, 1994; Meisels, 1995; Pearson Early Learning, 2002b). Like the PLR and the OS, this system includes a concern for positive language (it provides guidelines on word choice for report writing) (Pearson Early Learning, 2002a), although parents are not as fully involved as in the PLR. Because of the broad scope of the system (e.g., language and literacy is only one of seven domains at first grade), the emphasis on checklists is greater, and reading is reduced to a three-level rating scale: not yet, in process, or proficient. At first grade, reading is rated in the areas of "interest," "understanding of concepts about print," "decod[ing] unfamiliar words," using "strategies to construct meaning from print," and "comprehend[ing] and interpret[ing] fiction and non-fiction" (Pearson Early Learning, 2002b). The breadth of coverage is at once an advantage (representing the overall picture of the child's development) and a disadvantage (e.g., reducing the child's knowledge and use of print conventions to the three-level rating scale, with the portfolio component providing examples). Although complex systems, such as the PLR and the Work Sampling System, require a serious professional development investment on the part of a school system, they are being successfully adopted (Falk, 1998; Falk & Darling-Hammond, 1993; Meisels, Bickel, Nicholson, Xue, & Atkins-Burnett, 2001; Meisels, Liaw, Dorfman, & Nelson, 1995; Meisels, Xue, Bickel, Nicholson, & Atkins-Burnett, 2001).

Portfolios, too, are successfully being implemented in family literacy programs to evaluate individual and family progress (Johnson, McDaniel, & Willeke, 2000; Johnson, Willeke, & Steiner, 1998; Paratore, 2001), with the advantage that "all participants are active in their own assessment" (Hoffman, 1995, p. 594). For instance, in the Home–School Literacy Portfolios created by the Intergenerational Literacy Project (Paratore, 2001), parents, with the guidance of their family literacy teachers, documented their children's literacy at home and shared the portfolios with the children's classroom teachers, who had participated in professional development about family literacy and collaborating with families. Paratore found that parents were able to affirm and share their home literacies and literacy experiences. Further, classroom teachers were able to recognize the parents' and children's literacy learning experiences, as well as to provide suggestions for building on them. Children's learning was enhanced, both at home and at school, by the cooperation among families and family literacy and school staff. Teachers reported more productive conferences with parents, and both parents and teachers reported better understanding of the students and their progress (Paratore, 2001). Although the PALS and the OS detail specific areas of literacy, in portfolios, the breadth and reduction of standardized components yields valuable, but perhaps less focused, information about young children's literacy.

ASSESSMENT AND PSYCHOMETRICS

The traditional scientific or psychometric view of assessment has become the center of the national dialogue on education. For example, programs applying for Early Reading First[3] funds must "acquire, provide training for, and implement screening reading assessments or other appropriate measures that are based on scientifically based reading research to determine whether preschool age children are developing the early language and cognitive skills they need for later reading success" (U.S. DOE, 2002a, p. 15). Further, Early Reading First screening assessments must be "valid, reliable, and based on scientifically based reading research" (NAEYC, 2002, p. 4)[4].

However, current ways of thinking about reliability and validity differ from the more traditional views represented in this legislation. Reliability is coming to be thought of in terms of the extent to which an indicator, score, or judgment can be generalized across observers, over time, across contexts, and so forth (Shavelson & Webb, 1991). Validity has come to more centrally include the consequences of assessment practices (Messick, 1994; Moss, 1992, 1998), because of the increasing realization that assessment is always a social practice and that a perfect diagnostic test, whose administration hurts the student and trivializes the curriculum, is probably not a good one.

Sometimes, the consequences of assessments are not what we might expect. For example, current approaches to early literacy assessment that emphasize fairness and accountability require testing every student. This approach in turn requires a limited form of assessment, because of time and other constraints. A teacher learning more complex assessment strategies, however, might only complete them on a third of the students in the class. Darling-Hammond, Ancess, and Falk (1995) document the ways assessments, such as the PLR or the Descriptive Review of a Child (Carini, 2001), used on even a few children in a class, affect the teacher's understanding of other children's literacy development, and the ways such instruments affect the school as a learning organization. They point out that:

> Assessment reforms can increase student success only if they change both the kinds of tasks students are asked to engage in and the kinds of inquiry schools and teachers are called on to undertake as they bring assessment into the heart of the teaching and learning process. (p. 253)

---

[3]"The overall purpose of the Early Reading First Program is to prepare preschool-age children to enter kindergarten with the language, cognitive, and early reading skills necessary for reading success, thereby preventing later reading difficulties. Early Reading First will transform early childhood programs into centers of excellence that provide a high-quality education to preschool-age children, especially those children from low-income families" (U.S. DOE, 2002a, p. 5).

[4]A screening test is further described as a "brief procedure designed as a first step in identifying children who may be at high risk for delayed development or academic failure and in need of further diagnosis of their need for special services or additional reading instruction" (NAEYC, 2002, p. 4). As we discussed earlier, this can be problematic.

Documentary assessments also approach consistency or reliability through frequent sampling and observation of literate activities in context; traditional assessments aim for agreement among judges, by restricting the context, domain, and sample (Gipps, 1994). The most reliable documentation is not necessarily the most valid, because important dimensions can be complex and less easily agreed upon. For example, children's self-corrections while reading are the least reliable aspect of running records (Clay, 1993a), but arguably the most important. Furthermore, some disagreement across observers or situations is expected because literacy is complex, and performances will differ across situations. Indeed, rather than indicating measurement error, such differences are not only expected as legitimate variability, but, like differences between observers, can be viewed as useful grounds for dialogue about literacy and a student's development. Such dialogue is a constructive source of learning and instructional improvement—the ultimate purpose of the assessment.

There remains, however, a range of different stances on assessment qualities. Compare the requirements of the authors of the PALS test with those of the PLR. The validity information provided with the PALS emphasizes content, construct, and concurrent validity. Content validity requires that the assessment constitutes a representative sample of the domain. Based on their model, for the authors of the PALS test, the domain means "children's knowledge of sound and print and . . . tasks that assess the wedding of the two" (p. 48) or "a representative sample of tasks found in other measures of early literacy" (p. 41). Construct validity refers to the extent to which the assessment reflects the underlying theoretical constructs—in this case, literacy defined principally as word recognition. Concurrent validity requires that the assessment correlate well with an independent indicator of the same construct, which is usually, as in the PALS case, another standardized test. The test validity is examined independently of the consequences of its use.

The authors of the PLR take a different stance. Although they address content validity, construct validity, and concurrent validity, their emphasis is on consequential validity, that is, the implications of the assessment in use. Teachers' ongoing assessments are more about change in performance than consistency, and classroom documentary assessments are more likely to affect change. Regular classroom samples of reading and writing are not as difficult to generalize to regular daily performances as are test performances. Most important are the trustworthiness of interpretations and the effectiveness of instructional responses—the consequential validity.

There are several reasons traditional psychometricians might wince at assessments such as the PLR. First, it assesses literacy in all its complexity. This is a matter of construct validity not encountered by assessments based on more limited views of literacy, but assessments of more complex performances are distinctly more likely to reduce agreement across judges (Shavelson, Baxter, & Pine, 1992). Second, the centrality of teacher expertise has a similar, and compounding, effect on reliability. The PLR addresses these potential problems with reliability by building inter-rater agreement through regular collaborative negotiation of case examples (called *moderating*) among the participants in the immediate assessment community, including parents. Moderation requires participants to reach agreement on ratings, based on specified criteria and through reference to collected data. Moderation assumes that disagreements are not always simply negative indicators of assessment quality, as they would be with traditional reliability, but, sometimes, that they are useful grounds for dialogues that deepen the understanding of all parties and move them onto the same discursive page. These practices take some time, because they are not simply training judges in a highly constrained domain, but they have been used in state-level assessments (Hewitt, 1995) and in other projects in which the nature of the process is evolving (Blythe, Allen, & Schieffelin, 1999). Nonetheless, societal pressures on parental time, particularly pressures that keep parents too busy to participate, and teachers too concerned with accountability tests, will impact these necessary and ongoing moderating procedures.

CONCLUSIONS

The International Reading Association's and the National Council of Teachers of English Joint Task Force on Assessment's, *Standards for the Assessment of Reading and Writing* (1994) asserts that "the interests of the student are paramount in assessment" (p. 13), that "the primary purpose of assessment is to improve teaching and learning" (p. 15), and that, consequently, "the teacher is the most important agent of assessment" (p. 27). In relation to family literacy, the *Standards* argue that "assessment must be based in the school community" (p. 33), and "all members of the educational community—students, parents, teachers, administrators, policy makers, and the public—must have a voice in the development, interpretation, and reporting of assessment" (p. 35). This involvement of families and students is important, not merely for ownership and accommodation of local variation, but because "the assessment process should involve multiple perspectives and sources of data" (p. 29) so that it will "reflect and allow for critical inquiry into curriculum and instruction" (p. 17). In particular, the document argues that "parents must be involved as active, essential participants in the assessment process" (p. 37). Teachers, students, and parents must work collaboratively towards appropriate assessment and plans for learning. These standards set a high bar for literacy assessment. Although there appears to be wide agreement in the *Standards* and elsewhere (e.g., FairTest, 1995, NAEYC, 1991; Phye, 1997) that literacy assessment should serve children's interests first, there are serious disagreements over what those interests might be and how assessment might best attend to them.

Current government policy increasingly insists on a traditional psychometric approach, with comprehensive testing of every student and with high stakes attached to motivate students, teachers, and schools. The argument presented is that

> too many of our nation's schools have not measured up because our measures for success have been ineffective. That's why under the *No Child Left Behind Act of 2001*. . . . states are required to use a method of measuring student progress that teachers use in their classrooms every day testing. (U.S. DOE, 2002d, para. 6)

The document compares testing to going to the dentist, which nobody likes, but "it's the right thing to do" (para. 7). In addition, current policy insists on a less-than-complex, cognitive view of literacy—what Street (1995) terms "autonomous" literacy—concentrating almost entirely on reading. The literacy assessment that arises from this view presumes little expertise on the part of the teacher. It makes no accommodation for variations in the language and culture that children bring with them to school (Au & Jordan, 1981; García & Pearson, 1991; Heath, 1983; Volk, 1997), and the norm-referenced framework readily brings with it a discourse of deficits (Poplin, 1988; Taylor, 1993). Further, as Carini (2001) points out, "When the focus is on measurement, we are forced to substitute small, static, additive units for events which, as they are enacted in life, are animated, layered, textured, complexly interlaced, and educationally potent" (p. 173).

Consider again the *Standards* assertion that assessment must "recognize and reflect the intellectually and socially complex nature of reading and writing and the important roles of school, home, and society in literacy development" (International Reading, 1994, p. 19). Assessment instruments differ in this regard, with a normative psychometric approach to assessing autonomous literacy being the most narrow and currently riding the pendulum back into prominence. The combination of narrow assessments and high stakes will diminish the curriculum children experience and, consequently, the literacy they acquire. This combination will also represent and position some teachers, children, and families in ways that will not serve them well.

With this in mind, the *Standards* assert further that "the consequences of an assessment are the first, and most important, consideration in establishing the validity of the assessment"

(p. 25). As we have discussed, assessment practices, particularly those attached to high stakes, can have powerful effects on teaching practices, the learning community, and the language through which children and their literacy are represented (Johnston, 1998; McNeil, 2000; Sacks, 1999; Smith, 1991; Smith & Rottenberg, 1991). Indeed, the curriculum-distorting power of assessments might lead us to adjust the current mantra to "no child, or part thereof, left behind." Unfortunately, those policies that represent narrower and more authoritarian views of schooling, literacy, learning, linguistic diversity, assessment, and research are politically expedient because they conform to the discourse of schooling and literacy with which the public is most familiar, and they can be easily transformed into sound bites such as "testing for results."

Professional organizations concerned with the literacy learning of young children currently press in another direction, taking a broader view of literacy as centrally social and bound up with other learning and social practices.[5] Kagan (2000), speaking as president of the NAEYC, has suggested that assessments, "if done well, should enable us to teach more reflectively and with more intention. They should honor children's full range of development" (p. 4). This stance is the one taken with assessments such as the PLR, which are productive in part because of their effect on the participants in terms of their learning, teaching, and relationships, and in part because of the intimate connection among assessment, teaching, and learning. Such instruments approach assessment as a system, integrating assessment with instruction, development of professional learning communities, and communication with children, their families, and other school personnel.

This view of assessing early literacy development emphasizes the consequential validity of assessment practices, the agency of the teacher and the student, and the need for ongoing, in-context assessment. Teachers must essentially become action researchers (Kemmis & Wilkinson, 1998; Noffke, 1995; Zeichner & Gore, 1995), researching their own practice, as well as their students' learning, to connect teaching, learning, assessment, and professional development. In other words, thinking of early literacy assessment in terms of the instruments selected is not sufficient, although that selection is important. Rather, we have to think about the learning community and how assessment practices affect the teachers, parents, children, and families involved.

REFERENCES

Allington, R. L., & Johnston, P. H. (Eds.). (2002). *Reading to learn: Lessons from exemplary fourth-grade classrooms.* New York: Guilford.

Allington, R. L., & McGill-Franzen, A. (1989). Different programs, indifferent instruction. In A. Gartner & D. Lipsky (Eds.), *Beyond separate education* (pp. 75–98). Baltimore: Brookes.

Allington, R. L., & McGill-Franzen, A. (1995). Flunking: Throwing good money after the bad. In R. L. Allington & S. A. Walmsley (Eds.), *No quick fix: Rethinking literacy programs in America's elementary schools* (pp. 45–60). New York: Teachers College Press.

Allington, R. L., & Woodside-Jiron, H. (1999). The politics of literacy teaching: How "research" shaped educational policy. *Educational Researcher, 28*(8), 4–13.

Athey, I. (1990). The construct of emergent literacy: Putting it all together. In L. M. Morrow (Ed.), *Assessment for instruction in early literacy* (pp. 176–183). Englewood Cliffs, NJ: Prentice Hall.

Au, K., & Jordan, C. (1981). Teaching reading to Hawaiian children: Finding a culturally appropriate solution. In H. Trueba, G. Guthrie, & K. Au (Eds.), *Culture and the bilingual classroom: Studies in classroom ethnography* (pp. 139–152). Rowley, MS: Newbury House.

---

[5] An exception to this direction is the position adopted by the American Federation of Teachers, which has moved to a progressively more restrictive view of literacy teaching, learning, and assessment.

Auerbach, E. (1995). Deconstructing the discourse of strengths in family literacy. *Journal of Reading Behavior, 27*(4), 643–661.

Bahrmann, A. (2000). *Painting a picture in your head: Using mental imagery with first grade writers.* Unpublished manuscript, The University at Albany, State University of New York.

Barrs, M., Ellis, S., Hester, H., & Thomas, A. (1989). *The primary language record: Handbook for teachers.* London: Inner London Education Authority/Centre for Language in Primary Education.

Baudanza, L. (2001). *Disabilities of a child or disabilities of the system?* Unpublished manuscript, The University at Albany, State University of New York.

Bean, M. S. (1997). Talking with Benny: Suppressing or supporting learner themes and learner worlds. *Anthropology and Education Quarterly, 28*(1), 50–69.

Blythe, T., Allen, D., & Schieffelin, B. (1999). *Looking together at student work: A companion guide to assessing student learning.* New York: Teachers College Press.

Bourdieu, P. (1991). *Language and symbolic power* (J. B. T. [Ed.] & G. Raymond & M. Adamson, Trans.). Cambridge, MA: Harvard University Press. (Original work published 1982)

Bredekamp, S. (Ed.). (1987). *Developmentally appropriate practice in early childhood programs serving children from birth through age 8.* Washington, DC: National Association for the Education of Young Children.

Broikou, K. (1992). *Understanding primary grade teachers' special educational referral practices.* Unpublished doctoral dissertation, University at Albany, State University of New York.

Brozo, W. G., & Brozo, C. C. (1994). Literacy assessment in standardized and zero-failure contexts. *Reading and Writing Quarterly: Overcoming Learning Difficulties, 10*, 189–200.

Bush, G. W. (2002). *Good start, grow smart: The Bush administrations early childhood initiative.* Retrieved May 24, 2002, from the White House Website: www.whitehouse.gov/infocus/earlychildhood/earlychildhood.pdf

Carini, P. F. (2001). *Starting strong: A different look at children, schools, and standards.* New York: Teachers College Press.

Chester, M., Maraschiello, R., & Salinger, T. (2000, April). *K–3 assessments in Philadelphia: Innovation and realities.* Paper presented at the annual meeting of the American Educational Research Association, New Orleans.

Cirino, H. (2001). Journal journeys: An exploration with young writers. In E. Duckworth (Ed.), *"Tell me more": Listening to learners explain* (pp. 79–92). New York: Teachers College Press.

Clay, M. M. (1991). *Becoming literate: The construction of inner control.* Portsmouth, NH: Heinemann.

Clay, M. M. (1993a). *An observation survey of early literacy achievement.* Portsmouth, NH: Heinemann.

Clay, M. M. (1993b). *Reading recovery: A guidebook for teachers in training.* Portsmouth, NH: Heinemann.

Clay, M. M. (2001). *Change over time in children's literacy development.* Portsmouth, NH: Heinemann.

Cochran-Smith, M., & Lytle, S. (1993). *Inside/outside: Teacher research and knowledge.* New York: Teachers College Press.

Crooks, T. J. (1988). The impact of classroom evaluation practices on students. *Review of Educational Research, 58*, 438–481.

Darling-Hammond, L., Ancess, J., & Falk, B. (1995). *Authentic assessment in action: Studies of schools and students at work.* New York: Teachers College Press.

Deci, E. L., Siegel, N. H., Ryan, R. M., Koestner, R., & Kauffman, M. (1982). Effects of performance standards on teaching styles: Behavior of controlling teachers. *Journal of Educational Psychology, 74*, 852–859.

Dichtelmiller, M. L., Jablon, J. R., Dorfman, A. B., Marsden, D. B., & Meisels, S. J. (1994). *Teacher's manual: The work sampling system.* Ann Arbor, MI: Rebus Planning Associates.

Dressman, M. (1999). On the use and misuse of research evidence: Decoding two states' reading initiatives. *Reading Research Quarterly, 34*(3), 258–285.

Engel, B. (1990). An approach to assessment in early literacy. In C. Kamii (Ed.), *Achievement testing in the early grades: The games adults play* (pp. 119–134). Washington, DC: National Association for the Education of Young Children.

Fairclough, N. (1992). *Discourse and social change.* London: Longman.

FairTest. (1995). *Principles and indicators for student assessment systems.* Retrieved August 1, 2002, from http://www.fairtest.org/princind.htm

FairTest. (n.d.). *Achievment tests for young children.* Retrieved July 18, 2002, from http://www.fairtest.org/facts/ACHIEVE.html

Falk, B. (1998). Using direct evidence to assess student progress: How the Primary Language Record supports teaching and learning. In C. Harrison & T. Salinger (Eds.), *Assessing reading 1: Theory and practice: International perspectives on reading assessment* (pp. 152–165). London: Routledge.

Falk, B., & Darling-Hammond, L. (1993). *The Primary Language Record at P.S. 261: How assessment transforms teaching and learning.* New York: The National Center for Restructuring Education, Schools, and Teaching: Teachers College Columbia University.

Fennimore, B. S. (2000). *Talk matters: Refocusing the language of public school.* New York: Teachers College Press.

Feuerstein, R. (1979). *The dynamic assessment of retarded performers.* Baltimore: University Park Press.

Fletcher, J., & Lyon, G. R. (1998). Reading: A research-based approach. In W. Evers (Ed.), *What's gone wrong in America's classrooms?* Stanford, CA: Hoover Institute Press.

Fletcher, J. M., Lyon, G. R., Barnes, M., Stuebing, K. K., Francis, D. J., Olson, R. K. et al. (2001, August 27–28). *Classification of learning disabilities: An evidence-based evaluation.* Paper presented at the Learning Disabilities Summit: Building a Foundation for the Future, Washington, D.C.

García, G. E., & Pearson, P. D. (1991). The role of assessment in a diverse society. In E. H. Hiebert (Ed.), *Literacy in a diverse society: Perspectives, practices, and policies* (pp. 253–278). New York: Teachers College Press.

Gates, A. (1937). The necessary mental age for beginning reading. *Elementary School Journal, 37,* 497–508.

Gee, J. P. (1996). *Social linguistics and literacies: Ideology in discourses* (2nd ed.). London: Falmer Press.

Gee, J. P. (2000). Discourse and sociocultural studies in reading. In M. L. Kamil, P. B. Mosenthal, P. D. Pearson, & R. Barr (Eds.), *Handbook of Reading Research, Vol. 3* (pp. 195–207). Mahwah, NJ: Lawrence Erlbaum Associates, Inc.

Gesell, A. (1925). *The mental growth of the preschool child.* New York: Macmillan.

Gipps, C. (1994). *Beyond testing: Towards a theory of educational assessment.* London: Falmer.

Goodman, Y. (1978). Kidwatching: Observing children in the classroom. In A. Jagger & M. T. Smith-Burke (Eds.), *Observing the language learner* (pp. 9–18). Newark, DE: International Reading Association.

Graue, M. E., & DiPerna, J. (2000). Redshirting and early retention: who gets the "gift of time" and what are its outcomes? *American educational research journal, 37*(2) 509–534.

Gregory, E. (1997). Introduction. In E. Gregory (Ed.), *One child, many worlds: Early learning in multicultural communities* (pp. 1–8). New York: Teachers College Press.

Grossen, B. (1996). Making research serve the profession. *American Educator, 20,* 7–8, 22–27.

Hallahan, D. P., & Mercer, C. D. (2001, August 27–28). *Learning disabilities: Historical perspectives.* Paper presented at the Learning Disabilities Summit: Building a Foundation for the Future, Washington, DC.

Heath, S. B. (1983). *Ways with words: Language, life, and work in communities and classrooms.* Cambridge, England: Cambridge University Press.

Helm, J. H., Beneke, S., & Steinheimer, K. (1998). *Windows on learning: Documenting young children's work.* New York: Teachers College Press.

Hewitt, G. (1995). *A portfolio primer: Teaching, collecting, and assessing student writing.* Portsmouth, NH: Heinemann.

Hicks, D. (2002). *Reading lives: Working-class children and literacy learning.* New York: Teachers College Press.

Himley, M., & Carini, P. F. (Eds.). (2000). *From another angle: Children's strengths and school standards: The Prospect Center's descriptive review of the child.* New York: Teachers College Press.

Hoffman, J. L. (1995). The family portfolio: Using authentic assessment in family literacy programs. *The Reading Teacher, 48*(7), 594–597.

Hubbard, R. S., & Power, B. M. (1993). *The art of classroom inquiry: A handbook for teacher-researchers.* Portsmouth, NH: Heinemann.

Huber, G. L. (1994). Travelling in the triangle of theory, empirical research, and practice: Guides for classroom investigation. *Teaching and Teacher Education, 10*(4), 453–459.

International Reading Association. (1999). *High-stakes assessments in reading.* Newark, DE: International Reading Association.

International Reading Association and National Council of Teachers of English Joint Task Force on Assessment. (1994). *Standards for the Assessment of Reading and Writing.* Newark, DE: International Reading Association.

Invernizzi, M., & Meier, J. (2000). *PALS 1–3: Phonological awareness literacy screening 2000–2001: Teacher's manual.* Charlottesville, VA: The Virginia State Department of Education and The University of Virginia.

Invernizzi, M., Meier, J. D., Juel, C., & Swank, L. (1997). *PALS II: Phonological awareness and literacy screening: Teacher's manual.* Chartlottesville, VA: Virginia State Department of Education and University of Virginia.

Johnson, R. L., McDaniel, F., II, & Willeke, M. J. (2000). Using portfolios in program evaluation: An investigation of interrater reliability. *American Journal of Evaluation, 21*(1), 65–81.

Johnson, R. L., Willeke, M. J., & Steiner, D. J. (1998). Stakeholder collaboration in the design and implementation of a family literacy portfolio assessment. *American Journal of Evaluation, 19*(3), 339–354.

Johnston, P. H. (1987). Teachers as evaluation experts. *The Reading Teacher, 40*(8), 744–748.

Johnston, P. H. (1989). Constructive evaluation and the improvement of teaching and learning. *Teachers College Record, 90*(4), 509–528.

Johnston, P. H. (1992). *Constructive evaluation of literate activity.* White Plains, NY: Longman.

Johnston, P. H. (1993). Assessment as social practice. In D. Leu & C. Kinzer (Eds.), *Forty-second yearbook of the National Reading Conference.* Chicago: National Reading Conference.

Johnston, P. H. (1997). *Knowing literacy: Constructive literacy assessment.* York, ME: Stenhouse.

Johnston, P. H. (1998). The consequences of the use of standardized tests. In S. Murphy (Ed.), *Fragile evidence: A critique of reading assessment* (pp. 89–101). Mahwah, NJ: Lawrence Erlbaum Associates, Inc.

Johnston, P. H., & Rogers, R. (2001). Early literacy development: The case for informed assessment. In S. B. Neuman & D. K. Dickinson (Eds.), *Handbook of early literacy research* (pp. 377–389). New York: Guilford.

Kagan, S. L. (2000). Making assessment count.... What matters? *Young Children, 55*(2), 4–5.

Kemmis, S., & Wilkinson, M. (1998). Participatory action research and the study of practice. In B. Atweh, S. Kemmis, & P. Weeks (Eds.), *Action research in practice: Partnerships for social justice in education* (pp. 21–36). New York: Routledge.

Lyons, C. A., Pinnell, G. S., & DeFord, D. E. (1993). *Partners in learning: Teachers and children in reading recovery.* New York: Teachers College Press.

McDermott, R. P. (1993). The acquisition of a child by a learning disability. In S. Chaiklin & J. Lave (Eds.), *Understanding practice: Perspectives on activity and context* (pp. 269–305). Cambridge, England: Cambridge University Press.

McDermott, R. P., & Varenne, H. (1995). Culture as disability. *Anthropology and Education Quarterly, 26*(3), 324–348.

McGill-Franzen, A., & Allington, R. L. (1993). Flunk 'em or get them classified: The contamination of primary grade accountability data. *Educational Researcher, 22*(1), 19–22.

McNeil, L. M. (2000). The educational costs of standardization, *Contradictions of school reform: Educational costs of standardized testing* (pp. 229–271). New York: Routledge.

Mehan, H. (1993). Beneath the skin and between the ears: A case study in the politics of representation. In S. Chaiklin & J. Lave (Eds.), *Understanding practice: Perspectives on activity and context* (pp. 241–268). Cambridges, England: Cambridge University Press.

Meisels, S. J. (1995). *Performance assessment in early childhood education: The Work Sampling System* EDO-PS-95-6. Urbana, IL: ERIC Clearinghouse on Elementary and Early Childhood Education. (ERIC Document Reproduction Service No. ED382407)

Meisels, S. J. (1998). *Assessing Readiness* (CIERA Report No. 3-002). Ann Arbor, MI: Center for the Improvement of Early Reading Achievement.

Meisels, S. J., Bickel, D. D., Nicholson, J., Xue, Y., & Atkins-Burnett, S. (2001). Trusting teachers' judgements: A validity study of a curriculum-embedded performance assessment in Kindergarten to Grade 3. *American Educational Research Journal, 38*(1), 73–95.

Meisels, S. J., Liaw, F.R., Dorfman, A. B., & Nelson, R. F. (1995). The Work Sampling System: Reliability and validity of a performance assessment for young children. *Early Childhood Research Quarterly, 10*(3), 277–296.

Meisels, S. J., & Piker, R. A. (2001). *An analysis of early literacy assessments used for instruction.* Ann Arbor, MI: Center for the Improvement of Early Reading Achievement.

Meisels, S. J., Xue, Y., Bickel, D. D., Nicholson, J., & Atkins-Burnett, S. (2001). Parental reactions to authentic performance assessment. *Educational Assessment, 7*(1), 61–85.

Messick, S. (1994). The interplay of evidence and consequences in the validation of performance assessments. *Educational Researcher, 23*(2), 13–23.

Moll, L. C., Amanti, C., Neff, D., & Gonzalez, N. (1992). Funds of knowledge for teaching: Using a qualitative approach to connect homes and classrooms. *Theory into Practice, 31*(2), 132–141.

Moss, P. (1992). Shifting conceptions of validity in educational measurement: Implications for performance assessment. *Review of Educational Research, 62*(3), 229–258.

Moss, P. A. (1998). The role of consequences in validity theory. *Educational measurement: Issues and practice, 17*(2), 6–12.

National Association for the Education of Young Children. (1991). Guidelines for the appropriate curriculum content and assessment in programs serving children ages 3 through 8. A position statement of the National Association for the Education of Young Children and the National Association of Early Childhood Specialists in the State Department of Education. *Young Children, 46,* 21–38.

National Association for the Education of Young Children. (2001). *NAEYC Guidelines Revision: NAEYC Standards for Early Childhood Professional Preparation Baccalaureate or Initial Licensure Level.* Retrieved March 21, 2002, from http://www.naeyc.org/profdev/prep_review/preprev_2001.htm

National Association for the Education of Young Children. (2002, January). *Early Reading First: A new federal literacy program for preschool-age children.* NAEYC. Retrieved May 24, 2002, from http://www.naeyc.org/childrens_champions/federal/2002/erf_q&a.pdf

National Association of Early Childhood Specialists in State Departments of Education (2000). *Still unacceptable trends in kindergarten entry and placement (Discussion of Principle 5).* Retrieved May 15, 2002, from http://www.naeyc.org/resources/position_statements/psunacc.htm

National Education Goals Panel. (1998). *Principles and recommendations for early childhood assessment.* Washington DC: Aatho.

National Reading Panel. (2000). *Report of the National Reading Panel: Teaching Children to Read Reports of the Subgroups* (NIH Pub. No. 00-4754). Washington, DC: U.S. Department of Health and Human Services, Public Health Service, National Institutes of Health, National Institute of Child Health and Human Development.

Neuman, S. B., Caperelli, B. J., & Kee, C. (1998). Literacy learning: A family matter. *The Reading Teacher, 52*(3), 244–252.

Noffke, S. E. (1995). Action research and democratic schooling: Problematics and potentials. In S. E. Noffke & R. B. Stevenson (Eds.), *Educational action research: Becoming practically critical* (pp. 1–10). New York: Teachers College Press.

Paratore, J. R. (2001). *Opening doors, opening opportunities: Family literacy in an urban community.* Needham Heights, MA: Allyn & Bacon.

Paris, S., Turner, J., & Lawton, T. A. (1991). A developmental perspective on standardized achievement testing. *Educational Researcher, 20*(5), 12–20.

Pearson Early Learning. (2002a). *Complete developmental checklists.* Retrieved July 11, 2002, from http://www.worksamplingonline.com/School/ResourceCenter/Articles/show_article.cfm?Action

Pearson Early Learning. (2002b). *Work Sampling Online.* Retrieved July 19, 2002, from www.worksamplingonline.com

Phye, G. D. (1997). Epilogue: Classroom assessment: Looking forward. In G. D. Phye (Ed.), *Handbook of classroom assessment: Learning, adjustment, and achievement* (pp. 531–534). New York: Academic Press.

Poplin, M. S. (1988). The reductionist fallacy in learning disabilities: Reproducing the past by reducing the present. *Journal of Learning Disabilities, 21,* 389–400.

Pressley, M., Allington, R. L., Wharton-MacDonald, R., Collins-Block, C., & Morrow, L. (2001). *Learning to read: Lessons from exemplary first-grade classrooms.* New York: Guilford.

Project Zero & Reggio Children. (2001). *Making learning visible: Children as individual and group learners.* Reggio Emilia, Italy: Reggio Children.

Rogers, R. (2002). Between contexts: A critical analysis of family literacy, discursive practices, and literate subjectivities. *Reading Research Quarterly, 37*(3), 248–277.

Rogoff, B. (1995). Observing sociocultural activity on three planes: Participatory appropriation, guided participation, apprenticeship. In J. Wertsch, P. D. Rio, & A. Alverez (Eds.), *Sociocultural studies of mind* (pp. 139–164). Cambridge, England: Cambridge University Press.

Roskos, K., & Neuman, S. B. (1993). Descriptive observations of adults' facilitation of literacy in young children's play. *Early Childhood Research Quarterly, 8,* 77–97.

Sacks, P. (1999). *Standardized minds: The high price of America's testing culture and what we can do to change it.* Cambridge, MA: Perseus.

Scientific Learning. (2002a). *FastForWord.* Retrieved August 3, 2002, from www.scilearn.com

Scientific Learning. (2002b). *Scientific Learning achieves revenue goal of $3.2 million in first quarter (Business Outlook).* Retrieved August 3, 2002, from http://www.scilearn.com/info/index.php3?main=invest/pr1q02&cartid=

Scientific Learning. (2002c). *Scientific Learning achieves revenue goal of $3.2 million in first quarter (Deferred revenue increases 120% Year-Over-Year to $7.4 million).* Retrieved August 3, 2002, from http://www.scilearn.com/info/index.php3?main=invest/pr1q02&cartid=

Scientific Learning. (2003). Scientific Learning Reports Record Revenue of $6.4 Million in First Quarter: Revenue Increases 100%. Retrieved October 2, 2003, from http://www.scilearn.com/annc/index.php3?main=../info/invest/prlq03.

Scrivens, G. (1998). Nursery children as emerging readers and writers. In R. Campbell (Ed.), *Facilitating preschool literacy* (pp. 169–191). Newark, DE: International Reading Association.

Shavelson, R. J., Baxter, G. P., & Pine, J. (1992). Performance assessments: Political rhetoric and measurement reality. *Educational Researcher, 21,* 22–27.

Shavelson, R. J., & Webb, N. M. (1991). *Generalizability theory: A primer.* London: Sage.

Shepard, L. A. (1994). The challenges of assessing young children appropriately. *Phi Delta Kappan, 76*(3), 206–212.

Shepard, L. A., & Smith, M. L. (1986). Synthesis of research on school readiness and kindergarten retention. *Educational leadership, 44,* 78–86.

Shepard, L. A., Taylor, G. A. & Kagan, S. L. (1996). Trends in early childhood assessment policies and practices. Washington, DC: OERI.

Smith, M. L. (1991). Put to the test: The effects of external testing on teachers. *Educational Researcher, 20*(5), 8–11.

Smith, M. L., & Rottenberg, C. (1991). Unintended consequences of external testing in elementary schools. *Educational Measurement: Issues and Practice, 10*(4), 7–11.

Stallman, A. C., & Pearson, P. D. (1991). Formal measures of early literacy. In L. M. Morrow & J. K. Smith (Eds.), *Assessment for instruction in early literacy* (pp. 7–44). Englewood Cliffs, NJ: Prentice Hall.

Stanovich, K. E. (2000). *Progress in understanding reading: Scientific foundations and new frontiers.* New York: Guilford.

Street, B. (1995). *Social literacies: Critical approaches to literacy in development, ethnography, and education.* New York: Longman.

Stuebing, K. K., Fletcher, J. M., LeDoux, J. M., Lyon, G. R., Shaywitz, S. E., & Shaywitz, B. A. (2002). Validity of IQ-discrepancy classifications of reading disabilities: A meta-analysis. *American Educational Research Journal, 39*(2), 469–518.

Taylor, D. (1993). *From the child's point of view*. Portsmouth, NH: Heinemann.

Taylor, D., & Dorsey-Gaines, C. (1988). *Growing up literate: Learning from inner-city families*. Portsmouth, NH: Heinemann.

Teale, W. (1991). The promise and the challenge of informal assessment in early literacy. In L. M. Morrow & J. K. Smith (Eds.), *Assessment for instruction in early literacy* (pp. 45–61). NJ: Prentice Hall.

Tolbert, K. (1999, November 25). Tokyo's tots face important, early test after 2 years of cramming, kindergartners take private school entrance exams. *Washington Post Foreign Service*, pp. G01.

U.S. Department of Education. (2002a). *Draft guidance for the Early Reading First program*. Retrieved May 22, 2002, from http://www.ed.gov/offices/OESE/earlyreading/erfguidance.doc

U.S. Department of Education. (2002b). *The facts: Reading achievement*. No Child Left Behind. Retrieved May 20, 2002, from http://www.nochildleftbehind.gov/start/facts/reading.html

U.S. Department of Education. (2002c). *No child left behind*. Retrieved April 29, 2002, from http://www.nochildleftbehind.gov/

U.S. Department of Education. (2002d, February 14). *Testing for results: Helping families, schools, and communities understand and improve student achievement*. Retrieved February 17, 2002, from www.ed.gov/nclb/testingforresults/

Valentine, P. V. (1990, November 16). Baltimore tries to stop abuse over grades. *Washington Post*, p. B04.

Vasquez, V. (2001). Constructing a critical curriculum with young children. In B. Comber & A. Simpson (Eds.), *Negotiating critical literacies in classrooms* (pp. 56–66). Mahwah, NJ: Lawrence Erlbaum Associates, Inc.

Vellutino, F., & Scanlon, D. (1998, April). *Research in the study of reading disability: What have we learned in the past four decades?* Paper presented at the annual conference of the American Educational Research Association, San Diego, CA.

Vellutino, F. R., Scanlon, D. M., Sipay, E. R., Small, S. G., Pratt, A., Chen, R. et al. (1996). Cognitive profiles of difficult-to-remediate and readily remediated poor readers: Early intervention as a vehicle for distinguishing between cognitive and experiential deficits as basic causes of specific reading disability. *Journal of Educational Psychology, 88*(4), 601–638.

Volk, D. (1997). Continuities and discontinuities: Teaching and learning in the home and school of a Puerto Rican five year old. In E. Gregory (Ed.), *One child, many worlds: Early learning in multicultural communities* (pp. 47–61). New York: Teachers College Press.

Vygotsky, L. S. (1962). *Thought and language*. E. Hanfmann & G. Vakar. Cambridge, MA: MIT. Press. (Original work published, 1934).

Vygotsky, L. S. (1978). *Mind in society: The development of higher psychological processes*. M. Cole, V. John-Steiner & E. Souberman (Eds. & Trans.) Cambridge, MA: Harvard University Press.

Whitmore, K., & Goodman, Y. (1995). Inside the whole language classroom. *School Administrator, 49*(5), 20–26.

Zeichner, K. M., & Gore, J. M. (1995). Using action research as a vehicle for student teacher reflection: A social reconstructionist approach. In S. E. Noffke & R. B. Stevenson (Eds.), *Educational action research: Becoming practically critical* (pp. 13–30). New York: Teachers College Press.

27

Standardized Assessments of Children's Emergent Literacy Skills

Christopher J. Lonigan, Kimberly D. McDowell,
and Beth M. Phillips
Florida State University

The assessment of children in the areas of basic concepts, oral language, phonological processing skills, and print awareness provides family literacy programs with the ability to determine which children may be at risk for developing reading difficulties, compared to those children whose emergent literacy skills are developing at a rate consistent with their peers. During the past decade, a growing body of research evidence has highlighted the significance of the preschool period for the development of critically important emergent literacy skills. Data from these research studies indicate that oral language, phonological processing skills, and print knowledge are strongly predictive of how well and how easily children will learn to read and write once they are exposed to formal reading instruction from kindergarten through the third grade. Many children arrive at kindergarten with low levels of these skills, making it less likely that they will benefit from instruction they will receive in the early elementary grades. These data also emphasize that these skills are very stable individual differences, in the absence of targeted intervention (Lonigan, Burgess, & Anthony, 2000; Storch & Whitehurst, 2002).

Accurate assessment of skills involved in the causal chain of learning to read and write is important, because early identification can lead to focused early intervention. Data from a variety of sources indicate that prevention of reading difficulties is far more efficacious and cost effective than remediation. Children who experience early difficulties in the acquisition of reading receive less practice in reading than other children (Allington, 1984), miss opportunities to develop reading comprehension strategies (Brown, Palincsar, & Purcell, 1986), often encounter reading material that is too advanced for their skills (Allington, 1984), and may acquire negative attitudes toward reading (Oka & Paris, 1986). Children with limited reading skills rarely catch up to their peers (Torgesen, Wagner, Rashotte, Alexander, & Conroy, 1997) and continue to experience difficulties throughout their school years and into adulthood. Children who have difficulty acquiring the alphabetic principle, and who continue to experience difficulty with decoding, lose the opportunity to develop the fluency required to become a skilled reader. Early identification of areas in which children need targeted intervention is essential if the cycle of failure is to be broken.

In this chapter, we outline some of the advantages of using standardized assessments for identifying strengths and weaknesses in children's emergent literacy skills. We briefly describe the four skill areas that are related to later reading and writing, and review the purpose, characteristics, and qualities of standardized tests in these four areas. Family literacy programs serve a broad age range of children. Not all these skill areas are appropriate to assess at all ages. Moreover, even though the number of tests for younger children has been increasing in recent years, there is greater availability of tests for older children. Our primary focus is on the assessment of emergent literacy skills. Therefore, we do not extensively review the broad array of assessments of children's reading and writing skills that may be most appropriate for elementary school children; however, we do review a few tests that are appropriate for use with older children. Near the end of the chapter, we discuss issues in the selection and use of standardized assessments in family literacy programs. Finally, we briefly examine alternative assessment procedures and modifications to standardized assessments for special populations.

STANDARDIZED ASSESSMENTS

A *standardized test* is one in which a common set of stimulus materials and questions, a consistent set of administration procedures, and conventional scoring procedures are used, and the scores are based on a norming sample. Standardized tests have a number of significant strengths: They allow meaningful comparisons among children, because they have (a) clear and consistent administration and scoring criteria (i.e., the test is always given and scored in the same manner), (b) generally good reliability and validity, and (c) raw scores are converted into scores that reflect a child's performance relative to the performance of a normative group. Because the test is the same for each child who is administered the test, resultant scores have consistent meaning across children, examiners, and testing sites. Standardized tests are usually normed within relatively large representative samples, in which the distribution of scores approximates the normal curve, with 66% of those taking the test scoring between -1 and $+1$ standard deviations from the mean.

Although some have questioned the fairness of using standardized assessments in assessing emergent literacy skills (e.g., Plante & Vance, 1994), because of poor administration or inadequate reliability, standardized testing is arguably the most reliable, valid, and fair way to contrast a child's performance to his or her same-age peers or to establish that a child's performance is significantly different from other children's (i.e., to identify a meaningful strength or weakness). Nonetheless, tests chosen for use should meet accepted criteria to be considered psychometrically sound; test results need to be interpreted properly and judiciously; and the tests should only be used for their designed purpose. Standardized tests are most often not intended to identify specific goals for intervention; however, they do identify domains in which a child may benefit from intervention (e.g., a standardized assessment may indicate a required focus on vocabulary development, but will not indicate which words should be a focus of an intervention).

CONCEPTUAL AND EMPIRICAL FRAMEWORK ON EMERGENT LITERACY

Emergent literacy includes the skills, knowledge, and attitudes that are presumed to be developmental precursors to conventional forms of reading and writing (Whitehurst & Lonigan, 1998). From an emergent literacy perspective, reading, writing, and oral language skills are seen as developing concurrently and share an interdependent relationship from an early age, even in the absence of formal literacy instruction. Consequently, an emergent literacy perspective views prereading behavior occurring during the preschool years as an authentic and legitimate aspect of literacy. Although many emergent literacy skills have been described in the literature, evidence for the independence or predictive significance for many of these abilities is either negative or currently lacking (e.g., Gough, 1993; Lonigan et al., 2000; Masonheimer, Drum, & Ehri, 1984; Purcell-Gates, 1996). Our primary goals in this chapter are to highlight those areas of emergent literacy that have evidence of being predictive of later reading and to provide a review of standardized measures that could be used to assess the development of these skills, including oral language, phonological processing, and print awareness (see Whitehurst & Lonigan, 1998; see chapter 4 in this volume, for description and review). Skills in these three areas provide the foundation for learning how to read and write. In addition, children's basic concept knowledge has been identified as providing the background knowledge needed for building the vocabulary, comprehension skills, and conceptual knowledge necessary for becoming a skilled reader.

EMERGENT LITERACY ASSESSMENT INSTRUMENTS

As with any educational domain, there are several ways in which emergent literacy skills can be assessed. It is important to choose the measure that is most appropriate for the given situation and one that will yield the desired information. Family literacy programs span the age range from birth to 7 years of age, and no single test assesses all of the emergent literacy skill domains across this broad age range. There are several commercially available standardized measures used to assess the components of emergent literacy. A brief summary of these measures is included in Tables 27.1 through 27.4. In the following sections, we provide a brief description of the emergent literacy domain assessed by the instruments, brief descriptions of the measures, descriptions of their use and standardization information, and descriptions of the psychometric characteristics of the measures.

Psychometric Considerations

Accuracy of results should be considered paramount when determining the value of any particular test. Obviously, decisions made on the basis of inaccurate information will be of little benefit to a child, may be unfair or harmful to a child, and may prevent more beneficial decisions from being made. One of the strengths of a standardized test is that the consistency of administration and scoring procedures enhances its psychometric characteristics, or the accuracy of the test. In addition, because of this consistency, the accuracy of a standardized test is known. The two key psychometric characteristics of a test are its reliability and validity.

Reliability refers to consistency of measurement. A test is reliable if it produces the same score over multiple administrations. Variation in test scores across administrations reflects error, because stable constructs are not expected to show significant fluctuations over the short term (e.g., children's vocabulary does not change greatly in 2 weeks). Reliability is typically assessed by correlating scores from two administrations of the same form of a test (*test–retest reliability*) or from administration of parallel forms of the test (*alternate forms reliability*). Reliability is indexed by a coefficient that can range from 0 (*no reliability*) to 1.0 (*perfect reliability*). Low reliability implies that the score provided by a test includes a large degree of variance that is unrelated to the construct of interest. A second type of reliability, *internal consistency* reliability, refers to whether or not a test or a scale assesses a single construct (e.g., all test items measure receptive vocabulary). Internal consistency reliability is typically assessed by examining how well subsets of items in a test correlate with each other (e.g., split-half reliability, Cronbach's alpha). Low internal consistency reliability implies that the items on a test are not good indicators of a single construct. A test is generally considered to have adequate reliability when reliability coefficients are at or above .70.

Validity refers to the degree to which a test measures what it is intended to measure. Validity is a concept that cannot be separated completely from the theoretical underpinnings of the construct being measured, because the theory specifies the expected pattern of relations involving the construct. Establishing the validity of a test typically involves demonstrating that the test (a) correlates with other measures of the same or a highly related construct or that it identifies known groups (*convergent* or *concurrent validity*), (b) predicts construct-related outcomes over time (*predictive validity*), and (c) is unrelated to different constructs (*discriminant validity*). For example, the validity of a test of print awareness would be supported if it correlated with a measure of letter knowledge (concurrent validity), correlated highly with a concurrent or later measure of decoding (predictive validity), and was not highly correlated with a measure of receptive vocabulary (discriminant validity). Identifying the point at which a test becomes valid is difficult, because of the multitude of possible theoretical relations (most of which are not evaluated) and the strength of relations specified by the theory. Tests of similar constructs can be more or less valid than each other, depending on the sizes of their validity coefficients with theoretically specified constructs. However, in general, tests with low concurrent or predictive coefficients, or high relative discriminative coefficients, would not be considered valid (i.e., a print awareness test, which correlated as highly with a measure of general intelligence as it did with a test of letter knowledge, would have poor discriminant validity). A test with low reliability also would not be considered valid. The validity of a test is tied to its reliability, because a test cannot be expected to correlate with related constructs higher than it can correlate with itself (i.e., the more error in a test, the less able it will be to predict important outcomes accurately).

Basic Concepts

Basic concepts, according to Kagan (1966), are the fundamental agents of intelligence. For individuals to communicate, there must be societal agreement on the meaning of these agents. For a young child to communicate effectively, the child's understanding of the most basic concepts must reflect socially accepted meanings. Research has demonstrated consistently that the attainment of basic concepts is related significantly to achievement in the early school years (Estes, Harris, Moers, & Woodrich, 1976; Piersal & McAndrews, 1982). Although knowledge of basic concepts is not one of the core components of emergent literacy, children's conceptual knowledge and their knowledge of the world are important when assessing oral language. As noted, knowledge of basic concepts provides the building blocks for developing vocabulary and comprehension skills. There are several standardized basic concept instruments. Two of the more widely used ones are reviewed in this section (see Table 27.1).

Bracken Basic Concept Scale (BBCS).   The BBCS (Bracken, 1984) is divided into two separate instruments: a diagnostic full-scale instrument that measures 258 concepts, and two alternate-form screening tests. The diagnostic scale allows for an in-depth assessment of an individual child's conceptual knowledge through 11 subtests: Color, Letter Identification, Numbers/Counting, Comparisons, Shapes, Direction/Position, Social/Emotional, Size, Texture/Material, Quantity, and Time/Sequence. The diagnostic scale of the BBCS is appropriate for preschool and primary children from $2\frac{1}{2}$ to 8 years of age. The screening tests are appropriate for children from 5 to 7 years of age.

Standardization of the diagnostic scale was conducted according to a format that would allow for selection of children across the United States, in a fashion closely representative of the 1980 U.S. census. There were 44 standardization sites across large metropolitan areas, suburbs, and rural locations. In all, over 1,100 children were involved in the standardization of the BBCS.

TABLE 27.1
Summary of Basic Concept Measures

Measure	Skill Area Assessed	Age or Grade Range for Use	Time to Administer (min)	Reliability	Validity
Basic concepts					
Bracken Basic Concept Scale	Colors, letters, numbers/counting, comparisons, shapes, direction, social/ emotional, size, texture, quantity, time/sequence	$2\frac{1}{2}$ to 8 years	Unreported	.47 to .98[a] .67 to .98[b]	.68 to .88[c]
Boehm Test of Basic Concepts–R	Space, quantity, time, misc.	K through 2nd grade	15–20	.77 to .87[a] .85 to .88[b]	— .58 to .64[d]

Note. [a]Internal consistency reliability; [b]test–retest reliability; [c]concurrent validity; [d]predictive validity.

Reliability for the BBCS ranges from inadequate to excellent, depending on the subtest. Internal consistency coefficients range from .47 (Size subtest performance by 6-year-olds) to .96 (Direction/Position subtest performance by 4-year-olds) for subtests and from .94 to .98 for the total test. The median subtest and total test reliabilities are .85 and .97, respectively. Test–retest reliability ranges from .67 (Size subtest) to .98 (School Readiness Composite), with a median test–retest reliability coefficient of .91. Test–retest reliability for the total test is .97. Support for the validity of the BBCS is found in how well the BBCS correlates with other similar tests. Correlation coefficients range from moderate to high (.68 to .88), when compared with performance on the Boehm Test of Basic Concepts–Revised (Boehm–R; Boehm, 1986) and the Peabody Picture Vocabulary Test–Revised (PPVT–R; Dunn & Dunn, 1981).

The screening tests, although not as in-depth as the full diagnostic scale, might provide useful, initial information about children in the classroom who are performing lower than their classmates. The BBCS manual (Bracken, 1984) provides instructions on how to administer the screenings, which can be done in a group setting. A classroom or school-based cutoff score is determined, based on the mean obtained within that classroom or school. As noted in the BBCS manual, however, the screening might over-identify children as at-risk, because of the shorter length of the screening measures than of the full diagnostic scale.

Boehm Test of Basic Concepts–Revised. The *Boehm–R* (Boehm, 1986) is designed to assess children's mastery of the basic concepts. The test, which has two alternate forms, is read aloud by classroom teachers and is appropriate for use with children in kindergarten through second grade. Each form consists of 50 pictorial items arranged in approximate order of increasing difficulty and evenly divided between two booklets. Each booklet contains three sample questions, followed by 25 test questions. Each of the booklets requires approximately 15–20 min to administer to a kindergarten class. Older groups should require less time. The manual provides directions on how to establish classroom norms as the means of comparison.

Standardization for the Boehm–R occurred with over 6,000 children in kindergarten and in first and second grades, at the beginning of the school year, and with similar groups at the end of the school year. The sample design was based on national statistics published by the National Center for Educational Statistics (1981).

Reliability for the Boehm–R ranges from adequate to good, depending on the sample. Split-half reliability coefficients on Forms C and D range from .77 (kindergarten, high socioeconomic level, for Form D) to .87 (in kindergarten, low socioeconomic level, for Form D). The median split-half coefficient is .77. Test–retest reliability coefficients, with a 1-week interval between testing, range from .85 (kindergarten, Form D) to .88 (kindergarten, Form C). Support for the validity of the Boehm–R was determined by comparing raw scores achieved on the Boehm–R with measures of academic achievement obtained 1 year later in three school districts. These correlation coefficients ranged from .58 (when compared to performance on Form C of Comprehensive Test of Basic Skills; Herman, Huesing, Levett, & Boehm, 1973) to .64 (Form D of Comprehensive Test of Basic Skills).

The Boehm–R is not as extensive a measure as the BBCS. It does, however, provide an efficient way in which a teacher can assess the entire classroom in a limited amount of time. The fact that classroom norms are the yardstick of comparison is helpful, in that the teacher will know how each student performs in relation to their classmates. However, if the class as a whole is functioning at a lower or higher level, this information would not be as useful as using the national norms presented in the manual.

Oral Language Skills

A substantial body of evidence links oral language skills with later differences in reading skills (e.g., Bishop & Adams, 1990; Butler, Marsh, Sheppard, & Sheppard, 1985; Scarborough, 1989; Share, Jorm, MacLean, & Mathews, 1984). Children who have larger vocabularies and greater understanding of spoken language have an easier time with reading. Reading is a process of translating visual codes into meaningful language. Children's vocabulary skills seem to have a relation to their early decoding skills, as well as to the development of their phonological skills. Oral language skills, including both semantic and syntactic skills, play a significantly larger role later in the process of learning to read, because of their impact on reading comprehension (Whitehurst & Lonigan, 2001a; see chapter 4 in this volume). There are several standardized measures for the assessment of oral language skills, ranging from those that focus on single aspects of oral language (e.g., receptive vocabulary) to those that provide an assessment of a range of oral language skills (e.g., receptive and expressive vocabulary, listening comprehension). Several of the more commonly used oral language measures are reviewed in this section and are summarized in Table 27.2.

Peabody Picture Vocabulary Test–Third Edition (PPVT–III).   The PPVT–III (Dunn & Dunn, 1997) is an easy-to-administer test that provides an assessment of a child's receptive vocabulary skills. It is not, however, designed to provide a comprehensive assessment of receptive language. Like the 1959 edition and the 1981 revision, the third edition is an individually administered, untimed test that is available in two parallel forms. Each form contains four training items and 204 test items grouped into 17 sets of 12 items each. The item sets are arranged in order of increasing difficulty. Each item consists of four black-and-white illustrations arranged on a page, and the task of the child is to select the picture that best represents the meaning of a stimulus word presented orally by the examiner. The test is designed for children and adults between $2\frac{1}{2}$ and 90 years of age. Testing time averages between 11 and 12 min, because only five sets of items (i.e., 60 items) of appropriate difficulty are administered to most individuals (i.e., basal and ceiling procedures are employed). The PPVT–III can be used both as an achievement test of receptive vocabulary attainment for standard English and as a screening test of verbal ability.

TABLE 27.2
Summary of Oral Language Measures

Measure	Skill Area Assessed	Age or Grade Range for Use	Time to Administer (min)	Reliability	Validity
Peabody Picture Vocabulary Test–III	Receptive vocabulary	$2\frac{1}{2}$–90 years	10–20	$.92-.95^a$ $.90^b$	$.63-.92^c$
Expressive One-Word Picture Vocabulary Tests–III	Expressive vocabulary	2–18 years	10–15	$.93-.95^a$ $.88-.89^b$	$.64-.71^c$
Preschool Language Scale–III	Auditory comprehension, expressive communication	2 weeks to 7 years	15–40	$.85-.94^a$ $.82-.94^b$	$.66-.88^c$
Clinical Evaluation of Language Fundamentals–Preschool	Expressive vocabulary and syntax, receptive vocabulary and syntax	3–7 years	30–45	$.49-.93^a$ $.60-.97^b$	$.31-.93^c$
Oral and Written Language Scales	Listening comprehension, oral expression	3–21 years	40–60	$.84-.91^a$ $.80-.89^b$	$.46-.91^c$
Test of Language Development–Primary:3	Vocabulary, syntax, verbal memory	4–8 years	30–60	$.81-.96^a$ $.77-.92^b$	$.52-.97^c$

Note: [a]Internal consistency reliability; [b]test–retest reliability; [c]concurrent validity; [d]predictive validity.

Standardization of the PPVT–III was conducted during 1995 and 1996 on a sample of 2,725 individuals between $2\frac{1}{2}$ years and 90 years of age, who were selected to proportionately match the U.S. census data from the March 1994 Current Population Survey. Test sites were distributed throughout the United States and were balanced across central cities, suburban and small town communities, and rural areas. Between the ages of $2\frac{1}{2}$ and 6 years, the standardization sample was divided into 6-month intervals; between the ages of 7 and 16 years, whole-year intervals were used.

Reliability for the PPVT–III is excellent. Internal consistency ranges from .92 (3-year-olds, Form IIIA) to .95 (4- to $5\frac{1}{2}$-year-olds, Form IIIB), with a median value of .95 for both forms. Alternate-forms reliability coefficients range from .88 (2 years, 6 months to 2 years, 11 months) to .95 (several age groups). Split-half reliability coefficients range from .86 ($6\frac{1}{2}$-year-olds) to .96 ($4\frac{1}{2}$-year-olds), with a median of .94 for both forms, and test–retest correlations are in the .90s. Evidence concerning the validity of the PPVT–III comes from demonstration of an increase in scores over the age span of the instrument. In addition, criterion (concurrent) validity is supported by correlations ranging from .63, when compared to Oral and Written Language Scales (OWLS; Carrow-Woolfolk, 1995), to .92, when compared with performance on the Wechsler Intelligence Scale for Children–Third Edition (Wechsler, 1991). A normed Spanish-language version of the PPVT is available.

Expressive One-Word Picture Vocabulary Test–Third Edition (EOWPVT–III). The EOWPVT–III (Gardner, 2000) is a measure of expressive vocabulary standardized for individuals between the ages of 2 years, 0 months and 18 years, 11 months. Examinees are presented with stimulus pages containing an individual color picture and asked to correctly label the appropriate object, action, or concept depicted. Items are arranged in order of increasing difficulty. There are 170 items in total, although, because basal and ceiling procedures are used, no examinees are presented with all items. Total administration time is approximately 10–15 min.

The current edition of the EOWPVT–III was conormed with the Receptive One-Word Picture Vocabulary Test–Third Edition, for ease of comparison. Norming took place with a sample of 2,327 individuals in the United States, representing 220 different sites in 32 states. The sample was stratified on age, gender, geographic region, ethnicity, level of parent education, and community size.

Reliability of the EOWPVT–III is excellent. Internal consistency values for 2- to 5-year-olds range from .96 to .98 for split-half values and from .93 to .95 for Cronbach alpha values. Test–retest reliabilities over a 20-day interval are .88 and .89 for 2- to 4-year-olds and 4- to 7-year-olds, respectively. Several findings also support the validity of the test. The measure demonstrates a steady increase in scores across the relevant age range, as would be expected for a vocabulary measure. The test manual reports a number of studies showing concurrent correlations, ranging from .64 to .87 with other language measures and from .67 to .90 with other specific measures of vocabulary. Many of these measures are appropriate for an older age range or for a very wide age range. However, in a sample of 59 preschoolers, the correlations with the Preschool Language Scale–Third Edition (PLS–III; Zimmerman, Steiner, & Pond, 1992) were .64 for the Expressive Language score of the PLS–III and .71 for the Total Language score of the PLS–III.

Receptive One-Word Picture Vocabulary Test–Third Edition (ROWPVT–III). The ROWPVT–III (Gardner, 2000) is a measure of receptive vocabulary standardized for individuals between the ages of 2 years, 0 months and 18 years, 11 months. Examinees are presented with stimulus pages containing an individual color picture and are asked to correctly point to the appropriate object, action, or concept depicted, after the examiner says the stimulus word. Items are arranged in order of increasing difficulty. There are 170 items in total, although, because basal and ceiling procedures are used, no examinees are presented with all items. Total administration time is approximately 10–15 min. The ROWPVT–III was conormed with the EOWPVT–III for ease of comparison. Norming took place with the same norming sample of 2,327 individuals.

Reliability of the ROWPVT–III is excellent. Internal consistency values for 2- to 5-year-olds range from .95 to .97 for split-half values and from .95 to .96 for Cronbach alpha values. Test–retest reliabilities over a 20-day interval are .89 and .80 for 2- to 4-year-olds and 5- to 7-year-olds, respectively. Several findings also support the validity of the test. The measure demonstrates a steady increase in scores across the relevant age range, as would be expected for a vocabulary measure. The test manual reports a number of studies showing concurrent correlations, ranging from .50 to .83 with other language measures and from .38 to .87 with other specific measures of vocabulary. Many of these measures are appropriate for an older age range or for a very wide age range. In a sample of 59 preschoolers, the correlations with the PLS–III (Zimmerman et al., 1992) were .71 for the Receptive Language score of the PLS–III and .65 for the Total Language score of the PLS–III.

Preschool Language Scale–Fourth Edition (PLS–IV). The PLS–IV (Zimmerman, Steiner, & Pond, 2002) was developed to provide clinicians with a diagnostic instrument capable of measuring the language development of young children. The PLS–IV, an individually administered, untimed test, is organized into two standardized subscales: Auditory Comprehension and Expressive Communication. The Auditory Comprehension subscale evaluates a child's receptive language skills in the areas of attention, semantics, structure, and integrative thinking skills. The Expressive Communication subscale evaluates a child's expressive language skills in the areas of vocal development, social communication, semantics, structure, and integrative thinking skills. The PLS–IV also includes three supplemental measures (an articulation screener, a language-sample checklist, and a family information and suggestions form).

The PLS–IV was designed to be used with infants (i.e., 2 weeks of age) through young children (up to 6 years, 11 months of age). The administration time ranges from 15 min to 40 min, depending on the age of the child. Standardization for the PLS–IV began in March 2001, on a sample of more than 1,500 children (between the ages of 2 weeks and 6 years, 11 months) in 48 states. Within each age group, 50% were male and 50% were female. The sample was representative of the U.S. population based on the 2000 U.S. census. Normative data for PLS–IV are reported at 3-month intervals for infants and at 6-month intervals for all other age groups, illustrating developmental progression of scores.

Reliability of the PLS–IV is good. Internal consistency coefficients for the total test range from .81 (9 months to 11 months) to .97 (3 years, 6 months to 3 years, 11 months). Test–retest reliability coefficients, with between-test intervals from 2 days to 2 weeks, range from .82 (Expressive Communication in the 2 years to 2 years, 5 months group) to .95 (Expressive Communication score in the 4 years, 6 months to 4 years, 11 months group). Inter-rater reliability was computed and the percentage of agreement between scorers was 99%, and the correlation between scores was .99. Concurrent validity of the PLS–IV is good, with correlation coefficients ranging from .65 (compared with Auditory Comprehension scores on the PLS–III) to .79 (compared with the Expressive Communication scores on the PLS–III).

Although the PLS–IV provides useful information regarding a child's expressive and receptive language skills, the materials needed for the testing process can be a distraction for some children; therefore, careful management and planning is required. In addition, the supplemental measures (i.e., articulation screener, language sample checklist, and family information and suggestions form) can be used to provide additional information on a child's communicative competence. Finally, a normed Spanish-language version of the PLS–IV is available.

Clinical Evaluation of Language Fundamentals–Preschool (CELF–P). The CELF–P (Wiig, Secord, & Semel, 1992) is a clinical tool for identifying, diagnosing, and performing follow-up evaluations of language deficits in preschool children. It is an untimed, individually administered test that assesses receptive and expressive language ability through six subtests: Linguistic Concepts, Basic Concepts, Sentence Structure, Recalling Sentences in Context, Formulating Labels, and Word Structure. It is designed to be used with children from 3 to 7 years of age and takes approximately 30–45 minutes to administer, depending on the age of the child. Standardization of the CELF–P began in 1991, with more than 1,500 children in 42 states. The standardization sample was nationally representative, based on the 1980 U.S. census information (1988 update) and was stratified on the basis of age, gender, race/ethnicity, parental educational level, and geographic region.

Reliability for the CELF–P ranges from marginal to excellent. Internal consistency reliability coefficients range from .49 (6- to $6\frac{1}{2}$-year-olds on Basic Concepts) to .93 (4- to $4\frac{1}{2}$-year-olds on Recalling Sentences in Context). Test–retest reliability coefficients, with between-test intervals at 2 to 4 weeks, range from .60 (3- to $3\frac{1}{2}$-year-olds on Recalling Sentences in Context) to .97 (3- to $3\frac{1}{2}$-year-olds for the Total Language score). Finally, inter-rater reliability was calculated, with a mean percentage of agreement greater than 90% for all raters.

Evidence concerning the validity of the CELF–P comes from comparing scores on the CELF–P with scores obtained on other language measures. Correlation coefficients range from .31 (6- to $6\frac{1}{2}$-year-olds on Basic Concepts subtest) to .93 (6- to $6\frac{1}{2}$-year-olds on Total Language scores). The CELF–P was also able to identify children as having language disorders or not having language disorders 74% of the time.

In addition to the full measure, the CELF–P includes a Quick Test, which is comprised of the Linguistic Concepts and Recalling Sentences in Context subtests, and which enables one to make an initial determination of the presence or absence of a deficit in language development.

Instructions for computing a Quick Test score are provided in the test manual. This Quick Test might provide a useful means of screening children in need of administration of all of the CELF–P subtests.

Oral Written and Language Scales.   The OWLS (Carrow-Woolfolk, 1995) was designed to cover a wide spectrum of language tasks (i.e., lexical, syntactic, and supralinguistic skills). It is an individually administered test intended for use with individuals 3 through 21 years of age. The test is divided into two core components: Listening Comprehension scale and Oral Expression scale. Each subscale takes approximately 20–30 min to administer, depending on the age of the examinee. The Listening Comprehension scale consists of 111 items arranged in order of difficulty. The examiner presents each item by reading aloud a verbal stimulus, while the examinee looks at a plate of four black-and-white line drawings that are numbered 1 to 4. The examinee must select the picture that best depicts the verbal stimulus. The examinee responds either nonverbally by pointing or verbally by saying a number. The Oral Expression scale consists of 96 items arranged in order of difficulty. Presentation is the same as for the Listening Comprehension scale; however, for some items, the examiner describes the first picture and the examinee responds by describing the second, and in other items, the examiner provides a verbal model for the examinee. Standardization for the OWLS began in April 1992 and concluded in August 1993, with a sample of 1,985 examinees age 3 through 21 years, tested at 74 sites nationwide. The sample was representative of the U.S. population, with socioeconomic status, gender, and ethnicity balanced in proportion to the population.

Reliability for the OWLS is good. Mean internal consistency coefficients are .84 (Listening Comprehension scale), .87 (Oral Expression scale), and .91 (Oral Composite score). Test–retest reliability coefficients, with between-test intervals at 20 to 165 days, range from .80 (4 years to 5 years, 11 months on the Listening Comprehension scale) to .89 (4 years to 5 years, 11 months on the Oral Composite score). Finally, inter-rater reliability coefficients for the Oral Expression scale were reported to be .99 for 3- to 5-year-olds.

Evidence for the validity of the OWLS is provided by the developmental progression of scores and intercorrelations of the scales, with coefficients ranging from .72 (6-year-olds) to .77 (4-year-olds), with a mean of .70. When compared with other language assessment instruments, the correlation coefficients range from .46 (compared with the Test for Auditory Comprehension of Language; Carrow-Woolfolk, 1985) to .91 (compared with the Kaufman Assessment Battery for Children; Kaufman & Kaufman, 1983).

A relative strength of the *OWLS* is that it can be versatile in terms of the population to which it can be administered. It provides an overview of a child's receptive and expressive language skills; however, because the subscales assess a broad range of verbal skills, it cannot provide information regarding the particular category of expressive or receptive language skill in which a child may have a strength, delay, or deficit.

Test of Language Development–Primary:3 (TOLD-P:3).   The TOLD-P:3 (Hammil & Newcomer, 1997) was designed to assess three core linguistic features (i.e., semantics, syntax, and phonology), through three linguistic systems (i.e., listening, organizing, and speaking). The test has four principal uses: (a) identification, (b) determining a child's specific strengths and weaknesses, (c) documenting progress, and (d) measuring language in research studies. The TOLD-P:3 was designed to be used with children between the ages of 4 and 8 years of age. There are six core subtests: Picture Vocabulary, Relational Vocabulary, Oral Vocabulary, Grammatic Understanding, Sentence Imitation, and Grammatic Completion, as well as three supplemental subtests: Word Discrimination, Phonemic Analysis, and Word Articulation. The time required to administer the core subtests varies from approximately 30 to 60 min. The supplemental subtests require about 30 min, and it is recommended that they should not be given at the same time the core subtests are administered. Standardization of the TOLD-P:3 began in the spring of 1996, with a sample of 1,000 individuals from 28 states. Standardization testing was completed by experienced examiners residing in numerous cities and rural areas across the country.

Reliability for the TOLD-P:3 ranges from adequate to excellent. Internal consistency reliability coefficients range from .81 (4-year-olds on Picture Vocabulary) to .96 ($4\frac{1}{2}$- to 6-year-olds on Spoken Language Composite). Coefficients for the composite scores were all greater than .90. Test–retest reliability coefficients, with an average of a 4-month interval, range from .77 (Word Discrimination) to .92 (Spoken Language). Finally, inter-rater reliability coefficients for the subtests and composites are all .99.

Support for the validity of the *TOLD-P:3* is illustrated by comparing performance from 30 first- through third-graders on *TOLD-P:3* subtests to performance on the Bankson Language Test–Second Edition (BLT–II; Bankson, 1977). Correlation coefficients range from not significant (for Word Articulation and Semantic Knowledge) to .97 (for Oral Vocabulary and Semantic Knowledge). Finally, validity was supported by the developmental progression in scores.

The TOLD-P:3 can provide a wealth of information regarding a child's language skills. If skilled in interpreting this information, the volume of information can be an advantage; however, if one is relatively new to formal testing or is unfamiliar with this assessment, this volume of information might be overwhelming. The Profile/Examiner Record Form provides a graphic representation of the child's score, so that performance can be represented visually and confidence intervals illustrated.

Phonological Processing Skills

Phonological processing refers to the use of the sounds in words to understand spoken and written language. Research in the past two decades has revealed that almost all poor readers have a problem with phonological processing (Stanovich, 1988; Stanovich & Siegel, 1994), and that early phonological processing skills are strongly predictive of later reading skills (Lonigan et al., 2000; Wagner, Torgesen, & Rashotte, 1994; Wagner et al., 1997). There are three domains of phonological processing skills (Wagner & Torgesen, 1987): phonological sensitivity (often called "phonological awareness"), phonological memory, and phonological access to lexical store (phonological access). *Phonological sensitivity* refers to the ability to detect and manipulate the sound structure of oral language (e.g., syllables, phonemes). *Phonological memory* refers to short-term memory for sound-based information. *Phonological access* refers to the efficiency of retrieval of phonological information from permanent memory. This section reviews measures that either were designed to assess, or include components or subtests that assess, one or more of these phonological processing skills, and a summary of these measures is included in Table 27.3.

Preschool Comprehensive Test of Phonological and Print Processing (Pre-CTOPPP). The Pre-CTOPPP (Lonigan, Wagner, Torgesen, & Rashotte, 2003) was designed as a downward extension of the Comprehensive Test of Phonological Processing (CTOPP; Wagner, Torgesen, & Rashotte, 1999). The test was designed for use with children from 3 through 5 years of age. Like the *CTOPP*, the Pre-CTOPPP provides assessment of all three areas of phonological processing: phonological sensitivity, phonological memory, and phonological access. Phonological sensitivity is assessed by the Blending, Elision, and Initial Sound Matching subtests. Phonological memory is assessed by the Word Span and Nonword Repetition subtests. Phonological access is assessed by the Rapid Naming subtests. In addition to the phonological processing subtests, the Pre-CTOPPP includes a Print Awareness subtest (described later) and a Reading Vocabulary subtest, designed to assess children's

TABLE 27.3
Summary of Phonological Processing Measures

Measure	Skill Area Assessed	Age or Grade Range for Use	Time to Administer (min)	Reliability	Validity
Preschool–Comprehensive Test of Phonological and Print Processing	Phonological sensitivity, phonological memory, phonological access	3–5 years	20–30	.57–.89[a] .50–.89[b]	.41–.43[c]
Comprehensive Test of Phonological Processing	Phonological sensitivity, phonological memory, phonological access	5–24 years	30	— .68–.97[b]	.25–.74[c] .42–.71[d]
Woodcock–Johnson III Tests of Cognitive Abilities and Achievement	Phonological sensitivity, phonological memory, phonological access	2–90 years	2–10 per subtest	.82–.98[a] .57–.77[b]	.46–.49[c]
Phonological Awareness Test	Phonological sensitivity, decoding	5–10 years	40	.72–.96[a] .45–.98[b]	Contrasted groups[c]
Lindamood Auditory Conceptualization Test	Phonological sensitivity	Any	Unreported	.96[a]	.68–.75[c] .88–.98[d]
Test of Language Development–Primary:3	Phonological sensitivity	4–8 years	30	.89–.94[a] .77–.87[b]	.65–.78[c]
Developing Skills Checklist	Phonological sensitivity, phonological memory, letter knowledge	Pre-K–K	20–30	.81–.92[a]	.41–.57[c]
Phonological Awareness and Literacy Screenings–PreK	Phonological sensitivity, phonological memory	4–5 years	10–15	—	.70[c]
Dynamic Indicators of Basic Emergent Literacy Skills	Phonological sensitivity, decoding	K–3rd grade	1 min per subtest	— .72–.97[b]	.36–.79[c]

Note: [a] Internal consistency reliability; [b] test–retest reliability; [c] concurrent validity; [d] predictive validity.

knowledge of words that they are most likely to encounter in text during beginning reading instruction.

Internal consistency reliabilities for the phonological sensitivity subtests of the Pre-CTOPPP are moderate to high for 3-year-olds (.88, .78, and .57 for Blending, Elision, and Initial Sound Matching, respectively), 4-year-olds (.89, .87, and .67 for Blending, Elision, and Initial Sound Matching, respectively), and 5-year-olds (.86, .85, and .73 for Blending, Elision, and Initial Sound Matching, respectively). In a sample of 41 children, 4- to 5-years-old, test–retest reliability for the phonological sensitivity subtests, with a 3-week interval, was .89 for Blending, .79 for Elision, and .50 for Initial Sound Matching. Internal consistencies for the phonological memory subtests are moderate to high for 3-year-olds (.76 and .87 for word Span and Nonword Repetition, respectively), 4-year-olds (.79 and .83 for Word Span and Nonword Repetition, respectively), and 5-year-olds (.76 and .83 for Word Span and Nonword Repetition, respectively). Concurrent validity is demonstrated by the intercorrelations among the phonological sensitivity subtests (average $r = .41$ across all ages) and with a measure of print awareness (average $r = .43$ across all ages).

The Pre-CTOPPP is in the final stages of development, with national standardization to commence in spring 2004. The test was constructed according to the developmental progression of phonological sensitivity (i.e., from word sensitivity to phoneme sensitivity), and both recognition (multiple choice) and expressive formats are used. A Spanish language version of the Pre-CTOPPP's phonological processing and print awareness subtests has been developed and validated in a moderate-size sample of preschool-age children.

Comprehensive Test of Phonological Processing (CTOPP). The CTOPP (Wagner et al., 1999) is an individually administered test designed to assess phonological awareness, phonological memory, and phonological access skills. Two versions of the test exist. Version 1 was developed for children between 5 and 6 years of age. Version 2 is for individuals between the ages of 7 and 24 years of age. The first version contains seven core subtests and one supplemental test. Phonological sensitivity is assessed by the Elision, Blending Words, Sound Matching, and Blending Nonwords subtests. Phonological memory is assessed by the Memory for Digits and Nonword Repetition subtests, and phonological access is assessed by the Rapid Color Naming and Rapid Object Naming subtests. The test takes approximately 30 min to administer. Standardization for the CTOPP began in the fall of 1997 and involved a total of over 1,600 persons in 30 states, ranging in age from 5 to 17 years. The normative sample was selected to adequately reflect the demographic status of the U.S. population in 1997.

Reliability for the CTOPP is adequate to excellent, depending on the age group. Test–retest reliability coefficients, having a between-test interval of 2 weeks, range from .68 (5- to 7-year-olds on Blending Nonwords) to .97 (5- to 7-year-olds on rapid letter naming). Inter-rater reliability for 5- to 7-year-olds ranges from .95 (Nonword Repetition) to .99 (Sound Matching, Memory for Digits, and Rapid Color Naming).

Support for the validity of the CTOPP comes from comparing performance on the CTOPP with performance on the Woodcock Reading Mastery Tests–Revised (WRMT–R; Woodcock, 1987) 1 year later. Coefficients range from .42 (kindergarteners and first graders on Phonological Memory) to .71 (kindergarteners and first graders on Phonological Awareness). Additionally, performance of kindergarten through fifth-grade students on the CTOPP was compared with performance on the WRMT-R and the Test of Word Reading Efficiency (Torgesen, Wagner, & Rashotte, 1999), to calculate criterion-predictive validity. Coefficients ranged from .25 (Word Analysis on WRMT-R with Rapid Color Naming on the CTOPP) to .74 (Word Analysis on WRMT-R with Elision on *CTOPP*).

Woodcock–Johnson III Tests of Cognitive Abilities and Achievement (WJ–III).   The WJ–III (Woodcock, McGrew, & Mather, 2001) is a comprehensive battery of cognitive and achievement tests designed for individuals between the ages of 2 and 90 years. The WJ–III was standardized on a sample of 8,818 individuals from 100 diverse geographic locations in the United States. The sample included individuals representing a stratified random cross-section of the population, with respect to age, sex, ethnicity, socioeconomic status, community size, and education level. The preschool subsample included 1,143 participants between the ages of 2 to 5 years, who were not yet attending kindergarten (McGrew & Woodcock, 2001).

The Tests of Cognitive Abilities include subtests grouped into the three broad areas of Verbal Ability, Thinking Ability, and Cognitive Efficiency, as well as several supplemental subtests. The Tests of Achievement include an array of over 20 subtests representing measures of basic reading and math skills and tests of various academic applications. Only subtests from the two batteries with direct relevance to emergent literacy and reading achievement are reviewed here, and there are several oral language subtests that are not included in this review. Each of the described subtests requires between 2 and 10 min, on average, to administer. Basal and ceiling procedures are used, so most examinees receive a subset of the total items on each subtest.

Four subtests from the Cognitive Abilities battery assess phonological skills. The Sound Blending subtest (phonological sensitivity) is presented by audiotape to the examinee. On this measure, 33 common words are presented orally in segmented parts, first at the word level for compound words, and then at the syllable and phoneme level for increasing difficulty. The examinee must correctly pronounce the word as a single spoken unit. Split-half reliability, for ages 2 through 5 years, ranges from .90 to .93. The Incomplete Words subtest (phono-logical sensitivity) is presented by audiotape and involves 44 words spoken with one or more phonemes missing. The examinee must correctly pronounce the word with all phonemes. Split-half reliability, for ages 2 through 5 years, ranges from .86 to .92. Test–retest reliability, for ages 2 through 7 years, is .76 with a 1- to 2-year interval and .77 for a 3- to 10-year interval. The Memory for Words (phonological memory) subtest is also presented by audiotape and requires that the examinee repeat back words in the exact order presented. The items include single words, then two, three, and up to seven words, with three items at each difficulty level. Split-half reliability, for ages 2 through 5 years, ranges from .82 to .94, decreasing with age. Test–retest reliability, for ages 2 through 7 years, is .57 with a 1- to 2-year interval and .77 with a 3- to 10-year interval. The Rapid Picture Naming subtest (phonological access) involves oral naming of a series of pictures presented in 5×6 item grids, with 4 grids total (i.e., 120 total pictures). The examinee must correctly name as many pictures as they can, in the correct order, within 2 min. Correct Spanish responses are provided in the manual, as well. Split-half reliability, for ages 2 through 5 years, ranges from .91 to .98.

On the Tests of Achievement battery, the Sound Awareness subtest is comprised of four brief subsections that assess phonological sensitivity (i.e., rhyming, deletion, substitution, and reversal) skills. Rhyming is assessed with both oral and pictoral stimuli and requires the examinee to either select the two stimuli that rhyme or to provide a free response of a rhyming word. The other three subsections are presented by audiotape. Deletion requires the examinee to orally pronounce what would remain if syllables or phonemes were removed from a stimulus word (e.g., "Say hat without /h/"). Substitution requires the examinee to orally pronounce words after replacing target phonemes (e.g., "Say penny, and then say what you would get if you change 'pen' to 'sun'"), and Reversal requires the examinee to reverse the order of phonemes in words to get new words (e.g., "Say 'drop-rain' backward" or "Say 'fine' backward"). Split-half reliability, for ages 2 through 5 years, ranges from .81 to .93.

Validity data for the WJ–III subtests comes from a number of sources. Validity is demon-strated by the gradual increase in scores across the age and grade ranges of the tests. Also, corre-lational and factor analytic examination of subtests within the battery indicate that they adhere to the content and construct clustering patterns anticipated by the test's theoretical model. Validity is also indicated by significant concurrent correlations with other standardized measures of similar content areas. In a preschool sample, significant convergent correlations and some evidence for discriminant validity were found between the Stanford-Binet total and cluster scores and WJ–III Cognitive Abilities cluster scores. Concurrent correlations were also significant between the Cognitive Abilities scores and the Differential Abilities Scale (DAS; Elliot, 1990) and the Wechsler Preschool and Primary Scale of Intelligence–Revised (WPPSI–R; Wechsler, 1989). Of particular note, the Phonemic Awareness cluster correlates .46 and .45 with the DAS General Ability and Verbal Ability scales, respectively. This cluster also correlates substantially with the Full Scale (.49) and Verbal IQ (.48) scores of the WPPSI–R.

Phonological Awareness Test (PAT).   The PAT (Robertson & Salter, 1997) is an individually administered test designed to diagnose deficits in phonological sensitivity and phoneme–grapheme correspondence through eight subtests: Rhyming, Segmentation, Isolation, Deletion, Substitution, Blending, Graphemes, and Decoding. It was designed to be administered to children 5 years of age and older, with administration time being approximately 40 min, depending on the age of the examinee. Because of the time involved in administration, the test may be too long for some younger children. Standardization for the PAT took place between September and November 1996, on a sample of 1,235 students from 175 elementary schools; children in the standardization sample range in age from 5 years to 9 years, 11 months. Children were selected randomly, with consideration for ethnicity, gender, age, and geographic location.

Reliability for the PAT ranges from low to excellent. Internal consistency coefficients range from .72 (5 years, 6 months to 5 years, 11 months on the Substitution subtest) to .96 (5 years to 5 years, 6 months on the Isolation subtest). Test–retest reliability coefficients range from .45 (6 years to 6 years, 6 months on the Rhyming subtest) to .98 (several age ranges on the Decoding subtest). The validity of the PAT was established by the methods of internal consistency and contrasted groups. Internal consistency estimates are reported with 99% of the items showing statistically significant average correlations with the total test scores. In addition, contrasted groups validity was established by comparing the test performances of randomly selected individuals from the normative population with a matched sample of students who had been identified as at-risk for reading difficulties. The PAT correctly discriminated between the two groups for each subtest (38 of 40 comparisons) and for the total test (5 of 5 comparisons) in the 5 years to 5 years, 11 month group.

Lindamood Auditory Conceptualization Test (LAC).   The LAC (Lindamood & Lindamood, 1979) is an individualized test designed to measure auditory perception and conceptualization of speech sounds (phonological sensitivity) through two subtests: Isolated Sounds in Sequence, and Sounds Within a Syllable Pattern. The test is suitable for administration at any chronological or functional age and at any academic level, with individuals who understand the concepts of sameness and difference, numbers to 4, and left-to-right progression. The test can also be used as a diagnostic instrument at the remedial level. In the LAC, the examinee manipulates wooden blocks of various colors, to indicate their conceptualization of speech sound patterns spoken by the examiner. By using the blocks to represent individual speech sounds, the examinee tracks the order of sounds in pattern sequences. This method allows the examinee to show number and sameness and difference of sounds and to visually represent changes in spoken patterns. Standardization for the LAC took place in the Monterey, California area, with a sample of 660 students in kindergarten through the 12th grade. A full range of socioeconomic status and ethnic groups were represented. School district administrators selected 15 regular classrooms from each grade level. Teachers in these classrooms divided their classrooms into four quadrants, based on classroom performance (upper and lower half boys, upper and lower half girls). One student was randomly selected from each of the four quadrants (in grades 7–12, 10 children from each quadrant were randomly selected for participation).

Reliability for the LAC is excellent. The correlation coefficient between Form A and Form B is .96 for kindergarten through high school. The validity of the LAC in predicting at or above grade-level reading versus below grade-level reading and spelling achievement was determined by reference to scores on particular reading tests, spelling tests, or both. Correlations of the LAC and these reading or spelling measures range from .68 (in grade 1, compared with scores from the Wide Range Achievement Test [WRAT; Jastak & Jastak, 1978]) to .75 (in grade 2, when compared with the scores from the WRAT). Predictive validity of the LAC (i.e., whether LAC Total Test performance at the beginning of the first grade is predictive of reading achievement at the end of first grade) was reported to range from .88 to .98 (September LAC scores compared with May WRAT scores, across three different classes).

The LAC's scoring system is different from other standardized measures. Instead of providing raw scores, standard scores, percentile ranks, or age equivalents, the LAC provides a set of minimum scores that serve as cutoff points for differentiating between those with appropriate phonological processing skills and those with deficits: "Individuals who score below the recommended levels have a dysfunction that disrupts the spelling/reading process and interferes with the acquisition of spelling/reading skills" (Lindamood & Lindamood, 1979, p. 27). The use of a minimum score may result in overidentification of children possibly at-risk for developing reading difficulties. In fact, the manual states that "the purpose of recommending higher minimum scores is to aid in early identification of students whose auditory-conceptual judgment needs further development" (Lindamood & Lindamood, 1979, p. 27). Finally, the use of the manipulative blocks makes the process visual, which some may find beneficial; however, the blocks may prove to be a distraction during testing with young children.

Test of Language Development–Primary:3.   The TOLD-P:3 (Hammil & Newcomer, 1997), as noted earlier, includes three supplemental subtests that assess a child's phonological sensitivity skills, including Word Discrimination (a 20-item phonological subtest that assesses a child's ability to recognize the difference in significant speech sounds), Phonemic Analysis (a 14-item subtest that assesses an aspect of auditory processing skills—the ability to recognize phonemic units that constitute words), and Word Articulation (a 20-item subtest that measures the child's ability to articulate English speech sounds). Internal consistency coefficients for these supplementary tests range from .89 (4-year-olds on Word Discrimination) to .94 (5-year-olds on Phonemic Analysis). Test–retest reliability coefficients, with between test intervals at 4 months, range from .77 (Word Discrimination) to .87 (Phonemic Analysis). Finally, support for validity comes from comparisons between the supplementary measures and the BLT–II (Bankson, 1977). These correlation coefficients range from *not significant* (Word Articulation on TOLD-P:3 with Semantic Knowledge on BLT–II) to .78 (Phonemic Analysis on TOLD-P:3 with Semantic Knowledge on BLT–II).

Developing Skills Checklist (DSC).   The DSC (CTB-McGraw Hill, 1990) is used to evaluate the skills that children develop from prekindergarten through the end of kindergarten. The full DSC assesses three skill groupings: Mathematical Concepts and Logical Operations; Language and Memory; and Motor, Visual and Auditory. In addition, there is a Concepts of Print and Writing supplementary test. The DSC is an untimed test that takes approximately 10–15 minutes for each of the three skill groupings testing sessions. The Auditory, Memory, and Concepts of Print subscales assess components of emergent literacy. On the Auditory subscale, children are required to identify same or different sounds in words, segment sentences, segment words into syllables, and to identify rhyme (phonological sensitivity). On the Memory subscale, children are required to repeat digits, name letters, identify letter sounds in words, and blend three phonemes to form a word. Items on the Print Concepts subtest assess children's familiarity with books and print, as well as providing an assessment of early writing skills.

Standardization of the DSC took place between the fall of 1988 and the spring of 1989. The norming sample included 3,985 participants (633 from pre-K) from diverse geographic areas of the United States. The norming sample was selected to be representative of the population regarding sex, ethnicity, socioeconomic level, and type of preschool or school setting. Internal consistency reliability of the Auditory, Memory, and Print Concepts subscales is good, with values ranging from .81 (Print Concepts, winter of kindergarten assessment) to .92 (Memory, spring of pre-K and winter of kindergarten assessments). No test–retest reliability is reported. Evidence for validity of the DSC is provided by concurrent correlations between DSC subscale scores and scores on similar subscales of the Early School Assessment for children in kindergarten. These correlations range from .41 (Auditory subscale) to .57 (Memory subscale).

The DSC provides an overview of a child's emergent literacy skills, but the emergent literacy skill domains are mixed within the subscales; for example, the Memory subtest assesses children's phonological memory (digit recall), letter knowledge (naming letters, identifying letter sounds), and phonological sensitivity (blending). Uniquely, the DSC provides a standardized assessment of children's early writing skills. Additionally, *La Lista* is a supplement available to assess the developing skills of Spanish-speaking children. *La Lista* uses standard Spanish common to all dialects and incorporates positive references to Spanish-speaking cultures.

Phonological Awareness and Literacy Screenings–PreK (PALS–PreK).

The PALS–PreK (Invernizzi, Meier, Juel, & Swank, 1997) is a literacy screening component that assesses alphabet knowledge, letter-sound knowledge, word recognition in isolation, concept of a word, and sense of a story, through two broad groupings of skills: Phonological Awareness and Literacy. Phonological awareness is assessed through rhyme and beginning-sound recognition subtests. Literacy is assessed through alphabet naming, verbal memory, print knowledge, concept of word, and name writing subtests. The PALS–PreK is individually administered, and it is designed to be used with children between 4 and 5 years of age.

Reliability of the PALS–PreK is difficult to ascertain because only inter-rater reliability was reported in the manual. The resulting median coefficient is .90. Support for the validity of the PALS–PreK comes from how strongly performance on the PALS–PreK is correlated with another preschool criterion-referenced measure. The resulting median coefficient is .70.

Dynamic Indicators of Basic Emergent Literacy Skills (DIBELS).

The DIBELS (Good, 2000) are a set of standardized, individually administered, measures of early literacy development. They are designed to be short (i.e., 1 min) fluency measures used regularly to monitor development of prereading and early reading skills in students from kindergarten through third grade. The skills assessed through DIBELS include Initial Sound Fluency, Phonemic Segmentation Fluency, Nonsense Word Fluency, and Oral Reading Fluency. Local norms are created to provide benchmark levels of achievement in each grade level. The DIBELS manual does provide approximate benchmarks, but no standardization or normative information. There are no components of DIBELS that can be used with preschool children. DIBELS provides a way for teachers to monitor progress (or lack thereof) in a specific set of skills. Ease and speed of administration make it a helpful tool in the classroom; however, it is limited in scope and may not be the most valid of instruments. The restricted set of skills it assesses, although important, are not the only predictors of ease of reading acquisition.

TABLE 27.4
Summary of Print Awareness Measures

Measure	Skill Area Assessed	Age or Grade Range for Use	Time to Administer (min)	Reliability	Validity
Test of Early Reading Achievement–3	Alphabet knowledge, print conventions, print meaning	3–9 years	15–45	.82–.95[a] .86–.99[b]	.34–.98[c]
Woodcock Reading Mastery Test–R	Letter knowledge, decoding	5–18 years	10–25	.94–.99[a]	—
Preschool–Comprehensive Test of Phonological and Print Processing	Alphabet knowledge, print conventions	3–5 years	5–10	.89–.94[a]	—
Developing Skills Checklist	Print conventions, writing	Pre-K–K	20–30		
Phonological Awareness and Literacy Screenings–PreK	Alphabet knowledge, print conventions, writing	4–5 years	10–15	—	—
Phonological Awareness Test	Invented spelling	5–10 years	Unreported	—	—

Note: [a] Internal consistency reliability; [b] test–retest reliability; [c] concurrent validity; [d] predictive validity.

Reliability for DIBELS ranges from good to excellent. Alternate-form reliability coefficients range from .72 (Initial Sound Fluency) to .97 (Oral Reading Fluency). Evidence for the validity of DIBELS comes from concurrent criterion-related validity coefficients. These range from .36 (Nonsense Word Fluency, compared with performance on the Woodcock–Johnson Psychoeducational Battery [Woodcock & Johnson, 1987]) to .79 (Phonemic Segmentation Fluency, compared with performance on DIBELS in May of the children's kindergarten year).

Print Awareness

Print awareness involves an understanding of the connection between writing and the language it represents. In alphabetic writing systems, decoding text involves the translation of units of print (graphemes) to units of sound (phonemes), and writing involves translating units of sound into units of print. Knowledge of the alphabet at school entry is one of the single best predictors of eventual reading achievement (Adams, 1990; Stevenson & Newman, 1986). Print awareness includes knowledge about letters (e.g., letter names, letter sounds) and other aspects of print. In this section, measures are reviewed that were designed to assess print awareness or that include components or subtests that assess print awareness, and a summary of these measures is included in Table 27.4.

Test of Early Reading Ability–3 (TERA–3).   The TERA–3 (Reid, Hresko, & Hammill, 2001) was designed to measure children's ability to attribute meaning to printed symbols, their knowledge of the alphabet and its functions, and their understanding of the conventions of print, through the use of three subtests: Alphabet, Conventions, and Meaning. The TERA–3 measures early reading in children from $3\frac{1}{2}$ through $8\frac{1}{2}$ years of age. The test takes approximately 15–45 min to administer, depending on the child's age and ability. Standardization for the TERA–3 began in February 1999, on a sample of 875 children from 22 states. Children between the ages of $3\frac{1}{2}$ years and $8\frac{1}{2}$ years were tested at each major site. The characteristics of the sample were based on the U.S. census data from 1999.

Reliability for the TERA–3 is moderate to high. Internal consistency coefficients range from .82 (6-year-olds, Conventions subtest) to .95 (4-year-olds, Meaning subtest). Test–retest reliability coefficients range from .86 (4- to 6-year-olds, Convention subtest, Form B) to .99 (4- to 6-year-olds, Reading composite, Form A). Support for the validity of the TERA–3 comes from correlating scores obtained on the TERA–3 with scores on similar measures. Validity coefficients range from .34 (Conventions, Form A) to .98 (Reading composite, Forms A and B). Finally, construct validity is illustrated in the relation between chronological age (rs = .82 to .95) and test score increase, as well as correlation with later school success.

As one of the only tests devoted completely to print awareness, the TERA–3 is a valuable tool. The time required to administer this test is reasonable, and the materials are minimal, creating fewer distractions for the examinee. In addition, there is a software scoring system available from the publisher to assist in scoring the test, which also provides classroom-wide and school-wide data (to be used like local norms).

Woodcock Reading Mastery Tests–Revised.   The WRMT–R (Woodcock, 1987) is a test battery designed to measure reading readiness and achievement in individuals from age 5 through older adulthood. Standardization of the WRMT–R took place between 1983 and 1985 and included 6,089 participants from 60 diverse geographic areas of the United States. The norming sample was chosen to be consistent with population distribution information from the 1980 U.S. census regarding age, sex, ethnicity, socioeconomic and education levels, and community demographic variables. The kindergarten through 12th grade sample included 4,201 participants. The test has two parallel forms, with norms for kindergarten to age 75 and older. Form G includes four tests of reading achievement, two readiness tests, and a supplementary letter-knowledge checklist. Form H does not include the readiness tests or the supplement. Basal and ceiling procedures are used, so most examinees only receive a subset of the total items on each subtest.

Within the achievement battery, there are two Basic Skills subtests—Word Identification and Word Attack. For Word Identification, the examinee is presented with a series of words of increasing difficulty, which must be correctly pronounced. For Word Attack, there is a similar presentation of pronounceable nonwords presented, which must be correctly read aloud. Each form includes 2 practice items and 45 test items. Together, the Basic Skills cluster requires approximately 10 min to administer. The other two achievement subtests compose the Reading Comprehension cluster. These subtests are the Word Comprehension and Passage Comprehension measures. Because these two subtests are not considered appropriate for young children who are not yet reading words, they are not discussed in detail. The two readiness subtests include Visual–Auditory Learning and Letter Identification. The first of these measures involves the presentation of icons meant to represent words. The examinee must remember the meaning of each successively presented icon and must correctly orally label novel combinations of these icons. Letter Identification requires the examinee to correctly label upper- and lowercase letters presented on the stimulus pages in a wide variety of print and script type fonts. Together, these two subtests require approximately 15 min to administer. The Letter Checklist subtest requires oral labeling of the names and sounds of upper- and lowercase letters presented in typical fonts on the stimulus pages.

Internal consistency reliability (i.e., split-half reliability) and validity data on the individual subtests, clusters, and total scores are provided in the manual, for selected grades and ages.

For the first grade, internal consistency values for the various individual and total scores are all excellent, ranging from .94 to .99. Evidence of the validity of the WRMT arises from the gradual increase in scores across the age and grade ranges of the battery. Concurrent validity data for first grade indicates significant correlations with subtests and composite scores from the Woodcock–Johnson Achievement and Cognitive Abilities battery (e.g., Letter–Word Identification, Total Reading). However, no reliability or validity data are provided for children in preschool or in kindergarten.

Woodcock–Johnson III Tests of Cognitive Abilities and Achievement.

Two subtests in the WJ–III Tests of Achievement battery (Woodcock et al., 2001) assess print skills. The Letter–Word Identification subtest includes visual presentation of individual letters, then words of increasing length and difficulty that must be read aloud by the examinee. The first six items require selection of a target letter from among other letters and pictures. There are 76 items in total. Split-half reliability, for ages 2 through 5 years, range from .97 to .99. Test–retest reliabilities, for ages 2 through 7 years, are .91 for 1- to 2-year intervals and .87 for 3- to 10-year intervals. A sample of 4- to 7-year-olds, tested at a 1-year interval, yielded a test–retest coefficient of .92. The Word Attack subtest is designed for examinees age 4 years and older and requires correct pronunciation of readable nonwords of increasing numbers of syllables and difficulty. The first several items involve identification or pronunciation of individual letter sounds. There are 32 items in total. Split-half reliabilities, for ages 4 and 5 years, are .93 and .94, respectively. Test–retest reliability for ages 4 to 7 years, over a 1-year interval, is 79. Concurrent validity for the Achievement Tests has been supported by significant correlations between the subtests and selected scores from other achievement batteries. For example, the correlations with the DAS Verbal Abilities score are .39 and .36 for Letter-Word Identification and Word Attack, respectively. Correlations with the WPPSI–R Verbal scale are .40 and .35, respectively, for the same two subtests.

Phonological Awareness Test.

The PAT (Robertson & Salter, 1997) contains a subtest that assesses a child's emergent writing/spelling skills. Invented Spelling is an optional subtest on the *PAT* that does not yield standardized information. According to the manual, it may be used for diagnostic information about a student's encoding ability. It is appropriate only for those students who have been "introduced to writing" (Robertson & Salter, 1997, p. 37). The examiner reads a list of words to the examinee, who is responsible for spelling the words on a sheet of lined paper.

The PAT manual provides a spelling analysis system for determining which stage the child is at in terms of encoding. The stages include (a) prerepresentational (no sounds logically represented), (b) developmental (some sounds logically represented), (c) representational (most sounds logically represented), and (d) conventional (virtually all sounds accurately represented). As one of the few spelling instruments available, the Invented Spelling subtest of the PAT provides some useful information. It also provides a starting point for educators in determining areas of strength and need within students; however, no reliability or validity coefficients are reported.

Preschool Comprehensive Test of Phonological and Print Processing.

As noted earlier, the Pre-CTOPPP (Lonigan et al., 2003) includes a subtest designed to assess children's print awareness. This 36-item subtest assesses children's knowledge of print concepts, letter discrimination, word discrimination, letter-name knowledge and letter-sound knowledge. Internal consistency reliability is excellent, with alphas of .89 (3-year-olds), .94 (4-year-olds), and .95 (5-year-olds).

ASSESSMENT GUIDELINES

The information value of scores on standardized tests is diminished if the correct procedures are not followed or the testing environment does not allow optimal performance from a child. Test administrators should be familiar with the test, so that the testing process moves smoothly. Manualized test guidelines need to be followed exactly. For example, test directions should not be changed because an examiner thinks a child could do the task with altered directions. Standardized tests must be administered in the standard procedure.

Assessment of children from culturally or linguistically (i.e., limited English proficiency) different backgrounds poses several challenges. Children with limited English proficiency are likely to have significantly lower scores when tested in English, either because of constructs assessed or inconsistency of performance. It is important to recognize the distinction between a difference and a disorder. A *disorder* is typically defined as a significant discrepancy in skills from what would be expected, given a child's age or developmental level; a *difference* reflects a rule-governed style that deviates in some way from the standard usage of the mainstream culture (Paul, 1995). In determining whether there is a difference or a disorder, the issue of language dominance is key. A child's primary language must be identified, so that unbiased assessment can occur. The Individuals with Disabilities Education Act (Part B) requires that testing be provided in the language or mode of communication in which a child is most proficient. Observation of the child in the classroom, as well as in informal settings, and the use of structured questionnaires are two ways to establish a child's dominant language (Kayser, 1989). If English is found to be the child's primary language, testing in English can proceed with sensitivity to pragmatic, experiential, and dialectal differences. If English is not the child's dominant language, Kayser (1989) suggested testing in both English and the dominant language, so that comparison of the two performances would be possible.

Although it would be ideal to use tests that provide equivalent versions in English and a child's dominant language, this is often not possible, because few standardized tests of emergent literacy have equivalent forms in different languages, and those that do are typically for children whose dominant language is Spanish. Although translating a standardized test into the child's dominant language might seem a viable option, translating invalidates the test, because the effects of this altered administration procedure are not known. Moreover, words and concepts common in English or the mainstream culture may be unfamiliar to the child (Cheng, 1993). Kayser (1989) suggested modifying or adapting the test items, rather than translating them directly; however, when such modifications are made, the test becomes a criterion-referenced test, instead of a standardized test (and results cannot be interpreted within the test's norms). Although this method can provide information regarding what skills the child does possess, it cannot provide information regarding the identification of a significant skill deficit.

CHOOSING ASSESSMENT INSTRUMENTS

Although standardized tests have a number of positive features, the value of the information derived from an assessment is dependent on appropriate test selection and administration. Salend (1984) and Thorndike and Hagen (1977) recommended that evaluators ask the following questions to determine if a test is appropriate for the situation: (a) Does the test manual provide a clear statement of the purpose and the qualifications needed to administer the test and to interpret it properly? (b) How are the test items presented? (c) How are test items responded to? (d) Is the test free of gender and ethnic biases? (e) Are the test and its component parts reliable? (f) Is the test valid for its stated purposes? (f) Are the directions for administration and scoring clear and complete? and (g) Are the scales used for reporting scores clearly and carefully described? The answers to these questions will help the examiner determine whether the test is an appropriate one to use with a child, depending on the situation and information desired.

Test selection also can, and should, be guided by the information summarized in Tables 27.1 through 27.4. That is, given the range of skills and ages that may be the focus of family literacy programs, test selection should be guided by questions concerning the domain assessed (i.e., basic concepts, oral language, phonological processing, print awareness); the match between the ages of the children to be assessed and the age for which the test was developed, normed, and has adequate psychometric properties for use (i.e., a test with adequate psychometric properties for 5-year-olds may not have good psychometric properties for 3- and 4-year-olds); and the time required for administration of the test, relative to the planned use of the information derived from the test (e.g., the time required to complete a comprehensive diagnostic assessment for a child probably is not justified, if the obtained information will not be used to specifically target identified weakness in specific skill areas). Additionally, test selection should be guided by the qualifications required of the examiner to administer the test. Publishers of many standardized tests require that the examiner have specific levels of training (e.g., a master's degree in an appropriate field), to ensure valid administration and interpretation of their tests.

Alternative Forms of Assessment

Our focus in this chapter is on standardized measures, but other forms of assessment may be more appropriate to achieve the purpose of the assessment. Most often, different types of assessment are used at different points in an assessment–intervention process.

Criterion-Referenced Measures.   Criterion-referenced tests determine if a child can attain a certain level of performance, and such tests can be used to establish baseline functioning, to identify targets for intervention, and to determine if intervention goals have been met. Criterion-referenced tests can be informal and naturalistic, because, unlike standardized tests, they do not have to be administered according to a standard set of rules. They allow in-depth examination of specific behaviors and individualization of an assessment for a particular child. They are often considered highly useful in planning remediation and monitoring progress in intervention (Paul, 1995).

Developmental Scales.   Developmental scales are interview or observational instruments that sample behaviors appropriate for a particular developmental period. Although there are some exceptions, developmental scales often are not standardized and do not provide standard comparison scores. Developmental scales, however, typically provide clearly stated guides for administration and usually provide an equivalent score. Developmental scales can be useful in establishing baseline functioning, by illustrating the general age-equivalent at which the child is functioning.

Informal Assessments.   Informal assessments are neither standardized nor typically highly structured in nature. They provide no comparison or equivalent scores and may be difficult to use in determining baseline functioning. Such assessments can include teacher-created checklists, other checklists, observation of children with anecdotal notes, or portfolios of children's work products. Because of their informality, they are relatively easy to create and use; however, they are often not a reliable and valid means by which to assess a child's skills. They might provide useful qualitative data on a child or provide critical information for use in scaffolding interactions with a child (e.g., making use of informal assessment is using a child's immediate responses to instructional interactions to increase or decrease the difficulty level of the interaction). However, in terms of identifying a deficit or monitoring progress on goals, informal assessments are likely to be ineffective and inappropriate. Because informal assessments typically do not utilize a standardized procedure, the conditions of elicitation of children's skills are not uniform across children. Therefore, whether or not a child exhibits a particular skill may result from the child's skill, the eliciting context, or both. Moreover, the meaning of skills observed is unknown with respect to reliability or validity.

SUMMARY AND RECOMMENDATIONS

Standardized assessments can be used to provide a wealth of information about children's development in the skills that are the important building blocks for learning how to read and write. The key advantages of using standardized assessments include the following: the reliability and validity of the information they provide is known and they allow comparisons of children's skills to a normative context. Hence, standardized assessments can allow meaningful and accurate determination of the emergent literacy skill areas in which a child may have strengths or weaknesses. The key disadvantages of using standardized assessments are their costs, both in terms of financial costs of purchasing the test and in terms of the time required to administer the test to individual children, and in the level of training or expertise required to administer the test and interpret the results. Hence, there should be a plan for the use of the information derived from the assessments.

As reviewed in this chapter, there are several measures that provide reliable and valid information about children's emergent literacy skills in each of the three core domains of emergent literacy (oral language, phonological processing, print awareness), as well as in basic concepts. Availability of preschool measures with strong psychometric characteristics is most evident for oral language, although there are currently available, or are soon to be available, measures of phonological processing skills (e.g., WJ–III, Pre–CTOPPP) and print awareness (e.g., TERA–III; Pre–CTOPPP). Although there are some measures that can be used with Spanish-speaking children, the availability of standardized assessments for English-language learners is very limited. However, if the language of instruction is to be English, it may be useful to know how English-language learners or limited English proficiency children perform on measures of emergent literacy in the language of instruction.

Selection and use of particular measures should be based on resources available, the availability of qualified individuals to administer the assessments, and, perhaps most important, the ages of the children to be assessed. The acquisition of emergent literacy skills is a developmental and sequenced process (Whitehurst & Lonigan, 2001a; see chapter 4 in this volume). Assessment of all three core domains would not be appropriate for all ages of children. For instance, although some 2-year-olds demonstrate phonological sensitivity skills (Lonigan, Burgess, Anthony, & Barker, 1998), this is a skill that most children acquire in the late preschool period. Hence, assessments for younger children (e.g., 2- to 3-year-olds) should focus on oral language, and assessments for older children (e.g., 3- to 5-year-olds) should focus on all three domains.

A sequence of formal and informal assessment is likely to create the optimal educational context for children. Every child in a program is unlikely to need an extensive battery of standardized assessments. One mechanism for selecting children who may be in need of more extensive assessment is the use of a screening measure. At present, however, there are no validated screening measures for preschool children's emergent literacy skills. One measure that may be used to provide the type of snapshot assessment typical of a screening measure is the Get Ready to Read assessment (GRTR; Whitehurst & Lonigan, 2001b). This 20-item measure was developed by the National Center for Learning Disabilities to provide a brief, accurate assessment of 4-year-olds' emergent literacy skills, and it was designed so that it could be administered by individuals with minimal training in assessment. Hence, it is well suited to be used by preschool teachers and others to assess children's emergent literacy skills.

Although the GRTR assessment predicts scores on more comprehensive assessments of emergent literacy skills (i.e., it has concurrent validity), screening measures typically are judged in the context of how accurately they identify children who will demonstrate significant strengths, weaknesses, or typical performance on a more comprehensive assessment. Additionally, there is typically a score at which children are judged to be in need of more extensive assessment, and there is no such established cut off point for the GRTR assessment. However, the broader norms provided could be used to identify children most likely to benefit from a more extensive assessment, for example, children scoring in the below-average range on the GRTR assessment. Such children could be administered a battery of standardized tests to determine the exact nature of their strengths and weaknesses in emergent literacy skill development. Educational activities designed to promote development in areas of identified weakness could then be employed.

Informal assessments could be used more frequently to ascertain children's progress, both for children who received more extensive formal assessment and for children who were determined to not be in need of more extensive formal assessment. Such informal assessment allows teachers to track children's abilities to perform within the educational context, and it allows teachers to adjust the nature of their interaction to children's abilities in that context.

Assessment is not an end in and of itself. It is one part of an identification, intervention, and evaluation sequence. Standardized assessments can be powerful tools for acquiring information, but they are only truly valuable in the context of a well-developed intervention program that translates the information obtained into curriculum modifications and specific instructional tactics and goals. That is, these assessments can more clearly focus family literacy programs on key emergent literacy skills, enabling them to accurately target those skill areas in which children need the most help, and to provide a means for determining whether program goals have been achieved.

ACKNOWLEDGMENTS

Preparation of this work was supported, in part, by grants from the National Institute of Child Health and Human Development (HD/MH38880, HD36067, HD36509, HD30988), the Administration for Children and Families (90YF0023), and the National Science Foundation (REC-0128970). Views expressed herein are the authors' and have not been cleared by the grantors.

REFERENCES

Adams, M. J. (1990). *Learning to read: Thinking and learning about print*. Cambridge, MA: MIT Press.

Allington, R. L. (1984). Content, coverage, and contextual reading in reading groups. *Journal of Reading Behavior, 16*, 85–96.

Bankson, N. (1977). *Bankson language test*. Austin, TX: PRO-ED.

Bishop, D. V. M., & Adams, C. (1990). A prospective study of the relationship between specific language impairment, phonological disorders and reading retardation. *Journal of Child Psychology and Psychiatry and Allied Disciplines, 31*, 1027–1050.

Boehm, A. (1986). *Boehm test of basic concepts* (Rev. ed.). New York: Psychological Corporation.

Bracken, B. (1984). *Bracken basic concept scale*. New York: Psychological Corporation.

Brown, A., Palincsar, A., & Purcell, L. (1986). Poor teachers: Teach, don't label. In U. Neisser (Ed.), *The school achievement of minority children: New perspectives* (pp. 105–143). Hillsdale, NJ: Lawrence Erlbaum, Associates, Inc.

Butler, S. R., Marsh, H. W., Sheppard, M. J., & Sheppard, J. L. (1985). Seven-year longitudinal study of the early prediction of reading achievement. *Journal of Educational Psychology, 77*, 349–361.

Carrow-Woolfolk, E. (1985). *Test for auditory comprehension of language.* Allen, TX: DLM.

Carrow-Woolfolk, E. (1995). *Oral and written language scales.* Circle Pines, MN: American Guidance Service.

Cheng, L. (1993). Asian-American cultures. In D. E. Battle (Ed.), *Communication disorders in multicultural populations* (pp. 38–77). Boston: Andover Medical.

CTB-McGraw-Hill. (1990). *Comprehensive test of basic skills.* Monterey, CA: McGraw-Hill.

Dunn, L. M., & Dunn, L. M. (1981). *The peabody picture vocabulary test* (Rev. ed.). Circle Pines, MN: American Guidance Service.

Dunn, L. M., & Dunn, L. M. (1997). *The peabody picture vocabulary test* (3rd ed.). Circle Pines, MN: American Guidance Service.

Elliot, C. D. (1990). *Differential abilities scales.* San Antonio, TX: Psychological Corporation.

Estes, G., Harris, J., Moers, F., & Woodrich, D. (1976). Predictive validity of the Boehm test of basic concepts. *Educational psychological measurement, 36*, 1031–1035.

Gardner, M. (2000). *Receptive one-word picture vocabulary test.* Novato, CA: Academic Therapy Publications.

Good, R. (2000). *Dynamic indicators of basic literacy skills.* Eugene, OR: University of Oregon.

Gough, P. B. (1993). The beginning of decoding. *Reading and Writing: An Interdisciplinary Journal, 5*, 181–192.

Hammil, D., & Newcomer, P. (1997). *Test of language development–primary* (3rd ed.). Austin, TX: PRO-ED.

Herman, D., Huesing, P., Levett, C., & Boehm, A. (1973, March). *A follow-up study of the BTBC standardization sample: Correlation with later measures of achievement.* Paper presented at the meeting of the National Association of School Psychologists, New York.

Invernizzi, M., Meier, J., Juel, C., & Swank, L. (1997). *Phonological awareness and literacy screening.* Charlottesville: University of Virginia.

Jastak, J., & Jastak, P. (1978). *Wide range achievement test.* Wilmington, DE: Jastak Associates.

Kagan, J. (1966). A development approach to conceptual growth. In H. J. Klausmeir and C. W. Harris (Eds.), *Analyses of concept learning* (pp. 97–116). New York: Academic.

Kaufman, A., & Kaufman, N. (1983). *Kaufman assessment battery for children.* Circle Pines, MN: American Guidance Service.

Kayser, H. (1989). Speech and language assessment of Spanish–English speaking children. *Language, Speech, Hearing Services in Schools, 20*, 226–244.

Lindamood, C., & Lindamood, P. (1979). *Lindamood auditory conceptualization test.* Hingham, MA: Teacher Resources.

Lonigan, C. J., Burgress, S. R., & Anthony, J. L. (2000). Development of emergent literacy and early reading skills in preschool children: Evidence from a latent variable longitudinal study. *Developmental Psychology, 36*, 596–613.

Lonigan, C. J., Burgress, S. R., Anthony, J. L., & Barker, T. (1998). Development of phonological sensitivity in 2- to 5-year-olds children. *Journal of Educational Psychology, 90*, 294–311.

Lonigan, C. J., Wagner, R. K., Torgesen, J. K., & Rashotte, C. A (2003). *Preschool Comprehensive Test of Phonological and Print Processing.* Austin, TX: PRO-ED.

Masonheimer, P. E., Drum, P. A., & Ehri, L. C. (1984). Does environmental print identification lead children into word reading? *Journal of Reading Behavior, 16*, 257–271.

McGrew, K. S., and Woodcock, R. W. (2001). Technical Manual. *Woodcock–Johnson III.* Itasca, IL: Riverside.

National Center for Educational Statistics. (1981). *Common core data.* Washington, DC: Author.

Oka, E., & Paris, S. (1986). Patterns of motivation and reading skills in underachieving children. In S. Ceci (Ed.), *Handbook of cognitive, social, and neuropsychological aspects of learning disabilities* (Vol. 2, pp. 116–145). Hillsdale, NJ: Lawrence Erlbaum, Associates, Inc.

Paul, R. (1995). *Language disorders from infancy through adolescents: Assessment and Intervention.* New York: Mosby.

Piersal, W., & McAndrews, T. (1982). Concept acquisition and school progress: An examination of the Boehm test of basic concepts. *Psychological Reports, 50*, 783–786.

Plante, E., & Vance, R. (1994). Selection of preschool language tests: A data-based approach. *Language, Speech, and Hearing Services in Schools, 25*, 15–24.

Purcell-Gates, V. (1996). Stories, coupons, and the *TV Guide*: Relationships between home literacy experiences and emergent literacy knowledge. *Reading Research Quarterly, 21*, 406–428.

Reid, D., Hresko, W., & Hammill, D. (2001). *Test of early reading ability* (3rd ed.). Austin, TX: PRO-ED.

Robertson, C., & Salter, W. (1997). *The phonological awareness test.* East Moline, IL: LinguiSystems.

Salend, S. (1984). Selecting and evaluating educational assessment instruments. *Pointer, 28*, 20–22.

Scarborough, H. (1989). Prediction of reading dysfunction from familial and individual differences. *Journal of Educational Psychology, 81,* 101–108.

Share, D. L., Jorm, A. F., MacLean, R., & Mathews, R. (1984). Sources of individual differences in reading acquisition. *Journal of Educational Psychology, 76,* 1309–1324.

Stanovich, K. E. (1988). Explaining the differences between the dyslexic and the garden-variety poor reader: The phonological-core variable-difference model. *Journal of Learning Disabilities, 21,* 590–612.

Stanovich, K. E., & Siegel, L. S. (1994). Phenotypic performance profile of children with reading disabilities: A regression-based test of the phonological-core variable-difference model. *Journal of Educational Psychology, 86,* 24–53.

Stevenson, H. W., & and Newman, R. S. (1986). Long-term prediction of achievement and attitudes in mathematics and reading. *Child Development, 57,* 646–659.

Storch, S. A., & Whitehurst, G. J. (2002). Oral language and code-related precursors to reading: Evidence from a longitudinal structural model. *Developmental Psychology, 38,* 934–947.

Thorndike, R., & Hagen, E. (1977). *Measurement in evaluation in psychology and education* (4th ed.). New York: Wiley.

Torgesen, J. K., Wagner, R. K., & Rashotte, C. A. (1999). *Test of word reading efficiency.* Austin, TX: PRO-ED.

Torgesen, J. K., Wagner, R. K., Rashotte, C. A., Alexander, A., & Conroy, T. (1997). Preventive and remedial interventions for children with severe reading disabilities. *Learning Disabilities: An Interdisciplinary Journal, 8,* 51–62.

Wagner, R. K., & Torgesen, J. K. (1987). The natural of phonological processing and its causal role in the acquisition of reading skills. *Psychological Bulletin, 101,* 192–212.

Wagner, R. K., Torgesen, J. K., & Rashotte, C. A. (1994). Development of reading-related phonological processing abilities: New evidence of bidirectional causality from a latent variable longitudinal study. *Developmental Psychology, 30,* 73–87.

Wagner, R. K., Torgesen, J. K., & Rashotte, C. A. (1999). *Comprehensive test of phonological processing.* Austin, TX: PRO-ED.

Wagner, R. K., Torgesen, J. K., Rashotte, C. A., Hecht, S. A., Barker, T. A., Burgess, S. R., et al. (1997). Changing relations between phonological processing abilities and word-level reading as children develop from beginning to skilled readers: A 5-year longitudinal study. *Developmental Psychology, 33,* 468–479.

Wechsler, D. (1989). *Wechsler preschool and primary scale of intelligence* (Rev. ed.). San Antonio, TX: Psychological Corporation.

Wechsler, D. (1991). *Wechsler Intelligence Scale for Children* (3rd ed.). San Antonio, TX: Psychological Corporation.

Whitehurst, G. J., & Lonigan, C. J. (1998). Child development and emergent literacy. *Child Development, 69,* 848–872.

Whitehurst, G. J., & Lonigan, C. J. (2001a). Emergent literacy: Development from prereaders to readers. In S. B. Neuman & D. K. Dickensen (Eds.), *Handbook of early literacy research* (pp. 11–29). New York: Guilford.

Whitehurst, G. J., & Lonigan, C. J. (2001b). *Get ready to read!* Columbus, OH: Pearson Early Learning.

Wiig, E., Secord, W., & Semel, E. (1992). *Clinical evaluation of language fundamentals–Preschool.* New York: Psychological Corporation.

Woodcock, R. W. (1987). *Woodcock reading mastery tests* (Rev. ed.). Circle Pines, MN: American Guidance Service.

Woodcock, R. W., & Johnson, M. B. (1987). *Woodcock–Johnson psycho-educational battery* (Rev. ed.). Itasca, IL: Riverside.

Woodcock, R. W., McGrew, K. S., and Mather, N. (2001). *Woodcock–Johnson III.* Itasca, IL: Riverside.

Zimmerman, I., Steiner, V., & Pond, R. (1992). *Preschool language scale* (3rd ed.). San Antonio, TX: Psychological Corporation.

Zimmerman, I., Steiner, V., & Pond, R. (2002). *Preschool language scale* (4th ed.). San Antonio, TX: Pscyhological Corporation.

28

Evaluating Parent Participation and Outcomes in Family Literacy Programs: Cultural Diversity Considerations

Douglas Powell,
Lynn Okagaki, and
Kathryn Bojczyk
Purdue University

The growing cultural diversity of families participating in family literacy programs offers significant challenges and opportunities for program design, implementation, and evaluation. The extant research literature on family contributions to children's literacy development is based mostly on middle-class Euro-American populations. Far less is known about the literacy environments of lower income, culturally diverse families increasingly served by family literacy programs.

This situation has generated a range of responses in the scholarly literature regarding the content of program work with parents. At one end of a continuum are rationales for sharing with lower income, ethnic minority families what we know from research on how primarily middle-class families successfully support children's early reading success (e.g., Edwards, 1994). At the approximate midpoint are illustrations of how family literacy programs can learn about and accommodate the interests and preferences of culturally diverse parents, while supporting practices known to foster children's literacy development (e.g., Neuman, Hagedorn, Celano, & Daly, 1995). At the other end, scholars argue for organizing the content and methods of family literacy programs exclusively around and within the sociocultural contexts of participants (e.g., Auerbach, 1989, 1995). The question of how best to respond to issues of cultural diversity in family literacy programming has created considerable tension in the field about the appropriateness of various program approaches (Wasik, Dobbins, & Herrmann, 2001), but there is limited research to guide decisions.

Culturally responsive research on parent participation and outcomes in different types of family literacy programs offers promise in identifying program designs and practices associated with positive child outcomes. This chapter identifies parenting beliefs and behaviors that often vary by cultural background and provide a context for how culturally diverse parents may engage a family literacy program and respond to measures of parent outcomes. It also provides guidelines for considering implications of cultural diversity in evaluations of parent participation and outcomes in family literacy programs. We are interested in program practices and parent outcomes directly associated with the goal of strengthening parents' competence in supporting their child's early literacy development (see chapter 9 in this volume).

IMPORTANT DIMENSIONS OF DIVERSITY

In this section, we describe three dimensions of parenting beliefs and behaviors related to family literacy that have been shown to vary by social class and cultural background: parental goals and expectations, approaches to literacy, and family roles and relationships. The intent of our selective review of studies, here, is to illustrate the salience of parenting beliefs and behaviors for family literacy interventions. Because many participants in family literacy programs are recent immigrants to the United States, we conclude with a discussion of how parenting beliefs and behaviors are influenced by immigration and acculturation.

Parental Goals and Expectations

Because family literacy programs are designed to help parents actively support their children's literacy development and early school success, practitioners and evaluators must be sensitive to the variation in the goals and expectations that parents have for their children. Some differences emerge because cultural groups have different ideas about the desirability of specific child attributes (Hoffman, 1988). People have children for a variety of reasons and have different ideas about what constitutes an ideal child. For instance, although many Euro-American traditions in the United States have emphasized individualism, independence, and self-reliance in childrearing (e.g., Spence, 1985; Triandis, Bontempo, Villareal, Asai, & Lucca, 1988), many Latin American and Asian cultures value interdependence, cooperation, and collaboration (Harrison, Wilson, Pine, Chan, & Buriel, 1990). Socializing children to develop desired cultural traits means that, across cultural groups, parents may strive for different childrearing goals. For example, in a study of immigrant and U.S.-born parents of young elementary school children, Okagaki and Sternberg (1993) found that immigrant parents from Cambodia, Mexico, the Philippines, and Vietnam believed that it was more important for parents to teach their child to comply with adults' requests and expectations than to foster their child's independence. In contrast, for U.S.-born Euro-American and Mexican American parents, helping their child become independent and autonomous was viewed as being more important than teaching their child to be obedient.

Culturally based beliefs also undergird parents' understandings of their children's developmental needs. For example, among some Native American peoples, a traditional childrearing practice is to carry infants on cradleboards during the first several months of life and to drastically limit infants' physical activity (Garcia Coll, 1990; Joe & Malach, 1997). In contrast, many Euro-American parents find playpens to be too restrictive for infants because they want their infants to be able to explore and move around their environments with greater freedom.

Parents' goals and expectations provide the cultural lens for parents' interpretation of their children's behavior. For example, consider parents' interpretations of children's responses to novel objects and unfamiliar situations. Some children are relatively relaxed in unfamiliar situations. Other children react to new situations and novel objects with high anxiety, and they stay close to their mother and do not try to explore the new situation. These actions are indicators of behavioral inhibition. Researchers have found that the meanings parents place on their children's behaviors vary across cultural groups. In a study of Canadian parents of European descent and of Chinese parents, researchers examined parents' interpretations of young children's responses to unfamiliar situations (Chen et al., 1998). In the Chinese families, greater behavioral inhibition was associated with mothers having more positive views of their toddler and being more encouraging of their child's achievement. In contrast, Canadian mothers' responses to behavioral inhibition were quite different. Among Canadian mothers, behavioral inhibition was negatively associated with maternal acceptance and encouragement of children's achievement. With respect to discipline, Chinese children who displayed higher levels of behavioral inhibition had mothers who were less likely to believe that physical punishment was the best way to discipline the child and who were less likely to feel angry toward the child. In Canadian families, however, higher levels of behavioral inhibition were associated with stronger belief in physical punishment.

Although the perspectives on behavioral inhibition just described are opposite from each other, each perspective is consistent with the broader values of its culture. Chinese families have traditionally valued interdependence. From this perspective, the Chinese mother may interpret her young child's desire to stay close to her as an expression of the closeness of their relationship. In contrast, Canadian families of European descent have favored an individualistic orientation, so that Canadian toddlers' eager exploration of a new setting may be viewed by their mother as first steps in becoming an autonomous person, rather than as a reflection of the quality of the mother–toddler relationship.

Culturally based parental goals and expectations are linked to different childrearing approaches. In a series of studies comparing Euro-American mothers and Puerto Rican mothers, Harwood and her colleagues (Harwood, 1992; Harwood, Schoelmerich, Schulze, & Gonzalez, 1999; Harwood, Schoelmerich, Ventura-Cook, Schulze, & Wilson, 1996) have found that mothers' goals, interpretations of children's behaviors, and childrearing strategies are associated with the individualistic–collectivist difference between Euro-American and Latin American cultures. In general, the Euro-American mothers in their studies have wanted to encourage their child's personal development and self-control (e.g., developing talents and abilities, being confident and independent, not being selfish or aggressive). In contrast, Puerto Rican mothers expressed more concern for their child being respectful, behaving properly, and becoming a decent, hardworking adult. Euro-American and Puerto Rican mothers interpreted children's behaviors according to their cultural models of the ideal child. This difference in childrearing goals was reflected in mothers' interpretations of children's behaviors. In response to descriptions of hypothetical children, Euro-American mothers were more likely to describe a particular behavior in terms of personal development (e.g., the child who waits for her mother to give permission to play with toys in a doctor's waiting room is not being assertive or independent). In contrast, Puerto Rican mothers were more likely to interpret a given behavior as some aspect of proper demeanor (e.g., the child waiting for permission to play with toys is being respectful of others).

In addition to finding that mothers interpret children's behaviors in ways that accord with their goals, Harwood et al. (1999) have observed that mothers' interactions with their child differ in ways that are consistent with their goals and expectations. In that study, middle-class Euro-American and middle-class Puerto Rican mothers were observed while they interacted with their 1-year-old infants in multiple situations. In general, the Euro-American mothers engaged in strategies to encourage their infant's autonomy and provided more praise in response to their infant's efforts to be active and independent. Euro-American mothers were more likely to offer indirect suggestions to their infant than to give the infant direct commands. Euro-American mothers let their babies attempt to feed themselves. During a free play session, the Euro-American mothers were more likely to sit back and watch their babies play. In contrast, the parenting strategies of the Puerto Rican mothers might be described as efforts to enhance the social connection between mother and infant. Compared to the Euro-American mothers, the Puerto Rican mothers were more likely to provide verbal affection to their babies (e.g., using terms of endearment). They maintained more continuous interaction with their infants by saying the infants' names and drawing the infants' attention back to the mothers. They were much more likely to spoon-feed their infants and to give the infants direct commands. In these studies, the Euro-American and Puerto Rican mothers were socializing their children according to different goals and expectations.

Broader cultural values are also related to the ways in which parents understand and evaluate their own parenting abilities. For example, Bornstein et al. (1998) conducted a multinational study of mothers of 20-month-old infants in countries representing different cultural perspectives, including Argentina, Belgium, France, Israel, Italy, Japan, and the United States. An example of a difference that emerged is the contrast between Japanese mothers' evaluations of their parenting and U.S. mothers' perceptions of their parenting. The Japanese mothers were more likely than other mothers to attribute parenting successes to their children's behavior and parenting failures to their own lack of effort. Although the Japanese mothers rated themselves as high in their investment in parenting, they rated themselves as low in terms of their competence as parents. Rather than reflecting the Japanese mothers' actual parenting ability, compared to mothers from other countries, these ratings may be more appropriately attributed to the emphasis Japanese culture places on being modest and on the importance of working hard. U.S. mothers, however, consider themselves to be relatively competent in their parenting skills. When U.S. mothers feel that something is wrong in their parenting, they are much less likely than Japanese mothers to attribute the problem to something that they have (or have not) done.

Approaches to Literacy

Researchers have identified important class and cultural differences in how families use reading, writing, and language in the home, and in parents' understandings of how children learn to read. Much of this research information comes from qualitative investigations, including Heath's (1983) classic study of the uses of language in different communities in the South, Teale's (1986) research on literacy environments in low-income homes, Taylor and Dorsey-Gaines's (1988) exploration of literacy development in low-income African American families, and Purcell-Gates's (1995) case study of a mother and son learning to read and write together. A general theme emerging from most qualitative studies is that literacy experiences in lower income, culturally diverse families are different from, but not deficient in relation to, middle-class Euro-American families (e.g., see chapters 21 and 22 in this volume).

A number of studies have documented social class, race, and ethnic group differences in approaches to reading at home. For example, national survey data indicate that 89% of White, non-Hispanic children, 71% of Black, non-Hispanic children, and 61% of Hispanic children were read to three or more times in the past week by a family member in 1999 (Nord, Lennon, Liu, & Chandler, 1999). Some evidence suggests that lower income parents tend to emphasize skill development (e.g., recognize letters, practice reading words from cards) in reading interactions with their young children and that middle-income parents tend to view reading as a source of entertainment (e.g., show child reading is fun, encourage child to pick out books about things of interest to the child) (Sonnenschein, Baker, Serpell, & Schmidt, 2000). This pattern is consistent with studies that have found, for example, that mothers with lower levels of education were more likely than mothers with higher levels of education to promote didactic, performance-oriented instruction with their young children (Stipek, Milburn, Clements, & Daniels, 1992).

Findings on the tendency of lower income parents to emphasize skill development in reading with their child may reflect larger understandings about how children learn to read. For example, a study of African American mothers of children attending early childhood programs in schools enrolling large numbers of low-income children, found that mothers believed that children learned to read through a graduated instructional approach. In their view, children should first learn to say and then recognize their ABCs, then learn the sounds associated with each letter, then learn to put them together through a sounding out method (Harry, Allen, & McLaughlin, 1996). The mothers' emphasis on phonics instruction was part of a general expectation that preschool education should provide their children with a head start in academics, through acquisition of basic skills in the three Rs.

Family Roles and Relationships

Besides having different ideas about children, social class and cultural groups vary in the ways in which they understand family roles and relationships. For example, what responsibilities do parents have for their children? Chao (1994) has observed that Euro-American mothers and immigrant Chinese mothers think about their roles in different ways. In contrast to the Euro-American mothers, the Chinese immigrant mothers felt strongly that young children should only be cared for by their mother or, at least, by some other family member. The Chinese immigrant mothers also focused on training and teaching their children. A good mother was one who started training her child as soon as the child was ready to learn. In fact, Chinese immigrant mothers believed that the primary way in which mothers demonstrated their love to their child was by helping the child succeed, especially in school.

Contrast the emphasis of the Chinese immigrant mothers on training and teaching the child to the view that Smith-Hefner (1999) described in an ethnographic study of Khmer Americans. The Khmer American parents explained that the first responsibility of the parent is to observe the child; that is, a good parent is one who knows his or her child. Parents needed to understand the child, including looking for clues to the child's past lives, based on prior reincarnations. According to Khmer Buddhist beliefs, the infant enters the world with traits and abilities carried over from past lives. The Khmer Buddhist infant is not a blank slate, but rather an individual who comes with innate characteristics and personality, which the parent must discover. The task of the parent is to observe the infant carefully, to identify and encourage further development of interests and abilities from these preexisting lives.

Another example of cultural differences in family roles can be seen among some Native American nations, in which responsibility for the care and upbringing of the child extends beyond the parents. Tribal elders are viewed as having an important and legitimate voice in what happens to a child to the extent that parents may need to consult with tribal elders before making a decision regarding the child's welfare (Joe & Malach, 1997). Grandparents, aunts, or uncles may have primary responsibility for the discipline of the child (Machamer & Gruber, 1998). Among these Native American nations, parenting is defined in a much broader way than it is in most Western models of parenting. There is a stronger sense of community involvement and responsibility in caring for children.

Immigration and Acculturation

Finally, we conclude this section with an illustration of parenting issues that emerge when traditional approaches to parenting and family life are abruptly exposed to alternative demands because of immigration. Several researchers have provided examples of the conflicts that result when families have immigrated to the United States and found their family values and roles to differ from those of majority culture (e.g., Dinh, Sarason, & Sarason, 1994; Nguyen & Williams, 1989; Segal, 1991). These conflicts often become particularly salient when children are exposed to American culture through school, friends, and the media.

In an ethnographic study of Vietnamese immigrants living in Philadelphia in the early 1980s, Kibria (1993) described family problems that arose because of immigration to the United States. Both younger and older Vietnamese Americans reported that intergenerational conflict increased as a result of generational differences in acculturation to American society. Younger Vietnamese Americans were adopting the practices and speech of their mainstream American peers. From their parents' perspectives, the Americanization of their children resulted in a lack of respect for elders and in more materialistic attitudes. In addition, parents expressed helplessness in their ability to discipline their children because some parenting strategies common in Vietnam (e.g., corporal punishment) were viewed as being unacceptable in the United States. When Vietnamese American children reported instances of physical punishment to school authorities or to the police, intervention in the home undermined parental authority, although the underlying tensions between parents and children were unresolved. Parents had to give up traditional parenting strategies before learning alternative socialization practices. As is the experience of immigrant families from many countries, these Vietnamese American children often developed proficiency in English-language skills more quickly than their parents. As a result, many children assumed the role of liaison between the family and the larger community. Because of this role, and because the Vietnamese American parents were not gaining new parenting strategies, the balance of power in families shifted. For many parents, this shift in power meant that they no longer had a useful understanding of what it means to be a parent.

GUIDELINES FOR EVALUATING PARENTS' PROGRAM PARTICIPATION AND OUTCOMES

In this section, we consider implications of cultural diversity for evaluating parents' program participation and outcomes. These two domains of information—how parents participate in programs and what impact programs have on parents—represent recommended components or levels of evaluations of family programs (Jacobs, 1988) and educational practices (National Research Council, 2002). We offer examples of ways in which social class and cultural variations in parental beliefs and practices may influence parents' receptivity to and understanding of the goals and strategies endorsed in a family literacy program.

Parents' Program Participation

Uses of Descriptive Data.   Examination of the inner workings of a family literacy program may contribute to advances in the literature on the uses and fate of program information aimed at parents. Systematic description of an intervention is essential to careful analysis of outcomes, including the consideration of differential program effects and interpretations of why a program did or did not work. A detailed understanding of program implementation is particularly needed in evaluations of multifaceted interventions, such as family literacy programs, in which different pathways of program participation may be associated with the magnitude and/or types of program outcomes (Powell, 1988, 1994). Descriptive information on parent participation also can be used to inform program improvement efforts and to ensure intervention fidelity in replication studies.

More generally, we know little about what happens to childrearing information or advice offered to parents. Research and theory suggest that parents' uses of expert knowledge may be influenced by factors such as the clarity of the message, the credibility of the information provider, the nature of the relationship between parent and information provider, the compatibility of parent and program goals, the timing of information in relation to phases of child and/or parent development, whether the parent lives in a culture that values the pursuit of new ideas or tradition, and the extent to which recommended actions are consistent with the parent's ideas about appropriate parenting roles and behaviors as well as with established routines and patterns of interaction in the family (for a review, see Goodnow, 2002).

Dimensions of Program Participation.   A description of what actually happens in family literacy programs requires information about the major settings or activities designed to influence parents' support of their child's literacy development. These include parent–child interaction time, parenting classes or discussion groups, home visits, and early childhood classrooms when parents are present. Data on parents' uses of program suggestions or materials at home also are valuable as discussed in the next section.

Information must be collected at the individual level, so that variations within a parent population or cohort can be considered. Data collected at the program level of analysis are helpful in answering basic questions about fidelity of the program plan (e.g., Did the program offer the number of planned sessions for parent–child interaction time?), but are not useful for examining within-group differences. For certain, population groups with similar characteristics do not represent homogeneous ways of thinking and behaving. For example, a study of African American adolescent mothers' beliefs about children's literacy development and learning found important within-group differences in theoretical perspectives on child development and learning (Neuman et al., 1995).

What aspects of participation should be measured? With minimal resources, evaluators can record and analyze parent attendance at program sessions. This information can be used to depict patterns of attendance across settings (e.g., Are the number of home visits and frequency of attendance at parenting class sessions negatively correlated?) and can provide an indicator of the dosage of program received (e.g., number of program sessions or hours attended). With reliable attendance data available, evaluators can determine whether particular patterns or levels of attendance at a family literacy program are associated with stronger program effects. Examination of this topic is problematic, in the absence of random assignment to different levels of program intensity, because there are no controls for variables (e.g., family stress) that may contribute to both frequency of program attendance and indicators of program outcomes (e.g., frequency of reading to child).

Although economical to gather, attendance is limited as an indicator of program participation. Quantity of program participation does not appear to be related to quality of program participation and to program outcomes. For example, an evaluation of a parenting education program serving low-income parents found that frequency of program attendance was not related to the quality of parents' program participation, such as type of verbal contribution to parenting group discussions (Eisenstadt & Powell, 1987). Another evaluation of a different parenting education program found that frequency of parent attendance at program group meetings about parenting was associated with increased knowledge about certain aspects of child development, but not with child outcomes. In contrast, quality of participation in the program was associated with improved child performance on tests of intellectual competence (Pfannenstiel & Seltzer, 1989). In general, a closer look at indexes of program participation seems essential to securing insight into how culturally based norms and expectations of parents might contribute to their program experiences.

Some indicators of the quality of program participation, such as active versus passive engagement of a session or activity, might be sufficiently general to apply to all program settings involving parents. Other indicators, such as the number and type of storybook-related questions a parent generates in planning a shared book-reading experience with their child, are specific to a program activity. Whether universal or setting-specific, indicators need to accommodate the range of participation opportunities in a particular setting and reflect the program's assumptions about the types of parent participation expected to promote positive outcomes.

Sensitivity to cultural differences is critical to gathering and interpreting parent participation data. For example, parents who believe that adults should determine the structure and content of children's learning experiences may have difficulty accommodating the parameters of the parent–child interaction component of the widely used Kenan model of family literacy promoted by the National Center for Family Literacy. The model calls for the regularly scheduled parent–child interaction time at the program to be child-led and play-focused. Children are to decide and communicate what they want to do with their parents. If children change their plans, parents are to "follow their lead" (Potts & Paull, 1995, p. 177).

By design, family literacy programs vary in the extent to which they seek to learn about and/or accommodate parents' perspectives, as noted earlier. Descriptive information on parents' program experiences should include documentation of planned and unplanned shifts in program goals, content, or methods in direct response to parent preferences and interests. In what ways does the program acknowledge individual differences and within-group variability among participants? How do staff members communicate respect for parents' views and uses of literacy, then move toward shared goals for their work together? Respectful responses to parents' goals, preferences, and concerns are now a common standard of professional practice (e.g., Bredekamp & Copple, 1997). Data on the specific ways family literacy program staff attempt to develop supportive relationships with parents would help professionals move beyond what is often little more than rhetorical acknowledgment of cultural and social class diversity in program services.

Information on the roles and behaviors of staff in helping parents support their child's literacy development is essential to include in a description of parent participation. For example, what strategies do staff members use to encourage parents to strengthen or incorporate literacy-related experiences in existing, everyday routines with children? Data on the range of staff actions can yield a rich chronicle of core messages to parents. These messages may or may not match the intentions of program designers, and staff intentions may or may not be obvious to parents. For instance, one study of the Parents as Teachers program, which is used as a parenting education curriculum in many Even Start Family Literacy programs nationally (Tao, Gamse, & Tarr, 1998), found that home visitors emphasized their social support role and generally did not discuss parenting behaviors that seemed to be in need of change or improvement despite program goals emphasizing both confidence-building and parenting knowledge and skill improvements. Although home visitors and parents offered similar views on many aspects of their relationship and visits, they differed on two key dimensions: Home visitors talked about the parents as the real experts, but parents saw the home visitors as experts; and parents viewed the time the home visitor spent interacting with the child as a direct intervention that would enhance the child's development, but the home visitor saw the same interaction as modeling for the parent (Hebbeler & Gerlach-Downie, 2002).

Staff records and reports can be a source of data on parents' program participation. For example, one program evaluation secured assessments from staff on the quality of parent participation in each session, to supplement attendance records (Pfannenstiel & Seltzer, 1989). Parents' perspectives are critical to measure because, as just indicated, parental understandings of a situation may differ from those of staff members. Observation of program settings can be especially informative, although resources most likely will be needed for measure development because little work has been done in this area. Existing observational studies of home visits (e.g., McBride & Peterson, 1997) and parenting discussion groups (e.g., Powell & Eisenstadt, 1988) may provide helpful background information on measurement approaches.

Participation information must be collected at regular intervals for the duration of parent involvement. Both program content and the level of parent participation can be highly fluid. For example, a longitudinal study of a parent–child education program serving low-income families found dramatic changes in the frequency and quality of participation of highly stressed parents over time (Eisenstadt & Powell, 1987), and observations of parent discussion groups, in which topics were determined by parent interests, pointed to significant differences across 1 year in the content of discussion and especially the allocation of time to formal and informal discussion (Powell & Eisenstadt, 1988).

Uses of Program Ideas and Materials.   Family literacy programs expect that parents will practice program suggestions at home. Whether this outcome is achieved depends partly on whether parents see value in the recommended practice. How parents respond to program suggestions, then, is a valuable aspect of program participation to assess.

Measurement of parental responses to program ideas or suggested practices may need to entail more than observations of parents' reactions to an activity or key message during the program session. Specifically, parental endorsement of a recommended family literacy practice during a program session may not be a reliable indicator of likely implementation of the practice in the privacy of the home. Consider the experiences of a family literacy program known as Parents' Roles Interacting with Teacher Support (PRINTS) enrolling working-class parents (Anderson, Fagan, & Cronin, 1998). During program sessions on the uses of play to promote children's literacy development, leaders described and demonstrated how Playdough could be used by children to make storybook characters and to form letters and make words with the material. Mothers communicated excitement about these activities and indicated they could see how children would learn from this type of hands-on activity. However, as the program progressed, mothers complained that Playdough was dirty and their houses became untidy as children left books, papers, and other literacy artifacts lying around. Some mothers kept the messy items out of their children's reach. Mothers reported engaging in few or no play-based learning activities at home, such as using puppets to read a story, dramatize a character, or retell a story, even though mothers appeared to enjoy these types of interactive activities during program sessions. When program activities or games were focused on print, however, mothers enthusiastically reported how they participated in print-driven activities with their children at home. From the broad range of literacy activities promoted by the PRINTS program, then, mothers appeared to selectively carry out a traditional set of literacy activities with their children (Anderson et al., 1998).

The PRINTS program learned about parent actions (and inactions) on program suggestions through interviews with mothers. In an evaluation of a home-based parenting program known as Ready for School, Segal (1985) developed an instrument used by home visitors to record time spent by family with child on program-suggested activities. Curriculum developers generated a scale for estimating the amount of time each activity (learning game, craft, song) was likely to require.

In addition to selective action on program messages, parents may use program resources or ideas in ways not intended by the program. Consider the common practice of providing parents with children's books and other literacy items with suggestions on their use at home. Findings of a study by Goldenberg, Reese, and Gallimore (1992) suggested that Latino parents' use of literacy materials sent home by kindergarten teachers reflected parents' understandings of how to help children learn to read. Parents in one set of classrooms received storybooks in Spanish (*Libros*) that teachers had read to the children at school. During the fall parent–teacher conferences, teachers suggested to parents that they engage their children in repeated readings of the books and in conversations focused on the meaning of the texts. Teachers in the comparison classrooms sent home packets of phonic and syllable worksheets developed by teachers with extraordinary success in helping young students begin to read and write (Goldenberg, 1994). Home observations of parents' uses of the books and phonic worksheets revealed that parents used these resources in similar ways. Regardless of whether the *Libros* or worksheets were used, parents engaged their children in repetitive, drill-like activities aimed at helping children memorize letters or words and gave little attention to the meaning of the text or word. Interviews with parents indicated that they equated learning to read with learning to decode and not with learning to construct meaning from written texts. They attached less importance to children hearing books or "pretend reading" or talking about books, and assigned greater importance to children remembering the sounds of letters and identifying letters and words (Goldenberg, 1988, 2001).

The Goldenberg et al. (1992) study illustrates how data on what parents actually do with program suggestions and resources can improve our interpretation of outcome results. Goldenberg et al. found that the frequency of home use of the *Libros* was unrelated to children's literacy outcomes, but the frequency of home use of the phonics worksheets was strongly related to children's literacy outcomes at the end of the school year. The investigators speculate that congruence between the worksheets and parents' beliefs about how children learn to read led to their more effective use at home. The plausibility of this interpretation is significantly enhanced by findings from yearlong observations of parents' uses of the materials at home and from interviews with parents.

Parent Outcomes

No simple answers exist to the question of how evaluators should measure the outcomes of parent participation in a family literacy program while being sensitive to differences in social class and cultural norms and expectations. Decisions need to consider program goals, activities, and population characteristics. We offer guidelines below in two major decision-making areas regarding the selection of variables and measures.

Links to Program Goals and Actions.   Existing measures of family literacy environments, found to be predictive of low-income children's literacy outcomes, are promising candidates for use in assessing parent outcomes of a family literacy program. Evaluators and program staff need to ensure that the variables assessed in a family literacy measure are the direct focus of change or support in program goals and activities aimed at parents. For example, parental warmth and control are the focus of two of four subscales of a parenting instrument found to be predictive of children's early literacy outcomes in elementary school (Morrison & Cooney, 2002), yet value-laden dimensions of parenting, such as discipline strategies, may not be a central concern of staff work with parents in a family literacy program. Even when a variable, such as level of maternal education, is a clear goal area of a family literacy program, it is unlikely that, within the usual 1- or 2-year time frame of most evaluations of family literacy programs, maternal education would be altered in sufficient magnitude to have measurable impact on children's literacy outcomes. Thus, a family literacy environment measure that includes an item on years of maternal education—such as the Stony Brook Family Reading Survey (Whitehurst, 1993), shown to be strongly predictive of low-income African American children's literacy performance in elementary school (Storch & Whitehurst, 2001)—would need to be adapted for use as a measure of program impact on parents.

The practice of linking parent outcome measures to program goals and activities requires thoughtful attention in culturally sensitive evaluations of family literacy programs. A basic task is for both program staff and evaluator to consider the degree to which desired parent outcomes are consistent with the cultural norms of the participants. For example, among other goals, program staff may expect participation in their family literacy program to increase parents' feelings of efficacy and confidence in their ability to read to their child. Accordingly, the evaluator uses a measure of parental self-efficacy and confidence in reading to a child, but evaluation results show no program effects on parents' feelings of efficacy and confidence. After talking with some parents, the staff comes to realize that the parents from the cultural group served by the program believe that expressing confidence in one's ability is inappropriate. Moreover, analysis of the evaluation data indicate that the measure of parental efficacy and confidence is not correlated with the number of times parents read to their child each week.

In this example, the parental efficacy measure is not a good outcome measure for the program and is also not related to the primary outcome goal that the intervention is designed to change. Program staff can easily eliminate the goal of improved parental efficacy and confidence as an indicator of the effectiveness of their program.

Some decisions about program goals and parent outcome measures are more complicated. As an example, consider a family literacy program in which parents are taught the importance of encouraging their child to talk about the book, to ask questions, and to be active participants in the book-reading process. Unfortunately, this style of parent–child interaction goes against the cultural norms of the parents who are participating in the program. In their evaluation of the intervention, the staff learns that, although parents are reading to their child more often, they do not encourage the child's active participation in the process. In addition, program staff discovers that children's early literacy skills have not improved as much as they would have liked. After talking with some of the parents, program staff realizes that the parents believe that children should be quiet and fully attentive when an adult reads. With this feedback, program staff has a choice. Based on the empirical evidence and theoretical rationale supporting the intervention, program staff may decide that encouraging active participation of the child in shared book reading is critical to fostering children's early literacy development. Consequently, they decide to teach parents about the importance of allowing children to be actively engaged in joint book reading in a way that explicitly acknowledges parents' cultural values. Alternatively, the program staff might try to develop other ways to foster children's early literacy knowledge and skills that do not require parents to actively engage their child in the joint book-reading activity. If the staff can generate an effective process, then their original anticipated outcome of having parents encourage children to be actively engaged in shared reading is no longer a goal.

In addition to attending to the important nuances just described, evaluators of family literacy programs need to respond to unplanned, midcourse changes in program goals and activities. For instance, family literacy programs commonly promote parents' use of the local library with their children, and evaluators often include family library use as an outcome variable. One local Even Start Family Literacy program, however, abandoned this goal and corresponding activities after the local library imposed relatively steep fines on program parents who did not return books the program helped them borrow (Powell & D'Angelo, 2000).

Reliable and Valid Measures.   As implied, strategies for collecting data on program outcomes need to be appropriate for the cultural and social class population under study. This is a challenging guideline because many measures of parenting beliefs and behaviors have not been examined across different subgroups. Still, a recent review of measures of parent attitudes toward childrearing noted a significant increase in research on cross-cultural comparisons and in subculture differences within the same country in the past 10 years (Holden & Buck, 2002). For example, researchers have effectively measured mothers' beliefs in the efficacy of their parenting in rural single-parent African American families (Brody, Flor, & Gibson, 1999) and in a Head Start sample of predominantly Mexican American mothers (Machida, Taylor, & Kim, 2002).

Growing interest also is evident in the cultural appropriateness and utility of established measures of parenting practices. For example, racial/ethnic differences in the psychometric properties of the early childhood version of the widely used Home Observation for Measurement of the Environment (HOME) inventory, developed by Caldwell and Bradley (1984), have been examined. Results pointed to few differences across Euro-American, African American, and Hispanic families, although the measure was better as a predictor of child outcomes generally for Euro-American than for Hispanic and African American families. This finding suggests that, although certain aspects of parenting appear common across these three groups, dimensions of parenting are not equally important in explaining child outcomes for different racial/ethnic subgroups (Sugland et al., 1995). For instance, Berlin, Brooks-Gunn, Spiker, and Zaslow (1995) found that two cognitive stimulation scales of the HOME measure related in different ways to children's receptive language abilities in White and Black samples. In the Euro-American sample, the HOME Learning subscale was positively associated with children's receptive language abilities; in the African American sample, both the HOME Learning subscale and mothers' Quality of Assistance scores predicted children's receptive language skills.

Evaluations of family literacy programs that include an assessment of parenting outcomes typically rely on self-report measures because of resource limitations. A persistent issue is the accuracy of self-report data. For example, the frequency of parent–child joint book reading is a common item in parent questionnaires and interviews, because it represents a major goal of most family literacy programs. Questions often are raised about the possibility of social desirability in parents' responses to this and other self-report items, even though studies generally find significant differences in the self-reported frequency of shared book reading between higher and lower educated parents.

Sénéchal, LeFevre, Hudson, and Lawson (1996) addressed this measurement issue in a study of better educated, middle-class parents by developing a list of titles and authors of children's books that contained both real and made-up book titles and author names. Parents were asked to identify familiar titles and names and were informed that the list included foils. The researchers reasoned that parents who read often to their children will know more about children's literature than parents who read less often to their children. Results indicated that this measure of storybook exposure at home, and not parents' reports of how frequently they read books to their children, was a significant predictor of children's vocabulary skill. The feasibility of this measurement strategy with a lower income population is not known.

Parental cognitions—particularly beliefs, knowledge, and expectations—regarding literacy and children's learning, are another common set of outcome variables, in part because research evidence suggests that beliefs are predictive of parenting behaviors supportive of children's literacy development (e.g., DeBaryshe, 1995) and of children's language and literacy outcomes (Galper, Wigfield, & Seefeldt, 1997) in lower income populations. The belief–behavior connection is tenuous at best (Holden & Buck, 2002; McGillicuddy-DeLisi & Sigel, 1995), however, and evaluators need to be clear in their understandings and communications regarding what is assessed and not assessed in measures of parental cognitions.

Evaluators with sufficient resources may wish to gather observational data on parent–child shared book reading and/or family literacy environments as outcome variables. Existing observational research on lower income families, regarding shared book reading (e.g., DeTemple, 2001; Pellegrini, Perlmutter, Galda, & Brody, 1990), conversations during mealtimes (e.g., Beals, 2001; Snow, Barnes, Chandler, Goodman, & Hemphill, 1991), and pretend play with young children at home (e.g., Katz, 2001), offers informative starting points for decisions about culturally appropriate approaches to measurement. One critical factor to consider in observations of shared book reading involving parents with limited literacy proficiency, for example, is how type of text contributes to the quality of parent–child storybook reading (Pellegrini et al., 1990). Neuman (1996) found that low-proficiency parent readers tended to engage children in chiming and repeating text and that more capable readers involved children in recalling and higher cognitive demand behaviors. Further, low-proficiency parent readers in that study appeared to benefit the most, that is, exhibited an enhanced sense of efficacy and enjoyment in fostering their children's reading skills and their own when using highly predictable books with clear illustrations.

CONCLUSIONS

Decisions about how best to respond to the growing diversity of participants in family literacy programs would benefit from research on parent participation and outcomes in family literacy programs. Parents' cultural and social class backgrounds may be important predictors of the quality and quantity of their program participation and of the nature of their responses to program suggestions. Yet, there is a paucity of scientific information on interactions between programs and parents to inform program design decisions.

Our consideration of this topic suggests that three dimensions of parenting beliefs and behaviors—parental goals and expectations, approaches to literacy, and family roles and relationships—are promising for inclusion in evaluations of how family contexts are linked to parents' program participation and outcomes. For example, how are program messages filtered or reworked according to parents' prevailing images of the appropriate balance of power in the parent–child relationship or according to parents' desired identity and status in relation to their child? These culturally driven parenting variables have special significance for family literacy program participants who have recently immigrated to the United States.

Our review also suggests that indicators of the quality of parent participation in a family literacy program are likely to be more productive than measures of participation quantity in examining the relation of parenting beliefs and behaviors to parent program participation and outcomes. Because staff and parent perspectives on program experiences have been found to differ, it is also important for evaluators to use multiple sources of data and to consider participation similarities and differences across the range of program settings involving parents. Whether and how parents act on program messages and resources in the home is a critically important domain for evaluators to assess.

Research on parent participation and outcomes in family literacy programs has a valuable opportunity to contribute to methodological advances in the use of existing parenting measures with different population groups. There also is opportunity to address existing measurement limitations, such as self-report data on family literacy activities, and to extend our understanding of connections between parental cognitions and behaviors regarding children's literacy development.

Perhaps the greatest potential yield of research on parent participation and outcomes in family literacy programs is systematic information on the assumption that direct work with parents maximizes program impact on children's literacy outcomes. Both program participation and outcome data are required for a thorough examination of program→family→child pathways of influence, and, ultimately, for scientifically based improvements in the design and implementation of family literacy programs serving culturally diverse parents and their young children.

REFERENCES

Anderson, J., Fagan, W. T., & Cronin, M. (1998). Insights in implementing family literacy programs. *Literacy and community: Twentieth yearbook of the College Reading Association* (pp. 269–281). Carrollton, GA: College Reading Association.

Auerbach, E. R. (1989). Toward a socio-contextual approach to family literacy. *Harvard Educational Review, 59,* 165–181.

Auerbach, E. R. (1995). Which way for family literacy: Intervention or empowerment? In L. M. Morrow (Ed.), *Family literacy: Connections in schools and communities* (pp. 11–27). New Brunswick, NJ: International Reading Association.

Beals, D. E. (2001). Eating and reading: Links between family conversations with preschoolers and later language and literacy. In D. K. Dickinson & P. O. Tabors (Eds.), *Beginning literacy with language* (pp. 75–92). Baltimore: Brookes.

Berlin, L. J., Brooks-Gunn, J., Spiker, D., & Zaslow, M. J. (1995). Examining observational measures of emotional support and cognitive stimulation in Black and White mothers of preschoolers. *Journal of Family Issues, 16,* 664–686.

Bornstein, M. H., Haynes, O. M., Azuma, H., Galperin, C., Maital, S., Ogino, M. et al. (1998). A cross-national study of self-evaluations and attributions in parenting: Argentina, Belgium, France, Israel, Italy, Japan, and the United States. *Developmental Psychology, 34,* 662–676.

Bredekamp, S., & Copple, C. (1997). *Developmentally appropriate practice in early childhood programs* (Rev. ed.). Washington, DC: National Association for the Education of Young Children.

Brody, G. H., Flor, D. L., & Gibson, N. M. (1999). Linking maternal efficacy beliefs, developmental goals, parenting practices, and child competence in rural single-parent African American families. *Child Development, 70,* 1197–1208.

Caldwell, B. M., & Bradley, R. H. (1984). *Home observation for measurement of the environment.* Little Rock: University of Arkansas at Little Rock Press.

Chao, R. K. (1994). Beyond parental control and authoritarian parenting style: Understanding Chinese parenting through the cultural notion of training. *Child Development, 65,* 1111–1119.

Chen, X., Rubin, K. H., Cen, G., Hastings, P. D., Chen, H., & Stewart, S. L. (1998). Child-rearing attitudes and behavioral inhibition in Chinese and Canadian toddlers: A cross-cultural study. *Developmental Psychology, 34,* 677–686.

DeBaryshe, B. D. (1995). Maternal belief systems: Linchpin in the home reading process. *Journal of Applied Developmental Psychology, 16,* 1–20.

DeTemple (2001). Parents and children reading books together. In D. K. Dickinson & P. O. Tabors (Eds.), *Beginning literacy with language* (pp. 31–51). Baltimore: Brookes.

Dinh, K. T., Sarason, B. R., & Sarason, I. G. (1994). Parent–child relationships in Vietnamese immigrant families. *Journal of Family Psychology, 8,* 471–488.

Edwards, P. A. (1994). Responses of teachers and African American mothers to a book-reading intervention program. In D. K. Dickinson (Ed.), *Bridges to literacy: Children, families, and schools* (pp. 175–208). Cambridge, MA: Blackwell.

Eisenstadt, J. W., & Powell, D. R. (1987). Processes of participation in a mother–infant program as modified by stress and impulse control. *Journal of Applied Developmental Psychology, 8,* 17–37.

Galper, A., Wigfield, A., & Seefeldt, C. (1997). Head Start parents' beliefs about their children's abilities, task values, and performance on different activities. *Child Development, 68,* 897–907.

Garcia Coll, C. T. (1990). Developmental outcome of minority infants: A process-oriented look into our beginnings. *Child Development, 61,* 270–289.

Goldenberg, C. (1988). Methods, early literacy, and home-school compatibilities: A response to Sledge et al. *Anthropology and Education Quarterly, 19,* 425–432.

Goldenberg, C. (1994). Promoting early literacy achievement among Spanish-speaking children: Lessons from two studies. In E. Hiebert (Ed.), *Getting reading right from the start: Effective early literacy interventions* (pp. 171–199). Boston: Allyn & Bacon.

Goldenberg, C. (2001). Making schools work for low-income families in the 21st century. In S. B. Neuman & D. K. Dickinson (Eds.), *Handbook of early literacy research* (pp. 211–231). New York: Guilford.

Goldenberg, C., Reese, L., & Gallimore, R. (1992). Effects of school literacy materials on Latino children's home experiences and early reading achievement. *American Journal of Education, 100,* 497–536.

Goodnow, J. J. (2002). Parents' knowledge and expectations: Using what we know. In M. H. Bornstein (Ed.), *Handbook of parenting: Vol 3. Being and becoming a parent* (2nd ed., pp. 439–460). Mahwah, NJ: Lawrence Erlbaum Associates, Inc.

Harrison, A. O., Wilson, M. N., Pine, C. J., Chan, S. Q., & Buriel, R. (1990). Family ecologies of ethnic minority children. *Child Development, 61,* 347–362.

Harry, B., Allen, N., & McLaughlin, M. (1996). "Old-fashioned, good teachers": African American parents' views of effective early literacy instruction. *Learning Disabilities Research and Practice, 11,* 193–201.

Harwood, R. L. (1992). The influence of culturally derived values on Anglo and Puerto Rican mothers' perceptions of attachment behavior. *Child Development, 63,* 822–839.

Harwood, R. L., Schoelmerich, A., Schulze, P. A., & Gonzalez, Z. (1999). Cultural differences in maternal beliefs and behaviors: A study of middle-class Anglo and Puerto Rican mother–infant pairs in four everyday situations. *Child Development, 70,* 1005–1016.

Harwood, R. L., Schoelmerich, A., Ventura-Cook, E., Schulze, P. A., & Wilson, S. P. (1996). Culture and class influences on Anglo and Puerto Rican mothers' beliefs regarding long-term socialization goals and child behavior. *Child Development, 67,* 2446–2461.

Heath, S. B. (1983). *Ways with words: Language, life, and work in communities and classrooms.* Cambridge, England: Cambridge University Press.

Hebbeler, K. M., & Gerlach-Downie, S. G. (2002). Inside the black box of home visiting: A qualitative analysis of why intended outcomes were never achieved. *Early Childhood Research Quarterly, 17*(1), 28–51.

Hoffman, L. W. (1988). Cross-cultural differences in childrearing goals. In R. A. Levine, P. M. Miller, & M. M. West (Eds.), *Parental behavior in diverse societies* (pp. 99–122). San Francisco: Jossey-Bass.

Holden, G. W., & Buck, M. J. (2002). Parental attitudes toward childrearing. In M. H. Bornstein (Ed.), *Handbook of parenting: Vol 3. Being and becoming a parent* (2nd ed., pp. 537–562). Mahwah, NJ: Lawrence Erlbaum Associates, Inc.

Jacobs, F. H. (1988). The five-tiered approach to evaluation: Context and implementation. In H. B. Weiss & F. H. Jacobs (Eds.), *Evaluating family programs* (pp. 37–68). Hawthorne, NY: Aldine de Gruyter.

Joe, J. R., & Malach, R. S. (1997). Families with Native American roots. In E. W. Lynch & M. J. Hanson (Eds.), *Developing cross-cultural competence: A guide for working with young children and their families* (pp. 89–119). Baltimore: Brookes.

Katz, J. R. (2001). Playing at home: The talk of pretend play. In D. K. Dickinson & P. O. Tabors (Eds.), *Beginning literacy with language* (pp. 53–73). Baltimore: Paul H. Brookes.

Kibria, N. (1993). *Family tightrope: The changing lives of Vietnamese Americans*. Princeton, NJ: Princeton University Press.

Machamer, A. M., & Gruber, E. (1998). Secondary school, family, and educational risk: Comparing American Indian adolescents and their peers. *The Journal of Educational Research, 91*, 357–369.

Machida, S., Taylor, A. R., & Kim, J. (2002). The role of maternal beliefs in predicting home learning activities in Head Start families. *Family Relations, 51*, 176–184.

McBride, S. L., & Peterson, C. (1997). Home-based early intervention with families of children with disabilities: Who is doing what? *Topics in Early Childhood Special Education, 17*, 209–233.

McGillicuddy-De Lisi, A. V., & Sigel, I. E. (1995). Parental beliefs. In M. H. Bornstein (Ed.), *Handbook of parenting, Vol. 3,* (1st ed., pp. 333–358). Mahwah, NJ: Lawrence Erlbaum Associates, Inc.

Morrison, F. J., & Cooney, R. R. (2002). Parenting and academic achievement: Multiple paths to early literacy. In J. G., Borkowski, S. Landesman Ramey, & M. Bristol-Power (Eds.), *Parenting and the child's world: Influences on academic, intellectual, and social-emotional development* (pp. 141–160). Mahwah, NJ: Lawrence Erlbaum Associates, Inc.

National Research Council. (2002). *Scientific research in education*. Committee on Scientific Principles for Education Research. R. J. Shavelson & L. Towne, Eds. Center for Education. Division of Behavioral and Social Sciences and Education. Washington, DC: National Academy Press.

Neuman, S. B. (1996). Children engaging in storybook reading: The influence of access to print resources, opportunity, and parental interaction. *Early Childhood Research Quarterly, 11*, 495–513.

Neuman, S. B., Hagedorn, T., Celano, D., & Daly, P. (1995). Toward a collaborative approach to parent involvement in early education: A study of teenage mothers in an African-American community. *American Educational Research Journal, 32*, 801–827.

Nguyen, N. A., & Williams, H. L. (1989). Transition from East to West: Vietnamese adolescents and their parents. *American Academy of Child and Adolescent Psychiatry, 28*, 505–515.

Nord, C. W., Lennon, J., Liu, B., & Chandler, K. (1999). *Home literacy activities and signs of children's emerging literacy, 1993 and 1999*. National Center for Education Statistics. Washington, DC: Office of Educational Research and Improvement.

Okagaki, L., & Sternberg, R. J. (1993). Parental beliefs and children's early school performance. *Child Development, 64*, 36–56.

Pellegrini, A. D., Perlmutter, J., Galda, L., & Brody, G. (1990). Joint reading between black Head Start children and their mothers. *Child Development, 61*, 443–453.

Pfannenstiel, J. C., & Seltzer, D. A. (1989). New parents as teachers: Evaluation of an early parent education program. *Early Childhood Research Quarterly, 4*, 1–18.

Potts, M. W., & Paull, S. (1995). A comprehensive approach to family-focused services. In L. M. Morrow (Ed.), *Family literacy: Connections in schools and communities* (pp. 167–183). New Brunswick, NJ: International Reading Association.

Powell, D. R. (1988). Toward an understanding of the program variable in comprehensive parent support programs. In H. Weiss & F. Jacobs (Eds.), *Evaluating family support programs* (pp. 267–285). Hawthorne, NY: de Gruyter.

Powell, D. R. (1994). Evaluating family support programs: Are we making progress? In S. L. Kagan & B. Weissbourd (Eds.), *Putting families first: America's family support movement and the challenge of change* (pp. 441–470). San Francisco: Jossey-Bass.

Powell, D. R., & D'Angelo, D. (2000). *Guide to improving parenting education in Even Start family literacy programs*. Washington, DC: Office of Educational Research and Improvement.

Powell, D. R., & Eisenstadt, J. W. (1988). Informal and formal conversations in parent education groups: an observational study. *Family Relations, 37*, 166–170.

Purcell-Gates, V. (1995). *Other people's words: The cycle of low literacy.* Cambridge, MA: Harvard University Press.

Segal, M. (1985). A study of maternal beliefs and values within the context of an intervention program. In I. E. Sigel (Ed.), *Parental belief systems: The psychological consequences for children* (pp. 271–286). Hillsdale, NJ: Lawrence Erlbaum Associates, Inc.

Segal, U. A. (1991). Cultural variables in Asian Indian families. *Families in Society: The Journal of Contemporary Human Services, 72,* 233–241.

Sénéchal, M., LeFevre, J., Hudson, E., & Lawson, P. (1996). Knowledge of picture-books as a predictor of young children's vocabulary development. *Journal of Educational Psychology, 88,* 520–536.

Smith-Hefner, N. J. (1999). *Khmer American: Identity and moral education in a diasporic community.* Berkeley: University of California Press.

Snow, C. E., Barnes, W. S., Chandler, J., Goodman, I. F., & Hemphill, L. (1991). *Unfulfilled expectations: Home and school influences on literacy.* Cambridge, MA: Harvard University Press.

Sonnenschein, S., Baker, L., Serpell, R., & Schmidt, D. (2000). Reading is a source of entertainment: The importance of the home perspective for children's literacy development. In K. A. Roskos & J. F. Christie (Eds.), *Play and literacy in early childhood: Research from multiple perspectives* (pp. 107–124). Mahweh, NJ: Lawrence Erlbaum Associates, Inc.

Spence, J. T. (1985). Achievement American style: The rewards and costs of individualism. *American Psychologist, 40,* 1285–1295.

Stipek, D., Milburn, S., Clements, D., & Daniels, D. H. (1992). Parents' beliefs about appropriate education for young children. *Journal of Applied Developmental Psychology, 13,* 293–310.

Storch, S. A., & Whitehurst, G. J. (2001). The role of family and home in the literacy development of children from low-income backgrounds. In P. R. Britto & J. Brooks-Gunn (Eds.), *The role of family literacy environments in promoting young children's emerging literacy skills* (pp. 53–71). San Francisco: Jossey-Bass.

Sugland, B. W., Zaslow, M., Smith, J. R., Brooks-Gunn, J., Coates, D., Blumenthal, C., et al. (1995). The early childhood HOME Inventory and HOME-Short Form in differing ethnic groups: Are there differences in underlying structure, internal consistency of subscales, and patterns of prediction? *Journal of Family Issues, 16,* 632–663.

Tao, F., Gamse, B., & Tarr, H. (1998). *National evaluation of the Even Start Family Literacy Program. Final report.* Washington, DC: U.S. Department of Education, Planning and Evaluation Service.

Taylor, D., & Dorsey-Gaines, C. (1988). *Growing up literate: Learning from inner-city families.* Portsmouth, NH: Heineman.

Teale, W. H. (1986). Home background and young children's literacy development. In W. H. Teale & E. Sulzby (Eds.), *Emergent literacy: Writing and reading* (pp. 173–206). Norwood, NJ: Ablex.

Triandis, H. C., Bontempo, R., Villareal, M. J., Asai, M., & Lucca, N. (1988). Individualism and collectivism: Cross-cultural perspectives on self-ingroup relationships. *Journal of Personality and Social Psychology, 54,* 323–338.

Wasik, B. H., Dobbins, D. R., & Herrmann, S. (2001). Intergenerational family literacy: Concepts, research, and practice. In S. B. Neuman & D. K. Dickinson (Eds.), *Handbook of early literacy research* (pp. 444–458). New York: Guilford.

Whitehurst, G. J. (1993). *Stony Brook family reading survey.* Stony Brook, NY: G. J. Whitehurst.

29

Assessment of Adult Literacy Skills

Barbara Van Horn
The Pennsylvania State University

Lori Forlizzi
Tuscarora Intermediate Unit II

Regardless of the participants' ages, education programs seek mainly to develop their skills and knowledge. Ideally, administrators work with teachers to specify the types of skills and knowledge their programs convey. As they identify these skills and knowledge, they may also question learners or potential learners, especially if they are adults, to identify the topics that interest them. In this way, instructional content, along with the skills and knowledge taught, match the educational needs and interests of the adults enrolled in the program. Teachers then adopt the appropriate curricula, instructional materials, and teaching strategies that help learners acquire, then apply the specified skills and knowledge.

Teachers also identify and administer assessment instruments that help to screen and place learners, identify learning goals, plan and guide instruction, and document achievement. Throughout this process, teachers share assessment results with interested parties, such as funding agents, to inform them of learner outcomes, and with the learners themselves to keep them involved in the process of assessing their learning needs and defining goals. Carefully planning the overall instructional program—with its curriculum, materials, and assessments— to meet the educational needs of the participating adults clarifies and articulates the program's goals and improves educational outcomes. The following discussion examines the implications of these general steps for family literacy practitioners and their meaning for adults enrolled in family literacy programs.

As mentioned, administrators, teachers, and learners all need to understand the goals and purposes of the educational program. In a family literacy program, participating adults expect to develop basic or foundation skills that lead to further education, to employment and economic self-sufficiency, and to becoming full partners in their children's educational development. Thus, the focus here is on building foundation skills and applying them to such meaningful adult roles as family member, employee, and community participant.

We traditionally define basic skills as communication (i.e., reading, writing, speaking, and listening) in English, math (or numeracy), and problem solving. But, in the last decade or so, these basic skills have come to include such skills as observing, planning, using technology, reflecting and evaluating, and taking responsibility for learning and interpersonal skills (more precisely, guiding others, resolving conflicts and negotiating, advocating and influencing, and cooperating with others) (Secretary's Commission on Achieving Necessary Skills, 1992; Stein, 2000). Faced with appraising learner gains within this broad range of skills, family literacy providers may sometimes feel overwhelmed and frustrated. But planning instruction and assessment to meet the educational needs of participants usually helps to reduce these feelings and results in improved outcomes.

As part of an integrated approach to family learning, family literacy programs build on existing resources to provide education and support services to parents and other members of the participating family. Most family literacy programs depend on state or federal funding or on grants from private foundations. As a result, funding agents usually specify, at least in part, the structure and expected outcomes for the participants. The federally funded Goodling Even Start Family Literacy Program, for example, bases its expected academic and employment outcomes for adults on core indicators established in the Workforce Investment Partnership Act of 1998.

On the other hand, most programs also enjoy enough local flexibility to use assessments for purposes beyond reporting and accountability. These purposes include screening and placing learners, identifying their needs, diagnosing their skill gaps, helping them set realistic goals, and tracking their progress. Although providers usually rely on standardized instruments to report learner outcomes to funding agents, they may also select or develop informal instruments to collect additional information to guide the instructional process and to document learner gains and outcomes less evident in the results of standardized instruments. For example, an informal assessment might require learners to perform a task that requires them to apply knowledge or certain skills to solve a problem or to make a decision (Mislevy & Knowles, 2002; Salvia & Ysseldyke, 1995).

Focused as it is on the assessment of adults' academic skills and knowledge and related educational outcomes in the context of family literacy, this chapter includes a summary of federal accountability requirements; definitions of different types of assessments, along with their advantages and drawbacks; purposes of assessment; and assessment planning. Because informal assessment plays such an important role in many adult and family literacy programs, this chapter also discusses strategies for developing and using these instruments effectively. It offers suggestions for assessing English-language learners (ELLs), and, finally, it addresses the importance of a supportive test environment—an increasingly important issue at a time when programs face significant accountability requirements.

FEDERAL ACCOUNTABILITY REQUIREMENTS

Although far from being the only funding agent, the Even Start Family Literacy Program is the largest supporter of family literacy in the United States. All Even Start programs are required to establish indicators of program quality to guide state funding decisions and to improve local efforts. These performance indicators focus on outcomes among participating parents and their children. Even Start aligns its outcomes for parents with outcomes established in the Workforce Investment Partnership Act of 1998, for adults served under Title II, also known as the Adult Education and Family Literacy Act. (During 2003 and 2004, this Act is being reauthorized and may include changes related to learner outcomes.) These indicators support the purposes of the Act, namely, to help adults develop literacy skills and to obtain the knowledge and skills they need to complete a secondary school education, to enter postsecondary education, and to gain or keep employment. At their discretion, states may also include such purposes as helping adults obtain the educational skills to become full partners in their children's educational development. As Table 29.1 shows, the alignment of expected outcomes for adults in the two pieces of legislation is clear. Moreover, aligning outcomes and

TABLE 29.1
Required Outcomes for Adults

Even Start Family Literacy Program [Sec. 1210 (20 U.S.C. 6369a)]	*Adult Education and Family Literacy Act* [Sec. 212 (b) (2) (A)]
Achievement in the areas of reading, writing, English language acquisition, problem solving, and numeracy	Demonstrated improvements in literacy skill levels in reading, writing and speaking the English language, numeracy, problem solving, English language acquisition, and other literacy skills
Receipt of high school diploma or GED	Receipt of a secondary school diploma or its recognized equivalent
Entry into postsecondary school, job retraining, or employment or career advancement, including the military	Placement in, retention in, or completion of postsecondary education, training, unsubsidized employment or career advancement
Other indicators as determined by the state	Other indicators as determined by the state

establishing a common definition of family literacy have been useful at the state and local levels for coordinating educational services across departments and agencies.

Table 29.1 also shows that such expected outcomes as a high school diploma, or entry into postsecondary education, or the procurement of employment, although often difficult to assess across systems, include clearly defined criteria for documentation. On the other hand, documenting an adult's achievement of basic skills can be complicated. In fact, a good deal of controversy surrounds the assessment of these skills in adults. Although they use various standardized instruments, many researchers and practitioners consider these instruments inadequate (Kruidenier, 2002). Nevertheless, federal legislation requires the documentation of gains in basic skills. Accordingly, states often provide guidelines for both adult basic education and family literacy programs and specify the acceptable instruments for reporting gains. For example, Maine's adult learning indicators require that programs use the Tests of Adult Basic Education (TABE) or Reading Evaluation Adult Diagnosis for reporting gains among native English speakers in basic skills, and that they use the English as a Second Language Oral Assessment or Basic English Skills Test (BEST) for reporting gains among speakers of other languages (Maine State Department of Education, 2002). On the other hand, Connecticut's performance indicators for adult learning gains mandate the Comprehensive Adult Student Assessment System (CASAS) for documenting and reporting the gains (Connecticut State Department of Education, 2002).

TYPES OF ASSESSMENT

Assessments generally fall into two categories: standardized and informal. Regardless of category, most assessment instruments have both advantages and drawbacks, which one should consider when selecting an assessment for a specific purpose (Jackson, 1990; Moran, 1997; Van Duzer, & Berdan, 2000). An outline of these advantages and drawbacks appears shortly.

Standardized Tests

To be standardized, a test should use a standard set of materials and procedures under standard conditions. For example, one should use the same stimulus materials and items with each administration of the test. Such administrative procedures as directions to learners, procedures for scoring, and procedures for interpreting scores, must remain unchanged each time the test is administered. Results for learners located in different programs, and in different parts of the country, can bear comparison, as long as one has followed the standard procedures and the learners are among the population the test appropriately measures.

Standardized tests also have demonstrable reliability and validity. *Reliability* refers to the consistency of the assessment. Theoretically, if the test were administered repeatedly to an individual, the score obtained would be the same each time. *Validity* refers to the veracity of the measure: A valid test measures what it is supposed to measure. One typically determines the reliability and validity of a test with statistical procedures performed on test score data from hundreds of individuals.

Standardized tests also use a standard score scale and standards of comparison for interpreting scores. For example, one can compare the scores of individual learners (converted to a standard score) to those of a group of individuals with similar characteristics who have previously taken the test (a norming group). Scores on the TABE fit this description. Also, one can compare the scores of individual learners, converted to a standard score, to a particular criterion for performance, as is done with CASAS scores. The standard score scale allows one to compare performance across different levels and forms of a test.

Not all standardized assessments are based on a norming group, or are norm-referenced. Criterion-referenced assessments, such as CASAS, or performance-based assessments, such as the instrument emerging from the National Institute for Literacy's Equipped for the Future (EFF) project, increasingly serve as alternatives to norm-referenced achievement tests. EFF provides a standards-based and systemic assessment of adult education that focuses on the skills and knowledge adults need to fulfill their roles as parents and family members, employees, and citizens. The EFF development team has so far defined content standards focusing on performance that are observable and measurable and specific enough to guide the assessment and instructional process. They have also begun to define various performance levels and to identify or develop relevant assessment tools (Stein, 2000). This assessment system will focus on the proficiency of learners in completing realistic tasks within a specific context and to offer tools to adult education providers to improve their programs' accountability and to offer learners access to portable and meaningful credentials.

Examples and descriptions of standardized assessments for adults, including the TABE, the BEST, and the CASAS Employability Competency System and Life Skills System tests, appear in Table 29.2.

Informal Assessments

Informal assessments typically lack the qualities that make standardized tests standardized. For example, they may lack a standard set of procedures for administering, scoring, or interpreting. They rarely come with documented reliability and validity, and they often lack a standard score scale or a method for interpreting learners' scores or for comparing the learners who complete the assessment. Informal assessments vary in their informality, ranging from the highly structured, like those using a fixed set of interview questions or observation categories, to the casually open-ended, as when a teacher spends the last few moments of class with learners each week to gather current impressions of their progress and current needs. Informal assessments may include published instruments or teacher- or program-generated tools (Knell & Scogins, 2000; Salvia & Hughes, 1990). Short descriptions of various informal assessments appear in Table 29.3, with examples of how one can use them in family literacy programs.

TABLE 29.2
Standardized Assessment Instruments Appropriate for Adults

Instrument	Appropriate Audience	Areas Assessed	Competency-based and skills-focused	Publisher Information
Tests of Adult Basic Education	Beginning to advanced ABE/GED	Reading, mathematics, spelling, language	Skills-focused	CTB/McGraw-Hill 20 Ryan Ranch Road Monterey, CA 93940–5703 800–538–9547 www.ctb.com
Adult Basic Learning Examination	Beginning to advanced ABE/GED	Vocabulary, comprehension, spelling, language (levels 2 and 3), number operations, problem solving	Skills-focused	Harcourt Brace 555 Academic Court San Antonio, TX 78204–2498 800–211–8378 www.hbem.com
Woodcock Reading Mastery Test–Revised	Beginning to low-intermediate ABE	Word identification, word attack, word and passage comprehension, total reading	Skills-focused	American Guidance Services 4201 Woodland Road PO Box 99 Circle Pines, MN 55014–1796 800–328–2560 www.agsnet.com
Wonderlic Basic Skills Test	High-intermediate to secondary level ABE/GED, work-focused	Verbal skills, quantitative skills	Skills-focused	Wonderlic 1795 N. Butterfield Road Libertyville, IL 60048–1238 800–323–3742 www.wonderlic.com
Comprehensive Adult Learner Assessment System (CASAS) Employability Competency System	Beginning to advanced ABE or ESL, work-focused	Reading, math, listening	Competency-based	www.CASAS.org *Note*: CASAS requires that agencies be trained in order to purchase or use CASAS materials.
CASAS Life Skills System	Beginning to advanced ABE or ESL	Reading, math, listening	Competency-based	www.CASAS.org *Note*: CASAS requires that agencies be trained in order to purchase or use CASAS materials.
Basic English Skills Test	Beginning to low-intermediate ESL	Oral skills, literacy skills	Competency-based	Center for Applied Linguistics 4646 40th Street NW Washington, DC 20016–1859 (202) 362–0700 best@cal.org

Note: ABE = adult basic education; ESL = English as a second language.

TABLE 29.3
Types of Informal Assessments and Informal Assessment Techniques

Published informal assessments

Curriculum-based assessments match the content of a specific lesson or unit and are used to determine learner's mastery of content (e.g., a curriculum-based assessment might determine a learner's ability to make inferences while reading before and again after a lesson making inferences)

Examples:

Pre- and postlesson tests or quizzes in the *Challenger* series (New Reader's Press)
Pre- and postlesson tests or quizzes in GED instructional materials
Pre- and postlesson tests or quizzes in other instructional materials

Informal reading inventories, typically a word list and set of graded passages. Learners read the word list aloud, and their performance indicates where they should start in the graded passages. Learners then read the passages orally or silently, so that the administrator can obtain measures of reading miscues and/or comprehension.

Examples:

Reading Evaluation Adult Diagnosis (New Reader's Press)
Whole Language for Adults: A Guide to Initial Assessment (New Reader's Press)
Jerry Johns Reading Inventory (Kendall Hunt)
Ekwall Reading Inventory (Allyn & Bacon)
Bader Reading and Language Inventory (Prentice Hall)

Inventories: Learners are presented with list of items and indicate items that apply to them.

Example:

Published learning-style inventories are very common.

Other published informal assessment instruments

English as a Second Language Oral Assessment (New Reader's Press)
Assessment, Instruction, Mastery (State of Oregon)

Teacher- or program-developed or initiated informal assessments and techniques

Interviews — face-to-face questioning of learners, allowing interviewer to obtain learner opinions or perspectives (e.g., teachers may use interviews to track learners' changing perceptions of how they use literacy outside of the classroom)

Questionnaires — usually presented on paper, as opposed to interview questions, but also a good approach to obtaining learner perspectives or input (e.g., a teacher may distribute a brief questionnaire during a class each week, in which learners respond to questions about what they felt they learned during the week, how they plan to apply their learning, and so on)

Inventories — learners presented with list of items and asked to indicate how items apply to them (e.g., on inventory may be used to allow learners to indicate specific skills they would like to learn)

Reflections/journaling — learners or teachers may periodically reflect in writing on general or specific learner progress (e.g., learners and teachers may independently note gains made at the end of the week)

Anecdotal records — learners or teachers record descriptions of situations that illustrate change or achievement (e.g., a learner can keep a record of changes in interactions with their child's teacher)

Observations — teachers record observations of learner performance, by writing notes or using structured observation guides (e.g., teachers record observations as they watch learners work on a task, such as following a set of procedural directions)

Charts — may show frequency of an activity over time (e.g., number of times per week that learner engages in independent reading may be charted)

Logs — lists of completed activities (e.g., lists of books read in a month or lessons completed in a week)

Checklists — more structured than logs (McGrail & Schwartz, 1993; and Auerbach, 1992, include examples of checklists for various purposes)

Retell Exercises — learners repeat what they have read in selected passage, providing insights into text comprehension, prior knowledge, metacognitive strategies, facility with language (Hermann, 1994, includes format for recording learner responses)

Portfolio Assessment — collections of learner work over time that are evaluated to demonstrate learner progress (e.g., teachers keep folders with learner writing from various points in time and review to determine areas of growth and areas in need of additional work) (Bear, 1987, and MacKillop & Holzman, 1990, provide criteria for evaluating writing samples)

Advantages and Limitations of Standardized and Informal Assessments

All assessment instruments have advantages and at least some limitations, and, before selecting them, family literacy providers must carefully consider their assessment purposes and the intended use of the assessment results. Both types of assessments provide useful tools for family literacy providers, if used with skill and sensitivity.

Standardized Assessments. Standardized assessments often serve accountability or evaluative purposes, but, to be useful for those purposes, the administration of the assessment should follow standard guidelines. More specifically, any violation of the standardized administration protocol (e.g., ignoring time limits or reading aloud directions intended to be read silently) can invalidate the results for comparative purposes. Also, tests with multiple levels require that learners be placed on the appropriate level, and most leveled instruments have an accompanying locator or appraisal procedure to guide this placement. One should also use alternative forms—with their administration separated by a considerable number of instructional hours—with each retest, to reduce familiarity with the forms. Finally, if one intends to compare test data across learners in a program, one should accumulate a predetermined number of instructional hours before retesting. At the very least, instructors should track the number of hours between test administrations, to hold the number of instructional hours equal when analyzing learner gains.

The results of standardized procedures can be remarkably valuable. If administered as intended, for example, they yield comparable results, regardless of program location or type. Therefore, funding agents and policymakers often rely on them for program accountability. Another advantage is that gains on standardized tests may be useful to program administrators and teachers seeking an objective measure of their learners' progress, compared to an external norming group. Given an appropriate design, the assessment may show learners' progress toward meeting specified criteria or acquiring specified competencies.

On the other hand, standardized tests define the trait or characteristic they measure from a definite perspective. Thus, they may have only limited applicability or relevance for particular programs. For example, a workplace literacy program that focuses on work-based literacy skills may find inappropriate a standardized assessment that measures the targeted skills. Standardized tests may also reflect the performance of a particular norming group. As a result, the extent to which the characteristics of the learners at hand match those of the norming group affect the relevance and applicability of the test for these learners. Finally, standardized assessments may recall unpleasant memories for learners who have been unsuccessful in traditional school settings.

Informal Assessments. With their own advantages and limitations, informal assessments may be selected or developed to match program or learner needs and goals. They may be capable of tracking skill development and movement toward goals that standardized test scores fail to reveal. For example, a writing sample portfolio may demonstrate a learner's development from disconnected sentences to coherent paragraphs to several connected paragraphs. Or a reading log might demonstrate changes in the amount and type of reading one does outside of class. Also, informal assessments can be selected or developed to link closely with instructional activities. Herman, Aschbacher, and Winters (1992) added that informal assessments often involve higher level thinking and problem-solving skills, as well as real-world applications. As such, one can use them to continually monitor or direct instructional activities for learners, and they can come to seem, for learners, an almost seamless extension of instruction. Auerbach (1992) noted also that informal assessments are often process-oriented, open-ended, and ongoing, and this inherent adaptability, in terms of format and procedure, invites learners in a supportive environment to become more deeply involved in the assessment process in a way rarely feasible with standardized assessments.

Informal assessments have, however, several drawbacks. They often lack a clear purpose or are poorly designed and organized, confounding efforts to collect meaningful information about a learner's skills. These instruments may also lack reliability, making it difficult to ensure that the scores accurately measure improvement. In addition, results from informal assessments can rarely be generalized across programs or even across learners in the same program, making it difficult for administrators to identify trends or areas for improvement. Finally, the lack of statistical reliability and validity precludes their use for providing broad, or many, comparisons across programs. Although this failing may be of little interest to local teachers, it is of great interest to researchers and funding agents. As a result, informal assessments are valuable tools but hardly replace standardized instruments for the purpose of accountability.

PURPOSES FOR ASSESSMENT

Whether a family literacy program selects standardized or informal assessment instruments, it should administer the instruments consistently, so that the results provide information useful to instructors, learners, and funding agents. Funding agents increasingly base funding decisions on assessment data, which reliably reflect learner outcomes, In fact, inadequate or invalid assessment data, which purport to measure participant outcomes, may well result in serious funding cuts. Accordingly, one of the most compelling purposes for assessment in family literacy programs is program accountability. And, as we have seen, providers must select and administer assessment instruments in a manner appropriate for state and federal reporting.

But test information is critical not only at the federal or state level but also at the program level. Unfortunately, learners (and, too often, their teachers) perceive testing as a necessary evil, gathering essentially meaningless numbers intended solely for program reporting and accountability. Assessment should, of course, be meaningful and an essential component of instruction. At the program level, one should use test results to refer learners for additional services, to place them in appropriate educational settings and on appropriate instructional levels, and to diagnose their strengths and weaknesses in order to guide their instruction and help them set realistic goals.

Screening and Placement

A primary purpose of assessment in family literacy programs is screening participants for initial program or level placement. Adults entering a family literacy program should receive an immediate, honest, and supportive response to the questions about the program's ability to help them achieve their goals. Such assessment activities usually take place during intake, early in the learner's contact with the program, and they may take only between 5 and 20 minutes to complete. Still, they help a provider determine whether the applicant is an appropriate candidate for the program's services and, if so, where in the program's offerings the applicant may best fit. Screening may involve such informal approaches as one-on-one learner interviews or program-developed reading assessment. It may involve administering the locator for a standardized instrument, such as the locator test in the TABE or the screening instrument based on the BEST. In any case, one must remember that initial screening is a first step in assessment, that the results will provide only a global view of a learner's basic skills, rather than a diagnostic profile, and that the instruments are inappropriate for accountability or general reporting.

Setting Goals

Assessment information also can help learners set more realistic educational goals. Although teachers should routinely discuss assessment results with their adult learners, helping them to use this information to set goals is an effective way to engage them in the educational process itself. For example, an adult in a family literacy program may express the desire for a GED. Screening may indicate, and further testing may confirm, however, that the learner's skills are low and that it may take many months, if not years, to achieve this goal. Teachers can use such information to help learners set realistic short-term objectives and long-term goals. The short-term objectives should be oriented toward obtaining the GED, but they should also allow the learner to reach clearly defined learning successes along the way. This progression, in turn, fosters in a learner responsibility for the learning.

Guiding Instruction and Documenting Changes

A third purpose of assessment is to gather more detailed information about a learner's specific strengths and areas for development. This information helps one set instructional goals, plan a specific course of instructional activities, and select relevant materials. Programs often develop individual educational plans or individual learner plans to record this information for later reference. Gathering more detailed assessment information can ensure an appropriate placement within the program. Diagnostic assessment may include such standardized instruments as the TABE Complete Battery, providing a diagnostic profile of specific skills, or such informal instruments as the Reading Evaluation Adult Diagnosis, which is an informal reading inventory.

Other informal instruments, such as reading inventories or retell exercises, can also provide instructors with detailed information about a learner's word recognition and comprehension skills. Holistic scoring of a writing sample can identify skill in using grammatical structures and the ability to produce a cohesive paragraph. Teachers can also observe and record a learner's application of literacy skills in a particular context. For example, the teacher might observe the ability of a parent to read instructions for an over-the-counter medication and determine the correct dosage for her child. The conduct of this task could question or confirm the parent's vocabulary, comprehension skills, and knowledge of math concepts.

These types of diagnostic assessments can provide an instructor and learner with initial instructional plans, but they should be revisited regularly with the learner to revise the plan and identify alternative instructional strategies in areas where the learner has failed to progress. When revisiting and revising instructional plans, it is often useful, as well, to retest the learners to document changes in their skills. Typically, the same assessments used for initial pretesting are readministered to track any growth in specific terms. One may use this information to adjust and develop the learner's educational plan. If one uses standardized instruments, the results will also provide assessment data appropriate for state and federal accountability purposes.

The strengths and weaknesses of standardized and informal instruments make them more or less appropriate to various assessment purposes. Screening and placement, diagnosis, and individual learner progress may be accomplished with the guidance of standardized or informal instruments. Program accountability, however, usually requires outcomes from standardized assessments.

ASSESSMENT PLANNING

When developing an assessment plan for adults in family literacy programs, one should begin by identifying and actually listing the purposes for the assessment and the specific population the program serves. One may select the instruments likely to meet the identified purposes and to provide comprehensive assessment information. The plan might list for various learner populations the instruments to be administered, when they are to be administered, and where the resulting data are to be routed (e.g., to a learner file in the main office, to a data entry person, or to the teachers). Instructors may want to develop an assessment procedures manual as a one-stop reference, to keep everyone current and consistent with important assessment procedures. This manual may include directions for matching new parents entering the program with the most appropriate tool used by the program, directions for administering standardized tools, and directions for completing and routing assessment data summary forms.

Selecting Standardized Assessments

Family literacy programs required to administer standardized assessments should ask specific questions when selecting appropriate instruments for adult learners. Factors to consider include administrative, technical, and content issues.

First, examine the administrative aspects of the tool and consider these 10 issues:

1. How long does it take to administer the instrument?
2. Can it be administered to whole groups, only to individuals, or to either?
3. Are the administration and scoring relatively easy?
4. Is the administration manual clear and comprehensive?
5. How much staff training will be needed to use the instrument?
6. What type of scores does the instrument yield?
7. If multiple levels of the instrument are available, how will learners be placed on the appropriate levels?
8. Do alternative forms exist for retesting?
9. Is the cost of the instrument reasonable?
10. What purposes for assessment could the instrument address?

Second, examine the technical aspects of the instrument and consider these two questions:

1. Do I have information about the instrument's development, its norming data or criterion selection, and its reliability and validity?
2. Is the norming group a good match with the learners in my program?

Third, examine the content of the instrument in relation to these four programmatic and learner needs:

1. What specific literacy skills does the tool assess?
2. Does the focus of the instrument provide a good match with the program's instructional approach and philosophy (e.g., a program that takes a skills-focused approach may find little relevant information coming from a competency-based or criterion-referenced assessment)?
3. Are the directions for the learner easy to follow?
4. Is the content age-appropriate and culturally appropriate?

A family literacy provider will find it difficult to locate one assessment instrument that meets all of the desired characteristics. However, it should be possible to identify two or more instruments that provide assessment information necessary for effectively achieving accountability, as well as for diagnosing skills and tracking learning gains. One can also, when necessary, supplement standardized instruments with appropriate informal assessments.

Selecting Informal Assessments

Programs may select from a variety of published informal instruments or may develop their own. Many of the considerations useful for selecting standardized instruments hold true for published instruments, especially regarding administrative aspects and content. Publishers' catalogs and conferences are good sources for new or unfamiliar published informal instruments that may meet a program's needs. Published instructional materials that programs may find useful often include informal assessment instruments keyed to lessons or units.

In addition, teachers may develop informal assessments. In fact, teachers often involve adults in casual, classroom-based activities that really constitute informal assessments (although neither party may realize that is what it is). One way to explore the development and implementation of such activities within a program is to center a discussion among teachers on what types of informal activities they use, why, and what seems successful. First, good ideas can be noted, shared, and expanded upon. Second, needs can be identified that form the basis for a program improvement activity (specific strategies for developing informal assessments receive attention later in this chapter).

Samples of informal assessments that teachers have developed appear throughout published reports and manuals. For example, frameworks for recording observational records can be found in McGrail and Schwartz (1993) and Holt and Van Duzer (2000). Adult learners, too, should be encouraged to reflect on their learning and explore how and why their work shows progress or seems to lag. The process of reflection engages learners in the educational process, bringing to the surface a need to evaluate their own work, think of possible solutions to identified problems, and take some responsibility for their progress toward personal goals (Bingman, Ebert, & Bell, 2002; Fingeret, 1993). Self-assessments can take various forms, including, for example, unstructured interviews, reflective journals, checklists, or open-ended surveys. Holt and Van Duzer (2000) included several examples of open-ended surveys and questionnaires focused on adults who were ELLs and on family literacy programs.

DEVELOPING INFORMAL ASSESSMENT INSTRUMENTS

Many family literacy programs adopt informal assessment instruments to supplement the information they acquire from standardized instruments. Portfolio assessment, the checklists and self-assessments teachers develop, curriculum-based assessments, program-designed interviews, and commercially available rating sheets all can be used to collect information about a learner's progress and achievement.

Reliable assessments provide useful information about learner progress, but family literacy providers who develop informal assessments should approach the process carefully and should involve administrators and, if possible, learners as they reach decisions concerning the purpose of the assessment, the key outcomes, the processes to be measured, administration procedures, and guidelines for scoring items and interpreting the results (Marshall & Rossman, 1999; Patton, 1990). Without this discussion, teachers often find themselves disagreeing on definitions of progress or success (e.g., How is "little progress" or "much improved" defined? Do staff members agree on the meaning of an individual's score of "4" on a checklist?). A lack of agreement on these issues can easily undermine the instrument's reliability.

Designing Informal Assessments

Curriculum-based assessments may seem easy to design, but only if they rely on a simple vocabulary and include recall comprehension questions. Developing more complex questions (e.g., summaries, inferences, and analyses) can be time-consuming and often difficult. These more complex questions are essential, however, for building critical literacy skills. Meanwhile, the disadvantages of informal assessments stem from their lack of clear purpose, meaningful design and organization, and reliability. To reduce these drawbacks, plan carefully before developing the instrument.

One should consider various design issues before trying to develop an instrument. Identifying a clear purpose for the assessment, identifying specific goals or expected outcomes, and selecting criteria for measuring a learner's level of success are essential. To identify the purpose, consider what is to be measured and how the resulting information is to be used. Expected outcomes should include descriptions of what tasks learners are expected to complete, how competence will be demonstrated, and what short-term objectives and long-term goals must be reached. Finally, the criteria for measuring performance or gains should include definitions of performance or progress, as well as milestones on the path toward a goal. For example, a learner might be expected to write a cohesive paragraph consisting of a topic sentence and three supporting details. The learner might pass a milestone when they write a coherent sentence on a single topic. A second milestone might consist of writing two coherent sentences on a single topic with a thesis statement or topic sentence.

Standardizing Informal Assessments

Some programs attempt to standardize their informal assessments, and, although these efforts might improve the assessment's reliability and, therefore, its usefulness for reporting purposes, the assessment may also lose some of the flexibility that initially made it effective. In addition, standardizing informal measures can be time-consuming and expensive.

Some programs prefer to use locally developed assessments that match their curricula. Few funding agencies, however, accept data from these assessments as the only evidence of effectiveness. Nevertheless, these assessments may provide a local program with enough usefulness to justify the effort to standardize them. Once standardized, moreover, the assessment may become useful to other programs with similar learners and curricula.

Standardizing a locally developed assessment requires time and expertise. The first step is to specify items that precisely measure what the curriculum teaches. If the items assess what is being taught, the assessment will be valid for program use. If the assessment is criterion-referenced, learners who have been taught the assessed skills, and presumably mastered them, should score almost 100% on the assessment.

Next, one should write standardized directions that all teachers and tutors can use to administer the test. The assessment need not necessarily be timed, but it should be administered consistently. Procedures for scoring and reporting the data should also be standardized.

One can ask colleagues to examine the assessment and to suggest refinements in the wording, directions, and format. After revisions, pilot the instrument to reveal any directions, or items that are unclear or otherwise poorly expressed. Ask learners about the items they miss to determine why they answered as they did.

Collect data (i.e., the items answered correctly and missed by each learner) from a minimum of about 50 learners who take the assessment. Even on paper, patterns may begin to emerge (e.g., learners with a certain level of competence tend to miss certain items). The formula for calculating reliability is influenced by the number of items in the assessment; therefore, a longer assessment is more likely to be reliable (one may be in a position to ask a local university for data analysis help in determining the reliability of an assessment).

Some computer programs come equipped with item analyses that reveal how closely an item correlates with a learner's total score and that, thereby, calculate reliability. If the test is a mastery or criterion-referenced test, one should include those items that learners with high total scores get right and eliminate or reword those items that learners with high total scores miss.

To create local norms, collect data over an extended period. Ultimately, it will become evident that learners with different mastery levels score differently on the assessment. At that point, the assessment can help determine the instruction that a new learner needs, as well as demonstrate program effectiveness when it is used after instruction.

Using Qualitative Data for Program Accountability

The effort to standardize a locally developed assessment may seem daunting, which is why programs so often rely on commercial standardized instruments, but one might use qualitative information for program accountability, if it is quantified or used to supplement required data. In fact, one quantifies qualitative data specifically to enhance reporting to funding agencies and other external audiences. Along with changes in standardized test scores, qualitative data that have been quantified can highlight those changes attributable to the impact of the program.

Sometimes, programs may include case studies of selected clients who have, for example, gone on from adult basic education classes to obtain the GED or high school diploma, and then gone into satisfying employment. These qualitative data can provide important evidence of program effectiveness, but they can also provide quantitative data useful for program accountability.

By collecting evidence of a program's effectiveness over time, one can quantify qualitative data. Funding agencies already expect such data as numbers of learners who have found jobs or who have moved to the next educational level. Some data are more subtle and may require some effort to collect, such as a parent becoming able to help a child with homework, to ask the child's teacher questions about the skills being taught, and to administer a child's prescriptions accurately. In all these cases, notice how an adult's ability to perform reflects demonstrable literacy skills.

One might usefully interview learners who are succeeding in their educational programs or who are recent program graduates, to determine how the program has affected their lives in both large and small ways. Compile, on a list, all of the outcomes learners mention, leaving space for others to come. Then, systematically and periodically collect this information from learners through interviews and record it on a summary checklist. Be sure to collect documentation for each outcome. For each learner, one now has both the results of assessment instruments and a list of reported outcomes attributable to class participation.

When asked to provide program accountability information, one can aggregate outcomes data for learners by saying, for example, that 80% of the learners reported themselves better able to help their children with homework. With access to a database program like *Access* or *Filemaker Pro*, one can enter data about each learner into the system and later search the database for particular outcomes, such as "Child's homework." It will then list the number of times learners mentioned that particular outcome. Quantitative data like this also can be accompanied by case studies that illustrate the accomplishments of the learners.

ASSESSING ELL ADULTS

No single test or type of test can address the complex assessment issues facing instructors of adults learning English as a second language (ESL) (Wrigley & Guth, 1992). Commercially available, standardized tests, such as the BEST or CASAS, provide quantifiable information, such as an adult's listening comprehension proficiency, but they may not accurately reflect the ELL's true communicative abilities in real-life situations. And, although informal assessments may provide a more accurate picture of what learners actually can do and say in English, they rarely provide data that administrators and funding agents need to demonstrate and compare program effectiveness.

In addition, assessment practices used for ELL adults vary with the vision and scope of the program, the specific kinds of services it provides, and the cultural and educational backgrounds and needs of its learners. For example, assessment practices in an ESL family literacy program, which teaches beginning English skills to recent immigrants so that they can communicate with their children's teachers, may differ from those in an employer-sponsored workplace literacy program.

Despite the different purposes one encounters in English-language and literacy programs, current research and practice suggest that the more effective programs for ELL adults use a combination of commercially available standardized tests and program-developed informal assessments. In any event, when choosing assessments, family literacy providers must consider their learners' cultural and educational backgrounds and levels of English proficiency. They also should consider whether or not to test in a learner's native language.

Initial Interviews for Intake and Placement

Family literacy providers can collect essential information with appropriate intake and place-ment procedures, diagnostic testing, and progress tracking for assessing their learners' back-ground and educational needs, as well as by monitoring their English proficiency. Individual interviews help a staff collect relevant background information about a learner's oral language proficiency, native language literacy and education, previous English-language instruction, reasons for enrollment, and learning preferences. Questionnaires can help one collect this in-formation systematically. In addition, placement tests, such as the CASAS ESL Appraisal Test and the oral component of the BEST, can help one place learners on the appropriate instruction level. Additional diagnostic testing can identify areas of strength and weakness in such spe-cific skills as oral proficiency, grammatical knowledge, listening and reading comprehension, and writing competence. Finally, the periodic monitoring and recording of academic gains, achievement of learning goals, and attainment of competence can help one track a learner's progress in acquiring English-language skills or basic literacy skills, either in the adults' first language or in English, but standardized instruments and locally developed informal tests can also support this work.

Culture and Educational Background

One should, of course, consider the cultural and educational backgrounds of the learners, when one chooses assessment instruments. If the learners are well grounded in their first language, they can rely on their existing knowledge of an oral and written language when learning a second language. But, if the learner's native culture lacks a written language or provides no public educational opportunities, the learner is unlikely to perform well on a standardized achievement test.

Consideration must also focus on the development and content of the test. Was it normed on ELL adults? Do the test items require cultural background knowledge unfamiliar to the learners at hand? At the very least, learners should be familiar with the testing procedures and the structure of the test items. Be sure to consult the test manual before selecting the instrument. It should include information on norming, test bias, and appropriateness for selected audiences.

English Proficiency

One's choice of assessments for ELL adults should also depend on the language proficiency levels of the learners. A complicated grammar test would be inappropriate for a beginning

TABLE 29.4

English Language Proficiency Descriptions

Beginner	A learner at this level may have little or no ability to speak, read, or write English and would be unable to function independently using the language. In listening, only short utterances, simple courtesy expressions, and main themes are comprehended. In writing, this student can copy, list, and label concrete terms and may be able to fill in simple autobiographical information on forms.
Advanced beginner	This learner will have some ability to operate in a limited capacity and to satisfy immediate needs in English. In listening, this learner will be able to decipher the main idea of a dialogue. A writer at this level will be able to produce simple paragraphs using familiar materials and may read short passages with general understanding.
Beginning intermediate	A learner at this level will be able to satisfy survival needs and minimum courtesy requirements. The learner can understand easy questions and answers and hold simple face-to-face conversations. In reading, the learner will be able to read for information and identify supporting details. The learner can write letters and short compositions, using simple grammatical structures.
Intermediate	The full intermediate learner will be able to converse with native speakers and will be understood when discussing familiar topics. Listening may be selective, and the listener can identify mood and attitude of the speaker. Polite expressions are mastered at this level. In reading, the use of context clues and the skills of skimming and scanning are possible. Writers are able to take notes in class, and to write using common terms and vocabulary comprehensible to the native speaker, but would be labeled simplistic.
Advanced	This learner can communicate well at work and can adequately satisfy the social demands of conversation, with some sensitivity to both informal and formal language. Listening comprehension now can include abstract discussion and the details of everyday nontechnical conversation. Abstract material can be comprehended in reading as well. Academic reading in history, cultural and moral issues, and politics is within this ability range. This writer can use both informal and formal prose, paraphrase and summarize, and produce complex sentence structures with adequate accuracy.

Source: Rance-Roney, J. (1995). Classifying ESL proficiency. In T. Reiff (Ed.), *The Pennsylvania adult basic and literacy education staff handbook* (p. 25). Harrisburg, PA: Pennsylvania Department of Education.

student. Similarly, a simple verbal assessment would provide an inaccurate measure of an advanced student's ability to read and comprehend a complex technical manual. Those who make effective ESL assessment decisions consider what students can do with the language, not just what they know about the language. In addition, demonstrating that students have moved from one level to another provides an appropriate assessment of progress. Table 29.4 illustrates various English-language proficiency levels.

Testing in a Native Language

When choosing assessments, family literacy providers must also consider whether to test in a student's native language. This decision rests, in part, on the reason for testing. If a student is being tested on their knowledge of a particular content area, such as history, testing might be appropriate in the native language. For example, the results of the Spanish version of the GED test should accurately assess a Spanish-speaking student's subject knowledge. On the other hand, if one is assessing a student's competency in English, rather than subject knowledge, the testing should probably proceed in English.

The decision whether or not to test in a student's native language also depends on the scope and mission of the program. Programs that follow a bilingual literacy model tend to test in a student's native language. The TABE, for example, is available in a Spanish version, to measure the basic reading, math, and language skills of Spanish-speaking adults. Many programs also develop informal tests in the student's native language and rely on a multilingual staff to administer assessments.

Using Assessments Effectively with ELL Adults

Assessment purposes for ELL adults are the same as they are for other adults. One uses the assessment data to place students at appropriate educational levels for instructing them, for diagnosing skill strengths and weaknesses, and for determining progress. The issues of English-language proficiency, educational background, and cultural issues should, however, be considered within each purpose to ensure the appropriateness of the assessment procedures.

Placement.   During an initial interview, the program staff can collect preliminary information about a learner's native-language literacy and education, oral English-language proficiency, previous English-language instruction, reasons for enrolling in the family literacy program, and learning preferences. If the program staff see that a new student has only a limited skill with the English language, the program should make a translator available to help with the interview. To simplify the intake process, one can use a questionnaire to guide this initial interview. Students with more advanced levels of English proficiency can complete the questionnaire independently, thereby providing additional information about their writing skills.

In addition, one can use placement tests, such as the CASAS ESL Appraisal or the oral component of the BEST, to place students at appropriate instruction levels. This step usually involves a short survey or locator test, to place the student tentatively within a broad ability level, such as beginner, intermediate, or advanced. The initial placement also helps a program identify appropriate instructional materials.

Diagnosis.   After the locator test suggests an appropriate learning level, further testing serves to adduce baseline data for measuring progress and collecting diagnostic information. Diagnostic testing provides information about an individual's strengths and weaknesses in such specific skill areas as oral proficiency, grammatical knowledge, listening and reading comprehension, and writing competence. The BEST, for example, provides diagnostic information one can use to develop individual education plans. An item-by-item review might indicate that a parent can correctly fill out forms but may have difficulty reading information that a child brings home from school.

Measuring Progress.   Periodic assessments of academic gains, achievement of objectives, and attainment of competence serve to measure individual and group progress and to provide accountability. One should administer the same assessments used for pretesting and posttesting. In addition, alternative assessments for measuring student progress can help one evaluate a learner's educational plan. ELL adults often respond positively to such informal assessment strategies as audiotapes, writing samples, journals, and checklists. These informal methods also provide simple yet relevant information for adults, who can see their progress more easily than they can by reviewing results from standardized instruments.

PROVIDING A SUPPORTIVE TESTING ENVIRONMENT

Most adult learners, whether learning English in a family literacy program or being native speakers, experience some test anxiety. They may become visibly uncomfortable when placed in a testing situation, especially those who have avoided a return to education because of unpleasant associations from past test results. Many have not taken a test in years, and some may abandon the program if they are tested too soon or too rigorously.

Family literacy educators must, therefore, provide a testing atmosphere both comfortable and reassuring, yet likely to yield an accurate picture of the adult learners' educational achievements, strengths, and weaknesses. Various factors influence the testing situation, but one can use effective strategies to address these factors in ways that help provide a supportive testing environment without compromising the reliability and integrity of the assessments.

Test Anxiety

Test anxiety, both a physical and emotional response, may hinder an adult's ability to concentrate and perform well. The physical responses may include sweating or trembling, an upset stomach, or an accelerated heart rate. The emotional responses may include panic, negative self-talk ("I can't do this" or "I hate taking tests"), or an exaggerated dread or avoidance of the testing situation. For many adults, test anxiety reflects earlier experiences. These learners may have endured repeated school failures (either real or perceived). They may have received discouraging responses from teachers, peers, parents, or spouses about their ability to do well on tests or in school, and their self-esteem may accordingly be low. Some ELL students may have had little formal education in their native countries and may be unfamiliar with the testing situation itself. Finally, many adult learners may never have developed simple test-taking strategies to ease their anxieties. Some or all of these factors can combine in varying degrees to create an exaggerated dread of the testing situation.

Orientation Sessions to Reduce Anxiety

Ideally, a family literacy program provides opportunities, early and often, for parents to learn how to take tests comfortably. If feasible, orientation sessions or workshops should address test anxiety and test-taking strategies. These opportunities can be particularly important for adults who have been out of school for a long time or who have serious test anxieties. In these sessions, one should discuss test anxiety and allow the adults to discuss their testing experiences, and one can explain how and why testing complements a family literacy program. This openness helps students understand that taking a test can be a positive and informative experience and that the consequent information will help them succeed in the program. In general, one should explain test-taking strategies to the students and provide opportunities to practice them.

Effective Assessment Strategies to Reduce Anxiety

If the program cannot schedule orientation sessions or workshops, it can still provide a supportive testing environment to help students ease or overcome their testing anxieties. Providers can design appropriate assessment schedules based on the program's structure, its assessment plan, and the needs of the various stakeholders. Additionally, these three strategies can help design effective assessment scheduling: (a) establishing consistent guidelines, based on the purposes for assessment; (b) involving learners in the assessment process; and (c) reviewing testing procedures to evaluate their appropriateness and effectiveness.

Consistent Guidelines.   Family literacy educators should have a common understanding of their particular program's assessment guidelines, and they should comply with these guidelines to ensure consistency across the program. Administrators should provide all counseling and instructional personnel with an orientation that includes a review of these guidelines. The staff members should be aware of the assessments their program uses for screening, for diagnosing strengths and weaknesses, and for documenting learner progress. They also should understand and use appropriate procedures for administering standardized and informal tests and for recording data.

Learner Involvement.   As part of the learning process, assessment requires instructors and students to meet regularly to discuss assessment results and to plan or revise educational plans. Effective assessments help learners identify learning goals and help instructors and learners plan meaningful instruction. Adults are more likely to recognize the importance of testing when they play an active role in using the information for instructional planning.

Testing Procedures.   Family literacy providers should consider the review and evaluation of their program's various components to be a required, ongoing process of renewal and improvement. Both internal factors (e.g., staff turnover) and external factors (e.g., funding requirements) influence a program's ability to meet the needs of parents who participate in the program. Therefore, a family literacy staff should review its testing procedures, along with the other components in its instructional system at least annually.

SUMMARY

Family literacy programs must select a variety of standardized and informal tests according to their assessment purposes, the information needs of all the stakeholders, and the strengths and limitations of the various assessment instruments. Assessment practices should measure and report, more or less quantitatively, what is taught, and they should help document program effectiveness. They should also suggest program changes, if those are necessary. For example, intake and screening assessments provide a starting point for instruction. Diagnostic tests guide ongoing instructional planning. Program administrators and funding agents use standardized test data to document and compare program effectiveness. Finally, all family literacy staff members and administrators should consistently and carefully reexamine and document their assessment practices. Family literacy programs also must consider the administrative and technical aspects of a test, along with its audience, purpose, content, and format when choosing assessment tools. All of these factors must be judged in relation to their appropriateness for the family literacy program's assessment purposes, program structure, and learners. Commercially available tests should come with a technical manual that clearly explains all aspects of the test.

Most funding agents seeking program accountability prefer standardized, norm-referenced test data that document learner progress, but other types of tests, when properly administered and reported, can also provide data suitable for program accountability. For example, a standardized and criterion-referenced assessment, such as CASAS, indicates a student's mastery of specific skills and can be a reliable indicator of their progress during instruction. Programs may also standardize a locally developed test, although the process requires considerable time and expertise. Finally, programs may also use qualitative data (e.g., case studies) that have been properly analyzed to document program effectiveness.

In contrast to funding agencies and outside stakeholders, instructors and learners are interested in individual progress. As a result, they often supplement standardized test data with information gathered from informal assessments, which can range from portfolios to teacher-developed checklists and self-assessments to curriculum-based assessments or to commercially available rating sheets. Informal assessments tend to involve both instructors and their learners in the assessment process, to help parents set education goals for themselves, to guide the actual instruction, to document changes in a learner's self-esteem, and to direct gradual progress toward larger goals. These tools are valid within a program; however, the resulting data do not readily translate across programs, nor are they rigorously reliable. As a result, informal assessments, although valuable tools, rarely meet all the requirements for program reporting and accountability.

Test results are immediately critical to a program, because assessment is integral to instruction. Programs should use assessment data to refer learners for additional services, to make appropriate instructional placements, to guide instruction, and to help learners set attainable goals. Family literacy providers may try to find one assessment instrument to fit all purposes, but the quest is unrealistic. The ideal one-size-fits-all test does not exist. Rather, providers should carefully consider the purposes of assessment and select instruments that accommodate each purpose. For the purpose of screening learners and guiding instruction, one single assessment may be appropriate, but it is generally more realistic to select several valid instruments that meet both the instructor's and the learners' informational needs.

Meanwhile, although effective assessment practices benefit all learners, assessments for ELL adults tend to vary with the scope and vision of the program or the specific services it provides. All family literacy programs serving ELL adults should, however, select and use assessment instruments based on their learners' cultural and educational backgrounds, on their English proficiency levels, and on programmatic decisions regarding assessment in the students' native languages. A complete assessment plan should include various commercially available standardized tests as well as program-developed informal tests that address all its assessment purposes.

Finally, family literacy programs can provide a supportive productive testing environment by addressing both the learner and program factors that affect the testing situation. For example, discussing testing procedures, test anxiety, and test-taking strategies soon after students enroll, provides a supportive testing environment. One can address all of a program's assessment procedures by establishing consistent guidelines for testing based on the assessment purposes involving learners in the assessment process, and frequently reviewing these practices carefully. These strategies can help provide a comfortable and reassuring testing environment, yet one that yields an accurate picture of the learners' educational abilities and achievements.

REFERENCES

Auerbach, E. R. (1992). *Making meaning, making change: Participatory curriculum development for adult ESL literacy.* Washington, DC: Center for Applied Linguistics.

Bear, D. R. (1987). *Teaching adults to read using language experience and oral history techniques.* Reno, NV: Reno Center for Learning and Literacy. (ERIC Document, Reproduction Service No. ED 294155).

Bingman, M. B., Ebert, O., & Bell, B. (2002, March). *Documenting outcomes for learners and their communities: A report on a NCSALL action research project* (NCSALL Reports No. 20). Cambridge, MA: National Center for the Study of Adult Learning and Literacy.

Connecticut State Department of Education. (2002). *Guide to Even Start performance indicators for adults and children* (Rev. ed.). Hartford, CT: Author.

Fingeret, H. A. (1993). *It belongs to me: A guide to portfolio assessment in adult education programs.* Durham, NC: Literacy South.

Herman, J. L., Aschbacher, P. R., & Winters, L. (1992). *A practical guide to alternative assessment.* Alexandria, VA: Association for Supervision and Curriculum Development.

Hermann, B. A. (Ed.) (1994). *The volunteer tutor's toolbox.* Newark, DE: International Reading Association.

Holt, D. D., & Van Duzer, C. H. (Eds.) (2000). *Assessing success in family literacy and adult ESL* (Rev. ed. Washington, DC: Center for Applied Linguistics.

Jackson, G. B. (1990). *Measures for adult literacy programs.* Washington, DC: ERIC Clearinghouse on Tests, Measurements and Evaluation.

Knell, S., & Scogins, J. (2000). *Adult literacy assessment tool kit.* Chicago, IL: American Library Association.

Kruidenier, J. (2002). Literacy assessment in adult basic education. In J. Comings, B. Garner, & C. Smith (Eds.) *The annual review of adult learning and literacy, Vol. 3: National Center for the Study of Adult Learning and Literacy* (pp. 84–151). San Franscisco: Jossey-Bass.

MacKillop, J., & Holzman, M. (Eds.). (1990). *Gateway: Paths to adult learning.* Philadelphia: Philip Morris.

Maine State Department of Education (2002). Family Literacy Performance Indicators. Augusta, ME: Author.

Marshall, C., & Rossman, G. B. (1995). *Designing qualitative research.* Thousand Oaks, CA: Sage.

McGrail, L., & Schwartz, R. (Eds.). (1993). *Adventures in assessment: The tale of the tools.* Boston, MA: World Education/SABES.

Mislevy, R. J., & Knowles, K. T. (Eds.). (2002). *Performance assessments for adult education: Exploring the measurement issues. Report of a workshop.* Washington, DC: National Academy Press.

Moran, J. J. (1997). *Assessing adult learning: A guide for practitioners.* Malamar, FL: Krieger.

Patton, M. Q. (1990). *Qualitative evaluation and research methods* (2nd ed.). Newbury Park, CA: Sage.

Rance-Roney, J. (1995). Classifying ESL proficiency. In T. Reiff (Ed.), *The Pennsylvania adult basic and literacy education staff handbook* (p. 25). Harrisburg, PA: Pennsylvania Department of Education.

Salvia, J., & Ysseldyke, J. E. (1995). *Assessment* (6th ed.). Boston: Houghton Mifflin.

Salvia, J., & Hughes, C. (1990). *Curriculum-based assessment: Testing what is taught.* New York: MacMillan.

Secretary's Commission on Achieving Necessary Skills. (1992). *Learning a living: A blueprint for high performance.* Washington, DC: U.S. Department of Labor.

Stein, S. (2000, January). *Equipped for the future content standards: What adults need to know and be able to do in the 21st century.* Washington, DC: National Institute for Literacy.

Van Duzer, C. H., & Berdan, R. (2000). Perspectives on assessment in adult ESOL instruction. In J. Comings, B. Garner, & C. Smith (Eds.), *Annual review of adult learning and literacy* (pp. 200–242). San Francisco: Jossey-Bass.

Wrigley, H. S., & Guth, G. L. A. (1992). *Bringing literacy to life: Issues and options in adult ESL literacy.* San Mateo, CA: Aguirre International.

30

Continuous Improvement in Family Literacy Programs

Robert G. St.Pierre, Anne E. Ricciuti, and Fumiyo Tao

Abt Associates

Collecting data as part of a systematic, continuous improvement effort allows federal, state, and local staff involved in implementing family literacy programs to assess programmatic strengths and weaknesses, make changes that enhance program functioning, and determine the effects of program improvement activities. This chapter focuses on the Even Start Family Literacy Program, the nation's largest family literacy program, describing evaluation activities at the national, state, and local levels, and the extent to which data collected from these studies are used for program improvement. It ends with recommendations on how to do a better job at continuous program improvement.

NATIONAL STUDIES AND PROGRAM IMPROVEMENT

Methods

A strong evaluation requirement is a key feature of the Elementary and Secondary Education Act (ESEA) (No Child Left Behind Act of 2001, Title I, Part B, Subpart 3, Sec.1205). Since Even Start began in 1989, legislation has required, and the U.S. Department of Education (DOE) has sponsored, a national evaluation. Although the legislative mandate has changed slightly over the years, the national evaluation's basic purpose has remained the same—to examine the performance and effectiveness of Even Start projects nationwide and to identify effective Even Start projects for program improvement and technical assistance (section 1210, ESEA). Three 4-year cycles of national studies have been completed, and a new—and very different—federal study now is underway. Substantial continuity exists across the first three national evaluations, but each has its own special focus and challenges. The methods and uses of each evaluation are described in the following.

First National Evaluation (1989–1990 Through 1992–1993). The legislation establishing Even Start, which mandated an ongoing national evaluation, led the DOE to contract a 4-year study of these programs (St.Pierre et al., 1995). In this first national evaluation, the National Evaluation Information System was developed to collect data from all Even Start projects. The evaluation broadly addressed the following three areas: participant characteristics, project implementation, and participant outcomes. Each project completed a set of data forms and sent these to the national contractor for analysis. In addition, a literacy measure was administered by local program staff to one child and one adult in each family.

Part of this first evaluation was an analysis of five sites, referred to as the In-Depth Study. Families were randomly assigned to Even Start or to a control group. This study called for a series of assessments, first at entry to Even Start; then 9 months later, at the end of the school year; and a third assessment 18 months after the pretest. Outcome measures included the Peabody Picture Vocabulary Test (PPVT), the Preschool Inventory (PSI), and an emergent literacy task (for children); the Comprehensive Adult Student Assessment System (CASAS), education and employment level (for adults); and income, parent–child interactions, and home resources (for families).

Although this first national survey provided useful information about Even Start's early implementation, it did not provide solid answers about Even Start's effectiveness. Outcome data collected from all projects showed consistent gains over time, but no data were collected from families not in Even Start, making it impossible to know if the gains made by children and adults resulted from participation in the program. The In-Depth Study, designed to address these issues, had a small sample size (only five projects were able to commit to the experimental design, with a resulting sample of about 100 Even Start and 100 control group families) and sample attrition, which further restricted conclusions that could be drawn.

Second National Evaluation (1993–1994 Through 1996–1997).   After the first 4-year evaluation of Even Start, the DOE began a second national evaluation (Tao, Gamse, & Tarr, 1998). The national survey data collection system was improved, was renamed the Even Start Information System (ESIS), and was used to collect program and participation information from all projects. The administration of literacy measures was restricted to children and adults from a sample of 10% of Even Start projects (approximately 60 of 600), called the Sample Study.

The Sample Study was intended to provide a national snapshot of the outcomes of Even Start over 4 years and to establish a link between Even Start practices and outcomes for use in designing technical assistance for local projects. Although the Sample Study allowed aggregation of data to assess Even Start's outcomes across the sampled projects, it did not prove as useful as hoped in identifying effective practices. Small within-project sample sizes, project and family attrition from the sample, and uneven quality of some of the data collected by local project staff, all left the Sample Study unable to provide reliable information on the outcomes of individual Even Start projects or on effective practices. Because this second national evaluation did not include a control group, the Sample Study could not address continuing questions about Even Start's overall impact.

Third National Evaluation (1997–1998 Through 2000–2001).   In the late 1990s, the DOE funded a third national Even Start evaluation. The national data collection system was again updated and renamed the Even Start Performance Information Reporting System. A major improvement over the two earlier evaluations was an additional survey section asking parents in all Even Start projects to report the types of literacy-related activities and behaviors they engaged in with their children and to report the kinds of literacy competencies that their children possessed. The evaluation also provided for an Experimental Design Study to test the effectiveness of Even Start in 18 projects involving a total of 463 families, who were randomly assigned to Even Start or to a control group (St.Pierre et al., 2003; Ricciuti, St.Pierre, Lee, Parsad, & Rimdzius, 2003).

Classroom Literacy Interventions and Outcomes Study (CLIO) (Beginning 2003–2004).   In the fall of 2001, the DOE funded a very different Even Start evaluation. First, the federally sponsored national data collection system was set aside, with states taking over the responsibility for collecting performance and progress data from each local project. Then new federal-level study, profoundly influenced by the No Child Left Behind Act of 2001 and its central principle that federal funds should support educational activities backed by scientifically-based research, was designed to assess the relative effectiveness of different family literacy curricula at promoting improved language and literacy outcomes for children and their parents.

Uses for Program Improvement

First National Evaluation.   Although required by Congress to determine the performance and effectiveness of local Even Start programs, the national Even Start evaluation has a varied audience, including the DOE, states, local projects, technical assistance providers, and evaluators. The first national evaluation did not provide firm answers to questions about Even Start's impact, but it did help the DOE to determine the extent to which these early Even Start projects were able to implement the program as intended. Documentation of program implementation helped the DOE and grantees agree to definitions of key program terms, by answering such questions as, What counts as adult education in Even Start? and Who counts as a program participant? The DOE also used data from the first evaluation to identify areas in which Even Start projects needed technical assistance, in particular, in improving the literacy focus and intensity of their parenting education components, developing strategies for engaging adults in adult education, and recruiting and retaining families.

Finally, information from the first national evaluation was used to improve the program through legislative changes. Findings that showed a fairly low year-to-year participant retention rate were used to modify legislation to require year-round services to help retain families in Even Start throughout the summer and into the next program year. Other substantive changes made to the legislation, which were informed by the study, included targeting program services to the neediest families in a given service area, requiring that projects serve at least a 3-year age range of children, and expanding project services to young teen parents.

Second National Evaluation.   The second national evaluation provided the DOE with useful information to improve the program. Implementation data collected through ESIS—the system used in the second evaluation—allowed the DOE to track changes in the population served over an 8-year span, and the Sample Study provided data on the size of gains made by Even Start participants. Early ESIS data provided evidence corroborating the positive relationship between service intensity and family outcomes, which was found in the first national evaluation. The finding of a positive correlation between the amount of participation in Even Start and child and adult test gains, coupled with similar early findings from the first evaluation, provided evidence that resulted in an amendment in 1996 requiring Even Start services to be intensive to promote a higher participation level. The DOE used this information as the basis for designing and providing technical assistance at the state and local levels.

The second national evaluation also provided feedback to individual projects. Even Start grantees could begin to use national data at the local level by taking advantage of a computer program that generated summaries of ESIS data. Another innovation was the development of annual profile reports for each Even Start project. These reports were first sent to each project and state coordinator in the fall of 1997. They compared each project's data on several important variables to all projects in their state, to data on projects at a national level, and to other projects with similar characteristics. This feedback informed projects of important comparisons that they then could use to design improvements in their programs.

Third National Evaluation.   The third evaluation provided longitudinal data by tracking changes in projects and participants over time. Increased emphasis was placed on understanding the outcomes of Even Start, for the benefit of the DOE policymakers, and state and local officials. In an effort to improve project management, the third evaluation used two procedures to promote an increased use of evaluation data at the state and local levels. First, the evaluation emphasized the use of software that allowed local projects to easily generate summary reports based on their own data. Second, the evaluation provided annual project profile reports that compared local project data to state-level and national-level data on key implementation and outcome variables.

Classroom Literacy Interventions and Outcomes Study.   Rather than extending the decade-long series of national Even Start evaluations, the CLIO study is specifically designed for program improvement purposes. It will provide information to Even Start projects about the relative effectiveness of different family literacy curricula for enhancing the literacy levels of children and parents, so that they can improve the effectiveness of their own instructional services.

STATE STUDIES AND PROGRAM IMPROVEMENT

In 1992, administrative responsibility for Even Start was transferred from the U.S. DOE to states, which currently administer the program by holding subgrant competitions, distributing funds, providing and coordinating technical assistance and staff training, and monitoring grantees. During the mid- to late-1990s, the number of projects and families served by Even Start grew rapidly, and earlier worries about appropriate program design and development shifted increasingly to concerns about program performance and improvement.

Methods

State-level studies or evaluations are not required by law and occurred infrequently until recent years. However, recent legislation has emphasized the quality and intensity of Even Start services, pointing to the importance of continually striving to improve local projects. With this background, state Even Start agencies have begun to play a more active role in a range of studies and evaluation activities. The U.S. DOE currently is conducting a study of state administration of the Even Start program (Tao, Ricciuti, & St.Pierre, 2003), which has collected information describing how states administer the program, rather than evaluating how well they administer the program. State agencies could build on this federal study by assessing the effectiveness of Even Start operations in their own state. This effort could mean studying how well they administer the Even Start program, including the effectiveness of state policies and procedures used to select, fund, and monitor subgrantees. It is not clear that any states are currently conducting this type of self-assessment.

State agencies might also assess how well their local projects are doing at improving family literacy. During the late 1990s, some states began to plan and conduct evaluations of the projects that they funded, completely separate from the national evaluation. These evaluations have been funded either by using a state's administrative funds, or by coordinating local evaluations, so that data from these studies can be used to support a state-level study. States have taken a number of different evaluation approaches, such as (a) collecting and analyzing local evaluation reports, in order to prepare a state-level summary; (b) working with local project directors to agree on a common set of research questions to be addressed in each local study; (c) meeting with local project directors to agree either on a complete set of common measures to be used in all local evaluations, or on a partial set of common measures that still allows local projects flexibility in assessing the unique parts of their projects; (d) designing and implementing a state-level management information system, in which each local project completes a common set of data collection forms and returns them to the state for analysis and compilation into a state report; (e) providing guidelines and training for good local evaluation practices; (f) hiring a single local evaluator for all projects in the state to use; and (g) designating benchmark data from the national evaluation as the basis of comparison for all local projects within a state.

The 1998 Reading Excellence Act amendments to Even Start exerted a major influence on state-level assessment activities, by requiring states to develop results-based indicators of program quality and performance (performance indicators), which will be used by states and local projects as tools for program improvement. Specifically, the law requires each state to provide its subgrantees with uniform guidelines for assessing their program performance based on six kinds of outcomes: adult participants' improvements in basic and literacy skills, completion of basic education, employment or further education/training, and child participants' reading skills and school readiness, school attendance, and grade retention/promotion. States may also develop additional indicators to assess service quality and/or participant outcomes.

States were required to submit descriptions of the six performance indicators by June 30, 2001. Currently, states vary considerably in the extent to which they have progressed in implementing the required performance indicators. A few states have developed computerized systems to be used by subgrantees to collect performance indicator data, have held staff training to assist subgrantees in implementing this system, and have piloted the systems and data reporting procedures. Some states expect to complete such activities in the near future, but many states are still refining the details of their six required indicators and performance standards.

States will need to pay special attention to several tasks involved in implementing a performance indicator system: (a) training local staff to administer assessment instruments and to collect other types of data; (b) providing technical assistance to implement the system at the local level; (c) developing and providing clear and detailed documentation of assessment instruments, data collection methods, and schedules; (d) monitoring data collection and reporting activities and schedules; (e) providing guidance to local projects on the use of performance indicators for program improvement; and (f) providing guidance on how to coordinate the collection and use of performance indicator data and project-specific local evaluation data.

Uses for Program Improvement

The Even Start legislation does not require that states submit performance indicator data to the federal level, nor does it provide guidelines on how performance indicator data should be used, either by local projects or by states. However, collection of performance indicator data at the state level, especially with addition of optional, state-specific indicators, could become a highly useful evaluation and improvement tool for states. Potential uses of performance indicator data at the state level may include (a) identifying problems at the local level and providing project-specific technical assistance; (b) identifying high-performing local projects and facilitating sharing of effective practices among subgrantees; (c) using the indicator data for decisions about continuation of funding and evaluating recompetition applications; (d) assessing program performance across subgrantees, to make decisions on whether to distribute available funds across a large number of projects or to award larger grants to a smaller number of projects; and (e) using program performance data to promote the Even Start program (increase matching funds and program support) to existing and potential new collaborators.

With sufficient federal–state collaboration, widespread implementation of Even Start performance indicators could serve as a vehicle for collecting key program data for federal, state, and local evaluation/monitoring efforts. If all states and federal program administrators could agree on a small, common set of data that are needed for program management purposes, and if all states agree to collect the minimum, common set of data from each subgrantee, compilation of such data by each state, and reporting them to the federal level, would help minimize duplication in data collection and reporting activities, would minimize local staff burden, and would provide a consistent system for assessing program performance across local projects within each state, as well as across states. Careful coordination between the state and federal levels could bring them closer to realizing this type of streamlined evaluation approach.

LOCAL STUDIES AND PROGRAM IMPROVEMENT

Even Start's legislation calls for each grantee to conduct a local evaluation, and guidance on how to conduct those studies has been provided by the DOE as noted here. Each Even Start project is required to provide for an independent evaluation of the program to be used for program improvement (see section 1235 [15] of the ESEA). These evaluations provide local projects with critical information on areas of strength and weakness and are used to improve program services and participant outcomes. These evaluations also provide local projects, states, the U.S. DOE, and the Congress with objective data about the activities and services provided by the project, the participants served, the retention rates of those participants, and the achievement of the families in the project (U.S. DOE, 2002). In addition, the DOE has distributed a document titled *Guide to Local Evaluation* (Dwyer & Frankel, 1998), which provides guidance on how evaluations might be conducted to help improve local projects. Some of the topics covered by the guide include setting evaluation questions, designing an evaluation, selecting an outside evaluator, choosing appropriate measures, and interpreting data.

Methods

Because there was little systematic information available on the characteristics or findings of these local evaluations, the DOE recently funded a synthesis of local and state Even Start evaluations (St.Pierre, Ricciuti, & Creps, 1999). The synthesis project gathered and reviewed state and local Even Start evaluations, described the types of evaluations that were conducted, summarized findings about the impact of Even Start programs, and provided guidance on improving state and local evaluations. We draw on findings from that report for the remainder of this discussion on the Even Start local evaluations.

By asking Even Start state coordinators for copies of local evaluations conducted in their states, we obtained and reviewed a total of 122 evaluations from 19 states, of which we judged that 113 (93%) contained information about the implementation of the program being studied and that 94 (77%) contained some information on program outcomes.

Analyses of Implementation Studies. The results of the implementation studies are presented in Table 30.1 Almost all of the 122 local implementation studies (95%) described the project structure and activities with families served by Even Start. These descriptions ranged from simple one-paragraph statements about the project and its services, to detailed, multipage charts showing the exact length and nature of the planned services in each component, as offered or delivered by a number of different service providers.

Almost two thirds (62%) of the local implementation studies provided information about the level of family participation in Even Start. Typically, this information included data on the average number of months that families participated. Less often, the data included the average number of hours per month that families participated. Many studies commented on the difficulty

TABLE 30.1
Implementation Studies: Description of Local Even
Start Evaluations ($N = 113$)

Study Characteristic	% (n)
Study design	
Project structure/description/activities	95 (107)
Level of participation	62 (70)
Sample	
Project director	81 (91)
Teachers	
(All)	72 (81)
(Random/representative sample)	2 (2)
(Convenience sample)	1 (1)
Parents	
(All)	70 (79)
(Random/representative sample)	0 (0)
(Convenience sample)	4 (5)
Measurement methods	
Project director report	75 (85)
Teacher report	72 (81)
Abstraction from project records	66 (75)
Parent report	40 (45)
Log of activities/level of participation	32 (37)
Observation	23 (26)
Report from Early Start Information System	15 (17)

of recruiting and retaining families in Even Start, but none contained a systematic accounting of the number of families contacted, the number that showed up for at least one contact, the number that officially enrolled in Even Start, or how long families stayed in the program.

Data for understanding local implementation issues most often came from the project director (81%) and from studies that assessed all Even Start teachers (72%) or all parents (70%). Local evaluations rarely called for samples of teachers or parents because the maximum number of respondents in each Even Start project is usually small enough to warrant collecting data on each participant.

Self-reporting was the most common measurement approach for local implementation studies. This strategy was used to obtain information from project directors (75%), teachers (72%), and parents (40%). Other commonly used measurement methods included abstraction of information from project records (66%), participation/activity logs (32%), and observation of classrooms or home visits (23%). Only 15% of the local implementation studies relied on data collected for the national evaluation. The limited use of participation/activity logs and observations is not surprising, given the high level of effort they require.

Analyses of Program Outcome Studies.   Local projects used many different evaluation designs for studying program outcomes. These designs and methods of measurement are presented in Table 30.2. In this discussion, the designs are categorized according to their experimental design characteristics. To test the Even Start Family Literacy model requires a relatively sophisticated experimental design, namely, a randomized, two-group design with an experimental and a control group. Using this kind of design is costly, time-consuming, and

TABLE 30.2

Outcome Studies: Description of Local Even Start
Evaluations ($N = 94$)

Study Characteristic	% (n)
Study design	
Randomized experiment	None
Quasi-experiment (two groups)	10 (9)
One-group pre-poststudy	76 (71)
All project families	60 (71)
Random/representative sample of families	None
Convenience sample of project families	6 (6)
One-group post-only study	31 (29)
All project families	31 (29)
Random/representative sample of families	18 (17)
Convenience sample of project families	1 (1)
Time period covered by study	
Families followed for 1 project year	75 (70)
Families followed for more than 1 year	11 (10)
Measurement method	
Child direct assessment	64 (60)
Adult direct assessment	70 (66)
Adult report on child	38 (36)
Adult report on adult	65 (61)
Adult report on family/home	42 (39)
Teacher report on child	29 (27)
Teacher report on adult	27 (25)
Record abstraction	35 (33)
Parent report of satisfaction	48 (45)
Observation of child and/or adult	19 (18)
Observation of family/home	11 (10)
Report from Even Start Information System data	9 (8)

requires considerable expertise. It was not surprising that we found no local programs using this design. More manageable designs that could be conducted at the local level can involve the use of a control or comparison group (e.g., the quasi-experimental two-group design). Other manageable designs look only at data on Even Start participants (the one-group pretest–posttest design and the one-group posttest design). Because these latter designs can be constructive in providing information on program improvement, we review their use within Even Start.

Ten percent of the local outcome evaluations used a quasi-experimental two-group design, in which the gains of Even Start families were compared to the gains of families in a nonequivalent comparison group (e.g., families in a parallel program or children in Head Start). Although these designs provide a basis of comparison for any gains achieved by Even Start participants, the nonequivalence of the comparison group makes it difficult to attribute any outcome differences between the groups to the program.

The most common design for local evaluations was the one-group pretest–posttest study, used in 76% of the outcome studies. In this design, families were assessed first as they entered the program and then at a later point in time, often at the end of a school year, or when they left the program. This design did not include control or comparison group families. Although this design allows a calculation of gains made by Even Start families, knowing how much the families would have gained, if they were not in Even Start, is not possible.

Even though the lack of a comparison group makes the one-group pretest–posttest study a weak design for estimating the effectiveness of Even Start, pretest–posttest data can be used to assess a project's effectiveness in helping families meet a preidentified set of literacy standards (e.g., at entry to kindergarten, 80% of the children who participated in Even Start will be able to perform tasks a, b, and c). Although program staff would find this analysis useful, it is rarely included in local evaluations, mostly because it is difficult to agree on performance standards to be met by program participants. These data can also be used to determine whether parents and children achieve above, at the same level, or below the levels of parents and children in national normative groups on tests of literacy skills.

Finally, 31% of the outcome studies used a one-group posttest design in which Even Start families were administered only a posttest. This design, the weakest for drawing causal inferences, calculates whether Even Start adults and children achieve at a given level, but not how much they gain. However, data from this design could possibly be used to assess the performance of Even Start participants against a set of literacy standards.

In 75% of the local outcome studies, families were followed for 1 project year; in 11%, families were followed for more than 1 year. In general, these multiyear studies tracked children into the public schools in an attempt to learn about school-based child performance. The greater focus on performance over a 1 year period is reasonable because about half of all families participate in Even Start for 1 year or less (Tao et al., 1998).

Measurement Methods.   Local outcome evaluations used many measurement methods. Children were most often assessed by administering a test such as the PSI, the PPVT, or the Preschool Language Scale (PLS) (64%); through parent interviews about the child's behaviors or progress (38%); or through teacher reports (29%). Adults were most often assessed by administering the CASAS or the Tests of Adult Basic Education (TABE) (70%); through self-reports (65%); or through teacher reports (27%). Some of these instruments (the PPVT, PLS, and TABE) have national norms that can be used as one basis of comparison for gains made by Even Start adults and children. The PSI has its own Even Start norms, based on developmental data collected in the first national evaluation.

Other data collection methods included abstraction of data from school or project records (35%), observation of the child/adult (19%), observation of the family/home (11%), and use of data from the national evaluation (9%). Given the high cost, data collection through observation is rare. Collecting follow-up data from teachers is also costly. Even though teachers can, relatively easily, complete a rating scale for a child, substantial resources are required to track Even Start children into many different public schools and to obtain the time of teachers to do these ratings.

Continuous Improvement in Local Even Start Evaluations

Ideally, Even Start projects would collect and use data as part of an ongoing continuous improvement effort that would also guide the development and implementation of local evaluation activity. The evidence contained in the local reports shows that Even Start projects rarely engage in the systematic use of data to manage and improve their programs. One reason data are not used is because program improvements or alterations are typically made on the basis of anecdotal evidence obtained through observations and stories gathered from the personal experiences of program implementers. A few reports, however, noted recommendations from the previous year, described whether they had been addressed, and provided additional recommendations for the current year.

A reason for the apparent lack of data used to improve Even Start projects may be the distinction between the work actually done for a local evaluation and the information presented in the local evaluation report. Based on discussions with Even Start project directors and evaluators, local evaluations may focus more on program improvement than is indicated by reading the resulting reports. When faced with limited time and resources, a local evaluator is likely to prepare a report that attempts to document the gains made by families, rather than the types of programmatic improvement needs that the evaluator might have identified and recommended, and the response that was made by the project.

This approach to conducting local evaluations and preparing evaluation reports makes sense because the effort of preparing a written report is spent in areas in which the report is perceived by local staff as doing the most good—generating support for the program by documenting positive outcomes. Although formative evaluation activities are done by local evaluators, often the outcomes are provided in discussions between the evaluator and the project staff and may not occur in a written report (St.Pierre et al.1999).

Finally, an important gap exists between the data and the conclusions of many local evaluation reports. Local evaluations almost always report very positive conclusions about the effectiveness of Even Start projects, but other readers of the data may come to different conclusions. These conflicting interpretations of the same data occur for two reasons. First, as described, data gathered in local evaluations are almost always collected only on participants in the program. Those data typically show that children and adults improve over time on relevant outcome measures, and local evaluators generally report that the program helps participants. However, without a control group to assess the size of the normal developmental gain, one must be cautious in concluding that these gains resulted from participation in the Even Start program. Alternative explanations may account for the gains. For example, children and adults make gains on measures such as the PPVT, the PSI, the TABE, and the CASAS as a result of normal development and maturation. A second reason for the discrepancy between the conclusions reached by local evaluators and unbiased readers could be that local evaluators are not objective evaluators. Furthermore, continued funding often rests on a local evaluator's ability to draw positive conclusions. These evaluation issues have implications for using data for continuous improvement. If it is politically unacceptable for an evaluation to point out program weaknesses, to state that a program is not meeting its goals, or to demonstrate that children or parents are not attaining desired literacy skills, then evaluators may be reticent to conclude that a program needs improvement.

RECOMMENDATIONS ON USING DATA FOR CONTINUOUS IMPROVEMENT OF FAMILY LITERACY PROGRAMS

Improving Studies

Some recommendations follow for improving family literacy programs and for enhancing the ability of Even Start state coordinators and local grantees to conduct continuous improvement efforts.

1. *Change the Even Start guidance to refer to "local continuous improvement efforts," instead of "local evaluations."* Terminology is important, and the past and current use of the term *local evaluation* has become synonymous with a study of only program outcomes, with the implication that local projects will be in trouble if they cannot demonstrate positive outcomes. Use of the term *local continuous improvement effort* would more clearly signal the understanding that Even Start is a difficult program to implement and consequently projects are expected to engage in a systematic, ongoing assessment of the strengths and weaknesses, as well as the outcomes, of their approaches, and to use evaluation data to improve their programs.

2. *Provide guidance to state coordinators and/or local projects on the amount of funding that needs to be spent for a local evaluation that focuses on program improvement.* Without such guidance, new projects have little knowledge of the amount of funds to allocate for this

activity, and some do not include a local evaluation line item in their budgets. Suggesting a set amount or a percentage of the total project's budget that should be allocated to evaluation will signal the importance of evaluation and data collection to local program staff.

3. *Help establish a community of local evaluators.* This effort would facilitate the exchange of information about useful evaluation approaches by establishing communication links among local evaluators and by having sessions for local evaluators at annual Even Start conferences. The DOE has begun this effort, through the provision of technical assistance on continuous improvement at the local level.

4. *Help state coordinators implement performance indicator systems.* This objective can be met by training local staff to administer assessment instruments and to collect other types of data; by providing technical assistance to implement data systems at the local level; by developing and providing clear and detailed documentation of assessment instruments, data collection methods, and schedules; by monitoring data collection and reporting activities and schedules; by providing guidance to states and local projects on the use of performance indicators for program improvement; and by providing guidance to states and local projects on how to coordinate the collection and use of performance indicator data and project-specific local evaluation data.

Improving the Use of Data

Evidence presented in this chapter suggests that the federal government has used data from the national Even Start Family Literacy evaluations to make many improvements in the Even Start program, through legislative changes and the provision of technical assistance to state agencies and local projects. The emphasis of the fourth Even Start evaluation, on assessing the relative effectiveness of various family literacy curricula, shows that federal evaluation efforts are now being specifically targeted at program improvement. Because programmatic improvements at the federal level tend to be broad in nature, work at the state and local levels may have the greatest chance of affecting the literacy levels of participating families through continuous improvement. Unfortunately, the evidence reviewed here indicates that local family literacy projects rarely engage in the systematic use of data for improving their programs. One important reason for the lack of systematic use of data is a need for guidance and information on the value of research, evaluation, and continuous improvement in family literacy programs. Although program directors are keenly interested in delivering the best possible services, the skills required for identifying program difficulties, collecting systematic data, selecting data to collect, analyzing data, and implementing recommendations, all pose potential obstacles for a director's administration of local improvement efforts.

In recent years, researchers have paid attention to this problem and have provided guidance on how the staff from individual family literacy projects could improve their programs by the systematic application of evaluation methods and data. There are many ways to approach this task. Here we describe one strategy, using a set of five principles that local projects could incorporate to effectively use evaluation data for program improvement. The DOE, in its observational study of 10 well-implemented Even Start projects, has facilitated and assessed the use of a continuous improvement approach based on these principles:

1. *Collaboratively set outcome goals for children and families.* Staff, evaluators, and families enrolled in the program should work together to set concrete outcome goals.

2. *Devise an intervention to achieve set goals.* The family literacy intervention should be designed to achieve the specific outcome goals that are set. The intervention should be based on practices shown to be effective in prior research.

3. *Set intervention thresholds necessary to achieve goals.* An assumption underlying all family literacy programs is that, if a family is to achieve its goals, it must participate in the program for a sufficient period of time at a sufficiently high level of intensity. Program staff

need to define, ahead of time, the minimum intervention threshold that they believe is needed for families to achieve their goals.

4. *Assess progress toward goals with sound measures.* To determine whether families have achieved their goals, programs need to assess progress on a periodic basis, by using sound measures (i.e., measures that have adequate reliability and validity, that have a history of use in similar studies, and that are available in appropriate languages).

5. *Use evaluation to monitor program quality and results, and to target areas for improvement.* A comprehensive evaluation needs to be implemented to help program staff monitor the quality of their family literacy program. Such an evaluation also will help staff keep track of each family's level and duration of participation in the intervention and wil help assess progress toward goals. Knowing the quality of each program component, the extent to which families have participated, and the degree to which they are making progress will allow program staff to understand why some families do not achieve their goals (e.g., they did not participate at a sufficient level, or program components were of low quality), to identify program components that need improvement, and to target resources accordingly.

This continuous improvement approach ought to be helpful to local Even Start projects. Federal resources could be used to provide guidance and technical assistance to state and local staff in using data to improve family literacy programs. Three procedures for doing so are listed here:

1. *Provide guidance to states on using state-level performance indicator data to provide a broader perspective on program improvement.* State-level data could be used to identify problems at the local level and to design appropriate technical assistance; to identify high performing local projects, so that information about effective practices may be shared; to make decisions about continuation funding and evaluating grant applications; to assess performance across projects, to help decide whether to distribute funds broadly across many projects or to award larger grants to a smaller number of projects; and to promote the Even Start program (increase matching funds and program support) to existing and potential new collaborators.

2. *Provide training for local grantees in using data collected at the state and/or national level for continuous improvement at the local level.* Local family literacy projects often regard participation in state- and national-level studies as a responsibility that offers little or no return. State and national evaluation sponsors could promote local use of data by helping local staff access data collected for state or national studies, understand what those data mean at the local level, and use those data to assess the performance level of their projects and to improve unsatisfactory performance.

3. *Provide guidance to local projects on the use of data/evaluation for program improvement.* Continuous program improvement procedures at the local level occur through a variety of procedures that range in utility because most local staff have had opportunities for experience or training. Consequently, we recommend helping programs conduct systematic continuous program improvement efforts. Such efforts have been described by Haslam and Steif (1998) in the *Observational Study of Even Start Family Literacy Projects*; by Alamprese (1996), in studies of workplace literacy programs; and by Appel (1998), in her work with local Even Start evaluations.

CONCLUSIONS AND RECOMMENDATIONS

Several conclusions and recommendations can be drawn from this review. When looking for evidence of continuous program improvement practices, we have considered federal-level legislative changes and program refinements and evaluation activities taking place at the local, state, and national levels. From this review, we concluded that it is likely that overlap and duplication in these evaluations occur, and that there is a lack of distinction in the purpose of each evaluation level. We recommend that decision makers determine whether separate evaluations are needed at each level. If not, then evaluation requirements can be combined, with a resulting cost savings and increased efficiency in the use of data. If separate evaluations are needed, then the three levels of evaluation can be better coordinated, so that federal, state, and local evaluations each have clear and, if possible, nonoverlapping roles and responsibilities.

The second conclusion drawn from this review is that the current set of family literacy evaluations often concentrate on assessing program outcomes instead of improving program operations. This focus should remain a responsibility for federal-level studies (as it does with the Classroom Literacy Interventions and Outcomes study), but we recommend that local evaluations, in order to better benefit local programs, concentrate on continuous improvement of program operations based on outcome assessment. We have described ways of moving local evaluations in this direction.

A third conclusion is that additional technical assistance needs to be provided at the state and local levels. We recommend that additional responsibility be assumed at the federal level for providing assistance at the state and local levels to coordinate the construction of state-level performance indicators, to push for commonality in indicators across states, and to advance the ability of states and local projects to obtain and use evaluation information for program improvement. Implementing these recommendations has the potential to move the field significantly forward in understanding and using data for continuous program improvement.

REFERENCES

Alamprese, J. (1996). The role of data in program management and accountability in program management and accountability in education. In T. Reiff (Ed.), *The Pennsylvania ABLE adminstrators handbook* (pp. 43–44). Harrisburg: Pennsylvania Department of Education, Bureau of Adult Basic and Literacy Education.

Appel, E. (1998, April). Keynote address. Presented at the National Even Start evaluation conference, Baltimore; Houston, TX; Denver, CO.

Dwyer, M. C., & Frankel, S. (1998). *Guide to local evaluation: Even Start Family Literacy Programs.* (draft) Portsmouth, NH: RMC Research.

Haslam, M. B., & Steif, E. (1998). *Observational study of Even Start Family Literacy Projects.* Washington, DC: Policy Studies Associates.

Ricciuti, A. E., St.Pierre, R. G., Lee, W., Parsad, A., & Rimdzius, T. (2003). *Third national Even Start evaluation: Follow-up findings from the experimental design study.* Washington, DC: U.S. Department of Education, Institute of Education Sciences.

St.Pierre, R., Ricciuti, A., Tao, F., Creps, C., Swartz, J., Lee, W. et al. (2003). *Third national Even Start evaluation: Program impacts and implications for improvement.* Washington, DC: U.S. Department of Education, Office of the Under Secretary, Planning and Evaluation Service.

St.Pierre, R., Ricciuti, A., & Creps, C. (1999). *Synthesis of local and state Even Start evaluations.* Washington, DC: U.S. Department of Education, Office of the Under Secretary, Planning and Evaluation Service.

St.Pierre, R., Swartz, J., Gamse, B., Murray, S., Deck, D., & Nickel, P. (1995). *National evaluation of the Even Start Family Literacy Program: Final report.* Washington, DC: U.S. Department of Education, Office of the Under Secretary, Planning and Evaluation Service.

Tao, F., Ricciuti, A., & St.Pierre, R. (2003). *State administration of the Even Start, Family Literacy Program: Structure, process, and practices.* Washington, DC: U.S. Department of Education, Office of the Under Secretary, Planning and Evaluation Service.

Tao, F., Gamse, B., & Tarr, H. (1998). *National evaluation of the Even Start Family Literacy Program: 1994–1997 final report.* Washington, DC: U.S. Department of Education, Office of the Under Secretary, Planning and Evaluation Service.

U.S. Department of Education. (2002, February). *Guidance for William F. Goodling Even Start Family Literacy Programs.* Washington, DC: U.S. Department of Education, Office of Elementary and Secondary Education.

IX

What the Future May Bring

In the previous chapters, authors have raised issues with the procedures and outcomes of family literacy programs, while also making valuable recommendations for improving practice and conducting research. In this section, Sharon Darling and Barbara H. Wasik review developments in family literacy.

Darling reviews the evolution of family literacy programs over the past two decades, noting the progression from a set of co-located educational services to a structured educational approach that encompasses many theories and methods. She identifies key areas that will guide future development: innovative, high-quality services that meet the needs of populations at risk; staff development that includes a focus on working with families; policies that support and sustain high-quality services to families; interagency collaboration and research; and research that addresses topics relevant to family literacy programs. She describes initiatives designed to resolve serious questions in the field, including asking whether services are reaching those who need them and, if so, whether they are doing so effectively. Echoing other authors, she argues that the value of professional development "cannot be overstated," but she also stresses the need for high-quality preservice training. She concludes with a view of an ideal family literacy system of the future.

In the concluding chapter, Wasik finds common ground among authors, even as they explore topics ranging from the roots of emergent literacy to how adults become literate. She identifies common theories and themes, especially the focus on a systems perspective. Authors called on a systems perspective either explicitly to organize their writings or implicitly as they discussed parent–child or teacher–child relationships or the interactions of family practices and program expectations. Wasik writes that a systems perspective provides a framework for understanding interactions within families and the relations between families and programs. She describes two major theories—those of Bronfenbrenner and Vygotsky—and their strong implications for family literacy programs. Within the systems perspective, other subthemes emerged, including the centrality of the family, the importance of relationships, individualization, and the home and program environments. Wasik reports that the authors highlight program quality issues, and she cites continuous improvement efforts, professional development, and high-quality experimental studies as crucial for improving quality across program dimensions.

These two chapters show a strong convergence of beliefs about future needs. Though family literacy programs have many strengths, the authors emphasize a full agenda for researchers and practitioners for these programs to reach their potential.

31

Future Directions for Family Literacy

Sharon Darling
National Center for Family Literacy

FAMILY LITERACY: TODAY AND TOMORROW

Over the past two decades, family literacy services have evolved, from a discreet program of colocated services for adults and children, to a structured educational approach that embraces the ideologies and methodologies of multiple disciplines, to work with diverse at-risk populations under a variety of circumstances. As the scope of family literacy services has expanded, so too has the intricate network of delivery and support systems to meet escalating needs of both the field of family literacy and the families themselves. The further development of this network, which includes families, educators, training institutions, policymakers, and researchers, is crucial to the vitality of family literacy in the coming years.

From the start, family literacy programs sought to bring together concepts based on family systems theory and sound instructional practices for both adult learners and children. This objective may sound simple, yet it is this very objective that has so complexly layered the family literacy approach. Padak, Sapin, and Baycich (2002) point out that "views about family literacy and parents' involvement in children's education have changed radically in the past 30 years" (p. 1). They point to two causes for this change: First, research has revealed that adults in the home and home-based literacy practices are important influences on children's literacy development; second, the emergence of federal programs, such as Head Start and Title I, established as part of President Johnson's War on Poverty, "paved the way for different thinking about homes and schools, about parents, children, teachers, and literacy learning" (Padak et al., 2002, p. 1).

But change is never easy. The journey to bring about this fundamental shift in thinking about children's education and, subsequently, adult education, placing both in a family context, has been a long one. It is also a complicated journey. In their review of family literacy-related research, Wasik, Dobbins, and Herrmann (2000) describe one of the biggest challenges currently facing the field of family literacy.

We see the study of family literacy as a broad one that is inclusive of (1) descriptive studies of literacy and language practices with families; (2) studies of family and parent influences on children's literacy, language and reading; and (3) studies on family literacy interventions, including children, parents, and the family as a whole. Family literacy includes studies about specific intervention procedures, such as adult education, early-childhood education, and parenting education, as well as programs for learners of English as a second language. Family literacy may also encompass studies of emergent literacy, reading, and school performance. (p. 445)

All of the categories and subtopics that those researchers mention have warranted and received intensive study (Wasik et al., 2000). The field of family literacy strives to incorporate this research and the practices it implicates to positively influence sustaining change in families at the lowest ends of the economic and educational continuum. To accomplish this goal, the field must constantly draw on a variety of support systems at the local, state, and national level.

Family literacy has made great strides throughout its developmental years, and many of those accomplishments are described throughout this handbook. One strategy that has directed much of the development of family literacy is an emphasis on constant, ongoing improvement (see chapter 30 in this volume), a strategy that also guides the content of this chapter.

Several key areas will set the tone for the future development of family literacy services:

- Ongoing program development that ensures the delivery of innovative, high-quality services that meet the specific needs of at-risk populations
- Staff development that focuses on working with families, especially families facing multiple barriers to success, in addition to teaching individual child or adult learners
- Policy that supports and sustains high-quality services to families, provides avenues for interagency and cross-program collaboration, and facilitates research
- Research that is specifically focused on family literacy and, more important, is specifically tied to family literacy practice.

This chapter briefly examines the populations that family literacy programs intend to serve, discussing economic and educational issues that have developed, or are likely to develop in the future, and how family literacy is facing those issues. In the following sections, current and promising practices in the areas of programming, staff development, policy, and research are discussed.

WHO FAMILY LITERACY PROGRAMS SERVE

In considering what populations family literacy services target, two issues need to be addressed: What is the need for these services? and, Is the need likely to continue? The relation between intergenerational poverty and intergenerational undereducation is complex and intertwined. One can ask how a lack of literacy abilities perpetuates poverty, or one can ask what impact poverty has on literacy development and the family literacy field.

According to the U.S. Census Bureau, the population growth of 32.7 million people between 1990 and 2000 represents the largest census-to-census increase in American history (Perry & Mackun, 2001). The poverty rate for the nation in 2000 was 11.3%, or about 31.1 million people (Dalaker, 2001). Despite a decrease in child poverty (from 16.9% in 1999 to 16.2% in 2000), people under age 18 continued to have a higher poverty rate than other age groups, and most of those under age 18 who live in poverty can be assumed to live with adults who are also impoverished.

Because family literacy services have traditionally targeted families considered most at-risk of economic or educational hardship, it is significant to note the percentage of the population living in profound poverty. From 1995 to 2000, the rate of people living below 50% of the poverty level increased from 3.7% to 4.4% (U.S. Census Bureau, 2002).

There are three categories of people within these poverty statistics who warrant a closer look in determining what populations family literacy can expect to serve in the coming years: (a) the working poor, (b) Hispanics and others for whom English is a second language, and (c) single parents, particularly female-headed families. Traditionally, family literacy programs are already serving families within these categories. What is significant to note, however, is where these categories fall along the economic continuum.

The first category, the working poor, is a population group that has become more prevalent since the 1996 passage of welfare reform. Despite overall poverty rate declines, a greater percentage of the poor in 2000 has one full-time worker in the family than in 1993. According to Dalaker (2001), "Even though people with working family members were less likely to be poor in 2000 compared with 1993, the poor were more likely to have a working family member" (p. 8).

The second category, speakers of languages other than English, is a population confronted with both educational and economic challenges. According to the National Institute for Literacy (2003), the International Adult Literacy Survey, 1994–1998, found that the average composite literacy score of native-born adults in the United States was 284 (level 3), and that the average composite literacy score of foreign-born adults in the United States was 210 (level 1). In 2000, the Current Population Survey (National Institute for Literacy, 2003) reported that 33% of the foreign-born population were not high school graduates, compared to 13.4% of the native population. The Children's Defense Fund (2001) states that 28% of Hispanic children were poor in 2000, compared to 12.9% of White children. Furthermore, the National Council of La Raza (2000) reports that, in 1999, one of five Hispanic families was poor.

Certainly, many family literacy programs have seen an influx of foreign-born students over the past several years, which mirrors the national trend. According to Schmidley (2001), the foreign-born population in the United States has increased from 9.6 million in 1970 to 28.4 million in 2000. As of March 2000, 55.9 million, or approximately 20% of the population, were of foreign stock (i.e., foreign-born, native-born with foreign-born parents, or native-born with one foreign-born parent). Schmidley further reports that

> the foreign stock population is likely to increase in the future as recent international migrants form families. One indication of this is in the increase in the proportion of births to foreign-born women residing in the United States: from 6 percent in 1970 to 20.2 percent in 1999. (p. 3)

Increases in populations speaking languages other than English have already had an impact on family literacy programs and will continue to do so in the near future.

The third population category often singled out in poverty data is female-householder families. Although at an all-time low, there are still 3.1 million poor female-householder families in the United States. People in these families, both those who lived with other adult workers and those who did not, had a poverty rate at least four-and-a-half times greater than their counterparts in married-couple families. Not surprisingly, people in female-householder families with no workers had the highest poverty rate: two thirds were poor (Dalaker, 2001).

Why focus on poverty in an examination of family literacy's effective practices? There have been many correlations made between families' economic status and educational attainment (e.g., see the U.S. Department of Education's *America's Kindergartners* [2000] and *The Condition of Education* [2001]), but few have summed it up as eloquently as Hart and Risley (1995):

We could see in the welfare families the nation's continuing failure to eradicate poverty. We saw the welfare parents' isolation from the world of working-class parents and from opportunities to see and talk about the parenting styles that were providing so much more cumulative experience to the average classmates the welfare children would meet in school. We saw poverty of experience being transmitted across generations. (p. 179)

This poverty of experience, characterized not only by diminished socioeconomic status, but also by differences in the home literacy environment and parental support throughout a child's educational endeavors, is what places children at risk of school failure and is what places the nation at risk of perpetuating a cycle of intergenerational underachievement.

This poverty of experience becomes an even more pressing issue when considered in conjunction with those population categories mentioned previously and the potentially overwhelming barrier of sheer physical poverty that they face. In light of the current emphasis placed on increasing children's reading abilities, the cautions of Snow, Burns, and Griffin (1998) are worth noting: "It is the concentration of poor readers in certain ethnic groups and in poor, urban neighborhoods and rural towns that is most worrisome, rather than the overall level of reading among American schoolchildren" (p. 98). These are the populations family literacy programs most frequently serve.

Based on this brief overview, we cannot assume that the 31.1 million impoverished people in the nation require educational intervention. Even if we want to make this assumption, we cannot then assume that the most effective intervention they could receive is family literacy. We can, however, look to see if family literacy is indeed reaching these populations and, from there, determine if it is doing so effectively.

According to a recent U.S. General Accounting Office report (2002), Even Start served approximately 31,600 families and 41,600 children, in the 1999–2000 program year, excluding migrant and Native American programs. It is of note that only 14% of parents participating in Even Start programs had completed high school. Even though Even Start is the largest national family literacy program, bear in mind that it is not the only family literacy initiative reaching out to impoverished populations.

Providing educational services to low-income families, in which one or both parents work, has proved challenging, as adults, affected by the landmark passage of welfare reform in 1996, struggled to meet increased work mandates, thus decreasing time for educational activities. However, it is significant that, in terms of work experience, less than 8% of adult Even Start students enrolled in 1996–1997 had participated in employment or vocational training before or at the time of enrolling (Tao, Gamse, & Tarr, 1998). Creighton and Hudson (2002) note that:

Virtually every group of adults examined increased their participation in adult education between 1991 and 1999, often in ways that reduced disparities in participation that had existed in 1991. But a closer look at participation in specific activities reveals some troubling signs of groups being left behind—especially Hispanics, those with lower levels of education, those with lower status jobs, and those who are employed part time. Even after accounting for other factors, all of these groups have relatively low rates of participation in work-related courses, an adult education activity that is likely to have economic payoffs. (p. ix)

There are tremendous challenges to ensuring that working parents have continuing opportunities to improve their education. Family literacy programming has tried to adapt quickly to the work-first attitude that swept the country following welfare reform, providing more work-related instruction in all of the components (helping children also adjust to their families' new world of work) and offering more flexible scheduling. But it is likely that further efforts, along with policy support, will be necessary to provide skill development for working parents.

Both Even Start and the National Center for Family Literacy (NCFL) have noted a marked increase in program participation by Hispanic families. During the 1996–1997 program year, 39% of participating families in Even Start were Hispanic, compared to 22% in 1992–1993 (Tao et al., 1998). In program year 1999–2000, 44% of participants in Even Start were Hispanic, and about one third of Even Start children spoke Spanish as their primary language (U.S. General Accounting Office, 2002). Similarly, data on more than 9000 families participating in NCFL's partnership programs from 1991 to 2000 show an increase in the percentage of participating Hispanic adults, from 17.9% to 47.7%. Participants whose primary spoken language is Spanish have increased from 12% to 52%. Significantly, data also show that the average highest grade completed by Hispanic adults, enrolled in the 2000–2001 program year, was 8.6, compared to 10.0 for all races (NCFL, 2002).

The increase in program participation of Hispanic families has implications for both the design and delivery of family literacy services, particularly in terms of the availability and appropriateness of materials, curricula, and instruction. However, although Hispanic families represent a large portion of the English-language learners who enroll in family literacy programs, there are certainly many other cultures and native languages represented in programs throughout the country. The final report on the national evaluation of Even Start also points out that 31% of 1996–1997 new enrollees had limited English proficiency, but only 12% had participated in English as a second language program before enrolling (Tao et al., 1998).

Finally, 36% of families participating in 1996–1997 Even Start programs were single-parent families at the time of enrollment (Tao et al., 1998). Again, this statistic, especially when considered in light of welfare reform, may have implications for the delivery of family literacy services, particularly in the areas of child care, transportation, and flexible scheduling.

Family literacy programming has the potential to reach diverse segments of the overall impoverished population. One advantage family literacy offers to the working poor and single-parent households is that it provides services to children as well as to adults, which is a program characteristic that may minimize transportation and child care worries. The involvement of children may also have appeal to Hispanic and other foreign-born parents, who can learn how to navigate American educational systems and access other community services through participation in family literacy programs. Furthermore, family literacy services are free to participating students. Although the fundamental purpose of family literacy is to improve the literacy skills of children and adults, family literacy also works to address noneducational needs of families.

Will the need perpetuated by poverty persist in the future? It is unrealistic to assume that there will be dramatic reductions in the poverty levels in the next 5–10 years. Within the context of poverty, the question now becomes, Can family literacy make a difference in the lives of families, and if so, how? The next section describes some current family literacy programming, in an effort to demonstrate what family literacy is already doing, and can do, to address the literacy and educational goals of families disadvantaged by income levels.

FAMILY LITERACY PROGRAMMING: THE POTENTIAL
TO MAKE A DIFFERENCE

How significant is family interaction in the literacy and emotional growth of a child? In their study of language development in children according to family socioeconomic status, Hart and Risley (1995) determined that just to provide an average welfare child with an amount of weekly language experience equal to that of an average working-class child would require 41 hours per week of out-of-home experience as rich in words addressed to the child as that in an average professional home. (p. 201)

Or, to put it another way, a child from a welfare family would have to participate slightly more than 8 hours a day, 5 days a week, in some sort of intervention program that provided language-rich interactions with adults, to have experiences similar to their more advantaged peers.

Consider now the amount of time spent by American children in school, where they may or may not receive intensive, high-quality, language-rich interactions. Children who attend kindergarten through 12th grade, on a 9-month schedule, will spend approximately 15,840 hours in school. Compared to the total hours in a child's life through age 18, this time spent in school equals about 10.05% of their life. Clearly, we cannot expect schools and teachers alone to provide the totality of language experiences for children that will balance any shortfalls that may occur in their home environments.

Hayes (2001a) finds that children who participate in family literacy services increase their likelihood for success, but adds a qualifier that is crucial for ongoing family literacy programming:

Almost any study of correlations between demographic characteristics and school performance leads to the conclusion that without effective interventions, children from at-risk families dispro-portionately would be categorized as not ready to enter school when they enrolled or be retained by grade four. However, this is not the case for children who attended well-implemented family literacy programs. (p. 1)

Here, the key phrase is *well-implemented*. Hayes defines well-implemented programs as

high-intensity, integrated, four-component programs such as those advocated by NCFL and Congress, validated by the National Research Council (NRC) as an effective model for preventing reading difficulties in children, and specified in the Guide to Quality Even Start Family Literacy Programs. (p. 1)

One particular challenge to implementing high-quality family literacy services goes back to the statement made earlier by Wasik et al. (2000). Family literacy programs, to be truly effective, must incorporate quality research-based practices that serve adult learners and children, independently, and, in addition, must integrate those services with interactive activities that take full advantage of the model.

Hayes (2001b) further highlights one element of family literacy services that should not be ignored in discussion about effective literacy interventions for children.

A variety of outcome data indicates that parents made significant short-term gains while enrolled in family literacy and the follow-up studies demonstrate a number of significant long-term effects.... While separate early childhood and adult education programs alone can cause significant long-term effects for many families, reports from families enrolled in the family literacy programs indicate that most would not have attended those separate programs to a point of completion. (p. 2)

One of the primary motivators for families to participate in family literacy programs is parents' desire for their children to succeed. If parents are to be primary teachers of their children, their participation is vital. Family literacy programs may be particularly adept at gaining this commitment from parents who are facing multiple barriers to participation in an educational program.

Recent NCFL Initiatives

Does family literacy truly reach those most in need and, if so, does it have an impact on families' educational attainment, economic status, and literacy-related behaviors? Three NCFL initiatives may offer some insight.

The Family Independence Initiative (FII) was begun in 1996 in response to welfare reform legislation. The initiative was designed to study the impact of this legislation on family literacy programs and to monitor family literacy programming adapted specifically to meet new mandates and to accommodate families adjusting to change. The project incorporated research, training, and technical assistance, over a period of 5 years, working with several established family literacy sites across the country.

A study of adult learners who participated in FII programs revealed that 51% participated in job shadowing, mentoring, internship, or volunteer work during their enrollment. Sixty-five percent received job skills training, 67% went on field trips to job sites, 79% received work preparation activities in class, and 79% received computer training. From the time of enrollment through 1 year after receiving FII services, 26% of participants took and passed one or more of the GED tests (Tao & Alamprese, 2001).

The same study showed that, 1 year after receiving FII services, 79% of adults participated in their children's school activities, 58% were serving as volunteers at their children's schools, and 35% volunteered at other community organizations. Ninety-five percent indicated that participation in FII was important and helpful to them, and 95% also planned to continue their education or enroll again to take classes.

An analysis of data collected on the Careers for Families initiative, initially implemented in Louisville, Kentucky, reveals similar results. In this program, the average education level for enrolled adults was the ninth grade. Pre- and post-Tests of Adult Basic Education scores showed gains in both reading and math. According to the levels determined by the National Reporting System, the students' gains in reading indicate a capacity for learning basic computer skills and software. Gains made in math indicate that students would be able to perform jobs that involve simple written instructions and diagrams (NCFL, 2001).

Also significant, 63% of parents participating in Careers for Families reported having their library card when they entered the program, but only 29% said they took books home on a weekly basis. By the end of the school year, all the parents had library cards, and 71% took books home on a weekly basis. Upon entering the program, 24% of parents reported reading to their children every day, compared to 70% who were reading to their children every day, at year's end (NCFL, 2001).

Both the FII and Careers for Families initiatives targeted parents who wanted to improve their job skills and whose children were likely to be ill-prepared to meet the challenges of school. Not only have these programs provided job training for adult learners, but they have also had an impact on the literacy interactions between parents and their children.

A third initiative is the Toyota Families in Schools program, which seeks to improve academic achievement for children ages 5 through 12 by providing family literacy services in the elementary school environment. The initial approach of family literacy focused on models that addressed the needs of families with preschool children, but it was never assumed that children past preschool age did not need services. Efforts to aid families with children who are already in school are an important focus of family literacy programs.

Data collected from year three of the Toyota Families in Schools initiative, conducted in 45 elementary schools, show that almost two thirds of adults enrolled in the program were in the two lowest literacy levels, as defined by the National Reporting System, when they began the program. Throughout the course of this initiative, parents made considerable gains in reading skills and English-language acquisition, and children demonstrated positive changes in attendance, classroom behavior, and other performance-related variables (Tucker & Hill, 2002).

This brief overview of three family literacy initiatives demonstrates that well-implemented family literacy programs can reach populations facing economic and educational barriers. Further, it offers a glimpse at the kinds of gains that families can make through participation in family literacy programs and the types of skills they can expect to learn and practice.

What do these initiatives, and others like them, indicate for the future of family literacy programming? There are several conclusions we may consider:

- Parents who are focused on obtaining gainful employment for themselves are often willing to combine this objective with educational opportunities for their children.
- Children and parents can improve their skills simultaneously.
- Efforts to target services to the particular needs of families can be successful.
- Those family literacy programs will thrive that meet both short-term and long-term goals of families.

To build on the premise that family literacy services are an appropriate intervention for some families, the next challenge is how to ensure the quality of those services. Three areas are of vital interest to the field of family literacy, in its quest to improve and sustain quality programming: (a) staff development, (b) policy, and (c) research.

Staff Development: Learning to Work With Families

The quality of teaching is as influential to the success of a family literacy program as are other practical essentials, such as ongoing funding and adequate facilities. Teachers are the primary point of contact for parents and children who participate in family literacy services. Unlike some other educational services, participation in family literacy programs is usually voluntary. Consequently, the quality of teaching affects not only the pursuit of academic goals, but also a program's ability to retain its students—an ongoing challenge for some family literacy programs.

Yet, there are few formal preservice opportunities for family literacy educators that prepare them to work with the families who enroll in family literacy services, namely, at-risk families who are often facing complex, deeply rooted issues and multiple barriers to their participation. In-service opportunities for family literacy practitioners are also limited, and yet are essential to allow educators to keep pace with new information and research. Furthermore, few training opportunities exist that specifically provide guidance in the unique collaborative effort required to integrate curriculum and instruction across the four components of family literacy. Finding ways to expand these opportunities for teachers will probably be a focus for the family literacy field in coming years.

Even outside the boundaries of family literacy, teachers are more frequently being encouraged to engage parents in their children's education (see chapter 8 in this volume). However, in their study *New Skills for New Schools: Preparing Teachers in Family Involvement*, Shartrand, Weiss, Kreider, and Lopez (1997) are quick to point out that few states include family involvement training in their teacher certification requirements. They also note that school personnel, including teachers, often have negative attitudes toward family involvement.

Adding to the complexity of working with disadvantaged families is the challenge of working with culturally diverse populations, as is frequently the situation for family literacy programs. These populations may represent cultures that are very different from those a practitioner has previously experienced. Gadsden (1996) illuminates:

The critical questions here are bound to culture and to context: Family literacy practitioners, like other practitioners, enter their classrooms with assumptions and beliefs about their students. Work in family literacy must unravel assumptions and encourage strong learning contexts respectful of the lived experiences and goals of parents, children, and other family learners. (p. 18)

Working with at-risk families requires passion and commitment, and appropriate training could prepare educators to channel that passion and commitment effectively. Training at the formative level of an educator's career potentially would have the greatest impact on how educators work with families in the future. One initiative seeking to bridge this gap is a program currently being developed through Pennsylvania State University, in partnership with NCFL, to offer a certification in family literacy. This sort of direct instruction for educators is an ideal opportunity to enhance teachers' understanding of working with family systems, but more avenues are needed for new teachers to explore the merits and complexities of working with families.

The field of education, in general, demands that teachers and administrators stay abreast of new theories and practices. Like any other professional field, education is not stagnant; it grows and adapts to meet the current needs and, it is hoped, anticipate the future needs of its clients. As Snow et al. (1998) state:

> Professional development should not be conceived as something that ends with graduation from a teacher preparation program, or as something that happens primarily in graduate classrooms or even during in-service activities. Rather, ongoing support from colleagues and specialists, as well as regular opportunities for self-examination and reflection, are critical components of the career-long development of excellent teachers. (p. 10)

The value of ongoing professional development cannot be overstated and is probably one of the critical factors in the success of the Family and Child Education (FACE) program, which has served American Indian families for more than a decade. This unique family literacy partnership intentionally and specifically incorporates professional development into the program design (see chapter 25 in this volume, for a description of the FACE program). According to Yarnell, Pfannenstiel, Lambson, and Treffeisen (1998), the training system within the FACE program has contributed significantly to the program's student outcomes.

> During the initial planning for the FACE program, designers recognized the necessity of providing staff development that is sustained, continuous, and intensive. Through collaborative efforts of trainers from each of the three programs (Parents as Teachers, High/Scope, and NCFL), a comprehensive FACE training program was implemented. Group training sessions and on-site technical assistance are provided. The training program serves not only to provide professional development and guidance in program implementation, but also to provide support to program staff in addressing local challenges. The comprehensive training supports the integration of the program components and the emergence of the FACE model of American Indian family education. (p. 2)

Gaining this level of commitment to ongoing professional development, from both practitioners and administrating agencies, will likely result in higher quality programming for families.

Both preservice and in-service training opportunities can also address an area of study and practice essential to the implementation of high-quality family literacy services: staff collaboration. The structure of comprehensive, four-component family literacy services consistently requires the interaction between adult learners and children. Consequently, to provide these services, family literacy requires the collaboration between adult educators and children's educators. This sort of teamwork among teaching staff is unique to family literacy and does not necessarily come about naturally.

To facilitate collaboration among staff, a commitment to collaboration, from both teachers and supervisors, is essential. Not only are family literacy staff expected to work with one another in providing and integrating services for both parents and children, but often they collaborate with other agencies to be able to offer a full range of services to families in need (see chapter 20 in this volume). Furthermore, many funding streams—federal, state, and local—encourage collaboration as a way to sustain programming. As Hinkle (2000) puts it:

> Coordination across programs requires leaders who respect, listen to, and learn about and from each other. It is important for child care, Head Start, and school leaders to identify the goals and objectives that they have in common and to understand the unique niche filled by each program. Teachers and administrators need training and professional development to work through conflicts and across program, cultural, and historical boundaries. (p. 35)

Professional development opportunities for educators, which are tied to both the theoretical and practical elements of working with at-risk and culturally diverse families, will only improve the quality of family literacy services. These opportunities can be offered during preservice and in-service experiences. Efforts to include training about teamwork will help facilitate the level of collaboration that results in integrated and cohesive family literacy services, which in turn will likely bring about greater gains for families.

The Political Landscape: Potential for Ongoing Support

Having well-trained staff working directly with families will go a long way toward helping those families achieve their goals. But staff, like families, need ongoing, stable support to work effectively. Although many programs receive private funding, most rely on public funding to sustain programming. In addition to funding, however, policy also provides direction for program collaboration across both agencies and research.

Family literacy has benefited from considerable support at the federal level, but that support should not be taken for granted. Wasik et al. (2000) recognize the delicate position that has characterized family literacy's development.

> Though questions have been raised since the 1960s on the beliefs underlying many early-intervention programs, the debate on interventions for family literacy programs appears especially intense. We believe this intensity has arisen from theoretical differences about the role of pedagogy and becomes more visible as the number of programs increase. (p. 451)

This debate is likely to continue, as the field of family literacy continues to advocate for the relevance of parental education in the context of improving outcomes for children. To determine how the political landscape may change for the future of family literacy, this section briefly examines some of the policies at the federal and state level that currently affect programming.

At the federal level, it is significant that family literacy services receive support from legislation that directs programs through the Departments of Education, the Interior, Health and Human Services, and Labor. This variety of support confirms an emphasis on collaborative efforts. This support may also demonstrate a belief in the ability of family literacy programs to meet the needs of a variety of at-risk populations, including those affected by welfare reform, families with children from birth through elementary school grades, and culturally diverse families.

Federal support for family literacy was solidified when the 105th Congress (1997–1998) passed several pieces of legislation, which included a consistent definition of four-component family literacy services. The 106th Congress (1999–2000) further supported family literacy through amendments to Even Start that extended the period that local grantees may continue to receive federal funding, and the Literacy Involves Families Together Act, which encourages the use of Title I funds to implement family literacy services in qualifying schools.

Can family literacy programs expect this sort of continued support at the federal level? Some recent signs are promising. The Elementary and Secondary Education Act (ESEA) is the cornerstone of national educational policy. In December 2001, Congress passed the No Child Left Behind Act of 2001, reauthorizing ESEA, and the bill was signed into law in January 2002. Family literacy is mentioned in seven different titles in the act, including Title I: Improving the Academic Achievement of the Disadvantaged; Title II: Preparing, Training, and Recruiting High Quality Teachers and Principals; and Title III: Language Instruction for Limited English Proficient and Immigrant Students.

Although the inclusion of family literacy in this law is encouraging, the legislation also indicates some future directions for family literacy programs. Clearly, accountability and research-based practices are high priorities at the national level, as is improving the academic achievement of children. The field of family literacy will need to demonstrate and document outcomes that are directly tied to practice in order to maintain ongoing federal support.

Through statewide Even Start and other initiatives, states are developing systems of collaboration and support for family literacy. In Kentucky, for example, Kentucky Adult Education (KYAE) which in 2003 became part of the Council on Postsecondary Education, funds 120 family literacy programs by providing support for the adult education, parent education, and interactive literacy (or Parent and Child Together Time) components of family literacy. Programs then collaborate with preschools or elementary schools to provide the children's education component. Kentucky agency guidelines defining family literacy are similar to the federal definition, thus helping smooth transitions between multiple funding streams. Also, the KYAE and Even Start use the same performance indicators, which helps to foster collaboration.

To further facilitate interagency collaboration, Kentucky established the Kentucky Institute for Family Literacy, as an independent coalition charged with coordinating and integrating existing federal, state, and local resources. The Kentucky Institute for Family Literacy collaborates with representatives of the Kentucky Department of Education (where the Even Start program is housed), Kentucky Adult Education, the Head Start Association, the Cabinet for Families and Children, and the Governor's Office of Early Childhood Development.

There is no denying, however, that policy often boils down to funding. St.Pierre, Gamse, Alamprese, Rimdzius, and Tao (1998) identified a crucial outcome that results from reliance on public policy: "State coordinators and local project staff have noted that uncertainty in future funding poses challenges to establishing healthy long-term collaborative relationships with school districts and other providers" (p. 11). That is, funding does not simply affect the stability of services offered, but also has consequences for the quality of services that can be provided to families.

Will family literacy continue to be supported by policy? Family literacy is by no means in the clear as far as future funding opportunities are concerned. Positive, replicable results from strong research studies will be the best advocacy tool for the field in the coming years.

Research: Connecting to Practice

Research can and should guide program quality, staff development, and future directions for public policy. One of the biggest challenges facing the field of family literacy in the area of research is the complexity of comprehensive services. Wasik et al. (2000) reveal multiple areas of program quality that research can help inform:

> Research needs to focus on specific individual characteristics, family variables, and setting variables, such as the classroom and the community in relation to outcomes. The effects of program variables such as intensity, duration, teaching strategies, and integration of program components need to be explored more in depth. (p. 453)

These effects, particularly if studied in high-quality programs and disseminated systematically, could contribute significantly to family literacy programming.

Research can also be used to help determine future directions for staff development. New research-based strategies for instruction certainly must be incorporated through preservice and in-service opportunities, to ensure that families receive the highest quality instruction available. Program evaluation can also be used by administrators and school leaders to help identify areas for staff improvement.

Policy is also keenly interested in, and influenced by, research; legislators want to see the outcomes of their policies. An example of policymakers' interest in research is the establishment, through federal funds, of the William F. Goodling Institute, which will work to build capacity for the delivery of research-based instruction, developing a research base to guide practice and policy.

Evaluating family literacy services at the local level continues to be challenging. As St.Pierre et al. (1998) indicate, some states "allow each project complete autonomy to conduct their own local evaluation, and as a result, projects within a single state often conduct widely different kinds of studies" (p. 11). Obviously, this situation makes it difficult to assess family literacy's effectiveness nationally or to determine what key elements promote quality from community to community.

As for the difficulties intrinsic to collecting longitudinal data on families, Hart and Risley (1995) sum up this challenge: "Such a study runs on the hope that the families and staff will not quit, on the faith that the child's cumulative experience is being accurately captured in the measures, and on the charity of funding sources" (p. 23). Furthermore, as Snow et al. (1998) point out,

> A review of family-based literacy projects quickly reveals the complexities inherent in attempting to describe, much less evaluate, these programs. The variations among them are enormous; in fact, a hallmark of a successful program is that it is tailored to the needs of the specific population it serves. (p. 146)

A critical research question then becomes, How do we evaluate family literacy programs without losing this hallmark of individualized instruction that builds on the strengths and life experiences of families?

The field of family literacy has historically used research and evaluation findings to justify its services. Today, and in the future, it will be essential that research focus more specifically on what makes family literacy work—What are the standards of quality that determine a high potential for success for families and how can programs achieve those standards? One hopes that research will be used to improve practices. Furthermore, evaluation methods specific to family literacy's components and the integration of those components need to be developed and utilized to their maximum potential.

AN IDEAL FAMILY LITERACY SYSTEM

Rather than conclude with what family literacy services will look like in the future, let us envision what an ideal family literacy system could look like. Ideally, there will be a program in every community of need. Educators and other program staff will have access to staff development and mentoring that cuts across agency boundaries. Programs will be funded and supported by multiple sources, both public and private, that have a vested interest in the well-being of families. Federal laws and policies will encourage an integrated program approach, and states will provide structures of support. Finally, research will be tied directly to practice, through dissemination streams that reach educators at the preservice and in-service levels.

Can this ideal system exist? Yes. In fact, there is evidence the field is headed in this direction. Is this system necessary? Again, turning to Hart and Risley (1995), we see an ongoing need for family literacy services:

> Our data showed that the magnitude of children's accomplishments depends less on the materials and educational advantages available in the home and more on the amount of experience children accumulate with parenting that provides language diversity, affirmative feedback, symbolic emphasis, gentle guidance, and responsiveness. By the time children are 3 years old, even intensive intervention cannot make up for the differences in the amount of such experience children have received from their parents. If children could be given better parenting, intervention might not be necessary. (p. 210)

But how do we give children better parenting without reaching out to parents themselves? Parenting that promotes children's literacy and language development will not happen for some children without interventions designed for their parents. Improving parenting skills and adult education are early childhood interventions.

Programming, staff development, policy, and research are important factors to the development of family literacy, but the most influential factors for the future of family literacy are the families. To this end, one quintessential question remains: Does family literacy positively impact families and bring about sustainable changes for future generations?

To be sure, this question can and should be answered by closely examining student outcomes and long-term program impacts. But it is also hard to deny the testimonials of participants about the effects family literacy has had on their lives and the lives of their children. To conclude this chapter, an excerpt from a speech given by Berta Perez (2002), a former family literacy student in Washington, DC, who is now employed in the Even Start program in which she was once a student, is presented.

> It is such a great feeling to be able to work in the same family literacy program that taught me to become the person I am today. Every time we get a new student, I see myself standing in the doorway, unsure of my future, unable to speak English, but longing for a better life. I am so happy that I can be a living example of the power of family literacy. They can look at me and say to themselves, if she can do it, so can I. Most of all, my children, particularly my daughter Kimberly ... will one day look back on this evening and say, I am so proud of my mom. Kimberly is eight years old, in second grade and reading on a third grade level. My children will know that determination, hard work, and education will open doors and allow you to fly like an eagle. (¶ 16)

REFERENCES

Children's Defense Fund. (2001, December). *Frequently asked questions: Basic facts on poverty.* Retrieved February 3, 2003, from http://www.childrensdefense.org/fs_cpfaq_facts.php

Creighton, S., & Hudson, L. (2002). *Participation trends and patterns in adult education: 1991 to 1999.* Washington, DC: U.S. Department of Education, National Center for Education Statistics.

Dalaker, J. (2001). *Poverty in the United States: 2000.* U.S. Census Bureau, Current Population Reports, Report No. P60-214. Washington, DC: U.S. Government Printing Office.

Gadsden, V. L. (1996). Designing and conducting family literacy programs that account for racial, ethnic, religious, and other cultural differences. Retrieved March 13, 2002, from http://www.ed.gov/pubs/FamLit/design.html

Hart, B., & Risley, T. R. (1995). *Meaningful differences in the everyday experiences of young American children.* Baltimore: Brookes.

Hayes, A. (2001a). *High-quality family literacy programs: Child outcomes and impacts.* Wilmington: University of North Carolina at Wilmington, Watson School of Education.

Hayes, A. (2001b). *High-quality family literacy programs: Adult outcomes and impacts.* Wilmington: University of North Carolina at Wilmington, Watson School of Education.

Hinkle, D. (2000). *School involvement in early childhood*. Jessup, MD: U.S. Department of Education, Office of Educational Research and Improvement.

National Center for Family Literacy (NCFL). (2001, November). 2000–2001 Careers for Families project school-year program analysis. *Momentum*, 4.

National Center for Family Literacy (NCFL). (2002). [Primary language spoken; percentage of Hispanic adults; Highest grade completed by adults for 2000/01 program year]. Unpublished raw data.

National Council of La Raza. (2000, November). *Census information center: Hispanic poverty fact sheet*. Washington, DC: Author.

National Institute for Literacy. (2003). *English as a second language literacy*. Retrieved February 3, 2003, from http://www.nifl.gov/nifl/facts/esl.html

Padak, N., Sapin, C., & Baycich, D. (2002). *A decade of family literacy: Programs, outcomes, and future prospects* (Information Series No. 389). Columbus, OH: ERIC Clearinghouse on Adult, Career, and Vocational Education. (ED465074)

Perez, B. (2002, March). Speech presented at the Eleventh Annual National Conference on Family Literacy, Albuquerque, NM.

Perry, M. J., & Mackun, P. J. (2001, April). Population change and distribution: 1990 to 2000 (Census 2000 Brief No. C2KBR/01-2). Washington, DC: U.S. Department of Commerce.

Schmidley, A. D. (2001). *Profile of the foreign-born population in the United States: 2000* (U.S. Census Bureau, Current Population Reports, Report No. P23-206). Washington, DC: U.S. Government Printing Office.

Shartrand, A. M., Weiss, H. B., Kreider, H. M., & Lopez, M. E. (1997). *New skills for new schools: Preparing teachers in family involvement*. Retrieved February 20, 2002, from http://www.ed.gov/pubs/NewSkills/title.html

Snow, C. E., Burns, M. S., & Griffin, P. (Eds.). (1998). *Preventing reading difficulties in young children*. Washington, DC: National Academy Press.

St.Pierre, R., Gamse, B., Alamprese, J. A., Rimdzius, T., & Tao, F. (1998). *Even Start: Evidence from the past and a look to the future*. Washington, DC: U.S. Department of Education, Planning and Evaluation Service.

Tao, F., & Alamprese, J. A. (2001, November). Work-focused family literacy programs: A natural progression. *Momentum*, 1–2.

Tao, F., Gamse, B., & Tarr, H. (1998). *National evaluation of the Even Start Family Literacy Program: 1994–1997 final report*. Washington, DC: U.S. Department of Education, Planning and Evaluation Service.

Tucker, J., & Hill, H. (2002, February). An analysis of families in schools research. *Momentum*, 3.

U.S. Census Bureau. (2002). Table 22: Number and percent of people below 50 percent of poverty level. Historical poverty tables. Retrieved April 3, 2002, from http://www.census.gov/hhes/poverty/histpov22.html

U.S. Department of Education. National Center for Education Statistics. (2000). *America's kindergartners*. Washington, DC: Author.

U.S. Department of Education. National Center for Education Statistics. (2001). *The condition of education 2001*. Washington, DC: Author.

U.S. General Accounting Office. (2002, March). *Head Start and Even Start: Greater collaboration needed on measures of adult education and literacy* (Report No. GAO-02-348). Washington, DC: Author.

Wasik, B. H., Dobbins, D. R., & Herrmann, S. (2000). Intergenerational family literacy: Concepts, research, and practice. In Wasik, B. H. (Ed.), *Synthesis of research on family literacy programs*. Chapel Hill: University of North Carolina.

Yarnell, V., Pfannenstiel, J., Lambson, T., & Treffeisen, S. (1998). *Bureau of Indian Affairs Family and Child Education Program: 1998 evaluation report*. Overland Park, KS: Research & Training Associates.

32

Family Literacy Programs: Synthesizing Across Themes, Theories, and Recommendations

Barbara Hanna Wasik
University of North Carolina at Chapel Hill

Like a kaleidoscope, this handbook has looked at many different facets of family literacy. The authors have provided a rich set of information on theory, research, and practice. Collectively, they have explored the roots of early literacy and the struggles of adults to become literate, examined how literacy develops both informally and in formal educational programs, and focused on issues ranging from how children acquire phonological awareness to the larger realm of family culture and language. In the process, they have made recommendations that will help guide the field over the next decade as it addresses how to foster early literacy, satisfy parent and adult needs, improve program quality, and expand our empirical foundation.

Each chapter makes a special contribution, one that is best captured through the authors' own writing. Consequently, this concluding chapter will not summarize the chapters but will strive to identify theories and themes across authors. Many authors address multiple topics. For example, those writing about children or parents also discuss program implementation. Those writing on literacy development tackle culture and language as well. Chapters on evaluation and assessment include information on program quality and family diversity. We see debate, at times intense, about intervention's effects on program participants. From my reading of these chapters, I have observed recurring themes across writers as they address family literacy programs. As such, they merit special consideration as we look to the future of family literacy services.

The most salient is a systems perspective. Within such a perspective, the following subthemes emerge: (a) the centrality of the family; (b) the importance of relationships (parent–child, teacher–child, adult–adult); (c) individualization and relationships; and (d) the importance of the environment, including (i) the home environment and (ii) the environment of the family literacy program. Authors also give considerable attention to program quality issues, including engagement and participation, responsiveness to culture and language, program intensity and duration, curriculum, content, instructional procedures, professional development, and integration with other community services. The authors also make recommendations for research and evaluation efforts, and here, too, common themes emerged, such as the need for continual evaluation of program effectiveness and the need for large-scale studies to address major questions. All these themes overlap and interact, like the parts of a system.

THE IMPORTANCE OF A SYSTEMS PERSPECTIVE

Systems are all around us, from the solar system to educational systems. Systems are about connections, but connections that merge or come together in a special way. Within a given system, parts are related to each other in specific or defined ways and frequently follow a predictable order. Systems are also characterized by structure and by repetitive patterns. The increasing use of a systems perspective in family literacy programs is consistent with its increasing prominence in developmental psychology (Bronfenbrenner, 1986; 1995; Sameroff & Fiese, 1990) and family therapy (Gurman & Knishern, 1991; Minuchin, Colapinto, & Minuchin, 1998) as well as the growing use of an ecological approach in early intervention programs (Garbarino & Ganzel, 2000; Meisels & Shonkoff, 2000).

The family unit itself is also a system. Every section of this volume makes references to the family as a dynamic unit and stresses its importance in planning for family literacy programs. Family systems are dynamic; they experience transition and growth, disorganization and unity (Minuchin et al., 1998). They have structures, such as common communication pathways, and repetitive patterns, such as routines.

A fundamental principle of systems theory is that parts of a system influence other parts of the same system. The ecological contexts in which parents and families live their daily lives enable or hinder their ability to help each other's growth. The authors of this handbook illustrate numerous ways that individuals within families affect each other. Powell describes many parenting behaviors and beliefs associated with children's literacy and school-related competence. Those writing on adult education, including Comings, Alamprese, and Askov, identify barriers and facilitators within families that influence decisions about education, parenting, or work.

Other questions arise when we begin to consider the family as a unit, such as asking which family members participate. We know, for example, that fathers are underrepresented in family literacy programs. As a result, examining the circumstances surrounding father involvement becomes important. Marital status and presence in the home are two factors that can influence fathers' contribution to children's home literacy development. Siblings of the child or children enrolled in the program are typically not included in the program's activities in meaningful ways, yet many of these children have their own literacy needs.

Families also have subsystems, typically related to role, age, and gender. Thus, parents form their own subsystem, siblings another (Gurman & Knishern, 1991). The subsystem that family literacy programs most often address is the parent–child relationship. This focus derives from the basic belief that literacy is transmitted intergenerationally and that family literacy programs provide parents with additional knowledge and skills to enhance their children's literacy development. A parent–child focus is integral to family literacy programs, in general, and to the federal Even Start Family Literacy Programs, in particular. Such programs move beyond promoting the adult's or the child's performance through participation in an educational program to focusing on parenting and how parents can promote children's literacy development long after their participation in the literacy program.

A systems perspective also encompasses individual response systems and the environmental settings within which children and parents carry out their daily lives. For example, a child's behavioral, cognitive, and emotional responses are not isolated from each other but work together as a system. Children who are hungry or afraid may learn less than those who are neither. Authors writing about adult learners constantly remind us that it is important to keep in mind the multiple responsibilities of adults, as well as each individual's personal strengths and resources.

External systems also affect the family. Participating in a family literacy program brings new influences on the family and can have consequences for all its members, as these influences interact with family values, beliefs, traditions, and expectations. Many other systems within the community are also relevant to a discussion of family literacy programs. Social services, employment organizations, educational systems, transportation systems, and job training agencies, just to mention a few, can affect both the family and the family literacy program. Opportunities in the community such as access to employment, libraries, and health care directly affect the family's functioning and often support the family literacy program's work. Harbin, Herrmann, Wasik, Dobbins, and Lam highlight interactions with these systems when they write about the relations between family literacy programs and the myriad of other local service organizations.

Family literacy programs themselves, like other systems, have structure, communication pathways, and repetitive patterns, and what goes on in one component, such as parent education, can have a direct effect on the parent–child literacy interactions or the adult education component. Indeed, the very premise of family literacy programs, namely, the intergenerational transmission of literacy from one family member to another, is grounded in a systems perspective. This grounding explains why, regardless of the topic they address, the authors of this handbook subscribe broadly to systems theories. Each section, whether focused on participants, programs, or culture, articulates the importance of systems thinking. Some authors use systems theories to give their writing both rationale and structure, including Harbin and her co-authors; Pianta; Vernon-Feagans, Head-Reeves, and Kainz; and Roskos and Twardorz. Other writers incorporate a systems perspective more implicitly as they discuss influences between parents and children, or between homes and schools.

Two theorists who have expanded our understanding of systems in relation to development are Bronfenbrenner (1986, 1995) and Vygotsky (1978, 1987). Bronfenbrenner (1995, p. 620), expanding on his ecological model, has identified two propositions. In the first he writes the following: "Especially in its early phases, and to a great extent throughout the life course, human development takes place through processes of progressively more complex reciprocal interaction between an active, evolving biopsychological human organism and the person, objects, and symbols in its immediate environment." He adds that for these enduring interactions to be effective, they must occur "on a fairly regular basis over extended periods of time." Parent–child interactions are a prime example. In his second proposition, he elaborates on the proximal processes that affect development, writing that the form, power, content, and direction of these proximal processes "vary systematically as a joint function of the biopsychological characteristics of the developing person; of the environment, both immediate and more remote, in which the processes are taking place; and the nature of the developmental outcomes under consideration" (p. 621).

In chapter 1, alongside Bronfenbrenner, I identify Vygotsky (1978) as a major influence on the authors of this volume. Vygotsky's contributions were primarily published in the 1920s and 1930s, but not translated into English for many years. Thus, only in the past 25 to 30 years has his work been more widely available, but it has gained considerable acceptance for its implications for education, especially that of young children. Vygotsky describes education as part of a larger sociocultural system and identifies the relationship between the adult and the child as central for the child's learning. Thus, his writings spoke to a systems approach related to children's learning and education before others were writing from such a perspective.

Of particular interest here are Vygotsky's (1978) tenets about how young children learn. His most prominent concept related to children's learning has come to be called the *zone of proximal development*. This concept illustrates how adults, by attending to and recognizing children's level of competence, can provide prompts and encouragement for children to move beyond their current level of functioning but not beyond their capacity. The zone can be thought of as the child engaged in a collaborative activity in a specific social environment (Moll, 1990). Thus, adults can assist children through demonstration or modeling; prompting, such as by asking leading questions; or "introducing the initial elements of the task's solution" (Vygotsky, 1987, p. 209). These instructional methods are not limited to adults in the child's life; any more competent individual, including a peer, can provide the scaffolding for children to advance. Though Vygotsky's examples of adult behavior do not include all the ways adults

FIG. 32.1.   The family system influences and is influenced by other systems.

can encourage children's development (see Tharp & Gallimore, 1990), his understanding of the developmental process has significantly enriched our instructional procedures with children.

Furthermore, Vygotsky's concepts are not limited to children, but also come into play when a more competent or skilled adult facilitates the learning of another adult. Practitioners in family literacy programs need to help parents respond to their children's abilities, and they can do so by providing scaffolding so that parents learn new skills. Modeling, prompting, and scaffolding new skills are valuable in facilitating learning by adults just as they are in facilitating children's learning. And practitioners must know parents' level of competence in order to give individual instruction based on parent skills and other sociocultural considerations. All those writing about both adult and parent education, including Powell, Rodriguez-Brown, Comings, Alamprese, and Askov, stress the need to account for parents' own competence levels.

Beginning with the family

Not only must we see the family as a system, but also we must pay attention to family character-istics. At times, our gaze will be directed toward individuals or family subsystems, especially the parent–child dyad. But keeping the family as the central focus reminds us of the need to attend to culture, patterns of interactions, social supports, and hindrances within the family that affect participation in family literacy programs. Keeping the family at the center also keeps us aware of potential short- and long-term benefits for families. Figure 32.1 illustrates the family's centrality. Here, I have placed the family in the center circle with other proximal settings surrounding it. The family and the surrounding settings are part of Bronfenbrenner's microsystem, but I have put the family in the center to keep our attention on the purpose of these programs: the need to keep the complexities and interactions of the family and their goals prominent. Earlier, Bhola (1996) proposed a similar model for family literacy, observing that the family should be seen as the core of family literacy efforts. A family-centered focus will help programs take into consideration family strengths and dynamics that influence individuals within the family as well as participation by family members.

Arguably, the most important consideration in working with families is to begin with an understanding of culture and diversity. Literacy and language are not independent of family traditions, values, beliefs, and practices. Rather, they are intrinsically related to these aspects of family life and heritage. Literacy and language are not only cognitive phenomena but also social phenomena. Learners, both children and adults, internalize family traditions, beliefs, and practices that have a direct bearing on their learning styles and the meanings they make of their educational experiences. Narrowing in too quickly on the educational needs of an adult or child without recognizing broader sociocultural contexts can hinder an individual's ability to relate to and become engaged in the learning process. Gadsden; Vernon-Feagan, Head-Reeves, and Kainz; Strucker, Snow, and Pan; Emberton; Rodriguez-Brown; and Wrigley all show that for programs to be effective, we must understand family characteristics and needs. The authors also make numerous recommendations for learning about and responding to the families these programs serve. Gadsden, discussing how practitioners can engage and enrich literacy instruction and learning, notes that selecting just a few facts about a learner's cultural or ethnic group will not be sufficient to bring about meaningful programming. What is required is to understand "what the role of these facts—and the traditions and practices associated with them—has been in a group's history, how they are understood within the learner's family, and how they might be used by programs and practitioners to build a knowledge base for all learners within a program."

Powell identifies the need first to understand parent beliefs about how children learn and how parents view their role in the process. Then we need to consider how these beliefs and practices relate to parental goals or participation. Involving parents early in the process, asking them about their family practices, and discovering what they would value for themselves in the family literacy program are essential for bridging the home and school environments in ways that make families feel comfortable and welcomed into the educational setting.

Emberton illustrates one way that the needs of a particular culture have been effectively integrated with a program's goals, procedures, and curriculum. She describes how a family literacy program incorporated diabetes prevention for Native American families, integrating in an extensive manner gardening, menu planning, diabetes education, and even exercising into the curriculum.

Family home language also needs to be respected and family wishes related to the home language included as appropriate within the program. Providing literature in the parent's home language is one way of respecting the home language. Numerous other ways are illustrated by Rodriguez-Brown; Strucker, Snow, and Pan; and Wrigley. Their examples show the creative and meaningful ways that programs can bring families' experiences and values into the curriculum, integrating fundamental concerns within the culture with positive experiences in an educational setting. We are just beginning to explore the challenges and possibilities of this goal. Progress will come as programs engage in dialogue with families. Gadsden encourages what she calls an inquiry approach for practitioners, a way to engage families in discussions and interactions that help educators learn about the goals families have for themselves and see the strengths that families can build on. Learning about a family's culture serves not only to help bring families into the learning environment, but also to provide practitioners with important knowledge for engaging them in new learning opportunities.

Relationships

Relationships are intrinsic to systems; they are the connections and transactions between and among a system's parts. Relationships between children and adults are the pathways along which interactions that bring about developmental change occur. Researchers have long recognized that these interactions affect children's literacy and language development, as evidenced by their extensive focus on parent–child book reading and by an appreciation of the emotional tones of these relationships. Over half of the writers in this volume explicitly address relationships within family literacy programs; others do so implicitly. Throughout the literature of developmental psychology, the parent–child relationship is fundamental. Through this relationship, children develop not only language and literacy but also social and emotional skills. Their development springs from parents' emotional responses and informal instructional efforts. Both Sparling and Pianta underscore that responsiveness and emotional availability by parents and other caregivers are crucial for young children. Such relationships promote not only social and emotional development but also literacy and language. Children who have positive relationships are more attentive and engaged in book reading with parents than are less securely attached children. As Pianta notes, parent–child relationships facilitate mastery of basic task-related skills, such as attention, conceptual development, and communication, as well as motivation and interest. This cluster of skills establishes the communicative and motivational infrastructure for literacy growth.

Our consideration of parents' role in children's literacy development cannot begin with the preschool child. These relationships begin in infancy, and the patterns established during that time influence later parent–child interactions. Thus, for family literacy programs that focus on infants and toddlers, parenting education needs to include a focus on helping parents interact with their children responsively and positively. Facilitating these parenting skills will provide a strong basis for parental encouragement of children's literacy development. Practitioners working with school-age children also need to help parents recognize the role these relationships play in their children's social and academic success.

The parent–child relationship is so germane to family literacy programs that the federal Even Start program requires a parent–child literacy interaction component. The child development literature and numerous theories of development emphasizes this relationship between parent and child. Hart and Risley (1995, 1999), in their intensive study of parent–child talk, obtained strong support for the idea that positive verbal interactions between parent and child promote children's language development and later literacy skills, including vocabulary. Five different models of literacy development described in this volume identify parent–child relationships as an essential part of the home literacy environment (Powell; Roskos and Twardorz; Leitchner; Britto and Brooks-Gunn; and Wasik and Herrmann). Others writing about the home also stress the need to address parent–child interactions. Bryant and Wasik elaborate on how home visitors can help promote positive parent–child relationships.

Good parenting comes about through many routes, including learning from role models as one is growing up, from other parents and supportive individuals later in life, and from written information. Not everyone, however, has had these opportunities. Also, parents who are struggling with their own literacy needs and did not grow up in homes where literacy was supported may have less understanding of what is important for early literacy development. Adults without models or other sources of encouragement and support for positive parenting can benefit from family literacy practitioners who provide guidance and opportunities for discussion and practice. The staff, however, must be sensitive to the family culture and expectations. Staff can develop flexible strategies to respond to family practices while increasing children's literacy and language skills. They can attend to these dyadic interactions and build their own instructional procedures accordingly. Fortunately, family literacy programs include exactly the kind of opportunities that make such individualization possible, especially parent–child literacy interaction time and home visiting.

Teacher–Child

High-quality parent–child relationships are not only inherently beneficial for children, they also provide a foundation or infrastructure for those children to build on with teachers. Such relationships with preschool teachers are both important for children's learning in these settings and predictive of children's development in the early elementary grades (Peisner-Feinberg et al., 2001). Thus, providing teachers with knowledge and skills for establishing strong positive relationships with preschool children needs to be an integral part of teacher preparation. Furthermore, as Pianta observes, these positive relationships must be intentionally used to help foster literacy and language as well as social skill development for children who are behind their peers in such skills.

Parents and Programs

Other important relationships include those between parents and program staff. Fuligni and Brooks-Gunn observe that such relationships are an essential feature of participant involvement, and many other authors give examples to back them up. Hammer and Miccio observe that successful communication between staff and parents can reduce cultural misunderstandings between families and professionals and help tailor interventions to an individual family. Participants frequently report that their relationship with one or more staff members was a determining factor in their remaining involved and completing the program. Rodriguez-Brown notes that Hispanic children's literacy knowledge is highest when teachers and parents maintain frequent contact with each other. Powell, Okagaki and Bojczyk, however, point out that we have little data on how family literacy program staff develop supportive relationships with parents, though such information could help us develop these relationships more effectively.

Relationships among participants are also important as they come to know and support each other. Parent–parent relationships form as parents interact with each other during the program activities. These interactions often become a significant social support for parents and can help adults become more comfortable in the program and stay engaged.

INDIVIDUALIZATION WITHIN RELATIONSHIPS

Within instructional relationships, competent adults must be continually assessing and planning for the needs of the individual learning. A child's language skills, speech delays, attention delays, difficulty attending to instruction, or difficulty regulating emotions can all influence the child's ability to respond to and learn from adults. Vygotsky's writings (1978, 1987) address the need for individualization in helping children develop. The adult must be able to assess each child's competence and then provide support through encouragement and prompt the child to move ahead. When children lag behind their peers in early literacy development, as most children in family literacy programs do, staff need an understanding of each child's skills in areas such as oral language, letter knowledge, and phonological processing, and they need to identify strategies to help these children progress. One-on-one language interactions, as Lonigan observes, is one such strategy for children to develop strong oral language skills. Vast differences in skill levels among adult learners also have to be considered in program development and assessment. We also lack clear information about the effectiveness of adult basic education programs, making it difficult to call on this literature for family literacy programs.

When addressing individualization, assessment plays a significant role for both children and adults. Johnston and Yanoff discuss ways to gain information about child learners using more informal or individualized procedures, whereas Lonigan, Keller, and Phillips also discuss the value in obtaining individual data from standardized instruments and criterion-referenced instruments. Though they differ on the value they give to different approaches, these authors all emphasize the importance that quality assessment can add to planning for individual children. Assessment data are also of value in planning for adult learners. Van Horn and Forlizzi discuss both informal and formal assessment and provide information for adult educators on how to select and use different instruments. Common to all their chapters is the value given to information on each child or adult and the need to use this information in selecting and using materials and instructional approaches. Tailoring adult instruction to the needs of each adult learner is also emphasized by Comings, Alamprese, and Askov, and all provide additional suggestions for how practitioners can implement individualized instruction.

Other strategies for responding to individual needs are noted by Kelly, who discusses how the parent and child literacy times can be individualized for each parent–child dyad to accommodate parent work schedules. Because most family literacy programs provide home-visiting services as well as center-based programs, they can use these opportunities to discuss ways to individualize aspects of the program that make it more responsive to family needs.

ENVIRONMENTS

A systems perspective recognizes one's environment as a significant influence on behavior. Thus, physical and social resources in our everyday settings influence whether, when, and how we engage in certain actions. A considerable body of research has focused on the relation between environment and child outcomes, including both broad categories such as socioeconomic status and more specific variables such as parent–child verbal interactions.

Physical resources include materials, space, and time. Social resources encompass relationships and interactions with others, including instructional interactions. Numerous writers in this volume address the importance of the home and classroom environment, and they note common features across both settings. These environmental influences are often distinguished as proximal, those in the immediate environment, or distal, those that are farther away.

The critical role of the environment is illustrated by the behaviors of infants whose initials behaviors are very undifferentiated but who move toward more behavioral differentiation in development through interactions with their environment. Adults are critical in helping young children's undifferentiated behaviors become more distinct. Sparling writes that scaffolding, prompts, and feedback help literacy skills gradually develop through everyday routines as well as more formal literacy practices. Parents, through their verbal interactions and by using literacy materials in the environment, help promote children's early language and literacy development.

Purcell-Gates, and Morrow and Temlock-Fields observe that the physical resource almost always identified as important for literacy development is the presence of storybooks for young children. These authors and others point to crucial features of the physical environment: a place to store books, having books in more than one area, and having a quiet, accessible space in which to read to children.

As Hammer and Miccio note, participants in family literacy programs generally have few literacy materials in the home and may know little about the ways in which these materials can be used to foster children's development. Helping parents obtain such resources and use them with their children is a fundamental part of many parent education programs. Family literacy programs work to help parents increase the number of available books through activities like book making and obtaining library cards. They also encourage parents in the use of these materials by helping parents find times to interact with their children around literacy activities.

As Hammer and Miccio observe, such encouragement needs to be sensitive to ways that are comfortable for parents.

Roskos and Twardosz observe that we know a lot about literacy materials in the home—indeed, many authors of this handbook write about the topic—but we know much less about other physical resources, especially time and space. Several authors call for comfortable and quiet spaces to help make parent–child storybook reading a quality experience. These physical resources, however, need to be examined if we are to understand how the family environment influences events such as the frequency of storybook reading and children's later reading success.

Social resources are also fundamental to literacy development. We have seen the importance of interpersonal relationships for both children and adults. Parents also need help in instructional interactions with their children. Some parents have models in their everyday life; others do not. Materials alone without training are not enough to bring about change in children's skills. Parents of children whose environments do not provide literacy-rich experiences need to learn how to use materials in the environment, including specific literacy materials such as storybooks and writing and drawing materials to encourage children's skill development. For children, social resources include not only positive adult–child interactions but also adult–child instructional activities focused on helping children master language and literacy skills. Recent findings from the home show that specific maternal behaviors in the proximal environment, including properties of maternal speech, are more important sources of influence than more general and distal environmental events such as family income (Hoff, 2003).

Literacy richness in the preschool classroom in relation to children's early literacy development is a consistent theme among this volume's authors, especially Dickinson, St.Pierre, and Pettengill; Morrow and Temlock-Fields; and Fuligni and Brooks-Gunn. Physical, social, and instructional resources are all essential. Other writers also acknowledge that the classroom environment affects literacy development (Cryer, Harms, & Riley, 2003; Cost, Quality and Child Outcomes Study, 1995; Peisner-Feinberg, et al., 2001). Certain physical characteristics are especially important for classrooms that seek to promote children's early literacy, such as having writing centers and placing books and writing materials where they can be used in connection with other activities (e.g., Neuman & Roskos, 1993). Morrow and Temlock-Fields report on the effects of other environmental characteristics on children's book reading, including the number of books per child and the physical design of the library area.

Dickson, St.Pierre, and Pettengill, drawing from observational studies of family literacy programs, show that programs' classrooms often lack sufficient literacy materials to bring about effective gains for children. For example, the literacy materials in many such classrooms are not different from those in preschool classrooms that do not have a literacy focus. They also discovered that staff members are not always engaged in the kinds of literacy interactions with children that have been found to promote literacy and language competence. Many resources are available to help staff consider alternative ways to organize their classrooms, and such information can be a valuable part of professional development opportunities.

Materials in the environment also have other significant influences. Many authors write compellingly about the need to make classrooms inviting to families from many cultures. There are many ways to reach this goal. Multicultural posters, cultural artifacts, and books in different languages that portray family diversity all send a message of acceptance and support.

Program Quality

Program quality is one of the most frequent themes of this handbook. Authors raise quality issues with every program characteristic, from procedures for recruitment and instruction to assessment of child and parent outcomes. They agree that programs must offer quality, literacy-rich programs, and they make numerous recommendations to enhance quality. Similarly, Hayes (n.d.), one of the first individuals to stress program quality, proposed a set of comprehensive guidelines to help develop quality programs. Publications from the Even Start Family Literacy Program (Dwyer & Frankel, 1998) and the National Center for Family Literacy also offer strategies to enhance quality.

To think more systematically about program quality, I propose the following three categories as an organizing framework: continuous program improvement, professional development, and evaluation and research.

CONTINUOUS IMPROVEMENT EFFORTS

Though some questions in the field can only be addressed through experimental studies, each local program has both the opportunity and the responsibility to continually evaluate its own efforts, a process known as *continual program improvement*. Previous emphasis on local evaluations resulted in an almost exclusive focus on program outcomes. St.Pierre, Ricciuti, and Tao describe continuous program improvement for local programs as engaging in a systematic, ongoing assessment of strengths and weaknesses of their approaches and their outcomes and use the data for program improvement purposes. Family literacy programs must continually ask whether their procedures are effective and, if not, how they might be modified. They must examine such variables as coordination with other organizations, recruitment and retention, instructional effectiveness, staffing patterns, relationships between staff and parents and between teachers and children, individualization for children and parents, the program's fit with parent needs, cultural responsiveness, home–school relations, and assessment procedures.

The program staff is often so overloaded with work that finding time for program improvement may seem impossible. Yet there is no other way to make informed changes. Adopting a commitment to continual assessment and improvement will help assure that ineffective procedures are either modified or discontinued and that effective ones are maintained or enhanced. States also have a significant role in this regard. They can provide training and technical support for evaluation efforts so that each program will not have to develop these on their own.

Participation

Family participation will be used here as an example of how program improvement efforts can occur. Many authors of this handbook see participation as one of the most important factors affecting program quality, a conclusion supported by research studies that show a relation between program participation and program outcomes in early childhood and adult education. Consequently, programs must pay attention to enrollment and retention data. Low rates of participation signal a need to carefully analyze other program components. Many variables affect participation, including, as Fuligni and Brooks-Gunn observe, program and parent relationships.

Another consideration is the program's fit with the family's needs. Adult lives are not organized around schooling, but rather around family, work, and community. Family literacy programs, however, are organized more like schools, with classes that meet at specific times. Thus, programs may need to adapt to the daily lives of adult learners. Many other considerations come under the heading of program fit. Wrigley and Strucker, Snow, and Pan, writing on second-language acquisition, identify many issues that could contribute to adult participation. Comings and Alamprese writing about adult education, identify personal variables that can influence participation and describe ways of helping to address these during the early stages of participation.

Another ingredient in participation is the balance between parent nonliteracy needs and parent literacy and adult education needs. Programs will, of necessity, become involved in family concerns that are only indirectly related to literacy learning but directly related to family members' well-being. Sometimes staff must deal with these concerns because there are simply no other community resources nearby or available; this is to be expected in any comprehensive program serving families. It behooves programs, however, to arrange in advance ways to integrate services with other agencies so that others can provide help with nonliteracy concerns. Many communities have well-organized procedures in place, such as joint administrative boards and shared enrollment procedures designed to facilitate service integration. Even Start Family Literacy programs that identify collaborative partnerships during their planning stages will have already made valuable linkages.

Though service integration has been described as fundamental to family literacy programs, Harbin and her colleagues observe that barriers stand in its way. Communities may have different systems for different target groups in a community, or services for some situations may be lacking. Yet precisely because family literacy programs are comprehensive, providing direct services to parents and children, both in the center and at home, they will most likely be the first to learn of a family's concerns. Sometimes programs encounter family situations that do not fall under any other agency, yet the issues cannot be ignored. Programs must constantly find the balance between providing literacy services and assuring that parents have the other social supports they need to participate.

PROFESSIONAL DEVELOPMENT

Professional development is not only a consistent theme but also integral to program quality. Writers give many reasons to devote serious effort to professional development. Demographic change has meant that staff members often lack prior experience with the populations they serve. When participants and staff come from different cultures and speak different languages, practitioners need opportunities to learn more about participating families and to examine their own beliefs.

Writing about England, Hannon and Bird identify professional development as one of the four most important issues facing family literacy programs in their country, stressing its importance for both early childhood and adult educators. They point out that early childhood teachers are not prepared to work with adults, and vice versa. Yet these individuals must work together to plan an integrated program. Hannon and Bird describe professional education as piecemeal, with a short-term outlook, and not linked. They see making professional development a national priority with adequate funding as necessary for the current status of professional development to change.

Other writers identify the critical need for professional education in the United States. Strucker, Snow, and Pan stress that professional education must prepare educators to address the special demands of children with low proficiency in English literacy. They also observe that we lack information about how to design and provide such professional development effectively and efficiently. They argue that practitioners should understand literacy learning in a second language, obtain information about immigrant groups, and gain knowledge of the differences between traditional basic education learners and immigrants. Adult education is further compromised by the fact that qualifications for adult educators vary widely across the country. Early childhood educators are often trained in areas such as social development, not in the skills needed to promote English-language learning for non-native-speaking children.

The Families and Child Education program (FACE) for native Americans provides an example in which intensive professional development was planned from the beginning and adopted as a goal by all program developers. Emberton and Darling note that this program also provides professional and social support for program staff, an ingredient mentioned by others who call for professional education. Conveying information is important, but so is providing understanding and encouragement for educators who are learning new knowledge, skills, and attitudes related to their work, a feature of professional development noted by many writers.

Professional development has other advantages. Dickinson, St.Pierre, and Pettengill, as well as Strucker, Snow, and Pan, call for professional development to better understand how language and literacy develop in order to improve instruction in ways that promote children's skill development. Potts writes that team learning and coordination can facilitate integration of the curriculum across components. Johnston and Yanoff observe that appropriate professional development can give teachers knowledge about alternative ways to document children's learning other than formal assessment procedures.

Technology is another area where professional development has a direct effect on program participants. As Askov notes, lack of training is one of the most serious obstacles to more widespread use of technology in adult education. Providing technologies for the classroom will only make a difference if teachers know how to use these tools and can support their students in doing so.

EVALUATION AND RESEARCH

Across authors, we see congruence in their calls for the study of issues that can lead to enhanced quality and effectiveness. They call for the use of multiple research methods for examining important questions, including intensive descriptive studies, quasi-experimental studies, and randomized experimental studies and the continual development of assessment instruments. Though the particular topics they emphasize arise from their different areas of expertise and knowledge, collectively, their recommendations create considerable guidance for future research directions.

The authors left no topics sacrosanct when it came to identifying research needs. Areas identified for research include determining the characteristics of those who might best benefit by these services; testing the value of each program component and its contributions to outcomes; and intensely examining processes and quality within each program component. Specific recommendations ranged from more closely studying benefits for children in different age groups to examining adult work experiences and their influence on young children.

Authors raise many questions for research efforts directed toward content and instructional strategies. Yet, many noted that we often know what strategies are linked with positive outcomes, but we have less knowledge about how to provide effective professional development. Given the numerous professional development needs authors identify, understanding how to increase the effectiveness of professional education, as Strucker, Snow, and Pan observe, would make a considerable contribution, a contribution that could benefit the broader field of education.

Though research on diversity and culture has been increasing, Gadsden notes that questions about culture and diversity are at the margins of research endeavors, rather than at the center. She observed that culture and diversity are often included as variables when examining topics such as parent participation, but are not often included when developing curricula or in developing indicators of progress. Integrating these concerns with other central research questions will expand the application of research findings to more diverse groups.

Family literacy programs provide an exceptionally rich setting, as Powell observes, for examining areas of broad interest, such as studying parenting behaviors and beliefs or contrasting strategies of parenting education. Information gained from such studies will inform not only family literacy programs but also a much larger audience concerned with parenting education. Other areas where research is needed could also inform a larger audience, including early childhood education, early literacy, English-language learners, adult education, and parent–child interactions.

At times, research might need to be focused on individuals outside family literacy programs. Alamprese, for example, noted that one of the difficulties of studying adult education within family literacy programs is the limited amount of research on the effectiveness of adult education in general. Lacking clear information about the effectiveness of adult basic education programs, local programs cannot draw definitive conclusions about the outcomes of their adult education component. Thus, research on adult education in stand-alone programs can inform efforts within family literacy programs. Thus, we see that benefits of research travel a two-way street; research within these programs have a broader audience, and research on other groups have a direct bearing on features of family literacy programs.

In this volume, St.Pierre, Ricciuti, and Tao report on findings of the three national evaluations and report how changes in practice were called for as a result of the evaluation findings (see also St.Pierre et al., 2003). The original legislation called for Even Start programs to build on existing community resources to create new services and to assist children and adults from low-income families to achieve challenging standards. Over time, Even Start legislation has been amended to include many specific guidelines designed to increase program quality and intensity. For example, in 1996, legislation was passed requiring Even Start instructional services to be intensive. In 2000, legislation called for projects to use instructional procedures based on scientifically supported reading research and the prevention of reading difficulties.

As many authors observe, some questions require large-scale experimental studies. One effort now underway is the Classroom Interventions and Literacy Outcomes study (CLIO) funded by the federal government. This study has its roots in the findings of the three national evaluations of Even Start. For a long time, developers have believed that family literacy programs derive their efficacy from the combination of components; in other words, providing services at the same time across family generations would provide a beneficial synergy. Yet this hypothesis has not been demonstrated by the national evaluations. Data from the national evaluations have also shown that quality and intensity are related to child and parent outcomes. Building on these data, CLIO will implement a randomized experimental design to test the effectiveness of two promising early-childhood interventions, evaluating each of the two interventions with and without a parenting component.[1] This study has been designed to yield information on Even Start outcomes when high quality curricula and professional training are provided to participants. It will also provide information on parenting outcomes under two conditions.

CONCLUSIONS

Family literacy programs have been ambitiously designed to address complex issues of adult and child literacy, parenting, and life-course outcomes for adults. They are inherently more complex than stand-alone programs. Because they serve low-literacy and low-income families, many of whom are immigrants, they have a larger share of English-language learners than many other education programs and thus must address all the issues related to mastery of English as a second language, bilingual families, and supporting the home language. Immigration and its associated issues of adjusting to the United States are also part of this complex picture. Programs also enroll many minority families whose traditions and beliefs are not always congruent with those of our educational system; such differences call for program responsiveness to cultural differences.

---

[1] Awards to develop the curricula for these interventions were made to the University of Texas at Houston and the University of North Carolina at Chapel Hill.

As we strive to make essential program features more effective, we must also keep in mind that the adults for whom these programs are designed have many barriers in their paths. Learning more about what makes it possible for families to participate and remain engaged will help us tailor the necessary social supports. Thus, family needs and characteristics must be an integral part of program enrollment decisions. When we layer on top the fact that we are still grappling with determining the best structures, curricula, and teaching strategies for assisting multigenerational family members together in a learning environment, we gain a better sense of how large a mission these programs are managing.

Some of our initial assumptions about these programs do not assure program quality and effective outcomes. Providing the four most often linked components—early childhood, adult, and parent education, as well as parent–child literacy interaction time—is not sufficient in itself to produce strong outcomes. Staff and researchers must work together not only to see that content and instructional strategies facilitate language and literacy acquisition but also to evaluate how other program features affect outcomes, including enrollment, engagement, duration of participation, responsiveness to family needs, and relationships with parents and children.

A review of relevant theories suggests that these programs have many of the right ingredients to make a difference in the lives of young children and their families. But some features are not as strong as they need to be, including literacy instruction and the use of literacy-rich environments. Evidence also suggests that many programs are not sufficiently intense, and many participants do not remain involved for sufficient lengths of time. Though many theories provide support for the existing four-component model, to advance the field we must intensify our efforts to obtain strong empirical data on the effectiveness of this model and changes that might be necessary to provide educationally significant outcomes for children and adults.

As local and state programs continually examine their efforts, as high-quality professional development becomes increasingly common, and as researchers and evaluators tackle systematically the major questions identified by authors throughout this handbook, we will move forward to a better understanding of the role family literacy programs play within the wider range of services for families and children. As these programs have expanded, we have grown in our knowledge of what features appear fundamental for positive outcomes. Much, however, still needs to be accomplished in determining effective program procedures and matching them with families. Even when we identify procedures that work, we do not always know how to bring about change on a large scale. Thus, the future offers many challenges. Meeting these challenges will increase educational and social opportunities for the families we serve and increase our knowledge base across a broad array of educational concerns.

REFERENCES

Auerbach, E. R. (1989). Toward a socio-contextual approach to family literacy. *Harvard Education Review, 59,* 165–181.

Bhola, H. S. (1996). Interconnections, reconstructions. *Convergence, 29,* 34–45.

Bronfenbrenner, U. (1986). Ecology of the family as a context for human development:

Bronfenbrenner, U. (1995). Developmental ecology through space and time: A future perspective. In P. Moen, G. H. Elder, Jr., & K. Luscher (Eds.), *Examining lives in context* (pp. 619–647). Washington, DC: American Psychological Association.

Cost, Quality and Child Outcomes Study Team. (1995). *Cost, quality, and child outcomes in child care centers.* Denver: Economics Department, University of Colorado at Denver.

Cryer, D., Harms, T., & Riley, C. (2003). *All about the ECERS-R.* Lewisville, NC: Pact House Publishing, Kaplan Early Learning Press.

Dwyer, M. C., & Frankel, S. (1998). *Guide to local evaluation: Even Start Family Literacy Programs* (draft). Portsmouth, NH: RMC Research Cooperation, Prepared for the U.S. Department of Education.

Garbarino, J., & Ganzel, B. (2000). The human ecology of early risk. In J. P. Shonkoff & S. J. Meisels (Eds.), *Handbook of early childhood intervention* (2nd ed., pp. 76–93). Cambridge, United Kingdom: Cambridge University Press.

Gurman, A., S., & Knishern, D. P. (Eds.). (1991). *Handbook of family therapy* (Vol. 2). New York: Brunner/Mazel.

Hart, B., & Risley, T. T. (1995). *Meaningful differences in the everyday experiences of young American children.* Baltimore, MD: Brookes Publishing.

Hart, B., & Risley T. (1999) *The social world of children learning to talk.* Baltimore, MD: Paul H. Brookes Publishing.

Hayes, A. (n.d.). *Assessment of the quality of family literacy programs.* Wilmington, NC: University of North Carolina at Wilmington.

Hoff, E. (2003). The specificity of environmental influence: Socioeconomic status affects early vocabulary development via maternal speech. *Child Development, 74*(5), 1368–1378.

Meisels, S. J., & Shonkoff, J. P. (2000). Early childhood intervention: A continuing evolution. In J. P. Shonkoff & S. J. Meisels (Eds.), *Handbook of early childhood intervention* (2nd ed., pp. 3–31). Cambridge, United Kingdom: Cambridge University Press.

Minuchin, P., Colapinto, J., & Minuchin, S. (1998). *Working with families of the poor.* New York: Guilford.

Moll, L. C. (1990). Introduction. In L. C. Moll (Ed.), *Vygotsky and education* (pp. 1–27). Cambridge: Cambridge University Press.

Neuman S. B., & Roskos K. (1993). Access to print for children of poverty: Differential effects of adult mediation and literacy-enriched play settings on environmental and functional print tasks. *American Educational Research Journal,* 95–122.

Peisner-Feinberg, E. S., Burchinal, M. R., Clifford, R. M., Culkin, M. L., Howes, C., Kagan, S. L., & Yazejian, N. (2001). The relation of preschool child-care quality to children's cognitive and social developmental trajectories through second grade. *Child-development, 72*(5), 1534–1553.

Sameroff, A. J., & Fiese, B. H. (1990). Transaction regulation and early intervention. In S. J. Meisels & J. Pl. Shonkoff (Eds.), *Handbook of early childhood intervention* (pp. 119–149). New York: Cambridge University Press.

St.Pierre, R. S., Riccuiti, A., Tao, F., Creps, C., Swartz, J., Lee, W., Parsad, A., & Rimdzius, T. (2003). Third national Even Start Evalaution: Program impacts and implications for improvement. Cambridge, MA: Abt Associates. Prepared for the U.S. Department of Education, Planning and Evaluation Services.

Taylor, D. (Ed.). (1997). *Many families, many literacies: An international declaration of principles.* Portsmouth, NH: Heinemann.

Tharpe, R. G., & Gallimore, R. (1990). *Rousing minds to life: Teaching, learning, and schooling in social context.* New York: Cambridge University Press.

Vygotsky, L. S. (1978). *Mind in society: The development of psychological processes.* Cambridge, MA: Harvard University.

Vygotsky, L. S. (1987). *Thinking and speech.* In L. S. Vygotsky, *Collected works* (Vol. 1, pp. 39–285 (R. Rieber & A. Carton, Eds,; N. Minick, Trans.) New York: Plenum.

Author Index

Note: Numbers in *italics* indicate pages with complete bibliographic information.

A

A Day in the Life, 277, *282*
Abbott-Shim, M., 142, 143, *151, 152*
Abi-Nader, J., 215, *227*
Achenbach, A., 311, *326*
Ackerman, C., 386, 393, *396*
Ackerman, D., 360, *370,* 374
Adams, C., 60, *76,* 530, *548*
Adams, M. J., 58, 62, 63, 64, 65, 66, 73, *75,* 442, *445,*
    455, *465,* 472, 473, 475, *480,* 542, *548*
Adler, T., 279, *283*
Adult Literacy and Basic Skills Unit (ALBSU), 24, 28,
    29, *36, 37*
Agranoff, R., 373, 374, *394*
Ainsworth, M. D., 179, *189*
Alamo Navajo School Board, Inc., 497, *500*
Alamprese, J., 254, 257, 258, 261, 262, 263, 265, 266,
    267, *268, 269,* 355, *370,* 374, 375, 386, 387,
    391, *394,* 598, *599,* 609, 613, 614, *616*
Albom, J. A., 221, *228*
Albritton, R., 387, *394*
Alexander, A., 525, *550*
Alexander, K. L., 65, *75,* 434, 435, *445*
Allen, D., 517, *520*
Allen, L., 66, *75*
Allen, N., 554, *564*
Allen, V. G., 83, *97*
Allington, R. L., 58, *75,* 505, 508, 509, 511, *519, 522,*
    523, 525, *548*
Allison, D. T., 4, *19,* 183, *189*
Almasi, J. F., 90, *96*
Altwerger, A., 84, 88, *96*
Amanti, C., 214, *228,* 504, 509, *522*
Amos, K. J., 383, *397*
Anastastopoulos, L., 139, 143, 145, 147, *152, 153*

Ancess, J., 516, *520*
Anderson-Yockel, J., 311, *325, 337, 345*
Anderson, A. B., 66, *75*
Anderson, J., 559, *563*
Anderson, M., 65, *77*
Anderson, R. C., 58, 66, *75, 78,* 91, 92, *96, 97*
Andrews, S. R., 169, *170*
Angell, A. C., 54, *56,* 68, 72, *81*
Angell, A. L., 62, 66, 68, *79, 81,* 105, *115,* 162, 168,
    173, 177, 181, 182, 183, *191,* 443, *448*
Anthony, J. L., 60, 62, 63, 64, 66, 68, 70, *75, 78,* 525,
    527, 535, 547, *549*
Apel, K., 11, *21*
Apfel, N., 123, *135,* 169, *172*
Appel, E., 598, *599*
Apple, M., 455, *465*
Applebee, A., 213, *227*
Aram, D. M., 11, *19*
Armstrong, W. B., 197, *211,* 241, *250*
Arnold, D. H., 68, 72, *75, 81,* 162, 168, *173,* 293, 296,
    301, 443, *448*
Arnold, D. S., 68, *81,* 144, *151,* 177, 181, 182,
    183, *191*
Aronowitz, S., 455, *465*
Arsenio, W. F., 159, *171*
Asai, M., 552, *566*
Aschbacher, P. R., 573, *585*
Askov, E. N., 273, 275, 277, 278, 281, *281*
Athey, I., 509, *519*
Atkins-Burnett, S., 515, *522*
Au, K., 408, 420, *423,* 518, *519*
Auerbach, E. R., 8, *19,* 23, *37,* 93, *96,* 101, *114,* 166,
    170, 287, *301,* 360, *370,* 429, 431, 441, *445,*
    453, 454, 456, *465,* 508, *520,* 551, *563,* 572,
    573, *585, 630*
August, D., 308, 320, *325*

Subject Index